MAIL ORDER KNOW-HOW

by Cecil C. Hoge, Sr.

1⊕ TEN SPEED PRESS

To and For

My grandson, Joshua Hoge, with
his tugging hand and sudden
bright smile.

My deep gratitude to my wife,
Fritzi, and son, Cecil, who
made our business grow faster
while I wrote than before . . .
to my sister, Barbara Obolensky,
who did so much research . . . and
to Deborah Padron, my typing
boss.

🏃

TEN SPEED PRESS
P O Box 7123
Berkeley, California 94707

Library of Congress Catalog Number: 82-050903
ISBN: 0-89815-015-9 (paperbound)
      0-89815-016-7 (clothbound)

Cover Design by Brenton Beck

10 9 8 7 6 5 4 3 2 1

Printed in the United States of America

Quotation on page xiii © 1981 by the New York Times
Company. Reprinted by permission.

Thanks to Edgar Guest for his wonderful poem, "The Catalog." Special thanks to the many from when it all began who were concerned with the old-time mail order ads scattered throughout. These ads are unrelated to stories herein. Long gone are prices featured, most of the firms and almost all of the products.

Particular thanks to Sears, Roebuck and Montgomery Ward for the use of advertising for items. Those not otherwise identified are from Sears and Ward catalogs of close to a century ago.

In working on my upcoming book, "Mail Order Nostalgia: A Pictorial History of Direct Marketing," I ran across these ads. "Nostalgia" will feature ads from 1742 up to recent years that started industries and famous companies, changed mail order most and led to today's direct marketing . . . including many directly related to stories in this book. Perhaps you'll read it . . . if you like this one.

And much thanks to the staff of the library of the State University of New York at Stoney Brook who have helped and are helping me so much.

Preface

This book is for companies . . . who want to go into mail order or use direct marketing, to start or acquire a division in it, or to provide a service to mail order firms.

It is for those who want a job and to get ahead faster in a career in mail order or direct marketing . . . for anyone who makes or sells any product that those in mail order can resell to the public . . . for anyone in any media who provides advertising for mail order.

It's for companies which want to use direct marketing methods to advertise anything better and increase sales . . . in the non-mail order mainstream of its business. It's for companies which want to launch a product via mail order . . . and then quickly use mail order to force distribution and then to switch entirely from mail order to store distribution.

It's for top management who are non-mail order people and seek background on mail order. It's designed for sophisticated direct marketing firms to orient their young people in mail order. Its endeavor is to help the Fortune 500 and the smallest boutique and any retailer . . . the importer and wholesaler. . . the bigger manufacturer and smallest moonlighter (who wants to grow bigger).

It's for mail order specialists. Direct marketing's size is so great, its growth so fast, its proliferation so broad that any expert in any part of it is usually far less so in other parts. There are ways of using mail order so sophisticated and expensive that the very small can't consider them. There are simple ways ideal for the small but quite impractical to the big.

In my book, I tell in brief outline what I know of the history of mail order, its size, scope and growth and possible future. I introduce you to some of the most interesting people in mail order from the super big to very tiny and tell how they made it—and of their quite different backgrounds and kinds of abilities.

No single book, course or limited series of seminars could possibly get into depth on each of the varied and constantly increasing number of paths to success in mail order. But there is a wealth of help, of more kinds than you perhaps realize, available to anyone who knows whom to turn to and where to find it.

My hope is that among the case histories and stories that comprise the majority of the book there is one uniquely useful to you. If so, you may then desire more thorough, specific information about the person, the firm, the area of direct marketing concerned. In the Help Reference Section I try to refer you to just that, to sort of zero you in to the special kind of help you may then need.

In my book are listed over 150 pages of help sources in a variety I hope can fit most of the myriad of ways possible to start and advance your career and to start up and use mail order and direct marketing today.

No case described here is a blueprint for another success. The last decade's or last year's mail order opportunity may be little related to next year's. But the strategy is eternal. For mail order newcomers to get more advantage from the stories, advice and help in this book, read the first few background chapters thoroughly.

This book is a study of mail order success and its roots. It does not analyze in great depth mistakes in mail order. One of the first brief chapters, "The Mail Order Graveyard," is devoted to failure. I suggest that each of you considering going into mail order as a career or as an entrepreneur carefully read it, particularly after reading the many stories in this book of extraordinary mail order success.

Good luck in your mail order career or business.

—Cecil C. Hoge, Sr.

To the Reader

You must be interested in mail order—or direct marketing as it has now become fashionably called—to be reading this remarkable book by an equally remarkable man. And you have good reason to. For, although in and of itself the book is full of fascinating reading, it is more importantly an extraordinarily intelligent volume on this particular business—and, while I have always maintained that there are no geniuses in the mail order business, Cecil Hoge comes closest.

How many of us have learned from him—and how many of us has he helped to make rich! His alumni and pupils have made literally millions of dollars from mail order in an amazing range of products—from books and records to real estate and general merchandise.

In the late 1930's, Huber Hoge and Sons was pioneering electronic mail order. In the 1940's, Cecil Hoge was one of the very first to use network radio and network television for mail order. In the 1950's, he was a pioneer in multi-media, combining the use of broadcast, publications and direct mail for mail order.

In the 1960's, he began to apply third-party sponsorship, running proven mail order copy under trusted department store names and with presentation in character with them. Later he became a consultant to me. He did this along with operating Huber Hoge and his own mail order business, Harrison-Hoge Industries, Inc.

I am one of his pupils and, yes, I worked hard and I made some good decisions, and I was lucky. But without Cecil Hoge I would never have made it as big. It's that simple. So I recommend him to you—if you are lucky enough to get his help. The next best thing is this book.

Read it well, and you will be a long way along the road to mail order success.

Edward R. Downe, Jr.
March 1982

(Mr. Downe started as a moonlighter with a one inch ad, via mail order built a Fortune 500 company—and then, in his early forties, sold out and retired.)

Table of Contents

MAIL ORDER SAMPLER
Seminar II

MAIL ORDER SAMPLER
Seminar III

MAIL ORDER SAMPLER
Seminar VI

Reference Section V

*How they started; problems, difficulties; how success
came; what helped most; advice of owners, managers to
others in or starting in mail order; over 100 in
varied fields.*

Reference Section VI

*A small indication of mail order's growth industry, its
support system; direct response agencies, consultants,
list firms, printers, fulfillment houses, lettershops,
computer service bureaus, services referred to in this
book and its reference sections.*

Reference Section VII

*What brings it all together: the direct marketing clubs,
the Direct Marketing Days, the courses, seminars, publications, the conferences, the shows, the associations
that help direct marketers, the DMMA.*

THE CATALOG

* i know the markets of the earth and
   wondrous tales i tell
of all the new and pretty things the
   whole world has to sell.
and those who sit with me awhile and
   roam my pages through
may see the pageants of mankind set
   out in open view.

* i know the realms of happiness
   for little girls and boys
i swing the gates which lead into the
   magic land of toys.
i am the window of the world at which
   is kept displayed
the best of everything men do;
   the best of all they've made.

* oh, whether it be north or south
   or distant east or west
i show the dwelling beautiful and
   fashion at its best.
i am a thousand shops in one;
   gay stall and quaint bazaar,
the glamour that is paris and the
   charm of zanzibar.

* they know me as a catalog and yet on
   lonely nights
i bring them dreams and fancies and
   a wealth of real delights.
for often when the day is done and
   duty's flags are furled
i take the family shopping round the
   markets of the world.

—Edgar A. Guest

A Brief Overview

Becoming an expert on anything requires mulling it over, touching and smelling it from many different angles and carefully filing away its various facets in the tool chest of the mind.

— Malcolm W. Browne

The University of the Night

THE young Lincoln, poring over borrowed school-books far into the night—seeking in the dim light of his log fire the transforming light of knowledge—eager to grow—eager to do—here is a picture that has touched the hearts of men in every country on the earth—here is an example which, for three score years, has inspired the man who strives against the odds of circumstance to make his place in the world.

To-night, in cities and towns and villages, on isolated farms and on the seven seas—thousands of men will drop their daily labors to fight, beneath the lamp, the battle that Lincoln fought—to wring from the hours of the night the education of which circumstance deprived them in the days when they might have gone to school.

Up from the mines, down from the masts of ships, from behind counters and plows, from chauffeurs seats and engine cabs, from factories and offices—from all the places where men work they will go home and take up their books because they yearn to grow, because they seek higher training, greater skill, more responsibility, lives more profitable and work more satisfying.

Some of them are men who work in one field whereas their talents and desires are in another. Some, happy enough in their field of work, are halted in their progress because they do not understand the higher principles of their business or profession. Some of them left school in boyhood because poverty made it necessary; some left because they did not realize then as they do now the value of an education. And some have need of special training which they could not have anticipated, or which they could not have obtained in public schools.

Fifty years ago these men, some of them married, all of them with a living to earn by day, would have had no place to turn for the courses of study and for the personal guidance that they need.

Thirty-two years ago there was founded a school to help them—a school created for their needs and circumstances—a school that *goes to them* no matter where they are—a school whose courses are prepared by the foremost authorities, whose textbooks are written for study in the home, whose instructors guide their students by personal correspondence.

Created in response to a need, the International Correspondence Schools have developed their scope and usefulness with the growth of that need. Beginning with a single course in coal mining, these schools have become to-day an institution with courses in 304 subjects, covering almost every technical field and practically every department of business.

In the thirty-two years of their history the International Correspondence Schools have furnished instruction to more than two and a half million men. Many of them now occupy positions of leadership in their fields. Most of them have been helped to greater earning power, to higher skill or craftsmanship, to the added responsibility, character and good citizenship that come with increased knowledge.

For the most part, these Scranton Schools have served men who could have been served by no other type of educational medium. They have served a larger number, and in a greater number of fields, than any other educational institution.

INTERNATIONAL CORRESPONDENCE SCHOOLS
Scranton, Pennsylvania

Offices in leading cities of the United States and Canada, and throughout the world

Chapter 1
Mail Order Osmosis

Aiding direct marketing success by exposure to and absorption of know-how.

In this book are the stories and advice of people who have made billions of dollars of sales by mail order for giant companies, and of those who have found small, secure mail order niches allowing the lifestyles, pace and balance desired.

Here is told how they made it, what helped them most to make it, what they do, what opportunities they see coming up, what they think anyone starting out in, or considering, mail order might best do for best chances in a career or to start or build a business in mail order.

Essentially, I try to introduce the readers to examples of success and to forms of mail order activity. My interest has been to balance the big with the small, the sophisticated with the simple. Each story tries to cover a different facet of mail order, whether it be a lettershop, a list maintenance firm or about an entrepreneur in a specific field. I try to bring my readers on a visit with the people who can help them most.

Jerry Hardy, founder of Time-Life Books, in his story and interview in this book says he learned mail order by osmosis. That's the way this book endeavors to teach it . . . not by blueprint but by immersion, not by secrets of instant riches easily obtained but by growing familiarity.

I try to write about those who can be role models to others, those with integrity as well as ability . . . with taste and restraint instead of the opposite. This is a study of success traced back to its roots, of a field where jobs came easier, raises faster and bigger and where there's more security, where profits can come when others have losses.

Those who made it tell what helped them most to start and rise, to get raises, customers, their first mail order hits. They tell of the qualities in themselves they found most useful, of the qualities they seek in those starting out. They tell of what previous training and experience helped most, what books read, seminars attended and courses taken along the way helped most.

For each story I tried to talk to more people in an organization, to ask each person interviewed about others interviewed. I try to have about one-third of a story on how he or she made it, one-third on what he or she does and one-third on what he or she advises . . . a sort of mini, mini-seminar.

For a single story I've often had several interviews, read several hundred pieces of material and taken over a hundred pages of notes. Each illustrates a facet of mail order. Sometimes, several stories touch on one important phase. There are stories on small entrepreneurs in collectibles, retirement mail order and least risk small ventures. The concept is to do a story on success via TV or with direct mail . . . by one-step or two-step. Each story tries to arouse interest, tell how and stimulate interest for further research.

The concluding pages comprise a Help Source Guide which lists specialized background material on or related to each story in the book. Tapes of speeches and reprints of articles are often listed when available from whomever . . . also, several thousand pages of booklets available free and several thousand more for a token fee. I've tried hard to avoid useless ones and to indicate which are for beginners and which give more sophisticated help.

I visited computer bureaus, incoming fulfillment houses and outgoing lettershops. I talked to the highest official I could, whether for the Sperry Univac 0777 or Bell & Howell's AIM, made by its Philipsburg Division. I did stories on computer modeling, people research and statistical research.

I review the books on direct marketing, the newsletters, the magazines, the seminars, and the courses. I review even the tapes of speeches concerning direct marketing which I feel will be helpful. I describe the direct marketing clubs, the Direct Marketing Days, Direct Marketing Magazine and the Direct Mail/Marketing Association. I write of the history of mail order and of the mail order future.

My hope is that the combined wisdom of the masters of mail order will help anyone starting out in his or her career, any firm opening a mail order division, any supplier to a mail order firm and any new entrepreneur far more than I can alone.

Their collective word is that mail order is not a quick, easy, lazy way to riches. Instead, mail order know-how can be a scientific tool. It's becoming as universal as computers. It can help sell more profitably a surprising variety of products and services.

It's all a bit encyclopedic, but not arranged in an orderly way. I introduce people in mail order to you as I interviewed them. The reading order and how much you care to read may vary with your situation. I'll try to sign post ahead a little of what's coming.

Glance through the table of contents. Look up anything in the index that you're curious about. Browse a bit. Riffle through the pages. Start anywhere. Skip to anywhere. Inhale gently. Absorb a little at a time. Apply as much or as little as desired. Let's begin.

Chapter 2
Your Best Mail Order Opportunity

—most perfect for traits, interests, training, experience, situation, lifestyle, pace.

Suppose that you completed your education in 1970 and started to work for the outdoorsman catalog of L.L. Bean just as it started to multiply its size twelve times in eleven years.

Suppose that you enjoyed the idyllic country life of Freeport, Maine, where Bean is located. Now let's assume that, if a woman, you were creative; had ideas on designing clothes and were interested in women's and men's outdoor sportswear. Or suppose you were a man who likes to hunt and fish and try out products for these sports. Or that you were a canoeist, or hiker, or interested in other outdoor participation sports.

Perhaps you graduated as an MBA with a flair for systemization of a fast growing business; or you were imaginative, could write and became excellent at catalog copy or direct mail promotion. Suppose you got interested in new printing processes; or developed a special ability to work with computer programmers; or got the mail order bug, and became fascinated with the relationship of incoming orders to promotion techniques used. Suppose you were good at dollars and cents, bookkeeping and then accounting; or you could think up new products to develop; or you found yourself a natural negotiator, excellent at buying products.

If some of this were so, you might have been quite a find for L.L. Bean, and Bean might have been an extraordinary opportunity for you. Mail order might not have been suited to you. You might not have liked it. You might have joined a firm that went broke. Or you might have gotten in on any of many exciting mail order opportunities described in this book.

Suppose in 1976 you were in Chicago, in the credit department of a Montgomery Ward store. You liked city life and figures. You got the chance to be transferred to a new Ward subsidiary—in the specialty mail order business, called Signature Corp. You might have been a great help to Dick Cremer when he founded Signature with one employee that same year. And you would have been in on the ground floor. You could have been working personally with a mail order genius—as he built a network of four subsidiaries of Signature Corp. and built up to $150 million a year in 1981. By then Ward's Signature Groups was selling insurance and publishing magazines. They were also running travel, health and personal computer clubs.

If, in the 1970's, you had gotten interested in mail order and in the mail order method, your chances to make it in marketing would have been a good deal better than if not. Most Fortune 500 companies began, if even in a small way through a subsidiary, to move into mail order. You might have gotten in on the start of what often becomes faster growing parts of big companies. If you were in retailing and had mail order know-how, you would have been particularly needed—as mail order sales for retailers grew faster than all retail sales.

If you had started in mail order publishing or mail order record clubs, you would have been in the parts of the publishing and record business that grew faster than store sales and proved more profitable and stable. In the magazine business, you would have been needed to help launch any of the biggest proliferation of new and specialized magazines in history.

In any business dependent on salesmen you could have participated in the use of the mail order method to supply qualified leads to salesmen—and to take over the sale of products and services where personal sales calls became too expensive to make. To sell many products or services to business firms the use of mail order methods gave additional and faster growth. For an ever-increasing variety of consumer products mail order firms proved a faster growing source of sales than overall business.

Many companies selling products through stores increased sales by helping customers sell their products with mail order methods. They provided proven ads or mailings dealers could use to sell the company's goods with all advertising keyed, traced and measured. Many companies provided inquiries for follow-up by dealers. Companies that did this grew faster. Executives with the mail order know-how to help their companies do this benefited.

Since 1970, mail order generally and companies overall that used the mail order method have grown dramatically. Success was not universal. Be sure to read my chapter in "The Mail Order Graveyard". There was no guaranteed road to raises or riches. Often raises did come faster and were bigger, with more job security—and often there were more new job opportunities in the direct marketing activities of companies than in general marketing.

Often working in mail order was more exciting and more fun; there was more chance to use and develop a talent suited to the business; talent contribution could be measured more precisely (by the mail count) which brought more recognition, appreciation and money.

Will this continue? Those written about in this book expect that overall it will accelerate, but not uniformly; that mail order will grow far bigger; that the use of the mail order method will grow far bigger still; that it is still an imperfect instrument; and that the biggest opportunity is that so few, even in 1981, have used it to near its full potential.

With all its imperfections in application, the mail order method has been a slowly gathering force that has constantly proliferated with gathering momentum. As the trend broadens and accelerates, it creates more than average opportunities for companies, divisions and entrepreneurs to direct market and to service and sell direct marketers. In depression, recession, stagflation or boom, mail order methods can change a company's life; and not using them can lose business and risk a job.

Mail order is the way of least investment to start a business or a new division. It's the fastest way for any non-retailer to bring in cash. Mail order can be the safest way to cut the pattern to the cloth and keep expenditures within budgeted percentages. It's the fastest way to find out what is selling, how much the customer will pay, whether a price is right, what models, colors and sizes sell the best and to turn on a dime and proceed the way results indicate is best.

Making a mail order fortune from a tiny beginning has always been tempting, possible, difficult and dangerous. More tiny mail order ventures are now succeeding than ever before . . . many described in this book. One chapter is "The Mail Order Moonlighters" about those who have successfully done what I teach in my book, "Mail Order Moonlighting". Another chapter capsules stories of those who start with and use mail order classified ads. But consider the opportunities, with *no* promotional risk, to supply services or sell products to direct marketers.

The percentage of total printing . . . from printing circulars to personalized letters to catalogs . . . sold to the mail order and direct marketing field keeps growing. Two stories of building such businesses are in this book.

If, ten years ago, you had gotten into printing labels or computer addressing them, into a computer service bureau to maintain lists, or a lettershop or a mail order fulfillment service, you would have been in a fast growing field. Or suppose you had gotten into the list business. There are stories in this book of seven firms which did. The numbers of names rented by mail order companies has multiplied many times in 30 years. There are list brokers, list compilers, list managers and list advisors, with considerable opportunity for anyone with a flair for whichever specialty.

For magazines, newspapers, broadcasting stations or any logical advertising medium, more and more of the advertising sold is to mail order people and direct marketers. Sometimes mail order accounts for most of the advertising. Often it's the difference between profit and loss. Usually, it's the fastest increasing form of advertising sold. If you sell advertising for almost any medium, more of it will be direct response advertising. Mail order know-how may affect your income. In this book is the story of the man who has sold more mail order ads than anyone in the world.

If you are in the advertising agency business, you will find direct response methods revolutionizing all advertising. More accounts now go to those agencies with direct response know-how. Seventeen of the top 20 general advertising agencies now own direct marketing agency subsidiaries. The biggest in the U.S. (Young & Rubicam) owns four. In this book are the stories of 11 direct marketing agencies. Bob Stone tells how he and Aaron Adler started Stone & Adler with $500 each, built it up to the biggest independently owned direct marketing agency and then merged with Young & Rubicam.

But, of all this array of opportunities, which is best for you? Maximum success in mail order is dependent on more perfect mating of prospects to product, product to company, manager to organization, specialist to problem and each person to the one opportunity most suited to him or her.

In mail order marketing the problem is now far less whether the product will sell by mail order. It's how to sell it by mail order the correct way; to marry people who want to buy whatever to firms which want to sell it. The ideal is to match you—with your interests, abilities and training—to the mail order opportunity most suited to you, and which will be most rewarding and satisfying for you. This book is so long because it tries to expose you to enough opportunities to select one more perfect for you or to help you decide that mail order is not for you.

This is a sort of adventure how-to book. In it are stories of many people who made it in some way connected with mail order. Some chose careers, some to go on their own. Some went after and achieved huge, and others limited, success. Some sell by mail. Some sell to or service those in mail order.

In education, they ranged from some high school drop outs to more MBA's. Their IQ's ranged from average to more often very high. Previous motiviation had sometimes been low but was often high. Previous self-disciplined habits of work had sometimes been poor and more often very steady. They came from the widest possible variety of background and experience.

Yet, many interviewed in this book may not be models for the rest of us. They are brighter, more organized and with a greater feel for making money. Some of these people were in quite high percentiles of their class in school and college. Some took special courses for years thereafter. Many worked a good deal more than normal business hours. Many were highly ambitious and competitive. Each of us have our own interests, objectives, limitations and ways of doing things.

If you have a friend who is not all that bright, or motivated, or self-disciplined—what are the chances for career or entrepreneur success in mail order? All this is exactly my problem. My marks in school were poor. I had neither the ability nor the will to win competitively. I was mentally lazy, had a grasshopper mind and was completely disorganized. I avoided thinking, thoroughness in anything and left carrying through to others.

My solution has been to aim for more limited success and to allow myself to be tempted to work harder than planned because I could do what I liked and could do best. I teamed up with others who could compensate for my weaknesses. I learned to be lazy more efficiently.

We live in a gardener's cottage, not a palace, and drive simple, low-cost cars, eat a cheese sandwich each day at lunch, at our desks, and philosophize. The richest man can drive only one Mercedes at a time, wear one Brooks Brothers suit at a time, and eat one $100 lunch at a time. Many of my richest friends won their wars but now rest quietly beneath the earth.

So I study workaholics and complex successes to find simpler, easier, more limited success segments and a life style away from city smog, dust and smell—as have many others who tell how in this book. There are stories of unusual, off-beat success . . . in obscure hamlets and big cities . . . in mass mail order and in quite small, limited fields. One story, "Fun Mail Order", is just about being in mail order for fun.

Those written about have a message for you. Each protests that he or she has made many mistakes, often failed to do what later proved to be correct . . . and is not all that bright, doesn't always work that hard and is subject to human frailty. They do

not profess to be without flaws . . . or guides to be slavishly followed. They suggest that any of their advice in this book be taken with a grain of salt; that your own careful study of your mail order situation be added . . . and then good common sense applied.

My message is that this book is about people who try, accomplish, help others and want to help you—to decide if mail order is for you and, if so, to find the best mail order opportunity, for you. Finally, if you're uncertain of what to do, have not even thought about mail order before and never trained for it, consider this.

Almost none interviewed, including biggest successes in mail order, had beforehand trained for mail order, planned to go into it, or been familiar with it. Often they had never heard of it. The favorite phrase was that they had "stumbled into it".

There is a chance for many of the rest of us. Within each of many readers of this book, quite new to mail order, may lie the seeds of a direct marketing career or business. We can look into ourselves and find ways to go in our own way at our own pace into and up with mail order.

Chapter 3

Help Available In Mail Order

*For careers, businesses; Fortune 500 or kitchen
table; starting, growing, update.*

Some in mail order are self-taught loners who keep to themselves. Some who are knowledgeable hoard their know-how but try to pick the brains of others. But more succeed through mutual help.

There is help available in mail order—of an astonishing variety . . . for the unsophisticated beginner and the experienced and for any size of business. There is free help, cheap help, expensive help . . . worthless help and dangerous help to avoid. Fortunately, there is also a tradition of help in this business from those most reputable and successful.

Almost everyone I interviewed for each story in this book told me of one or several or many who helped each start, and along the way. Most had multiplied know-how by exchanging information with others in mail order. Each felt that helping newcomers was a way of paying back those who had helped each of them.

This is a book of help by some of the finest, most reputable and most successful people in this business, big and small . . . plus a good deal of reference to a world of reputable help beyond this book—a surprising amount of which I never, before this project, realized existed.

There is so much help available that the problem is to select the most useful to you. At eight hours a day, seven days a week, it would take over two years just to listen to the tapes of the 7,000 speeches which concern direct marketing and have been taped by Hoke Communications. I've listed several hundred most relevant to the stories in this book and other classics greatly praised over the years.

In this book is the story of how Henry Hoke founded what is now Direct Marketing Magazine; how his son, "Pete", transformed it—and created a new kind of publishing business with new magazines, newsletters and the creation and marketing of taped cassettes, all concerned with direct marketing; how the third generation has come into the business; how Hoke Communications, Inc. has become one of the two greatest sources in mail order of possible help; and how readers of this book can use this help most effectively.

There are many help services available through the other greatest source, The Direct Mail/Marketing Association—so many that few members fully realize how much and how many. It took me months of research to find out—and to determine the maximum help the smallest DMMA member can get for least cost . . . and what is available from the Association to non-members, all told in this book. From a variety of sources far more effective help is available to the small, large and medium than taken advantage of. Many in mail order don't realize the scope, are confused by the multiplicity, or think they can't afford it.

Each year more people attend direct marketing shows, Direct Marketing Days and join the direct marketing clubs. But few are aware of how to benefit most. I interviewed attendees and members and did considerable research on shows, clubs and Days. I pass along background information to help readers decide for themselves the practicality for them of each, and the possible priority in time and money to be spent.

Creative people in mail order, copywriters and art directors, help each other with their own organization—The Direct Marketing Creative Guild—both to get started and get ahead in careers. The Women's Direct Marketing Group helps women in any mail order marketing job to rise and women without experience to start. I report how and in what ways each helps.

Each year more people at the entry level in mail order have some amount of specialized training for it. Although still a small minority, these prople now get ahead faster and obtain more top jobs. More and more experienced mail order people update their know-how and extend it by attending seminars. The trend is to specialized seminars on specific areas, but basic seminars still flourish. I review courses and seminars.

In this book, many who made it tell how each got that first job. Many who hire—and top executive searchers specializing in mail order management people—tell what training and experience each looks for. I also tell in this book how to get a wage and salary guide to jobs in the field.

Hardest of all in mail order is to start a business. The first question that comes up is whether the founder has what it takes to make it. From then on it's a problem of what kind of mail order business to start, what items to sell, how to offer them, the creative aspects to get orders and fulfillment nitty gritty. The experience of others can be invaluable help. Each story of each mail order business in this book tells how it started and, step-by-step, its difficulties and ways of overcoming them.

Tiny firms often start with tiny ads and simplest follow-up material—a method called two-step. More big firms use one-step or use a far more sophisticated form of two-step. In this book is help on all of these methods with considerable reference for more detailed help on each. The big can help the successful small to become bigger. But the small help the big even more, as told in this book. The biggest mail order companies, with the latest methods and newest technology, can test far more variations of approach than the small. They can help the small tremendously. Much of what they've learned is available at token cost.

The executives of Time-Life Books, for instance, have passed along in lectures and speeches much of what many millions of dollars of testing have taught them. All this is available on tape or in printed form. In this book one story is "The March of Time-Life Books". Another is on Jerry Hardy, the founder of Time-Life Books. The Help Source Section tells how to get enough tapes and articles by Time-Life Books executives to be a course in mail order.

Consultant experts and top direct marketing agencies help make the mail order rich richer, and create mail order new rich. There are idea people who keep coming up with quite new ways of making money in mail order. There are technology specialists who come up with new automated ways to warehouse, pack, ship and handle mail order customer correspondence—in less space with less people. Such cost-saving specialists have made it possible for some big firms to stay in mail order.

In my book are stories of and about each—and how to get tapes and articles by them to help you. I visited computerized warehouses, shippers and mailing houses and watched them perform every fulfillment function of a mail order business. They cash checks, deposit money, mail literature, ship products, keep mail count records, even do light assembly outside your operation . . . and some for a moonlighter.

If you're rich and don't care for the nitty gritty of mail order, you can have a turn-key situation with everything done for you.

The product is presented to you and shipped for you. You don't have to read the ads or the mail. Others write and run the ads for you and process the mail, warehouse and ship for you.

Many are in the business of helping those in mail order. There are list brokers, managers and consultants . . . media reps who specialize in direct marketing . . . and experts in shipping and fulfillment . . . service bureaus and direct marketing advertising agencies . . . and printers, lettershops, free lance copywriters and a good deal more. I write about many and list more.

Many authorities have contributed much expertise in this book. But even the longest story here can only be an overview. There is far more wealth of help available to those starting out and rising in mail order than can be included. I list a great deal including several thousand pages of free information and several thousand more available at nominal cost.

There are magazine articles, taped cassettes and transcribed speeches which can all help. Some come from magazine files, some from association files and some from files of experts and companies. I've listed how to get each of many of them in the Help Source Guide in this book.

There are some very important and helpful books on mail order marketing and technology. A number of books on advertising are vital to mail order. There are useful books on TV; on catalogs; publicity; legal safeguards and copy cautions; and a range of media buying directories. There are excellent booklets as well as books on list selection; saving money on printing; direct mail; industrial mail order; and telephone marketing. I review a fair number, some in great detail and list a good many more. I indicate which are more sophisticated and which most basic, and how to get them.

I have a story on the DM News and ZIP, in addition to Direct Marketing Magazine. I tell how to get articles at nominal, and for some, no cost—with suggestions of important articles to get. There are also good newsletters which I recommend in the book.

There are far more help sources than written about or listed here. "The Direct Marketing Market Place", which I review in this book, is far more complete. But I do write about or list here at least several representative sources in each of many areas. In my stories and listings is a wide variety of help needed by anybody going into mail order as manager or trainee . . . or even considering a career in it or selling to those in it. There is written and spoken advice from usually expensive experts—yet which can be obtained for very little, or even read or listened to in a library. Some information is free. Sometimes, those sending information even pay the postage or sometimes send for nominal cost.

There's really no need to start in mail order with no information, too little information or misinformation—the reasons for many, if not most, mail order failures.

Chapter 4
My Mail Order Life

Mistakes, lessons and people along the way.

This is my forty-third year in some form of mail order activity.

Our family has been in the advertising field for over seventy years. My father, Huber Hoge, started in the magazine field in 1905. He later joined one of the several then largest agencies, the Frank Seaman Agency. There, he handled some of the largest accounts of the day and stayed for some years until, in 1920, he founded Huber Hoge, Inc.—an advertising agency.

My first job was selling personalized printed letters to direct mail advertisers. Then I worked for the New York Sun. Then I had two other jobs in advertising media and started moonlighting with Huber Hoge and Sons just as my brother John started full-time. John was four years older. First John, and then I, became fascinated with mail order. John got the agency into working for mail order clients. He was my senior and taught me mail order. We developed expertise working with small and then big accounts.

During World War II, John left to run another business owned by another brother, and I ran the agency. Several years after the war, John came back and we ran the business together until he died, at 44, of a heart murmur in 1953.

In the 1950's, I got us into our own items, first in mail order, but then quickly in stores. Our business became largely store distributed. For years a big share was in the fish lure business. Our lures are sold in most logical outlets and sales have increased every year for over twenty years. But in 1982, sales of our Sea Eagle inflatable boats are passing those of our fish lures. We sell our inflatable boats through very fine sporting goods outlets and catalogs. We sell L.L. Bean, Eddie Bauer, REI, Eastern Mountain Sports, Sears and many others. And we sell boats in volume by mail order.

All in all . . . for Hoge clients, Hoge products and before, I've had a fairly diversified experience. I've sold direct mail advertising, bus card advertising and magazine advertising. I've bought magazine, newspaper, TV, radio and direct mail advertising. I've written thousands of ads in every form of advertising. I've worked in our advertising agency for big firms and run our own small businesses. I've sold books for Doubleday, roses for Jackson & Perkins, correspondence courses for American Schools and hundreds of items for other clients.

Whatever I've learned has gone into our business. We've helped our customers sell our products by mail order. It has helped us in sales literature, advertising, even store displays. Everything my family has today comes from what we have made and learned—from mail order.

Today, Huber Hoge & Sons Advertising is chiefly the advertising agency for and a subsidiary of our small, family-owned business, Harrison Hoge Industries, Inc. The Harrison came from Harrison, New Jersey, where at one time our factory was located. We've built a solid net worth for our modest business. This year mail order sales, which are a minority of our business, are running several million dollars. My wife and son now own and run it equally.

The know-how gained has given us a good life. My wife and I live on Long Island Sound, as does my son and his wife . . .

minutes from the factory. Everyday, I walk an hour on the beach. My wife gardens each day. My son takes a paddle. He runs rivers on weekends or surf canoes with an inflatable. My wife is now designing garden products and my son marine items. In business, we sell things we're proud of in a way we're proud of. I find it a joy to sit at a desk across from my wife with my son and sister working in the same room.

Many of our graduates have been more successful than we have. Often they started (from widely different backgrounds) with no knowledge of mail order, learned the business from me and went on to make it in mail order on their own.

One trainee worked for us for nothing for a year . . . but later built up several mail order businesses, one of which he sold for $3,250,000 cash. Another started as a messenger, became general manager and later built a scientific educational toy business which he sold for $700,000. A former accountant became our comptroller and then general manager and went on to organize a mail order sales agency with a contract to handle mail order sales for Walt Disney Records. He built up a business of $5,000,000 a year and sold out for $1,000,000 in cash.

One messenger boy in our firm became a star copywriter for us. Since then, solely from working in mail order for himself and others, he has assembled a modern art collection worth $500,000. Three former partners built (with a fourth partner) and sold out a record business for $505,000 each. One Hoge alumnus became publisher of Soap Opera Digest. One became direct marketing head of Hammacher-Schlemmer.

Great copywriters have graduated from our small advertising firm for over fifty years . . . going on to top jobs in biggest advertising agencies. Some have specialized in broadcast advertising, some in direct mail and some in publication advertising. One of our graduates for years headed the mail order division of Ogilvy & Mather. Another became the creative head of Benton and Bowles. Another became a top writer for Ted Bates . . . three of the ten biggest advertising agencies.

Other graduates used mail order know-how to prosper in other fields. A former general manager became promotion manager of a sizeable record company. One of our copywriters became a war correspondent, another a novelist, another a poet and one a psychiatrist.

Some started small mail order ventures, became mail order consultants, or applied mail order know-how to organizing store distribution businesses. Each taught me as I taught him or her.

In this book, I interview some Hoge alumni. I interview Jack Oldstein who is the biggest list broker in the world (Dependable Lists), Malcolm Smith who did $30 million last year selling records and tapes via mail order, and Gene Schwartz, whose copy launched "Board Room Reports". I tell of a number more.

I am 69 and, in 1975, took a year off to write a book, "Mail Order Moonlighting." By summer 1982, it was in its sixth printing and had over 60,000 copies in print. I call it a professional book on primitive mail order. It has received good reviews.

For readers of "Mail Order Moonlighting" my role is that of an authority on mail order based on over 40 years of experience in it. But in "Mail Order Know-How" I never forget that I'm an observer taking a look at each phase of mail order and direct marketing for any of you who want to get into it and up in it.

My effort has been to ask more people more questions than had ever been asked before about mail order and to pass the answers on to you. For almost four years, seven days a week, writing "Mail Order Know-How" has been for me, taking a Master's degree in today's direct marketing. In each interview I learned something I did not know, after 40 years in this business. I interviewed over 400 people. What I learned changed some of my basic concepts about mail order. The updating of know-how proved immediately applicable to our family business . . . run by my son and wife, with me as a consultant while I wrote the book.

I hope that your reading my book will benefit you as much as writing it has already benefited our business, which has grown dramatically as I've passed along what I've been learning.

Chapter 5
The History of Mail Order

How the mail order method was transformed, widened, became more scientific . . . until enthusiasts said it could sell and advertise almost anything better.

Maxwell Sroge has made a study of it. Bob Stone has written a fine article in Advertising Age on it. Lester Wunderman made a great speech on it. Nat Ross has written for the 1982 Direct Marketing FACT BOOK of the DMMA the most complete history of direct marketing I've read and a splendid one.

Oral ordering of individual items . . . for delivery later by peddler or sea captain . . . started when trade did, long before writing was invented—after which there were orders on clay tablets and papyrus. When the ancient Persians built the first postal service, the first mail orders started.

But for the postal service of the Persians and then of the expanded one of Alexander the Great . . . and then of the empire-wide one of the Romans . . . permitted use was largely for officials. Mail order was for the very few. In the Dark Ages, the post office service deteriorated and then stopped. Then things began to get better. By the 14th century there was a postal renaissance.

First the art of paper making arrived from China and then printing from Korea. After Gutenberg, by 1500, twenty million books were printed in Europe. In the 16th century, printed lists of merchandise were sent as catalogs to mail order buyers for future delivery. The public post office followed all over Europe. In books, one or more pages began to advertise other books, by mail order. In the 17th century came printed newspapers and then magazines. In the 18th century, universal education started. People could read mail order ads.

In Colonial America, postmasters frequently became publishers. They could mail out periodicals and advertising, for themselves, free. Ben Franklin ran the post office in all the colonies for the king, and then the U.S. post office. In 1792, a special postage rate started for magazines, periodicals, books, pamphlets and circulars. But for 60 years, great limitations discouraged mail order.

In 1832, when Abe Lincoln was postmaster . . . at New Salem, Illinois . . . a letter was one or more sheets of paper folded and sealed. The sender paid no postage. The recipient paid 6¢ for each sheet up to 30 miles and up to 25¢ a sheet for more than 400 miles, one dollar for four pages. There were no envelopes.

The British post office put in one penny universal postage. In the U.S., in 1847, came postage stamps. In 1848, the predecessor of the Republican Party had a platform of "Free Labor, Free Land and Cheap Postage". Abe Lincoln, in 1863, brought 3¢ a half ounce postage to anywhere in Union held states. Envelopes, city mail and third class mail started, including packages up to 12 ounces and more for books.

The telegraph created news agencies and an appetite for newspapers, magazines and Brady's photographs. New technology made paper, printing, newspapers and magazines cheap. The stage was set for cheap catalogs, low cost advertising, postage and shipping. Railroads and steamships gave farmers a world market, money and desire to buy. A lack of stores encouraged mail order.

Abe Lincoln was the father. Chicago, closest to most farmers, became the mother. Montgomery Ward, in 1872, became the first healthy child. In 1886 came Sears and later Aldens and Spiegels, all in Chicago.

Later, the post office introduced C.O.D. Suspicious buyers could see a package and then pay. It had the impact of credit cards today. Chicago mail order firms pioneered it. Then mail order came to the cities which, by now, had big population and huge city newspaper circulation. A bigger percentage of magazine circulation now came from the cities.

From here on, stories elsewhere in this book tell much of the history of mail order, and intermingle. Max Sackheim, who wrote great mail order ads, started a great mail order advertising agency and co-founded the Book-of-the-Month Club, shares memories of a career from 1905. Max recalls Nelson Doubleday (Sr.) whose story starting with his first mail order tests before World War I, is also told in this book.

By the 1920's, the New York News became the first picture newspaper, and the movies had made people picture-minded. The News reached people who had not read books, magazines or newspapers before. It used giant pictures, huge headlines, quick captions and street language. It had comic strips with balloons. It concentrated on crime, sex and sports. It was raw. It had mass appeal. It had an explosive effect on advertising.

Ruthrauff and Ryan, in New York City, was then the leading mail order advertising agency. For years Max Sackheim was copy chief. It adapted the Daily News editorial techniques to mail order and created a new mass mail order market and then a new mass way of advertising anything. They created ads with Daily News techniques but ran them in mass magazines as well as newspapers, with tremendous success. Then the Crash changed mail order dramatically.

To be saleable, a mail order offer had to perform a big service. It had to change somebody's life and be a big bargain. To operate profitably in mail order was hard. Mail order companies which started this way in the 1930's had a leanness, a frugality, an efficiency that decades later still gave them advantages. Many big companies today started in a tiny way then.

The depression became the crucible in which the tools were forged that began to make mail order more of a science. There was a survival of the fittest people, companies, products and methods. There were two worlds, the shrinking, shrivelling world of the old methods for the many and the exciting, innovative, booming world for the imaginative few. For them, new trends, new media, new methods offered endless opportunities.

Mail order became much more efficient. The Book-of-the-Month Club, which had modest success in the boom, became a big success in the depression by the use of giveaway books. Many other book clubs today started in the depression and succeeded. New media, like back covers of the comic sections (and, as they appeared, the national magazine supplements), began to work.

New publishers, like Walter Black, became big successes. Direct mail began to pick up.

In this book I tell the story how John Crawley then built Wm. H. Wise and Co. Inc. into a successful how-to publisher which sold more how-to books by mail order than ever before.

The publishers and magazines were in New York. Mail order became more and more a tale of two cities. Ruthrauff & Ryan then adapted the techniques for national advertisers from Lever Brothers to Plymouth cars. Many were so desperate in the depression they'd try anything. John Caples became famous explaining mail order methods. The recency-frequency-monetary formula of analyzing mail order customers changed the way catalogs were distributed. Schwab & Beatty became a great mail order agency with success and integrity.

After World War II, returning soldiers burst into civilian life. With the GI Bill of Rights, so many went to college that in several years more college educated men and women came into business than all through the depression. More women were in business. It was a new wave of vitality.

One thousand new radio station transmitters went on the air and over two hundred TV stations soon followed. Now magazines and newspapers had unlimited paper. Media were hungry for advertising. New families formed, moved into the suburbs, raised families, started gardening, bought shelter magazines and needed everything.

Now there were young optimistic entrepreneurs. Many brought back ideas and even items from overseas. Many were very bright. Some were MBA's. A lot became fascinated with mail order. They thought differently from the depression veterans. They made mail order bigger than it had ever been before, sold far more kinds of products and used new media while using the old more than ever before.

In this book, Milton Runyon tells of a career that started in the 1920's working for Schwab & Beatty and then for Doubleday—assisting Nelson Doubleday (Sr.)—and then, shortly after World War II, running the mail order and book club business of Doubleday as executive vice president. Elsworth Howell was starting to create and build a hundred and fifty million dollar business for Grolier and tells how in this book. John Stevenson had travelled around the world at 21, by mail order, in the 1930's, and brought English book promotions to American newspapers. Later, at Doubleday, he assisted Nelson Doubleday and Milo Sutliffe. After World War II, he started on his own and later launched the first book continuity program. He tells about it in this book.

Then the post war crop of mail order beginners came straight from school. More came from college. By the 1950's, more began to come from graduate schools. By the 1960's, the MBA's began to arrive in greater numbers and far more so in the 1970's.

Mail order firms became bigger. Bigger companies went into mail order. Concepts of what mail order was began to change. In this book are individual stories of many of the people who have made mail order and direct marketing history ever since. I've tried to cover the changes of each decade—the forties, fifties, sixties and seventies, and now the eighties, by stories of some of the mail order people and direct marketers most active in each. I've selected some active as entrepreneurs and in services, tiny and huge, using most heavily direct mail, space advertising or TV—people and companies whose activities can teach us about the areas they each know best.

All through this period, Chicago mail order firms again pioneered much that was new in mail order—direct mail solo pieces and syndication, big ticket merchandise on credit and credit card selling, radio and TV mail order, two-step inquiry from space ads and closure by direct mail and far more.

In this book Maxwell Sroge tells of his mail order mission-ary activities converting big companies such as Bell & Howell, Phillips of Holland and Armstrong Corp. to mail order. Andy Andrews tells how he applied the most scientific direct marketing methods to slash the cost and multiply the response of fund raising. My story on him is called "How to Raise a Billion Dollars."

As Fortune 500 mail order grew and grew, so did New York as a mail order center. It was the money capital, the management capital, the media capital and the list capital. Then, gradually, mail order centers started on the West Coast, in Texas, in Boston and in the South. But world mail order meant mail order centers all over the globe. It's still expanding and developing.

In October 1980, Direct Marketing magazine included a supplement on Chicago, with a history of mail order and direct marketing in the Chicago area. It included a reprint of an article by Henry Hoke Sr., originally published in 1967. It gave an overview of the history of direct mail and first lettershops, as well as of the early days of the trade associations and magazines.

Mike Manzari, of the Kleid Company, gave me some background on the history of the list business in mail order. Montgomery Ward began renting lists from owners over 110 years ago. Before that there was informal swapping of names by mail order firms. Some of the first in the list business were list compilers. Some began in 1890. Ponton & Company, whose story is in this book, started in 1894. Robert Mosely, in Boston, was the first modern list broker starting in the 1920's.

The post office has a history of postal services. Montgomery Ward has a story of the origin of Ward. Two books tell the story of Sears Roebuck. "The Americans, a Colonial Experience", by Daniel T. Boorstin, contains some fascinating stories of the development of mail order from colonial days through the 19th Century. It tells of Ben Franklin's mail order efforts, of Aaron Montgomery Ward and of Richard Warren Sears.

The Direct Mail/Marketing Association asked the equiv-alent organization in each of a number of countries to tell the mail order history of that country. The most complete with earliest references came from the German Association. It's all in the DMMA Manual. In my story on "Pete" Hoke in this book, I tell in detail of the sound archives of Hoke Communications, a non-stop, continuing oral history of the direct marketing world.

In my business lifetime in mail order, the concept of mail order has gradually and then rapidly changed until, in its present direct marketing form, it's quite different—mainly in this way: Mail order was a trial and error way to find out of countless possible products and services—each with different ways of offering, pricing and presenting—an occasional success. The idea was to test in pennies and project the rare success in dollars . . . to wash out many small losses on testing with quite big profits on projections and thus make an overall profit.

Most people thought of mail order as a possible way to make a great deal of money. Anyone might start in a tiny way and make a killing, maybe. For most it was still mysterious and chancy. But segmentation, analysis and research aided by the computer have made direct marketing far more of a science which vastly broadens the variety and numbers of items which can be sold by it.

Direct marketing is now considered a part of all marketing. The concept is now that if a product can be sold profitably through stores, it can also be profitably sold by mail order—by marrying people who want to buy whatever it is to the firm which

sells it. In this book Bob Kestnbaum tells how numbers science can make it safer to select a mail order project or product to offer to present customers and sell it. Much of this book is about many of those who have caused this metamorphosis, and how it all happened.

Advertising to sell mail order or via direct marketing is now called direct response advertising. Direct response advertising is used not just to sell but to get inquiries to follow up, leads for salesmen and for dealers. Direct response advertising, keyed and measured, is used more in the mainstream marketing of biggest companies—to increase sales via stores. More direct response campaigns are created by companies for retail and catalog customers to use.

One latest phenomenon in the history of mail order is world direct marketing. In "The March of Time-Life Books" story in this book, I explain how Time-Life Book sales outside the U.S. have climbed to 58% of total sales. And so the history of mail order proliferates.

In the Help Source Guide in this book, I give details on how to get books, tapes and reprints of any of the historical material on mail order and direct marketing referred to in this chapter. Also listed are tapes and articles concerning world mail order.

Chapter 6
Direct Marketing's Size

*How big is it? What is
it? Not all agree.*

From the beginning of estimates of the size of direct marketing, attaining accurate figures has been a battle. Some say that total sales cannot be measured. "Pete" Hoke, publisher of Direct Marketing magazine, says that direct marketing is not an industry but a concept . . . a method of marketing that is a subdivision of all marketing. Some estimate the total size of direct marketing with a grain of salt.

But the effort to measure direct marketing sales continues. "Pete" Hoke and his Direct Marketing magazine staff constantly gather growth data on the field. The Direct Mail/Marketing Association (DMMA) has been assembling such data. It pub-lishes and Bonnie DeLay edits the Fact Book On Direct Response Marketing, an important research help.

Maxwell Sroge has been making estimates of the size of key segments of mail order, and of its total size, since 1972. Sroge studies largest mail order companies. He combines statistics from annual reports with hard data and estimates he gets directly. Each year Sroge publishes "The United States Mail Order Estimates".

"There is no doubt that the mail order method of selling is growing faster than over-the-counter sales," says "Pete" Hoke. "Retailers are selling more by mail order. More now have catalogs. Department stores are getting more sales increases from mail and telephone than from walk-ins."

The DMMA estimates that direct marketing sales created by direct mail are 28 times bigger than 35 years ago . . . that specialized catalogs of smaller firms (often of carriage items) are now increasing . . . that telephone marketing is up . . . that newspaper reprinted inserts used in direct marketing jumped from 8 billion to 20 billion in one 5-year period—and have continued to jump . . . that credit card buying after hitting an all time high with over half a billion cards out is, despite credit curbs and reduction of gas cards, holding its own.

Maxwell Sroge says, "Mail order is growing faster than the economy." Year after year, Sroge compares 15 publicly owned mail order companies with 13 publicly owned retail chains and with publicly owned manufacturers. Sroge states that these comparisons show for mail order companies higher increase in sales, better profits and higher return on investment.

Direct marketing has been called the "unknown giant" by Bob Stone, author of "Successful Direct Marketing"—because so many firms and executives are still unaware of its power.

But truer words may never have been spoken about its size and growth. No one has ever obtained from every firm in direct marketing the sales of each. Today most direct marketing dollar sales come from companies which also sell in other ways. Many do not release figures of sales. Many who do release only figures of total sales including direct marketing and other sales.

Mail order has so expanded and changed it's hard to recognize, and harder to measure. Today a "mail order" item may be advertised on TV, ordered by telephone and shipped by UPS. Soon you can pay for a "mail order" by instantaneous electronic fund transfer from your bank.

Today only 3% of Sears Roebuck catalog mail orders come by mail. The rest come by telephone from catalog desks in stores and other ways. Today, 97% of mail order firms report they ship by UPS, not by mail. You can still call it mail order . . . or direct response . . . or direct marketing . . . or direct response marketing.

"The common denominator," says "Pete" Hoke, "is the list produced by direct marketing—which can be keyed, allowing results of tests and projections to be measured." Here is the DMMA definition:

> Direct marketing is the total of activities by which products and services are offered to market segments in one or more media for informational purposes or to solicit a direct response from a present or prospective customer, or contributes by mail, telephone or other media.

The umbrella has become so wide that many now considered part of direct marketing don't know it. In its broadest definition, direct response marketing includes areas never dreamed of by yesterday's mail order people . . . from telephone marketing to coupon distribution to sales from inquiry advertising closed by salesmen. The understanding of the definition is probably clearest in the direct mail field and nowhere near equally in all other areas.

Up to 1982, direct marketing sales were estimated in any of three ways. The first accepted the $29 billion figure in a 1959 U.S. Department of Commerce study and has adjusted it yearly to the Consumer Price Index. The second estimated yearly all advertising and direct mail expenditures and multiplied by five. It assumed the advertising cost averaged twenty percent. The third took sales figures of large, public mail order companies if published. It guestimated sales for other big companies. It then guestimated sales for the rest of a field other than the big companies. Sales figures were totalled for each field examined (many have not yet been examined).

Each method was rough but they seemed to support each other. Two methods worked out to similar annual grand totals. The third might if all fields could be examined. So far, no other method has been available. The hope for each method was that errors might balance out.

Most media keep records of ads running by product classification and do not separate direct response advertising. Even if separated there can be confusion as to what to separate. In the past, for example, if a retailer ran a newspaper coupon ad and featured telephone orders in the ad, it was considered to be a mail order ad. If the same retailer ran the same ad without a coupon, it was not.

Separating telephone service calls from telephone selling calls is also difficult. Incoming WATS sales usually have already been credited to the form of advertising which generated them. Duplication can be a problem. And over half the volume of direct response marketing has been attributed to telephone marketing.

Another estimating problem is overlap. One reporting service can in some part duplicate another's data. Another is the reporting period. The Post Office reporting year ends September 30th. Most media report calendar years. Public company fiscal years may end any month.

Actual costs of advertising can vary dramatically from rate card in one medium and be close to rate card in another. In some media such variation will be more or less from period to period and from one publication or station to another. Just assuming actual cost paid for advertising becomes difficult.

Estimating direct marketing sales from direct mail by assuming that advertising cost is 20% of sales volume may work. The same formula may not work in some other media where 20% advertising cost seems low.

The emphasis in measurement is how to get broader agreement defining the field and measure accordingly; to estimate primarily those segments where data is now available and accurate; to get more cooperation and data from industry, government and media; to avoid overlap from data supplied from different sources; to standardize 12-month data reporting periods (to end the same month).

Most media other than direct mail may only gradually provide equally detailed, accurate reports of all direct response advertising in it. But more segments can now be calculated more accurately. Groundwork is being laid to estimate still more segments more accurately and hopefully for overall direct response marketing—at a later date.

Direct response advertising may have grown more rapidly in TV than in any other form of advertising. Now there is an extra bonanza of cable TV mail order. Most station managers and TV sales reps agree there's been a tremendous increase. For Wunderman, Ricotta & Kline, the world's biggest direct marketing advertising agency, TV mail order for clients has been the fastest growing segment of its billing. Lawrence Krutcher, corporate vice-president of Time Inc., in an internal presentation to Time executives, showed that not only was the volume of TV subscriptions a growing proportion of all subscriptions to Time Inc. magazines but that the quality of those subscriptions was excellent - as indicated by renewals of those subscriptions.

But TV mail order volume is still a small proportion of all mail order and TV response advertising is still a small percentage of all TV advertising. A top executive of CBS Columbia House told me that TV mail order sales were only 6% of all Columbia House mail order. In this book, Malcolm Smith who sold thirty million dollars worth of records and tapes by TV in 1981, explains why many still fail in mail order TV.

Previously, direct marketing sales via magazines may have been substantially underestimated. This is despite a possibly over-optimistic assumption that sales from direct response ads in magazines are five times advertising cost. It's despite the drop in recent years of shopping column mail order in some mass women's magazines and shelter magazines. Often in the same magazines, front of book, full-page mail order was gaining. Such ads represent most magazine mail order dollars spent. Yet, the Magazine Publishers Association tabulations show as mail order shopping column and mail order section ads only.

The actual figures of mail order ads run by Family Weekly, Better Homes & Gardens, National Geographic, Woman's Day, Parade, TV Guide, Reader's Digest and Time have probably averaged 50% more than the figure attributed to all magazines. By 1982, business and professional magazine publication advertising was over $2 billion. The Industrial Equipment News produces over one million inquiries a year. T. Richard Gascoigne, Publisher, says: "Ten percent convert to orders but only five percent of these to mail orders. 95% of inquiries are turned over to salesmen, distributors, jobbers or dealers. But almost all advertisers keep track of inquiries and sales produced from them."

Years ago, McGraw-Hill Research found that 23.1% of advertisers used business and professional publications to get direct sales, inquiries for mail follow-up or leads for salesmen. "It's much higher today," says Gascoigne. "Today every McGraw-Hill publication but Business Week uses bingo cards. Most advertisers keep careful records of sales closed."

Today, direct response marketing's surging growth is viewed differently by some experts. Instead of a steady "no surprise" slant on the growth chart, many now see a more irregular pattern. Growth is seen to be flexible, responding to changing conditions. Blocked by higher costs here, it expands there. It slows expenditure in media with sharpest cost per thousand increase. It moves in where opportunities are greater.

Direct marketing's growth is a record of overcoming and getting around obstacles. With more analysis a changing perspective of its size and shape takes form. Inflation is an obstacle race. In a twenty-year period, postage increased over six times. But improved technology, from printing to computers, slowed inflation in every other direct mail area except paper. In the same period, overall costs including postage only went up at the general rate of inflation.

Meanwhile, in many cases, computerized purging, compiling and segmentation of mailing lists increased their percentage response. A Post Office survey made in two different years during this period showed a drop in all classes of mail received per household. Less advertising pieces produced more business with less competition for readership.

Each sharp postage increase caused an immediate sharp reduction in mailing. Then, after careful testing, volume gradually came back. The increase became acceptable, just in time for another increase. Skyrocketing postage has dramatically changed the use of catalogs. The number of one-pound or over catalogs of biggest mail order houses dropped over one-third and then gradually climbed back slightly.

The big catalog houses did more sales than ever. They mailed fewer big catalogs to better customers less frequently and more in peak seasons. They supplemented big catalogs with smaller, specialized ones mailed to customers who had purchased similar items. There are now more small catalogs. "Pete" Hoke estimates there are now a billion yearly.

The right specialized catalogs are growing faster. Herrschner's needlework catalog has grown 25% a year for years. So has R.E.I., (Recreational Equipment Inc.), for camping and backpacker equipment; L.L. Bean went from $8 million to $130 million in 12 years.

It will take years, work and many dollars before most of the entire picture emerges . . . but more segments of direct marketing,

trends, potential opportunities and growth are becoming clearer.

The DMMA got so many inquiries asking for statistical facts about direct marketing that it began to make an increasing effort to research such information. This led to publishing the "Direct Marketing Fact Book", a very unusual project.

Bonnie Rodriguez was the first editor and had the back-breaking job of gathering together for the first time statistics estimated, guestimated and calculated by a wide variety of fact-gathering organizations. The next year, under Bonnie Rodriguez, facts gathered had been sifted, compared and correlated. Under Bonnie DeLay this process has continued and accelerated.

Gradually, the DMMA is drawing on its own resources to get some estimates. In her work with DMMA councils, Bonnie Rodriguez has been working with fact-gathering projects by councils in different fields. There is real hope that statistical relief is on the way. The DMMA Fact Book is developing, too.

The 1982 Fact Book was totally new. The DMMA Statistics Committee met with the Department of Commerce. Editor Bonnie DeLay says, "Martin Baier, Arnold Fishman and 'Pete' Hoke were members of the committee who visited the Census Bureau. They asked that three questions pertaining to direct marketing be included in the next Business Census. The Census Bureau was quite receptive."

The Fact Book has steadily improved in coverage and accuracy, edition by edition. The Department of Commerce cooperation could be all important. They can ask in the Business Census questions which will identify marketing sales and dollar volume of those sales of companies using direct marketing for all or only some of their sales.

The task of the DMMA was to work with existing sources of

such statistics, to encourage sources to develop improved statistics, to get the Census Bureau cooperation in getting new statistics, and finally, to start developing its own estimates from member sources. This is a continuing long-term plan.

"We're working on the Magazine Publishers Association and other media associations. We're going to our media owning members. Up to now the publishers and broadcasters had no vested interest to keep records separately of direct marketing advertising expenditures."

My impression is that the DMMA is determined to strive for an all encompassing figure for sales generated in every industry from direct marketing; that this will be apparent with each issue of The Fact Book; also that until overall figures can be more accurately measured emphasis will be on areas the DMMA feels can be measured more accurately; further, to do so, that the DMMA will control all of the research functions.

For individual offers, companies, fields and media advertising percentage of sales varies . . . from a fraction of the 20% estimate to three times or so the amount. To estimate the average percentage requires estimating total sales versus advertising for each variation.

"We have three volunteer committees working on this. Mary Craven and I have been researching. Rose Harper, Nat Ross—people of that caliber, leaders in the industry—are working on this. It's not easy. So many people perceive direct marketing in so many ways.

"The telemarketing Council has surveyed DMMA members' use of telephone marketing. The figures are just being compiled. The DMMA is making a study of direct marketing sales and advertising of its own members. Bob Hupplesberg, a statistical consultant, is conducting the study. We'll have this information soon.

"The Fact Book will constantly get more complete and more encompassing figures and statistics. As fast as we get data that changes our estimates, we'll adjust future Fact Book editions. From the first edition it has brought together available facts in a much needed way."

The DMMA is working hard to solve the problem of accurate measurement of the size and growth of direct marketing. It can be done. Media can keep records (to their own advantage) of direct marketing advertising. Media salesmen almost invariably know when they are selling advertising to direct marketers. The first step for any media to go aggressively after such business is to keep records of this fast-growing classification.

Even if only key media keep proper records of direct advertising, a good guestimate can be made of similar figures for all media in a classification.

While the average selling cost for direct marketers varies for different forms of advertising from that in direct mail, a reasonable guestimate can be made for each form. Once the selling percentage is assumed, a more accurate multiple is available to project estimated sales from estimated ad expenditures for direct marketing in each form of advertising.

To sum up, direct marketing and mail order sales are growing fast. Growth and size estimates in the past have probably been more accurate in some areas (particularly direct mail) then in others. Errors in segments sometimes may cancel out each other.

But estimates of segment size are becoming more accurate and, year by year, will become more so. Meanwhile, it's reasonable to be dubious about exact figure total direct marketing estimates. And the more detailed and specific such estimates are, the more cautiously they should be considered.

Chapter 7
The Mail Order Graveyard

It's quiet there, rarely talked about—and getting more crowded all the time.

Occasionally, a few big mail order bankruptcies are briefly publicized. Most die quietly with no obituary. For each thriving, healthy mail order venture born there are many more that perish with their first gasp for air. And, for each of these, there are numerous mail order projects aborted before birth.

The stories of success in this book can teach much about what it takes for such achievement. But not one person written about in this book wishes any reader to be misled by the number of successes and lack of failures mentioned here. Instead, they collectively warn you that mail order can be dangerous to the financial health of your company and yourself.

Similarly, the ever-increasing number of newspaper stories and magazine articles of mail order success can overtempt. Trade articles and newsletter reports of constantly increasing direct marketing activities can overexcite. Speeches at meetings and the proliferation of activities and organizations devoted to direct marketing create a gold-rush feeling. Just listening to the more enthusiastic brethren can give an impression of near universal success for anything sold by anyone through mail order.

The truth can be far different. Tiny mail order dreamers start their little ventures with no present customers to sell related products to . . . with no concept of what to sell—when, how and to whom . . . with no experience, advisors or sophisticated tools. Many perish. Many lose much in mail order, with the big often taking the biggest losses.

Westinghouse bought Longines-Wittenauer and the Capitol Record Club for over ten million dollars, lost close to ten million more and closed it down. General Foods had high hopes for Fabrizaar-Creative Village selling creative stitchery, invested millions in it and closed it down. With all its sophisticated know-how, Time-Life Books paid over $1,000,000 for Haverhill's, a mail order catalog, and then decided it didn't fit and closed it down.

Western Union started Gift America, with great plans to build a gift mail order house business by telephone . . . but then stopped it. John Blair launched "Books by Phone" but later gave it up. At one time, Damar, Greenland and Foster and Gallagher Catalogs were distributed by the tens of millions. Now they are no more. Publishers Clearing House operated a merchandise mail order operation and then dropped it. Douglas Dunhill was a big syndicator of mail order items for oil companies but went out of business.

The list is endless and keeps growing. Klein's Sporting Goods was successful for years with a mail order catalog and then went bankrupt. Kaleidoscope, with its gorgeous color catalog of lush fashion gifts, closed in bankruptcy. So did Holiday Gifts and Griffin Ltd. American Consumer advertised with full pages everywhere before going bankrupt. Sports Liquidators distributed ten million catalogs a year and then went bankrupt.

Initial mail order success and intriguing potential do not guarantee continued mail order prosperity.

Mail order ads, mailings and catalog pages are becoming

business. The business did not make a profit. The average sale was not high enough. There were no related follow-up items to create more sales to original customers.

For many companies successful in mail order, many new products fail. For many companies beginning in it, all efforts to sell by mail order fail. When mail order success does come, it may seem perpetual and be only temporary. Even a non-fatal mail order disaster can take most of a business lifetime to recover from. I could write a book far longer than this one on mail order failures.

"The Mail Order Graveyard" need not be so crowded. To avoid it, always keep aware of it, study how others stay out and do likewise. And if you get carried away by any success described in this book, reread this chapter.

Chapter 8
Mail Order Entrepreneurship

Can it be taught? If so, how?

more and more evident all around us. The impression is of their seemingly constant, ever-growing success. Yet, all that glitters is far from mail-order gold. The mortality of items, offers and approaches—in any media, by even the largest companies—is tremendous.

Sears Roebuck, in September 1980, launched in its catalog a 16-page section promoting gourmet foods. Sears offered a luscious feast of gift packages from king crab legs to fresh fruit and imported cheese. The expected piece de resistance was the offer of luxury steak cuts. The 16-page section was mailed separately to 350,000 businesses, but meat orders did not amount to anywhere near the sales hoped for. Even the mighty can fall.

And the small can march like lemmings to the sea or, if in a greater hurry, fly like moths into the flame. I called 25 people who advertised, with a classified ad, recipes for a dollar or so. Twenty-two of them lost most of the cost of the ad. These were first-time mail order entrepreneurs, drawn irresistably to run the ads they did because so many others were running recipe ads. Sometimes mail order items sell—with some success, but simply not enough to continue. This was the experience of one man who started a retirement business based on his professional career.

He was a travelling circus performer in the 1920's and 1930's . . . an aerial bar artist in the big tent. He photographed it all . . . Belgian horses pulling circus street parade wagons, elephants unloading from circus trains, cowboys and cowgirls with mounts . . . bareback riders, lion and tiger trainers in action . . . ponies, dogs, monkeys . . . clowns, acrobats, flying acts . . . beautiful girl aerialists and much more.

He put it all in Circus Life In Pictures, 100-page book . . . 6"x9" . . . with each picture enlarged. He was publisher, ad writer and ad buyer. He ran in circus and horse magazines he subscribed to. He started with small space and then tested a full page in Band Wagon and White Tops circus magazines and in Western Horseman. Five dollar orders came in until he had only 52 copies left . . . but not enough to print more books and continue the

What are the traits of a mail order entrepreneur? How can you recognize one, become one or become a better one? What background and experience is most conducive to entrepreneurship?

For almost three years I've talked with major (and smaller) entrepreneurs for this book. Before that, I talked for another book to smallest mail order entrepreneurs. Before that, I grew a few. I believe that the traits, the experience and the background of a mail order entrepreneur can be observed and noted. The effectiveness of a mail order entrepreneur or kind of entrepreneurship can be measured by mail count.

My belief is that entrepreneurship has deep roots. An entrepreneur draws on experience, background and instinct. It's an ability to relate something in the past to the future . . . and to apply concepts gradually developed to new opportunities discovered.

Mail order entrepreneurship makes it all happen, from gleam-in-eye to bottom line. It comprises many abilities to spot the trend, see the chances, pinpoint the opportunity and get the idea to cash in on it; to recognize surmountable obstacles—and stone walls not to bang heads against; to realize limitations and drawbacks; to compare these with potential volume and profit and determine practicality; to see the high costs of low volume tests and translate them into the low costs of big projections when judging results.

It's the ability, then, to point the way; persuade bosses, backers, associates, employees, vendors to join in; to plan it, man it, do it . . . pull it all together, make it happen. The dictionary calls this the role and function of the entrepreneur.

An entrepreneur, the dictionary says, is the organizer of an economic venture; one who organizes, owns, manages and assumes the risks of a business; one who promotes, a practitioner; one who serves as an intermediary, a middleman, a go-between. Entrepreneur is derived from the French verb, entreprendre—to undertake. But let us not be mail order undertakers.

An entrepreneur is responsible for operation of a business . .

, choice of product, raising capital, deciding on price and quality, hiring and firing, expanding and reducing facilities. He or she runs the risks, present and future, and is responsible for and benefits or suffers from profits or losses. The entrepreneur seeks out and takes the risks of introducing more efficient methods. An entrepreneur sees possibilities and potentials others don't, and makes things happen that otherwise could not. He has the insight to zero in on the just-right-for-us aspect of mail order.

The manager is an entrepreneur. He's often a generalist who must make decisions after analyzing the recommendations of specialists. Successful companies organize participation management and develop an entrepreneur spirit. The internal entrepreneur is the organizer and monitor of the flow of interactions in an organization. One approach in training managers is to place a man immediately on a job in which he has responsibility for results, and is highly interested in.

Quality of entrepreneurship can determine greater or less success of an individual, a company and even a country. Mail order entrepreneurship is simpler, quicker, lower cost and more measurable.

In "Mail Order Moonlighting", I describe the entrepreneurial ingredient needed in mail order as "Fingerspitzengefuhl", a feeling at the tips of the fingers for what to do and not to do. It's a German phrase which referred to Rommel in the desert in World War II, when he sensed when to attack and when to retreat and when the British were about to attack or withdraw. There is an instinct for mail order but the traits most effective for its application differ.

There are many roads to Rome. Entrepreneurs vary widely in their traits, experience and background. The kind of entrepreneurship needed varies substantially with different businesses and even different stages of the same business.

In this book are stories of many great mail order entrepreneurs. Some have an uncanny feel for what to sell and how to present it. Often, it's the sum of their previous life experience, of what Father, Mother, or both, gave. Many were brought up with good working habits. Most have great imagination. Many are highly competitive. Some almost instantly see product promotion possibilities. Many are good at figures, organized and pragmatic. Some have a special talent to identify with their mail order customers in their needs and wants.

A trait I've noted as important is simplicity. Lowest middle management often uses big words. The biggest boss usually uses the smallest words. Simplicity leads to selectivity of the most important, to streamlined projections to the maximum.

Some have a rare sense of timing and of opportunity and a driving, intense energy when needed. One important trait is the ability to concentrate, be self-sufficient, use time effectively, and project success to the maximum. Some combine much needed skills, for instance, to be a dogged, thorough researcher, a superb copywriter, an able buyer and a careful cost watcher.

As a company grows huge and the team becomes more important, entrepreneurship tends to become more discrete. An internal mail order entrepreneur may walk the plank if ads don't pull or, high above, policies change. Being too successful can be dangerous. Bravery becomes a vital trait.

Some have strong gut feelings and enthusiasms. They like to sell what they like. Some have a talent for selecting, training and leading people. Some are analytical, some adventurous, and some mathematical. Some remarkable mail order entrepreneurs are all three.

Some entrepreneurs have found success by concentration on a single product or a single field, by doing one thing at a time and doing it to perfection. Others seem to thrive on diversity, on a variety not just of products but of partnerships, joint ventures and businesses. Some work steadily with a definite but limited schedule, others pour out their efforts until it would break most people. And some do so until they suddenly sell out or retire.

Some can be friends with and work closely and personally with a number of people in various ventures at the same time. Interlocking activities sometimes make them safe. These entrepreneurs thrive on complexity.

Some can carry their businesses in their heads and do business on the phone, all day long. Some have an unusual ability to buy and sell items, media and even businesses. Some write almost all their own copy. Some have a great feel for picture elements. Others are great editors of mail order copy. Some rely creatively on others.

On rare occasions, an entrepreneur finds sudden, enormous success with a breakthrough others consider inexplicable or a temporary aberration and that surely must collapse tomorrow . . . and yet, which becomes even more successful.

Some know how to sense the opportunity, how to form the offer, create the copy and give elegance and credibility. Some have a flair at getting the maximum information from the test and can project and proliferate the smallest initial success.

Some have audacity. Many are perfectionists. Some make all entrepreneurial decisions and do everything possible themselves. Some attract top talent. Some are great at delegating. Most have a lot of ideas and a flair for persuasion of associates. Entrepreneurship often starts in childhood. Some seem to know how to do almost anything right, the quality way. Some are strong in timing when to drive, plunge and proliferate.

In this book, I've told the stories of many entrepreneurs with quite different traits, training and experience. Which trait is most important? Some say it's the killer instinct. The story of each entrepreneur told in this book gives more clues to what traits in yourself may give entrepreneurial strength. For some it's been missionary ability . . . carrying the mail order word to others . . . seeing the mail order method as a form of marketing far more universal than mail order, for instance.

Often mail order entrepreneurship is perceiving quite new mail order opportunities in existing situations, as stories in the book show. Jerry Hardy saw how to sell sets of books to Time and Life magazine subscribers. Others saw how to use new computer applications to create opportunities in list brokerage.

Eddie Bauer got an idea for insulated jackets and sleeping bags, using down material . . . and became father of the many-

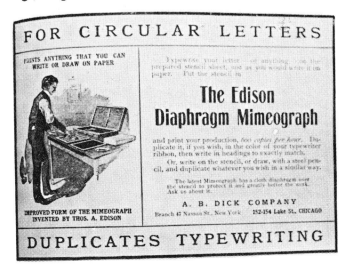

billion-dollar padded coat industry—and of a great mail order catalog. Henry Harris saw how to form his stamp collecting hobby into a mail order business . . . when he was 14 . . . with a free classified ad given by the Washington Post to any teenager-owned business. The Talbots saw how to turn a flair for selecting fashion merchandise for working women and their small specialty fashion shop into a mail order catalog. All three became General Mills subsidiaries.

An entrepreneuse is a woman entrepreneur. Women, as told in this book, have proven to have a special feel for mail order entrepreneurship. I call Joan Throckmorton "the lady with the laser mail order mind". Rose Harper, President of the Kleid Company, uses her accounting background to be a great entrepreneur for her list clients, even making up a profit and loss balance sheet for each campaign. Robin Smith, President of Publishers Clearing House and former president of ten Doubleday book clubs, feels that women have risen in mail order management because entrepreneurship can be measured by the mail count and prove their ability.

Entrepreneurship in direct marketing is needed by any Fortune 500 company that goes into it and by the tiniest moonlighters who start with a classified ad. I've talked at length to many of the smallest and tell some of their stories in this book.

These people taught me that entrepreneurship can be used for limited objectives in mail order to sell Italian Queen Bees, castle guides to Europe, harpsichord kits and stained-glass window kits.

The kind of entrepreneurship needed varies from small companies to big ones, from new companies to established ones. The kind needed by executives to further careers varies—and the kind suited to and possible for them. It even varies by time of life, by home situation and by temperament.

A company and an individual can customize entrepreneurship to objectives and limitations. I used to think that only certain products sold a certain way could succeed in mail order. But with today's direct marketing, it's no longer a question of finding products but of fitting right ones to appropriate companies. Prosaic items can be the most profitable, when offered to those precisely needing them. And each company and each executive can look inside at past history for the entrepreneurship most needed.

The qualities and traits needed for entrepreneurship are so many and varied that almost all of us have some of them. The opportunities for entrepreneurship are so different and require such different specific qualities that each of us possesses some traits ideally suited to some situations.

Within each of most readers of this book is the seed of some possible mail order business, and probably a number of them. The trick is selectivity to choose the entrepreneurship situation particularly opportune to your personality, character traits, background, upbringing, interests, training and experience.

This is a book of mail order entrepreneurship. Read the stories of success, whether in a specialized, small niche or on a huge scale. Compare your traits and experience. Find a success by someone most similar to you in likes and dislikes, abilities and life style. Then consider that area.

Chapter 9
The Mail Order Scientists

They analyze, advise and plan . . . predict, compare . . . signal to stop or go, speed or slow . . . make mail order bigger, safer, more universal.

They moved in from a dozen disciplines and use new technology from dozens of fields. They have changed mail order completely. Many practitioners today feel that the mail order method has become a science that can sell and advertise almost anything better.

Many tell how in this book: by segmentation, the matching by computer of those specific people who most need and want a specific kind of item to the maker and seller of it; the matching of items most likely to appeal to the tastes of present customer lists; the matching of the most appropriate offer, appeal, presentation to these lists; applying the scientific selection of whom to sell what to in the choice of outside lists and media.

To puzzled old-timers, they seem to have changed the street signs in mail order. They brought with them a new nomenclature—necessary to learn before reading direct marketing magazines, newsletters and books. The terms used in the business graduate schools came with the MBA's. The computer programmers and systems analysts brought theirs. Each science borrowed from added more.

Orlan Gaeddert is a statistical scientist who works almost entirely for those in mail order. He has created a mathematical model to develop break-even points. It's so simple it works on a palm-sized calculator. Bob Kaden, president of Goldring & Company, has—for largest companies—pioneered research in mail order: to find and develop items, create offers, develop copy, select copy and headlines; to resurrect a failed test and make it a winner; to trade up a company while increasing sales—all by asking customers and prospects research questions, quite aside from making mail order tests.

In World War II, a psychiatric profile was made of Hitler for the Allies. When Kennedy met Khrushchev at Vienna, the Russians had psychoanalyzed Kennedy, and the Americans Khrushchev. It became standard operating procedure in diplomacy, and them domestic politics. Since then, the psychologists and psychiatrists have moved into mail order, bringing their vocabulary.

From sociology came factor analysis to determine which of many traits each of us has that are shared by others; and to arrive at personality profiles, based on shared traits of specific groups: of readers of a certain publication; viewers of a certain TV show; of those comprising a list of buyers of certain mail order items; of residents of a zip code area. Computers speeded it all up: all this brought a smorgasbord of new words.

Borrowing from astronomy, came the study of population growth; then actuarial studies of insurance. Then came mail order probability scientists. Professor Robert C. Blattberg teaches statistics and marketing at the University of Chicago. He is an authority on setting up mail order tests more scientifically. He assists management to project successful tests with more certainty that roll out results will hold up. To do so, he helps design tests and judge results.

At Printronic Corporation of America, which produces personalized letters for mail order firms, laser-printed words pour out of computers . . . faster than ever printed in the history of the world, before lasers . . . on paper that moves at twenty miles an hour. The process can print the Bible in a minute, with each page in a different language, and personalize each paragraph.

More science in mail order can confuse newcomers and make seasoned veterans wonder about what they don't know. It causes more new expertise to become more specialized. It means that everyone in mail order needs at least touch base with mail order know-how. Some do. Others use latest words and phrases glibly which can befog and make mail order less, rather than more, exact. But the elite that understand most prosper most.

Bob Kestnbaum is a Harvard MBA. With a staff of seven more MBA's, he's a "super consultant" on mail order to the Fortune 500. He believes that with numbers science, virtually no mail order disaster need happen; that most mail order losses need not occur; that sales and percentages of profit of profitable items can often be sharply increased.

AIM is a computer robot system, the intelligent mail order machine. It reads blip code computer marks and then selects inserts at high speed. It inserts into Mrs. Rich's bill a fur coat ad and into Mrs. Plain's one for a plain cloth coat. AIM uses scientific segmentation to insert less and sell more at lower cost. MAGI is a group of scientists, physicists and mathematicians out of atomic laboratories—and into mail order to provide solutions to problems of list maintenance, list selection and computer letters.

Art Blumenfield is a programming systems analyst who, as a consultant, has pioneered the computerization of mail order. His specialty is programming practicality, determining what computers can and cannot do better in specific mail order situations and how best to use them.

Dr. C. Fremont (Monty) Sprague founded Policy Development Corp. PDC computer models prepare for mail order firms detailed cash flow predictions, when assumptions are fed in: for various several-year plans, with complex variables. Models analyze a five-year buying history of customers from different sources, compare and evaluate. Models compare personality profiles of past customers and future prospects. They help match lists to products and new products to present customers.

In direct mail, biggest medium of biggest mail order firms, technological change and the new mail order science has been biggest—from printing to list selection. But even on the periphery, the way mail order can be conducted is being altered. Suppliers, consultants, creative people and specialists in many areas are affected.

The scientists have been a part of an evolution. The transformation of the mail order method into direct marketing took place as the computer was introduced and developed and was greatly aided by it. Each is becoming more and more universally used and more necessary—although often misunderstood, misused or not used to its potential.

The mail order method, now called direct marketing, is not an industry. Rather, it cuts a swath through almost every kind of business. It is a form of selling which constantly accelerates . . . for manufacturers and importers, wholesalers and to business—to widest markets and small, specialized ones . . . in the U.S. and world-wide. There's a simple reason. Those who use it effectively prosper more than the economy, sometimes when the economy shrinks and often more than competitors.

This can be so for the small as well as the large. Mail order can make the smallest, local retailer a national business. The most specialized jobber in a limited field can become a catalog house. The smallest manufacturer can launch a new product with national advertising—which, instead of being an expense against trade sales, can make a profit in mail order sales. Properly used, the mail order advertising can force distribution.

Mail order can pioneer new kinds of products before retailers accept them or are even aware of the field. Mail order tests for a quite different product can catapult an enterprise into an entirely different business. Mail order can provide increased volume for a small business and lower overhead and production cost.

Retailers give more counter space to fields of products which are growing. When growth flattens, counter space shrinks. Customers no longer get adequate choice of color, sizes and model. Mail order can preserve for loyal customers availability of product in a shrinking field by organizing a specialized catalog business.

Mail order know-how has become important to growth in almost any business. It's a way to make advertising, the universal salesman of business, more efficient. A salesman who does not effectively ask for the order is considered of far less value than one who can. More and more, efficient advertising is expected to ask for an order or an inquiry which is then followed up—and results are traced to individual advertisements, direct mailings or commercials . . . and then analyzed to modify future advertising for improved effectiveness.

This can be done for a florist, boutique, department store, wholesaler, manufacturer, for just about any kind of product or service sold to people, industry or the trade. Direct marketing can provide leads for salesmen or for follow-up by literature on a two-step method, often a series of mailings to close a sale. It can raise funds for charities and non-profit organizations. It can sell theater tickets, get concert subscriptions, solicit members for a resort club.

A car can be driven and a TV set watched with almost no knowledge of what is inside the motor or set. Performance still satisfies and is reasonably standard. But a computer or direct marketing must be custom adapted to the user's needs to be effective.

Many still fail in mail order. So few use the new methods to anywhere near potential effectiveness that those who do comprise an elite. They are members of the mail order club, an inner circle. They have a considerable advantage over others. They consistently succeed in their careers and businesses. Some of them tell how in this book.

Some own big ventures. Most are professional managers, specialists, members of a unique talent pool for biggest companies with big advantages—a famous, trusted name . . . a big organization . . . big buying power, and a far greater advantage, latest know-how which they constantly update, exchange and thus multiply.

Members of this group do not consider themselves mail order people as much as direct marketers who use methods as directly measured as mail order but far more sophisticated. In this group are the very bright, very motivated and most self-disciplined. Some are surprisingly young and have acquired know-how surprisingly fast. The group includes a rapidly increasing number of women.

I'm not referring to any actual club of formal membership but to those who ride the ever-growing wave of direct marketing, accelerate it and benefit from it. This wave started when mail order did. It gathered speed when computers, credit cards and telephones transformed every aspect of making money by mail order. Each year it makes mail order more of an art and science.

Most members of this inner circle know and work closely with each other. Once in it, members generally prosper for life. Executives rise and companies grow faster. Success is more stable and opportunities for further, faster success more frequent.

The primary advantage of each in the group is the know-how he or she possesses. But there is no desire to keep it to themselves. Instead, the only barrier to still more and faster growth seems to be the problem of finding new talent to pass along know-how to. Much of this book comprises an effort by members of the inner circle to pass along to you the know-how advantage each has. Direct marketing technology and technique keep changing. Methods that worked last year often don't this year. Keeping updated is a constant process.

Mail order science costs money but is often very cost efficient. Sometimes it's impractical. Often it's a substitution for testing which sometimes can be as expensive as, or more expensive than, testing. It's not a way to fly in mail order on automatic pilot. It can tremendously aid an entrepreneur but is no substitute for entrepreneurship. It's not a substitute for brains or hard work. It usually requires more of both to benefit.

Is scientific mail order a monopoly of the big? Can a small or tiny mail order firm wanting to grow big have access to it? Is it a monopoly of the technically super-educated? If you're ambitious and want to use it in your career, how can you master it?

While much technology is patented, there is no patent on the scientific method in mail order. It is not kept a secret. The elite that is most informed about it has chosen to be. Its availability and practicality is not confined to the super big. The super bright and super trained do have a big advantage in understanding and benefiting from it but often become super specialized.

Often such specialists work for natural entrepreneurs with less brains and specialized training but who are highly motivated, driven and self-disciplined and have a good overview education of all mail order. Of course, the more the natural entrepreneur is a mail order scientist the better his or her chance.

But far from keeping such know-how to themselves, biggest companies and authorities make it surprisingly available to anyone who wants it, and encourage all to take it—as is specified all through this book.

In this book I tell the story of Policy Development Corp.; of Orlan Gaeddert; Bob Kaden; Professor Bob Blattberg; Printronic; Bob Kestnbaum; AIM; MAGI; Art Blumenfield; and printing technology change. In most interviews with executives of biggest firms I discussed just how scientific each considered mail order to be, as done by their firms, by their bigger competitors—and by average to smaller firms. I particularly asked executives and experts to compare actual vs. potential use of latest scientific mail order methods available.

Almost all felt that few in mail order yet use scientific mail order to the degree they could. Most executives felt that their own firms were doing a pretty good job but could do better, but that most other larger firms were not and that almost all smaller firms were not. Some experts felt that many in largest firms were not aware of, did not feel comfortable with, did not believe in, did not use, or misused latest scientific aids.

My conclusion is that scientific mail order near its full potential is an ideal more talked about than attained. It's an indication just how profitable mail order often is that big businesses are still being built using far less scientific methods

than possible. But those that are most scientific overall do far better.

But what chance does a small newcomer have to succeed without the aid of the mail order scientists? Curiously, excellent—under certain circumstances to start in a tiny, small or limited way. I tell how, in detail, in my story "Big vs. Small in Mail Order". The big disadvantage to the tiny and small is that they rarely can become big without learning and applying the scientific mail order methods used by the most successful big.

Chapter 10
Mail Order Risk

How some reduce it,
sometimes avoid it.

Risk is part of mail order life. But biggest mail order successes rarely have biggest risks. Big mail order risk takers sometimes have big bankruptcies. Any way to avoid or diminish mail order risk, any example of doing so can be worth studying. Let's examine the problem of risk, under the most difficult of mail order conditions, particularly how the small survive.

One way is to avoid risk. Boynton (Tony) and Michele Selden are moonlighters whom mail order got started . . . whose business has been profitable every year, has sent three children (now grown) to prep school and then to college and is busily building up a tidy net worth right now. Yet, the Seldens have never taken a mail order advertising risk.

The Seldens began as moonlighters with the Needle Easel. Tony invented it as a favor for a needle-pointer friend. Tony is an electronic engineer. The friend found it hard to hold her needlepoint on a frame when she needed one hand on top of the needlepoint and one hand on the bottom. The Needle Easel is made of wood. Tony engineered it to support the needlework project and allow stitching with both hands. The friends, and other needlepointers, liked it a great deal.

Soon needlepointers wanted to order Needle Easels. Tony arranged for a Shelter Workshop to assemble and pack it. Michele submitted it to Parade Magazine's new product column, "Parade of Progress". Parade ran a fifty word and picture story at no cost. It quoted prices and gave ordering information with the Seldens' address.

From this one story in Parade, readers ordered over one thousand Needle Easels. Dollar sales totalled over $21,000. Needlework dealers also ordered as did wholesalers and companies from foreign countries (asking for distribution rights). It became a no-risk bonanza. The Seldens have been prudent. They have never bought a mail order consumer ad.

They methodically followed up the opportunity the Parade write-up made possible. Some of the same retailers, jobbers and foreign companies who originally answered the free Parade write-up are still buying the Needle Easel . . . and new sister products. Six or seven jobbers buy regularly. One jobber mails 5,000 retail accounts.

Michele runs the fulfillment end of the business. Each day she writes up orders, goes down to the Shelter Workshop and gets orders packed and ready for United Parcel Service to pick up. Each day's orders go out the next day.

Tony's original work was with jet engines and jig borers. He continues in electronics. But he has found moonlighting as a needlework accessory designer just as challenging. The Needle Easel's patent number is 3730077. Three sister products have two more patents. The new products are a latch hooking stand, a floor stand and six sizes of frames.

For years Tony has been learning more about needlework problems, and often developing solutions. One product, brought out in August 1981, helps the needleworker's eye to see more clearly and work more easily with fine detail projects. It is a simple clamp-on with two flexible goosenecks mounted on a spring clip to grip round or flat surfaces. At the tip of one gooseneck is a small flood light which provides glare-free white light . . . and of the other a five inch diameter magnifying lens for undistorted magnification. Both lamp and magnifier can be adjusted separately for perfect focus.

The combination enlarger and light proved an instant success . . . when introduced to needleworkers without risk by editorial write-ups, and by a simple black and white mailing to retailers who already have been purchasing from NEEDLE-EASE. This time Tony and Michele had a product with applications far beyond needlecraft. They sent a glossy photograph and suggested editorial write-ups to over a hundred specialized publications.

Free write-ups brought in orders. A dental journal described and showed it. Orders came from dental labs. The same thing happened with a magazine on electronic production and one for fly fishermen. The Enlarger-Lite is a handy eye-saver for engraving, electronic asembly, modelmaking, or other close-in work. It sells for $49.95. Tony's father-in-law uses it to read The Wall Street Journal, suggesting another market as a reading lamp and lens for anyone who has difficulty reading small type.

The Seldens carefully make only the number of items experience has shown they can sell. They are obligated to the Shelter only per unit made and shipped. They have no employees and no overhead except use of their home and phone. Selling expenses are usually only a little travel cost.

From the first mail order from Parade to the store orders received by mail each day, it's been a no-risk business.

The big are not averse to reducing and avoiding mail order risk. Sometimes for biggest companies, it is not politically possible internally to get an important project budgeted. Or it may be very difficult to do so. Getting started without risk can be the answer. It has sometimes been so in mail order.

Of the top ten of Fortune 500 companies, five started in mail order without risk. They are the oil companies . . . Exxon (2), Mobil (4), Texaco (5), Standard Oil of California (6), and Gulf (8). Because there was no budget . . . and no desire for one . . . syndicators took the risk for the oil companies. They still do (to their profit) . . . even when the oil companies each profitably make up to tens of millions of dollars of sales a year by mail order.

A no-risk start is often desirable for the big and necessary for the small. Pat Schatz is a Malverne, New York, housewife who has made it in mail order using seemingly unrelated advantages . . . and a flair for no-risk promotion.

Pat's first advantage was her hobby. It started when she was a child. Her parents took her to the Danbury Fair in Connecticut and let her buy some Swedish huck weaving designs demonstrated there. Starting with making "finger tip" guest towels with the huck designs, Pat made a lifetime hobby of huck weaving. Twenty years later, her huck weaving skills became the basis of her present mail order and retail business.

Pat is a former teacher, another big advantage. This gave her the ability to instruct others in her hobby. At Brooklyn College, she developed a third advantage, the ability to write interestingly . . . and persuasively. But "more valuable than a college education" and a tremendous advantage has been Pat's experience working her way through college . . . in the public relations business.

Everything helped, particularly Pat's mother, Frances Gordon. Pat's upbringing made her a hard worker, frugal and organized. She had an instinct to be cautious and to avoid risk, as did her mother.

First, Pat wrote three beginner instruction booklets on Swedish huck weaving and self-published them (she is now completing research for her own book on huck weaving). Next, Pat and her mother started The Huckery, P.O. Box 59, Malverne, NY 11565.

The Huckery sells everything necessary for Swedish huck weaving . . . from materials to Pat's booklets; from Pat's award-winning designs to complete project kits designed by Pat. It's the only company in the U.S. to specialize solely in huck weaving.

It wasn't all easy. For the first five and a half months, Pat concentrated on a retail shop. Then Pat discovered mail order, but not from buying ads. She used her publicity flair to get free advertising through editorial write-ups. It started slowly. "The first year was rough. We lost money."

By the second year, Pat's publicity stories got so many inquiries followed by orders, it put the shop in the black. It then made mail order the big end of the business. Aside from the cost of printing simple brochures to follow-up inquiries from free publicity, The Huckery has still spent a bare minimum on mail order advertising!

McCall's Needlework has run a free shopping column write-up. Creative Craft's Magazine ran a four-page article written and signed by Pat and her mother. House & Garden ran one of Pat's articles, Women's magazines ran stories. "Any magazine that runs an article must make a brochure offer." When inquiries come, brochures are mailed back. Then the cash comes.

The key to Pat's success is her design and promotion ability. Pat never studied art after junior high and high school. "I just passed it." But in Pat's hobby, she found she had a gift for design. Pat has created over fifty innovative variations of huck designs.. . from the simple to complex . . . towels, placemats, pillows, skirts, you name it. "We keep adding, practically weekly."

Pat has become a recognized authority in her field. Home Sewing Trade News states that "practically through her efforts Swedish weaving is once again assuming its rightful place as an exquisite craft with daily practicality."

Pat's mother now designs and produces kits, frees Pat to create and promote . . . and makes it all possible. Pat and her mother have become top designers in their field and Pat an excellent writer on it. She has developed a knack of creating the kinds of designs and stories that particularly appeal to each publication.

A busy lady at 36, Pat has appeared on a mini-series on cable TV and is full of plans for more stories, designs and books. She has many new product ideas to develop. Each has a new publicity possibility. She credits her success to her hobby, her school teaching and her mother. But Pat will always remember that no-risk promotion permitted The Huckery to survive . . . and succeed.

In this book, Montgomery Ward's Dick Cremer tells how he tested almost without risk to Ward an entirely new mail order project which led to the future formation of five Montgomery Ward specialty mail order companies. Dick is president of each. Together, in 1981, they did over $150,000,000 in sales.

Domus Ltd. of Kansas City will transform your Volkswagen Bug into a unique pickup truck . . . by mail order. It all started in 1970 when Drake Koch, fresh out of design school, started work on this unusual idea. He designed and built a fiberglass kit that converts any Bug into a sporty pick-up. Installed in one weekend using only hand tools, it offers VW economy with pick-up versatility.

A friend of his, Jim Tharp, ran a successful VW shop with an expanding parts business. He was a natural marketer. As a Bug owner himself, he loved the kit and immediately had ideas how to market it by mail order. Another friend, Tillar Swalm, was a Bug owner, a mechanic and had a flair for writing and layout. A business, owned and managed by Jim Tharp, but sharing profits with all three was formed under the name, Domus.

Drake had only planned on a flatbed kit. Jim decided that a camper version should be introduced simultaneously. Jim had a machine shop. The three worked together to improve and perfect the kits which were finally ready to market in 1972. Each kit originally sold for a little over $400. The converted Volkswagens had style and quality. Tillar created a press kit and literature with the same feeling. There were lots of pictures, plenty of detailed engineering drawings and brief but clear explanations. Both were professionally done in layout, typography as well as specification copy; each came across with sincerity and enthusiasm.

The press kits and literature went out to magazines which seemed logical as prospects to run news stories on the kits. Thirteen magazines ran stories. Road & Track and Motor Trend ran a one-half page each. Hot Rod ran a full page and Popular Mechanics a small story as did Volkswagen fan magazine. Popular Science ran a full page.

Inquiries began coming in from the stories. The same press kits and literature sent to the magazines now went to those inquiries. Mail order sales started immediately, at no advertising cost. The Popular Science story was the most successful of all. Inquiries and then sales kept coming in from the stories, all from the free publicity. For two years Domus did no advertising while selling all the kits that could be made.

Then Domus ran a four-inch ad in Hot VW's and VW/-Porsche and later in more magazines. For five years the business grew, owned and managed by Jim Tharp. Overall, in nine years Domus did $585,000 all via mail order. Actual manufacture was by an outside company. Domus overall had very little advertising cost. Cost could be subtracted from selling price. The difference was largely profit, almost without risk.

Meanwhile, for several years Drake Koch and Tillar Swalm had been investing their share of profits in their own business, a small industrial design and fiberglass business called Drake Design. In 1979, Drake and Tillar were joined by John C. Koch, fresh out of business school, as a third partner. Together they developed the Volkswagen Rabbit Kit (the Flatback II) for Domus for a royalty. In 1980, Domus expanded its ownership to include the three Drake partners. In 1981, Drake, John and Tillar bought out Jim's share. The Rabbit kit was mail ordered the same way; press kits were sent out. Seven magazines ran stories. Playboy ran a substantial story with great success. Some of the VW fan magazines ran feature stories.

Domus has prospered. The new management bought out the fiberglass plant that manufactured the Domus Kits in Windsor, Missouri. It has become a larger scale manufacturing company with many more employees than the working partners.

President John Koch says: "Now the sales of the flatback kits are a drop in the bucket to sales of our other manufacturing business but it has been a foundation from which we expanded. The manufacturing business is now called Drake Design, Inc., and it has grown to dwarf the VW kit business of Domus, which has continued under the name Domus. It's not as easy as a moonlighting-mail-order business run by one person 1-2 hours a week, but it's more challenging and profitable at the same time. New products out of R&D are being finalized and mail order again will be the key to sales.

"Mail order is more profitable per dollar for us than most of our other activities and you can't beat the cash flow—people send in their money before you send out your product. And now, for the first time in Drake Design/Domus history, we are exporting. We've shipped kits to Canada, Germany, and Central America, with constant information requests from all over the world. Although there's more paperwork, it's a vast market we haven't even begun to tap." Not bad for starting by mail order with a no ad risk.

In Seminar VI, Chapter 8 in this book, I tell how Harrison-Hoge Industries, Inc. our family firm did business without any promotional risk for four years.

It was an old house in Brooklyn, not a landmark, not even elegant . . . but built in 1883 . . . run down, yet still with character.

Then Clem Labine and his wife, Claire, bought it. Clem had a fine job with McGraw-Hill . . . working in editorial and promotion for chemical Engineering Magazine. But the old house ended all that by tempting Clem and Claire to restore it, not just to renovate it.

That changed Clem's life. To learn how to restore the house, Clem needed information about the construction methods and materials as well as the decoration of the period. Little was readily available. Clem researched in depth. He traded information with anyone interested in restoration. Friends, and friends of friends, came for advice.

Then Clem had his idea . . . a newsletter to widely exchange such information. He would publish it on his own. Instead of moonlighting, Clem decided to resign and go into it full time. "I took the plunge. We were a two-income family. Claire is a TV writer. While I launched The Old-House Journal newsletter out of savings, Claire provided all family income . . . for some time."

In October 1972, Clem left his job. For almost a year, he worked on the restoration and on research. Then he wrote the first issue. "I laid it out on my high school drawing board I hadn't used since." He printed 2,000 copies.

The next month, Carolyn Flaherty became the first staff member, "when there were 18 subscribers" . . . obtained by sampling free copies. To increase circulation was slow going. "I'd take a booth at a flea market and physically hand out copies." A few subscriptions came in. It was a lot of work with almost nothing coming in. Claire was "immensely helpful", also writing for "The Journal".

Clem experimented with more sampling, with classified ads and tiniest display ads. The expenses of such efforts came first. Clem sent a publicity release and a sample to newspapers and magazines. Some ran a mention. A few inquiries and subscriptions came in. It was obvious that the little income produced would be too little for "The Journal" to survive indefinitely.

Then Clem came up with the solution . . . giveaway booklets so useful and of such real value that publications would want to offer them to their readers as a free srvice.

He wanted them related to old houses so that recipients would be receptive to a subscription offer. For his booklets, Clem created four-page digests of past issues. The most popular has been "The Inspection Checklist for Vintage Houses - A Guide for Buyers and Owners". It was first offered for 50¢ and then free.

The booklet offers have been so successful that each year— from free write-ups in publications—they pull in over 30,000 inquiries. The subscriptions that recipients have sent in may have saved "The Journal's" life and enabled it to survive to its present success.

There are now 55,000 subscribers. "Each year we get about 20,000 new subscribers. About 16,000 old subscribers do not renew. We get a net gain of about 4,000." Once Clem had found the formula, "everything I learned at McGraw-Hill helped tremendously."

Clem began to hone and refine his techniques. "My scale of operations was tiny. But the principle was the same as at McGraw-Hill. I knew what to do. Where I didn't, I knew where to get advice. But a lot I had to learn from trial and error."

Advice from top experts in circulation particularly helped in preparing and sending follow-up material converting inquiries into subscribers . . . in renewing subscribers . . . in getting subscribers to buy additional subscriptions as gifts for friends . . . in mailing outside lists a subscription offer . . . and even in swapping lists, to save list rental charges.

With help from others in publishing and on his own, Clem found more ways to increase sales and profits. Clem began to sell

back issues . . . from October 1973 to last month. "They add 25% to our gross." Single issues cost $2.00 each, but few order them. More take 12 back issues at the yearly subscription price of $16. A surprising percentage accept the "Buy Everything Package" of all back issues for $59.95.

Back copies and the catalog are sold by enclosures in mailings and in "The Journal" and by house ads in "The Emporium" ad section which also carries classified ads but only for current subscribers who get ads free. "We treat it solely as a reader service."

"The Journal" also sells its own items in "The Emporium". Its best is "The Master Heat Gun" to remove paint. It has done well in a one-third to a full page ad, enough to keep repeating but not to buy outside ads. "The Journal" sells books such as "Century of Color" but not yet as successfully as "The Heat Gun". "The Old House Journal Catalog" carries advertising (solicited only by mail) which adds more extra revenue.

But all the successes of Clem's entrepreneurship were made possible by his editorial ability. If you like old houses, you'll like "The Old-House Journal". The Victorian flavor comes across with your first glance. The logo-type, subhead typography, initial letters and design blocks all convey a period feeling. The cream yellow antique paper, the selection of drawings and photographs all give the atmosphere of a hundred years ago.

Clem gives more value for less dollars than most newsletters do. There are 32 pages, each 7" by 10". The subscription, originally $12 for 12 issues, is now $16. "We want to make money, but also to do good."

It took 18 months and $8,000 to turn the corner, and much more. "It took 6½ years for my actual draw from the business to come up to what it would have been if I had stayed at McGraw-Hill." The difference in income not drawn was the big part of Clem's investment.

Until Christmas of 1978, Clem operated the business from his home. Then he moved into another brownstone, 21' by 60' and four stories, built in 1872. Clem restored this building also and converted it into a small office building. Profits from "The Journal" paid for the building, restoration, furniture and equipment, with no mortgage. Rent from tenants occupying three floors pays all expenses. "The Journal" has one floor rent free. As of mid-1981, "The Journal" took over a second floor in the building and will be taking over a third floor in the building by mid-1982.

The business has matured. Clem is editor. There's a full-time staff of 12 now. Fifty percent of all editorial material is from outside. Although half of the articles are now contributed, all articles are edited, laid out and pasted up by "The Journal's" four editors. Clem gets a good living, a good net worth and a good deal more out of the business.

For CBS owned stations, Clem does a syndicated radio program, "Weekend Around the House with Clem Labine." Clem has been a consultant for an old-house TV show which PBS ran regularly. Parade Magazine included "The Journal" in its page of recommended information booklets in a March issue.

"The Journal" is a recognized authority. Clem has the satisfaction of doing good. The business keeps making more money. "We survive and succeed by getting most of our subscriptions partly at no cost and partly at no risk." Congratulations!

The age of syndication has developed many forms of mail order joint ventures to share risk. There are other advantages, too. When a trusted company recommends and offers on credit your product to its credit customers, sales jump much more than if you rented the list and mailed cold.

To enclose a brochure of someone else's product in your mail order shipments may only have the risk of inserting a proven piece . . . or only the cost of a small part of a big printing run and inserting . . . or only the cost of reprinting, (avoiding production costs) plus inserting. You may be able to avoid entirely the risk of inventory and work out of the manufacturer's stock, perhaps drop-shipped for you.

If you have a product you've succeeded with in mail order now in inventory, and have a successfully tested brochure with ad production cost already paid for, you may be able to get extra sales; perhaps in big volume, at no risk to you . . . if someone else inserts your brochures in his package.

The same principle works for billing inserts, mass solo mailings and mail order advertising of any kind where one firm has a special advantage. In any of these cases, it's good sense to get together.

Risk can vary from none to all and anything in between. The more risk you take, the greater your chance of doing business and the bigger your potential profit. The less the risk, the less chance of getting together and the shorter the end of the stick. But not always! The best horse trader can come out with the ideal mix of least risk and most profit; so negotiate such arrangements with care. Syndicators that take most risks grow fast, and sometimes go under financially . . . as do mail order firms risking too much.

Aside from subscriptions, almost every magazine sells some house mail order items . . . sometimes in major volume . . . but usually avoiding all risk but its own paper and ink. One that succeeds and limits risk is Hearst.

Gil (B.J.) Gilman is Director of Product Development for Hearst Magazines. Gil quietly and consistently finds items which he sells profitably via space in each of the Hearst Magazines. Often the items are specialized and particularly productive for the specialized Hearst Magazines most suitable, such as decorative art prints for House Beautiful.

The objective is limited. It is not to create a mail order empire, not to find winners to project in every form of advertising or even to risk outside dollars in any way. It's to use space in Hearst Magazines profitably and with least risk or overhead of any kind.

Gil's office is small. His operation is tight. He has catalog experience and is accustomed to make each square inch of space pay its way. He uses Hearst Magazine space frugally. He operates simply . . . using Hearst facilities as little as possible. His ads ask only for checks and money orders. "We prefer not to cope with processing credit cards or direct credit payments." He watches pennies in ad production, and keeps advertising claims mild and presentation tasteful.

"We're billed for each ad we use." Gil buys his products in small increments and rarely carries over inventory from a promotion. He attains his company's objective of adding volume without substantial commitment of resources or risk.

John Mack Carter, editor of Good Housekeeping and a pioneer in magazine editorial mail order, is one of Hearst's greatest assets. John is the only man in women's magazine history to have been editor of Ladies' Home Journal, McCall's and Good Housekeeping . . . at different times . . . and to the great competitive advantage of each as long as he has been with each.

John is interested in editorial mail order as a way to keep a warm and personal service contact with readers. A typical editorial mail order offer is a stitchery kit. John's service editor selects the kits. John is famous for his use of superb color photography and layout and he uses his skills to devote a color editorial half-page or page to a specific design and kit. The mail order coupon seems incidental.

John runs two color pages a month on editorial mail order items. So do other leading women's magazines. John is not concerned with greatest profit per order but with most striking designs and greatest value to readers. Over his editorial lifetime, again and again, John's editorial staff has come up with the concept of the design of the kit. John does not press his staff to bargain for lower prices. He keeps the outside designers and suppliers on his team.

And John Mack Carter avoids risk of product development, of inventory, of product company staff. His objective is to attract and keep more readers . . . although, consistently, editorial mail order brings in to almost any magazine far more revenue per page than any house mail order items.

I know one man who started a newsletter with almost no risk. He swapped his promotional writing for a printer to print his letters for services, not cash. In exchange for ad space, he swapped his services by writing articles for trade magazines appropriate to his newsletter for ads for it. He swapped some ownership in his newsletter to obtain the services of a professional trade magazine editor to write his newsletter with him. The part-time editor's wife typed labels and mailed out the newsletter as part of the deal.

This man used his publicity ability to get free write-ups and his negotiating ability to get advertising on a percentage of sales no-risk basis. Soon he had $1700 in the bank and then sold out at a handsome profit.

In TV and radio, inventory disappears daily if not used. In the best of times, some broadcasters take on mail order risk for advertisers some of the time. Most who do lose. Some regularly get more than card rates this way. Huber Hoge has spent as much as $100,000 in one year on one station on a percentage of sales where payments were $10,000 over rate card.

But almost all TV stations who consider gambling want a video tape or film of the commercial. To do this properly costs more than the TV time for a small test. So most TV entrepreneurs prefer to take test risks and find out if the offer is safe to project on other buys. If it is, they then prefer to avoid risk only where the station is weak. But some prefer PI's (Percentage of Income). Caution: *Most TV offers tested fail.* A station that runs a loser PI quickly drops it. The cost of setting up failure after failure in time spent isn't worth the effort.

There's always something new cooking. Almost every major company subsidizes the introduction of new products with the profits of existing ones. Some direct marketers nurse new products with no-risk mail order. The book publishing divisions of most magazine publishers were started by in-house mail order ads. Few of the titles can pay out by mail order when space is bought in other magazines. Yet often the mail order book divisions started this way have produced very important profits.

This is true of The Outdoor Life Book Club, The Popular Science Book Club, The Yankee Book Department and for publisher after publisher. The back issue sales so vital to so many magazine publishers started with no-risk use of their own paper and ink.

And mail order company after company has added products this way . . . with an add-on coupon, package or billing insert, or however . . . *but with little or no mail order risk.* The opportunities to get more sales with less risk keep coming up for the resourceful and imaginative. We suggest that you continue to take risks but never stop asking, "Is this *much* risk necessary?"

Chapter 11
Big vs. Small

*What are the advantages of
each in mail order?*

It has been said that the day of the small entrepreneur building a mail order fortune from a kitchen table is over; that the future in mail order belongs to the Fortune 500 and other large companies; that they have the capital, the staying power and the organization to stay and survive.

Many agree. In recent years in many areas of mail order small firms and moonlighters have suffered most. To the big it has always seemed unlikely that the small could have a chance, without the know-how of the big. To help kitchen table entrepreneurs have a chance, I tried to put whatever I had learned from a business lifetime in mail order into my book "Mail Order Moonlighting".

Since then I've done more actual research into exactly how small mail order entrepeneurs have done than I believe has been done before. Many people who have read my "Mail Order Moonlighting" wrote or telephoned me. For "Mail Order Moonlighting" I was interviewed on over 200 TV and radio stations. On radio talk shows I'd be on the air one to three hours. On the air questions were phoned in. The most frequent question was: "How can I start for the least money?"

For clients and then for Hoge products our objective had been to make tests of ads and mailings definitive enough to proceed to a good sized projection. Typically, we'd test a full page ad. But a tiny venture could not consider that. I decided to research the smallest mail order businesses I could.

At the same time I got interested in another project, to research the latest most sophisticated technology and methods in mail order and the biggest company use of mail order. I ended up writing two books. One is "Mail Order Know-How", which includes case histories of the biggest and latest. The other is "The Mail Order Underground" for which I corresponded with the world's tiniest mail order entrepreneurs, users of mail order classified ads. I ended up interviewing over 400 people for each book. In "Mail Order Know-How" I devote one chapter to capsuling case histories from "The Mail Order Underground".

Let me summarize what I learned about the big and the small. Mail order can be dangerous for each. To make it safe the big have overwhelming advantages: Scientific method, know-how and a famous, trusted name; technology, organization and buying advantages to obtain far better position in media, at better discount structure—and obtain volume savings in product buying or manufacture; money to hire and monopolize most experienced and skilled advertising agencies, consultants and staff specialists.

Advantages for the big seem overwhelming. There are two methods by which launching a mail order division can be extraordinarily safe for big companies. One way is to zero in by as many tests of items and services as well as offers and presentations as necessary. Inevitably, some tests succeed. Projection can be so big as to wipe out all test losses and provide an overall profit—but most direct marketing experts now feel this method to be outmoded . . . too slow, too expensive, too unscientific.

The other method, far more scientific, is described in some detail in my story and interview with top direct marketing planner, Bob Kestnbaum. For Fortune 500 companies, Bob Kestnbaum has a remarkable record of pre-test selection of profitable areas to start a mail order division in and of specific products to sell profitably. He tells in this book why he feels that most losses in mail order can be avoided and how his clients often have avoided losses and made increasing profits in mail order.

For the small these advantages may be unknown, unavailable or impractical. They must substitute far more frugal trial and error testing on a tiny scale, ingenuity and persuasion of others to take risk. Yet they persist. More tiny mail order ventures are starting and succeeding than ever before, often in ways impractical for the big . . . and sometimes in ways the big are unaware of. Often the little lead and the Fortune 500 follow. But the tiny are restricted in general to mail order methods now found outmoded by the big.

While big companies are doing more and more of total mail order sales, their mail order ventures are a tiny minority of all mail order businesses. And the non-big company mail order sector is growing as all mail order gets bigger. Smaller companies in mail order are the bush leagues from which the major leagues of biggest companies hire up and coming talent and buy promising businesses. Many of the divisions operated by big companies and many companies now big in mail order started as tiny ventures.

In this book my story, "General Mills Mail Order Mix", tells how each of five subsidiaries started in a tiny way—one with a classified ad . . . were acquired years later . . . and are now the fastest growing part of General Mills.

Periodically, it is said that starting small and building big can no longer be done. As World War II ended, paper, publication space and broadcast time were short. The big got first access to product manufacture and advertising space. Media often restricted or turned down mail order ads altogether. The end of the small mail order firm was feared.

This was just before innumerable, small mail order successes burst upon the scene . . . and for tiniest entrepreneurs mail order classified got underway. (Today more mail order businesses start this way than any other.) By 1981, with new sophisticated mail order methods, some said the future was for the big.

But as opportunities closed off for the small and tiny, far more specialized opportunities occurred. The mail order minnows still survived. They grew and showed the way for the bigger mail order fish.

Always, mail order minnows dart away faster from rising costs . . . and dart in where new opportunities lie. Many are now leaving mass media . . . and darting into new specialized publications. Where the items advertised are the right fit they are thriving.

The big often pay to have their people attend seminars, take courses and go to trade meetings all concerning mail order and direct marketing. They are members of the direct marketing clubs, of the Direct Mail/Marketing Association and often join in helping organize the Direct Marketing Days. They often start in-house libraries of books most logical and helpful to orient personnel to direct marketing. Some endeavor to update know-how of personnel in specific specialties often with the aid of specialists in each important facet of direct marketing.

Then why do big companies ever fail in mail order? When a big company starts a mail order division or buys a profitable mail order business and loses money, the reason is usually in its management. The advantages to the big are so great and the specialized know-how for anything it wishes to do in mail order so available that success can be the norm.

Usually the reason is lack of commitment by top management to the mail order project. This, in turn, usually comes from disagreements within management. Some are in favor and some not. The project is gone into half-heartedly. Its potential has not been worked out in advance fully enough, nor the necessary growth period for it to mature.

Sometimes it is ill-suited to the company's basic business or its image. Sometimes it's gone into hurriedly and casually. Sometimes the appropriate outside expertise is never brought in, or, if brought in, listened to. Sometimes top management of the parent company changes. The new broom sweeps clean, the mail order project of the old management along with much else.

Those who start in mail order without knowledge or money have certain advantages. The use of scientific methods can be costly. Advice from those who profess to be expert can be wrong. The tiny avoid much possible loss. They usually escape the danger of misinformation. They know nothing about and no one in mail order. They're usually unaware of books, seminars, magazines and authorities. If they know consultants they couldn't afford them. They don't realize how complex mail order is. They've never heard of direct marketing.

They escape 90% of normal testing cost. With little money and credit they make microscopic tests. They don't misuse latest technology. They never ran across it. With no computers they have no computer disasters. They usually sell for cash with no credit losses or logistics. They have no employees or fee specialists to mishandle anything. Overhead can't sink them; they have none.

Most mail order firms still start this way, with a classified or small display ad in a small circulation or inexpensive publication. They can do what the big can't, a very limited business, for a very specialized item or catalog in a very specialized medium.

Many fail and quit but usually lose very little. Percentage of failure to sell Italian Queen Bees in a bee magazine is lower than for new mass items in mass media for giants. More succeed now than ever . . . in innumerable niches, nooks and crannies. They innovate more. Some get big. Most don't and suffer in that they can't use sophisticated methods needed for most lucrative opportunities. Their success is *very* limited. The MBA's, the experts, the trained can carry small success to very big success and with less worry, stress, fatigue and work.

Those in between big and tiny have most risk. They have more to lose and more overhead than the very small. They lack the resources, organization and top experts of the very big. Their consultants may be the blind leading the blind. They may get misinformation and confusing information.

More mail order businesses start with a classified ad than in any other way—and almost all without joining an association, going to a seminar, reading a direct marketing trade magazine . . . and without using an advertising agency or consultant, buying an expert's book or even reading a direct marketing magazine. But a common denominator of the many businesses which succeed this way, without help, is how limited the success is and how great the potential growth and increased profit not perceived.

The big have the tanks, planes, rockets, laser weapons and missiles. The tiny have the guerilla weapons fighting their war in an age-old way. The big are the developed nations using latest technology. The small are the undeveloped nations, using the same mail order methods as first created mail order.

For the big, the maximum use of the most scientific methods is the ideal rarely attained. Their big muscles, unexercised, can get flabby. Specialists, as direct marketing grows more and more

complex, are more apt to be fuzzy outside of their specialty—yet may be given overall responsibility. As businesses grow bigger, it takes more courage to be an internal entrepreneur who innovates. It can seem safer to copy. Desire to show more profits or less losses this quarter can cause the search for quick bucks in mail order, even in projects unworthy of association with a great corporate name.

The biggest advantages of the small are greater closeness to the product, the mail count and the profit or loss. Often there's more respect for the product or service and its importance, to fulfillment, to pleasing the customer. The small can spend more time in making a product better and in careful shipping with far less on advertising. With no pre-opinions, the small are often more innovative.

How do the small start? Usually in simple ways, easy ways and ways offering the chance of bootstrapping and pyramiding. Each ad must create an increase of capital to run further ads.

More mail order businesses probably start from publication ads than from direct mail advertising. More start with single items than with catalogs. More new items starting with ads in any form of advertising do so without benefit of experts than with them. This includes classified and display publication advertising, TV and radio and literature through the mail. Even advertising in direct mail, more new items start—without, or with little—knowledge of latest methods or technology. Some of the most dramatic, huge, and almost instant mail order successes from TV occur with no expert presiding.

In mail order there is ample room for both big and small. This book is an effort to bring the small the know-how advantages of the big but to help anyone connected with the big to observe and benefit from the experience of the small. To update personnel of the big and familiarize the small with latest methods there are more case histories of big companies, sophisticated technology and advanced specialists.

But I love the stories of small beginnings and big growth . . . how Ed Downe started in mail order with a one-inch ad for a fun gag item and then, based on mail order know-how, built a Fortune 500 company . . . how Lillian Katz, to save baby sitter fees worked at home on her own and launched the Lillian Vernon Catalog. All through this book the big successes are balanced by the niche successes which never stop.

Every new medium and field of media becomes a nursery for new fields of mail order advertisers. There are new small advertisers in each new specialized publication whether in hang gliding or personal computing. 90% of Yankee Magazine advertisers are mail order ventures so small they buy ads direct and Yankee sets type for them. There will always be a place for the small.

The small can learn from the big. But generally, the big cannot do some things the small can. The successful all too often start to freeze their ideas from the moment of first success. They determine what cannot be done and avoid it . . . and what is most profitable to be done and stick to it. The small, unknowing and unburdened, try anything . . . and are usually the innovators of the business. The big benefit when they study the small.

However small your endeavor in mail order, there may be stories here quite applicable to you. There are reviews of helping organizations and publications and careers. There are listings of information and literature, much free and much at modest cost.

However big your business, there are case histories vital to you. And for those growing from tiny to small to big, here is help at each stage of the way.

Chapter 12
Fortune 500 Mail Order

*Beginning to move from periphery to mainstream,
direct marketing comes of age among the superbig.*

Shades of John D. Rockefeller!

Exxon is competing with Standard Oil of California . . . #1 Fortune 500 company with #5 . . . with a travel club . . . in the mail order business.

Ma Bell, Fortune's #1 listed utility, is going great guns against General Telephone, Fortune's #2 . . . selling telephones mail order. The Ford Motor Company is going into mail order combat with Mobil Oil . . . #6 in the Fortune 500 against #2 . . . in the travel club business.

Virtually every Fortune 500 company probably sells via mail order, sometimes in a small, peripheral manner. Many, like Dupont, sell seminars mail order. Many, like G.E., sell programmed instruction mail order or, like Westinghouse, sell manuals mail order. But who are in it seriously?

Sears and Ward's were born of mail order. The eyes of most giants opened to mail order by Bell & Howell's famous movie projector and camera offer, the first tremendously successful big ticket mail order item. In this book, Maxwell Sroge (then Director of Sales of Bell & Howell) tells how it all happened. Then Time-Life Books with its huge overnight success built interest in big company mail order. In this book Jerry Hardy, founder of Time-Life Books, tells of the beginning years.

I asked Paul Sampson, a grand master of mail order who has been mentor and guide to many of the big, how giant company mail order came about. Paul answered: "Fortune 500 mail order was a reaction to forces from the consumer . . . not a process from corporate boardrooms. It was a buying revolution. The harassed, busy consumer turned to mail order. Working women had less time to shop. The consumers forced Fortune 500 companies into mail order.

"Hewlett-Packard's fantastic success with their first pocket calculator for engineers, at $397, had great effect on big company interest in mail order." Bob Kestnbaum, consultant to Hewlett-Packard from the time its mail order department had one employee, tells the founding and early growth story in this book.

"In recent years, probably the most exciting Fortune 500 success story has been that of Montgomery Ward's subsidiary—Signature Financial, Inc. It's due largely to one person, Dick Cremer, president and founder of Signature. Dick is a rare person, an idea person entrepreneur coming out of a big company." In this book Dick Cremer tells how from one employee and one mail order service Signature Financial, Inc. grew to five companies and a 150 million dollar a year business in eight years.

Paul considers IBM Direct another success story. "Bob Hutchings at IBM in recent years recommended phase one of a direct marketing approach, selling office supplies for its own equipment. It's gone exceptionally well. IBM is now selling products mail order." Jerry Coyne, manager of IBM Direct, in this book tells how IBM, in one year, produced several hundred thousand orders and inquiries (to salesmen) by phone alone. Now since the success of IBM, National Cash Register has set up its own mail order business. NCR is aiming at over $100,000,000 in annual sales of office products by mail order.

It isn't all roses. Some Fortune 500 ventures fail. Some succeed but have set-backs. When, in 1980, the dollar rose it caused the foreign profits of Time-Life Books to drop considerably. High interest bills that same year were hard on big catalogs. Beneficial Finance sold out its ownership of the Spiegel Catalog to German interests. General Mills reported that, in the fiscal year ending in April 1981, pretax earnings of its mail order companies were only about half the previous year; particularly because of a drop in sales of its collectibles business as well as coins and stamps.

At Time Inc., cable TV had by 1981 become the new, big, glamorous profit earner and growth potential. But its book sales by mail order were still strong. The Spiegel catalog has been pioneering what may be the most exciting concept of the 1980's in catalogs. The General Mills mail order companies may grow in the future faster than General Mills overall, as they have done since first mail order company acquisition—except for 1980.

In 1981, American Can decided to sell a quarter of its business, and to find different ways to grow. Its 1980 earnings had dipped to 85.7 million dollars from $127.3 million in 1979. But American Can's mail order subsidiary, The Fingerhut Corporation, reported record earnings in 1980, selling everything from stout women's fashions to imports from China of handcrafted items. Yet, Fingerhut, several years before it was acquired by American Can in 1979, had its bad years—after some mail order over-expansion.

But Fingerhut bounced back and its success was enough for American Can, in late 1980, to buy 20 percent of the stock of Franklin Mint—only to find that Warner Communications then bought 100 percent, including American Can's stock. And earnings of Franklin Mint (now the Direct Response Division of Warner Communications) in the first quarter after acquisition by Warner were one quarter of Warner's earnings. Joe Segel, the founder of Franklin Mint, tells in this book how it got its start and first huge success.

More and more of the top 500 companies use mail order. The new mail order for big companies is highly visible. Anyone can see it in mail received, ads in publications, commercials on TV . . . in hybrid ways—envelopes of inserts in newspapers, in postcard magazines, in direct mail . . . or hear it in radio commercials or even by telephone.

A driving force behind the first tremendous use of telephone marketing by Fortune 500 companies was Lee Iacocca, then sales director of Ford and later president of Chrysler. In this book Murray Roman, who for Ford made 20 million phone calls, tells how it came about and how telephone marketing later swept through the Fortune 500 as a marketing tool. The Ford phone campaign was probably the opening wedge of the use of the mail order method in the mainstream marketing of big company products through normal trade channels.

The Ford Auto Club wants to give Mobil Oil's Montgomery Ward Auto Club (which has enjoyed phenomenal success) a run for its money. Each club is pure mail order and by any mail order measurement the stakes are big. The scope and interest by such superbig companies in mail order has been a long time coming . . . but this type of mail order by the Fortune 500 is still not in the mainstream of either company's acitivities.

The Ford Auto Club is being marketed by a subsidiary . . . of a subsidiary . . . of a subsidiary of Ford. The Montgomery Ward Auto Club is also being marketed by a subsidiary . . . of a subsidiary . . . of Ward, which is owned by Marcoa which is 54% owned by Mobil. However big the potential of either auto club its maximum success is peripheral to its final parent corporation.

For some Fortune 500 companies mail order has been very big and for others very important, if not huge. In this book Pierre Passavant tells how Don Seibert, now Chairman of the Board, planned the growth of J.C. Penney into its present two billion dollar a year mail order business and how Gerber baby foods got started in the mail order insurance business.

Much Fortune 500 mail order is still peripheral. Some is in big volume. But the method of scientific mail order and direct marketing is getting into the mainstream of parent company product advertising. The automobile and appliance companies for several years have been selling mail order extended service contracts directly or through dealers to buyers of their products, chiefly by direct mail. This adds to customer satisfaction and creates a new profit center.

Eastman Kodak has developed a data base of 10 million camera owners. Kodak offers photo developers anywhere a choice of ten creative packages. It arranges to send the mail selected to the names selected by the photo developer. Each can cover names nearest facilities. Both of these uses of the mail order method are mainstream.

In the years of the first rush into the mail order by Fortune 500 companies, top management of parent companies was sometimes divided about, sometimes hostile to and sometimes not fully informed about mail order.

A retired, senior executive of one of the top 100 of the Fortune 500 told me this story of years ago: "Our company now makes some peripheral sales via mail order but essentially we missed the mail order boat. At one period we operated some services which got a 500 to 800 percent increase in activity via direct marketing. But no system or method of keeping track was ever installed.

"We were split into several companies. I was staff, giving advice and counsel—which was not wanted or taken. The divisions of our company had become decentralized. Subsidiaries, in turn, were decentralized. We seemed to flounder in communications. Divisions went in different directions. Each company became a self-contained hierarchy.

"We once operated a corporation-wide industrial direct mail campaign. It was all done internally and resulted in orders and inquiries. I tried to measure and calculate results. We tried to trace the relationship between dollars spent to promote and orders placed. We never established a connection between bingo cards and sales. We did see that publicity got about 95% of inquiries, and ads about 5%. We sent inquiries that looked significant to divisions for phone follow-up by salesmen. We never got reports of what happened. The potential of mail order and direct marketing via computerized tracking of inquiries and sales existed. But management was not in the mood to take advantage of it.

"We then made a many million dollar acquisition of a mail order business—just when a philosophy for decentralization existed, which made every manager a king. Some executives of one subsidiary wanted the acquisition because in some ways it seemed related to some of its activities. The acquired firm had been successful but no one in our company knew anything about mail order. It was all part of our over-merge and over-decentralization phase. Maybe the seller played us for a sucker. The result was a fiasco—costing several million dollars more in operating losses.

"Our top management did not want to know about mail order. It was not familiar with the fundamentals. I brought in mail order experts like Maxwell Sroge. He was in college. We were in kindergarten. He was smart, full of ideas. He spoke fast.

We had to slow him down—and still could not understand what he was talking about.

"Here we were, a company doing business in billions of dollars but passive to mail order and direct marketing. Management would say 'Not for us'. They wouldn't listen. It's a sign of less flexibility and adaptability than in the big Japanese or German companies. Any effort toward direct marketing became secondary. They'd end up buying the cheapest help. Operations would be by those least qualified."

This story concerns a time when mail order was quite new to many Fortune 500 companies. This same company has since dramatically changed its approach to mail order. It has invested heavily in people and acquisitions to position itself in a big way in the mail order future. Fortune 500 mail order has come a long way since then.

CBS was one of the first Fortune 500 companies to succeed in a big way in mail order. Goddard Lieberman, then president of CBS Records, came to Lester Wunderman over 20 years ago and told him he wanted to start a record club. Lester Wunderman came up with the winning offers, copy and the successful use of double spreads and insert cards, free-standing inserts and pre-prints, as told in my story in this book on Wunderman, Ricotta & Kline.

CBS and WR&K proved an effective combination. One reason was that Columbia was an exciting account to work for. One WR&K creative person described it to me this way: "Of all the accounts I worked on, Columbia Records was the most fun. There was a challenge in the development of the ad, the new formulas, the new types of layout, new graphics. We were always encouraged to try new things, as far out as we wanted, provided the effect projected the image Columbia was trying for."

WR&K and CBS have worked in mail order tandem for over 20 years. Ben Ordover, who in 1979 became president of Columbia House (the mail order arm of CBS) had even worked for years at WR&K. He knows mail order as few do. His first job was as a copywriter at Prentice-Hall where he learned the business from George Costello (now president of Prentice-Hall). The co-founder and then Chairman of the Board of Prentice-Hall was Richard Prentice Ettinger and he demanded results, and got them, from his mail order division.

Anyone who worked for George Costello at Prentice-Hall got a sound mail order education. Ben Ordover got more than that. He went on to work for Richard Prentice Ettinger himself— for a mail order business Ettinger owned in partnership with William Casey. This was many years before William Casey managed the 1980 Reagan Campaign and, in 1981, became Director of the CIA. Both Ettinger and Casey were mail order realists and produced a super realist in Ben Ordover. By the time Ben graduated and became advertising director of Famous Artists, he was very numbers-oriented. WR&K handled the Famous Artists account. Ben later became an account executive at WR&K and then joined, and climbed the ladder to the presidency, of Columbia House.

Columbia House is the subsidiary of CBS which operates its record club and sells records and tape albums mail order with great success. Ben Ordover is considered one of the most able men in direct marketing. He has a flair for knowing when to get Columbia House into a business and when to get out. Columbia House paid eight million dollars in cash, in 1969, to James Wooters for National Needlecraft, and millions more to others to assemble a very big mail order crafts division. The division was highly profitable year after year. Then it started to become marginal. Finally it lost money and, in 1980, Columbia House dismantled the entire division and closed down the National Handicraft Institute.

Columbia House sold X-Acto to Hunt Foods, at a big profit over the price paid for it. It sold Needle Arts to Meredith Publishing and part of Model Builders to Parent's Magazine. The crafts area was no longer booming as it had been. Now, Columbia House is concentrating on its specialty . . . selling records and tapes and closely related products.

Those who worked with Ben Ordover describe him as very creative. He likes to give people coming up a chance, and considers it good business. He has been responsible for CBS-Columbia House sponsoring an affirmative action program described in my story on the Direct Mail/Mail Order Educational Foundation which conducts it . . . a summer apprentice program for young blacks. Ben considers it a small, starting program.

Ben has proved an astute business man in building a huge mail order record and tape business . . . and so effectively that on November 30, 1981, he was made president of CBS Toys, another important CBS subsidiary.

Today there's far more Fortune 500 expertise to go around. William Willett joined Avon Fashions in late 1972 when it was founded by Avon Products. In December of 1976 he was named president.

Avon Fashions quickly built up to over $100,000,000 a year in sales. Bill Willett has ample expertise. He has only worked in mail order and only for Fortune 500 companies. "I came from school straight to Time Inc. It was very comfortable. There was somewhat of a courtly club atmosphere. It was a sort of fraternity." At Time, Bill Willett sold subscriptions mail order and learned his mail order from Wendell Forbes, whose story I tell in this book.

"After Time, Inc. I worked for Downe Communications. I arrived along with two others from Time. At Downe, I was vice president in charge of circulation for Ladies' Home Journal and for American Home. Ultimately, I had a small ownership in American Home. In 1972, I sold my interest and took a job with Avon. Avon mail order started in 1972. I was president of Avon Fashions, but when we passed $100 million in sales I became vice-president of Avon Products, the parent company, where I now work in finance and acquisitions.

"To create Avon Fashions, I didn't use the Avon customer list. We sent the catalog to good mail order lists. Renting the right names did it. Presentation was important. We gave the best service to customers. But the real secret of Avon Fashions has been credibility. Avon Fashions succeeded primarily because of the power of the Avon name."

Mail order made some Fortune 500 companies happen. James West, later Vice Chairman of the Board of Tandy Corp., told me this story: In 1947, Charles Tandy, back from World War II, started work for his father, a small leather findings jobber. James West was general manager and Charles reported to him. "Charles came out of the Navy full of mail order ideas. In 1948, he made a test of an $84 one-inch ad in Workbasket Magazine. The ad offered the Little Moc Kit with pieces of leather, a pattern, instructions and a simple tool to make a set of children's moccasins.

"The test changed the Tandy business completely and mail order gave Tandy its first big growth after World War II. Charles ran a lot of classified ads and inch ads. Then Charles ran bigger ads. Later, it taught us where to start stores and what to sell in stores. Mail order provided cash to start stores. This proved vital when Charles got the joint venture idea. Tandy would train a manager and give him an interest in a separate corporation." In those days, no matter how many corporations with the same majority ownership, there was a minimum tax on the first $25,000 in profits of each . . . providing someone different in each owned 25% or more of it. The first 100 stores, each making $25,000, could save over a million dollars in tax, and so forth.

Tandy got its growth in the stores, and then when it acquired Radio Shack it really took off. It's well over a billion dollar company now. It's out of the handicraft business now. But mail order was there when Tandy needed it.

Bell & Howell was a tiny fraction of its present size when it first made its movie projector offer by mail order. Now it's a Fortune 500 company which sells mail order technology products (among many others to many fields) to mail order companies. Another Fortune 500 company, the Mead Company, the huge paper conglomerate, developed Mead Dijit, the first laser printer accessory offered by IBM. R.R. Donnelley is the biggest printer in the world and for many mail order companies, as Dick Hodgson describes in this book. Boise Cascade sells envelopes to mail order companies. And many other Fortune 500 companies have divisions which sell to or service the mail order field.

Selling to the Fortune 1,000 has become big mail order business. Ed Burnett, whose story is in this book, has shown that with all subsidiaries, divisions, departments and executives that there are as many as 131,000 key people in the Fortune 1,000, important to mail for some products.

When the Fortune 500 moved into mail order one growth industry was helping them do it. Direct marketing advertising agencies and direct marketing consultants launched many of them into mail order. Then came marketing planning consultants and people trainers; then list consultants, managers and brokers; and copywriters and mail order executive head hunters; and experts in telephone marketing and sweepstakes; specialists in mail order law and others in customer handling; and mail order acquisition experts and later experts (often the same) at mail order divestitures; mail order computer programmers and systems analysts. Now recent graduates of the big are finding a growth industry in teaching the rest of us how the Fortune 500 succeed in mail order.

James W. Hinkley IV worked on new products at Grolier Inc. and is now a consultant to Western Publishing, a division of Mattel Inc., the Fortune 500 toy company. In his first year doing so, Jim Hinkley came up with a major hit, The Sesame Street Book Club. It had the impact that the Dr. Seuss Reading Program had had many years before. By 1981, it was substantially bigger than The Betty Crocker Recipe Card program and almost as big as Betty Crocker was at its height.

The Betty Crocker program in 1981 still ran at almost half its top volume, and at a good profit. Western's program of house plant cards was tapering off but still making money while one of its competitors, SRA (an IBM subsidiary), had closed down its plant card operation. At one point, TV was very productive for Betty Crocker but, in 1981, it's been selective direct mail and space. Sales are almost all U.S. with some via the Western subsidiary in Canada and a partnership in Australia.

Now Jim Hinkley (who also numbers the Hearst Corporation, Warner Books and Macmillan among his clients) is on the prowl for more continuity programs.

"Today the editorial investment to develop a book continuity program is over $1,000,000. As a result I look for existing editorial properties which can be adapted for mail order sale under a licensing arrangement with the original publisher. Mail order selling in the 1980's demands careful targeting of product, audience and media to be successful. Shrewd selection of new programs for testing is a key element.

"Right now Mattel is looking into mail order for its toy and game products, including some cross-pollination with Western. In 1981 Western took on Kobs & Brady (whose story is in this book). We like them, their attitude and approach. Their first creative packages for us are now being tested. They will create most of our direct mail and space, and also work with us on research and media planning." And so, professional management, an able consultant and an able agency continue Western Publishing's mail order activities.

Wunderman, Ricotta & Kline have been developing for Fortune 500 clients new forms of direct marketing and helping to make direct marketing far more important to them. One client, the New York Telephone Company, now advertises new services as though mail order items. Ma Bell has Dial-A-Joke, Sports Phone and Off Track Betting Results. It has the Dow-Jones Report, the New York Report and Music Line. It has Time and Weather Reports—and even Horoscopes with a different number for each sign. Ads ask you to dial each. When you do, Ma Bell's computer bills you. It's instant direct marketing.

Mail order and Fortune 500 companies are now married— and neither may ever be quite the same. Fortune 500 companies may make mail order bigger than yet dreamed. And scientific mail order advertising methods may change the mainstream of Fortune 500 product advertising. It is well to study Fortune 500 mail order and much of this book concerns it.

In the Help Source Guide in this book are listed over a hundred articles and speeches on Fortune 500 mail order and how to get copies and tapes.

Chapter 13
The Mail Order Moonlighters

They started successful mail order businesses from home - part-time. Perhaps you can, too.

In 1974, a 22-year-old male nurse who was a vegetarian became a mail order moonlighter and launched the Vegetarian Times for $17. He is Paul Obis.

The $17 paid for printing 300 copies of a single 11″ x 17″ sheet newsletter folded to make four pages. In a small part of Chicago where Paul then lived, he persuaded health food stores to give away copies free to customers. Mail order coupons in the newsletters brought back subscriptions . . . with cash . . . enough to print 300 copies more . . . and then another 300. The 900 copies brought in his first 51 subscriptions, at a profit.

Next, Paul ran a classified ad in Rolling Stone Magazine . . . for $18 . . . offering a sample copy free. Again, enough inquiries and then cash subscriptions came in to make a profit. Then Paul projected. He bought more classified ads and then display ads. He kept growing. By 1981, The Vegetarian Times had become a fat 84-page magazine, loaded with ads and with 50,000 circulation and growing. It is sold in 1200 health food stores. Its subscription ads run widely.

Life has changed for Paul. He has moved to Oak Park, Illinios, with his wife, Clare, whom he met in the hospital where both worked. Paul works full-time for his magazine and walks to his Oak Park office. Associated Business Publishers has become Paul's senior partner, giving full financial backing.

Paul is doing what he loves . . . spreading the word about something he believes in. "As editor I meet interesting people, get a chance to write, travel a bit and find satisfaction." The dream is to grow still more . . . to sell copies in far more of the USA's 6,500 health stores . . . advertise subscriptions in direct mail, perhaps on TV and then get more advertising. Atheneum has published "The Vegetarian Times Restaurant Guide" and Paul is thinking of more books. Clare syndicates a newspaper column distributed by Copley News Service. Who knows what else may be on the way!

For every Paul there are other moonlighters who fail but more and more constantly go into mail order from home, part-time, and make it. Those who do realize that with more know-how chances of success can be better, losses less, profits more and long-term benefits greater. Still more important, strain, work and worry become less. But most still start with no help and succeed by becoming self-taught by trial and error.

Scattered through this book are stories of moonlighters who have made modest to comfortable successes and some who started as moonlighters and later built big businesses.

Dave Rago was a college student who became an authority on antique art pottery, and from home started in mail order with a 6-inch $60 ad in the Antique Trader. He did $400,000 in sales by the time he was 25, earning good money. I tell his story in my chapter, "Mail Order Collectomania". In the same chapter, I tell of the school dietician who collected plates . . . then started in mail order with a $35 ad in Plate Collector Magazine—and then built a hundred-thousand-dollar-a-year business; and of a nuclear physicist and his wife who collected antique maps . . . then tested an inch ad asking for inquiries and mailed typewritten descriptions and photographs of maps . . . and in several years built up to earnings comparing with the physicist's salary.

Jack Scaritt was a research chemist for a subsidiary of Gulf Oil. He was also a backpacker, a hang glider and a kayaker. He taught wind surfing. Then he combined his professional abilities and hobbies and became a mail order moonlighter from his home in Gardner, Kansas.

After hours Jack invented a closure that makes a tight, waterproof seal for plastic bags and then two unique products using it. Each is for kayakers. The first is to keep sleeping bags or spare clothes dry in a kayak. The second is to keep cameras safe, cushioned and dry in a kayak. The first has two bags, polypropylene outside and polyethylene inside. The second is made of foam-lined heavy vinyl.

In 1969, Jack opened his moonlighting business with a $49 small ad in American Whitewater Magazine. It succeeded. Jack tried classified ads in Sports Afield, Outdoor Life and Field & Stream. He used the name Voyageur's Ltd. Since then, he's proliferated into a variety of business activities, each an offshoot of his favorite hobbies, and works full time in his own business.

In 1973, Jack opened his own 600 square foot retail store catering chiefly to each of his hobbies. "The store was an outgrowth of the mail order business. My basement became crowded with backpacks, stoves and canoe gear, and local residents were bugging me for gear and only one other store was in town at the time. So I opened the store to supply a strong local need." By 1979, he built sales up to $336,000 for the year and sold out.

"In essence, the mail order business was sort of part time up until November 4, 1979, when the store was sold, and we had to 'make it' on mail-order manufacturing.

"In 1979, the mail order volume was $116,000. We really worked at it, and 1980 volume was $214,000. Using mailing lists, exhibiting at the National Sporting Goods Association show in Chicago, and selective ads in magazines which cover the sports we manufacture for, we were able to achieve a volume of over $300,000 in 1981, despite a generally slack economy."

But Jack was now building his mail order sales a new way too. "We have de-emphasized our own retail mail order and concentrated on getting dealers, and a few distributors. Our line of boating related gear and accessories seems too limited to do very well in retail mail order, especially as postage rates increase. We have just installed a computer to handle invoicing and all accounting, and believe this will increase accuracy and speed of service." Jack has no sales reps. He sells by mail order to stores.

"We are continuing to expand our product line of manufactured goods as well as those we distribute. Prospects look good for continued growth, as we are one of perhaps three companies in the U.S. which manufacture and design similar equipment. Thus, we fill a comfortable niche in the mail order business." Jack has licensed a Florida company to use his closure to bag potato chips. He sees expansion ahead. He explains the difference he finds being on his own.

"There's no comparison. With Gulf I could forget my job after hours. But this is more rewarding. I control more of my destiny. If I make a good move, I get immediate personal benefits. It's more exciting."

In Kansas City, WDAF-TV produced a half hour show interviewing me and sending in a camera crew to film two business enterprises in operation which started by mail order moonlighting. One was in the plant of Voyageur's Ltd., interviewing Jack Scaritt. The other was with Tom Pugh who had worked as a typesetter, went into selling computer typesetting systems to newspapers and became a mail order moonlighter. He liked brass beds, decided he'd make a better one and sell it. He started with a $14.50 classified ad. I tell his story in my book, "The Mail Order Underground".

There is risk for moonlighters. You can lose . . . a lot. For top experts and the biggest companies, most mail order items tested fail. Often, experts fear for the average moonlighter's chances. But without knowledge, experience or experts, more and more moonlighters succeed. More successful mail order businesses and more fresh, innovative and imaginative products are started by moonlighters than by giants. I continually learn from the ingenious ways some moonlighters survive and prosper.

Sal Fusco, a moonlighting baker used his coin collecting hobby to go into mail order. Sal built up The Old Roman Coin Business, in Hicksville, New York, to $5,500,000. He sold out and retired at 42. Four years later, he started an old coin retirement business, Shoreham Enterprises. He did $3,500,000 in mail order last year. "It's fun retirement . . . and sure beats baking." I tell much more of Sal's story in "The Mail Order Underground".

Joe Segel, at 15, started a little mail order catalog selling by mail order advertising specialties to magicians. By the time he was 20, it had expanded far beyond magicians into a variety of flourishing activities. I tell how he did this; how, at 34, he founded and built what became the several hundred million dollar a year Franklin Mint—in my chapter, "Making a Mint in Mail Order".

Boynton (Tony) Selden is an electrical engineer who for a friend invented the Needle Easel, a frame to hold a needlework project with both hands free to stitch. He and his wife, Michele, started in business with a 50-word free write-up, did $21,000 in sales from it and have done business for years with no mail order risk. I tell how in my chapter, "How to Avoid Mail Order Risk".

James and Jean Bird live in Connecticut. Along with raising four children, Jean is a mail order moonlighter and publisher of the Factory Outlet Shopping Guide.

Jim is an investment analyst for a major pension fund. In his spare time he helps Jean. "For two years, Jean has made more money than I have." In 1971, Jean began to compile a directory of factory outlets—first for herself, then for friends and then to sell.

"We printed at an instant copy store 500 copies of a thirty page typewritten directory at a cost of $201." Word-of-mouth recommendation got orders. A coffee-klatch friend sent her copy to the Bergen County Record which did a story on it. 3,200 orders poured in. In 1972, the Birds brought out a regular annual edition in expanded form. Volume printings kept the cost per copy down.

Jean had worked as a secretary, a retail clerk and in a bank. Now she became editor and publisher and a production, shipping and public relations executive as well as a writer and buyer of advertising. Jim was a part-time partner in it all.

A small ad in Yankee Magazine was so successful they began to expand. The Philadelphia Inquirer, Sunday Living Section did a nice article. This brought an ABC network TV interview with Jean on "Good Morning America" and a New York Times story. From each story more orders came in.

In 1976, Jean and Jim had expanded the first edition to over 500 listings and had published six different regional guides from South Carolina through New England each of 500 listings. As the guides were expanded the price was gradually raised from $1.95

to $3.95 still selling a mail order item for less than $5 on a profitable basis which is unusual in mail order. For the Birds a small ad in the national edition of Southern Living, with most circulation wasted, made money. Even paying a premium cost per thousand for Eastern regional circulation in Family Circle and Woman's Day made good money.

Each step, each publicity story led to the next. Both ads and publicity increased. Joan Hamburg interviewed Jean on WOR radio. One TV station has scheduled a profile of Jean. Retail bookstores began to order, quickly sold out and reordered as did more and more. Today bookstore sales are 60% of the business.

Over a million Factory Outlet Shopping Guides have been sold. Sales volume is over $250,000 a year, but with much work. Jean puts great editorial care into each new annual edition of her guides, constantly updating and enlarging them. They now have a mailing list of over 70,000 mail order customers. There's a bonus income from renting the mailing list to other companies. Three and a half years ago the Birds began to publish The Factory Outlet Shopping Newsletter with eight issues for $5. Each year about ten percent of The Guide mail order purchasers also subscribe to the newsletter.

"We've tried selling by mail order other books, records and various items. But nothing worked out." So the Birds keep concentrating on The Guide. "There was more publicity last month than any previous month." And it keeps growing.

Today, in most financially comfortable families, both husband and wife work. More and more, mail order moonlighting is a preferred alternative. A moonlighting mother can work at home, and be with the children. Wife and husband can work together as a team. It gives added security, a feeling of dignity and fulfillment. When husband and wife both have jobs the big tax bite of the second salary is a surprise. Most moonlighters are surprised at the tax advantage the business gives. It may pay part of home rent or carrying charges and part

of telephone bills. It may need a car, entertainment, travel—at business expense.

But be careful. You can lose—plenty. Ralph L. Woods of Ramsey, New Jersey, was 75 years old when he self-published and sold by mail order "The Book for Family Facts and Records". It was beautifully done, filled a real need and lost Ralph Woods over $8,000. Ads in the New York Times, Rotarian Magazine and others produced a total of 32 orders for $8.95 each. And a lot of moonlighters lose each year.

Ralph Woods is a successful writer and intelligent man. Knowing what his experience has taught him the next time he would lose far less. But any item can fail. It may sell for too much . . . or too little. It may have the wrong ad . . . or an ad in the wrong place, or at the wrong time. It may simply not be wanted. Orders can come in nicely, but moonlighters still lose because they did not include all costs or miscalculated in estimates. Some moonlighters are not suited to mail order, perhaps losers at any business. Those with the worst chance are desperate to make money in mail order selling . . . anything . . . fast.

But most losses can be avoided, and many do surprisingly well.

An Episcopalian priest I know has earned a quarter million dollars from a book he first sold by mail order as a moonlighter. Each year trade publishers take over more books from moonlighter authors. We've paid over $100,000 in royalties to one fish lure inventor who was a mail order moonlighter. For years we've paid good royalties to other inventor moonlighters. We just took over a garden item from a new moonlighter.

Carpet salesman John Hanes raised orchids, then crossed one orchid with another to produce a new hybrid. He began to exchange with other hobbyists. Then he started a little mail order moonlighting. Then he retired and now sells root seedlings worldwide. Growing and shipping is done by a partner. Everything else is done from home with almost no overhead. I tell the story in more detail in my chapter, "Retirement Mail Order".

In the same chapter, I tell of retired TWA pilot Roderick K. Penfield, of East Setauket, New York, and of his two mail order moonlighting businesses. One sells slides he makes of photographs he mostly takes of different types of airline planes, his hobby. He started with a $51 ad. The other is the Greek Fisherman's Cap started by mail order, selling also to dealers and giving a good income.

Lillian Katz became a housewife mail order moonlighter rather than take a job and spend her salary on baby sitter charges. Her first very small ad in "Seventeen" Magazine brought in over $16,000 of orders for a monogrammed leather belt. This led to her Lillian Vernon catalog business which, in 1980, did over $30,000,000. I tell her story in this book.

Contest Newsletter is a mail order moonlighting business which did over $5,000,000 in 1980 by mail order . . . from home, part-time. In one story in this book I tell its story; how Roger and Carolyn Tyndall, an air-traffic controller and housewife, started it; of their early difficulties and first success; and of its tremendous expansion with the aid of Dick Benson, the top direct marketing consultant who became their partner. In this book I have a separate story on Dick.

Adele Bishop became an interior decorator, researched early American wall designs with stenciling and with a partner developed a stencil design kit using transparent plastic. This led to a mail order ad for a brochure for 25¢ which offered kits of tools, designs and selected items . . . with business done from a Vermont country home. Adele became an authority on stenciling, author of a book on it and her business now does over

$300,000 a year by mail order. I tell the story in more detail in my chapter, "The Stenciler", in this book.

Many, many mail order moonlighters succeed. More people seem suited to mail order than to most businesses. Average I.Q. seems sufficient. Limited education is often not the barrier. And not sex, background or age. Beginners from teens to 70's have succeeded. The main barrier seems lack of practicality and lack of money sense. Sometimes, ivory tower scientists seem to have a worse chance than housewives ... and a better chance with their wives. Most women watch their costs better in mail order than men. They're accustomed to make dollars stretch. More and more women mail order moonlighters succeed.

Many who succeed in mail order avoid staples, heavy or bulky items, extremely expensive or under ten dollar items. They usually don't copy but originate unique items or catalogs. Far more moonlighters I have talked to have succeeded with inquiry and follow-up (two-step) than by selling in the ad itself (one-step)—but only with an item or items getting a high enough average order to support it—higher each year. Often those with simple black and white catalogs, often a list with prices, of highly needed items in a quite specialized and often new field have done well.

More who succeed in one-step, avoid middlemen, self-manufacture or import. Most with catalogs buy from manufacturers or importers, more rarely from wholesalers. With more items in a catalog, particularly where the field is specialized and sales per item small, most moonlighters make less mark-up per item; if so they may buy from wholesalers.

For most the first use of direct mail has been to follow up inquiries. When this has been very successful some have succeeded with a mailing to a few thousand names using lists highly specialized and suited to the product. Almost all avoided self-billing to start, selling all cash first and via credit cards if ads produced enough volume to justify setting up for it. But as the trend has been to more expensive specialized items and catalogs of them appealing to those with higher incomes, credit cards have sometimes been necessary to start.

Most moonlighters look for items quite superior to others, difficult to get in stores and not yet explained or demonstrated properly. Most, at first, avoid the broad appeal items, full page and lavish color ads, complex direct mail pieces or TV commercials used by the giants.

They can't afford all this. Instead, they succeed in ways most giants can't. They go into highly specialized products, limited volume, small display ads or even classified. Those who continue with the same product or catalog after finding it unprofitable usually concentrate on improving, modifying and changing the product or catalog. They often try to get others to take risk in manufacturing it or promoting it.

They crawl before they walk. But some do walk, then run and make a fortune ... and use credit cards, computers, telephone, elaborate mailings, full page ads, TV, or whatever. Malcolm Smith, who sells records and tapes on TV and whose story I tell in this book, started his TV mail order advertising schedule for 1979, 1980 and 1981 spending over $1 million a week. Maybe, one day, you will, too.

But, however small your moonlighting business and success may be, there's no thrill like the fun, excitement and money in mail order. It can start as a hobby, become a game ... then an addiction. Once you're hooked, you're in it for life. My book, "Mail Order Moonlighting", in 400 pages tells what I've learned that can be useful to mail order moonlighters. You can read it free in most business libraries or get a low-cost paperback edition at a book store. But, if you don't, I suggest you carefully read the following ten suggestions for new moonlighters:

1) Investigate mail order gradually, don't rush. Look at mail order ads in publications, or TV and in direct mail.

2) Write down your job experience, hobbies, sports, interests, any activity you're good at. Select areas you feel suited for.

3) In that area, write down any idea for a new item, service or business—or to improve one. Select best. Research further, develop, try to perfect.

4) If you're creative, practical, with feel for money—go it alone. If a dreamer, team up with a doer. If not creative, but practical, find a creative partner.

5) Limit your objective. Specialize in product (or catalog). Avoid commitments for merchandise, components, molds, dies, employees—any overhead, initially.

6) Keep studying mail order. In this book, I recommend courses, seminars, books, magazines, newsletters, booklets, articles and tapes of speeches that can help.

7) Learn as you go to create ads. Specify advantages, broadest in headline. Tell how to order or inquire. Be clear, complete, brief. Inquiry ads can be tiniest, even an inch, or several line classified ad. Simple black and white brochures even typewritten and photocopied may do to start. Avoid advertising production costs.

8) Substitute time and persuasion for money and risk when possible. Seek free write-up directing orders to you, or try to get others to take risk.

9) Advertise with one small ad, once. Try one publication, specialized to suit your product and in which mail order ads repeat. Sell for all cash, for several times your cost.

10) Give up on product if test ad fails, but not on mail order. Set aside monthly or annually sum you're willing to lose as if spent on hobby. Keep testing new ads or new items as above or get free write-ups; or get others to take risk until you succeed. Then run successful ad elsewhere—cautiously.

CAUTION: I have found no fool-proof blueprint to a mail order fortune. Following the above guideline will help you to start, survive in mail order and succeed modestly. At first, it will keep you from considering many kinds of more sophisticated products and advertising which later on you may find far more profitable, but perhaps can't afford now.

"If only I had known more, earlier." I've heard many successful moonlighters say this ... convinced success would have been faster and easier. I've seen moonlighters do the hard part ... creating or finding unique, innovative products or catalogs ... testing ads successfully for them ... improving products ... working nights and weekends—yet never get a fraction of what they are then entitled to.

For a small club of top experts there is far less risk. Testing is an art and expanding a near science. Rather than big money or big size, know-how is their secret. Know-how can increase the percentage of those who succeed and cut the losses of those who fail. But above all the know-how of this elite allows maximum projection at least risk. That is why a moonlighter, once successful starting, has far more need of the expertise many in this book can supply. Some sections of "Mail Order Know-How" concerned with more sophisticated methods can then be worth re-reading.

But now let's discuss moonlighters who use the simplest, lowest cost methods not practical for the big.

Chapter 14
Notes From The Mail Order Underground

How most mail order businesses start

It's mail order's other world, the way most mail order businesses start. It's the world of over one million classified ads run each year worldwide . . . a fascinating world of successful, little-known ventures. For over a year I researched this world. I studied over 10,000 classified ads, corresponded with over 1,000 entrepreneurs using them, and talked at length to over 400 of them.

Novice entrepreneurs told me how they built their businesses. I talked to those who failed as well as those who built businesses of a few thousand to millions of dollars a year . . . often starting with ads of a few words . . . often offering to send more information to get the final sale. One entrepreneur began with an ad costing $1.56, another for $2.07, others for $5 to $10 and many for from $15 to $85 in initial cost.

Those who failed told me what they felt they had done wrong. Entrepreneurs who succeeded advised of the steps they found most important to success. It was quite an eye-opener to me.

We had worked for big clients as an agency. Our clients couldn't afford to keep mail order counts of such tiny cost ads or keep track of such a small-scale operation at the start. And the more ads they ran, the more the overhead of functioning in a widespread, mail-order Lilliput became unprofitable. We had gone into our own products in much the same way as our clients did.

But here, in the mail order underground, I found a new world . . . one in which it was customary to go into business for the price of dinner, possible to do it for the price of breakfast and had been done successfully for the price of a tip.

A few months ago I had lunch with two of the authorities in mail order known most to biggest firms. I asked each this question: "Which publication in American ran more mail order ads than any other last year?" One answered, "Popular Science" and the other, "The National Enquirer".

The correct answer is Linn's Stamp News, a magazine for stamp collectors. It ran 22,000 mail order ads last year. 20,000 of them were classified ads. Most of the thousands of mail order businesses that Linn's Weekly launched are small hobbyists having fun; but almost every major stamp company started with a classified ad. Henry Harris was 14 when he started . . . with a free classified ad the The Washington Post, offered to any teenage businessman. The Harris Stamp Company is now the world's largest and a General Mills subsidiary. I tell its story in this book.

Ralph Garcelon was fired, in 1931, as a bookkeeper and started Garcelon Stamp Company as a mail order collector-dealer. It's now a substantial stamp company run by his son, Bill Garcelon. Maynard Sundman, in 7th grade, started buying stamps wholesale to sell in school retail. In 1935, he ran his first classified ad for Littleton Stamp as a mail order entrepreneur. Now Littleton has a hundred and fifty employees, a stamp division, a coin division and a rare coin division, and operates in the U.S. and Canada. All three stamp companies have made it . . . out of depression . . . through wars . . . and in inflation. Stamp collecting, and they, should continue and prosper.

Do you remember the flower children of a number of years ago who adorned themselves with beads? I know a couple who designed more imaginative, better quality beads . . . at precisely the right time . . . and advertised them with a classified ad. Inquiries flooded in, and sending samples resulted in a high percentage of orders. Sales produced profits of many times the cost of the ad.

For years they continued to own and operate their small but profitable business, located in Chicago. Mail order classified ads ran in Craft Horizons, Mother Earth News and Decorating Ideas. The profits bought an entire building with an art studio. The husband is a professor of art, and his main income never came from the mail order business. Now life is simple again. They both enjoyed the experience, but have no new mail order plans.

Of course, there were quite a few failures. For most, the losses were very tiny and they quickly stopped. But if classified ads were run widely and continuously in the hope that results would improve after the first test failed, losses mounted.

A truck driver had a hobby of woodworking. Tired of driving, he and his wife started a newsletter for fellow hobbyists . . as a future retirement business. They invested their entire savings in it. They ran classified ads in 45 publications, spent $8,000 in advertising and got less than 100 subscriptions.

Some did not particularly want to make money. It was a hobby. Thirty years ago, one of the most famous western singers on radio quit, and became rich in cattle and ranching. Then, after retirement, he began to make records again . . . and to sell them mail order with classified ads.

Others found ways to use their classified ads to lead to other sales. Robert Long was a trade magazine editor. He and his wife had a hobby . . . to find and visit castles in Europe that were also inns. They now publish a book, "Castle Hotels of Europe", and sell it by mail order . . . as their retirement business. It led to a cottage industry publishing business with several titles. The Longs handle mail order sales themselves. Hastings House Publishers has taken over trade sales.

Those who, on an average, have done best have done so with very simple catalogs, often in black and white, sometimes typed out and photo-offset or even photocopied to start with. Classified ads were used to get inquiries.

Carven Woll is a fisherman. In 1965, he ran a 12-word ad in Field & Stream for $14.50, to sell game cock necks to fly fishermen. Enough wanted game cock necks, for the fine-quality feathers for hackle, for it to pay off. Carv then sent customers a simple catalog of other fly fishing items. The business now does over $100,000 a year. Carv has been gradually retiring and his son, Alan, taking over.

Some have found fulfillment as well as a living from small businesses brought into being by stepping into the "Mail Order Underground", with a classified ad.

Ed Rich, of Norwich, graduated from Brown University in 1938 with an engineering degree, and worked for an oil company. But, years ago, he found fulfillment as a wood carver, first part-time and now full-time. He has a reputation for superb quality carving, from his eagle on Airforce One to the nameplate of the America. It all started with a tiny $21 ad in Yachting, brought him out of a depressed, nervous exhaustion and gave him a new, rewarding and profitable career. Ed has a country showmanship and integrity.

Some have built surprisingly large businesses starting with

classified. Nancy Crosby and Pat Baker are partners in Bacchanalia, in Central Village. Nancy worked in a bookstore. Pat is a chemist who put his chemistry know-how to work making his own wine and then his own beer . . . and then for others. Now Nancy and Pat have a mail order catalog, a retail store and a wholesale business selling to other wine and beer equipment stores and even a publishing business. Bacchanalia does over $500,000 a year but started with a $15.50 ad, as a moonlighting venture. Nancy runs the business full-time now, and Pat still works at his job. Their enthusiasm and vitality comes across to any visitor. After eleven years, they see even bigger growth ahead.

For many, a mail order business via classified has been an ideal retirement activity. Often it's been possible to go at almost any pace and with whatever hours a retiree feels up to. At modest risk, a comfortable extra income has been secured.

Since 1975, Charles and Ida Thoraldson have sold travel slides as their retirement business. They started with a classified ad. Their catalog is a typewritten list, inexpensively reproduced. Orders come in every day. Charles and Ida have customers from every state in the U.S. "Now, in addition, we have coverage from European suppliers who supplement our GAF coverage of every major country and continent in the world."

The company, WORLDWIDE SLIDES, of 7427 Washburn Avenue South, Minneapolis, Minnesota 55423, now publishes two additional special order catalogs . . . for slides not usually carried in stock but available on a special order basis. "Our catalogs now are very professional and produced in large quantities. We have tried other forms of advertising, but have found the classified ads to be our best source. Repeat business and referrals are the keys to our success."

The business has paid for numerous trips to Europe and to Mexico. A hard life!

Warning: Retirees who have little business experience and are not quite practical often lose. Even a small mail order venture has risk and makes demands on time and vitality and requires self-discipline.

Those who have the best chance have the most directly related experience. West Fork, Inc., of West Fork, Minnesota, is a catalog house offering backpackers', hikers', campers' and canoers' equipment. For Will Johnstone, former manager of Herter's Sportsman's catalog, it's a mail order retirement business. Will has two partners, including his son, Henry. West Fork started in 1976 with 1,000 catalogs and tested classified ads to secure inquiries. The next year he ran in 23 publications and display ads in three. By then he was printing 50,000 catalogs. Since then West Fork has continued to expand further.

For those advertising a single item with a classified ad, I found a very high mortality. Most failed. Those with a business potential, something they could sell continuously to the same mail order buyer, had far more success. This was pariculary so for the right related products in the right specialized field. A very specialized offer in the appropriate, very specialized magazine did well with a high percentage of success.

But there were considerably broader fields than that; selling begonias or boat plans or exotic computer accessories for computer buffs did well. The more people I talked to the more I learned and the more I respected their know-how versus top mail order professionals. I believe that if every trainee of the biggest mail order companies was forced to make classified ads work before progressing further, it would be the least expensive way to start training for most life-long effectiveness.

Some small to medium retailers have launched mail-order departments via classified. Leonard Katz owns Huning's De-

partment store in St. Charles, Missouri, near St. Louis. With a loose-leaf catalog of a few pages and a weekly classified ad in Grit, Huning's started a mail-order division in 1974. Its books are kept separately. It makes a profit each year. Leonard plans to expand into display ads and run widely. One camera store doing $200,000 a year in sales in a small town ran a classified ad statewide. It led to a $4,000,000 national mail-order business which, in turn, jumped the local store business to $500,000 annually.

A favorite story of mine is of Frank Hubbard who taught, at Harvard Music School, a course on "The Harpsichord—Its Role in Music, Society, Science, Technology, and the Decorative Arts", and another course on "Harpsichord Making in the Renaissance and Baroque Era". As a hobby, he made replicas of some of the harpsichords made by the masters. Then he got the idea of making kits of harpsichord replicas for others. He ran a classified ad and started a business. This was many years ago. His widow, Diane Hubbard, now runs it and it's close to $1,000,000 a year in volume.

Quite a few have told me of a new security, a flexibility, a quality of life they achieved. Success can be anywhere, often from a hobby or interest. Countless niches the big can't fit in become opportunities for the small.

John Caples, one of the greatest authorities on mail order advertising, used to experiment with classified ads for his mother's tutoring school. He thought them important enough to write a column, "How to Write a Classified Ad".

Every beginner and every expert should master classified ad mail order. It's the easiest, fastest and cheapest way to learn for big as well as small success.

Mail Order Sampler
Seminar I

"ENCORE" is the word, after hearing an "IVERS & POND."

IVERS & POND PIANOS.

Wherever in the United States we have no dealer, we send Pianos on trial (on **easy payments** if desired) and guarantee to suit you as well as if you lived in Boston. If unsatisfactory, we pay railroad freights both ways. This may seem risky to you — it has ceased to seem so to us. If you are unacquainted with our house we will gladly give unquestionable references as to our financial responsibility, the high merit of our piano, and our reputation for honorable dealing. The New England Conservatory of Music has bought since 1882 over 250 Ivers & Pond Pianos. We refer to this and the other 200 schools and colleges now using our Pianos. Old Pianos taken in exchange.

Catalogue and personal letter quoting lowest prices, with valuable information about piano-buying, including our unique easy payment plans, giving from one to three years to complete purchase, free upon request.

IVERS & POND PIANO COMPANY,

112 Boylston Street, Boston.

Chapter 1
Mail Order's Grand Old Man

*He was in at the birth of and nursed more
mail order businesses than anyone.*

It was his ninetieth birthday, September 25, 1980. His son, Bob, had come from Connecticut to Clearwater, Florida, for the celebration. His son, Sherman, who is in real estate in Clearwater was there, of course. As for his wife, Mary . . . she gave the party.

There were old friends in mail order who were visiting Florida. From all over the country others phoned good wishes, wrote or sent Mailgrams. I called days before and we spent almost an hour talking about mail order—before my time, during my time and right up to the moment.

Max Sackheim was the co-founder of the Book-of-the-Month Club. He may well have made any book club possible by coming up with the concept of negative option, whereby the monthly selections keep coming unless you notify the club you don't want them. Three-quarters of a century ago, Max Sackheim started working at his first job for a mail order advertising agency. He helped others start and build in mail order ever since.

He was born in Russia, but grew up in Chicago, a city boy. Yet, still in his teens, he could write mail order copy to farmers as if he were one. Every word was farmer talk. It was specific, factual and plain. It told exactly what the farm implement would do in a farmer's words. It sold.

Max, from the beginning, was a prolific copywriter. He never lost the habit. He wrote in his office, at the desk of a client, on the train, at home. There were few things he did not do.

He was the mail order creative director of Sears Roebuck before World War I. A half century before top ten advertising agencies bought mail order subsidiaries, he launched a mail order division for one of the three biggest, J. Walter Thompson. Thirty years before the first Reader's Digest sweepstakes, he used contests to sell books.

He was copychief of Ruthrauff and Ryan, the leading mail order advertising agency in the East, in New York City. He was a co-founder of Sackheim and Scherman, which became Schwab & Beatty, and which, in turn, for almost fifty years has been one of the great mail order advertising agencies.

He founded and operated in the 1940's and 1950's, the Maxwell Sackheim, Inc. advertising agency. From this agency came all three founding partners of what is today the biggest direct marketing advertising agency in the world, Wunderman, Ricotta & Kline. So did most of the first personnel and most of the first accounts and the majority of billing for years.

Max Sackheim made a top income most of his working life from mail order. He accumulated a big bank account of respect and affection from many along the road. He found a lot of personal satisfaction. But he did not make a great fortune in mail order.

Twice he came close to becoming very wealthy, each time in association with a brilliant intellectual. The first time was with Harry Scherman as partner in the Book-of-the-Month Club. Max sold out too soon, for $150,000. Harry Scherman persevered, through the depression, World War II and into the post war boom. Now it's owned by Time, Inc.

The other time was when Lester Wunderman worked for Max. Had Lester become a partner in Max Sackheim, Inc., there might have been no Wunderman, Ricotta & Kline. Instead, Max Sackheim, Inc. might have grown as WR&K did. It might have been sold to Young & Rubicam (as was WR&K). It might, itself, now be the world's biggest direct marketing advertising agency.

When Huber Hoge and Sons was starting in mail order Max Sackheim was a dean of mail order. He had written the first copy for Arthur Murray to sell dance lessons by mail order. We were first to put the Arthur Murray dance studios nationally on radio and then on television.

Max started Jackson & Perkins selling roses mail order with ads. We did so with garden programs on radio and television. Max had started Maxwell Sackheim, Inc. in 1942 with the Literary Guild as his first account. He had his first office in the Doubleday book store building on Fifth Avenue, above the store. Sackheim was one of the Doubleday agencies handling space advertising. We were the agency handling Doubleday radio and television advertising. (We did handle space for the Doubleday Book Stores.) Max Sackheim handled a good share of the space advertising for Greystone Press. We did the radio.

So I knew first-hand of the impact Max had on mail order and of his great ability. I learned from him just by sharing accounts with him. For anyone starting in mail order one of the first three books I recommend to read is "My 65 Years in Advertising," by Max Sackheim.

There is no way to prepare yourself better to understand and benefit from the most sophisticated, most up-to-date books and articles on direct marketing than to get the basic principles first from Max. His book is the story of his life and the story of mail order and America as it was. It's a nostalgia album of great ads written by Max. It's a history, a visit, a joy, a romp. It's easy, yet *must* mail order reading, and a course in basic copy.

For readers of this book I asked Max some questions which he has kindly answered.

Q. *Can the lessons learned in mail order be successfully applied in non-mail order businesses?*

A. Absolutely. My son, Sherman, applies mail order methods every day to the real estate brokerage business, in Clearwater. It helps him with classified and display ads to pull in leads. It helps in sales letters to close them. It helps in presenting the story for each house sold and in asking for the buying decision.

Q. *How interchangeable is the ability to run a mail order and a non-mail order business?*

A. If you can run a mail order business profitably, you can run any business profitably, but the reverse is not so.

Q. *Who was the client who was the most interesting to work with?*

A. Many were. Nelson Doubleday (Sr.) was a wonderful guy. He was so big and I was so short I had to take a step ladder to reach his ear. He was a client at Ruthrauff & Ryan, At Sackheim & Scherman and at Max Sackheim, Inc. He was really the father of the mail order book business. He tried a lot of original things in mail order even before he came to us. He was the most interesting, most effective and best person to deal with in all my years of work for Doubleday.

Q. *Can you recall Nelson Doubleday's first test through Ruthrauff & Ryan of the Lillian Eichler Book of Etiquette?*

A. Nelson Doubleday had taken some remainder etiquette books, with 1868 art. I had hired Lillian Eichler at Ruthrauff &

Ryan and trained her. She wrote the ad. When it sold people returned the book as too antiquated. Then Nelson Doubleday had her write the book. It sold over two million over the years.

Q. *How do you recall the Ruthrauff & Ryan advertising agency?*

A. Working there was wonderful. Ruthrauff was a patent medicine copywriter. Fritz Ryan was the son of a dentist, an entrepreneur and a great businessman. He had a lot of business experience and knowledge.

Q. *Did R&R sell many items, themselves, mail order?*

A. A few items, but very successfully.

Q. *What were Harry Scherman's strengths in mail order?*

A. He was a good businessman and a good book man. I think I was probably stronger in copy and advertising. The agency name was "Sackheim and Scherman"—not "Scherman and Sackheim."

Q. *Today they call mail order methods direct marketing. When direct marketing is applied to the advertising of any business for non-mail order activities they call it main stream direct marketing or action advertising. What are your views on this?*

A. All advertising is based on the mail order principle: Attract, convince, give benefits, give satisfaction, get action. Mail order know-how can make any advertising better—for anything.

Q. *Whom do you recall as the most able copywriter you trained?*

A. Vic Schwab. We both attended a course of instruction in advertising production. He was 18 or 19 and bright. He knew shorthand. I hired him as my secretary, at $15 a week. He learned and wrote great copy and, with Bob Beatty, continued as Schwab & Beatty after Harry Scherman and I turned Sackheim and Scherman over to them.

Q. *How do the opportunities today in mail order seem to you compared with the early days?*

A. Better. It's more of a business. Then it was more often a promotion. Now there's more variety of product sold at higher prices. American Express now sells merchandise at prices from $500 to $1,000.

Q. *If you had it to do all over again, would you be a mail order advertising man?*

A. I'd be in management and ownership, where the money is.

But then, Max, you would have specialized. We never would be able to study the tremendous variety of ads you've written. Your ads like "Do You Make These Mistakes in English?" are in every advertising copy course and included in the "100 Greatest Advertisements." You probably wouldn't have had time to write "My 65 Years in Advertising" or your other great book, "How to Advertise Yourself." And the readers of this book wouldn't have the chance to read them.

Note: Both are listed in the help source section in back of this book. For mail order wisdom that seasons with age, read them.

Chapter 2
Direct Marketing's Multi-Media Voice

It's run like a radio station, publishes magazines and newsletters and offers 7,000 tapes of speeches and lectures.

If your company or you start to consider seriously going into mail order and direct marketing, a most important man to help you is "Pete" Hoke. He is president of Hoke Communications, Inc., whose business is providing more information about mail order and direct marketing than is available anywhere. It publishes magazines and newsletters. It's an audio cassette producer. It's a fascinating mail order business.

"Pete" Hoke has been described as a teacher of direct marketing. His greatest satisfaction has been teaching classes of beginners, for nothing. His magazines, newsletters and cassettes are his continuing course in all phases of direct marketing. I have never seen an equivalent service in depth and variety in any industry.

His Direct Marketing magazine and Friday Report newsletter are essential to direct marketers. Hoke subscribers include sophisticated giants and users of latest technology and most advanced techniques. More than any other man, "Pete" has given Fortune 500 the research facts needed to get into and benefit from direct marketing.

Yet, it's still not a huge enterprise. "Pete's" father started it in a very small way in May, 1938. It crawled, walked and then ran. Even then, it had to face and survive unexpected adversity. It overcame, grew and prospered. It's proof a small family-owned mail order business can be simply run and make it.

"Pete's" real name is Henry Reed Hoke, Jr. His son, Hank, is Henry Reed Hoke, III. The business started with Henry Hoke, Sr., who got into it by accident. In Pittsburgh during the early 1920's, Henry Sr. wrote some sales letters to get inquiries for his employer's salesmen who then made more sales. They boasted about their letter writer to other salesmen. Soon Henry Sr. was moonlighting, writing letters for other companies, which grew to a creative in-house lettershop. It grew until his boss invited Henry to start his own business, with his boss as his first client. He discovered other lettershops by attending a national convention in Pittsburgh of the Mail Advertising Service Association. He met John Howie Wright, publisher of "Postage and the Mail Bag", a magazine covering direct mail. John heard Henry make a speech at a later convention and asked him to come to New York as editor. And he did, in 1929.

In the depth of the Depression, the Board of DMMA (then Direct Mail Advertising Association) asked John Howie if it could borrow Henry to be their executive director. Henry was manager of DMMA until 1938 and put DMMA on the map with road shows to many cities, introducing direct mail. (When "Pete" was in high school, he worked summers in the DMMA mail room.)

In 1938, "Postage and the Mail Bag" folded. The employees asked Henry Sr. (still at DMMA) to start a new magazine. Key suppliers guaranteed 12 pages of ads for a year if Henry Sr. would do so. He did. The first issue was called "The Reporter of Direct Mail Advertising".

Direct marketing was then unknown. Mail order was far smaller than now. "The Reporter" covered mainly direct mail used for selling to businesses. It was a tiny publication running about 36 pages per issue. In the 16 years Henry Sr. ran it, "The Reporter" became trusted, controversial, respected and successful. It grew along with direct mail and mail order. It was intimate and personal. It still covered direct mail but with more emphasis on mail order. Henry Sr. wrote most of it. He had close friends in the field who were masters of their specialties and who contributed.

"Pete" had learned a great deal from Henry Sr. and from his father's associates as well. When "Pete" took over "The Reporter" in 1955 he made a gradual transition to a new generation of contributors . . . his own close friends who had grown up in the field with him. As the field of direct mail and mail order expanded, the magazine began to cover its many new forms in all media, with emphasis on new technology and techniques.

Today, many years after "Pete" bought out Henry Sr., Direct Marketing magazine (named in May, 1968) is almost entirely different . . . from name to content. "Pete" too, spent his four years at the Wharton School of Business. When he first became involved with The Reporter, it was as a space salesman, not a writer. He had his own ideas. "Pete" is a futurist. He studies the economy. He senses change. How his doing so changed the Hoke family business is a more exciting mail order case history than any he has ever reported.

Lew Kleid, an old friend of Henry Sr.'s, may have planted the first seed for the concept that changed the Hoke business. In 1956, Lew wrote a series of classic articles in The Reporter, each in question and answer form, each interviewing a top leader in the field. Later, the series was published by "Pete" as "Mail Order Strategy", a 150-page book.

Years later, Al Migliaro, then editor of The Reporter, interviewed Postmaster General Blount in the magazine using the same question and answer format. "Pete" liked it and wondered whether more articles could be written that way. Then he had a great idea. Why not apply this technique of interviewing to tape recording? He had watched a young couple with their tape recorders taping meetings. "Pete" got them involved. Then he, himself, began to tape and set up a studio for mastering and duplication.

At first, he taped for later rewriting. Reel tapes were expensive, but taping technology was making startling improvements in reproduction. Then small cassettes were introduced and new equipment was developed to facilitate duplication. Reproduction quality was stable and excellent, and the new tape was inexpensive.

Then "Pete" hired John Hicks (the famous voice of "The Shadow" on the Mutual Broadcasting System radio network) to head up a new editorial-cassette department. They were a great team. "John and I developed the present interview technique and system" explains "Pete". "He had the voice; I had the direct marketing background."

"Pete" created a new income stream, starting with a $2,000 investment in tape equipment. He felt his way into, developed and proliferated the cassette library idea to form the base of his publishing pyramid. "Pete" became a compulsive taper of anything connected with direct marketing. It went far beyond dollars and cents. In the early 1970's he began to go beyond direct mail and beyond the U.S. to cover all media, to travel the world.

At luncheons, meetings, seminars and university courses from New York to Los Angeles, the tapes began recording it all. Some days, at almost any given hour, anywhere on the globe, a Hoke tape is being recorded or listened to. On such days, the sun never sets on "Pete's" audio network.

His cassettes are tiny time capsules of direct marketing, the audio journal. In the Hoke archives are over 7,000 tapes of direct marketing speeches and lectures. In 1972, "Pete" published a tape catalog, "Ideas in Sound", and has issued a catalog every six to twelve months since. It takes over 600 catalog pages just to list and describe the tapes. The 1981 catalog contained 92 pages listing tapes produced in 1980 alone.

Direct marketing is vast and constantly changing and proliferating. Even the best once-a-week university course is an overview. A several-day seminar, while more intense, has much the same limitation. Only "Pete" has an endlessly updated encyclopedia of direct marketing in sound and print. For the superb New York University direct marketing course alone, "Pete" has taped over 250 lectures by top authorities. He has taped hundreds more lectures on different phases of direct marketing delivered at top courses of leading institutions. He has taped great seminars and classic speeches by most respected authorities.

"Pete's" audio reporters also interview by telephone top executives of the biggest companies in direct marketing, taping it all. They also tape small, kitchen-table moonlighters. Often the reporter returns at a later date for updates. "Pete" is the audio historian for the big and the small, for the authorities and the newcomers in each aspect of the field. Over 60 tapes are made each month. About a third of them are interviews. Of about 200 to 250 interviews a year, 25 to 30 are transcribed and printed in the magazine. Of 500 or so *talks* taped each year, perhaps only 10 to 15 are then printed.

In 1981, the typical tape was offered for $10. Longer tapes were $12, and the longest were $15. To buy them all would cost over $50,000. To listen to them all would take an hour a day, 7 days a week, for 20 years! If all "Pete's" tapes were transcribed and printed in book form, over 40,000 pages would be needed. Perhaps 10% are priceless classics. These include great lectures on subjects that never date, such as copy and strategy. They include most instructive case histories. For $5,000, the same tapes can be used by any firm to train each new employee at modest cost. What a master course!

From "Pete's" 7,000 cassettes can come a variety of custom courses, varying in depth, complexity and specialty. "Pete's" personnel can custom blend the right combination for any firm or individual. No matter what the field, from a boutique wanting to sell by mail order to industrial direct marketing, "Pete" has highly specialized tapes perfect for the specialty.

At times, a cassette buying customer will give "Pete" a budget of $500 to $1,000 to custom select the tapes most suitable for the situation. But benefits may be gained in other ways, as well. These tapes are the information bank for "Pete's" publishing. Some of the very best are available in printed form for far less cost.

It was the cassette concept that so completely changed Direct Marketing magazine. The cassettes created such an evergrowing flow of information that they made possible an entirely new approach. Under John Hicks and "Pete", all reporters were trained in the audio medium. The magazine now draws heavily on the cassette base. Always 1 or 2 of these transcriptions appear monthly in the magazine.

In 1964, "Pete" started attending international meetings in Europe and, in 1970, in Australia. The recording of meetings worldwide made Direct Marketing magazine international, now with approximately 2,000 subscriptions from overseas.

In 1953, with less time to call on advertisers, "Pete" started a free newsletter to keep in touch. When the mailing list reached to 3,400 and costs in the mail jumped, he asked for paid subscriptions. When he began to tape, the newsletter became a perfect vehicle to tell subscribers about cassettes. Friday Report, as it is called, has a staccato, flash bulletin style. Taping so much in so many places provides "Pete" with so much latest, fast-breaking information that a growing percentage of Direct Marketing magazine subscribers are also newsletter subscribers.

In the late 1960's, fund raising by mail became a more important part of direct marketing. Churches, alumni councils and other organizations wanted much more information about more efficient methods of fund raising. For them, "Pete" launched Fund Raising Management magazine in 1969. This led to FRM Weekly newsletter for the same field. In 1979, "Pete" issued a separate tape catalog for fund raising.

Audio cassettes are the input for all four publications. Fastest breaking news goes into the newsletters. Ordered cassettes are made and mailed within 48 hours. The magazines come later. The same audio reporters service them all.

Hoke Communications, Inc., is a successful publisher. It is diversifying and not all based on tapes. "Pete" has an open mind for any business publication for which he feels there is a need. Marketing Information Guide was a government publication that later became a private enterprise. It covered economics and research. When the owners couldn't make a go of it, "Pete" took it over and has published it for years with no tie-in to taping.

However, the tapes have greatly expanded "Pete's" publishing activities. They give him a simple low-cost method to feel his way in any area. The tape concept may lead "Pete" further in directions beyond direct marketing. The tapes made Direct Marketing magazine more of a magazine of record. It made back issues more important. Many subscribers buy them and some even buy a bound volume (at $36) every year for library use.

Cassettes led to Advercassettes. Anyone with a reputable service for direct marketers can be interviewed by a Hoke reporter to advertise their service. The advertiser pays nothing to be taped but $8 for each tape shipped. Each tape gives the advertiser's name, address and phone number. For some advertisers, results have been excellent. The cassette buyer pays only one or two dollars. People who buy Advercassettes value them. I, for one, like paying $1 instead of $8 for a cassette on a subject I need information on.

Under Henry Sr., and into the 1950's, Hoke published some splendid small books of 100 to 150 pages. But the cassettes have made Hoke more of an educational institution as well as publisher. Now Hoke does sound publishing while selecting and selling the printed books of other publishers.

Understandably, "Pete" is convinced of the benefits of cassette listening. Before taking a long trip by car, "Pete" checks his latest catalog for cassettes containing new ideas and takes a dozen along. "There's absolutely no greater thrill than driving while hearing the voices of friends, acquaintances and newcomers talk about an exciting new breakthrough." The tapes stimulate "Pete". "They're a great way to pick up profitable ideas in your down time. It's a rare day that dozens of idea's don't come forward."

John Hicks died of cancer in 1979. "Pete" and the audio staff trained by John carry on. New reporters are selected for voice effectiveness, reporting ability and aptness in handling tape equipment as well as in the interview technique.

"Pete" has created a publishing hybrid. It has prospered while most family-owned business publishers have sold out to conglomerates or folded. "Every year from 1964, we've turned down take-over offers. More important is the fulfillment and satisfaction serving constituencies gives."

But success hasn't come automatically. In 1963, "Pete" suffered a real disaster. Fire destroyed his building. Insurance coverage couldn't begin to make up for all indirect losses. But "Pete" built a fine new four-story building. He rents out two floors and uses the other two. With high ceilings, large rooms and beautiful furnishings, there's a quiet, restful and creative atmosphere.

It's a real family business. Jean Demment Hoke, "Pete's" wife, became treasurer in 1968. As a housewife and mother of two, she had watched pennies at home. Now she does so in business. Everyone calls her by her nickname, "Demi". The most effective promotion Hoke has ever done came not from "Pete" or any expert, but from "Demi's" common sense. She clipped mail order ads of firms not yet subscribers to follow up in her own way, with sample magazines and simple letters. It's not uncommon that she converts up to 20% of carefully selected names for a "mass" mailing of, say, 200 letters.

"Pete" is training a new generation of the family. Henry "Hank" Hoke, III has two children. "Hank" now heads the tape cassette division. He came up with the idea that is now helping to solve "Pete's" greatest problem: finding the time to hear all new cassettes.

"Hank" discovered "Teknicon". It's a variable speech recorder without "Mickey Mouse" effects. With it, an audio reporter can play back tapes up to twice as fast and hear each word distinctly. He can slow down hurried talkers. Secretaries can type from the tape quickly and accurately. It's been so effective for the Hokes that they have offered it to cassette buyers. Now "Hank" is investigating video programming and colorful cassettes.

Daughter Wendy is busy raising two children. Her husband, Stuart Buysen, has joined Hoke Communications and has developed computer operations.

Not everything works. In 1978, "Pete" published in portfolios from selected winners of DMMA award ad campaigns with case histories and sales results. "It was a disaster," says "Pete". But his batting average is good.

Henry Sr. found a need in a highly specialized field and filled it with a service not available elsewhere. "Pete" Hoke anticipated direct marketing's growth and proliferated additional specialized services that can't be duplicated.

"Pete" is a catalyst and synergist intertwined with all direct marketing. He is a staunch supporter of the association, the DMMA. He promotes direct marketing clubs and direct marketing days in many cities. Often he helps launch them. He has helped in the birth and growth of equivalent organizations and events in other countries. He publicizes seminars and reviews books. He orients, teaches and familiarizes us all with each other. He often writes his own very effective subscriber promotion.

In his magazine and with his cassettes, you can sample a seminar, a course or the thought of an expert before paying anything substantial for the expertise. Often you can go on to read more articles, listen to more cassettes or read a book by the same expert for little expense and sometimes in a library for nothing. The next step can be to attend a seminar, subscribe to an expert's newsletter or attend workshops conducted by the same experts. Later you may choose to pay a personal consulting fee or become an advertising agency client for a minimum fee. Often it all may start by reading Direct Marketing Magazine or listening to "Pete's" cassettes.

There are probably ample case histories in or close to your field, whether you are a retailer, manufacturer, wholesaler or in service. There's expert advice on a wide range of subjects from new product selection to creating attractive new offers to the mathematics of profit and loss in mail order.

There's a lot of creative help ... from a stream of articles on writing profitable copy to creating more effective graphics. There's help in media and list selection. Whether the subject is telephone marketing, latest technology or technique or world mail order, top specialists in that field are interviewed to give you answers.

"Pete" is at his best when reporting on latest and future anticipated developments. He is at his happiest when setting up new technology in his own business as with his cassettes or latest computer, a Datapoint. In 1980, he put in a new Datapoint with 120 megabytes (120 million characters) capacity and many applications from billing to typesetting to segmenting his cassette catalog for custom recommendation for cassette purchasers.

Of all tapes, some on strategy, copy, approaches to creative work, buying media, overhead control, history of mail order and direct marketing and the best of case histories are timeless classics.

"Pete" is particularly intrigued with electronic mail and in any way to maintain banks of information in any field with access available to subscribers via telephone or TV. Meanwhile, advertising in Direct Marketing Magazine has grown like Topsy. It's jumping in Fund Raising Management. Back copy sales, book sales and list rentals add further to income. The newsletters prosper. Cassette sales grow and grow.

Cassettes are used by regulars to keep up with anything missed. They are credited by Jim Kobs as part of his research for his great book, "Profitable Direct Marketing". They have been invaluable to use to back up my own research. They're used by salesmen before making a call. They're used for training and for reference.

"Pete's" catalogs listing them represent a who's who of direct marketing greats. Each catalog is arranged chronologically and indexed by company and name of speaker or interviewee.

For those entering the field, the best first step is to read selected articles and to listen to selected cassettes. I've selected, out of 7,000 cassettes, about 300 that are available either in magazine reprint form or in cassette form. These are listed in Reference Section IV and V of The Help Source Guide in this book.

I've also asked "Pete" Hoke to have his staff recommend, personally, for anyone starting in the field and reading this book, a custom selection of reprints and of cassettes suited to the situation of each company or individual phoning or writing Hoke.

For anyone reading this book and short of money, I suggest asking for Direct Marketing back issues or cassettes at your nearest business library or university or business college library. Leading ones may have some Hoke cassettes. Some subscribe to Hoke magazines and newsletters. If so, you can read or listen at no charge.

If you go into mail order and direct marketing as a career, want to sell a service or merchandise to those in it, if your firm starts a division in it or if you become an entrepreneur in it, you'll need "Pete". We all can be grateful that Hoke Communications exists.

Chapter 3
List Success Strategy

It worked for aristocrats of mail order to launch new direct marketers. It can work for you.

It's solid, unromantic bookkeeping. It's treating a new direct marketing campaign like a new business. But this strategy, plus some unusual abilities, made Rose Harper first president and then principal owner of the Kleid Company. Kleid is a leading list broker, manager of lists and consultant on lists. Its clientele includes direct marketing major firms from Time-Life to Grolier Inc.

She is Italian. Her smile is gentle. Her mind is purposeful. She is a compassionate intellectual. She has avoided woman's traditional business role. "In school and later in all my courses I took no shorthand ... to avoid becoming a secretary." Instead, Rose studied accounting and became a self-made female capitalist. She bought her firm back from the big conglomerate the founder sold it to. Under Rose's management it has tripled its size in the last ten years.

Rose has helped many get into and ahead in direct marketing. Each is a young man or woman recipient of a Kleid scholarship to learn direct marketing. Kleid has given over 500 of these scholarhsips. Rose may be able to help you.

This is more likely if you'd like to work for or sell to big direct marketers . . . or if you are one. If you have a small newsletter or self-publish books, you can benefit. For any woman who wants to make it in direct marketing, Rose is a living lesson that it can be done. Her strategy will work for anyone in mail order.

Rose first worked for an accounting firm, then audited for Liberty Mutual Insurance and next became comptroller for a relief organization. Then Rose found the right firm, in the right field, at the right time and with the right boss. In 1950, Rose started as comptroller for the Lewis Kleid Company, a direct mail letter shop.

Lewis Kleid was a pioneer and leader. His company could perform almost every function connected with direct mail . . . planning it, laying it out and writing it . . . buying printing . . . selecting lists, then addressing and mailing them. He had grown up with his cream accounts and learned with them.

For years The Reporter of Direct Mail Advertising (now the Direct Marketing Magazine) printed a series of interviews conducted by Lewis Kleid with top direct mail leaders. These were collected and published in a book, "Mail Order Strategy", distributed by the DMMA. They are still recommended by Richard S. Hodgson in his "Direct Mail and Mail Order Handbook" as must reading for anyone entering direct marketing.

Lewis Kleid sensed that direct mail advertising now required more specializing. In 1951, he gave up creative work. In 1960, Rose submitted a business plan which made it clear that concentration on lists was the way to go. Lewis Kleid gave up the letter shop business to concentrate on list brokerage and management. And concentrating paid off. The list business grew.

Rose recalls: "Lewis Kleid was marvelous to me. He let me do anything. I quickly went beyond being comptroller." Working under Kleid, Rose had now learned each aspect of the list business as he knew it. "My turning point was when Lewis Kleid let me make list recommendations to a client."

"I looked at the problem from an accounting viewpoint. I studied every list the client had ever bought from us. I took notes of every list the client repeated and presumably made money from. I did the same for every list the client had tested and dropped, presumably because unprofitable.

"I then analyzed possible lists to buy, by categories. I picked kinds of lists as similar as possible to the successes. I avoided the kinds of lists that had failed. My recommendations made money for the client. I had a new job."

From then on Rose played a bigger part in the business. She studied changing technologies and methods of list selection along with Kleid's clients. Because Kleid worked with larger direct marketing firms, she had access to new developments at early stages.

"Lewis Kleid was fair, but not easy. He was innovative and very open to suggestions and ever cautious. But he did have a very strong personality of his own. We complemented each other. He was creative . . . truly so. He could write well . . . and was superb in graphics . . . and had a flair in working with people. Actually, he preferred to be active with the written word rather than be active personally in associations and organizations. It was not lack of interest, but rather a personality trait."

Rose, too, could write . . . well and with great clarity. In the early 1960's, Rose wrote a prophetic article predicting a number of requirements of the coming zip age. Big list houses had early computers. The first big mail order companies were converting lists to magnetic tape. But, by 1967, when the post office began to require zip coding less than 10% of lists were on computer.

Direct marketers were fearful. Rose recalls, "Mailing zip code would be too expensive . . . the costs would drive anyone into Chapter XI . . . but, immediately, computerization of direct mail and the list business became a necessity . . . a major marketing revolution was forced on us . . . and direct marketing prospered as never before.

"Zip coding led to the computer . . . and through it to data processors, statisticians and market analysts. The computer helped us to indentify duplicate names . . . which resulted in zip analysis . . . which in turn gave us the first chance to segment the lists and to analyze them far more precisely than before."

In 1968, Rose took a course in computer programming. This and her accounting background gave her an edge with the new tools. She began to be interested in probability theory math as a possible tool for more scientific list selection.

In 1970, Lewis Kleid sold out to a big conglomerate, Dart Industries, Inc. Shortly after, Lewis Kleid retired. Rose ran the company for Dart, as the first woman president of any Dart division. When she found that Dart had scientists, advanced mathematicians and physicists, she persuaded top management to assign several to a special project.

An IBM 360 computer at UCLA was programmed by Dart scientists according to probability theory in a manner to make list recommendations. Rose supplied characteristics of lists profitably mailed for a specific item . . . plus those of a variety of lists under consideration. She gave sales results of other items mailed to each list considered. The scientists fed the facts into the computer. The computer analyzed facts received, determined probability of successful use of each list considered and made list selection recommendations.

The experiment was first reported in an article in Direct Marketing Magazine. Rose recalls: "The Dart scientists, Anthony

Posgny and Marcel Tyzler, wrote the majority. I wrote the introduction and close and tried to simplify and clarify it."

Today, leading list companies have computer data banks. Comparison of results from list selections made by computer versus buying lists without a data bank have shown dramatic jumps in results. But Rose's bank was one of the first. "The Kleid Mailing List Selection Guide was a new technique to improve by a substantial margin results from lists."

Since then, more and more, Rose has become a middle person between scientists and mail order executives. She works with specialists to come up with the right formula for the situation to reduce mailing costs and to boost results. Kleid has the exclusive in the list brokerage and management field for the RESPOND computer modeling method of direct mail analysis described in this book in the chapter on "Computer Modeling for Mail Order Decisions".

Rose's next opportunity came when Dart Industries decided to relinquish several acquisitions including Kleid. In 1975, Dart sold 100% of Kleid to Rose. Now Rose could take on a more creative, guiding role and project more of herself into her business and direct marketing.

"Running your own business despite what would appear to be simplicity because of size . . . is a 24-hour a day job. And sometimes the rewards don't seem worth the headaches! You love what you're doing . . . but as your business grows, you've got to spread yourself thinner and thinner. That's dangerous.

"During my life in a small business—initially I found it necessary to learn a great deal about taxes, legal matters, anti-trust exposure, because, unlike a big company, these matters could not be referred to 'legal'. Running a small company means you call the shots. It also means that sometimes you must execute the shots you call.

"One of the real problems I have seen is that many small enterprises are kept from growing larger because of their failure to adapt the proven operational methods of big business— research and development, budget plans, cost accounting, cash flow analysis and corporate structure. 'Big Business' has the right idea and you can't ignore these management concepts. Small companies seem to have to devote more time to getting the job done. This is not enough. In our company, we regularly spend a great deal of time in quality control and examining every step of our operation to see if it can't be done a little better or faster.

"Each time you set a new goal for your business, you've got to view its achievement—that is, your company's further growth— as an occasion for delegating authority . . . not just dumping a responsiblity onto somebody else.

"A good solution is to make it possible for key employees to have a stake in the business. I found it practical to develop that personal stake by letting key people purchase equity in the business. I did not give a share. Like everything else in life, equity is valued and cherished proportionate to our personal investment in it."

Kleid has grown with its accounts. Some of its oldest accounts have, in time, become some of the biggest and most sophisticated direct marketers, for example, The Kiplinger Washington Editors, Inc. "But we don't discourage smaller clients. Architectural Digest, Bon Appetit and others started with us when quite small. We will turn down a conglomerate if we fear it can't pay out. We turn down shabby, get-rich-quick or pornographic items. We've turned down clients we felt were not organized to benefit from direct marketing.

"The profitable use of big volume direct mail is sophisticated. Computers, data processors (human and machine), statisticians, mathematicians and market analysts are needed. We have three strong mathematical people in our organization. But we advise clients to call in their own specialists to help them get the most from available technology.

"We like to treat a new marketing campaign like a new business. It's my accounting background. We help the client make a forecast . . . actually a pro forma financial estimate of sales and profit objectives, even before the first test. As the campaign progresses we keep comparing results with forecasts.

"When the campaign is over we like to make a report exactly as if a company's financial statement. Then we compare the final balance sheet and income statement with the original pro forma statements. This brings us more into their organization. For Time-Life we were in on preparing tests for Sports Illustrated when it was Project X. We've worked closely with Grolier, Book-of-the-Month, Meredith, Smithsonian, Time Inc. Magazines, Time-Life Books, U.S. News, Natural History, just to mention a few.

"Today there's new technology. There's more concentration in list management to deliver more revenue per name. We've pioneered in both . . . and in the concept of a list consultant. We initiated the fee system for list brokers. We prefer it. The relationship is more comparable to that of an accountant, lawyer or advertising agency. We do more list buying for the client exclusively, while cooperating with other brokers. Kiplinger was the first to work with us this way."

An accountant is thought of as cold, dry and with eyes only for hard facts. Rose is warm, with her eye on the future as well as the present. She has practicality and curiosity, organization and imagination. She has a balanced life. "I love what I do in business but have many interests. I get involved in many animal causes, from the Animal Protection Institute to the ASPCA."

Rose reads a lot. Favorite subjects are philosophy, logic and reasoning as well as economics and business. She is moral and urges others to be. She has a desire to help others. Her husband shares these feelings and, in turn, has inherited an intellectual outlook from his father, a Ph.D. from Columbia.

Rose and her husband, Rondel, now retired from management in Rockefeller Center, have always been interested in investment. Rose has a mix of the ability to think in money terms and on an intellectual level, of a drive forward and sympathy for others.

Just out of school, Rose wrote articles in Italian for the Italian Tourist Bureau. Her math background has helped to organize her creative research, thinking and writing. Rose is articulate. She can explain very well very complex technology and techniques. She can give a speech or write an article or newsletter constructed like a Swiss watch. She has never worked or trained as a copywriter. She is self-taught. She writes simply, easily and in down-to-earth terms . . . with utmost clarity. She knows copy and has a feeling for headlines and subheads.

Her newsletter, *Immediate Release*, is pragmatic, fact-loaded, stimulating and sometimes poetic. Who but Rose would quote Maurice Maeterlink to underline the problem of over-high cancellations or Henry James to stimulate the imaginations of direct marketers. It's all a mix of imagery, simple basics, the complex and down-to-earth, practical advice and eloquence.

"Our business—yours and the Kleid Company's—is not for the weak, the lazy or the shortsighted. We're in an enviable position . . . we can measure just about everything to find a profit—that is the task." When Rose writes of "a feast of profits"

you want to draw up a chair. When she discusses "blackest anthracite bottom-line figures", it's a clarion call.

All this is part of much solid, practical help. In one issue, Rose asks the greatest direct marketing writers, one-by-one, what they want to know, before they write, about the people to whom their mailings will go. Each answers, explaining the importance. Rose goes on.

"All of us have to understand demographics, psychographics, regression analysis, return on investment and the wealth of other tools we can now field as armament in the war for profits. It's a war which the smart and the tough, those who offer reliable products and services, will survive."

Rose keeps reporting latest ways computers, zip codes and analysis of ordering record make possible more scientific use of direct mail. "Today each time someone buys by mail, it's a personal statement. You can know your customer's preferences and find people like them to mail to. Selectivity is the essence of direct mail." Rose reduces it all to "mail less . . . pull more". Kleid's study on seasonality (when biggest mailers mail—month by month—according to the field) is a classic.

Rose's talks and lectures on list selection are in the same vein. Rose has for many years participated as a lecturer or moderator at DMIX annual meetings, Direct Marketing Days, DMMA Conferences and other activities in the field.

Rose credits this philosophy of help a great deal to Lewis Kleid. "Lewis first contributed to start the DMMA Educational Foundation." For seven years the Kleid Company, solely, supplied foundation scholarships. Kleid has fully paid transportation, room and meals for over 500 students who then pay nothing for the one-week course. This is a staggering gift.

"It's exhilarating to see what the course means to those taking it. It's one full week. The students work hard. I've taught at the Institute, myself. Many students have told me that they have never had a week of training so exciting. They became absolutely fascinated."

This foundation is in its thirteenth year. It has over 50% women enrolled. Minorities are well represented. "Many of those winning scholarships have gone on into direct marketing, some with great success."

During her career Rose has seen the number of lists offered by brokers jump from a few hundred to over thirty thousand. She has seen the use of direct mail, the numbers of list users and the number of mailing list brokers and managers multiply as well. She has been a prime leader in direct marketing. For four years she served as Treasurer of the Direct Mail/Marketing Association. In the Fall of 1981, Rose became the first woman to be elected Chairman of the Association.

Rose sees new direct mail opportunities for the small. "Package billing and co-op mailing inserts have become a new medium." Specialty catalogs for the unusual, like architectural items, found direct markets exactly suited to the specialty. Lewis Kleid was very bearish on the chances of small mail order beginner entrepreneurs. And so is Rose. Rose has never taken a mail order flyer, herself. "I'm too busy."

If you want to start a career in direct marketing, heed these words of Rose. "A college degree is the minimum for a fair chance in direct marketing—with some emphasis on statistics and finance. Direct mail is becoming sophisticated in the development of campaigns. Much of this depends on statistical evaluation, proper budgets and projections. I don't see how anyone can move up on the management echelon without an understanding of financial fine-point."

Rose Harper has kindly made available a copy of her newsletter at no cost. For the most recent issue, write the Kleid Company, 200 Park Avenue, New York, New York 10017.

Any student of a business college or university marketing course may apply through his or her class instructor for a Kleid Scholarship to The Direct Mail Marketing Educational Foundation, 6 East 43rd Street, New York, NY 10017.

Rose's parting recipe for direct marketing success is "hard work, talent, perseverance . . . and to keep on learning the business." Rose, where are your thorns?

Chapter 4
How To Start a Catalog

*—grow carefully in the mail
order business and survive.*

She seems living proof that anyone . . . without experience or real capital . . . can start in mail order and catapult to unexpected, big success. Her success seems a blue print for easy mail order riches. Instead, it's the result of unusual qualities and background, hard work and strong will . . . and circumstances that may not recur.

At 10, she arrived in New York City, an immigrant not speaking English. At 24, to save babysitter charges, she started a home mail order business with a monogrammed leather belt she designed herself. Her first ad cost $495 and in six weeks pulled in $16,000. At 54, she did over $40 million yearly in sales.

Her 35,000 square-foot headquarters is in Mt. Vernon, New York. Her 44,000 square-foot office for order processing, telephone ordering and customer services is in New Rochelle. Her 100,000 square-foot warehouse is in Port Chester, and her showrooms are on Fifth Avenue in New York City. Her wholely-owned subsidiary manufactures her copyrighted items—and an extensive line of costume jewelry—in Providence, Rhode Island.

Each day, her computer typically reports 7,500 orders received for over $25 each. She is the biggest receiver of mail in Mt. Vernon. Each day, her creative staff of artists and writers are busy on the next of her eight different catalogs, 30 million copies of which are mailed yearly. Her buyers are interviewing salesmen offering new items while her bookkeepers tote up profits. She is the largest shipper of packages in Port Chester, shipping a total of 1,850,000 packages in 1981 alone. Her shipping facility is a model of computerized order handling and automation. From August through December, she has 550 employees, and 225 in other months.

Her married name is Lillian Katz. But tens of millions know her as Lillian Vernon, the name of her catalog house. Lillian credits her first ad's success to a good item, a good price, an exciting new magazine, *Seventeen*, and the strong appeal of personalization to the kids. It was a belt for $2 and belts were big in 1951. The timing was perfect.

She used her bonanza profits for a self-taught mail order education. She ran more ads and found and developed more items. She made up a leaflet and inserted it with each order. She shipped out of the back of her first husband's store. Then he gave her a space 14 feet square, as an office. Then she rented her own space.

For years Lillian, herself, packed and shipped each order. Her first real catalog started in 1960 with 16 black and white pages. For years she wrote every word. She sold to other catalogs, then stores, even manufacturers and manufactured herself . . . until non-mail order sales became 80% of her business. Her first husband, Sam Hochberg, helped. Then, in 1955, he quit his retail store to join her. The business grew to $5 million a year.

In 1970, they divorced and divided the business . . . with his part 50% and hers 50% . . . comprising the mail order business and items she sold to other mail order firms. Then her total business was $1 million yearly. In ten years, she multiplied it 40 times. To see how, let's look at her catalog.

It's different! It's a cut above her competition. Photography, typography, paper and reproduction are excellent. The layouts indicate a top art director. There are large pictures, more white space and yet more descriptive words. Copy is clear and effective. Each page pleases. But the stars are the items. Lillian is a queen of items.

Many of her items are exclusive. She sells for modest prices articles of better taste. Everything conceivable is personalized. Most seem made by known names. More seem unusual and some unique. About 60% are imported . . . from countries synonymous with quality, style and originality.

You see kitchen, bathroom and bath housewares; toys and adult games, costume jewelry and garden items; stationery and gift and gourmet items. But you immediately notice Lillian's specialties. Collectibles are throughout, including her favorites . .

34 kinds of thimbles, each quite different. There are a great many Christmas ornaments including many she makes herself. There are her angels, most of which are ornaments. There are angels from Italy, Spain, Germany or wherever . . . wooden, ceramic, pewter or glass angels . . . or on luminous stained glass material. I like the mail order angel . . . with mail box. My favorite is "The Sleepy Angel" in a quarter-moon cradle.

Let's meet Lillian. She has iron in her and elegance. She's organized and pragmatic, with a feel for money and sympathy for others. She has culture and taste and a quick mind, a strong back and feet that walk beyond fatigue.

She was born in Leipzig. The name she was called as a child was the German diminutive of Lily, "Lilychen". In 1967, Lillian started what promptly became the most profitable end of the business . . . Lillikins, Christmas ornaments with Lillian's special name . . . changed for Americans. They were two-dimensional . . . stamped, plated, personalized and usually in brass . . . and each about 3½ inches tall.

Lillikens took off like rockets. "I've sold 100 million of them, 80 million to other catalogs and stores." For others Lillian calls them "Twinkles". She even custom makes special designs for competitors like Walter Drake. Customers order Lillikins year after year. A grandmother gives each of twenty grandchildren a different Lilliken yearly, each with the child's name, the date and signed "Grandma".

There are three Norman Rockwell Twinkles® and six Walt Disney. There's Superman and Tweety . . . Christmas scenes . . . Santas, the creche, The Night Before Christmas . . . a bridge, church and bells . . . babies, children, birds and animals . . . and naturally, angels. One hundred and fifty Lillikins do 5% of Lillian's business and contribute 10% of profits. They have financed much of Lillian's growth.

Lillian's father manufactured children's clothing in Leipzig, ladies' housecoats in Amsterdam and dresses in New York. Later, he made leather belts, bags and accessories. He was always successful. He died in 1962. "Father said loud and clear that a woman can be as capable and talented as a man. He said that a woman had the right and duty to succeed and to contribute, just as much . . . in business as well as at home. My mother always worked along with Father.

"We had fun, too. Father was an opera buff. He loved sports and beautiful cars. We had a Mercedes and a Daimler. He was a skier. We travelled to Switzerland, Paris and Rome. I was taken to concerts and museums. Our home always had beautiful things.

"Without Father I could not have started in mail order. He helped me design my belt. He made it for me for one dollar." Lillian's father and mother gave her far more than a start. They gave her good taste and good working habits. They started her in a kind of personal life that's intertwined with her business and is a key to her success.

Lillian collects modern and impressionist paintings. She visits museums and goes to the ballet, theater and opera. She's religious and goes to Temple. "I'm an enormous entertainer. I like pretty clothes. I like to have my hair done, I take care of myself. I love to cook. I get up and make my husband's breakfast. On weekends we drive out to our new country house in Greenwich, Connecticut. I bought $2,000 at retail value for it from my catalog."

She has an innate feel for right items, fields of items and item trends. She has a sense of timing of when to get in and out and when to stay in. Each page, item, picture and word is geared to Lillian's friends, her customers. They are 98% women, usually between 20 and 40. They are upward mobile. Husband and wife work. Family income is over $25,000. There are two children. There's little time, lots of desire for a better life and pennies to watch. She brings individuality, identity, touches of nostalgia, culture and taste.

She and they think alike. She brings them items she knows are uniquely useful. She does not overtempt. She has items at prices they can pay . . . from several to a little over seventy dollars. The majority are $5 to $25. Lillian selects for her friends little things, bits of culture and individuality yearned for and psychologically needed. For them she seeks exclusives. Her catalog is a gift shop of items directly imported by her or often made by her.

She often gets exclusives and never stops trying . . . she tries for a longer and, if not, a shorter period . . . she tries for an item, for an exclusive model, color, size or variation . . . or at least for mail order only. She asks for lead time over competitors. She has a flair for combining an item with another item for an exclusive combination. And, finally, while few stores personalize, she does wherever possible.

Lillian has imagination, the ability to suggest modifications, give specifications, even design or invent items. Often she suggests highly profitable ideas to manufacturers for product variations. She does them favors. They do her favors. It all helps get exclusives. Her ideas come in the night, at breakfast, at a country stand, a restaurant or store . . . in a plane or wherever.

She came across a strawberry pattern English china set. She offered it 16 different ways in a double spread . . . from 5-piece place settings to a pitcher. She persuaded the maker to let her use the strawberry artwork for stationery and for Christmas wrapping paper. She gave away a set of stationery with each $10 of anything bought. She featured the offer next to her order blank.

Lillian saw a canister in Italy with two cherub angels on the top. One was blond and one brunette in soft blue coloring. In England, she found a pot pourri of dried flowers in a long white frill. She put the pot pourri and frill into the tin and called it nostalgia in a tin.

Lillian finds winners in items others pass by. She looks for

unknown, talented designers and capable new, small suppliers. The product may be unadvertised, poorly packaged, not yet in stores or even have failed in stores. But Lillian may instantly see in her mind the way to show or explain it . . . how a color picture, the right words and placement near related items, perhaps as an add-on, can give it new life.

I enjoy her catalog. I like the jigger that pours like a pitcher and the ceramic cannon with the nine-inch matches about to be fired and ceramic little man with his hands in his ears. I like her idea items, nostalgia items, the things to put things in and fun items.

Lillian is not alone. She has built an organization. In 1971, she began to computerize. "I recruited good talent and trained people. We kept trading up. I took the NYU Direct Marketing Course. I began to send employees. This year we have five in the course. In all, I've sent twelve. I joined the DMMA and the DMIX. I began to attend DMMA seminars at the annual meetings."

Lillian imported very little for years. In 1970, she began to do so. In 1973, she began to go to Europe to buy, just as others began to be afraid of imports. Lillian loves Europe and is the perfect middle woman to bring bits of it to America. All the life she had lived with her parents helped her to select what is now the heart of her catalog.

Lillian speaks fluent German and "poor Dutch". She and her buyers criss-cross Europe. "We all scout together but I'm very influential in the final decisions." She buys a full season's estimated needs for an item. She keeps expediting promised shipments. She concentrates on shipping promptly orders received. Inquiries and complaints are handled within 48 hours. Refunds are 1.7% of sales (very low). Of refund checks, half are returned by customers and applied to new orders.

What about buying mistakes? She can run the item again at full price if first results came close. If worse, she can offer at 20% to 25% off and if necessary, 35% to 50% off. She may be able to exchange with the manufacturer for new items. She has four bargain surprise packages in her catalog. She can sell at whatever markdown necessary in her quite successful factory outlet discount store.

"We have a fabulous copy department." Copy must describe every possible use for an item. Clarity is all important. Confused customers write for answers. Answering any letter takes away profit on the sale. The copywriter must anticipate every possible question a customer might ask about how an item feels, looks and functions. The copy also sells, and in good taste, with image captions and demonstration words. It attracts, intrigues and persuades. It has style, restraint and taste. Every word works.

The art department designs Lillian's product ideas, stages photographs, specifies type, lays out the catalog and determines the positions items get in the catalog.

"We divide responsibilities. We don't have personality clashes often . . . but certainly sometimes. I don't overrule once responsibility is given. I'm close to my people. We're friends." Lillian puts the same drive into supplying employees a service like detecting breast cancer or testing for hypertension as she does to making money.

She has built a trusted team of suppliers. As an incentive, when possible she buys clusters of items. "In turn, suppliers come up with ways to create exclusives for us. Our families visit each other. They're our friends and will check on a new supplier for us."

Products she designs and makes have best profit margins. In 1956, she designed a metal clip book mark. Later, she invented a metal arrow book mark that points to the line as well as page. She invented a brass golf tee and flag. "Tee bends 90 degrees when ball is hit." She invented a better blotting paper flower press. She keeps coming up with new ideas.

"Six months after my divorce, I met my husband, Robert Katz. He's very successful in his business. He runs it. I run mine. We don't interfere with each other's. He's an engineer. He's strong on product development. He is great for making the best product for the price. He makes mainly Lucite and wood products." When Lillian gets ideas of items to make in Lucite and wood, Robert makes them. "Then he gets sales from other outlets. It's all in the family."

Lillian's sons are taking on their share. Fred is Senior Vice President Marketing at Mount Vernon headquarters. David runs the Lillian Vernon Sales Corp. Wholesale Division. "They've got their own ideas. I can tell others. I try more persuasion with them. They're bursting with ambition and ideas to do more volume, make more money and build the business to the sky."

There are always problems. Each expansion has growing pains. Space ads don't pay out as they did. TV hasn't worked. Special catalogs for garden and gourmet items had to be dropped. Sky-high interest hurts everything. In the new building, there was a leak in the cafeteria roof and the heating system didn't work right. The money in fixed assets could be used in inventory.

Lillian conquers all. "I'm good at figures. I can do a cash flow. I've taken no bookkeeping or accounting courses. But I can watch costs." Meanwhile, the business keeps growing and making more money. "There are many ways to grow we've hardly tried." Lillian is testing telephone selling. She's investigating doing more export. She's emphasizing U.S. items. Sne's looking at new technology and making more non-mail order sales.

"There was a time I thought if I could ever have a million

dollar business, it would be my dream. Now I think if I had concentrated on the business from the day I started the same as since my boys grew up, I'd be doing $100,000,000 a year." But, Lillian, you will! (in 1981 Lillian Vernon did $47,000,000).

Note: In the Help Source Section are listed speeches and articles (along with information on how to get them) by Lillian Katz and by her son, Fred Hochberg, which can give great help to anyone considering a career or a business in the catalog field. And for some wonderful items, send to Lillian Vernon at 510 South Fulton Street, Mt. Vernon, N.Y.; telephone (914) 699-4131.

Her advice to mail order newcomers is to narrow your horizons. "Success comes from real specialization" in an area the mail order entrepreneurs know intimately.

Chapter 5
Getting a Job in Mail Order

How best to do it - without experience - when beginners are turned away.

It's not easy if you're starting out or changing careers. Direct marketing growth predictions may be more and more bullish. Lack of good people may be the only bar to even faster growth for direct marketing companies. Still, those without experience may be turned away.

Employment agencies may prefer not to interview beginners. Want ads may specify requirements you don't have. Standards for those starting out may seem overhigh. To understand the problem and how best to overcome it, please understand the situation of the direct marketer.

The better business is, the faster growth is, the more reluctant successful direct marketers are to stop in mid-stream to explain to beginners what the experienced already grasp. The big are inclined to pay more for already trained people. This makes it harder to break in but easier to rise once in. To understand how to break in, it's necessary to know how the direct marketing boss thinks.

Most of the most successful mail order people and direct marketers I interviewed are very bright. They have high IQ's. More and more of the most recent big successes came from the highest percentiles in their class at school. Most were college graduates, often in the top 5% of the class. More and more completed graduate school. Quite a few are MBA's. And more and more of them seek to recruit as beginners the very brightest and most business educated.

Your best chance as a beginner is if you are brighter than average, more highly educated and more motivated—particularly if you like this business and want to get in it and ahead in it. If you have average brains, you'll need to work harder than average. If you have less than average brains, you'll need to limit your objective, do something simpler and work very much harder.

In mail order and direct marketing, the jobs for those not so smart or not ambitious for careers are being replaced each year faster and faster by smart machines. Of those on the top, I have found very, very few—almost none—who started in a manual

mail room job on the very bottom. I found little mobility from these disappearing manual jobs to the money-making mental jobs in the business.

Employers may not be aware that some of their manual employees are quite capable of more interesting, mental jobs. They may not know which ones are most so. Most manual work employees are unaware that jobs exist for the same employer that they might fill. Even when job openings are posted in the shipping departments of big catalog houses nothing much usually comes of it.

Success in any job usually comes from intelligence, self-discipline and motivation. Things even out because the brightest often have little self-discipline and motivation. Self-discipline is greatly increased by motivation which can only come in something you like. You can only tell if you like something if you know something about it.

This book proposes to tell you how others made it in a mail order career, in the widest possible variety of situations. My hope is that each story will help you decide whether you really want to go into mail order, and particularly into what phase of mail order discussed in that story.

If you get interested enough in any job you'll get motivated. If you get interested in it enough and if you're motivated enough you'll get ahead. I've tried to include in this book advice, information and sources of far more detailed advice and information on any area of mail order or direct marketing you'd care to learn more about. If so, my hope is to help you get that first job.

First, to me, direct marketing is not an industry or business but an expertise that can be used in virtually any business. Probably, if you're now employed, it is or should be used by your employer. If so, expertise can be the difference between profit and loss, between survival or closing of a business or division. This expertise can be acquired by experience or training or both. It can be acquired by anyone by self-education alone. It can be applied by anyone, to any business, for any employer.

A prospective employer can select another with more expertise but no one can ban you from acquiring that expertise. To an employer, experience is the number one requirement. Business and direct marketing educational training, alone, is a poor second. Expertise in direct marketing is getting scarcer in relation to growing demand for it.

More beginners are being hired. More will be. But the employer is seeking the bright and most motivated, the most practical and purposeful, the most business educated—and in ways most suitable to direct marketing.

For any field, for any company, some kind of expertise is a passport to a better life. In a larger company there are different levels . . . top, middle, and lower middle management—and the lower depths. Upward mobility seems to start with lower management. Below that, jobs seem to be for the lesser educated and the less smart—and to be constantly replaced by smart machines.

I'd like you to meet in these pages people in different aspects of the field. Find out what they do, how they made it, how they like it, what they look for in those they hire and what they advise you to do to start and rise in the field. You'll find many kinds of jobs, careers and businesses to consider.

Start now to make a hobby of gaining direct marketing expertise. At first, spend no money on this hobby. Get the books I later recommend at your business library. Then, if your interest builds, make the first small expenditures for booklets, magazine subscriptions, books—a direct marketing course.

Don't worry if you don't immediately get a direct marketing job. If you start to acquire expertise, you will then find ways to apply it. If you have a job not in direct marketing, very likely the company you work for uses direct marketing or will soon do so. As you acquire expertise, it can be a tool for your company and for you to progress in it.

It is easy for you to study not just direct marketing but the kind suited to your present employer or any prospective employer to whom you apply. Often, you can study the direct marketing activities of the very company which may interview you, in time for the interview—and also of its competitors. To do this, you might have to buy back issues of a magazine or a tape of a speech, but it might help get the job. For this purpose the help source section in this book can be particularly helpful.

Few applicants for jobs are thoroughly briefed on the business of the firm interviewing. You'll be surprised how quickly you will speak their language and what a better chance it gives you. Remember, if you get enough expertise and are capable of using it, you are certain to get a job. Don't be in a hurry. Take any job to eat and pay rent—and keep applying. Then become selective.

As you develop your hobby of studying direct marketing, you will become familiar with companies, jobs, people in the field. Now you choose those that interest you. This is the method advocated in "What Color is Your Parachute." This is a splended job book I recommend strongly.

Look at each interview as a two-way negotiation. Explain that you're less interested in an immediate job than in joining the organization when a job is open. Tell them of your self-study activities. Get their advice for further courses, books to read, seminars. Keep in touch. Regard each as a possible second job in direct marketing to get later if they insist on experience.

The more you learn, even before your first direct marketing job, the more options will open up for you. You'll find it easier to get a job in a smaller company. You'll find it easier outside of New York and Chicago which are direct marketing centers drawing the most experienced from elsewhere. Often, the smallest areas are best of all to start in. A bigger percentage of direct marketers off the beaten track take beginners and train them.

If you can gamble all or part of your time, consider it. It's your way to buy experience. Work part-time at a menial job and gamble your part-time for an entrepreneur in mail order. You may learn more, faster than in any other way. But negotiate. Get a commitment that if you gamble your time for a specific period, you'll get paid thereafter and ask how much, beforehand.

The woods are full of eager beaver, underfinanced, new mail order ventures. Even if you worked for six months or a year and found that your employer was not meeting the commitment or even folding, you still would have a bit of experience to show for your loss with a much better chance at your next job interview.

You have other choices. You can use direct marketing expertise even for a non-profit organization. One branch of direct marketing is fund raising. The expertise is to a degree interchangeable. You can help your local church, hospital, college or political candidate to raise money and contribute your time. You can study case histories of how it's done. The same skills are involved in writing copy and in list selection. While helping you can be learning and acquiring experience which you can add to your resume.

Now you have the choice that everyone in America had a hundred years ago. Then, anyone could reject any employer's offer and go west, pioneer, homestead. The same could be done if no job offer were obtainable. Mail order as a business anyone can

go into is the last frontier. If you don't get or can't get the job you want in it, you can start a business in it as I describe in my book "Mail Order Moonlighting." And that experience can become the most valued you could possibly bring to a prospective direct marketer.

You have still another choice. You can work for the small or yourself, continue self-study of direct marketing—zeroing in on some specialty you feel suited to and interested in. You can then start in a tiny way to freelance. If you charge very little, you'll probably get someone to try you out, as a writer, an artist, whatever. This, again, goes on your resume.

It is by one of these various ways that many who have succeeded first began in mail order. Don't give up a steady, stable job with a substantial firm. Inform each desired prospective employer of any experience you're acquiring. You will find that most respect every effort you make to self-educate yourself in direct marketing and each small bit of experience you add . . . and particularly the ingenuity you show to do it.

Finally, you can use direct marketing to direct market yourself. One book I recommend and list in the help source section is "How to Advertise Yourself," by Max Sackheim. A favorite story among mail order people in how Karl Dentino broke into direct marketing in just this way.

Karl took a marketing course in college. His professor recommended him for a scholarship for the Collegiate Institute, the one week direct marketing course run by the Direct Mail/ Marketing Foundation. Karl was selected and attended. With what he learned he prepared a direct mail piece selling himself just as if he were selling a mail order product. He paid the cost to produce a simple black and white mailing piece. He wrote a letter that itself proved his mail order copy writing ability. He mailed it to largest direct marketers and agencies, got a selection of job offers and accepted his choice.

And you can do all this, too. In the chapter on "The Direct Marketing Courses," I tell how to apply for the same scholarship and what are the qualifications needed. So, if you care to accept it, welcome to a direct marketing career.

Chapter 6
Making a Mint in Mail Order

The phenomenon of Joe Segel; his success with the Franklin Mint.

At 34, his first ad for commemorative medals started generating profits of $10,000 a month. Then mail order ad after ad brought in orders for other commemorative series, jumping profits, booking business for years in advance.

At 36, two years later, Joe was worth over a million dollars. At 40, in another four years, he had made a bigger fortune than most dream of. At 42, two years after that, he retired. Franklin Mint has since multiplied its sales and profits, offering more and more kinds of collectibles, all over the world, and is now diversifying into other fields.

At first Joe Segel's success seems a mail order dream. It's an idea anyone might have had . . . with a product that has an excellent profit margin and is habit forming. It seems the lazy way to mail order riches—developing one concept and forever after happily cashing checks from your mail box.

But the reality of Joe Segel's success is quite different. Timing and circumstances and abilities developed from years of experience made it possible. You will quickly see that Joe Segel has more ideas, has worked harder and is more of a perfectionist than most of us.

But his story can help any of us achieve more in mail order— even if we are only capable of and care to go after a more limited success. It can encourage any of us who are considering changing careers in mid-stream. He did it, and perhaps we can.

Joe Segel was a born entrepreneur. When he was 13 years old, he started his first business. He bought a small printing press and sold calling cards to his school buddies for five cents a hundred. He was also interested in magic. When Joe was fifteen he started a mail order business, a little catalog selling advertising specialties to magicians.

He could write. He was sports editor of his junior high school paper. He was a leader. At West Philadelphia High School, Joe was president of the Students' Association. He had business sense. He always seemed to have some business idea in mind.

At 16, he entered the Wharton School of Business Administration at the University of Pennsylvania, majoring in accounting. And, while going to college, he continued to build his advertising specialty business, creating many promotional ideas for local businessmen.

By his junior year, his advertising specialty business led Joe to publish a directory for the industry. "None existed. It was very difficult for advertising specialty jobbers to find out who the manufacturers were and vice versa. So, I felt that many people in the industry would be interested in a directory that would help identify manufacturers of advertising specialties by product and trade name and identify jobbers by area served. But I did not expect it to be more than a one-time publication."

The Advertising Specialty Register, as Joe named it, was an instant hit. Immediately, the jobbers and manufacturers who subscribed to it urged Joe to continue publishing it on a regular basis. To do so, Joe formed the Advertising Specialty Institute during his senior year at the Wharton School. He subsequently graduated from the University with a degree in economics and went on to Wharton Graduate School, while continuing his business and starting other services for the advertising specialty industry.

The professors at Wharton were aware of Joe's business entrepreneuring. When a professor of marketing then died suddenly, they had to shift around class assignments and Joe was invited to become an instructor.

Joe taught Marketing I and Marketing II. It was part of a tight schedule. He was taking a full course load as a graduate student, while also running an expanding business. Joe doesn't think he did very well at Wharton. He recalls: "I never got a graduate degree. I was too involved with my business ventures to write a thesis. And I don't think I was a good instructor. I concentrated too much on talking about my own small-scale business experiences." He never did any formal teaching after that.

But, in 1980, I asked members of the Wharton faculty about their memories of Joe. He was described to me as "The classic American entrepreneur." Wharton is proud of his success. He was still talked about and had become a folk hero. The Wharton Account, the graduate school magazine, ran a feature story on him. When he can accept an invitation to speak to groups at Wharton, he is greatly appreciated.

After leaving Wharton, Joe's activities accelerated. The Advertising Specialty Institute evolved into the central information service for the advertising specialty industry. "Each activity I went into led to something else." Joe formed a credit interchange service, a trade association, a trade show and various sales training programs. He also started a trade magazine called The Counselor, which has since become quite large and recently passed its 25th year of publication.

People in the advertising specialty field still talk with awe of what he did. He was a fountain of ideas. He was a perfectionist in carrying out each project. He had drive. He came to a business of small salesmen and manufacturers and gave them a sense of pride as professionals.

Many people in the advertising specialty industry feel he multiplied the size of the industry. It is now eight times larger. The magazine he started, The Counselor, is superbly edited. The association he started opened up the field to an entire new generation of specialty advertising counselors. Some say today, "I don't know how he did it." An entire industry benefitted. He's in the industry's Hall of Fame.

Then Joe overexpanded. "I started a new division to provide a service I thought was badly needed by advertising specialty distributors." It was a selective gift catalog that businessmen could send out to customers, to select their own Christmas gifts. It involved buying and warehousing of merchandise, which was new to Joe. He grossly underestimated the gross margin required to operate that type of business, a mistake he would not make again. But this time he was in trouble.

Joe then had a number of inter-related companies. He even had a color printing business that did all the color printing for his publishing company. The selective gift business drained capital from his other, more successful businesses. And now he was short of cash.

"As a result of a couple of very bad years, I had to seek a loan to keep our heads above water." Joe negotiated a loan with a group of thirteen Small Business Investment Companies. "These thirteen SBIC's soon divided into two camps. About half of them had great faith in what I was doing, and the other half had no

faith at all. There was continued bickering between the two factions. Eventually, their dispute encumbered our operations and took all the fun out of the business. So, I decided to step out."

First Joe sold off the Selective Gift Institute. "I could have held on to Colorcrafters and the Advertising Specialty Institute, but a year later, I decided to sell those operations also, just to get the SBIC's off my back." Joe stayed on as Chairman of the Board of Directors and Chief Operating Officer of National Business Services, Inc., the corporation that was formed by the new owners to continue these businesses.

So, 21 years after Joe Segel started his first business at 13, and 14 years after he started in the advertising specialty field, he had little in the way of financial assets to show for all his creativity. With no equity any longer in any of the companies he had founded, after saving them he began to lose interest and to look for something else. "Then I got the medal idea."

"In June of 1964, I saw an article in Time magazine about the last U.S. silver dollars that were being sold by the government. A picture showed people lined around the block waiting to buy silver dollars from the United States Treasury Department in Washington. That gave me a brainstorm.

"My idea was to issue a series of solid sterling silver medals, a little larger than a silver dollar, of the highest quality. Each medal would be designed by a different, famous sculptor. And the edition would be extremely limited. Only one numbered specimen of each medal would be available, at a fixed price, to each member of a society formed to issue the medals. Membership in the society would be open for a short period of time. After the membership rolls were closed, then the total edition of each issue would be exactly equal to the number of members of the society. And members would vote on what to commemorate. There were various other features such as a monthly newsletter, and so forth. I called it The National Commemorative Society.

"I had no experience in coin or medal collecting. I knew of several manufacturers of promotional coins. So, I thought it would be relatively easy to have my sterling silver medals produced.

"And I had never seen any coin publications until about two months before I placed the first ad. I went to the library and read a year's worth of issues of each of the four major coin publications to get a feel for the field. I particularly noted that almost all the ads in these coin publications were very cluttered, small-space ads.

"I decided my ad had to be an impressive promotion with a clear headline. I felt that a multi-page ad with a lot of open space would stand out. So, I laid out a four-page ad to introduce The National Commemorative Society. The first page of the ad consisted only of the headline, swimming in an enormous amount of white space. The next three pages consisted of a letter, set in a typewriter typeface, and a subscription form. It was a very simple presentation. But it had a very clean, quality appearance. And it worked."

The Society's ad ran one time only, during the month of June 1964, simultaneously in several publications that reach coin collectors.

The cut-off date was one of Joe's most valuable ideas. The deadline for joining the society was eight weeks after the first ad was placed. There was a sliding scale of charter membership fees which favored urgency. If your membership application was postmarked within the first two weeks, your membership fee would be $10. In the next two weeks, $15. The next two weeks, $25. And, in the final two weeks, $40. After that, *no* additional memberships would be sold by the society.

The ad emphasized that the number of members in The National Commemorative Society would be permanently limited to the number of charter members who signed up by that date. But the memberships would be freely transferable, so members could sell their memberships if they wished. Each member had the right to acquire just one sterling silver medal each month, of the subject commemorated by the society in that month, for $6.60.

The ads did stand out. The program was instantly successful. Joe obtained 5,250 members just through that one-time ad campaign. The $6.60 price per medal was held for several years, even though silver kept going up, and the members appreciated that policy. By late 1980, members found that the NCS medals were worth very much more than $6.60 because each contained almost a full ounce of silver. And at the height of the silver boom, they were worth about five times their original cost.

He invested about $10,000 in the NCS promotional campaign. A number of his friends thought it was a crazy idea. But the program initially generated a profit of about $10,000 per month, one hundred percent return of the original investment, every month for several years thereafter. And the members loved what they got from the Society. Later, the National Commemorative Society was sold to the Franklin Mint.

Joe assumed it would be easy to produce a proof-quality sterling silver medal about the size of a silver dollar. So, he gave the manufacturing order to a promotional coin supplier he knew from his advertising specialty days. But that coin manufacturer had great difficulty in producing the first NCS medal to the quality standards Joe felt necessary.

"After we shipped the first medal, many collectors wrote to say that they thought it was quite beautiful and well made. But I was not entirely satisfied. It did not come up to what I expected. Yet, the coin manufacturer said they could do no better.

"I ignorantly believed that making a proof-quality coin was a relatively simple process. I felt a jewelry manufacturer could certainly produce a medal of the quality I desired. So I gave the order to produce the next four medals to a jewelry manufacturer in Rhode Island. But they had a lot of difficulty, and I felt that the finish was still not perfect. Finally, I decided that I might as well set up a small, high-quality minting operation and control the quality to my satisfaction."

Gilroy Roberts was then chief sculptor of the U.S. Mint. Joe had commissioned him to produce the design for the second NCS medal, and Joe learned that Gilroy was about to retire. So, Joe contacted Gilroy again and this time convinced him to join in establishing General Numismatics Corporation, the company that would eventually become the Franklin Mint. Initially, it would be very small, starting with one press and a small machine shop to mint high quality medals for the National Commemorative Society and for other commemorative societies.

Soon after, Joe started the Brittania Commemorative Society with friends in England. His mother and aunt formed another society to produce a series of medals commemorating famous women. "So there were three commemorative series to start minting and others in the wing."

Joe had planned his mint as a private business but soon decided to make it a public company. He developed a prospectus and showed it to stock brokers in Philadelphia. None wanted to underwrite it, even on a "best efforts" basis. So he did it himself, with an SEC exemption, by direct marketing. Joe sent the prospectus to NCS Members and to other known coin collectors. Only $33,937 of stock was sold in 1965, and $209,429 in 1966. It was just enough to get the mint started.

Experienced manufacturers had difficulty delivering the quality Joe originally demanded. Now it developed that the new mint would find it even more difficult.

Joe then began to understand what his former suppliers were trying to tell him, that the quality standard he was stubbornly trying to achieve (a "two-tone proof finish") was practical for small coins but not for coins or medals as large as a silver dollar. The breaking point was about a half dollar size. Above that size required such high tonnage (about 200 tons pressure) to form the coin that the stress tended to create stress marks which marred the proof finish and also frequently cracked the die after only a few coins were struck.

Gilroy Roberts' U.S. Mint experience had been producing smaller coins, so this was a surprise to him, too. "Because we didn't know it couldn't be done," Segel recalled, "we continued to attempt to do what others thought was impossible. We cracked many, many dies in producing the first medal at the Franklin Mint's facilities. It was very expensive and very frustrating. I couldn't get solutions from anyone. So, I either had to give up or plunge into the technology myself. I studied books on tool die making, heat treating of die steel and other areas of die making. I even stayed up all night trying new methods to preserve the proof finish.

"We slowly solved the problem through trial and error and experimentation. The number of impressions we got from each die gradually increased, as did the quality. Eventually, we got the process to a high degree of perfection. But in the early days, it was very rough. We would spend a week making a set of dies. Put them in the press. Push the button. And 'POW'. The dies would crack, setting us back another week.

"One of the things that kept me going was that I had picked up a 'two-tone' proof set minted by the British Royal Mint, and I figured that if they could do it, we could, too.

"Much later, I learned that the British Royal Mint was getting only about fifty impressions from a set of dies. The dies were then repolished and maybe run for another fifty or so impressions. After several repolishings they were scrapped and a new set of dies made. Yet, we were ignorantly attempting to mint 5,250 medals of equal quality from one set of dies.

"Some years later, the British Royal Mint, which I had first used as my standard, sent a delegation to learn how the Franklin Mint was producing finer quality coins with greater die life. And to learn the same technology, the U.S. Mint eventually hired away one of our technical people.

"All this would never have happened if I had been more experienced in the coining field and shared the general belief that it couldn't be done. In fact, if I knew before I started the Franklin Mint how difficult the manufacturing process is, I would probably never have started it. So, I am very thankful for my ignorance at that time."

During its first year of operations, General Numismatics Corporation functioned primarily as a mint for its captive customers, the commemorative societies. The initial manufacturing problems were gradually brought under control. In 1965, GNC did $391,564 in sales and lost $11,644. But Joe had been very conservative in figuring depreciation and amortization. There had been pre-operating expense of $104,404. Operations had really been almost a wash.

A lot had been accomplished. The mint expanded into 15,000 square feet of space and built the first "clean room" for proof-quality coining. Joe's gifts of persuasion were showing. He acquired the Jewel Die and Mold Engraving Company for stock. The proprietor, Edmund Becker, became engraving supervisor.

Brian G. Harrison (who later became president) joined the company as technical director.

Gilroy Roberts was chairman. Joe was president. Martin Walsh, a former plant controller of Lear-Siegler, was vice president. Joe wanted the best in people, equipment, supplies, services. He wanted business; he was exploding with ideas. In 1965, there were 27 commemorative issues. In 1966, there were 73. Joe found a new "major source of business", Nevada gaming casinos. They had used tons of silver dollars. Now there was a shortage. Joe was glad to fill the gap, by designing and minting a new type of dollar gaming token.

Meanwhile, Joe had a much broader appeal interest than coin collecting (rapidly increasing) to satisfy. He had a mail order smash hit, ripe to expand. He had discovered a readiness to subscribe to a commemorative series. It could be for national or ethnic pride, prestige or history. A set of medals could be a prideful possession. Joe kept coming up with new concepts, variations and proliferations to stimulate the trend in more and more variety. Medals could commemorate all kinds of things. They could be beautiful works of art. And when made of precious metals, they could be true "stores of value".

Creeping inflation had begun to accelerate. There was a beginning of unease about the value of paper currency. Gold and silver were beginning to rise. Tangible objects of value were beginning to be more desirable than money. When Joe offered medals in a choice of bronze or silver, more and more people began preferring silver. Those with foresight recognized at the time that silver would be a hedge against inflation.

In 1967, the name of the General Numismatics Corp. was changed to Franklin Mint Corporation. Its gamble in equipment and personnel now began to pay off. Joe was creating more and more Franklin Mint customers by coming up with ideas for additional commemorative societies. He would persuade a group to promote an appropriate series to its members at its risk. Often he came up with the idea of a new association to commemorate something, organized it, and then turned it over to others. He manufactured customers as well as medals.

Joe was a busy man. He wrote the copy for the first ads, and for several years thereafter, edited all the copy written by others. Joe selected media, negotiated, hired, fired, ran the business. "I did everything myself, at first. But as the business grew, I had to delegate. Initially, doing so came hard to me. But I soon learned that if you give good people increasing authority and responsibility, they quickly rise to the occasion.

"We did not use an advertising agency except to place some space advertising. Our creative work was always done internally. I always had an interest in graphic arts and advertising. And, for several years, I was somewhat of a terror because I insisted on editing every piece of copy myself—and often had it rewritten many times until I was absolutely satisfied."

Gradually, Joe built a creative team. A number of very talented people joined the Franklin Mint and contributed. Dick Hodgson was one. Joe hired the best writers, artists, managers and technical people he could find and rewarded them handsomely. The policy paid off. "I never cut corners by trying to hire people cheaper or hire less qualified people than the best I could find." It proved an important element to Franklin Mint success.

The time was now. Others began to see Joe's success and copied. But none grasped the huge potential as Joe did. Joe innovated. They followed.

Every mail order person with a hit wants to project, before others do . . . to overcome every obstacle, to win the race. Joe proved to have an ability to do so. He could mesmerize others with his plans . . . bankers, financial analysts, organizations to affiliate with—the more prestigious the better. He recruited able employees. He acquired mints in other countries. He began to extend his medals to the world.

The Franklin Mint was becoming a "hot" growth company on Wall Street. The annual report for 1967 showed sales of $2,677,435 and net income of $136,293. But far more important, the stage was being set for skyrocket growth. Again the report was very conservative. $122,804 was written off for depreciation and amortization. Working capital dramatically increased from $105,675 to $537,920. One reason was the sale of $553,630 of stock to shareholders. The net worth had doubled to $1,177,419.

In addition to the first plant at Yeadon, Pennsylvania, Joe had leased two and a half times more space, 40,000 square feet, in four buildings in Folcroft, Pennsylvania. There was more new equipment. And many new programs were in the works.

From the annual report for the year, you learn something else. Joe was a good provider. On January 1, 1967, a profit sharing plan started, with 20% of profits to go to key employees. There had already been a stock option plan. Joe was just warming up. Sales were about to leap, with profits and public issues to multiply capital.

Underwriters in New York sold a second issue and then a third. "Beginning with the fourth public issue, C.E. Unterberg Towbin & Co. became our underwriters. They have a great reputation as investment bankers, and that brought prestige to our stock." There were no more "best efforts" offerings. Every issue after that was sold out.

In April 1968, Unterberg privately placed 33,000 shares of FM stock, which brought in $736,000. In October, they sold a public issue of $2,522,000.

Joe was beginning to show another element of his make-up, audacity. The first large-scale national advertising by the Franklin Mint "History of the United States" series—an unprecedented series of 200 medals, two a month for a hundred months. Each sterling silver medal was ten dollars. The commitment was for over eight years. The ads ran everywhere. It was the first big, significant FM promotion. "The success was most gratifying. This one promotion brought in thirty-five million dollars worth of advance subscriptions for the 8-year period.

The ads for the "History of the United States" series, and then for one Franklin Mint offer after another, were run without testing. "At that time, I didn't think testing was desirable or reliable. I just went by intuition, one promotion after another, and almost every one was successful. Whether it was good timing, good concept, good copy, good luck or whatever combination, it just worked. And it kept working."

Sales for 1968 leaped to $19,268,000. Net earnings were $629,679. And while Joe was taking promotional risks, there was no inventory risk. Everything was minted against orders, and all Franklin's metal purchases were hedged.

Then Joe came up with another market for Franklin Mint products—coin games as traffic-building promotions. Shell Oil tested the "Mr. President Coin Game". Results convinced Shell to run in nearly every one of its marketing regions. They ordered millions of aluminum coins. After that, Joe came up with another coin game, "Famous Facts and Faces". Toward the end of 1968, he signed up Sun Oil for the "Antique Car Coin Game". Total sales in 1968 for the two oil companies amounted to $4,600,000, all out of Joe's head.

From here on in, doubters more quickly became believers. The same year, the First Pennsylvania Bank and Trust Company gave Franklin a loan of $3,500,000.

Joe attributes some of his success to his philosophy . . . to always give people more than expected . . . to put a little something extra in a shipment . . . to give a larger, heavier, better quality medal, or additional and unexpected collateral material. "Many times, surprised people wrote us to say they received more than they thought they would get. That brought a great deal of loyalty. Every new FM collector was a potential long-term customer. Concentrating on quality and giving more then expected were the important ingredients of Franklin Mint success."

By the end of 1968, Franklin Mint had 900 employees vs. 200 the year before, and occupied 13 buildings. The number of collectors rose from 10,000 at the beginning of the year to about 75,000 at year end. There was approximately $4,000,000 of bullion in storage for Franklin Mint. Franklin had purchased enough silver bullion, silver futures and copper futures to fully cover commitments. Brian Harrison became vice president in charge of operations.

In the 1968 annual report there is a picture of a line of people (it extended around the block) before the Delaware Trust Company in Wilmington, Delaware. A Franklin Mint medal commemorating the opening of the Delaware Memorial Bridge was on sale. The bank had to limit each customer to one silver medal a customer, and was sold out in two hours. It was another typical idea out of Joe's head.

Sales in 1969 went up to $28,600,000. Earnings were $1,649,000. Lots of things happened. Ground was broken in January, a cornerstone laid in August, for a new 175,000 square foot plant at Media, Pennsylvania, to replace all present facilities.

Equipment and production staff were getting more efficient. Bigger volume was cutting costs per unit. There was a good gross margin. There was no problem of rises in metal costs. Silver was hedged to cover all subscriptions, even years ahead. In the "History of the United States" series, each $10 sterling silver medal weighed over an ounce. In September 1980, silver was over $22 an ounce. The $10 price was maintained to the very end. The silver was committed for eight years. "Collectors who bought those series did quite well." At the height of the silver boom, each medal was worth in silver about five times the issue price.

In 1969, a subsidiary was formed to manage the foreign operations. Joe made a flying tour of Europe. He acquired the John Pinches Organization, the oldest medal manufacturer in England. He negotiated successfully and, in 1970, acquired Le Medaillier, in France, manufacturers of the basic engraving machine used worldwide in government mints. Le Medaillier also made medals. And he acquired the Wellings Mint, in Canada.

In May 1969, Franklin Mint sold four million dollars of fifteen-year, six percent convertible debentures through C.E. Unterberg Towbin. Half was used to retire bank loans. The rest bought more equipment. Stockholder equity went up to $7,100,000. Direct sales to collectors by mail order were $19,000,000. By the end of 1969, there were 300,000 Franklin Mint subscribers.

Joe didn't use outside lists very often. "We just built up our own lists, promoting through media. We then mailed new offers regularly to our own growing list." FM customers were very responsive.

In 1970, sales were $45,885,000. Net profits were $2,413,000. The "Genius of Michelangelo" series was launched. Franklin began the minting of Tunisian and Panamanian coins, each for a special series of proof editions. Thus, Franklin became the first private mint in the U.S. to mint foreign coin-of-the-realm in fifty years. Franklin began to sell etchings, open stock jewelry, coin jewelry, silver and gold pendants.

The American Express Company sent test mailings of Franklin Mint offers to card holders. Chuck Andes (now Chairman of the Board) became vice president and marketing director. The new 200,000 square foot plant was in operation, with a thousand visitors a week. Franklin Mint had a hundred thousand new collectors and a backlog of fifty million dollars of orders by the end of 1970.

There were only two million dollars of foreign sales in 1970. Initially, foreign operations were a drag. Eventually, they became very important to FM profits. Brian Harrison contributed most to the foreign expansion. Brian was born in England. He started with FM as a metallurgist. He moved back to England to run the international operation, and then later returned to the U.S. to become president under Chairman Charles Andes.

In 1971 and 1972, Franklin Mint kept expanding. It turned out medals and broadened into fields far beyond medals, but always collectibles sold in limited editions. It also produced coin-of-the-realm for the British Virgin Islands, Jamaica and several other countries.

Joe Segel often obtained the imprimatur of a prestigious sponsor to add appeal to a program. It might be a medal series of the U.S. Olympic Committee, the Royal Shakespeare Theater or the White House Historical Association . . . or a group of eminent historians to select the subjects to be commemorated in the "History of the United States" series.

There was pride and patriotism, art and culture. You could participate with others in shared memories. You could hold up your head and point to your class, race, profession. To each group, Joe brought heroes and events to be proud of—to pharmacists and to dentists, to doctors and to lawyers, to women and to postmasters, to Italians and Scotch, to hunters and bird lovers, fishermen and baseball fans.

Not surprisingly, certain medals modestly popular in one country were far more so in another. He had something for every country. Treasures of the Louvre did well here and even better in France, as did Napoleon. Michelangelo did well all over, and particularly in Italy. The Kings and Queens of England did well in Canada and far better in Great Britain. General MacArthur and Samuel Adams and Andrew Carnegie and Pearl Harbor and Benjamin Franklin were all for us.

Even as Joe proliferated in every possible way into more medal series, he was planning for the contingency that coins and medals might be nearing the peak and then be on the downward side of their life cycle. He determined that Franklin Mint should move faster into other areas of collectibles. "I concentrated, during the last year of my administration, on starting the book program." When the Franklin Mint came out with the "One Hundred Greatest Books of All Time" promotion, the mint instantly became one of the largest book publishers in the world. They booked close to $100,000,000 in sales from that one promotion.

By now, Franklin Mint stock was climbing faster. The stock split eighteen times. A lot of people made a lot of money with it. Segel did well by selling stock periodically within the SEC limits for insiders.

"After about five years of existence, Franklin Mint became quite a different company than it had been. I continued to be involved in creative work. But I also became much more involved with stock analysts, budgets and administrative details. I did not enjoy that as much." At 39, in 1970, he decided to retire but first to prepare the company for it. After publicly announcing his intentions and spending 3 years grooming his successors, in 1973, a few days before his 43rd birthday, he retired.

Why, in a totally different field, did he suddenly make it so big and so very much bigger than he had before?

Before, in the advertising specialty industry, Joe Segel had an unlimited imagination in a limited field. All his creativity was bound by a very small universe of 2,500 hundred wholesalers and 1,000 manufacturers. For the Franklin Mint the same brain could think in the same way for, in comparison, almost unlimited markets . . . first in the U.S. and then in the world.

Before, Joe had often worked with tight margins between what a product cost him to make or to buy and what he sold it for. Franklin had bigger margins. There was more room for fluctuating product or promotion cost or even miscalculation.

Before, Joe, had been underfinanced. Now, with the Franklin Mint, he was able to obtain financing from stockholders and, later, banks.

Before, Joe had built a big overhead in relation to a small field. Now Joe first made money with almost no overhead and, as big as overhead became, always kept it lower in relation to sales.

And with unlimited growth potential there could be unlimited employee incentive potential. Joe had always been able to attract others with talent to him. But with Franklin, he could offer stability and multiplied opportunity.

All his experience and contacts could come into play. His first sources came from the advertising specialty field, as did Chuck Andes, present chairman of Franklin. He had learned to do things right, the quality way. He had class and style. He grew and traded up his objectives.

Above all, it was the right time to do it, to plunge, drive and proliferate as he did.

When Napoleon launched the Legion of Honor, he reputedly said: "With these bits of ribbon I'll build an empire." And with his medals, Joe Segel launched many legions of honor to create his empire on which the sun never set.

Joe Segel became a patron of the arts the Medicis would envy. He may have hired more sculptors than anyone in history. He won the founders' race for making a mint in mail order—bigger, faster and when younger.

And, in all of mail order, I have never before encountered anyone so prolific in ideas who executed so many of them, and with such perfect standards.

Analysts tended to comment that Franklin Mint was a one-man company, that it was all Joe Segel. "I was flattered, but I disagreed. I had excellent managers. I felt I had done more than build a one-man company. I felt I could gradually step out of the business and that it would continue even better after I left. It was a challenge to prove this, to work out an orderly succession. Gradually, I delegated more and more and, finally, virtually everything. In the last couple of years that I was there, I had little to do but to complete phasing myself out of the business.

"I guess one of the proudest recollections I have of what I accomplished with the Franklin Mint was not just developing the company but being able to have a very orderly transition of management without skipping a beat, being able to phase myself out of the company while laying the groundwork for it to grow even faster after I left than when I was there."

Retirement

For years Joe Segel had been on the Board of Governors of the United Nations Association. Now he could devote more time to it. "The Association does very important work to help the American public better understand what the UN is all about. There are great misconceptions about the UN. Many people think it's just a debating society. They don't realize that 90% of the UN budget is directed toward international cooperation in essentials like air traffic, telecommunications, world health and economic development . . . and the good works of the UN never make the headlines. You mostly hear about the acrimonious debates."

Joe developed a public information program for the United Nations Association and got it adopted by The Advertising Council. He became Chairman of the Board of Governors of the United Nations Association. President Ford, in 1974, appointed Joe Segel as a member of the United States Delegation to the 29th General Assembly. As a U.S. delegate, Joe worked for the State Department and had an office at the U.S. Mission to the UN (in New York City).

In 1970, Joe had stayed at a hotel in Switzerland, liked it and bought it. It's now Le Mirador Hotel and Country Club. Le Mirador overlooks Lake Geneva near Montreux. Joe has developed it into a major international conference center. Harvard Business School now maintains their international headquarters and a year-round staff at Le Mirador. Joe built special classrooms for Harvard executive seminars, which are eight weeks long and twice a year. ITT, General Electric, General Motors, Shell, IBM and many other multinational companies regularly hold high-level executive seminars there.

Le Mirador is not large, only 110 rooms, but it's one of a kind. Joe had made it a collector's piece of European hotels, with Joe's touch—from its elegance to the perfection of its facilities and the style of its literature. One of the greatest assets of Le Mirador is its magnificent view over Lake Geneva.

Even heads of state come to Le Mirador. Joe has flown over to welcome personally the Emperor and Empress of Japan. Kurt Waldheim, Edward Heath, Willy Brandt have all been there. Jimmy couldn't make it, but Roslyn Carter stopped at Le Mirador during an official visit to Switzerland in 1979. Even the Swiss government brings important diplomatic functions to Le Mirador because of its superb facilities and standards of service.

Once again Joe is giving the joy of joining, prestige and perfection—this time for the most unusual club in the world, for leaders.

Joe now spends most of his time in photography, his prime interest. He has been an active photographer for almost thirty years.

In 1979, Joe took a trip to Africa. "I shot a lot of pictures of animals which came out nicely." Joe printed them in his own darkroom, which is equipped with the latest and most sophisticated equipment. "I got interested in reviving some of the old concepts of masking color transparencies for contrast control that I had learned 25 years ago. And I found that I was able to produce better prints that way than with any other method."

Originally, Joe produced color prints just for his own enjoyment. But Franklin Mint has now launched an offer of a limited edition of a series of Joe's wildlife prints for collectors.

To introduce the Segel Wild Life Photography Series, the Franklin Mint gave Joe the Segel treatment. There's a photograph of Joe on camera safari in Kenyan bush country. Another shows him working in his darkroom. The story is of Joe's perfection in stalking and photographing each subject, of weeding out all but around 1% of the shots that are developed, and then rejecting print after print until he is perfectly satisfied with the color balance.

"With photography and my own darkroom, I'm now able to create things myself with my own hands. I've always wanted to do that. In a way, it's a lot more fun than running a big business."

Note: For readers of this book the following questions have been answered by Joe Segel.

24784 Road Cart
A perfect
model, made
of iron and nick-
el plated. Single
horse and driver.
Length of toy,
10¼ in.
Price......$0.50

Q. *Could you do it all over again, from scratch?*

A. I don't know that starting from scratch and creating a new market for quality collectibles could be done today. It's quite different than when I did it in the mid-60's. But, if the Franklin Mint did not exist, and no one else had stepped in to create this new market, it probably could be done today. However, to be realistic, since that market has been created and is being well cultivated, I would say that one would have to dream up a different new market to create. That's more difficult, but by no means impossible. In fact, at least one important new market— previously unthought of—is created each year in the American economy.

Q. *Do you collect?*

A. No, I'm not really a collector, although I did subscribe and pay for every new issue and new series started by the Franklin Mint during its first ten years. I wanted to have that complete collection. But I don't collect anything else.

Q. *How important was recruiting others, training them and delegating to them?*

A. I was very fortunate to be able to recruit exceptionally competent management people. To motivate and keep these people, we paid them very well, provided opportunities for rapid advancement, stimulated innovation and delegated huge doses of responsibility and authority. For instance, I recruited Chuck Andes as executive vice president, then moved him up to president, and then chose him to be my successor as chairman— all within around 3 years. Obviously, I had great confidence in him.

Q. *What areas did Franklin Mint get into after you left, aside from those already started by you?*

A. I worked on the first big book program and the first big record program, but the other areas of porcelain, crystal, furniture, jewelry, etc., all came after I left. Chuck Andes deserves most of the credit for the great diversification of products that the Franklin Mint now markets.

Q. *How do you compare the methods you used to build Franklin Mint to those used by present management?*

A. The Franklin Mint is operating differently today than when I ran it. They test virtually everything and operate very scientifically. They have grown soundly since I've left. I was able to bring the business from zero to $100,000,000 in sales in the first 8 years. But my successors have tripled the sales in the succeeding 7 years. My methods may have been appropriate to get the business established; but I think the present methods are better to generate continued growth.

Q. *What advice do you have for anyone who wants to get into direct marketing?*

A. Read all the good books on direct marketing. Study the promotions that are currently being offered. I certainly think that studying and researching trade publications is very important. I

still receive Direct Marketing magazine, and I'm sure that the articles in there would be just as valuable to a beginner as they are to a current professional.

Postscript

By the time Joe retired, the Franklin Mint plant, complete with flags of nineteen countries it operated in, looked like the United Nations Building. The Franklin Mint Museum alongside looked like an improved version of the Guggenheim.

A tour of the plant and museum told much about Joe Segel as impresario, showman, businessman, fountain of ideas and perfectionist about carrying them out.

The Franklin Mint Museum is a reflection of all that subscribers sought from the Franklin Mint, aside from hedging against inflation. Joe had even given each subscriber a vote telling Joe what to put in such a museum.

In the museum each piece of memorabilia was a bit more background for the people and events Franklin medals had been based on. From Will Rogers' lariat to a letter from Einstein, there was something for everyone. It was the collectible history of the world, complete with a slide and sound show.

It was also a powerful new medium to make each related Franklin series more desirable. It was a three-dimensional catalog of the all-time hit offers of Franklin Mint. It was a means of public relations, a source of prestige and of business as tangible and even more immediate than a magazine coupon. It was another promotional idea carried out with perfection and originated in Joe Segel's head.

The plant, itself, was an exhibit, spanking new, efficient, smooth-running. Parts of it seemed a combination of a Star Wars command center and a hospital operating room. You could see the minute details of the original sculpture of a medal, reducing it from a 10-inch diameter sculptor's mold to the 1½-inch diameter medal. You could see the minting process, the brick of silver being transformed into medals and ingots and plates and spoons.

The Franklin Mint from any aspect . . . the magazine for members, "The Franklin Mint Almanac", to the award-winning film on the Mint, "The Ultimate Achievement" . . . was a reflection of Joe Segel. He was a hard act to follow. But after Joe, Franklin Mint sales and profits did grow, faster than ever.

The very success of Franklin in the years to come created problems for it. The outpouring of offers, the omni-present ads, the constant stimulation to collect, collect, collect. A book was published independently which annually listed quoted values of past and present medallic issues. Some serious collectors wondered how long it could last. It seemed a bit too much, a sort of Franklin Mint-O-Mania.

In each field Franklin had entered, the old-timers scoffed and doubted. Mail order people predicted that the offers would prove temporary promotions and die. Publishers said books sold at that price would soon prove impossible to sell. It was the same in ceramics or jewelry or art prints, or whatever. To veterans in each field, Franklin Mint success was suspect, doomed to collapse.

Sunday, November 12, 1978, was Franklin Mint's Pearl Harbor. On that date, CBS-TV newsman, Morley Safer, made two statements on the CBS-TV show, "Sixty Minutes". "The coin business has never been better . . . had you begun collecting only a few years ago, you would have made a tidy profit by now." He went on to say: "There is one area of collecting in which you almost certainly would have lost your shirt and that's in the material sold and advertised by the Franklin Mint . . . more than 75%, to be conservative, of all Franklin Mint issues have decreased massively in price."

Franklin stock, which had gone up like a rocket, came down like a stone. Subscriber cancellations peaked. Ad results plummeted. Headquarters became a beleaguered fortress. The media pressed from every direction for exposé interviews. Chuck Andes and Brian Harrison had to refuse interviews even to The New York Times and Wall Street Journal. The stability of the company was threatened.

Franklin maintained that it did not stress investment potential, that people bought their products primarily because they sought beauty and satisfaction. As for investment, it was best to take the long view. Skeptics pointed out that Franklin profits came after adding to metal cost the processing cost of the medals, the advertising and the overhead; that the raw silver in a silver medal cost a fraction of the price of the medal when sold.

But sales held up surprisingly well. While medal offers were hardest hit, other Franklin Mint offers did better than projected. The crown jewels of Franklin Mint were the subscriber lists. The procedure of constantly testing new offers mailed to their list continued as did tests in other media. New offers tested well, were projected and produced profits. It emerged that many, many people still had enough faith in Franklin Mint to keep buying, for whatever reason.

Then events took an unexpected turn. A new lurching leap in inflation, weaker currencies, rising gold, OPEC, the Arabs and the Hunt brothers, all joined to help vindicate Franklin Mint. The price of silver skyrocketed. In sixty days, "Sixty Minutes" started to be disproved.

At the height of the silver boom, untold numbers of Franklin Mint collectors turned their sterling silver medals in for melting down, often for much more than the purchase price. Meanwhile, kinder words began to be spoken about Franklin Mint.

The editor of Coins magazine told me: "The value of Franklin Mint issues has fluctuated. In earlier years there was a down trend. Many subscribers sold out at a loss. But they were short-sighted. Overall, I'd say Franklin was vindicated. There's never been a question in my mind that some Franklin issues could be cherished and valued.

"Of course, with the boom in silver, so many have been melted down that today their numismatics issues are, overwhelmingly, over the issue price. It's not always been the same for the silhouettes and the statues. But a lot of these have been melted down. This pulled a lot off the market, particularly those that had been a drug on the market. Overall, the last big jump in silver prices made all these go up in value. The tremendous number of medals melted down made those remaining scarcer and more valuable for collectors. So the 'Sixty Minutes' expose didn't hold up in the end."

This discussion was after the price of silver had collapsed from its wild highs. Since then, silver has steadied. Franklin Mint stock has started to go up again. Sales and profits are up. Chuck Andes calls Franklin Mint "a new business." Coins and medals are only 22 percent of sales. Fine porcelain, leather-bound books and proof-quality records are now the biggest volume producers. Franklin is all over the board in luxury products, and now diversifying with acquisitions, as well.

In the Fall of 1980, American Can announced that it had acquired 9.9% of Franklin Mint for about $12.3 million—and was considering raising its investment to 20%. In spring 1981, Warner Communications Inc. bought all shares of Franklin Mint (including those of American Can) for $206 million. In the first quarter of combined operations, Franklin Mint contributed about a quarter of Warner Communications' overall profits.

Chapter 7
The $5,000,000-A-Year Newsletter

By mail order, from home . . . part-time

That's Contest News-Letter. In 1975, Roger and Carolyn Tyndall started it, without a subscriber. "We were complete amateurs," says Carolyn, a housewife and former chemist. Roger is an air traffic controller and former accountant.

Roger and Carolyn are contest and sweepstakes buffs. "Both Roger and I liked entering contests. We've won over a hundred prizes in contests and sweepstakes. Even now, we keep entering them and winning them. We've won a total of 12 trips over the past 10 years. We went to Switzerland for a 3 week vacation in September and enjoyed a brief vacation in San Francisco in November. We've won two color TV's, pearls, money, food, small appliances, toys, a bunch of radios and some minor gifts. Sometimes, we take cash instead of prizes. We like to win.

"I was reared in MacClenny, Florida. My husband was brought up in Greenville, North Carolina. We met when we both worked at Cape Canaveral. Roger had a degree in accounting. He was tracking money spent on missiles. I had majored in chemistry and worked as a chemist for six years. At Canaveral, I tested missile fuel and all other chemicals associated with the missile industries except solid propellants.

"Roger and I got married. Roger only worked at Canaveral for a year. Then, he worked as an accountant for the IRS. But, he didn't enjoy IRS work. He's not nosy. He didn't like asking personal financial questions of taxpayers. He always loved planes and wanted to fly. A vision problem keeps him from being a pilot; so, the next best thing was to become an air-traffic controller, and he did.

"To keep up with contests, we subscribed to a newsletter published by a man in Texas. Then, he put in the newsletter that he was retiring and going to stop it. We tried to get in touch with him and buy his newsletter and subscription list. But it was no use; he wouldn't do it. So, we started our own.

"We had friends who liked contests and we got names of people interested in contests from the Win Lists that contests published with names and addresses of previous winners. That was all we had to go on. We ran a classified ad in *Southern Living* and got three inquiries. We ran other ads, and each was a failure.

"Then, we found two ways to get subscribers that worked. We located win lists amounting to 20,000 names. In September 1975, we sent out 20,000 free sample copies. We didn't even enclose an order form. We didn't know any better.

"We got in with contest clubs and sweepstakes clubs. We'd write them about our newsletter. People would write back and subscribe. Our subscrition was $6.50 for 10 issues. Now it's $12 for 12 issues.

"Then, we were mentioned in *Changing Times* magazine. We got 10,000 inquiries. When we sent sample issues, we converted one out of ten. That was a thousand subscribers at one time. Then we got mentioned in a lot of publications. A lot of people began to see our letters."

By 1977, Roger and Carolyn had got the circulation of Contest News-Letter up to 8,000 subscribers. Then, they met

Dick Benson. After a bit, they became partners with Dick who has since got them up to 400,000 subscribers. And how all this happened is quite a story. Carolyn tells it.

"We live in Amelia Island Plantation. It's a resort residential community located near Jacksonville, Florida. There are now about a hundred homes and some condominiums. It's very small. People know each other. But, when we moved in, there were only fifty homes.

"Roger loves cars and particularly Rolls-Royces. We noticed a silver and black Rolls-Royce with red trim driving around Amelia Island Plantation. We kept wondering who owned it. We heard he was in publishing and very smart and successful. Neighbors said that he was a mail order consultant, lived two streets from us and that his name was Dick Benson.

"My husband was fascinated with that Rolls-Royce. He'd watch Dick drive around. We sure thought he might be the man for us to talk to about our newsletter. We phoned him and asked if we could talk about his being a consultant for us. Dick told us we couldn't afford him. We thought about that and phoned him again to ask whether we could hire him for one day. Dick had seen the newsletter, but he explained he didn't work for people for one day. We even met him once but gave up the business idea.

"Then, one day, Roger and I were out on our bicycles. We didn't have ten speeds, just three speeds. Dick was jogging. We said, 'Hi, Mr. Benson.' He stopped jogging a while. We kept talking. He said, 'If you're ever interested in financing, let me know.'

"When we got home, Roger said, 'What does he mean? We're not broke. People send us the cash and then we print the letters.' We called up and asked him. Roger said, 'Let's have dinner sometime.' We knew this meeting could be important. We had a problem. We had no furniture in the living room. But, we decided, 'We're young. We have chairs in the dining room. We'll just have him.'

"So, Dick came to dinner. All through dinner, he didn't say anything. After dinner, he looked around the living room with no chairs. He remembered talking about financing. He said, 'If you're ever interested, let me deal.'

"We had an appointment in New York City with Publishers Clearing House. We flew up and stayed at the Waldorf-Astoria. That was all at our expense, but we loved the trip. PCH sent a limousine to pick us up. They treated us well and were wonderful. They liked everything about Contest News-Letter and us. They wanted to include it on the sheets of stamps they enclose with a mailing, each for a separate magazine, or in this case, a newsletter. Anyone getting this letter could tear off a perforated stamp for any magazine or newsletter, paste it on a return order card and include it in the order to PCH.

"But PCH explained they were afraid of us. We were new. We might not be able to deliver subscriptions they sold for us if we went broke later. They knew Dick. 'If you ever deal with Dick, let us know.'

"Then, we met Dick again. He explained what a partnership would be and how it would work. We'd just keep doing what we were doing. He'd expand the circulation. We were up to almost 8,000 subscribers, but he thought he could make it bigger.

"Then, we became partners and life changed. We had had a good idea. But it was a lot of work. We fulfilled on the dining room table. We got all our renewals working from there. Of course, now with Dick and his plans, we couldn't do it that way. We knew it as soon as we realized how big Dick's plans were and how fast he operated. There was no way we could keep up with

him. We couldn't possibly handle such a flood of subscriptions, by ourselves.

"Dick saved our life. He got outside services to do everything but write the Contest Letter. Roger does that which also takes research. We also promise readers a lot of services. I do that. And my mother works at it part-time. She's our only employee. The mail for the free services we offer comes here, nothing else.

"Dick has all the direct mail that goes out to solicit subscriptions printed outside. Then, he has a mailing house mail it out. He got us Neodata, in Boulder, Colorado. All the subscription orders and inquiries come to Neodata. They open the mail and bank the money for us. Then they sent the mail to Ireland . . . for processing in their plants there. Each name is put on magnetic tape in Ireland and flown back to Neodata.

"They send out the newsletters, the literature to convert inquiries, the bills, the renewal notices and letters, and maintain the list file and send out the names for rentals. We work with Biff Bilstein and Karen Reynolds there.

"There are 21 air route traffic control centers in the U.S. Roger works in one in Hilliard, Florida. It's a big center open 24 hours a day. 600 people work there. Probably 2,000 to 3,000 people lived in Hilliard. The center does the air traffic control for part of Florida, part of Georgia, and part of Alabama, North Carolina and South Carolina.

"Roger works full-time at his job. He won't give it up. But he works more than 40 hours a week on Contest Newsletter, as well. Every air controller worries. They're supposed to be worried. The Air Traffic Control Center asked the wives to talk to psychiatrists at the center. The psychiatrists made a study and found out that controllers with outside interests are better off, even though air traffic controllers in the U.S. work more hours than anywhere in the world. Roger finds air traffic control and mail order a good mix.

"Our friends think we're interesting. They're impressed. For a long time, they called us the 'mystery couple' because we worked all the time. We have no children. And we have no time for anything else. As far as making money, Roger and Dick take care of that. I do mainly service and proofread what Roger writes. I do write feature paragraphs. We do a lot of research. My mother is 66 and does the service fulfillment. I'm 38, and my husband is 43. My mother loves the business. For me, mail order is better than chemistry.

"We're good friends of our subscribers. They write us and phone us. They tell us of their medical problems and of their children. Some are fantastic winners. One subscriber won twelve cars. Another won a $300,000 island and a completely furnished home in central Florida. They often write us and say we helped them win. Some even ask what percentage to send us. Of course, we can't accept anything. Some send us presents. One subscriber, in his 80's, sends us a Christmas gift each year.

"Of course, without Dick we'd still be very small. He got us the subscribers and got us the services to handle most of the work. And he makes good suggestions. We depend greatly on Dick's advice. He's the most honest man we've ever met. But, we never know what he's thinking. After we were partners with him for a year, we asked if he liked us. He said if he didn't, he wouldn't still be a partner.

"We're pretty happy living this way. We have a half acre here. We grow pine trees on the side. We have 120 acres of pine trees we bought two years ago. It takes 18 years to harvest them. My father is in the pine trees business, and he's done well. We hope to, too. It's nice to have 400,000 subscribers and do

$5,000,000. And it's fun to keep going into and winning contests and sweepstakes."

If you want to have a five-million-dollars-a-year business, get a good idea and become a mail order moonlighter. Then, succeed with it on a small scale and move to Amelia Island Plantation. Keep your eye out for a silver and black Rolls-Royce with red trim driving around. Take up bicycling or jogging until you meet Dick Benson. And, when you ask him to dinner, make sure there are no chairs in the living room.

Chapter 8
The Direct Marketing Computerman

A pioneer's story; advice when to use a computer . . . in-house, outside or not at all.

Art Blumenfield is a specialist in the use of computers for direct marketers. He's the founder and president of Blumenfield Marketing, Inc. He's a programmer, a systems analyst and consultant on computer problems. He has computerized the Direct Mail/Marketing Association, Direct Marketing magazine and many large direct marketers.

"We've consulted for American Express, Revere, Fingerhut and Van Heusen. We did work for the American Civil Liberties Union and for Richard Viguerie. For computer installations our clients include Walter J. Black, Inc., American Can Co., Pepsicola, Seton Name Plate, Alfax and the Franciscan Friars of Atonement." Art has been working on computer applications for direct marketing since 1964 and with computers since 1953.

"At Standard Oil of New Jersey, I was an office boy. We got one of the first IBM computers, and I was one of the group in the new computer department. I attended CCNY nights, starting in engineering, and switching into economics. I minored in accounting. It took me 9½ years, from 1953 to 1962, to get my degree in economics.

"I stayed seven years at Standard Oil and ended up in charge of operations. We did all sorts of computer operations. We did inventory control. We worked out a degree day system to determine when a home owner needed a refill and when to send a truck. Esso credit was keypunching sixty million credit slips a year. Another fellow and I suggested the use of two credit card imprinting machines which would punch the tickets at the gas station. Esso adapted the idea of imprinting.

"In 1960, I went to Lever Brothers, working with computers in production scheduling. Then I worked for Computer Sciences Corp, a California-based consulting group—now the largest firm of computer consultants in the world, specializing in government work. For two years I worked for a pharmaceutical firm with their computer, then for a CPA firm in charge of their new computer consulting section. It was my first exposure to retail inventory control and to inventory control forecasting.

"Then I learned that two blocks from my home a new computer firm was starting—in Hartsdale, a suburb of New York City. It's now called MAGI, the Mathematical Applications Group. The founder was Dr. Philip Mittelman, a physicist. All the executives were engineers and physicists. They were masters of computers for scientific purposes but had no experience dealing with businessmen. Their first contracts were with the Government. MAGI became my first really big opportunity. (The MAGI story is in this book.)

"My experience was very complementary to theirs. We made a deal. I'd try to set up a division selling their computer capabilities for business use. From an idea I had, MAGI came up with what turned out to be a superior form of merge-purge, a duplicate identification we called Mail Save. It appealed so strongly to direct marketers and proved so effective for them that MAGI thereafter concentrated on the direct marketing field, in my division. MAGI bought a computer service bureau. We got contracts to maintain lists and to produce computer letters.

"While at MAGI, I began making speeches about our computer activities, and through this I met Murray Miller. Murray had had a successful fulfillment shop, was growing fast, had been forced into merge-purge, and suddenly had a lot of sophisticated requirements. I had been with MAGI seven years. Murray and I seemed to fit in our backgrounds. I joined him in 1972 in Office Electronics, Inc. which is now American Express Direct Response Division.

"Murray was wonderful to work with. He was a pioneer in the computerized fulfillment house business. People from overseas came to study the operation. He was just starting the International Direct Marketing Symposium, in Montreux, Switzerland. John Dillon was writing his 'Handbook of International Direct Marketing.' Murray and I wrote the chapter on the computer and direct marketing.

"While with Murray, I got one idea on my own time, for computerized and personalized children's books. I mentioned it to Rose Harper. She suggested talking to Dart (who then owned Kleid). Dart paid me for my contribution to what later became their 'Me Books' division, which they have since sold.

"After OEI, I took a very attractive offer for a one-year assignment . . . to take over a list brokerage and management business that was sick, learn the business, reorganize it and then leave. Then, on June 18, 1976, I started Blumenfield Marketing.

"By this time, I knew many people in direct marketing. From the start, people came to me with computer problems and became clients. I've never had to look for a customer. We have no literature. I've never reprinted my articles or printed my speeches. But we deal with the best.

"Ed McLean, Jack Oldstein and Murray Miller had all suggested that I become a consultant and they all helped me. Datapoint, whose equipment we work with a good deal, has sent us customers. Many people helped me. For 15 years, I've been close to 'Pete' Hoke, and he helped.

"We have gotten clients from speeches at other direct marketing days in the U.S. and in Europe, and some from working with the DMMA. We installed the computer system for the DMMA and gave them approximately $25,000 of software. I've spoken at many DMMA seminars and I'm asked to write for the DMMA publications which I do because I believe that each of us should do what we can to help our industry, thereby helping ourselves.

"We have a good but small crew. There are seven in the organization. I'm hiring two more programmers. Tony Toogood is our technical head. He was in data processing in England for years and has been with us for 3 years. Before joining BMI, he did support work for users of IBM equipment."

Note: For readers of this book Art Blumenfield has been kind enough to answer the following questions I've asked him.

Q. *When do clients (before they are) find that they need to computerize?*

A. Someone comes to us and describes a problem, losing track of their business, needing more accurate information, or whatever. Then, once the problem is defined, we can come up with the solution and it's not always a computer.

Q. *What is an example of a mail order situation in which you recommended against use of a computer?*

A. For Landau, the Icelandic Woolens Firm, I recommended an order processing plan using photocopy machines to process handwritten orders and use of a service bureau. Doing this was enough to solve the paper work mess. Each company has a very different problem. It can be simple to handle lots and lots of orders, but can be very complex to handle a few. I keep an open mind as much as I can to determine the best way to handle a given situation.

Q. *How do you determine when a client should use a computer in-house and when to use computer services outside?*

A. Generally, I advise clients not to do their own list rental fulfillment or merge-purge. I advise clients, almost always, to do their own order entry in-house. But because of the decrease in the cost of computers, there are few aplications that can not be done cheaper on the client's own computer rather than outside.

Q. *What are your views on computerized list selection?*

A. One must be very careful. Obviously, the computer has given us the ability to make "Recency/Frequency/Amount" selections quite readily. There are a lot of charlatans selling schemes which use computers for "sophisticated" list selection. Selectability of lists is related to information you have. You need a good data base. Computer selection can look good, but it's not always possible to duplicate successful tests on projections. One can take a list, break it into random segments and show significantly better results with one test segment than the other.

Q. *Why is that so?*

A. The samples are too small. For example, you can break a list down by the letters of the alphabet and show significantly better results for one letter of the alphabet than others. But it won't hold up in a rollout. I don't have a lot of faith in many of the computer selections or life style marketing selections that are currently being promoted.

Q. *How about analyzing your past orders to see what kind of zip code areas they came from and then selecting lists accordingly?*

A. I've had people say 'I know where my customers are. Why can't I use that to select by zip code?' The answer is that unless you relate the number of customers to the number of pieces mailed into the zip code, you can't project its responsiveness. Two zips with the same number of customers are not the same if you mailed four times as many pieces into one than into the other. And you won't have any customers from a zip you never mailed to, even though it may be quite responsive.

Q. *What do you think of computer modeling?*

A. If properly used, it's fine. It should be used for business projections. American Express and CBS Publications both use computer modeling this way.

Q. *How about computer modeling for list selection?*

A. I'm cautious. Once we drew off several segments of 500,000 names each from an 8,000,000 name list for special tests. Because of a last minute change, two of these segments were sent the same mailing piece with the same offer, mailed the same day. Yet the results were statistically different. What this shows is that you must never forget that you are dealing with people, not statistics, and people are not that predictable.

Q. *Do you ever get into computer situations for clients where computerization does not work as anticipated.*

A. None of us come up with the right answer, always. We bombed on Dependable Lists. Jack Oldstein wanted to computerize and start full blast on a data processing system that handled all of his company's activities. We automated his system. But the Datapoint hardware kept breaking down. It was all leased equipment. Ultimately, Jack had Datapoint remove the equipment. But since then Kleid has computerized using Datapoint hardware. So has "Names in the News", and an number of other organizations (not through us). Apparently, Datapoint has worked for them, but not for Jack. Now Jack plans to try again, but cautiously.

Q. *What do you suggest for direct marketers starting or upgrading uses of computers?*

A. Do so prudently. Don't attempt to do too much at once. Principals should get into the plans deeply and early. Personnel should be indoctrinated thoroughly.

Q. *Will computers that talk together become a business to business advertising medium and a new form of direct marketing?*

A. It's wise not to live too far in the future. The ability of computers to talk to each other isn't quite here yet. As for taking programs from one machine to another, we're a long way away. Many blades can fit a Gillette razor. But one company's computer software doesn't work on another's equipment; and one company's disks can't be read on another's machine. Only magnetic tape works on all computers, because everybody adopted IBM's method. But computer manufacturers, when they copy each other, change computers enough to get around patents. Usually, the change means they can't take the first company's software.

Q. *How do you charge for service?*

A. I charge per diem for consulting. We implement small, well defined systems for a total fixed fee. When objectives are nebulous and change, we charge by the hour.

Q. *Do direct marketers now use computers as effectively as they could?*

A. The post office forced mailers to automate when they introduced zip codes. Now a very large proportion of direct marketers use computers effectively.

Q. *How do you see the use of the computer developing for direct marketers, particularly for smaller mail order firms?*

A. In the future, every company that has a copy machine will have a computer. The word processing capabilities are fantastic. I'm most fascinated with computer systems for correspondence. For Pepsi Cola we created a customer correspondence system with a couple of thousand paragraphs. The operator just defines the problem to the computer. The computer selects the appropriate paragraphs, just as a private secretary would, and personalizes it. The system can theoretically answer 10,000 letters differently and appropriately.

Note: Art Blumenfield is down-to-earth, open and non gobbly-gook. Most days you'll find him at Blumenfield Marketing, 300 Broad Street, Stamford, CT 06901 (203) 359-2080.

Chapter 9
The Direct Marketing Clubs

Members help each other become
more mail order experienced.

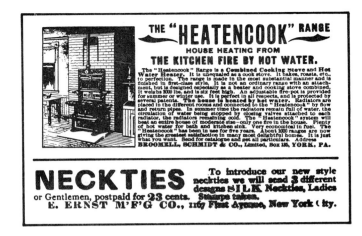
They are all over the U.S. and all over the world. Once a month they hold their dinners and luncheons. They are the Rotary clubs of the mail order community. Speakers are those prominent locally and travelling through. The clubs provide a circuit for top authorities with a flair for showmanship and a story to tell.

There are clubs from Atlanta to San Diego, from Philadelphia to San Francisco, from Boston to Seattle, from Houston to Des Moines. Often, the first introduction to mail order is an invitation to lunch or dinner and a talk.

The biggest clubs are in New York, Chicago and Los Angeles. But let's visit a small one, LIDMA—The Long Island Direct Marketing Association for a dinner at Stouffer's restaurant in Garden City.

Each direct marketing club is warm and friendly. People who don't know each other quickly get to. LIDMA is no exception. Members and guests begin to gather at 6 PM. By 6:30 there's almost a full house. Each new member gets a free drink. Everyone get a chance at a door prize.

At a LIDMA meeting, there are usually 60 to 70 people with 6 to 8 at a table. For most it's been a few minutes drive from office or home. Most member companies are located in Long Island's Nassau County where Garden City is. Some are from Suffolk County, further out on the Island. Because Long Island is bedroom to New York City, some work in the city. Most memberships are company paid.

To giant mail order firms like Doubleday and Publishers Clearing House, membership is an excellent way to orient trainees in mail order marketing and to keep staff veterans up with the field. Suppliers and services find it effective to teach salesmen the business of their mail order customers.

Just as a singles bar can start a romance, each table is a meeting place for buyer and seller, for the experienced consultant to become a guide for the firm considering direct marketing. A casual meeting now might mean business later.

To the small entrepreneurs there's the hope that some application of some idea stimulated here will brainstorm the next mail order hits. And for most employees there the meal is free, on their company. The ladies are not cooking. An employer may find that brighter, more eager and more knowledgeable employee dreamed of and each employee may meet his or her next boss.

But, beyond all this, there is a hunger on the part of all to learn, to become more mail order experienced. And each club meeting has a special meaning to all in mail order who attend. It's like the team's pep meeting before the big game. It reinforces the conviction that mail order is where the action is, growing faster than retailing, giving more opportunity to everyone in it and that the future may be more wonderful still.

Of all direct marketing clubs now in existence, the oldest is The New York Direct Marketing Club, better known as the Hundred Million Club. It was established in 1926. The Philadelphia Direct Marketing Club was established in 1943 and The Chicago Direct Marketing Club in 1955.

Each of the local clubs are independent but there is considerable cooperation between the Direct Mail/Marketing Association and the clubs. Ed Pfeiffer, Communications Director of DMMA, is the liason with the Direct Marketing Officers' Club, which has a representative from each club in a liason committee. The DMOC started in 1979 and came out of a joint effort of Ray Brennan and Ed Pfeiffer working to help the various clubs.

A direct marketing club usually starts informally. Two people in the fraternity have lunch together every so often, then three and then more. The idea comes up casually of getting more people to meet for some occasion, and then regularly. The more experienced give advice. The founders usually get advice from another club, and often from "Pete" Hoke.

"Pete's" father, Henry, ran the DMMA and later launched "The Reporter of Direct Mail", now Direct Marketing Magazine. In the 1920's, 1940's and early 1950's, he helped in the organization of the "Direct Mail Clubs" and Direct Mail Days. Almost all direct marketing club founders come to the DMMA and "Pete" Hoke for suggestions when starting. In LIDMA's case, "Pete" Hoke was a lot of help. "We did not talk to the DMMA until later."

Larry Chait, a past chairman of DMMA, lives in nearby Valley Stream. While not now an officer or director, he has been a speaker at LIDMA meetings and helped the founding group. "Pete" Hoke is in Garden City itself and is always accessible. The principal founder was Irwin Le Bow of Four Star Associates, a creative printing firm and lettershop. Irwin ran LIDMA before there was a president. LIDMA was founded in 1977. Don Kilstein, of 21st Century Marketing, was the first president.

Irwin Le Bow recalls: "It was Larry Chait's idea. He thought that enough direct marketing people lived and worked in Long Island to want and support a club. Several of us got interested. Bernie Lande and I are on the Board of Directors of MASA.

That gave us enough experience to draw up a constitution. Marie Fiero of Doubleday helped on the by-laws. We sent out an announcement of LIDMA's opening meeting to about 500 people in direct marketing on Long Island. Sixty-four people showed up. In the first year, we got seventy paid members. Now we have 97. This year will be the big push for membership.

"In getting members, so far, we haven't cared about balance. We just wanted anyone in the field to join. But the balance is good. We have agencies and lettershops, publications and financial institutions. We'll get banks. We're strong in book publishing. We have Doubleday and Walter Black. About 40% of members are direct marketers. The rest are services and vendors."

Hank Rossi is Vice President in charge of membership. Hank is Executive Vice President of Hy-Aid, a big fulfillment house. "I joined LIDMA last year, when one of the two owners of Hy-Aid retired, and I replaced him as a member."

LIDMA has thus far had individual memberships only. Now it is starting corporate memberships. A corporate member may put in the LIDMA mailing list five members. Anyone coming to dinner or to any LIDMA event will get the company rate.

The purpose of LIDMA is: 1) to provide a way for the direct marketing fraternity on Long Island to get together, exchange information and become more professional; 2) to provide a very low cost way to expose to those in the fraternity the top pros in the country. Most bigger direct marketing clubs in bigger cities get biggest guests. Those clubs in smaller cities have a harder time regularly getting biggest name speakers. But LIDMA is a small club that gets big guests.

"We get the calibre of speakers usually heard in New York. But here everything is better. There's no parking hassle or cost. You park free right outside. The meal is $10 cheaper. There's no bother. A scotch is $1.75 and wine $1.00. About 50% of members are within twenty minutes driving time. Some are within a half an hour to forty minutes drive. A lot come from New York City on the way home.

"So far, LIDMA has made no push for new members. The plan was to get a track record, get good guests, create a good club publication, organize and execute events properly. In any new direct marketing club the first members have a substantial percentage of vendors. That happened here. But the board of directors are primarily direct marketers. We expect the same balance of mail order firms, services and vendors as in other clubs and within the coming year.

"The big companies are now sending a number of people to LIDMA. Marie Fiero of Doubleday is Secretary. David Glass of Compton Direct Marketing has been Vice President. Doubleday sends six or seven people over. I send six or seven Hy-Aid trainees over on specific nights. Wherever I think a specific speaker can help a specific trainee develop, I send him or her over. Some members have brought clients to hear an important speaker like Jerry Pickholz, president of Ogilvy & Mather Direct. But most members come for personal learning. The biggest number we've had attend was 86, for Larry Chait."

LIDMA members work at it. There are a number of committees. There's ample opportunity to contribute time and expertise. As in many clubs, there's a desire to help out in any reasonable way with club activities. At $30 for membership, it's the lowest cost education you can get in mail order. This is typical of membership costs in other, smaller cities. Because most clubs can be reached through their officers, who are elected at different intervals throughout the year, it is wise to check Direct Marketing Magazine or the DMMA for latest information on the club nearest you.

Chapter 10
The Patrician Entrepreneur

An aristocrat who had an uncommon ability to sell the common man, by mail order.

He came up with very simple ideas and ways to present them very simply and to make mail order proposals very tempting to average people . . . and always in publishing. Edna Ferber called him a genius at selling books to the un-bookish.

"He was a rich man's son who very much wanted to make it on his own. He did it, at 22, in mail order publishing, from a small office in Oyster Bay, Long Island. Oyster Bay had no post office. The influx of orders was enough to force the building of one. Over a ten year period, he succeeded dramatically in two mail order publishing ventures, without his father's money. Then, when his father was in ill health and the family business needed direction, he joined it. He then transformed it almost completely and made it grow into "The General Motors of Publishing." He was Nelson Doubleday (Sr.).

His father, Frank Nelson Doubleday, had founded it in 1897 and had run it very successfully as a very genteel magazine and book publishing business. It had a strong base of the right magazines and the right books for the right people. The first Nelson added mail order sales of books and book clubs appealing to average people. Doing so, he multiplied its sales and profits. And management since (now the present Nelson) has made it branch, blossom and grow into perhaps the most scientifically run all-round publishing house in the world.

Before he started on his own, Frank Doubleday had climbed, over a period of twenty years, up close to the top rung of the distinguished publishing house of Scribners. When he left, he went into business with S.S. McClure. He brought in top authors. McClure brought in top magazines.

Then Frank Doubleday persuaded Walter Hines Page, editor of the Atlantic, to leave, join them and become editor of World's Work, the company's lead magazine. The company became Doubleday-Page. Page had great prestige. He was concerned with the magazines and Frank Doubleday with books. Particularly, the company sought the British authors and, more and more, got the cream of them. Walter Page became Ambassador to Great Britain, which helped. Country Life and their other magazines kept their own presses busy. Later, when magazine sales slowed after World War I, Frank Doubleday considered the drop temporary.

As time passed, Nelson Doubleday saw things differently. By the late 1920's, weekly news magazines made World's Work obsolete. Mass magazines and newspapers were flourishing. The class magazines were still too small in circulation. Costs were going up. They weren't contributing enough to overhead.

Nelson was 6'5" tall, weighed almost 200 pounds and was a powerful agent of change. Douglas Black, president of Doubleday after Nelson, said that under Nelson some of the changes were violent, but necessary.

Nelson's surgery and his mail order saved the day. He changed everything and started new growth. He weathered the Depression, jumped sales during World War II, and laid the foundations for booming post-war growth. First, the Literary Guild, then the Book League of America, the Doubleday Dollar Book Club, the Mystery Guild, and then one club after another were launched. Fortune magazine quoted Nelson as saying, "The book clubs are my magazines."

By shortly after the war, some said, "Mail order does 90% of the volume and makes 110% of the profit." It was an exaggeration but the mail order book clubs had changed Doubleday into virtually a different company. Entrepreneurship, drive and shrewd decision-making were the elements that brought it about.

Fueled with mail order profits, Doubleday could take advantage of change as no other publisher could. And Nelson did. He ploughed profits into plant and equipment. In World War II, he planned and, in 1946, opened the most modern book printing plant in the world, specially designed to produce the exact kind of books needed by his book clubs.

Part of his time he spent in the literary world with croquet at Oyster Bay with top name authors of books selling to the trade... and part in the mail order world. Nelson Doubleday died of cancer, but since then Doubleday's tremendous growth has only been possible because of his mail order entrepreneurship in those early days.

During Nelson's lifetime everything had changed at Doubleday. Its name had been Doubleday, McClure ... then Doubleday-Page, and then Doubleday-Doran. It's now Doubleday. It had published magazines and then none. It had sold its plant at Garden City to the manager. When he died and his estate could not carry out the acquisition, it took the plant back. Then the company built four more plants.

The first Nelson was a born entrepreneur, born into publishing and into an old family descended from French Huguenots. The Doubleday family name was derived from the French Dubaldy. He grew up among ideas, authors and publishing talk at the family home.

He made his first entrepreneur deal when he was eight, between Rudyard Kipling and his father, Kipling's publisher. He read a Kipling story in St. Nicholas magazine. He wrote "Uncle Rud" and suggested that Kipling write more children's stories and let his father publish a book of them. Kipling wrote and Frank Doubleday published the "Just So Stories" and Nelson received a penny a book for his lifetime. At 14, with a friend, he formed an employment agency getting people who needed work jobs on estates of those who needed help.

For the mail order business he started at 22, he sold subscriptions at sharply cut prices for magazines he delivered two months late. He got the idea the summer before from his father's complaints that magazine copies returned were almost worthless.

The business boomed. It was a great mail order hit, until 6 years later when the post office forced him to stop mailing at the very low magazine postage rate. He closed the business down and soon after went in the Navy in World War I.

After World War I, he started his second mail order book business, starting with remainder books—some from his father's firm. He tested an etiquette book and used Ruthrauff & Ryan as the agency. Lillian Eichler wrote the ad which succeeded. But the book was out of date. Returns were substantial. Lillian, whose son later worked for me, told this story.

"You wrote the ad. Now write the book," said Nelson to Lillian. In three months, she did it, for $500 outright. Then Nelson sold 600,000 copies at $3.95 each, and gave her a royalty anyway. It was Nelson's way. The ads, such as "Again She Ordered Chicken Salad," became part of the culture. They also helped make Ruthrauff & Ryan famous.

Another Ruthrauff & Ryan client of that day told me this story. He was Arthur Murray, later a Hoge client for radio and TV, who finally was earning $2,000,000 a year from his dancing school classes. But then Arthur Murray was selling dance lessons by mail. He heard that Nelson Doubleday's next venture would be dance lessons. He expected to be wiped out. He was desperate.

He told me: "I wracked my brains. I tossed in bed in the night. Finally, I went to see Nelson Doubleday. There were pictures of his ancestors on the wall. I looked at him and said, 'Since when have the Doubledays had to be dancing masters?' He looked and laughed. He felt sorry for me and forgot the dance lessons course idea. I went ahead."

After World War I, Nelson had spent more time at his father's company. After his father became sick, in 1921, Nelson became a director and vice-president. In 1922 or 1923, Doubleday-Page bought Nelson Doubleday & Co. to get still more of Nelson's time.

Still later, Nelson took on another mail order venture, on his own. And this one then created the modern Doubleday. It was the book club business.

Within a year of the launching of the Book-of-the-Month Club, Harold Guinzberg, of Viking Press, started The Literary Guild with Nelson Doubleday as a part owner. Viking didn't understand mail order and soon wanted out. Nelson did understand and soon took over control personally. Doubleday-Doran bought 100% of it in 1934, when Guinzberg agreed to sell his interest and Nelson felt free to sell his share, as well.

When Nelson saw an opportunity, he acted, often very fast. During World War II, books could be sold more easily than ever before. Book clubs pulled at low order costs. Credit collections improved. But supply was the problem. Every book publisher had a paper quota. And then Nelson bought Blakiston, a publisher of the Red Cross Manual and other medical books... with the biggest paper quota in the United States. Doubleday had to hire a special medical book editor and a medical book sales force. This would take time. Meanwhile, Doubleday book clubs and trade books could use some of Blakiston's paper.

Profits from mail order helped buy Blakiston. Paper from Balkiston helped fill mail orders for books and book clubs. It also helped Doubleday sell 1,600,000 copies of "A Tree Grows in Brooklyn," turned over to Doubleday for a reprint edition by Simon & Schuster because S&S lacked the paper after 400,000 sold. And all this helped supply the money to build the new post World War II plant which manufactured books for book clubs at the then lowest price possible, for bigger mail order profit.

And it has been Doubleday's ability to change, to adjust to and profit from change that has caused it, powered by mail order profits, to expand and proliferate ever since. Nelson put Doubleday into mail order books. He got Doubleday to reprint its own books, with Garden City Publishing Company. He put Doubleday into book clubs. He kept coming up with new ideas and carrying them through.

"Nelson Doubleday was the one who was always driving for expansion and new ventures . . . his greatest strength was as an innovator . . . he kept on being a financial backer in making reasonable tests of new ventures." That's how Milton Runyon, for years a right arm to him, remembers him.

Now another Nelson is president and chief executive officer, the son of the first Nelson. He, too, is said to have a strong will and new ideas and to have brought in new people and gone into new ventures. Again the winds of change are blowing and Doubleday is off to a new surge of growth.

Chapter 11
Guiding Direct Marketing's Growth

How a remarkable leader of an unusual organization can help you.

He joined an organization which had been established 42 years. Under his direction in the next 21 years, it grew faster than inflation, faster than any organization which does the same work in any field, faster than direct marketing. It grew over 37 times its size when he took over.

In all my mail order life, I have never seen any organization of its size every year launch and run so many different direct marketing operations simultaneously. Much of its activities are forbidden to make a profit. Yet, under him it's never had a losing year.

The organization is the Direct Mail/Marketing Association. All through this book are stories of people who belong to it, work with it and benefit from it. Each of its activities is designed to help direct marketers. Whether to join it and how to get most benefit from it is discussed in another chapter. First, I'd like to tell you about the man who runs it. Since he's been president, direct marketing has exploded and the activities of the DMMA have proliferated into every medium and all over the globe.

He is Robert F. DeLay, a remarkable leader of an unusual organization. The constant growth of DMMA and the continuing tight control of all its operation by Bob DeLay is an achievement any manager or owner in direct marketing can envy. He has built an able managerial team, a high calibre staff and an organizational morale and excitement rarely found.

The DMMA gets its members by direct marketing, markets its Conferences the same way, sells its books and publications mail order and direct markets all its seminars. For a constantly growing array of projects, it relies entirely on direct marketing. For most of us the testing costs and overhead of often quite small operations would quickly put us out of business. Yet, Bob DeLay runs the DMMA on the principle that in every year it cannot lose. How he does it is quite a direct marketing lesson, we'll shortly take up.

He was born in South Dakota. He was in the top 5% of his class while holding after school jobs. He was and is a competitor. His main interest was in sports—football, basketball and baseball.

Bob went to South Dakota State University and majored in journalism, with two years studying printing. "I started out to be a sports editor. It took me only part of a year to decide there was no money in it, but I found I could write. I got the habit of it, of reading newspapers, of seeing opportunities to get stories in papers of clients. I applied whatever writing ability I had to advertising. I'm a promotion writer.

"My first real job was with the Victor Adding Machine Company, in Davenport, Iowa. Alexander Victor, the founder, was inventive and creative. At Victor, I first heard of the DMMA. At that time, it was solely concerned with direct mail and its more efficient use. It had started as part of the World Association of Advertising Clubs, in 1914 . . . and officially, on its own, in 1917.

"Victor had a 16-millimeter movie camera and projector. I had to write a direct mail campaign for distributors. I knew nothing about direct mail until I joined DMMA. From it I got sixteen portfolios by mail of direct mail campaigns. I studied them and wrote my own, with my own layout. Later, I successfully sold for Victor its sixteen-millimeter projectors and cameras, by mail order, helped by what I learned from the DMMA.

"I began to spend more time exchanging information with DMMA members, and even more in my next job with American Air Filter in Louisville, Kentucky—where I was responsible for a lot of direct mail. By now, I was in quite close touch with others who were members. We helped each other. In 1955, I was put on the DMMA Board. More important to me was that I met and married my wife, Bonnie. She was in Graduate School at the University of Louisville.

"My next job was in Chicago, from 1955 to 1959, with Waldie and Briggs, an advertising agency and public relations firm. The agency principally had industrial clients who used direct mail and space advertising. A big client was Whiting Corp., selling construction cranes. I did a lot of industrial mail order selling for clients. Keeping up, via the DMMA, with what others did was still more important.

"Still, when the DMMA, in late 1958, made me an offer to be president, I had no idea of the future growth of mail order. I took the job because it seemed an opportunity to be on my own—almost as though I were to run my own business. More than financial reward, it was the fascination of working with the talented people who had created business with mail order know-how.

"In 1959, the DMMA had its office at 3 East 57th Street, above Stouffer's restaurant. You'd just walk upstairs. There was plenty of space, about 4,000 square feet. We had a man who ran one-day seminars, a librarian, a bookkeeper, a multilith operator, two secretaries and me. Now we have close to 70 people. In 1959, we had an annual budget of $158,000. For the fiscal year starting in October 1980, it was over $6,000,000.

"Mail order and the use of direct mail had been growing fast. Membership had grown to 1,800 people from about 100 in the depths of the depression. But each member paid about $35 to belong and expected very little for it. There were no company members then, just individual members. In 1959, volunteers ran the organization. A few zealous members did all the real work."

Bob brought with him to the DMMA one bonus, his wife, Bonnie. She had a master's degree in music and became an actress in The Children's Theater—a non-business background. But Bonnie wanted to help and be with her husband. "I've always been active in the DMMA ever since Bob became president, twenty years ago, but never on the payroll. When there were very few people I helped where needed. I would stuff envelopes or whatever. I used to assist the bookkeeper."

Bob continues: "At that time, I thought of the people in a trade association as about the same as in a big government office, without great drive. I've always worked pretty hard. I like to be busy and to work with busy people. I found the DMMA had good people. My job was to keep them busy and, when growth required, get more.

"There was no chance I could pay people the big money available in private industry. My job was to find brighter, more able people who felt as I did. I would explain to each that here was a chance to work with exciting people who generated businesses from their ideas; people that we might otherwise never get to know so well. Money isn't the main incentive. It's the excitement."

As soon as Bob started at the DMMA, he dove into his work and has never stopped. Bob looks back: "Bonnie and I have had a reasonable social life; but, mostly, it's been a 24-hour job, nothing else.

"The first thing I did at the DMMA was to go out into the field to find out from members what could help them most. I asked where the growth in mail order and direct mail was coming from, probably would come from and how we could help this growth.

"It was the help I got from the people in this business, their ideas and talent—the volunteers—that gave me a chance. I had to analyze their suggestions and my own abilities and put them to work. Then I had to communicate to each staff member, to each prospective employee I hired, the excitement I felt.

"A few helped a great deal. Ted Bihler did. He had been Chairman of the Board of the DMMA in 1957. He was the business manager of the Journal of Commerce, a Ridder publication. He saw and persistently made plans for future DMMA growth. He helped me for years.

"One of the early things we did was to reduce the number of volunteers working with the DMMA member committees. A committee would meet twice a year and committee members would talk. We abolished most of the committees but kept those most active.

"In my first five years, we built up to 2,500 members. Then we changed the DMMA from a professional to a trade association. That meant changing from personal to corporate member-

ships at several times the membership fee. At once, we lost 600 members—some of whom upbraided the board members.

"But now we could do things for members. Mail order was growing with tremendous speed. Direct marketing was about to begin. We had a number of fund raisers. We had some magazine circulation people.

"Changing to corporate memberships made all future DMMA growth possible. Before that I was collecting money from individuals. Angelo Venezian was Board Chairman. He was for it. Jim Kobak was managing partner of J.K. Lasser. He set it up organizationally. Now with $100 a member we could make it. When mail order turned into direct marketing we began to get bigger companies as members. That was around 1968. Even then, we didn't have some of the biggest mail order firms.

"When the post office began to make its first really big postal increases, we spoke up on behalf of mail order people. Spiegel was spearheading the fight to reduce these big increases. In 1970, Spiegel joined the DMMA, *and* also Alden. Montgomery Ward & J.C. Penny did not join until 1974. Sears only joined in 1978. But we did have a lot of smaller and very fine catalogs, the ones that have been showing the best returns in profit in sales and which are unusually innovative.

"Grolier was a strong book publishing member. Doubleday came later. The book publishers were much slower to join than the magazine publishers. We had the biggest magazine people much earlier.

"In 1970, we began to get more insurance companies. There was a lot of criticism of the mail order insurance business. The mail order insurance companies which were honorable and offered a good value suffered from the sins of the bad actors. They wanted to do something about it, to join together, tell their stories, do some public relations. They needed a home for a joint effort. We put them together in an Insurance Council and showed them how to use it to launch a public relations campaign. At first it was tough. There was a lot of political wrangling. But the Insurance Council did raise $60,000 for its campaign. The insurance people liked getting together.

"Other groups wanted to set up councils. They'd say to me, 'We don't want to raise a public relations campaign. We do want to get together.' They did. We now have eight councils. We may form a new council on electronic direct marketing soon and still others later.

"Then, in 1973, the DMMA went beyond direct mail. Then we really began to grow. We enlarged our franchise to represent any direct marketer using any form of advertising. Since then, growth of direct marketing has accelerated to even faster speed, and the DMMA has grown, too.

"When the Canadian Direct Marketing Association began, the DMMA helped it organize. We gave it ideas and advice. Back in 1968, we started making marketing missions to Europe. We would spend twenty days and visit four entire cities. We did this every other year through 1972. Starting in 1974, we ran our own International Conferences. That led to memberships from all over the world. Our sending of seminars first to Europe and then to Australia and elsewhere accelerated international membership. Our Paris office is further increasing it.

"Who helped me most? A college professor who taught me to write. Max Sackheim, early on, in one hour on the phone made me realize the basics of mail order at a time when I knew nothing about it. Ted Bihler did, before and long after I became DMMA president. Each Chairman of the Board with whom I worked with did. Each of many talented people in direct marketing helped and each brought me something different.

"Each chairman taught me. Bob Clarke was president of Grolier, and a financial genius. Lew Kislik was president of Publisher's Clearing House. He's now a busy consultant. Paul Sampson was and is a good influence. Reed Bartlett, of Proctor and Gamble, was tremendous.

"Two chairmen who had their own businesses were Earle Buckley and Bernie Fixler. Earle had a direct marketing agency in Philadelphia. An important client was IBM's office equipment division. Bernie Fixler owned Creative Mailing Service on Long Island.

"All these people and a lot more gave me a lot to bank on. Ed Roll was great at presentation. He knew advertising. He had organizing ability. Colin Campbell, of Campbell-Ewald, in Detroit, was the great pioneer of automobile advertising. Arthur Dembner was circulation manager of Newsweek. Giles McCullum was a top man at R.H. Donnelley. Angelo Venezian was vice president of McGraw-Hill.

"To realize how much each helps, you must know how much each Chairman of the Board of the DMMA gives to it. Dave Heneberry is a very articulate idea type of guy. He was just wonderful. He was supportive. He went out of his way to help. And he kept on top of the situation. For two years I reported to him every two weeks of the year for almost half a day. He spent much time at many other meetings with us. RCA and other big companies encourage their top people to do this sort of thing.

"From the needs of members and the ideas of staff things began to develop. Ruth Shea was here when I came. Members would ask her questions. She was marvellous. On her own she'd find out what she didn't know and then call back and answer. Members liked that.

"Ruth was one of the best. She's retired now but first Ruth trained Bonnie Rodriguez and Karen Burns to answer questions, as a department called Information Central. Bonnie later worked on the DMMA book bibliography of recommended books for direct marketers. Then she helped assemble the books for the first DMMA catalog of direct marketing books. She was the first editor of the first books published by DMMA including the FACT BOOK. Karen currently is director of Information Central. I found we could get very good people from libraries, and later from schools."

The DMMA staff was good. Bob DeLay had a flair for finding them, enthusing them and getting them to work effectively together. He sensed ability even when there was not a strong background. In 1970, he needed someone to run the Conference Department and organize the Annual DMMA Conferences which were getting bigger and bigger. He hired Sue White.

Sue White does not have an MBA. She took no postgraduate course. She had no special training or experience. She went to San Jose State College, in California, and majored in psychology. She was a Phi Beta Kappa. She graduated with honors. She got along with people.

"I was very fortunate to get the job. The DMMA was much smaller then. It was great working with Bob DeLay. He's an advertising man and a public relations man. He always has a lot of ideas. He's a real promoter. But he just suggests. He doesn't insist. He gives leeway. Do I take all his ideas? No, lots of times I don't."

In 1980, a third of the DMMA's $5,000,000 income was produced by the Conference Department run by Sue White. The Department sold more services in dollars to members than any other activity did. It produced almost 40% of all new members. It sampled, promoted and advertised to and dangled before members and non-members almost every service and product the DMMA offers. Bob DeLay is constantly concerned with its success and growth.

In 1974, the DMMA Board of Directors decided to start the Marketing Department for memberships and service. Ray Brennan was hired as Director. Before that he was a management executive with IBM for 13½ years. The DMMA's atmosphere caught his imagination and gave him a chance to more fully express his own ideas.

"Here it is exciting. Direct marketing is growing so fast. There's so much technological change. It's faster moving all the time. I like planning for expansion. I like new programs. I like mail order and direct marketing—finding out about it, keeping up with it." At the DMMA he could help shape the services given members, help create the reasons to join the DMMA and stay in.

Ray's emphasis was on delivering services to members and keeping members. He could then concentrate more on getting members. "But before talking to or promoting to members I wanted to learn everything possible.

"I did learn. First, I took the Basic and Intermediate Institute five-day seminars taught by Ed Mayer. I took a dozen more seminars. I've never stopped. Even when, three years ago, I started Pierre Passavant, I attended all three of his basic seminar series. I've read a lot of books. I meet, talk with and listen to top direct marketers."

The DMMA is a direct marketer of educational courses. It teaches science in direct marketing and applies it in its own business. It has the problems of any other direct marketer with a limited budget, with time and organization effort fragmented in many endeavors. But, in addition, it's not allowed to make money, but must break even. The seminar operations of the DMMA are run by Dante Zacavish. He was hired not just because he is a highly professional educator but because he succeeded in his own mail order education business, building it up and then selling it off.

Bob DeLay has an ability to sense what makes a person unhappy working in a public or private bureaucracy and then to provide a more stimulating environment. He has created a team, a team objective and a team harmony—an animated beehive. There are meetings, lists of things to do, and follow-up. But he's developed a team flexibility, too.

Bob DeLay is always in a hurry and he has his people feeling that way. But in a business that forever expands, and keeps coming up with new projects, new overhead and more promotions, how can Bob DeLay control it? "I've got to be sure we don't lose. We never had money up front. We have no venture capital. We do have a budget director, Jasvant Mahedevra. He was vice president of a bank in Bombay but came to New York and we were lucky enough to get him. He's fantastic. He's in my office every day reporting on something else we'll lose money on if we don't act at once. And we do. Jasvant watches everything as if we were a bank. It's very important.

"Rose Harper, president of the Kleid Company and chairman of DMMA was formerly DMMA treasurer. She has always had the concept that every direct marketing project and campaign should be regarded as a business. We try to encourage each department to proliferate in activities members need but also to become a profit center.

"We try to run a tight ship. We put up each year to the Board an annual budget to approve or revise. We seldom get turned down. We have a fantastic approval rate from the Board. As treasurer Rose was exceptionally good at interpreting the budget to the Executive Board. She watched carefully what we did. She did a masterful job. She and I reviewed the budget. She took the pertinent facts and presented them. She was spectacular.

"It's my responsibility to operate within the budget. With Jasvant's help I do it. There are Board meetings four times a year. He gives about eight days to them. There are Executive Committee meetings four times a year. That takes seven days a year. He spends perhaps three or four days in a year meeting with key direct marketers. We're in touch by phone probably twice a week.

"This means the Chairman, Treasurer, Executive Committee, other officers and the members of the Board of Directors have a pretty good idea of how things are going. Basically, they trust me to watch over everything.

"We always have a contingency plan. Our fiscal year starts November first. Of our budget, about 80% consists of pledged or fairly predictable income. For next year this includes dues revenue for a little over $1,000,000. Total pledged income is $1,100,000. We can estimate pretty accurately what our income will be from conferences and seminars and even some small income source such as book sales from our Catalog. But about 20% of the budget is for new projects that may produce very little of the guestimated income or beyond it. Here is the main risk.

"One way we handle this is to schedule a substantial part of our new projects to start after May first. If first six-month income is below expectations, we can cut out some projects after May first and cut down on others . . . after that we can cut down on travel. Finally, if necessary, we can let go employees and cancel still more projects. But we know we must live within our budget and income for the fiscal year. And, so far, we always have."

Part of Bob's secret is his attention to nuts and bolts and the way he encourages each department to use each project to test out the next. Bob DeLay has found the questions phoned into Info Central an invaluable guide as to what the DMMA should do next. It gave the idea for The Fact Book and later for The Law and Direct Marketing Book. It showed where seminars might be needed.

Ray Brennan is vice president of marketing now, in charge of three departments. He has done effective DMMA recruiting. "As the DMMA grows, we structure more. We do more long-range planning. We try to attract bright, capable people. Few plan for a career in association work. We have to convince them that it's challenging, diverse and rewarding.

"We're getting good people . . . Ed Pfeiffer, Jack Cavanaugh, Ann McGuire. We need directors to run departments. I knew Dante Zacavish. I live in Westport and met him there. Through Dante we got Dick Montessi. We're building an executive staff. We try to tell them what we're doing, to get across the big picture—how big direct marketing is and how fast it is growing, the fascinating people that are in it.

"In 1980, the DMMA acquired 700 new members, bringing membership to 2,200 firms who joined for 4,000 individual members. We had a new growth of close to 500 members. We're looking for 3,500 company members versus the 2,200 we have. We have a good many Fortune 500 members.

"Direct marketing is growing overseas. We're getting members there and now have a Paris office. Our international newsletter and other promotions are translated into French and German. In the U.S. and all over, direct marketing and mail order are expanding in many different ways. The future is electronic. We're working on a cable TV report and other reports. We're adding a researcher-writer."

At the DMMA offices at 6 East 43rd Street, in New York,

the atmosphere is fast-moving. Ruth Troiani, who heads up Administrative Services to back everyone up describes it: "Here there are high expectations of what you can and will do. This comes right down from Bob DeLay. We attract the best. We look for people who seem to be able to work on their own. Our executives travel a lot. Our people work as well when the boss is away as they do when the boss is in the office.

"The DMMA has many projects that grow. Year after year, we get new young people working. They develop. They get interested. They want to know more about direct marketing. My job is to help and encourage the starting personnel I'm concerned with. We motivate our people. They get involved. They work with each other. There have always been good opportunities for women in the DMMA. There's no discrimination. We encourage all the staff to go to seminars and conferences. Almost all have."

The DMMA has the direct marketer viewpoint. It trains its own personnel with its own seminars. DMMA staff members are entitled for the most part to attend the Passavant seminars and the Basic Institutes as they relate to their jobs. Most do, on their own time. Dante Zacavish did.

"I like attending seminars, attending conferences and other direct marketing meetings. I like each weekly DMMA staff meeting. From every meeting, every contact, I learn more of the how-to of mail order. Being here is to stay on the cutting edge, to meet innovators, to get ideas."

Dante came up with and found ideas for seminars of most interest to members and to non-members. He made alliances to lessen the risks of launching new seminars. He sought out associations who needed to teach some form of direct marketing to their members—and then convinced them to join forces. "We did this to bring the DMMA seminars overseas. All these DMMA overseas seminars have been co-sponsored. We prefer to go in when hosted, but not to walk in and walk out. We work closely with each co-sponsor."

Seminars are an important source of DMMA new members. Each member attending becomes a prospect to join an appropriate council. Membership follow-up solicitation is personalized, segmented and geared for each non-member attendee specialty. Bonnie Rodriguez, after running Information Central, starting the book catalog and editing the first Fact Book, coordinates the eight councils.

To Bob DeLay, all DMMA activities are one vast research project to select most needed, least risk future projects. Everything interrelates. A question asked enough times by phone to Information Central may lead to a special report, a book, a seminar, a council, a special fund-raising campaign or whatever. Tests are made unendingly, more tests at a tinier average test cost than any mail order organization I know. Bob DeLay uses each tiny test as an exploratory tentacle for something bigger, and often far bigger.

Government Relations and public relations, ethics and legal positions—each facet of DMMA activities has a life of its own. Each project is a risk. "We try to be right always but can't be. We try to figure out what we can do with what income we've got. We must always adjust outgo to income.

"It takes vigilance and work. But each year we do keep within the budget. And the confidence we've earned makes us determined to keep it that way. Each vice president and each director of a department feels that way. We're all very close."

In a later chapter I tell in more detail what the DMMA does for members and advise when it pays to join and how joining can best pay off.

Chapter 12
The Man Who Wrote A Billion Letters

What helped him most to write successful copy . . . how he mastered his craft.

Over one billion letters written by Maxwell C. Ross have been mailed out by direct marketers. Over 6,000 keyed tests of his letters have been made. His letters have been keyed and tested against many of the top direct mail writers in the U.S.

He is a master of mail order. He is one of the very few consultants who are the very best—and one of the greatest copywriters in mail order. He is considered one of the ten best direct mail writers. Many consider him number one as a writer of sales letters. His "rules" of mail order copywriting are accepted guideposts. He is quoted by just about every professional book on mail order.

Max Ross sold insurance for Old American Insurance Company where he was advertising director. He sold magazines for Cowles publishing where he was subscription promotion director. He has sold magazines, books, food, insurance and a wide variety of products since—for a variety of clients . . . as a consultant, strategist and creative team of one.

His reputation has attracted clients from all over. From his home in Kansas City he flies to various parts of the country to meet with those clients he handles. They include insurance companies, associations, publishers and others. Creatively, he's a one-man band. His wife does the billing and bookkeeping, and serves as a direct marketing sounding board. How did he start? Let Max tell it.

"I grew up in Des Moines. In 1936, I went to work for the country circulation department of the Des Moines Register and Tribune. After a year of getting my feet wet, the Cowles organization invited me, as a callow youth, to look after the few subscriptions that had trickled in for their new magazine, Look. At first, Mike Cowles did not want subscriptions, but intended to concentrate on newstand circulation. Somehow, the subscriptions arrived anyway.

"As the months went by, I absorbed more and more about the circulation business—much of it from Floyd Hockenhull, publisher of Circulation Management. I persuaded Mike Cowles and the rest of Look's management staff to let me make a few direct mail tests.

"They worked—and by the end of 1937 we had 50,000 mail-sold subscriptions in the house. This began to look good to management. If a youngster not yet dry behind the ears could do this, what would happen with a seasoned pro at the helm? So Les Suhler was hired from Rand McNally. Lester Suhler was one of the great circulation men of all time and exerted a powerful and profound influence on me."

Even before Suhler arrived, Max Ross had absorbed a great deal from master copywriters like Robert Collier and Henry Hoke, Sr. . . . from marketing strategists like Frank Egner and Jack Lacy (for their influence with formulas) . . . from Richard Manville . . . from Maxwell Sackheim, who was excellent on headlines and opening sentences . . . from Arthur Kudner, a strong advocate of small words. Ross is a strong believer that you

never stop learning. As he said in each of his books, "Learning is a process that begins with the cradle and ends with the grave."

"For help in writing copy, I looked for the writers and publications with the ability to speak to, reach and persuade average people," Max explains. "For example, I studied the style of Reader's Digest. I read, in particular, examples from 'Toward a More Picturesque Speech' in the Digest. This helped me develop picture-building words for copy. One might call it 'photo speech'. I studied Time magazine's style and even its favorite space-saving device: the colon."

More than the skill of writers, Max Ross studied the reactions of people. He studied psychology, human nature, human reactions—what people want most, in order—what persuades and convinces them most, in order; what blocks, fears and suspicions keep people from buying, in order of importance.

"Early, I learned the importance of exchanging information with others—of asking questions—of getting more than one opinion. Martin Baier and Bob Stone were among my close friends and we learned a lot from each other, especially about the techniques of *learning*. Perhaps no one in direct marketing has helped so many people as has Edward Mayer, Jr. He helped me become a better direct mail practitioner and the experience of putting on seminars with him, as we did together, was unforgettable.

Ross early learned the value of teaching, and he himself taught at Drake University in Des Moines as a member of the evening faculty. Like many instructors, he learned the value of studying books like Strunk and White's "Elements of Style" . . . John Opdycke's "Say What You Mean" . . . Bob Stone's earlier book, "Successful Direct Mail Methods" . . . and all of the Rudolf Flesch books. To him, Max gives credit for the Ross Short Word Formula of 75% of all words being five letters or less.

"Dr. Flesch had a profound effect on American writing," Ross explains. "From the moment he turned his Ph.D. thesis at Columbia into the best-selling 'The Art of Plain Talk', his influence was unmistakable. His formulas on 'reading ease' and 'human interest' unmistakably worked. Dr. Flesch explained how to pick samples of your writing, count the number of words, figure the average length and then count the number of syllables. That determined your 'reading ease' score. Counting the number of personal words and personal references gave your 'human interest' count.

"But I learned that listeners in the audience had difficulty applying the Flesch formulas. So I set about to reduce the Flesch teachings to a simpler scoring device that said:

FOR EVERY 100 WORDS YOU WRITE, MAKE SURE THAT ABOUT 75% ARE WORDS OF FIVE LETTERS OR LESS.

"It seems that the length of the word rather than its syllabication is more important."

Max Ross tested this formula under actual marketing conditions and in his own words, "The Short Word Formula helped every letter we ever wrote. Letters written to conform to the formula always outpulled those that didn't—every time—without fail."

"At Look—Henry Cowen, Marvin Barckley and I, along with our staff members, tested mailing elements—and because of the huge quantities we mailed, there was ample opportunity to find out what worked and what didn't. It was a remarkable testing laboratory and everyone who took part put that knowledge to good use, not only for Look but throughout their careers later."

Cowen, Barckley and Ross developed a reputation for

originating "busy" mailings—order forms with borders, stamps, boxes and all manner of devices that helped the reader "get into the act". They learned that multi-page letters usually worked—until it came to renewals and collections. There, one-page letters seemed to do the trick. As Max points out, "The only good collection letter is the one that collects the money AND keeps the customer."

Henry Cowen tells a story about Max Ross of the time when a research organization offered to save Look magazine the trouble of testing copy. They would select by research methods, asking people's opinions, which letter and mailing piece would pull best. Max offered to give them last year's tests to research which would be the winners. The offer was not accepted.

But Max Ross is one of the first mail order copywriters to recognize the benefits of research—particularly in learning how readers react to mail order copy. "We used the Look Eye-Camera to study the reading habits of people as they looked at a printed page. The camera photographed each eye movement to determine exactly what pattern was followed.

"We discovered the erratic movement patterns of most people reading a mail order letter, broadside or ad. In a letter there would be a glance at the lead, a hurried look at the signature, then the P.S., then back to the start—*If* interest warranted." Since then, these same reading patterns have been confirmed by researchers thousands of times.

Ross, Cowen and Barckley engineered many great direct mail pieces for Look. Max spent sixteen years with the Cowles empire. Together with Les Suhler, these men helped build Look circulation to more than seven million subscribers. Around 1950 they helped launch Quick, a pocket picture magazine, and Flair, an up-scale women's fashion magazine.

Elsewhere in this book, Henry Cowen tells how he was taught mail order by Max. To this day, top pros talk with wonder of mail order subscription mailings produced and results secured by the Look team. But by the sixties the picture magazine party was over, and for big circulation general entertainment magazines, TV did them in. One by one, Look, the Saturday Evening Post and Life went down the drain.

Maxwell Ross left Cowles 18 years before this in 1953. He was hired by Old American Insurance in Kansas City. Elsewhere in this book, Martin Baier, marketing head of Old American, tells of Max and their work together there. It was a marriage of talents for fourteen years.

At Look, the job was to get trial subscriptions, convert them and then keep renewing them. At Old American, the job was similar—to sell policies and build business by selling different policies to present policy holders. At Old American, Max did two-step mail order, as well as one-step—getting inquiries and converting them. Inquiries were secured from different media using direct mail to convert inquiries to sales.

"At Look, I learned to edit my copy twice—once to make sure I covered the selling points and once more to improve reading ease. But at Old American, I edited both of those ways—and a third time for a legal check, because of so many state and federal regulations of insurance advertising. I spent 14 happy years with Old American."

Then, in 1967, he launched Maxwell Ross and Company, himself, with his wife as moral support. "This is an age of specialization, and so my work takes me into the fields of publishing, insurance, associations, travel and religion."

Max Ross had made mail order techniques work—under changing and challenging conditions—for more than four decades. He works in all forms of advertising, but his expertise is particularly strong in direct mail copy and mail order strategy. I asked Max how his track record could be so good when direct mail costs have literally skyrocketed. His answer:

"The creativity and open-mindness of the people I work with is a vital factor. And don't give up. If you can't get through, go over. If you can't go over, go underneath. If you can't do either, go around. And if you have to, go back to square one and start over.

"Computer letters and now laser letters have been great. But the art is to use them in a way that conveys sincerity and not phoniness." Max sees mail order success as requiring constant development and use of new methods . . . but with basic professional skill.

Max has always kept ahead of the times in each new direct mail development. What does he expect for the future? "There will be more targeting, more elimination of less desirable names. Before merge-purge you would find the same customer on six or seven lists. Out of this came the multi-hit process.

"This development—creating lists of people who have bought a number of mail order offers—has been very important. These names and better producing lists can be mailed more often than they generally are. If you pay out the first time, don't stop at one mailing. Go out of your way to mail again. Find a reason or excuse to mail, and explain it in your copy. If you pay out on a multi-hit list, you should mail at least three times."

Max Ross is a top recognized authority. His fees from clients have built a substantial equity over the years. He has trained and helped others. He has lectured, written articles and spoken before groups. He helped originate the DMMA Manual with monographs on letter writing and direct mail.

Max keeps one room at home just for writing. He types all his copy. "I try to start each job with a clear mind and a clean desk—except for notes, paper, books and other material I need to refer to. I keep carbon copies of all projects. I don't throw away any false starts. Some of my best ideas have come from past rejects.

"Over the years, I've painstakingly worked out a 20-point check list. After I write a rough draft, I still go down my check list, point by point, and see where my letter needs strengthening. It is only by being ruthless and impartial in this kind of self-discipline that I've been lucky enough to come up with copy that sells."

Max believes strongly that the sales letter, from opening to P.S., can make or break the entire mailing piece. "The letter is usually *the* basic element in the direct mail package. Without the letter, a seller is simply putting an advertisement in the mail. The letter is basically a 'me to you' communication. There is a unique flavor and style exclusive to letter writing which makes it an art unto itself." And Max is the master of that art. His little manual, "How to Write Successful Direct Mail Letter Copy" is a small masterpiece. Never in direct marketing have so few words said so much. "What I tell is the sum of what I've learned and the way I work." The DMMA has it and you should read it.

Note: Maxwell Ross solves problems in direct marketing, creates his sales letters and direct mail, and dispenses his mail order wisdom from 3 Crown Center, 2440 Pershing Road, Kansas City, MO 64108.

P.S. He can help you. Check the Help Reference Guide in back for material by him and about him available to you.

Mail Order Sampler
Seminar II

Electric Launches

Newest Types—all motive power beneath flooring.

Safe,   Simple,   Reliable
No Heat, Smoke, nor Smell.   Fully Guaranteed

Can't Explode   Can't Sink

Can be USED EVERYWHERE with our New
PORTABLE CHARGING PLANT

Illustrated Catalogue mailed on request.

THE ELECTRIC LAUNCH COMPANY, Morris Heights, N. Y. City.

Chapter 1
How the Book Club Business Grew

Recollections, wisdom, humor,
advice from Milton Runyon, retired
boss of Doubledays's mail order.

Since his retirement as executive vice president of Doubleday, Milton Runyon has been a consultant to publishe s in two hemispheres.

In on-the-job training, more people new in top jobs of mail order publishing have learned more from him than from anyone. Under him, as it prospered, Doubleday became a school for rising young stars in mail order. Entire mail order divisions of companies have been the product of people who learned how from Milton Runyon.

Mail order at Doubleday was started personally by Nelson Doubleday. On his own, Nelson Doubleday went into mail order, made money and proved to his father, Frank Nelson Doubleday, that mail order book selling should be added to the family business. On his own, he went into one of the first two book clubs, succeeded and then, later, made mail order book clubs the base of the Doubleday business. To do so, his first lieutenant in mail order was Milo Sutliff whom many called a mail order genius.

But it was when a third man, Milton Runyon, was added to form a mail order triumvirate that the biggest proliferation of Doubleday mail order began. As mail order most transformed Doubleday . . . Milton was first the stabilizer and then the guiding hand. This started with Nelson and Milo and went on for two decades after both were gone.

Gradually and quietly, Milton, under Nelson and Milo, contributed more and more to Doubleday mail order success. He had a way of side-tracking an impractical brain storm. He would cut the losses of an unprofitable test. Projects Nelson started and Milo carried forward, Milton made happen safely and profitably.

The creative talent Milton developed carried on after Nelson and Milo, and built further mail order growth. And Milton's continued creating of creative talent kept accelerating growth. He was the bridge from depression, over war and through the boom that followed to further mail order change . . . while mail order was most important to Doubleday.

To buy the great presses that gave Doubleday such competitive advantages . . . to expand world-wide . . . to acquire other publishing companies . . . or to proliferate into so many publishing activities no public stock issue was ever needed. Mail order profits provided the money.

To attract authors, Doubleday book clubs provided extra big royalties, instant and huge distribution, and, with far bigger promotion, much more exposure. Book store sales of titles featured in book club promotions jumped.

Mail order contributed most to Doubleday's growth. Overall, Milton Runyon contributed most to the transition from Nelson Doubleday's entrepreneurship to today's management. And his recollections, wisdom and advice can help each reader of this book, all with Milton's quiet humor. I'd like to introduce him to you. First he talks of his roots and start.

"I was born and brought up in Plainfield, New Jersey. My father, David M. Runyon, worked in a bank all his life, working up from office boy to cashier of the First National Bank. He wanted me to go into banking and got me a job one summer as an office boy at the bond house of Harris, Forbes. He later made contact with a friend at the Federal Reserve Bank in New York. But I 'went my own way' and got into advertising agency work and then into book publishing—especially the mail order and book club side.

"My mother was Alice Spangenberg, of the then-popular occupation of housewife. I was an only child and had the tender loving care which probably helped me into lifelong obesity. I went through Plainfield High School and a few years later married the Valedictorian of my class, Alleyne Macnab, who had become a research scientist at Rockefeller Institute.

"An early hobby was printing. I bought a Kelsey hand press and later a pearl treadle-operated foot press, earning a fair amount at general printing. I also did greeting cards and other personal items. I have been an amateur printer all my life, so I began to read magazines like Inland Printer and learned much about production. I started a small stamp business with a classmate. I had summer jobs.

"My father wanted me to go to Princeton and I tried it for a couple of weeks, but found that such subjects as Greek and chemistry had no appeal, so I went to the Dean and asked to change to economics and similar real-life subjects. When he said no, I packed my bags, went to New York and enrolled in the NYU School of Commerce at Washington Square. I studied accounting, business English, advertising copywriting and direct mail—with such teachers as Charles Gerstenberg, Gerald Seboyar and Earnest Elmo Calkins. Since I commuted from Plainfield, and earned some money with job printing, I took four years for what was normally a three-year course. I had no time for school activities and did not take any graduate courses, but went directly into business upon graduation.

"My first job was as a copywriter with Robinson, Lightfoot & Co. I wrote copy. When the production manager quit, I also began to do production—ordering typesetting, engravings, art work, electrotypes, mats.

"One of the Robinson accounts was The Crime Club, Doubleday's mystery-novel publishing venture, serviced by an account executive who specialized in creating 14-line ads. When he left permanently, I took over the Doubleday contact and began weekly trips to their Garden City office. I worked with an artist, Richard Porter. Our principal contact with Doubleday was Dan Longwell, who later went to Life Magazine. Dan liked our Crime Club ads and later gave us the Doubleday general book advertising.

"The Robinson Agency fell on hard times even before the Depression began, and they went broke in 1928 after I had been with them just two years. Dick Porter and I packed up our belongings and joined Schwab & Beatty who were then doing the advertising for Doubleday's Garden City Publishing Company division—"Star Dollar Books" and occasional mail-order ads for individual titles, Etiquette books, Home Medical books and the like. Their main accounts at that time were Book-of-the-Month Club, Simon & Schuster, Walter J. Black. Harry Abrams was production manager, Mac Gache was art director, Bob Beatty the media man, and Vic Schwab, of course, the copy chief. I certainly learned a great deal from all four of these people.

"In addition to Doubleday, I developed some minor book accounts for S & B—University of Oklahoma Press, University of Chicago Press, University of Pennsylvania Press.

"In 1937, I was invited to join Doubleday. My first job was as advertising manager for the trade book department. I reported to Malcolm Johnson who then headed the division.

"In many ways, I carried on many of the same activities but as part of the publishing business. I gradually got interested in mail order. I began to come into contact with Nelson Doubleday, who always reviewed the mail order result cards every morning, Bob DeGraf (head of Garden City Publishing Company) and Charles Sherman, chief copywriter for the book clubs. I worked closely with Milo Sutliff who was Nelson's mail order chief, and John Stevenson who assisted him."

By three years later, Doubleday was expanding and Milton Runyon's job. On November 1, 1946, a front-page and follow-up story ran in the New York Times on "The Dramatic Success Story of Doubleday-Doran". It called Milton a "surprisingly young and indefatigably industrious graduate of the Schwab & Beatty Agency." It described paragraphs of duties and went on. "Quiet and even-tempered, Milton plows through like an excavating machine. He's one of the few who work on Saturday. The lights in his office are usually the last at night."

About those early days and those of his mail order leadership and about the people in mail order who impressed him most, I asked Milton many questions. Milton kindly, for readers of this book, answered each one.

Bob Beatty was co-partner of Schwab & Beatty, one of the really great mail order advertising agencies, now a subsidiary of Marsteller, Inc. About him, Milton recalls: "Bob Beatty was the real mathematician of mail order. He taught me a lot about how to forecast the pull of ads in various media, and the keys to profitability. I remember that we had once scheduled a back cover in American Weekly for a 69¢ book, and Nelson Doubleday phoned from South Carolina to question the wisdom of such a risky investment. I came in to the office on Thanksgiving Day and phoned Bob Beatty and others to get the ammunition to convince Nelson that the risk was good. The ad ran—and it paid out!" (Please don't try this in a supplement today. 69¢ books now would be after inflation the equivalent of 10¢ each, for probable mail order suicide.)

I asked Milton about the great copy copywriters. He answered. "Max Sackheim and Harry Scherman were top copywriters. I would say that Max might have had more diverse abilities as a copywriter than Harry. But Harry Scherman not only *wrote* Book-of-the-Month Club ads, but he also created and dictated the styling which kept his distinctive touch as long as he lived. He was probably the greatest 'stylist' in mail order copy and typography. He worked principally with publication ads and did very little with direct mail. Harry was also the better rounded executive to deal with business matters as well as creative work. Vic Schwab was a great copywriter.

"I probably learned from them, but never aspired to concentrating on copy. Perhaps my one memorable achievement was a sales letter for Best-in-Books which was so successful that we mailed many millions. (I was once questioned by the FBI because one of the letters, signed by me, had gone to the Soviet Embassy and they obviously thought that I might have included a microdot message in it.)

"Walter Thwing and Dave Altman were long responsible for the Dollar Book Club ads, in what would now be considered a pretty hard sell manner, with big Gothic headlines and strong copy. Sackheim gave somewhat similar treatment to Literary Guild ads, but when Wunderman, Ricotta & Kline took over, their agency used a more imaginative, lighter tone."

Milton Runyon continues: "At Schwab & Beatty, Dick Porter, as art director, carried out Harry Scherman's styling in ads. The agency became Schwab, Beatty & Porter. Dick Porter became the chief contact with Book-of-the-Month Club. (Schwab & Beatty is now a subsidiary of Marsteller, Inc., which is a subsidiary of Young & Rubicam).

"Harry Abrams carried out Harry's styling in Book-of-the-Month Club direct mail. I originally worked with him when he was production manager at Schwab & Beatty, at the start on a no-salary basis as he learned. Then I often saw him when he was art director at Book-of-the-Month Club. He was the one who developed the idea of having paintings on the covers of Book-of-the-Month Club News. And when Harry started his art book and art print business, I made some deals with him to use his products in Doubleday clubs."

Note: Harry Abrams became, with his own company, "Harry Abrams, Inc.," the largest art publisher in America. Harry Abrams, Inc. is now a subsidiary of the Times-Mirror Company.

Milton recalls: "We had strong, creative talent internally. Charlie Sherman was a top copywriter and idea man; unfortunately, he died some time before normal retirement. George Weiss, a classmate of mine at NYU, was one of our steadiest producers of sound copy. Warren Levy did good work for us before he left for Famous Schools and then Franklin Mint. Tom Stasink was an outstanding Art Director and he could write copy with his other hand.

"All direct mail was done in-house, but for publication advertising we used a number of different agencies over the years. The in-house staff began with a handful but grew to probably a hundred (mail order creative and marketing) by the time I retired in 1970.

"Jack Cassidy was our wiz on the fulfillment side. Doubleday did all fulfillment operations in-house. The mail room at Garden City opened all incoming mail, banked the remittances. They sent new enrollments for each club to that club's section for label typing and forwarding to the shipping department, originally in the same building. In my earliest days, all Club fulfillment was by the use of Elliot punched stencils, with the punch marks indicating shipments, payments, etc. All initial collection methods were handled in-house, using collection letter series prepared mainly by Jack Cassidy's assistant, Margaret Cody. Collection agencies and lawyers were used for hard-to-collect items of worthwhile amounts, and some fraud cases were referred to postal inspectors. "When I got into the Doubleday mail order activities, the most specific help with knowledge about methods and results came from Milo Sutliff, John Stevenson, Tom McElroy, and Jack Cassidy.

"Nelson Doubleday always had ideas for expansion into new projects and fields and kept pushing them.

"Milo Sutliff was excellent at carrying out Nelson's plans. He watched the figures closely and often had a hand in the creative work. We had a term—"Sutliffing up the Coupon," which meant to lure the customers with attractive bait.

"I guess I was something of a 'stabilizer' for Nelson Doubleday and Milo Sutliff. We used to have 'idea' sessions at the Doubleday plantation in South Carolina during the winter, and then I would come back to New York and get things moving.

"It was when Milo Sutliff left Doubleday in 1948 to join John Stevenson at Greystone Press, that I was ready to step in as principal executive for the mail order division, reporting to Douglas M. Black, President, and Nelson Doubleday, Chairman.

"Since Douglas Black was principally concerned with overall management of Doubleday's very diversified business,

including the development of three new manufacturing plants, he left the management of Book Clubs and Mail Order principally to me.

"In turn, I tried to organize all the help I could get. To the extent that my organizing ability existed, it depended on much delegation of authority—to John Beecroft and then Ed Fitzgerald in Editorial, to Jerry Hardy for advertising, to Charlie Sherman for Direct Mail, to Jack Cassidy for Fulfillment. And I had great staff help from Laura Orford (later Mrs. Runyon, organizing my home life), and Vilma Bergane, who worked with me for twenty years.

"In this way, many ideas came from Jerry Hardy, Charlie Sherman, product managers such as Ruth Buchan and Marian Patton, and from Bill Havercroft—head of Doubleday, Canada. Some ideas came from our advertising agencies and the agencies helped in shaping and testing many of them.

"Walter Thwing was a great garden enthusiast. He started a magazine called The Home Garden, which Doubleday later purchased. The American Garden Guild was stimulated by Walter, his magazine and his publication of books by such noted gardeners as Montague Free and Fred Rockwell. Walter Thwing had a lot to do with starting the Garden Guild for us.

"One of my contributions was BEST-IN-BOOKS, a club which offered a volume each month consisting of one full-length current novel, and excerpts from other current books—maybe a short story, a chapter from a non-fiction book, a short novel, etc. It was intended to compete with Reader's Digest Condensed Books, but with the advantage of having all the material complete in the author's own words, without being chopped up by editors for 'condensed' reading. It was quite successful for many years, but like many other propositions, began to be unattractive because of increased costs of acquisition of material, higher manufacturing costs, higher costs of maintaining membership.

"There were three book clubs in operation when I joined: The Literary Guild, started by Harold Guinzberg and Nelson Doubleday and purchased by Doubleday & Company in 1934; The Book League of America which offered one new title and one classic each month; and the Doubleday One Dollar Book Club, originated at Doubleday in the early 30's. The Literary Guild had started in 1926, the same year as Book-of-the-Month Club. "The first addition was Mystery Guild, which was an idea of Milo Sutliff's although possibly based somewhat on The Crime Club which Doubleday started in the late '20's but promoted more as a Trade imprint rather than a mail order club. Next came the Family Reading Club which emphasized 'wholesome' books. It grew effectively in the early War years, with the many inspirational books available from Norman Vincent Peale, Fulton J. Sheen, et al. By the time I left there were 30 clubs, mail order programs and other such mail order ventures.

"The developments in those years were to expand the number of book clubs to cover many special interests. The present tendency is to shrink down the number and concentrate on getting the largest possible membership for the most successful clubs. The present practice makes very good sense today, because manufacturing and fulfillment costs are much lower as quantities increase. In Britain, however, the policy is to have a large number of specialized clubs; that seems to work most effectively in the U.K. where there are probably a greater number of specialized interests in reading (History, Biography, Natural History) and where book manufacturers are more accustomed to dealing with smaller quantities.

"Jerry Hardy had quite a lot to do with the inspiration for Doubleday's first 'Program'—Around the World Program—booklets with gummed color illustrations printed on a sheet of stamps so the the recipient could complete the book. It had wide appeal to families, at $1 a booklet, and led to a series of similar programs—Nature Program, Science Program, Know Your Bible Program, Know Your America Program, Success Program. Testing was done by direct mail so any projects that didn't work out could be abandoned at comparatively small cost.

"Not all ideas tested out. Charlie Sherman created a plan for a Music series, a combination of books and records, which might have beaten Time/Life to this market, but we didn't have the knowledge of resources to mount it successfully. "We had one book club which worked through banks. Collections were marvelous, but the plan was difficult to administer (pretty much through a separate staff) and was soon abandoned. We also tried a paperback book club which did not work and was never retested.

"We have had many propositions which were successful for a number of years and then had to be abandoned for economic reasons. These were certainly not 'failures' but perhaps they could be said to have failed ultimately. The Doubleday Programs are a good example. It became impossible to make a profit at the $1 price and the format would not stand a higher price. Meanwhile, Time/Life had come into the field with similar products in hardbound form with which we could not compete.

"The Doubleday One Dollar Book Club had to be re-named The Doubleday Book Club when we could no longer maintain the $1 price. It is still one of the most successful clubs.

"We kept experimenting with different ways to market successful clubs. For many years, Literary Guild booths in department stores were very effective. The stores handled billing which worked very well because the cost of the books was usually well smothered by the sheets, pillow cases and dresses which the customer bought in the same month. There were also some experiments in supermarkets, but not very successful.

"Ads on some match-book covers pulled successfully for a while, mainly on male-oriented clubs like Mystery Guild. Some oddball ways tried did not work. We sampled book club selections in hotel bedrooms. A guest could read a book and mail in a membership coupon. The offer was a dud.

"Increasing sales per member became a high priority because of the vastly increased costs of publication advertising, direct mail material and postage required in recruiting new members. These were the principal ways of bringing this about:

- Making the books offered as attractive as possible.
- Offering the 'lead' books which reflected the kind of books the member would receive after joining, rather than offering attractive 'bait' and then giving quite different material as selections.
- Offering a very wide variety of books that can be bought by members in addition to the regular selection. This does

mean that, whereas we once could sell 50% or more of the members the Main selection, we now sell 20% or so, but we do sell a great many more books overall.

- We have found that it is useful to send as many enclosure offers with the Advance Announcement as postal weight will handle, and that the use of many enclosures does not detract unduly from the main offers.

"Non-selection offers to members were almost entirely created in-house. We established a small editorial department to create suitable books. Some of them have been:

Encyclopedia of World Travel

Best Recipes from the Cook Book Guild

Know Your America

A Treasury of Modern Mysteries

Encyclopedia of Child Care and Guidance

"We also mailed syndicated offers, such as a mailing by the Literary Guild on a book like Harry Abrams' big Norman Rockwell volume, or on a series such as Stuttman's Home Medical set. Yes, I think your figures are right, that such an offer coming directly from the Guild could pull at least double what the same offer mailed over the names of Harry Abrams or Webster's Unified would pull. My impression is that such offers are probably declining now, because there are fewer people originating suitable products. Stevenson is out of the business, Abrams appears to be concentrating more on Trade sale, Stuttman is concentrating on its own mailings rather than mailing through others.

"We put great effort into testing effectively at modest cost. Testing new club offers was frequently a matter of testing the agency's best ideas for space ads and our direct mail department's best mailing outfits (often more than one in each case). Then we could cross-fertilize—adapt a successful d.m. outfit for a space ad, and vice versa.

"Usually direct mail material started with the copy man's rough sketch and pretty-well-finished copy being given to an art director to put into final form for art and typography.

"You have asked about the origin of continuity programs, sets of books a subscriber can take once a month or so and cancel at any time. I do not have detailed knowledge of the start of continuity sets. I think it had some relation to the start of 'Parts-In-Work' in Britain and other European countries. They could be sold effectively through the nationwide suppliers of bookstalls and stationers. They were usually sets of books broken into many volumes in magazine format and usually issued at the newstand once a week. A similar product, developed for the U.S., could not be sold in the same way, so mail order, at a higher price, was experimented with and became successful. More recently, the magazine format sold through newsstands and backed by TV has been tested in the U.S. with some success in several cases.

"Doubleday's only extensive test of continuity programs was with Dr. Fishbein's medical set. The principal reason why Doubleday did not pursue these programs was that the books were unsuitable for manufacture at Doubleday's book production plants, and a good part of the profit in book clubs was in the manufacturing of the books by wholly-owned plants. FTC and credit problems also played some part.

"John Stevenson, who left Doubleday in the middle 1940's, operated Greystone Press. Particularly after Milo Sutliff joined him, he had considerable success with various continuity programs. I did not know very much about the Stevenson operation, but I did watch closely the H.S. Stuttman development of

continuity sets, and helped him in the creation of many of them by licensing to him the Doubleday materials on which he based his Medical set, Nature set, Bible set, Child Care set.

"Over the years, we kept dealing with many of the same advertising agency people but often the agencies evolved. Max Sackheim and Harry Scherman had worked together as copywriters at J. Walter Thompson Advertising in Chicago, then at Ruthrauff & Ryan, the first major New York mail order agency. They also moonlighted together in the 'Little Leather Library,' small sets of classics in leatherette binding. Later, they started their own advertising agency, Sackheim & Scherman . . . and then the Book-of-the-Month Club. Harry Scherman with the Club then became a client of Schwab & Beatty. Max Sackheim joined the Brown Fence Company as part owner and stayed in the midwest for 16 years.

"Nelson Doubleday had used Ruthrauff & Ryan. I'm not sure that Sackheim and Scherman ever did any Doubleday ads, but Schwab & Beatty did. I'm sure that Nelson Doubleday became acquainted with Max Sackheim at Rutherauff & Ryan.

"It was when Max Sackheim resigned as president of the Brown Fence & Wire Company and returned to New York, that Nelson and Milo agreed to let him have a crack at Literary Guild ads. The first ones were disastrous, but Max and his art man, Ed Ricotta, soon got the hang of it.

"When, later, Wunderman broke off from Sackheim, he took the Literary Guild business right away. I believe that some minor business stayed with Sackheim for a while, but Max soon retired to Florida and left Bob Sackheim to run the business. This was about the time when I began traveling overseas to start Doubleday book clubs in Australia, New Zealand, France and England, so I was not too familiar with U.S. details. I know that Ed Fitzgerald had great confidence in the development of the Wunderman agency. I have met their people in Paris and London and have been very favorably impressed. I have watched Lester Wunderman operate a brainstorming session and heard him talk at the Direct Marketing Symposium in Zurich. I have the impression that he's very brilliant. Jerry Hardy had most of the contact with the agency, Wunderman, Ricotta & Kline.

"The Walter Thwing Agency became Thwing & Altman, when Walter took David into partnership. And when Walter retired, the agency became David Altman & Company. Later Dave joined Frank Vos and for a time the agency was known as Altman, Vos & White. Frank Vos had started with Doubleday writing direct mail. Stan Rapp worked with Altman and Tom Collins was a Schwab & Beatty man. They got together to form their own agency, Rapp & Collins. Tom was the copywriting strength, and Stan the general executive strength, in my opinion.

"What changes contributed most to Doubleday success? Probably the two most important were the building of the new manufacturing plants and the introduction of computers. Doubleday's new manufacturing plants . . . first at Hanover, Pennsylvania, then at Berryville, Virginia, and an offset plant at Smithsburg, Maryland, and then at Orange, Virginia . . . made the biggest difference in *profitablity*. The computers made the biggest difference in *efficiency*.

"The rubber-plate rotary presses at Hanover provided Book Club editions at far lower cost than the sheet-fed printing at Garden City or the book manufacturing available from other traditional plants. This plant produced only a single trim-size, so the later addition of Berryville, making 3 sizes available, was another step forward. Orange has been the ultimate, producing a completely bound, jacketed book, in a single operation.

"The computers gave better information about members

performance, response from different media and mailing lists. They made it possible for us to know that low cost responses from certain publications were very much less valuable than higher-cost enrollments of better quality from other publications, and the same with mailing lists. We could also test such things as the results from Advance Announcements containing no extra enclosures against those with 1, 2, 3 or more enclosures. It began to require Harvard Business School graduates to operate the systems, but they really worked and contributed much to the financial success.

"Doubleday began using computers in a modest way, in the late 40's, I think, with IBM equipment and punch cards. This equipment, and Scriptomatic, took the place of the Elliot system. The next step was an experiment with a Univac system which didn't work out; it couldn't get up enough speed to be cost effective. We then called in all the main companies for research and consultation—IBM, Honeywell, Univac, Burroughs. We were advised by the computer experts at our auditing firm, Scovell Wellington which merged later with Ross Brothers and Montgomery, and finally with Coopers & Lybrand. The decision was in favor of IBM and the original installation rented at about $80,000 per month. We hired an expert named John O'Neill to run it, and it has been performing miracles ever since. The computer became essential partly because it was impossible to hire enough people in the Garden City area to deal with the handling of club member accounts by other methods. Cost saving has been less of a consideration than the increased effectiveness possible through assessing the values of different sources of members, different offers and that sort of thing.

"Source analysis was always important, but in the early days had to be done by laborious hand counts and the charting of sample memberships over a period of time. Computers have made it much more practical. Many publications have had to be dropped from use entirely. The same with many types of mailing lists. I rate it of primary importance.

"Automation of inserting helped a great deal. I expect that Doubleday had one of the first Phillipsburg inserting machines marketed but I can't remember the date it was installed.

"One advantage Doubleday had was that it had become big enough in direct mail to have experts available on list buying and rental of lists and on production, so that I rarely had to participate in such matters except in a general supervisory capacity.

"Another advantage was doing so much in-house, for cost and control. But only in the earliest days of my experience was much direct mail produced in Doubleday's own plant in Garden City, on letter press equipment. We very soon began doing most of the mailings with various lithographers, although we brought all the material into Garden City for addressing, folding, inserting, mailing.

"Another development that helped was the use of insert cards with ads. Insert cards in publications have been used for a very long time in Britain because postal regulations there do not forbid the use of loose inserts. My first recollection of use in the U.S was by Book-of-the-Month Club, probably in the early 40's; they used a full-page bind-in on card-weight stock, with a business reply card, scored at the bottom. I don't remember the date of Doubleday's first use of newspaper free-standing inserts, but we did make some use of them as soon as they became available.

"Clearly, the novelty hyped the results at first and now that they are so common, it becomes a matter of cost effectiveness against normal space. Doubleday found that one way to get the greatest use out of the best media was to run double page spreads, instead of single pages, and often multi-page ads, such as the 6-page center inserts in TV Guide. Often this larger space results in a bit higher cost per member, but the advantage is in getting so many *more* members from the publication. This is especially true when dealing with publications with limited availabilities on premium positions such as back covers.

"During my time, we never found computer letters worthwhile. We used letters printed through ribbon which gave a very successful look of typing. We never used telephone selling in my time, although I once made a trip to Stockholm to visit the advertising agency, Schonkopf & Westrell, which had done considerable pioneering in selling by phone in Sweden. I was not convinced that it could produce a book club customer of good quality.

"How about the direct mail spectaculars? I have some feeling that the over-size, lavish pieces are over-done. It seems to me that a greater *variety* of approach is likely to give the best results. One of our most effective pieces for a while was a simple multi-page letter with pretty persuasive copy. (Life once used a similar letter for the Life History of World War II.) Maybe Franklin Mint requires such pieces for its high-priced items, and Time-Life for the lavishly illustrated Garden series and others, but I wonder whether some recipients aren't put off by the obvious high cost of the material and the impression that they'll be paying for it when they buy the product.

"What success did Doubleday have in selling merchandise? Doubleday has always concentrated on selling its own products to club members to the greatest extent possible. There were a number of experiments with merchandise, even merchandise catalogs, but none succeeded well enough to make as much profit as Doubleday's own self-manufactured books and booklet series. At present, most months there is a single envelope-style enclosure for a syndicated product used with enough succes to make it worthwhile.

"Developing international sales was important. Even by 1950, Doubleday had 160 employees in Canada and, more or less, each operation successful in the U.S. was set up there, plus some others.

"From 1961 through 1969, I made many trips to Australia, New Zealand, England, France and Germany to discuss possibilities for joint ventures in the book club field with local companies, and Laura and I lived in London most of 1967 through 1969 in working out the joint venture between Doubleday and W.H. Smith & Sons, which has become the highly successful Book Club Associates. It was interesting to note that the opposition of British publishers and booksellers to book clubs was much the same in the 60's as it had been in the U.S. in the late 20's and early 30's. Much persuasion was necessary to induce the Publishers Association to change the restrictive rules and to obtain the co-operation of publishers. As the club memberships grew, and royalties to publishers increased, the opposition began to vanish.

"We noted many differences between mail-order methods in Britain as compared to the U.S. Mailing lists were virtually unobtainable, so we depended heavily upon publication advertising, where it was very useful to have the nationwide distribution of the Color Magazine sections of the London Times, London Observer and the Telegraph. We found that club members were much more 'touchy' about service than their counterparts in the U.S., and we found it often advisable to answer complaints by telephone rather than wait for a reply to arrive by mail. A device which proved especially useful in getting the confidence of advertisement readers was to use a logo which

read 'This is a book service of W.H. Smith and Doubleday'. Since there are W.H. Smith shops and bookstalls throughout Britain, readers felt they were dealing with a well-known firm that they could trust.

"When I retired from Doubleday at the end of 1970, the new electronic technologies were just beginning to be talked about. I have, of course, kept on reading about them and get the impression that they have been making more headway in the U.K. and Europe than they have here. I don't doubt that many of them will be successful. But since Doubleday's essential business is in selling *reading*, it seems logical to keep major emphasis in selling by the printed word.

"No, we did not then do much research, as such. The research was mainly in the testing of various offers, different lead books, different prices. Originally, results had to be hand-tabulated, with new hand counts at intervals in the life of memberships. Computers made it far easier to do such testing. We never had much faith in any kind of interview-testing—feeling that the only thing that counted was the response from the ads or mailings. Split-run tests in publications were very widely used. (Now Doubleday uses a good deal of research.)

"You have pointed out that a lot of women have done well at Doubleday and asked me whether Laura, having worked at Doubleday, made me value more the potentials of women. Yes, I'm sure that Laura's abilities helped show me the potential that women could have in mail order. Since Laura (whom I married in 1949, after my first wife died of cancer) was Milo Sutliff's assistant and worked in various aspects of mail order, her success did influence me. Jerry Hardy's secretary, Joan Manley, became his assistant and went on to her great success at Time-Life. Vilma Bergane, who started as my secretary, is now a vice president at Book-of-the-Month Club. Robin Smith, who began in Double-day's Research Department and then transferred to Book Clubs, became president of the Doubleday Book Club division. On the retirement of Charles Marshall, Patricia Fitzsimmons took charge of the Literary Guild's Department Store operation and was especially effective in dealing with department store executives.

"By and large, the Doubleday women worked up through the ranks rather than being hired on an executive level. I knew Robin Smith only slightly in her original research job; her rise up the ladder began just about the time of my retirement, but I know of her activities and get the impression that she is a brilliant mail order person. She later had a lot to do with the Doubleday activities overseas, many of which I started.

"Joan Throckmorton worked principally with Charlie Sherman and I knew only that he had high regard for her writing ability. I have followed her activities with Throckmorton Satin Associates."

Who are the most interesting people I've worked with?

Among advertising agency people: Max Sackheim, Vic Schwab and Bob Beatty, Walter Weintz, Stan Rapp, Dave Altman, Frank Vos, Lester Wunderman. Jim True was the only list broker I knew well. Outstanding publishers: Harry Guinzberg of Viking, Bennett Cerf of Random House, Dick Simon and Max Schuster of S & S, Arthur Thornill of Little Brown.

"Others included Elsworth Howell who began to do many innovative things in selling merchandise to people who had bought Encyclopedias and other books, Harry Stuttman who was great in creating books that would sell by mail and the mailing outfits to sell them—he designed and wrote them all himself, Walter Black who had great stories about his shoe-string start, but played his cards very close to his chest and never told any of his results. His son Ted has carried on the success.

"One of the most interesting was Harry Scherman. I got to know Harry quite well for several reasons. He was a close friend of Thomas B. Costain, a Doubleday editor who became an author and wrote The Black Rose, The Silver Chalice and all those successes. Laura and I often joined the Costains, the Schermans and the Rosins (the Scherman daughter, Katherine, who married Alex Rosin) at dinner parties.

"What were Doubleday personnel requirements and training methods? When the business was simpler, we looked for intelligent young people, were usually content with liberal arts degrees, took some who did not graduate from college and looked particularly for some mail order experience.

"Lester Ohrtman was head of personnel at Garden City most of the time during my tenure. He had, himself, been active in mail order at Doubleday, and had been with Reader's Digest for a time, so he was well acquainted with talent requirements. Almost all of Doubleday's personnel training was in-house, but the activities were so diversified that the training tended to be in specific areas. In recent years there has been a tendency to hire more graduates of Harvard Business School and similar institutions, as the business becomes more sophisticated.

"I didn't get as much chance as I would like to go to association meetings and seminars. Jack Cassidy was the Doubleday executive who attended DMMA meetings and some employees attended Hundred Million Club. I think they are both useful, the DMMA especially in dealing with government authorities and regulations. Direct Marketing Day in New York is, of course, quite a recent invention. I have been to two of them and rated them both quite good, certainly of most help to people new in the business.

"It was only after retirement from Doubleday that I went to such meetings as the Canadian Direct Mail Association, the Seminar in Switzerland. I did give a couple of lectures on aspects of direct mail, one at NYU and one at the New School, and one usually learns something in putting together such talks.

"As for books I've read, I'm sorry that I haven't kept the books I used at NYU and I don't remember the specific titles. I purchased most of the Direct Mail books as they came along.

"I read DIRECT MARKETING regularly and also subscribe to The Friday Report. I have purchased only one of the Tapes, because I find it much more useful to *read* rather than to listen. I am sure that quite a number at Doubleday have been DMM subscribers and use the magazine regularly.

"At various times, I was Executive Vice President of Doubleday & Co., Inc., I was President of the Literary Guild of America, Inc. and Vice President of Nelson Doubleday, Inc. I had various titles in other subsidiary corporations.

"Would I choose the same career again? Looking back, I can see the disadvantage of spending one's entire life as an employee.

Even though the rewards in salary and bonus can be very good, there is certainly nothing like the success possible in developing one's own business. If I had it to do over again, I'd give real thought to that possibility.

"I think there are fine opportunities in small mail order businesses where the product is right. I wince at some of the ads which promise millions of dollars in easy money, and I certainly warn starters about proceeding incautiously. I am sure that a great many advertisers in publications like Yankee magazine do very well. It's when people get too ambitious, try to expand too rapidly, that the numerous failures which we have been reading about recently start occurring.

"What did I enjoy most? Probably the most enjoyable part of my career was in meeting the exciting people who create books. I remember especially Thomas B. Costain, Sinclair Lewis, Herman Wouk, Dr. Morris Fishbein (and his wife, Anna), Ilka Chase (I was one of the angels for her play, 'In Bed We Cry'—but I did *not* cry all the way to the bank; the show folded after 47 unprofitable performances), Gertrude Lawrence, Daphne du Maurier. It's been a great pleasure to keep up many of these friendships in retirement—meeting the Fishbeins in Chicago or London, visiting the scenes of Rebecca and Jamaica Inn with Dame Daphne du Maurier.

"Yes, I have really enjoyed retirement and it has been made pleasant by the ability to keep on traveling and to 'to keep my hand in' as a consultant.

"My activities have included these: I helped get Farm Journal started in publishing books to sell to their subscribers and to distribute through Trade and mail order sales via Doubleday. When I retired, they asked me to be a consultant and I have helped them attain sales of well over 10 million books. A similar thing happened with the H.S. Stuttman Company. I licensed certain Doubleday materials to Harry for his use in creating continuity sets. After my retirement, he invited me to make contacts outside the U.S. for these sets and I was successful in making some sales in Australia and England. I was involved, early on, in Franklin Mint's creation of the Franklin Library and I helped them clear publication rights for many of their sets before it became necessary for them to have staff help for the purpose. I did some advisory work for International Correspondence Schools in Australia and the U.K. I now have several clients abroad to whom I supply information about U.S. mail order catalogs, space advertising and direct mail.

"Laura and I have been getting to England once a year and last winter we had an extensive trip to New Zealand and Australia. We are off to London again on September first to visit the extensive new offices and warehouse which have just been opened by Book Club Associates, the Doubleday/Smith joint venture. After ten years of such activity, we may begin to slow down a bit.

"My older son works for IBM in the Washington D.C. area. My younger son has given us two grandchildren, a girl and a boy; he teaches mathematics at Rochester Institute of Technology. I read lots of magazines and books, still do a little photography.

"For young people starting out, I'd recommend some liberal arts training; I have always been grateful for 4 years of Latin, perhaps just because it helps in doing the Times crossword puzzles. The new sophistication of equipment and methods and financial management suggests the desirability of college and graduate school work. At the proper stage there would need to be specialization, since few people are capable of being expert in all the diverse aspects of mail order.

"I think one can rise through minor jobs to the top with

enough application. A good example is Bill Tynan, now in a top job at Xerox; his start was as an assistant list man at Doubleday. Maybe one of the keys is simply hard work. That's what I credit with much of my own advancement at Doubleday. There were nights when I was at the New York Times at 4 a.m. reading proof on a publication-set ad which took advantage of some timely event. I worked a great many evenings, Saturdays and Sundays, and probably accomplished quite a few things which 9 to 5 application couldn't have done."

Note: You have met or will meet in the pages of this book many of those referred to by Milton. There are stories on Jerry Hardy, on The March of Time-Life Books and Joan Manley, on Robin Smith, Nelson Doubleday, Max Sackheim, and Wunderman, Ricotta & Kline.

Jerry Hardy, who launched Time-Life Books and then Dreyfus Liquid Assets Fund and went on to create a billion dollars in sales in 18 months, tells in some detail what Milton Runyon's teaching and guidance meant to him. Elsworth Howell, who built 150 million dollars of sales from zero for Grolier and was a competitor to Doubleday, calls Milton "a particular hero of mine." There are many in direct marketing today who admire and are grateful to him for advice and help.

I'm sure that each reader of this book joins with me in thanking Milton Runyon for helping us, too.

Chapter 2
Joining the Direct Marketing Establishment

How it can help you.

If you're about to start as a mail order entrepreneur with a tiny ad, you're not ready for it. If you are (or work for) a small or large, successful direct marketer or if you sell or service direct marketers, you should know about it.

It started in 1917, at first concerned with direct mail; then mail order via direct mail; then direct marketing by direct mail; finally direct marketing in every form, wherever on the globe. It's the Direct Mail/Marketing Association.

The DMMA has drawn to it big and smaller direct marketers. Its members are active in direct marketing from TV to catalogs, from telephone marketing to free-standing inserts in newspapers, from couponing to radio. Through the DMMA, the expertise is passed around. If your company pays for a membership with you as a representative, you may be lucky.

Can the DMMA help a career in direct marketing? Yes! Because you meet people you should. There, everybody meets everybody else. Outstanding accomplishment anywhere is known everywhere. It's a help to any supplier of a better way to do anything in direct marketing. Young talent gets seen. By volunteering for jobs that need to be done, newcomers meet old hands. Beginners meet, become friends with and get advice from the more experienced, established and successful. It's often a meeting place that leads to alliances and joint ventures whether in a new area or another country.

"I never started to really make money in mail order until I joined the Direct Mail/Marketing Association." That's what the owner of a quite profitable publishing company, located in Tucson, Arizona, told me years ago. The workshops, seminars and conferences he attended, the DMMA recommended books he read, the stream of mailings he received, all helped him keep in touch with opportunities he might otherwise have missed.

His name is Ronald Weintraub. His company is Communication Skill Builders, selling educational aids for exceptional and disadvantaged children to schools by mail. Another division, Lawyers and Judges Publishing Company, sells legal books to the profession.

Quite recently, I asked Ronald whether he felt the same today about the DMMA. "Very much so," he said. "It's the best way of training our young people I know. Tomorrow we're sending two of our people to a DMMA seminar on catalog economics in Dallas. We're in the desert, not in New York, Chicago or Los Angeles. But through the DMMA we're in contact with the mainstream of direct marketing activity."

Ronald traces increased sales and profits (and savings, too) to DMMA help. "But, anyway, I'd belong just for the work the DMMA does to present our case as an industry at rate increase time to the Post Office—and to the public, too."

As I researched this book, I asked each person interviewed whether he or she had heard of the DMMA, joined it—and, if so, benefited from it. I talked to the big and the tiny. The majority of the big did belong. Most of the tiny had never heard of the DMMA. From members I heard two or three negative reactions. The big majority ranged from moderate to strong praise. A number felt that their careers could never have been so successful without belonging to and participating in the DMMA.

From members I learned much about the DMMA that I, as a member, was not aware of. I then interviewed the present and six previous Chairmen of the Board and the president. I interviewed vice presidents, department directors and members of the Board of Directors and the Executive Committee and individual department staff members. Many big members I talked to had joined for specific purposes. They knew other benefits existed but had not gotten around to using them. Only after I completed my research did I realize the full extent of services—and how the smallest new member could get most membership value for least cost.

Many DMMA members are the giant firms from American Express to U.S. Steel, Avon to Xerox, Book-of-the-Month Club to Montgomery Ward. They include G.E., IBM, NCR, P & G, RCA, Doubleday, Exxon, Ford, J.C. Penny, Kodak and General Mills. There's also Colgate, McGraw-Hill and Reader's Digest. There are the biggest advertising agencies specializing in direct marketing, the most important list brokers, the top mailing houses, the biggest direct mail printers.

The majority of DMMA income comes from large members. The Chairman of the Board, Directors, Executive Committee, other committees and task forces are recruited from the big and those who service the big. At first, it may seem only for the big. But the majority of DMMA members are smaller companies. And many larger DMMA members started in a tiny way.

Of DMMA members, Edmund Scientific, Harris Stamp (General Mills) and Littleton Stamp started with a classified ad. Tandy Corp. started its leap from leather findings jobber to a billion-dollar-a-year company with a one-inch mail order ad. Nelson Doubleday, Sr. started on his own selling by mail order and later merged with and then took over his father's business. Lillian Katz, founder of Lillian Vernon, was a moonlighter. So were Lyman Wood and Ed Robinson (Garden Way), both from

J. Walter Thompson. Many DMMA members started in services in a small way, and then grew big.

It's been said that DMMA members account for 65% of direct marketing. Yet, the DMMA has a majority of small members. It wants to keep this balance. The result is that the big subsidize the little. The smallest can join for an almost nominal cost compared with the biggest.

For any firm, however small, which is seriously in, going into, or exploring direct marketing, the field has to be studied. There's no escape from the cost of learning any new field. You can learn by making your own mistakes or for a fraction of this cost you can learn from the experience of others. Usually, it takes a combination of both.

Any new mail order firm which can afford it should spend one to several thousand dollars in research and study before launching the business. For the smallest retailer, wholesaler, manufacturer, importer or service business, doing so will increase chances of profit and reduce chances of a disaster.

If you do proceed with research and study, you'll go to seminars, attend conferences, read books produced by the DMMA. You can do much of this as a non-member, but members pay less. Free services for members and savings in costs of services for members can at some point make membership free. And there are times when special offers for starting members are made when you can join and go to the Annual Conference, for example, for little more than attending the Conference as a non-member. And the DMMA also has its Spring Conference, and List Day and the Government Conference and the International Conference.

For bigger firms, to me, DMMA membership seems a prudent must, if serious about going into direct marketing. For smaller firms, I have a caution. Joining the DMMA results in your receiving frequent DMMA mailings to participate in more DMMA activities, almost all of which cost more money and require time you may not have. To get your full value for each dollar spent with the DMMA, you should use fully services free to members. You should be very selective about the use of any further paid service, using what you need when you need it. Direct Marketing magazine is free to members. Read it.

Years ago, surveys showed that one of the prime reasons for joining the DMMA was the ability to phone in or write in questions and get answers. Today the free service most used by members is still answering questions. 25,000 questions on direct marketing are answered each year, 80% by phone. Now so many questions pour in from members the DMMA must turn away non-members who ask questions.

Members can ask any question. For some questions the answers snap back. Usually, turn-around time to answer a question is one to five days. For most asked questions requiring detailed answers, copies of answers are run off and a copy mailed the same day anyone inquires. A question may require a complex answer. The DMMA may know of detailed treatment of it elsewhere. If so, a form response is sent with the reference source.

The service is called "Information Central". It's a reservoir of statistics, data, regulations, rates, contacts and almost any information you might ask a question about on direct marketing. Info Central has rates and data on every postal classification and copies of statutes and postal requirements which may affect your mailing pieces. It can usually give you notice of upcoming postal rate increases and changes.

It can give you the FTC regulations for conducting a sweepstakes or the names of list brokers or direct marketing firms in your area. Info Central can lead you to literature on any direct marketing subject. All the staff are college graduates, some cum laude.

Everyone in Information Central is bright, imaginative and works hard. To be hired, each must be inquisitive, have a friendly personality and be able to write. She or he must be organized, learn complex information and then pass it on to members. Each has taken the New York University Direct Marketing Course. Each has attended about as many really worthwhile direct marketing seminars as offered. Information Central work is at a fast pace. The complexity of a request for information can slow the process. But progress is constantly checked to see that the work is turned around in the proper time.

It's set up along the lines of a professional library. Information of every type, from transcribed speeches to articles, books, periodicals, other literature—even portfolios of direct marketing award-winning campaigns—is catalogued and arranged efficiently. Many of the member questions are very sophisticated.

Non-member questions are usually much simpler. Advice for a non-member is to spend some time with a professional reference librarian at a business or university library. The librarian can almost always help them to find the source to help them. There are superb business libraries in largest cities, such as the Brooklyn Public Library and the New York Public Library. Bigger business colleges have good business libraries. Almost any big university library contains needed titles. But any professional reference librarian in far smaller libraries can tell where to go to get reference books needed.

From Information Central there have been many ripple effects which, in turn, required enlarged activities. Its capabilities drew jobs. As it felt the pulse of direct marketing, it became a constant research project finding out, from the horse's mouth, member needs. It led to the DMMA Marketing Manual. At first, the Manual was a looseleaf binder of reprinted articles and transcribed speeches of subjects most asked about. Then the idea came of asking authorities to write on subjects where information was most sought after, to re-edit and revise completely the entire Manual up-to-the-minute. It was a huge project. Every article was new.

A Manual Review Committee coordinated with Information Central in putting together the manual. An outline and parameters were decided on. Volunteers to write it were chosen. Editing was done by Karen Burns, to achieve a similarity of style and unified appeal. This was done surprisingly well. I review it elsewhere. It's only available to members, free to them, and a good reason to join.

There are over seventy authors. Each is an expert in a direct marketing specialty who has contributed his or her work. The Manual is continuously updated. Work on it never stops. It includes results of DMMA research, articles and transcribed speeches. Each individual "Manual Release" is forwarded to members, punched and ready to slip in the Manual looseleaf ring binder. Each is available to non-members at a modest price, as part of a section in its own folder.

The top five manual sections in popularity are: 1) Legal, Ethical and Regulatory—9 releases; 2) Creative—19 releases; 3) Fulfillment & Operations—8 releases; 4) Testing, Analysis and Economics—6 releases; 5) Production—10 releases.

Members in joining get well over 100 releases free and a continuing stream thereafter. I added up the price to non-members for all "releases" given a member on joining the DMMA. The total cost to outsiders almost pays for the minimum membership. Actually, a non-member is only allowed to buy one Manual Section, ever. The savings on the member price to buy multiple copies versus the non-member price would be important for bigger member companies with a number of employees, subsidiaries and offices to indoctrinate.

One activity is the DMMA ECHO Awards campaign. ECHO Awards are direct marketing's Oscars, given for most effective selling campaigns. One important service of Information Central is a by-product. Each entry has submitted a portfolio of the advertising of one direct marketing campaign. Each was asked for dollar-and-cents sales figures versus product margin available and advertising costs. Some entrants provided more information than others. Each gave permission for the portfolio to be available to other members.

In the DMMA research library are files of almost 3,000 of these campaigns. They can be borrowed by members like library books. It is possible to analyze and study a past success in fields close to your own. The DMMA will send any of them to members anywhere in the U.S. You multiply your own experience. The DMMA has many more classic direct marketing campaigns available in its warehouse for call-up, going back to the 1960's.

Also in the DMMA Library are 400 books important to direct marketers. There are magazine articles and speech transcripts on direct marketing. Those considered "classics" are kept on file for years. The Library has business and financial directories. It subscribes to sixty periodicals including important direct marketing newsletters.

One plus service of Information Central is a list of executive search firms which specialize in direct marketing job opportunities.

Another plus is that on joining, the membership roster is given to every member. The roster is also broken up and listed by fields. The DMMA is valuable in finding sources for direct marketing services. Members may buy a list of DMMA member list brokers, of direct marketing agencies, of consultants and of lettershops and printers, or of mail order firms . . . all members.

The most prolific mother of more new kinds of activities has been Information Central. First the samples of direct mail campaigns from the DMMA's annual ECHO Award contest were available in the library. The next step was a travelling exhibit of award-winning campaigns of a given year. Next 500 awards—winning campaigns since 1969—were put on microfiche. They can be purchased for a few dollars per campaign or by product/service/service category or, for several thousand dollars, all 500.

As Information Central staff members did more and more research, they found another way to apply research, writing and editing skills. Info Central prepares and publishes special research reports and directories, one on print advertising and another on broadcast advertising use by direct marketers and many more. Updating the Manual brought out the need for specialized information in less pages than a book but which members gladly paid for.

For the library, Info Central began to collect catalogs. From a collection of 1980 catalogs, a catalog directory of 200 pages was prepared. It prepared booklets, one listing list brokers and compilers, another direct marketing agencies, another direct marketing consultants and one for lettershops and printers. It collected approximately 25 articles each for special loan kits for telephone marketing, fund raising, creative direct response copy and mailing lists.

Information Central specialists can ask, record, write, edit,

They can take on a subject, investigate it, produce a report and publish it. All offers are made to all members. But for offers the DMMA membership list is also segmented for just the right membership group for the Catalog Directory, the Microfiche Library, the Slide Presentations, the International Source Directory or the Monograph Reports. In all its research, Information Central keeps pencils poised for any facts that can help, for any new areas that deserve books.

Then the book publishing operation that Info Central gave birth to graduated to its own division under Bonnie DeLay. In this book I review "The Fact Book" and "The Law Book" published by the DMMA Book Division. I recommend both.

George Wiedemann, president of Grey Direct, wrote the new DMMA Professional Development Program, a media direct marketing course. It's a multi-faceted kit with lessons, exercises and cassettes. There's the Max Ross Letter Book, telling as only Max can how to write direct mail letters, and other titles. Then there's the DMMA mail order catalog of direct marketing books which is a mail order business in itself. All this is done by volunteer Bonnie DeLay and staff assistant, Merry Craven.

In addition to more and more specialized seminars, the DMMA has organized eight special interest councils which none but members can join. Each came about as a result of a number of members wanting to exchange information with others in an area of interest. At this point, the DMMA researches how many other members desire to do so and then, if enough wish it, helps them do it.

When you join, be prepared to also join a DMMA Council appropriate to your direct marketing activities. If you have even a very small mail order catalog, join the Catalog Council, assuming it is to grow. If you're in the list business or use direct mail extensively, consider the List Council.

In addition to those on catalogs and on lists, there is the Marketing Council, on any selling aspect. There is the Council for Business and Industrial Direct Marketing and one for Telephone Marketing. For magazine and newsletter publishers there's the Circulation Council. There's the Fund Raising Council and the Direct Marketing Insurance Council.

About half of DMMA members belong to a council. Most of these belong to one council only. Each is a do-it-yourself cooperative group, with some DMMA staff assistance. The most popular is the Catalog Council. At press time for this book, there were 196 members out of 450 DMMA members in the catalog business.

Each council operates as a Dutch Treat Club. Its cost covers the DMMA cost of administration staff devoted to it. Each event is operated to break even. A council operating an all-day workshop uses volunteers to provide the program.

For work put in there are compensations. As in most small no-frills clubs, the atmosphere is open. The natives are friendly. Important secrets are guarded but any other information that can help others is surprisingly freely given. Newcomer companies to mail order have marvelled at how much they learned how fast. In some cases, following meeting in a council a newcomer will later visit other council members to ask or even see how things are done.

The degree of cooperation between council members and towards newcomers, particularly, has been called a "phenomenon". One form of member cooperation is often for a larger member to invite others to a tour of facilities as, for instance, a catalog house.

In each council certain veterans from bigger and larger established companies tend to become guides for younger, newer

members. But more experienced members enjoy contact with young, imaginative new comers. A new member may establish contact with a number of those who have just the needed information he or she is after. Then it's easy to pick up the phone later and get more advice.

There is the intimacy of the quite small direct marketing club. But here everything discussed in every meeting and communication may be particularly pertinent to information badly needed for an immediate, specific purpose.

You quickly learn that the more secretive you are about your business the more guarded others will be about theirs. You find that the more open you are the more they are. Those that benefit are those who give as well as receive. Newcomers who know nothing have, of course, most to gain.

Each council is now much as the DMMA, itself, was in its own infancy—when the field was small. The idea has been to establish smaller groups for narrower segments. Studies have shown the number one reason to join the DMMA and to attend a conference has been to meet people. This is best done in small groups. Getting to know well others in a council gives a core of people you know when you attend a Conference.

Joining a council may be more rewarding than any course or club or other DMMA activity . . . but only with work. Each council annually elects a chairperson and vice chairperson for a one-year term. Either can be re-elected only once. A chairperson has a lot of work starting with selecting and recruiting a committee which acts as a Board of Directors. Most of what the directors decide to do they must then do, themselves; or they must then persuade other council members to do it.

The DMMA membership has grown dramatically. It's international. Although there are many volunteers, it's so complex that it must be run by a professional staff. Each council, on the other hand, can be run like a neighborhood club, largely by itself.

Each council is self-supporting. It is run by its members. Its newsletter is written by them. Some of the newsletters are quite good. Each event is planned and staffed by them. The Marketing Council has lunch meetings with speakers. About 20 to 35 people attend. Other councils have day-long workshops which from 25 up to 120 attend. An event can result from or graduate beyond council activities, as did List Day.

The Fund Raising Council has put on a two-day "Fund Raising Fair", its own trade show. The Direct Mail Insurance Council was interested in improving the image of mail order insurance and raised $60,000 from its own members to do so. The Catalog Council has put on an all day finance workshop, "How to Set-Up and Control Annual Budgeting for a Direct Marketing Company". It also put on a seminar on the creation of a catalog from scratch by a beginner company.

Membership in a typical DMMA council gets you a newsletter, on the mailing list, special council event rates for attending council events and often more. It depends on you and your fellow members of the council you belong to. You can do anything, yourself.

It takes a great deal of time for each chairperson and quite a bit for each member. Council members register for their own workshops. They volunteer. When they do, they pay all their own costs, even phone calls. But exchange of know-how, this way, is a very effective form of mail order education.

Two meetings a year of the council are at the Annual and Spring Conferences. At the Fall Annual Conference each year, the councils hold their elections.

The workshops are growing and beginning to travel, to get more members. The Insurance Council recently had a meeting in Toronto. The Catalog Council has had a one-day workshop in Dallas and one in Chicago. The Business Industrial Council has had one in Boston.

For all eight councils the DMMA administrative staff consists of Bonnie Rodriguez and one assistant. Merrill Tomlinson (a lady) is assistant director. But various DMMA departments also help to some degree.

Bonnie originated the idea of statistical research by the councils. "I recognized the need for statistics." Bonnie had previously been the first editor of "The Fact Book" and found that it was difficult to rely on others to gather statistics. The obvious thing to do was for the DMMA to ask members to cooperate in creating statistics of size and growth. And the councils are an ideal, informal place to start.

The Telephone Council has completed a survey of all DMMA members on their use of telephone marketing. The Business Industrial Council has conducted a survey of industrial companies' use of direct mail and direct marketing. Bonnie reports: "The Catalog Council surveys many catalogs members' mail and what sales were produced. Of all catalog companies 450 belong to the DMMA, 196 to the Catalog Council and 80 have answered, still not enough to be a reliable statistic. Sears, Ward's and Penney's always answer us but we don't yet include their figures as they would overwhelm statistics all the others are answering."

Bonnie Rodriguez, as she helps shape the Councils, never forgets the importance of statistical facts to the members of each Council and to the DMMA. The grass roots statistical research she is encouraging and initiating can greatly strengthen DMMA efforts to measure the size and growth of direct marketing. There is also the Statistical Committee and the Publications Committee. Such activities are reasons why some council members have found council membership alone valuable enough to justify all costs of DMMA membership, as well.

Once you join the DMMA and a council you can begin to select appropriate books from the DMMA catalog and from the most logical seminars for your situation. And after joining the establishment, as you find yourself established, you will send your assistant to the DMMA—as has been done many times before.

In this book the present menu of DMMA services is described. Get an update on what is available when you join. Be cautious in considering each service offered. Give priority to what fits you best. If new to direct marketing, take a Basic Institute seminar. Consider specialized services in the area in which you're active.

In this book there are stories on some who give DMMA seminars, on many who write for the Manual, and on a number who have shaped the DMMA. To sum up, the DMMA is one of the two most important sources of help any direct marketer can find. The other is "Pete" Hoke, his Direct Marketing Magazine and the Hoke Sound Archives, about which there is a chapter in this book.

Chapter 3
Egg Head Mail Order

*Direct marketing's extraordinary
marriage with science.*

MAGI came out of atomic physics . . . into mail order. Its full name is MAGI, Mathematical Applications Group, Inc. In 1966, Dr. Phillip S. Mittelman gathered together a group of scientists, physicists and mathematicians to form the Company.

He worked as a physicist in 1948 at Brookhaven National Laboratory. He taught atomic physics from 1949 to 1953 at Rensselaer Polytechnic Institute. He worked at United Nuclear on nuclear reactor design from 1954-1966. When he started what is now MAGI, no one there had the slightest knowledge of mail order or any idea they would be concerned with it.

Today, MAGI is a mix of computer service bureau, servicing direct marketers and a high technology science company with exotic products of the future in the present and a constantly growing stream of more exotic products to come.

Dr. Mittelman describes it this way. "Direct marketing takes two-thirds of our personnel time. It's the majority of our dollar sales. It's good profitable business. But we expect the most profitable side of our business to eventually come from the activities that were a financial strain earlier."

The marriage of mail order and science has been extraordinary. Dr. Mittelman and his physicists and mathematicians provided solutions to problems that had plagued direct marketers using computers for list maintenance, list selection and computer letters. The steady and constantly growing income from servicing direct marketers helped finance potentially far more profitable long-term growth in exciting new technical products they invented.

MAGI is also a remarkable mix of talents and abilities, particularly of President Phillip S. Mittelman and Executive Vice President Warren Weinberg. "Phil is a conceptual genius," says Warren. "He can calculate what will be needed four years from now, and apply what, to him, are obvious solutions to the problems. Our physicists, engineers and mathematicians go to work. Then, three years of programming later, we get the solution in practical form to market. This means we're always putting money into research projects for years ahead. Had we just wanted to marshall profits and avoid such expenses, the profits would be far larger, but the future - much more bland."

Phil Mittelman is the scientist-creative genius. Warren is the practical, dollar-and-cents profit man, with no scientific background. "We can make considerable money in our computerized slide business for which we've licensed sole distribution rights to Xerox. Xerox is our partner in this. Our income is just beginning. Much of it will be in royalties with no present personnel time or overhead to apply to it."

Another activity of MAGI is licensing software for the computer aided design field - SynthaVision. The "Design News" describes it this way: "It can cut untold hours out of the conventional design engineering and analysis routine or can reduce engineering costs per job, if it can be given enough work to justify the initial $150,000 cost of the program license." The first customer was Boeing Corporation's Computer Service Company, who uses it to model complex aircraft parts and systems to generate line drawings, shaded pictures, exploded drawings.

As a result, the Company's volume went from two million eight hundred thousand dollars in the fiscal year ending in March 1979, to four million five hundred thousand dollars in the year ending in March 1980 to ten million dollars for the year ending March 31, 1981. A good deal of the non-direct marketing revenue will be royalty income in the future where there are almost no costs against it and the gross is virtually the pretax profit.

It wasn't always this way for MAGI. It took a long time to get to this stage, accomplished principally by servicing mail order clients. The first office was in Hartsdale, a suburb of New York City. "We were working heavily in research and development for the Government," remembers Dr. Mittelman. "This was mainly in developing requirements for shielding from nuclear radiation for nuclear power plants. Our scientists were specialists in working with computers toward this end.

"Through an acquaintance, a former president of Lafayette Radio, I met Art Blumenfield. Art asked for a commercial job and discussed the possibilities of computer commercial applications using our equipment and scientists. He was hired." A short time later, Art Blumenfield received two duplicate free catalogs from Sears. Art wondered if a duplicate identification system could avoid the waste of multiple mailings to a single household or company. The problem was given to Dr. Mittelman and his scientists. One advanced mathematician in the group with computers came up with the answer. It was called MAILSAVE and was the first system of duplicate elimination employing a mathematical equivalency system.

The question then was - how to begin the marketing. "Pete" Hoke of Direct Marketing Magazine suggested an ad in his magazine," recalls Art Blumenfield, now a computer consultant. The ad pulled over six hundred responses.

The new division grew rapidly. "We couldn't keep up with the direct marketing business and gave up the idea of other commercial applications. The government contracts had no risk factor and the profits generated enabled the company to buy the initial heavy hardware needed for the new division."

The Company first worked with the Hodes-Daniel letter-shop on its new MAILSAVE product. A service bureau called Data Recording, Inc. had done most of the direct marketing work for Hodes-Daniel. When MAGI's scientists and mathematicians got into the mathematical coding of addresses, they did so in a very sophisticated way. "Our method was dramatically better."

In 1967, MAGI bought Data Recording, Inc. and retained its founder and President for several years to run it for them. Contracts to maintain lists and to produce computer letters followed.

When the Company first received inquiries from Direct Marketing Magazine, it simply offered to run their names and charge only for the duplications uncovered. "This generated the interest of the direct mailers and we began to learn some of their problems first hand. And, one by one, our computer scientists got into them. The results have been rapidly increasing work with an expanded line of programs geared to solve the needs of the people who use the mails most."

"Leon Malin was first in charge of our business management. We had the problem of investing in equipment for computer service bureau business, plus heavy investing in the rest of our business. Over the years, we put almost a million dollars into a system for designing business slides and into SynthaVision. This

resulted in heavy losses during the development years and some cash-flow problems, to be sure. But the banks were good to us.

"Of course, physicists are not such great business men. When our cash was getting to its lowest and our direct marketing staff was growing, we hired Warren Weinberg as Executive Vice President. Since then, we've had quite a dedication to the direct marketing industry."

Though Warren Weinberg had no background in computers or direct marketing, he was a business man and he had come to the right place—MAGI. It was running out of money and out of banks. Its stock was selling for under a dollar a share. There has since been a 50% stock dividend and it sells for 17 dollars.

Direct Marketing sales were growing but losing money. Some of the scientific projects were also losers. Warren Weinberg's cost techniques helped define direction. MAGI got rid of unproductive projects, and streamlined and changed pricing formulas. New programs for direct marketing were added with the help of outside specialists and consultants. The Company now has a bank of new programs to service the rapidly growing direct marketing industry.

Marcella Lieberman, recently promoted to General Manager of the Division was originally in purchasing. Her talents in Customer Service relations and in serving in a liaison capacity between sales and production resulted in her heading that department prior to her recent promotion.

Warren Weinberg was in public accounting, a CPA, until he was 29. Then, in 1951, he joined a company called J.E. Plastics as controller. It was a packaging company doing pressure forming and vacuum forming. It expanded profitably and went public. Years later, with Warren as President after being listed on the American Stock Exchange, it merged into a substantially larger company, Metal Edge Industries. In 1974, after a successful few years as President of the merged company, Warren left to devote himself to a life of golf and tennis.

But that lasted nine months. A mutual friend introduced him to Phil Mittelman. Phil had a company full of geniuses, software talent and exotic programs. Basically, his company, MAGI, was in computer service.

In April 1975, Warren Weinberg came to MAGI as Executive Vice President and Chief Operating Officer. MAGI had just lost $300,000 in the fiscal year ending March 31, 1975. The following year the loss was cut to $40,000. It has been increasingly profitable ever since then. Phil and Warren recall the $240,000 due Central State Bank of 24 West 48th Street, New York City, and their preparations for their meetings with Bob Bradley and John Tierney to resolve their cash shortage dilemma.

Bob Bradley, whom Central State had just brought in as Executive Vice President turned from negative to sympathetic. "We really did a preparation job. We had prepared thorough projections for all divisions and asked for a meeting two months before the loan was due. Our financial fate was really in their hands.

"By the end of the meeting, Bob Bradley asked us whether it would be too harsh for us to repay the loan, not with the lump sum of $240,000 due, but to repay $5,000 a month (a four year payout) with extra payments should any redundant cash develop. The loan was repaid fully in less than two years."

The Direct Marketing division was then structured to be MAGI's bread and butter division. However, since it was making little money, there was nothing to support increased R & D. The Company was trying to promote SynthaVision movies. "The effort took five people. The road to profitability called for a heavy focus on direct marketing. It could and should make money. We put SynthaVision on the back burner cutting the staff to just one person instead of five."

Further analyses of MAGI's problems just pointed out how similar all custom businesses can be. MAGI had a lot of similarities to even a J.E. Plastics in problems and solutions. Each had marketing problems and financial problems and even manufacturing problems - with MAGI's computer room being, in a sense, its manufacturing plant.

Now and for the past few years, Direct Marketing has supported an expanded internal development effort and shown a healthy profit besides. "We rewrote the MAILSAVE program. We added a sophisticated list maintenance system. Then came new large IBM and Control Data computers. We just get deeper into it all the time by learning more of direct marketer's needs. We meet with clients, listen to their requests and react. Sales in the division have increased 500% in 5 years just by listening and responding.

"It's quite a mix," says Phil Mittelman. "We've gotten into more equipment for direct marketing. We're into demographic response analysis. The basic idea is to combine demographically similar zip codes into larger, more manageable MAGI Groups. This enables mailers to define, select and locate his buyer with greater ease and accuracy, thus pinpointing his mailing effort."

Marcella Lieberman is very happy with the growth of MAGI sales to the direct marketing field. "We now have a tremendous file maintenance business. Five years ago we were maintaining three files. Now we maintain fifty to sixty files. Our smallest file is thirty thousand names. Our biggest is thirty million. We probably maintain a total of fifty million names.

"Computer letters and forms are probably ten percent of our business. We're best suited to smaller runs. We're now considering getting into ink jet or laser printing, more suited to long runs, but have not yet decided if that represents an expansion area into which we wish to direct ourselves.

"Many mailers come to us because they need help. They're often unfamiliar with computer maintenance of names. We work with them and show them and they come to count on and trust us."

The Company is proud of its lead fulfillment program. It's a way of handling, directing, tracking and following up inquiries. Advertising brings in the leads, directed to a special Post Office box that has been set up. Then the system takes over.

In addition to MAGI's use of nixie banks for undeliverable third class mail and positive match files for address correction, it has put together a data bank of information for general mailers and one for catalog mailers. Terminals are placed in the location of the list owners. They are able to access information and communicate with MAGI. There is no need for tapes. The computer houses the data bank. MAGI keeps coming up with more new developments at the Company.

Today, license agreements such as those with Xerox, Control Data and Applicon account for an increasing share of the revenue, and more particularly, the pretax profit of MAGI, Dr. Mittelman related. And the royalty impact is just beginning. Additional contracts are in negotiation now and all include clauses calling for minimum royalties. The Company's Syntha-Vision programs have also been licensed to General Electric, U.S. Bureau of Mines, Pacific Electric Pictures, and Boeing, etc. Other licenses are expected. The movie production work is growing and some major feature film work is expected.

Though the bulk of the work has been done on the business

slide program licensed to Xerox, new developments continue to keep them number one in the field. "Because we have the ability to develop more and more concepts directed toward high profit activities, we have licensed the scientific marketing rights to these developments to those more qualified to develop the marketplace.

"Do we have any problems? Only to get good people to grow with us. We try for the best. We look for higher IQ's but also for determination. Will can overcome lack of a higher IQ."

Phil is a happy man, too. "We have a sound business. We keep coming up with exciting products, generally for big companies and for direct marketers. We've never developed a consumer product. Art Blumenfield developed for us a computer calendar personalized for the individual. But we never tested it."

Meanwhile, Phil Mittelman and his scientists keep coming up with new, exotic science products and new computer service bureau techniques for direct marketers, while MAGI continues to grow like magic, now at 3 Westchester Plaza, Elmsford, N.Y. 10523 (914) 592-4646.

For an outlet Phil has now gotten into square dancing. And that's a good mix, too . . . mail order, exotic science products, and square dancing.

Chapter 4
Mr. Direct Marketing

*Most written about,
talked about authority.*

Bob Stone is Chairman of the Board and Chief Executive Officer of Stone & Adler, Inc. which became the biggest independently owned direct marketing advertising agency in the world—and is now a subsidiary of Young & Rubicam, Inc., the biggest general advertising agency in the world. He's done close to 200 columns on direct marketing more faithfully read by more people than any other articles on direct marketing. He is the author of the most praised book in the world on direct marketing.

From the Direct Mail/Marketing Association, Bob Stone received the DMMA Hall of Fame Award in 1979 and the Ed Mayer Award in 1980. The Wall Street Journal has run several full-page ads quoting Bob in direct marketing. He was a founder of the Chicago Direct Marketing Association. He served as its second president.

He's a kindly man who has a talent for teaching and a hobby of helping those starting direct marketing careers. He's given his time in many ways all his business life to pass along know-how to others. In the last five years, he's given more cash dollars for scholarships to take introductory direct marketing courses than anyone in the field. He can help you now. For this book, he tells readers of his start, early days and rise in direct marketing—an experience that can help each of us.

"I am a Chicagoan by birth. I was born on September 5, 1918. I have lived in and around Chicago all my life having moved to Wilmette, Illinois—a suburb of Chicago—about 25 years ago.

"I was a Depression child, graduating from high school in 1936. My college education was attained at Northwestern University night school where I attended classes three nights a week for five years. My first interest in direct mail came as a result of my taking a course on the subject of Sales Letter Writing. The professor was Mr. Cy Frailey, who was on the staff of Dartnell Corporation, in Chicago—a firm specializing in business services.

"This nurtured my interest in direct mail and in mail order. Having become fascinated by the subject, I set out to read books published at that time on the subject and systematically set out to meet the important people in the business. My favorite trade publications at the time were Printer's Ink, the leading advertising publication of the day, and later, Advertising Age.

"I have had five jobs in my life: 1) a used car salesman for my father's business, Stone Auto Sales, from 1936 to 1940; 2) the advertising manager of American Bandage Corporation, in Chicago—a family-owned business specializing in the sale of surgical bandages to manufacturing firms; 3) starting in 1945, I became direct mail manager of National Research Bureau, a business service organization specializing in business services on such diverse subjects as advertising and marketing, personnel management, economics, publicity and sales training; 4) in 1960, I sold my interest in National Research Bureau and started my own firm called National Communications Corporation. This firm specialized in sales training recordings for sales organizations; 5) on December 1 of 1966, Aaron Adler and I started Stone & Adler, Inc.

"I took the letter writing course when I started my job with the American Bandage Corporation which, at the time, was doing poorly. The self-adhesive bandages weren't selling. Once I learned that letters could produce orders and learned how to do it, I put that training to work to sell bandages. I sent letters to manufacturing companies, suggesting the bandages for first aid kits. The orders came rolling in, the business was saved, and I had a career.

"I joined the Direct Mail Advertising Association in 1939 and attended my first National Convention in Atlantic City. (I have attended every National Convention of the Direct Mail Advertising Association, now called Direct Mail/Marketing Association, since 1939 with the exception of one or two conventions during the war years.) Starting in 1939 I became an avid reader of "Reporter of Direct Mail Advertising", a trade publication, which was published by Henry Hoke, Sr.

"As a result of my having become active in the Direct Mail Advertising Association, I met Mr. Edward N. Mayer, Jr. who was a stalwart in the Association for many years. Ed Mayer became a close friend of mine, and was a big factor in the development of my career. He was elected to the Direct Marketing Hall of Fame, following his death.

"The most significant book I came across at that point in time was the "Robert Collier Letter Book". I also read a significant book on direct mail advertising written by Homer J. Buckley who, at the time, was the president of Buckley Dement & Company, a mailing organization in the city of Chicago. I also read the Hopkins book and later met Homer J. Buckley who rather adopted me as a protege.

"I was inspired by my 'father image'—Homer J. Buckley—to start writing articles for various publications. I submitted articles on direct mail advertising to *Printer's Ink, Forbes* magazine, *Industrial Marketing* and others. Most of these articles were accepted and I started to gain a reputation of sorts in the direct mail field.

"The first book I ever wrote was titled 'Profitable Direct Mail Methods', which was published by Prentice-Hall in 1945. My good friend Homer J. Buckley reviewed the manuscript chapter by chapter and made many suggestions which greatly improved the book.

"Very early in my career I had come to the realization that I had a moral obligation to give back some of what I had learned to others. Again, I was inspired by what Homer J. Buckley had done in his career. I exchanged information, answered questions freely and began to talk to groups.

"The first major speech I ever gave was at the Direct Mail Advertising Association Convention, in Philadelphia, in the fall of 1948. Since that time I have delivered speeches in most major U.S. cities and several European cities including Paris, Munich, Amsterdam, London and Copenhagen.

"I wrote a second book in 1955 titled 'Successful Direct Mail Advertising and Selling', which was also published by Prentice-Hall. This book went through eight printings and sold something like 18,000 copies.

"Based upon the concept that I had an obligation to give back to others what I had learned as a result of those who had helped me along the way, I started teaching brief courses on the subject of direct mail and later direct marketing. Under the auspices of the Direct Mail Club of Chicago, I taught a course at the University of Chicago night school.

"My prize student turned out to be a young man by the name of Thomas Nickel, who later headed up a company called Baldwin Cooke. Baldwin Cooke has been a personal client of mine for a good 15 years. At the time he was in the course, Tom Nickel had a little mail order business doing about $35,000 a year. Today, Baldwin Cooke is a multi-million dollar operation and five years ago my 'student', Tom Nickel, turned down $4 million for his business.

"Stone & Adler was founded on December 1, 1966. The story behind the Agency was rather interesting, I believe.

"Aaron Adler and I had known each other for a number of years, having met at various direct mail functions in Chicago. About once a month Aaron and I would have lunch together and during the course of one of these lunches we both agreed that the time was ripe for a *full service* direct marketing agency in the Middle-west. Multi-media—the use of one or more media to get a direct response—was coming into vogue. The term 'direct marketing', which includes all media when used to get a direct response by mail, by phone or by personal visits, was also starting to be used.

"At this point in time I was president of National Communications Corporation, a firm I owned which sold sales training recordings direct to business. Aaron Adler was with a general advertising agency, heading up the direct response division. In addition to my sales training recording business, I personally handled a few direct response accounts, including Sunset House, the specialty mail order house in Los Angeles, Baldwin Cooke Company, headed by my friend Tom Nickel, and one or two minor accounts. Aaron Adler had about four direct response accounts, including Standard Oil Company of Indiana. We decided to start Stone & Adler.

"Aaron Adler bought out the accounts he headed up with the general advertising agency and I brought accounts I had into the picture. Thus, we started with a small base. Our total investment—we never put in another dime—was $500 each.

"In launching the Agency, we agreed that under no conditions would we take any account, no matter who the company might be, that would not sign up with us for at least a minimum of a six-month period, agreeing to pay a minimum monthly retainer. At that point in time, our minimum retainer was $1,000 a month.

"We started with a total of five people, including Aaron and I. The very first month after announcing our Agency we got our first account—Wincraft, of Winona, Minnesota, a company who sells fund raising supplies to high schools. (We still have WinCraft as an account 14 years later.)

"We grew rather rapidly. Our profit for the first year was $25,000 and we have never had a losing year in our 14 years in existence. One of the concerns we had was whether we would be able to attract personnel with direct marketing experience to accommodate our growth.

"The thing that surprised us was that we became known as a 'hot' agency and attracted a number of people who wanted to get in on the excitement of a rapidly emerging direct marketing agency. In 1967, we landed our first Fortune 500 client— Polaroid. The very first mailing package we did for them won a major DMMA award—the Gold Mailbox.

"That same year, I started a column for Advertising Age titled 'Direct Mail/Marketing'. Since that time I have written 185 articles for Advertising Age. (The Column later became 'Stone on Direct Marketing'.)

"Stone & Adler continued to grow. By 1970, our capitalized billings were approximately $4 million. Aaron and I decided that while we were growing rapidly, there was little chance that we would acquire any major clients in the New York market unless we were associated with a New York direct marketing agency.

(We had decided that having a New York office that would be serviced out of Chicago would not suffice.)

"I had made it a practice to know all of the principals in direct marketing agencies, and I was most impressed with Stan Rapp and Tom Collins, of Rapp & Collins. I had a number of conversations with them and told them that we were interested in growth in the East, having decided we would never get it from Chicago. They told me candidly that they were interested in growth in the Midwest, but had likewise decided they would never get it from New York. From these admissions the concept of merging came about. We announced Rapp, Collins, Stone & Adler in October of 1970. At that time, our combined billings were approximately $10 million.

"It was a fine association and both offices grew to combined billings of $20 million within three years. At that time, Doyle, Dane, Bernbach talked to us about acquiring Rapp, Collins, Stone & Adler.

"There were problems as related to Stone & Adler: There were three major client conflicts between Doyle, Dane, Bernbach and Stone & Adler. There were no client conflicts between Rapp & Collins and Doyle, Dane, Bernbach. Thus, the Rapp & Collins Division was sold to DDB and Stone & Adler returned to becoming an independent. At that time, billings of Stone & Adler were up to $10 million—equal to the combined billing when the two agencies got together.

"In 1974, Sid Bernstein, then president of Advertising Age, approached me with the idea of writing a book on the subject of direct marketing. I signed a contract and in 1975 the first edition of 'Successful Direct Marketing Methods' was published. This edition went through 7 printings and ultimately sold 35,000 copies. The second edition of 'Successful Direct Marketing Methods' was first published in May of 1979. The first printing of 10,000 copies sold out by December 31, 1979, and the second printing of the second edition is now in print, with another 10,000 printing.

"Stone & Adler continued to grow and prosper. The articles in Advertising Age and the publication of 'Succesful Direct Marketing Methods' were undoubtedly factors in attracting new major entries into direct marketing. By 1978, Stone & Adler numbered Fortune 500 Accounts such as Allstate Insurance Company (Sears Roebuck), Montgomery-Ward (Marcor), SRA (IBM), United Airlines, AT&T and Southwestern Bell, Amoco (Standard Oil Company of Indiana) and Armstrong Cork.

"Without taking any initiative, we started hearing from major general advertising agencies in the summer of 1978—by that time, capitalized billing had surpassed $20 million—each expressing an interest in acquiring us. We established a price for our agency and were in the enviable position of having this price accepted by three of the top ten general agencies in the country. So it was a matter of us deciding which agency we'd like to be associated with.

"We checked this out very carefully, checking with agencies that had been acquired by each of the three suitors. Y & R came out as the best choice by far.

"At this writing, we have been a Y & R agency for three years. They have been everything they said they would be. They have let us run our own ship, but whenever we have needed help in media buying, research or business management, they have been available and of invaluable assistance. Being a member of the Y & R family has helped us to gain major accounts because we have been able to offer their complete back-up facilities. By the end of this year we expect to be billing $40 million.

"Being a sister agency with Wunderman, Ricotta & Kline

has also been a boon. We have been extremely helpful to each other: WR&K has outstanding expertise in direct response television—Stone & Adler has outstanding expertise in lead producing programs and catalog development and distribution. Each of us has been in a position to fill in voids for the other.

"You asked what are the strengths of the agency and myself respectively. I guess if I were to describe my strengths they would relate primarily to business management, development of executives and the ability to build the image of the agency.

"We are particularly proud of our management staff. I would like to review briefly the members of the Executive Committee:

"Jerry Wood—President and Chief Operating Officer. Jerry comes to us from Young & Rubicam Corporate where he was vice president-director of Corporate Business Planning. It is his charge to bring professional management capabilities to all levels of the agency.

"Bill Waites—Vice Chairman and Creative Director. Bill had been at Y&R/Chicago where he was director of Creative Services.

"Marshall Edinger—Senior Vice President and General Manager. Marsh has spent his entire life in direct marketing, having served Bankers Life for many years. He is a superb General Manager, setting standards for hiring and training of personnel. It is his charge to make certain that all of our personnel are well compensated, motivated at all times, that they have incentives for career growth and that they are treated as professionals. He accomplishes all of these things.

"John Mecchella—Executive Vice President. John is highly organized. He has a rich background in direct marketing, including many years with the Dartnell Corporation of Chicago.

"Jim Rose—Executive Vice President. Jim Rose has a unique background in direct marketing, having started with his father who was an entrepreneur in that field. His greatest strength is in the new business area and Jim was instrumental in developing new business presentations for such accounts as IBM, Samsonite and Stauffer Chemical Company.

"Mark Weinstein—Executive Vice President. Mark Weinstein started with us many years ago as a Production Manager. He then left our agency to get experience as an Account Executive with a much smaller agency. Having gained that experience he returned to us and is now an Account Group Manager. He services such accounts as United Airlines and Sears Roebuck.

"Ed Leiman—Controller and Vice President. Ed comes to us from the Kansas City Y & R office. As controller, he is instrumental in setting up realistic budgets and profit goals. He has set up systems tying into the Y & R computer which measures productivity of all personnel and profitability of all accounts. He is an outstanding member of our Executive Committee.

"We are particularly proud of our management group. Capitalized billings for this agency have increased 51% over the last two years and I have set a goal of compounded growth of 25% a year through 1983.

"All departments of our Agency are charged with developing and maintaining ongoing training programs, whether it be for assistant account executives, account executives, writers, artists, media people or accounting. We try at all times to create an atmosphere of excitement and we try at all times to promote from within. I am high on the futures of our young people.

"You asked if we might be amenable to taking on general advertising acounts. We are definitely against this. We have built our reputation as a full service direct response agency. We are in a tremendous era of growth and we feel very strongly that should we 'branch out' to general advertising, we would stunt our growth in the area we know best.

"Over the years we have only lost one top management person. This is no reflection on him, but to this day we have never found it necessary to replace his position. He did take one account from us, but as I understand it, this account was subsequently lost.

"I see the future as very bright. We definitely have no plans for going into other ventures such as the publication of newsletters. We are going deeper and deeper into research on behalf of our clients.

"We feel that we are in an ideal position to ride the wave of new electronic media. There surely will be clubs promoting video discs. Cable is finally maturing and, by the end of 1981, it is highly possible that 30% of the TV homes will be wired for cable. This will open tremendous opportunities in Direct Response TV. And there is a whole area of Interactive TV such as Viewtron and QUBE. Being a wholly owned subsidiary of Y & R, we are definitely organized for the future.

As stated above, we feel that the breakthroughs in electronic media will very much play to our advantage. Video discs do offer great opportunities and they won't be used solely for movies. We see great opportunities in training programs on video discs, all of which lend themselves to sale via direct marketing methods. Certainly there is a possiblity that there will be video disc catalogs and magazines.

"We see the American home being set up as an entertainment center and an information access center. There is little question in my mind that the larger direct response agencies will benefit most simply because they will be dealing with giants in these new developments who require major agencies with all of the necessary facilities.

"You asked what I have enjoyed most. The thing I have enjoyed most is to see people grow within our Agency. We started with 5 people and we now have just over 100. We are blessed with what I feel are the cream of direct marketing talent. In my heart I know we are creating an atmosphere which will allow them to grow to the heights to which they are capable.

"One of my personal satisfactions has been the respectability that has come to direct marketing with scores of major corporations entering this discipline. As recently as January 21, I saw Advertising Age publish a 38-page supplement devoted solely to direct marketing. Even 10 years ago the thought of this happening would have been ludicrous. It has been wonderful to be a part of the growth and the recognition. But I sincerely feel, 'We ain't seen nothing yet.'

"It might sound ridiculous but I find it very difficult to think of any particular worries. It is true that in a personal service business clients tend to want to deal with the principals. Aaron Adler and I always follow the practice of keeping our hand in account work. And we do make it a point to sit in on meetings of clients on occasion.

"From the very beginning we set up a program where the principals of the Agency become involved in account reviews. Thus, we are always pretty much on top of things. As you get bigger, major clients, in particular, realize that there is no way in the world that the principals of the Agency can sit in on every meeting. But they do know that when a major problem arises the principals are responsive.

"Included in my outside activities has been a long-term relationship with the Ethics Committee of the Direct Mail/Marketing Association. I felt strongly that business ethics were important to the future of direct marketing. As a member of this committee, later the chairman, I have felt the satisfaction of bringing some of the bad actors into line.

"My most satisfying outside activity over the past 12 years or so has been as a director of the Direct Mail/Marketing Educational Foundation. This foundation was formed some 12 to 15 years ago when Lewis Kleid, of the Kleid Company of New York City—a prominent list broker—stated that he would fund such a foundation initially if my friend, Edward N. Mayer, Jr., would teach courses on direct mail/direct marketing to college students. Ed Mayer agreed and, thus, the Foundation was started.

"My personal involvement in the Foundation goes back about 12 years. Twice each year the Foundation pays all expenses for 35 college students selected from universities across the country to come to a central location and partake of a five-day intensive course on direct marketing. It has been my privilege to address the groups twice each year—the brightest of the bright marketing students—and, as I have said, it has proved to be my most satisfying experience.

"Direct marketing is growing at a tremendous rate and I am thoroughly convinced that the only deterrent to continuing rapid growth is availability of personnel who have an interest in this discipline. The prime source for such personnel is, without a doubt, college students with an academic marketing background. It has been my privilege to contribute all of the royalties I have received from the sale of 'Successful Direct Marketing Methods' to this cause. As of the end of 1980, this came to an excess of $60,000. Thus, in a small way, I have been able to help acquaint college students with the opportunities and the challenges of direct marketing.

"Another source of gratification resulting from outside activities has been the lectures I have given at Roosevelt University, in Chicago, where they teach a full credit direct marketing course and at the University of Missouri/Kansas City.

"The direct marketing courses taught at UMKC have come about as the result of a long time friend of mine—Martin Baier, Vice President Marketing, Old American Insurance Company, Kansas City. Martin teaches night courses at UMKC, and he has been the prime mover in making direct marketing courses available not only to students but to business people in the community, as well. It has been my privilege to address each one of his classes."

Note: The following are answers by Bob Stone to questions asked by me for readers of this book.

Q. *What attracts the gifted and talented of direct marketing to it?*

A. I think the superbright of direct marketing are attracted by two things: 1) the challenge; and 2) the fact that their input can be measured precisely.

Q. *Who are some of the more talented copy free lancers, agency executives, list brokers and direct marketing consultants whom you have known?*

A. There are a number of outstanding copy free lancers, including Hank Burnett and Bill Jayme. I consider Lester Wunderman, of Wunderman, Ricotta & Kline, to be an outstanding agency executive. The most outstanding list broker, in my opinion, is Rose Harper, of the Kleid Company. Among outstanding direct marketing consultants are Dick Hodgson and Bob Kestnbaum. A truly outstanding systems consultant is Roy Hedberg, formerly president of Sunset House.

Q. *What is your policy on hiring women and minorities?*

A. We started hiring talented women and so called minorities about 10 years ago. Today, better than 50% of our Creative Department is peopled by females. Our media director, Ms. Marilyn Gottlieb, is a vice president of the Agency. Of four account group managers, one is a female. We are very high on females. They are bright, aggresive and anxious to learn. They seem to have a particular capacity for the massive detail so much a part of direct marketing.

Q. *Who is the woman most successful in the direct marketing field?*

A. The most outstanding female executive in direct marketing, of course, is Joan Manley, Chairman of Time-Life Books.

Q. *What are the opportunities for young people considering direct marketing as a career? What are educational requirements? How important is a high IQ? What qualities are most important?*

A. I'm convinced that the future of direct marketing belongs to the young. Dramatic growth requires that there be a steady influx of young people who become excited about "accountable advertising". Most of these will come from marketing majors. I don't believe that a higher IQ is essential. Curiosity, challenges, ability to learn from failures are key ingredients.

As direct marketing is growing there will be continuing need for people interested in research, "figures people" who understand profitability theories and economics. At this point in time, an MBA degree certainly is not essential.

Q. *How do job opportunities in direct marketing compare in pay with those in other fields? How are they in a direct marketing advertising agency versus a general advertising agency?*

A. Up to 10 years ago, pay scales were on the low side. That certainly is not the case today. We regularly check our job titles against average income for comparable job titles in all agencies of our size. We are usually 10 to 20% higher. Because of the specialization a top copywriter, a top account person can demand and get a much higher income than he or she would realize in the general advertising agency.

Q. *How about on-the-job training and advancement opportunities?*

A. We have a continuing on-job training program going on for all departments of our Agency. We have a number of Agency people who have developed training programs, plus we use many of the training programs provided by Young & Rubicam on such subjects as "Techniques of Client Presentations", "Business Management", "Print Advertising", and so forth, and so forth.

We have a policy of advancement from within wherever possible. I am not aware of any aptitude tests for direct marketing people and we have not developed one up to this time.

Q. *What are the starting jobs in a direct marketing advertising agency?*

A. The best entry level for newcomers at Stone & Adler is assistant account executive. This entry job enables the newcomer to learn about the importance of marketing plans, trafficking, production, reverse time schedules, media plans, budgeting, research and analysis.

From this entry level an assistant account executive can move into Copy, Production, Art or up to account executive.

Many of our outstanding account executives today started as assistant account executives.

Because of rapid growth, I do believe that raises come faster than in a large general advertising agency.

Q.   *What are the opportunities today for the small entrepreneur in mail order?*

A.   In my opinion, there is always an opportunity for the small entrepreneur in direct marketing. What he needs is a "big idea" and the determination to learn everything he can about direct marketing.

Q.   *What advice do you have for direct marketing entrepreneurs just starting out?*

A.   There are books available. The Direct Mail/Marketing Association runs scores of seminars throughout the country teaching the basics of direct marketing. There are a number of good consultants who can be hired at a reasonable rate. Just reading the leading trade journal—Direct Marketing magazine—can keep the entrepreneur up-to-date on developments. Pete Hoke's newsletter, Friday Report, is another low cost way to learn about what is going on.

Also there are always scores of potential investors looking for new ideas which can be developed through direct marketing methods.

Q.   *How important is direct marketing as a creator of jobs?*

A.   It is estimated that approximately one million people in this country owe their jobs to direct marketing. I rather guess that the figure is higher than that. Certainly, direct marketing growth indicates that the discipline is an outstanding job creator.

Q.   *How does the pulling power of customer lists compare when billed directly versus via credit cards?*

A.   A customer list built by credit card puchases will pull every bit as well as a customer list obtained by direct billing. Using a credit card for payment does not obviate the name of the company from whom the purchase is made.

Q.   *Is New York City taking over from Chicago as the center of direct marketing?*

A.   I don't think that any particular city takes the spotlight away from Chicago when it comes to direct marketing. Actually, there is little evidence that the locale of the firm selling via direct marketing methods has a positive or negative effect upon sales.

Q.   *How does direct marketing in Europe compare with the U.S. in expertise and use of new technology?*

A.   I've been to Europe many times and I am continually impressed with their knowledge of direct marketing. About 15 years ago, the United States was way ahead of Europe in direct marketing expertise. In my opinion, they are still ahead, but the margin has narrowed.

As things develop I can see the day—probably not far off—where there will be worldwide telephone ordering services. I see Europe and the U.S. coming closer together all the time.

Q.   *How important are successful formulas in coming up with direct marketing individual product hits? Do formulas that are successful dictate the choice of new items?*

A.   It is certainly true that successful formulas do seem to develop. The interesting thing to me is that a formula which works for Time-Life Books will not necessarily work for Book-of-the-Month and vice versa. Thus, each has a successful formula for their promotion packages and ads and develops a uniqueness.

I don't think that there is necessarily a relationship between product development and a promotion formula. Time-Life Books will research what subjects have potential. Then they apply their promotion formula to the sale of these subjects. But they don't look for a product that will fit their promotion formula.

Q.   *Have you personally been in the mail order business aside from your early success in your family's business selling bandages to manufacturers?*

A.   Yes, I have been involved in mail order. I was a principal of the National Research Bureau which sold business services by mail. I was sole entrepreneur of National Communications Corporation, a firm which sold sales training and employee development recordings by mail and space advertising.

Q.   *What geographical area of the U.S. pulls best for direct marketing?*

A.   There is no one specific geographical area for direct marketing. However, there are great differences in response by geographical areas depending upon the type of product or service. Each organization must learn their own best geographical areas.

Q.   *How reasonable do you consider sales estimates of direct marketing made in recent years?*

A.   The Direct Mail/Marketing Association has worked with the Commerce Department and the Census Bureau in developing figures. I don't believe anyone feels they are 100% accurate, but they have been using the same formula for developing figures for a number of years and, thus, growth from year to year as reported has to be fairly accurate. The estimate for 1979 is in the area of $87 billion. I estimated a few years ago that total sales would reach $120 billion by the end of 1982. I still believe this will happen.

Q.   *How does the growth of mail order compare with that of other businesses?*

A.   It is generally agreed that mail order has been growing faster than retail sales.

Q.   *How does the trend of more married women holding jobs affect mail order?*

A.   I think mail order is benefitting tremendously from the new lifestyle of married women, better than 54% of them being employed. Some estimate that this will reach over 70% within this decade.

Q.   *Are you raising any new direct marketers in your family?*

A.   I was first married in 1942. Our first child, Karen, was born in 1945. My wife died suddenly at the age of 23 when our daughter was 8 months old. I remarried in 1948. My wife, Dorothy, and I have had four sons. Here is a brief rundown of the five children:

Karen, our daughter, is married to a fine attorney, Tom Gillick. Karen is a partner in the personnel firm of Gillick, Ridenour & Associates, Ltd., a highly successful executive search firm specializing in direct marketing personnel.

Jeffrey, our oldest son, married, is the manager of a real estate firm in Cary, Illinois. He became a member of the "Million Dollar Circle" in real estate in the first year in business. Rick Stone, the second oldest son, is in the stained glass business. He and his wife, Jane, have twice made Dorothy and I grandparents.

Willie, our third oldest son, met his wife, Marybeth, at Marquette University, in Milwaukee, from which they both

graduated. Upon graduation, Willie was hired by Proctor & Gamble and at the age of 23 is in management capacity in their Milwaukee branch. Larry, our youngest son, is in his second year at St. Louis University. He is majoring in physical therapy.

Q. *In your memories of all whom you've known in direct marketing, whom do you recall as particularly outstanding?*

A. There are six people who particularly stand out over the period from my starting in direct marketing until today.

Aaron Adler—who co-founded Stone & Adler with me on December 1, 1966. Aaron Adler is one of the best creative direct marketing people I have ever known. He has a genius for picking products which have potential for direct marketing. He can look at an ad layout and immediately spot deficiencies.

There were many others along the way, of course. People like George D. Gaw, who taught me the importance of color in direct response advertising. Max Sackheim, co-founder of the Book-of-the-Month. And many others. All of these people have had one thing in common—they have freely given of their knowledge and time. They have stimulated others to enter the direct marketing stream.

Robert Collier—his "Letter Book" became my bible and stimulated me to explore the possibilities of selling by mail. I was intrigued with the wide variety of products and services that he was able to sell profitably by mail.

Homer J. Buckley—he coined the phrase "Direct Mail". He adopted me as a protege and was of tremendous help to me in learning the fundamentals of direct mail advertising.

Leonard J. Raymond—he was the founder of Dickie-Raymond and brought "class" to direct mail advertising and promotion. His agency was based upon the premise that major advertisers should have two types of agencies: a general advertising agency and a direct mail agency. His methods of operation brought a professionalism to direct mail.

Edward N. Mayer, Jr.—Ed Mayer was the greatest "teacher" I have ever known. He, along with Lew Kleid, launched the Direct Mail/Marketing Educational Foundation. He was a fountain of knowledge about direct marketing developments. He helped to bring the gospel of direct marketing to Europe.

Lester Wunderman—his agency, Wunderman, Ricotta & Kline—also a subsidiary of Young & Rubicam—has been a driving force in bringing full service activities to major corporations entering the direct marketing stream.

Lester Wunderman and his agency have developed many of the innovations which we take for granted today. One of his innovations was the development of magazine and newspaper

inserts. Another innovation has been the development of "gold box", which is a method of measuring the impact of television upon a newspaper insert or magazine insert.

Q. *Over your business lifetime, what have been the key developments in mail order and direct marketing?*

A. The most significant developments in direct marketing over the decades—without identifying them by exact decade—are these:

A) Development of the free trial offer
B) Development of installment credit
C) Development of commercial credit cards
D) Development of the negative option plan
E) Development of newspaper and magazine inserts
F) Use of TV for direct marketing
G) Development of interactive TV
H) Development of the recency-frequency-monetary formula for mail order enterprises
I) Development of the computer for maintenance of prospect and customer lists
J) Development of computer letters, laser beam letters and so forth.

Note: Bob Stone can help you in many ways. Read any article he writes anywhere. Read his book, "Successful Direct Marketing Methods". I review it elsewhere in this book and strongly recommend it. In the Help Source Section of this book I tell how to get reprints of some of his most outstanding articles and tapes and transcripts of some of his most famous lectures.

Bob Stone is liked, trusted and known personally by more people in direct marketing than any other successful practitioners. His life is a lesson in how to make it in direct marketing.

He is a thorough, polished and meticulous professional. He had from early on an ability to doggedly inquire into what works and why. He went to the leaders to learn more. He continued learning until it blended into his own teaching of others. He exchanged information with anyone and everyone in direct marketing. He started giving, early on, lectures and talks and in work in associations, institutions and clubs.

Giant companies respect not just his know-how in Fortune 500 direct marketing but his background as an entrepreneur, as a principal and as a sole owner taking his own risks. A particular reason for Bob Stone's success and that of Stone & Adler has been loyalty to associates and accounts. Many a success shakes off earlier profitable but small associates. Stone & Adler values each.

What will Bob stone do next? His agency will grow more. He will give more. And he will do more. He'll write more, travel more. Perhaps "Successful Direct Marketing Methods" will be on video disc with Bob on the screen and his words coming from his lips in each of many languages. But Bob Stone, above all, will continue to help more people get on the first rung, and move up rung by rung in direct marketing.

Chapter 5
The World's Biggest List Broker

By helping new entrepreneurs grow.

His coat is off. His shirt sleeves are rolled up. His pipe is in his mouth. He's on the telephone. He is Jack Oldstein.

He has the corner private office of a huge floor of private offices at 257 Park Avenue South. It's like Merrill Lynch, or a big real estate brokerage office. He's getting reports by phone from his offices in Chicago and Washington, talking to customers, competitors, friends.

Meanwhile, the whole beehive at 257 South is humming. In each cubbyhole office a list broker is on the phone or seated with a client. Each office is immaculate, organized for instant referral to information on any of the 15,000 buyer lists and an encyclopedia of compiled lists.

This is Dependable Lists of which Jack is founder and president. In one area is Dependable List Compilation where you can select any compiled list or have one compiled for you. You can select patent lawyers or rock gardeners . . . chest physicians or sugar beet technologists, gynecologists or daffodil growers, bankers or puppeteers, every possible compiled list from agricultural engineers to zoologists.

In another area of the big floor is the list management division. It manages a list just as a real estate management company manages an apartment house. Here two clients new to mail order but already successful are arranging for Dependable to computerize their lists at Dependable's expense—against future list rental income. Competitive but friendly list brokers are phoning Dependable and Dependable list managers are phoning brokers arranging for rentals of Dependable managed lists.

In Washington, the big emphasis in election years is political lists. In New York, there's been a big push for magazine subscriber lists, books and book clubs, credit card lists and so on. In Chicago, insurance and catalog lists have been having a big play.

All over the country, 9,500 direct marketers have just received the latest issue of Dependable's List Marketing Newsletter. Many are putting the reference information—practical, meaty, factual—into ring binders for permanent reference.

It's another normal day for Dependable Lists and for Jack Oldstein, whose entire career I've observed and admired. He's my friend and alumnus and he got into direct marketing by waiting on tables at a resort in the Catskills. Later he became a gym teacher but then joined the Hoge mail order business started as a result of our family advertising business.

Two of his former co-waiters had jobs in our mail order operation. They recruited him to join and, before he knew it, he was given the assignment of list selection for direct mail campaigns. He's been doing that ever since, now with the Dependable List empire.

From Hoge he went on to select lists for others, first for Hoge alumni. What he really wanted was to get into list brokerage, working for a number of clients. The list brokerage business was small and tightly knit, almost a club. "I didn't have enough contacts with enough large mailers to get a job offer."

Instead, in 1955, with no business experience he opened a one-room office at 381 Fourth Avenue, now Park Avenue South. He went to the super and through him got some second-hand, old equipment . . . a beat up desk, an old typewriter for $15. The super's son fixed it. An old Heyer duplicator with purple ink. Some data cards to present for recommendations.

"My first problem was the name for my business. I submitted to the state of New York three names. The first two were fancier but were already taken by others. The last name was plain and simple, 'Dependable Lists'. It got through.

"I sat in that little office and typed and filed seven days most weeks. My big expenditure was one telephone. There were about 400 or 500 lists then. You needed permission from a list owner to represent his list. I had to write each. Often a list owner said he had three reps and didn't need another.

"I was not at all confident I could make it on my own. I didn't know how to approach list owners or how to persuade list users to work with me. I felt unsure of myself in answering questions beyond my previous experience. I was advised to tell anyone asking too tough a question that I'd get back to them shortly. Then I'd call the most knowledgeable Hoge alumnus for the question, work out an answer and call back.

"The first year was a total disaster. At the end of the twelfth month, I told my friends I was ready to throw in the towel, but was persuaded to try another month or so. The thirteen month was the turn around. Recommendations made months before began to come in as test orders. Tests made for clients before now suddenly projected. I hadn't really realized that the first year had just been testing. The second year I had some clients projecting.

"Most big mail order companies using direct mail had long-time, very close connections with old line brokers. It was very hard to break in. I began to analyze my strengths and weaknesses. I knew mail order and I knew how to select lists profitably. At Hoge and Hoge alumni-owned companies I had worked a lot with gardening and automotive names as well as household items. At Hoge, we mailed certain states at certain times according to the planting season. I knew all this.

"I did not have contacts with really big mail order companies. I did not know how to break in. I would have to grow with companies new to direct mail mail order. If I wasn't one of the establishment, if I didn't have the biggest old line accounts, I'd just have to grow with the new entrepreneurs. My first clients were offshoots from Hoge. My first growth came from accounts new to mail order or from mail order accounts new to direct mail. And ever since, the big growth has been that way. I matched my ability to pick winning lists with new rising entrepreneurs, and still do.

"It had been suggested to me to contact Charles Kasher at Charles Antell, in Baltimore. They were pitchmen and were selling lanolin by TV, and a host of other items, with enormous success. They wanted to use direct mail, took my recommendations, paid out and became a big client. Of course, I got tests from some major mailers. I did from Popular Science, which had formerly placed some advertising with Huber Hoge.

"I enjoyed psychologically making the right recommendations. To see them work was my greatest satisfaction. I had sincerity. I saw that the business made sense. I also realized that getting the client only began the process. I was dead if I couldn't get the list to him on time. I grasped that if I knew a file was not coming in time, I had to call the client. I had to tell the truth. I couldn't make up stories and report wrong information.

"I was very conservative, and I did lots of back room work. First I was a one-man band. Then I hired one girl part-time. I had a hundred square feet. I got two more desks. Then I began to expand. I added two people the second year for order processing. They were good people and helped organize the set-up.

"I had the ability to select names that made money for my client, and I had to see that the lists were delivered and on time. Always, I relied on choosing the right people and then letting them do their job. One lady I hired started giving me orders. Then I knew I had someone who could direct other people. There are lots of girl Fridays for one boss Friday. After that lady took over, the fur began to fly. She developed systems.

"My sister, Betty, came in as full-charge bookkeeper. Then she did a little phone selling and then did it full-time. She was my first account supervisor. By the fifth year, Dependable had five employees. And only after those first five years was I accepted as a member of the National Council of List Brokers, although I had made application years before. Now I could sit with the leaders, the six major brokers.

"But Dependable was still not able to crack the major book and magazine publishers. I couldn't get the Book-of-the-Month Club or Time-Life. Doubleday, for years, used one broker. Each major old account seemed to belong to somebody.

"We dealt with owners, proprietors who often would never let anyone select lists. We reviewed their past selections and made recommendations which were successful. An entrepreneur would have an idea. We'd select lists. From tests together we sometimes exploded to millions of pieces. Success here came with the entrepreneurship of beginning clients.

"I began to get good management people. I got new salesmen. In 1964, my seventh year, Philip Boehm joined me. He had been an encyclopedia salesman for 18 years. He was an entrepreneur. I needed that. He became sales manager. He had a number of titles. We had about 11 or 12 people then.

"In 1964, Jules Sherman came with me. He worked for Walter Drey, who had an unusual list compilation operation. Jules was very creative. When he split with Walter and came with me, we went into compilation, another division. List compilation is a business of specialties. Let's say you want a list of wholesalers for your sales reps. It seems simple enough but the problem is immense. Here's a directory. But what is the date of compilation? It could be once every three years. It carries for three years. Companies move, start, fold all the time. The deliverability may not be what you're looking for.

"Compiling has always been necessary in many forms of business to business mail order. It became huge in the consumer field for car registrations, retired people on social security, births, home owners and so on. In business lists now some of the biggest compilers are Dun & Bradstreet and National Business Lists. Metro Mail, R.L. Polk and Donnelley are the giant consumer list companies and larger than many of us. We're in business, consumer, professional and just about all kinds of compilation. Over the last twenty years, dollar rentals of compiled lists have grown considerably.

"Our compilation business is important to us. But it's an adjunct. We make a better percentage of the dollar on our own compiled lists but we handle as a broker all good compiled lists. We never forget we're a broker. Each of our salesmen knows which service is best for his client. He has to. It's his protective environment. If he wants teachers, he'll select from all teachers' files on the market. Ours is just one of the many available. Our salesman knows which works best for the client.

"List brokerage, list compilation and list management are the three major legs to our stool. I didn't originate the concept of any of them. I study new developments in our business and when

I feel it's the time to go into it, I do. As I recall, Ed Burnett conceived the list management concept. One professional compiler said you can't be a broker and compiler at the same time. I saw it as a list transaction and, as such, we should become involved.

"We discovered the secret of list management the day we managed our first list. It was to offer full commissions to other brokers. Cooperation was the idea, to get all brokers to help us rent names we managed. We were now able to get the maximum return in rental income for the list owner and we shared in it. At that time, we became one of the largest list managers in the business.

"But when we started to manage lists, I'm sorry we didn't open up our own computer service. Second party services give the same headaches. But if it were internal, it would deliver. Now we're in the stages of getting back into it. In the beginning, I attempted the same thing by investing in an operation. But we eventually became the flea on the elephant's back. They got that big. I got out. It was a good investment but not what I was looking for. We may go to our own in-house computer service. It boils down to this. Do you want to be in control? Eventually, it may be wise. A vendor can do a good job but he also may have many other accounts. We can be account #427.

"From the early years, we had grown 25% to 30% a year. Just prior to computers the real explosion started. We were the first to develop the idea of account supervisors in a big way. We have seventeen account executives now, each one a specialist in a category. That helped us grow. The list compilation did. The list management did. Promoting the business with mailings did.

"At the start, I knew how important list selection could be to any mail order business and that I could contribute. But I realized that no matter how good I was at list selection, copy creativity, the offer and the item were just as important. I saw Gene Schwartz (a great copywriter Hoge alumnus) change a headline that raised results 50% and let us rent lists that before we couldn't make pay out.

"This probably made me believe in using direct response methods to promote Dependable Lists. Often we mailed every day, never hard sell—just telling people about new lists ahead of others. I used telephone marketing personally and trained the account representatives to do the same. Often we got there first to tell of a new list.

"And, overall, we have a wonderful crew. We have some 72 people now. I have total trust in my people and in Philip Boehm as general manager. More and more, I've taken a back seat on day-to-day operations. You're dealing with Dependable, not Jack. Each salesman is his own profit center, but just part of Dependable's total team effort. The organization is more important then me or any salesman.

"We must do something right. We do over 8 figures a year and are still growing." Dependable does a lot that's right. Jack has grown by helping entrepreneurs in mail order start using direct mail effectively and then growing with them. He has taught what he knew about effective use of direct mail. He has constantly updated his knowledge and passed it along. He has attracted talented people who knew and others who learned and kept passing around more know-how.

Another good name for Dependable would be practical. It teaches in a practical way. Each issue of Dependable's List marketing newsletter is meaty, simple and practical. Each booklet of Dependable's five classic booklets on the use of different facets of the use of direct mail is simple, practical and so meaty it seems a digest of a full length book. The newsletter and

booklets are reviewed elsewhere in this book. How to get copies of each is explained in the Help Source Section.

Jack is a kindly host who gives a friendly welcome to new mail order entrepreneurs. He has a smiling, open attitude. He gives practical advice. He helps and backs it all with an organization that's competent, up-to-date and highly organized.

Note: For readers of this book Jack has answered the following questions I asked him for you.

Q. *Did you dream when you started in business that it might grow to be as big as it is?*
A. No. When I couldn't get a job with a list broker, I became one.

Q. *What would you do if you were starting out all over again as a list broker?*
A. I have a few clients who are engines of ideas. They generate them. They study market places, pick categories and then create a product. Usually, it's printed. They let others fulfill. They use direct mail as a marketing vehicle. I'd be tempted to do that if I were starting out. I'd pay specialists, utilize people in the field, pay each his or her profit. I wouldn't get into their specialties. Of course, they'd make mistakes. But I would avoid the headaches. I'd love to have a few clients and be a one-man business that way.

Q. *Have you ever gone into mail order yourself or gambled with Dependable mail order clients?*
A. I've never been a mail order entrepreneur. But I believe that mail order is a constant gamble.

Q. *In the early days, when mail order entrepreneurs were important to you, did any of them badly hurt you by non-payment?*
A. I've had my share of bankruptcies. But they also served my continuing business education. Overall, the loss was small.

Q. *What changes in the list business have been most important?*
A. It's a very different business today, much bigger and more complex—with computers, list management and far bigger and more buyer lists, more sophisticated compiling and new data bases. In the early days, each broker did it all with someone to back up.

Q. *Who in the list business in the early days was the most fascinating?*
A. Lew Kleid was probably the most interesting and remarkable of all. There was little interaction or interchange between brokers, but I'd study his techniques. He was his own salesman. He had a tremendous sense of organization. He was a strict perfectionist. Everything had to be in place. If he found a typo on an order, it would have to be retyped. He was shy and rarely would speak to groups of people. He established himself as the list authority by his writings. He had a penchant for this.

Q. *Anybody else really fascinating?*
A. George Bryant was another interesting personality. He knew how to live. He specialized as broker in lists for religious fund-raising. He'd book his business in two months of the year. Then, for the rest of the year, he'd go on safari. He'd go to the Indianapolis Speedway. He was a great auto enthusiast. Perhaps you've heard of the "Bryant Special".

George had certain exclusive lists. Once I negotiated to buy his business. When I looked at his books, I found he did more business in two months of the year than I did for my first four years.

Q. *What is the most important factor in the list brokerage business?*
A. Caring about your clients *total* marketing plans and maintaining a continual involvement in their acquiring a customer at the lowest cost per order.

For example: Several years ago, we began with a client selling vacuum cleaners by mail. We began a limited campaign designed to reach the industrial business executive at his office. Then, as quantities grew to over a million pieces a year, we utilized "merge/purge" and "wave" techniques to keep him mailing all year. At the same time, we started to mail to the consumer market and also continued a program to sell various back-end products until a catalog of high ticket merchandise emerged. We also experimented with package inserts and helped to develop a "deck" or postcard mailing. The company today has over 700,000 customers and is growing quite nicely.

Q. *How effective are computerized methods of list selection?*
A. The computer is a remarkable tool, but the computer won't tell the current make up of a file. A change of a list source can be very rapid. The entire make up of the file can change. The historical record of which mailer used which list and how successfully is still one of our most important research tools.

Q. *Is the computer today a must for anyone in mail order for inside application?*
A. Computer applications have changed the business. The computer is not for everyone, but the cost of computerization is now less than plating lists. I'd recommend a small computer for anyone starting in business today.

Q. *House advertising agencies are often set up by mail order advertisers. What about advertising agencies and mail order firms setting up house list brokers?*
A. Most advertisers and advertising agencies have been glad to leave list selection to the brokers. Compiled lists do pay a 15% commission to advertising agencies. Otherwise, the agencies have to add a commission or fee on top.

Q. *Who do you think is outstanding as a teacher of direct mail for mail order?*
A. The DMMA does a good job in education. Ed Burnett has also done a job. He's an excellent writer and lecturer on the list business.

Q. *What do you think of the chances of women in mail order and how have they done?*
A. Women in mail order are tremendous. They take on more and more executive jobs. They also own businesses. There's

more of them in it all the time. This can only accelerate in the future to the good of mail order.

Q. *How have your family and business affected each other?*

A. I've worked at this business some 26 years and my usual schedule is up at 5:30 to be in the office by 7:30. Usually I'm not home until 9 or 10 PM, and that's 6 days a week. As you can see, it doesn't allow much time for family life or outside interests except an occasional tennis game. My wife has not only been my support and inspiration over these many years, but she's also raised our children and has had to find her own interests and activities to fill the gap.

We live in Scarsdale now. We have three children. Our daughter got her master's degree and lives in Arlington, Virginia. Her husband is in computer science. Our son now works for Dependable after his recent graduation from the University of Colorado. Our daughter is at SUNY, in Binghamton, New York.

Q. *What do you think of the future of mail order and the opportunities for a career in it or to start a business in it?*

A. It keeps growing, and in startling new forms. It keeps proliferating. It will get tougher as it always has in the old ways and easier in new ways, some of which we don't even now know about. That's what makes it fun. I strongly recommend going into it as an entrepreneur or for a career.

There's some gray in Jack's curly hair. But his energy and enjoyment of each business day seems increasing. His eyes twinkle. He smiles, relaxing in the controlled hum of his hive. Right now, very probably, he's helping somebody else new in mail order and having fun at it. It's a nice way to see that Dependable continues to grow and prosper.

Chapter 6
The Mail Order Recruiter

How he pre-selects his candidates.

He has grown 135 kinds of begonia—and collects art and every conceivable variety of direct marketer. At any one time, he knows of more jobs in direct marketing . . . and of more people suited for them . . . than anyone in the world.

He's placed more people in direct marketing jobs . . . paying $20,000 to $200,000 a year . . . than anyone in the job business. There's a good reason. It takes one to catch one. Hal Crandall has been a direct marketing consultant. He's written mail order copy. He knows and is known in the field.

"About 25 years ago, I was a partner in a small direct mail advertising business. I handled accounts and wrote copy. Our clients were investment advisors, financial brokerage firms, a firm that sold paintings by mail, another that sold industrial products mail order, and so on.

"Before that I was a newspaperman. After that I was a stockbroker. Then I used the entire combination of everything I knew to help good people rise to the top in direct marketing—and top direct marketers to find top people.

"I started in the personnel business with an employment agency, placing people for a wide variety of jobs in many fields of communication and marketing. I got started working with direct marketing personnel with an assignment from Prentice-Hall to find them a direct mail copywriter.

"Prentice-Hall did not give me an exclusive and a number of employment agencies sent over candidates. Mine got the job. Prentice-Hall called me again and the same thing happened. They began to call me more often to find people for other direct marketing jobs. My candidates kept winning over those sent over by others.

"This made me think. If Prentice-Hall needed people, other direct marketers should. And I knew how to select and prepare the right people for interviews, because of my own previous experience in the field. I approached other firms, never got any exclusive job orders, but kept getting jobs for my candidates.

"That was back in 1966. I knew direct mail. I required candidates to read books on direct mail and come back. I kept a pile of paperback editions of David Ogilvy's "Confessions of an Advertising Man". They cost me 75 cents each. I gave copies away to anyone I had hope for. But interviewees who had not bought and read some book on direct mail—on their own, after our first session—I didn't consider as serious candidates.

"For the interested ones, I'd take out of my desk drawer a direct mail package . . . consisting of outer envelope, letter, broadside, free gift flyer and return order card and envelope. I'd point out the strategy behind it . . . the frequency of the word 'you' in the copy . . . the action picture in the broadside . . . what the P.S. could do in the letter, and so forth. I sent over to the client interviewees who understood, were interested and had a chance of mastering direct marketing.

"My candidates were more carefully pre-selected than other candidates. They talked more sensibly to the client because they were well prepared. They got jobs. They and the clients were happy. I got more interested in direct marketing and began to realize that recruiters and employment agencies knew little about it.

"I had been concentrating my recruiting for public relations firms and big, national advertising agencies. But now I felt I could concentrate my activities. I saw that direct marketing was growing far faster than other fields. I decided to give everything else up and switch to and concentrate on direct marketing. I began to study intensely.

"I read books and attended seminars. Then, when Publishers Clearing House or any other direct marketer called me, I could talk intelligently. My clientele began to grow by recommendation and word of mouth. In 1968, I became the partner and manager of an employment agency and specialized in direct marketing. Then I started Crandall Associates, Inc., in 1972.

"This was a major move for me because I made the big decision to become a recruiter. I would charge the client, never the applicant. I'd concentrate on finding the best applicants for the best jobs for the best companies in the business. I would build a data bank of talent. I would undertake to write, phone, travel, do whatever necessary to match the right position and person—whatever the time and cost to me. And I would make money at it.

"I would secure people of caliber but charge 25% of the first year's salary as a fee. (Today, recruiters in some fields charge one-third.) Again my friends, and a lot of direct marketers, thought I was crazy. But I made it for several reasons.

"Direct marketing was growing so fast and the opportunities were so great that the one principal handicap to even greater growth was the lack of people with mail order know-how. There was and is no substitute for experience in direct marketing. And now the need is even greater. Direct marketers must know where to find the best people, not average ones. Those with the know-how must know where and how to get full value for it. I'm the middleman.

"We have built an internal list of names of over 15,000 people in the U.S. and over 1,000 people in Canada in direct marketing positions. We compile these names ourselves. They may be seminar attendees or mentioned in trade magazines, the Wall Street Journal or local direct marketing newsletters. They may answer ads. We may get their names in dozens of ways.

"We categorize these names, breaking them down by kinds of direct marketing and kinds of jobs each holds. This way, from the beginning we've built our mail order know-how file. We've identified 700 people in insurance direct marketing, alone. Then when we get a job offer, we go in and screen.

"We just mailed 12,800 pieces to find the right person for a specific job. We make telephone calls continually to identify people more accurately on our list. Early on, I realized that direct marketing people in Detroit knew each other but not people in Philadelphia. Employees looked locally to find candidates. I created a national market.

"For the right person I might find a job anywhere in the country, and I might fill a job with just the right person from anywhere in or outside the country. The more I concentrated on direct marketing the greater I found the need for new people. And so measurable are the results of what someone in direct marketing contributes that the most dollar-conscious employer could see a fast, happy pay-off . . . my applicant's entire salary, plus my fee.

"The higher the position the more know-how is needed. After I go into the field and do recruiting. I may have 100 to 200 interviews to find just the right person—for instance, a Spanish-speaking director of direct marketing. This was for the Mexican subsidiary of an American company.

"My copywriting experience is a great help in finding productive copywriters. I can read any applicant's copy and tell if there is anything there. I look for someone who can come up with a new package, concept or breakthrough. It's no trick to repeat a sweepstakes.

"People think they know direct marketing when often they don't know simple things about it. I ask them if they use the RFM formula? They have no idea what it is. I ask if they've tried a publisher's letter? They don't know what it is. I have recommended more copies of Bob Stone's book than anyone can believe.

"We work on direct marketing jobs ranging from operations to creative. We work for the biggest firms and often help the very small grow. Twenty percent of our business is with direct marketing agencies. Eighty percent of our business is with direct marketing companies.

"Once I place people in a position I never talk to them—unless I get a letter stating they would like to change their job. Only then will I work with that candidate again. All employers know my policy and understand it. I avoid helping applicants leap-frog. But often they come back in the course of their careers. One man came to me for his first job in direct marketing. He was a carpenter. I put him into Prentice-Hall. Then he came back. I placed him at Scholastic Magazine. Then, on his own, he went to Rapp & Collins. Now he's with Ogilvy & Mather. Each move was at a nice increase.

Direct marketing experience is such a shortage commodity that the average pro who accepts a new job gets 28% more. Most experienced people today will not leave for another job for less

than a 20% to 25% increase. If relocation to another city is required, the company often pays the difference between a lower interest rate on a mortgage and the higher rate in the home moved to . . . usually for three to five years.

"Companies need me to talk to people they want. They often don't want to make a direct approach. They clear through me. Direct marketing talent in all areas need me. And the higher up they are, the more so. A person may have a top job that's hard to duplicate money-wise, but still be unhappy for a particular reason.

"If so, he or she wants to be most discreet—to have a minimum chance of any job hunting effort getting back to the boss. I can describe and recommend someone . . . and only disclose when I get very real interest. But I always discuss the position with the applicant first.

"Sometimes, a large company will want to start a direct marketing division. Or a European direct marketing company will want to set up here. Either may ask me to help find people. Generally, if I get the general manager, he'll hire people he or she knows. After a while, they come back to me for help.

"A direct marketing advertising agency may come to me for any job. For one direct marketing agency, I found 18 people in five years, of whom 15 are still there. I fill jobs from creative people to supervisors to account executives. I find general managers and directors of marketing, people for jobs of every description.

"As regards requirements for applicants, I don't care about education. An MBA, even just a college degree, while desirable, is not a necessity. Some clients like MBA's. Some insist on college degrees. But otherwise, good experience is my measuring rod. I only work with people after their first direct marketing jobs, preferably after at least two years. The kind of experience is important. If trained by a pro, I can do a lot more for my candidate. If they're copywriters, my interest is in their ability to write good copy.

"If someone with just two years direct marketing experience is good, I'll get him or her $20,000. I interviewed a woman with three years experience. She was good. She had learned her trade. I got her $32,000. Several years ago, a good copywriter could start a new job at $25,000. By 1981, it became $35,000. A top writer who several years ago would start at $35,000 can start at $50,000 today. Art directors earn less. There's a bigger supply and more competition.

"In some situations, I don't charge anything. I try to help beginners. I refer them to the Direct Marketing Education Foundation, which places beginners informally. I also suggest they contact Prentice-Hall and Doubleday who sometimes start beginners. If I know of beginner jobs, I refer them out of courtesy, for nothing. Sometimes all that's needed is to give someone a start. Then executive positions open up in the same company.

"With free lancers, it's the same situation. Often, I bring together one with an assignment, for no fee. I've referred consultants without charge. If I do it, I may benefit in the future. The companies are grateful to get them and they, to get assignments. A company benefiting may later use me on a paid basis for an assignment I might not have otherwise gotten.

"Women in direct marketing are very interesting. There's absolutely no resistance. Pay and opportunities for men and women are indistinguishable. Some women still feel that discrimination exists. Occasionally, there's static about a job that didn't come through. But, one recruiter who had made a study, states that the situation is now weighted in favor of women when they apply for a job.

"One difference I have found between men and women: If a new job opportunity means the family must move, usually the man can persuade his wife to move and go after a new job in the new location. But when a woman is offered a job in another city, she can seldom persuade her husband to move and look for a new job, but I'm sure that will change. I placed one man at the Franklin Mint, near Philadelphia. His wife worked in New York City. They compromised. They moved halfway between. One commuted to the Franklin Mint and the other to New York City.

"My newspaper experience gave me the background to do my own PR. I can sit down any time and write a new article to submit to the trade media. I do about four major ones a year. I lecture, particularly at Hofstra in Hempstead, Long Island, and Hunter College in New York City. I write and produce the promotion for Crandall Associates.

"I also publish 'The Direct Marketing National Salary Guide.' Very likely, I'll do this yearly, if inflation continues. In it are listed a wide variety of executive and creative jobs. For each I estimate average pay for small, medium and large companies. I give the low, medium and high figures earned for each job.

"Anything I go into I do with enthusiasm. I live in Port Washington, Long Island, with my three children, Wendy, Matthew and Joshua. I'm a member of The American Begonia Society and of the Nassau Museum of Fine Arts. I was more into begonias at one time. But now I'm a small art collector and take courses at the New School. If I don't get to an art gallery, it's a lost weekend. If I have a two-hour gap on a recruiting trip, I hop over to the local museum. I'm a widower, but direct marketing and hobbies keep me busy.

"The longer I'm in direct marketing, the more astonished I am at its growth, proliferation and ability to grow faster than before.

"I have a secretary, an assistant and two recruiters beside myself. I have one office, in New York City. But we have a tie-line to Chicago. People there can now reach me with a local call. It's helped business quite a lot."

Note: For readers of this book Hal Crandall has answered the following questions I have asked.

Q. *Is it hard to get a job after 40?*
A. No. In direct marketing, experience is valued. Often, for years after retirement, free lancers earn a consultant income—and sometimes more than they earned before.

Q. *Do direct marketing employers pay as little as they can?*
A. Some may. But wages are determined by supply and demand at each experience level . . . plus the desire of the employer to keep people happy enough not to look for another job during lunch.

Q. *Is it smart to exaggerate past earnings in an interview?*
A. It's said that 82% do. But they often get trapped by competing over their heads. There's no better lie detector than direct marketing. Job performance can be measured by results, as ads can. So, when asked your last salary, don't lie. It's far better to keep yourself competitive.

Q. *How important is a resume in looking for a direct marketing job?*
A. Usually, essential. Some people do get jobs without one. Your direct marketing experience is your stock in trade. Each added bit of experience adds to your value. Your resume documents your know-how. Keep it up-to-date. Always show a clean, typed copy.

Q. *Should an applicant put a job objective on a resume?*
A. Usually, it's unwise. It limits your possible opportunities. A summary of experience is better.

Q. *Is it disastrous to be unemployed when looking for a job?*
A. It is sensible to look with a paycheck coming in. But you also have advantages in being unemployed. You can start at once, often when someone is needed in a hurry.

Q. *How can a small company, in a small town, locate good direct marketing help in a tight market?*
A. Competent, professional direct marketers are not easy to find and tougher still to woo away from their present position. But some don't like big companies, big cities and long, tiring commuting. A friendly, small company in a near rural setting has something to sell in obtaining good people . . . particularly those starting out—and often free lance help from top mail order people who have retired.

Q. *If an applicant is willing to move anywhere, does he or she have a better chance?*
A. Yes. But more than 70% of candidates willing to relocate tell us they mean within 25 miles. Others mean only to a major city—sometimes to Florida. Those willing to move anywhere have far less competition, and often more challenging careers.

Q. *Are divorced and single people less desirable to hire than married people?*
A. No! They usually can work longer hours and are freer to transfer to any kind of job or location.

Q. *In what area of direct marketing does an applicant start with little experience and have the most chance of getting the job and then getting ahead?*
A. Telephone marketing. It's growing very fast, yet is still so young many beginners get ahead rapidly.

Q. *Where are the best direct marketing job opportunities?*
A. New York and Chicago remain the hubs, with Pennsylvania a strong third. Washington, D.C. is rapidly coming into fourth place. Boston has opportunities but high living costs. California has the same problem. But both appeal to young, single direct marketers. Small states and cities have some of the best mail order job opportunities. Salaries are good and the cost of living lower. Couples often prefer them.

Q. *Is it customary to have a contract drawn up between direct marketing firms and executives?*
A. List brokers are heavy on contracts as a form of protection. For other direct marketing jobs, interest in contracts starts at jobs paying $75,000 or so.

Note: The latest "Direct Marketing Salary Guide" and reprints of "Hal" Crandall's articles in Direct Marketing Magazine are available without charge to readers by writing Crandall Associates, Inc., 501 Fifth Avenue, New York, New York 10017; New York (212) 687-2550; Chicago (312) 726-2977.

Chapter 7
Mail Order Collectomania

How little people created a boom.

In each field, first came small collectors . . . then tiny dealers . . . then self-published price guides and obscure trade publications and more and more little mail order dealers.

Collectors pointed the way for investors . . . small mail order dealers for the big, for the Bradford Exchange and the Franklin Mint . . . the self-publishers for the giants, for the Time-Life Encyclopedia of Collectibles.

Collectors run tiny mail order ads offering to buy a single piece. Other steps may soon follow. It's only a slight step to sell a piece, the second—and a small further step, to buy items not just to collect but to resell. Profit made makes it possible to buy again.

Many collectors become dealers . . . to feed the habit. They already have some inventory. They can start with a classified ad. Collecting is America's most universal hobby. Some say there are 150 million collectors of something in the U.S.A.

"Depression glass" became a big mass collectible. Stamps alone have 15 to 22 million collectors. Investors favor stamps, autographs, old automobiles, antique furniture and coins. Coin collectors have multiplied in the last 25 years from half a million to 8 to 12 million. They compete for and force upward the prices of a limited number of coins. There are countless collectibles from china dolls to cigar coupons.

There are more mail order entrepreneurs in collectibles than in any other product classification. In every field, collectors become mail order dealers. The first price guides and reference books in any field are usually published by mail order collector-dealers. So are almost all new periodicals for specialized collectibles. With specialized collector shows they create the market place. They quote latest prices, picture items and publicize club meetings, shows and seminars.

A determined collector negotiates better than most. Expertise in advertising is usually aquired by trial and error. Often ads are classified. A catalog is often a typewritten price list, photocopied. Choicest media is usually the most highly specialized for the field.

Collector plates have become the most collected art form in the U.S. At 55, Violet Krispien retired as school district dietician. Her children were grown. She was bored. Vi Krispien decided to turn her ten-year-old hobby of plate collecting into a business. And at 57 she did, from home.

Vi became a plate collector-dealer, exhibiting at antique shows. At 58, she started to sell mail order with a $35 ad of four inches in Plate Collector Magazine. Now, not yet sixty, Vi has had a full-time career and sold her business for a substantial capital gain.

At 59, she did $150,000. "Then the year I sold out we did close to $200,000." It was all from home. Two-thirds was mail order. Each year it was comfortably profitable, with one 4-day-a-week employee; but Vi did draft her family.

Daughter Karin was a French teacher in high school. Daughter Toni worked as an Air Canada agent at La Guardia Airport. Both were college graduates. Both pitched in where needed for mother's business. Vi bought, wrote the newsletter, worked with the customers, spoke before groups and exhibited at collector shows.

Husband Robert had his own full-time business in nearby Melville, Long Island . . . as an insurance agent for Equitable Life. For his business he had studied some law, taxation, investments and annuities. For Vi's business, Bob packed each order for next day shipment. He handled all advertising, made out the income tax returns and advised on buying. "The pay was rotten but working conditions were good."

Bob liked working for his wife. Bob's business was flexible. He also worked 10 to 15 hours a week for Vi. "I could always take off for a show." The family room at 8 Burrwood Court, East Northport, NY was the showroom. "We had special shelving and lighting to set off our plates, figurines and bells. We got all the leading limited editions; it all made a beautiful room. People were surprised and delighted when they came.

"We started buying from distributors. Then we bought from manufacturers. We started mail order with little ads. We went up to half columns, then quarter page and full page and double page ads. Each ad paid for itself.

"There were retail dealers in collector plates who were in trouble, behind in bills or with credit cut off. But we kept things safe. We didn't worry. We were liquid at all times. It was the dealers with stores, employees and overhead who had problems. We were careful in buying. We first bought in a small way and paid cash. Then when we got credit we paid fast. We sold the middle class who were looking for beauty. Collector plates are art forms. We sold limited editions that would come up in value. The business kept growing. The key was honesty."

Vi and the entire family found a new life, and then a fine retirement bonus.

Collector media are very effective. Linn's Weekly (for stamp collectors) carries more mail order ads, about 22,000 a year, than any other publication. Coin World is not far behind. Then comes Antique Trader. But other collector tabloids and magazines unknown to Standard Rate and Data are potent in their fields. There's the Plate Collector Magazine, Antique Toy World and Baseball Hobby News (baseball cards) . . . Depression Glass Daze and Coin Slot Magazine . . . The Antique Bookman's Weekly and The American Postcard Journal.

There's a tab or mag . . . or several . . . for almost any collectible field. Each provides rifle shot segmentation for collector-dealer ads. Just one publication can build surprisingly substantial mail order collector-dealer business.

By the time Dave Rago was 25 he did $400,000 annually in sales—much of it directly and indirectly from mail order.

He's an authority in antique art pottery, is spending his time and his money on it, and is making money from it. To do the entire business takes one room in his house. He's been an antique trader for only 8 years.

It all started from cleaning out cellars while working his way through college, working at a supermarket and acting as a finder for his father who was collecting Roseville pottery. And to combine doing all this took only about 100 hours a week. An all night flea market made it possible.

"The only way to start a business in my situation . . . the only way to perpetuate it . . . was to work as and when others wouldn't. But it was only a sprint. Looking back and judged against my entire life, it was for a very short time. It didn't hurt me. It got me what I wanted. I don't need to put in those hours anymore. My health is good. I play a lot of tennis. Life is good and I don't work that hard now and plan never to again."

Dave was a student in Trenton Day College but didn't graduate. To get through college he worked in a supermarket. "I hated the job I had but it started me off. In college, I was a full-time student, 25 hours. The supermarket job was a normal 37 hour week. Then I also began to clean out cellars."

Whenever Dave found someone with a crowded attic, cellar or garage, he offered to clean it out, take anything saleable to the all night Englishtown Flea Market and sell it for a one-third of the proceeds commission. Englishtown got him into his present business. Some days, Dave had a busy schedule. Some were 24-hour days.

"Early in the morning, I would clean out an attic and load a truck. I'd attend classes from 9 AM until 2 PM and then work in the supermarket from 3 PM to 11 PM. Then I'd drive the truck to Englishtown. It would be bright as day with floodlights at 1 AM when I arrived. I'd set up the booth in time to start selling at 2:30 AM, man the booth all night until 9 or 10 AM, and then go home for a little sleep."

Dave found he could do a little better than that. By arriving a half hour earlier and setting up in half the time, he could visit other booths for an hour between arrival and set up. Dave noticed that here and there in booths there were pieces of Roseville pottery of the type his father was collecting. He quickly made a deal. On anything he found that his father liked, he could make a dealer's profit, if he bought it at his risk.

"From cellars and attics, I was getting old radios, beat up chairs, whatever. My gross sales for a night might be $125 to $150. I'd make $40 to $50 for my time, gas and truck wear and tear. And I made a little buying pottery to sell to my dad. But it gave me a little, very little, spending money. Then I discovered mail order."

Dave's first ad ran in the Antique Trader and featured 10 pieces of antique pottery. It was 6 inches, cost $60 and was instantly successful. Ever since, Dave has run the same size ad featuring about the same number of items, every month. It now costs $100 a month. "I didn't have much expertise then except what I had learned buying for my father. But I began to swap services for expertise. I'd do anything to help anybody who in return could teach me about antique American art pottery."

Meanwhile, Dave's ads kept pulling. Now he began to exhibit at Englishtown pottery items he bought, and then to exhibit at other flea markets and antique shows. Running the first ad was the big step. Gradually, Dave began to specialize more and more. "My field was and is American antique pottery from 1880 to 1920."

Dave's strategy was to work closely with customers who need to keep coming back. These were usually dealers. To work with them he had to learn their needs, what they bought and to work on a small profit. "I might buy for $100 and sell for $115 as a broker. I'd have the average item sold almost before I bought it. And if I didn't sell it, I'd take an immediate loss to do so."

Today, the monthly ads and antique shows Dave attends seven times a year continue to bring Dave's first time customers and inquiries. "I run ads not to sell pieces but to get names." Dave concentrates on inventory turnover. "I prefer to sell for 20% less than others, make a smaller profit—and go back and buy more."

"For a big collector, time may be too valuable to search out personally each need. He or she may be too busy. Normally, a big collector doesn't want to deal with me. I'll sell the dealer who sells him. When an item comes along that fits an avid collector, I may get it and sell it to a dealer who sells it to the collector. There may be a chain of 3 or 4 people selling and reselling it. The key is knowing and scouting needs and then working with a small profit

for quick turnover. This keeps me constantly on the telephone. My telephone bill is $500 a month."

Dave has no employees. Dave does it all. Each week he types or handwrites forty to fifty letters. "I type 70 words a minute on a manual typewriter and 85 on an electric, with maybe 6 or 7 errors before correction." Dave has a little over 500 customers. "But I do 90% of my business with 20 to 25 people." Dave sells "an average of $10,000 or so" to each. But, of these, Dave deals mostly with the top ten who give Dave about half his business. "I prefer to deal with people who know what they're doing. I'm constantly developing those who do."

Each Antique Trader ad solicits sellers as well as buyers. Dave runs classified ads in other antique publications just to attract sellers. From these, Dave gets many calls offering to sell. From these he developed 10 to 15 sources for most of his needs. Volume selling means volume buying, which helps get consideration when Dave buys. "The more you buy from a source, the more you will get in the future."

Dave's constant mail order ads generate a continued stream of new sellers and new buyers with new wants. Dave works with a small group of volume dealers to sell to and another to buy from, marries buyers and sellers at modest but constant profit to himself, and does it all himself . . . with one typewriter, one telephone and in one room of his house.

Dave has to subtract from modest gross profits a variety of costs. His annual ad bill is small, about $1,500—but the telephone bill is $6,000. "I spend almost $20,000 on travel . . . to shows, to close sales and to buy." Carrying inventory means bank loans and interest. "I usually carry about $50,000 of inventory.

"For all this work, my accountant figures I'm making about $28,000. It's not a bonanza, but it's sound. A lot of my friends aren't willing to work this hard and this carefully and for such modest profits. In my teens, I was forced to make a choice between their way and the way I now live. My grandfather influenced me a lot. He's 84 now, retired and mainly works in his garden. But he rented his place to us and I got to know him.

"At some point, I understood what I had to do. I had to put all my spare time and energy into this business. While I was working at the supermarket and moonlighting, I had to put in 50 to 60 hours a week after hours. That included travel and phone. After I quit the job for a while I had to put 100 hours a week into the business, for very little return. It was the only way to guarantee my future. From here on in, I'll work less and make more. I'm already easing up. By the time I'm 30, I'll cut down to 25 or 30 hours a week. I've worked harder when younger to take it easy later."

Dave expects his business to grow a good deal, to become more profitable per dollar and still to require no employees. "I'll use the same techniques for bigger transactions." Right now, Dave is swapping services to get know-how in other fields as well as pottery.

"I'm interested in acquiring knowledge about oriental rugs, silver, mission furniture, and Lenox china." Dave hopes that this will sharply increase his profit per minute of negotiating time. He feels strength in his youth and flexibility. If recession or depression comes, he plans to switch to whatever activities necessary. "But I enjoy art and hope to stay with it.

"My advice for those starting out is to endure short-term misery for long-term leisure. Most want to rise to the top immediately. That becomes more likely with a solid foundation. This isn't novel but it works.

"What mistakes did I make? I made basic errors in protocol and judgment, for starters. I didn't always define the parameters and understand how to work within them. Most of those with whom I deal understand sincerity and honesty when it is in front of them. In developing long-term relationships, these two traits are the most enduring. Many older businessmen with whom I deal see themselves in me and are generous in giving me sound, tested advice. Others sometimes react negatively out of dissatisfaction with their own level of success. It doesn't take long to see through them, though.

"I like mail order. It makes all this possible. The pressure is past now. I'm spending more time with my wife, Elaine, and our children. And for the rest of our lives, I can do this more and more."

Note: Dave Rago is located at P.O. Box 3592, Station E, Trenton, NJ 08629; phone (609) 585-2546.

Why is collecting so big: It's nostalgia. It's social activities. It's shared pleasures. You don't need physical dexterity or enormous time. It's the chance to become expert and looked up to fairly fast. It's a hedge against inflation.

For 19 years Chinese ceramics and rare books have gone up in value more than gold . . . stamps and coins more than crude oil . . . and defunct stock certificates and non-legal tender money more than stocks and bonds.

Careful mail order collector-dealers have done well. But it can be risky. In collectibles, as in all mail order, those who know the least risk the most. Combining collectible misjudgment with mail order misinformation can be a disaster.

Collector-investors may fall in love with what they wrongly invest in. A price guide, a tab or mag, a few dealers can create a false market with reports of overhigh sales that can't be duplicated. Too many collectors can become dealers . . . changing collecting into get-rich-quick speculation, almost like a chain letter or a pyramid plan. A thin market can collapse.

From Amsterdam, Holland: "WILD SPECULATION IN TULIPS! SINGLE BULB SELLS FOR $3,000! Dutch Government forced to Intervene". It happened in the 17th century . . . a wild boom and terrible crash. Dumas wrote a book about it, "The Black Tulip". Before getting too enthused about most odd-ball collectibles look in the dictionary . . . for the word "TULIPOMANIA". It says it all.

Experts in investment, collectibles and mail order are concerned about the fads and fancies of collectibles. "Collectibles have had a heyday which I believe is coming to an end."—Dawne Schultz, investment advisor.

What is the future for collectibles? Many experts feel that today's tangible assets are now over-valued compared with stocks and bonds. Many agree that when deflation comes the collectible investor will depart. Collectibles might seem wild, eccentric fancies in a stark depression period.

Art for the rich had its heyday between the 1850's and the 1920's. Will the 1970's go down as the high for other collectibles? In mass media, mail order collectibles may already have passed their peak.

Some limited edition offers have been too unlimited. Some private mints are in trouble. Some are diversifying . . . out of collectibles.

Long before, the tiny antennae of the small were flashing caution signls. It is the little people in collectibles who are finding the future . . . what to get out of . . . when to hunker down and hang on in . . . and where collectibles will be bigger than ever.

Collectibles range from the sublime to the ridiculous . . . from the probably conservative investment to the possibly treacherous speculation. Some collectibles seem so sound they might go on forever. The adhesive postage stamp is 150 years old.

Collecting started almost as soon as printing them . . . and has gone on ever since.

Almost every stamp company was started by a mail order collector dealer. Henry Harris was 14 when he started . . . with a free classified ad in The Washington Post, offered to any teenage business man. The Harris Stamp Company is now the world's largest and a General Mills subsidiary. Its story is told elsewhere is this book.

Let's examine another sound collectible field and business. All their married life Jo-Ann and Richard Castén have shared a hobby, collecting antique maps.

Jo-Ann has been a teacher and a real estate broker. Richard is a nuclear physicist. When they lived in Denmark, where Richard had a laboratory job, Jo-Ann had ample time for their hobby. There were wonderful buys in antique maps, limited only by savings and where to put the maps.

Richard suggested they sell some. To do so they tested an inch mail order ad asking for inquiries. Jo-Ann then mailed typewritten descriptions and photographs. First orders and checks came back.

Now their hobby could be more fun. Now they could buy more maps . . . while travelling at business expense. They could gradually buy older, more desirable, more expensive maps. With no children, it was a wonderful way to spend week-ends together.

Two years later Richard began work at a Long Island scientific laboratory, and they moved to Wading River, Long Island. They became mail order collector dealers, concentrating in scholarly fields . . . from home (516-929-6820) . . . and joined The Antiquarian Booksellers Association of America, Inc. They won a loyal clientele. They began to sell a good deal to universities and libraries. Earnings from their hobby started to exceed Richard's salary. Then their business grew more dramatically. By 1981 they did $500,000 yearly.

But their first love is collecting. "Being in love with what we sell has advantages. We know what we're doing. It has limitations. We won't break-up an atlas that is whole or that we can repair . . . for whatever profit. And cutting out each map and selling it separately can be lucrative.

"We purchase for immediate resale, to augment our stock and for our collection. If anyone wants a map we bought a week ago, we'll usually sell it . . . and at a smaller mark-up. But we really want to keep each . . . at least for a while. We have a rotating collection we could not otherwise afford.

"As capital generates we collect more for ourselves. It's almost immaterial whether we sell any single map or not. The value of our maps has steadily gone up faster than inflation."

There are no employees. Jo-Ann works about half of each weekday on their business. The business leaves leisure time for Jo-Ann and doesn't interfere with Richard's lab work. They still devote most weekends, some evening time and working vacations to their business.

The Castens have mastered their trade. They've learned what to buy and where, how much to pay, what an item can be sold for and where to advertise. They once ran an inch ad twice in the Wall Street Journal. It proved too general with lots of inquiries, but few closures.

Initially they built much of their business on "The Antique Bookman's Weekly" in the U.S. and "The Map Collector Magazine" in England. Four times a year, they ran a quarter page in each for $85 and $90 each for an insertion. They have also run in "Antiques Journal" in the U.S. Now they run mainly in The Map Collector.

They have a more expensive catalog now. It's typographer

set, professionally written, with a handsome logo and good photos. Jo-Ann publishes the catalog, wraps, packages, quotes, and is the chief buyer. "I'm not good at numbers, accounts and selling but Richard's abilities complement mine."

It's a business both like. "We enjoy the time we devote to this business . . . maybe more than the money. We like the travel. Richard just visited nine countries in eight days, on a working vacation. We go to Europe regularly."

The Castens are making more buying trips as the business grows and buying becomes more important. The Castens offer to buy as well as sell in each ad and at each show exhibited. On the way to a show or back they may stop off to buy or sell. "We like the flexibility of mail order. In teaching I had regular hours. In real estate I was away from my husband on weekends. But our business is anytime."

Most map collectors with little to spend start with mid or late 19th century and then go into the 18th century. Still more desirable are the 17th and 16th centuries. The Casten maps date from the late 1400's to about 1800.

• "The higher the quality and price the smaller the margin." But historically, maps have gone up overall. The technology of preserving and restoring old maps is dramatically improved. Institutions will continue to buy old maps in bad times and good. Prices can drop and probably come back."

The percentage of ad cost to sales keeps getting lower. Total magazine cost is now under 1% of sales. More cost is the catalog. Most is in travel and shows. More business each year comes from repeats, referrals and bigger customers. "They trust us. Some give us lists of what they want. We look for them. We specialize in maps of America, the World, the Holy Land and the Far East. The business keeps making more profit. We don't see it. The money goes into buying and collecting."

The Castens feel that the business is sound, that the inventory is a sound, long-term investment, and they are confident about the future.

For many a collector his or her hobby is getting expensive. Many long for a quieter day. Investors and giants may leave, but a hard core of collectors will remain.

The big can cash in on collectibles (and also overstay). . . in a big way. Unlike the stock market it is the small who get in first . . . who sense first it's time to get out . . . who find the times, areas, nooks and crannies where they can outcompete the big. The number of advertisers and subscribers to Antique Trader hit highs several years ago, dropped and then began growing again.

Frank Barning, publisher of The Baseball Hobby News, points to baseball cards he bought for pennies that are now worth quarters. He is holding them until they're worth dollars. He's not looking for the rare baseball card that last sold for $4800.

This may be the future of mail order collectibles . . . closer to earth. Opportunities may be smaller and more specialized, yet continue. As long as little people can start with baseball cards for pennies, move into stamps and coins and on up into antiques, collectibles will prosper.

There is safety in know-how. Some do have a flair for finding collectibles that keep going up in value. Others acquire the ability . . . chiefly by study and familiarity. Collector and mail order know-how can create profits from the first tiny ads, then multiply them.

With expertise it's possible to buy some, keep some and sell some . . . often from classified ads. Some, for surprising profits, project to small and then larger display ads, then pages and then several in an issue. More often it's possible to find a safe, profitable niche for a small, steady income.

Collectibles risky for some can be surprisingly safe for others who know when to get out . . . and often for the small versus the big. As for depression far more experts still predict stagflation. And in stagflation things may still do better than money and things collected better than other things.

There are determined collectors in many fields. Many a collector would bet on his or her expertise in collectibles more than in other investments. Many collectibles have done well over long periods. In the future in collectibles, as in the past, the little people may well lead . . . and the Fortune 500 follow. And meanwhile, more and more mail order collector-dealers are making more and more money.

Chapter 8
Magazine Mail Order's Happy Brain

The numbers man who has looked into the innards of more magazines than any consultant.

Jim Kobak is a specialist in bottom line profit improvement for magazines. He assists at births. Biggest publishers come to him for his analysis of the chances of a new publication being considered. Others come with only an idea for a magazine seeking help to launch it. He won't gamble his money. He will his time, if convinced survival and success chances justify it. When he does, knowledgeable backers get interested in risking their money.

He is a reorganizer of businesses, particularly magazines. He's a marriage broker for magazines, assisting in mergers and acquisitions. The firm he was with for many years were tax experts and helped draft the tax laws that are most favorable to magazine publishers.

Overwhelmingly, most of the magazines he helps and guides are dependent on mail order results for life, itself. And Jim Kobak is one of the shrewdest analysts in the world of mail order and direct marketing's latest methods available to magazines.

He's a physically strong man, the original healthy mind in a healthy body . . . a high IQ combined with high vitality. He has a morning metabolism and an afternoon one, and an evening one. He gets up at five a.m. and bounces through the day. He travels world-wide wherever publishers need his magazine doctor skills. He writes a stream of articles, conducts seminars, lectures and trains middle management of clients to develop to the top and do without him.

He's not shy and does not lack confidence. He often shocks the tradional conservatives he deals with. It's an opening gambit he prefers. He cheerfully admits that anyone can get almost free much of the advice he sells simply by reading reprints of his articles or listening to tapes of his talks . . . as he constantly recommends the same principles, and does for readers of this book.

He was born to success. Brains, motivation and drive insured it. His father, Ed Kobak, was vice president of McGraw-Hill, NBC and the ABC Radio Network when it was part of NBC. Later, Ed Kobak was head of the largest radio network, Mutual Broadcasting System. He has been named to the Advertising Hall of Fame.

Jim went to The Hill School in Pennsylvania. He managed the football team. He was editor of the school paper and of the year book. He went on to Harvard. "I liked bridge, beer and girls." To get extra money, he wrote for the Boston Herald-Traveler; he was paid by the inch and earned more than a salary. He graduated with a liberal arts degree in 1942 and went into the Army.

In Artillery School, the outer limit of IQ measured was 160. He hit the top, finishing the achievement tests in half the time allotted. He broke the record in the school by making no mistake in any quiz written or oral given every day for eight weeks. "I enjoy winning."

He got out of the Army in 1946, found he had a wife and two children. He had no idea what to do. J. K. Lasser was a friend of his father's and suggested: "You should come to work for me in the day and take accounting at night." Jim did.

He started in the checking department. "I checked the numbers in everything typed, before and after typing. It was the best training I could possibly get." Soon he progressed from it. In 1946, he started taking accounting at night. In 1949, he graduated. With three years experience at J. K. Lasser he was eligible to take the CPA examination, did so and passed in late 1949.

As a trainee, Jim went on to the tax department. He compiled statistics for publishers. He did auditing, particularly of magazine and book publishing. That became his specialty.

J. K. Lasser & Company found that income taxes for publishers were being figured differently by different tax examiners.

"About 1950, some of the partners went down to Washington and got provisions into tax law favorable to publishers. To do so required that Congress pass a new law. It pertained to subscription income. Some publishers took it into income at once, some over the life of the subscription as it was paid. It was the same with expenses. Some did so immediately. Some deferred them. They got two provisions into law making it legal to do it either way for tax purposes even if for accounting purposes the alternate choice was made."

This proved very attractive to public companies. They could show immediate income and profits and deferred expenses for financial statements, greatly improving the impression made on stockholders. They could show low or no earnings for the immediate present to the IRS. It was the best of two worlds. "They could spread income over the subscription term. They could write off expenses at once. They could defer taxes yet, as public companies, they could show immediate income. It made possible an attractive tax shelter while showing the public attractive earnings."

For publishing companies, it had a lot to do with making possible the go-go years to come in the sixties. And the accounting firm that understood it best was J. K. Lasser & Company.

There were plenty of publishers interested in becoming clients. Jim Kobak became sought after and he sought after new business. "Enough clients were handled badly and left that I got into internal management." The problem was to grow in staff and services as clients grew; to become more effective in handling each client rather than less; to maximize growth and efficiency and profit for J. K. Lasser & Company. And the time was ripe for Lasser to grow.

The J. K. Lasser Tax Book had been published by Simon & Schuster. It was introduced by mail order with instant success. It was then distributed in outlets everywhere and new editions were brought out yearly. Probably, of all accountants in the world, the name J. K. Lasser was best known. Yet the firm was small compared with giant accounting firms. It had only one office. They had many. It was in the U.S. only. They were often international. Jim Kobak set out to remedy that situation.

At first he got interested in internal growth. Because of the book, inquiries came in from all kinds of potential clients. Almost any prospective client had heard of J. K. Lasser. The desire to avoid overpaying taxes was universal. Lasser's specialty of tax accounting for magazines was attractive to largest publishers. And once they worked with magazine publishers, they got into every aspect of their business including profitable acquisitions of subscribers by mail order.

It was inevitable that Jim Kobak would get interested in mail order and advertising as it related to magazine publishing. It was mail order that made the J. K. Lasser Tax Book known and the future growth of the J. K. Lasser accounting firm far more possible.

J. K. Lasser & Company worked with McGraw-Hill, among others. They also worked with all the associations in the field, then including Associated Business Publications, National Business Publications, Magazine Publishers Association, Agricultural Publishers Association, American Book Publishers Association and others. Angelo Venezian was vice president in charge of circulation of McGraw-Hill and became Chairman of the Board of the Direct Mail/Marketing Association. He asked Jim first to develop for the DMMA certain statistics of advertising expenditures. From these figures estimates were made of the direct marketing advertising expenditures and sales from it by business firms.

Next, Jim was assigned the job by the DMMA of drawing up a plan to convert the DMMA from a professional association to a trade association, a project favored by Venezian and others. The plan switched from individual to company memberships. Membership had been about $35. They were put on a sliding scale ranging from modest charges for small firms going to thousands of dollars for big ones including contributions for various purposes.

The result catapulted the DMMA over a few years from a dozen or so people to over seventy. The operating budget went from several hundred thousand dollars to over six million dollars. The services delivered jumped to make membership more and more of a bargain. "Everyone had a little trepidation but Bob DeLay was superb and it all worked out."

Meanwhile, Jim had a plan for another kind of growth for J. K. Lasser & Company, by merger. He had a simple idea. Accounting was growing and becoming more complex. American business was becoming more and more international. Publishers all over the world were growing. Accounting problems and business management problems all over had many similarities. International accounting firms were growing. Jim and J. K. Lasser & Company moved into the race.

"We expanded to forty offices in the U.S. and in thirty-nine other countries. This was the result of sixty to seventy mergers. I ran a merger school. I developed a regular pattern. I'd phone, explain, meet, persuade other accounting firms to join us. Finally, I was doing it by push-button. The routine was almost by rote.

"By now, I was international administrative partner and overall boss. I had been at J. K. Lasser & Company for twenty-five years. Somehow it was all the same old thing, committee meetings, business, growth and more and more people. I was tired of it. I decided to do the very opposite of what I was doing.

"I resigned from J. K. Lasser & Company in 1971 and started a cottage industry with two partners. But after a few years, they left. I had a simple plan. I'd give the world, anybody and everybody, the benefit of what I knew—but without an organization.

"My first assignment was to reorganize Young & Rubicam for Ed Ney, Y&R president. Y&R had been one of the largest advertising agencies in the world but for a few years had not been doing anywhere nearly as well. Ed Ney wanted help in evaluating the problems and correcting them. It took two years spending about a quarter of my time on it. It all worked out. Now Young & Rubicam is the number one advertising agency, world-wide."

Over the years Jim became interested far more deeply than ever before in launches of new magazines. He examined each magazine before birth. He was not interested in the pocketbook of the publisher. Instead, he asked: Did it have a reason for being? Should it exist? If not, however wealthy the publisher, he would recommend against it. If it did, if the would-be publisher did not have a penny, he'd consider it a project worth considering. The criteria were largely Jim's based on all the experience he had working with magazines for over twenty-five years.

"I've roughly counted the number of magazines I've investigated before birth. Probably two hundred should have been launched. Of these, about 100 (50%) didn't have the money and were unable to raise it. The average publisher had trouble communicating with investors who had money. Yet, of those magazines which did raise money, about 90% succeeded in their mail order subscription tests. And most magazines which survived the tests succeeded thereafter."

Jim Kobak set about to systematize magazine launches. He wanted to avoid bringing out new magazines which had little chance and to test those with a real chance. He wanted to investigate more thoroughly and scientifically a magazine's chances before launching. If chances looked poor, he wanted to investigate if any changes editorially or in marketing plans would give it a chance.

Most magazines Jim works with are very dependent on subscriptions for circulation. The problem is to develop and test successfully a mail order subscription offer.

Once a launch got underway, an evergrowing size of the dollar commitment was required. Therefore, Jim made more and more efforts to determine from the start whether to test at all. Jim Kobak has been a pioneer in pre-test research which is now becoming far more accepted as sound procedure in mail order far beyond magazine publishing. Jim's first step is to require that the magazine dream be reduced to more reality. This means the selection of a possible editor, art director, possible staff and contributors. The more concrete it is, the better. He demands that articles be written and layouts made. For real consideration, he requires the printing of a pilot issue complete with editorial and advertising. However expensive, all this costs far less than actual publishing. With the pilot, research can begin. The idea is to show the issue to the kind of people it is intended for and to get reactions. Sometimes, it's shown to other kinds of people who unexpectedly might like it.

"We use different research methods but focus group studies have been best. I make the entrepreneur do all the work. Focus groups are nothing new. They started twenty years ago.

"It's possible to get very excited about projects. And I have been night and day, year after year. The most important problem and a very hard one is to determine if the entrepreneur is sound. Some are nuts. I find I must work closely with each, find out what each is planning at each step and determine if it's wise. A good plan is not enough. If I turn my back, the entrepreneur may change something. He may take a foolish, wild chance. That can kill the project."

Folio magazine, edited for publishers, has run a series of articles by Jim Kobak in which he describes his methods thoroughly. "It's all been written down there. It's available for anyone to read. But of those who pay me fees, very few have taken the articles and read them carefully. Often, they pay me to say the same things they could have read for nothing."

Jim Kobak found that ideas for magazines that had best chances often came from those who had no money. One thing seemed obvious to him. "They couldn't waste money on advice. They needed any cash they could raise for that first mail order test—or to eat.

"Instead, I decided to take a piece of the company.

Originally, I'd work with an entrepreneur on a launch for a $5,000 fee (sometimes waited for) and 2% of the company. Now I do it for $7,500 plus 3% of the company.

"I've been in on the launches of Psychology Today, New York, Book Digest, Firehouse, Pacific Fishing and many others. I've done a lot of newsletters, such as Hazardous Materials. I'm not particularly interested in publishing my own magazine or newsletter. I don't want to operate. I've had that. I prefer to juggle 300 projects at a time. It's very exciting.

"I'm a morning person. I'm up at 5 AM until 10 PM. My wife, Hope, is a partner. She spends a quarter of her time working. She's superior to me at editorial and getting people to focus on a subject. She's been doing this for six years. The children are grown. Hope went to Syracuse University School of Journalism. She's been an editor at Appleton-Century. She has written one novel, one essay, one poem, one screenplay, one broadway play, but none have been published.

"We have had three sons. One is a trial lawyer and has three children. One was in the VISTA program, got cancer at 22 and died at 25. Losing him was one reason I left Lasser. He finished his education at Harvard, got married and had one child, Zeke, after the cancer started. Our third son is Tommy. He's with Kobak Business Models.

"About Kobak Business Models—I had always made up projections, proforma profit and loss statements, advance guestimates in great detail on 14 column spreadsheets, or whatever. It was time-consuming and relatively inaccurate.

"I hired a genius programmer, David Webber, to do what I had been doing by hand, by computer. He did. It worked for clients. We decided to see if we could sell it to the magazine industry. I own half and David and Mary Staples, David's wife, own the other half. That's Kobak Business Models.

"David and Mary operate it. Mary is great at selling. She learned at IBM. They now do about four million dollars a year

and are growing like mad. They have as clients magazines, book clubs and continuity programs. They have big and little clients on time-sharing programs all over the world. In addition to the model are programs for advertising analysis, list and media selection, for long-term planning, for accounting, for handling single copy sales.

"And new programs are being developed all the time. We started with magazines and have been kept so busy that selling in other parts of the direct response business has been postponed although Grolier and Rodale Press use models of continuity programs and book clubs.

"A few direct marketers are scientific and do a great deal to become more so. Most are in the dark ages. It's not that difficult to be scientific. But most business men delude themselves. They think they are scientific when they are not."

Jim Kobak has looked at the bottom line of more businesses than anyone I've met. He has strong opinions. "Most publishing businesses should be cottage industries. They never should be in a big building. This automatically results in the business being run like an empire. Instead, it should be broken down into little groups. A big central location leads to a big central bureaucracy, a big circulation department, a big editorial department, etc. I am against functional breakdowns into big departments which then have lives of their own which become more important than the magazines themselves.

"The best way to run a magazine is with editorial, circulation, advertising, production and accounting in one group. Many big companies do it exactly the opposite. They have a self-destruct button built in. They build personnel far beyond needs. Every business has an optimum size. An accounting office needs thirty to fifty people. You need somewhat more for an advertising agency. But some big businesses build and centralize beyond optimum levels.

"I reorganized Playboy when it was in trouble. It had one hundred and seventy-nine people in editorial. I asked Hefner how many editorial people would be needed to turn out the same magazine if he were starting it from scratch all over again. He told me about forty would easily do it. We didn't get down to forty. We did get down to seventy and improved the magazine editorially.

"Owning more magazines does give financial strength, particularly because it provides a mix of life cycles. Each business, each magazine has a birth, life and death. But the overall publisher can keep growing and succeeding by recognizing the growth patterns of each magazine and providing replacements and additions so that as one fades, another takes its place and still others start for further growth. A publishing company has to keep starting and buying magazines to keep growing soundly, overall.

"The magazine publishing business has never been better. Magazines don't exist for themselves, but are the result of peoples' interests. There is now more education, more real affluence, more new technology, more travel, people interested in more fields.

"TV did not really hurt magazines. Each new medium helps because it arouses new interests. All the new electronic publishing will come much slower than expected. People's habits don't change that fast. It's a struggle to get people to use a microfiche. People want a book or magazine or newspaper in their hands.

"My work goes beyond numbers. The Young & Rubicam reorganization was a problem of management and spirit, how to change the morale, give confidence, provide motivation. It was so in Playboy.

"A lot of people have invested in magazines. The problem is that they often invest for the wrong reasons. They fall in love with the project. It's often very difficult to raise money for some magazines that deserve it and provide the safest bet for investors. It's often easy to raise money for magazines that have far less chance of success.

"You never know who is particularly suited to becoming an investor in a specific magazine. We use computer modeling to prepare forecasts of what alternate plans of mail order promotion might require, different cash flows, when the turn might come and no further investment be needed, potential profits. Investors feel safer if it is spelled out. I put out a lot of data for them. It does give a sense of security. To raise the money usually takes nine months to a year.

"Newsletters can often be smaller and safer investments. A newsletter can be launched for fifty thousand dollars. Look magazine, to have been brought back correctly, would have needed twenty million dollars. The normal special interest magazine requires two million or three million dollars to launch. A city magazine may take two hundred thousand to a million dollars. A business trade magazine or newsletter is not as exciting or as expensive to start. The computer determines the ballpark figures needed. We just feed in the data. It adds and subtracts.

"I do a lot of things. I reorganize companies, mostly magazines. I develop acquisition programs. I consult all over the world. I'll spend two days to ten days with a client. I don't care if it's Little Rock or Stockholm. I also, for clients, buy and sell. I negotiate, I value properties about twice a week. I've probably seen 2,000 magazines intimately.

"I've had a lot of fun with Rodale Press. They just started in the book business in a sizeable way around 1972 or 1973. Now they have a twenty-five million dollar book business, built from mail order, soundly done. Bob Rodale is an excellent business man. I deal with him and Marshall Ackerman and Bob Teufel and others. They started with a philosophy. They are believers. You may not agree with all they do and say. But they have a mission and they are good at it. Two weeks ago, I ran a retreat where I explained to thirty second-level managers of Rodale a breakdown of company operations, mistakes and right steps, profits and losses of departments, a detailed breakdown most companies only give to top managers. The experience was very enlightening.

"I do seminars of one or two days each ten times a year. I cover buying, selling and merging of magazines mostly for Folio. I've lectured at the Radcliffe School of Publishing. I've started quite a few people in publishing, kept up with their careers and I'm still friends with them.

"What suggestion do I have for beginners? Go into an area where you can find out everything. In magazines, most people are specialists. Start out in financial first, circulation second. Get into a medium-size company. It's best to go with a new magazine, great for a kid.

"What should a would-be magazine publisher read? Everything that Folio puts out is excellent. There is nothing to read in the way of a book. There is no book yet on accounting for magazine publishers. I'd like to get around to writing one.

"We don't just work. I play golf and do body surfing—no flippers. We have an apartment in New York and a home in Connecticut. We have a house in St. Croix and go to Bermuda. We travel all over. We're both very sociable. I don't read much. I don't plan on retirement. I'll just keep on advising, as long as it's this much fun.

Chapter 9
Ruby Reds From Alamo, Texas

How a grapefruit farmer made it big starting by writing to two hundred people.

Forty-five percent of the envelope . . . front and back . . . is in red. Fifty-five percent is in contrasting white. The straight, vertical dividing line starts just to the left of the window. A stylized crown is half in each section. Three words in reverse jump out of the red section: ROYAL RUBY REDS.

On the back of the envelope is another crown, half in white and half in red. In script, reversed against the white and red, are the words: from Frank Lewis - - - Alamo, Texas 78516. To find out what it all means, just open the envelope.

Inside, the stationery is white. On top, there is a logotype of a red half grapefruit. It is against two larger and three smaller outlined grapefruit. All are in color, sitting on a grapefruit leaf. The name, Frank Lewis, is in large red script. Phone and post office box numbers are in very small type. The words "Alamo, Texas" are in red, followed by the zip, small and black. Then come four words in red: ROYAL RUBY RED GRAPEFRUIT.

Frank's four-page letter to you is in black typewriter type. In his opening words, he tells you of the "miracle" grapefruit he's sending you, in time for Christmas and the holidays.

It seems delicious, enough to read on, at least for the next two deeply indented paragraphs. The first says a package of 16 to 20 grapefruit . . . now tree-ripening . . . is coming prepaid. The second states how rare, how sweet and how big each is.

"But wait a minute" starts the next two-line paragraph and tempts you into the "development" story . . . starting in the next paragraph a story that seems out of the Reader's Digest. The story of the "miracle" . . . nature's accident that produced the first strange fruit . . . brilliant ruby red goes on.

Your appetite for the grapefruit is being whetted just as your interest in reading more . . . of the surprise of the good doctor who stumbled on it . . . and of its perfect, juicy and luscious flavor . . . not sour like other grapefruit . . . but naturally sweet without sugar. And this in only the first page.

The story tells of the budding, the grafting of grove after grove of this fruit not one in a thousand has tasted. It goes on to the royal Ruby Reds so rare that only 4% to 5% of the crop qualify. Frank tells how "I check for 'natural sugar', low acid balance and high juice content" . . . even that the fruit is "plump and meaty" and the skin thin. The copy is personal and folksy.

As he tells of the "picking ring" . . . "each of us" uses to screen out too small grapefruit, you can just picture Frank out there harvesting in the grove . . . carefully inspecting . . . sizing . . . grading even for beauty . . . rejecting occasional "wind-scarred" fruit or those with a "bulge" on the stem. He tells you just how he does it. So far, for over two pages there's been not a mention of cost.

But now for the "turn". When the Ruby Reds come, just cool four in your refrigerator, cut them in half and have the family sample. The offer is "you decide" . . . keep the fruit and join Frank's Winter Fruit Club, or return at Frank's expense. Pay nothing now. Be billed or charged via your American Express credit card. Each winter month, December through April, get 16 to 20 Royal Ruby Reds passed through Frank's tough tests. Pay only after each shipment. For a taste test on Frank send the postage-paid card today . . . as supplies are limited. The price is never mentioned.

The letter ends "Sincerely" with Frank's signature and a P.S. grateful customer quote stronger than anything Frank has said.

The order card is in color. A big open box of Royal Ruby Reds slants down like an arrow to the signature blank. It's all as American as apple pie . . . planned in Florida, written in Connecticut and mailed from Alamo, Texas by Frank to you. Frank is a farmer who has made it big in mail order as Frank Lewis, the grapefruit man from Alamo, Texas. And his name is Frank Schulz. He's a good man and very able.

"I never got very far in life. I was raised just a mile and a half away. My folks were citrus growers. During the early 1940's, it was so difficult it seemed impossible to sell grapefruit, and my Dad looked for some way out.

"My uncle was in an advertising agency in Dallas. It was Tracy, Locke and Dawson then. Now it's just Tracy-Locke. The agency had a list of two hundred to send Christmas presents to and one year sent our grapefruit. Later they gave us permission to write those two hundred people and ask if they'd like some more. We did. Some ordered and we were in the mail order business. The first printed brochure sent to those two hundred people was in 1945.

"Then Dad tried telephone books in Northern Texas towns and sent letters to a thousand or so such names. That didn't work. But Dad got some other firms to send our grapefruit as Christmas presents, in bigger quantities. He got permission to mail the list his brochure and kept mailing the first two hundred each year. Each year, Dad got some customers this way, and began to get some by recommendations. Gradually, it began to grow a bit faster.

"Then I was in high school; and, later, I went to college at the University of California, at Berkeley. I finished in 1954. Then, in 1955, I worked in Medford, Oregon, for a firm called Pinnacle Orchards. They were successful in selling apples by mail on a far bigger scale then we had sold grapefruit. Pinnacle mailed 100,000 names. Later they dropped most of their mail order sales. But, in that year, I learned a great deal about how to sell fruit by mail. The next year, I went into the air force.

"In 1958, I came back to my family. The business had grown some. It was shipping out about 4,000 to 5,000 packages for about $6 each, about $25,000 to $30,000 a year. Of course, I had ideas by then. After two years, my parents were ready for semi-retirement and gave me a free rein. That was in 1960.

"That year, I met the man who really showed us what mail order could be for us, M.P. (Merritt) Brown. He was always called M.P. Brown. He had founded, run for many years and sold out his own mail order business. When I met him he had become a mail order consultant.

"This was our turning point. For the first time, we were on a professional basis. M.P. Brown was a good friend to us. He taught me more about mail order than I learned anywhere else. He wrote the first outside copy we ever used. It succeeded better than anything we had ever done. He selected names. He knew about lists we didn't even realize existed. We knew very little about buyer lists. He knew a lot and picked winners for us. We went to mailing over a million names. Year after year, we tried to write a better letter and mailing piece and paid outside writers to try. But it took us thirteen years to come up with a better letter than M.P. Brown wrote for us.

"You need outside consultants, other viewpoints. I wanted to find the good ones. I wanted to meet other people who sold by mail. I joined the DMMA. That was sometime between 1965 and 1970. I went aggressively slowly. Every year, without exception, our volume is larger. It's pretty orderly and considered. If you're patient and test up-front, you learn and grow. We test each year in various ways. Across the years, we've found that what we test this year will usually hold for next year.

"When we started, we sold Christmas gifts. We shipped the first twenty days of December and then we were through. Now we sell on a personal basis, as a club. We send a shipment a month. We let them skip or cancel. Still, the club plan gives an even workload. Over the years inflation keeps raising the price. Dollars don't make much difference. We go up a dollar year. Now we have a $16.98 package. We always test each price increase.

"We have fresh fruit six months a year. Then, in summer, we ship tree-ripened juice. Then we go back to fresh. If they like our grapefruit, they want it every day. They convert to juice. We sell on a negative option. We tested that twelve to fifteen years ago. Now we don't go after gift business. We don't do two-step to get inquiries and send literature. We do pretty well on the direct deal.

"Seven years ago, Dick Benson became our consultant. He's fantastic, bottomline and good for us. Dick got us Bob Jones as a direct mail writer. Bob was the first person to write a letter and mailing piece that outpulled M.P. Brown's piece, thirteen years later. And, since then, nobody has written a direct mail piece for us that has outpulled Bob's. Even Bob couldn't when we tested new pieces he's written for us since.

"Some of Dick's best help has been to get us to not do things like nit-picking or testing trivia. He's sound. He's practical. We used to have a one-color letter and a four-color brochure. Four years ago, Dick suggested testing the letter without the brochure. We still kept a four-color reply card. It did better, and we've saved that four-color printing cost ever since. And, in space, we've never used color.

"Three years ago, I spent $2,000 to attend Joe Sugarman's seminar. It made a deep impression on me. On the way back, I wrote an ad to sell grapefruit paraphrasing the way Joe sells micro-electronic items. I got my $2,000 back almost as soon as we tested the ad. The first year, it did beautfiully. It was my first success in space. Joe made me pay out in space. The next year, it was marginal. The cost of space is up. I've tried testing three or four differend ads. Now, we're back to break-even or worse.

"We ask for no money in advance. We advertise in upscale lists and magazines. For new, first-time buyers, our credit loss

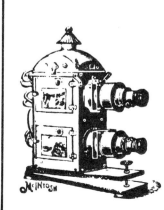

runs 3.8% to 4%. But for those who have paid for the first shipment, our credit loss on further shipments is one-half of one percent. In space for the Wall Street Journal, the New Yorker and the Christian Science Monitor . . . our credit loss is about the same as direct mail and almost as low for the New York Times magazine. We end up with an annual sale of $40 to $45. We have a big drop-off after the first month. Those that continue average twenty-eight months.

"Direct mail lists hold up better and longer for us than space. We test thirty or forty lists a year. Dick and I talk over the lists every year. The same list will stay consistent. Each year we keep 90% of last year's prospect lists, and each year we find new ones out of those tested for the first time.

"But some lists surprise us. One is Fingerhut. We take recent multi-buyers. This is a very big list. There's a little larger no-pay. When analyzing results, we're careful to charge no-pays to the list. The Fingerhut list still makes money. It's our fourth best list. A very steady list is Ambassador Leather. It's not among our greatest. But it's always in the re-run schedule. One I never expected to pay out was a list of contributors of more than five dollars to the D.A.V. It's a fantastically large list. It was a hit.

"Naturally, lists with a food connotation do best. And credit stands up best for lists of customers for upscale items. We usually stay away from big lists. We like personal lists. We try for hot-line names, recent buyers who have spent $15 or better. We mail outside names once a year in early fall, usually in September. We mail our own list eight or ten times a year.

"Our best offer is to try six of our grapefruit on the house and take five dollars off the shipment when paying for it. We've tested different ways of offering almost the same price—a higher price with postage and handling included versus a lower price with postage and handling extra. The lower price plus has pulled better in direct mail.

"We keep trying new methods. Our WATS phone to previous cancellations worked out. We've been developing it for five or six years. We convert by phone over one-third of all those who cancelled our service and they decided to continue. But phone has been no good to follow up cold mailings.

"The vast majority of my time is spent on long-term promotional planning. We have one man, Dick Hamilton, full-time on production and to get promotion into operation. Dick Benson and I make all list decisions and Dick works with outside writers and me. We have a good crew for everything else. We have several hundred at peak, during juice canning time. At the lowest period, we're down to thirty or forty people.

"We try to find other products, fresh fruit for customers own use, canned juices, grapefruit sections. These sometimes worked for our own lists but never succeeded for outside lists. For a while, we owned Mission Pack Oranges, in California. it didn't work for our list. One of our problems is there appears to be a limited universe for our business. We've gotten pretty close to what seems to be our potential and are kind of hung up there."

Frank has told me how many direct mail pieces he mails every year, how many shipments he makes, and how much dollar sales, but has asked me not to quote them. But Frank is a very successful and sound businessman and a very fine gentleman. To find out more about Royal Ruby Reds . . . with perfect, juicy and luscious flavor . . . not sour like other grapefruit . . . but naturally sweet without sugar, phone or write Frank.

Chapter 10
The Intelligent Mail Order Machine

. . . that decides what to mail to whom and custom inserts into each envelope.

Its name is AIM, and it puts billing inserts into bills, selectively. It places an ad for a mink coat along with the bill to Mrs. Richwitch, and for a plain cloth coat with the bill to Mrs. Plain. A lawn mower ad only goes into the bill of a home owner or renter, not into bills of apartment dwellers—and so on.

The Philipsburg, the most widely sold inserting machine in the world, pioneered the business . . . made possible an entire advertising medium of billing, and cooperative mailing inserts— and entire divisions and subsidiaries of biggest mail order companies dealing with advertising inserts. Bell & Howell makes the Philipsburg and its computerized variation, AIM. John Jenks, president of the Philipsburg Division explains:

"The lettershop units are standard. The intelligent billing insert machines are electronic. They're custom-made for the customer. For example, we have one machine with fourteen stations and another with ten. They can select and also trim, burst, cut, fold, pick out. These machines run $80,000 to $100,000. We just shipped two very special units to the State of Illinois for $247,000 each.

"All this evolved. The need came. The computer came. The more elaborate machines are responses to the constantly increasing fire power of the computers. The computer jumped its speed. Companies centralized their accounting, billing and inserting. More segmentation and selection of lists became possible. It became more profitable to mail special advertising to appropriate parts of lists. Electronic inserting machines came from the need.

"The big growth came as hand labor became prohibitively expensive and as computerization came in. Credit cards required the machine for billing inserts. New York Citicorp uses six machines for VISA. The oil companies all used to stuff by hand.

"Montgomery Ward has four billing centers and a master file of millions of accounts in account number sequence with Alpha capability. They can find an account by number or name. They can pull out names locally for their retail stores, sectionally or nationally.

"They want to stuff inserts depending on the part of the country each name is from. They want to stuff inserts advertising sleds in the bills of people living in Minnesota, not Florida . . . to stuff inserts advertising a tire sale in the bills of people living near the stores where the sale is—maybe in Utah, but not New Mexico . . . to stuff inserts advertising garden items in the bills of people who have bought garden items—and so on.

"They want to stuff reminders with bills, gentle if 30 days, tougher for 60 days, and maybe a little fiery for 90 days. They may want to group envelopes sent out, also, for timed release, to post offices to coincide with TV advertising.

"They also want to get the pre-sort discount from the post office. This means they want to print names by zip code sequence and group all stuffed envelopes accordingly. They want everything shipped to the post office in zip code sequence.

"The more of this complexity, the more dizzy it gets to do by hand. It used to require armies of girls. At Wards, behind each non-electronic machine was a board showing what inserts were to go with the 26 different batches of statements. A tired or careless or lazy girl could insert the wrong pieces for a particular batch. Today, with all the options needed, handwork is just not feasible. The custom variations needed are endless. AIM can be programmed to insert as desired.

How did machines develop to do all this? The accounts started by telling their troubles to salesmen, then salesmen coming to engineers and, then, computer programmers coming in. To cope with the computer, the computer was put into the machine. How did all this start?

"Bell & Howell, in December 1958, bought the Philipsburg Machine Company. It was the first company bought at the start of a diversification program that has never stopped. I came May 5, 1958, as one of the first four sales reps. Now, 22 years later, I'm president.

"We believe that the Philipsburg Machine derives from the Sague Mailing Machine, first made in the late 1920's. We found an ad in a 1927 magazine for the Sague Machine. We believe that, at first, Sague had proprietary rights and that American Bookbinding, in Pennsylvania, first made it for Sague and then owned it. We know that when American Bookbinding went belly up in 1933, they gave the rights to manufacture the machine—as severance—to the plant superintendent. His name was Williams.

"He lived in Philipsburg, across the river, and called his business the Inserting & Mailing Machine Company. It was the Depression. Labor was cheap. We don't know any lettershops or mail order firms that bought the machine then. He sold mostly to banks, utilities and some department stores.

"During World War II, his machine became the V-Mail Machine. V-Mail was microfilmed in the U.S. and the microfilm sent overseas. There it would be blown up to V-Mail letter size, and the V-Mail Machine would insert it into envelopes for forwarding to the GI's. All his production went for that. After the war, the Inserting & Mailing Machine Company began to sell inserting machines in bigger volume.

"R.H. Donnelley, in Mt. Vernon, New York, was probably the first major mailing house to buy Philipsburgs, in 1946 or 1947. Almost immediately afterward, the Kleid Company put two Philipsburgs into its lettershops. Others followed, but in no rush. In 1948, while in high school, I worked in a lettershop. Operations were still all by hand. Meanwhile, Williams kept developing and improving his machine.

"At first, the machine had been entirely friction fed. Next, Williams made the insert stations vacuum. Then he went all vacuum. The speed of the machine kept increasing. Until 1953, it was a fixed speed of 60 envelopes a minute or 3,600 an hour for one girl with one machine. Some machines could do 4,200 an hour. As a comparison, a girl without a machine could do 125 an hour if six inserts were involved. In 1957, the machine was built with a variable speed. At maximum, it would go up to 6,000 an hour. The first Philipsburg machine took a number ten envelope only. In 1953, Philipsburg also made a machine for 6" by 9" envelopes.

"We had a ratchet that would fall into a pall. It was like a gear. It was just a round piece of level flanges coming up like a little gear. There were 6 of them instead of a gear. Each had a flat edge on one side. It would pull, come back, drop down, give a forward hit and drop down. Each hit of the flat edge would drive the machine. The machine would be motionless. It was like a kid sitting on a wagon. You'd push the kid forward, stop, and push again.

"Then we used the conjugate cam drive. That took the violence out and the maximum speed went up to ten thousand an hour. We still sell the ratchet type that operates up to 7200 envelopes per hour. We also make the conjugate cam drive that does 10,000 6" by 9". For the 9" by 12" envelope with ratchet and pall, the unit can do 4,500 an hour and, with conjugate cam, 6,250 an hour.

"In 1957, it took about thirty minutes to set up each machine for each job change, and it was hard. Today it takes five to ten minutes, and it's easy. Then it required 21 adjustments. Now it takes two. Then it took a lot of special tools. Now it doesn't take any.

"Inserting machines began to pay for themselves faster as labor costs jumped. Fifteen or twenty years ago, we'd make time studies to show the savings. Someone like Briggs & Stratton, sending out 60,000 pieces of mail a month, could pay for a machine in six months. If they mailed more, they could do it faster. Now we scarcely have to make time studies. It's generally accepted. Anyone can realize that for humans to each pick up six items and put them in an envelope hour after hour is a waste of resources.

"A big department store stuffs inserts with statements. Today, very few department stores stuff by hand. Some people kept sending such work to the handicapped. But either the handicapped get very little or it's very expensive.

"In 1957, Pitney-Bowes started in the inserting machine business. That year, Williams sold Bell & Howell his manufacturing operation. Don Williams, his son, kept the lettershops. None is now in operation. We've modified the product with little changes every year. In 1959, we brought out a machine for 9" by 12". In 1962, we got rid of the tools needed to set up and adjust the machine. We also increased its speed from 6000 envelopes per hour to 7200. Now it's not anything like the machine as we bought it.

"People use the same machine differently, even our standard ones sold to lettershops. Some run the machine slowly so the girl can zip sort manually. Some have trays. But, however used, overall productivity has probably doubled for the same type of use twenty years ago.

"The average life of our machines is fifteen to twenty years. We rebuild others, too. There are plenty of older machines in use. The oldest I know of in use were out, originally, in 1957. So, we haven't gotten much of our volume from replacements. It's mostly growth to support the use of the machines.

"We've had competition. There is a Pitney Bowes unit that does 7,500. We are 5% higher on one and appreciably higher on the other, but have advantages. We do much more business. At one time, Frieden, when part of Singer, handled the Ertma from Switzerland. Almost ten years ago, Cheshire picked up Kern out of Europe; but it's mostly Pitney-Bowes and us, with us appreciably bigger.

"We do business worldwide, with a plant in Germany, in addition to Phillipsburg, New Jersey. Overseas we've had a very handsome growth. But our sales here are still larger than those abroad."

The standard Philipsburg machine is unintelligent. It's largely for basic mailing operators. It's also for promotional mailers who send out major mailings on individual or several items. It's to insert the same material in each envelope.

"At first, our machines were very simple. With customer needs, they grew more complex and constantly became more so. The first thrust in inserting machines was mechanization. Quite a few years ago, the Ma and Pa machine we installed at the U.S.

Treasury did things our machines hadn't done before. If the U.S. Treasury sent a husband and wife a check each the same day, it used separate envlopes. They asked us to put them in one envelope. First, our machines would get Pa, and then Ma. We did it.

"In the early 60's, the phone company toll tickets were manually associated. There were three trays. The first was for the cash card which was slipped into the statement. Then the toll pages were similarly handled. Then the machine pulled the entire pack out, along with some advertising inserts and the return envelope. Subsequently, the machine was modified to match each toll page, the cash cards with the statement eliminating the need of any manual association. We were the first to do this."

Department stores were the first to use billing inserts. At first, they sent all the same inserts to everyone. Then they would sometimes sort bills by groups for each of which they would manually prepare a somewhat different group of inserts. Later the inserting machine would first insert the correct pack for one group, then stop for reloading with the next pack and insert it. It was a stop and start beginning of segmentation, still with plenty of handwork.

The next thrust was intelligence. This started in billing operations circa 1968. The first inserting machines used by credit card companies were not yet intelligent. The first truly intelligent machines were used by American Express. This was the beginning of sophisticated segmentation.

"At first, we got the machine to recognize a certain hole in an insert card, then a certain mark on it, and gradually to scan different marks, to read it and decide what to do, reach out, pull out, to act as needed. Could we match a bill to a certain card? Could we make a sequence verification? Every problem looked different, needed a special configuration, its own bells and whistles.

"If we saw we didn't lose, we'd do it. All this evolved into machines that can read computer marks, then select at high speed. The computer goes into the machine. The machine becomes kind of a friend of business.

"It can plug in the zip code, in present sequence, see that every envelope has the correct insert combination to go with the accounting documents. As the computer increased fire power, we tapped in. We have developed a lot. We have patents on a lot of things. Each electronic mailer has different computer equipment, different needs. These big, complex units are so specialized they don't really have resale value or trade-in value for later use by others."

AIM, the name for Philipsburg's intelligent mail order machine stands for Automated In-Line Mailing System. AIM is so custom designed and custom modified for each customer that it differs widely in size, shape, form, method of use and capabilities. It never stops changing. It keeps doing new things it never did before.

Montgomery Ward has four huge billing centers to bill for over five hundred stores and all catalog sales. At first, each center used automatic but non-intelligent Philipsburgs. "A center would simply bill all Fort Wayne or all Madison, or whatever, enclosing proper inserts. It would then readjust and repack the proper inserts for the next store's accounts. Next, Ward put in an intelligent machine at each center, AIM. At first, AIM selected different batches for different stores but did not select different, individual pieces.

"Now AIM can machine pick individual inserts—both to suit the geographical area and the individual customer. If you've just bought a stove, AIM won't give you an insert on a stove, and

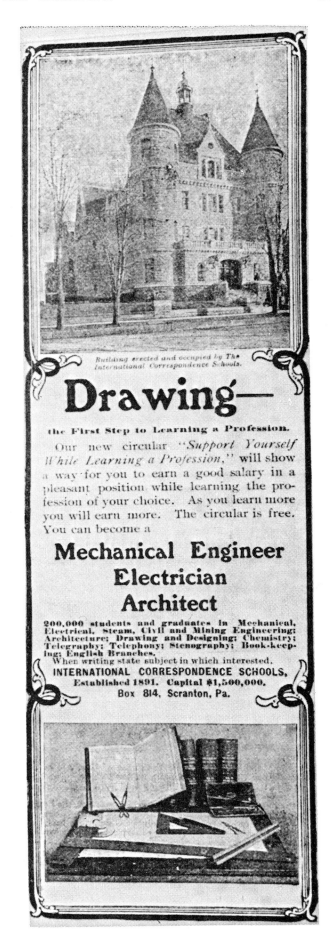

so on. Montgomery Ward sells its credit life insurance policy to customers in many states with different insurance regulations. It often sends its policy holder customers copies of new regulations and laws and changes in them. AIM decides to whom to send what.

AIM selects from the proper station and to join the customer's bill just as it's moving down AIM's raceway. AIM moves the statement and regulation along . . . automatically releases, slides down and assembles just the right other inserts for the customer . . . and then assembles and stuffs it all in an envelope.

If the next bill requires a different regulation, AIM automatically ejects it from another stack. If the next statement requires no statement, it gets none. At the same time, AIM is moving along in zip code sequence any statements which qualify for a 2¢ postage discount. For doing so, AIM saves well over $2,000,000 a year in postage this way.

All the while AIM is reading a blip code that is printed by computer on each customer statement. The blip code is triggering the ejection of the proper inserts from their stations. AIM never tires and keeps taking on more and more jobs as it is programmed to do so.

AIM puts into the typical Montgomery Ward envelope containing a bill six inserts. It gives catalog customers some different inserts than retail customers. It changes inserts for any customer as instructed. AIM sees to it that no envelope in a group qualifying for a pre-sort discount weighs more than an ounce, diverting the overweight envelopes before the postage machine.

AIM varies, almost with every installation. Some AIM stations may have both select and match capabilities. Others may only be able to select. Inserts correct for each envelope can be triggered automatically, one after the other and carried down to the spot where the assembled inserts are put into one envelope. For a set a mother insert can be coded to trigger the inserts at other stations. The exact number of inserts to be triggered can be pre-programmed by the computer print-out.

Completed envelopes move down the conveyer while the machine operates at high speed. An envelope moving down the raceway gets a special red slash from a marketing device to indicate where a new zip code is beginning. The electronic marking device automatically separates the envelopes. Envelopes are flipped over after flaps have been moistened. Then they are sealed and metered in zip code sequence. They are taken from the moving belt and stacked into containers.

Zip codes are placed into trays. Computer printed labels are then slipped into place to identify the trays which will then be shipped to the Post Office. Each morning a summary sheet can be compared with tray labels. The summary shows exactly how many envelopes should go into each tray. The first zip code in each new grouping is checked particularly carefully, to avoid sending any tray to the wrong city.

Each AIM operator works from one side of the machine—replenishing envelopes and inserts, removing the finished product, etc. But AIM is in charge. AIM's control panel signals with flashing lights when attention is needed for some step along the way. If there is a mix-up, the machine stops. Lights pin-point the problem so that the operator can find and correct it.

Mr. Howard Hunlock, Manager of Montgomery Ward's Credit Operating Center, calls AIM a little short of amazing. "It's the closest thing to an error-free system that we have seen. The machine stops and a light goes on when a station runs out of inserts or when two inserts are mistakenly ejected from one station."

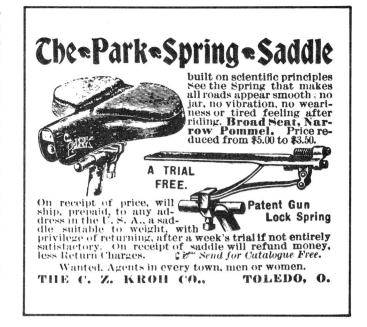

Many foreign post offices won't use a regular two-window envelope. Ward even tailored a system for AIM to switch envelopes for those which won't. The machine stops automatically. The operator is alerted that foreign mailings are coming and to switch from two-window to one-window envelopes.

Howard Hunlock describes the situation before and after AIM: "The change was dramatic. The Chicago Center had four six-station mailing machines with no selectivity. We had 33 different handling codes and 16 credit services . . . up to 528 inserts to change. We were contantly pulling out and putting in new inserts by hand. Every insert in every station went into every envelope. Statements were not in zip code order. We could not get the postage discount. We had manual errors. With AIM, errors have virtually been eliminated."

Larry Olsen, manager of Procedure Analysis of The Famous Insurance Group, describes what AIM does for them: "We can break down insurance policies according to price and include a flyer on earthquake insurance just to those homes in a specific range, say $60,000 and over. We can send special flyers just to owners in areas where heavy flooding occurs periodically, where hurricanes are a threat, and so on. The savings are more than enough to justify the cost of the machine, about $93,000."

After AIM, mail order may never be quite the same. AIM may cause far more mail order change than most in mail order in 1976 dreamed of and perhaps more than Bell & Howell contemplates.

If AIM is used by a giant consumer co-op insert program, as Dick Cremer uses it at the Signature Financial Companies of Montgomery-Ward, there may be a new ball game. Scientific segmentation and AIM may make it possible to insert less to sell more at lower cost.

AIM may increase the use of co-op inserts for mail order, with couponing and without, and in enormously greater volume than all package inserts and billing inserts used in 1981. It may make it possible for small mail order entrepreneurs as well as greats to benefit. The insert is a simple, lower production cost ad. It can be projected in increments. Using it can make the small grow, and maybe become big.

As for the mail order rich, with it they're liable to get richer.

Chapter 11
The Stories Behind Mail Order Stories

"We seek, investigate, report them."

"We publish news. We specialize in investigative reporting." It's *DM News*. It's new, it's brash, it's controversial. Headlines and subheads are breezy. There are plenty of pictures. Its writers are on the street, on the phone and constantly digging for exclusive stories, which they sometimes get.

It's the new publishing kid on the direct marketing block. Its first issue was September 1979. Its staff and its editor looked at direct marketing with new eyes. It reflects the competitive drive of its owner-publisher, Adrian H. Courtenay III. It's full of sass and vinegar. It strives . . . in every issue . . . to be Numero Uno.

Its aim is to be more up-to-date, deeper in coverage, wider in scope—to give anyone a fast look at everything. Each month it gives a bonus, a special section with considerable coverage on one facet of direct marketing. This makes each current and back issue particularly useful to anyone starting out.

In how-to info in direct marketing, there is no greater bargain. Anyone new to direct marketing can get a free copy of any back issue. Until such time as DM News goes "paid", any qualified user of direct marketing or supplier to direct marketers can obtain a free subscription. Shortly, I'll describe the special section for each month of 1981 and give details how to get DM News free.

From its first issue, DM News came on strong—shadow boxing down the street . . . almost with a chip on its shoulder . . . spoiling to prove itself to anyone. In six months it was in the black and deep into direct marketing. By early 1981 it was making better and better profits and accepted as essential by more and more direct marketers.

How did all of this come about? Adrian remembers it this way: "It happened as many enterprises do . . . an entrepreneur spotted a niche and filled it. In this case, my interest in journalism and experience in publishing happened to provide me with just the qualifications required to fill the niche.

"The financing for DM News came from profits of my trade publications business, where I had used direct marketing to build the circulation of another publication. Having been a space salesman and publisher, I knew all the 'ins' and 'outs' of sales promotion and rate cards and using the telephone and sales letters to supplement personal visits. When I hired sales reps for DM News, I made sure that they knew these rudiments, too.

"My background in sales served me in another way. I appreciated the critical importance of a superior editorial product. That's why I chose an editor who knows marketing inside and out. He's Joe Fitz-Morris who was founding editor of ANNY, now know as Adweek/East. He's been a reporter, an editor, an author and an advertising executive. Joe and I each have strong views on journalism, but we agreed entirely on making DM News a true newspaper, on hiring only able staff people, on honest reporting, on using only strong contributions of any editorial material."

Ed Burnett compiled the list for the charter circulation, which is now being converted to Request status. The first issue was sent to almost everyone in the field—the association and club members, the pros—including the list people, agency people, consultants, copywriters, media people, printers, mailers, and above all, every substantial user of direct marketing. The first issue was September of 1979.

The tabloid page was 100% bigger than the 7" by 10" page of competitors. It packed in more news. It jumped into direct marketing. Adrian jumped into planes and into any activity of direct marketers. Staff reporter Linda Miller at once took the Nat Ross New York University course on direct marketing. Editor Joe Fitz-Morris knew advertising backward and forward but set out to expand his contacts in direct marketing.

At first, some old direct marketers didn't care for it, were amused by it or even resented it. But most felt that DM News was adding coverage. If a subscriber or an advertiser complained about anything in a letter, it could become a lead story. Once, Adrian ran a simulated interview of himself by a simulated reporter (with whom he got into a testy argument) of a simulated magazine. The simulated reporter's name was one letter of the alphabet off from Larry Kofsky, of Direct Marketing Magazine. Adrian explains why he positioned DM News as he does.

"From the moment I considered the direct marketing field, I realized it was an exciting, dynamic growth market for the eighties, full of fast-breaking news, a perfect candidate for my brand of publishing. After ten years of space selling for various trade journals, I made the transition from salesman to publisher in 1974 when I founded Laundry News, another newspaper which is now the undisputed leader in its field.

"In the process, I fell in love with journalism in general, and the tabloid newspaper format in particular. Unlike a lot of publishers who come from the advertising side of the business, I take my journalism very seriously. Most of my efforts these days are devoted to the quality of my editorial products.

"Direct marketing, by the way, is a reporter's paradise, bursting with activity . . . achievements and success stories right alongside of failures, frauds and bankruptcies. New technology, new media, new marketing ideas are popping up all over the place. So are new lists, new people and new companies, not to mention a new publication here and there.

"DM News is not a passive propaganda sheet for direct marketers and their associations. It's an aggressive news medium that reports the good news along with the bad. It tells you what's happening now in direct marketing. It has a fresh new outlook. It's hard-hitting, honest and independent."

To Joe Fitz-Morris, the emphasis is on news. To Adrian, it is aggressively and competitively so. "Our reporters are always looking for the exclusive, the story-behind-the-story, the news before it happens. They turn up in places where they're not expected. They cover the country from bases in New York, Boston, Chicago and Los Angeles. Even when a newsworthy event crops up outside the country you'll probably find a DM News reporter there.

"DM News is by, for and about big-time direct marketers. It's written for the pros. It presents in-depth coverage in special feature sections. Each focuses on a particular aspect of the business. Leading experts write by-line articles; contributing editors write monthly columns of 'how-to' information."

News stories in every issue report on campaigns by users of direct marketing—the publishers, catalog and mail order firms . . the fund raisers, financial and business marketers and other direct marketers. Adrian is equally proud of his stories on the abusers of direct marketing. He obviously enjoys having DM News assume the role of the newest and most irreverent publication in the field.

Some very able people have written for it. Just reading the Stan Fenvessy feature, "Questions on Fulfillment" can be invaluable. For upward strivers, Hal Crandall—direct marketing recruiter—writes articles on how best to get a job. He also advises employers on how to hire. Stories on both Fenvessy and Crandall are elsewhere in this book.

Stan Rapp, Al Eicoff, Robert Sawyer, Richard Viguerie and Ed Burnett have all written for it. But mainly, the content is news. Adrian says: "We cover all facets of direct marketing—the people, the companies and the campaigns—hard news from mergers to technology."

Adrian emphasizes: "DM News is in tune with direct marketing as utilized *today*. We cover campaigns and promotions either before they start or while they're in progress. People want to know the state of the art, *today*—and what the leading practitioners are doing today. We cover *many* current mailings and other campaigns in every issue.

"We also keep our readers up-to-date on speeches, club and association activities, legislative developments and postal rates. Once again, there are numerous stories in each issue on these subjects.

"The common denominator is that we have professional reporters, real journalists who distill the important news into articles that contain the essential information and do not take forever to read.

"We edit. We separate the wheat from the chaff. We save our readers the trouble of reading for an hour in order to get a few kernels of information that can be transmitted in a crisply written news article that takes ten seconds to read. *We* read the long speeches and attend the meetings and then report on the worthwhile points.

"We have no interviews with pussycat questions, no extraneous biographical information, no irrelevant pleasantries—no trivial fillers. We use journalistic judgment. We don't attempt to please our advertisers or interviewees in our editorial columns. We feel it would be an insult to our readers' intelligence.

"An independent survey has shown a perception in the marketplace already that DM News is 'most up-to-date' and 'more in touch with the marketplace'. . . 'more entertaining' and characterized by 'more investigative reporting'.

"Most direct marketing campaigns these days are conceived and created by direct marketing and advertising agencies. This is constantly reflected in DM News. Joe Fitz-Morris has lifelong contacts in advertising and total familiarity with the subject. As a result, DM News has been the first direct marketing journal to acknowledge and explain the important role of agencies in the campaigns of the major direct marketers of the eighties."

In 1982, Adrian Courtenay put DM News into a new activity, a library of video tape instruction for direct marketers. The first production was the Ed Burnett seminar on lists taped at Pace University. But his main interest has continued to be developing the DM News itself.

Adrian emphasizes that DM News is primarily for experienced and substantial direct marketers. I think it is also particularly helpful for any newcomer, however big or small. DM News special feature sections can be very helpful to anyone getting started.

The 1982 special feature sections are:

January 15 - Subscription Marketing by Publishers
February 15 - Direct Response Travel Advertising
March 15 - Progress Report on Interactive Video
April 15 - Review of Chicago and New York Direct Marketing Days
May 15 - Financial Direct Marketing
June 15 - The DMMA Spring Convention
July 15 - The State of the Art Report: Current Computer Applications
August 15 - The List Business
September 15 - Direct Response Ad Agencies
October 15 - DMMA Annual Conference
November 15 - Telephone Marketing
December 15 - Retail Direct Marketing.

To get a free copy of any back issue or, as explained earlier, a free subscription, write or call DM News at 19 West 21st Street, New York, NY 10010. Telephone: 212-741-2095.

If a back issue is out of stock, a microfilm copy on microfiche can be purchased from University Microfilms International, 300 N. Zeeb Road, Ann Arbor, MI 48106.

Mail Order Sampler
Seminar III

BURPEE'S NOVELTIES FOR 1888

This year we are particularly fortunate in being able to introduce some grand novelties of more than usual merit, prominent among which are the two New American Peas, BURPEE'S QUANTITY and BURPEE'S QUALITY, which we have selected and developed from a number of crosses obtained several years ago, and BURPEE'S WHITE ZULU BEAN, described below. We would also mention as especially noteworthy THE VANDERGAW and EXPRESS CABBAGES, THE BLUE-PODDED BUTTER BEAN, CALIFORNIA CREAM-BUTTER LETTUCE, THE CELESTIAL PEPPER and QUAKER PIE PUMPKIN. None of these are catalogued upon the representations of others, but all from our own personal knowledge as to their real worth. We annually test and discard many more new varieties than we introduce, preferring to offer only those of distinct character and actual value. Thus we constantly aim to hold the confidence of our customers, who have learned to rely absolutely upon our representations.

We would ask careful attention, also, to our list of TESTED SPECIALTIES, described on PAGES 19 TO 30 and to our FLOWER SEED NOVELTIES, pages 84 to 95. On ALL SEEDS IN PACKETS the purchaser is entitled to select TWENTY-FIVE CENTS' WORTH extra for each ONE DOLLAR'S WORTH ORDERED.

BURPEE'S WHITE ZULU POLE BEAN.

In Rhode Island, three years ago, we found a very distinct and handsome Pole Bean in the possession of a market gardener near Newport. Obtaining the entire stock, we have grown it with great satisfaction for the past two seasons, and now have pleasure in introducing BURPEE'S WHITE ZULU as a most valuable New Pole Bean. It is so named because of the mammoth size of its white pods and the jet blackness of its dry beans. It grows quickly, clings well to the poles, foliage very healthy, with leaves of immense size, and *produces pods ready for the table in seven weeks from date of planting.* The pods are remarkably handsome, of a waxy appearance, nearly *pure white* in color, *very broad* and yet *very fleshy* and *perfectly stringless.* Our illustration is exactly *natural size* of a matured pod. Even when fully grown, eight to ten inches long and proportionately broad, the pods still retain their exceptionally fine quality, having a very rich flavor equaled by but few varieties of string beans. Their white color when cooked is very attractive on the table. THE WHITE ZULU is *wonderfully prolific,* the vines bearing continuously, so that a few poles will keep a family supplied with string beans of the finest quality for a long period. *Sold only in sealed packages.*

Per package 20 cts.; 3 packages for 50 cts.

BURPEE'S LOUISE STRAWBERRY.

We would call particular attention of all lovers of fine Strawberries to this superb new variety, now offered for the first time. It is illustrated and described on the last page of this Catalogue.

BURPEE'S WHITE ZULU

Chapter 1
How-To Mail Order's Biggest Pioneer

*In toughest times he sold more how-to
books by mail order than ever before.*

Walter Black, Milo Sutliff, Elsworth Howell, John Stevenson, all publishing mail order greats, admired and respected him. Whenever I had a chance I listened to his every word. He was John Crawley and what he did to turn tough times into real opportunity—by mail order—could help you, if really tough times ever come again.

Very few publishers are as old as Wm. H. Wise & Co., founded in 1888. W.H. Wise was a very successful salesman of books and organizer of door-to-door crews. Two close friends were Fred. C. Dolan and Elbert Hubbard. All three grew up in Bloomington, Illinois. Dolan was a partner in the Bloomington daily newspaper with the family of Adlai Stevenson. He owned a printing business, too. Elbert Hubbard became famous as an inspirational author, editor and publisher. They were three young Turks.

Wm. H. Wise became president and Fred Dolan treasurer of Wm. H. Wise. The company published and sold house-to-house sets of books of name authors, including Elbert Hubbard. In the 1920's, Wise sold sets at prices as high as $400 to $600 on time payments and was very profitable. It went public, with 500 stockholders. It always made money and seemed a Rock of Gibraltar.

Then the depression started and each year got worse and worse until families were lucky if they had money for food. Most of those who had bought sets of books couldn't pay for them. Sales plummeted. The Hanover Bank for years had loaned money to Wise on the receivables of these house-to-house sales. Now more and more of the receivables were worthless. They had been guaranteed by Wise, which now had to, but could not, pay the bank. Big overhead had continued, with the inevitable result.

John Crawley was a cost accountant put into Wise, when depression struck, by Adam Luke who controlled the two largest creditors. Adam Luke was said to be one of the richest men in the world. He controlled West Viginia Pulp and Paper and The Hanover Bank. Crawley was a protege of Luke's whom Luke had put into half a dozen or more different companies before. Crawley would go into a company for a year or so, tighten up accounting procedures and then go on to another company.

Crawley discovered in the stricken company a tiny core of profitable business, by mail order. Much as Grolier and Brittanica later mailed mail order offers to encyclopedia subscribers, Wise had in a small way sold books by mail to its door-to-door customers.

Wm. H. Wise & Co. was prostrate. Many years later, John Crawley told me: "The public could not afford any of our sets of books. There was no money. Most of the employees had been laid off. We owed every supplier. We were cut off because of bad credit from buying paper and printing. We were counted out. I persuaded the creditors that I could make a success of it, and to make me president. They did—at $67 a week."

Fred Dolan was a friendly Midwesterner and helped in the transition. Stock in Wise of the principal owners had been pledged to the Hanover Bank. The creditors arranged to give Crawley bonuses of stock and to give him an option to buy stock on notes. Eventually, Crawley acquired 90% ownership. He knew nothing of mail order. He first studied everything Wise had ever done in mail order, each mailing piece it had sent out and took inventory of books left.

He found mailing pieces for a 26-volume set of Joseph Conrad, with a 9-volume set of Stevenson as a gift; O'Henry complete in 18 pocket volumes; George Bernard Shaw in 12 volumes; Bret Harte in 20 volumes; The Little Nature Library in 4 volumes and Marvels & Mysteries of Science in 5; Myths & Legends in 4 volumes; Emerson in 2 volumes. There were The French Immortals, a set of Ingersoll, 2 books of John Gunther and the "Poetry of Youth", edited by Edwin Markham. In the depths of the depression these offers were mostly unsaleable by mail order at a profitable price.

Except for one or two books, inventory of these and all other Wise titles ranged from small to tiny. Crawley made up a bargain sale mail order offer and mailed it to those who had previously bought by mail and door-to-door. This sold out almost all the inventory and gave him the cash to get going. But the chances to sell anything at a profit by mail order seemed very bad.

A quarter of the population was out of work. Income for the rest was sharply cut. Anyone out of a job got a new one for less, and the next time, lower still. It was leap-frogging in reverse. But life went on. Babies were born, although less of them. Children grew up. People married, although later.

Crawley was convinced that how-to information was more needed than ever, and only needed to be published in a form and at a price suitable for the times. He determined to give the public, for $2.98 to $3.98, as much content as had been in a Wise many volume set. He would compress big sets into single books of 1300 to 1500 pages. Each page would have twice as many words as an average book, but in smaller type.

Crawley wanted books suited to mail order. Usually Wise had no proprietary rights but paid plate royalties to the original publishers for the sets it sold house-to-house. He wanted proprietary rights. He preferred not to pay a continuing royalty. He saw his opportunity in England. Wm. H. Wise had been the American importer and distributor of certain books from England published by Odhams Press. Wise had dealt with Mr. Stevens and his assistant, Harold Grigsby. This same Grigsby taught John Stevenson the mail order business and many, many years later became the English consultant to Ed Downe (whose story I tell in this book) in a mail order business he conducted there.

John Crawley took some of the cash received from selling off old Wise inventory and took a trip to England. The book business in England was just as bad, if not worse, than in the U.S. The English had little hope of big U.S. sales. John got from Odhams Press some of his first mail order books.

Crawley also got something far more valuable than the books themselves from Odhams Press. Harold Grigsby told him which books were selling in England despite the depression. He showed Crawley the offers and gave him the successful ads and mailings. All Crawley had to do was to adapt the copy and offers to the U.S. market. Crawley took from the few dollars coming in enough cash to get out the simplest mailing to Wise names. When successful, he imported his first books. Then he tested outside lists and space, and then projected.

First he imported, at very advantageous prices. The British were willing to sell U.S. publishing rights for fairly small outright sums. John Crawley even persuaded them to take a small portion down and to stretch out the remaining payments. He took the plates and printed in the U.S. Then he began to re-edit, update and broaden coverage for more appeal to U.S. readers.

He was a big, determined man with a charismatic personality. He persuaded a free lance copywriter and then a free lance artist to create mailing pieces for tiny fees. He talked The Circle Press into giving enough credit to print test mailings. He got prices for paper and printing, for both books and direct mail, so low they seemed impossible. He got longer credit than Wise had previously. He offered the public how-to information at a fraction of the price the same information previously sold for.

Without having the books in stock, he began to test offers that would, if successful, require more capital than his hand-to-mouth operation could bring in. His first really successful test was on The Garden Encyclopedia. He had no books. He would have to create the Garden Encyclopedia from scratch. It would be a huge project and take a lot of time and money. But he was making money with his imported books. The time had come for him to see Adam Luke.

John Crawley said he drove for miles on empty roads through a remote, wild area to see Adam Luke who lived in a great manor house in a huge forest. Luke felt it was time to get back some money and payment commitments. John Crawley told me this story:

"Wise owed $250,000 to West Virginia Pulp and Paper. I explained that Wise could not pay a cent. But I said that I knew that sales of paper to book publishers for how-to books had dropped down close to bottom, that no one knew how to sell how-to books to the public anymore—but that I did." Then Crawley showed Luke his proof. He had brought with him all the figures on tests to date and a huge barrel of orders which he upended all over Adam Luke's desk. "Very impressive," said Adam Luke.

John Crawley told me: "I walked out with enough credit to get paper for a new edition of 'The Garden Encyclopedia' and a commitment for a $250,000 line of credit. This was enough to pay all editorial and typesetting costs, provide some money for advertising and to pay for postage to mail direct mail pieces in volume. But I needed much more credit from others."

Crawley convinced creditors that only by cooperating and actively helping him reactivate Wise could they get their money. He also persuaded them that Wise could soon become a very big customer...at a time when business seemed very difficult to get.

It took two years to re-edit the Garden Encyclopedia from a previous many-volume set and print it as a giant, one-volume encyclopedia, in 1936. But, at $2.98, it sold and sold. He convinced Sidney Satinstein, who owned American-Book Stratford Press, to print books on 90-day credit and West Virginia Pulp and Paper to give 90 days. He persuaded Louis Silverstein, of Circle Press, to give 90-day credit to Wise and prices so low other publishers had difficulty matching them with any supplier. On the basis of this, he got 90-day credit from more and more suppliers.

In every way, John Crawley capitalized on the hard times of the depression to persuade others to work with him and for him, to give Wise some help because he convinced them that only Wise was able to deliver more business in hard times. He even got his book, "American Wild Life", royalty-free from the U.S. Government. The editorial material was produced as a project of the Works Progress Administration—to provide jobs.

Franklin D. Roosevelt had brought in a new breath of hope. Entirely new people were making a quite new start on the

No. 18K16000 Ladies' or misses' stylish Street or Suit Hat. Is made of fine quality satin finished Jap braid in short front mushroom shape. Hat is trimmed in front with a large natural wing in large twist of fine quality Jap silk, this silk extending in folds around the base of crown. Hat is finished with a half round bandeau of silk velvet and is silk lined. Colors, white, brown, navy or champagne, all with trimming to match. Be sure to state color wanted. Price....(If by mail, postage extra, 24 cents.)....$1.19

humblest of scales. People were pouring into the night schools and libraries. More were finishing high school. College enrollment was rising. Education was cheap. People were getting accustomed to a lower scale of living. But more people were beginning to get some minimum income. There was a thirst for more how-to information, at a bargain price.

The first really big John Crawley success was the National Educational Alliance—a magazine a week for 35¢ each, and ideal for the depression. Each issue contained lessons in about 20 of 57 courses on high school and college subjects. Subscribers could not select some subjects and reject others but could cancel at any time. Magazines were mailed Second Class, much less than book rate—four issues a month for 12 or 18 months.

Many of the subjects came out of John's head and were tested on his mimeograph. Since subscribers could stop at any time, this meant constantly reselling the selections of coming months. John used the preferences of subscribers for each book in the series as a test of a possible proliferation of more material on that subject. He constantly checked results.

This excited John Crawley. He called his buyers "my constituents". He felt they were constantly voting whether he should expand in publishing books on a certain subject, to contract or stop...that he was their public servant. The National Educational Alliance had an encyclopedic scope of how-to subjects. If a lot more people paid for a 35¢ magazine book on any subject, this electrified Crawley.

Willard Morgan edited the photography course in the National Educational Alliance Series. It was accepted so enthusiastically that John Crawley had Willard Morgan produce a magazine type photography course at 35¢ an issue, 4 issues a month. This was very successful. Many years later, when short of cash, Crawley sold it to John Stevenson. John made a hard-cover continuity library outfit with tremendous success. This was long before Time-Life Books brought out its photography series.

Subscribers who took the entire 57 courses each, and those who went quite a way and paid well, were "renewed" into a second Popular Educator Literature Series, under the same National Educational Alliance name. The Literature series was followed by the N.E.A. Popular Mathematics Series and one on

Our Special Soft Hat for 1902.

Full Shape.
No. 33R2094 Men's Full Shape Hats, similar in style to the one above but larger shape. Crown, 6 inches; brim, 2¾ inches. A shape that is particularly desirable for tall or heavy men. The quality we will send you will be found equal to hats retailing for $3.00. Fine nutria fur, fine silk band and binding. High open curled brim, as shown in the illustration. This style will please you. Colors, black or steel. Sizes, 6¾ to 7¼.
Price, each..... **$2.25**
If by mail, postage extra, each, 25 cents.

Aviation. Later, Wise published the original High School and College Courses as a 10-volume set, "The Popular Educator".

John Crawley went to Mortimer Berkowitz (son Mortimer is now a magazine advertising representative). Mortimer was publisher for Hearst, of American Weekly and Puck, "The Comic Weekly" . . . the funny papers. He wanted to sell national advertisers to run in what were then exotic media. Advertising in comic sections for adult products seemed foolish.

What was worked out between the two of them no one but they knew. But after the first back cover of American Weekly proved a huge success for Wise, back cover after back cover of American Weekly and of Puck blossomed with full page color ads for Wise books. And then Mortimer built an impressive easel presentation with page after page of dollar sales results of Wise books. At lunch after lunch, twenty to thirty advertising prospects were a captive audience for the Wise and American Weekly Puck story. Wise sales soared and national advertisers were sold by Berkowitz almost as fast.

With no previous knowledge of mail order, John Crawley developed a genius for it as he went along. Two people began to help him greatly. One was Walter Thwing, who owned his own advertising agency and shared the Doubleday account with others. His hobby was gardening. The Walter Thwing Agency became the agency for Wise starting with The Garden Encyclopedia. It was a fine choice of Crawley's. Thwing brought a lot of expertise. His gardening know-how helped. At first, Crawley bought free lance copy and art for his direct mail. One writer who supplied him with successful mailing pieces was Fred Breismeister—so successful that Crawley turned his mesmerizing skill to persuading Fred to work for him.

Fred recalls: "John Crawley enticed me back to New York' in 1938 from Chicago, where I had gone to work. John Crawley, with his tousled gray hair, presented a strong, dominating character. When I came with Wise, I heard it still had net debts of a quarter million dollars, aside from current obligations mostly on 90-day credit. John Crawley and I were quite compatible and hit it off right from the start.

"Probably one reason was that I produced results right away and took on more responsibility. We grew fast and John made me his General Sales Manager and Vice President. When I came Wise had about 125,000 names of mail order buyers. We grew and grew until we had lists of over 5,000,000 paid-up book buyers and were doing $10,000,000 a year.

" 'The Popular Educator' was already started when I got there. John had me write a newspaper ad in connection with the Walter A. Thwing Agency on it—and immediately prepare mailings on it. It was then in magazine form. Later, I did mailings on it as a ten-volume set. We mailed many million pieces on 'The Popular Educator' as a magazine and as a 10-volume set."

As soon as Crawley began to buy outright the plates and publishing rights to books and sets, he began to persuade young editors of appropriate how-to magazines to edit free lance for a larger sum the acquired sets and books. This worked particularly well when he bought outright the plates of how-to books published in England.

The editor would make emergency changes and corrections, delete the hopelessly archaic, make minimum editorial changes and then add as necessary, covering newest developments in the field. Often a book taken over would be just the skeleton. The free lancer would flesh it out. Crawley carefully avoided royalties and paid as little as possible outright. But he gave credits generously.

"John Crawley always tried to give extremely terrific value for the buyer's money," remembers Fred, "sometimes too much. An extreme example of this was 'The Garden Encyclopedia'. John began selling this with its 1400 pages and 10,000 articles at $2.98. I remember one time, when he was hard pressed for cash he sold it for $1.98."

Crawley cut every corner and Fred helped. "I made my own layouts, specked my own type faces and layouts." Even before Crawley, Wise had an artist, Robert Rotter, who did some illustrations for one of its books. Crawley used him and then Fred. Fred said, "I had Robert Rotter do a great deal of finished art. He was great on books and on color circulars on fish, birds, animal life, flowers and vegetables for the books dealing with those subjects.

"In those early days, working out of the Depression Thirties, at Wise we put selling efforts into the mails, consisting of 2-color, 16" x 11" circular, letter, order card and carrying #9 envelope for $23.00 per M, including hand-inserting and $10.00 per M postage. That's why we could sell single volumes at $2.98 (and $3.98 for Deluxe Edition) and make a profit. Sometimes we sold, profitably, books for a single dollar."

In the 1960's, I read an article in Direct Marketing magazine by a vice president of the European operation of T-L Books. It described a wonderful way of testing—without testing. The article called it "Quasi-testing". The description was of the method used by John Crawley in the 1930's. Perhaps both re-invented the wheel.

Fred Breismeister recalls: "We used quickie tests to save thousands of dollars and valuable time. At Wise we developed a method of testing new offers, without employing the usual elaborate color circular and other items in regular mailing; instead we used a simple letter and business card."

Crawley would send to his customers a mimeograph letter describing the latest book idea that came into his head. He asked the advice of each as to whether he should go ahead. Each could check one of three boxes. One was "don't publish". One was "go ahead". The other was "If and when you publish, ship me a copy C.O.D." The method worked. "The answers to questions 1 and 2 would be very revealing and the answers to 3, we found, would closely parallel the numbers of orders we would get on the finished mailing."

White Duck Rain Covers.

37486 Team Rain Covers, made of heavy 10 ounce white duck. They are 78 inches long and 66 inches wide, all one piece. Have trace leathers with patent hook snaps, line pockets on the back and 3 inch by 11 inch hame leathers. Only made in one size. Per pair (two horses) .. $3.50 Weight, per pair, 8 pounds.

Fly Nets.

No Flies on This Horse.

Cut shows styles of nets quoted as "Body and Breast" nets.

NOTE.—Our quotations for fly nets are not by the pair, but for one single net for one horse.
37490 Upper Leather Team Nets, to head, standard weight, 5 bars, 84 lashes, body and neck. Weight, each net, 3¼ lbs. Each $1.85

"The tests could be put out almost overnight, saving many days of priceless time. Not only that but various prices could be tested, and the price most worthwhile and practical would clearly show up. The astute John Crawley saved author royalties by these tests. We could gauge the market and offer to authors handsome flat fees for the complete rights for such books as 'The Home Handyman's Guide', 'Machine Shop Practice', 'The Encyclopedia of Sewing', 'Your Dream Home - How to Build it for $3500 or Less', and others."

John and Fred had a wonderful ability to come up with unusual giveaways. The quickie would even describe the give-away. And what wonderful give-aways they were.

"The Modern Home Physician" was the Wise doctor book. Fred's copy said that, next to the family Bible, it was the most important book a family could own. The give-aways were two mannequins of the human body, one male and one female, each with layers. They were flat, die-cut to unfold as if a striptease of all inside. First, there was a discrete nude body, then the organs, then the blood system, then the nerve system, and finally the skeleton—all with named parts. To get the mannequins (which you could keep and return the book) was irresistable.

Then for the Modern Encyclopedia there was the flat globe. You could visualize huge presses flattening globes. It was a big cardboard disk with one hemisphere on one side and one on the other. You could hang it, twirl it, even look at it in all its full color. And for every book there was a giveaway which John Crawley found or thought up. Later, Fred Breismeister developed many of them.

Harold Grigsby at Odhams taught what he knew to John Crawley, in correspondence and in personal visits on his trips to the U.S. . . . suggesting new titles, giveaways and passing on any mail order method that worked in England . . . much as he had taught John Stevenson. Fred remembers:

"We enclosed in every shipment and with every separately mailed resell letter, a hand-this-to-a-friend and a Companion-Sales leaflet, which we copied from similar circulars used in England. When filling out the order form, the English publisher would make the customer not only sign the order but also print his own shipping label, plus another label that was used for a follow-up mailing. We did the same. These leaflets were highly profitable. The more closely related the Companion Sale was to the book bought by the customer, the better it pulled. I remember some pulling over 30%. Example: Selling American Wild Life buyers 'Wild Life the World Over'; selling 'Garden Encyclopedia' buyers 'Favorite Flowers in Full Color'. In each case, the companion offer effectively increased the price of the unit sold.

Huber Hoge & Sons Advertising started to work for Wm. H. Wise in 1940, when Wise had gotten into big volume . . . but was still a bit short on cash and still watching pennies . . . and still working with old everything. The Wise offices were in an old six-story building at 50 West 47th Street, opposite the Jewelry Exchange.

The outside was a sort of tired Elizabethan, with simulated wood beams and graying plaster. The inside was musty. The walls had not been painted for many years. The old elevator and the wood floors each creaked in their own way. You stepped off into a corridor. Directly opposite was John Crawley's office. Ceilings were high. It all was quiet and roomy with the feeling of the past. Dickens would have been at home.

John could usually be found behind his big desk, on the phone. In a glass-doored bookcase were Wise and competitors' books and a few of his favorites, such as "The Robber Barons". When the mail excited him, he'd get up, stride around his office, down the hall and often into Fred Breismeister's office.

Often, he'd grab up actual mail orders. He could project in his head probable final counts from the first few days' mail counts from a test. At the same time, he would calculate mentally the projection potential. He'd talk and plan as he walked, often holding a cluster of orders in his hand. "Do you realize what these 18 orders mean?" Then he'd plan full color supplement pages, mailings to several million outside names, and of course, his 3,500,000 house names. He'd plan the step-up to deluxe, the companion volume, the follow-ups to mail to the great new customer lists this would produce.

He'd speak to Fred Breismeister because it was Fred's job to make John's dreams happen creatively. Crawley would restlessly pace, think to himself and then aloud, bounce ideas off the wall—on Fred or whomever. Fred had a large corner office in the back with only low buildings behind—so that the quite big windows let in plenty of light. In Fred's office, there were usually two or three copywriters, often trainees.

John Crawley personally made all space advertising decisions and worked with the Walter Thwing Agency. Fred and his staff created all direct mail. John made the big decisions on list and printing buying. Jack Maher followed through with lists and Fred with printing purchases. Miss Guthman was editor. And, as more and more mail order tests paid off, how-to books came out like an assembly line.

Malcolm Smith had written to John Crawley about the wonders of radio mail order which Huber Hoge was pioneering. John Hoge and Malcolm had arranged the first test. I took over and was handed over to Fred Breismeister by John Crawley. After that, we worked together on and off for a good part of our business lives.

Years later, Fred took on, for John Stevenson, the same role he had with John Crawley. For John, Fred created—in much the same way—one mailing package after another for the first book continuity programs for Greystone. Still later, he became president of Downe Publishing, working for Ed Downe to whom I had introduced him.

Out of an English set of twenty books, excerpts of a hundred "World's Greatest Books" were created. Fred showed them pouring out of a great horn of plenty, with covers in full color. Success was huge. It was the first time the mass space and mass mailings were used so widely for the World's Greatest Books. Since then, many have featured the concept. The greatest of all was the Franklin Mint with its over $100,000,000 of sales from the first campaign.

John Crawley had a great feeling for cycles. John Crawley had remembered the publishing of history books of World War I. He told me that interest in such a book had been very great while World War I lasted, that it had stopped almost completely the day the war ended, and that it then, a number of years later, came back. All this came true for Pictorial History of World War II.

Fred Breismeister recalls: "'The Pictorial History of World War II' was a failure when we first tested it by letter. That was before the U.S. got involved in the war. We were testing the British two-volume set. A little more than a year later, the U.S. got into the war and millions of Americans were in the Armed Forces. The tables were reversed. Virtually the same letter effort was an outstanding success."

In July 1940, John Crawley had Huber Hoge & Sons test on radio "The History of the World - through the Fall of France". The fall had occurred a few weeks earlier. The offer didn't sell. We tested 'Pictorial History of World War II' on radio in early 1941 and had borderline results. But a year later it became the first book offer which we sold in tremendous volume on radio. In 1944, on radio we spent over $100,000 on one station in one year and sold several hundred thousand dollars worth of volumes I and II. We used hundreds of stations.

We used the top news commentator programs. We created our own commentators, hiring a writer and then the voice. We supplied program material related to the book to programs we were on. We created a program, War Quiz. We used any trusted air personality who liked the book and would say so. But when the war ended, general interest in the war did, too.

Fred Breismeister recalls: "Wise had a colossal flop right after the war, until we turned it into a huge success. The two-volume 'Pictorial History of World War II' was a tremendous money maker. Both John Crawley and Walter Thwing were sure that a book on the U.S. Navy's part in the war would be equally so. John went slam bang ahead with a 100,000 edition of 'The Navy, Queen of Battle'. The ads just didn't pull as expected. We were stuck with 80,000 sets of unbound sheets.

"We took a gamble and bound up 10,000 and shipped them out as Volume III to buyers of our 2-volume set—on a free examination basis with return privilege. And also with the privilege, if they chose, to count it as Volume III of a multi-volume 'Pictorial History of World War II'.

"I added the further privilege of examining volumes of 'Pictorial History of World War II' as they were produced as the government released war photos and stories of battles from their highly secret and classified files.

"Result . . . we cleaned out the 80,000 sets of sheets on the Navy book, printed many more, and built the 2-volume 'Pictorial History' into a 10-volume set and one of our very biggest money-makers. You can turn a failure into a success if you search for the right sales angle."

John Crawley with his restless mind and Fred Breismeister with his relentlessly thorough carrying out of creative projects worked extremely well together. Fred's activities were usually the base of all promotion in other media. Almost invariably, first tests and projections of any offer were in direct mail. This meant that Walter Thwing or Huber Hoge had the tremendous advantage of translating a present success in one medium into another.

Walter Thwing did it with great skill. A Thwing ad for Wise was extremely well constructed. Thwing had an excellent art director. A Wise ad would have an extraordinary number of elements of different size, with 1800 or more words. Yet, it would have a clean look.

We had a different problem. We had to use talk words instead of print words. We had to make something said as clear and understandable as in print. We had to make it simpler and friendlier. We had to use related programs and trusted personalities who could recommend and be trusted enough to get the order. And we had to come up with the ways to do this step-by-step, learning as we went. How we did it varied with the book we sold.

One book that succeeded very well was the Wm. H. Wise Book of Knitting. Crawley followed with a sewing book. He was a master of the add-on. An extra check off in the coupon or a 50-word box of copy could sometimes get 20% or so to take the selected book and 12% to take a deluxe edition of each.

Looking back, it seems as if there was almost no subject, on a really mass how-to field, we didn't sell—"Recipes of the World", "American Wildlife", "Wild Animals of the World", "The Wm. H. Wise Handy Man", "Your Dream House", the "Popular Decorating Book". The books were not handsome. Color was usually lacking. Photographs were often poor. But every Wm. H. Wise book gave extraordinary value in the huge amount and scope of information for its very low price. Often the editors who worked for so little were catapulted into such overnight fame that they became consultants, magazine editors and authors of more books for other publishers at full royalties.

One offer I remember well was the "Marvels and Mysteries of Science". During World War II, Fred wrote some very imaginative copy on it. "Right now, scientists all over the world are racing to harness the power of the atom—one spoonful will power a car for a year. Laboratories are working on atomic explosives so incredibly powerful that the winner nation in this race may wipe out the other side in this war." The copy pulled very well—three men from the FBI. Fred had been born in Berlin. The Manhattan Project was under wraps. It took a little doing to explain that Fred was just a mail order futurholic.

Years after the war, in the boom that followed, John Crawley—who had prospered in depression—went broke. While others sold for much more, he kept his prices low. But it was the competition of the continuity programs that proved most difficult. More than anything his health failed. He became an ailing grand master of mail order. For the last fifteen years of John Crawley's life, he suffered severely from emphysema. He had great difficulty in breathing and was quite debilitated from it.

Fred Breismeister remembers: "A lot more bothered John. With the improvement in the economy . . . the UOPWA (United Office & Professional Workers of America) was attempting to unionize Wise employees. In the meantime, one of the accountants embezzled $50,000. And postage began to increase.

"When the first of the third class postage rate increases went

The Farmer's Friend.
You can scarcely believe it possible to secure such a large, roomy rocker as shown in this illustration, for the extremely low price quoted. It is hand carved and polished and has heavy steam bent arm posts and slat spindles; it is well braced in every way and has dark golden oak finish. The large seat and high shaped back makes this chair very comfortable and desirable.
No. 1R321 Our special price, wood seat....................$2.95
No. 1R322 Our special price, cane seat....................3.40
No. 1R323 Our special price, genuine leather seat...$4.35

into effect, we thought it spelled our doom. We were mailing at the giddy pace of almost a million pieces every week. In a good year we netted about $500,000 in profit. But the third class postage rate increase would wipe that out—and, we thought, us. Of course, as third-class postage and our other costs rose, we managed to prosper by finding ways to increase our dollar prices per unit of sale. And so did most other mail order firms."

But Wise did not accumulate the capital that more and more big volume mail order required. It did not have the cushion if things went wrong. And any misjudgment caused instant big problems. Fred Breismeister remembers one such mishap and warns readers: "You will lose your shirt if you overestimate your market.

"Consider, for instance, Wise & Co.'s '100 World Famous Paintings'. This volume was a colossal bargain and a huge success. One hundred of the world's most famous paintings were reproduced in full color, and each individually tipped into a huge volume which I described as 'Over 11 inches deep, over 2½ inches thick—and nearly half a yard wide when opened'. It sold at $2.95—Deluxe edition at $1.00 extra.

"John Crawley took the bull by the horns and printed 300,000. Influencing him, of course, was the full-color printing. You just couldn't produce 25,000 or 50,000 sets of 100 full-color paintings and tip them into such a giant volume, and make a profit selling at those prices. To shorten a long story, 275,000 sold like hot cakes at a very handsome profit. Then, we suddenly ran out of lists that paid off. So we took a terrible beating moving the last 25,000.

"If we weren't forever depending on a high volume cash flow, and could have held those 25,000 volumes inventory for a year or two, or three—we would have moved those also at a profit as we developed new lists of book buyers, and found other lists to rent."

More important, cash problems caused concentration on moving inventory of present offers and began to slow development of the kinds of offers particularly suited to the post war boom and changing life styles. The opportunity was to upgrade, to sell more quality at higher prices, to sell sets rather than single volumes, to do it in new ways. Fred remembers:

"Wise had the makings of a great continuity library but failed to assemble contents in the most appealing way. For such a set, Wise had the 'Practical Home Handyman', 'The Amateur

Builder's Handbook', 'The Wise Handbook of Home Plumbing', 'The Practical Home Furniture Builder', 'Masonry', 'Electrical Wiring and Carpentry' and 'Machine Shop Practice'.

"When we tried to make a continuity program of the Wise books it would flop when it hit the 'Electrical Wiring' volume. That book scared them off. What a difference the correct type of presentation can make. Years later, long after I left Wise, I found the way to present a handyman's continuity library—by featuring all the most pleasing *end products* that would or could result by the buyers' use of those books: such as vacation cabins, fishing boats, sand boxes, attic apartments, garden patios, beds, tables and summer furniture. This approach made the Greystone Handyman's Library the biggest continuity library success John Stevenson ever had.

"But we missed out on this at Wise and on other opportunities, perhaps because we were constantly getting over a hump. Because of our rapid growth and our method of financing that expansion, we were constantly dependent on a big volume, quick cash flow to meet our ever-increasing bills for paper, printing, binding, postage, and space and radio time. I think this became a further strain on John's health. It was on mine. I finally had to take two months leave of absence and then work under conditions of less tension. This meant I regretfully had to leave John, after 15 years with him.

"I like to remember John at the height of his vitality when he and John Stevenson and Milo Sutliffe would lunch together, each trying to pick the others' brains, while revealing nothing of his own plans."

John Crawley had a summer home in Hampton Bays, Long Island, on the Great South Bay, across from which was a stretch of dunes and then the ocean. He loved it. He would sit on the big veranda at night and look out, thinking. He said he got his best ideas that way. Finally, the emphysema struck him down.

For Wm. H. Wise, with Fred Breismeister and John Crawley, we pioneered broadcast mail order. We created question and answer information radio shows and later how-to TV shows. We put Wise on network radio and then on TV, and made them the first publisher to do so. On one subject, sewing . . . on one network, ABC . . . in one year . . . we wrote and produced over a million words of sewing how-to shows.

The mail order know-how we acquired by association with Wm. H. Wise proved priceless. We later used it for other publishers and to sell over 300 how-to titles. We did so for John Stevenson and still more for Doubleday. The same kind of garden programs we had created to sell 'The Garden Encyclopedia' for Wm. H. Wise, we later used to sell roses for Jackson & Perkins.

As Fred Breismeister did, we went on from Wm. H. Wise. Whatever we did for Wise benefited us for our work for other clients later and still later for our own products, for our space ads and direct mail. Even the concept of the encyclopedic content of this book came from what I learned at Wise.

John Crawley blazed many trails that the biggest how-to book publishers have followed. Each time I see a mailing or an ad for a how-to book or series for a subject Wise first published on, I think of John Crawley and the framed lines from Rudyard Kipling, which he kept opposite his desk on the office wall:

"They copied all they could follow
    but they couldn't copy my mind,
and I left 'em sweating and stealing
    a year and a half behind."

Thank you, John Crawley.

Chapter 2
The Direct Marketing Shows

National and International

The Annual Conference of the Direct Mail/Marketing Association is direct marketing's biggest event. Almost as many attend Direct Marketing Day in New York but for one day. They're at the Conference for three and a half days. The DMMA Annual Conference is more than the biggest Direct Marketing Day. It's more in-depth, more versatile, more intimate.

The Conference is primarily for professionals in the field. It's for any company that sells to or services direct marketers or could do so. It's for any company or individual able to spend at least a few thousand dollars to get started in mail order or direct marketing.

Many in mail order feel that there is no better way for a newcomer to begin than to go to it. But you have to be able to afford it, use it and understand it. For anyone already in mail order or going into it—substantially, it can be invaluable.

A tiny entrepreneur with little money hoping to start in mail order with a classified or inch ad cannot afford or benefit, initially, from the Conference. For most people hoping to get a starting job in mail order or direct marketing, going to the Conference is also impractical. In my chapter on The Direct Marketing Courses, I discuss how marketing students who qualify may attend, without admission charge, career days at the Conference. In the help source section in back of this book I tell how anyone can attend the Conference by cassette.

To get maximum value from a DMMA Annual Conference a beginner should first get some orientation in other ways. The ideal is to first join a local direct marketing club and then the DMMA. This would give a free subscription to Direct Marketing Magazine. The beginner would do well also to read books on the field, look at a newsletter, listen to tapes of some speeches and perhaps attend a seminar or course or both. If money is a problem, try a business or university library. Consult the back of this book for the source reference help section and talk to the reference librarian.

If you've been in a career or business in mail order, even for a few months, the Conference will do you more good. If you've got one to three years under your belt, the Conference will do you far more good. You'll understand more. You'll perhaps go with people you know. You will benefit greatly from business contacts. You can attend basic seminar sessions, meet others in the field and perhaps get new ideas. At the Annual Conference are users and suppliers, salesmen and consultants, services and middle and upper management of direct marketers.

The Annual Conference particularly concentrates on the big picture, the overview of everything in direct marketing. It's a report on change, present and coming. Old timers attend advanced learning sessions to update themselves on change. They renew old acquaintances. They maintain contact with clients.

It's been going on since 1918—first as the Direct Mail Show. Only 9% of those attending the conference are not DMMA members. And 70% of these join. This is largely due to a combination offer usually made. For slightly more than the non-member registration fee companies can join the DMMA and attend the Conference. There are many other reasons to join and the combination offer gives that extra push to do so.

Each Conference is a family affair. The success of each depends on tremendous efforts by the staff and also by volunteer members. The councils help a lot. The Board of Directors do; also the International Advisory Board and the Exhibit Advisory Council.

All 70-odd DMMA staff members are called on in some way to work for the Annual Conference. Almost every DMMA project in some way gets into it. For every department it's a demonstration. For eight councils it is a showcase. The result is an outpouring of variety. With the members it's the same way. Top leaders from every field are tapped. From the Chairman of the Board, the entire Board of Directors, the executive committee and the long-range planning committee—from the Conference Task Force to the Exhibit Committee, members work throughout the year to prepare for it.

The annual DMMA Conference and Trade Show is the culmination of all this. At the Conference at a general meeting for DMMA members only, officers are elected. Each Council has a closed meeting at the Conference to elect its officers. At a typical annual conference, you can go to a TV direct marketing workshop or one on the new technology of filling orders. There is always something on telephone marketing and on list selection. You can attend seminars for one day or every day. It's a many-

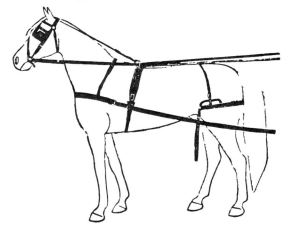

Single Pony Harness.

Russet Leather Only.

This harness is made of Fair Russet Leather of the best oak tanned skirting.

It can be adjusted to fit a pony weighing 500 lbs or a small horse weighing 900 lbs. It is not suitable for anything larger or smaller than we mention.

We make it in *one style only*, and we insure satisfaction to every purchaser.

It is well made and well finished; is complete in every respect, and is decidedly nobby in appearance.

37000 Single Pony Harness, all fair russet leather; breast collar, 1⅜ inch wide, folded with layer, box loops for traces; traces 1 inch, double and stitched, to buckle to breast collar; blind bridle with overcheck and round winker stays; breeching, 1½ inches wide, folded with layer; saddle, 3½ inch with leather pad and leather covered seat; round dock, flat back and hip straps; folded bellyband with Griffith's patent buckles; flat lines; full nickel mountings. Per set....$13.50 Weight, per set, packed in box, 19 pounds.

ring extravaganza. You could spend all your time at the exhibit booths. It's a living catalog of mail order.

But attending it is expensive. You first have to be able to spend a working week of time including flying to and from it. This means travel expenses, plus the hotel expenses, four days with taxis, convention-priced meals and incidentals. You need over seven hundred dollars more to get most benefits. You can then join the DMMA, join one council appropriate to your interest and attend the Conference. If you do, you can then plunge into the inside of the world of direct marketing. At the Council meeting you can be in a smaller group where people get to know each other rather than only being a spectator.

You can be introduced to the gamut of all direct marketing and mail order. You can have a concentrated direct marketing lecture course every day, a sort of saturation Berlitz of mail order. If a member, you can attend the annual meeting of the DMMA. You can attend the annual meeting of any of the eight Councils of the DMMA you may have joined—each an intimate club within a club for those with special interests. You can drop by exhibit after exhibit—from computers to inserting machines to printing . . . from services to vendors of products.

There are other DMMA shows. At the Spring Conference there are again users and suppliers but mostly upper management. Only 3% of attendees are non-members. The Spring Conference concentrates on learning workshops. But to attendees, program context and information are again second in importance. It's a big show. Many prefer its size and feel there's more mixing in smaller groups, more learning and more accomplished. But almost all who attend it go to the Annual Conference, almost four times bigger.

List Day is usually in August and often in New York. It's the size of a medium-sized or larger Direct Marketing Day, but it's entirely on direct mail. It is organized by the Conference Department with the great cooperation of the List Council from which it came. If you use direct mail in any volume, you should go.

The first International Direct Mail/Marketing Conference sponsored by the DMMA was held in Montreux, Switzerland, in 1974—complete with simultaneous translation into French, German and English. Only 15% of those attending were from the U.S. At this point, the DMMA began to get European members. By 1980, only 23% of those attending the International Conference in London were non-members. And, of those, 15% then joined the DMMA. At the International Conference, members are from upper management from the U.S. and overseas and learning and program content are most important.

Direct Marketing has its own Oscars, the ECHO Award for most effective direct marketing campaigns. All spring the DMMA drives to get campaigns submitted. In the summer, a panel of judges selects winning campaigns. Actual dollar-and-cents results are asked for along with entries. Awards are made at the Annual Conference.

The Government Affairs Conference has, as attendees, management involved in government relations. Learning and content are most important. It's a report in person on attitudes of the government toward mail order and direct marketing. It's a place to get together and plan steps to self-regulate rather than be regulated. It's not for the new careerist or new small entrepreneur.

Outside the U.S. there are other international direct marketing shows. One of them, The International Direct Marketing Symposium, has been running every year since 1968, first at Montreux, Switzerland, and now at Lausanne. Close to 2,000 direct marketing executives attend. It's a three-day show preceded by two days of seminars. Murray Miller, of American Express, had the idea of bringing American know-how in direct marketing to Europe. He and Walter Schmid and Chris Eibel are partners in the venture. The majority of lecturers and attendees are European. Each speech or lecture is simultaneously translated into English, French or German, as needed, available via headphones.

In November 1980, the first World Congress of Direct Marketing took place in Singapore. The Australian Direct Marketing Association asked the DMMA to be responsible for U.S. attendance. The British Direct Marketing Association joined in. Meanwhile, "Pete" Hoke's Direct Marketing Magazine joined forces with another group for still another international direct marketing show, this one in Argentina.

The International Shows are for big international direct marketers, big national direct marketers in countries nearest the show location and for suppliers to them. Each of them is far more expensive to attend as well as to get to than the U.S. shows. They are important as an indication of how sweeping the international direct marketing field has become. They are particularly important for anyone who in any country has come up with a new, big mail order success.

It is possible to start small in one country, succeed fast and go international very quickly thereafter. Each show is a meeting ground for alliances between anyone with a new successful offer in one country and direct marketers in other countries. But for the unprotected it can be dangerous territory.

Encouraging Note: Direct marketers overseas are getting better and better. But direct marketing is one area where the U.S. still leads the world. There are reputable direct marketing firms all over the world which value associations with U.S. firms with currently successful offers.

Chapter 3
Mail Order's In-House Entrepreneur

*"The most exciting case history today
of Fortune 500 entrepreneurship."*

"It's the most exciting case history today of Fortune 500 entrepreneurship."

That's what Paul Sampson, Chairman of the Board of Garden Way, told me about Montgomery Ward's specialized mail order subsidiary . . . Signature Financial . . . and Dick Cremer, its president.

For Montgomery Ward he started an entirely new mail order business—without risk. He built $150 million annually of mail order sales, in seven years from scratch. He took the lowest cost form of Ward advertising and made the greatest possible science of using it. Dick Cremer has put Montgomery Ward into the credit insurance business, the magazine business and into operating clubs. He's put Ward into the travel business and into vitamins.

On sales of the five Montgomery Ward subsidiaries, of which he is president (Signature Financial and its four subsidiaries), he has consistently delivered an average profit of 20%

before taxes. He's done it by offering to Ward customers add-on services with a higher profit margin than average Ward items, but with a lower selling cost than competitive items. He's run all five subsidiaries with far less overhead per dollar of sales than average for retailers including Ward's.

"In college, I studied accounting. I came out of school determined not to be an accountant. Instead, I got into credit work—first for Household Finance, then for International Harvester and then for Montgomery Ward. On August 17, 1953, I started as credit manager of one of the four Montgomery Ward stores in Detroit. I knew nothing of mail order. I didn't dream of running a mail order business."

Credit led Dick Cremer to mail order. He studied every aspect of credit. This involved not just cutting credit losses but putting on more credit accounts and selling more on credit to each credit account. He studied Ward's entire history of using credit sales to grow. He became convinced that Ward's two greatest assets were public faith in the integrity of Ward and its list of charge customers, to whom he felt more and more could be sold by mail order.

"I saw that, selling for cash only, it had taken Ward fifty-five years to grow to fifty-five million dollars. In the next twenty-five years with stores and credit it went to over seven hundred million dollars. Since then, Ward's has grown to over four billion dollars. I don't know anyone who'd disagree that credit selling enormously accelerated Ward's growth."

The lowest cost method of mail order selling is the use of a package insert and of a billing insert. Use of billing inserts in bills to store accounts to sell by mail order is not new. But Dick Cremer came up with a way to use billing inserts more scientifically than they had ever been used before, at lower selling cost, for a higher percentage of profit and in bigger volume than had ever been achieved before.

"After a few years at the job in Detroit, I was moved to Chicago, with a job in Ward's corporate credit office. That was in 1961. There I learned something that later made possible everything we've done at Signature Financial. Craig Lovesay, circulation manager of Look Magazine, called on me.

"He said: 'You send out millions of bills. Let me give you business reply envelopes to use as billing inserts offering subscriptions to Look. We'll pay Montgomery Ward to insert them. It will be extra income for Ward.' When I saw how well these inserts in Ward bills pulled for Look, for the first time I realized the potential of inserts. If inserts worked for Look, they could work for us, inserting our own mail order offers to our own charge account names.

"We inserted the BRE's inserts manually. Even then, the use of billing inserts was profitable. The inserting machines didn't make the use of inserts profitable. They made it a lot more profitable. Just after the Look test, we began to use six-station Philipsburg inserting machines. The machines were first used to save money in envelope and bill inserts. Their dramatic cut of the cost of inserting advertising was a side benefit. Now we have twelve-station Philipsburg machines with scanning heads. We keep working with the manufacturers to improve them further.

"Years ago, one operator could insert thirty times as many pieces an hour. Today, under optimum conditions, an operator can insert up to eighty times as many pieces an hour as manual. The bills have to go out anyway. The cost of printing and inserting an insert is a small fraction of the cost per thousand of any other form of Ward advertising.

"The amortizing of any machine only gradually pays off. Computers first were very expensive and more expensive to operate than manual operations. Inserting machines were the same. It's always the same. But, sooner or later, the lines cross. There's the kissing curve. The new way is lower cost and then it can get lower and lower in cost very rapidly.

"The speed of the inserting machines gradually made the use of inserts much more feasible. There was another plus. After we switched to machines to cut billing cost for years we had plenty of open insert positions. We could insert for others, as for Look, at so much a thousand and get extra revenue. We could insert for our own mail order items and make extra profits, for a number of different inserts each month. But now, there is keen competition for one of the five available positions. Now I fight for just one station for Signature."

Ward was growing fast. So was Dick Cremer's career, and his mastery of credit. In 1963, he joined the North Central Regional Headquarters, in Chicago, as assistant regional credit manager. In 1964, he became regional credit manager for Ward's Eastern region in Baltimore, Maryland. In 1966, he was promoted to assistant corporate credit manager and returned to Chicago.

"Paul Sampson introduces me at seminars with what he considers a compliment. He will describe the success of Montgomery Ward's new mail order subsidiary. Then he says how remarkable it is that it has all been created by just a credit man. *Just a credit man!*

"You don't succeed in direct marketing without a high regard for numbers and a good grounding in scientific management. Credit is the same. It's a numbers business. Direct marketing is. I'm a numbers man. Ward credit sent out millions of collections letters. They also sent out millions of invitations offering to open up new credit accounts. The credit collection manager and new credit account sales manager each reported to me. Each complained about the other. I had to set policies. Even before Signature Financial marketing, Inc. was formed, we were spending millions of dollars a year on credit promotion direct mail.

"Retailing had a very strong trade association of retail store credit managers which, over the years, had taught me a lot. Therefore, when I became interested in direct marketing, I sought out a trade association. I found the Direct Mail/Marketing Association. It, too, was very strong. It was very similar. I went to DMMA meetings to see and hear what others did. It was like going to college again. It all helped. People were willing to share experiences. I always exchange information. All credit managers do."

Dick was now actively in mail order for Ward. He looked continually for mail order items that could yield most profit with a billing insert. Some items came from the catalog or store successes. Others he found were not currently sold by Ward until use of Ward inserts. He began to form opinions as to which items could sell best. He started to think about creating items with maximum appeal and margin.

Mail order was just beginning to be referred to as direct response marketing. Zip codes were coming into play. There was talk of demographics and the beginnings of conjectures about psychographics. The computer was being applied to mail order in many ways. Segmentation of lists was being experimented with. And, in his exchange of information, Dick Cremer began to realize that at Ward was the basis of far more mail order science than elsewhere.

"Our involvement in selective marketing started for an entirely different purpose. We began to use multivariate linear regression analysis (MLRA), developed in 1962, to select good credit risks on a point scoring system. It all came about from the questions we asked each applicant for credit. In 1968, we began putting all this data on computer.

"The format of the Charg-All master.file now contains 70 demographic and other characteristics on each of our 20 million accounts. It costs millions of dollars more to do it this way. It costs us a half a million dollars each year just to input data for new accounts and update existing ones. But the information not only paid off in keeping credit losses low, it gave us invaluable information to sell more scientifically by mail order to selected credit accounts.

"We used a scientific, statistical research method called multivariate linear regression analysis to compare what people who for us were good credit risks had most in common; and what those who for us proved bad credit risks had most in common. We found out much more. Other credit granters computerized only name, address, city, state, zip and financial billing information. We computerized seventy different characteristics. MLRA determined points for attributes for each characteristic. To be accepted for credit you needed a passing score. Our credit losses dropped. Our new credit accounts jumped.

"We created a panel of a hundred thousand good credit customers selected at random on an Nth name basis. This meant taking every Nth name right through the list up to 100,000. Then, before mailing a big outside list to offer charge account privileges, we tested it sufficiently to obtain at least 1,000 buyers. Then with MLRA, we averaged out the characteristics of the buyers and scored them. Only if the projected response was high enough did we mail the offer to a selected portion of the entire list.

"Then we began to add the buying record of each customer to the file. Now we knew which Ward customers would more probably want what. We could not only use inserts at least expense, we could insert them precisely into the bills of those customers most receptive to the item offered. We were ready to go into mail order more intensively.

"The next requirement of success was to find products with more chance of success and better margin and to build offers for them that would be hard to resist. My entire experience in credit for Ward shaped my attitude toward mail order. It even gave me my first mail order item for Ward. As an old bill collector, I knew most delinquent credit customers don't intend not to pay. They are not dead beats. Their accounts become delinquent mainly for two reasons: Their income is destroyed or they suffer unexpected financial loss.

"That gave me my great idea. It was to find an insurance company to insure each credit account and pay accounts for anyone who couldn't. I scouted around for a company that would issue this insurance. I talked to Maurice Olsen, Chairman of the Board of Central National Insurance of Omaha, in Omaha, Nebraska.

"I came up with the insurance policy concept. He underwrote it. He made me the exclusive agent. I got him to participate in the test and put up the money to print the literature under Ward's name in a statement insert. In return, I made CNO our exclusive underwriter. Ward incorporated Signature Agency, Inc. to collect the commission and to handle it. I was made president.

"We called our credit account protection program Charg-all Security Plan—CSP for short. (Charg-all is Ward's name for its revolving credit program.) A few other large retailers and banks offered customers credit insurance.

"We took the best of what others offered, improved on it, and came up with some new wrinkles of our own. So far, over 2 million Ward's credit customers have enrolled for credit insurance protections, paying a monthly premium based on their current outstanding balance." Richard Popel was Signature's first employee and is now the V.P. and General Manager of Signature Agency, Inc., the insurance agency that administers CSP.

Ultimately, Dick Cremer had to give up wearing his credit hat. In 1976, Signature Financial/Marketing Inc. was formed. It became the holding company for Signature Agency, Inc. and for three other mail order subsidiaries. Dick became president of Signature Financial and of each subsidiary.

"Once in a lifetime a really brilliant idea pops into your mind. It happened to me. A man had an auto club and came to me with a proposal. 'I'll pay $10 per member and provide all materials.' I asked how many he expected to pull from our list. He said 2%. I decided that I'd better get into the business. His club was the U.S. Auto Club. The Ward club was started on the basis of being run for Ward by U.S. Auto from the outside. It became another Signature Financial subsidiary.

"I decided that in the auto club business, as in any other, I'd have to know my competition and build a better mouse trap. I joined fifty auto clubs. They were all alike. Some gave a little more and some a little less. I gave all the important benefits they did plus more. I had the idea of a 10% discount at all the best hotels. We wrote 18,000 hotels and got 6,000 to sign up. Later, in 1976, we added a service to enable members to get a new car at $125 over dealer cost."

I recommend strongly that you read the detailed story by Dick Cremer, himself, of Montgomery Ward Auto Club, as told in an article in Direct Marketing magazine and listed in the help source section in back of this book.

Dick found the use of inserts to Ward charge accounts far more successful than anticipated. He had a smash hit—a mass appeal, universal offer . . . with ample margin. He used all his number skills. He tested one method of advertising after another. He projected each that paid out—safely, scientifically, with showmanship and to the maximum.

He ran inserts to his entire active charge list. He made selective solo mailings to active and inactive charge names. He ran a 14 million mailing. He used 11 million inserts in R.H. Donnelley co-ops. He ran a four-color, four-page center section in TV Guide. He ran in Parade. Magazine media amounted to 41 million circulation outside of Ward's customer list. He used support (hype) TV. He featured Zsa Zsa Gabor in direct mail ads and in store and supermarket personal appearances. He used take-one literature in Ward stores and in supermarkets to solicit orders. He tied it all in with a giant sweepstakes offer.

"We ran sweepstakes with big prizes to get the envelope opened. We ran three in a row. We used TV mostly for support. We used one-minute spots with a phone-in offer. Sweepstakes were essential for outside lists. Without sweepstakes, it would have been impossible."

Dick Cremer had become for Ward's the U.S. exclusive official ticket distributor for the Summer Olympics in Montreal, in 1976. He then sponsored racing cars. "We generated three 30-minute TV specials for ABC. We got two free 30-second spots in each."

From outside media, to become a member each applicant had to open a Ward's account. These campaigns resulted in over 500,000 new account applications in 1977 alone. These new Ward accounts opened have bought as much merchandise from Ward per account as the average Ward credit account.

"With over 1,300,000 members, the Montgomery Ward Auto Club is the world's fastest growing auto club. It's the third largest full-service auto club in the country. It's gaining ground fast on Number Two."

Then the club started a two-color newsletter which came out quarterly to members of the Montgomery Ward Auto Club. Later, it became a four-color magazine members got every other month. Now it has 1,300,000 circulation and averages 64 pages—all in four color. It costs 35¢ an issue to produce. "If I could sell space for $14,000 a page, 18 pages would subsidize it. When I found I couldn't sell 18 pages, I started a subsidiary to sell products in the space."

The Montgomery Ward Enterprise Marketing Services Division was largely devoted to finding and selling products first in the magazine. It has become a test medium. "We consider an item if its service fits our image, if it's a good value, if it can make at least 20%. Montgomery Ward Enterprises Marketing Services tests hundreds of items every year in the club magazine. Those that do well enough are further tested in co-op mailings. Those that do very well are tested in solos. From these items we get perhaps a dozen good solos a year."

Meanwhile, Dick developed another mail order hit, done this way. "Signature offered Ward's customers a credit card registration service for all credit cards. We assessed what everyone else in the credit card registry field was doing and tried to do it better. We offered an alert, 24-hour around-the-clock notification service for lost or stolen credit cards. We covered all credit cards, not just our own Charg-all cards. Ward's Credit Card Registration Service has competitors. But we try to give more with our service. We now have a million members.

"For our Ward's Credit Card Registration service, we run inserts and a solo mailing and co-ops. We're also in the Carol Wright mailings of R.H. Donnelley. We also use free-standing inserts.

"By now, quite a large number of our charge accounts are members of the Ward Auto Club. For those people we want to offer other clubs and policies. To do that, we're coding statements. Our software programs have the logic to know from the coding which offer the statement needs inserted and sends the message down. We're starting more new promotions. It's in the process of evolution. When promoting the Ward Auto Club, Ward's is starting to include other offers. One is for an accidental death insurance policy. Another is for a hospitalization policy.

"We're testing a pre-paid legal service plan. We made a small test with six cells to lists totalling 25,000 (each cell was a sub-test). We also included in the test telephone selling to get quick results. We're encouraged. Now we're proceeding far further. That's a service consumers will pay a price for."

Dick does not live for numbers science alone. He has gut feelings. He has enthusiasms. He likes to sell what he likes. He likes health. He likes travel. He believes strongly in and practices fitness. He's gregarious. He likes clubs. He enjoys his magazines. But he does it all with science.

"Another new division is our direct response vitamin club. I purchased all the different kinds of one-a-day vitamins in the world. Then I developed one with more as the maximum potency. We call it FIT. We've got 100 M members we're sending these vitamins to. Now we're in the roll-out. I bought Vital magazine to become its vehicle. We've more bells and whistles to come.

"Our publication division is a growth area. For our travel club, we have our magazine, Going Places. We're developing magazine subscriptions. We have a full-scale publishing operation.

"We also have the Family Aerobic Exercise Program. It's one contribution to mankind I'm very proud of. Results are not strong enough yet to project.

"Three years ago, I was quite a smoker. I went to 227

Ten Nights in a Bar Room.

6774 Ten Nights in a Bar Room, And What I Saw There. By T. S. Arthur. A new edition in large type of this famous book, 12mo. Illustrated. Retail price.....$1.25
Our price reduced to......... .45
Postage .... .10
6775 Home Stories. 6 vols. Sold only in sets.
Sowing the Wind.
Hidden Wings.
Sunshine at Home.
Not Anything for Peace.
The Peace Makers.
After a Shadow.
Price $2.00

Alcott's, Louisa M., Stories.
Series No. 6768.

"Miss Alcott is the benefactor of households".
Little Men.
Little Women.
Eight Cousins
Jack and Jill.
Work.
Moods.
Life Letters and Journals.
Hospital Sketches.
Modern Mephistopheles.
Rose in Bloom.
Jo's Boys.
Old Fashioned Girl.
Under the Lilacs.

Each 12mo., c'oth. Retail price, each $1.50
Our price, each................................. .98
Postage........................ . :........... .12

Bolton, Sarah K., Works.
Series 6827.

All uniform binding, large type and cloth. Illustrated. Large 12mo.

Famous Types of Womanhood.
Famous English Statesmen.
Famous English Authors of the Nineteenth Century.
Famous European Artists.
Famous American Authors.
Famous American Statesmen.
Famous Men of Science.
Girls Who Became Famous.
Poor Boys Who Became Famous.
Famous Leaders Among Men.
Famous Voyagers.
Retail price, each $1.50
Our price 1.00
Postage extra, each ...... .12

pounds. I'm six feet one inches, too. I was heavy. The ony reason I smoked was because I was stupid. I couldn't quit because I was weak. Then I kicked the cigarette habit. It's one of the most gratifying experiences possible.

"I always wanted to climb a mountain. I always wanted to be on a ridge with unlimited visibility. I never did climb a mountain until, in November 1978, I made a trip to the Himalayas and did climb my mountain. I had lost 23 pounds getting ready for the climb. On the trip I lost 18 pounds more. Now I weigh 185. I don't smoke. I run 4 to 7 miles a day. Today, I ran 10 miles. Dr. Ken

Cooper, of Dallas, gives me my physicals. He has Aerobic International Research Society (AIRS). I'm trying to start a good healthkeeping club for Ward's.

"I encourage fitness for my five hundred plus employees. At the 1979 ribbon cutting ceremony of our Demster headquarters, we had an open house. We had an inter-facility fitness program run between the old office and our new office. It was 3.8 miles. Ten percent of the employees signed up. Each entrant made it. We then entered the Corporate Cup relay race. It's sponsored by Brook shoes and Runner's World magazine. We competed against twenty corporations. Thirty of our employees, including me, entered. It's a fifty/fifty deal, men and women.

"We're building an 8,000 square foot fitness laboratory for our staff and to test equipment. We'll have treadmills, an indoor track, lots of test equipment. We'll have lots to report to Good Healthkeeping Club members. We hope it will be of general interest, institutional interest and editorial interest. It's a fun way to do it.

"We're looking around for other new ventures. When I find time, Ward's has given me authority to look into anything which fits Ward's image where there is an opportunity for profit. We're very selective. We study each possibility carefully to determine if we really belong in that particular business. Once we know we want to consider it seriously, we test it very scientifically.

"We've got the most sophisticated mailing list available in direct marketing and an active testing program to help us get the most out of it. Our 18 million active and inactive names can be segmented in a surprising number of ways. We know each customer. Purchases show their hobbies, likes, dislikes. When each courts, marries, has children, we see it in the buying record. We can see the change in buying a divorce makes. We can match specific products with people who need and want them, when they do.

"We've developed our testing programs to the point where we've had a significant reduction on our overall testing costs. By using Multivariate Linear Regression Analysis (MLRA), we've managed to identify and select parts of our master file that are three to ten times better than others. Thus, we've been able to keep our tests small enough to minimize cost and still maximize the returns on roll-out mailings.

"We do all direct marketing on a very selective basis. For selection of outside lists and media we did a lot of regression analysis. We cut down on response but got better quality credit applications. We do a lot of source analysis. The source of mail order credit orders is important. For business generated by TV, for instance, credit quality is lousy. Applications from TV are substandard. Ward's won't approve bad ones.

"The Montgomery Ward Auto Club was so successful it allowed us to use outside media. This greatly built up the lists of mail order buyers of the Signature Group. When we have another hit that big, we'll do it again.

"We concentrate on small ticket offers of widest appeal. We need quality names, our own. We have our own magazines. Our statements go to 8½ million credit accounts with an outstanding balance each month.

"Each separate Signature company and division is a profit center. Within each Signature company, separate profit centers can and will develop. We already have ten profit centers. As we succeed in certain directions, we tend to grow in related directions."

Dick Cremer did not do all this by himself. He's a numbers man who has a flair for selecting many good people and motivating them. "I have drive and enthusiasm. I surround myself with those who also have it. First we built our team using a great many people out of Ward's. That was good up to a point. Then we started to look for those with direct response experience. Now, at the lower level, we take on graduates from marketing courses. I get a lot of applications from bright, young people.

"We have enthusiastic professionals in key management positions. When Lawrence Chait closed his agency, we were fortunate in being able to retain his president, Saul Mills. Saul is very talented. He's a genius, really! He's been with me since the beginning. At first, we thought he would work only one day a week, but then he worked more and then full-time for me.

"Dave Clarke is a computer sciences genius. He developed and at first headed our multivariate linear regression analysis program. His old boss at a former employer was then at J.H. Whitney, the car item catalog. When it filed bankruptcy, Dave and I hired him. I moved Dave up as vice president of planning and research and gave him a small staff. Bob Sebastian took over Dave's old job. He has a dozen people working for him now. He works on list segmentation. In addition, he's just getting into programming software."

All scientific methods do not always work out as hoped for. "When I was still in credit, we developed a computer model. I became disenchanted with it. Maintaining it was quite burdensome. And a test destroys the model. It's really not on line. We have a few models. We have a profit simulation model. We can get a picture in about ten minutes of what a project can develop to under different future conditions. Carl Noble, of Kellogg Graduate School at Northwestern University, is helping us learn how to use models. There's not just one way feasible, only one way of going.

outside. Since then, our tendency has been to do more and more of each operation ourselves. We are starting some vertical integration doing everything possible ourselves. We have no promotional lettershop operations. We do no promotional mailings inside. We use dozens of lettershops for all that. We do a lot of our list maintenance ourselves. We have our own systems development group. We have full time systems analysts and programmers. Heading up all operations, systems and our chief operating officer is Harold F. Drew, Executive Vice President and an outstanding executive that I've known for over 25 years.

"We work with Murray Roman, of C.C.I., in telephone selling. We use MLRA to select lists to phone." Dick Cremer used multivariate analysis of his nine million list of Ward Charge-All Customers to produce the best segments to phone. Calling such segments enrolled at the rate of 20% when offering Ward's Credit Card Security Service. The same method was used even more successfully by Signature's FIT vitamin club.

"We have a good team and strong talent. But the faster we grow the more strong direct marketing talent we need. Getting them and training them is not easy. We use a number of outside agencies on spot assignments. Our future growth problem is acquiring the number of people with expertise and motivation that projected growth takes. Most people don't like the unusual. I've hired seven hundred people to net five hundred. For our five-year projections, I'll need to hire another 1,000 employees for volume projected. Hiring the right people and motivating them is the challenge. I look for bright, young people. I get some from the marketing classes including some colleges with a limited curriculum. I get some from Roosevelt University's direct marketing class. I get some from the Collegiate Institute of the Direct Mail/Marketing Educational Foundation.

"We have success stories. We have several young men and women who've taken to our business like ducks to water. One we took from graduate school, from Kellogg School of Business at Northwestern. He was a student of Professor Philip Kotler. Carl Noble, Director of Information Services, helped us by recommending this young man.

"Would I value someone who had experience owning or running a very small mail order business? I certainly would. I interviewed a man who had owned five shoe stores. I spent the whole time talking about his business. I hired him. His name is Syd Klevait, and he runs our marketing services division. I don't personally interview as many people as I did. I wish I had time. I have a vice president in charge of employee service and career development whose name is Eric Freesmeirer.

"I value associates who share our philosophy. Two other senior officers of Signature are our Financial V.P., Len Hollenbeck, and our General Counsel, Fred Zeni, both top men that I've known for 15 years.

"At Signature, we promote products we've tested that we like and think our customers will like. Our way is enthusiastic but does not fudge truth. It has zing but no exaggerations.

"Our illustrations both flatter and honestly depict the product. Photos are retouched only to bring up details, not to make the product look like something it isn't. We don't say the price is special unless it is. The proposition of sale is stated very clearly, generally two or three times in the piece. We have our own legal division of four lawyers.

"Every product we promote must be first evaluated and okayed by Ward's own testing laboratory. Every service must meet extensive value criteria. Every sales proposal must have integrity and clarity. Only after we phone buyers from a test mailing to see if they think the item is 'as advertised' and a good value do we schedule a big mailing. Our executive vice president of marketing is George Swiorczynski. He is a winner. He's studying nights to get his MBA from Kellogg Graduate School at Northwestern."

Montgomery Ward doesn't rent lists of customers. Every credit applicant is informed that data from filled out applications may be used by Ward in determining specialized products to offer each by mail. Each is asked to notify Ward if doing so is not desired.

Dick Cremer is an inside entrepreneur with a rare, natural talent. He's an imaginative accountant with a feel for numbers, items, offers and mail order. He's a pioneer. "To succeed you must have the know-how to succeed, the desire to succeed and the need to be a pioneer. To turn a large corporation three degrees is difficult and can be dangerous. A retail manager perceives competition. More success for the pioneer means more exposure to being shot down. To succeed, I've had to put my job on the line."

Dick Cremer is a company man, with infinite faith in Montgomery Ward. "It was the first U.S. mail order business. Its growth has constantly accelerated for its stores, its catalog and now its specialized mail order sales. I could not have done what I've accomplished at other big retail companies. They're too bureaucratic. Ward created the atmosphere to permit it to happen. My principals gave me latitude. Ward had the leadership to value it. Ward is unique. Only Ward's top management could have been so supportive. They made it possible. They let me be an entrepreneur for Ward but as if I were on my own.

"Recently, profits for Signature Financial companies have seemed strong. High interest and high overhead have knocked down overall profits of Ward, Sears and Penny. But, in the future, the Signature Group and Ward overall will do well. Ward is a strong, sound company. I never forget that the Signature Financial companies exist as satellites. Their high profitability comes from the power of Ward.

"Retailing has huge investments and is traditionally a small margin business. Direct response and mail order has been at Ward the traditional catalog—as for Sears, Spiegel, Penney and Alden's. The catalog is a form of retailing and also has a narrow mark-up. It's labor intensive. Overhead is high. When interest rates go sky-high, it becomes very difficult to maintain good catalog profits, just as it does for mass retail stores.

"In the direct response industry, the catalog business represents about half of the total sales. But it is the other half of the mail order business that is quite different. It operates with a bigger margin, with less overhead and with less labor. It's objective is a bigger percentage of profit, up to 15% to 20% before taxes. That's the field the Signature companies are in."

With the Signature Group Dick does better than that. He does so because so much of Signature volume comes from the cheapest form of mail order advertising inserts; because the Ward charge list is 18,000,000 and the trust in Ward is great; because he has such a flair at product selections and creation, and of offer development; because he is so extraordinarily scientific in testing and projecting; because he has assembled so remarkably effective a direct marketing team; because of his unending, ever-accelerating driving energy; and because of his willingness to dare, to do what can be done, even if it has not been done.

"Ward is domestic. Ward has a policy of non-involvement with companies in other countries. But, I'm interested in expanding the Signature Group beyond the U.S. I'm looking at one auto club in Puerto Rico and at one in Canada. We'd like to go further."

Dick Cremer sees the Signature operation as a small balance to the giant Ward one. It may soon become a bigger one. The overall sales of Montgomery Ward are thirty-three times those of the Signature Group, but with two hundred times the number of employees. 1981 was Signature's most profitable year. In 1982, Dick Cremer began to open up new universes to expand into. Signature began to offer Ward Auto Club Insurance via banks, loan companies and other credit granters.

He is realistic, constantly watches mail order vital signs of all Signature operations and acts accordingly. In January 1981 analysis convinced him that selling merchandise to Signature buyers of services was requiring a disproportionate share of personnel and overhead and yielding too marginal a profit. He expanded sales of services but dropped sales of merchandise to customers who bought services. He found he could reduce staff sharply but then personally went to work with his executives to help place elsewhere those for whom the new policy meant loss of jobs.

Dick Cremer is a very busy man. He also gives his advice freely to those entering the business. He helps the young start careers. He lectures at universities, talks at direct marketing meetings. He's been on the Board and Executive Committee of the DMMA and is currently chairman of the Inter-Council Task Force for DMMA's eight special interest councils. He's also a member of DMMA's long range planning committee.

When will he slow down? "I'm aiming to take it easier when the Signature Financial Companies do $700 million a year. That was the volume all of Montgomery Ward did the year I started with the company."

Chapter 4

Stimulating Direct Marketing Careers

*The one-man catalyst to faster,
bigger career success.*

He has taught more people, helped more people and been a catalyst to greater direct marketing success for more people than anyone I know.

Nat Ross conducts New York University's Direct Marketing course. He founded The Direct Marketing Idea Exchange (DMIX), a discussion group of leaders. He aids a variety of activities for the Direct Mail/Marketing Association, various Direct Marketing Days, Direct Marketing clubs and whatever.

He is the conscience of direct marketing. Quietly, year after year, he has been reforming, remolding and changing it for the better. Nat has always been a reforming progressive . . . since graduation as a Phi Beta Kappa from Columbia. Yet unreconstructed conservatives and every shade of opinion have warm affection for Nat . . . even as he reforms them. It was at Columbia that his fundamental philosophical and political views began to crystallize and he became part of the student left of the 1920's.

In the late 1920's, Nat taught in the New York High School System. He became interested in educational and statistical research. He became a labor organizer and a "premature" civil rights activist. He helped organize the Share Croppers Union in the Deep South. Later, he went to Minnesota where liberal reform politics are a tradition.

He helped Hubert Humphrey win his first election as a mayor of Minneapolis in 1944 and start his march to the political top. Nat was associated with the political reform leaders of the state . . . Governors Elmer Benson and Floyd Olson, the great commoner.

Nat worked with well-known labor, civil rights and political leaders nationally. He was a friend of Howard Fast, author of "Freedom Road", "Spartacus" and other historical novels, and of John Howard Lawson, first president of The Screen Writers' Guild. Lawson wrote the standard university text book, "Theory and Practice of Playwriting and Film Writing", and the play "Processional", the most successful Broadway play of 1927, produced by the Theatre Guild, as well as about 20 movies. Nat gave lectures on current events to students at The University of Minnesota and has spoken at a number of universities. He appeared on radio station WCCO, in Minneapolis, and received 150 favorable responses to his address.

Then, at the age of 51, he went into a new way of making a living, a new world . . . advertising and selling . . . mail order marketing . . . business competition . . . free enterprise.

In 1956, Nat started with Harry Green, owner of a New York City lettershop. A year later he joined Lincoln Letter Service, founded in 1950 by Norman Eisner and Leo Swedler. In 1965, it enlarged as Lincoln Graphic Arts. Today, it consists of Lincoln Web Offset, Lincoln Lithograph and Lincoln Letter Services with its plant at Farmingdale, New York. Customers range from Mobil Oil to Crown Publishing. Annual sales are over $12,000,000.

Nat's job was selling big run, direct mail printing to sophisticated, knowledgeable direct marketers and to those getting into the field. How did a crusading reformer fit into all this? From his first day, he found excitement in it . . . and has ever since.

"For me, it's been an ongoing learning process, an indescribably rewarding and fulfilling personal experience." He fell in love with the numbers, math, science and art of it. Measuring test results and from them predicting future projections intrigued him. Above all, he was fascinated by the many wonderful people he met in direct marketing.

He brought to direct marketing a professionalism, a new viewpoint. Surprisingly, his interests, abilities and even past experience did fit. He sought knowledge everywhere possible. He became a student, later a research scholar and then a master of direct marketing.

Gradually, subtly and indirectly, Nat's know-how paid off. He began to help his customers as a bonus. More and more, he sold printing while acting simultaneously as an unpaid consultant. More and more, customers relied on his help. His reputation grew and became an asset to Lincoln Graphic Arts. Nat has been with Lincoln for 25 years. He is vice president. To me, his successful switching of careers in his fifties is impressive.

At 51, he went into direct marketing and, at 54, began to participate in the DMMA. At 56, he took the New York University Direct Marketing course, then conducted by Jerry Hardy. At 63, he took over conducting the course. At 66, he founded the Direct Marketing Idea Exchange. At 70, he became a full adjunct professor of advertising promotion . . . while continuing his business career.

When Nat took over the NYU course, all he had done before seemed to come together. He had taught, reformed, organized, led, persuaded and helped. His restless intellect had been a magnet and sounding board for bright minds. Now, in two hours a week for ten sessions a semester, he began to change people's lives . . . and all of direct marketing.

He was a perfectionist in teaching presentation, guest lecturer recruitment and administration. The 1982 Spring Session is Nat's 30th semester and sixteenth year. Through the Fall of 1982, the NYU course has had 474 lectures. It is direct marketing's oldest continuous course. Over 2,600 have attended it. From the first, it earned mounting praise.

Jerry Hardy, who went on from Doubleday to head Time-Life Books, then Life Magazine and then Dreyfus Corporation, says: "If all the alumni of the NYU course ever met together, they would include a large percentage of those who hold major executive posts in the direct response business." NYU's Dean Stanley Gabor calls Nat "one in a million in organizing a course."

"Nat Ross' professionalism is unsurpassed," says Roy Abrams, President of Margrace Corporation. "Nat has gathered together leaders of field after field of direct marketing . . . then seen to it that they arrive with lectures better prepared than elsewhere."

It is a course not just of beginners but of presidents and top executives, because that is what so many students later become. Adolph Auerbacher became publisher of annuals and semi-annuals for Better Homes & Gardens; Sally Reich, marketing manager of the Literary Guild; Lee Van der Waal, Direct Response Manager for J.C. Penney. All are Nat's graduates.

John Caples, one of the all-time great names in advertising, who pioneered in mail order in the 1920's, took the course in the spring of 1970, as a refresher. He didn't miss a lecture. Tim Sharpe became Senior Executive Vice-President of McCann-Erickson-March Direct Response, Inc. Roger Lourie is owner of Devin-Adair Co., Inc. All graduated and later lectured at the

course. "Pete" Hoke, of Direct Marketing Magazine, has taped and distributed internationally over 300 lectures, from 1969 through 1981.

Dick Cremer, President of five Montgomery Ward companies, has lectured for Nat. So have Robin Smith, President of Publishers Clearing House, and Dave Heneberry, President of T-L-K Direct. Lillian Katz, founder of Lillian Vernon, has too... as has Lester Wunderman, President of direct marketing's biggest advertising agency, Wunderman, Ricotta & Kline. So have many others, young and old. Joan Manley, President of Time-Life Books, describes the NYU course: "What a cast! Chosen from the best of the 'old pros' and the talented rising new stars!"

Originally, the course was attended mainly by white males. But Nat has always fought to open top opportunities in the field to women and minorities. Changing enrollment reflects this.

The late Omar Persons, Vice President of CBS-Columbia House, was the first black to take the course ... and then Ann Killian, now a consultant. Other pioneer women taking the course were Fran Keegan of Book-of-the-Month Club, consultant Ginny Daly, Nancy Merritt of Business Week, Patricia O'Callahan of Popular Science and Sally Reich, all smart women. 56% of the students in the Fall 1981 Semester were women. Originally, the course was 90% on direct mail. Now it's 60%, with all media covered by top authorities. Through fall 1971, Nat gave the first and last lectures, later giving the opening lecture in the fall and

closing in the spring. He doesn't lecture now but participates in each session. He often plays the part of devil's advocate in order to stimulate dissent, discussion and thought among the students. From the start he helped students personally, often to get jobs and then advance in them. Often he has kept close contact afterward.

Most enrollments are paid for in whole or in part by the employer. I urge the boss of any company near New York going into direct marketing to enroll himself or herself or to send a promising employee. If you're an employee and interested, get your boss to enroll you.

If you can't, and can't afford the course, two fully-paid scholarships are available. Apply to sponsors. One is the NYU scholarship. For information write to Evelyn Deitz, Treasurer, Direct Marketing Idea Exchange, c/o CBS-Columbia House, 1211 Avenue of the Americas, New York, NY 10036. The other is Howard Flood, President of Hundred Million Club, c/o McGraw-Hill Publishing Co., 1221 Avenue of the Americas, New York, NY 10020.

You can buy any of over 300 NYU lecture audio tapes by writing Direct Marketing Magazine, Garden City, NY 11530 (telephone: 516-746-6700). Or ask your library or business college to buy them. Many lectures have been transcribed and printed in Direct Marketing Magazine and short excerpts are in its Friday Report Newsletter. You can buy back copies. Some business and college libraries subscribe Ask the reference librarian.

If in the New York City area, you may go to the Direct Marketing Magazine library and listen to tapes or read back issues. Phone first for permission. Also try the DMMA Library, 6 East 43rd Street, New York, NY. Call 212-689-4977 first for an appointment. Or get in touch with Nat Ross at Lincoln Graphic Arts, 475 Park Avenue South, New York, NY 10016.

In the fall of 1979, Nat initiated and became the consultant to a new Advanced Course in Mailing Lists, held at noon time at NYU's new midtown center, 11 W 42nd Street, and conducted by Richard Vergera of the Kleid Co.

In 1970, Nat started another project as a discussion group of a dozen friends. It's the Direct Marketing Idea Exchange (DMIX). Attendance is still by invitation only. Invited members may not bring guests, except under special circumstances and by prior clearance. Membership is limited, and not just to the eminently successful. One hundred members is considered the optimum size for this type of discussion group.

The DMIX constitution states: "Any individual direct marketer who has shown an interest in the exchange of ideas and who espouses ethical business values, a respect for the consumer and a sense of social responsibility, is eligible for membership." The board wants active participation. "Members are nice people, able people, the cream of the crop," says Founder and President Nat Ross. "We don't want any fast buck operators."

The first four years each speaker was a member. Today speakers range from great editors like Clay Felker or Pat Carbine, economist Fabian Linden of the Conference Board, former Postmaster General J. Edward Day, iconoclastic advertising great, George Lois, noted author Cleveland Amory, and outstanding direct marketing professionals. The executive board and executive committee speakers who are true professionals often speak of the unusual.

The DMIX meets at the Yale Club in New York City. The board expects 24-hour notice if a member does not attend. No-shows are swiftly dropped. There have been over 100 DMIX sessions. Currently, there are 100 resident members and 15 non-resident members. Once, at a dinner at the Advertising Club in Nat's honor, he was asked to identify each of over a hundred attendees. He did, without an error.

For both course and DMIX, Nat runs a tight ship. He makes things happen. He has standards. He's interested in practicality, profit and success, but in a lot more. One direct marketer, Jim Howard wrote a poem describing Nat as "historian, professor, humanist, friend and mentor".

Nat is an amateur historian. At Columbia, he won the Chandler Historical Prize writing on "The Anglo-Japanese Alliance in the Far East", and the Carolyn Phelps Stokes Historical Prize on "Criminal Syndicalist Laws in the U.S." He is interested in the past of mail order and the present and future of direct marketing... in its impact on society... and the impact of our changing culture on it... and in the impact of new technology on the use of direct marketing and on opportunities in it.

Few of us can see the mail order forest for the trees. He sees it all, from the mountaintop, with a different eye. He views in perspective the history of mail order as a moving panorama of America, itself. Nat sees Aaron Montgomery Ward, who, in a period of great populist agrarian unrest, founded modern mail order in 1872, as the answer to the National Grange slogan, "eliminate the middle man".

He sees Harry Scherman's Book-of-the-Month Club as the natural outcome of wider interest in good books and an inability of a limited number of book stores to supply these needs. He sees the broadening of mail order in the 1950's and 1960's into direct marketing as a part and result of technological, economic and cultural changes of those years. "It was an inexorable evolution and sprang from the warp and woof of a changing American society."

Nat is an intellectual. His vision gives an electrical charge. He sees the impact on direct marketing of economics and social background of politics and literature, of psychology and cultural trends and particularly of changing ideas. "Above all, a market is changing values, behavior and life-styles. The progress and growth of direct marketing depend on and derive from a comprehension of the nature of change and the impact of societal change on the marketplace."

He sees, before others do, changing behavioral patterns, new methods and emerging techniques. He was one of the first to grasp the new concept of psychographics which analyzed customers and prospects by their life styles and their wants and preferences. "Today psychology and science give us remarkable tools to research and understand what makes the consumer tick."

Early in the computer age, Nat initiated a seminar on the Computer and Direct Marketing at NYU. It was conducted by Leo Yochim, President of Printronic Corp. Nat has a nose for the new and different, as his choice of speakers indicates. Whether it's world mail order, telecommunications, or whatever technology, Nat is into it early. In the '70's, he helped to initiate the outstanding DMMA seminars given by Pierre Passavant and John Henry Achziger.

He is prolific. He's given over 250 lectures. He's been a speaker at direct marketing clubs and at direct marketing days in various cities, as well as at symposiums and university meetings. For over ten years he has reviewed in Direct Marketing Magazine the top books on and for use in the field, and has authored numerous articles.

He's been frequently interviewed by publishers in the field. For a number of years, Nat was Program Coordinator for the Annual Direct Marketing Day in New York, and was a pioneer in advancing the role of women and young people in the committees.

Nat seems to be picking up all the time. He's "deeply involved" in the NYU course and in DMIX. He is very active in the DMMA. He contributes to the DMMA Fact Book. In letters to the editor of Direct Marketing Magazine, he raps knuckles where it seems warranted. For him, it's all a continuing labor of love.

For the past decade, Nat has been very active in the DMMA working with Bob DeLay, Sue White and Bonnie DeLay. He believes strongly that the DMMA deserves the wholehearted support of all direct marketers and every local club in the direct marketing field. Under his leadership, the DMIX has come forth vigorously to support the DMMA public affairs programs, its campaigns on privacy, its Mail Preference Service and Mail Order Action Line efforts and its Ethical Guidelines, as well as helping to build DMMA membership. He has conducted *Idea Exchange* programs at the past nine Annual DMMA Conferences and *Information Please* panels at the last 8 conferences. These programs have involved about 400 speakers, and over 5,000 registrants have attended.

Nat is not unappreciated. NYU's Division of Liberal Studies has given him its first annual Award for Outstanding Service. He received The Leadership Award from New York's Hundred Million Club, The Ed Mayer Award from the Direct Mail/ Marketing Educational Foundation and a special award from Direct Marketing Day in New York, and a number of special awards from the DMMA. On his birthday eulogies, poems and affectionate messages often come in from one big name in the field after another.

The words paint a portrait of "candor, ethics and discipline. .. knowledge, awareness and wisdom... unswerving loyalty and steadfast honesty . . . clear-headed thinking and standard of excellence . . . of the Diogenes of direct marketing."

Raymond Zelasny, Director of Continuing Education for Queens College, states: "Probably more than any other individual, he has changed the image of direct marketing from one of nuisance junk mail to a respected career opportunity." "Pete" Hoke, of Direct Marketing Magazine, calls Nat "The incomparable, indefatigable professor . . . a catalyst in direct marketing without peer." Nat is also appreciated by his wife, Johnnie West Ross, to whom he has been married for 48 years, and who in her own right has had successful and challenging careers both here and abroad.

Nat likes people. Nat has a heart. He is for the underdog. He's fought to widen opportunities for women and blacks. Probably 100 to 200 men and women now important in the field have come to him for personal career help and gotten it. In 1979, he helped to found, together with Bob Jones, Norm Eisner, Stan Rapp and Ray Lewis, the *Direct Marketing Minorities Opportunities Committee* which is making progress in minority employment in Direct Marketing. "In my early days, others helped me. Now I can help. The greatest contribution of my whole life's work has been to help people move forward. I have never lost my belief in human progress and historical progress since my student days—and I never will."

He hasn't just helped people advance in the field, often he's helped them solve a job, production or marketing problem. You'll like Nat. He's the kind of person who, after meeting him for a few minutes in the day, leaves you feeling better all day.

He has some advice for you if you're getting into direct marketing . . . whether as a career, as an entrepreneur or as a supplier. He advises you to get acquainted with knowledgeable marketers, keep abreast of current events, to be honest and keep a sense of social responsibility. He advises that you join the DMMA and learn with the leaders.

He tells young people in his NYU course who want to advance in direct marketing to learn about the careers of the foremost professionals in direct marketing who have risen to new heights. He cites Joan Manley, Robin Smith, Rose Harper, Florence Peloquin, Jeramy Lanigan, Dick Cremer, Lester Wunderman, Bob Stone, Lillian Katz, Jerry Hardy, Tom Collins, Pierre Passavant, Norm Eisner and others. And what do they have in common? "Integrity, broad knowledge, respect for their colleagues and associates as well as the conscience . . . and above all, they *care*.

"There is little doubt that changes in direct marketing will be more drastic in the decade of the 80's than in the entire period since the founding of Montgomery Ward and Sears Roebuck. This will be brought about by the exponential advance of the 'compunications' revolution, ie. the merger of the computer as the information machine, with the new communications technology, and the advancing multi-media transformation with its increasing interdependence and interrelationship. It will come about by the continuing differentiation of the marketplace, as women tend to be the majority of the workforce and life styles continue to change and the consumer becomes more interested in self-realization as well as self-gratification. And it will be brought about by the continuing energy crisis, and as the period of unlimited resources and growth of production recedes. This challenging time ahead can be met only as true professionalism becomes the central focus of direct marketers."

In 1981, Nat was the coordinator of New York University's first one-week advanced seminar in direct marketing. It was a summer session so star-studded that Robin Smith (President of Publishers Clearing House) said: "Never before, and perhaps never again, will this level of experience and talent be assembled for a concentrated 5-day period." For the 1982 DMMA Fact Book, Nat wrote "A History of Direct Marketing", a superb accomplishment. His parting word is: "As long as I can work, I'll be active in this field."

Note: Quite a number of particularly outstanding NYU course lectures and DMIX talks are listed in the Help Source Guide with information how to get tapes and when published how to get copies.

Chapter 5
"SuperStation" And Cable TV

How Ted Turner opened a new horizon for mail order TV.

When Ted Turner launched the Cable News Network, it immediately broadcast more TV news than any network or station in the world. His Atlanta "SuperStation" is, itself, another TV network. It broadcasts a varied TV schedule and emphasizes sports. It transmits programs 24 hours a day—via microwave relay, an earth station and a space satellite to 1,500 cable TV systems, which reach 10 million subscriber homes. It's a Ted Turner idea.

Ted is a fighter, a competitor and a winner. He is also an innovator. He does what others don't. He often wins where others lose. He captained the Courageous which won the 1977 America's Cup Sailing Race. He owns the Braves, the Hawks and the Chiefs . . . the Atlanta baseball, basketball and soccer teams.

With no previous mail order experience—and one idea—from his "SuperStation" and Cable News Network, he created a torrent of TV mail orders—that with less and less advertising has kept growing bigger and bigger. He changed the concept of what TV mail order could be.

The Sun Belt made it a century late. Ted Turner is an empire builder of a breed of over a hundred years ago. He looks like Rhett Butler, has the iron will of Scarlet O'Hara and a headquarters that looks like a movie set—of a remake of "Gone With The Wind". He's Barnum with his "SuperStation" as his Jumbo. His Cable News Network is the first transcontinental railroad. He has the fervor of Billy Graham. His mail room looks like Oral Roberts', with mail orders flooding in.

Ted inherited an outdoor advertising company. Then he moved into radio and afterward TV. He took over sick properties, for their troubles and their debts. He took and doctored an ailing TV station and then sold it for twenty million dollars. He took over another TV station by assuming $2,000,000 of debts. In ten years, he made it make five million dollars a year in profit, while transforming it into his "SuperStation"—WTBS-TV, Atlanta.

Before Ted, it had been a local station . . . UHF (Channel 17) . . . traditionally unable to compete in a VHF market. Ted did not accept this. By buying local teams in sports and televising their games over his TV station, he offered what other stations didn't. From there, he offered more sports, signing up rights as he went along. His audience ratings and advertising grew. His station got in the black.

This got Ted interested in cable, its growth, its technology. Then he discovered earth stations and satellites and transponders and began to realize that they would revolutionize Cable TV and vastly speed it and make it more immediately profitable. He began to make trips to Washington D.C., to talk to RCA and to investigate each aspect of it.

He fell in love with satellites. He ultimately got his private earth station. He first dreamed of his "SuperStation" in 1974 (he even copyrighted the name). By 1976, everything was in place. Ed Taylor, of Southern Satellite Systems, had rented transponders on the RCA satellite and, in turn, was making them available for the "SuperStation's" use. Ted Turner was beaming the "Super-Station's" programs 24 hours into space. The transponders on the RCA satellite, 22,300 miles above the earth, were picking them up and bouncing them back. The result was a new advertising medium.

Southern Satellite Systems charged ten cents per home to deliver the WTBS signal to cable systems. Ted banked on charging more for advertising. But he found it impossible to charge local Atlanta advertisers more. And to charge national advertisers more, he would have to prove his national audience. He knew how many cable TV stations actually took his "Super-Station" programs and broadcasted them. He had rating information on the "SuperStation's" national viewing audience. Yet national advertisers moved slowly to sign up as "SuperStation" advertisers. Then Ted turned to mail order advertisers. They could judge results.

At first, Ted was blocked here, too. Most of the orders were by telephone. If orders were telephoned in to a phone service from a "SuperStation" cable viewer far away, the mail order company recorded the call as miscellaneous response and credited to its general advertising. It only credited to WTBS-TV calls in the VHF coverage area around Atlanta. Then Ted Turner got his mail order idea.

Ted put in his own 800 number to take orders phoned in to his "SuperStation" from anyone seeing one of its commercials anywhere in the U.S. Then, to convince mail order advertisers they should pay the "SuperStation" a lot more money, he gambled. Instead of charging normal advertising rates, he began to charge for each telephone or mail order or inquiry the station produced for the advertiser.

The effect was to make WTBS-TV overnight a huge producer of orders for its mail order advertisers. Before the 800 number, people anywhere who ordered by telephone had to pay to make an Atlanta call. Further, too many calls would flood the local answering services. There were no facilities to handle them. But National Data Corp., which provided the 800 number and operators, could handle almost unlimited calls. Overnight, Ted Turner proved to national advertisers that the "SuperStation" had a tremendous, responsive, national audience, and that cable was ready for national advertising on a big scale.

Incidentally, Turner Communications could now, for 24 hours a day, use every minute of unsold time to sell mail order. This brought in a lot of money. Because the "SuperStation" already made money, almost all gross profit of new mail order income added net profit.

Ted Turner had created a tremendous success for his "SuperStation" which he later repeated for his Cable News Network. And he also tamed TV mail order. With his staff he selected offers, already proven to pay out on TV. He screened out those that a careful check indicated had poor product quality, a bad company reputation or a failing delivery record. He rejected mail order commercials he felt were too high-pressure.

Then he gambled all the way to put in the selected mail order offers and commercials. He did it a new, low-key way. He insisted that tags by his announcers asking for orders be short, mild and delivered without urgency. He never allowed mail order to become too major a factor in his station or Cable News Network income. He used it to prove that the audience was there and responsive while aggressively going after national advertisers. Almost incidentally, he opened a new world of TV direct marketing.

Mail order led. National advertisers followed, more each

month, with less mail order commercials shown. Meanwhile, more people subscribed to cable. More cable systems took on the "SuperStation" programs. More people watched each "Super-Station" commercial. By the end of 1980, for weeks before Christmas, there were almost no mail order commercials, yet for 1980, the "SuperStation" sold much more by mail order than ever. Less and less commercials for mail order were selling more and more by mail order.

By 1981, over ninety percent of "SuperStation" viewing came from cable homes. Mail orders from cable homes were in proportion. These homes were the cream, the affluent minority of TV homes able to subscribe to cable. Mail order proved their higher quality as customers. The "SuperStation" successfully sold more expensive cookware sets, sets of Time-Life books, subscriptions to Smithsonian and other quality offers. A comparison of the renewal rates of subscribers for better class magazines showed far better renewals for those secured from the "Super-Station" than for those secured via VHF-TV.

Don Lachowski, vice president of sales of both the "Super-Station" and CNN, recalls: "We started the 800 number mail order in May of 1977. For a while, advertisers bought a schedule at a given rate. This was a minimum guarantee. We had no interest to be a test vehicle. We wanted the advertiser to take part of the gamble to discourage experimentation and attract already proven TV offers.

"Now we've learned the business better. We find it simpler to sell on a straight per order or per inquiry basis. But we don't take on offers on this basis which are not already tested and successful on TV. If anyone else with an offer we can legally and ethically approve wants to buy time entirely at risk for a test, we'll sell the time. But few try, and most who try fail.

"Susan Snead runs the mail order operation. She makes judgments as to which offers to take. She watches performance to determine which to drop, which to use less spots for, and which to increase schedules. I have some involvement watching this.

"Of course, each mail order spot is pre-emptable by a regularly scheduled advertiser. This can leave less desirable spots for mail order. But, so far, in increasing mail order we have found daytme 8 AM to 5 PM as good as at night. Of course, we span seven time zones.

"We envisioned all kinds of sophistication. In practical application, we haven't gotten around to doing what we'd like. We book mail order schedules by going into the log. We look for holes and plug in any empty hole. Only in a very obvious case do we put an offer into a hole specially suited to it rather than another one. We did this for Time-Life Books for their World War II picture books. We were running 'Victory at Sea' and used spots there. Time-Life Books and Time-Life Records have done well.

"We're selective in spots. We've found some direct response spots that are better produced than general advertising spots. One two-minute spot is often preferable, audience-wise, to four or five national spots adding up to two minutes. Then too, we handle asking for the order quite differently. On VHF-TV, the phone number is drilled in. It's repeated several times. There's pressure in the announcer's voice. We never repeat our phone number, but it's well known by our audience. We ask for the order in a low-key way. There's no pressure. We have no screaming. Our tags are low-key.

"In Atlanta, people assume that our number is where to order a TV mail order item. When Elvis Presley died, the first week we did not carry the commercials for Presley albums but other stations in Atlanta did. We had hundreds of orders a day for Presley albums, without advertising them. From all over the country we get very good mail order sales. We probably sold over $500,000 worth of Slim Whitman records. About half our mail order sales are records.

"We have found mail order sales on the 'SuperStation' increasing in volume—with less time used for it. But it should increase. There were one million potential viewing homes when we started the '800' number in 1977, and ten million in 1981. It's been a unique situation. No station or publication has had such a growth rate in advertising and circulation. Mail order added income. It proved our audience and pulling power." By the end of 1981, there were 18 million potential 'SuperStation' viewers."

On June 1, 1980, Ted Turner launched the Cable News Network, rushing in where Time and Newsweek feared to tread. He determined to produce news in depth superior to network news of ABC, CBS, and NBC, all of which he called "headline services". It was the race and gamble of his life.

His expenditures for future months were known to him. His income for future months was far less known. He bet that CNN advertisers would start with him, stay with him and grow with him and that, month by month, more and more advertisers would join the pioneer advertisers on CNN. He hired a former president of CBS-TV, a former head of TV production for NBC and the former head of the Washington News bureau for ABC. For president he hired the former president of the biggest supplier of news to independent news stations. He hired 50 TV news journalists. He opened news bureaus in six cities and shared others around the world. He exchanged TV news with stations in all principal cities.

Against these expenses he signed up some cable systems to pay him 20¢ a viewer a year, and only 15¢ if the system carried programs from the "SuperStation". He signed up some contracts with big national advertisers. He would have some income from offering items mail order on the network as on the "SuperStation". One problem was that the overhead of the Cable News Network was many times that of the "SuperStation"—while at its start the potential homes CNN would reach would be one-tenth those reached by the "SuperStation". Mail order offers run on the "800" number could only pull in proportion. This was the least of his problems.

The RCA satellite CNN rented space on got lost in space. RCA said it had no room on its other satellite. Turner sued RCA for 34.5 million dollars (Turner's pre-launch investment in CNN.) It persuaded the FCC to order RCA to give it the satellite space without which it could not start. Turner persuaded 14 of the top 15 largest cable TV systems to accept CNN programs, but most on a here and there test basis. Turner had to hold out until cable, itself, increased. More cable systems would have to take on CNN more fully and run more CNN programs, more subscribers would have to view them, and more advertisers would have to sign up at higher rates.

All three of his teams were financial losers. One was losing two and a half million dollars a year. Ted Turner estimated that CNN would lose two million dollars a month for a year, but meet expenses in late 1981. The word was out. TV consultants clucked. Network TV executives chuckled. Ted Turner couldn't make it. No way. He was overextended and over his head.

Ted Turner describes himself as a turtle, slowly and laboriously plodding ahead. He says he's not a natural sailor, that he lost every sailing race for eight years, that he mastered sailing as a swimmer trains him or herself, slowly, gradually, with endless

self-discipline. In business, too, he says it's the same, but he has a sense of inevitability of success. To him, to start with seemingly impossible odds makes, in sport or business, a reasonable handicap. Always, he expects gradually to overcome it.

After winning the American Cup race sailing the Courageous, he entered the British Fastnet Race. It took place in the storm of the century. Thirty boats were lost. Nineteen sailors in the race drowned. Turner won the race, and not to his surprise. To him, to make a success of the Cable News Network was a similar problem. All that was needed was to convince TV owners to subscribe to cable, cable systems to carry more of his programs and advertisers to sign more contracts. To persuade them, his first step was to become the biggest media figure in American business.

In doing so, he says he learned the journalism he needed to operate CNN—from the world's top reporters, who covered him. They found him a master interviewee—passing out a book on cable and cable news and Ted Turner. The New York Times got one chapter, the Wall Street Journal another—to be continued in Forbes and Fortune. Everybody got something different . . . each magazine and newspaper, radio station and network—even TV news shows, network and local. He was prolific and inexhaustible. There was surprisingly little duplication.

The one-man whirlwind campaign was buttressed by the impressive executive and broadcasting talent of CNN and by growing faith in Ted Turner as a winner. He personally tremendously advanced the acceptance of cable by TV set owners. He personally advanced the serious consideration of cable by giant advertisers as an advertising medium, by years. About it all he had no doubts. After launching CNN on June 1st and nursing and promoting it (for free) through June, he took off July and August for something more important—training for and then racing the Courageous for the 1980 International America's Cup sailing races.

Then, in September 1980, he set out to win the war. He resumed his crusade to sell America cable, to sell cable systems full use of his Cable News Network and to sell advertisers for it. And he began to win. By the end of 1981, he had increased coverage of CNN to 10,000,000 TV homes. He and his cohorts secured an even more impressive array of Fortune 500 advertisers.

Those most in the know in the cable business, in TV, in advertising—began to talk of another secret Turner weapon, his mail room. They said that far more orders were pouring in, that the monthly deficits—because of more receipts from cable systems, advertisers and mail order—were less than half each month those original estimates of Ted Turner. The word was that Ted would make it, that it was time to get on board—as a cable system or advertiser.

The attitude of Ted Turner and his organization was casual. Don Lachowski reports: "We're happy with our business. We're delighted with our news product. We've had excellent advertising acceptance. It's been overwhelming. Advertisers are coming in for a mixture of motives. Some feel a need to get involved early in the game. We're getting traditional and new advertisers. A brokerage house is sponsoring financial news. Some advertisers are buying very long contracts to get rate protection for inevitably rising circulation.

Everyone at Turner Communications underplays mail order. Don Lachowski says: 'We can get along without it. It fills a role. It's insurance of extra income. CNN has special features like pets suited to specialized mail order new to TV. But we still refuse products without a track record. We limit mail order spots.

"Our main interest has been to create a superb product of network news and to set a base of national advertisers on CNN. We're very happy with the product and with the amount of national advertising already secured. We've done better than anticipated but have worked very hard to do so. We've been too busy to think too much about developing mail order. We use mail order primarily to convert unsold inventory into money."

Susan Snead was in charge of traffic before she began dealing with mail order PI advertisers. "To me, it's another form of traffic. We don't seek mail order. It comes to us. We have a procedure. We ask for a history—what stations and time bought versus results. We check it. We check the product and its quality—then the company's reputation and shipping record. We check the FTC, Post Office, and the Governor's office.

"If we get a clean bill of health, we put it on the waiting list. Then, when time is available, we put the offer on TV. Time becomes available because we pull off offers that pull less gross revenue versus spots used than average. We try a new offer. It may pull a lot—but less than average. If so, off it goes."

Ted Turner checks Susan Snead from time to time as to how new offers are pulling. He likes mail order—if it pulls and if it's clean, but in its place. He's even stricter in his acceptance policies for CNN than for the "SuperStation".

To Ted Turner, by 1981 the issue of CNN was not in doubt. He was still a booster for it as for his teams, for cable, for the "SuperStation" and for Atlanta. He spoke of making it a media center as big as New York or Los Angeles. He talked of producing in the 30 acres of Turner Communications—movies, drama, situation comedies and documentaries. In 1980, the "SuperStation" billed over 30 million dollars. In the first six months of 1981, it billed 34 million dollars.

In January 1981, Turner Television Stations—a subsidiary of the Turner Broadcasting System—filed applications with the Federal Communications Commission for the right to operate 25 low-power TV stations in 15 states and the District of Columbia. And Ted Turner had other new plans. He scarcely mentioned mail order.

But in a crunch, his contact with his own Cable News Network and "SuperStation" viewers may be the extra to insure success, by mail order. Once when his Charlotte TV station was in dire straights, he asked viewers to help by each sending in the price of two theater tickets. $36,000 came in and saved the day, that week. He later sent back every dollar, with thanks. This was the TV station he later sold for $20,000,000.

In August 1981, Westinghouse and ABC announced their own jointly owned cable news network to start in 1982 . . . backed by the enormous resources of each. It offered each network affiliate a wealth of news just for its region in addition to national news—thus outbidding Ted Turner, who couldn't have been more delighted. Ted Turner announced that he would launch his second Cable News Network to compete differently . . . and a month earlier, in 1982 . . . with a 30-minute "wheel" of hard news, and a 5-minute "window" for cable systems to insert local news.

Ted Bates convinced its clients to transfer 5% of their network prime time budgets to Ted Turner's "SuperStation." Ted Turner then turned up with an association with Warner Communications, getting invaluable transponder space on an Amex Satellite and with Warner Amex taking over advertising representation of the "SuperStation" and both Turner Cable News Networks. Westinghouse and ABC had the money, Ted Turner was the pioneer. He had his advantages and kept adding more. In September 1981, Ted Turner leased space on Satcom I from Warner Amex for CNN-2. By New Year's Eve 1981, he had built a

Banquet Lamps.

The demand for Banquet Lamps increases every year, and this season we offer a very attractive line, carefully selected from the several leading factories

55635 Gold Finish Metal Banquet Lamp, cupid center piece, extra heavy cast foot: cast open work head, removable oil fount, with 80 candle power, central draft burner, 18 inchs fancy silks bade with 8 inch chiffon border embroidered in colors. An extra heavy, massive lamp and one of the handsomest designs brought out this season. Height to top of chimney, 31 inches.
Price.. $10.50

20,000 square foot headquarters for CNN-2 and it started operation.

CNN lost $16 million in 1980 in start-up costs and seven months of operation. It lost $10 million in 1981. And Ted was predicting that CNN-2 would lose a million dollars a month in 1982. But, for the month of November 1981, CNN-1 had come within $100,000 of breaking even. Some estimated that in 1981 CNN took in between $16 and $17 million. By spring 1982, CNN was expected to grow to $40 million in 1982. The "SuperStation," WTBS-TV, had total revenues of $55 million in 1981 and expected (in Spring, 1982) to take in $125 million in 1982. Turner Broadcasting overall was expected to be in the black for 1982 and money fund managers were betting that Ted would make it.

With Satcom, Ted Turner had beat ABC-Westinghouse to the punch; their Westar IV satellite had been delayed. And when it went into orbit many more cable systems were equipped to receive Satcom than Westar. Ted said: "Ours was a pre-emptive strike. We wanted to keep them from establishing a beachhead in cable news." By January, 1982, CNN-1 was available to over nine million CATV subscribers and CNN-2 to 800,000. On March 1, 1982, Ted Turner started a 24-hour all news radio network. An attempt to unionize CNN had failed. There were rumors he might buy a movie company.

Without perhaps fully realizing its future consequences, even for himself, Ted Turner opened a new horizon for mail order TV. He opened a door to a new world of high-ticket, prestige mail order via cable TV. The time could come when this could save him. He may amortize his huge news organization by mail order. He may launch a laser printed customized news magazine via cable and get a million subscribers at triple Time's price. Or, he may become a view data provider of his own computerized news file to your TV set via telephone.

Or, Ted Turner may become the country's first really big

video disc how-to publisher. He may form a cable viewer club with benefits and savings for members and membership fees pouring into the "SuperStation" and CNN. He may bring out one stock issue after another he personally sells to viewers, mail order via cable. But Ted Turner will overcome. Quite incidentally, he'll change mail order more and more. And maybe it will all be a warm-up—to run for president of the U.S. . . . and, tomorrow the world.

Chapter 6
Safe, Sound Success - By Mail Order Moonlight

Ed Stern is the owner of one publishing company . . . an executive of a second . . . and receives royalties from a third.

Mail order moonlighting gave Ed Stern his business. Mail order and publishing experience gave him the idea for the books he wrote and created. Mail order know-how, acquired over many years, made success happen. And talent and a natural entrepreneur's feel made it possible.

He owns Hilary House, publisher of the much praised "Direct Marketing Market Place", reviewed in this book. He's a senior executive of New Century Publishing, which is launching a series of health, physical fitness and reference books. He was vice president and marketing director of Grosset & Dunlap (where he spent ten years). For them, with the encouragement of then President Harold Roth, he created the best seller, "Prescription Drugs and Their Side Effects".

He got the idea from personal experience and that of friends. Some prescriptions from doctors when used had side effects quite unexpected to patients, yet known and documented medically. Why not list all commonly given prescriptions and the documented side effects for each? Why not let each patient know what he or she is getting into?

He conceived it, created it, entrepreneured it. In every way, he did it as though it were his own business—but inside Grosset & Dunlap and for them. He researched the entire book. He wrote it. He wrote the ads for it. He selected the media. He watched every phase like a hawk, from production through sales of over 650,000 copies. Maybe it will go on forever. Its beautiful royalties were Ed's biggest step to independence.

Ed made a lot of money for Grosset & Dunlap. He became a needed man. He earned flexibility. He gained security and an unlimited future potential. It came about because Ed Stern was a pro. He had mastered the art of writing a book, writing an ad, buying advertising profitably and watching pennies. He thought like a entrepreneur for Grosset & Dunlap. And his book was only a small part of his work for them.

After the prescription book, Ed got an idea for another book. It was outside of Grosset & Dunlap's field. He became a moonlighter. By day, he did an increasingly valuable job for Grosset & Dunlap. At night, he did all the research for, and became the publisher of "The Direct Marketing Market Place". It's the address book, by classifications, of the direct marketing world—much like The Literary Marketplace for publishing.

Under the name Hilary House (Hilary is Ed's daughter's middle name), Ed launched his business. He did it from home— by mail order to mail order people. Direct marketers welcomed it with open arms. It carries advertising. It is revised annually. It's not only successful, it looks like a lifetime business—with an ever lower selling cost per copy. In 1981, the price per copy went up over 30% (from $25 to $40 per copy) without a murmur. Advertising in it jumped, too—over 52%. In 1982, the Direct Marketing Market Place began to be distributed exclusively by Gale Research Company, the biggest publishers in the U.S. of directories by industries.

Ed explains: "In 1980, the Direct Marketing Market Place listed 2,200 organizations. For 1981, we got back 700 additional completed questionnaires. This required 80 more pages. Paper and printing cost went up 13%. We had to increase the price to $40. In August, we made a pre-publishing offer at $30. We got a good number of orders, and then went to $40. The fun part is that my wife and kids all help out. I'm training three more mail order pros.

"When I left Grosset & Dunlap, I launched New Century Publishers, Inc. with Charles Walther. We started it in October 1980. It's a subsidiary of New Century Education, which sets up learning centers and reading centers in schools throughout the country.

"We're testing five titles to start—health, physical fitness and other reference titles. I won't write the books. We're taking on the marketing of books for mail order and creating books for mail order, assigning projects for writers and packagers of how-to books. We won't distribute through stores. We'll sell off trade rights. We don't want problems of book returns. When we established New Century, I already had one book in progress. It's a salary and career guide, and will be published by Hilary House.

"I still get royalties on the Prescription Drug Book. We live comfortably and eat regularly. I love what I do. I'm teaching, too—something I'm very interested in. For two years, I taught a course in advertising and book promotion at NYU, once a week. It became a little too much as my activities increased. Now I do seminars throughout the country for the American Association of Publishers—about six a year. It's a joint venture. I cover the same subject—mail order. These seminars seem to take less of my total time."

Ed Stern was brought up in New York City where the first reason for his mail order success turned up early. He's bright. Ed went to George Washington High School, in Manhattan. He graduated from New York University in 1957 and went on to graduate school—getting an MBA in marketing from NYU in 1960.

While at graduate school, Ed worked for two years at his first job for a small advertising agency . . . Lifton, Gold and

Asher. They published furniture and jewelry catalogs, on a co-op advertising basis for department stores and their vendors. "I first wrote the copy for the catalogs and then sold space in the catalogs to vendors."

His next job was for four years with a direct mail envelope and printing company. Ed was assistant to the president. The company was a publisher, a printer and an advertising agency. It specialized in special formats, like Reply-O. Ed wrote copy, originated format ideas and mastered printing production enough to help him ever since.

"Then I went to Doubleday and for two years wrote direct mail copy selling books and book clubs. Charley Sherman, Warren Levey and Tom Stasink all taught me a great deal at Doubleday. Then I worked for Newsweek for four years. I was copy chief for the circulation department. When Red Dembner started Newsweek Books, I became Marketing Director.

"After that I went to Grosset & Dunlap." This proved Ed's first really big opportunity. All his previous experience came to fruition. He proved a great entrepreneur for them and then began moonlighting his own business from there.

The growth of a direct marketing firm requires, more than any factor, personnel who think like mail order entrepreneurs. You who work for direct marketers consider this: Learn more about your employer's business and you'll be appreciated. Gradually master some phase of direct marketing needed by your employer and you'll be needed more.

And if you act like an entrepreneur on behalf of your employer, you may become another Ed Stern—first for others and then for yourself.

Chapter 7
People Research To Sell More By Mail Order

*Why responders inquired or bought
. . . why non-responders didn't.*

Bob Kaden is a marathon runner. "I ran the Boston Marathon in 1980. In 1980, I also ran the New York Marathon in 3 hours 31 minutes, my best time." Meanwhile, Bob is off and running in the research business, in a constantly bigger way. And his latest kick is applying it to direct marketing. "Direct marketing is new for market researchers. We got into it in 1975. It's exciting.

"We were working for United Airlines, a client. Stone & Adler was their agency for direct marketing. Through United, we were recommended to Bob Stone. We started with Stone & Adler working with Aaron Adler. After we had worked for Stone & Adler for two years, they asked me to put on a seminar for Stone & Adler. Some of the material in the seminar is in Bob Stone's latest edition of his book.

"For Ward's Signature Corp. division we've worked extensively with President Dick Cremer on direct marketing. He's a very exciting guy. We work in direct marketing for Spiegel—with Ted Spiegel. He is most imaginative. It's a wonderful relationship. The job is to help them develop a position, to become the 'Bloomingdale's of catalogs.'

"They take propositions, claims, promises. We do testing in a group of 300 or so. The group has seemed to show interest in fashion, variety of merchandise, convenience and ease. Then the ads are created. The ads are to get catalog inquiries while promoting an upscale image.

"One day, we got a call from the DMMA. Don Kantor, of Stone & Adler, had recommended us for research. I was invited to New York to talk to the planning comittee. They had been involved with someone who couldn't seem to get off the ground. I suggested studies. The result was 'Direct Mail in Focus', a published study of a focus group interview on attitudes toward direct mail. Now I'm giving speeches all over the world for the DMMA.

"The focus group goes back to Ernest Dichter and his Center for Motivation and Research. Out of the work they did came the first focus group. It proved a great tool. It's a theory producing technique. It's not evaluative. The Creative Educational Foundation, in Buffalo, has done interesting work in creativity that has stimulated us. Take brainstorming. We're way beyond, maybe three or four generations beyond brainstorming as usually practiced. We've done a lot of work in how to stimulate creative thought.

"For direct marketers we've done background research, pre-testing research and post-testing research. We've done some fascinating work with responders, why they inquired or bought—and non-responders, why they didn't. We make psychographic promise studies to determine what appeals are most important. We make all forms of surveys by mail, phone, one to one and in small groups."

Bob Kaden was born and brought up in Chicago. "I wasn't a great student. My IQ was middle of the road. I didn't have much in the way of special interests. I didn't really develop until later in life. But I was an A-type achiever. I wanted to succeed and in busines I drove myself to do it. I was compulsively competitive."

Bob went to Lincoln College, in Lincoln, Illinois, and then on to Miami College in Miami, Ohio. He took accounting at Roosevelt University. He then attended the School of Communications at Columbia College, in Chicago, as an undergraduate and got a degree in communication.

"But I learned my specialty of research on the job. I was never taught." Bob got into his career by first playing on the BBD&O softball-baseball team, which led to a summer job in their research department. "That was in 1962. I started in traditional consumer research."

After that, Bob went to work for Young & Rubicam in their research department, and then in research for J. Walter Thompson. "In six years, I became a pro." From there Bob got a top job at Earle Ludgin Advertising, in Chicago. "I became the research director at 30." At 31, he became a member of the Board of Directors.

"With each job, I learned. Two clients at agencies I worked at had great impact on my career. Don Johnson was research director of Alberto Culver. He was a strong help. Richard Hammett is now president of his own research business in St. Paul. But when he was research director at Hamm's Beer, he helped me develop. He relied strongly on me and that gave me a great deal of confidence.

"By the time I was 33, I had thoroughly mastered the marketing research business. I was successful. But I was bored and restless." Bob had done some free lancing for Norm Goldring, a management consultant who was also in acquisitions. "One day, months later, I saw him at lunch." Bob and Goldring had enjoyed working together previously. "I asked Goldring how

Goldring and Company was doing in research and was told that operations were dormant. Goldring was busy in other things. 'Why don't you hire me and let me run it,' I suggested." Goldring did, giving Bob a salary and stock options.

That was in 1973. Today Goldring is a minority stockholder. Goldring and Company has 18 employees, is successful and Bob is president of Goldring. The business has come largely from clients served by Bob with ideas from Bob. "When I got into Goldring, I was full of plans. I wanted to conceptualize programs I had never done, to be highly creative, to do the unusual. We've tried to be different. We've succeeded. I like it . . . research, my own business and my applying it to direct marketing. What I've liked, I've done well at.

"We work for both Sears and Wards but for assignments other than mail order. For Wards we research why people buy furniture—things like that. For Sears we do research on price testing, feature price optimization. Let's say a refrigerator sells for $200. Our work indicates what extra features would make it a good value at $220, say, or $230, or whatever. Eighty percent of our business is with non-direct marketers. G.D. Searle, the drug people, are clients. So is Ovaltine and Kraft, Texas Instrument and Frito-Lay. But we expect big growth in the mail order client area.

"What I really want to do is to come up with more and more unequivocal proof of what research can really do for direct marketers. I know of only one direct marketing agency which has a full-time research director. Of course, those direct marketing agencies which are subsidiaries of biggest general agencies have access to their research managers. But it's every bit as hard for a top research man without direct marketing experience to help effectively, as for a general copywriter.

"I want to do much more mail order testing of ads and mailings based on our findings versus controls. Research is powerfully effective in finding items, developing items, creating offers, developing copy, selecting headlines and subheads. It can resurrect a failed test and make it a winner. It can trade up a company while jacking up sales. But so little of what can be done has been done and measured, that few grasp the potential. I hope to do it, get it measured and get the numbers.

"Some are succeeding with research in direct marketing. Allstate Insurance is very sophisticated in their use of it. But for most direct marketers, so much more can be done with it. If you want to sell computers to business people, you can test different pieces so effectively this way."

To old mail order pros, the results from each ad were the research. They usually laughed at other research. But as mail order has become direct marketing, people research is turned to more and more, particularly by Fortune 500 companies. Direct marketing is starting to be considered as a legitimate branch of marketing with some of the same needs for research.

General Mills has done it to find out the attitudes and opinions of customers for each catalog house they now own— and used the research as a guide for merchandise selection, pricing and presentation—with considerable success.

Working with Kaden, the Direct Mail/Marketing Association has used focus group research to explore how people feel about shopping by mail, itself—even about individual reactions to advertising received through the mail. People have told what mail they open, what they throw away, what they keep. The findings are not considered a final answer but are detailed and eye opening. Anyone in or about to start a mail order business, anyone on the creative side, should study it . . . also, attitude research concerning individual products, ads and companies.

Research is still new for most direct marketers. But direct marketers are now starting to use market research pretesting methods. And research specialists are studying mail order. Bob Kaden says, "I learned a lot attending seminars. Now I try to exchange with others some of what we're finding out about direct marketing research. I gave a three hour speech on it at the Direct Mail/Marketing International Conference, in London, in February of 1980, and spoke at the national DMMA in Chicago in October of 1980. I also spoke at the DMMA conference in Paris in 1981.

"We've got good people, unusual people. We have some we utilize free lance, people who have talent but will only work out of their homes. And some we use just about full-time that way. I have a fine statistician I'm bringing in. We'll do early stage prediction. We are doing computer modeling. We'll do a lot more things. Our entire organization is getting much more direct marketing minded."

Meanwhile, while Bob gets ready to run his next marathon, I strongly recommend that managers of businesses substantially in or going into mail order send to Hoke Communications for a tape of Bob's London or Chicago speech. It's an education on research for direct marketers. Details on getting it are in the help source section in this book. And you can always reach Bob at Goldring & Co., 919 North Michigan Avenue, Chicago, IL (312) 440-5252.

Chapter 8
Taking Advantage Of Change - By Mail Order

The story of a man who has done it . . . for some of the biggest companies in the world.

He is Lawrence Chait. What he has written and spoken about the mail order future, for over 25 years, has eventually come true to a surprising degree. And he has a very detailed view of how you can benefit most from future mail order change.

Some extraordinarily talented people have been associated with him, learned from him, been helped by him and gone on to become some of today's most successful direct marketers. For years he operated one of the first and most successful direct marketing agencies, Lawrence G. Chait & Co., Inc. He's a top direct marketing consultant. He co-founded the Canadian direct marketing agency, March/Chait & Associates, Ltd. He's Associate Publisher of "International Moneyline" Newsletter.

His major organizational activity these days is as Chairman of the Research Committee and a member of the Board of the Sales Executives Club of New York - the largest aggregation of sales management professionals in the world.

Ed Mayer, Jr. - considered the greatest teacher of and a top practitioner of direct mail was, before his death, an executive of the Chait organization. Mildred Semler was one of the first women to make it really big in direct marketing. She did - with Larry Chait.

Other now famous names in direct marketing were part of the Chait team . . . Saul Levine and Jack Stern as Directors of Art and Design pioneered new direct mail formats which became legendary, such as direct mail in burlap bags, plastic boxes, see-through envelopes, mailing tubes and metal cans. Norma Roberts, Murray Rosenberg, Fred Borden and Malcolm Labat-Simon were brilliant copy stars. Hal Drucker was the shining light in Account Supervision and New Business.

Joan Throckmorton is principal owner of Throckmorton Assocs., the most successful direct marketing agency founded by a woman. She says she got her direct marketing finishing course at the Chait Agency.

The agency served such clients as Standard Oil of Indiana for its Imperial Casualty Insuance subsidiary . . . American Airlines for the development of both passenger and freight business . . . Montgomery Ward and Alden's in the big catalog field for credit account activation and many other activites . . . 3-M for such divisions as photocopy equipment, microfilm, printing and paper products, educational products, etc.

To anyone innovating anything promising in direct marketing, Larry Chait has had an open office door. Murray Roman recalls how Larry would listen to his ideas and encourage him in the earliest days of telephone marketing. Leo Yochim went to him for advice when Leo was first starting with computer letters.

There are those who came to Larry Chait underfinanced and unable to pay an adequate fee - but with a concept he felt should be given a chance. He helped them and became their father figure. He can help you - thanks to what he has written and to his taped speeches.

Larry Chait is an intellectual. He is a scholar and more informed in economics than many holders of a Master's degree. "I'm a voracious reader, and not a fiction reader. I read heavily in history and a lot of economics. I must write and speak. I've given many lectures outside the direct marketing field on economic and political developments."

For 25 years he's given talks and lectures and been on and chaired panels on mail order and direct marketing. He's probably done more of this than anyone outside of those professionally giving seminars. He was one of the last volunteer presidents of the Direct Mail/ Marketing Association. He was founder and first president of The Association of Direct Marketing Agencies. He's been president of "The Hundred Million Club." LIDMA, the Long Island Direct Marketing Association, started as his idea.

Larry Chait was born and brought up through his high school years in Scranton, Pennsylvania. Larry never went to college or post-graduate school. But he got two degrees even more important. Each was an education, a cachet and passport. He was a Circulation Executive for the Wall Street Journal and Barron's and later for Time Inc.

His education started early. Larry's father was a retail merchant in Scranton, just about wiped out in the Depression when Larry got to high school. After hours and summers Larry worked for the Scranton Republican. "I did everything . . . wrote ads and sold them." Then, Larry worked for a local advertising agency and, again, did everything and anything.

The Depression was ending when he went on to live in New York and got a job with a newspaper in Hackensack. Then he worked for a point-of-purchase display firm, The Manders Company. It was started by executives who had broken away from Einson Freeman, the country's leading point-of-purchase display manufacturer. "I wrote copy and ideas for displays . . . and then went out to sell them."

Then, for 4 years during the war, Larry, who had been interested in short-wave radio, became a radio officer in the Merchant Marine! "Three weeks after I got off my last ship of the

Men's Toupees

To measure for a Toupee or top piece, cut a piece of paper the exact size and shape of the bald spot, mark the crown and parting, enclose a lock of hair, and state if hair is to be straight or curly.
No. 18R4418 Men's Toupee, weft foundation. Price, each. (If by mail, postage extra, 8c)..$5.50
No. 18R4422 Men's Toupee, ventilated foundation. Price, each.................................$10.00
If by mail, postage extra, each, 8 cents.
Red, Blonde and Gray Hair cost extra. Allow one-half more than above prices.
Remember, we guarantee a perfect fit and match if you follow instructions, or your money back.

war I was working for the Wall Street Journal. I became direct mail manager for the Journal and Barron's. I knew nothing of mail order to begin with but benefited from the wisdom of some great colleagues.

"The Wall Street Journal was about to have the greatest turn-around in publishing history. I was privileged to be there. Three young executive near-geniuses were responsible. One of the three was Barney Kilgore. He came up with the editorial formula that made the Journal have such immense appeal. Bob Feemster built the advertising revenue. My boss was Leslie Davis, the third of the trio who took responsibility for circulation.

"It was a remarkable story, an incredible turn-around. Leslie Davis was an accountant. He had no mail order background; but he was very imaginative. He could evaluate a list. He studied mail order. He was a great copy critic. He took me under his tutelage. He was a fantastic analyst. At the end of the war, the circulation was 45 thousand. By the early-fifties, it was 165 thousand. And I learned from him every day I worked for him.

"Essential to the early circulation success of the Wall Street Journal were two advertising agency representatives . . . both were to become legends in their own time. The incredible John Caples was our account supervisor at BBDO and prepared all of our space ads.

"Our creation and preparation of direct mail received the immense assistance of Leonard Raymond, the principal owner of Dickie-Raymond - the earliest of the full-service direct response advertising agencies.

"A similar contribution was made to Barron's by Anshel J. Gould, the account supervisor representing Albert Frank Gunther Law. In toto, what a team!

"At the same time, I had been free-lancing for Arthur Wiesenberger - a leading stock broker and investment banker. Mass interest in investments was starting again. Arthur had written a fine book, 'Investment Companies'. He had some ideas about working cooperatively with Mutual Funds on a reciprocal

basis. After free-lancing, I went with him full-time. My job was to sell the book mail order and to provide lead-getting ads for Mutual Funds.

"There were a lot of copy restrictions. We were members of the New York Stock Exchange and the Curb and the Security Dealers Association. We cleared copy with everybody. I got to know them all. I did this for a year and a half.

"Then, I joined 'Time Inc.' in 1951. There, I had a horizontal staff job in circulation. There was a corporate circulation department. I worked on every existing 'Time Inc.' magazine and, at the end, on the launch of 'Sports Illustrated.'

"We had an organization of tremendous talent. Bill Jamie and Bill Baring-Gould were there and Frank Johnston, who later launched 'American Heritage' and 'Horizon' . . . and Nick Samstag, father of Chris Stagg. Nick was an incredible idea man, then in his late 40's. He headed the advertising promotion department and had 200 people in it, and developed all ad promotion themes. Wendell Forbes, who later became 'Life' Circulation Director was there. Red Dembner, who went on to become a top 'Newsweek' executive was there. Ed Miller was there. He was head of research. Later, he became president of Alfred Politz. Politz had worked with him on Life Research.

"Bernie Auer was circulation manager of 'Time', and then publisher, and then a group vice president. Bernie was very able. The initial thrust for demographic study came from him. He started a really scholarly approach to circulation growth/analysis.

"I left 'Time' to become vice president of R.L. Polk, in charge of Polk offices and plants of the Eastern seaboard. Polk controlled automotive registration lists and published 800 to 900 city directories. My recommendation was to put all that vast information resource about people into one unified computerized file. The end result came to be known as 'The Polk Market.'

"Later, under Julian Hayden and Walt Gardner (President of Polk), and Fred Zimmerman, it was all broken down by zip code areas. Polk had truly gigantic information resources. The auto lists were big. Polk went to each state for the lists. The dealers needed them. Polk rented lists to auto companies. The auto companies put up enough money to guarantee the cost of compilation. It took a lot of political footwork to get the okay from each State Motor Vehicle Department. The auto companies and dealers interceded to get lists for Polk.

"Meanwhile, O.E. McIntyre was being encouraged by 'Reader's Digest' to put phone books on computer. At that same time, Jack Cole out in Lincoln, Nebraska had an approach to reversing phone books into street address order. He did it first in Dallas and then in Kansas City, Missouri. He asked if I was interested. I looked and said 'Yes,' if it could be related to address area demographics. Then I went to the Census Bureau for an okay to overlay their data on computer tape. Now, the Census Bureau will do it. Then, they thought it was an awful idea.

"The Sanborn Map Company had a fantastic neighborhood mapping system for fire insurance companies. They provided a vivid picture of each neighborhood. Fire insurance companies financed it. I worked with Sanborn, using Sanborn maps to get at the problem of quality-of-neighborhood selection.

"So, there was Polk with its city directories and auto lists and McIntyre with its alphabetical phone books and Jack Cole with his street-address-sequenced phone books. All of these pioneers contributed greatly to the current sophistication of mailing effort. The Census Bureau finally capitulated in the 1970's to provide data. I think Congress passed a law to do it. In the 1980 Census, the Census Bureau has gone all out to provide data which direct marketers can employ.

"I launched my own direct marketing advertising agency in 1958, in the Seagram Building in New York. In the mid-sixties I opened up a second office in the John Hancock Building in Chicago. On a capitalized basis, we finally got up to the equivalent of 15 million dollars billing, as big as anybody then."

Larry has seen mail order turn into direct marketing. He recalls earlier days of the Direct Mail/Marketing Association.

"When I was president, the DMMA had a budget of $300,000 or so a year, and maybe 500 to 600 members. It had a paid staff of four. But volunteers did most of the work.

"The DMMA is enormously bigger now. Bob DeLay has been a dynamo. He's hired very good people. He has 65 on staff with a major Washington office. He's done a magnificent job. The field has broadened on an international scale. Walter Schmid and Murray Miller of American Express have had an international symposium going in Switzerland for 12 consecutive years. For several years it was in the red. Murray helped finance it. But now it's a big business and a big profit maker. Many developments have expanded membership possibilities for the DMMA . . . the growth into special TV and telephone marketing and internationally as well.

"Since 1974 I've done consulting for various corporations, organizations and governments. My office is five minutes from home. I also work with March/Chait in Canada. My Canadian partner is the Vickers & Benson Advertising Agency. I fly up to Canada two or three days a month for client meetings and planning sessions. But we've built a strong Canadian organization. They're doing a good job. It's succeeding. Now we're talking of a second international office.

"I have one book on the fire. It's an anthology of the best writing in the world on direct marketing, the best lectures and the best research. I'm doing a job in great depth, researching it, going back many years."

Larry is already the author of four widely read monographs: "Multi Media Direct Marketing"; "Consumer Credit 1970-2000";

"The Problems of Marketing Management in a new Era of Social Responsibility", and "Building Business by Mail". Some of this work is excerpted and digested in the DMMA Manual.

Larry Chait first mastered direct mail selling before going on to all media. What he has to say about direct mail is urgent, succinct and applies to all mail order.

"Don't consider direct marketing if you think it's quick and easy. Successful direct marketing operations are built on the basis of careful, thoughtful, long-range planning and development . . . as is any business.

"Mail order demands step-by-step experimentation, evaluation and projection. You experiment at each step. You develop productive mailing lists by a combination of experience, judgment and experimentation. You develop successful mailing packages the same careful way. You develop a relationship between the initial sale and eventual customer value based on extensive experience tables.

"You determine how much you can afford to get a customer via study of your experience tables. You determine how much you can afford to spend on intensive cultivation of a customer once you have received his first order.

"You study the whole problem of developing new products and new services you can sell to existing customer groups. This takes time, development and careful planning. You 'key' everything. You don't guess but, instead, test when feasible and practical.

"Successful mailing lists become your 'machine tools'. Your input becomes the foundation of your 'direct mail machine' which will spin out volume and profits once it has been successfully prototyped and put into production.

"For most products and services the initial mailing effort is at best a break-even or a loss operation. The question is usually how much you can spend to put a customer on your books. This requires experience tables to provide information on the ultimate profitability of new mail order customers as they remain on your books over a period of months or years.

"A satisfied customer can be expensive to acquire and then become the goose that lays the golden eggs. It's not enough to have one brilliant promotion planned. You should have your next five or six lined up in advance. Make your new customer a target for repetitive sales and profit-building efforts.

"Build your lists. Warranty cards can be splendid. Using inserts in your bills and statements can be gold. Programmed direct mail to your list is the answer. It's cheaper to do more business with current customers than to acquire new ones. Acquire every possible customer name. Then keep everlastingly at the job of retaining and extending that customer's loyalty to you."

Larry combines extreme practicality with being a tireless visionary. Very early he foresees what is coming, what will be its effects and how to cash in on it—by mail order. He did so with what he calls the three big C's—credit selling, computerization and continuity programs. He did it with multi-media—and with the use of direct marketing methods in mainstream marketing.

A favorite Chait concept was the "Troika" . . . letter, phone call and salesman's personal call follow-up. Before Ted Turner, he was a believer in the coming boom in cable TV. Before Qube, he was talking to anyone and everyone about interactive TV. He enthusiastically recommended telephone marketing to clients long before their competitors heard of it.

More and more, he's been a bull in world mail order. At a Pacific Direct Marketing Symposium in Australia, he predicted: "Interactive cable TV will increasingly replace mail and phone as the prime vehicle between buyer and seller. This will lead increasingly to marketing beyond national boundaries."

For world marketing, as in each development he studies, he sees ways to benefit that others often don't. "Not all national economies suffer as much at the same time. With world mail order you can diversify internationally. If business at home is bad, run your mail offers where business is better, and beat your own recession. Pick your spots. When it's tough here, market there."

He takes the same attitude about the business you're in. "In shifting economies, take a hard look at the new large opportunities that will create entirely new businesses and industries. Move in fast—by mail order. Success is based on seizing opportunities represented by a world in change. Reach for the brass ring yourself.

"Direct marketing technology, itself, constantly changes. Techniques that work change with conditions. Understand the degree to which marketing is moving in the direction of direct marketing. Get into direct marketing, then use the direct marketing tools that are coming in and not fading out."

Larry Chait emphasizes that it takes imaginative creativity to take advantage of change—and to create great copy, and that this takes plain, hard work. "Direct response copywriters should spend 80% of their time researching, investigating and planning—and 20% of their time creating packages. They should remember that in spite of future changes, certain copywriting elements remain.

"From your headline deep into your copy, for example, announce the *new* now. Simultaneously announce to readers that everybody wins—whether by sweeps, gifts or whatever method. Make a third-party offer to somebody else's customers, under their name.

"For the core of your copy, detail practical and service advantages—in price, quality, availability and durability. Emphasize the 'security blanket', your guarantee, and strongly enough to overcome suspicion, fear and doubts. Offer credit, if not yourself directly, then via credit cards—available to even the smallest direct marketers.

"Give an endless chain of benefits—this, this and also that—pluses, extras, unexpected bonuses. Try "The Lock-In", the continuity program—automatic shipment, cancellable at any time . . . multiplied business at the same advertising cost. Finally, limit your offers with a "cut-off" date. When it's given and a follow-up mailing arrives 10 days before the date, the follow-up virtually always exceeds the response of the original effort."

Larry Chait writes constantly on the subject of money. He is a student of inflation's effects. He worries that mail order people who can adjust prices faster than others don't do so. He recommends that you do it quickly and continuously - as fast as inflation increases your costs. For credit sellers he suggests that as inflation increases you tighten credit criteria. He suggests replacing your own direct billing with the use of credit cards on a non-recourse basis. "In any event, keep a tight credit rein. Provide inducements for cash-up-front to long-term or large-volume purchasers. And take advantage of inflation. Sell purchase of your product as a hedge against inflation, a tangible asset."

One of Larry Chait's greater speeches was on "The Psychology of Mail Order Promotions and Consumer Purchasing", of which he is a master. I recommend it highly. The text appears in the book "Direct Mail Advertising and Selling for Retailers" published by the National Retail Merchants Association.

But even better is a lecture Larry Chait gave at New York University's Direct Marketing course: "Direct Marketing as a

Scientific Process of Business Growth and Profitability"- how 30 years of industry experience in applying computerization to the lifestyles and purchasing characteristics of the consumer list . . . plus a knowledge of media interdependence in marketing . . . and an increase in interactive communication technologies . . . have created a new phenomenon in our distributive economy in which professional direct marketing people have become "the scientists of advertising and selling."

This, one of his more elegant efforts, sums up nicely Larry Chait's philosophy and his life in and contribution to direct marketing.

In the help source section of this book are full details how you can get any or all of Larry Chait's accumulated mail order know-how in print or on tape—from Hoke Communications or your business library. Coming: Larry Chait's anthology of mail order greats. Read it when it arrives.

Chapter 9
The List Maestro

*He has helped select one billion
names for mailers*

Ed Burnett has trained many knowledgeable and successful list brokers and list managers, including Stan Woodruff and Robin Black who are now executives in the largest list business. He has helped hundreds of list users personally and has taught over 2,000 in seminars on the basics of the list business.

"Pete" Hoke, publisher of Direct Marketing magazine, calls him "the most articulate of some very articulate people in the list business." His seminars are not just highly instructive. They are theatrical productions. He knows lists as few do. His particular specialty is business to business direct marketing. But what he teaches applies to all lists and all direct marketing and mail order.

Ed does most of his consulting on the telephone. Words fire out as from a machine gun, then slow for emphasis, then change tone for effect. He's an actor all day long. He's a writer, he's an intellectual. He plays the piano, loves music and art. He's a part-time economist and probably one of the most knowledgeable statisticians in the field; his writings include much data on testing and the mathematics of Direct Mail. He pours out words in articles, booklets and literature. He gives ten seminars a year and also lectures.

His vocabulary is his palette. Each word is a touch of his brush. Each speech, each article, each piece of promotion is organized like a lawyer's brief. He is extraordinarily thorough and very perceptive. He prides himself on being helpful; that he cares and that he sees that each person in his organization cares; that he will give as much time to a neophyte just starting out as to a professional looking for guidance for one of his customers.

"I've not always had success. I've had my share of grief, too. I spent 15 years building Ed Burnett, Inc., and sold it for stock in a conglomerate. The conglomerate went bankrupt, with what I had built up over 15 years. I started over again, from scratch. Now my business is just a good and solid as it ever was."

Burnett cites the success of his clients, many of whom started as modest mailers. "A father and son combination in the

Materials Handling trade tried direct mail on their own, with what help they could find, and could not make any progress. Five years ago, they came to me, doing a bit over $500,000 in gross volume, hardly enough to keep afloat. This business is now doing over $5,000,000, and expanding. I've picked every name they have mailed, helped them see the worth of penetration analysis, and we have together brought the cost to buy new customers down by over 90%."

Most of the words that pour out from Ed are facts about lists and adages. Ed is not unaware of the extent of his list and marketing know-how. His mailing list adages are usually management-oriented. A whole host of list users have heard Ed say:

"It is better to send a poor mailing to a good list than a good mailing to a poor list."

"Direct Mail is a business for pros who know the product, markets, media, the mathematics of marketing, the mystique of computers and back-end control. The beginner needs a good deal of luck, a great deal of stick-to-it-ivity and a number of helping hands to keep him from continuous disaster."

"Customer files are not sacrosanct. I've never seen a list I could not improve in some way."

Ed is forever making lists of lists, ways of using lists, do's and don'ts, types of lists, sources of them, of demographic and psychographic factors, of changes, of what you should know about list management—including the fact that Ed started it— about major and minor compilers, kinds of census data, standard industrial classifications.

When he talks, he warms to his subject—how to get rich from astute use of lists. As he goes on, he takes pleasure in attempting to forecast the future of mailing lists, computerized printing, government, the post office, list brokers, managers and compilers. He nurses beginners, tutors those who need help, coaches experts, teaches them all and lectures to anyone. He never stops giving his know-how away.

Custom consulting is his pleasure—to lay out a plan—how to create a mailing list from within and uncover one outside, each compiled from scratch for you . . . to explain and demonstrate the art of the compiler.

Ed Burnett was brought up in Highland Park, a suburb of Detroit. He grew up during the depression. He worked for a cigar wholesaler for $7.50 a week when he was 15 years old. He worked for a small Detroit advertising agency. He came to New York in the mid 1930's with no money and a letter of recommendation to a man for whom he thought it had been arranged for him to work. There was no job. He survived, got a job and an education. He started as a proof press operator. He got the job because he threw in being a proof reader. He became a student of type.

He went to and graduated from New York University at night. At NYU, he got a degree in business and marketing. Then, he did graduate work in economics and statistics, which has led to doing penetration analyses (a form of measurement of market share) for most of his major customers. His first job was creating the first set of reports on what commodities at what price were likely to move by air. At the age of 30, Ed became a business consultant with the then largest management engineering organization in America.

He got interested in marketing by mail and began to write direct mail copy. He put out his own shingle. "I went to a number of people in promotion who knew me, and shortly had 6 clients, at $200 per month each. Within months, I found I was more interested in solving the list selection problems of my clients than scribbling about their product line. I straddled for a couple of years and then turned my complete attention to the list field."

He presently is president of the B'nai B'rith Direct Mail Marketing Unit. He never hesitates to take a stand on issues of importance to his industry. He had a strong view on the imposition of the 9-digit zip code, wrote a series of articles and letters on it and testified before Congress. In 1978, MASA honored him by making him their "Man of the Year." He plays a first-class game of tennis, adequate golf and agile squash.

Ed is both a compiler of names and a merchandiser of names compiled by other major compilers. In his early years he was instrumental in building a substantial base for national Business Lists in the East. He created the concept of the 5th-digit S.I.C. to add 2,500 new classifications to the somewhat confining 1,000 classifications in the U.S. Commerce S.I.C. system.

The Burnett Organization works very closely with Reuben H. Donnelley. Burnett pays Donnelley to run through its entire file of 67,000,000 households twice a year and carve out for his province such lists as Doctors at Home Addresses, Pastors at Home Addresses and Armed Forces at Home Addresses. Burnett says: "The gem of all I have compiled is the list of Members of Boards of Directors at Home Addresses and their near neighbors, the highest level large list of affluents available in the country. This is the list used regularly by top banks and stockbrokers."

Ed Burnett is computer oriented. His partner, Paul A. Goldner, gives seminars on the use of computers for direct mail, from merge-purge to construction of data banks. Burnett and Goldner have been in business for 12 years. "I utilized the computer for what must have been one of the earliest computer letters back in 1963, before there was even a chain for upper and lower case. It came out looking like a long telegram."

"Twenty years ago, I recognized that half of all the business generated by list brokers comes from just 100 or so lists—and there are 15,000 lists to choose from. Brokers get their commissions from list owners, but owe their fealty to the mailer, the list user. So I created a new business—the List Manager or List Merchandiser for list owners. Today, better than 70% of all list usage goes through the hands of 25 to 30 list managers, a good number of them well-respected, Burnett-trained alumni.

"We do not run a list brokerage operation. And we are not a direct marketing advertising agency. We are both list compilers and list managers, but mainly we are list consultants. That means we must utilize the brightest, cleverest brains we can find. We talk to young, bright people with research instincts. We use a pragmatic approach to find them. We're listed as a market research house. Research-minded young people see us listed and come to us for a career.

"When someone new comes aboard, he or she spends several months learning, absorbing, listening and probing. We start at square one with the order, and each of our people is trained, thoroughly, to trace everything that happens to that order from analysis, checking, clearance (if a managed property) through production, shipping and billing. Those who wish to know more are sent to seminars and schools. Those who wish advanced degrees have access to the greatest file of knowledge on lists and list usage available anywhere—the reports and analysis of top consultants from our staff, a goodly number by me, through which they can 'go along' and get inside dozens of organizations.

"At least twice a week, someone at our shop refuses to rent lists to a willing, usually overwilling, prospect. If the order margin—not the mark-up—is too small, such a mailer can only produce disaster for himself, and for us, if he mails. All of us here go through the simplistic arithmetic to show what is required for breakeven. And, usually, the prospect thanks us—and perhaps returns another day with a more viable proposition. At least we sleep better this way."

What are Ed Burnett's predictions?

1. Direct Mail is here to stay. Ink on paper, delivered to selected homes or offices is a form of selective marketing that machine or machines will impinge upon but not replace. Yes, interactive TV is coming, yes, newsbriefs can be screened or printed through telephone wires. But the mails offer a form of inexpensive selectability that other media are not likely to match.

2. Lists are likely to become data banks. AMA and Penton already have millions of outside names merged into their files. The Kodak file has 15,000,000 logical users of photographic prints; D & B has built a base of 8,000,000 executives. NBL & MDR each have over 6 million establishments. Direct Media has collected several million business mail-order buyers. This points to fewer but larger list originating entities - both business and consumer.

3. Direct Mail will be invaded, more and more by big companies who will see it as a means to contact customers, and build customer bases in ways other than through conventional industrial and retail outlets.

4. Postage costs and overall costs of mailing will increase. Historically third class postage rates have increased at 9% per year (not compounded) for over 20 years - and there is nothing on the horizon which indicates this thrust will not continue.

NOTE: Ed Burnett has answered the following questions I have asked for the benefit of readers of this book.

Q. *Have compiled lists or buyer lists grown faster?*
A. The mail-order buyer lists grew fastest in the fifties. Since then, compiled lists have grown faster.

Q. *As a business opportunity, is a business supplying direct marketers superior to the list business?*
A. Many who have made the best living are in the supplier lines. Look at the average person in the list business. The largest factors are changing the role of the smaller, for small list retailers are now mainly marketers, really dealers.

Q. *Will direct marketing advertising agencies buy lists in the future with a list buyer as they buy other media and without a list broker?*
A. Agencies are best off working with list brokers for mail-order lists; they have that precious ingredient; they know which lists work best on given offers. Agencies do work with brokers and will continue to do so.

Q. *How much do clients pay for a list when they buy from a list broker who buys from a list owner?*
A. Clients should pay the same price as if they went directly to the list owner. But this is another of those "it depends" areas. Large mailers often work out special relations with brokers and compilers.

Q. *What happens when you get an order from a broker who, in turn, acts for an advertising agency who acts for a client?*
A. We provide the list to the broker less the standard 20% commission. When we get an order this way, we have no idea how much the list is marked up along the way. This could be for a client from an ad agency, a list consultant, a broker with a

mark-up at each step. Generally, advertising agencies should deal with brokers for buyer lists and buy compiled lists direct.

Q. *How many lists are available to rent?*
A. In commercially available lists, some 15,000.

Q. *How many names are rented a year?*
A. About 13 billion names are rented for prospecting each year.

Q. *Today, what do all costs of a mailing in the mail add up to?*
A. About $250 per thousand of which about $35 is for list rental. The balance is for printing, fulfillment, and postage.

Q. *Who are the major compilers of consumer names?*
A. Donnelley today is the only compiler of all names from alphabetic phone books; they currently sell a copy to Metromail. Metromail, which may shortly begin compilation from the phone books itself, sells a copy to R.L. Polk. Polk compiles all available registrations of automobiles (some 40 states), and turns over a copy of this source to Donnelley. Polk also compiles some 24,000,000 names through City Directories. It is a rather fascinating roundelay.

Q. *What about compilers of business lists?*
A. There are four principal business list compilers. They are National Business Lists, Market Data Retrieval, Dun & Bradstreet and Ed Burnett doing a majority of the business.

Q. *How does the list brokerage of buyer lists break down among brokers?*
A. Six brokers dominate, renting something over 500 million names a year each. At $35 a thousand, this comes down to an average of 17 million dollars each in rentals. The average broker does half its business on 100 lists.

Q. *How effective is research in direct marketing?*
A. The best and only really valid research in direct mail comes through mailing. What a person does with an offer, not what he says he will do is significant. Advertising Agencies which promote pre-research on offers have been able to narrow down the number of offers worth testing by mail. But if that same research is utilized to provide the ultimate "winner," actual market tests often prove such research results can be indicative only. It is costly to produce two different packages - but by grid testing, a single mailing can determine which package is best, which of several prices is best, which premium, if any will pull best. The right answer is "Test and find out - not research & hope."

Q. *Do you ever take a flyer yourself in a mail-order business?*
A. I don't invest. But I have gambled by consulting for future royalties. An insurance company agreed to pay me $2 per thousand mailed on my projection of a test. When one million were mailed, the $2,000 paid seemed reasonable to them. But when 30 MM were mailed and $60,000 would be the tab, the client tired of the idea.

NOTE: A wealth of Ed Burnett list know-how is obtainable in cassettes, transcribed lectures and reprints of articles. I particularly recommend "Effective List Marketing—The Key to Direct Mail Profits" recorded on four cassettes, from Hoke Communications. Next I suggest you ask Ed to send you a copy of his elegant directory of mailing lists, called, appropriately, "The Source." This provides a very good idea of the universe available for

almost every classification of business, every institution, every office of every professional in America. Ask him to add to that his chapter, often reprinted, on Direct Mail Lists which is a key section of the Folio book on circulation, plus the analysis of "Big (Very) Business." If you wish to reach people of means, ask for data on Affluents. Attending a seminar is far better. Ed Burnett Consultants, Inc. is located at 2 Park Avenue, New York, N.Y. 10016 (212) 679-0630. Their WATS line is 800-223-7777.

Chapter 10
The Roman Empire

He pioneered Fortune 500 telephone marketing.

Murray Roman is responsible for organizing more telephone calls than anyone else in the world. He is the man who has motivated over a hundred million phone calls to persuade someone to do something . . . to give to a specific cause, vote for a specific candidate . . . buy a car, join a club, or whatever. He has organized successful phone programs for clients all over the world.

He has directed telephone campaigns which helped elect three presidents and dozens of senators and congressmen since 1968. He made telephone marketing a new medium for direct marketers—his name is synonymous with it in the industry. He launched today's telephone selling age back in 1960, with a campaign beyond imagination. One man made it happen, Lee Iacocca, then head of Ford Division for the Ford Motor Company. He authorized a program to make twenty million phone calls to secure prospects for Ford salesmen.

It was the largest continuous sales promotion ever conducted by Ford or any automobile company. It lasted two and a half years. Murray Roman was president of the company that made the calls. "This was the first time telephone selling had been used as a management tool for sales by a major company. We made twenty million calls to consumers, each one accounted for, to get people into their local dealership for a test drive. And those leads created sales."

Today, Murray Roman rules a telephone marketing empire. Calls are always being made by his "communicators", somewhere in the world, 24 hours a day, every day, for the most prestigious organizations and companies in the world. Murray's communicators, all trained according to his demanding standards, make another fifty thousand calls each day. With the current operation running smoothly, Murray says that now, "I spend most of my time building for the future. It blows my mind what telephone marketing is going to develop into. This is only the beginning."

Murray recalls, "Years ago, most businesses wouldn't touch telephone selling. There were horror stories in every Better Business Bureau office. There were boiler rooms and bucket shops. There were phone calls to sell penny stocks, land, oil deals." How did all this change? How did telephone selling become telephone marketing? Murray Roman changed the concept and use of the telephone as a selling tool.

Today, the Direct Mail/ Marketing Association credits over half of all sales created by direct marketing to telephone marketing. Not all agree on that figure, but everyone admits that sales from telephone marketing are enormous. How did today's telephone marketing, Murray Roman and his Roman Empire start?

Murray Roman was born in Russia, coming to the U.S. when he was three. "First we lived in Springfield, Massachusetts, then we moved to Jamaica, Long Island. Dad had a department store, but lost it in the Depression—it burned down, and he had no insurance. He had two more dry goods stores later on.

"I went to Jamaica High, where I helped in the school store. I was very active in student organizations. I was a reporter on the school newspaper, and learned how to reach professional newspaper editors. That was when my interest in publicity really started. These were Depression years though, so I couldn't stay and finish high school. I decided not to work in dry goods—instead I worked in factories and on the docks.

"I got married before World War II, then joined the Army when the war broke out. I transferred to the Air Corp and flew fifty-seven missions from Italy to Germany. When I got out of the Service in August 1945, I got a job in publicity for the Railway Express Agency. I moved on to another job in publicity for the American Cancer Society, where I became National Director for Special Events. Then I went into movie publicity for 20th Century Fox, and then United Artists.

"My interests shifted to fundraising when I became Western Regional Director for the first State of Israel Bond campaign. Starting in 1953 and for the next ten years, I was a National Director of what is now the National Asthma Center. I used direct mail pieces, which I wrote, to raise funds, and was pleased to find that my words were drawing a hefty response. Then I tried the telephone. I started using telephone volunteers to call other people and ask them to become fundraising volunteers. If the person we called agreed to help raise funds, we'd mail a kit telling them how to go about it. We made many calls, got many volunteers, mailed many kits, and received many envelopes with checks. It was highly successful. Over the years, our volunteers made several million calls. This campaign became another model for the 'Women's March for Polio'.

"Then I met Eugene Gilbert. He was brilliant. While he was a student at the University of Chicago, he did research on the mores and habits of students. This had never been done before. He wrote a book on student marketing—he was the pioneer in that whole, booming field. He had a lot of vision—he was ahead of his time in many of his ideas. And, ironically, with all his insight into marketing to the young market, he died young, at 40 . . . but that, of course, was later.

"When I met Eugene Gilbert, he had just sold Ford on the idea of the twenty million phone call campaign. Lee Iacocca had said "Go." But Gilbert didn't know much about telephone selling. When I met him, he said, 'Look, you've been in fund raising. You know telephone work. Now how about trying it for industry?' He formed a new public company, Communicator Network, Inc., to handle the Ford telephone campaign, and I became the president. This was in 1960.

"Two people helped me tremendously at this time. Thomas Parker, who had gotten the Ford business for Gilbert and was extremely close to it, was a consultant. He got me started and taught me a lot. George Brown taught me a great deal also. George was Director of Research for Ford Motor Company at the time, and later became Director of the 1970 U.S. Census. Today, he's Secretary of the National Conference Board.

"There I was, suddenly thrust into the enormous Ford phone campaign. I learned new refinements at each testing stage. We started with three cities, then went to eight, and then went national. We used home workers, and had to figure out how to control them, so that the leads they produced would be high-quality, measured, and accountable. We had an army of people working for us, each being paid per call, yet the campaign had to produce predictable, accurate results.

"We found that handicapped people were dependable and stable workers. Shut-ins, people in wheel chairs, the legally blind—all people who might not otherwise get a job—could make phone calls for us. I worked closely with the United States Department of Vocational Rehabilitation. The department sent notices to their offices all over the country for applicants. Our people then interviewed them. At one point, we employed more handicapped people than any other single employer in the country—five thousand people! We had fifteen thousand people in all working at one time. To get this many as an average, over 25,000 different people worked on the campaign at one point or another. And it all had to be controlled and accountable every day. If anything went wrong, we heard from Top Management at J. Walter Thompson or Ford very quickly. It had to be managed efficiently.

"We had to have a system of controls. It was all based on statistical averages. One person could dial 40 calls an hour, and reach 27 people. Out of the 27 talked to, 15 to 17 were qualified decision makers. Out of these, 3% said they were each planning to buy a car in 3 months, 7% in 6 months, and 11% in 12 months. We derived and verified those figures in the first three tests.

"We structured the operation with a supervisor for each 10 to 12 people calling. We had 2,000 supervisors. Each phone communicator called her supervisor every day. Each supervisor

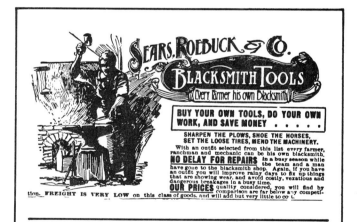

took the calls, totalled the results, and called them into her city or area manager that night. We had 20 to 22 of these regional managers, who called us each morning with the previous day's results.

"We could tell, just looking at the numbers, what was happening. If someone didn't achieve the norms we'd know it fast—we could tell in 3 days if we were being ripped off. And we were just as systematic about getting each lead into the hands of the dealers and their salesmen within 24 hours, so it could be followed up quickly for maximum results.

"It was Ford's longest-running program to motivate car dealers and salesmen. Then Iacocca changed his strategy overnight. He went for a youth image, a speed image. Ford entered the LeMans Auto Races with 'souped-up' cars that won. By contrast, ours was a family image. We were cancelled in the middle of making 2,000,000 just-authorized calls.

"After the Ford campaign stopped, the New York Times wanted a half-million-call campaign to introduce its West Coast edition—a nice program, but nothing compared to Ford's 20 million. Out of Gilbert's business, 95% was from Ford, and now that was cancelled. It was my learning experience, but it was time to move on. I bought up my non-compete clause, resigned, and became a telephone marketing consultant to R.H. Donnelley.

"I began to get into all kinds of uses of phone. Donnelley was extremely successful selling ads in the Yellow Pages over the phone—in fact, they are to this day. At that time, I worked with Curt Frank and Ham Mitchell for Donnelley clients, and for Duke Drake of Donnelley on the West Coast. Ham Mitchell was President. Duke Drake is now Chairman of the Board. We all hoped that the Donnelley salesmen would sell clients on telephone marketing.

"But, despite the Ford campaign, telephone marketing was still ahead of its time. The salesmen could make more commissions faster selling direct mail. Donnelley management decided it would be unwise to continue in telephone marketing beyond the 'Yellow Pages' activity. Telephone marketing didn't really look like a growth industry in the 60's! Donnelley wanted out, but I decided to set out on my own, and they helped me—in a way none of us realized would have such startling results.

"One of the last campaigns through Donnelley was for the National Democratic Committee in 1964. We recruited volunteers for Lyndon Johnson by calling lists of voters block by block. It was highly successful in helping to elect Johnson President, and also worked for Democratic congressional candidates in the 1964 election. We asked for volunteers, and 25% of the people we contacted volunteered. In Chicago, we did the same for Barry Goldwater, and 2% volunteered. Clearly, that one failed. But we built a reputation in political circles of both parties.

"This experience gave my wife and me our big idea—a political mail order catalog. It would offer anyone running for political office almost any promotional materials required for successful campaigning. We'd do it for the 1968 elections. We started CCI in November 1967, with just a few consulting clients. The catalog would have only expense to start with—any income only many months later—and might bomb. We had to earn enough money elsewhere to hedge our bets.

"My wife, Eva, and I lived at 50th Street and Third Avenue. Eva is a psychotherapist, and used one bedroom to meet with patients. In the other bedroom, I was a telephone marketing consultant. We had a part-time seretary. And everybody—Eva's patients, my clients, the secretary—were in that little apartment, switching bedrooms for meetings.

"Elsworth Howell, of Grolier, was the first true mail order man to hire me. Elsworth was fascinated by the use of the phone. He and I spent a lot of time putting together a phone marketing campaign. Bob Clarke, who's now Chairman of the Board, worked with me, too. I drove them crazy asking questions. We started selling Dr. Seuss books on the phone and followed up with other offers. It took a while to find a formula that worked. Nothing became very succesful, but I'm very grateful to Elsworth Howell. He was a pioneer. And I was learning. It was the beginning of mail order telephone marketing.

"Meanwhile, Eva and I developed the political catalog. We took it on as entrepreneurs with our own money. I called my company Campaign Communications Institute of America— that's still our name.

"Our 'Communicate in '68' catalog offered campaign buttons, travelling exhibits, audio video programs, films, TV programs, direct mail, lists, research, telephone, fund-raising, anything a politician might need. We had it printed and collated it in our apartment. It was a mail order catalog, but we never bought a mail order ad. Instead, I remembered everything I knew about publicity and used it to get the word out, to generate inquiries for free. My public relations experience proved invaluable. Timing was right—press and TV grabbed the new idea—you could charge it all to your AMEX card!

"My wife and I were the subject of a special program on NBC Network TV with Edwin Newman—'Somehow It Works'—on May 10th and September 13th, 1968, at 10 PM. We explained and demonstrated our best political items. The NBC interview flooded us with inquiries from politicians of both parties running for national, state and local office. We did more TV interviews, network and local. We had article after article—over 300—in national publications. We were interviewed on radio. We did seminars. Inquiries arrived in a greater and greater torrent, and out went our catalog, and back came orders by phone and by mail.

"I was a consultant for both the Democrats and Republicans. We conducted big telephone campaigns for all sorts of candidates. We made political movies in association with Philippe Halsman. In the '68 elections, we did 60% of the political promotion business in many categories at the national, state and local level.

"Suddenly, in less than a year from start up in November '67, we were making a lot of money, and killing ourselves doing it. We worked in congressional and senatorial and presidential campaigns. We operated out of three offices. By Election Day, including all telephone communicators, we had a total of 4,000 employees. We were even selling to foreign politicians running for office in their countries. Things were wild.

"In the middle of the campaign, Gordon Grossman called from Reader's Digest and said that he wanted to see our telephone operation. When we asked why, he said he wanted to see if we could handle a telephone selling campaign for Reader's Digest. Gordon came with some of his executives. He was 'Mr. Big', Director of Marketing, but I was busy. I really had no idea of his importance, nor any clear approach to why Reader's Digest was interested in our political calls. What was there to see?—just hundreds of people on the phone. He spent twenty or thirty minutes. Then one of his men said thanks, and they left.

"On November 20th, we closed the operation. We turned over the business to our employees and said thanks. We said goodbye. My wife had convinced me to 'go see the world' and relax. We decided to take off for a year and travel to the Far East. We became advisors to UNICEF, and consultants for TWA and Hertz. We were also invited by the Australian Broadcasting System to visit their country.

"We were honored guests wherever we went. Top government people in every country had heard or seen the publicity on the 'New Ways' to get elected, and knew that we were experts at it. We were wined and dined and greeted by Ambassadors and Heads of State in the Philippines, Japan, Malaysia, and Cambodia. We toured through the wilds of the Philippines into remote villages, where the government wanted to know how to teach with audio-visual slide show machines powered by simple gasoline motors. We were even taken to Angor Wat in Cambodia.

"We stayed in Australia two months. We went into business there, which lasted as long as we stayed. After five and a half months, we reached Bangkok. We were just about to leave on a trip around the horn of India with the Far Eastern Manager of TWA when we got a call from Gordon Grossman: 'Get your rear back to New York'. I said 'Forget it'. Gordon said, 'Come do a campaign for Reader's Digest'. I discussed it with Eva. We were both pretty tired. We decided to come back.

"I called my assistant at our apartment, 150 East 50th, where she was finishing up our bookkeeping and told her to rent a floor, we'll be back (at the time, there was plenty of space in the building). We were back in three days and started up in two weeks! We've never stopped since!

"First, we expanded to the Grolier Building, then to 641 Lexington Avenue. Now we're at 555 West 57th Street. CCI just kept growing. Through R.H. Donnelley I had met some people in direct marketing, including Walter Wientz. He helped us get started in that area, and introduced us to the right people.

"In 1970, 'Pete' Hoke called and asked me to do a talk for Direct Marketing Day in New York. I was asked to give many more speeches—which in turn led to my first book. It was published as *Telephone Marketing: How to Build Your Business By Telephone*, by McGraw-Hill in 1976.

"Our direct marketing phone business grew quickly. First came Grolier and the Reader's Digest—they were our first mail order clients. Then we learned how to apply a technique I had used in political telephone campaigns, the concept of the taped telephone presentation introduced by a communicator, to marketing programs.

"Politics had been the beginning for us in the use of tapes in telephone work. We would tape a political figure. Our communicator would phone someone and ask him or her to listen to this famous politician. The tape gave us complete control over the presentation, but we had no way to measure the effect of each call. The results came out in the election, and the politicians' success or failure could not be traced individually to our calls. The opportunity to apply the tape technique on an accountable, economically sound basis to sell by mail order came years later, sparked by a call from Ed Miller, a client of ours, who was President of Berlitz Language Schools.

"Ed said, 'Murray, do you know Norman Cousins? He's starting a new magazine, and I think you can help. Will you talk to him?' I said I would. Norman had been editor of The Saturday Review for 40 years—the magazine was his baby. But now it had been sold, and the new owners wanted to change it into four separate magazines, which Norman wasn't happy with. He had decided to go out on his own and raise money to start his own magazine, called World. He came to see me to discuss a marketing program.

"Norman was very persuasive, very impressive. He said, 'I'm starting a new magazine. How can you help me?' I said, 'I haven't the slightest idea. But you're known and accepted by special kinds of people and they will respond to whatever you do. We can get the demographics of these people based on using select lists. We can test their response to your new magazine. A few hundred calls will provide some answers.' Norman said, 'Let's go'.

"Then I told Norman, 'We've got nothing to sell but you, so let's put your voice on tape and play it to our prospects'. Norman said, 'No, that's invading my privacy. I won't do it' I said 'It's the only way we can do it—you're the only real asset we can talk about!' Finally, Norman said 'Yes'. We wrote a script. He wrote a better one! Five or six test scripts later, we taped it. He sounded great! Now, everything depended on the quality of names we could call.

"Peter Tagger ran 'The Center for the Study of Democratic Institutions', a CCI client. I knew he had sent mailings to the Saturday Review subscriber list and had gotten a good deal of response from it. I said, 'Peter, you've got all your contributors' names coded by their source. Give me your Saturday Review names.' We tried 5,000 Saturday Review names first. I still remember the list code number—it was 905.

"Norm was seen as one step lower than God by his Saturday Review subscribers. We pulled up to 40% on that list with direct subscriptions by telephone. Norman would come in every night while we were calling, talking to our communicators. He was going crazy! He was thrilled with the results, going to his backers with them, and making plans for the future.

"I said, 'Wait a minute, Norman! We've only got a total of 12,000 Saturday Review names from CSDI. No other names will pull like this.' We tested Common Cause names, Harper's names, other logical names, all from Peter's file. Of course, they didn't pull as well as the original list, but they did pay out. Then we rented outside lists. We tested Smithsonian. It worked. We went to more tests. We averaged 28% across all lists used, the bad and the good.

"Based on the economics of phone solicitation, we set 15% as the minimum acceptable response rate. As our testing progressed, we could look at the phone response rate for each list, and predict the response rate Norman could get by mailing to that list. The cost for telephoning was higher than the cost of mailing, but phone consistently produced 2½ to 5 times better response from each list. In direct mail, it was highly profitable for Norman to pull 3% to 5%. That meant that, if phone pulled less than 15% on a particular list but close to it, we would stop phoning that list and Norman started mailing. In all, we made more than 500,000 calls for Norman.

"The campaign to launch Norman Cousin's World magazine was a big success, and the success of World led eventually to Norman's regaining control of the four Saturday Review magazines from the new owners, combining them and merging with World—and once again publishing Saturday Review in its traditional way. This dramatic evidence of phone's power fascinated direct marketers, and led to a big acceleration of my business. All sorts of people got interested in the new sales power of the telephone when used the way we used it, particularly with the control of the pre-recorded tape. It made telephone marketing a new advertising medium.

"About this time, Dr. Theodore Levitt of the Harvard Business School wrote an article called 'Marketing Myopia'. He also wrote an article in the Harvard Business Review on 'The Industrialization of Service'. When it was brought to my attention, I got very excited. Levitt was writing about bringing the kind of systemization to business that we were already using in telephone selling.

"I called him. I explained what we were doing with the phone, and told him, 'Dr. Levitt, I'm thrilled with what you've written. You've provided a theoretical basis for our telephone concepts. My company is a nuts-and-bolts numbers business. But we do what you've been writing about.' He became fascinated, wrote about our work, and even agreed to write the introduction to my book.

"Then the most brilliant people in direct marketing got interested—people like Bob Stone, marketing pioneer and Chairman of Stone & Adler. Lester Wunderman, Chairman of Wunderman, Ricotta & Kline, began to work with me on setting up telephone marketing for their clients. Richard Zeldin, President of Xerox College Publishing, did also.

"McLean-Hunter, the publishing giant, went into business with CCI in a Canadian telephone marketing company. We also began to operate in other countries, with the UK, France, Holland, Finland, Switzerland for starters. In 1980 we made several million calls for the Republicans. I conducted seminars for the American Management Association, NYU, the University of Chicago and the International Direct Marketing Symposium in Montreaux and Australia. I became the founder of the Telephone Marketing Council of the Direct Mail/Marketing Association and the CCTU (Committee of Corporate Telephone Users), an industry watchdog organization to monitor changes in government regulatory policies and AT&T rate structures.

"Many of our clients have been with us for years. For example, we have a long-running program selling the Bull Worker exerciser for Sam Josefowitz. He runs mail order inquiry ads with soft coupons. He mails them literature, then we call them immediately to follow up and take the order. We've been doing this successfully for nine years. We make calls for Citicorp, IBM, Xerox, McGraw-Hill, and a host of others. We work for 20-30 accounts at any one time."

Bob Muller, Vice President Marketing of McGraw-Hill, introduced Murray at a McGraw-Hill executive seminar in 1979: "In 1970 Business Week called him the Marco Polo of telephone marketing. In 1980 Fortune calls him 'The Toscanini'." Eva Roman, Murray's wife, was in the audience. Murray got up, bowed and said, "And there is Mrs. Beethoven". Murray Roman feels that Eva is the "conductor" responsible for their success.

Murray is grateful for the acceptance of telephone marketing by the nation's largest direct marketers, and of direct marketing by Fortune 500 companies. He feels that it was all capped by the Fortune magazine article of April 21, 1980, on direct marketing and telephone marketing. "The entire Fortune article was the best publicity yet" he says. "Certainly the best for CCI."

What is so remarkable about Murray is the degree of trust in him shown by so many people in top positions at giant companies. "I see no purpose in doing anything crooked" he told me. "I believe in what I do."

"We work only one way, our way, and our clients appreciate that. The telephone is now over a hundred years old, making it one of the oldest instruments used in business today. It has been misused in every nook and cranny of the country by fly-by-night operators ranging from exterminators to rug cleaners, dancing schools, land salesmen and oil well schemers.

"From the start, we did it a different way. We practiced telephone marketing with integrity. We made it a projectable marketing tool for business. We fostered accountability. We look at the telephone as a machine, and telephone selling as a structured use of that machine, just the way you would use a punch press in a manufacturing operation. A piece of steel is put into a punch press and something happens, the same way each time. The result can be anticipated. That's exactly the approach we bring to telephone marketing. It was the only way to utilize 15,000 people in the Ford campaign, the only way to use the

phone in political campaigns. It's controlled. The end result is predictable.

"To successfully use the telephone in direct marketing, I had to learn the art of scientific list selection. I learned the hard way. I first learned lists from Peter Tagger, most of all in the Norman Cousins campaign. Peter is now a consultant in fundraising. Gordon Grossman taught me a great deal. I didn't make many moves without him. But Dick Cremer, President of Montgomery Ward's five specialized mail order companies, surprised me the most with what he taught me.

"Dick Cremer taught me what happens when we use regression analysis to select lists. I had never heard of it, didn't understand it, and thought he was crazy when he insisted on using it. I wanted to select the best of his lists for phone testing based on his results from previous marketing efforts. He refused.

"Dick said, 'Do it my way. Just keep calling until you can give me 500 orders. I'll give you some random lists to call.' Of course, doing this just couldn't work! Against my will we did it, and pulled 7% to 8% response. This *couldn't* be profitable. But we sent the results to Dick. Then, a month later, Dick sent me some names and said 'Now call these'. We got 28% response! Dick had analyzed the first 500 orders by regression analysis and then selected lists with the same characteristics. I became a convert— and, I've been a true believer ever since!

"For list selection today, Gordon Grossman is still our advisor. His methods are scientific and sound. He regards selection of lists for telephoning as the same problem as selecting names to mail.

"By now, we've tested dozens of uses of telephone marketing. We've tested it to convert from small trial orders to bigger commitments, to reinstate cancelled orders, to renew subscriptions for present buyers, to convert inquiries, to sell for dealers and to dealers. We know where it works and where it has failed. We are always getting new ideas to test a different way, and sometimes we succeed. We've experimented with using telephone marketing for the biggest and some of the smallest businesses. We've never stopped work for our political clients. We used Theodore Bikel on tape to reach Jewish voters in the Bronx, and Herman Badillo on tape to address his own Puerto Rican community, conservatives and liberals, republicans and democrats, each in segmented ways to reach their constituencies.

"The cost of a personal sales visit can exceed $140. A simple letter costs $6 or more. 'Reaching' a visitor at a trade show can cost $60 and direct mail costs soar with each paper and postal increase. That's why we get clients. A lot of them are biggest companies like Hertz, GTE, and Montgomery Ward; or Merrill Lynch and NCR; Monsanto, American Express, IT&T and Equitable Life. We deal with the U.S. Postal Service and the Salvation Army, with J. Walter Thompson, 3M and Hoffman-LaRoche."

"I think the smallest entrepreneur we've dealt with was a fellow from Wisconsin who called me just after he read my book. He said, 'I'm a real estate salesman. I'm working on cornering the wild rice market in my state. If I can get 500 restaurants to order from me, I can control the crop of wild rice. I can buy, warehouse, and ship, if you can get the customers. I'll put all my eggs in your basket. I trust you. When can I come to New York?'

"I said, 'Hold on—you can't'. He said, 'I'm prepared to do it'. I said, 'This will cost $10,000'. There was a dead silence. I could hear the gulp. There was a pause. Then he said, 'If you say so, I'll go get it.' Then, in a week, a letter arrived from him. It was four or five pages long, with a complete marketing plan. It was brilliant. My staff didn't want to do it, but we managed. I said, 'I like his plan. Maybe it can be a special case history that can be a new milestone.' I called him and said, 'OK.'

"We developed a list from Holiday magazine listings of restaurants. We called and offered a sample of wild rice. He had a small local agency do a brochure for him to go with a sample. It was a beautiful job. He sent me the wild rice samples and the mailing. We called restaurants and asked them to try a sample. If they agreed, we sent the rice and the brochure, then called back after they received their samples and took orders. At the same time, he sent out a mailing offering a sample, and we followed up those sample requests by phone as well. It was a great success— we sold him out. And, as a side benefit, we got lots of cases of wild rice, and still get them."

When asked about the crucial testing phase in the phone marketing effort, Murray's advice is straight forward and clearly well-rooted in experience." How many calls do you have to make in your first test? I'd generally say a thousand or so for a program reaching consumers, and approximately 500 completed calls for businesses—that will give you a feel. If it's a success, then go ahead with a confirming test—you'll need at least a few thousand calls for projectable results. For business-to-business phoning, we know that 500 completed calls in any SIC is enough.

"How much does a test cost? It's going up, but the maximum is $15,000 to $20,000 to get a clear cut answer. And that's only because all our creative and planning costs are up front. We have to create the script, plan the test and projection, select lists, train the communicators, and we do all that whether we're making one call or one million calls."

The headquarters of the Roman Empire, with its 18,000 square feet and 380 employees, is at 555 West 57th Street, New York, NY 10019, (212) 957-8520. The company continues to make over 15 million phone calls a year for its clients. And Murray never stops. "I find telephone marketing challenging. Telecommunication in the future is exciting—the sky's the limit! The telephone marketing age has just begun. We commissioned an Arthur D. Little study. It blows my mind, everything that's about to happen in the 'interactive electronic media age'. And, it's all built around the telephone."

Chapter 11
Getting A Better Job In Direct Marketing

"How to Reach Your $50,000 Goal"

That was the speech and Karen Gillick the speaker . . . at the Chicago Association of Direct Marketing. For anyone starting a direct marketing career and aiming high, Karen is someone to know. Her specialty is finding people to fill $20,000 to $100,000-a-year jobs . . . in a wide variety of direct marketing areas.

Karen is president of Karen Gillick & Associates, a Chicago personnel agency specializing in direct marketing. She deals with people and firms all over the country. What she knows about how to get a better job in direct marketing can help anyone in it, anywhere. She has helped many do it.

She has an ideal background for her chosen field. Karen was born into and brought up in direct marketing. She is the daughter of Bob Stone. She has an advertising background. She worked for Leo Burnett and before that for Needham, Harper & Steers. She was assistant manager of the McCann-Erickson personnel department in Chicago. Karen has Bob Stone's integrity, a lot of know-how he taught her and some special qualities of her own.

"Each assignment we regard as confidential. We are discrete, for applicants and for client firms. Business is business. There are many matters I can't divulge, even to my father—because they concern competitors." Karen is talking. "We're 99% in direct marketing and work with over 75 direct mail/marketing firms. We match needs to strengths.

"Our business has quadrupled in the last three years. We can't stop the phone. Employers keep calling to fill jobs—but almost always for experienced help. We try to get resumes from those with at least three to five years direct marketing experience. About 50% of our placements are for direct marketing agencies and almost 50% for direct marketing firms.

"For one very big company we're looking for someone to head up their house agency. For another it's someone in the advertising department. For another we're looking for a corporate director of direct marketing. Right now, we're looking for a president and chief executive officer for a catalog business, with experience and background in the garment field. The job pays $50,000 to $70,000. I'm looking for an account executive for a direct marketing agency.

"Direct response writers are always in demand. Employers constantly ask for them. Good ones are harder to find. We've got jobs for four good writers. We also place free lancers. Art directors are becoming more desired, but also comptrollers and accountants.

"Some clients give us an exclusive for a month. They may call us first. Then if we don't come up with someone to fill the job, they give the assignment to a competitor.

"We get exposure. I had an article in Advertising Age in October 1980. We're members of the Chicago Association of Direct Marketing and of the Direct Mail/Marketing Association. We get a lot of referrals from our clients and from the associations. Now we get 20 to 50 resumes a month from our ads in Direct Marketing magazine. Eighty percent of them are good people.

Life Preservers.

48897 "Never Sink" Cork Jackets, adopted as standard, and the government inspector's stamp on each one, and easily put on, durable and has great buoyancy. Weight, 9 pounds; each............$1.25
Per dozen........ ......13.50
48898 Life Belts, in squares, similar to the "Never Sink," and buckles on the same way. One of the best in the market; safe and durable.
Weight, 9 lbs. Each ...$1.10
Per dozen 10.20

"We do try to help beginners. But even when we offer to place them at no fee to us, we've had very little luck. We have to turn away eighty percent of beginners and tell them to call back when they have had some experience.

"Once you're in direct marketing it's important to update knowledge. The more you learn the more marketable you are. We recommend going to the Basic DMMA Seminars. For those in Chicago, we recommend the Roosevelt University course. Also, John Flieder and the CADM has a 12-week course that we recommend.

"Direct marketing keeps growing faster. There are more and more jobs to fill. We keep growing with it. It's a full-time job. The pace is increasing but I still have plenty of time for my husband, who is a lawyer."

Future growth of biggest direct marketers is largely determined by ability to secure the trained, experienced direct marketing specialists to make it possible. Widely different types of training, experience and traits are needed for different jobs. This is when the training you received in school and college, plus your first experience, begins to pay off.

Post-graduate business school—and night school logical business courses—improve further your chances for a better job. . . after experience is added. Even the least experience gives a great advantage over none. More experience . . . of a type desired and for a boss respected . . . makes you more desirable. If your actions in your job create profits, avoid losses or cut costs, you'll have a bright mail order future.

Doubleday, in one ad, offered jobs for accountants, financial analysts and market research analysts. All had to be MBA's. The same ad offered jobs for copywriters and artists and advertising production assistants . . . and even for mechanical engineers and electrical engineers. What is needed is this kind of specialized training, plus experience applying it in direct marketing.

Companies which get much of their sales from direct marketing usually grow faster than the economy. This forces the creation of new jobs. It is cheaper to fill these jobs from inside. Direct marketing methods, applied scientifically, can usually sell more of most products more profitably. For a good company and product, with a good organization, all that is needed to add is direct marketing know-how. If you have it, you may qualify for a job opening up where employed—or you may even propose to your boss a direct marketing plan that creates your new job opportunity.

Many people in direct marketing think of getting a better job in it as a form of direct marketing yourself. In May 1977, an article by Morris Rosenblum and Judy Ocko appeared in Direct Marketing magazine. The title was "How Each Marketer Can Best Promote Himself". In August 1980, a panel discussion on hiring and finding a creative staff was the feature of the monthly luncheon meeting of Direct Marketing Creative Guild. The speakers were Suzanne Ridenour and the presidents of two other personnel agencies, Greg Freson and Toby Clarke. Anyone creative in direct marketing can get a tape from Hoke Communications. Details are in the Help Source Guide section of this book.

Most successful people in direct marketing are of one or two basic types, creative people and marketing people. Some have both abilities and, if so, are usually hugely successful. But you can make a lot of money, if you're strong in either area and weak in the other. Other types succeed as well—often most of all . . . the entrepreneurs and the organizational persuaders who gather about them those with special talents.

However bad you are at anything in direct marketing, there may be something else in it that you're good at. From your first day at your first job in it, you can start looking for the areas you like working in and are best at. This book is designed to introduce you to a wide variety of successful people in direct marketing, often with quite different traits, experience and ability—and in quite different careers. You might be interested, yourself, in one of these. If so, you can get far more detailed information on it. Just refer to the index in the Help Source section.

As soon as you find something you like and are good at—and start acquiring more expertise in it than others—you get an advantage. This book lists and reviews the courses and seminars, publications and books, articles and tapes, newsletters and organizations where you can get a good deal of specialized know-how.

Adding unpaid, extra hours for the boss can greatly increase this advantage. Often, this quickly results in specific, measurable contributions. And these can lead to higher paying jobs. If your boss doesn't value them, others will. The more of a specialized know-how you master the more you have to offer to someone who needs it . . . particularly in an area that is becoming more vital to direct marketers.

If you've been with a successful company, you are still better off, and if trained under a master of direct marketing, more so. But even if you started away from the big centers or with a small, struggling firm, such accomplishments make you desirable to the big—who constantly recruit from the bush leagues. Conversely, experience and first career success in New York or Chicago makes you even more hotly desired away from these cities where there is more mail order talent.

The February 1980 meeting of the Direct Marketing Idea Exchange was devoted to direct marketing careers. The agenda included discussion of the data gathered from a career questionnaire filled out by DMIX members.

That panel is a fascinating study of career strategy in the highest brackets of direct marketers. Sixty percent of DMIX members are presidents or vice presidents of major DM companies. Twenty percent are managers, Thirteen percent are directors and eight percent are consultants. Seventy percent earn more than $50,000 a year.

An excellent report on this meeting is in the March 15, 1980, DM News, which I suggest sending for. A tape of the entire panel discussion can be obtained from Hoke Communications.

As in any field, the brighter, more driving and harder working do better. The organized and practical, those with a "feel" for what to sell and how to sell it, the persuasive and innovative all do well. And so competitive is the drive to recruit in direct marketing that it's hard to hide talent under the mail order bushel. But exposing talent to wider view multiplies possible offers. A little politicking can go a long way.

Throughout this book are described the organizations and places where anyone can meet others in direct marketing. You may meet your future boss at any such meeting, with a better opportunity. But remember, your boss may meet someone better than you for your present job. To play safe, master your job as first priority. Then meet others and when offers come, let your boss join in the bidding. I describe the direct marketing clubs and Direct Marketing Days.

From the smallest direct marketing club or Day to the biggest—and to the DMMA conferences—one contact might change your career. Volunteer work for such groups causes you to meet others, any of whom may later help you. Sharing know-how will gain respect. Your first speeches and articles may, while helping others, get a customer or a job for you.

To form friendships with others in the field can be rewarding—personally and in business. Exchanging information adds know-how to each. Friends can help. Tips of sources, items, media buys, copy slants, fulfillment methods or whatever can often make or save instant money. Job tips and recommendations can make big career differences.

So, if you're in that league or aiming at it, you'd better send for both the DM News story and the Hoke tape. See details in the Help Source Guide Section.

Note: Karen Gillick & Associates is located at 221 North La Salle Street (Suite 3306), Chicago, Illinois 60601; (312) 236-4666.

Chapter 12
Family Success In Free Lance Copy

They write copy for the mail order giants, but not just giants.

They write for products and services they like, for people they like, for companies they like, and they charge what you like in a way that is your choice and your pleasure.

And they only take on products and services that challenge, that they believe they can make succeed and that they believe they can make good money working for. But every year they write more and more copy for nothing at all, for causes they feel are important and to which they contribute their professional talents.

Head of the family, president of the free lance copy firm and undisputed boss is Henry Cowen. The family business is The Cowen Group, Inc., at 205 East Main Street, Village East, in Huntington, New York 11743.

Year in and year out for over twenty years, Henry Cowen has been considered by many as one of the very few great writers in the U.S. of direct mail order advertising. He learned his trade on the job but got into it because of a course he took at New York University. Before that he had found no direction in school or college that caught his interest.

"I was an immature college student. My marks were mediocre. I looked for simple courses. But in my senior year at New York University, I took a course not given before and given

up the next year. It was a course in direct mail which I had never heard of. It was taught by Earl Manville. He fascinated me and what he taught changed my life.

"The next year I stated a job writing direct mail. To get it, I wrote Lester Suhler in charge of circulation at Cowles Publications, for Look and all other Cowles publications. He became my mentor. He didn't really teach me to write copy. Max Ross taught me.

"But Lester Suhler guided me and influenced me as he did many others. There are many people in direct marketing today who learned from him and picked up all his mannerisms, his way of talking, his way of walking, his way of carrying a briefcase. He was that kind of a guy.

"Max taught me. Max would take a red pencil and go over my copy until it had measles, and send me back to the drawing board. But they used my copy. I could see what worked. I could learn by just being there. A copywriter at Cowles in those days did everything from figuring costs and order margins to lists.

"Lester taught a lot and expected a lot quite aside from copy. He expected successful copy to be produced. In bad times he told me people would stop buying outside the home and stay home and subscribe to magazines to save money on entertainment. In good times, he told me people had plenty of money to spend on magazine subscriptions. There were no MBA's around to show us how to make money for the company. It was our job to do that.

"Lester taught me responsibilities beyond business. He felt I had a duty to use any talent I had outside of business for public good. He saw to it; he expected me to help worthy fund-raising efforts.

"What's the most fun I've had in business? I think it was when I went to work for Publisher's Clearing House. It was and is owned by the Mertz family. Harold E. Mertz was the guiding force then. He started mail order in early 1953. I knew him. I had told him to save his money. But he started and was making money and growing when I left Cowles after 18 years. This was 1960. Marvin Barckley came over from Cowles at the same time.

"Harold Mertz started PCH as a listing of magazines with the subscription price of each and a return order card. It was a way to gamble that he could pull subscriptions for his clients at an advertising cost low enough to be satisfactory to the publishers and profitable for him. It worked. The business grew. He mailed more and brought us in to help.

"We started to show Harold how to go for the full potential. He was mailing in big volume. He was making a very nice living. But we began talking about mailing a hundred million, to project his success to the maximum. Postage was going up. Subscriptions began to jump in price. But PCH increased sales didn't come from this. The gross volume from a list doesn't jump when prices jump. You usually get the same dollars but less orders.

"The big gains came from better creativity. I did the first contest for PCH in 1967. I did the first support TV for PCH in 1971 or so. I was with them for fifteen years. Harold let me do what I knew would work, and it did. It was fun to see the business grow so tremendously.

"I loved my jobs. Look was great. Publishers Clearing House was very nice to work for. They were very fair. They paid me a lot. I left in 1975 to form The Cowen Group. That's me, my son-in-law and my son—plus a secretary. PCH was our first client and still is a client. They're good friends.

"My son, son-in-law and I are all three copywriters. My wife is the part-time bookkeeper. My son, David Cowen, had worked for my son-in-law, Lewis Tobak, in Lew's clothing store. Neither had ever written copy or been in direct mail. When I first

Waterproof Horse Covers.

Black Oiled Waterproof Hame Horse Covers. These goods, as we have them prepared, are absolutely rainproof. The coating applied to the canvas contains nothing that will in any way injure the fabric, but is rather a preservative. Our covers extend on the neck twelve inches in front of the collar and can be used over either single or double harness. They are made with hame leathers, trace straps, and straps across the breast.

37476 Made of black oiled 8 oz. duck in sizes from 5 feet to 5 feet 6 inches from collar to tail. Each..$2.00
Weight, each, about 8 lbs.
37477 Made of black oiled drill in sizes from 4 feet 8 inches, to 5 feet 4 inches, from collar to tail. Each.. 1.75
Weight, each, about 5 lbs.

suggested it, I was amazed that they said yes. But they like this better. They make more money.

"And as I write and they write I teach them a trade. It must be hard to work for a father or father-in-law, but we get along well, which merely means they are good guys. I'm tough. I read every word and change any word I don't like. They're good. We produce. We have to. We have an organization and an overhead.

"We've worked for a lot of people. We've had a lot of clients. We work for Exxon Travel Club, for TV Guide, for the Xerox Educational Division. We work for a French book club, Le Grand Livre du Mois, and for a French record club. In the job we're doing now we write, translate and make the mechanical with all type set in French.

"I love mail order. I loved it when I worked for others. I love even more being in our own family business. It's great to work for the biggest. It's a thrill to see smaller clients grow.

"Consumer's Digest, in Chicago, had 180,000 circulation after 18 years. Arthur Weber hired me. I flopped. He said try again. I flopped again. He was tough, determined and he said he had faith in me. We seldom fail. I tried again and this time found the key. Apparently, (he told me) people didn't buy the magazine as a magazine but as an overall service. I presented it just that way and it clicked. I admit I did something else, a contest.

"They say contests need big prizes, that they're only for bigger companies, that you have to have professional contest people to run it. All this helps but I played the copy differently. The grand prize was two Superbowl tickets or a night on the town for two. Just incidentally, I added that, as the winner, you'd also get a car to drive home with and a thousand dollars in American Express checks. It was 1976. It was a low-priced car. All the prizes were several thousand dollars. Arnold Weber did it all himself. Now we do a contest every year for him.

"We work for a variety of businesses. The three toughest things to sell are books, magazine subscriptions and insurance. We've sold more of all three than anything else. We work for low-end consumer products for a catalog like Foster & Gallagher.

We work for the National Law Journal. I just had lunch with a lithographer specializing in mail order. He wants us to create advertising to tell about his specialty and he's willing for us to make some money for doing it. How do we get business? Mostly over the transom.

"How do we charge? Any way people want. For some, we're on retainer. For others, we charge for the package. For others, we charge nothing down, but a commission forever as long as the copy is used. It's a charge per thousand for pieces mailed. For a tiny test, it's a tiny cost. For big roll-outs later, there's no limit. Of course, we normally make more money this way. One magazine got so tired of writing the commission check. This was my son's first piece. So far, we've made $70,000 on it. But people who pay us this way don't complain; most are as good as gold.

"The most gratifying thing about my work has been the chance to teach people and to help people. One year, I taught a night course in direct marketing at Drake University. Max Ross had taught the same course before. I've tried to help people wherever I worked. I've helped people find jobs.

"John Mienick was president of Publishers Clearing House. He trained with me. Of course, I can't take all the credit. He learned from others, too. Dale Steiger has a consulting agency at 488 Madison Avenue, in New York. Mike Kauffman was with me learning at Look. Ed Bartlett was. They've all succeeded.

"I don't think I can remember all the organizations I've written fund-raising copy for. I've never charged a cent for it. Because of Lester, I started. I've never stopped. Out here on Long Island, I worked for the North Shore Animal League. Now they mail 16 million names. I've built them up just lke an account. I've done it for years for the America the Beautiful Fund, for the National Conference of Christians and Jews, for Drake University and Manhattan College.

"I believe in creativity more than research. Look did research why subscribers subscribed, why non-renewals did not renew, and why 60% of new subscribers didn't renew. People had difficulty giving answers. They wouldn't or couldn't tell. Their answers didn't help us.

"I'm not pro research. One time, Cowles had a big national agency for advertising to advertisers. The agency offered to save money on testing. They would submit our mailings to special panels of consumers. For a fraction of the cost of a test, they would find out which would fail and which succeed, and which succeed best. That was the idea. We were ordered to submit test mailings to them. Max Ross said, 'Let's give them last year's.' That was the end of it. The agency decided not to try.

"I'm more concerned with creativity than with computers. I work long and hard to plan tests and project what will happen, but not with computers. In the old days, Look didn't do modeling. Our clients today do not hire us for that sort of thing. They hire us for a sales plan, for advice or to create packages. When I work for a TV Guide or R.L. Polk, they don't want us for anything but to make money for them by our creativity.

"I believe in creativity and creative people even over the numbers people. MBA's are okay until they cut down on creativity. They tend to set up rules. The rules can limit the use of imaginative ideas. They tend to throw out an untested creative idea if it causes a change in the way they think is the most efficient way to process an order, to print, to mail. They limit amounts available for testing. They create sameness because they favor playing safe.

"What does it take to succeed for someone starting new? Creativity and work. There's a shortage. And both are needed badly."

Chapter 13
Helping Direct Marketing Beginners

*Major hobby of managing partner
of one of biggest U.S. direct
marketing advertising agencies.*

That's a major hobby of the managing partner of one of the biggest direct marketing advertising agencies in the U.S.—with over a hundred employees.

He's Freeman Gosden, Jr. His column on Direct Mail/Direct Marketing is a great book on direct marketing in the making—with each column a chapter. He devotes more time to lecture to and orient those starting out than almost any top executive in the field.

He created the concept of the United Airline Executive Air Travel Club. He sold 2,000,000 personalized "Me Books" for children for Dart Industries, Inc.—and ran the division. For five years he was president of Market Compilation and Research Bureau, a Dart subsidiary. Previously, he headed advertising and public relations for Dart.

"My first job was in the oil business, starting as a roughneck and working up to a petroleum engineer. A co-worker was George Bush, now Vice President of the United States. The year before the Salk vaccine was developed, I came down with polio. I recovered enough to walk by myself and play most sports, but it still affects my back muscles.

"In 1953, I was back at work, starting my business career over—in the mail room of Young & Rubicam, in Los Angeles. Then I joined BBD&O in Los Angeles. The Rexall Drugstore chain was an account. I decided, on my own, to moonlight at night and on weekends—working in a Rexall Drugstore. It changed all my ideas of how the account should advertise. Because none of them worked in a drugstore, everyone started to listen to what I had to say. After a few years at BBD&O, I became head of advertising and public relations for Rexall, which then became Dart Industries—now a billion dollar conglomerate.

"For Dart, I started a business, Bonus Gifts. It was a coupon plan for participating manufacturers, and highly advertised to the consumer. For Bonus Gifts, we spent sixteen million dollars in a 20-week period, probably the largest consumer test campaign ever. We ran all kinds of advertising and kept track of results. The direct mail pulled best—which sold me on direct mail as a powerful advertising tool. I was on this project for three years. Dart sold the business. I was offered a job to run it, but would have had to move to Connecticut which I declined.

"Then I really got into direct marketing with both feet. Dart asked me to head up their subsidiary, Market Compliation Research Bureau. MCRB had been founded by Lew Rashmir, who became head of all direct marketing activities for Dart. MCRB compiled names and rented them to direct marketers. I was president for five years. We also created a lot of computer letters, had a computer service bureau and maintained lists for direct marketers.

"While at MCRB, I created an entirely new product—'Me Books'. These are children's books done by computer. We took the child's name, plus address, names of relatives, friends and pets and wrote a personalized book all about the child and various friends. I set it up as a separate company. We sold two million 'Me Books' by mail order. Later, Dart sold the 'Me Books' division.

"One day, I got a call from a well known direct mail agency president, Bob Hemmings. He told me that his partner, Eric Smith, had retired and he would like someone to take over and run his company, Smith & Hemmings Advertising in Los Angeles. I came in as executive vice-president. Smith and Hemmings had been in business for 34 years and had a stable growth. We had 35 people when I joined. S&H had a printing operation. We later disbanded all this and now rely on other printers. Our reasoning was that while copy hadn't basically changed over the years, graphics technology was changing daily. Now, using the proper specialist, we can specify newest paper or type and keep up with most sophisticated, latest developments.

"The business is quite different today. Now it's Smith, Hemmings and Gosden. Our business is all direct marketing. Ninety percent is direct mail. The rest is space. We have very little business in Los Angeles, as our clients are all over the U.S.A. The potential was already there when I arrived. We've worked well together and have grown considerably. The billing and staff are several times larger. And our growth is continuing to accelerate.

"How do we do it? We go out and sell. Our people are on the road constantly. One of our people just flew around the world in eight days. We go all over, because there are no really big direct marketing companies in Los Angeles. We have eighty clients. They include commercial business to business accounts, fund raising and consumer mail order accounts. When a company is run by the same internal people for a long time, an outsider can often bring in a broader exposure and knows where good people can be found.

"My main strengths are the abilities to come up with the big idea, to hire good people, to teach and train. I can't draw. I'm poor at grammar. I've never been a copywriter. At one time, about 30% of my time was devoted to buying media, but I've never been a full-time media buyer. I had done account handling and supervising.

"I'm luckiest at quick creative reaction. My office is open to anyone in our organization. I'm open to listening to any problem for any account. Usually, in thirty seconds, I can come up with a solution, or at least a good direction. I'm tough and run a tight ship. Everybody works from 8:15 AM to 5 PM.

"To start work for a client, we first get the facts. We break the facts down into parts, as many as possible. We write down suggested solutions, then all possible alternatives, then alternatives to alternatives, until we come up with the right alternative that becomes the right solution. I'm a brainstormer. I learned it at BBD&O, which originated it.

"We have two rules. The first is, 'What is important is not what you want to sell, but what the customer wants to buy'. The second is Ed Mayer, Jr's '40-40-20 Rule'. Forty percent of success or failure is who you are, what your product is, and what the price or deal is. Forty percent is the media choice or list sub-selection. Only twenty percent is the copy, the theme, the graphics, the printing quality and postage rate. This last 20% is most visible, but still only 20% of the factors that determine success or failure.

"We don't just develop a mailing package for a product. We go back to square one and develop the market background, the first 40%. We concentrate on media and lists, too. The 80% is the important part. Most of our work is not in huge volume or in mass mailings. We have a broad range of client needs. We have one program of only 1,600 pieces and another of 25 million pieces. Both are important. Each client is really different and we must convert their needs into direct marketing opportunities. I review all advertising of our clients. I love my work.

"We view testing differently for different clients. One client may have little money, must start out small, and then branch out. In this case, we test only factors such as lists that have a high probability of success. A large corporation, on the other hand, is more concerned with determining how big a volume can be ultimately attained. The big firm needs to know fast not only if a test is successful, but if the roll-out potential is big enough to justify going into the venture at all. Therefore, it is necessary to test a sample of the entire universe to see the total potential. We use sophisticated overlap testing to test many factors at one time. In one 40,000-name test we're running, we have over 1,200 different mailing package variations.

"My father created 'Amos 'N' Andy'. He played Amos, Kingfish and many other characters on the show. I grew up in Chicago and Los Angeles. I went to high school in Indiana. I went to Princeton University and graduated in 1950 (in the top third of his class). I was cadet major of ROTC on campus. While my father paid for my high school and college, I also sold items on campus to students. Since then, my success has been on my own, without support from my father.

"When at college, I was a stammerer. I grew out of it. I enjoy helping young people overcome problems. I speak a good deal to groups of young people, usually for one hour. Each time, I've had some come up and tell me it was the most exciting hour that they ever spent. I personally do a good deal of educational work. To me, it's an obligation to help others. It's also a personal hobby. I teach one course on direct marketing for the Direct Marketing Club of Southern California. It's somewhat equivalent to the Nat Ross course at NYU, in New York.

Twice a year, I lecture at California State University at Northridge for the adult educational program. Each time, it's an all day session, for seven straight hours. Attendence is 50 to 175 students who are either just going into direct mail or mail order or would like to.

"I also do the all day Business to Business Mail seminars, lecture at fifteen to twenty colleges a year, and talk on direct marketing at advertising clubs. I organized Career Day at the DMMA Spring and Fall Conferences. We had 160 college students at Colorado Springs this year and 200 in Chicago. Now we're adding a session for professors. We try to turn them on to direct mail and mail order so they give it more attention on campus.

"My hobbies are paddle tennis, crossword puzzles, building TV sets and writing magazine articles. Another hobby is teaching younger people how to start off in this business. I show them how to market themselves. It's like a direct marketing problem. First the students must do research on themselves as to what each offers, what each wants to do, in what field and where to get help.

"Then comes the media analysis. How do you reach the smaller companies who can't afford to send personnel people to campuses. Do you visit, phone or do an ad . . . how to find lists, whom to reach at each company, etc. Then comes copy . . . what are your strong points; what is the interviewer interested in. Then comes graphics—what should the resume look like—letter versus card, quality and color of paper, etc. I don't believe in standard resume formats for anyone seeking a position in a creative organization.

"Now comes the budget affordable—savings by doing it yourself. Then the timetable—start early and stagger mail.

Finally comes the analysis—whether it's working, how to improve it and the basis for follow-up.

"I tell young people looking for jobs to check eight points: 1) If you're going to be in this business, be a self-starter. 2) Do a marketing plan on yourself, covering all essential points. Analyze the facts—what's good? Who is out there? 3) Remember, it's not what you want to sell that counts. It's what the customer, interviewer, donee wants to buy. 4) Master anticipation. 5) Develop a concept of perception. In direct mail, you don't see, feel or touch the product. It's a different dimension. 6) Use common sense. 7) Read, read, read. Do your homework. 8) You've got to develop a capability to be good with numbers."

Note: Freeman Gosden, Jr. has answered the following questions I have asked for readers of this book.

Q. *Do you recommend that young people today consider direct marketing as a career?*
A. Very much so—if willing to work harder than most, learn more than most and if reasonably intelligent.

Q. *How high need a student's marks be in school and college to have a chance?*
A. I don't care that much about marks. I judge motivation and self-discipline on the job. Working while going to college means more than anything.

Q. *To really get ahead, is it necessary to be an MBA?*
A. I've got two MBA's in our financial department. But an MBA is not necessary. It's preferred by Proctor & Gamble type companies, but I value more a good IQ, ability to learn, memory reflex, aptitude, common sense and the ability to anticipate.

Q. *Is it important to graduate from a top college? Is a liberal arts degree better or do you advocate business courses?*
A. We find that our people who do best came not from the best liberal arts colleges, but from state colleges. They've taken practical courses . . . advertising, journalism, marketing, research, statistics, public speaking, selling, that sort of thing.

Q. *What chance do women have in direct marketing?*
A. I just wrote an article for Ad Week, "Women Will Take Over the Whole Business".

Q. *What changes over the years have you found most important for your clients?*
A. The changes I've found most important for our clients have been the advent of the credit card and the 800 phone number, and for business-to-business mail order, the increased sophistication of segmentation of business lists. For fund raising, segmentation has been all important, and personalization.

Q. *How effectively do most direct marketers sell by mail or get inquiries for follow-up, compared to potential?*
A. There are two kinds of firms in direct marketing. The first are new to the business and have no knowledge of it. The others are already in the business. Of these, some, perhaps 10%, are very competent and scientific in their use of available tools. The rest are not. Because we have over 100 clients, we know more of what is going on than any one company can.

Q. *How effective do you find the use of focus group research for direct marketers?*
A. I've been doing focus groups for twenty years. Many times, they're wrongly used as a form of research to find how viable the product or service is. That is wrong. They can't tell you

that. I use them to stimulate ideas for copy. I've done this fifteen to twenty times in the last few years. I'd rather do a dry test or a small test to see if the prospect really pays for the product or service.

Q. *If a test fails for a client, what do you then do?*

A. We try to limit failures to test efforts with minimum exposure. We learn more from failures than successes. We spend more time analyzing failures than successes. We take immediate action. Direct mail is expensive and tests give us the numbers to be able to use it to maximum efficiency.

Q. *In your career, who have helped you the most?*

A. Ed Mayer, Jr., by far. I was very close to him for the last several years of his life. He taught me more than anyone. He was the best teacher of direct marketing the DMMA ever had.

Rose Harper helped me a great deal. Chris Stagg is a great help; we use him a lot, as he is both a great writer and thinker.

Q. *What publications have you read and recommend to new direct marketers?*

A. I read and recommend Friday Report, Direct Marketing, The DMMA Fact Book, Bob Stone's book, Jim Kob's book, Dick Hodgson's book and Jaffe's book, which is good for small enterprises.

Note: Smith, Hemmings, Gosden, Inc. is the largest direct mail advertising agency in the West. It is located at 3360 Flair Drive, El Monte, CA 91731; (213) 571-6600. If you send $2.00 to Freeman Gosden, Jr. at the agency, he will send you a packet of reprints of his Adweek column. I strongly recommend that you do so—if you're in a direct marketing business.

Chapter 14
Upward Toward The Stars —By Mail Order

*An unusual business started by a
man who loved stars and wildlife.*

Questar Corporation manufactures the Questar® Telescope, a scientific instrument made and priced for the general public . . . and sold by mail order. Questar Corporation was started by Lawrence Braymer, an artist and illustrator for big national advertisers. Co-founder was his wife, Marguerite Dodd Braymer.

His hobbies were photography and fine instruments, particularly telescopes. He was an amateur astronomer. This led him to invent a small, portable telescope he could look through and photograph through. He created a scientific instrument that, while expensive, was soon recognized as the finest small telescope in the world and, because of its versatility, a worthwhile investment for a serious hobbyist and for use in education.

Marguerite Braymer was and is equally creative. She started as a very young woman in the copy department of N.W. Ayer Advertising Agency, in Philadelphia. N.W. Ayer was the first great national agency and has graduated a procession of creative talent ever since, including the founder of a number of great New York agencies. Marguerite later became editor of one of the departments of Women's Day. She was very skilled in creating do-it-yourself projects . . . decorating, design and new creative editorial ideas of every kind.

Marguerite and Lawrence proved a superb team when they together started Questar Corporation in the early 1950's in a little manufacturing shop in New Hope, Pennsylvania; just themselves and one or two helpers for the assembly work. Together Lawrence and Marguerite ran the whole operation although neither had run a business before.

Questar's first ad was a one-third page in Sky & Telescope asking for inquiries and following up with a simple black and white brochure. It succeeded in stirring up a great deal of interest. For over 25 years Questar has advertised in every issue of Sky & Telescope with a full page and in Scientific American with a two-thirds page ad. "These are still our best showcases."

Along the way, Questar has added other showcases and now uses twenty publications ranging from Sky & Telescope and six or more other consumer magazines to industrial publications in the electro-optical and surveillance fields. Ad sizes range from full-page (inside cover) in Sky & Telescope to one-sixth page in more general publications.

For almost twenty years the Braymers worked together building their business. Marguerite Braymer recalls that owning their own business offered them flexibility in working hours . . . "The opportunity for longer working hours." But from the first their little shop was quite separate from their home, and they always maintained that division.

One requirement the Braymers greatly enjoyed, the necessity for business trips—which came with business growth. It was a nice life. Lawrence Braymer was an accomplished painter and Marguerite a creative writer. Together they had created a prestigious business. And then, in 1965, Lawrence Braymer died.

It was a sad and difficult adjustment to continue alone an activity which had always been conducted together. Lawrence had been president. Now Marguerite took over and ran the business for eleven years, as president and advertising agency. In 1976, Douglas Knight became president and Marguerite chairman, still sharing in major decisions and continuing to do all the advertising, including catalogs and booklets. Meanwhile, her son, Peter Dodd, had grown up and joined the firm.

For Marguerite Braymer, Questar is more than a business. For her there are other pluses. One of them has always been to meet customers who travel to their offices in New Hope and to get letters from customers all over the world who write as friends.

Questar has discreetly built a success in more ways than money. A visit to Questar—tucked away in New Hope, Pennsylvania—gives a new view of business accomplishment. A very old barn has been tastefully reworked into interesting space to house originally an office and a shop section for assembly workers. As operations have grown, a second assembly building has been blended into the landscape with equal care. Recently, a small observatory dome has been added, which displays larger models of the Questar telescope, developed over the years.

Quality mail order advertising of a quality specialized product, a creative dedication rather than only the effort to maximize profit, has made friends of and won the respect of customers . . . and growth and profit have followed. There's a combination of integrity and showmanship. Advertising is two-step. A Questar ad suggests: "With a Questar, you can be a wildlife observer from your patio armchair." To prove it, Questar Corporation sends a booklet with photographs in color by Questar owners.

Questar depends solely on inquiry ads. Readers write in for a booklet which was priced at one dollar for many years but is now two dollars. The first request is answered by a comprehensive packet of material with price list and photos. Inquiries are studied carefully and judged for the weakness or strength of interest. The majority of the list gets a second follow-up with, perhaps, more elaborate follow-up for more serious inquiries. A third follow-up is often by telephone.

Inquiries are generated almost entirely by ads and, in turn, generate the bulk of sales. Inquiries are kept for as long as two to three years. A consumer luxury buying decision is often planned well ahead of the actual purchase date, when the money becomes available. A Questar telescope ranges in price from $1,200 for the Questar 3½ to a shade under $6,600 for the Questar 7, fully mounted. In addition, there are special models of many kinds designed and built for government and industry and priced accordingly.

The Questar is offered for cash, on credit or on time payments but not via credit cards. "Most optical products have a 50% margin and can afford credit cards, but we can't. The cost is too high. With our tight margin, we can't afford it."

Marguerite Braymer writes the advertising, selects the photographs for it, is the creative force behind the advertising and supervises it entirely herself. Her advertising and editorial training has provided the springboard for promotional ideas to build company growth.

Her mail order ads pinpoint the child's market for Questar with the teaser, "What other tool could you buy a child that not only would enchant and amuse, but continue to serve for a lifetime?" The copy suggests a purchase for a child could mean a future scientist. And letters from customers say it has done just that. Questar uses its "private advertising agency" not to save money with a house agency but because advertising is Marguerite's profession. Nobody can do it for her product like she can. And the house agency gives a tight control she would lose if handled any other way.

There is now a line of Questars with variations in capabilities, prices and appeals. Questar telescopes are in demand for first beginners, advanced hobbyists and professional scientists, astronomers and photographers and for surveillance and industrial applications. Each area has sales expansion potential.

Major editorial stories about Questar, although never sought, have from time to time run. Questar has been featured on TV, on good shows including The Today Show. But from all types of such mass media there has come no rush of inquiries and from inquiries received, only occasional sales. Questar's audience is found in more highly specialized media.

Questar Corporation keeps careful records, eliminates losers and constantly explores new magazines. But some decisions have been made without testing. Three decades of keyed results have caused Questar to make certain general judgments about media and to act accordingly.

"Modern Photography magazine seems to pull better than Industrial Photography magazine but this may be an unfair judgment. We're not currently in Industrial Photography. The bulk of our media is definitely profitable. We avoid 'short term' publications which get quickly thrown away. We prefer publications that are kept around rather than daily's or weekly's. We have never advertised in the New Yorker magazine. We don't use a billing enclosure . . . nor even a product enclosure . . . we don't use direct mail to outside lists." Not all experts (and probably not Marguerite or Douglas) will consider this the final word.

What intrigues Questar Corporation currently is the inter-esting results they're obtaining from smaller space. "It seems to do very well." The immediate plan is to add more one-sixth page and smaller ads to the present Questar schedule of larger ads, both alternating in existing publications, and to test new publications. If small space is now working, even tinier space may work in more general publications.

Mail order has led to retail distribution. It's now harder to trace just which retail outlet business originally came from mail order ads. "The demarcation line is still too shadowy and too new to define what percent of the dollar volume is attributable to the mail order initiated retail distribution versus that created by straight mail order ads."

For years, many potential purchasers have been getting into their cars and driving to New Hope so they could actually see the telescopes before making their decisions. They had usually read the ads and received catalogs first. Gas shortages stopped a good bit of that. For some time, Questar Corporation has been studying and changing its market strategy to meet the needs of a new economy.

The new plan is to continue mail order advertising at the same rate, keep an eye out for new publications but also to develop further retail distribution already gained from previous mail order advertising. Questar will use reps on a countrywide basis and believes that sales through retailers will grow considerably.

Marguerite Braymer may be one of the few women of her age in the country still so active in such a demanding position. Douglas Knight describes her: "She is highly capable but extremely reserved about her own skills and accomplishments. She has always avoided the limelight." She has no plans to stop work. Resigning from Questar might be like resigning as a member of a favorite club. But it could be a nice place to retire from gradually, someday . . . maybe.

Marguerite Braymer can retire as she chooses partly because she planned a transition, partly because of the success, soundness and simplicity of this unique mail order business. Meanwhile, Marguerite, as chairman of the board, is a very busy lady.

Note: If you love stars or wildlife or both, Questar Corporation is located at RD #1, New Hope, PA 18938; phone (215) 862-2000.

Mail Order Sampler
Seminar IV

On entering an apartment the first thing that strikes the eye is the Mantel, especially if a fire is burning on the hearth. If first impressions are lasting, how important is it that Mantels should be handsome and harmonious.

We supply Wood Mantels for new or old houses, with all the accessions of baskets, grates, tiles, frames, etc. We send printed directions, so that Mantels can be set by an ordinary mechanic. We quote prices which include cost of delivery at nearest railroad station. Sketch Book of Mantels sent free on request.

Chapter 1
The Mail Order
Continuity Man

*His extraordinary success in
selling books and records.*

The continuity program has made billions of dollars of mail order sales of books, records and tapes.

The first to launch a continuity program in the U.S. for hard cover books was John Stevenson. He has been extraordinarily successful in conceiving, launching and building one continuity book program after another . . . and later in liquidating them one after another—for attractive capital gain.

John Stevenson's success as an entrepreneur-owner is important to study—for any present or potential direct marketer. He has achieved many mail order firsts. He sold books a new way on three continents, before world mail order existed. He was the first publisher in the U.S. to use a contest to sell books in huge volume.

He launched and built a 650,000 member record continuity program. He was first to sell language records in really big volume by mail order, and then to use his mail order ads as co-op ads—to create a big store distribution business as well, for "Living Language Courses". He was the first in mail order to carry third party sponsorship to its full projection potential.

A continuity program is a way to buy a set of books, records or tapes—one at a time—with the right to cancel at any time. When cancelling, the buyer keeps books previously received but has no obligation to complete the set. The commitment is open-ended. The publisher can keep adding titles to the set.

How did John develop the continuity program for books? John explains it this way: "The credit for creating the concept of the continuity program can be shared by many. When publishers first brought out sets of books in England, the idea of 'parts in work' developed. The publisher could print a few chapters in magazine format and sell it on newsstands—and then print and sell groups of successive chapters the same way. It was a form of pay-as-you-go publishing. The 'parts in work' sales helped finance the publishing of the set. The works of Charles Dickens and many authors were sold this way."

In the U.S., newsstands were not interested and there were not enough book stores. The closest thing to the English method was The National Educational Alliance series of educational course booklets published by Wm. H. Wise & Company under John Crawley. "I decided to sell, in this way, series of clothbound, high-quality books."

John Stevenson's entire previous career had prepared him to see and take advantage of the opportunity. His father was editor of the London Daily Herald. (The John Stevenson of Wunderman, Ricotta & Kline, formerly with American Express, is American and not related.)

"My first job was with the Odhams Press which owned the Daily Herald. My boss was a man called Harold Grigsby who knew more about mail order and newspaper promotion than any man in England. It was 1933. Circulation promotion was at a low point. Grigsby had a lot of free time to teach me how to write mail order advertising and in greater detail than he ever could have otherwise.

"At the time the newspaper barons had made a truce in a fierce circulation war where newspapers gave away china, sheets, anything as premiums to secure subscribers. The newspaper circulation people were getting itchy from the truce and seeking a way around the truce agreement. Then someone, I'm not sure who, got the big idea . . . to make one promotional offer after another selling books at a few pennies over cost. Only if you would read the paper each day and clipped a daily coupon could you qualify for the bargain. The object was to increase circulation for the Daily Herald.

"A new phase in the circulation war was about to start, and Harold Grigsby and I became part of it. I was 19.

"By this time, I had learned to write copy—and write it well. Grigsby would give me an assignment in the morning to write copy for a mail order book or set. I'd write my ad or mailing piece. The afternoon would be a critique. It was private tutoring by a master. The ads were house ads in the papers. The mailings were to house lists, owned by Odhams, of mail order customers. When we first ran ads offering books pennies above cost, we had a runaway success. We did it again and again. The ads sold tons of books and circulation soared.

"This was in 1934. It was exciting but I was young. I got another idea . . . to travel all over the world, writing about my travels and sell my writing to newspapers in cities I visited. Thereby, I'd pay for my trip. My savings got me to Ceylon (now Sri Lanka). The paper in Columbo, Ceylon, published a column by me—'As it Strikes a Stranger'—but this did not keep me busy enough so I said: 'Look, boys, I can show you how to sell a lot of books and get a lot more circulation, the way we do it in London.'

"They liked that and we made a deal. I stayed long enough to find a stock of cook books, write an ad and for the paper to run it. It was a smash hit and the paper paid me enough to go on to Australia. From there on, it was around the world by mail order.

"In Melbourne, Australia, I went to the Melbourne Herald, owned by Sir Keith Murdoch (father of Rupert Murdoch). For them, I set up book promotions just as we had done for the London Daily Herald—and with just as great success. Sir Keith then secured a similar job for me with Frank Packer in Sydney. I stayed until I made enough money to go on to the United States. Then I went visiting and researching ideas from newspaper to newspaper from the West Coast to the East Coast and ended up talking to the New York Post.

"The Post circulation manager was Jacob Omansky and the promotion director was Paul Sarazen. Mac Gache was promotion manager. He was the most brilliant mail-order man I met in America, until I later met Milo Sutliff at Doubleday. I told my story and was hired to set up a plan to promote along the lines of the London Herald. The first offer I set up for them was for the Complete Works of Charles Dickens—four volumes a month for 93¢. It was a hit. I got paid and left for home.

"Soon, Frank Packer asked me to come back to Australia where I became promotion manager for his new morning newspaper—The Daily Telegraph in Sydney. I stayed through 1936. Then the New York Post asked me to come back and help them. Back at the Post I hired as a copywriter Fred Breismeister, who later worked for Wise and then again for me.

"The Post had had some rough going and was not in good financial shape. It was paying me partly in cash and partly in stock. I soon had a string of offers running and, according to the terms of the contract, was getting bonus money in proportion. But I was getting it in stock. Then Dorothy Backer (born Dorothy Schiff and later Dorothy Thackrey) bought the paper.

"Selling what little Post stock I had to Dorothy Backer, I

went into business for myself. This was October 1938. I did what I had successfully done—but for any newspaper anywhere and using books and records, I sold directly to newspapers and would run the ads under their name as a joint venture with the paper taking the promotion risk. Or I would buy the ad but still run under their name and I would take the risk. We'd try for a special rate because we were helping the paper increase circulation. Essentially, the entire hope of profit was to get subscribers to take a deluxe edition which cost a few cents more to produce and for which we charged 39¢ to 50¢ more per book. Enough did so for us to do very well.

"Gradually, while this happened, I met a lot of people in mail order. One was Milo Sutliff of Doubleday. We came to an understanding. I would come to Doubleday. I'd contribute everything I knew to sell books for them. I'd also learn the book club business and Doubleday's operation. I would continue being in business for myself. He cleared this with Nelson Doubleday and, in 1942, I became general manager of the Book Club Division and at the same time, with the knowledge and agreement of Milo and Nelson, I moonlighted in my own direct mail business, Book Presentations.

"Then I joined the service, went overseas and came back to be entirely on my own. While I was at Doubleday, Book Presentations made a lot of money. I sold single volume mail order books which, at that time, Doubleday had no interest in. It preferred to use its paper quota for its book clubs which they considered to be a more profitable use.

"Book Presentations continued to buy ads from newspapers and sell books either under the newspaper's name or as Book Presentations. Whenever I could get a back cover or page three in a national supplement, we sold 'The Complete Book of Sewing', 'The Complete Book of Crochet' and 'The Complete Book of Decoration' (my wife, Isabelle, edited both the Sewing and Decorating books). It became almost common-place to sell through The American Weekly $100,000 worth of Sewing or Crochet or Decorating books on any given Sunday.

"I was making a lot more than my former boss, Milo Sutliff. But my respect for his mail order talent was enormous and grew greater as long as I knew him. He and Nelson Doubleday each had great talent in mail order and in different and complementary ways. Nelson had a talent for determining what to sell and getting people to drive ahead to implement his ideas. He was a strong personality whose ideas people did not often contradict. Because I had my business on the side, I felt secure enough to say what I thought and often got into tremendous arguments.

"Working for Doubleday was something I greatly liked. I wished to find some way to do so and be my own man, too. One casual idea I had was to start an advertising agency and work for Doubleday as my first account, handling either The Literary Guild or The Dollar Book Club. Both were Walter Thwing accounts. It might have worked out but then Max Sackheim decided to return East and get back into the agency business. He approached Nelson Doubleday whom he had known back in the Sackheim and Scherman days and at Ruthrauff and Ryan when each agency had worked for Nelson. And out of loyalty, Nelson gave Max The Literary Guild. When Nelson gave one to Max I knew he'd never take the other from Walter.

"But I greatly liked Max and his agency and Lester Wunderman, his right hand man. Later, Wunderman, Ricotta & Kline handled the account of some of my own mail order efforts. Each Wednesday, for years, Lester and I would meet all day to plan campaigns for our record and art clubs. Years after that,

Lester became my neighbor in France, where we both own homes. I see him often.

"So it was Max who really was responsible for my going into the book business on the bigger scale I did after World War II. Instead of handling the advertising for the Dollar Book Club, I competed with it. I started the Fiction Book Club and, instead of a dollar, charged $1.39 a book. My advertising emphasized the books more than the price saving. It was closer to the type of advertising the Doubleday Bargain Book Club (the post inflation name of the Dollar Book club) switched to in more recent years.

"The Fiction Book Club did reasonably well. But when I used puzzle contests to promote it, the club took off. Essentially, I did what we had first done for the New York Post. Back in 1938, I was involved with the same puzzle contest method with huge success for Old Gold cigarettes. Now I did the same for myself.

"The grand prize I offered was $50,000, very big in those days. I had many other prizes. There were six levels of prizes. One subscription brought you to the second level . . . a third subscription to the third level. A paid-in-advance subscription counted as two subscriptions so that three paid-in-advance subscriptions qualified a contestant on all 6 levels. In the first seven weeks of the contest, we took in $1,300,000 in cash orders."

On a smaller scale John kept selling single volume books. Now with the Fiction Book Club he had a much bigger business. "But I wanted to create a longer term business than one based on pulling rabbits out of a hat, such as contests. I wanted something as ongoing as book clubs but not one as volatile as a contest based club. In 1948, Milo Sutliff joined me and we formed a new corporation, The Greystone Corporation, in which we were equal partners."

Greystone published a home medical set of books, a home law book and took over the Book Presentations Sewing Book and Decorating Book. But its new classical record club, "Music Treasures of the World", hit the jackpot. This became the biggest of its kind and went to 650,000 members. Subscribers received symphony records of the world's greatest composers. Then Greystone launched an art portfolio club, "Art Treasures of the World".

Greystone took over a children's record business and created the Children's Record Guild, a record club of children's records. Its success resulted in an expansion of sales via record stores. Greystone also ran the Catholic Digest Book Club—as partner with the magazine—fulfilling all orders. Greystone's organization began to build. Henry Goldsmith became office manager and later credit manager. Des Meehan was a copywriter, researcher and, ultimately, salesman. Dick Landsman came. He took over the job from Meehan of selling other organizations, whether media or publisher, to run Greystone offers under their own names and to work with Greystone in a number of ways. In 1954, John hired Fred Breismeister as a copywriter. They, with Milo and John, largely were the Greystone team.

The New York Post had proven, that tremendous numbers of starters could be secured for sets. But all these newspaper circulation-building, book-selling campaigns had a common denominator. Lots of books were sold but far less completed sets. People would start but might stop at any point. One of the perils for any continuity program publisher would be knowing how many of volume 14 to print vs. 8, 3 or 1.

John had sold sets for the New York Post. He had with Milo Sutliff helped upgrade book club advertising for Doubleday. He and Milo had created a stunning quality presentation for both "Music Treasures" and "Art Treasures". He felt that quality presentation and third person sponsorship could help any Greystone continuity program secure higher quality subscribers with less drop-off.

"The first Greystone Continuity Program, and I believe the first for any book publisher for clothbound books, was The Illustrated Encyclopedia of Gardening. There were originally 14 volumes. Ultimately, we sold over two million sets. Of course, from first starters there were sharp drop offs to completers. But it was very big and profitable."

John has been a master of complex mail order that few people in mail order understood as well as he did. Milo was the great brain of book club publishing who understood the mail order math of book clubs better than anyone else. Fred was the copywriter who had turned out hit after hit. Fred created for Greystone tightly packed, soundly built mailing pieces. Milo and John added their touch. Later, when Paul Michael became chief copywriter, he created the most valuable and highly creative direct mail order "plus" ever written. Under the name of Paul M. Greystone, he created the Publisher's letter, or "lift" letter, now used by almost everybody.

John Stevenson was the first direct marketer to use third person sponsorship on a really big scale. He had seen it used with great effect at Doubleday. Any time the Literary Guild mailed an outside syndicated circular with a letter on its own letterhead and a strong recommendation to members, sales were as much as twice or more those for the same offer mailed cold.

John was more systematic and carried out a more thorough campaign to do this than had ever been done before. He did so for the Garden Encyclopdia with Flower Grower Magazine and many other magazines, with book clubs and other publishers of sets. Often the majority of mailings sent out by John in a year were under the third party sponsorship of someone else.

The Illustrated Encyclopedia of Animal Life followed right after "Gardening". In 1963, John Stevenson bought the rights from John Crawley, at Wise, of the Popular Photographer and re-edited it into the Encyclopedia of Photography. The longest series was the 44-volume World and Its Peoples. The biggest volume and most profitable series was the Practical Handyman's Encyclopedia. The next was the Illustrated Encyclopedia of Decorating.

During this period, John Stevenson took over and successfully operated the Executive Book Club. Greystone's high culture contribution was its continuity program for Shakespeare Plays in Text and Recording by the Old Vic Players.

A big success was Living Language Courses. Selling courses on languages had been going on for over 30 years before, but in the expensive, bulky, many record sets which the old 78 RPM records required. John saw the opportunity of cutting 20 records down to 4 records. "Through the miracle of long playing records, $29.95 language courses for $9.95." The offer was so successful John quickly expanded from two languages to a wide variety of lanugages. He had a limited, good profit mail order success.

Then John Stevenson made a much bigger store distribution success out of it. The mail order ads became co-op ads, and run under dealers' names pulled better than by mail order, while forcing national distribution. Long after the mail order ads stopped pulling, the store distribution business prospered and does to this day.

All this required decisions—each a carefully calculated gamble involving caution and boldness. To get desired properties often took big guarantees of royalties, yet required fighting for each penny to keep down royalties per book. It once took a

36850   36851

36850 Dr. Warner's Coraline Corset, made of French cloth, 96 coraline stays, which are superior to bone or whalebone. Side steels *removable*, double front steels, a fine shaped bust; white, drab or, black; sizes, 18 to 30.
Per dozen. ....$ 9.00
Extra sizes, 31 to 36. Per dozen 12.00
36851 Dr. Warner's Health Corset, boned with coraline flexible coraline, bust; sizes, 18 to 30.
Per dozen, white or drab.......................$12.00
Extra sizes, 31 to 36. Each.................... 1.50
Black, sizes 18 to 30, Per dozen.....:..........16.50

$250,000 guarantee (by specific date) and $150,000 advance of royalties to reduce the royalty per book by 2½ cents.

Large advances could secure (and save on) a publishing property. But each could only return a profit if enough books were sold. A starter could cancel at any time. The more starters secured, the greater the dollar gamble. Yet without getting enough starters, enough books could not be sold. To reach desired minimums of starters huge additional gambles (often with marginal potential) had to be taken. Each commitment to go ahead with a set required a lavish use of Greystone funds.

For those subscribers who preferred to buy the entire set in one shipment, a huge build-up of inventory was required seven months ahead of use. In some cases, deferred payments were offered to customers who were committed for an entire set. This could mean gross receivables of several million dollars on one set, or far more, requiring borrowing.

Advance editorial costs came first. The least (immediately) expensive way to secure editorial was to find an existing set and pay royalties. The biggest outlay was to create a set from scratch. In between, there were opportunities to take over a set which required re-editing. Sometimes it ended up by being almost a new set. Sometimes the original publishers made the changes and sometimes Greystone did. When extensive changes were made, until the entire set was finally rewritten, there was always a question as to whether the final version would be acceptable.

Split operations and joint ventures were tempting. But each required careful examination. Tie-up of capital for one such co-venture could be enormous and prevent proceeding with the next wholly-owned venture . . . which the next successful test might make possible to project. One limited and specialized book club co-venture might take well over a million in capital.

Each had to be weighed separately. Another shortcoming could come later—in selling such a property. A wholly-owned property could be sold or liquidated—if profit justified—at will. A co-venture took each partner's agreement—and after much time and mutual negotiation—sometimes a series of negotiations, dragging on for months.

It was sometimes very difficult to get enough names which could pay out sufficiently. Sometimes publications counted on earlier, when carefully tested, brought in orders at several times the advertising cost acceptable. Often a failure of such a test eliminated the possibility of projecting an entire field of media.

Accrual profit and loss statements kept on a set sometimes showed an enormous loss before turning the corner . . . first reducing loss, then showing an overall break-even and finally a profit.

An accrual statement might show huge editorial preparation costs with only some books completed—and others in various stages in the pipeline—still a long way from completion of a set. To complete the set might then require getting a number of millions of dollars in sales and recapturing cumulative advertising expenditures. On a single set for many long months, editorial and plate cost would continue to a final budget in the stratosphere.

Sometimes first tests on a property were promising but average subscribers did not buy enough books to cover production and advertising costs. Editorial material could be concentrated in less books or stretched out to more books, affecting price per book for subscribers. It was necessary to give value and produce profit. Any change in plan had ramifications. To cut the dimensions of a book per page and leave the same number of pages could expand the number of volumes. But this would require new plates and require renegotiation of royalties per book.

A mailing made under the third-party sponsorship of a trusted name might require a profit sharing arrangement and a guarantee of minimum list rental. Yet, it might turn out that there was not enough profit to divide and that the joint effort was too marginal.

Mail order tests alone for a new property could run into substantial money. A few tests close together could tie up a lot of money, speculatively. Tests and projections in a single month could be very heavy.

Some foreign language sets required translation into English. English sets often required almost as much expense in editorial and plate costs to "Americanize" a British edition. The question was always whether there was a big enough market.

For each expansion there had to be added people, added space and added equipment. Often this meant making decisions as to whether to stay in New York City or move, in total or in part, to the suburbs. To make decisions might involve bringing in an architect, contractor or both. Decisions had to be made on fulfillment as to whether to do it all in-house, to accept or reject specific offers to share computer processing facilities. This meant feasibility studies.

In 1958, John bought out Milo Sutliff, but Milo and John continued much as before. John always considered Milo his partner and valued his advice on any mail order decision. "Milo Sutliff had the greatest mail order math mind of anyone I've ever met in my life. He sold out to me only because he had made as much as he cared to. It was enough for him. From then on, he was in it for fun, for income but not for risk. Yet he did everything in the business just as before."

After Milo Sutliff died, John never had the same interest in more expansion. Instead, he spent more and more time in other activities. He became a trustee of the National Association of Recording Arts and Sciences. He played both golf and tennis and dedicated more time to each—favoring golf. He spent time in Palm Springs and in Palm Beach and several months a year in the south of France.

He has made money in a wide variety of mail order enterprises and has a rare feel for when to get in, when to drive to the maximum, when to retreat in good order and when to get out. He has not attempted to make money in every conceivable way at all times in anything. He freely admits to missing the boat in specific areas.

"Our business has been overwhelmingly by direct mail, and in the U.S. We have had a very successful Canadian mail order business, running all our offers there. We've been successful in a joint venture in England but not as big relatively. We've scarcely touched other countries in Europe and elsewhere. We never really got into telephone marketing. There is much we've scarcely done." But John Stevenson is the master of what he has done.

John Stevenson prepared for retirement with special skill. His method was to build up and then liquidate one program after another for capital gain. At the same time, he successively cut down his operation to a smaller and smaller scale.

"We had experimented with the use of computers and then put in $350,000 worth of computer hardware after spending $300,000 more on software. This worked very well. When the time came to cut down, we sold it all to a fulfillment house for $100,000, payable in services. They then took over and have handled all fulfillment since—as it has diminished year by year.

Gradually, Greystone executives retired, went elsewhere or became consultants. "We cut office space from 40,000 square feet to 20,000 to 15,000 to 5,000—and now we're going down to 1,500. I've cut my own activities for the last six years. I've done almost nothing."

Yet, almost absent mindedly, the old master here and there shows his skill. In 1980, over 130,000 of John's home law books were sold at $12.95 a copy via TV. 'The Living Language' record business and the Children's Record business owned by his children keep prospering, both via store sales.

Future plans? "For the next five years, I plan nothing for business but to have active years in sports and other various non-business activities. Then, I'll come back and go into mail order again."

What is the trait most important for mail order success? "It's the killer instinct and drive. Without it, tests may pay off but really big profit projection won't come."

For beginners, what special training is most important for mail order success? "Math! Get all the math you can. Combine mail order math with the killer instinct and you've got it made.

"What would I do if I were starting over? Mail order. It's bigger than ever. I've picked out today's field of mail order I'd go in. But I'm not telling.

"One thing I would not do would be to go into a continuity program, not under high interest conditions. It's not an easy business to enter or one to bootstrap. It's profitability goes up and down with the interest rate. It demands a lot of capital."

In 1981, John Stevenson made his last shipment for the last of his continuity programs while successfully testing forms of mail he had never done before.

John Stevenson has brought fine music, fine art, fine theater, the far off world and nature everywhere to all of us. He has never been able to stay away from mail order. He has already successfully tested his new offer for his new field. Somehow, I don't think we'll have to wait five years to find out his new offer. We'll send in the coupon for it long before.

Chapter 2
The Advantages Of Using A Direct Marketing Consultant

*The easiest, safest, most profitable step
one consultant suggests first; more advice.*

Reader's Digest markets directly on a monumental scale.

Over the decades, Reader's Digest has made tens of thousands of mail order tests of magazine subscriptions, books and records. It has run thousands of magazine ads and TV and radio commercials, sent out billions of mailing pieces and received well over a billion entrants for its sweepstakes.

For years, Gordon Grossman was Senior Vice President and Corporate Marketing Director of the Reader's Digest. He was responsible for selling Reader's Digest magazine, Reader's Digest Condensed Books, general books, records and tapes, special products and home educational products—both in the U.S. and internationally. He was also Deputy Director of International Operations. He was a member of the Reader's Digest Board of Directors for his last seven years with them.

Gordon Grossman is a direct marketing consultant, one of the very best in the world. One reason is that from his early career he developed equal proficiency in creating advertising, buying media and planning strategy—while most top direct marketers can do really well in just one of the three. Another reason is his invaluable experience. "For 18 years, I worked in a laboratory of direct marketing, Reader's Digest.

"I graduated with an English major from Princeton. Walter Weintz hired me as a copywriter. Almost immediately, I became the only copywriter on the staff. Later, I became a product manager, then circulation director and then marketing director. Happily for me, the Digest tested everything." And so did Gordon.

For Reader's Digest, Gordon pioneered in the use of sweepstakes and computer letters, as well as TV support for direct mail offers. He was the first to use multi-variate analysis of census demographics in mass mailings, sharply cutting total names used while jumping response per thousand mailed.

"That was started in 1964. We worked with the telephone and auto lists of 45 million names and addresses each, which netted down to about 60 million non-duplicating names. We generally selected about 20 million of them for one mailing. The volume of compiled names used by the Digest was much greater in the late 50's and early 60's than it has been since then.

"The selection is now better. The use of sweepstakes has made response much better. The Digest has mailed less to get more. The pulling power of the sweepstakes has been remarkably durable and fairly steady.

"The Digest produces four sweepstakes a year. Each pulls in about 25 million entries, which adds up to about 100 million entries per year. A lot of companies now use sweepstakes, but Reader's Digest has been more advanced I think, than others in the use of them. TV support helped."

"The first use of support advertising by anybody was radio support for Reader's Digest. The first tests were in 1952. The pioneer who got Reader's Digest into it was George Perkins, at Schwab & Beatty. Since then, the Digest has constantly tested it, first for radio and then TV. It isn't easy to test. Not everyone who has tried it has succeeded.

"Support levels have become astronomical, and there really weren't many new ideas for years. Then, in 1977, Columbia Records came up with the transfer technique . . . offering in TV Guide 12 records for $1.95 and a thirteenth free if you indicated that you had seen the offer on TV. That has obviously worked well, for them and for others. I wish I'd thought of it. For seven years now I've been a consultant. I work for book and magazine publishers, catalog companies, record companies, industrial marketers, a couple of cosmetics companies—a wide range of clients, mostly (but not exclusively) large ones. How do I work? Generally, on retainer by the month. Country Journal was an exception. When Bill Blair started Country Journal, I had faith in it and in him. I worked for stock. It did well. That has been my only gamble. I've never gambled on selling my own items.

"My consulting can be on all aspects of direct marketing for a client or in just one area. I work as needed. Right now, I'm developing an entire marketing plan for a small company for next year. Their sales are less than $20 million a year. For large companies, I often work on very specialized projects, such as list selection or new product testing. For an overseas client, I picked a U.S. advertising agency.

"I've worked with Murray Roman quite a bit. I had nothing to do with Murray's famous first campaign for Norman Cousins for World magazine, but I later worked for Saturday Review with Norman on tape, selling renewals on the telephone. There's no doubt, Norman always had a close rapport with his subscribers. Usually, a renewal should be quick and simple; but Norman, with a minute or so on tape, really came across on the telephone, and it worked.

"What's the first thing I do for a client? In just about every case, I check to see if they're getting all the business possible from present customers, whether more can be had, and what to do to get it. It's obvious, but not always done; and it is the easiest, safest and most profitable thing for a client to do.

"Of course, there are other important things, but sometimes not as desirable in relation to risk and time as they first appear. At the Digest, for books and products, we worked mainly on our own list. Of course, it was tremendously successful.

"We tried just about everything else. More than once, we tried records on TV. We found that we could make more money with less risk and commotion selling more things to our own list. With every client, a good portion of opportunity lies in better development of existing resources."

Note: Gordon Grossman has answered for readers of this book the following questions I have asked.

Q. *What percentage of direct marketers use the scientific tools available to the degree available?*

A. Only a few do, I believe. For medium and small direct marketers, some of the tools may be impractical, but as the cost of computing time has come down, more and more people *should* be using them.

Q. *What has zip code area analysis done for direct marketers?*

A. I don't think it has as yet been worth all that much to anybody as a selection tool. The gains, when they exist, tend to be pretty modest. Some of the success stories have been overblown. The nature of the data, so far, has been severely limited. The big zips are too big, and the small ones too numerous. This will change. There will be 9- or 10-digit codes and new census data available by 1983! I can't wait for it.

Q. *How effective is working with census tracts and block groups to better select buyer lists and compiled lists?*

A. Working with census tracts and block groups is practical and effective. That's the way the best general data is available. Compiled lists have long been available by census tracts. Big buyer lists can use them, too, on top of their own data, of course. Mailers can work with Donnelley, Polk or Metromail. They do the demographic work for you; and when it is done right, it works. This is another area where the lower cost of running the computer makes it possible to do things today that we couldn't even seriously imagine a few years ago.

Q. *How do you compare for effectiveness the selection of lists by any demographic method versus the use of buying history?*

A. When you work with buying history, it's different and better, of course. I'm talking about using not just RFM but what products, what combinations, what rate of purchase, what multiples, what magazines subscribed to, and dozens and dozens of features. For response lists, the greatest tool (which is often unused) is *what* they bought last time.

Q. *What do you think of using multi-hit lists of people who have bought from several lists?*

A. It works. Renting only the duplicates was a specialty of Tom Foster, for Foster & Gallagher. The Reader's Digest has also done this. But few others have taken anywhere near full advantage of it. It's another example of something which used to be a big expensive deal, but is now eminently practical.

Q. *How much of a problem is list duplication today—sending mailings out more than once to the same name?*

A. There's still a lot of unnecessary list duplication. Those who use merge-purge have reduced it drastically. You can afford to buy 300 to 400 lists and put them all through merge-purge. The sophisticated new programs do a good job—far from perfect, but very valuable. Medium-sized mailers can save a lot of money if they're not now eliminating duplicates. Large mailers must, and most do, of course.

Q. *How much do you get personally into statistical research in selecting lists?*

A. I'm not a statistician, but I've become enough of a numbers man to have some idea of what I'm looking for. For statistical research in depth, I've relied on outside people. I have a couple of bright ones I use.

Q. *Is sophisticated statistical research for list selection now used substantially by the direct marketing agencies?*

A. I'm not aware of any direct marketing agencies who have such people. The agencies seldom get involved in list selection. They're apt to rely on a broker, who may or may not do much with sophisticated statistics. If you are talking about multivariate analysis, there aren't many places to go.

Q. *When a direct marketing agency calls in a list broker and the list brokerage commission is charged to the client, how is the direct marketing agency normally paid for their services?*

A. There are all sorts of ways for a direct marketing agency to base charges on direct mail. Many direct marketers would be reluctant to pay a 17.65% commission on top of using a list broker. The general method of compensation is fee-based.

Q. *What chance has the small entrepreneur in mail order today?*

A. The odds are tough. You have to accept testing on a tiny scale, learning and bootstrapping. This is hard work and it's best applied in specialized areas. With all the tools available, mail order takes a lot of judgment, careful record keeping and a lot else—and it's still risky. I'd certainly suggest a great deal of caution—but there's money to be made in the unique product or service promoted in a unique way.

Note: One way to be safer is to get Gordon Grossman's advice. Bigger companies form most of his clientele, but by no means all. And his advice is available free in two quite perceptive articles in Direct Marketing Magazine back issues. You can read them in a business library or purchase them from Hoke Communications. Also, you can get from Hoke tapes of Gordon's speeches. Details on how to order them are in the Help Source Section in this book. Gordon W. Grossman, Inc. is located at 606 Douglas Road, Chappaqua, NY 10514; (914) 238-9387.

Chapter 3
Building A Mail Order Fulfillment Business

From four employees in a basement . . .
to 350 at peak . . . in an industrial park.

Orders and money keep coming to 6 Commercial Street in Hicksville, Long Island, but never for anything anyone there makes or sells.

Every year hundreds of millions of pages of ads, and hundreds of millions of mailing pieces, instruct readers to send orders and payments there. Some of America's most prestigious and biggest companies do so. Each order and check is addressed to the giant company but always to 6 Commercial Street where no one from that company is. This is so for Johnson & Johnson, for Hearst Books, for Illustrated World Encyclopedia (a division of Bobley Publishing), for the Scholastic Magazine Children's Book Club, for Funk & Wagnalls.

At 6 Commercial Street people who work for Hy-Aid, Inc. open the mail, bank the money and do a good deal more. Hy-Aid is a fulfillment house for the mail order divisions of big companies who find it more profitable and efficient to use Hy-Aid than to do these functions themselves. To use Hy-Aid they must trust it. They do. Hy-Aid, for instance, is one of only a select few fulfillment houses in the U.S. that had been approved in 1979 by Gulf Oil to fulfill in this manner offers made in their monthly gas bills.

Hy-Aid opened in a basement in December 1969—with four employees. One secretary typed. One girl opened envelopes. Now it has 35,000 square feet in two buildings in Hicksville Industrial Park at 6 Commercial Street—and has over 300 employees at peak season. Today my wife, Fritzi, and I are visiting Hy-Aid and its owner, President Dick Levinson. Dick and his now retired partner, Sam Yang, were formerly at Grolier, Inc., as was Executive Vice President Hank Rossi. First Hank gives us the guided tour. Then Dick will tell us how it all began.

Hank worked at Grolier for 6 years. He became mail room manager. Then he became general manager of input and the central mail room, the payment department, customer service and the credit department.

"Before Grolier, I was with Greystone. Dick Landsman was there. Henry Goldsmith was consulting. I learned credit from him. Henry Goldsmith was looked up to at the New York Direct Mail Credit Association. It's a very important association. There are no vendors. Henry took the young fellows under his wing.

"Hy-Aid is a young business. We are all young. Dick Levinson and myself are forty. Dick Levinson's background is data processing. Ed Hughes works under me running clerical systems here. My background is manual. I'm a people manager. I had 300 people under me at McGraw-Hill. Ed is a specialist and a brain. I'm a generalist. I was customer service manager for the Diner's Club. I was heavy in book clubs, negative or no option. Ed and I complement each other."

Hank came out of business school. He got a master's degree in business and finance. He went to Seton Hall at night to get it. Before that he went to St. John's University. "My logic was the bottom line profit. I was taught that way.

"Hy-Aid fits in between the advertising agency which creates the sales and the shipper which sends out whatever is ordered. Where the advertising agency stops, we start. We work for the mail order client. We don't ship at all. We do no up front mailing. We do no creative work. We get out labels. We do all billing. We collect money and put it in the client's bank account. We do P & L studies for our clients. We do no marketing. We analyze up front. We will help design order cards but only for clarity in processing.

"We handle one shot promotions, book clubs—and continuity programs—also magazine subscriptions for agents. We handle mini-catalogs, up to several hundred item numbers. Typical is a choice of eight books. A full bloom catalog is not suited to us at this time. We don't handle premiums. That was Andy Sirocco who just went by. He's the fulfillment coordinator from SRA, Science Research Associates . . . the educational company of IBM. He's in here all the time for them. A typical account is Children's Choice Book Club (a division of Scholastic Magazines). For them, plus others, we have handled as many as 80,000 to 90,000 incoming orders a month. We work with top accounts. We have to.

"6 Commercial Street, as an address, is a brand name. If anything advertised with that address gets a lot of complaints, it reflects on each other account we handle. That's why, if we see any probability of slow delivery, we may not accept a potential client. It can happen with start-ups. One very fine client ordered calculators from Japan. One out of two didn't function. He opened every package, shipped only good ones and took a huge merchandise loss. But handling things this way slowed him up in shipping. He got complaints. We had to resign his account.

"For each new account, we first assign an account executive. He's not a messenger but a coordinator. The account executives act as our sales representatives and are headed by another Grolier alumnus who has more than 17 years experience in mail order. His name is George McGreol. We have operations and service people. Often clients have a fear of specialists and want the account man to be a generalist acting for them. For each new client we make a set-up memo. We start with a standard customer manual. It details everything we will do from the moment the mail comes in for the client. We ask each new client for all basic details needed for each specific mailing planned. Every step of procedure for each client goes into the book. Often it becomes 50 to 60 pages.

"SRA went into mail order to experiment with the sale of

ENAMELED IRON ONE-PIECE CORNER LAVATORY, REDUCED TO $4.64

$4.64

No. 42K3115 Enameled Iron One-Piece Corner Lavatories, with sanitary nickel plated brass soap dish, waste plug and coupling, rubber stopper, chain stay, nickel plated overflow strainer and wall brackets. Length, on sides, 16½ inches; back, 6 inches high. Size of patent overflow bowl, 10x14 inches. Shipped from our factory in Southeastern Wisconsin. Shipping weight, about 60 pounds.
Enameled inside, bronzed outside.   Price...........$4.64
Enameled inside and outside.   Price...............5.64
NOTICE—The above prices do not include faucets, traps or supply pipes.
No. 42K3165 Same as above, except furnished complete with two brass nickel plated compression basin cocks, 1¼-inch nickel plated trap with waste to floor and vent to wall, two brass nickel plated supply pipes to floor with flanges. Everything complete, as shown in illustration.
Enameled inside, bronzed outside.   Price.........$8.76
Enameled inside and outside.   Price..............9.90
We can furnish these lavatories, with all connections threaded for iron pipe at an extra cost of 75 cents over prices quoted.
If above lavatory is wanted without revent on trap, deduct 15 cents from prices quoted.

'learning' to the home. A declining birthrate and less schools and teachers could limit sales to schools. SRA sells Math Skills Ladder I and II, with flash cards. All orders come here. Each time SRA or any other client makes a mailing it has to give us an estimate of the number of orders expected from it. We have to be prepared, and for every other client.

"Each is different. Some clients are conservative. Some are overly optimistic. We check last year's performance. We can't do that for a new product. However a client operates, we go that way. Many people avoid mailing certain months and before certain weekends and holidays. We schedule our work to suit. For us, collections die during Thanksgiving week. We don't mail bills December 15th to December 23rd. We mail it all the day before Christmas.

"We're located in an excellent area. We have permanent key

people. 75% of our key people come to us. We have three crews. We have part-time people. We start at 7:00 AM and work until 10:00 PM. We have housewives in the morning, school girls in the afternoon and mostly Grumman wives at night. They're good. The most talented are in the morning.

"Housewives can work 10:00 AM until 2:00 PM. We get very high type people. It might be someone who was secretary to a president. They want something nearby to do that's creative. When people come through, they can't believe the quality of personnel we have. We're in the middle of middle America. We have excellent labor.

"The computer room works 24 hours a day. We have four operators for each shift and four supervisors who rotate shifts. We bring in computer people with some experience and train them more here.

"Incoming mail goes through slitting machines. Each can take 4,000 an hour. Then it comes to the mail extracting machines. Fifteen years ago, we were begging manufacturers for them. Now they're getting faster and faster. This one is a Mail Carousel. That's the brand name. It's made by Stevens Industries. It works by suction. The Mail Carousel handles all sorts of sizes, even those with coins.

"This mail opening machine is a Speed Trak. That's its brand name. It handles standard envelopes up to a #12, no coins. We open 80% of the mail by machine. But if the sort is complicated, a mini-catalog order where we have a number of items, we do it manually. Generally, our mail opening is more sophisticated. We have all standard stuff but we keep progressing.

"That girl is filling out a batch instruction sheet for the computer room. The sheet tells them what to do, encloses the batch and has written on it the number of orders in the batch. A batch has 50 to 300 orders depending on the client. It's based on simplicity. For fast information on tests, especially for space ads, we make a flash count. For this we make a special data entry on the computer. We get key counts in 24 hours. We use Entrex. That's the hardware.

"We phone the clients these figures daily. They then get mailed the key entry of the order. The batch control system lets us compare manual with the computer. We check the computer every day. 97% of the accounts in data entry are correct.

"We can do more of a check-up for more money. We use MOD 10, MOD 11 and MOD 12. It's a check digit system, a mistake catcher. For multi-client processing we use different digit numbers for each client. The computer is programmed to reject certain wrong entries. It makes a mathematical calculation of the first eight numbers. I use the system. I can't put a Johnson & Johnson's entry into Hearst. The computer throws it out. If I punch the wrong code, the computer doesn't show anything.

"How did all these methods come about? Mostly from common sense, from trial and error. But most of all, they developed from the suggestions of the auditors each client sent to audit what we were doing. Each wanted a different protection for the client involved. And from all those protection suggestions came a good deal of the fail safe methods we have.

"This is an OBM scanner. It reads orders, letters and payments. Each is a document and is printed in picking numbers, on line correct. We must do this for the auditors. We could run twice as fast but not on screen and would do so if it were our own business.

"This is a scanning sheet. The elements are key-punched on this computer. New sales go on through three sheets. Once on computer, they can go through a hundred times faster. For any computer work we usually switch girls every three or four hours.

It depends on the individual. Some will key-punch all day. Others get fatigued.

"The history of our growth is in our three computers. Each is double the speed of the other. Each is compatible. Each has more and more bells and whistles all the time. Our first computer was a Honeywell 115. We had used Honeywell at Grolier where Dick and Sam Yang, the founders of Hy-Aid, worked. There's the 115. Here's the next one we got, a Honeywell 2040. It's twice as fast as the 115. This one is the Honeywell 3200. It's twice as fast as the 2040. Now we're getting a mini-computer to replace the 115 which will be even faster than the Honeywell 3200.

"We make up a weekly computer schedule. Each job is scheduled for each client. We tell the computer room: 'Run these clients these times.' We estimate these quantities. We must accurately estimate the time required.

"We do updates. Let's say we generate 20,000 shipments and 13,000 bills. We have posting, credits, cancellations, changes of address. We put the names on computer tape. We act as a computer service bureau. We generate Cheshire labels. It's cheaper to copy every three labels. We give the names to the list manager. He puts them on a flow sheet.

"Each day we check the computer with the batch. If anything is missing, we re-run. The computer has all sorts of quality control instructions to throw out incorrect orders. The batch processing system is sequential, the old method of input. We can pinpoint the sales tax, or whatever.

"Every client is different. They may have edit programs, sort programs, label programs, statistical analysis, all sorts of different variations at once. We have five programmers. We get more help from Honeywell if we need it. We employ free lance programmers if we need them."

Hank now takes us to another building where the labels just off the computer are prepared for shipment to clients. "This is bursting, breaking the forms—separating the sheets of continuous forms run through the computer printer. We burst on this machine. There are the control girls. Each signs her code number.

"Over here are labels. They will be affixed to the product. These are going to Ware-Pack, a book shipper. This shipment is a total of 20,400 labels.

"In this room are 50,000 to 60,000 labels and invoices. It took a week from receipt of order to the labels here to be shipped out tonight. If we get an order Monday, we have it out Tuesday of the next week, with all controls. That's if we run one time weekly for clients.

"A cheap envelope can be shoddy and cause spoilage. It's cheaper to pay more for an envelope that doesn't jam in the equipment. We tell each client that. If envelopes jam because they're shoddy, we'll put the client on a labor hour rate. One client got a great buy on a million envelopes. They kept jamming. He then paid to insert by the hour. We could only process a thousand an hour instead of three thousand. The cheap, poor envelopes cost the client substantially more than more expensive, good ones.

"We don't inventory or ship merchandise. But our address is in the client's advertising. Orders come here and so do returns. On free examination orders, returns may be 10% or so of shipments made. These are returns. We strip the labels and put them on computer. We give each customer of each client credit for his or her return.

"We do all billing and collections for clients who sell on credit. Therefore, incoming mail consists of orders for us to process, payments for us to credit, returns for us to credit and complaints and correspondence for us to handle and answer."

We had missed one important operation which had already closed for the day. It was the caging department where payment checks are processed for each client and then deposited daily, each in the correct bank account for each individual client. We had seen everything else.

At this point, Hank Rossi brought me and my wife, Fritzi, to meet Dick Levinson in his office and left us there. Dick does not wear a coat and tie. He's an inside man and plans to keep it that way. He answered every question asked about his company, himself and how he made it.

"My biggest advantage was that I came from a poor background. My father earned very little money. He died when I was 17. My mother then worked to support us. She had to raise three children. I went to work early in life.

"What was my IQ? 148. But I did poorly in school and flunked out of college after one year. I went to Brooklyn Technical High School and got poor grades. I went to Hunter College for pre-engineering in the Bronx. My first job in data processing was at Grolier, Inc., the encyclopedia publisher. I never became important at Grolier. I was there six years and data processing manager before I left. I did learn a lot about computers. And I did begin to get ideas to use them differently for mail order.

"Next to being poor, the big advantage I had was that I had a burning desire to be in my own business. I always wanted to start up on my own. I thought about it. I planned for it. I worked for it. And when the opportunity came, I was ready.

"I did develop an understanding of and ability in using computers when it became very important to the fulfillment business. And I was interested. While I didn't work hard at school and college, I worked very hard at Grolier and much harder since, in my own business.

"I developed another ability. I learned to write—not books or articles, but detailed system specifications. I can write specifications in layman's terminology, something not often accomplished by a technician. This has been a big help, to communicate to the client—and more important, to do the job right and more profitably for the client and for us.

"At Grolier, Sam Yang was my boss. He was much more important than I was. He was a clerical systems expert. He is very brilliant, very honorable and a nice guy. He was very highly regarded by the top people in Grolier and by other direct marketers."

The opportunity to go into business came when Grolier decided to move to Danbury, Connecticut—over a hundred miles away. Some people didn't want to move away from New York. People began to think about alternatives, either getting jobs or starting businesses. Top people were thinking seriously about what to do.

"Grolier had a pretty efficient fulfillment operation. Occasionally, the idea came up of doing fulfillment for others. A lot of big companies were moving into mail order. They preferred to get a fulfillment house, at least at first, instead of going too far in overhead, themselves. I could see an opportunity for a fulfillment house as efficient as the Grolier house operation. There seemed a particular opportunity in Long Island.

"I lived in Douglaston, Long Island. I could see that Long Island had many big printers and very large mailing houses to send out enormous quantities of promotional mail. But to me there seemed a lack of a highly knowledgeable fulfillment house which could open mail, bank, bill, collect and handle customers for clients.

"I had researched the opportunity. I felt Sam and I could be partners. He was very strong in clerical systems. I was good on computers. I was a programmer and worked with programmers, as well as management. He had the strongest of contacts and of friendships. I felt I was practical and ready for tough conditions.

"Sam's family had money but I really didn't think about that. I didn't feel that going into business would be dependent on getting money from any one source or even on any specific set of partners. I saw an opportunity. I was strongly motivated to go after it. Sam was cautious. He thought about it and talked about it with others and decided he wanted to do it.

"I found a company willing to finance us. It was a conglomerate. We would be a subsidiary. Sam and I would have a lot of incentives and even the chance to buy the company later, on an earn out basis. Sam Yang was very conservative. He didn't like getting involved with new people he did not know. Sam said that he would get the money and did, from his family, I believe. It took us three years to pay it back, with interest. I also borrowed money for my share of the business.

"Sam's money started us. I appreciated it. But without that money, somehow I would have gotten it. If you have a burning desire and drive to do it, you can get money. I was confident I wouldn't fail. Anyway, we started, in a basement with four people. We had one secretary and one mail opener and ourselves. Meanwhile, a lot of Grolier executives went to Danbury, but not all. I was much lower down at Grolier than any of them. But Sam was up with them, and friends with them. Afterwards, there was a tendency for the Grolier graduates to help each other, and they relied on each other more than others they did not know.

"The first client we got was Western Publishing, recommended to us by Mike Kelly. The second was Marshall Cavendish, recommended to us by Bob Bull. The third was Mattel, recommended to us by Charles Munoz. All were Grolier graduates. Cavendish was very big right away. It was 70% of our business for two or three years.

"Sam took care of the dollar and cents side of the business. From the first, the people we dealt with trusted us as we did them. We did so much business that even when an occasional new client took advantage and a job wasn't profitable, overall we did fine.

"I costed jobs. Sam made final decisions on prices to customers. He owned the majority and I the minority of the stock, but we had equal voting rights. In practice, I accepted Sam as the senior in operations. We looked at things differently, but either could have run the business in the first few years and made a profit. Business was that good.

"But we were overly dependent on Marshall Cavendish, which then went out of business in America. It was an English company. Ed Bakal (since deceased), from Grolier, ran the U.S. operation. Marshall Cavendish had been very successful in England but in a way not really applicable to the U.S. Whether it was managed in the U.S. not as well, or with less financial acumen, or with more gambling in media, I don't know. Other companies had previously tested Marshall Cavendish products in the U.S. and had failed. Anyway, Marshall Cavendish didn't make money in the states, and we lost over half our volume. Luckily, when we lost Marshall Cavendish, Longine's was our next 70% volume client. This came to us through still another Grolier alumni—Bob Bartner. Another few years of prosperity and Longine's went out of business. We lost 70% of our volume with no one to replace it this time.

"Sam and I were totally different. He came from a cultured background. I was completely uncultured. Sam conducted business very much as his family did in China. He didn't bargain. He always lived up to his word. He was a gentleman in each transaction. He was absolutely open. He would go to a client and say: 'This is our cost. This is our profit. And this is our cost to you.' Although I thoroughly agree with his moral values, my business judgments are almost opposite to his. Naturally, we didn't agree on everything. Often, we were opposed. It wasn't easy for either of us to cooperate at all times.

"The next year or so things didn't work for us. We lost money. There was a possibility we could go out of business. In this business, a client can be a loser to handle if volume isn't a certain minimum. And the sum of a number of profitable clients can be unprofitable if there isn't enough total volume.

"An overly optimistic client can give hopes of far more than the minimum volume necessary and then deliver far less, yet fight any change in charges. Sam and I realized that we had different approaches to operations and that in bad times it became more important to each of us to want what seemed safest done. We felt that the 50-50-voting plan would be less effective than voting control by one or the other.

"If Sam should put more money back into the business, he should have voting control. If I should try to make the business succeed without additional money, I should have voting control. And whoever should have voting control should own the majority of the stock. Gradually, we realized that neither wanted to be a minority owner.

"I owed Sam respect for his senior status at Grolier, for the money he first put in, and for his contacts and friendships. Certainly, I didn't want him to lose face. But my feeling was 'I know how. Why shouldn't I make the business flourish?' I asked him to let me buy him out. That was two years ago. He decided to sell out and thought carefully how to do it. We made the deal a year ago.

"We've never had a harsh word. We would never do anything to hurt each other. I'd never hurt the next guy. In the last year, we had a big turn around. We made more profit than any previous year. We had more clients, and more diversification. Our biggest client was 12% of our total volume. We're optimistic for the future. And that's my story."

Note: For readers of this book Dick Levinson has answered the following questions.

Q. *Did you ever go into mail order, selling your own items?*
A.   Yes, with Sam. We went into items . . . books, merchandise. I learned a lot and paid a lot for the knowledge.

Q. *Who are some of the most creative people in mail order whom you have ever met?*
A.   Ed Bakal gave Grolier the "Beginning Readers Program." He was one. Bob Bartner was another Grolier vice president. He went to Longine's. He was a creative genius. We worked for Longine's, on books, records and the Capital Record Club. Another one is Peter M. Bobley, one of the shrewdest businessmen I have ever met. He is a surviver like myself.

Q. *What plans do you now have for Hy-Aid?*
A.   We plan to expand our computer power. We will diversify in mail order processing. We will use more sophisticated languages. We're going into catalog fulfillment processing. We'll start by the end of 1981 and be in production in 1982. Then we'll go into magazine subscription fulfillment. We'll grow bigger, but gradually.

Q. *What do you do to get business?*
A.   We go to the DMMA conventions. We advertise. We have a brochure. We get exposure and most important, we have an excellent reputation given to us by satisfied clients.

Q. *How much do you personally get into customer contact?*
A.   I go to the initial customer contact meetings. I discuss their business, their promotional plans and goals and I choose the proper clerical and computer system for their promotions. I discuss our operation with clients. I want to be friends with clients but I don't entertain for business. I'm not that sociable. But I'm cordial. I want to be with people because I like them, not because they are clients.

Q. *What do you do in the day-to-day business?*
A.   I get into computer and clerical systems. I discuss marketing plans and financial considerations with clients as well as to suggest credit and collection methodology that will maximize their potential. In addition, I plan, control and implement all Hy-Aid financial decisions and policy.

Q. *How important is new technology, such as the computer, to your business?*
A.   Clerical people still do the work. 20% of all overhead is the computer. But 50% to 60% is labor.

Q. *Why should a client come to you instead of fulfilling in-house?*
A.   A mail order company should be a marketing company. It should not build fixed overhead. It's better to use us.

Q. *What can you advise someone starting out, even if still in school or college?*
A.   Graduate. Get as much education as possible. Read. Talk. Look at the kind of career you like. The education and experience you need will vary for each job.

Q. *What do you look for in an employee?*
A.   Someone I think can quickly pick up what the job is—who has interests, who knows what he or she is talking about. Then I feel comfortable.

Q. *Will the mail order business keep growing?*
A.   The trend is for more and more growth. That's why we're growing.

Note: Hy-Aid and Dick Levinson continue to prosper at 6 Commerical Street, Hicksville, NY 11801, telephone number (516) 433-3800 . . . and so do their clients.

Chapter 4
How To Sell Mail Order Ads

He has sold more than anyone.

You quickly find that, in one way or another, it's cheaper to buy at least some media through him. But that's just the beginning. As soon as he meets you, suggestions and introductions start.

Through Dave Geller's offices stream customers, partners and associates. The most casual conversation becomes a conference. A lunch date with Dave ends up with a round table. In the office, the phone interrupts constantly. For years, he kept a ping pong table and challenged anyone to play at any time.

An attempt to buy an ad in Minneapolis can end up in a partnership in Canada, the use of cable TV, inserts in American Express bills, or a store distribution venture. Messages stream in usually on his biggest, latest deal such as putting up half the money to buy Helena Rubinstein from Colgate or selling to his partner in Collector's Guild his interest.

He has gambled more on other people's mail order business than anyone I know. He gambles in ads in his media sometimes all, sometimes part, of advertising cost. He gambles to help media new to mail order establish a track record and then a rate. He gambles to help those new to mail order get their feet wet.

He gambles for biggest, richest companies to induce them to try media they're dubious about. He gambles for the shaky, the tiny, the newest entrepreneurs. He gambles in mail order in the U.S. and all over the world.

He has financed more people to start new businesses connected with mail order than anyone I know, over a hundred businesses. Often he starts out as a big share owner and ends up with a small share or with no share at all, or he is bought out by his partner. He's flexible and quite content in any variation, modification or change arrived at if his objective is served.

That is to sell more mail order advertising. He views all else as a means to this end, as is his extension of credit. He bills and collects for advertising he sells. He grants credit sufficiently generously that, in almost any major bankruptcy of a mail order firm, he's one of the five biggest losers, losing over $250,000 on one transaction to over $500,000 on another.

It all sounds like a recipe for disaster. Yet, Dave Geller is canny, and his losses are insignificant compared to his gains. Sales of all activities he controls are close to one hundred million dollars a year.

He represents for mail order the Sunday supplements of most of the biggest circulation newspapers in the United States and a good share of biggest circulation magazines. He represents Paris Match and is partners with them in mail order in France. He's done this all over the world, going into mail order with a top publishing firm. His most successful effort is currently in Spain.

In Australia, he started a business as partner with Golden Books and Consolidated Press, Australia's biggest publisher, and has since sold out his interest. "We still get royalties."

I've known Dave for over thirty years. His mind works fast. He has an IQ of over 150. And it's worked faster and faster over the years. To Dave, from morning to night, it's a matter of new

partnerships, new joint ventures, new associations, all mixed together with those he's had over the decades.

Dave was raised in Brooklyn. He went to NYU. Then, he went to NYU Law School at night while playing in tennis tournaments all over (he was New York State Inter-collegiate College tennis champion) and selling advertising. Dave is a lawyer but his first job, in 1936, was with Secrets magazine and then with True Confessions. He went on to work for Ziff-Davis.

In World War II, he went into Counter-Intellgence as a private and came out as a captain. He returned to Ziff-Davis and stayed until 1948. He represented Ebony magazine when it first started, and still does. He also represented black newspapers and then comic magazines.

Somewhere along the line, he began to call on Huber Hoge & Sons and dealt with my brother, John, with Malcolm Smith, and with me. And early in the game he started to gamble. "Caesar Torrelli owned Foster-Trent. I wanted him to advertise in Fox Comics. He wouldn't. I gambled on a PI, and he paid me for each order. It was a smash hit. After four or five months, Caesar got tired of my profits and bought his own advertising."

Dave had found his formula. Gamble to get them started, encourage them to take over, and be happy to then earn a sales rep commission on an account that did not run before.

Dave got into representing Sunday supplement magazines by finding an unsuccessful one and gambling for those mail order advertisers who would be willing to try it. Sometimes, the publisher didn't know what to charge as a mail order rate. Dave's solution was simple—set a tentative rate agreeable to the publisher and then gamble, himself, for a mail order advertiser. By counting orders and comparing with other media, Dave could tell what mail order advertisers could afford. Then, the publishers could set such a rate or, if too low, forget mail order.

That was the second part of Dave's formula. Gamble to help the publisher. The publisher need never break the rate or gamble. Dave was the man between. Dave, at the least, would always gamble his rep commission. For a direct account, he'd place the ad through his own advertising agency and gamble both commissions. Or he might make up losses to the advertiser in ways that had nothing to do with the publisher.

Miscellaneous Parlor Games, Small.

Tiddledy Winks may be played by any number of people in any small table with a thick cloth on.

Each player is provided with four to six counters of the same color, and one larger one, the use of the larger one being to press to the edge of the smaller one and in that way cause it to jump into the cup, which is in the center of the table. The player who first gets all his counters into the cup wins the game.

25410 Popular edition, for four players		$0.20
Postage		.05
25411 Popular edition, for six players		.40
Postage		.08

Sometimes, Dave took payment in the most unorthodox of ways. He was particularly flexible when anyone went broke. While others quibbled, long before bankruptcy, Dave would take a swap payment. One way was to take the list the mail order firm owned in payment for a bill.

This led to the ownership of lists which Dave then rented to others, which led to a list brokerage business, Brookside, which Dave still owns and which is flourishing.

Dave might take merchandise, plates, art work, rights, products, other advertising, or whatever. Again and again, he has set up someone in business after a bankruptcy. Almost inevitably, if anyone fails using Dave and starts up, he bumps into Dave in the next business and, often, is helped again. The result is many losses totally down the drain come back in some new form. There's usually the desire to make it up by giving him a bigger share in the next joint venture. He rarely pushes, but simply helps people to start up and succeed; and if they fail, to try again. A better share in a new partnership may offset a loss in the last.

For many years, Dave's nephew, Mike Shapiro, has been with Dave and now runs more and more of the business. Dave taught Mike, and Mike learned well.

Dave moves with the times. He goes where the money profits in mail order are. For a while, he made more overseas than here. For a while, his TV operation was much bigger, relatively, than now, although he's never been a TV rep. For years, he was overwhelmingly in mass low ticket items. Now, he's switched gears into up-scale, not just here but all over. "In Spain, with credit card inserts, we're selling a $400 attache case, a $2,000 video recorder."

Right now, Dave is going big into credit and billing inserts and sales with third party endorsement. "Mostly items $100 to $400. We're doing more and more with American Express and with Citibank. Billing inserts are a new medium and are going to get bigger and bigger. Package stuffers are tougher. Too many never get inserted."

Dave has gotten out of C.O.D. in TV phone orders. "The drop in orders was abysmal, more than 50%. We got many less calls when we changed to 'send check' or 'give credit card number.' But with 30% to 35% refusals on TV C.O.D. orders, we had to get out. If the offer is strong, it will survive."

But Dave's big hope is cable. "The demographics are better. The average order can be much higher. Credit cards will pull." Dave is going into it more. He's representing people who own segments of some cable network programs and expects to represent more.

In Dave's head at all times are which mail order firms most likely to go under next, (even which kinds of mail order firms) the companies for sale, those that are slowing up . . . the danger signs . . . and not just in the U.S., but in England or wherever. He acts accordingly.

At all times, he views the economy realistically—when recession is coming, the threat of a real depression, when the next turn may come—and he's thinking what to do about it. Right now, he's optimistic for those starting in mail order, "if they try upscale items and the right media for it and in the right situation and items for the time."

For fifteen years, Dave has found mail order success overseas. For ten years, he's been big in supplements. He took over Argosy magazine when it went bankrupt, operated it and then sold it. He did the same for Camera 35. He still has an interest in Master Detective. His paths cross those of many. "We set up a separate corporation with Wunderman. I took the risks. We ran ads on a percentage for WR&K clients and others, too."

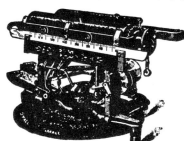

Dave helped some Hoge alumni start on their own, including Phil Steinberg, who later ran Disney Records' mail order operations, and Norm Roseman. Norm later became co-founder of Soap Opera Digest. He's helped many others. "I put up all the money for Walter Karl to start up his own list company. I put up the money for Dave Palgon to start Target Lists. I did the same for Victor Liss to start New Movers. I helped Al Nissim start Shore Direct Mail and then International Computer Services. For a while, we were in the printing broker business with Stern and Majestic. I was a partner in Merrin Jewelry mail order in American Express, and now do it PI."

Aside from Dave and Mike, the business is mainly run by women. Each of a number of Dave's girls run what is a separate business. Vivian Shapiro (no relation to Mike) is responsible for supplements. Tina Velchigo runs Blaine House and spends two million dollars a year of Dave's money on TV. Bonnie Gorman is responsible for most magazines under Mike Shapiro. Rosemary Senatore ran Romar Sales, named after her, and now a big mail order business in its own right. For twenty years, Mollie Cohen, as bookkeeper, has struggled to keep it all straight.

Of course, there's the Allegheny Drug Division selling through stores. "It's doing $16,000,000 this year and making $2,400,000 profit."

Dave never stops. "Yesterday, I met with Franklin Mint. They gamble a minimum. I gamble the rest PI." He's happy about mail order ads in premium coupon inserts. "They're very strong for $2, $3, and $10 items, usually household or garden." As for magazine launches, "I avoid them. I'd rather buy them a year later." The calls stack up. Dave jumps from one to the other. The day continues.

There are some who criticized products, copy, publications, offers and people he's been associated with. But Dave is associated with everything and everybody. He has been a true friend to many, including me. He's loyal. He lives up to what he says. He's traded up over the years more and more. He's generous in charity and a director of Southside Hospital, on Long Island.

If you're starting in mail order, he's a good man to know. One thing to remember—Dave is practical. He can sense a loser item and stays away from it like the plague. He's super cautious about the untested. Most with new items never get to see him. He stays away from dreamers, items that cost too much, have a built-in problem, or have already failed.

The best time to see Dave is when you have a winner in a test and need help to project it.

Chapter 5
"How Long Will Direct Marketers Ignore Marketing?"

Why not attain more of full potential, take fewer unnecessary risks, perhaps work less hard?

That was the subject of a lecture given by Professor Philip Kotler, considered by many to be the leading professor of marketing in the world.

It took place in London, in February of 1980 . . . at the International Direct Mail/Marketing Conference sponsored by the DMMA. It's available on tape from Hoke Communications. I suggest you get it. It's listed in the Help Source Section in this book.

He is the author of the most widely used economics text book in colleges today. His book MARKETING MANAGEMENT: ANALYSIS, PLANNING AND CONTROL, was voted the leading book in marketing in 1976. He was voted the leading academic marketing professor in the U.S. in 1975. He has written six books and sixty articles. His work has been translated all over the world. He has lectured extensively in the U.S. and in several countries world-wide.

On the one hand, Dr. Kotler has maintained that direct marketing should be an introduction to marketing in every marketing course in the country. He recommends a direct marketing project for students during their first course in marketing.

"Through a single such project they can learn the concepts of customer profiling, target marketing, market segmentation, consumer life style, media economics, copy development, vehicle testing, break-even analysis and other essential concepts in marketing."

On the other hand, he feels that direct marketers should master other aspects of marketing, particularly of strategically planning where their direct marketing sales can best come from over a period of time. Dr. Kotler says: "It is my observation that a good number of direct marketers know little or less about how to run a business from a marketing point of view."

He is Professor of Marketing at Northwestern University, J.L. Kellogg Graduate School of Management. Dr. Kotler received his Ph.D. in Economics at MIT and his MA in Economics at the University of Chicago. He did post doctoral work in mathematics at Harvard and in sociology at the University of Chicago.

Dr. Kotler has been a consultant to General Mills, Capital Records, Grolier and ITT. He is a particular specialist in model building for decision making, in the use of mathematical models in marketing, in modeling for media selection, in competitive marketing computer simulation, in applying operations research to marketing.

He is a futurist and, as such, a consultant to Fortune 500 companies in corporate planning for the next ten to twenty years. He sees direct marketing being used more and more in the coming decades by more and more giant companies. "There's no question. Direct marketing is a growing part of the overall marketing spectrum. The growth rate is impressive. This will continue. The cost of a sales call for IBM is now $210. As an overall average for companies it's over $100. As long as a sales call cost goes up, people will go to phone, cable and mail.

"When I first wrote my text book, MARKETING MANAGEMENT, in the middle sixties, I didn't include direct marketing. In current editions, I do. Now I have a session on a direct marketing problem in my marketing course. My course trains market managers for large companies. My students have gone everywhere—sales, advertising and marketing.

"I'm less interested in the tactical side of direct marketing. I'm interested in the strategic use of direct marketing. Direct marketing is a stepchild tool of the giant companies. It's overwhelmed by larger budgets for paid advertising and sales force. The Fortune 500 companies rarely use direct marketing to its full potential."

He does not talk with ivory tower words. His courses are overwhelmingly popular. He can dissect the complex with a verbal scalpel that immediately clarifies.

Dr. Kotler is very much aware of the moonlighting "mom and pop" start of many mail order businesses, of the trial and error, the "blood, sweat and tears". In the tape I want you to hear, he traces the evolution of such a mail order business, its survival and growth despite increasing hurdles at each stage.

He respects every bit of struggle, of dollars and cents lessons learned, of painful progress. He's simply concerned that, after all that agony, so many in mail order never attain anywhere near full potential and so often take unnecessary risk and perhaps work harder than needed.

Dr. Kotler wants to see more mail order businesses get past the phases of crawling and walking and when they run, that they do so safely. He wants them to see potentials, set goals, to see the forest, not just the mail order trees. Dr. Kotler would like to see direct marketers emphasize more opportunity identification, market research, segmentation, positioning, planning and strategy control.

"The Franklin Mint found it could sell its private mint concept. But it went further to conclude it could sell collectibles in different fields. It targeted the fields, tested them one by one. It broadened its base yet kept to the area of its expertise to build a big business. More direct marketers can do that."

Dr. Kotler feels strongly that each mail order business must do more than just project successfully current hit items. "Direct marketers should not use the excuse that they're too busy with today's problems to get to planning tomorrow." He feels that they must analyze their overall opportunities for some time to come, must plan, and soundly. "Too many direct marketers are waiting for a winner rather than working toward a winning strategy.

"What about modeling for direct marketers? I use decision modeling and modeling for economic analysis. Direct marketers should use it to start at the beginning, to determine things to cover, the offer, to figure out what is the largest target group."

He is provocative, stimulating and continually sought after. "I get several calls a week asking me to do something. I have to turn down four out of five. Often I'll turn down a direct marketer as being too specialized, small or immediate in objective. But I'm very excited about direct marketing. I include direct marketing as a part of overall marketing in my discussions with large companies.

"I work mostly for major corporations to develop competitive strategy on how to grow in the next twenty years. I work for hospitals and colleges, advising them how to survive in the eighties. I am a futurist and a strategist. I'm less interested in the shorter term factors.

"Direct marketers often have an inferiority complex. They want status and acceptance. They want to be scientific. They want business leaders to be more aware of direct marketing. And, more and more, they are."

Chapter 6
Making A Career As A Woman Direct Marketing Consultant

*How she learned to write
copy that sold.*

Betty Anne Noakes has made it in direct marketing. She has, on her own, been a successful direct marketing and circulation consultant since 1974. Before that, she was vice-president of the then biggest direct marketing consultant firm, whose clients included some of the most sophisticated and knowledgeable publishers and marketers.

"What should be tested for maximum and dramatic profit improvement?" That was the title of her talk before the Direct Mail/Marketing Association's Marketing Council and Circulation Council (she is chairperson). It's an astute summation of what testing can do for bottom line profits. It tells what to do and what not to do. In the Help Source Section of this book, I tell how you can get a copy. "She knows her subject," says Rose Harper, president of The Kleid Company. And Rose is right.

Betty Anne is a Canadian, born in Toronto. Her first job in publishing and direct marketing was with The Reader's Digest of Canada. "In 1965, I moved to the United States as advertising and promotion manager for Meredith Press book clubs in the U.S. and Canada—Better Homes & Gardens Family Book Service, Catholic Digest Book Club and Junior Book Shelf.

"In 1967 I joined Benson, Stagg & Associates, which later became Stagg, Dale & Archer. A wise choice, because I discovered I liked consulting—its variety and challenges. I worked with Southern Living, Harper's Magazine, Highlights for Children, Early Years Magazine, Scholastic Magazines, Time Inc. Book Clubs, The Theatre Guild, The Business Week Letter, The Craig Claiborne Journal, Old American Insurance, The Ayn Rand Letter.

"Stagg, Dale & Archer closed in February, 1974 when Chris Stagg moved to California. I've been on my own ever since—as a circulation and direct marketing consultant for such clients as: Early Years Magazine, New York, Leisure Books, Parents Magazine, Charles Schwab & Company, Ohio Magazine, New West, Financial Education Services, Highlights for Children, The MoneyLetter.

"I live in New York, in a co-op apartment with a big terrace. My hobby is gardening—flowers *and* vegetables.

"I work on a straight consulting basis although, if necessary, I may become the "circulation director" or "marketing director"

for a client until in-house staff is found or trained. This happens most frequently with a new magazine or product launch.

"As a consultant, I don't favor individual copywriters, agencies, design studios, or other suppliers. I try to give clients a choice of suppliers whose specialties are tailored to the needs of the individual client.

"There are excellent free-lance writers and designers. Most of my clients use the tested top producers. In 1980 a solo package cost $3,500 to $5,000 for copy and $1,500 to $3,000 for comprehensive layout.

"A lot of direct mail is written by free-lance talent. Some direct marketing agencies use in-house creative staff, but many promotion and marketing people feel that it's better to use free-lancers with expertise in their products and markets, for fresh, different sales approaches, and for maximum profitability from the promotion dollars spent. The name of the game, after all, is to beat the control and increase response and profit.

"Some direct marketers test several creative approaches or packages within a test matrix. Others test one new package only, or one new package component only—letter, outer envelope, brochure—to try to improve the control."

Betty Anne Noakes combines an analytical and creative mind. Her concept is to be scientific without reducing creativity, which she worries about. "There have been many changes in our business, a lot of them good, but creativity is being lost to 'rule by numbers', and is taking a back seat to printouts. Creative budgets have been greatly reduced in many instances. Such decisions can be penny-wise and pound-foolish, because top creative work may, and usually does, result in greatly increased response and profit.

"I recommend caution when launching a new product. Often, when asked to prepare a new product feasibility study, the results will indicate that the "dream product" as it is visualized has little chance of success. Maybe the concept is wrong, or the product is wrong, or the product cost is wrong, or the pricing is wrong, or the market is too limited, or wrongly defined. If modifications to product package and production costs, pricing and markups, market positioning, overhead, and so on, can be made, sometimes the dream does become reality, and the product is test marketed.

"Do I believe in testing? Yes, indeed. Ours is a totally measurable business. I believe in careful, measurable testing and careful, realistic projection fo the test results. And this includes equally careful monitoring at the back door, whether renewals, book or record club members, merchandise buyers, continuity program completers, or however the customers are defined. I believe, too, in knowing the value of a customer—the life expectancy, and the expected profitability during that life.

"Many new, exciting and viable marketing tools are available to direct marketers now that were not available, or widely used, when I started in this business many years ago. And there are marked improvements in one of our primary marketing sources—lists. There are more lists available now, with many more refinements. Mailers have become more knowledgeable about list usage and selectivity. And they're much more know-ledgeable about their own customers' demographics and psycho-graphics.

"Yes, I recommend telephone marketing to my clients, where applicable. Most magazine publishers have tested phone selling to cold names, to renewals, to expires, to donors. Many magazines find telephone marketing to be most cost efficient in renewal selling. Some book publishers use telephone marketing successfully to upgrade customers, or as holding efforts.

"In-WATS usage is, of course, very common. Very few cataloguers do not list an 800 number on their order forms. And many magazines use In-WATS for changes of address, for complaints, for new business, and for Christmas and other gift business.

"A career in direct marketing is no longer out of reach for women, and many women have done very well in the various direct marketing functions. The successful women I know started on the bottom rung of the ladder and learned their craft thoroughly and well, gradually expanding their knowledge and experience on their way to the top.

"Some were lucky and joined advertising agencies and companies with training programs for copywriters and direct marketers. I was one of the lucky ones. However, many companies cannot afford to continue training bright young people. It takes a year, I'm told, before there is a "return on investment" only, and all too often, to lose these bright young people to companies offering fancy titles and better pay.

"What is my advice to anyone wanting a direct marketing career? Start at the bottom if necessary and learn the basics. Change jobs if there is no room to expand knowledge and experience. Learn as many areas of our business as possible. Read. Many companies have extensive libraries on the "how-to's" of direct marketing. Subscribe to direct-marketing trade publications. Attend as many industry seminars, workshops and conferences as possible. Don't be afraid to ask questions.

"If hard, challenging, rewarding, exciting work is the goal— this is the industry to choose."

Chapter 7
Sound Mail Order

What is the most distributed disk in the world? No! It's not Elvis, the Beatles or Slim Whitman.

It's not even sold. It is a record given away by Time-Life Records as a sample of records and tapes offered. It's 4½ minutes. It's used to demonstrate the quality of Time-Life Records and plays up to 500 times. Yet, it's made on a plastic sheet so thin it weighs a quarter ounce.

Down on the warm, sunny coast of Florida, moved by mail order from cold Chicago, is the business that makes it, a business grown beyond its founder's dreams. The pressing is the Eva-Tone Soundsheet. The business is Eva-Tone, Eva-Type Inc., whose president is "Dick" (Richard) Evans, son of another Dick Evans, the founder.

Overwhelmingly, the field of Eva-Tone is business-to-business mail order. Eva-Tone Soundsheets are sold by mail order, using Eva-Tone Soundsheets as tools to do so. They are sold to companies which, in turn, use the Soundsheets to sell by mail order or in 1001 promotional ways. Institutions use them as fund raisers. They are used to get inquiries and to close inquiries, to demonstrate and to sell.

It all came about because business was getting mighty bad for Dick Evans, Sr., making and selling rubber stamps. He just had to come up with an idea for something to sell with less competition, something he could make with his same experience and technology. He did, and in 1962, started to manufacture Eva-Tone Soundsheets. And now, 400 million soundsheets later, the present Dick Evans presides over 90,000 square feet of space and facilities. These include a promotional advertising agency, elaborate sound equipment and high technology manufacturing operations which turn out Soundsheets by the millions.

Eva-Tone practices what it preaches. The key to its success is the use of its Soundsheets bound into trade magazines and in mailings and the use of Soundsheets to close inquiries secured from its ads. About ninety percent of its accounts have been generated from mail order. The $8,000,000-a-year Eva-Tone business is a double lesson in sound mail order, both selling with sound and soundly using mail order methods.

The telephone is used in tandem with the advertising and the Soundsheets. Ads get inquiries. Promotional material and Soundsheets are forwarded. Phone solicitation follows up. Objectives are discussed in the first such call. Requirements and budget are explored. Often the problem is thrown in the pot for internal Eva-Tone brainstorming to come up with exciting and suitable applications. Ideas are spelled out, proposals and quotes mailed and follow-up phone calls then close. Some such selling is done in-house and some face to face. But it is the advertising and the Soundsheets that power it all.

I talked to Dick Evans, to his son, Mark Evans, and to Director of Marketing, Larry Johnson. They told me this story. "In 1962, when this product was developed and ready, we had no market for it. We were very small. Larry came three years later. We had vulcanizing presses we used to make rubber stamps. Dick Evans, Sr., the founder, did not start his rubber stamp business mail order, but door to door.

"Dick Sr. would load up a trailer with a display work shop and small presses. He would go to merchants where he thought persons might want personalized or other rubber stamps. He would offer next-day delivery where usually it would take a week or two. He'd make the stamps overnight.

"Then Dick Sr. would go to some print shop or stationery store in the town and show copies of the orders. He'd say, 'Look what I did in your town!' He'd quote the cost of the equipment. He'd ask: 'How many stamps can you sell? After all, you live here.' He'd offer to turn over the profit he had just made to the buyer of the equipment. He'd set him up in the business and go on to the next town.

"That was his business. By 1962, he had a machine shop. He made equipment to make top-quality rubber plates and rubber stamps. Both rubber printing plates and the Soundsheets are molded with heat and pressure. Both need to be accurate to thousandths of an inch. About that time, letter press printing went to hell and rubber vulcanizing did, too. In 1962, when the first test was made, it had to succeed."

By this time, Dick Jr. had been in the business for some time. He had gone to Highland Park High School. He had no college. His father trained him in apprenticeship. Dick Jr., it soon developed, was creative, with a rare promotional flair. Dick proved to be a showman and a mail order man with a feel for how to come up with an offer, presentation and copy that could pull, and when to plunge.

For advertising of the new business, the company used an advertising agency. Dick Jr.'s concept was to run a full-page standing insert ad in Advertising Age and to bind-in a sample of the brand new Eva-Tone Soundsheet. He wanted to do so in the most dramatic way possible. Then he came up with an idea that proved to be the most sensational possible introduction for his Soundsheets.

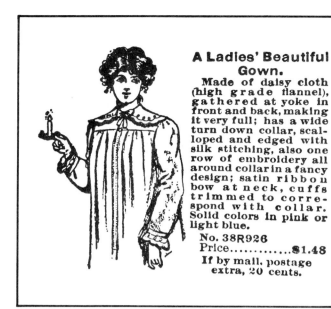

A Ladies' Beautiful Gown.

Made of daisy cloth (high grade flannel), gathered at yoke in front and back, making it very full; has a wide turn down collar, scalloped and edged with silk stitching, also one row of embroidery all around collar in a fancy design; satin ribbon bow at neck, cuffs trimmed to correspond with collar. Solid colors in pink or light blue.

No. 38R926
Price............$1.48
If by mail, postage extra, 20 cents.

A month before, John Glenn had orbited the earth. The first Eva-Tone Soundsheet was a mini-documentary, the story of his space flight with the actual sound track of his conversations with the Houston Space Control Center. It was royalty free. It tapped national pride and nostalgia. It could become a conversation piece and later a collector's piece.

Dick Jr. supplied Advertising Age with 45,000 Soundsheets to bind into the magazine, positioned with a space ad. The Eva-Tone Soundsheet story was told dramatically. Readers were urged to take off the Soundsheet, bring it home and play it on a record player. People listened, sent in requests asking for more information, and then asked for specific quotes.

That first Ad Age standing insert page combined with Soundsheet was expensive. But it was a major hit and the beginning of an ad approach that worked. Over 2,000 leads came in. Dick remembers, "We were swamped, but everything built from there." He had proved that people out there were intrigued enough to want to talk. Larry Johnson says, "It probably could not have paid out with space only. We still use Ad Age regularly."

Dick Jr. was busy producing for those first customers who bought Soundsheets. He designed any equipment required by the Soundsheet business, that could not be bought on the market. His object from the start was to keep customers, help them succeed with the use of Soundsheets and, thus, to grow into bigger customers. Sales converted from Advertising Age, alone, kept them busy for a while. But it was soon apparent that each inquiry needed follow-up, explanation and study. Only later did Dick Jr. hire a salesman.

Larry Johnson joined the company in 1965. He started out as a salesman of Eva-Tone Soundsheets working on the phone, calling advertising agencies and logical prospects. But to them, an Eva-Tone Soundsheet was just a gimmick they didn't need. What Eva-Tone did to overcome this can be useful to any manager, particularly of a business selling to business.

"I found that when I went to New York, Chicago or Los Angeles, people were hard to see, skeptical and difficult to sell from scratch. For us they were initially just too hard to convince. The phone was easier and I could make many worthwhile calls in a day. When I did go out to see those people, they were as happy to see me as I was to see them."

"We found that the solution was not to beat our heads against the wall. Instead, we helped whatever clients we did have to make a success out of Soundsheets. We got their repeat business. We got as clients those we were recommended to. We looked for people with promotional problems and opportunities. We then concentrated on helping them solve their problems and taking advantage of their opportunities, using Soundsheets."

Mail order and mail order methods became the solution. The Advertising Age insert idea could be used in other publications as well as repeated. It could be converted to a mailing piece and sent to appropriate lists. Small ads could be run to solicit inquiries. The Soundsheet mailing could then also be used as follow-up to such inquiries.

Most important, out of all inquiries received and followed up, some would be from people who could get less benefit and some, more from the use of Soundsheets. But out of enough inquiries would gradually develop some most ideally able to benefit. The key was to sort out the most ideal users and work closely with them, no matter how small. If users prospered the business would, and bigger and bigger users would follow.

Dick Jr. is just Dick now. He's president. His father has passed away. Larry is now director of marketing. Both have worked to use mail order methods in just this way. It has been built on small, right accounts, each nurtured to grow. Some did. The success of those attracted others. The success of the small led to bigger and bigger client companies. The advertising has been built to demonstrate the product, report successful use and to provide testimonials of profitability of use. Success stories developed one by one.

Sherman Christianson answered an ad and came to the small Eva-Tone, Eva-Type shop. He owned Advance Schools, now at 5900 North West Highway, in Chicago. He had an idea how to use Soundsheets for Advance.

Advance offered to veterans mail order courses which were government-approved and financed. Advance had secretarial, refrigeration, electronic repairs, small engine courses among others. Sherman wanted to combine oral with written and picture instruction. He created booklet and soundsheet lessons and tried his idea out, starting with hundreds, then of thousands and well over a million in a period of time. Through good, bad and good times again, he has continued as a customer.

Mail order advertising brought in many accounts, enabled Eva-Tone to survive and grow and made it far more known. Customer recommendations led to word of mouth pass-along recommendations. Gradually, more right users found the way to Eva-Tone.

In 1966, four years after introducing Soundsheets, Eva-Tone got an inquiry from a young man with an idea. He was Rudy Savage and only 26 from Denver. He had, thus far in his business life, worked in and was now running his family's paint distribution business. He had been innovative and aggressive. He had another business of his own, selling educational material. He was hard-working and responsible.

Now Rudy wanted to create a talking book to sell to the general public through book stores. Master tapes just right for his project already existed. The Listening Library of Old Greenwich, Connecticut, was producing cassettes for the educational market. The owner is Tony Ditlow, a very remarkable man. He is almost blind and operates his successful mail order catalog business selling to schools. He gave Rudy the rights to use his material on a royalty basis and some good advice.

"I wanted to create a talking book. I wanted each page to look like a real page from a book but to slip out and play, to actually be a very thin, flexible plastic record. My talking book had a nice cover and case, for store display purposes. Tony recommended that I get my flexible plastic records from Eva-Tone which alone, he said, could give me the quality and price I would have to have to survive. My idea was to make some talking books of one title and exhibit at the American Book Seller Association Show and feel out the market."

Larry Johnson continues the story. "Rudy Savage came to us in 1966 with tape masters for his sound book. He said, 'If it works, I have forty more.' We pressed five hundred pieces for him. It turned out to be the most important order Eva-Tone had ever recieved. It was the beginning of what in effect has become a partnership, a business marriage."

Rudy Savage picks up: "At the show some people from the Library of Congress came by and liked my talking book. They were already looking for something like the flexible Soundsheet idea. They liked the quality and the price. They were looking for something like this to supply the blind with a talking catalog of recordable products."

It took a lot of time, grief and perseverance by Rudy before any business came out of this interest by the Library of Congress. For the first step, Dick Evans and Rudy worked out an agreement for Rudy to become a special exclusive sales representative for Eva-Tone to provide Soundsheets for the blind.

The combination of Rudy and Eva-Tone has proved the best thing that ever happened to either. Dick Evans was a perfectionist in the production of Soundsheets. Rudy was willing to develop a team for recording the tape masters for the Soundsheets, as they later became needed for the Library of Congress. Dick had a stable business big enough to be considered as a serious bidder by the government. Rudy recalls: "Eva-Tone had built soundly on small contracts, one after another. Only Eva-Tone had the technology to produce what the Library of Congress wanted." The project the Library of Congress had in mind was the supplying of talking magazines to the blind, as well as talking books.

It started slowly, gathered speed slowly, but expanded. Rudy lived with the problems. He worked on every aspect, helping the Library of Congress in any way. When the problems were related to the discs, Eva-Tone worked them out. When the problem seemed to be producing the master tapes in the studio and proper standards editorially and of voice delivery, Rudy started his own recording studio and hired the talent himself. "I had to," he says.

"For Eva-Tone I now act in two roles. I'm the sales representative with sole rights to this field. I'm the production house that creates the master tapes from which Eva-Tone prepares Soundsheets of books and magazines for the blind. I've been able to devote the time and effort necessary. I sell for Eva-Tone. I'm a sub-contractor for Eva-Tone."

In Denver, in his recording studio, Rudy creates the masters for each talking book and each issue of each magazine. He forwards each master, as soon as produced, to Eva-Tone. He's built an organization of actors and announcers from Denver radio and TV stations. He even has PhDs on retainer to check scripts and finished masters for errors. Response from the blind has been very good, often enthusiastic.

"The Library of Congress has very high standards for the masters I make and for the Soundsheet books and magazine sound reproduction. There's just one other organization in the country with the ability to turn out a quality Soundsheet. Eva-Tone has the technology, the facilities, the volume and the efficiency needed."

Rudy and Eva-Tone are working closer together, more closely all the time. Larry Johnson recalls: "We've done at least 300 more books, 6000 sides. Now we're doing 100 a year. We're doing 300,000 copies of 35 different magazines each month. Rudy is very conscious of the need to deliver quality and value. He has our finest respect. He's a prince of a fellow. This project of books and magazines for the blind has come about because Rudy is a man who has believed so strongly in the concept, and because Eva-Tone backed the effort with technical know-how."

Thirty-five percent of the Eva-Tone business is now sound publishing for the blind. It's all done as a project of the National Library Service Division for the Blind and Physically Handicapped of the Library of Congress. It's a national service for the blind. Eva-Tone not only presses the Soundsheet publications, but does all fulfillment. It puts the Soundsheet in the envelope, labels it, does zip code sorting. Each magazine has a different closing date. Some require doing the entire Eva-Tone job, including recording, in five working days.

Rudy Savage is a sound entrepreneur. He's now testing a new idea, Newstrack, a talking newsletter. It's a business publication. "We buy editorial material from The Wall Street Journal, Forbes, Business Week and U.S. News." A subscription is $195 for a year. There's a short-term trial subscription for $45. "We'd like to get 10,000 subscribers. We've test-mailed 125,000 names. We are testing The Wall Street Journal and the Christian Science Monitor. If we do well enough, we'll then mail and advertise regularly. It's been done with my own money. So far, 86% of subscribers have indicated they plan to renew."

Years ago, Time Inc. got interested in Eva-Tone soundsheets to sell records. In one issue of Time, they used over four million Soundsheets. In one issue of Life, seven million.

The biggest success of Soundsheets for Time-Life Records was for their Swing Band Era Series. Here the Soundsheets sampled the series and demonstrated the difference in quality between stereo recreations done by today's musicians (with original arrangements but fresh technology) versus the old records made when the technology was inferior. The soundsheets were extraordinarily convincing. Reproduction quality of the Time-Life offering was superb. The big band originals were good but faded and scratchy in comparison. This Soundsheet is estimated to be the most widely distributed sound pressing ever made.

Bigger and bigger users have given Eva-Tone more and more volume. But the key has been more and more Soundsheet promotion, more and more use of mail order methods to bring in more and more inquiries from even more logical users. It has built its business with mail order methods. It has used Eva-Tone Soundsheets as its selling vehicle. It has put more and more effort into becoming more and more professional in its own use of Soundsheets to promote its own Soundsheet business.

As Eva-Tone began to promote on a bigger scale, it found itself more sound-oriented than the outside agencies interested in handling the account. In 1972, Eva-Tone formed its own house agency. "We had ten years working with agencies. Now we have our own. We're not trying for other accounts." Just a year after forming the house agency, one of the first campaigns was entered in DMMA's annual contest—and Eva-Tone took a Silver Mailbox for the year's best self promotion campaign.

One contribution Larry Johnson has made is to bring in professional name personalities to make Soundsheets advertising Soundsheets. The first was Ken Nordine. "He's a special breed of announcer. Ken is very creative. He can write extremely persuasively. He can create multi-media promotion and come up with a very special piece. Ken asked us how we felt about the business. What we needed was a way to prove the Soundsheet concept was correct by example, by testimonial and by shooting down typical objections. Ken did all that with great showmanship, professionalism and conviction."

Then Larry came up with the idea of using radio commercial comics, Dick and Bert. "They are very good." By using one side of the Soundsheet to promote Dick and Bert and one side to promote Soundsheets, it became a co-op promotion at no out-of-pocket talent cost to Eva-Tone. Dick and Bert primarily write and produce radio commercials.

Sooner or later, anyone in marketing is apt to tear off a Soundsheet, bring it home and get interested . . . particularly when it coincides with a just-right idea for it. The National Geographic bound in a Soundsheet, as a bonus to subscribers, of Winston Churchill with excerpts from his greatest World War II speeches. It was so appreciated that the Geographic has bound in a Soundsheet in each of two more issues, a total of close to twenty million copies.

Dick and Larry enjoy such huge business done so innovatively. But they also get a thrill out of small business ventures which come into being and succeed with Soundsheets.

A few years ago, a musician and arranger borrowed money to make a unique Soundsheet. His name was Jim Houston. He borrowed enough to mail a package to 20,000 high school band directors. That launched a music publishing business that has grown each year. Now Houston's Studio PR uses 250,000 Soundsheets a year. He mails band leaders of junior high schools as well as of high schools and does so frequently throughout the year.

So successful have sales been from playing the arrangements on a Soundsheet that Eva-Tone now makes Soundsheets for many music publishers including Hal Leonard, Warner Brothers Music, MCA, Columbia and Carl Fischer. Some uses just seem a natural. The Gregg Division of McGraw-Hill Book Company uses Soundsheets for dictation practice albums.

Word Publishing company has used Eva-Tone Soundsheets to spread the word. Starting in 1975, Word inserted a sampler disc in a package. It sampled religious tapes and records, a sort of religious sound catalog of Word's most popular hits. It was a big mail hit to increase sales in religious book stores. A dollar off was offered on Word religious albums to any listener to the Word Soundhseet catalog. It was profitable but a headache to trace. But it has led to Word Publishing ordering more Soundsheets.

And other religious publishers use Soundsheets . . . the Board of Publications of the American Lutheran Church in America, the Presbyterian Church, the Methodist Publishing House and Southern Baptist Convention, among others. So do over dozens of colleges and universities for fund raising and new student recruiting.

Ronald Reagan used Soundsheets in personal messages to the faithful, as have other candidates. Fund raisers from churches to symphony orchestras to museums to a wide variety of causes use Soundsheets. More and more Fortune 500 companies do. It's been used as a sound catalog to supplement a printed one. The U.S. Army, National Guard and Reserve have used them to recruit. A fellow in Philadelphia sells for $9.95 on TV a counting system, Soundsheets and a 16-page booklet to teach the material. Radio Yesteryear, which sells by mail order records of old time radio, buys 10,000 Eva-Tone Soundsheets at a time.

Eva-Tone made seventy-five different size Soundsheets in 1980. The biggest has 12 minutes of playing time on each side, a total of 24 minutes, almost half the playing time of an average LP record. In equivalent quantities, it can be manufactured for a quarter of the cost of an LP, a substantial saving per minute of playing time.

The company is computerized, automated and equipped with latest technology, constantly improved by Dick. Eva-Tone performs every possible task connected with manufacturing Soundsheets. It makes the master record, forms the dies, presses Soundsheets on plastic, prints on plastic and paper, with art prepared by its in-house art department. It die cuts. It folds by machine. It prints letter press and offset, and makes printing plates and negatives for each. It binds by machine and where needed, hand-glues. It can perform machine glue tipping automatically for inserting Soundsheets in multi-million runs. It has specialty bindery equipment for custom potential assemblies. It has a complete letter shop facility. There's no soundsheet facility like it anywhere. Eva-Tone's promotion never stops, almost always incorporating Soundsheets. It sends out a Soundsheet newsletter, "Soundstage". It sends out specialized Soundsheets and literature for special markets like fund-raising, training and direct mail. It has a superb Idea Kit crammed with Soundsheet samples, with every possible question answered, with full ordering information, so that Soundsheets can be ordered by mail. Dick and Larry have become masters in combining pictures, the printed word and the spoken word, each buttressing the other.

By 1980, 53% of the top 100 advertisers have used Eva-Tone Soundsheets, 75% of the top 50, 85% of the top 20, and 90% of the top 10, plus 3,000 other customers. Soundsheets have become accepted . . . to communicate, educate, motivate, train and sell.

Eva-Tone has not done all Dick has wanted it to do, or everything that Mark sees possible, or Larry. "We've neglected the creating of our own Soundsheet consumer products. In the last several years, we couldn't even think of it, until the new plant was built and operating. Now we have plans we can get to."

What about the future? What about the videodisc sheets manufacured the same way for playback over a TV Screen when videodisc players are widely available? "Yes, experiments in videodisc sheets have been made. They work. We have watched videodisc sheets we've produced perform in tests and watched the pictures on TV screens. We may need equipment and investment. There may be a lot of work and development. But we'll be there with Eva-Tone Videodisc Sheets in the new TV playback age."

The mind boggles at the concept of leaping over technological hurdles to videodisc sheet mailings at a fraction of the postage cost of printed catalogs, of videodisc sheet demonstrations of anything, of videodisc sheet mail order replacing paper and ink mailing pieces.

And all because a rubber stamp manufacturing business converted to manufacturing flexible plastic records, by sound mail order.

Note: Eva-Tone Soundsheets is located at 4801 Ulmerton Rd., Clearwater, Florida 33520; (813) 577-7000.

Chapter 8
Launching And Building A List Business

How to make big money with a no-risk start and quiet expansion in a simple way.

Within five years of learning of the existence of direct marketing and the list business, Dave Florence made $200,000 a year in it—on commission . . . as a list salesman. He then started a non-competitive list management business as a moonlighter, with a full-time associate.

He sold it and years later bought it back, for almost nothing, and then again made it prosper. Meanwhile, he had started a list brokerage business, virtually without risk. In a friendly transition, he continued to work with his former employers. Then he began to moonlight, from his list businesses, in the mail order business . . . without competing with any clients, and in partnership with several of them.

His business, Direct Media, Inc. and its subsidairy (List Management, Inc.) handle transactions for the rental of six hundred million names a year. "We do $22,000,000 a year in list rentals. List Management, Inc. manages lists with a rental income of close to $8,000,000." Dave has launched with partners mail businesses in Canada and in Europe.

It's done in a very quiet way. In any trade meeting panel discussion by top leaders on lists, Dave talks the most quietly. You have to strain a little to hear each word plainly. In any group picture of the company staff, you'd rarely pick him as the boss. He's at the back, on the side, and seems an observer. All he has he's gotten by observing, analyzing and then acting—in an orderly way. He was born in Texas. His family moved to Bronxville, in Westchester County, outside of New York City,

and then to Scarsdale. His father was in casualty insurance. Dave went to Scarsdale High School, then to Loomis preparatory school and then Dartmouth, in the class of 1953. There he took economics and liberal arts. But, in 1951, he went into the Marines. After two years in the Marines, he went to Columbia at night. "I had a fairly high IQ." He got an MBA in one year and spent another taking other courses.

In December of 1955, Dave had started in training at IBM. "I was in program data processing sales. We had an 18-month extensive training program. I learned a little programming. I started selling. I'm not very mechanically inclined. I learned mostly by osmosis.

"A father of a friend of mine had a friend at Royal McBee. They wanted to go into automatic data processing. I was introduced. They liked my IBM experience. They were in Port Chester. I took the job with them. Royal McBee personalized direct mail. My introduction to direct marketing was when we sold 100 machines to Oral Roberts. I had never heard of direct marketing. I was impressed with Oral Robert's use of our machines—sending personalized letters to his contributor list, for more contributions. Then I got interested in direct mail for our own use to get leads for our 25 salesmen.

"I met Milt Smoliar, of Names Unlimited. He took me to lunch. He got me very interested. I was intrigued by the mailing list business. I liked numbers. I was very analytical. Milt did for me what he has done for a number of people. He taught me, advised me and helped me. He could see I wanted to get into the list field. One day he sent me a blind classified ad advertising for someone to run a New York office for a Chicago list company. Milt told me that the advertiser was National Business Lists and suggested that I write directly to the president. I did, referring to the ad.

"Leo Gans called me wanting to know how I knew who advertised, interviewed me, and gave me the job. In 1964, I started, setting up a New York office. Ed Burnett had been a dealer for them but they had wanted their own office. At this time, most NBL customers were industrial. They mainly sold names to office equipment firms. I began to sell to people in the mail order field. I became very intrigued in the numbers and economics of mail order. I developed a clientele of mail order businesses. I built up a staff for NBL of 13 to 14 people.

"Originally, NBL had said they would pay me a very small draw but against a very attractive commission which they said they would never reduce. I made huge sales and was earning $200,000 a year. I'd fallen in love with it. But I was limited. My interests were to get into list brokerage to handle any list a client might want to buy. Now I could only offer NBL lists.

"I made a proposal to my boss. I would like to take my ten largest clients and represent NBL to them on a non-exclusive basis and give up all my rights under my contract to other clients. I would like to act as a non-exclusive broker for any other clients I might add in renting lists from NBL. I also asked my ten biggest clients if they would work with me, as broker, to select names for them from all lists I recommended to them, aside from NBL. Nine agreed to do so exclusively and one non-exclusively.

"It was good for everybody. Starting a list brokerage business was a no-risk thing for me. Getting released from a very expensive contract was good for NBL. My clients felt I could help them with other lists.

"I had a good deal of current commissions coming to me from NBL and a lot of receivables over the first six months from my ten clients. It was just myself and one girl. I never wanted to be very big. I just wanted these ten accounts. But everything went very smoothly. I could get all my business done for my ten clients fairly early in the day. Then I began to get bored, until I came up with an idea for a new project.

"NBL had been on punch cards when I came with them. I then helped them set up three and a half million names on punch cards it used to take days to pass and select.

"But several years after I started Direct Media (that was 1969) large consumer list companies started merge-purge. This was in 1971 or 1972. Some big clients asked if Direct Media could do this for them. Four line merge-purge was needed for business names. But it was much more difficult than the three lines used for consumer lists.

"Then the idea came up: Why not a perennial merge-purge? I wrote up the idea and made proposals to business mailers. In 1972, we got twenty-five to fifty mailers and put their names into one data bank. Since then, directly or indirectly, the data bank has been responsible for 35% to 50% of our volume in the business field, which in turn is 35% to 60% of our business. In the list business overall, the list management business is about 20%.

"Ed Burnett was the first list manager, back when I was with NBL. In 1966 or 1967, some of the mail order people asked us if NBL could market their lists. I went to Leo Gans and proposed that NBL get into list management. NBL was growing. It seemed to Leo to not fit and he decided not to.

"Fred Allen, who now is in his own list brokerage business in Texas, was then with me. I suggested we start in list management. We did, in Fred's kitchen. This was List Management, Inc. Fred sold via my contacts. I put up what money was needed for Fred. It was full-time for him and moonlighting for me.

"But when I started Direct Media, I felt I should concentrate on it and Fred too was getting busy with other interests. We sold LMI for 50,000 shares to a public company. This got taken over by another one. That got taken over. Our stock went to twenty-five cents a share. Then Fairfield Community Land, a hundred million dollar public company, took everything over. They didn't need LMI. They really gave it to me. I assumed the obligations in the fall of 1978. Now Kevin Aronin runs it. We have eleven people and it is successful.

"Several years ago, I became interested in becoming a mail order entrepreneur myself. I decided against doing anything in the U.S. I didn't want to compete with customers. I went into business out of the U.S. with several of my list customers in the U.S. One was Grayarc, the business products catalog. I trained a manager here and sent him to Canada. I put up the money for inventory. We built up the business and then sold out. I did the same in Canada with Ambassador Leather. They had an option to buy my share out and later did. I did the same with Ambassador in West Germany and in England.

Most of what I've done as an entrepreneur abroad has been with solo mailings. Basically, we just copied what we did in the states. I simply used the mailing piece successful in the U.S., translated where necessary. We mailed to the lists in Europe most directly equivalent to those successful in the U.S.

"I selected a couple of young fellows, trained them and sent them abroad. One was a German Swiss. He was ideal to build a West German business. But for another West German business, the young man I hired went to Berlitz for a couple of months and then picked up German in Germany. The enterprise worked out quite well. In each case, I started them out as employees for a year and a half or so and then made them partners. I'd made a lot with them, and I could give them something.

"Owning these mail order companies was an invaluable experience. I could finance and fulfill. I'd go to Canada five or six

times a year. I didn't go to Europe except maybe once a year. Perhaps four or five times, the European managers came to my office in New York. The European businesses were profitable and required, perhaps, six or seven days from me a year."

At each step, Dave used profits to create new sources of profits. "We've financed everything internally except for one major error when we went into compiling in 1974. This was Market Data Retrieval Corp. We lost money in it for three to four years. It was a real disaster. We had to go to the bank. We sold it to Houghton Mifflin in 1978. We almost broke even for all our losses in the price received. Part of the deal was getting the use, forever, of their compiled files for our business. So, we should come out all right overall."

His manner is mild. It all seems rather basic. Nothing sounds too difficult. But Dave's success would be hard for most of us to duplicate. He's very bright. Much of his effectiveness comes from what he chooses not to do, to avoid time wasting or money losing activities. He has an ability to select what to do in order of profit-priority.

His logical appraisal of list brokerage is that his survival depends on ability to produce more profits for clients from less lists bought. To do that, he found it more practical to work for fewer clients and essential to specialize. His only interest in building an organization was the add-a-specialist plan.

Dave is chairman of the board of Direct Media. He's also its specialist in Canadian lists, and in business merchandise and photography lists. "We have fewer clients but do more business per client than our competitors. For half our clients, we do 100% of their work. This is also true for Kleid and Names in the News. In one half of transactions, we're only brokers. We try hard to be specialists. Even our president, Larry Heely, is a specialist in hunting and fishing. Each of us, each in specific fields, specializes."

Clients describe Direct Media with such words as "integrity", "professionalism", "follow-through" and "honest". Growth has come far more from internal building of present clients than from new clients. And new clients have often come from new innovative projects unobtainable elsewhere.

"Our Executive Data Bank is one of the most exciting things I've done. Regional mailers badly need it. It's just starting." It includes several million executives from over fifty important business lists. It's primarily the seminar companies and financial institutions. It's possible to mail top executives (within a hundred and fifty miles of Atlanta, or wherever) from these important buyer lists, all merged and de-duped.

Dave sees an accelerating trend toward more and more data bases. "Data bases will occur in the consumer field, particularly to aid dealer programs. R.L. Polk and Metro Media have data bases. Eastman Kodak has put one together. The air conditioning people are into household data bases for sampling people. We worked on one for Noxell-Noxema for a denture cleaner. This was a data base of health and beauty conscious people."

In 1981, Direct Media launched a new division, Blue Chip Lists. Blue Chip only handled lists of purchases of a unit of sale of $50 or more. Kathy Duggan Jones is manager.

Another activity of Direct Media is representing co-op insert programs. "Jody Jaines is in charge of our package insert programs. They represent ten percent of our business. The economics of inserts are very different. A print run of two million inserts can run $7 to $8 per thousand. A print run of 25,000 will run $40. Of course, it takes time to insert. Fifty thousand inserts may take a year to insert. It needs very tight control. It's a terrific buy but ties up money for a longer period."

Direct media has kept growing, through good and bad

economic periods. "We've been through four recessions. In each case, for most clients response drops. Some go under. But we worked hard for each client to get better than average results by more scientific list selection to survive and succeed. Overall, clients have prospered. Direct media is still growing. Our problem is getting more good, qualified account executives."

Note: Dave Florence has answered the following questions I have asked for readers, based on his experience in the list business and as a mail order business owner.

Q. *What qualities do you seek in account executives?*

A. In the fields of servicing direct marketers, an understanding of the problems of direct marketing is needed. But to succeed as a salesman in any business, it is necessary to understand the problems of customers. Some in the service field for direct marketing are superb at it.

Alger, Horatio, Jr.'s Popular Juvenile Books for Boys.

12mo., cloth. Illustrated.
6786 **Ragged Dick Series.** 12mo., cloth.
Ragged Dick.
Fame and Fortune.
Mark, the Match Boy.
Rough and Ready.
Ben, the Luggage Boy.
Rufus and Rose.
Set of six volumes.............................$5.25
Single volumes, each.............................88
6787 **Tattered Tom Stories.** 12mo., cloth. **First Series.**
Illustrated.
Tattered Tom.   Phil the Fiddler.
Paul the Peddler.   Slow and Sure.
Set of four volumes.............................$3.50
Single volumes, each.............................88
6788 **Tattered Tom Stories.** 12mo., cloth. **Second Series.**
Illustrated.
Julius.   Sam's Chance.
The Young Outlaw.   The Telegraph Boy.
Set of four volumes.............................$3.50
Single volume, each.............................88
6789 **Campaign Series.** 12mo., cloth. Illustrated.
Frank's Campaign.   Paul Prescott's Charge.
                         Charles Codman's Cruise.
Set of three volumes.............................$2.50
Single volumes, each.............................88
6790 **Luck and Pluck Series.** 12mo., cloth. **First Series.**
Illustrated.
Luck and Pluck   Strong and Steady.
Sink or Swim.   Strive and Succeed.
Set of four volumes.............................$3.50
Single volumes, each.............................88
6791 **Luck and Pluck Series.** 12mo., cloth. **Second Series.**
Illustrated.
Try and Trust.   Risen from the Ranks.
Bound to Rise.   Herbert Carter's Legacy.
Set of four volumes.............................$3.50
Single volume, each.............................88
6792 **Brave and Bold Series.** 12mo., cloth. Illustrated.
Brave and bold.   Shifting for Himself.
Jack Ward   Wait and Hope.
Set of four volumes.............................$3.50
Single volumes, each.............................88

Q. *What qualifications are needed to succeed as a mail order entrepreneur?*

A. What is needed for success in mail order is intelligence, a product idea and a feeling for merchandising it, plus a feel for numbers.

Q. *Do you recommend direct marketing for young people starting out? In a mail order venture? In a career?*

A. Direct marketing is a great entrepreneurial opportunity. It's a great career. It's still not as hotly competitive as a career as elsewhere.

Q. *How about for women?*

A. There is more opportunity for women in direct marketing than practically any field anywhere in the world.

Q. *What courses have you taken that particularly helped you? What do you recommend?*

A. I've taken writing courses, public speaking courses, statistics and accounting. I took 2 to 3 courses in accounting. I suggest that anyone starting out in direct mail try such courses. For accounting, just one basic course is enough. I disagree with most on the value of more specialized courses. Almost everything else is not practical.

Q. *What helped you learn most about direct marketing and the list business? What about the books and other publications?*

A. I learned all along the way from others. I learned from the big and the small. My clients and I learned together. I read all the books, magazines and newsletters. I bought the Bob Stone book. We still have it and lend it. I bought the Hubert Simon book.

Q. *In business to business mail order what has worked best in recent years?*

A. The biggest area in the publishing field is in newsletters and books. Marty Edelson had a tremendous success with his Board Room newsletter.

Q. *In all mail order what kinds of mail order businesses have done particularly well?*

A. There's a trend to catalogs. Dozens of small companies have succeeded. A miniature doll house store in Chicago has succeeded. The key is the average order. Most success stories are the $90 to $100 items.

Q. *How do you compare mail order opportunities in the consumer vs. the business field?*

A. There are many more new consumer companies than new business product companies.

Q. *Is more capital required for a business products catalog? And how much is needed to launch one?*

A. In the business field, items are always sold on open account. To start a business product catalog and finance receivables, you need at least $500,000. Of course, many start with less than that, but with few items. If items are hot enough, they can succeed. Some get financing from banks. But a lot of banks don't understand.

Q. *How many names are rented each year by direct mail advertisers? Compiled? Non-compiled?*

A. Ed Burnett has estimated 2.3 billion consumer compiled names rented a year. Our company does 600 million names a year. We don't do anywhere near 25% of the business. I think that compiled consumer names amount rented should be four to six billion names. I think non-compiled consumer names should be five to ten billion a year. Ed's figures looked good for business names.

Q. *How many lists are there?*
A. We maintain files on 5,000 lists. 99% are not compiled. Probably, two to three thousand lists are really active. And we cover all logical, substantial consumer and business mail order buyer lists.

Q. *How many compiled lists are there?*
A. A lot less than listed in various directories. There are ten quasi-compilers. Each offers 500 lists. One compiles a list and sells to the others. Each then sells everybody else the same compiled lists.

Q. *How have buyer lists rental rates gone up over the last 20 years vs. those for compiled lists?*
A. Buyer list rental rates per M have doubled over the last 20 years overall, excluding high ticket gift lists. These are much higher now but scarcely existed then. Compiled list rental costs per M doubled in the same period, but for the biggest users probably only went up 20%.

Q. *How do you compare the pulling power of consumer buyer lists and compiled names?*
A. I've rarely run into an instance that somebody didn't do better using consumer buyer names than consumer compiled names.

Q. *Is the use of compiled consumer names going up or down?*
A. I think mass compilers of consumer names are doing less volume than years ago.

Q. *How do computer printing costs compare with traditional printing vs. a few years ago?*
A. Computer costs are lower. Printing costs have gone up less than inflation. Traditional printing is still cheaper for equivalent pieces than computer printing.

Q. *Are you concerned about government regulation of direct marketing?*
A. A lot of what government wants is good. Fighting government is more profitable for those paid to do it than for direct marketers.

Note: Direct Media, Inc. and List Management Inc. are located at 90 South Ridge Street, Port Chester, NY 10573. Their telephone numbers are (914) 937-5600 and (914) 937-4410 respectively.

Steam Trains.

24761 Weeden Steam Locomotive, Tender and Passenger Car, with jointed track on wooden sleepers. Diameter of track, 3½ feet, locomotive, 8 inches long; car and tender in proportion. Put up in wooden box. Weight, 4 lbs. Price, for train complete $3.50

Chapter 9
Developing Print Media For Direct Marketers

From catalogs to solo mailings

John Blair, Inc. started in radio, made its first profits in TV . . . and does the big majority of its volume in printing . . . with a big ever-growing share of it to direct marketers.

Blair owns 3 TV and 2 radio stations. It sells advertising for 125 radio stations and 48 TV stations. It's the biggest sales company representing radio stations and close to the biggest representing TV stations. It's a bigger and bigger commercial printer.

Broadcast profits funneled into high technology printing facilities—plus the Blair flair to develop print media as successfully as broadcast—has created over $200,000,000 a year in sales. The media mix of over $12,000,000 a year in profits (after tax) and of soaring growth with a heavy emphasis on helping direct marketers has proved irresistible to Wall Street—where Blair is listed on the New York Stock Exchange.

Blair bought and combined into its Graphics Group three big printers. It moved into a world of new hybrid media . . . of swiftly changing technology . . . of fast growing direct marketing as the key to fast growth of printing sales and profits.

The marriage of direct mail and publication advertising produced full, double and multi-page ads with return postcard attached in magazines. It resulted in free standing postcard stock inserts, in pre-print sections of two to sixteen and more pages, even of envelopes with solo or co-op mailing pieces—all delivered in newspapers. These formats were designed by, for and with direct marketers. Ever since, Blair has been there participating, pioneering and sometimes leading.

Much of the new print technology that Blair raced against competition to buy and create was specially valuable to direct marketers. Today, Blair's biggest printing subsidiary, The Alden Press, makes a billion printing impressions a year, mostly for mail order people.

The DMMA defines couponing as a form of direct marketing because each coupon can be keyed, redemptions can be calculated and traced to individual ads or mailings and pulling power of each couponing can be compared. Blair is big in couponing. Blair publishes a newspaper supplement of coupon offers (with some mail order ads). It has no editorial but is read by more people and is bigger in advertising volume than most magazines in the world. In 1981, Blair started a program called Prime Families Direct mailing coupon offers to 18 million homes.

Today much of Blair's business is manufacturing tools for direct marketers. These range from perfumed ink mailing pieces to invisible ink flyers. In some sweepstakes you have to scratch a square on a brochure. Then words appear which tell you if you're entitled to win or already have won a prize. While Blair's big thrust is developing print media for direct marketers, it's selling more and more TV commercial time to direct marketers. And each year, what Blair has on the drawing board in new print technology is so proprietary, it does not give details—only that it will save money for and save time for and be more effective for direct marketers.

John Blair started in 1933 as a small firm of radio station advertising representatives. Low cost radio sets had just created mass audience radio. Selling time to national advertisers was not yet mass audience radio. A radio time salesman was a pioneer. And it was the depths of the depression. At first, Blair represented good stations—but not stations in biggest markets and not the top station in a market. But Blair was a very competent sales rep firm.

In the late 1940's, Jack Fritz, now president of Blair, called on Huber Hoge and Sons Advertising. The audience, power and time sales of its stations were increasing. Blair was adding stations. Radio was the TV of that time, but TV was starting.

In 1948, Blair set up a separate organization, Blair TV— initially representing the TV stations of the owners of its radio stations. These first VHF TV stations proved goldmines for owners. Each became a Rock of Gibraltar in its market. Almost all were in major, although not the top several, markets. Blair was in on the ground floor. They were highly profitable to represent.

As TV stations multiplied and proliferated into smaller markets, Blair set up a separate organization, Blair TV Associates, to represent TV stations in smaller markets including UHF stations.

At the same time, possibly more than any other representative company, it grasped the impact of TV on radio station listening habits. The radio network program audience gradually faded away, day and evening, with soap operas clinging on longest. Older listeners were more loyal to network programs. Younger listeners wanted something else and John Blair knew what it was—top 40 hit records repeated as frequently as possible. Blair recommended this type for most of its stations. For stations which followed Blair programming recommendations, ratings soared.

Soon, in almost every market, a Blair station was the number one in audience. Each charged accordingly for its advertising which made Blair the biggest radio representative, as Blair added still more stations.

With TV and these abrupt audience changes, many radio station owners still operating in the traditional way were confused. Many felt the time of easy money was over and only wanted out. No one knew what would happen or which stations could survive in any market. There was big money then in acquiring at a low price a traditionally programmed station which had lost its audience—and reprogramming it the Blair way.

Blair knew which stations were for sale and had strong opinions as to how to program and run a radio station to survive and succeed. When Blair had a chance to buy a station at a bargain, it did. Blair tried out its theories with its own money. Its own station became a demonstration model for stations Blair represented in other cities. It also made Blair a bundle. Blair bought other stations and, each time, found success.

In time, Blair bought TV stations which, in turn, prospered. Blair became a growth company with exciting earnings. It went public. Growth and earnings kept jumping. It was cash heavy. But to buy more broadcasting stations would be to compete with stations Blair represented.

A corporate decision was then made to stay in media but diversify beyond broadcasting, to invest in and operate companies in the printing and direct mail areas. This has brought them into dealing with mail order firms and direct marketers on an ever-growing scale.

In 1945, Blair purchased American Printers and Lithographers run by Bud Lefton. AP&L was then sixty years old. It had always made money and was very well run. Wally Weinruf was president and principal owner—and sold it when he was a sick man with cancer. Bud Lifton was the number two man. Since then, Bud Lifton has run AP&L for Blair. His management ability gave Blair's new Graphics Division the strength, stability and respect to build further on. He also had ideas on other desireable acquisitions in the printing field.

In 1966, Blair bought the Alden Press, web offset catalog printers. It was also a successful company and as old as AP&L. Jerry Spier was with Alden, in sales. Jerry became president under Blair ownership. Jerry Spier was very farsighted. He saw direct marketing as one very big opportunity. He foresaw the coming triumph of the web press. He decided which way to go, what was needed—what equipment, what talent to take advantage of and the priorities. Web printing had been growing fast for 10 years. Jerry knew this growth was about to explode.

Jack Fritz saw the entire Graphics Group as a media opportunity. He recognized Bud Lifton and Jerry Spier as very able and backed them up in every way. The first step was to finance bigger presses for expected expanded volume, particularly for direct marketers. The emphasis was on bigger, faster web presses.

Then Blair found an opportunity. It bought City News Printing, a printing conglomerate which included Meehan-Tooker Printing, Springer-Tooker-Wayne and Stevens Direct Mail Marketing. It then bought FALA Mailmen (run by Lee Epstein) from Ted Bates and combined Stevens and FALA together. Stevens Direct Mail had a joint venture with Young & Rubicam. It was a co-op mailing called the Golden Envelope which went to 20,000,000 homes.

Now Blair had two solid printing companies and Meehan-Tooker, another sound one. But along with M-T, as a bonus, it had acquired a tangle of activities in printing and fulfillment. Only untangling and dissecting them could determine which should be kept, expanded, sold or closed . . . which fitted and which did not.

Jack Fritz felt that Blair should build and stick with printing activities that were part of a media concept—and to get out of activities which were not, such as the lettershop business of Stevens Direct Marketing. First it was decided to give it a go. Acquiring FALA was possibly advantageous. It was a bargain. It had lost money for Ted Bates. But combined with Stevens, a merged, bigger lettershop might make it. The object was a turn-around.

In 1970, Bob Hemm, who was sales manager of TV for 28 stations for John Blair, was given the job of getting into Stevens Direct Marketing and analyzing and reorganizing certain of its activities. Bob had started with Blair in 1956.

"I had no real knowledge of mail order. For our TV stations, I had worked with some TV mail order accounts. I had to study an entire new world." Blair had already sold off one division of Meehan-Springer, Tooker & Wayne—and one other subsidiary. Particularly, Blair hoped to make the combination of FALA Mailmen and Steven Direct Marketing work.

"I was 40 years old when I switched from TV to direct mail. It was a good move and all new to me. It gave me a completely different view of mail order. The vast bulk of TV advertising was *not* mail order but consumer advertising urging people to go to a retailer. TV commercials for mail order were then confined to times with little audience. Long pitches pulled. But in direct mail, the biggest advertisers were mail order people and the biggest growth opportunity was to increase business done with mail order people.

"To master all this, coming out of TV, I threw myself violently into it. I had to buy a little humility. I had been successful in selling TV time. A lot of things I had experienced applied. A lot didn't. Before—in TV—I had to know the agency and station way of functioning. Now the terms and technical background were different. In TV, mail order was then a very small factor. In Stevens Direct Marketing, 95% of the customers were direct marketers.

"Before, I had had only broadcast experience. Now I had to broaden my background. I was on the periphery. I had a lot to learn. I never did get involved in mastering the technology. Instead, I took a crash course, strictly internally, to learn everything I could about the business. I talked to everyone. I worked a lot of nights to catch up. I always attended the DMMA Conferences where I had a chance to meet with customers, get to know and learn more from them. There's nothing like knowing the customers. We had very innovative and creative ones. I met everyone of them I could.

"Milt Stevens had started in the compiled list business. He got into the lettershop business and then in the co-op mailing business. The Golden Envelope was a huge undertaking. We joint ventured it with Y&R Direct, a subsidiary of the Young & Rubicam advertising agency. It was a pretty good venture for a while, depending on the lists used. The Xerox list did well but petered out. The Golden Envelope contained coupons and sold about the same mail order advertisers as Donnelley did. The lists used were families with three or more children. Eventually, we dropped the Golden Envelope. Profits were marginal.

"We combined Stevens Direct Mail and FALA into one company, Blair Mail Marketing. We began to build up the mailing end of the business. As I got deeper into other activities, I turned over management of the lettershop more and more to the fulfillment people, who were quite capable. Fulfillment is not my business—and in the end did not seem to fit ours. Our concept is of direct mail as media. Fulfillment is service. We do fulfillment as a service in our printing businesses, from where we print. But in 1977, we sold the lettershop to La Salle Mailing.

"Since 1972, for years I had been largely concerned with another venture, John Blair Marketing. We started John Blair Marketing to sell inserts. We got into selling inserts because we had been printing inserts for groups selling them. We could see the growth. One company we printed inserts for went bankrupt. We took on the sales force. We slowly but surely got started ourselves, redesigned the program and made it a major business. We also placed solo free-standing inserts and pre-prints for individual advertisers in newspapers acting as space representatives. In all cases, a Blair Graphics company did the printings to insure security. But John Blair Marketing was solely concerned with dealing with newspapers and advertisers.

"Newspaper free-standing inserts and pre-prints have been quite profitable for mail order people. Prior to the late 60's, there was a problem inserting them in papers. The Philipsburg inserting machines had been necessary to make insert programs possible in envelopes. The Sheridan Stuffer made newspaper freestanding inserts and pre-prints possible, which proved tremendously profitable for mail order people. It can handle bigger insert material than a Philipsburg, as it was originally designed to handle newspaper sections and supplements. It came in during the late 1960's. Each paper handling inserts usually has one or more. We're heavy into inserts and pre-prints for papers.

"In 1972, John Blair Marketing launched Sunday X-tra. It was like the Golden Envelope but in newspapers instead of via direct mail. For both, we used Philipsburg inserting machines.

Their standard machine can drop as few as six pieces in an envelope. There are also 12 to 14 station machines. Two Philipsburgs are glued together. Then, to get 24 to 28 insert pieces in an envelope, two passes can be made with the machine."

For Sunday X-tra there were 12 to 13 inserts in the envelope for different advertisers. "We put 15 million envelopes in one day in Sunday papers. At first, it paid off, but the potential risks were greater than the rewards. Results then fell off. It still pulls profitably in smaller markets. Now it's only in C&D Markets, is all mail order and is three to five million per drop.

"Then John Blair Marketing found a big payoff, a couponing insert supplement—with no editorial. It consists of coupons and ads for coupons, except for remnant space—bought by mail order people." Couponing, inserts and supplements are very suited to me. The selling problems and opportunities are comparable to selling other forms of advertising. It's based on its competitive cost per thousand. It's an advertising promotion medium selling to many of the same advertisers who buy TV time.

"We started in November 1975. It's now a big operation. We pay heavily to the papers to distribute. We have 34 million circulation. We run 21 times a year. Insert programs in direct mail and in publications are growing. Couponing is growing and each couponing insert program also causes some mail order. In 1976, we were equal to any in it and we've been growing faster since—in five years, about 450%.

"Research studies have shown that Blair coupon inserts are noted, seen and associated 30% more than women's magazines, Reader's Digest, TV Guide or Parade. Coupons or direct marketers can split test, market by market—in full color. They can expand to over 100 metropolitan newspapers covering about two-thirds of the top 357 markets.

"Our newspaper inserts are effective in varied places. We have the same range of mail order advertising offers as in R.O.P. newspapers or in Parade and Family Weekly. Space size ranges from a full page, 9" by 11", to a 3½" by 2¼" space. Initially, we played with our own mail order items to use as filler. We don't do it now. We have some leftover space we prefer to sell at remnant rates rather than to use as filler space for our own offers.

"The use of insert programs, taking small to page space in coupon inserts in newspapers, is still a medium not fully tested by mail order people. It's a further diversification of direct marketing. We suggest testing at least 500,000 circulation. It's possible to further break this amount of circulation down to test formats and copy. You can test smaller cities such as Raleigh and Albany for this.

"Using insert programs scientifically takes a certain procedure. The creative people for direct marketers need to get into it more deeply. Just as for direct mail sales, the most sophisticated mail order users may test four or five packages, key results and then project. Some direct marketers haven't done inserts as seriously as solos. The best results are obtained by those specializing in such tests.

"I was in broadcast media. Now I'm in graphics media. Each Blair company falls into a category, is a teacher of its differences and is an individual profit center. Each Blair company has its own area and its own problems, but primarily, is creating sales for an advertising medium.

"We develop new direct mail media based on what we learn from our clients. We find out what they need, what ideas they have, what they want to publicize and promote in what ways. Direct mail is a business of constant new developments. Exciting new things keep being done. Often, new equipment makes a new development possible. Pop-up was quite a fad. But it's still pretty expensive. We're always experimenting with and watching something.

"We have tried some small mail order ventures. We published a book or two. We've worked for book publishers. Sometimes, you think you can get into someone else's business. But almost always you find it better to stick to your own. We did. But we're flexible. We work in a lot of directions.

"I'm interested in the new kinds of media improvements constantly being developed in direct mail for mail order people and direct marketers. One is the self-formed envelope in inserts. This is for mail order people who need to pull cash or a check. It pulls quite well. Right now it's going through a second renaissance. It's for larger people, looks good and we'll know more in several months.

"Alden Press and Meehan-Tooker are mostly web. American Printers and Litho-Graphers have more sheet-fed presses. But they're very innovative, using newer, three-dimensional sheet-fed presses.

"Alden Press makes about 50% to 60% of its sales to direct marketers. They are all big. There are very few big direct marketers or catalog houses we don't get into. Many of our customers do direct marketing as part of their activities, almost on the side. Since Blair bought the printing business, sales volume has increased considerably. The number of printing impressions a year is way up. We have more presses. Growth has been consistent.

"Most Alden Press production has been of mail order catalogs and of department store catalogs selling by mail order. Much of the remainder is printing for direct marketing. Alden Press can run 4 to 200 pages and from 4" x 6" to jumbo sizes.

"The Alden Press specializes in full-color catalog printing and mailing. It's deep into laser printing. On one continuous line are micro processors—laser and laser scanning. Catalogs go on press and in one press are machine printed, stitched, bound, put in a mailing bag and addressed; then they are sent to the post office according to postal service mailing priority sequence. The Alden computerized sorting system can get 3% to 7% more catalogs delivered by the post office, and gets quicker delivery, too.

"Other Blair plants can combine traditional and laser printing. One continuous press can print and personalize any or all of a solo's contents. It can form the envelope, insert all material, address and sort for zip coding—and then drop in post office bags to send to the post office.

"About 40% of sales of American Printers & Lithographers are to direct marketers for pre-printed magazine inserts, catalogs and direct response formats. It can print on plastic. It can make plates. It does its own binding. It handles sheet sizes from 11" to 77".

Meehan-Tooker is a large plant in New Jersey. Its sales are about 65% to direct marketers. In 1979, M-T bought the first Super Web press in the U.S. This press is German made, a Kaubau S-50, and is 42" wide. It operates at 1600 feet per minute and produces 25,000 32-page or 50,000 16-page signatures an hour. It has an ink-film metering system and automatic color adjusting. Meehan-Tooker also has sheet-fed, full color printing. For direct marketers it prints self-mailers, catalogs, preprints and solos. It prints inserts of the type in TV Guide, in huge volume.

When the printing companies were acquired, most of the management was kept intact. But Blair is an organization of, and believer in, salesmen. They have hired sales management people with a great deal of know-how.

Changing technology has made printing a capital intensive business. Some printers calculate that it takes one dollar of investment in equipment for each two dollars of additional annual sales. Since acquiring its printing business, Blair has made big broadcast profits—with an ideal place to employ them. It has proved a great mix. As a result, its printing companies now have 38 of the biggest, most modern presses, with latest bells and whistles.

Dollars put into latest technology printing equipment could be better than money in the bank, a hedge against inflation. The equipment could be written off and continued to be used. It would be possible to trade up equipment. The race to get latest equipment and then get maximum use and benefit from it would be won by the management which most thoroughly and rapidly investigated each possibility. The cost of doing so could be in pre-tax dollars. More recently, printing profits have been making it possible to buy broadcast properties.

In 1981, Blair went back into big scale direct mail inserts with Prime Families Direct, a direct mail co-op program to 18 million families with $26,500 and above estimated income and at least one child at home. It was mailed spring and fall, 80% in top 100 markets. It used a big 8" x 11" format, double normal size for envelope inserts.

"With our three present printing companies, we're the biggest or second biggest in commercial printing. This excludes biggest catalogs, magazines and books. Anyone with a press can be called a printer, including any copy print store. However, mail order people using volume printing go to more sophisticated, bigger printers. Web keeps getting more used. For big presses certain set-up charges are about the same for smallest or far bigger runs. Web, in particular, requires volume. But there are specialty web presses for shorter runs.

"It isn't all price that determines the best printers to use. Price is one factor. And the same printer is not always consistently lower or higher or the same in price as another. You might catch some printer with down time. Some printers would then break even or lose to keep the press running. That's the law of competition. At any time, for any job, for any reason, one printer may want the business more and underbid others.

"There has been inflation of ad cost for all media. Cost of paper more than doubled between 1975 and 1981. It has never been a minor factor in overall cost of a printing job; it's now far more major. Direct mail survives despite the tremendous increases in postage, and recently in paper, because of printing technology. There are more printing impressions per hour. The same press that got 20,000 impressions five or six years ago now gets 35,000 impressions per hour.

"The Blair Graphics Group has recently been reorganized into the Sheet Fed Division, with Bud Lipton as president, and The Web Division, with Jerry Spier as president. They have far more technological background than I do. But technological change is coming so fast and is so important competitively that we can't talk in too great detail of upcoming change at our plants. It's proprietary. But these changes will be most important in quality and in price to our customers. They will further help mail order people and direct marketers to use direct mail profitably.

"We will contribute in these ways to making mail order use of direct mail more profitable despite more general inflation. But our major contribution will, we hope, be in continuing to find, create and develop new and more effective forms of direct mail for direct marketers."

They must be doing something right. In 1981, John Blair sales were $265,303,000 up 20% over 1980. Net earnings were $13,637,000; up 17% over 1980. In the final quarter sales jumped

41% and net earnings 38% over 1980. In January, 1982, top money-fund manager Scott M. Black recommended John Blair stock as an investment.

Note: The Blair Graphics Companies and John Blair Marketing are located at 717 Fifth Avenue, New York, NY 10022; (212) 980-5252. Plants are in Chicago, Long Island and New Jersey.

Chapter 10
The Tall Ships

*The race to sell prints
before late becomes too late.*

In June 1976, my brother, Hamilton Hoge, brought over to the house we shared in Southampton, Long Island, an old friend . . . Kipp Soldwedel. We were discussing the upcoming July 4th gathering of tall ships in New York Harbor. All his life, Kipp had been a sailor and painter of sailing ships. He knew the famous sailing ships as few did. He had been a guest on some and served on the crew of others in the Bermuda races, or whatever.

To Kipp, each ship in the gathering was an old friend. He had painted almost all of them individually and in groups, some several times. He had just painted the gathering of tall ships in Bermuda and then at Newport, Rhode Island. All his life, Kipp had painted for a big fee or a royalty on prints sold, but now he had seen his chance. He had chosen this time to invest in making his own prints. He and my brother, Hamilton, were discussing a possible joint venture to sell them more widely by mail. Too late . . . that's what I told Kipp and my brother, Ham.

My brother had great faith in Kipp and in the prints. His 19-year-old son, young Ham, got interested. Together they organized a venture to hire street hawkers to sell the prints on July 4th. They got the rights to sell them on the ferry boats turned cruisers for the day.

July 4th was beautiful. The gathering was overwhelmingly successful but for Ham and his son the sale of prints proved a disaster. The ferry boats were so overcrowded they did not get off the shore. The crowds everywhere were so dense it was impossible to even hold up the prints much less sell them. Entire cartons of prints were stolen off the backs of trucks rented for the day. The venture had been a substantial loss.

My brother kept his faith in Kipp and the Tall Ships prints. Kipp had painted The New York Gathering. He kept painting the individual ships. He kept investing in the manufacture of more prints. At his expense, he ran a small ad in a Providence, Rhode Island, paper and reported that he had a mail order success.

The peak of the bicentennial was over. Why should mail order pay out after the big event? That a Tall Ship print offer could be a big success didn't make sense to me. My brother's background was in electronics. He had never been in mail order. Kipp Soldwedel was an artist. True, he had been an art director for J. Walter Thompson Advertising Agency. He had even had some engineering background. But artists were not supposed to be businessmen.

Reluctantly, and very much from Missouri, I arranged the first test ad for my brother of Kipp's prints. Huber Hoge and Sons placed a remnant ad at 50% off rate in The National

Observer for my brother's company, American-Ajax, a moonlighting venture. Ham never had any doubts. The $417 ad made $1,720 in profit—after costs of merchandise bought from Kipp and after cost of advertising, mailing costs and allowance for possible returns. He felt vindicated but not surprised.

It was arranged that Kipp would continue to advertise on his own, would sell the retail trade as before, would sell special markets such as banks, but that the bulk of the mail order would be done by American-Ajax, for whom Huber Hoge and Sons would be the advertising agency.

For a re-test, I determined to buy several publications at full rates . . . The Christian Science Monitor, The Louisville Courier, and the New York Times. Each paid out. For each dollar of advertising cost, there was more than a dollar of profit . . . after advertising, merchandise, shipping costs and allowance for possible returns. This was the classic objective. We spent several thousand dollars more and again confirmed. Results were remarkably steady and uniform.

So far, the ad tested was approximately the size of a one-third page in a standard magazine like Time. I wanted to test this size further and try a size the equivalent of a full page in Time. Ham and Kipp were pushing for expansion and eager to try the Wall Street Journal in which black and white prints of sketches of the Tall Ships had already been successfully sold by mail order. I was afraid that each day, each week after the July 4th gathering that response would drop and perhaps suddenly, at any time. It seemed treacherous. Ham and Kipp still had no doubts . . . and they were right.

Then a further test of the first size ad run in the New York Post appeared to be a loser. Perhaps it *was* too late to project. We had scheduled the equivalent of the one-third-page ad in Time in two editions of the Wall Street Journal. Warned by the bad results of the Post, I wanted to cancel the test of the page-size ad. My son, Cecil, and Ham wanted to proceed with the test. We did, and they were right.

First, other advertisers in the New York Post were reporting poor results in that issue. But then orders from the Post ad kept dribbling in until there was no loss. Meanwhile, the Wall Street Journal was a smash hit for the smaller ad and a bonanza for the bigger one. The impact of this was great. Now we could hope to buy ads with up-front position. We could find remnant buys usually far more available in page-size. We could achieve volume. It was time to move.

Now, I felt, was the time to expand. We decided to spend $50,000 on the next projection. It was a race. Almost all October issues and some November issues had closed and December was too late. But we put almost all of the $50,000 into the quickest closing dates. We got into issues past closing date not just within days, but within hours and even minutes of final, final closing. We kept some money for more tests in newspapers.

The weekly news magazines had quickest closing. We got a remnant page in Time at 35% off. It turned out to be on the page facing third cover. It was 84% of the circulation. This one ad sold over $100,000 of prints. Mostly, we had bought one-third pages. For a one-third page in U.S. News, we got the Table of Contents page—page two. Results were fantastic. We kept buying and, by Christmas, had spent over $125,000 with greater and greater success. What was going on?

America had taken the Bicentennial to its heart. The shame and humiliation of Watergate had made it very important for each of us to go back to our roots. The Bicentennial gave us back our pride. And the tall ships proved telegenic, photogenic, nostalgic, prideful and universal in appeal.

Washable Sailor. **Washable Sailor**

30946 Zouave Suits, fine navy blue flannel, front trimmed with neat black braid and small black buttons, buttons to match on cuffs. 3 to 7 years. Each.................................$2.50
30948 Zouave Suits, dark green corduroy, small button trimmings on front and cuffs, knees trimmed with silk ribbon, buckle and small button; an excellent suit. 3 to 7 years. Each...... 2.75

On TV, the tall ships were sailing across every screen. The National Geographic devoted 30 pages to them. The New York Daily News had a special issue on them. The Smithsonian ran 12 pages and, a month later, our one-third page produced the most fabulous profits of any magazine, to date, in relation to rate.

It was a time Kipp Soldwedel had been preparing for all his life. He was the right man in the right place. Here, past retirement age, he was catapulted into business success on a bigger scale than ever. The print stores were buying from him. The banks were offering his prints in their lobbies as a service to depositors. Kipp was selling mail order. And our ads were increasing each form of sales for him.

The problem was . . . how long would all this last? When would the inevitable drop off come? How sharp would it be? There were certain advantages to the situation. The professionals were like me. They assumed that the party was over. Ham and Kipp believed in the prints and that sales would continue. The competition was principally non-experts who weren't about to run on the scale we now had in mind.

There were three dangers. The first was that the offer would fall off or even die, suddenly, with big losses on ads still run. The next was that the offer had maximum appeal as a Christmas offer and would not pull after the first of the year even if it would succeed the following fall. The greatest danger was competition of cheaper prints of another painting of the same ship. Another artist might simply paint from the superb photographs taken.

We decided to spend $250,000 as early as possible after the first of the year. We had somehow to cushion the risk, to buy advertising so carefully that risk was minimized. In a few cases, the publications themselves took the risk but, primarily, it was the old story of the two most important things in mail order, what you say and what you pay to say it. In this case, showing it most advantageously was all important.

The race to spend money most cautiously was underway. Kipp's paintings were superb. Just reproducing the gathering of the ships made the ad. My son, Cecil, had honed and refined the copy until it sang. We had something to sell in our negotiations in buying magazine space.

Most publishers conceded that it was the most beautiful (or close to it) black-and-white ad offered for the issue scheduled. In any magazine, the second cover is almost invariably full color and the advertiser usually most anxious that the page opposite (page 1) be black and white. We presented our case that the Tall Ships ad was the most beautiful possible black-and-white ad to run on page one and did all in our power to obtain that position. In an astonishing percentage of cases, we succeeded.

Again we raced, negotiated, begged, pleaded, persuaded and made issues long past official closings . . . again within days, hours, minutes of final closing . . . the same old story.

We went after every attractive remnant rate possible. We looked for every possible special situation. People magazine had one issue over the Christmas and New Year holidays when the special year-end issue substituted for two issues. Circulation was all newsstand. It was getting almost double newsstand sales of an average issue, for the same one-issue ad cost. We bought it.

Rates were jumping. We avoided issues just following jumps and grabbed issues just before jumps whenever a big circulation bonus existed. Smithsonian had had a fabulous circulation increase. Its ad cost jumped from $8,000 in February 1977, when we ran, to $12,000 in March.

We did all we could. We set up tests of full-color ads. We planned to stop all further buys or go even further pending results . . . which we wanted for sleeping as best we could. We had fluttery stomachs.

Who in mail order does not marvel at the speed of transition of the changing buying reactions of the seasons? For a non-Christmas offer other than a special season one, January is the golden month, the first week of January the golden week, and the first Sunday after New Year's Day the golden day. And so it was—Happy New Year!

It had been impossible to peak expenditures in that first wonderful week. There had not been the leeway. It was impossible to schedule more than a few of the magazines for January issues. Instead, it was a rolling schedule that each week pushed up momentum.

The first results came from People, a big success. Next were the January issues which got some circulation out in late December. Then the first supplements . . . The Washington Post magazine, The Los Angeles Times magazine, The New York Times magazine. On the second Sunday in January was a good chunk of Parade. The following Sunday was a full-page color test in a small portion of Family Weekly. A small segment of TV Guide ran.

Orders were pouring in. Counting the mail was becoming a job. Two things were apparent. Each ad was pulling less in proportion to cost. But each ad was making money. And volume was enormous. We decided to keep buying . . . every desirable space purchase that we could get in quickly . . . but to count the mail faster and more furiously than ever . . . and be ready to stop as soon as counts dipped further.

In February, the really big parts of our schedule were to break. And now we were piling more purchases on. We were ready for anything. We were working on TV spots and on direct mail solo pieces. American-Ajax was testing running the mail order ad with a book store under its name in its local newspaper. The plan was to be ready to expand into TV, via direct mail,

Children's Reefer Suits.

We Have All the New and Nobby Styles. Sizes, 3 to 8 Years Only.

30910   Children's Reefer Suits, jacket and knee pants; brown and gray mixed diagonal cassimere; large plain collar. Each $1.90

30912   Reefer Suits made of dark gray diagonal cassimere; 3 to 10 years: same style as above. Each.................. 2.00

30914   Reefer Suits, gray and white cassimere, mixed with black; very pretty pattern. Braided collar and cuffs. 3 to 8 years. Each............ 2.75

30916   ReeferSuits, same style as above in dark gray melton cassimere. 3 to 8 years. Each.......................... 2.75

30918   Reefer Suits, fancy brown and tan mixed cassimere; hercules braid trimming on collar and cuffs. 3 to 8 years. Each............. 3.00

Reefer Suit.

through stores. We even prepared a radio commercial to test on WQXR and other classical music stations.

But all this was assuming that the ads continued to pull and did not suddenly drop. In the middle of it all, the snow began to fall, first just a heavy drop, then a bigger than average snow, and then an enormous storm striking in the heart of the Midwest and then again in the East.

Most in mail order remember the strange and eerie effect it all had on mail counts. Through the years, the post office seems ever slower. Now one storm followed another. A postal paralysis seemed to set in.

The storm was worse in areas affecting the magazine publishing business the most. Trucking slowed and then stopped to some of the nation's biggest printers and binders of magazines. Incoming orders to mail order advertisers slowed to a trickle. Outgoing magazines with mail order ads slowed. Big portions of some issues went out days, even weeks late and then sat in post offices.

Was it just the storm or was the offer dying? Queasy stomach was a common ailment for anyone in mail order, as many recall. We didn't know the answer. We had piled up purchases until, for 1979, the Tall Ships schedule had passed $500,000. But now we stopped dead in our tracks.

Neither Kipp nor Ham were unduly disturbed. They were not familiar with the mail order patterns. Nor were either as concerned with the day-to-day mail count as I. Each had deep faith in the offer and its continuing chances.

Then Kipp taught me a lesson I will never forget. We had a $44,500 ad for American-Ajax in the March National Geographic. The issue was mailed in early February, in the storm. First orders came in such disappointing volume that a huge loss seemed inevitable.

Meanwhile, Kipp had come up with a new project—a full-page ad in color offering, instead of the single print we offered, six different prints and with a most complex coupon. Customers could buy each print in four different ways and various combinations of prints including all six at a special saving.

While I was calculating possible losses from each ad still to run, Kipp decided to test his ad on his own . . . in the National Geographic . . . in the month of May. All I knew taught me that results were going to hell, that a repeat of any form of the same basic offer would drop in results . . . above all, within sixty days, and that running a mail order ad in May would pull far less, anyway, than in January through March.

Kipp's ad ran and was unbelievably successful. The average order jumped from $20 to close to $40. It meant that we could run for American-Ajax a four-color ad with the same combination offer in many magazines we had already paid out on in black and white. But we decided to be cautious, see how the huge campaign finally came out, test in the the fall and expand very carefully. Better be safe than sorry.

Ham, too, proved to have a calmer, sounder view of results than I did. The first comforting news was the extraordinary percentage of reorders . . . first from a mimeographed reorder form, then from a simple black-and-white folder featuring six of Kipp's prints. Then carry-over from most magazines came in far longer than usual, very late mail delivery.

Results from the winter campaign, in the end, were neither as disastrous as I feared nor as good as the fall 1976 figures. January was good but not as good as the fall. February was not as good as January and March more marginal than February. There were some bad busts. Results were more inconsistent. But, overall, all January made money, February made money, and even March made money—a soft landing.

It did take month after month of carryover through the long spring, summer and even the following fall to do it. But the National Geographic March issue ended by not losing money. Even the small miscellaneous counts not keyed to any publication built up as an extra cushion.

Kipp's color ad, when tested for American-Ajax, did pull successfully, but not always. In Americana magazine, in November of 1977, results were exceptionally good. A color mailing to the American-Ajax list offering a wider selection of Kipp's prints was extremely successful. More magazines made money in the fall of '77 and in January, February and March of 1978. But overall results were dropping for the color ad for sales in relation to ad cost.

The offer was finally getting ready to go to bed. In all, between American-Ajax and Kipp, considerable money had been made. It had all been very exciting. My brother, Ham had his 70th birthday in the fall of 1976. Few men I have ever known have his youthful enthusiasm, vitality and faith. American-Ajax continued to sell prints, Kipp's and those of others.

Kipp is more productive as a painter than ever and has continued to be a businessman. He keeps coming up with new paintings, making new prints and creating new ways to sell his prints. There is a continuing sale of Kipp's old and new prints to the print stores, wholesalers, catalogs, premium houses, banks and whatever. Kipp is apt to fly to Australia one week. to get things going there, to his old haunts in Palm Beach the next, or anywhere. Mostly, he's in his Park Avenue studio painting, planning and selling mail order.

For years the American-Ajax list brought in list rentals. Ham sold other prints. Both Ham and Kipp have many interests. Neither Ham nor Kipp will surprise me if either phones me next week and says, "We've got a new winner. It's ready to go national and let's get started."

To readers, one caution: "A bicentennial comes once every two hundred years."

Chapter 11
Selling Magazine Subscriptions By Mail Order

A master teacher tells how.

If you'd like to learn how to do this . . . for the smallest magazine or newsletter (and apply lessons to any mail order) . . . Wendell Forbes can help you. He is a Time Inc. graduate, a great teacher-boss who has trained many, and a top consultant to publishers.

The Ivy League university of Fortune 500 mail order is Time Inc. It attracts great talent, often for life. There are in this book more stories of successes of Time alumni than those of any other company. Time alumni are an informal club. A club within a club comprises those taught by Wendell Forbes.

Larry Crutcher is corporate vice president of circulation at Time Inc. He says: "Scattered around Wall Street, the fashion business, book publishing, pay TV . . . everywhere is Wendell Forbes' personal 'alumni association'. We owe Wendell a debt of gratitude for teaching us not just about direct mail techniques . . . but about ourselves, our surroundings, and how to understand."

Bill Willett, vice president of Avon Products, founded Avon Fashions which does $100,000,000 a year in sales. He was trained at Time by Wendell Forbes. He says: "Wendell is a great teacher. He always had a stable of trainees. He was a recruiter and groomer. He would bring in college juniors each summer. He was always working with two or three trainees."

Sandy Clark is the owner of the Clark Direct Marketing Agency. He says: "I was one of many young people he was always training from scratch. He gave us much freedom but expected each to develop ourselves and our job . . . and to do so with each promotion to a new job."

"Chip" Block is publisher of Games magazine. He says: "As a magazine subscription marketing consultant, Wendell Forbes is the best in the business, head and shoulders above anyone."

Wendell Forbes is considered by many top publishers to have contributed a great deal to new methods in gaining circulation more profitably; also, to have helped along the road a surprising number of those who are today close to and at the top of the magazine publishing world. He has even given editors some pretty good advice.

Today there are almost nine thousand different magazines, and probably two times as many newsletters. Every year the number of each grows. Despite mortality, a surprising percentage is started by amateurs who sensed a need. Circulation is obtained overwhelmingly by mail order methods. Circulation success goes most to those who know most about publication mail order.

The biggest publishing empires constantly break in new trainees to work in subscription promotion. However talented, much of the complex world of selling and renewing subscriptions is to them a mystery. On the job training alone can be too slow. Many giant publishers send their trainees and middle management to the School of Magazine Marketing, sponsored by the Direct Mail/Marketing Association—and taught by Wendell Forbes.

Wendell Forbes can help you in a number of ways. For this book, I have asked him questions for you and he has answered them. You will like him and how he thinks as he analyzes what helped him and might help you. You can attend his seminars. There are reprints of some astute articles he has written and tapes of his lectures. All are listed in the reference source section in the back of this book. The story of his career can help.

"I started out to be a doctor but after two-thirds of a year of pre-med, joined the RCAF . . . after which, in 1945, I had different ideas . . . and studied business at the University of British Columbia. At UBC I liked statistics, literature and Gilbert and Sullivan opera. Perhaps the combination gave me a balance between business and creativity and stood me in good stead throughout my career. While at college, I also worked underground as a coal box car loader. Most days I worked double shifts.

"In May 1948, I joined Time Inc., in Canada, as a newsstand representative, to monitor the distribution of Time and Life magazines in the Vancouver area. My boss noted my inclination to make sales graphs and concluded that my interests were in the business area. In August of 1950, I was transferred to Chicago to become business manager of the agent sales division of the company.

"I had excellent training in my agency job. The function had heavy reporting ties to the New York circulation business office and from there I was instructed on a highly professional level in the art of statistical reporting and analysis. I simply learned what I had to do in order to do the job."

He moved to New York and went up the ladder at Time Inc. For 22 years, Wendell Forbes was with Time Inc. in many capacities. He spent his early years in corporate circulation, then went to Life where he became circulation manager and director. Of all the many talented circulation managers at Time Inc., his represents one of the longest runs at the job.

There is a talent to working with talent. Time Inc. was loaded with talent. Wendell Forbes could work with the word people and the numbers people. He could pull together projects, plan, coordinate and develop. He didn't take credit. He preferred to give it. This way strongest creative egos could be recruited.

Bill Willett recalls: "Wendell Forbes was a pioneer in telephone marketing. He started in the 1950's when he was assistant circulation manager of Life and also ran Life Circulation Company, which largely did telephone selling. I worked for him. Wendell was responsible for and created big volume with the beginning of telephone subscription selling by magazines.

John Collins remembers: "I came into Life Circulation Company as Wendell's assistant when he was general manager. It became Time Telemarketing—after Life suspended. In 1975, it became 'Dial America Marketing Inc.' when Bill Conway (formerly Life circulation manager) purchased it." Now 'Dial America' has over 75 telephone marketing clients and makes over 25 million phone calls a year, with over 2,000 employees and over 40 offices."

He was always happiest working with others on a one-to-one basis. He carefully avoids claims of having been the sole developer of revolutionary changes or molder of successful careers of those who trained with him, or of having been a star direct marketing executive.

Bill Willett says: "Wendell was always ahead of others as an idea man. He could visualize ahead of others problems of the future. In 1960, we tested home delivery of Life magazine. That became popular with other magazines 15 years later. He initiated 'continuing subscriber service', a sort of negative option applying book club techniques to magazines—until the Audit Bureau of Circulation ruled renewals necessary."

John Collins says: "He could look into the future and articulate in detail what to expect and what to do about it." Sandy Clark says, "He was forward looking and years ahead. He taught us the future."

Now he began to mix creative supervision of circulation advertising with list and media decisions and watching costs. "Creative judgment came easily to me because I had analyzed the results of hundreds upon hundreds of tests and I knew what worked and what didn't work. I also knew that one must be very careful about saying that a given idea won't work. At Time Inc. we had a good working relationship and interchange with creative types. I did not, however, edit copy or change layouts. The creative staff was so competent and creative management so good that they were usually ahead of me."

Wendell Forbes could apply his way of thinking derived from his mail order know-how to non-mail order problems. Bill Willett recalls: "At Life, he was strong on calculating the numbers of copies to print, more scientifically than had been done before . . . with the same methods as to project mail counts, a form of probability theory."

He kept projects simple. He gave simple names to new methods developed. Some were industry firsts. One he called a "one list" program for mass mailings. It was born of the computer. Now it is called Merge-Purge and given more complex names for each variation developed. But Wendell doesn't take credit for it so much as to admit he was there at the time it happened.

He was responsible for developing offers, approving creative work and mailing up to a hundred million pieces of direct mail each year. This was when, more and more, the emphasis began to be to get quality circulation; to go after better quality prospects who might renew longer; to give them a more effective proposal to renew. Just one renewal offer Wendell developed resulted in hundreds of thousands of long-term subscriptions and millions of dollars in advance income.

Many people have credited Wendell Forbes with something else he is equally quiet about. "We had long, long sheets of paper on which we spun out the life cycle of a block of subscriptions, both in subscription dynamics and in costs pertaining thereto. It was not an invention as much as a fact of management that became possible through the computer. We hired a mathematician named Arnold Dumy, and he did most of the early work on this system." This was in the 1950's.

The idea was to judge not simply the promotion cost to get a trial subscription but to include the renewal history for several years and then to compare the total subscription income received over this period for different lists and media used versus original promotion costs.

Now it's called Source Evaluation used by every major magazine publisher and more and more large direct marketers. Arnold Dumy did it with a computer. One project was to guestimate different future situations, cases of better and worse rates of renewal, year by year. Now this is called Computer Modeling.

Wendell Forbes is very unassuming about it all. "I have always believed in statistics and research. Several of us at Time invented Source Evaluation. We didn't call it that but that's what it was." It was a breakthrough. It led to more scientific list and media selection . . . to emphasis on quality lists and media which might have higher promotion cost for the first trial subscription but produce better renewals. It led to seeking better quality parts of lists, and segmentation. It led to longer term planning, even years instead of months, for mail order. It changed the mail order business.

"It may have been another case of re-inventing the wheel. I suspect that many other magazines were working on Source Evaluation. The venerable financial vice president at Time Inc., Mr. Charles Stillman, told me that he used to fool around with such things 20 years earlier. So it was the computer that made possible what a lot of people wanted to do."

John Collins says, "He was the first to talk about source evaluation. He promoted that study. He and Arnold Dumy were among the first to come up with a computer model for circulation." Sandy Clark recalls: "For two years their source evaluation computer study was a team effort.

"We all began to use it soon after. We could then see the value of each source of subscription and compare it with another. We could value agent-generated subscriptions and those renewed by follow-up mailing series of different numbers of letters. It changed our thinking. We saw very differently the results or our renewal series. When we jumped from 7 to 13 letters, the renewals were still more valuable than those from outside sources."

Bill Willett says, "Wendell designed the renewal series of Life first as assistant and then as circulation director. It was a custom mailing plan with over 70 different renewal letters, sent as computer research indicated. The system was quite refined and extensively revised."

Somehow, Wendell Forbes was around when some pretty exciting new developements in mail order occurred. His art was contemplation and use of statistical research to stimulate creative ideas and quiet team work with others appropriately selected to help carry them to execution.

His ability at selling magazine subscriptions led to a broader application. Wendell Forbes was made manager of New Ventures for Time-Life Books. Each project, when launched, needed management to be watched, nursed and prodded for maximum, safe growth. Each enterprise was big. Each had its own area, its own set of opportunities. He managed the International Book Society. Under Wendell, each book sold 45,000 to 65,000 copies, for up to $45. It was like selling $100 books today. Most sold more than any similar book had ever done.

He managed the Time Reading Program in which Time editors selected books. He was in on the birth and beginning growth of what is now Time-Life Records. For it, he supervised all mail promotion and developed a space sales program. It was Wendell Forbes and Francis Scott who first used plastic records tipped on to the pages of Time, Life and Sports Illustrated. The story is told elsewhere is this book.

Wendell Forbes is versatile and modest. He comes out of statistical research but disclaims deep expertise in it. "You may have me pegged wrongly. You give me too much credit for knowledge about computers, flow charts and statistics." He uses all of them, but quietly and simply . . . and each in a reasonable way, in its place. He puts such things in perspective.

He used computers from their first availability to publishers. But rather than take credit for himself or even for direct marketers as publishers, he credits the computer hardware and software industry. He takes the same position in the use of new technology of any kind.

"Computerization and new technologies have had a great impact on the publishing industry. Because magazines use services provided by others, most of the pressure for technological change has come from suppliers competing to do a better job and striving to deliver a better product or service to publishers.

"Smart publishers simply evaluated new technologies and used them as needed. For the most part, however, technological advances are offered to the publishing industry. Publishers didn't invent the computer, they just used it when it was useful to them."

"Having gone through the days of doing budgets and analysis on endless yellow pads and reams of 16-column analysis paper, I do appreciate the luxury of computer application to the publishing business. I am not really qualified to discuss the history of computers or modeling beyond saying that as the technology becomes available, most businesses are smart enough to seize upon it. If they are not, their competitors do, and they play catch-up.

"I do believe computers were oversold or overbought by business. I still feel more comfortable looking at a final analysis in typewritten form because it gives me that confidence that perhaps a human being—a thinking, bright human being—has reviewed it.

"Computers will never make final decisions. They are only an aid to the process. The human brain is not in danger of being replaced. It is, however, in danger of atrophying due to lack of use. I am not really convinced that computers can do much that humans can't. Certainly they are quick and they do churn out tons of data. But I fear they are turning out more information than we can effectively turn into knowledge and wisdom."

More than computers and technology, Wendell Forbes credits those he worked with for helping him. It was their willingness to pass along and his to learn what they knew which, he feels, gave him his chance. Finding and benefiting from the specialists which he met first at Time and then elsewhere was his main support.

"Throughout my whole career and even in my consulting work, I have been fortunate in being associated with very capable people. In my early career, I always had mentors who were interested in teaching me and I was a willing student."

He found learning this way, by demonstration, superior to learning from books. "I can't say that I studied books. I found them too general and I preferred to move from the pragmatism of the specific thing that worked into careful generalizations. Generalizations are alright for the teacher but the operator must work with specifics."

In 1970, Wendell became circulation manager of McCall's magazine. Then for Y & R Ventures, a subsidiary of Young & Rubicam Advertising Agency, he did everything from research direct mail advertising agencies to buy, to becoming part of a "think-tank" to examine for clients new communications methods. And he acted as consultant for other clients, as well.

As Wendell progressed, learning became sharing of information. He became active in the Direct Mail/Marketing Association and met and talked with more and more direct marketers outside of Time Inc. Later he became Chairman of the Board of the DMMA. "By being active in DMMA, I met a lot of people and was further immersed in the business. It was through DMMA associations that I learned much about selling thngs other than magazines by direct mail. The principles were the same. In fact, a check list of points to be included in a good magazine sales letter is the same as for books, records and other products. It is perceiving what the needs of the customer are that makes a direct mail piece work.

"Learning and exchanging information led naturally to teaching others. I have always enjoyed teaching, and I come from a family of educators. I feel a great debt to those who taught me and one way of paying it back is to teach others. Also, teaching keeps ideas and outlook young, fresh and flexible."

Wendell Forbes has taken a narrow field of mail order, magazine subscriptions, and given it an encyclopedic coverage. He is thorough, practical, plain speaking and down to earth. He covers every aspect of circulation decision making. At the School for Magazine Marketing, he makes everything clear to attendees.

He draws simple pictures to illustrate his points. He sketches three-legged stools and faucets and garden hose and simple pumps or whatever to show how circulation works in and is part of magazine publishing. Attendees work all day, each day. But before they're through, he's seen to it that they grasp the nomenclature of circulation and know a great deal about obtaining new subscriptions profitably and renewing them that they did not before.

In each seminar, in each article, Wendell talks or writes in a mild, dry fashion. There's a quiet humor, kindliness and a little philosophy thrown in. His drawings are like copywriter layouts, penciled out by a non-artist. He has a non-Madison Avenue approach, a natural, almost country way of making the complicated quite understandable. He has a flair for teaching.

Chip Block analyzes the consultant abilities of Wendell Forbes. "His mind and character are tops. He's knowledgeable and understanding . . . very creative and completely open to new ideas. He grasps marketing problems. He will modify his marketing plans if warranted. He has good conceptual ability, excellent common sense and judgment. He's good with people. He's honest, gracious and courtly."

Wendell Forbes is also a good citizen in his same quiet way. He's volunteered his services to fund-raising organizations and other good causes. He's active in the Boy Scouts and the First Congregational Church of Ridgefield, Connecticut. One of his major consultant activities happens to be for a religious magazine, Guideposts, published by Norman Vincent Peale. He considers this a happy use of his talents. So does Dr. Peale, who says:

"I've worked closely with Wendell for several years. Mrs. Peale and I publish Guideposts magazine. Wendell started with us as a part-time consultant. He's done a spectacular job. We took all his time we could get. He became our deputy publisher.

"Under his leadership we've added 1,000,000 subscribers and now have 3,600,000. For us, he's in charge of 500 employees and is unusually beloved. He's very concerned for individual employees, down to the lowest. He is quiet, restrained and understanding of employee needs. He creates an attitude of enthusiasm. Yet, he runs a tight organization.

"He tries, makes an endeavor and gives it all he's got. He won't accept success but is constantly prodding us to plan two, five and ten years ahead. He has proposed and we're going ahead with a supplementary magazine.

"He's a very thoughtful man, very innovative. He believes that you have to carefully re-examine your objectives. Best of all, he's flexible, open to any suggestion or new idea."

Wendell Forbes takes the same position about Guideposts as about all his work. "Guideposts magazine was on a healthy growth curve when I joined them in 1975. I brought in a few new ideas but no brilliant breakthroughs. The magazine was and is immensely popular and needed only to be uncovered. I started out as a one-day-a-month consultant and later, at Dr. Peale's request, took over as deputy publisher. I still act in a consulting capacity and average about five or six other clients at any point in time."

Note: For this book, Wendell Forbes has answered some questions about magazine publishing.

Q. *How small a magazine has a chance today?*

A. Any magazine that fulfills a need can prosper if it is properly financed and managed. It is generally not possible for very small magazines to survive because they don't represent an advertising potential. If, however, a magazine went to absolutely every one of the 25,000 oil well diggers in the world, it would provide 100% coverage of an important market to certain advertisers. Unless a small magazine has a powerful advertising reason for being, it had best try its luck at having circulation income pay the freight. But not many magazines are enough needed by enough people to warrant the price that must be charged for a circulation-supported operation.

Q. *How much capital is required to launch a magazine? What percentage succeed? How much does testing it cost, just at the launch stage?*

A. To start a magazine of 200,000 will cost in the neighborhood of 3 to 5 million dollars before it turns the corner. I do not have figures on failure rates, but I'd guess that 20% make it. A new magazine can be properly tested for about $150,000.

Q. *What is different today about circulation methods and objectives?*

A. The biggest change in circulation has been to shift from mindless circulation growth at any cost for the purposes of generating advertising to the attempt to generate more revenues from the circulation side of the business. Publishers probably charge what they have to for circulation. They may not be able to sustain their present number of subscribers. I still believe that at least 20% of the circulation of many magazines is unreasonably forced.

Q. *Which functions can a magazine best do itself and which could better be handled by outside services? For bigger publishers? Smaller? Start-ups?*

A. The purpose of publishers is to communicate information, ideas, education and service to their publics. They are not printers, distributors, papermakers, etc., and should not try to be expert in every field. I favor outside suppliers for all supporting activities and especially in promotion.

Small publishers and start-ups should farm out all of their creative and even their list work and production. When larger, they can decide what is best for them.

Q. *Do creative people overspend to come up with imaginative, effective promotion? Do cost controllers stifle creativity? Is this a conflict?*

A. I don't find any problems between capable creative people and capable controllers. I find all sorts of problems between incapable creative types and incapable controllers. There is no need for such conflict. Even editors realize that their product will not sell itself.

Q. *How many magazines use computer modeling for planning? What is the trend for the future?*

A. I'd guess that about 30% to 40% of publications use some sort of computer-assisted planning. I believe the main area for improvement is in analysis and the computer not only encourages it but demands it as needed input. There is an opportunity for some good business person to help small publishers use computers.

Q. *When did Source Evaluation using computer modeling become generally available to magazines to aid them in more scientific selection of lists and media?*

A. Publishers Clearing House was the first company to offer Source Evaluation to its clients. They put on seminars in ten cities in 1976 and 1977. It was an important innovation and breakthrough in circulation management. All computer models offer Source Evaluation. There are several models available: KBM, Policy Development Corp., Ladd Associates. Time Inc. and Hearst have in-house models.

Q. *Can lists be selected more scientifically by analyzing zip code areas and mailing more to those zip areas with higher income and home value, etc.—that is, by demographics?*

A. Zip analysis certainly has some uses. Some of them are quite exotic. However, there is a limit to how much demographic analysis of any kind will contribute to the selling process. Psychographics will be the key to the future.

Q. *What about selecting from lists those who have purchased products which make them seem more logical to approach, segmenting them, and profiling them as the types of people you should reach—that is, by psychographics?*

A. Psychographics is, of course, the answer—but it is not all that simple. Selecting psychographic groups is difficult, if not impossible. Having psychographic groups select themselves by responding to an event that unifies them is currently the only way to do it. Special interest magazines are a psychographic selection of groups of people (regardless of the demographics) who like to do or are interested in the same thing. TV shows may someday be targeted in this manner.

Q. *Have you been able to use compiled lists (from directories, telephone books and services, etc.) profitably for small or large magazines?*

A. I have not been able to make compiled lists work for small publications, but they can work for a truly mass magazine or a mass product or service. Metromail is certainly doing some good work in refinement.

Q. *What do you think of the effectiveness of research by various methods to determine buying attitudes? How effective is this in the mail order business?*

A. I believe we can overdo research into why people buy and don't buy by direct mail. If the product is good and they have a need for it, they will buy it—perhaps not on the first mailing, but sooner or later depending on timing. If someone believes your product has value, he or she will buy it.

Q. *Has it been an axiom that you can't mix a subscription offer with a book offer (not a giveaway)?*

A. I have never been able to mix offers in direct mail. Simplicity is the rule and confusion is deadly. It may work for some but I would tend to examine the products individually to make sure each was reaching its full potential.

Q. *Some have said that the use of an 800 number and credit cards does not work for magazines. How do you feel about this?*

A. It's hard to prove that an 800 number doesn't work for any magazine. The idea of an 800 number being available for everything from complaints, change of address and order taking is very appealing. I've used it personally many times.

Q. *What is the response difference for an approval offer, credit card or cash?*

A. The best terms a magazine can be offered on are a cash/credit option with cards available. Cash only offers don't work in most cases. Billing privileges are a promotion stunt. If it pays off, use it; if it doesn't don't use it.

Q. *Do you avoid a choice of giveaways? In inflation, do you avoid long-term subscriptions? Do you avoid more than the alternatives in subscription length?*

A. I avoid a choice of giveaways. I avoid long-term subs. I use two-term options on the early letters in a renewal series, one in later letters.

Q. What chance do off-beat methods of getting subscriptions have? Is their use increasing?

A. Off-beat methods of subscription sales will produce some subs. Recently, we have seen more use of egg cartons, supermarket take-ones, etc. It is not that there has been a creative breakthrough, but that the economics of these high-cost, inefficient methods have become relatively viable. In other words, with the low response to high-priced offers in mail, the price many publishers are willing to pay for a sub has gone up thus bringing many methods back to life. Generally speaking, off-beat methods will not produce volume.

Q. *Of all offers you worked on, which gave the biggest thrill? What were disasters?*

A. Any mailing that comes in over budget is a thrill. My biggest disasters were in space testing.

Q. *Do you make decisions selecting one piece of creative work or another? Should you, as an overall consultant or the average client, defer to a specialized expert (on questions concerning the specialty)?*

A. Today, as a consultant, I am frequently called upon to judge copy and art and I feel comfortable doing this. I believe, however, that one must defer to the pro or get a new pro you can defer to.

Q. *To start in and succeed in direct marketing, what do you think can improve chances most?*

A. To succeed in direct marketing, you need to be bright, entrepreneurial and work well with people. In your early years, you must delve into detail, analyze everything and write good reports to the boss. A college degree is all one really needs and that only proves that one can probably read and write. The rest is enthusiasm and hard work—and it sure helps if you have a sense of mission in what you are doing.

Q. *Looking back, how have you found publishing as a career?*

A. Publishing is a most rewarding occupation.

One satisfaction that Wendell Forbes has found as a consultant has been the ability to avoid crises management and to be able to help his clients. He says that the purpose of publishing is not to make money. It is to be of service to the reader and then, if you are successful at this, you can't help but make money. It is the same, he says, with consulting. If your prime purpose is to help clients, you can't help but be successful.

Wendell Forbes has a lot of alumni out there applying what he taught. Sandy Clark says: "Wendell Forbes was my first boss and a terrific one." John Collins says, "He became the biggest influence in my life in my work in circulation."

Larry Crutcher says: "Wendell is a once-in-a-lifetime boss. I was lucky, and was exposed to him very early. Wendell was my first Time Inc. boss. Coming for the first time to New York and entering the flashy world of high-pressure marketing, I had preconceived him in entirely different terms.

"Wendell is an extraordinarily decent, loyal and moral man. His Calvinism sets him apart from most of the direct response industry, although it doesn't prevent him from understanding a good opportunity when it appears. He was, and is, consistently able to stand back from the swirl of today's problems and to visualize what is really happening in a situation.

"Another pleasant surprise about Wendell dealt with his large and devoted following of ex-trainees. He really cares about his employees and acquaintances, taking the time to be certain that they understand and are progressing."

Wendell Forbes can help you if you're in mail order, more so if you get into newsletters and most of all if you are in or go into the field of magazine circulation. If so, attend his "School of Magazine Marketing" seminars. If you can't afford them, listen to tapes of his lectures and speeches. Read his articles in reprints or back issues. Details of how to get them are in the Help Source Guide in this book.

Note: Wendell Forbes lives at 87 Peaceable Hill Road, Ridgefield, Connecticut 06877.

Chapter 12
The Direct Marketing Courses

*At college level, or after
work to get into and rise
in mail order; scholarships.*

Most of the people at the top in direct marketing got into it by accident.

Still, today, to get a job in it the best chance is to be in it. The idea of planning for it from the college level on has been recent, partially due to direct marketers' problems in raiding each other for experienced personnel.

There wasn't enough to go around. Those lucky enough to have experience were often hired away from one job to another, leap-frogging their way up. But companies found their growth was blocked by not enough experienced people. And they found themselves paying more than they felt comfortable with to get needed talent, when available.

The first step direct marketers have taken has been to trade up their existing employees who already had some experience in direct marketing. They encouraged nearby colleges and universities to set up courses and then paid for their employees to attend. This worked out pretty well.

In this book I tell the story of Nat Ross and the superb NYU course in direct marketing in New York City. In recent years, the Roosevelt University course on direct marketing, in Chicago, has won high praise. Dean Robert Snyder fathered it. Professor Ken Mangun taught it. John J. Flieder, assistant vice president of marketing for Allstate Insurance (Sears Roebuck) was one of the first graduates and later lectured regularly at it. In Los Angeles, the California State University School of Business and Economics started a direct marketing course. In this book, I tell the story of Freeman Gosden, Jr. and all the work he has done in conducting direct marketing courses at California State University and elsewhere in the area.

In New York, Nat Ross brought in as guest lecturers top direct marketers in every area. Each told the story of his or her firm, field and experience. Bob Snyder did the same in Chicago. Companies sending their employees to the courses discovered, not only were they learning beyond their previous experience, but they were getting more excited about direct marketing as they got the story.

The next step was for direct marketers to take promising people from non-direct marketing divisions of their companies and send them for courses, letting them learn from scratch, just as they were being transferred to direct marketing jobs or even before. Again it worked.

The final step has been to recruit beginners from the outside for direct marketing divisions. Requirements varied. Some, as does Doubleday, have usually required degrees as MBA's as a minimum. Others looked for bright, motivated young people with a liberal arts degree and preferably graduate schools. But particular preference was given by most to graduates of direct marketing courses.

At the same time, courses expanded. Now in the New York City area there are at least nine courses at eight universities or colleges on some aspect of direct marketing. There are more and more courses throughout the country on direct marketing. Many are credit courses. Others are given by the continuing education department of the college or university. Still more are conducted by associations and clubs.

Martin Baier has a splendid credit course at the University of Missouri, in Kansas City, Missouri. Philadelphia has two direct marketing courses. John Jenks has a fine course at the University of Wisconsin at LaCrosse. Professor David Perry has one at the same university's River Falls Campus. Details on these courses are in the help source reference section in the back of this book.

But the best place for you to get information on courses that is most up-to-date is the Direct Mail/Marketing Educational Foundation. The DMMA set it up as a separate entity, a non-profit corporation to encourage education in direct marketing at the college and university level. It's also located at 6 East 43rd Street, New York, New York 10017. One of its functions is to help colleges and universities set up direct marketing courses and to include direct marketing in general marketing courses.

Far more direct marketing courses than ever before are being taught. Many more general marketing courses now include direct marketing. Dr. Philip Kotler, of Northwestern University, is the author of the most widely used textbook on marketing. He has recommended that direct marketing be an introductory marketing course for all first year business school students. In this book, David Ogilvy—the most famous advertising man in the world—recommends that anyone starting a career in advertising begin by learning direct response advertising.

The Foundation strongly recommends that college students who are interested in direct marketing take marketing courses and advises that they go to business school and ideally get an MBA. If you take a marketing course and want to get into direct marketing, you might qualify for several Foundation programs.

College students can look into direct marketing by attending as a guest of the Foundation a "Career Day" conducted at a DMMA Conference or sponsored by the local direct marketing clubs. Some Direct Marketing Days, particularly New York, Chicago and Los Angeles, hold "Career Days". Elsewhere in this book activities of a typical direct marketing day and of a typical conference are described. Students are recommended by their professor to the Foundation. It can be an exciting experience. Since inception, over 1200 marketing students and over 400 marketing professors have attended "Career Days".

A variation of this is the "Lunch Bunch" which, if a marketing student, you also might qualify for. Each year the Foundation solicits and gets direct marketer sponsors to take a hundred to a hundred and twenty-five young men and women and professors to lunch at participating direct marketing clubs or Direct Marketing Days or at DMMA conferences. It's done on a one-to-one basis. The direct marketer explains direct marketing to his or her guest and introduces the guest around.

If you're a member of a minority and a college student, you might qualify for an internship program. The program started in June 1981 in a small way. The costs of transportation and room and board are underwritten with a $200 a week stipend by participating firms. Twelve students intern for eight weeks at New York area direct marketing firms. Interns benefit from on-the-job experience and meetings with experienced professionals in the field. The program is open to racial minority students after completing their junior year. There are no requirements for degree specialization. Applications are made through college placement officers or marketing professors or to the Foundation.

To get even a modest start took joint effort. Bob Jones and Nat Ross originated the minority program concept. Normai

Eisner and Ray Lewis helped shape it. Stan Rapp joined in and presented the plan to the Direct Mail Educational Foundation. Columbia House and other leading direct marketers became sponsors.

The Foundation program that has the history of having helped the most beginners get into direct marketing is the Collegiate Institute. It is a saturation five-day course that starts in the morning, goes all day and has lots of evening discussion. If you're a marketing student, you might qualify for a $750 scholarship that pays for travel, room and board.

"The most rewarding experience in my life." That's what Bob Stone told me about teaching at the Collegiate Institute. "Pete" Hoke, Rose Harper, Dick Cremer, and Paul Sampson told me almost the same.

It's a major activity of the Direct Mail/ Marketing Educational Foundation. Lew Kleid, founder of the Kleid Company, first underwrote it. Ed Mayer, Jr. first conducted the course. John Yeck, of Yeck Brothers, has given it the most time in recent years.

It's a magnet attracting the gifted and talented to direct marketing. 250 to 300 marketing professors recommend the best in their classes. Top marketer judges select 30 winning candidates from the marketing students applying.

These thirty are far above the average recruited by most direct marketing companies. Scholarships are awarded to each paid for by direct marketing firms and clubs. The scholarship pays for all expenses for a five-day crash course. The top leaders in direct marketing come to teach at their own expense for no payment.

This is done twice a year. Most of those attending the Institutes apply for direct marketing jobs, get them and do well. Most of those underwriting do it for the general good of the field and expect nothing in return. But backing the Foundation is often hard-headed good business. Often those contributing money and time meet candidates first, hire them and benefit at very low recruiting cost. A lot still don't realize the opportunity.

The professors who select candidates to recommend have their chance, too. Professors get the chance to win fellowships to attend DMMA Basic Institutes. Over the last ten years fellowships have been awarded to over one hundred and fifty professors. The hope is that these will return to their colleges and universities and include direct marketing in general marketing courses; and that these who already cover direct marketing will do so to a greater degree.

The DMMA Educational Foundation is strongly supported. It now has a total endowment of over $300,000 earning interest and contributing. Memberships start at one hundred dollars. Through 1980 Bob Stone has contributed close to $60,000. This represents all his royalties on his book, "Successful Direct Marketing Methods", and all his speaking fees. They never stop coming in and will continue. "The speaking fees come in all the time," says Foundation President Dr. Richard Montesi. "One check may be for $200 and the next for $2,000.

The Kleid Company has contributed over five hundred scholarships out of almost a thousand given. Kiplinger has contributed one hundred fellowships. RCA, Time-Life, Grolier, and Loo-Art have all been substantial contributors. The Direct Marketing Club of Southern California has contributed 100 fellowships. CADM has contributed ten. Dr. Richard Montesi is a top educational professional. Laurie Spar is Director of the Foundation. He's been a school superintendent in Pocantico Hills, New York (Rockefeller country), and in Connecticut, and in Scarsdale, New York. He's been superintendent of the district. He's been chief school administrator.

"I like very much the work I'm doing at the Foundation and the direct marketers and DMMA people I work with. The caliber of the young men and women getting scholarships seems high. My impression is that they are a very bright group. It's a self-selecting process. Close to 5,000 letters to teachers get about 300 applications for 30 openings.

"It's an opportunity for the kids and the field. Direct marketers need bright young people. Rose Harper has hired over a dozen for Kleid over a period of time. We need to expose the kids to more people who can hire. Paul Sampson raves about the graduates and Garden Way (of which Paul was Chairman of the Board) is always hiring them.

"I've taught at Fordham and at NYU in the School of Education. I've been in the administration of the school. I'm familiar with the caliber of college and graduate students. Those that the Foundation are attracting seem first rate."

Mike Manzari, Executive Vice President of The Kleid Company, says that Institute graduates are smarter than average and more ambitious. They have done well. One graduate, Joe Furguiele, is now Marketing Manager of Men's Group Lists at CBS Magazines. Another, David Carter, has been in his own mail order business for years. Another, Thomas Hood, is Marketing Director of Capital Cablevision, in Albany, New York.

RCA has hired graduates as has Stone & Adler. Dick Cremer, of Montgomery Ward, has told me he's always on the look-out for Institute graduates. One graduate, Carl Dentino, took the one-week course, created his own mailing to sell a product, himself, and used mail order methods to get a job in direct marketing.

Anyone with the requirements may apply directly to the Foundation for a scholarship. The requirements are: An applicant must be a college senior with a business-related major in marketing or a graduate student in marketing, advertising, journalism, news communications or almost any other field including art school. The Foundation also operates an informal placement service within direct marketing.

The trend by the Foundation is toward attracting specialized students high in their classes in accounting, higher mathematics, statistics, probability theory, computer programming, psychology, TV directing, advertising art and other specialties.

Another Foundation project is the "Visiting Executive" program. A top direct marketer visits a business college and lectures or talks informally with students about the field. More and more such meetings have taken place.

A set of direct marketing case histories and one of class guides for marketing classes were mailed to over 6,000 college professors in September 1980. A project planned is a library of transparencies and tapes. Summer work fellowships for teachers and key students are planned but not yet available. Freeman Gosden, Jr. and "Pete" Hoke are the impetus behind the case histories.

Dr. Montesi has further plans. "We want to establish a center, an institute for direct marketing at a university. Leonard Raymond, of Dickie Raymond (now the DR Group), and a former direct marketer is donating his files to the Foundation for such a center."

There are still other foundation projects. It encourages the formation of new direct marketing classes in a wide variety of forms. It supplies such classes and marketing clubs with teaching materials. Dr. Montesi is making a drive to develop better and better material. "We're hoping for new funding to bring out new course outlines. We'll then work on a variety of new course materials. Bob Hanford is now writing new direct marketing career booklets." One project Dr. Montesi is considering is a conclave of twelve professors of marketing and six direct marketers.

In direct marketing, big firms with best jobs still prefer to raid other firms for experienced personnel. When they take beginners they tend to select MBA's with highest grades and top IQ's, the cream. Small firms still start more average beginners. But each year a growing percentage of top direct marketing executives are graduates of direct marketing courses, an advantage available to you.

Chapter 13
The Lady With The Laser Mail Order Mind

Business Week called her one of the top 100 corporate women in America.

That was in 1976. By then, the direct marketing advertising agency she had founded in 1970 had become the most successful in America owned by a woman. Her name is Joan Throckmorton. The agency is Throckmorton Associates, Inc., which has grown far faster since.

Joan is super bright, super fast in reaction, super sure and overwhelmingly correct in her judgment. Her style is staccato. She thinks so fast, the ideas tumble out. It's sometimes hard to keep up. But Joan has extraordinary clarity. She sums up in three words what others need three pages for. She has no doubts. She knows exactly what she is trying to do. Yet she's friendly, thoroughly nice and doesn't frighten.

Joan's mind ranges like a hunting dog at top speed from right to left, forward, backward—but almost instantly racing back to the point discussed. She has an impatient mind. With Joan, it's superthink and shorthand speak. It is sometimes hard to keep up, but the reward is great; and if you're a client, you're liable to get rich. She'll only work for you if she sees such potential.

Everything Joan does and thinks is based on logical, orderly simplicity—the straight line is the shortest distance between two points. She has big clients. "Big clients don't cut off the funds in a recession. And every advertising entrepreneur knows—20 small clients equal loss; 10 big ones equal profit." From the day her agency opened, with $16,000 in the bank, it worked for big companies but also for growth potential smaller ones Joan believed in.

Joan is creative. She has business ability. She can initiate and carry out. What about writing, planning, recruiting, training, motivating, negotiating? "All of these are important aspects of the job. I love motivating and creating and selling."

Joan is an entrepreneur. She ran her own promotion business in Mexico. How did it happen? "I wanted to be independent financially." She once owned a share of a training film for women. She marketed the film by direct mail. It sold well. "We've seldom been tempted to be an owner or a partner in a mail order venture. We like what we're doing best. We have no time for the other."

Throckmorton Assocs. activities are 70% in direct mail and 30% in magazines, newspapers, TV, miscellaneous. "It functions 99% as a full-service agency. I do a little consulting on the side. We're marketers as well as an advertising agency in direct marketing.

Her father, Sydney Throckmorton, was in insurance and corporation pension planning. Her mother was an interior decorator. Joan has no brothers and one younger sister who is married, lives in Lima, Peru, and has three children.

Joan went to elementary school in Fort Lauderdale, Florida. She went to Miami Edison High School. Her favorite subject was English. She was Girls' Club president and a top scholar. She was in the top percentile of her graduate school and had the second highest marks in her graduating class. At Smith College she took English and graduated in Liberal Arts with Honors and was elected to Phi Beta Kappa.

In her career and business she had the advantage of a top brain and the disadvantage of being a woman. "When I started in the 50's, competition for good jobs was very stiff. In the male-oriented business world, it was necessary to do more homework, be more widely and deeply grounded and to follow through more thoroughly. I had to work longer and harder. Did I ever feel I lost a job or account because I was a woman? *Many times.*"

She started her first job at Doubleday as a trainee. Typing skills were required, but Joan never had to use them. Her first boss, Charlie Sherman, was mail order advertising manager for Doubleday Book Clubs. Her first chance to write was when she became assistant to the art director of Doubleday Book Clubs, when she got her first assignment to write blurbs and mailings to members of the Mystery Guild.

Staying put was never Joan's method. She moved over to Time Inc. for her second job where she started as a promotion writer for Life magazine working with Bill Baring-Gould. At Time Inc. she moved around a lot. A big break came when she became assistant to Chairman of the Board, Andrew Heiskell. She attributes her later success to "Andrew Heiskell and the fact that I changed jobs to move up. I didn't stick in dead ends."

Joan didn't. She, at different times at Time Inc., was circulation promotion manager of Sports Illustrated magazine and a promotion writer for Life magazine. Before Time-Life Books existed, she helped introduce the first major Time Inc. book, "The Life Picture Cookbook". Later, she became marketing project manager with the Time-Life Books Division of Time Inc.

In the course of working with talented promotion people at Time Inc., she mastered her craft. She did not accept do's and don't's without questioning. She was innovative. She wanted to test for herself. "Early in my career, I begged my boss at Sports Illustrated to let me put the coupon in the middle of the page. He did. It was a disaster. But it was a house ad. Sports Illustrated lived through it and I learned."

Joan's biggest learning opportunity came with her next job where she became associate promotion director of American Heritage. "American Heritage was a great place to work and learn. Jim Parton was a dynamo. Frank Johnson and I worked on the creative side, Dick Benson on the numbers." It was at American Heritage that Joan learned the fine points of the creative side of direct marketing. Frank Johnson was promotion director. "Frank taught me more about writing than anyone else."

From American Heritage Joan went back to Time Inc. for a brief stint, then down to Mexico for 4 years, back to New York and over to Lawrence G. Chait & Company, one of the several largest direct marketing advertising agencies at the time. She became Director of Marketing Plans and Programs, working under Mildred Semler.

"Mildred did crackerjack work for Larry Chait and deserves a lot of credit for his early success. She wasn't easy on me. She was a tough teacher, but she taught me to write proposals and make presentations. It was Mildred who showed me the art of organized marketing thinking. What is the primary purpose of the program . . . what is the objective? What are the logical steps to achieve it? What is the historical perspective? She taught me to think in an outline format, which is critical to good planning."

The icing on the cake of Joan's experience was her last job before opening her agency. She became a direct response executive for Cowles Communications, Inc. There, Joan was instrumental in establishing a direct marketing division for the publishers of Look and Family Circle magazines.

After she opened her agency in 1970, the first agency account was the LeeWards Division of General Mills. Joan's former employer, Time Inc., was an early account. Later, her first employer, Doubleday, became an account. For them, she worked on The American Garden Guild, The Mystery Guild, The Science Fiction Book Club and the Fireside Theatre Book Club.

An early account was GRI Corp. A big one was GAF Corp., for whom she worked for several divisions. Soon she was working for broadcasters, magazine publishers, newsletter publishers and book publishers. For clients she was selling collectibles, investment funds and hospital supplies. At first, Throckmorton/Satin handled special assignments and not necessarily entire accounts.

Now the agency handles entire accounts on a regular, month-by-month basis, although it still handles special programs for some giants such as the General Electric Major Appliances and AT&T Long Lines Division. One of the big regular accounts is the Special Interest Group of CBS Consumer Publications. Another is Citicorp Services, Inc. The agency also works for the MacMillan book clubs, Rodale Press, Inc., U.S. News & World Report and Current, Inc.

Looking back, success has come, says Joan, from her clients' success stories, from having talent in an industry that's short on new talent, from trust and friendship developed in good client associations. Public relations helped, also talks at DMMA, DMNY and other trade meetings and stories in Direct Marketing magazine and other media. Joan says: "Current clients always send us new business. They're our best PR."

Note: For readers of this book, Joan Throckmorton has kindly answered the following questions.

Q. *Do you find many direct marketers who pass up a success from improper testing?*

A. Yes. It's a constant battle. We push for scientific testing and *proof* of improvement via scientific methodologies. It's a direct marketer's primary means of survival. Improper testing is almost always due to a combination of "lack of budget" and "lack of time."

Q. *Do some direct marketers fail to project far more than a fraction of an offer's potential or accept a substantially lower profit on a campaign from projecting before sufficient testing?*

A. Our clients are usually well aware of the science of testing and projecting. This is particularly true of magazine publishers. Fifty percent of our billing is for magazines who are very much into scientific testing. Still, when we study past activities of a new direct marketer not yet a client, it is sometimes shocking to see what is not being done.

Q. *Do you ever interpret the results of a test differently than your clients?*

A. Rarely. One client felt a certain test was a failure. This wasn't true. The test was very successful. The product "died", however. The test had been highly structured to give as many answers as possible. In every case, test analysis was yes or no. It was clearly "No; don't do this." Or clearly "Yes; do that. This is your market." It showed at least six approaches that were disasters and others that were definitely a green light. It was an excellent test providing precisely the information needed at a low testing cost. Of course, the overall results were not optimistic and the client killed the project. But the test clearly prevented him from pouring more money into a poor investment.

Q. *When a direct marketer fails and then becomes your client and insists that you try again, what do you do?*

A. People come to us with problems. There's never been a question of our repeating what failed. Usually, we find a quite different approach to try. We search the history all the way up from the first inquiry or sale to judge overall success or failure; to find out what went wrong the first time. There can be no mysteries in good direct marketing.

Q. *Do some direct marketers jump too fast from over optimistically interpreted test results?*

A. Yes. They may not admit it but you can tell later. You notice funny little things. A publication can be out on the market. All reports are great. All of a sudden, it decides to reposition and cut circulation. Obviously, all those optimistic reports were overblown.

Q. *Is back-end follow up extraction of all possible profit from a first customer the key? Do you play a role in all these?*

A. Our entire agency philosophy is based on the concept of developing the customer dialogue. We're heavy on back-end. We're overwhelmingly concerned with its marketing aspects. We work on ongoing relationships. We try to help tighten the screws. Otherwise, it is useless to achieve breakthroughs up front.

Q. *Do you find this particularly important for magazine publisher clients?*

A. Naturally, it's critical to renewals—and renewals are critical to the magazine. One problem publications also get stuck with, in new subscriber prospecting, is the preview issue. It's the one where the offer says, "If you don't like the first issue, cancel and owe nothing." Even with efficient computer systems, this means serving three issues to a lot of deadbeats. Bills are going out, copies are being served and often no more than 40% convert to paids. The economics can be fatal.

Q. *Do you use research for clients as well as testing? If so, what kind and when? How effective has it been?*

A. Yes, we often do for new products or products in trouble. We believe strongly in focus groups, but only use them as qualitative research to help form copy platforms. We never overread them. We also believe in pre-testing "research" for new products. We can do 5-year projections on good pre-tests. We also do concept testing to develop appeals for space ads and for direct mail pieces.

Q. *For clients do you use demographic research? If so, do you find results of doing so to-date insufficient, promising or excellent?*

A. Since most of our clients maintain their own lists, we use little outside research. We find zip select methods largely helpful in making marginal lists pay. And we are doing some testing of new "lifestyle" demographics lists. Naturally, we feel that customer or reader studies are most helpful in selecting media in our client products. We encourage all our clients to compile such data in addition to or in combination with the basic customer record.

Q. *Do you use computer modeling for your clients? If so, do you find the investment worth it?*

A. For magazines, whether starting a new one or improving on an old one, modeling is critical. It cannot work without net subscriber figures. All our merchandise (catalog) clients are also heavily into modeling.

Q. *How effective are computer letters?*

A. Most effective in appropriate situations, used creatively.

Q. *How about laser letters?*

A. We're enthusiastic about laser printing. Particularly about laser letters and entire laser printed direct mail packages.

Q. *For whom are you using them?*

A. For several clients. For GE, we're using such letters with really heavy personalization. There can be over 15 variables on the order form alone.

Q. *How cost effective are they for most uses?*

A. Personalized laser letters are reasonable. You do need a run of 50,000 to 100,000, however; but this means the run necessary to amortize the programming cost. You don't have to mail all 100,000 at one time. If you have 10,000 inquiries coming in each month, you can use the same computer letter personalized for each inquiry and amortize over the year.

Q. *Is it practical to ask for inquiries or only for a one-step sale?*

A. It really depends on the product and its market. We have a project that shoots for an average sale between $400 and $500. We'll mail 50,000 names, not inquiries. We'll ask for inquiries. We hope that inquiry cost will run about $10. Then we send a follow-up series to get our sale at a profit. For this particular sort of thing and with the lists we're using, the personalized laser is ideal.

Q. *Do you believe in testing several direct mail packages for a client, each package created by a different writer?*

A. We do, but only with our close direction. We develop *packages*. What is of critical concern is that each represents clearly a substantially diffferent *concept*. Supposedly, if you take four writers with different styles and hire each to create a mailing piece, you will get four quite different mailing pieces. But it's not so. The style may differ but four bright people may all study the same problem and often come to surprisingly similar conclusions. If you want different approaches, it's unsound to think that just by hiring different people you'll get them.

Q. *How do you avoid this problem?*

A. Someone must see that each writer approaches the problem differently. Conceptually, stating the proposition doesn't accomplish this. Creative direction is needed. This direction must have the total overview in mind. But the professional approach of each writer requires a shift of emphasis within this overview. If you don't do this, you can have the right list, a good product and three good writers, but there won't be much difference in results. Give each writer a different approach and you then get a true test.

Q. *How do you determine what different approaches to test?*

A. Make sure you test important differences in approach, shifts in moral imperatives. You can't afford to test a whimsical approach against a straight approach or other variations of style only. It can be an outright waste of time and money to try variations other than clearly defined basic differences. In other words, if you can't define precisely what it is you're testing, don't. There's always a danger in any of this, of course—the danger of playing it too safe . . . keeping new approaches from being tested.

Q. *How does the creative process start when you work with clients?*

A. Marketing goals are critical as the first step. Agree on what you want to find out, where you're going and what you've learned to date.

Q. *Are contests productive?*

A. They're effective if used properly. Of course, the back-end can be weakened considerably by these "contest" customers.

Q. *What has impressed you most about changing mail order methods since your start?*

A. How long it takes new ideas to take hold.

Q. *Who have been the most interesting to work with and stimulated you the most?*

A. People who spark creative ideas—people with experiences to temper the enthusiasm, people you can count on who stimulate others, writers like Ken Scheck and Linda Wells, artists like David Gordon, teachers like Pierre Passavant, Mildred Semler, Frank Johnson and Bill Baring-Gould.

Q. *How long will direct mail, newspaper and direct mail advertising be pretty much the same?*

A. Possibly until the end of the '80's. After that I see a gradual shifting to electronic media, particularly the TV screen (or video player screen).

Q. *Do you see any changes in the use of the telephone in direct marketing?*

A. I see a major increase in the use of the 800 or toll free number. It will ultimately be used on network TV, as well as cable TV. Originally, 800 numbers, when used on network, have flooded and blocked the AT&T lines as to often make them unuseable. The answer is AT&T's new 900 number which can handle vastly more calls in a rush.

Q. *How do you see the growth of direct marketing?*

A. The field is booming. Business was never better. People who wouldn't consider it four or five years ago now want to get in.

Q. *What future changes will be most important in direct marketing?*

A. There will be more of a move into video. It will become less expensive, expecially when compared with magazines and direct mail (as new postal increases go into effect). Many who now use TV will get into cable and so will a lot of direct marketers who never used TV.

Q. *How should direct marketers prepare for change— video disc mailing pieces, video catalogs, 2-way TV?*

A. Listen to the kids—those who grew up with TV. They relate to electronic media. A lot of these young people would rather telephone than write—or read—a letter.

Q. *What is the best training in direct marketing for young people starting out? How can they best start?*

A. The best way I can think of is to work for a small agency. It gives you a taste of every part of the business and good on-line experience early on, if you're really willing to work hard.

Q. *What advice have you particularly for young women starting out?*

A. Stay out of traditional "female" areas of our business. Once you're in them, you're typecast. And don't be afraid to move around if you find yourself in a potential dead end job.

Note: Joan Throckmorton continues her success at an accelerating pace. Throckmorton Assocs. is at 152 Madison Avenue, New York, NY 10016; (212) 689-9230. In 1981, billing went to $4.5 million.

Mail Order Sampler
Seminar V

Chapter 1
Mail Order's Three Home Runs

*For three big companies he created
big mail order successes.*

For Doubleday Jerry Hardy came up with one mail order project after another, out of his head. For Time Inc. he created a book division which has since sold close to two billion dollars worth of books. For the Dreyfus Fund he created a billion dollars worth of sales in eighteen months. He did it with mail order methods never before used in the investment fund industry.

At each of these large organizations he has had a flair for working with others. He is a creative, realistic and practical man. He carefully points out that at Doubleday he rose from the ranks, worked with others as part of a team and that each contributed to each project; that he was only with Time-Life Books four years and that the overwhelming majority of its growth has occurred in the seventeen years since; and that Dreyfus as well as the other two had always been successful.

When Jerry came to Doubleday it was very successful, in a time of change. Nelson Doubleday had been the driving force but no longer could be. Due to cancer, he could only occasionally come to the office. He died the following year.

Doubleday had grown dramatically, powered by Nelson Doubleday. Milo Sutliff, his right hand man on mail order, had left. When Nelson died, Milton Runyon, who had been the third man of a mail order triumvirate, had to take over for all three. Milton had been a tremendously effective mail order administrator. Now he became executive vice president of Doubleday.

It was the beginning of a great mail order expansion under him. Milton had to form a new mail order team. There was an opportunity for bright new talent Milton began to find and develop. Milton recalls: "Jerry was a discovery of Ken McCormick, the Doubleday editor who first met Jerry when they were in service together in World War II."

Ken McCormick changed Jerry Hardy's life. Before the war, in 1939, 1940 and 1941 he had been in public relations. Except for World War II he might never have gone into mail order or into publishing. But through Ken McCormick's introduction, on leaving the service Jerry got a promotion job with Doubleday.

Jerry had always been bright, quick and a worker. He had started with after school jobs. "I've worked since I was fourteen years old. Always, when I was in elementary school, in high school and in college I worked after school and each summer."

For Doubleday Jerry started at the promotional bottom. He was a good soldier. "For one year I wrote blurbs on the inside flap and back of book jackets. I did it for 523 books." Milton remembers: "Jerry's next job was similar to my first job at Doubleday. He became advertising manager of the Trade department. It soon became apparent that he could turn his hand to many things effectively and we moved him into mail order where he was my right hand man until lured away by Time-Life."

Milton Runyon was a great influence in Jerry's development. Jerry recollects: "There was no better or kindlier or more patient teacher. I learned 90% of all I know about the basics of mail order, from him . . . the rules, the guiding laws. More, he taught me thoroughness in testing, great care in structure. It was an

extraordinary experience." Milton was expanding Doubleday's mail order activities and consolidating them. Jerry had a combination of imagination, drive and stability, all of which Milton greatly valued and Doubleday needed.

Milton continues: "Jerry was very good at developing people and new ideas. He was responsible for the development of the Doubleday 'Around the World Program' and of other Doubleday programs and of the development of such people as Joan Manley. She became Jerry's secretary at Doubleday." Jerry recalls: "Joan Manley first worked for Sam Vaughan. When I became advertising director of the company, including book clubs, I made Sam Vaughan advertising manager and stole his secretary." And at Doubleday, Joan became assistant to Jerry more and more.

It was a time when Doubleday was particularly open to new ideas, new sources of business, new talent. Milton was organizing mail order more methodically, bringing people together, getting new blood and giving encouragement to new projects, yet always doing so with care and supervision. Jerry was full of energy and ideas with plenty of drive to carry through any approved by Milton. Milton credits Jerry with getting Doubleday into one new enterprise after another.

"Jerry Hardy had quite a lot to do with the inspiration for Doubleday's first 'Around the World Program' booklets, with gummed color illustrations mounted on a sheet of stamps so that the recipient could complete the book. The program had wide appeal to families at $1 a booklet and led to a series of similar programs—Nature Program, Science Program, Know Your Bible Program, Know Your America Program."

The idea for the Nature Program came first. Jerry thinks back: "One day I went through the mail and found two mail solicitations that gave me the idea. The first was from the Book-of-the-Month Club for an art program it offered in cooperation with The Metropolitan Museum of Art. Enclosed were a sheet of stamps. Each was about twice the size of a postage stamp but a reproduction of a famous painting from the museum. You were instructed to paste stamps in the proper place in the accompanying booklet. It was well done.

"In the same mail was a mailing piece from The National Wild Life Society appealing for funds and offering nature stamps. I took both pieces in to Milton. I put down on his desk the Metropolitan Museum program. I put down next to it the wildlife stamps. I said, 'let's try this (the art program) with this subject (the nature stamps).' It took Milt about 26 seconds to see we had something."

Jerry and Milton felt that for a nature program the ideal organization to work together would be The Audubon Society. Making the arrangements to do so took a good deal of time. In the meantime, Jerry worked out another application, "The Around the World Program". Another Doubleday project that came out of Jerry's booklet-a-month concept was "The Personal Success Program" for which a free aptitude test proved an ideal giveaway.

Milton, Charley Sherman, as direct mail creative director, and Jerry became a product development triumvirate. Jerry goes on: "three of us discovered a good many ideas that became new book clubs. It was hard to determine which of us could be credited with what. It was a memorable team effort."

During this time, Jerry was developing himself as well and helping others get started. For a year, he taught the direct mail course at New York University. Several years later, he was one of those who recruited Nat Ross to conduct it as the present direct marketing course. Jerry met more and more people in direct marketing. He formed the friendships and found the associates whom he has worked with for the rest of his business life, at Doubleday, at Time-Life and at Dreyfus.

"I first took the NYU course from Al Leventhal before I took over from him. That's how I got to know him. He was brilliant. Many students were. Some of the top people today in direct marketing were students of the NYU course, mostly of the course that Nat Ross took and has conducted. A lot of help has been given by good people who have taken time to teach there and elsewhere. A lot of people helped me with their know-how as I worked with them. I learned by osmosis.

"Along the way, I kept getting help from good people." Jerry Hardy has an ability to suggest and to stimulate, to help creative people come up with their ideas or develop his further, to give recognition for contributions. He liked and got along with bright people.

He dealt with the advertising agencies servicing Doubleday and a good deal with the Max Sackheim Agency which handled the Literary Guild. He treated each person in each agency as someone who could teach him something. He remembers Max Sackheim. "Max was one of the originals, in the old tradition of mail order as it first developed. He loved long copy. He was very kind and generous."

Jerry also had a regard for new developing talent. Lester Wunderman felt that he and Jerry understood each other and had similar views on the future of direct marketing. Lester was coming up fast at the Sackheim Agency. Milton says: "Doubleday's contact with Lester Wunderman was, at first, principally through Jerry Hardy."

Lester Wunderman and Ed Ricotta, art director of Sackheim, and Jerry were all young and full of ideas. Jerry recalls: "Lester Wunderman was very bright. It was clear that he was the most important young person in the agency. I was also a good friend of Ed Ricotta. The best indication of my regard for Lester's abilities is that I almost started with Wunderman, Ricotta and Kline as a partner. Max Sackheim had two sons. Lester saw he couldn't have the agency after Max's retirement and Max was getting along in years.

"After Lester and his group had broken with Max and about the time they opened their office, they asked me to talk. I had several meetings with Lester and Ed but decided to stay with Doubleday. The Doubleday business stayed with Max Sackheim. However, WR&K did later become a Doubleday agency. About a year after starting Time-Life Books, I used WR&K for them and have worked with Lester and WR&K ever since, before becoming a consultant.

"Time Inc. had successfully sold books before I joined them in December of 1960. But I was the first person hired from outside who had a major publishing responsibility." Life was then close to its peak of circulation and prestige. Time Inc. had succeeded in magazines, newsreels and with its radio show. Some Time Inc. executives felt that it could expand its book sales from within. "I was the first to come from book publishing. It wasn't easy to come in as an outsider. When I started, I did not take Joan with me. I had no idea how it would work out.

"Time-Life Books was a different concept than the sale of books previously by Time Inc. It was not easy to convince some of the top people that a company which had sold $7,000,000 worth of one book in one year was not already seriously in book publishing and did not already have the right concept. My job was first to convince them that selling 700,000 copies of 'The World We Live In' at $10 each in one year, or $7,000,000 and then zero the next year, was not building a book business, but that our new plan was.

"This plan was to produce sets of books which could be sold as open-end subscriptions, and which capitalized on people's perception of Time Inc. as a creative organization. This meant a big emphasis on pictures. It meant subjects which could capitalize on the writing and photographic talents of Time and Life. It meant appealing to Time and Life subscribers with offers to which they seemed particularly receptive.

"The various divisions of Time Inc. worked a lot less together than might be supposed. We were pretty much on our own. Time Inc. supplied us with their house list as the number one contribution. Numbers two, three, four and five contributions consisted of the extraordinarily talented people available. It was not the morgue of pictures, the inventory of already written material. We used little or nothing of this. It was the calibre of the talent in the organization which we could gradually recruit and could call on."

The first set of Time-Life Books was "The Life World Library". The second was the "Life Nature Library" and the third "The Life Science Library". Walter Weintz wrote the first mailing pieces. He was a great choice. He had been creative head at Reader's Digest and had written first subscription offers and then the Digest book offers. He understood the attitudes of a magazine publisher going into the book business. Success was immediate and big. There was an instant need for a lot of people to help to create books and promotion.

"There's nothing new under the publishing sun. Every good subject has been done again and again. When I was at Time-Life Books we did subjects that had been done before. The sets we brought out were sound, stable and proven. But Time-Life Books added far more quality than had ever been done before. Time Inc. gave us a superb editorial staff. Time-Life Books, pictorially and in words, did each subject with extraordinary quality. I can't give enough credit to Time Inc. for this.

"We soon built a lot of promotion people in-house, particularly from the Time and Life subscription department. There was great talent there—Nick Samstag and Shel Gould and others. The same feeling for quality carried into the advertising both in direct mail and in space. With each presentation we tried to

produce a classier book and promotion than anything done by the competition.

"Success was not due to a technological breakthrough. For instance, the web press was coming in and available for mailings but did not, at that point, make the difference. The "Life World Library" books were the first Life books printed on offset. There was no creative breakthrough or any completely different approach. We just did everything better. We identified more completely with Life and Time, used pictures more effectively and had better copy. We used more color and used it better. It was the right time and the right offer to the right list.

"Early on, it was apparent that things looked very good as results from tests came in and confirmation tests were run. I called Joan in May 1960 and asked her to join me. I told her it seemed safe to come over. She gave immediate notice and came in two weeks. By the time she came, 'I told her, I've got a secretary. Just sit here, listen and do anything needed.' Joan picked up the pieces. Within a short time, she took over all direct mail. Then she took over advertising. Then she became sales manager."

The first year largely involved use of house lists and house ads. Then outside lists were used successfully. At first, space ads had mixed results. The second year Jerry Hardy gave Lester Wunderman a chance at the business. WR&K had enough success in magazines for the "Life World Nature Library" to project widely. Later, pre-prints did well in newspapers for a number of offers of Time-Life Books.

Time-Life Books had phenomenal sales the first year, and phenomenal growth for its first three and a half years, after which Jerry Hardy moved into other areas of Time Inc. Jerry points out that it has had phenomenal growth ever since. Currently, under Joan Manley—now in her twentieth year there—and including Book-of-the-Month Club and Little Brown, Time Inc. does a book business of over $400 million a year.

"I invented Time-Life Books. I founded it. I built it. But, in 1964, I left it. The overwhelming percentage of sales volume has occurred after I left. Joan has been responsible for all that has happened since. I'm not even familiar with a great deal that has been done. I see them socially, not on business. ' From the beginning, Time-Life Books made substantial contributions to overall Time Inc. profits. Jerry Hardy moved from books to become publisher of Life, where he remained for six years. Then he took on a new challenge.

In 1970, Jerry Hardy became president of the Dreyfus Corporation. "I joined Dreyfus on January 16, 1970, and left on January 16, 1980." Mutual funds are such a specialized form of mail order and so tightly regulated that few in mail order feel comfortable in it. Few copywriters are familiar enough with the legal strictures to write copy for it.

"For two or three years, I was learning. I familiarized myself with the SEC and other government and trade regulations. When the time arrived and Mutual Funds' shares had the possibility to be sold by mail order, I was about the only guy who had much direct marketing experience. Money market funds were the ideal product to apply my book selling experience to.

"At first, I wrote all the ads, the mailing pieces, the radio commercials. I even performed in some. First, we used WR&K. Later, we also used Rapp & Collins. Both were agencies I had worked with in selling books. We used book club techniques very similar to those used at Doubleday and at Time-Life." In a year and a half, Dreyfus sold a billion dollars worth of the Dreyfus Liquid Assets Fund.

Jerry spent ten years at Dreyfus Corporation, resigning as

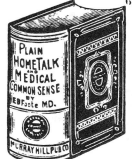

president on January 16, 1980. Since leaving Dreyfus, he has become a consultant and is in great demand. "I like it. Working for myself is quite delightful. It has drawbacks. I can't pass on paper work to others. I can't accomplish something and for a little while coast. If I slow up, income slows up."

Early in 1979, Jerry Hardy became part of a group that bought the H.S. Stuttman publishing business. "I'm 1%." Jerry is Chairman of the Board. Stuttman had been an outstanding syndicator of continuity sets. Stuttman had worked closely with Doubleday in developing many of them with Doubleday materials licensed to Stuttman, much of which Jerry had been in on in his Doubleday days. All this will now help Stuttman growth. "With Stuttman, I'm back to books."

"I find it best to do what I enjoy. I work on services, books and magazines. I never did much in insurance, but I do some now." In 1981, he became Chairman of the Board of Harper's monthly magazine, as well as advisor. He's a busy man.

Note: The following are a number of questions I asked Jerry Hardy which he has kindly answered for readers of this book.

Q. *How important have computers been in your career and how do you see their use by direct marketers in the future?*

A. They've been very important and will be more so. Way back, I saw Doubleday couldn't go on with Address-O-Graph, although volume using Address-O-Graph was enormous. When I was starting at Time-Life, computers almost killed the book department. There the programs had been designed for magazine fulfillment. The programs really didn't work for open-end selling.

The computer people didn't expect the kind of growth we had in Time-Life Books. When we expanded, they weren't ready. But they straightened it all out and we greatly depended on computer processing and billing.

Q. *Will specialized or general book clubs and programs prove most profitable in the future?*

A. There will be two markets. There will be very large clubs. There will be a proliferation of specialized programs. I believe that just as magazines have proliferated with narrower and narrower interests in specialized areas like golf and tennis, and with magazines like Science 82, book clubs will go that route.

Q. *What changes do you see coming in mail order?*

A. There will be vastly improved segmentation. You will know more and more not just about segments of a list but about individuals on a list. Already specialized book operations are taking advantage of this. The Los Angeles Times-Mirror, in the book operations of their magazines, has done so. Time Inc. has with open subscription series such as Cities of the World, Nature, Science, Cooking, Sailing and Boats.

Q. *What kind of future growth do you expect in mail order?*

A. The mail order business will get a lot bigger. There will be all kinds of more and more precisely segmented catalogs. Within five years, this trend will grow tremendously.

Q. *Will small mail order ventures have a chance?*

A. Everyone who has an entrepreneurial spirit will find a way. Bernie Goldhirsch did with his small business magazine, INC. Texas Monthly did. Entrepreneurs will always spring up and find a way in mail order.

Q. *What kind of education do you recommend for someone wanting to start a career in mail order and direct marketing?*

A. I would urge anyone wanting to get into this business to learn how to read and write effectively. An appalling number now

coming out of school and college can't spell or write. They're weak in grammar, semantics, spelling. I urge that those still being educated learn how to use language to communicate and persuade. Philosophy is a marvelous key to understanding what makes people what they are. And until you understand what moves people you can't help them persuade themselves. I recommend a liberal arts education. As to any business courses, they don't seem to hurt too much.

Chapter 2
General Mills' Mail Order Mix

Betty Crocker's recipe that made it grow faster than overall company sales.

The five mail order companies of General Mills grew faster than the overall company for ten years. Sales of the mail order group have gone up from under ten million dollars to over three hundred million dollars.

In ten years, sales went from a small fraction of one percent of overall sales to five percent. For the next five years the target has been to raise that percentage, perceptibly. It's all been happening because General Mills was so successful in its food processing business it decided to diversify.

Probably the one man who pushed hardest for launching and building a mail order division was Donald F. Swanson, who later became Vice Chairman of the Board. By 1981, the one man most concerned with overall mail order sales for General Mills was Robert Hatch, Executive Vice President, Specialty Retailing and Furniture.

By the mid 1960's, General Mills was becoming so large a food processor that any further acquisitions in the food business seemed an invitation to criticism. It was decided to take a diversification mode. The first step was to go into toys. That has become very large. The next steps were into fashion apparel, into restaurants and into mail order.

Back in 1970, late in the year, General Mills acquired its first mail order company. It was Lee Ward, a crafts catalog house. In 1971, General Mills bought Eddie Bauer, in outdoor sports equipment mail order. In 1973, General Mills bought two mail order companies—Harris Stamp and The Talbots—in fashion mail order. In 1974, General Mills bought Bowers & Ruddy, in rare coin mail order.

Whatever General Mills has paid in total for all mail order companies combined has been only the beginning of its investment in mail order. Each year, as growth has required, it has invested more, whatever it needed to meet objectives. And every year the mail order companies have grown. From 1975 to 1981, all mail order growth was internal—the years when the big majority of mail order growth up to 1981 occurred. Progress has not been without setbacks. For the fiscal year ending in April 1981, pretax earnings of General Mills mail order companies were only about half the previous year. But the previous year, Bowers & Ruddy had a big one-time mail order success, as described in this story.

Comparisons of the return on equity for General Mills' mail order versus overall sales have not been published, nor have the

---

Mechanical Arts Simplified.

6458 A work of reference for the use of architects, architectural iron workers, builders, blacksmiths, bookkeepers, boilermakers, contractors, civil, mechanical, hydraulic, mining, stationary, marine and locomotive engineers, foremen of machine shops, fireman, master mechanics of railroads, master car builders, machine shop proprietors, machinery jobbers, machinists, pattern makers, roadmasters, and business men generally. Compiled and arranged by D. B. Dixon, and with the most exhaustive electrical department by Thos. G. Grier, 480 pages. Retail price.... ....$2.50
Our price.................................... 1.75
Postage.. .14

Practical Draughting,
6459 A series of practical illustrations in draughting. By Pemberton. 12mo., cloth.......$0.75
Postage.. .08

Painters,' Varnishers' and Gilders' Companion.
6460 A most practical work on this subject. 12mo., cloth....................................$1.15
Postage.. .14

objectives as to what percentage its mail order should earn on equity. But, overall, General Mills has a very sound formula for growth. It's very balanced. By 1981, it had grown overall with increasing profits for twenty consecutive years.

The mills of the gods of General Mills grind very slowly— but exceedingly well. General Mills is a scientist of marketing. The company is accustomed to testing and projecting. One field of great expertise is its know-how in the use of premiums—the promotion of which has many similarities to mail order.

Lester Wunderman and other greats in mail order have reflected on the effect of mail order advertising on the 97% who don't buy from a typical successful mailing—and the 99½% who don't buy from the average successful mail order ad. General Mills saw a plus in the high percentage of sales a mail order firm spends on advertising, and a possible way to take advantage of it.

Each of the companies acquired was a catalog house. Four had owned one or more retail stores. Several had started as retailers and then gone into mail order. For each, retail store expansion—largely promoted by its catalog and magazine mail order advertising—might be accomplished . . . with the added ingredient of General Mills money.

The plan would be to buy soundly run companies, keep management and back them. They would only be replaced if things went wrong. At first, they would be given widest leeway. General Mills management would gradually develop a more detailed knowledge of each company, more mail order expertise, and more know-how in applying its great store of general marketing expertise to mail order.

After the advent of James Ruben, Group Vice President, Specialty Retailing, this process began to accelerate. The concept was to go through a transformation—to manage more as well as invest in the mail order companies. "We're not just a holding company for our mail order companies. We take a much more active participation in the group. We take a strategic interest. We try to contribute quite a bit on the marketing side.

"General Mills is happy with its mail order companies. We would not hesitate to acquire another if we liked the company. The expansion into retail is just a strategy that worked where it fit. We might or might not do so with another mail order company, if acquired. We have no policy against sticking to mail order only in an acquired mail order company. We don't consider mail order necessarily a stepping stone to a store operation. What we might do in other mail order acquisitions would depend on how the consumer reacts.

"Since General Mills took over each mail order operation, sales have grown dramatically for each. Harris is the world's largest stamp company; General Mills believes that Bowers & Ruddy may be the world's largest dealer in rare valuable coins. The formula of retail and mail order has been most dramatically successful for the other three mail order companies of General Mills. Overall growth of Eddie Bauer, LeeWards and The Talbots, using the catalog and stores combination method, has been most dramatic."

The Betty Crocker recipe, to bake a mail-order cake, has worked. Let's look at an acquired company . . . Eddie Bauer. By four years after acquisition, sales had tripled. By six years later, sales tripled again—nine times annual sales of the first year after acquisiton. Let's look at its history.

In 1920, Eddie Bauer opened a retail sporting goods store in Seattle, Washington. On and off, for most of the period between 1920 and 1924, he operated several retail stores in Seattle. At some point, he began to sell and got very interested in badminton equipment. He wanted to sell only the best in the world. He could

not find a shuttlecock satisfactory to him—and decided to make the best, himself.

That got Eddie Bauer into feathers. He got interested in goose down. He got an idea for an insulated down jacket . . . padded, quilted, enclosing down insulating material. He tried out the same idea for sleeping bags. In 1935, he started to manufacture both. In 1936, he got a patent for his method. In World War II, he supplied the armed services with both sleeping bags and jackets, bomber jackets. He negotiated an unusual contract. His jackets and sleeping bags became government issue, but with his label.

The label started Eddie Bauer in the mail order business, particularly with his bomber jacket. L.L. Bean started in mail order with Bean's Hunting Shoe and Eddie Bauer with his jacket. When bomber crews left the service, crew members began mailing in orders for bomber jackets. Then their relatives did, then friends, and then friends of friends—and their friends. Then Eddie Bauer began to run mail order ads and then to start a mail order catalog.

Eddie Bauer was the father of the many billion dollar padded coat industry. His bomber jacket was the concept for it all—for men, women and children. And his padded insulation garment concept was the basis for all Eddie Bauer manufacturing today. "It's all packaging of goose down insulating material," says Jim Casey, President of Eddie Bauer. "We restrict manufacturing to our own insulated line. We used to manufacture vests. We've dabbled in other things."

Jim Casey came to Eddie Bauer in 1975, from New York City. "I had very little knowledge of mail order. I had been general manager at Ticketron, a Control Data subsidiary. It did sell tickets mail order, as well as retail, for theatricals and sports. Before that I was a controller for several other Control Data operations. Most of my career had been financial.

"Before Control Data I was in management for General Mills. I became involved with the establishment of the Craft, Games and Toys Division. I assisted in acquisitions. Before that I was an accountant. I graduated from the University of Minnesota. After Ticketron, I returned to General Mills. There, I was thrust into Eddie Bauer which was having a problem."

Back in 1971, when acquired, Eddie Bauer had been in the process of opening its first modern retail store in downtown Seattle. The store was a success. For the next three years after the acquisition, with the aid of General Mills money, Eddie Bauer plunged ahead in opening more stores—too fast. It was a failure of control. In 1975, the president of Eddie Bauer and the controller resigned. Jim Casey came in as the new vice president of finance.

In 1977, an attempt was made to make the business more contra-seasonal. Eddie Bauer went into golf and tennis equipment. There was one problem. The Eddie Bauer customers didn't go for it. They weren't tennis players and golfers. They were campers, hunters, fishermen and outdoorsmen. The effort bombed. The golf and tennis equipment had to be worked off. The end result was that the profile of the Eddie Bauer customer became very clear. Future planning simplified and Jim Casey became president.

"Our mix of mail order and store business is roughly 50-50. Our five-year plan is to keep this mix. We have 16 stores now. In five years, our plan provides for roughly doubling the number of stores, increasing the sales of each and building the catalog business to keep equal to total retail. We figure inflation running at 9%. On this basis, we're looking for 16% to 20% growth each year. Whatever inflation becomes, we look for a real growth of 7% to 11% a year.

"We're emphasizing more business per store and per catalog. In the last years we haven't increased catalog distribution too much. In 1980, we distributed about 15 million in the U.S. and in Canada. We have close to 1,300,000 mail order customers. To develop more business per customer we make special mailings to our customers, quite aside from the catalog. We do so in a very focused way. Segmentation is very important to us. We try to mail the right offer to the right customer based on the previous buying record of each.

"Our stores run sales. Our mail order customers want to benefit and we want them to. We've had some success printing special brochures offering some of the same merchandise in the catalog at reduced prices, usually 4-page or 8-page flyers. Prices are reduced 30% to 40%. These are all our mark-downs. We do not ask our suppliers to sell to us at lower prices for such sales.

"Close to 50% of our customers buy via credit or bank cards. About 45% send in checks. Under 5% buy on open account. Above all, they buy our insulated wear. We're very wedded to apparel in the fall and winter catalogs and to hardware in our summer book.

"Our vice president of mail order is Richard Black. He's a financial man, an MBA. He and I feel very much at home in mail order. We like mail order. We like the ability to test and measure. Mail order is very analytical. It's not a classical marketing business. It's numbers. We devise tests, run them, analyze them, throw out the failures and build on the successes.

"We set aside 20% of our budget to test new products and items. If we have an item that pays out profitably, we keep running. If you see our item repeating, you can be reasonably sure we're doing well. We move quickly to cut expenditures if we're losing. The old time mail order entrepreneur sometimes plunged fast and hard, thinking he was making money when perhaps he wasn't. We think we can better define what is making money and act accordingly.

"The big contribution of General Mills to Eddie Bauer was first to bring money to the ballgame. It has also endeavored to aid in any way it could the growth and profit building of Eddie Bauer. Research has played an important part in overall General Mills marketing success. Research has not been an alternative for testing. It has been very helpful in starting a dialogue within our organization. It's been a challenge to old, fixed ideas. It's been a stimulation of our creative people."

Overall, the ten-year record since General Mills took over

has been very good—multiplying Eddie Bauer's size nine times and steadily making money in inflation and with ever-growing interest rates. "1980 had to be in many ways the worst year possible for retailers," says Jim Casey. "Interest rates were killing. But we had significant growth and improved earnings. We achieved our objectives. Not many retailers outside of catalogs have done this."

Eddie Bauer has character . . . integrity . . . a strong customer loyalty—and a specialized universe to appeal to. This is what General Mills has sought in each of its mail order acquisitions. Another of its mail order companies is The Talbots, a similar situation in a totally different field—fashion.

The Talbots, sells simple, classic clothes for women. "Basically," says President William De Jonge, "our business is built on style, taste and quality. As entrepreneurs we know exactly the kind of people we sell to—and what they need and want. We work hard to give it to them."

The Talbots started as a retail store, in 1947. It later began to run mail order ads in magazines and created its own mail order catalog. Mail order became the majority of the business. It still is, although The Talbots now has over 20 stores. The business is located in Hingham, Massachusetts. Its stores are in Massachusetts, Connecticut, New York, Pennsylvania, Maryland and Washington, D.C.

When General Mills acquired the company, in 1973, The Talbots distributed five million catalogs. By 1981, the distribution was fifteen million catalogs and there were 350,000 customers. The Talbots formula is "the timeless look that works for day or evening, season after season, investment dressing." Prices are modest, with a smattering of a bit higher priced tempters.

The Talbots succeeded in putting a small specialty fashion shop, with a flair for merchandise selection, into a very personal catalog. It was one of the very first of its genre, after World War II. No one has done it better. Others have gone into higher-priced fashion. The Talbots has stayed with its market, although it now devotes almost 10% of its catalogs to the equivalent type of men's clothes—which it does not stock in its stores.

Favorites for women are sweater dresses, Shetland pullovers, tweed blazers, flannel pants, shirt dresses. There's quite a variety of always tasteful sweaters, shirts and skirts. It's very suburban, but for working women who want to look nice and watch dollars.

Bill De Jonge had been with The Talbots before General Mills bought the company—and had a retail background before joining The Talbots. He's very low-key, but quietly confident. Those in mail order praise him highly as very effective. To Bill, The Talbots was successful, is successful and will be successful. But he's matter of fact and appreciates the benefits General Mills has given the company.

"One of the advantages has been capital for expansion. We do get encouragement to use new tools such as research and use of demographic information. Before recently, our small size didn't justify much investment in research. We do more now. We're constantly experimenting with new mail order methods."

One method The Talbots has developed is the encouragement of and handling of incoming telephone shopping calls—on an 800 number. When you call The Talbots, whoever takes your call works hard to help you shop by phone. "We train our people carefully to handle these calls effectively and properly." There's a great effort to answer any question about any item, to help a phone customer choose the right size—and particularly to inform the customer of any items on which there will be any shipping delay. After or before hours, a tape recorder takes your call and a nice lady phones you back the next day.

Bill De Jonge is guarded about growth plans but expects The Talbots approach will continue to work. "In inflation and when interest rates are high, it is harder to earn money. But people still need clothes. We'll still have them at good values and the business will still grow."

In my upcoming book, "The Mail Order Underground", I tell in some detail the history of another General Mills mail order subsidiary, The H.E. Harris Stamp Co. This book is entirely about mail order ventures that started with a classified ad. Harris Stamp Co. did—with a free classified ad, when Henry Harris was 14 years old.

Since 1966, six years before acquisition of H.E. Harris, Wesley Mann has been there. He's president. "I was sold with the company." H.E. Harris has not required capital after the original purchase by General Mills. "There's been no infusion of money. We've never required capital.

"We're in four hobbies. For 65 years, our entire business was in stamp collecting. Then in 1975, we got into banknotes—demonetized ones no longer in use. It's very small compared with the stamp business, a problem of supply. Then we got into stamp cover collecting—lastly in coins, mostly inexpensive foreign ones.

"The collectible craze had an effect on quality stamps. Investment stamps were hot. We do relatively little in this. Meanwhile, our main business, the hobby collecting of stamps, plods along. The other businesses we have are outgrowths of stamp collecting.

"Every stamp company was started by an amateur entrepreneur and stamp collector. I was the first professional manager in the stamp business. Before here, I was in retail sales in product management. I had some experience in mail order, in gifts. I was not strong in it when I came in to run the company, but now I love the mail order business.

"Before the acquisition, when Harris Stamp was a private company, the object was not growth. It was profit and taking out money. Since the General Mills takeover, the emphasis has been on growth and profit. Since 1973 to now, we've grown 12% to 15% annually. In this business there's no opportunity for unlimited growth. The size of the hobbies we're in determines our potential. We have steadily made the business more profitable in a variety of ways.

"We haven't increased our square footage during a period our business has grown five and a half times. During this period, we cut down from a peak of 410 employees to our present 375.

"We haven't been able to do this very much with automation. Our business isn't conducive to it. We do have more systemization. Mostly, we have better selectivity in what we sell. We anticipate better. We sell less widgets for more money. We've tremendously upgraded the stamps we sell, increasing our average sale accordingly. We used to be in the penny stamp approval business, making many sales to children. Now our business is directed at adult hobbyists to investors.

"The business was for most of its life based on sending to customers on approval shipments each month. We still have these continuity programs, but only when specifically instructed to do so do we ship this way to customers.

"As far as training our people goes, on the technical side of our business, the stamp know-how, we run in-house schooling. For specialists in data processing and direct marketing we hire already experienced people from outside. In adding to our marketing staff we're not concerned with educational background. We do look for people who have had mail order experience with smaller companies.

"We tried the concept of retail stores. We opened a store and closed it. We backed out. In collectibles, on-the-spot management is needed—to wheel, deal, buy and sell. A stamp and coin store is in a competitive, entrepreneurial environment. Someone comes in and wants silver melted down and to be paid. The manager has to use his or her judgment. This is not practical with the constraints and requirements of a public company. Overhead made the store unprofitable. We stopped it. We do better selling to stores.

"Our business is 50-50 mail order and non-mail order. Our non-mail order business will grow faster this year and thereafter. We're selling more to stores. The stamp and coin stores are not growing. The field is a sort of holding action. But for twenty years we've been selling stamps to supermarkets, drug stores and variety stores. It's a tremendous business. This fiscal year it's really growing. Over the next five years, we will increase this type of business. This field will improve. By 1985, mass market sales will be 65% to 70% of our business.

"We're looking at new ways of selling, new mail order communications. But we're careful. We're smaller than other General Mills mail order companies. We do about 10% of the group volume, about $30 million out of $300,000,000." And so, with its headquarters in Boston, Massachusetts, H.E. Harris continues.

Another General Mills mail order company, its first acquisition, is LeeWard's Creative Crafts—in Elgin, Illinois. Larry Kunz is president. When crafts were big, so was LeeWard's. When crafts had problems, LeeWard's did. Its mail order end was able to go with the tide and did relatively better than its retail end. In retail, it had found the short-term rental of space given up by supermarkets to be quite a bargain. But the cost of money to carry inventory in the cheap space was no bargain. Now the tendency is to go into small stores, with smaller inventory. The catalog is tighter. Things are better. Larry Kunz, president of Lee Ward, is discreet. "We keep a low profile in the mail order field. We have nothing to gain by publicizing our successes—or our future plans."

The fifth General Mills mail order company is Bowers and Ruddy of Los Angeles, California. It was the last company bought. It has particularly benefitted from the boom in collectibles. It sells expensive coins, much of them for investment. William Hawfield is president.

Bowers & Ruddy is the fastest growing of General Mills' mail order businesses, the biggest mail order coin business in the world and unlike most catalog businesses anywhere.

It advertises far less to get catalog inquiries, distributes a fraction of the catalogs and does far more dollars of sales per catalog distributed. Its average sale is much higher. Some transactions are huge. It sold the Brasher Doubloon for $715,000, the highest price ever paid for a coin. It gets more customers from word of mouth.

In 1974, General Mills acquired it—after it had been in business for only four years. But both principals—Dave Bowers and Jim Ruddy—had been well known and highly thought of in the coin field for twenty years. Jim Ruddy was president until 1977. Then David Bowers became president and Bill Hawfield became general manager. In 1978, Bill became president.

"Bowers & Ruddy was and is almost 85% mail order. The only retail is by appointment. Our mail order business principally comes from our catalogs and publications. We advertise to get catalog inquiries mainly in numismatic magazines—90% in Coin World and Numismatic News. Our ads vary from a quarter page to two pages. We follow up in a variety of ways.

"We send out monthly bulletins (8 to 24 pages) listing coins for sale. These go to over 20,000 collectors to whom we also send a quarterly catalog of about 70 pages. We also send auction catalogs which offer specific consignments. These run 75 to 100 pages and go to 10,000 auction customers. Our catalog publications are mainly written by Dave Bowers. He is a unique writer, better on coins than anyone in the world, and a big reason why we're looked up to.

"We have 14 numismatists. These are coin people who have been collectors since they were kids. They go out to coin shows, travel the country, read a lot and stay in touch with newest changes in the coin market. Our mail order customers call us. We'll discuss a coin and then often send it out for the collector to examine—registered, insured mail—and safely, all over the world. There is always a 30-day return privilege.

"Many people have come to us as investors, because of the record coins have had of appreciating 30% a year. We try to make collectors of them, to interest them in learning and reading about coins they own and then coins in general. We take the long view—to be in business twenty years from now. We grade conservatively and don't strive for the biggest mark-up. We're totally above board and try to act as a trusted advisor.

"We're not as large as the other General Mills mail order companies. From 1974 through 1978, sales went up about 20% a year. In 1977, sales went up 50% and, in 1980, sales went up 100%. There were three keys to the increase.

"Bowers & Ruddy had acquired respect and status among coin collectors. The market became right. We were in the right place at the right time with the right services. Then, in 1979, Bowers & Ruddy was offered the auction of the John Hopkins collection. The first three sections brought 22 million dollars. Overall, in the auction we realized over 30 million dollars. That was a tremendous burst of volume for those two years.

"It's been a help to be owned by General Mills. Mainly, they play the role of a board of directors, and very well. We get some management help, but a free hand in daily operations. When things go well, they don't interfere. If we make a mistake, they investigate and act. Otherwise, they get into plans, major decisions and most of all—controls."

Bill Hawfield went to VMI, then University of Virginia School of Business and, in 1969, to General Mills. "My first job was with the Kraftmaster Toy Division, selling computerized personal paintings." Kraftmaster sold them mail order, as well as paint-by-number kits (mainly sold in stores) . . . and accessories to people who bought kits in stores. "We had 120,000 mail order customers in paint-by-numbers and stitchery. We sold paintings via two-step. Print ads got inquiries and brochures followed up. We mailed our customers and experimented with many forms of mail order. I learned from it all.

"I never expected to get into anything like this but I enjoy coins and mail order a great deal. It's completely different in many ways than anything I did before . . . yet I still can use my accumulated experience. I've met many small businessmen in coins, and gotten great respect for them. I'm too busy in operations to become a real collector. I'm more of an accumulator, but I'm learning.

"We have growth plans in other numismatic areas. We plan to expand vertically and horizontally . . . into lower cost coins, bullion, maybe other collectibles." Bowers & Ruddy may prove to be the Brasher Doubloon of Betty Crocker's Mail Order Company collection.

Kent Larsen, Director Business Development, discusses the mail order strategy of General Mills: "We're consumer-oriented.

We believe in research. We're always interested in consumer perceptions, in how the consumer views our business. We like to determine who buys, finding out their attitudes and what they would prefer in types of new product. We like to analyze mail order operations as we would any business. We like the concept of store expansion from mail order but are not welded to it in all cases.

"In the merchandise selection area, products can be studied from the consumer point of view. Preferences can be learned. The present products can be compared with competitive products and with possible improved products by the consumer for us.

"We use many kinds of research. We have research managers in the subsidiaries and at the corporate level. We work in all types of research. We're not into red versus blue research or other theoretical research. We are much more involved in actual, actionable and more significant research.

"At Eddie Bauer, we manufacture a lot of the garments. Doing so improves margin. What we manufacture is important. Research helps guide us. It also helps us make merchandise selection. Ideally, we would use research in making every important merchandise selection decision. We don't always do this; but we depend a good deal on research. For this, we have used specialists in the kinds of research required.

"It's made a big difference in our mail order businesses. The biggest changes have been in appearance. Research on customer attitudes had led to an upgrading of appearance of merchandise in each catalog. Instead of flat studio pictures, we now have more on location. The overall changes have been great.

"We've found that our mail order sales lay the ground work for retail sales and that retail sales get new customers who often then buy by mail order, as well as from stores. Mail order companies spend a bigger percentage of sales on advertising. Smaller mail order companies often spend far more and become far better known than considerably bigger non-mail order companies. Opening stores is natural for a catalog house with a special market. The mail order advertising paves the way for the store.

"When a store for Eddie Bauer or another of our mail order companies opens, our share of the market in that area expands, but at first our store in the area takes away, to some degree, from our mail order sales in the area. Then our mail order sales in the area come back and expand to more than before the store opening. From then on, both store and mail order sales might increase. Some customers go more to the store and some buy more from the catalog.

"We haven't used all possible mail order methods. Could contests be used? Possibly. We never have. We've used laser letters to a minor extent. We use inbound WATS. It's working very well. We haven't experimented with outward WATS. We've never used a negative option plan in a mail order operation."

It may well be that as the new electronic and world mail order age dawns that General Mills management will be able to do what each subsidiary may not be able to . . . devote the time, the money and develop a core of this new kind of mail order expertise . . . and then multiply its mail order operation further.

Chapter 3
Retirement Mail Order

*Why more retirees are going into it,
and how; some cautions.*

Mail order business owners taper off in it. Direct marketing experts become proprietors in it. Ad pros, with no mail order background, find it the ultimate challenge. But most in it have never sold by mail order or been in advertising. They are beginners . . . from Fortune 500 executives to blue collar mechanics . . . housewives, salesmen and engineers . . . specialists, and those with no special skills.

Success can come through past career, hobbies or both. Some plan it for years. The best time to get into a retirement mail order business is before you retire. Here's one who planned retirement mail order for 28 years and did get in it early.

It started simply . . . just raising orchids. Then carpet salesman John Hanes began hybridizing . . . crossing one orchid with another to produce a new hybrid. He specialized in the Paphiopedilum, the slipper orchid.

This led to John Hanes' retirement business, "Hanes' Orchids of Distinction", at 6264 N. Bion Avenue, San Gabriel, California 91775. It is successful, substantial and ships bare-root seedlings world-wide. It started gradually. First, John began to exchange with other hobbyists. Then he started a little mail order moonlighting. It became a real business when John retired, in 1974.

Most growing and shipping is done by a partner. Everything else is done from home, with almost no overhead. Each year John comes up with something new and unexpected. He breeds in new features, new colors or an unusual variety of colors from one plant. He produces new shadings, gradations and nuances of a color.

His green orchids include green with rose mahogany lines, bronze green, green with white fringe, green gold or whatever. He breeds bigger greens, smaller greens, stemmier greens, greens with extra wide petals and greener greens. And he varies each new hybrid he brings out, in much the same manner.

From the first, John Hanes' hobby was practical and profitable. The first test ad John Hanes ran after retirement was in "The American Orchid Society Bulletin", cost $350 and made money. For four years, he has run in every issue profitably, now with full pages. The Orchid Digest has given more borderline results. The third magazine tried, Plants Alive, proved to have too broad an audience to be profitable.

The full page and other ads have no pictures. They're all type, and advertising production cost is relatively low. Total cost of all magazine ads is under 3% of sales. Clear, factual copy features six to eight varieties with prices. Mail orders range from a dozen to hundreds of plants. Usually the entire list of seedlings is also offered at no cost, as a catalog.

"Sure I could have a $50,000 catalog in beautiful four color. But it's not necessary." John Hanes does it with a list of 99 items typed on both sides of two pages and reproduced in black and white. The list is mailed to ad inquiries, old customers and people in the field.

The list includes a summary of seedlings. It also gives cross breeds being developed including the two parents used and expectancy of hybrid. "I mail customers twice a year. If any do not order within a year, I drop the names from my mailing list."

Each year total advertising expense of magazines is lower in percentage of overall sales, and sales are more world-wide. Most are now overseas. Each year the average order is higher, there's more repeat business and more referral business. The business was not entered into primarily for money. Yet it yearly becomes more profitable and satisfying.

Why do they do it? After being vice president of the U.S., Nelson Rockefeller sold art reproductions by mail order to find a new life, a new career and a new interest.

For David R. Williams, retired aviation systems supervisor, it's fulfillment. "I'm a mail order tinsmith. I work metal the same way they did in the 18th Century. I use finest quality pewter plate." David handcrafts lanterns, chandeliers, sconces and other authentic replicas. You'll find him at "Village Lantern", 598 Union Street, North Marshfield, Massachusetts 02059. His small ads run in Yankee, Early American Life, Americana and other magazines.

"I gross about $25,000 a year. But it's more satisfying than any executive supervisory work I've done."

Retirees go into mail order for many reasons; for the extra money . . . to be boss . . . as part hobby . . . to help a younger family member get started . . . or just to keep busy. Often retirees want only supplemental income, but to work at their own pace at home. There are failures as well as successes.

But often success does come. Roderick K. Penfield of East Setauket, New York, has been a retired TWA pilot for several years . . . and a mail order moonlighter before retirement, since 1970.

Pilots work intensively but have considerable time off. For years, this gave time for his hobby. He would photograph each

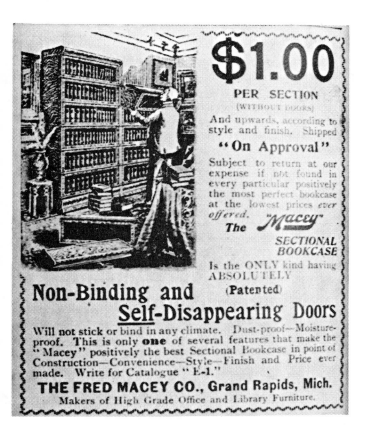

type of airplane used worldwide by most airlines. Rod found that collectors wanted such pictures. He made slides and began to sell them. In 1970, he started to sell by mail order with a one-inch ad . . . costing $51 . . . in Air Progress Magazine.

The ad pulled inquiries and forced Rod to make a simple catalog. This was simply a typewritten list of each slide he had, with a price . . . and inexpensively reproduced by offset printing. The catalog now lists 5,502 slides and sells for $1 in ads. These are still one inch and run in three American and in one English magazine . . . "Air Classics", "Wings", "Airpower" and "Air Pictorial".

Each slide sells for 50¢ and is made on Rod's own slide reproducing machine. "We get few inquiries . . . but seven out of ten buy." Most customers are collectors. They collect slides of all planes used by one or several airlines; they usually are men. The average order is about $10. Rod's photos account for 90% of slides in the catalog. At present small volume, it's breakeven, mostly a hobby. "But I'm running more ads. It should soon make money."

In 1973, Rod tested a mail order ad for The Greek Fisherman's Cap. It's knitted, woolen, nautical and jaunty. Rod ran a two-inch on two column ad in the New York Times Magazine . . . under the name, "Smuggler's Imports". For it, Rod used a photograph of his bearded dentist wearing the cap and looking like a sea captain. The ad cost $477 and made good money.

Rod ran his Greek Fisherman's Cap ad just once a year, the last Sunday in November, in The New York Times Magazine. He ran every other month in The National Fisherman. He ran the same ad in one other magazine, "Boating". It was a very small, profitable mail order business.

Then Rod quintupled the business at no extra expense. He added three words to his ad, "Dealer Inquiries Invited". Solely due to this, 80% of sales are now to stores and catalogs. Meanwhile, Rod began to import his caps directly from the Greek manufacturer. This gave a good margin for trade sales and improved mail order profit.

Rod keeps his inventory in the cellar of a Port Jefferson retail store. Mail is addressed to "Smuggler's Imports" at 140 East Main Street, Port Jefferson, New York 11777, the store's address. Mail is then forwarded to Rod who conducts all his business from one room in his home. Rod pays the regular mail order rate for ads.

Soon, "Smuggler's Imports" did over $90,000 in sales annually. It made over 15% in profits. Rod has no salesmen, makes no sales calls and spends no money in promotion to the trade. Most orders now come from stores . . . by mail. Rod still runs his same mail order schedule.

Rod likes retirement mail order. He likes the travel his business requires and pays for. He plans to expand the slide business, the cap business and go into new items.

Young & Rubicam is the world's biggest advertising agency. Frank Fagan retired as executive vice president in 1962 but began to prepare for retirement in 1957. He bought S.T. Preston & Son, Inc., Ship Chandler, a marine supply retailer in Greenport, Long Island.

Preston's was founded in 1882. When Frank bought it sales were only across the counter and at a loss. Frank's hobby was boating. He had once been a merchandise manager at Wanamaker's Department Store. He could buy, write copy and market. He decided to put Preston's into mail order.

Frank's problem was to apply his very sophisticated experience to a very small enterprise when he was very busy at Y & R. The answer was George Rowsom. George was Frank's son-in-

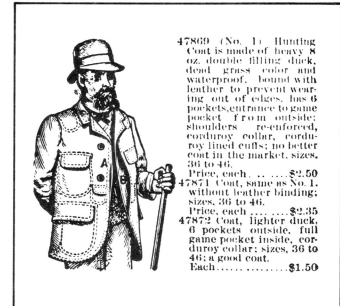

47869 (No. 1) Hunting Coat is made of heavy 8 oz. double filling duck, dead grass color and waterproof, bound with leather to prevent wearing out of edges, has 6 pockets, entrance to game pocket from outside; shoulders re-enforced, corduroy collar, corduroy lined cuffs; no better coat in the market, sizes, 36 to 46.
Price, each $2.50
47871 Coat, same as No. 1, without leather binding; sizes, 36 to 46.
Price, each $2.35
47872 Coat, lighter duck, 6 pockets outside, full game pocket inside, corduroy collar; sizes, 36 to 46; a good coat.
Each $1.50

law. In 1957, George worked for Preston's briefly but was drafted into the service. He came back in 1959 and has been there ever since.

In 1957, Frank began to run mail order ads for Preston's. First items failed. An early success was selling government surplus giant balloons. Then Frank found the items that made today's Preston's—art prints and then ship models.

Small ads asked for inquiries. A simple brochure for art prints expanded into a 32-page catalog including ship models. Gift items followed. For a while, ship model sales were so heavy they were 70% of all sales. They are now about 30%. Marine prints put Preston's into the black. Ship models made a tidy profit. Mail was contributing profits and increasing store sales. By Fall 1981, the catalog had grown to 112 pages.

Andrea, George's wife and Frank's daughter, helped from the start. Andrea had some art background and began to layout and design the catalog. Andrea began to go with George to marine and gift shows and still does. They selected merchandise as a team. The Rowsoms have five children, four boys and one girl; three got in the business. Two boys work now for Preston's in summer jobs. Another boy did for three years.

Frank retired in 1962 . . . to devote his full energy to Preston's. He could still enjoy other aspects of retirement, thanks to his family. He made the big decisions but gradually Preston's turned from his retirement business into a family business with George taking over more management.

Preston's, over the years, has built up a list of 600,000 customers and inquiries. To maintain and increase its inquiry list, it keeps increasing its advertising but carefully. Running more inquiry ads produces more inquiries, and catalog sales from them. Mailing the catalog to 100,000 outside names then started and has jumped sales. Preston's now issues 300,000 catalogs in the spring and 300,000 in the fall, a total of 600,000 catalogs a year.

Much growth has come from increasing the average order, from repeat orders and from referrals. Preston's does some business wholesaling art prints to other outlets. The retail store is growing. It does 40% of overall sales. "The catalog gave the store a second life. The advertising has pulled in a lot of out-of-town-people," says George.

Twice a year, Preston's runs a one-twelfth page ad in National Geographic. The biggest size ad has been a quarter page in House Beautiful. New publications are cautiously tested. Preston's currently runs in 15 magazines.

Preston's is a quite comfortably successful family business. George says, "Our big potential growth is in mail order. But we want steady, safe growth. We want to service our customers." Gradually, George has taken over policy decisions as well as running operations. Frank's retirement business has become the legacy he planned.

George and Andrea and their children have never known an industrial environment. Greenport is an old harbor town on Long Island Sound. It has a freshness of air, a nostalgia of history, a new face each changing season . . . and a lot of nice people.

It took the drive, experience and master plan of Frank and hard work of George and Andrea to build Preston's success. It brought out their abilities and gave them pride and fulfillment. It's a splendid business with products of integrity, and advertising with restraint and good taste—and a centennial in 1982.

When is it too late? I know one former big company executive who started in mail order at 64 and started a second mail order business in his late 70's. He's now 90 and still sole owner of both. I know one grandmother who ran her first mail order ad at 75, profitably.

In this book I tell the story of the Tall Ships Prints, which my brother, Hamilton Hoge, tested 2½ months before his 70th birthday. He had been an electronics manufacturer and it was his first mail order experiment. By two months after his 71st birthday, he had done over $1,650,000 in sales on the item, at a good profit.

Carol Brown, of Putney, Vermont, sold by mail order for fifty years. Her Sherlock Holmes capes and fine tweeds are known widely. She combined mail order with a shop, tea, conversation and designing. Carol kept it up until she was 91. Her niece and partner, Laurie, acted as her right arm and helping hand.

Not age but ill health, low vitality or severe disability determines when retirement mail order is impractical.

There is an art to reducing a mail order business for retirement. Fred Tyarks, an old Huber Hoge client, owned and successfully operated Harian Publishing for many years. Then he retired to Nice, France, and for years profitably operated it on a small scale from there. All fulfillment was done by a relative in the U.S., while Fred kept buying the ads from France.

Elsewhere in this book I tell how John Stevenson, owner of Greystone Press, has made a big and successful but demanding mail order business smaller and smaller and constantly simpler with less strain. He dropped all but most profitable continuity programs . . . and reduced mailing ad schedules to cream choices . . . all the while reducing overhead to a smaller base . . . all to retirement mail order size.

"Give a man a fish and he can eat for a day. Teach him to fish and he can eat for life."

—Chinese Proverb

Herb Bijur, retired former president of McCall Patterns, is devoting his mail order talents to the New York Botanical Garden. "I'm having more fun than I ever had in my life." For their Garden Shops, Herb has started a catalog. He gives his expertise.

Herb found The Botanical Garden short on budget, the new business demanding, and no-risk mail order as important as making tiny tests. Harper's Magazine ran at no cost a double spread in color featuring garden prints from The Botanical Garden. Results were phenomenal. He tested an inch ad in The New Yorker Magazine. "We got inquiries for 40¢." He bootstrapped their mail order, making each ad pay its way.

Herb watches Garden Shop sales closely. Successful items get into the catalog. He is constantly alert to new garden products. He sometimes arranges to have promising new products tested by horticultural use in the gardens with analysis of results and recommendation of improvements. Approved new items may go into the catalog. The tiniest space catalog item that pulls more sales per square inch goes into bigger space. Herb keeps experimenting with new ways to sell more in space ads and via direct mail.

Each year Herb's new mail order projects are more profitable for The Botanical Garden. And each year Herb teaches his associates to do more in mail order, without him.

If you know anyone retired or planning retirement and considering mail order, here are some cautions:

1) Consider if up to it physically. Ask self, family, friends and doctor.

2) If dependent on social security, small pension, modest savings . . . avoid risk.

3) 50% of the second $6,000 a retiree earns annually . . . if 65 to 72 . . . is deducted from social security payments. Risk some of this.

4) Check business library. Study mail order.

5) Appraise own career, hobbies, interests . . . for field with more know-how than most.

6) Consider younger or stronger, shrewder or richer partner.

7) Risk time, special expertise, least money . . . or persuade others to risk it.

8) Retire *early* . . . when younger, stronger.

9) Plan retirement years ahead. If possible, moonlight first.

10) Write or invent something . . . and mail order moonlight it . . . . successfully . . . *before retirement*. Then license bigger firm to sell it . . . with royalty to you (not deductable from social security).

Mail order can succeed in later years. The good life can come at any time of life. A retirement mail order business can give satisfaction, fulfillment . . . and pride in things accomplished. Many do make it.

I wish I had space to report on retirement business in golf balls, lead soldier molds, navigation chart holders, ceiling fans, genealogy books, stencil kits, spiral staircases, personalized luggage tags, marine art prints, craft patterns, peanuts, brass ware and many more.

With all dangers and risks retirement mail order businesses do start with little cash, experience or professional help . . . and succeed. More do each year. Limited health and strength can restrict efforts and hours. But it's easier to avoid the full speed wrong turns of earlier, busier years. There are advantages as well as disadvantages for retirees.

Vitality, time and risk can be rationed. An executive may be at the peak of business judgment at the very point of retirement. Experience can apply to the widest degree. Caution comes with age.

The quiet years can be late blooming ones. Retirement mail order can work . . . for pros and beginners.

Chapter 4
Business Mail Order's Free Consultant

If you sell to business, technical or professional firms, you may learn a lot from him.

His specialty is helping business, professional and technical magazines and newsletters get subscriptions profitably by direct mail. He has helped many start, survive and grow in business mail order. Angelo Venezian is the owner of a list brokerage business, a list compiling business, a list management business and a lettershop. His company also conducts a telephone marketing operation. He has advised for a fee but prefers to give his advice to customers of his services.

Angelo has the vitality of youth, the wisdom of age and experience in his field that would be difficult to duplicate. At various times at McGraw-Hill he was vice president of circulation, vice president of marketing and vice president of production. He is knowledgeable, practical and very wise. He has seen great changes take place. He relates to the future. He is practical, prolific, full of pep and a prodigious worker.

McGraw-Hill was and is one of the biggest publishers in the world of business, industrial and professional magazines and books. Many of its magazines are big businesses. All of them depend on getting subscriptions by mail

Even more than financial strength, it is shared know-how, watching pennies and maximizing each profit center's opportunities that makes things work. On each magazine, the top executive often has to wear different hats. Management applies the know-how of success from one publication to others—to know when to expand, contract, launch, acquire, stop and add new profit centers.

Following McGraw-Hill, Angelo had a successful career as a part-owner and manager in a business list service prior to starting his own company.

At McGraw-Hill Angelo Venezian was a walking compendium of marketing strategies and selling methods successfully used for handling business, technical and professional magazine circulation problems and for controlling production costs of mailings. "Ask Angelo" was the first tip many new circulation people were given.

He's old enough to have seen business mail order develop as few have. He's young enough in vitality to be starting new projects and planning still more. "When I was vice president at McGraw-Hill, the computer was just emerging and not yet on-line. Most business publications mailed to lists they kept on three-inch by five-inch cards. Most compiled their lists and matched them against their lists of subscribers manually.

"All this took large staffs of people and a great deal of space. McGraw-Hill had an overall list of five million or more names. To keep it up, one hundred and sixty people were needed and vast floor space. We had to stand up the cards and ship them to typing houses. Then we shipped the addressed envelopes from the typing houses to the lettershops.

"Today all that is a thing of the past. Few publications keep prospect lists. Compilers, list owners and computers do it cheaper, faster and more accurately and keep lists cleaner as well. The advent of the computer virtually eliminated the cards

the typing services they required. The computer also brought to the marketplace a variety of other services for mail order firms, including more selectivity in rented lists and making many more lists available.

"Often, before the computer, list owners just kept customer names for internal use. When list owners did offer their lists for rent, they often considered it too much trouble to avoid duplications in the list and to offer selections of parts of it. Publishers often mailed lists which included their subscribers and former subscribers.

"The computer helped eliminate subscriber names from lists mailed. It helped eliminate former subs. It gave more control. It was faster, more selective and more economical. Taking selectivity into consideration and waste names avoided, mailings have become more effective. In the mail, costs currently run around $250 per M vs. $150 per M then. There are many more lists. The mechanics are easier.

"To build a list today for an industrial, business or professional publication or newsletter, we recommend using lists of mail order buyers of items that would indicate interest in the field. We recommend lists addressed to individuals. Next, we recommend using lists of inquiries received by mail indicating related interest. Then we recommend using lists of attendees at trade shows in the field.

"Next in priority, compilation names can be valuable and useful. We do not recommend self-compilation. A business magazine like Textile World can get the names of textile mills a lot cheaper from a compiler. There are many hidden costs in maintaining a list. Using outside lists, the publisher has more control and he can be more selective.

"We do about seventy-five percent of our business with magazine publishers, mostly of business magazines. We have quite a few publishers of newsletters. Usually, newsletters have smaller circulations than magazines. This generally limits the number of names available to mail. Our experience is primarily with technical, business and industrial names. We have our specialties. For instance, we have one account executive spending full time on lists for seminar and workshop meetings.

"Something new we specialize in is the development of international lists. Standard Rate & Data Service, in their Direct Mail Databook, lists U.S. lists free but won't provide free listings for non-U.S. Lists. We arranged to buy listings for our European lists and have them included in the SRDS index. We now have eleven paid international listings.

"We keep developing new activities. We're thinking of Telex communications. A companion company, S & V Communications, does telephone research, telephone renewals and reclassification; sets up sales calls, etc. We've been doing this for several years. There are some twenty WATS lines manned 14 hours per day.

"In any business, previous contacts bring in business. We've helped and worked with many people who feel we've been a factor in their success. Some started with us in a small way. In business mail, it's possible to test with simple mailings. Some publishers can get by with one or two colors.

"The Computer Security Institute out of Massachusetts came to us some years ago—at the time they started. Their objective is to help prevent the misuse of computer facilities and records. There proved to be a good market and need for their service. Their first test was substantial—100,000 pieces. Total expense was probably around $25,000. Since then, the business of selling their services using direct mail has kept growing."

Angelo has worked for large organizations. He will often

work on small jobs for them and, of course, he also works for small organizations. "We have a lettershop geared for small jobs. Right now, we're doing one job of eight hundred and eighty pieces. We're doing another of six thousand pieces and another of twelve thousand. For us, twenty thousand pieces is a fairly large job. Odd size pieces are done by hand if not in large quantity.

"I enjoy advising and counseling. Sometimes, people have come in with small scale projects. I met Mr. Briggs at DMMA meetings. He published a magazine called The Catfish Farmer. It was distributed (7,800 copies) free. He had bought another magazine going to catfish farmers which had almost three thousand paid subscribers. He wanted to merge the two and come out with one magazine - and with 8,000 to 9,000 paid subscribers.

"This time I worked on a consultant basis. There was no list rental business involved. I decided to do the job using his own magazine to market the offer. Outside of my fee, his only out-of-pocket cost was the sending of direct mail to his own list. For the consulting fee, we wrote the copy and devised the format. We used the front cover and inside space. The problem was to convert to paid circulation. As you can imagine, it is difficult to convert from free to paid circulation. In case the offer fails, you want to be able to continue on a free circulation basis. So we decided not to say that if you don't subscribe the magazine will stop coming. Instead, we concentrated on the importance of insuring regular and continuous service thru a subscription. It made paying for a contractual subscription seem more reasonable and necessary.

"We published letters with the offer on the first cover of the unpaid publication just prior to the merger. We pointed out the greater volume and broader scope and that they would be getting the introductory subscription rate. It worked. Seventy percent of the 7,800 people receiving free copies subscribed. From there on in, we continued to build paid circulation and then began to test outside prospect lists. The conversion to paid circulation was successful at reasonable cost.

"We do creative work occasionally. But I don't believe much creativity is required for preparing renewal letters. I advise smaller publishers to write their own."

Angelo is a past president of the Print Advertising Association and a member of the Direct Mail Marketing Association. Initially he served as program chairman for one of the DMMA's National Conferences. Then he served on various committees. For two terms, he served as chairman of the Board of Directors. It was during those two years that the DMMA decided to change from a professional organization of individuals to a trade association of members. It was felt that a move to a trade association would allow for broader activities and therefore higher member fees, and a broader type of membership as well as multiple members per company.

In each activity he is in, Angelo keeps coming up with a flow of new approaches based on adaptations of past successes. He is always pragmatic. He extends help to newcomers to start more soundly in mail order. He supplies a printed mailing cost evaluation form. Just filling it out provides an analysis of net profit or loss per order.

He can answer just about any specific question about mailing to get inquiries or orders from business, technical and professional names; about past history; future trends; first orders; repeats; renewals; list selection or lowering printing production and mailing costs. Some have said that Angelo Venezian has come up with more winning promotions for business publications to get subscriptions than anyone in the business. For readers of this book, Angelo has kindly answered the following questions I have asked him.

Q. *When do you advocate the use of the web press to print a mailing piece?*

A. The web press can cut costs depending on the size of the run. The larger the run, the more efficient it beccomes. For 40,000 and up pieces of mail, it's practical. But not for five thousand. There's too much paper spoilage. Use it for big jobs.

Q. *Have you used your know-how to be your own mail order entrepreneur with your own items?*

A. I'm an entrepreneur in owning my business but I've never been one in mail order. Now I'm seriously thinking of doing it. Why shouldn't we use our own lists to be in our own mail order business?

Q. *Of your business activities, what do you concentrate most on?*

A. All our activities touch on the more effective use of lists. We develop customers with free consulting. We spend a good share of our time preparing marketing recommendations on what lists to use for each specific offer.

Q. *When the economy is bad, how does it affect your business?*

A. Up to now, not very much either way. We have found that when business slows, there's greater interest in more specialized areas. As a result, we get more rentals to help build business for our clients.

Q. *What will the future bring to direct marketing?*

A. I think there will be a great improvement in the industry's ability to maintain up-to-date lists.

Q. *In what ways?*

A. The technology is already here. Mead Digit can print the address with ink jet which does not then require a Cheshire label print-out. It gets away from the label. You save paper and labor. Phillipsburg can do the same thing.

Q. *How about other manufacturers?*

A. Xerox has a machine which can produce 8½" by 11" sheets of labels at tremendous speed - 48 names in a second. You can't feed those sheets into a Cheshire machine. But you can reproduce them on pressure sensitive labels which can be affixed semi-mechanically.

Q. *Any other wonders coming up?*

A. I believe there will be a practical way of photographically preparing full or partial pages of address labels at tremendous speed and less cost as compared with the current process of a computer printer which has to strike each character of an address label. The sophistication is already here. It is up to the companies such as Xerox, IBM and Kodak to implement it for the industry, which still struggles with the relatively slow strike on process of present equipment.

Q. *Do you have any advice for young people going into direct marketing?*

A. Yes! This is not a nine to five business, you will find it difficult to keep abreast without a lot of extracurricular effort.

Q. *What do you feel a starting job requires to master it?*

A. A lot of reading and studying in order to develop needed know-how, plan extra work on your own time. Come early. Stay late. Do more than you are paid for.

Q. *What else is required?*

A. The next requisite is to be practical. You should

develop analytical ability. Be able to do more than one job at a time.

Q. *Do you require prior experience in the field before hiring someone?*

A. We prefer someone with direct mail experience. Sometimes, however, the cost of experience comes too high for a particular person. In such cases, of course, we train from scratch. We've trained quite a few people who have gone on to be quite successful in the direct marketing field.

Q. *What education do you require in an applicant?*

A. We don't look for MBA's but we do look for good schooling experience.

Q. *How high an IQ do you look for?*

A. If you're considerably brighter than average, it helps a lot. If someone sits down with us for the first time and understands when we explain what standard industrial classification is all about and how it is used to classify markets, that's good. Then, usually, we feel they can move ahead. To be intellectually alert is what we want.

Note: Angelo Venezian makes available the Official Postal Zone Charts. These are 900 plus charts that enable users to determine the correct postal zone from any postal point of entry in the U.S. to any postal destination in the U.S. ($40 per set) Direct your request to A.R. Venezian, 10-64 Jackson Avenue, Long Island City, New York 11101—(212) 784-0500

Chapter 5
Women In Direct Marketing

Their present opportunities - what their own organization is doing about their future.

They do extraordinarily well in it—and better all the time . . . with only more opportunity in sight.

In my mail order lifetime, next to new technology the biggest visible change has been the emergence of women in the field. In variety of executive jobs, in speed of advancement, in degree of success, direct marketing has been good to women—because they have been good for it.

Elsewhere in this book I tell in detail of some remarkable successes of outstanding women in quite different direct marketing areas: Joan Throckmorton, direct marketing agency president; Betty Anne Noakes, talented direct marketing consultant; Robin Smith, former president of ten Doubleday Book Clubs and now president of Publishers Clearing House; Rose Harper, principal owner of the Kleid Company; the able women of the DMMA; and Lillian Katz, founder of the Lillian Vernon catalog. There are many more I wish I had interviewed for this book.

Linda Pawloski is president and owner of Damart Therma-Wear, the warm, woolen long underwear that looks like adult blanketsuits. Sandra Meyer is the corporate vice president of American Express, in charge of maintaining profitability of all American Express direct marketing activities and subsidiaries. I could go on considerably.

For one solid afternoon in November 1980, four of the most successful women in direct marketing each told the story of her rise. It was the "Winning Women" session of the Annual Conference of the Direct Mail/Marketing Association.

Rosalie Bruno, whom Dick Benson calls "one of the smartest people in direct marketing", told the success story of Architectural Digest and Bon Appetit and how she started as secretary and became senior vice president of Knapp Communications. "I learned what not to do, how to change the method of my work schedule, how to delegate responsibilities and to surround myself with stars."

Helen Sevier told the story of BASS (Bass Anglers Sportsmens Society). "It was a male dominated company but I was not intimidated. I got through obstacles to my ideas." Helen became executive president. Eileen Rhudy Sondheim, vice president of MCRB, a big list compiler, said: "I used four letter words to achieve success: Goal, gain, plan, join, work." Von Tucker, executive vice president of The Photographers, Inc., credited her success to creative approaches.

Any woman reader aiming for big time direct marketing success should listen to the tape of this session. Details of how to get it are in the Help Source Section.

Its tremendous growth has forced direct marketing to turn to women for added talent without which still further growth would have been slower. But before I lead any woman reader new to direct marketing down the garden path, let me caution you.

There are almost no women owners of biggest private mail order companies. There are almost no women controlling stock holders of biggest publicly owned direct marketers. There are almost no chairladies of the board, scarcely any presidents. And the situation in smaller companies is only a bit better for women. It's a bit better still in companies serving direct marketers.

Women are now moving ahead fastest in direct marketing, in the list business and in advertising agencies. But most list brokerage, management and list compiling firms are not owned or headed by women. None of the direct marketing agencies owned by top ten general advertising agencies are headed by women. Direct marketing agencies owned by women account for less than 2% of billing of all direct marketing agencies.

None of the biggest printing firms selling heavily to mail order firms is headed by a woman. Only a few bigger lettershops, fulfillment houses and computer service bureaus are. Most direct marketing consultants are men. But more sales and contact people for list, printing and service firms and for media now are women. There are far more women account executives and supervisors, administrators and managers. But usually they work for men.

More women are copywriters. Some are senior copywriters and copy chiefs. But far more men are. There are women art directors, but most senior art directors are men. There are women direct marketing consultants, but the vast majority and biggest earners are men. The same is true for free lance copywriters.

There are far more mail order businesses and direct marketing services owned by husbands and wives. But in the big majority of such jointly owned businesses, the husband is president. There are still quite a few mail order catalogs with women's names but with men as owners. But husband and wife ownership and ownership by women is increasing outside of the biggest businesses. The smaller the mail order business the more this is so.

For my book, "The Mail Order Underground", soon to be completed, I have interviewed over four hundred people who have started mail order ventures, and often built businesses, with classified ads. Here the percentage of husband and wife businesses

Meanwhile, women began to plan careers more, while in college. They began to attend business graduate courses and graduate from them and to take more business courses. They started with a different approach, to aim for the top—to get into creative work, media, account work. Women MBA's began to appear. More women began to take business courses at night, to read business magazines and business books.

Today slightly over 50% of enrollments at the New York University direct marketing course are usually women. The same pattern is true at the direct marketing classes at Roosevelt University, in Chicago, and at direct marketing classes in other cities. Slightly over half of the members of the prestigious Direct Marketing Idea Exchange, in New York, are women. Today, at almost any direct marketing club meeting, Direct Marketing Day or DMMA Conference, the percentage of women attending is increasing. Women are out to grow in direct marketing, to make equal pay (and they are doing it) and to acquire equal or better mail order know-how for further, faster advancement.

As assistants, women mastered the inner workings of mail order—sometimes better than male executives higher up and in the same office. This started in the secretarial days when an executive secretary to the top boss often was smarter and more knowledgeable than male vice presidents. That gave women their chance. Now the even faster acceleration of the growth of direct marketing is forcing more change. And now a new breed of woman is coming into direct marketing, out for something better—to go beyond the status of highest paid assistant to a male executive, to the top.

There's a real desire to become constantly more professionally skilled, to keep up with latest developments, to upgrade abilities further and compete still more for highest paying jobs. As those successful form friendships and help each other with tips and recommendations, they're beginning to start their own old girl network. An organization to help all this happen is The Women's Direct Response Group.

"We wanted to advance the interests of women in all levels of direct response management." This is Dorothy Pawlowski, the list buyer of Bantam Books—but talking for The Women's Direct Response Group. "We wanted to provide a platform, to determine

and of female-owned businesses was far higher than in big scale direct marketing. Many, many women told me that this kind of business was rewarding in more ways than money.

In husband and wife businesses, they felt a shared closeness more than before. Almost always the children pitched in and the family endeavor was a joint action the women felt good for the children. The businesses women owned, themselves, were often based on hobbies they were happy with. They valued small mail order businesses because the modest but extra income gave a feeling of independence. They valued the opportunity to make mail order income a part-time business which still left time for their husbands, children and hobbies.

And so, in different ways and with different objectives, more and more women are coming into direct marketing, a process that will accelerate.

You've come a long way, Baby—from secretary or clerk to lower middle, then middle and now upper middle management. In business, generally, women in such executive jobs for 40 years have been averaging 60% or so of money paid to men for the same jobs. But of close to 500 people I've interviewed in this book, from every area of direct marketing, almost all feel that pay for executive jobs in direct marketing is now far closer for men and women.

First, occasionally—then more often—more mail order executive jobs were turned over to women . . . but often for far less money than men. Women became mail order bargains. Acceleration of growth multiplied the key jobs taken over by women. Lack of experienced mail order people, male or female, made mail order know-how a shortage item. Pay became more equal.

our rights, to better locate opportunities in the job market, to improve our salaries, recognition and skills. We serve as a network for professional women to exchange ideas and provide encouragement to one another."

Shirley Stevens, now vice president of a new direct mail magazine subscription agency, Magazine Marketplace, recalls WDRG's start. "Several of us, who represented such top-notch corporations as Columbia House, Names Unlimited, Time-Life Records and Time-Life Books, were discussing how many women we had done business with over the years. It was decided to explore the idea of forming an organization of women in the industry to meet regularly as a group." An initial luncheon for approximately twenty women was given. Because of the interest expressed, two more luncheons followed.

A steering committee of thirteen women was then formed. A mailing went out to approximately 300 women announcing a luncheon. About 140 women attended and enthusiastically expressed a desire for more such meetings.

For guidance in setting goals and priorities, Dr. Margaret Hennig was consulted by the group. Dr. Hennig is a foremost management consultant and co-author with Dr. Anne Jardim of "The Managerial Woman". Emphasis was placed on raising the women's awareness of their position in the industry, as well as in their own companies. Creating a network for the exchange of information and know-how was also of primary importance.

Joanne Schindelheim is a sales representative with Shore Direct Mail, Inc., a lettershop facility. (Incidentally, Shore Direct is run by a woman). Her background includes creative and market services as well as production. Ms. Schindelheim is also the president of the Women's Direct Response Group, having succeeded Gloria Frumberg, the senior marketing manager for Encyclopedia Britannica.

All policies are determined by a 9-member Board of Directors, elected by the membership. The day-to-day activities of the WDRG, as well as special projects, are handled by committees reporting to the Board. The WDRG has monthly luncheons. Luncheon speakers have ranged from Lillian Katz to Joan Throckmorton (a WDRG Founder), from Judith Daniels, Editor of Savvy Magazine, to Paul Michaels, the great copywriter who invented the "Publishers Letter".

In addition, the WDRG sponsors 10 seminars a year. These are smaller and more informal than the luncheons, and offer an intensive 2-hour workshop in specific areas of direct marketing. Speakers at the seminars have run from Annette Brodsky (a WDRG Founder) to Rosemary O'Brien, Account Executive at Chapman Marketing, and from Shirley Stevens (a WDRG Founder) to Elaine Tyson, Circulation Director of Macmillan Professional Magazines to Lee Epstein, President of The Mailmen.

As of March 1982, the WDRG had 325 members. Although the WDRG is the only professional organization specifically geared toward women in the industry, membership is open to men. Ms Schindelheim: "We are a dynamic organization concerned with the growth and development of the industry as a whole as well as that of our individual members. The greater number of members, the greater their input, hence the WDRG offers greater information and contact for its members. Remember, we are essentially a network of women exchanging ideas and improving our position within the industry."

WDRG is a member of the DMMA Marketing Club Council. At the YWCA, 610 Lexington Avenue, New York, they participate in the Y's panel discussions, do career counseling, etc. The WDRG sponsors scholarships for the Direct Marketing Collegiate Institute of the Direct Mail Marketing Educational Foundation, for both spring and fall sessions. The WDRG will sponsor a qualified applicant who meets all criteria, regardless of sex.

How should a young woman still getting her education prepare for a career in direct marketing? Shirley Stevens suggests: "Take two or more years of liberal arts followed by business courses. Graduate school is always a plus—at night if necessary. On-the-job experience is invaluable. Technology and technique are constantly changing. To keep up, one should read the various industry publications and talk with as many knowledgeable people as possible.

"Two excellent books are: Dick Hodgson's 'Direct Mail and Mail Order Handbook' and Bob Stone's 'Successful Direct Marketing Methods'. Also, the DMMA has a library containing many reference books and portfolios of actual campaigns. Each portfolio contains write-ups of why the campaign was done the way it was, and the results. It is well worth many visits."

Joanne Schindelheim feels that women still have a long way to go in Direct Marketing." Women will start careers in DM. Unfortunately, many women become discouraged and leave the field. The luckier ones are able to start their own businesses. Within large corporations upward movement still seems to be closed to many women who have earned their credentials and have proven experience. The WDRG wants to have some part in reversing this trend. We want to assist women at all levels of the industry to find career opportunities and help them develop the appropriate strategies to gain recognition within companies and to attain those higher positions."

Note: WDRG membership is $30 per year. For information about joining write: Women's Direct Response Group, P.O. Box 5134, FDR Station, New York, NY 10150.

Chapter 6
How To Raise A Billion Dollars

*His clients raise more than that
each year . . . much of it by mail . . .
using methods he pioneered and perfected.*

If you are a member of the tiniest fund raising effort or the biggest, his words can help you. If you are concerned with any direct marketing creative work, you'll find much that applies.

Americans have been opening their pocketbooks to charity, by mail. They have been giving more, to more causes, more often . . . in response to a rising tide of requests by mail. The man who has more to do with helping the rising tide than anyone else in the U.S. is Francis (Andy) Andrews.

He is founder and president of American Fund Raising Services, Inc., which provides fund raising skills and facilities to aristocrats of charitable, educational and cultural causes. He has recognized and helped to accelerate a trend into a tidal wave.

"Fifty years ago, perhaps one out of a thousand third-class letters and cards was a solicitation for fund raising. Twenty years ago, this became one out of three or four hundred. Now it's one out of four. Fifty years ago, Americans gave generously to humanitarian causes, but largely in response to personal visits by volunteer canvassers, mostly women. Today, women are working. They don't have the time. And the recruiting of canvassers has become more difficult due to the fear of crime in the streets.

"Today, far more gifts are obtained by mail than by door-to-door solicitors. Direct mail raises from 10 to 12 billion dollars annually. Indirectly, it helps raise nearly all charitable dollars."

Andy Andrews' business is providing the know-how and facilities for nonprofit organizations to raise millions of dollars by mail at the lowest fund raising cost—often less than the costs of volunteer campaigns. The techniques he has pioneered are now widely used by all direct mail fund raisers. As a result, seven out of ten families in the United States contribute to charity by mail.

He does it all with letters and simple, response-style mailing pieces, friendly, in good taste, and almost always personalized. His mailing pieces help you feel good, by giving. His specialty is helping the charity make a new friend. Over the years, the gifts grow larger and the dedication to charity grows greater. He does it almost as personally as a canvasser's visit, and with less intrusion.

He uses computers to personalize letters and other computers to bring together people who like to give with the causes that need gifts. He has lists of people who give to charity and he has the ability to match the donor with the proper cause. His American Donor Profile contains the listings and characteristics of more than 40,000,000 Americans who provide the basic support of all American philanthropy.

Andy Andrews graduated from the University of Maine and received a master's degree in business from the Harvard Business School. He was a Phi Beta Kappa. In World War II, when the Army screened Harvard Business School graduates, Andy and eight of his business school associates scored the highest IQ's ever recorded by the Army.

The Army recruited many Harvard Business School graduates to form the new Transportation Corps. "We organized troop movements by rail and by water. The Army had far more boats than the Navy. We had to coordinate it all. We organized a national rail network to move soldiers from the training camps to the waiting troop ships. We moved millions of men.

"I was in the service for four years. After I got out, I worked for nine months for an electronics company. After my Army experience and a taste of business, I decided I did not want to work for others, but for myself . . . to start my own company."

He applied big business marketing techniques learned at the Harvard Business School to his tiny new business, making it succeed by working for the giants of business and charity. His specialty was the automatic typing of letters, producing letters in volume which looked like personally dictated and typed correspondence.

He stated with a partner (also from the Harvard Business School) and a one-girl staff. The corporate name, American Mail Advertising, described one of the very few creative lettershops. After five years of partnership, Andy purchased the other half of the business and proceeded to expand. From the day AMA opened, it relied on new technology. At first, it was automatic typewriters more advanced than in most lettershops. The company borrowed its $8,000 launch capital from the First National Bank of Boston, based on a sixty-page plan and projection of the type the Harvard Business School taught how to make for big business. But *this* sixty-page report projected a total first year sales of only $22,000!

At first, its tests for clients were microscopic, as few as 25 letters for $9. But each test and projection added to Andy's store of knowledge and ability to become more effective for the next campaign. AMA was learning from experience. For a year, it was a seven-day work schedule of 16 hours a day. The tiny sales were as predicted. So were the expenses and the loan was repaid.

For the first three years, the partners did everything. They made sales calls, designed campaigns, wrote copy and hired artists. They set up the machines and supervised their operation. They folded, collated, stuffed, sealed, stamped, wrapped and lugged to the post office their daily production.

AMA first went after—and got—blue chip accounts in the commercial field, like Monsanto, Gillette, Arthur D. Little and Polaroid. "I grew into fund raising from the very first account—the New England Council, a manufacturers' association.

"When I started, there wasn't much fund raising by mail. There were a few college campaigns and museum membership programs and, of course, the traditional Easter Seal and Christmas Seal mailings. The big fund raisers were still volunteer oriented. After World War II the United Fund made a drive in each community for money to support the combined needs of many causes. House-to-house canvassing and in-plant solicitation are still going strong, but no longer can raise enough money to satisfy the needs of so many diverse charities. The big trend has been to mail campaigns."

Another early account was the Children's Hospital of Boston, and this first experience with hospital fund raising led to the company's dominance of this field for more than three decades. Through his seminars for development directors, Andy personally trained more than 400 of today's hospital fund directors.

Since there was no precedent for raising funds by mail, Andy had to learn his trade from the commercial side of the business. "I was self-trained in direct mail and advertising. I read a lot. I took special courses. I trained as a writer. I joined the Direct Mail/Marketing Association and the Mail Advertising Service Association.

"I met and became close friends with many of the direct mail greats. Ed Mayer, Jr., Bob Stone, John Yeck, Henry Hoke, Sr. and many others were all my friends. I went to DMMA seminars and conferences. As I learned, I trained my own writers and designers. By mastering mail order methods, we were able to transfer sophisticated techniques directly to the fund raising business."

Meanwhile, AMA began to grow fast, doubling or almost doubling its sales each year. The company was successful and made good money. AMA could go back to the bank for more money as needed, and it did—continually—for newer, more sophisticated equipment. "We once had the largest installation of automatic typewriters in the world."

Andy Andrews mastered the personalized letter and was thus ready to transfer these techniques to the computer at the opportune time. He saw the computer as a super-automatic typewriter. When the computer made possible the revolution in personalized letters, he was in a unique situation to take fullest possible advantage of it.

"Years before the computer, I read an article by Ed Mayer, Jr., that the same letter with no changes could be sent periodically to the same list and pull about the same response. From this glimmer of an idea, I put two carbons in the autotype machine and mailed the carbons as follow-ups to the original letter. Often the carbons pulled better than the original.

"The original letter might cost as much as 50 cents to produce and mail. The carbon cost (at that time) was 5 cents. I could mail the same letter three times for 60 cents, 20 cents per mailing. The customers' resistance to the high price of personalization was thus broken and the flood of personalized mail began.

"We carried the same thinking over into computers. Computer letters had a dramatically lower cost in the mail than automatically typewritten letters—and they could be mailed at third-class postal rates rather than first class. For years we had proven again and again that personalized letters could out-pull form letter mailings, by margins ranging from three to one to ten to one. But automatic typing cost so much that personalized letters had to pull three times as much as a form letter to justify the cost.

"IBM's introduction of the upper and lower case printing chain changed the economics of personalization overnight. Computers could produce personalized letters at mass mailing prices." One computer took the place of 100 autotype operators and typists in Andy's plant. Since the cost in the mail of the computer letter was far less than the automatically typed letter, a huge increase in usage was possible. Since computer letters pulled at a higher response rate, the computer letter was vital for those with limited markets.

"Computer letters always cost more than printed ones. First tests indicated that computer letters were at best marginal when used on low-priced offers. But computer letter costs came down in relation to the printed letter. Methods of personalization improved."

From the beginning, Andy saw great possibilities for the computer letter for insurance, office equipment, banks, utilities, industrial concerns and for department stores. He saw the computer letter as the most effective form of direct mail for a variety of fields, but far more effective for some than for others . . . and most effective of all for fund raising . . . the direct mail equivalent to personal canvassing. While never accepted as the universal format, computer letters became a dominant force in all commercial and fund raising mail.

"The first computer letter used for fund raising was developed and produced in our plant. We developed the first fund raising computer system and did much of the early programming for such techniques as merge-purge, tape matching, upgrading, name dropping and segmentation. In 1961 and 1962, we were pioneering personalization in ways it had never been used before.

"We were the first to insert by computer names and personal references in a letter. By using this technique, we were able to obtain for the Massachusetts General Hospital up to 14 gifts from every 100 families mailed over telephone directory names. Other techniques followed. We developed the computer telegram and first used it for the Massachusetts General. We matched computers with the national telephone list."

As soon as computer letters were feasible, Andy made some exciting tests of computer letters, beginning with the landmark Massachusets General Hospital compaign which lasted for 13 years. "We tested the house list of former patients and donors. We selected top income census tracts in affluent suburban areas and we mailed the telephone book. We tested carefully selected lists of proven mail order buyers located within a hundred mile radius.

"We tested computer letters against printed letters in both one-part and series. We tested broadsides and envelopes versus a single non-personalized letter. The computer letter often pulled six times the printed control. For cold outside lists the computer letter mailings pulled over four times the percentage of response and secured about double the average gift, for about a quarter of the fund raising cost. In essence, the computer letter persuaded the recipient to read the entire mailing piece, thus multiplying response. The carbon copy got gifts at even lower cost.

"The cost of fund raising began to drop precipitously as those who gave were asked to give again, using personalized computer mailings. Today, the cost of renewal gifts is often as low as 3, 4 or 5 cents on the dollar.

"Our company introduced the concept of computerized record keeping and, for the first time, charitable organizations really knew what the fund raising costs were. Trained to buy the lowest priced mailing piece, fund raisers were amazed to see that the percentage of the donor's gift going to fund raising cost was far higher on printed mailings than on computer mailings, despite the difference in cost. The educational period was long and hard, and some fund raisers are still not aware of the fact that printed mailings can waste a charity's money."

By 1967, AMA had fifty fund raising accounts. By 1971, AMA concentrated 100 percent on servicing fund raisers and changed its name to American Fund Raising Services. Andy kept on innovating.

"In 1971-72, we developed a new technique, the Mini*Message, for the March of Dimes. The Mini*Message is a simple slip, one-third the size of a computer letter. The front side of the slip had only 20 to 40 words of copy, the suggested gift array, and a three-way address system which revolutionized national health and welfare fund raising.

"The computer printed the corner card address, the prospect or donor address, and the bank return address. By utilizing a unique arrangement of envelope windows and computer imprinting, it was possible for the computer to print the thousands of combinations required for a national mailing by 2,700 individual chapters. This capability saved more than $250,000 in imprinting

costs per year for the March of Dimes and opened up the feasibility of locally addressed mail for local chapters at a reasonable cost.

"By developing a low-cost computerized mailing package it was possible to make mailings over the large national lists of prospective donors—the Donnelley list of telephone subscribers and the National Business List. From this mating of the mailing piece with the list came the capability of building a large base of individual and business support.

"The March of Dimes became one of the top income producers in the entire field of national health and welfare fund raising. The mailing pieces which we originally designed for the March of Dimes are still in use, virtually unchanged."

Andy reserved the Mini*Message format for the use of the National Foundation for five years. Later he developed and refined the Mini*Message further for the American Cancer Society, the American Heart Association, Easter Seals, the American Red Cross, Multiple Sclerosis, Muscular Dystrophy and many other leading fund raisers. "When the Mini*Message was tested against the computer letter, the new format outpulled computer letters at far lower cost. A new revolution in fund raising was underway, more than a decade after my introduction of the computer letter.

"In our business we're creative doctors, always researching something new. We have already completed more than 3,000 research projects. One project is completed each day, on the average, just as a new one gets underway. It's an endless factory assembly line producing new ideas and techniques on a predictable basis.

"We're self-contained with our own creative staff, computer service bureau, list brokerage service and lettershop. We have a large staff of skilled experts. Many of the leading fund raisers were trained here and now conduct fund raising programs for various charities. According to our suppliers, we are among the leading purchasers of envelopes and computer forms—ranking up with the Federal Government, TV Guide and the Reader's Digest.

"There are about 175,000 fund raising organizations using the mails, of which probably 172,000 are local. A typical piece of mail travels under 1,000 miles, but a typical piece of fund raising mail travels under a hundred miles. Most fund raising is local.

"The techniques of fund raising are the same for the biggest or the tiniest fund raising campaign. But the tiniest must be run as a kitchen table entrepreneur runs his business. For the typical country church with 100 to 150 members, everything is usually done homemade, by volunteers.

"Letters are turned out on duplicating machines. While big national churches have central equipment and syndicated mailing pieces and other assistance which they offer to member local churches, the tiny, local fund raising effort without national affiliation is always a do-it-yourself, totally on your own, or help by mail alone.

"The Red Cross has thousands of local chapters, as do several national health organizations. For years we were not able to serve this important fund raising market because of the small size of lists and the cost of administration. We solved that problem with the introduction of a new and important national program called Mail*America.

"It's like a Sears Roebuck catalog offering a wide variety of mailing pieces, already designed and tested, covering hundreds of different fund raising situations, holidays, events and seasonal needs. The portfolio includes booklets on understanding computers and how they are used in direct mail.

"By reading the literature and choosing mailing pieces, a local chapter can order a complete direct mail campaign for only a few hundred dollars and enjoy the savings and convenience of computerized fund raising, once reserved exclusively for organizations with lists of 10,000 or more. Via syndication, the smallest fund raising unit can obtain the sophistication of researched programs, and the savings of mass purchasing of standard size mailing pieces.

"The original Mail*America concept was tested in pilot projects conducted for the American Cancer Society and the American Heart Association. Mail*America programs are now available for many different organizations—even for small hospitals and cultural TV stations.

"In the days when each program had to be designed and written on an individual basis AFRS could handle no more than 75 to 100 accounts at a time. Now, the Mail*America program opens up the opportunity for national growth and a clientele numbering in the thousands.

"I enjoy new projects and new ideas. And I like the challenge of new media. We are now in electronic mail, working with a company which is providing a competitive service to Mailgram. Telephone fund raising, now in its infancy, is a growth situation of the future. We have created a new service called Phone*America as a companion service to Mail*America. We are extending the benefits of a professionally managed phone campaign to the local fund raiser, just as we did for direct mail in the Mail*America program.

"While telephone fund raising is now a minor part of total philanthropy, college phonathons are gaining favor and telephone fund raising has become a proven part of political fund raising. Telephone fund raising has a much bigger potential, if properly used.

"Telephone fund raising has been limited largely to calling old donors, lapsed donors, or special lists. Calls cost up to $3 each on a professional basis, thus ruling out 'cold' calling for donor acquisition—where the real need exists. The Phone*America program utilizes local volunteers and trains them to become efficient. The use of volunteers is a natural for the clients we serve—national agencies with volunteers in the millions."

Cumulatively, over 35 years, Andy Andrews may have been the biggest single influence to stimulate giving in the United States. Few have studied anything in as much depth and with the intensity that he has studied everything about giving. He has assembled more case histories of successful fund raising by mail, in more detail and variety, with more step-by-step analysis, over a longer period than has ever been done before.

He has studied givers . . . who gives, how much, how often, and to what causes. He has explored the psychology of giving, why people give, what's behind the good feeling giving gives. He never stops researching the literature of persuasion or analyzing successful direct marketing of anything. He applies it all to fund raising.

"Fund raising deals with psychic satisfaction—a feeling of personal joy that one's small gift will make the world a better place to live. Charitable giving is a two-way process: money for the charity, and psychic satisfaction to the donor.

"The upper income group prefers educational, cultural and medical appeals. The middle income group supports the national health agencies, United Fund, youth activities and welfare organizations. The lower income group tends to support religious groups, primarily local churches. It gives so generously that over half of total charitable giving is to church or synagogue.

"Upper income groups tend to respond best to appeals supported by facts, examples and 'reason why' copy, and middle and lower income groups to emotional and simply stated appeals. Even educated people appreciate simplicity, clarity and ease of reading.

"All people want recognition, to join a group, to survive. They want in some small way, at least, to extend their life's influence—beyond the grave. It's the desire for immortality. Giving can help give recognition, even after we're gone. It involves us in a group. A donor gains by giving not just once but continually. Many donors give a tentative gift the first year—testing the charity, waiting for the 'thank you' and hoping for recognition. Twenty percent of donors will each year make a larger gift, if asked.

"Anyone opening a fund raising letter may just give it a glance to determine whether to read it versus anything else in the mail. In such a competitive readership situation, attention span can be measured in seconds. Even if the decision is favorable, the copywriter gets about sixty seconds to capture the reader. Twice as many people read the first paragraph as read the body copy. Readership declines rapidly after the first fifty words.

"Personalization can capture attention so quickly that the personalized letter or the Mini*Message has become the workhorse of fund raising. An effective fund raising direct mail package can be a personalized letter, enclosure and reply envelope in an outgoing envelope. Better known charities need less descriptive material and can omit the enclosure. Simplicity and brevity are the hallmarks of good fund raising—hence the success of the Mini*Message which combines personalization with brevity in a simple format. For Middle America, the fund raising package should be simple, direct and designed to stimulate impulse giving.

"The paragraph which specifies the suggested gift is vitally important—probably the most important single element in a fund raising package, and often the most overlooked. Suggesting a larger gift, if the suggestion is reasonable for the donor, increases income dramatically at no additional mailing or creative cost. Success combines securing a good percentage of response and an above average size gift. Dollars received per thousand mailed is a good measuring rod.

"There's no magic formula to direct mail fund raising. It is more and more a science. There are at least 600 *major* variations in creating a fund raising package. Experience and technical and research know-how, helped by the computer, can determine what to test first. Then test results can tell how to improve response percentages and increase average gifts, for minimum cost.

"The computer can segregate donors by gift size, geography, date of past gifts and in other ways. Tailoring copy to segments increases response and average gifts. Personalization is essential to attract and hold persons of high income and social standing. Their gifts go where requested and stay where appreciated."

Andy Andrews comes from an old New England family. He speaks the language of the patrician trustees of the great fund raising organizations of New England. He's an outdoors man. He likes to fish and hike and camp. At one time, he owned his own private lake and a square mile of wilderness. His oldest son is executive vice president of American Fund Raising Services and heads up the company's research activities in addition to his executive duties. His youngest son is a white water canoeing enthusiast and an outdoorsman, too. He manages the Andrews' family camping resort, Papoose Pond, located in North Waterford, Maine.

Andy has been one of the most imaginative chairmen the Direct Mail/Marketing Association ever had. He led the DMMA in launching 42 new projects. Among other things, his program started a huge seminar and book publishing business. "We divided the responsibilities. We formed task forces to decide what the Association needed for the future. We had a wealth of leadership talent. It was a matter of putting it together and giving it focus. And, without a first-rate professional staff, nothing would have happened. What *did* happen was to launch DMMA on its greatest period of growth and influence."

He's not only an organizer, creative thinker and extremely talented writer. He's very basic and practical. He's a good businessman, not just with an analytical eye but in watching pennies, and a good trader. He should be. "I came from a family of horse traders—four generations. Until World War II, we imported horses from the West and sold them in New England to farmers and lumber companies. Eventually, the tractor won!"

People in the mail order business think he could organize and succeed at anything. He chose to do it by making a science of raising billions of dollars to help human beings.

If you'd like to raise a billion dollars . . . or several thousand . . . you will find listed in the Help Source Guide in this book tapes of his speeches and articles by him, explaining how, in detail. In them, along with a great deal else, he tells you how to write a more productive fund raising letter. He details what to say paragraph by paragraph, from salutation to P.S. . . . to persuade people to give the first time and then again and again—and in larger amounts.

His writing about giving has the authority of a scientific report, the inspiration of a prayer and the excitement of a detective story. He writes with rare humor, eloquence and style, with every word right. I particularly recommend "Marketing For Human Needs", a special report published by DMMA and written by him.

Note: American Fund Raising Services is located at 600 Winter Street, Waltham, Massachusetts 02154 (617) 890-2870.

Chapter 7
The Anatomy Of Direct Response

It's a marriage of creativity and numbers.

It is his parting comment. For three days, at 180 words a minute, he has been dissecting direct response advertising with high intensity, considerable enthusiasm and involving each attendee.

Pierre Passavant is winding up another series of three one-day seminars. The first day he has been demystifying mailing list selection. The second, he has been building fires under those who create direct marketing advertising. The third, he has been rubbing the noses of direct marketers into mail order math, and making them like it. Throughout he has given a different perspective than most have ever experienced.

If you have a chance to attend any of Pierre's seminars, grab it. He's sharp, entertaining and knowledgeable. He's quite humorous, incisive and almost brutal in some of his judgments. He's precise and controlled. He gives a mathematical approach to copy and art and a creative approach to direct marketing numbers.

Pierre Passavant is a showman and a great teacher. He looks the creative part in turtleneck sweater, the professor with pointer and blackboard and the businessman with dark suit and tie and white shirt. He has MBA clarity, the sureness of success and the practicality of twenty years of day-to-day business experience . . . and a literary beard and a piercing eye.

There may be no one in direct marketing who can more effectively bridge the broad gap between the creative side and business side of direct marketing. He is a direct marketing rarity. He has been deep in research and analysis, has had to make personally the important stop, go, expand, contract business decisions, has personally written copy and is in love with the direct marketing creative process. He has been circulation manager of one of the three giant catalogs and has guided some of the biggest solo mailings in insurance and publishing. He's been with big companies but followed a yen to be on his own. His career and advice can help us.

Pierre Passavant was born in Paris and came to New York when he was 3½, in 1937. His father was a small importer of hides and skins for the kid leather tanneries. The family lived in Manhattan. Pierre went to Catholic schools, was taught with discipline by the Jesuits, was consistently first in his class and graduated from Loyola.

Pierre had a flair for absorbing information in a disciplined way, for analyzing it and for expressing himself. He enjoyed and was good at public presentation. He was always in elocution contests and any kind of oratorical or debating activites.

He graduated from high school in 1951, went to Fordham College for a year, then worked for a year in his dad's business, and started college at night. Next, he got a job on his own, at $45 a week . . . for a lingerie manufacturer, in the petticoat and panty business. He then spent two years in the Army, after which he returned to his father's business for another year, continuing night school . . . this time at NYU. It took him eight years to complete his undergraduate work. He graduated with a liberal arts degree in 1959 . . . cum laude and Phi Beta Kappa.

In 1958, he started with J.C. Penney as a management trainee. A year later he became one of the early members of the company's new Planning & Research Division. The stage was now set for a unique business-learning experience.

Mil Batten, president and later chairman of Penney, used the Planning and Research department as the moving force to transform Penney's from a chain of 1,700 small soft goods stores to the giant in all kinds of retailing it became. (It was doing 2 billion dollars a year in sales then, and is now over 12 billion). Pierre helped develop marketing plans for the introduction of insurance services, auto supplies, discount stores and other expansion lines.

At the same time Pierre was continuing his courses at NYU, at night, this time at the NYU Graduate School of Business, going for a master's degree. In 1961 he got his MBA.

About 1962, Batten put Don Siebert (later Batten's successor as Chairman of the Board) in charge of corporate planning where Pierre was now a Senior Analyst. "It was one of the most exciting places anyone could be and at the most exciting possible time. When I started there were five people in the department. When I left the department several years later, there were 85. It was tuned directly into the entire transformation." The department's job was to investigate, analyze, recommend and plan the transition of Penney. The company broadened out into hard goods, insurance and credit, enormous individual department stores, the acquisition of General Merchandise Company and building it into a giant Penney catalog business. When acquired the catalog was doing less than $100,000,000 a year. Now it does over $2 billion.

During 1964, Seibert was appointed Director of Penney's new—and struggling—catalog operation. He tapped Pierre for the key position of Catalog Circulation Manager. He believed in almost total delegation of responsibilities. "He assumed that I was smart enough to learn the job and when to go for help. He never looked over my shoulder. I didn't know a thing about catalogs or circulation but Don Siebert had confidence in me and thought I could learn. I did.

"During my last 3½ years at Penney's, I became increasingly aware of the scope of direct marketing. I learned from associates, from those who worked for me, from suppliers and by trial and error. The first step to expand circulation of the catalog was to give it free to anyone near a Penney store who asked for it. I wrote copy to induce them to ask for it. So I had to learn how to write copy. I loved it. In time, the creative end of direct marketing became my favorite activity.

"I took the NYU Direct Mail writing course which Ed McLean taught." Later Pierre lectured at NYU on eight different occasions at Nat Ross's Direct Marketing Course, the only guest lecturer for the course ever to do so. "Nat, by the way, has always been a great booster and has helped and encouraged me in my career many times. I've always read a lot and I began to devour anything to do with advertising, copy, catalogs and any facet of mail order. One of my favorites was Vic Schwab's 'How to Write a Mail Order Advertisement'.

"The Circulation Manager job at Penney's was demanding and stimulating. I began to master it. I really enjoyed mail order—both its creative side and the analytical parts. But I didn't feel comfortable in such an enormous organization. I decided I wanted to try the big-fish-in-little-pond route. After 10 years at Penney's, I was ready for something very different.

"My next job was as VP-Marketing with Gerber Life Insurance, right at the beginning when Joseph Morse launched it. He had been a big financial executive for ITT but wanted a business he owned part of. He was a true entrepreneur and talked Gerber into putting up most of the money to start Gerber Life Insurance but owned part of it. To start, there were three executives, Joe, me and an administrative VP. Joe was my boss and became another great influence in my life.

"Joe was the exact opposite of Don Siebert. He was totally inquisitive about anything I did and constantly looked over my shoulder. He was a second guesser, a non-delegator. Sometimes, it was exasperating, but I learned more about direct marketing in the next 5 years than I dreamed existed. A lot of my learning was on-the-job experience, from what we did, from suppliers, from others in the business. Bill Jayme created our first successful direct mail package. We used a lot of top creative people free lance and I learned from each. I did some of the solo package copy and learned by doing it. I also supervised list selection, media buying and so on.

"Joe Morse had incredibly high standards. He was almost a perfectionist. I find myself more demanding today, as a result of working under him. I also learned from Joe the art of skillful negotiation. I was extremely fortunate to have worked first for Don Siebert and then for Joe Morse. Each helped me in his own way.

"In 1972, I was 38. I was working 6 days a week at high pressure. I wasn't giving much time to life at home. I felt

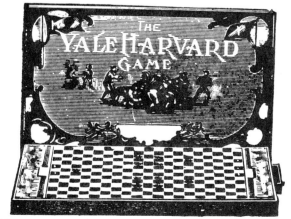

The Yale-Harvard Games.
A High Class Game for Thoughtful Players.

25345 A new game of skill of rare merit for two players. The basis of the game is foot-ball, the idea of each side being to carry the ball into the opposite goal. The pieces used are numbered, and can be moved as many spaces as their numbers indicate. New style of drawer game board. Price $0.85

successful business-wise but personally was unsure of my long-range direction. This led to a major personal decision. I decided to leave Gerber and try a less high-pressure life and do what I really enjoyed—write copy. I became a copywriter for Xerox Education Publications at about half my earlier salary, writing copy full-time for their children's book clubs. Almost from the beginning things took unexpected turns.

"My job as copywriter started in October 1972 and lasted four months. In February 1973, the promotion department was split in two . . . one part for home products and one for school products. The man who hired me kept half the department and I was made advertising manager of the other half. A year and a half later, the promotion departments were re-combined! The other advertising manager decided he'd rather be a copywriter and I became director of the entire promotion department with a staff of 35 people. Three and a half years later when I left, I was vice president of Promotion and Advertising, a job similar to what I had at Gerber. Again things were going great but I still wasn't personally satisfied. This time, though, I had a clearer picture of the right long-term direction for me.

"I wanted to do something independently—on my own. The idea of teaching direct marketing appealed to me. I had been deeply concerned with selling merchandise, insurance and books, with catalogs and solo mailings in huge quantity and the use of space media. I had to make media decisions, list decisions, creative and management decisions. I had worked closely with those on the business and creative side. I had for years been training people new to direct marketing for each of a variety of jobs in it.

"In mid 1977, I learned that the DMMA was interested in expanding its seminar activities. Gerber and Xerox had belonged to the DMMA. I had been a member for ten years. I had not participated intensively but had attended conferences once or twice a year. Andy Andrews, as Chairman of the DMMA, had set up the task force which identified education as a priority need of members."

Bob DeLay and Pierre negotiated an agreement under which he would do a series of seminars for the DMMA as an independent contractor, leaving him free to pursue other activities as well. It's been a happy, productive relationship. Thousands of members and non-members have benefited from Pierre's seminars. And he has benefited from the DMMA's sponsorship and the constant promotion of the seminars.

In 1978 and 1979, Pierre Passavant put on 18 3-day seminars for the DMMA in the U.S. In 1980 and 1981, the schedule was cut down to 12 each year, eliminating peripheral areas, but then expanded abroad. Under DMMA auspices, Pierre has done seminars in England, Holland, Sweden and France. "A thrilling but positively frightening experience for me was doing a seminar in Paris, in French. It was an emotion-filled moment to return to my birthplace in that way. There was no interpreter on stage, and my French was far from impeccable. But it was understandable and I did all right."

He's also put on seminars for AT&T, Dun's Marketing Services, for IBM and other giants. He's done specialized seminars for banks which he boned up for and for Market Data Retrieval, which is big in education marketing. For this his Xerox Education background came in handy. He does occasional mini-seminars of one or two hours each for the Direct Marketing Days of local direct marketing clubs, his samplers. All in all, Pierre does about 60 days of seminars a year, for which he puts in at least as many in preparation.

A Passavant seminar is encyclopedic but explained simply.

Pierre is a talking dictionary of direct marketing nomenclature but each term is made clear with plain words. Perhaps five percent of attendees find some parts a bit too hard and about five percent consider some too easy. Pierre is performing for the other 90% and by the time each seminar is finished, 96% to 98% of all attendees rate it excellent or good.

He is thorough and complete. He takes the fuzziness out. He's a creative person with an engineering mind. Whatever the area, attendees are expected to work, think, talk and participate, to learn by doing. He is dynamic and articulate. "He uses every minute, every word to its maximum. Nothing is wasted," says one attendee. Another calls him "tireless, with contagious enthusiasm". He quickly gets deep into the nitty-gritty of that days' area of direct marketing science.

The first day is usually on mailing list selection, starting with the very first fundamentals—defining everyone and everything in the list business. He's reviewing much of what most already know. He's filling in what they don't know or are unsure about. He's putting it all in logical order, making all the parts of the list selection puzzle fall into place.

He cites the 12-month mailing study of the Kleid Company, showing percentages of annual mail, month by month, for different categories of mail as recorded by Kleid's data bank.

He takes you through building a mailing plan. He cites how he did it and others do it, advising each attendee how to do it. "Maximize use of your house list and then of outside lists. Expand your outside list universe through testing. Achieve your profit goal within budget limits. Maintain a balance between successful lists and tests."

He recites many cautions: "Is your house list used by anyone else when your mailing is planned? Is your mailing sufficiently segmented? Have the sucessful outside lists you used before changed since then, particularly the offer made or the media mix used to produce these names? Is anyone scheduled to mail before you do a similar offer to your successful outside lists?

"Have you merged the lists you are mailing to eliminate duplicates? When were any inactive lists you are using last cleaned? Were your test samples properly selected? Are results of tests you are projecting valid, or are conditions now quite different from when you succeeded? Can the mailing really be made when planned or will it go too late? Are you prepared to record the response and performance of every list?"

He teaches old truths, brings you up-to-date, and leaves nothing vital out. He emphasizes do-it-yourself fundamentals. "Double check everything. Ask probing questions. Check every mailing list before it goes to the lettershop. Study 'Direct Mail List Rates and Data' yourself." It is startling how much you absorb from his rapid fire teaching, demonstration, participation way, and how much you improve future ability to select lists and make them pay.

The next day is Copy, Art and Promotion. "Direct response must pull orders or inquiries, be measurably successful and bring in enough responses at affordable cost. Your prospect very likely is too busy, not attentive and not actively shopping. He or she may be overbought, emotionally irritated, or seeking relief, pleasure, gratification or escape.

"Your ad must be noticed, be read and create interest and desire. It must get action, now if possible. Copy consists of the offer, headline and body copy. The art consists of paper, type, color, picture, format, layout, mood and image. You may use as involvement devices, tokens, stamps, tip-ons, or personalization. You may offer as gifts and prizes premiums and sweepstakes."

Pierre takes apart each element of a direct mail package

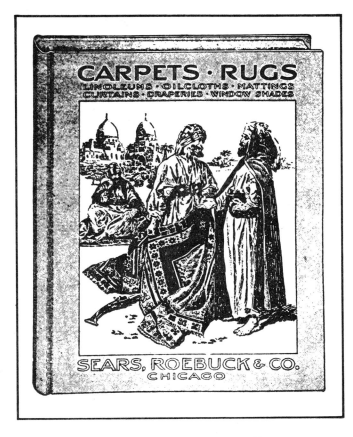

from outer envelope to main selling document, the letter to the main visual package, the broadside to the involvement device and the order device. He X-rays a mail order ad. He sums up the creative problems and opportunities of each medium.

"Direct mail has room to tell your story. It permits gradual unveiling and sequences. In any one day's mail, competition is limited. There is greater chance of being looked at. Great variety of creative techniques is possible. It has a high cost per thousand and requires high response.

"Space has limited room. You must boil your story down to essentials and get to the point fast. Usually, the whole thing hits the reader all at once. There's plenty of competition from ads, and even more from editorial. It's hard to be noticed. There's a limited range of creative techniques practical. The cost per thousand is far lower and a proportionately low response is okay.

"Promotion intensity requirement increases to the degree an ad's environment is less favorable, its position less accepted, its competition greater, the media less segmented to the product, its normal conversions from inquiries to sales lower, its promotion less frequent.

"For a mass product use a strong headline emphasizing benefits. Open with an enticing sentence or paragraph. Keep to an eighth grade text book reading level. Sell benefits before features. Appeal to emotions and self-interest. Take nothing for granted. Repeat key points. Describe products in a way that substitutes for seeing, touching, holding. Use specifics, not generalities. Tell what's special about your company and why your product is better. Long copy is okay. It's even desirable if interesting, readable and informative.

"A premium is often better than a discount but only for individuals, not institutions. The right premium can increase response 10% to 50%, but to get one you must keep testing premium items, number or premiums and the premium's offer. Never use an unsuccessful product as a premium.

"Sweepstakes can increase response 35% to 100% or more, with the right dream prizes to the right target audience, many chances to win, graphic excitement, involvement and simple mechanics. Sweepstakes are legal if you follow government regulations. Be sure yours complies."

Art establishes an image, mood and feeling. It can instantly communicate luxury, bargain or urgency. It can expand the meaning of words. It can help get and hold attention. Certificate borders, stamps and tokens usually help to increase response. Photos of products and prizes frequently are more effective than illustration.

"Know your audience's demographic and psychographic profile. Phrase your copy in his or her terms. Don't make your personal taste your sole criterion of advertising. Don't establish promotion rules by edict. Test to determine what's really effective. Then decide what to do. Realize that some promotional elements can substantially increase the demand for your product." Pierre covers in-depth testing, creative campaign planning, the product spectrum . . . which mail order items appeal to which instincts.

What Pierre says is peppered with examples of ads and mailings. He's describing tests and citing which worked and which failed. He's showing warning examples of the wrong way to do things, often by the biggest companies. He's asking opinions about headlines, subheads, coupon. People are citing the experience of their own companies. There's much discussion with Pierre keeping things moving along. No two days of the same seminar are the same. Pierre is teaching the same things different ways, with different words and different examples.

The third day is Math & Finance. Pierre explains, compares and shows how to calculate cost per thousand, orders per thousand and cost per order. He details how to make a profit and loss work sheet of every key factor in a mail order campaign. He compares fixed versus variable costs, particularly for small tests versus big projections.

For example, in determining the cost value of a large mailing of 100,000 as compared to a smaller mailing of 10,000, consider the following: per envelope, cost for 100,000 will be less than half that of 10,000; the cost of each 4-page letter will be cut in half; broadsides, flyers, order cards and other inserts will cost from one-third to one-fifth as much apiece. There will be a drastic reduction (to as little as one-tenth apiece) in the cost of copy, art and mechanical. In addition, costs of lists and lettershop processing will drop by 25%. Only postage remains as high per item.

Pierre figures the profit before tax per item after all factors. He compares profit of an offer with no premium, with one that costs fifty cents, a dollar and two dollars. He analyzes a sweepstakes with all its costs of prizes, handling and administration. He explains and shows how to calculate return on promotion and compare it with profit. He shows how to calculate the cost per page of a catalog in the mail, break it down per square inch and show the profit or losses of each item in a specific catalog. He shows the drop-off of starters in a book continuity program, book by book for 12 volumes.

Particularly important to the smallest direct marketer is Pierre's teaching of two-step mail order, getting an inquiry with an ad, and closing with direct mail follow-ups. "Direct mail can cost 20 times as much per thousand as space but for the right item it can produce inquiries at a comparable cost per inquiry, but

24789 Double Truck, with driver and two horses. Load consists of two boxes, two barrels and one sack of merchandise. Horses painted black, harness and running gear of truck painted a bright red, black striped. Packed one in a box; complete. Each............................$1.75

24790 Express Wagon with driver and two horses. Load consists of two boxes, and one sack. Horses painted cream color, harness black, hames red, collar black. wagon body red, black striped, gilt letters; gear yellow, black striped. Packed one in a box, complete. Each.............$2.00

24791 Barouche, with driver in coachman's livery. Cream colored horses, with fancy colored hip blankets, running gear, maroon, gold striped; body black. Both horses trotting when toy is in motion. A particularly handsome article. Packed one in a box. Each...........$1.85

only for higher priced items. The higher the price of the item, the more follow-up mailings can be used."

For a six-time follow-up by direct mail, a cost of one-half of the advertising cost to get the original inquiry is typical. But this can vary a great deal. A higher price item can mean a smaller percentage of conversion. If the original advertising cost to produce inquiries from an ad has been "paid off" by the margin from converted orders up to that point, the next follow-up mailing typically needs only to produce one-fifth of the response to "pay off" its costs in the mail.

Pierre charts out the value of a mail order customer for the first year, and year by year for five additional years . . . and cumulatively. He assumes the percentage of customers active each year after the first and the average sale for each year. He shows how a break-even the first year can yield a comfortable profit over a number of years—and how what looks more profitable the first year can actually be less attractive than other offers with great long-range customer value. Pierre shows how to discount future profits when comparing them with present ones, when each is created by present investment.

He explains the math of deciding how big the sample size should be for a test and the difference in sample size needed for a different estimated percentage of response. "The bigger the estimated percentage of response the smaller the sample size that is needed."

When the Math and Finance Session starts, perhaps half of the attendees seem uncomfortable. They're about to take their medicine from Dr. Passavant. As the session proceeds, there is almost audible surprise that it isn't all that bad to learn the numbers end of mail order. By the end there is relief, not that it's over but that at long last something long postponed and avoided is now clear, understood and mastered. Again, examples and involvement have made the dry and dull interesting. Pierre has been at the flip chart again and again throughout.

If you attend any Passavant seminar, I strongly recommend that you attend all three days. A top Doubleday executive told me that Doubleday encourages creative people to take the Math and Finance Session and business people to take the Creative Session. But the trend is for business people to avoid the Creative and the creative people to avoid the Math & Finance. Both groups should attend both sessions and anyone concerned with direct mail take the day on mailing lists.

Pierre's favorite is his two-day workshop for copywriters. Attendees can bring samples of their work. He critiques as many as he can. He gets the writers to write suggested paragraphs and to rewrite paragraphs of existing ads and mailings. Attendees compare efforts and discuss them. These are Pierre's people. He has been a copywriter and is a writer, has managed a promotion department and trained and stimulated writers and designers. The group is small. Pierre gives close attention and gets each involved. He uses concrete examples. He discusses the thought processes behind copywriting. He reviews and discusses creative solutions of attendees to problems he's given. It's the most highly praised by attendees of all his seminars.

Much preparation goes into whatever seminar Pierre gives. Each is the sum of his life experience in the subject synthesized for that session. He constantly seeks new examples. As an educator, he calls any direct marketers about any interesting test he observes and often gets much data about results versus objectives which helps to analyze and understand the promotion execution.

He is sought after as a speaker and prepares each speech just as carefully. He has spoken and written on the care and feeding of creative people, on testing, on legal do's and don't's and many other direct marketing subjects.

Pierre has delighted an audience by projecting slide after slide of boffs in direct marketing advertising by big name companies. And biggest companies regularly send their direct marketing personnel to Passavant seminars. The Bell System, every division of IBM, the American Management Association, Citibank, McGraw-Hill and many others send people who've been with them in direct marketing for a year or more.

Passavant seminar attendees are 75% new or lower management people in direct marketing with seminar fees paid by the corporate employers. Only a small proportion are new small entrepreneurs. "I don't position myself for them. Largely, I train direct marketing people for large and medium-size companies."

But Pierre is an independent man. "I like giving seminars. I also do consulting and have a little time left over for hobbies. I like fresh water fishing and listen to classical music and read. I enjoy my present work and plan to continue it for at least the next few years. I would like to do a book, but later, when I have time.

"In teaching seminars, I'm always learning. I've learned more about the mail order business in the last few years than in the previous twenty. I've learned about so many things— nuances, applications, approaches, unusual businesses like the company that sells and ships $50,000 worth of diamonds—by mail.

"I don't want to be an agency person or to run or own an agency. One day, I'd like to be in the mail order business, myself—but in a small way, from Middletown, and all owned by me so that I can remain my own boss."

In the Help Source Section of this book is listed information about Pierre Passavant's seminars you can arrange to attend through the DMMA; also at which Direct Marketing Days his mini-seminars are most likely featured; also the tapes of his mini-seminars and of his talks and the reprints of his articles available through Hoke Communications.

Every management and creative person should read his proposal on how each can best work with the other. I strongly recommend his report on profit analysis in the DMMA Manual. I also suggest that any creative person send to him for his checklist for copywriters and designers. Pierre Passavant is a smart pro who can help us all.

Note: Pierre Passavant is located at 505 Main Street, Post Office Box 1206, Middletown, CT 06457; telephone (203) 346-3003.

Chapter 8
Direct Marketing Public Relations

*The first mail order fraud hurt
everyone in the new business.*

Ever since, in mail order and new direct marketing, the bad guy made news. The ethics of the good guys did not. Today direct marketing is a universal tool used by just about every type of business. The biggest, most famous, most trusted names in American business are in it.

Everyone wants to be in a life activity he or she is proud of. Direct marketers do. They self-regulate to raise standards. They expose the bad guys and work with regulatory authorities to control them. They try to let the public see the overall picture of an honorable business.

The perception by the public of what direct marketers do is confused. The words "direct marketing" are unknown to the average person. Most people are puzzled as to exactly what mail order is. But they are very much aware of being taken advantage of in any form. Whatever mail order is to them, it has a tarnished image more typical of mail order's exceptions than the average.

Going after mail order sinners has often been good politics. Writing about them, talking about them or running mini-documentaries on them in news shows have been great for newspapers, radio and TV. Direct marketers believe that the growth, size and importance of direct marketing are under-reported and that the frauds and bankruptcies are over reported.

More and more individual mail order companies have built reputations for fair dealing and value. Yet, even the best known for quality and honesty feel that every mail order firm suffers from any unfavorable public perception of mail order as a whole.

Top direct marketers wanted to do something about this. If individual mail order firms could win a fine reputation by shipping promptly, giving value and servicing customers, so could mail order as a field, using its trade association, The Direct Mail/Marketing Association. The DMMA could provide services to the public, lead in corrective reform, drive for higher standards of ethics and work for self-regulation. A better reputation for mail order, itself, would follow.

Bob DeLay, DMMA president, comes out of direct marketing and public relations. For the ills of direct marketing Bob DeLay does not prescribe cosmetic public relations. The DMMA is the voice of reform, self-reform in mail order. Bob DeLay always has ideas for reform, of how to implement reform and how to let others outside mail order know that the reform is going on.

The DMMA has become the voice of mail order, a place to come to get the facts, a trusted source. One reason is that what is wrong with mail order is talked about frankly, and also what is being done to make it right. The DMMA offers any mail order business a model on how to communicate with the public, with the media and how to use publicity and public relations effectively and even to create traced mail order sales.

The reporter from the Los Angeles Times was working on a story—the mail order business. He wanted to research why people in Los Angeles were more and more ordering by mail. He wanted to know background, facts, comparison with retail business, future possible growth, impact on retailers. He was concerned about consumers and mail order whether it be rip-offs or privacy. And what was this telephone selling?

Research by phone and interviews got him a wealth of information. His problem was he had limited time to write the story and had to decide what was fact, what was fiction, of all he had been told. Then he heard of the DMMA and phoned New York headquarters.

In the next week he called three times and was given as much time as desired. He got answers to a variety of questions and a number of sources for facts and color background. He was referred to people in California, some right in Los Angeles. He got answers to all he asked about—the good and the bad.

Any writer about anything regarding mail order or direct marketing needing help in getting facts can get the same help. Any TV station news show or documentary, local or network, can get cooperation. The DMMA can arrange interviews with presidents and spokesmen of big companies or of the DMMA. It can bring any print or broadcast reporter into the heart of mail order. The concept is to establish the DMMA as the authentic reference source for anyone writing anything about direct marketing.

The DMMA operates on several fronts. It watches the media for any misinformation about direct marketing or lack or recognition of its importance. To do this, it monitors media through clipping bureaus and radio and TV monitoring services. It helps media to originate stories about direct marketing by supplying them with needed information when ncessary. It initiates accurate, favorable reporting by media by providing them with releases and facts. If it finds a story being written where the information is wrong or the attitude is of confrontation, it takes special pains to clarify facts.

The Communications Department communicates with members and urges them on to reform. It communicates with the public. Because Bob DeLay is a mix of public relations, mail order and businessman, DMMA publicity is action publicity, to get somebody to do something. He wants to measure the publicity, to know what the DMMA gets for dollars spent.

When the DMMA published its Catalog Directory, it sent out a fifty-word release with a description, the price, the address and instructions on how to mail in the order. It ran widely. Orders

came in and were turned over to the publications department. The orders were filled. The names went on the mailing list for future solicitation by general offers of books and seminars and DMMA membership and of specialized offers appealing to someone interested in catalogs.

This is done frequently. It was done recently in the new DMMA book, "The Law and Direct Marketing". This book is sold for $150 to non-members, and for $95 to members. Here the DMMA gets inquiries from prospects, many of whom are logical for and able to afford DMMA membership. If they join, they save $55 on the new book to start.

One public relations idea was a booklet, "Consumer Guidelines to Shopping by Mail." Another was to get a trusted authority to write the booklet. The contract for the use of her name was through 1980. The DMMA got the former Consumer Affairs Director of New York City, Bess Myerson, to write it. Bob DeLay raised money to promote it. He felt that the Communications Department should set up a Consumer Service Department. It did.

Money raised was used to pay for creation, production and mailing of the booklets. None was used for paid advertising. Yet ads for the booklet ran widely. Each ad was a contribution by a publication persuaded to do so by the DMMA, another DMMA idea. The same technique of sending a fifty-word release with a description of the booklet and mailing directions was used. It was sent out over the wire service, as well. Over 40,000 inquiries were received by the DMMA for the booklet.

In 1971, the DMMA and the DMMA public relations firm at the time had another idea. The DMMA calls it "The Mail

Camping Outfits Complete at $4.45 and $5.75.

KAMP KOOK'S KIT

Out of kit unpacked.

No. 6R10455 Pat. March 10, '96

No. 6R10455 Wilson's Kamp Kook's Kit. Just the thing for camping out. 53 pieces. Fire jack, two boilers suitable for using as an oven, fry pan, coffee pot and all utensils and tableware for a party of six. **Everything first class.** Boilers are made of 26-gauge smooth steel. **The entire kit nests in small space,** and when packed ready for shipment makes a package 14¼x 10¼x8 inches, **all nested together and can be firmly locked up by** ordinary padlock. Weight, complete, 20 pounds.

PAT. MARCH 10.96.

Price, complete...........**$5.75** No. 6R10455 Cut of **No. 6R10456 20-piece set,** con- kit packed for taining the fire jack and complete shipment. **apparatus without the tableware. Price......$4.45**

Preference Service". The DMMA advertises to the public asking anyone who would like to be taken off any mailing lists to request it or, if preferred, to be put on mailing lists and to indicate the kind preferred.

Again, money was raised for the booklet. Free ads were solicited. Again, releases were sent out with mailing directions. Then the unforeseen happened. Over 37,000 people asked to be taken off mailing lists and over 50,000 people asked to be put on mailing lists. The requests were forwarded to cooperating DMMA members, including the biggest mail order firms in the world. All requests are on computer tape. Close to 300 members have ordered the tape to update their mailing lists—as the public requests.

But now Bob DeLay and the DMMA had something to say to government legislators working on privacy legislation. There were two sides to the coin. They had proved that more people wanted to be mailed than not. The next step was another DMMA idea, the "Freedom to Mail" booklet as a form of freedom of speech. Now the DMMA has made a "Freedom to Mail" film.

Newspapers, radio stations and TV stations have found that their "Action Line" columns and program features proved to be very popular. Such action lines featuring a telephone number to call for help got heavily into obtaining faster service for mail order customers, getting refunds and exposing mail order frauds. Most action lines were local and had limited staff to put on individual problems.

Bob DeLay got the idea of a national service done better, the "Mail Order Action Line" of the DMMA. Anyone who didn't get delivery or satisfaction or felt ripped off in any way from doing business with any mail order firm could contact the "Mail Order Action Line". DMMA staffers took the written inquiries, expedited service and turned over mail order offenders to the Ethics Director of the DMMA. He, in turn, turned in incorrigible offending firms to government enforcement agencies. Again, the DMMA raised the money for MOAL, publicized it and let the government know what it was doing.

Attitude testing has proven an effective research tool for sophisticated direct marketers, particularly using small focus groups. One story in this book is on Bob Kaden and his use of focus groups to find out what people think of a company, its products and its way of doing business.

Bob DeLay got the idea of doing this for the very concept of buying by mail. Bob Kaden did the study. It was called "Direct Mail in Focus". It's excellently done. Copies are free to members and for sale to non-members for $25. But, primarily, it was to find out people's perception about mailings they received. A summary of the attitudes toward mail order sellers was then sent out in a release. Many stories resulted.

For member communication, the DMMA produces two newsletters, the Direct Marketing Journal and International Direct Line. To communicate, it also produces and sends out all types of press releases—trade, consumer and industrial. Various departments cover government relations, government affairs and consumer services.

Bob DeLay is a great believer in newsletters. He finds them a low-cost way to communicate. They get read. They pull people together, persuade and promote as well as inform.

Barbara Becker is editor of The Direct Marketing Journal in the U.S. and of International Direct Line abroad. The Journal's objective is to report anything in the field interesting to members, new postal regulations or whatever. The Journal also informs members of new DMMA projects such as the new book, *The Law and Direct Marketing*. The publicity is handled by the Com-

munication Department. Ruth Troiani and the Administrative Services Department supervise production, printing and fulfillment."

The DMMA has two kinds of specialized newsletters. Information Central and The Educational Foundation each have one type. The Communication Department advises and assists both with layouts and proofing. The other is the kind the Councils send out. Here the knowledge is specialized. There are eight councils and 36 newsletter issues a year for all eight. Each takes involvement, attendance at meetings and is produced by council members.

There is a staff of five in Communications plus three more in Consumer Service. The department works closely with all other DMMA departments to promote their activities and to help them in any way possible with whatever media coverage needed. The Department tries to function as the DMMA focal point in speaking to the outside world. Other departments come to it for advice. It functions as an internal public relations advisor.

"We are constantly sending out releases to all media. We use PR Aids, a computerized service. There is considerable contact of radio, TV stations, newspapers and magazines. It takes every publication and broadcast station and analyzes it, subject by subject, including who covers what. The Communications Department makes up summaries of each important speech at each important conference and sends it out to the press with a story. Where possible, it offers the entire text if needed.

The Communications Department gets a print-out of all publications that received a release. The list goes to the DMMA's clipping service which then watches for anything. In a typical year, the DMMA gets about 3,000 news clippings. The DMMA is now talking to a computerized service to analyze where each story appeared, how many took it versus how many received it and to grade each release as positive or negative on the basis of clippings produced.

"Summary reports of clippings produced versus the equivalent period a year earlier are made occasionally. Clippings are often up sharply in numbers of papers carrying stories with more features, longer stories."

But with all efforts to look good, there is even more effort to communicate and persuade the concept of self-reform, to influence direct marketers to be good—which we discussed in Chapter 1, Seminar IV . . . "Direct Marketing Ethics."

Chapter 9
Finding The Gold

A direct marketing statistical scientist describes his job.

"Although there is gold buried in those mountains of computer output, it is often obscured by the dross. My job," says Orlan Gaeddert, a top statistical consultant, "is to separate the significant from the meaningless and then to forge it into tools for practical decision making."

Orlan is a plain-talk scientist who applies his skills to direct marketing. He began his career at Time Inc. working with the circulation departments of the magazines. As the company interests broadened into new markets - notably in developing

Time-Life Books and Home Box Office television services - he was responsible for all of the start-up research and analytical support in these areas.

As Orlan puts it, "During my 16 years at Time-Life we developed a base of marketing facts and proven techniques that, by all accounts, continue to serve the company well. This is so, in part, because we invested in fundamentals and focused on strategic issues. We were building capital in the form of information."

In 1973 he established Orlan Gaeddert, Research. He refuses to name his clients. "It's a matter of confidence. To work most effectively, clients give me acccess to key figures vital to their business. Just say that I work for direct marketers large and small - mostly book and magazine publishers - some in New York City, some located elsewhere." Orlan graduated from Harvard and received an MBA degree from New York University.

He made the following points about statistical research and its effective application to business problems:

1. "Few businesses are prepared to cope with the data pollution of the computer age. Those marvelous machines produce jumbles, piles, mountains of numbers. Businessmen, however, seldom control the flow of what goes in or understand what comes out. Too often the marketer, who knows nothing about programming, depends on the programmer who knows nothing about marketing. The certain result of this confusion is decisions made on the basis of erroneous or misinterpreted information."

2. Research, properly conducted and interpreted, increases sales and profits. "I've seen my work bring back five to ten times its cost in the first year alone - and continue to pay dividends in later years." His examples include selectivity studies for refining lists and novel sample designs for probing special list universes. Also a unique analysis of newsstand sales and distribution.

   On the latter study he reduced a staggering pile of raw data down to one simple graph. "That graph proved to be a nugget of pure gold. Easily understandable, still actionable four years later, it distilled seven months of hard labor. It helps the publisher get the right number of copies - not too many and not too few - on the newsstand every issue."

3. Direct response marketers, he thinks, have a unique perspective on the sales process. "Because in our business selling and measurement and analysis are continuous activities. As a consequence, we demand - and need - much more precision than is customary in mass marketing. Off hand, can you think of any other business where the difference between bliss and misery is a mere quarter of a percentage point?"

4. On the subject of modelling, Orlan was enthusiastic. A model forecasts future results based on past experience and management judgments. "It's a way to evaluate past campaigns and to plan new promotions. A good model can, in fact, be a very creative tool. It helps us see our areas of ignorance and, thus, decide what we should be testing and what one can pay for information."

He has developed and used models in a wide range of business applications: A simple model which automatically finds breakeven points. (It works on a palm-sized calculator.) Models for continuity programs and "Total system" simulations for magazine publishers. A magazine system model translates the entire interrelated network of advertising and circulation revenues and publishing expenses into bottom-line results.

Most recently he developed - in cooperation with Ladd Associates, Inc. of San Francisco - a modelling tool for quick low cost list evaluation and campaign planning. Ladd and Gaeddert programmed their system to apply to almost any direct marketing campaign. Since it uses a time sharing computer, little more than a telephone and an inexpensive printer are needed to operate the system. It helps managers develop rational budgets backed up by efficient marketing plans.

Speaking about the role of consultants, Orlan observed that "Like the free-lance writer or artist, the consultant brings a fresh, independent viewpoint and seasoned judgment. So, even if you learn nothing else, the outsider helps you avoid the mistakes of others. It puts you on a faster track."

Putting his money where his mouth is, Orlan and his wife have started their own small publishing company, Milk and Honey Press, operating out of their country home in Canaan, New York. Their first book, *Survival Cooking for the Busy and Broke,* was written by Mrs. Gaeddert. (She is a professional writer.) They are selling this title to college book stores, health food stores, etc. solely by mail. "It's fun to adapt the techniques used by the big publishers to our own tiny mom-and-pop operation. We use calculators, not computers, in Canaan. Sure, it's a hobby, but it also has a serious side. This is my laboratory to test ideas."

Orlan Gaeddert pursues his quest for gold from 34-47 80th Street, Jackson Heights, NY 11372; (212) 426-8024.

Chapter 10
Selling Records And Tapes Via Mail Order TV

*An unusual company's unusual success
as it avoids some methods of the big.*

Slim Whitman is a country musician, first successful not in the U.S. but in England and Australia. In England, Slim holds the record for having a number one record for more weeks than any singer in history, including Elvis and the Beetles.

In twenty-one months, one million five hundred thousand Slim Whitman albums were sold by mail order on TV in the U.S.. .. not by RCA ... not by Columbia ... but by Suffolk Marketing Corp.

Suffolk Marketing sells only by mail order, almost entirely by TV. Its 1981 sales passed $30 million in its most profitable year from inception. Seventy percent of the business is done in two months, January and February. The peak week of advertising is usually the first week of January when often expenditures are slightly over one million dollars.

Suffolk Marketing is unknown to record stores. It's a family business in Smithtown, Long Island. Richard Huntley is the extremely able general manger. His wife, Jennifer—her two sisters, Helen and Cynthia—and brother Malcolm E. Smith, Jr. each own part of it.

And behind, over it and in it is Malcolm E. Smith, Sr., guiding, planning, driving . . . but against overwork, too-fast growth, over-complexity—and going into tempting, profitable but diversionary activities. He points out that it is still only five years old. Suffolk Marketing has sold over a million Guy Lombardo albums, over a million albums by Jim Nabors, over two million gospel albums . . . and several million more albums.

Malcolm Sr. founded it. He created, built and sold to Lin Broadcasting another mail order record company, for $3,500,000 cash. He was a partner in a third record firm sold many years ago to American Broadcasting for $2,100,000 cash. He's owned or been managing partner of half a dozen successful mail order businesses and been a radio station owner.

Suffolk Marketing has no computer. It does not use a giant direct marketing agency but Malcomn E. Smith Advertising, a house agency . . . which subscribes to no TV buying research services. President Malcolm Sr. is not an MBA. He never went to college.

Malcolm Sr. has never belonged to the DMMA, doesn't subscribe to direct marketing magazines and, for twenty years, hasn't read a book on direct marketing. He's never heard of most of the words so popular today in direct marketing. He is unacquainted with most of the coming miracles of telecommunications. He has never used laser letters. He's totally ignored all opportunities to sell overseas.

To know him is to marvel. I have for forty years. My brother, John Hoge, first trained him when Malcolm came to us. I worked with him. Over thirty years ago, we began to work for him as his advertising agency. Over twenty years ago, I became his partner. The fishing lure business our family owns today originated from that partnership.

I'm sure that Malcolm has a very high IQ. He's smarter than most of us. But the rest of us can learn much from him that can help us. I've learned more from Malcolm than from anyone in mail order. For decades, I've studied just what has made him so successful. It is his simplicity of word, his economy of time, his self-dependence, from typing to ability to write his own copy and buy his own time, or do any function—the directness of his thinking. It's what he avoids as much as what he does.

Malcolm sells records because they are the most sold mail order item via the biggest mass advertising medium, TV; because they can be bought virtually as they are sold, can be sold at a good value to the customer and bought with a good margin for him; because they can be sold on the merits of the artist and there are no excessive advertising claims.

Suffolk Marketing has sold 900,000 albums by Box Car Willie, half a million by Don Ho, half a million by Ray Charles and 400,000 by Jim Reeves. It has sold over 300,000 each by Kate Smith, Glenn Miller and Arthur Fiedler . . . by Otis Redding and by Brook Benton, by Ray Conniff and by Freddy Fender. It has sold over a quarter million by Nelson Eddy and Jeanette McDonald. It has sold the Big Bands, Disco's Top 20, Famous Stars and The Shirelles, all in big volume.

I'm pretty proud of Malcolm Sr. as a neighbor, friend and a good man. He has been trustee of Nissequogue, Long Island— and later the mayor. He has run for Congress. He's never permitted business to keep him from his family and spent more time with them thèn any successful man I know. He's a tennis player, duck hunter and deck tennis man. His greatest interest is the West, both going there and anything written about the Old West.

The Smiths are the Smiths of Smithtown, Long Island. The statue of the Bull on Route 25 from New York at the entrance of Smithtown commemorates Malcolm's ancestor, Bull Smith, founder of Smithtown. Malcolm Sr. lives in the home the original part of which was built three hundred years ago by his ancestor, Richard Smith. But Malcolm has always made it on his own,

Indiana Sawing Machine.

70413 This machine is sold at a low price, and is an efficient and easy running implement. Furnished with the very best Disston Champion Tooth Saw. Has all the advantages of any hand power cross cut saw made. The uncomfortable bent position when sawing in the usual way is overcome, and a natural upright position secured, enabling the full force and weight of the body to be thrown on the saw. Weight, 44 lbs. Price, with one 5-foot saw.....................$7.50

from the time forty-one years ago he worked for a year for nothing . . . for a small advertising agency, Huber Hoge and Sons.

There he worked in a windowless storeroom. He sat in a rickety chair writing copy on an old typewriter on top of an old telephone book on an old table, with the whole scene lit by a bare bulb . . . while he listened to mail order commercials on an old radio. He came in at six a.m. and left at nine p.m. At home, he read the books on the reading list my brother, John, gave him.

He read Claude Hopkins and John Caples and Kenneth Goode. He listened to radio late at night and early in the morning . . . to the mail order commercials from the country stations all over. These were the days when the clear channel ruled the air. From midnight to seven a.m. the mail order commercials from some of the most powerful clear channel stations never stopped.

Commercials were long and friendly. The words were simple and folksy. The voices were neighborly and concerned. Each was Malcolm's teacher. Guided by my brother, John, Malcolm (he was Jr. then) immersed himself in reading the books of the masters of copy who could help him most while listening to living mail order on the air. He combined it all in his own copy and added something of his own. His copy is natural and simple. It proved very effective on radio. He very successfully adapted it to publication advertising and then perfected it for TV mail order. Of all Huber Hoge copywriter alumni, for his specialty he is the master.

Malcolm Sr. is shy, retiring and does not throw his weight around. But at the start of his copywriting career he was determined that if he wrote a commercial properly, it be delivered properly. This got him into working with announcers and into production of commercials. The frustrations of getting a TV commercial made right made him a perfectionist. He struggled with each one. Even now, Malcolm Sr. will fly to Pittsburgh, Nashville or Los Angeles to tape commercials and then take eight hours to make one two-minute commercial. At the end, he may decide to make it entirely over or any part thereof, before testing it.

He learned to trust no one but himself to do anything. He would write the copy, pick the announcer, produce the commercial, personally deliver it to the station, personally pick up the mail and personally count it. Later, he carried this through to every phase of his business.

In the early days of his own business he sold many items for a dollar. He would go to the bank in a taxi full of suitcases. Somehow he'd get the suitcases into the bank, open them and make the tellers count in front of him the tens of thousands of dollar bills that burst out—and get his receipt, being sure it tallied with his own count. He was still in his middle twenties then.

For anything Malcolm Sr. buys he first asks question after question, sometimes at intervals and in different sessions as questions occur to him. His research digging is so dogged, so deep, so thorough he's the most able media buyer I've ever met. He is the same in a negotiation. He can sit in a meeting and hardly open his mouth to say a word, except the final one. He can ask, listen, analyze, conclude. His computer is his head.

He'll start a business with one employee or none. He's totally self-sufficient. I've seen him move from floor to floor in a huge office building, every several months, first from an office or two, each time to bigger space, and keep it up for years. Whichever office he's in, he'll sit in his private office at his desk, perch his typewriter on top of a telephone book on the desk and type while playing the radio or in more recent years, the record player. For years he would play his album, "The World's Greatest Music" (which he sold half a million of several businesses ago). All the while, he looked out the window and typed out copy for a new offer. In due time mail openers would take over his office until he expanded his space again.

Malcolm Sr. has a sense of timing, of pace, of stop and go. He can amble through days on end but then, when he smells a real opportunity, go for the jugular with a driving intense energy that can't be stopped. He can turn away from activities with never a backward glance, even giving a company he created to his employees and walking out the door. He may quit business entirely for months or years. He may then come back, ask what's new and, in months, outdo everybody else.

Often Malcolm Sr. has quietly, at crucial times, helped others with loans, jobs, and more important, advice. He has with me. His former partners and employees, of whom there are many, are almost a club. They talk for hours of his quirks and ways and

abilities. Malcolm Sr. prefers to hire already trained people but each who works for him later thinks back to it as a learning experience. In later businesses he built organizations to which he delegated more. But Suffolk Marketing is far more of an organization than any business Malcolm had before. And he delegates more than he ever has.

Because now it's a family business. Richard Huntley is superb in organization and Malcolm Jr. in copy and production of TV commercials. The entire family came up with ideas for albums. "Richard has ideas for younger people. Young Malcolm thinks of what appeals to younger people. Helen and her husband live near Boston and suggested Arthur Fiedler. We got the rights and have sold over three hundred thousand albums. They all think of artists I'd never think of and sometimes haven't heard of. I think of offers that appeal to those who are older.

"We work different ways. Young Malcolm likes to think of an offer, fiddle with it, and carry it through production. He's very good at it. Richard likes to do every aspect of the business. I really would like to devote more and more time to projects not in the business and do things not to make money.

"We could do more and make more money in more ways. But there's just so much to go into or think of. More can be highly dangerous. There isn't enough time in the day. We just try to do a few things, with concentration. The years are passing. I've a sign. It's something I saw in Reader's Digest. I blew it up and hung it on the wall over my desk. It reads: 'TIME FLIES - BUT REMEMBER YOU'RE THE NAVIGATOR'.

"I'm a media user. The media can be used by people like me to sell concepts, ideas, get across facts. I'm trying to do that with my Marijuana book." The Marijuana book is Father Malcolm Sr.'s message to all Young America. It's title is "With Love from Dad." The book and Malcolm Sr.'s copy and campaign for it is a labor of love . . . to stem the Marijuana tide . . . by mail order.

"We want to affect young people and parents who can influence pre-teen children in time and teenagers both. My hope is that beyond the effect of reading the book, which is admittedly hard to get young people to do, is the strength of the commercials. One hundred and fifty million people have seen it.

"So far, we've printed 150,000 Marijuana books. In it there are 768 short digests of facts about marijuana and the effects and dangers of its use. We are now printing 25,000 more books in a new edition. There are still 768 digests. But 200 are new, substituted for others.

"We have 20,000 books in stock. We've sold 130,000 by mail and through book stores. Walden's had our Marijuana book. It was number four or number five on the best seller list in March. Art Linkletter has made a two-minute TV commercial for it. He's anxious to help. We've run mail order ads for it in newspapers all over America.

"So far, overall, I've about broken even. I think it can do some good. I went to the American Book Sellers Association with it. I've a deal for a paperback pending with one of the biggest paperback publishers. I've offered to contribute all royalties to advertising. The publisher wants to go ahead.

"I feel I don't devote enough of my time yet to this. Right now, it's about ten percent of my time. I hope to get that up to twenty-five percent soon, and more later.

Note: Malcolm Sr. rarely, even when asked directly, answers with specific information about profit, loss, volume, items or whatever. For readers of this book I have asked him many specific questions which he has kindly answered in detail for which you and I can be grateful.

Q. *Many more mail order operators have gone bankrupt selling records via TV than have succeeded. Why is this so? And why do so many new mail order moths keep rushing into the flame?*

A. Because they're not careful enough. They become overly optimistic. They think they're more skillful than they are. They over-expand without sufficient testing. Each time a TV record commercial is aired new inexperienced entrepreneurs jump in, usually with the same result.

Q. *If they fail, why do you succeed?*

A. Ninety percent of offers we test fail.

Q. *Why?*

A. When we succeed, it's always because of the appeal of the artist. The appeal may be very strong even if to a special group, and even if, to others, the artist is unfamiliar . . . if the group is big enough. Ninety-five percent of mail order record artists are big names to their followers. If the appeal of the artist isn't there, we drop it.

Q. *How often do you originate the offers and how often do you just take an artist proposed to you by a record company?*

A. We think up most of the offers and then approach the record company. But often the company proposes an artist to us. RCA has suggested Mario Lanza to us. We've just made the commercial.

Q. *Are old-time, big name favorites the safest?*

A. Not always. RCA had the rights to Perry Como. They put it out for bid by the mail order operators, hoping for a huge guarantee. We bid. RCA decided all bids were too low. They decided to sell a Como mail order album through someone not skilled in TV, and failed.

Q. *With as big a name as Como, isn't there some way to succeed?*

A. Probably, but we couldn't. We thought we could do better and then got an option to test.

We did a commercial and tested. It failed. We studied it and figured we could do better. The album was a mix of upbeat and sentimental. We eliminated the upbeat and made a new commercial, all sentimental. It did worse. Then we dropped it. Afterwards, RCA told us we had been the highest bidder.

Q. *If you get a big name artist to deliver the commercial for his or her album, will that pretty well mean success?*

A. We've tried it both ways. We did this with Andy Williams from CBS. We put together a repertoire of the best hits Andy ever made. We went to Las Vegas where he was performing. We put him on camera and then on the air. The commercial didn't work. We put together another commercial with scenes to feature each song, and not Andy. This failed. We did another commercial with him on camera. When that failed, we dropped it.

Q. *Does getting the artist to deliver the commercial at least substantially improve results?*

A. Sometimes but not always. We get a lot of cooperation from artists because so much royalties are at stake, but often it doesn't help if the offer has failed without the artist.

Q. *When a TV commercial fails in a test, is there anything you can do to change the offer and re-test successfully?*

A. Sometimes, the way of presenting the songs, the artist, or group of artists can make the difference. We had a gospel

music album. I dreamed it up. It featured general gospel hymns. It didn't work. Then I heard of Billy Graham's success with his book, "Born Again," when I got one or two selections from Word, Inc., in Waco, Texas. I changed the name of the album to 'Born Again.' I changed the copy accordingly. This changed failure to success.

Q. *Why don't RCA and Columbia just sell their own albums and artists? Why do they and other record companies sell mail order operators?*

A. RCA doesn't do TV mail order on their own. RCA sells almost exclusively for TV to mail order marketers. Columbia sells a lot through Vista Records. It sold a lot of Mickey Mouse Disco albums mail order which it got from Disney. Columbia brought it out. It was a big success. But both RCA and Columbia feel that they do very well selling to mail order operators. There's no risk. We come up with ideas. We sell very often what they would never get to . . . or other record companies either.

Q. *What is the best price to sell records and tapes for on TV?*

A. Right now, $7.98 for records and $9.98 for tapes is our usual price, trying to keep under ten dollars. But now we're thinking of going to $9.98 and $12.98.

Q. *For your record offers how do radio, space advertising and TV compare for results?*

A. We use no radio but PI's. Radio is unsuited to two minutes. Virtually all of our TV uses two-minute commercials. We do little space. We'll buy a little in Parade, TV Guide, not much more.

Q. *How do your sales break down between records and tapes?*

A. Of the albums we sell, 60% are records versus 40% tapes.

Q. *How much record and tape inventory do you carry in relation to the advertising you run?*

A. To get the rights to an artist we give guarantees against which each week we buy albums. The week we bought a million dollars of TV time, our total commitment for TV included an extra five hundred thousand dollars and totalled a million and a half dollars. We bought enough albums to fill the anticipated demand for that million and a half dollar expenditure. We order each week and get delivery in one week. We deliver promptly orders received.

Q. *Why do you run such a big percentage of your year's advertising in January and February?*

A. There's more TV time available. Retailer use of TV is then lowest. National advertising on TV is down. Viewing is up. Yet, time can be bought more favorably. People stay home then and listen to albums more.

Q. *You sold Elvis Presley albums after his death, in space but not on TV. Why was that?*

A. Elvis was a peculiar story. Homestead Marketing had put out a Presley album by mail order on TV before his death. Usually, mail order rights are for a limited time. Apparently, RCA had neglected to put in a time limitation. After Elvis died, when RCA was approached for TV mail order rights, it discovered that Homestead still had them for TV. We bought some Elvis albums from Pickwick Records and sold them only in print as we could not do so on TV. Elvis mail order, after his death, was a fluke, unique in recording history.

Q. *Don't you usually have sole rights on TV for your offers?*

A. Usually we have proprietary rights. Sometimes not—sometimes an artist has recorded for two companies or records an offer himself. Sometimes the artist's contract with a major record company expires, and a mail order marketer will contract with the artist to make a special package.

Q. *Where do you get your artists?*

A. The sources vary. We may contract with RCA, Capital, CBS, United Artists.

Q. *What artists are most apt to succeed?*

A. Artists you'd expect to sell don't always. RCA supposedly got the rights to sell, by mail order, albums of a big rock group from another company to which it was under contract. It's said RCA had to guarantee a million sales, and that the offer then failed.

Q. *What kind of deal do you have to make to get rights to an artist for TV mail order?*

A. The commitment required varies. A lot of major record companies require purchase of five thousand or ten thousand records and tapes for a test. For this, they may give a three-month option. If we succeed in the test and take up the option, it may call for buying fifty thousand, one hundred thousand, or two hundred thousand albums, including tapes and records. Then we get exclusive TV rights but for a specified and limited time. Sometimes the commitment asked for can be very substantial. For Barbra Streisand, it's supposedly to buy in advance five hundred thousand albums. Cost of each record and tape varies widely, depending on demand for the artist.

Q. *What percentage of total mail order on TV comprise record offers and how much merchandise?*

A. On TV, generally 65% of mail order sales are for records and 35% for general merchandise. Only about 10% of our mail order sales on TV are not records and tapes and 90% are. For us, the reason is that it is very hard for us to find non-record offers which give a good value to the purchaser when sold on TV; but we can give excellent value on albums and have enough margin to work with.

Q. *How much of your business in on VHF stations, how much on UHF and how much on cable?*

A. Most of our business is on VHF stations. We do some UHF. Volume on cable is still small.

Q. *When will you use the new media like two-way TV and cable network?*

A. When media changes, we will—when the circulation is there.

Q. *When will Suffolk Marketing sell video discs?*

A. We'll be interested when distribution is meaningful, when there are video disc players in 25% or more of the homes in the area, with a strong appetite by new owners for video discs.

Q. *How many employees does Suffolk Marketing have?*

A. We have one hundred and fifty people at the peak of the season and twenty-five at the bottom.

Q. *Is it still practical and profitable to make C.O.D. record offers on TV?*

A. It's a big problem. We get a high percentage of C.O.D. refusals from the huge numbers of telephone orders received. Response can be so great and advertising cost for each order received so low that, even with 30% to 35% rejects on certain offers, it can be profitable.

Q. *Isn't it a tremendous headache?*

A. Yes, the rejects come back later, after the peak of the season, often after the offer has been saturated. It's not usual for the same offer to sell year after year. Inventory of rejects can pile up and then be unsaleable.

Q. *What do you do then?*

A. We try to save some markets that we don't use the first season and use them to sell the reject inventory the next season.

Q. *Is all this agony worth it?*

A. So far, C.O.D. has been necessary for telephone calls. We're thinking of offering only for cash or, if by phone, by credit card.

Q. *How complicated is it to buy TV time these days for mail order?*

A. It's not easy to buy TV time. The fact is that there usually isn't much time. It's limited. There are usually more people trying to buy time than there is time for sale. Mail order operators ask for lowest rates. In return, each spot scheduled can be cancelled by the station if it can sell it before broadcast for higher rates. You have to remember, you're at the bottom of the totem pole. Often you don't know you've been kicked off until the week after.

Q. *Is this always so?*

A. TV time does get soft—when automobile companies or others cancel. Then stations start calling.

Q. *Are there lower rating programs more suitable and more responsive to mail order than higher rating shows?*

A. We buy entirely based on past results of time availabilities and stations. But, better results coincide with better ratings. I had a study done by our six time-buyers. Each took three stations and compared the cost per order to ratings. There was a direct relationship between the cost per thousand based on rating and the cost per order.

Q. *How does TV news do for you?*

A. News shows are excellent. The CBS morning network news went up in audience, as did other network news, after the hostages. When we bought locally into CBS network news, the response was better.

Q. *Is the TV record business getting better or worse?*

A. It's harder to develop offers. It's more difficult to get successful artists. There are just so many.

Q. *For a test how long a commercial do you use, how many times and on how many TV stations?*

A. We always test a full schedule, seven to ten two-minute spots, on at least three stations. Usually, they just sell or they don't.

Q. *To keep up and increase volume how many tests do you have to make?*

A. Now is the testing season. We test ten, eleven, twelve packages. What will work? We go with the few that are successes. We don't try again on draggy ones. We may have to test more offers. We may rethink an offer and try again. We need three or four new hits for next season.

Thank you, Father Malcolm. We've learned a lot—and remember, readers, Malcolm Smith, Sr. has his alumni making money all over with what they've learned from him. I just look, marvel and wonder what he will do next.

Suffolk Marketing is a wonderful family business. Richard and Malcolm Jr. do more and more. Malcolm Sr. can, if he ever gets the urge, go West or wherever or into anything and safely disappear and leave them on their own.

But then, maybe a year or more later, there will be Malcolm Sr. somewhere in a one-room office hunched over a typewriter which is on top of telephone books, with the radio playing. He'll be looking out the window as he starts typing his first commercial to sell video disc music offers, or whatever.

Or maybe he'll just save the world, by mail order.

Chapter 11
Making A Career In Museum Mail Order

*He started from the bottom, rose through
the ranks and made it in direct marketing.*

He works for The Metropolitan Museum of Art of New York City—one of the great museums of the world, for its mail order business. Paul Jones is mail order operations manager. "I'm responsible for list selection , mailing and fulfillment for $12,000,000 a year of mail order sales. That's 65% of the Museum's $20,000,000 a year sales of products and publications."

Thomas Hoving, former director of the Museum, reports: "Various programs the Museum has presented in the past ten years have succeeded not only in drawing large crowds, but also in getting an overwhelming response from its direct marketing techniques. Through both its mail order and gift shop business, it now collects more than one-third of its entire operating budget.

Bradford Kelleher, vice president and publisher of the Metropolitan Museum of Art, says that the Museum went in to the mail order business for two reasons: "To make money to keep the doors open in the face of rising costs, and to permit more

of the public to experience world treasures outside the walls of the museum."

Paul Jones was born into America's intellectual elite. His father was a college president, his uncle a bishop. One brother was a university vice president. One is a professor at Massachusetts Institute of Technology. His sister is an analyst and training psychiatrist. He chose business. Twenty-five years after starting his first year, after mastering every facet of the fulfillment of mail orders, he started his Museum mail order career.

"Tom Hoving was director when I started. My boss, Bradford Kelleher, was and is publisher of all Museum publications and director of all Museum merchandise sales. My title is mail order manager. Under Kelleher, there are five managers—editorial, general merchandise, retail, finance and mail order manager. We each have specific responsibilities and interests in terms of overseeing and business management."

The Museum's Christmas catalog has a hundred and sixteen pages of over three hundred gift items, in every price range. Some are Museum publications. Most are reproductions of originals in the Museum's own collection. They are in gold and silver—pewter, brass and silk—and in glass, iron and porcelain. The MMA constantly advertises in consumer media to get more inquiry names to which it then mails catalogs.

"When the catalog of the Museum comes off the press, my responsibilities start with list selection. We have our own production department, our own computerized 1,200,000 list. It's all segmented. I can segment it down to almost anything on an RFM basis and demographically.

"I'm comfortable with computers. I grew up in the business around computers in lettershops. When I worked for St. John's Lettershop, it had a Data Line printer (no main frame). Later, when I was there, St. John's had its own computer. It wasn't my area, but I was curious. I was around, I asked questions. Later, I worked for subsidiaries of Ted Bates and John Blair. Each of the subsidiaries had access to the large computer operation of the parent companies.

"Mail order sales of the Museum were $3,500,000 when I came and have since grown almost four times. The growth has been gratifying. Marketing, using segmentation of our lists, has been important. It's exciting to trace results of list decisions. I have taken all my related experience, including dabbling in all areas, and used it for the Museum. Exchange of information is important. Since joining the Museum, I've been active in the DMMA Catalog Council. I'm on the Board of the Hundred Million Club. But more important to me than anything has been the fine people I met over the years.

"On May 20, 1974, I started with the Museum. It had a contract with Service Bureau Corp. which, at that time, did all Museum computer work. I had a broad stroke knowledge of the use of computers. But one of the first people I hired as a consultant was Leo Yochim. He advised me regarding work of the Service Bureau. I was the Museum's representative for the redesign of the computer operation, along with one of my co-managers and Coopers and Lybrand, our accountants. Leo was my personal advisor to make sure that the Museum got value from the new computer operation from a mail order standpoint.

"Other people helped me as well, such as Stan Fenvessey, who has done work for me in mail order at the Museum for the past five years. I've used him on a per job basis. Also, I've maintained a figure in my budget with room for me to use Stan Fenvessey. I'm a generalist. I know how to tap the specialists. Stan Fenvessey, Leo Yochim, John Kane and Lee Epstein have

worked for the Museum, but they've also done it out of friendship to help me do my job. We also use Robert Kestnbaum, of Chicago, a systems consultant on a retainer. Our advertising agency is Wunderman, Ricotta & Kline.

"We don't use outside lists. Out lists are built through two-step ads and follow-up mailings, with some sales from the ads. We invite people to send a coupon and a dollar for a year for catalogs. We track purchases. I am the liason with our data processing department, which is responsible to the treasurer of the Museum. I'm the one from the Publisher's office. Therefore, I get into tracking, conversion and calculating the value of a customer. The entire mail processing is under my direction— from receipt of order, data entry to cash receipts.

"We use telephone marketing." Along with Ernan Roman, Paul has been on a DMMA panel of telephone marketing case histories, at its Spring Conference. At the Fulfillment Management Association, Paul Jones has been a participant expert on a panel discussing cashiering, data entry, customer service, promotion and postal service. He has mastered many areas of mail order.

"I work hard. During our busy season, I may work from 8:30 AM to 8 PM. That's September to December. But then I can take ten days in winter. I get a six-week vacation. My wife gets all summer because she's a teacher. I'll never forget first getting used to that six-week summer vacation.

"This is the second marriage both for my wife and myself. We have five children between us. One is in graduate school. Two are in college. One is a senior in high school, and we have one child who is a freshman in high school. Today, only scholarhips and loans make college possible. All our children are achievers. Some have to work harder than others."

Paul Jones began in the mail order service field, from the bottom—then rose through the ranks. His mail order start was in Gimbel's Department Store in New York, in the Address-O-Graph department, in 1952. He came in cold, with one disadvantage, as he step-by-step progressed to director of mail order at the Metropolitan Museum of Art. Paul Jones is black, in a white mail order world.

"I was raised in a comfortable segment of society." Paul had black and white friends. His family environment was more established and secure. "But I still felt the difference of being black."

He was born in Greensboro, North Carolina, where his father was president of Bennet College, for black women. He went to a segregated black elementary school in Greensboro. But from earliest childhood he met the whites on the faculty, the white trustees. Bennet was church related.

He went on to junior high school, "A Horace Mann type school." It was in Columbus, Ohio, where his uncle was a Methodist bishop. From there he went to Mt. Herman Preparatory School in Northfield, Massachusetts. He then went into the service. On coming out, Paul went to Ohio State University, in Columbus. He transfered to Boston University but left at the end of his junior year. "I regret that I did not stay to graduate."

Instead, in 1950, he started to work in Detroit for a cousin who owned a chain of fifteen drug stores. "I did a little bit of everything from driving a truck to being a messenger. I was a Jack-of-all-trades."

From the Detroit drug store, Paul went on to work for Gimbel's in New York starting in the supply department. "I got to know a young man called Johnny Stevens, a white co-worker who lived in Queens, in New York. I had become his assistant in the Address-O-Graph department.

"Johnny left Gimbel's to join a puzzle contest mail order company, Rogers United, as production manager. A little later, I joined as supervisor of the Address-O-Graph department. This was late in 1953. Rogers United was in the same building as the Horace Mann lettershop. I became Rogers United's plant manager, assisting Johnny who was inside general manager.

"In 1955, Rogers United folded and I went with J.J. Berliner. They compiled lists and management reports. In 1957, I started work for Borkans Address-O-Graph. They sold reconditioned Address-O-Graph and embossed plates. I ran the shop. I did this until 1959.

"From there, I worked for Mailings, Inc., owned by Lew Kleid. I remember Rose Harper as very charming. I remember Lew as a very soft-voiced, very articulate, bright person. He was a perfectionist but not unduly so. A rule of the shop was never to throw away a label—always retrieve, type and mail. His attitude of integrity in conducting business was great. Much of the industry does not have that feeling to that degree. There are those who fight it. My job there was as a replacement for a young man who went into the service. When he returned in 1961, he replaced me.

"Mike Abbene, now at Scheduled Mailings, was production manager. When later, in 1961, Lew Kleid decided to get out of the lettershop business, he sold Mailings, Inc. to Mike. Kleid had Mailings, Inc. in New York. Kleid also had a business in New York called Research Projects. He sold this to Bernie Lande, who had managed it. Bernie moved it to Rockville Centre, New York.

"In 1961, I went with St. John Associates, a fine lettershop. It has been owned by three women. Two of them Ms. Hildreth and Ms. St. John, had since died. It was still owned by Helen Fisler. She's alive and is now eighty-eight. Her nephew, Bob Fisler, is circulation manager of Time Inc. I was manager of St. John's West Side plant (St. John had two) at 211 West 61st Street. I stayed eleven years and left in 1972. While there, I took the Nat Ross New York University course, just to get a feeling of direct marketing as a whole.

"Then I joined a subsidiary of Ted Bates Advertising Agency, FALA Mailmen. I worked for Lee Epstein. About that time, Bates sold Fala Mailmen to John Blair, which combined it with Stevens Direct Mail.

"With the John Blair acquisition of FALA Mailmen and merger with Stevens, it had become hectic. One night I came home to my wife and said: 'There's got to be a better way.' My wife is a teacher in the Port Washington, Long Island, school system. My wife said, 'Why not resign?' I said, 'I've never quit a job in my life.' We talked. The next day I resigned, without a job, and arranged to stay until I could be replaced.

"Lee Epstein has a hobby of helping people get jobs. He helped me. In the business, I've known a lot of people with integrity who respected me. I turned to them. Lee knew of the job at Metropolitan and called Bradford Kelleher for me. I talked to John Kane of John MacDonald Kane. I had known him at Mailings, Inc. He said, 'I have the job.' He was also talking about the Museum. He called Kelleher, too. I was hired. I had always been on the service side. I wanted to try the other.

"Of course, my exposure to the marketing areas of direct marketing and mail order has been more in the last six years than in previous years. I've been glad I could contribute my past experience to the Museum, grateful for the additional exposure I've acquired and happy to be there.

"I know few blacks in mail order. One reason is that most blacks are unfamiliar with it. Those that get into it do so by accident. I have one black friend working on a special direct marketing approach to black communities. This is for major corporations. It may not turn out to be all that different.

"Blacks in direct marketing should get together more and get more active in meetings generally. One of the problems blacks face is that the individual is often so hard-pressed to achieve, it seems difficult to take time off for meetings. I see that at DMMA conferences. Until direct marketers really think of themselves as professionals, people will stumble in. It's highly unlikely that blacks will see opportunities in a field they don't know about.

"Much of the momentum of the sixties for black entrepreneurship was doomed to failure. The opportunity can only come with correction of the basic problems. And they are getting worse. The inner cities are far more volatile. I try to do something. I was president of the local Community Action Program. Of course, some things are being done. There's a lot of creative entrepreneurship in the Bedford Stuyvesant arts and crafts projects. I don't know many black entrepreneurs or blacks in the creative side of mail order.

"I have friends of all races. The young men I grew up with in the South are doctors, lawyers, musicians, artists. I'm not a musician but I'm an avid listener to jazz music. Photography is my latest hobby. I've raised tropical fish. I love to sail.

"In any endeavor properly or improperly set up to give opportunity, you've got to learn to play the game, to understand it and how it operates, practically and technically. You've got to work. There are no short-cuts. I love my children, but I tell them this. 'You may not like the rules but that's the name of the game. You've got to learn that there can be lots of injustices and to overcome them.'"

Chapter 12
The Direct Marketing Missionary

*How he launched one Fortune 500 company
after another into mail order.*

His is an American success dream. He is Maxwell Sroge, and his friends call him Mac. He performs more kinds of services for his mail order super clients than anyone in the world. He has a fast mind and constant drive.

His company, Maxwell Sroge & Co., is the most unusual mail order expertise emporium in the world. He'll take a crack at doing anything for anybody he accepts as a client . . . usually in the Fortune 500. Shortly, I'll tell you all about it; but first, here's how he started.

"My name is Lithuanian, as it came out when my grandfather went through immigration. My father was an accountant for fruit and vegetable wholesalers. My mother was a housewife, and we lived in Brooklyn. I went to Stuyvesant High School, in Manhattan, from 8 AM to 12:30. Then, from 1 PM, I worked in the Garment Center, pushing hand trucks and packing dresses.

"I was not a good student. I didn't like the regulations, the controls or the conformity. I did badly in everyday grades, but well on tests and exams. I did skip a year and graduated from high school at 16½. Then, at 17½, in July 1945, I joined the Navy and became a photographer on the USS Topeka, a light cruiser in the Pacific.

"When I got out I started to work as a photographer (in 1946) for a company selling war surplus items, some by mail order. Its name was Benjamin's for Motors. They sold electric and diesel motors. I was paid $40 a week to photograph the motors and do any job asked. I was also made the advertising manager, so I registered in City College's night course, to study advertising. I went to City College, New York University and the New School for years but took business, not regular, college courses. I read then, as I do now, a lot of biographies and an awful lot of business books.

"My first creative contribution to Benjamin's was to suggest a new name—BFM Industries—which Benjamin's then took. BFM eventually grew. My boss told me to set up an in-house advertising agency, to save the 15% agency commission. I set up the Albert Maxwell Company (my father's first name and mine).

"To get inquiries for diesel engines, we ran ads in industrial magazines, factory maintenance, marine, etc. We then sent follow-up literature. I took the photographs, wrote the ads and had an artist lay them out and order type. By 1949, BFM was spending between $100,000 and $200,000 a year, and Albert Maxwell was a three-person ad agency.

"But I left to try for the big league. I got a job, in Chicago, at Hallicrafter as assistant advertising manager at $100 a week. That lasted a year. Then I heard that the sales promotion manager of Bell & Howell had just been killed in an accident. I got the job—for $90 a week, a $10 cut. It was 1950, and I was 23. Bell & Howell did $13,000,000. But Chuck Percy had been made president in 1949, and it was about to take off.

"I started as sales promotion manager but, to learn selling, I soon became a salesman. By then, I had met a Bell & Howell copywriter who later became my wife, June. For my year on the road, my sales territory was from Trenton, New Jersey, to the Canadian border. I was top man on beating my quota—and also courted June, mostly by mail and phone. Later, I became promotion manager for real—next, director of sales and then director of product planning.

"Home movie cameras were making great technological advances. Bell & Howell was in front with the first electric eye movie camera (I named it), the first automatic threading movie projector, the first zoom lens home movie camera, the first electric power-motor movie camera.

"By then, Bell & Howell consumer product sales were $60,000,000 a year. We sold Sears, Ward, Alden, Spiegel . . . all the catalog houses. But compared with sales to retailers, sales to them were not too important. Then, in 1954, I heard of Al Sloan, the pioneer mail order syndicator, who was interested in a movie camera and projector combination. He already had proposals from Revere and Keystone and our prices were higher. But I called on and sold him. I was lucky because, looking back, it seems we did all we could to be sure we would fail in mail order.

"Bell & Howell had a very important franchise with retailers. We had a one-third share of the market and a very close relationship with the retailers. Kodak created the demand with its advertising. But our relationship with the retailer was so good that he would recommend Bell & Howell movie cameras and projectors. We approached mail order selling, as planned by Al Sloan, very cautiously.

"We wanted to avoid any conflict with retailers. We sold Al Sloan a good camera but an obsolete one. We sold him a projector with a two-year-old design—and no advance features, one we could no longer sell at retail. We required that the set be offered to the consumer at $149.95, full retail price, versus flagrant discounting by many retailers. Everybody at Bell & Howell was skeptical about the project. We absolutely knew that there was only one way to demonstrate movie cameras and projectors. A customer had to come to the store.

"The first year we sold, via Al Sloan, 30,000 camera and projector sets. The second year, we sold over 90,000. Bell & Howell top management were amazed but still skeptical. We were concerned about customer satisfaction. Then Pete Peterson (now Chairman of the Board of Lehman Brothers) became executive vice president. He worked with me and we surveyed customers who had bought Bell & Howell cameras and projectors by mail order. The vast majority had never been in a camera store—and three out of four said they would recommend to anyone that they buy the same mail outfit in the same way.

"We had tapped a latent market. Today, this is still one of the primary reasons for mail order success. All that is then needed is to convert latent to active demand, simply to let people who already want something know where and how to buy it by mail order. To convert a latent market for stereos, slacks, pullovers, cars—whatever, it is not necessary to rely on or wait for the customer and the store to get together. The customers can be sold by mail order.

"When Al Sloan semi-retired, movie outfit sales by mail order had become very important to us. We took over the mail order operation and formed a Bell & Howell mail order subsidiary, the second business I started with my name. This time . . . because I had hired Bob Kestnbaum (whose story is told in this book), I called it Robert Maxwell. Later, Bob became president of Robert Maxwell. We were our own syndicator and also sold by mail order directly to consumers. I learned an important lesson when we sold on credit and lost money—how not to extend credit as well as how to.

"We tightened up credit handling yet Bell & Howell mail order sales kept growing and some years were 10% to 15% of the entire eight millimeter home movie kit market. We had worked cooperatively with more and more companies. Many got interested in doing mail order on their own products. I told Pete Peterson, by then president of Bell & Howell, that I would like to get into the consulting business, with Bell & Howell as an account, which I then did.

"First, I worked at Wunderman, Ricotta & Kline for nine months, with Bell & Howell as an account. Through Lester Wunderman I met the Eastern mail order establishment. I think I helped him meet a number of the kind of Fortune 500 companies which later became much of his client billing.

"Lester was very bright, talented, articulate, capable. There were top creative people there. Tom Collins was a fine writer. Irving Wunderman was brilliant. Ed Ricotta was a great art director and fine creative man. Harry Kline wrote the first ad for Physician's Mutual Insurance. He was extremely talented. I was used for organization, to come up with a chain of command. Everything then was Lester. People kept running into his office. I helped set up a system. At the same time, Lester kept arranging co-op mailings for Bell & Howell with new firms to us but important in mail order. We introduced each other to a lot of people. I learned a lot about the inside of an advertising agency. It was a wonderful experience.

"In 1966, I moved back to Chicago and started on my own as a consultant. Bell & Howell was my first client. That kept the doors open. I hadn't accumulated money but George Gregg, a friend, owned part of an art studio. In that studio . . . in a small office . . . with some furniture, he let me stay rent free and hang out my shingle.

"In my little office I started all by myself, with a bookkeeper/secretary several hours a day. As client fees came in, I began to pay a little rent. When more fees came in, I paid George full rent. At the same time cutting the pattern to the cloth, I hired my first people. I acted as a consultant and as an advertising agency.

"Elaine Erickson was my first full-time employee. She was account executive, art director and secretary. Then I hired a third person, my second full-time employee. She was Susan Kryl. She's now president of a Sroge subsidiary. She's also president of the Chicago Association of Direct Marketers. For two years, she was president of the Chicago Women in Direct Marketing Club. She's great. My wife, June, did some part-time work before she retired to raise our children.

"For Bell & Howell I began to work on future profit planning, solely for mail order. B & H began to expand in mail order beyond movie kits. I got them into stereo hi-fi. I sold hundreds of thousands of binoculars, which B & H still sells. In one way or another, I never stopped working for B & H. While not now a regular client, they occasionally still call me in.

"Our first client aside from B & H was American Photocopy (Apeco). Our first big project for a Fortune 500 company was in 1967, for Philco, which had a big inventory of stereo hi-fi equipment to move outside of retail channels. We sold out their production. We put together an offer, created a mailing piece and syndicated it. Fingerhut and other mail order houses grabbed it up.

"In the late fifties and early sixties, mail order began growing so big in the U.S. that giant European companies got interested, both for Europe and for more sales in the U.S. Philips, of Holland, came to us. They had no U.S. operation. They asked us to create a mail order business and run the business for them on a temporary basis. We set up the warehousing. We designed the package, did the advertising. We ran the business. Today, Philips owns a company on Long Island, Polygram, which grew out of that business we set up.

"We brought to America the superb classical records and tapes produced by Philips. At one time, Time-Life wanted to buy the business we had created. We created The International Preview Society. We created packages for American Express—The Festival of Great Orchestras, Great Awards, and so on. I love classical music. It was great.

"Then Bell & Howell Schools, a division of B & H, bought DeVry, a correspondence school in Chicago. After two other agencies had failed, we were called in to help. We felt that previous ads had been low type. We wanted a different, better image for a Bell & Howell company. We felt we could come up with a different, more profitable approach. We were given a space budget of $25,000. We produced enrollments so profitably that the budget kept growing until it was $7,000,000 in four years.

"One Fortune 500 company we got into mail order was General Foods. We helped them start Creative Village Fabrizaar, selling fabrics for home sewing. I learned an important lesson about giant firms going into mail order. Smart management, good talent, powerful management controls have great difficulty without enough experience. For even a giant, a mail order operation must start slowly and pick up speed gradually.

"General Foods was very committed to very rapid growth, to avoid or drop any operation too small and to decide on potential early in the game. This is very understandable for a large company, but the result can be as it was here—too much too soon. Often, there is disagreement and even conflict in big company management over going into mail order. It's often initially suspect, as it was at first to Bell & Howell.

"At any rate, General Foods started in a big way but then decided to get out of all mail order—Burpee Seeds, Alma Woodward Cosmetics and Creative Village. One faction had wanted it. One didn't. Our side lost.

"We were expanding our office a good deal by then. General Foods, Philips, Philco and Bell & Howell were all expanding as our clients. Another major client was Fox Photo (I'm now a director). Then, suddenly, I had my most difficult period, a blow few agencies could survive. Bell & Howell went out of the home study business, in 1974. We were never told of plans to close home study operations down; it just stopped. On Monday, we had $7,000,000 a year billing. On Tuesday, it was nothing. And we had 35 people for B & H alone.

"But we did survive and succeed. We were forced to grow, to develop new services and capabilities to go after new clients more aggressively. We were staffed up. The opportunities were there. We all simply worked harder. I went at an unbelievable pace—nights, weekends, constant travel.

"But I don't know of anyone who succeeded in anything who hasn't paid a price. I'm in at 8:30 AM. Often I've taken a plane at 7 PM to a client city, arrived at 10 or 11 PM and had five appointments the next day, taken the plane back that night and been back in the office at 8:30 AM the next day. Often, I wrote my best copy on the plane there and back. Otherwise, I write my copy mostly nights and weekends.

"I write a lot of advertising. I love to write. I've done it all my life, ever since my father wrote my Bar Mitzvah speech. I said it—but decided I'd rather do my own writing. I wrote in high school. I wrote advertising and promotion in my first mail order job. I've never stopped. When we needed to grow, I wrote copy as never before.

"Another asset helped me then. I've always been a good sales manager. I'm sensitive to people and needs. I've been able to see opportunities in mail order for big companies as I did for B & H and to help them get started in it from scratch. One of our organization's strong areas is the capability to work with a large corporation, to help it staff up and develop its own operation. When we start a client, we generate a lot of work—advertising and production, executive search group assignments, research, whatever. There is no greater mortality for advertising agencies and consultants than in start-ups, but I love them. Each is a challenge.

"Start-ups are very high risk. A start-up is the most difficult assignment in mail order. But half our business is in start-ups. They make tough demands. Since we divisionalized, we've become more organized for start-ups. Now we have the Consulting Division, Advertising, Publishing and Executive Search Divisions. We have very much like the product manager system. It provides more stability.

"Many start-ups don't make it. We expect clients to take over successful operations we start for them. IBM did it with its Science Research subsidiary. We start people. We help them grow and go on their own. A child develops and then walks. But, in one way or another, often the relationships continue. Clients come back with new problems. We have long-term relationships with many companies. I've had one for 30 years, as employee and consultant, with Bell & Howell.

"We've also kept our people pretty well. When good people go, they sometimes come back. Klaus Ruege did. He was in his own business for a while, Verbatim. Now he's back as executive vice president. He's very able. Susan Kryl left and came back. We're unique as an organization. We perform a great variety of functions. But they all share one thing. There's a common thread of mail order throughout. All our disciplines interrelate."

For a busy, big client, he will run a no-employee business with all functions done outside, under Mac's control. Just pay the bill. Or his executive search division will supply all the management executives needed, as needed. Or his merger-acquisition division will buy for you an existing mail order company. His advertising agency will handle your account. He has fine copywriters and a superb art director.

Before all that, he'll research for the kind of mail order most suited, the kind that benefits most from the company's reputation, from the consumer perception of it, from loyalty to it by users of present products through stores or however.

You need not originally be a client. You need not be a big company. You need not have a big budget. Just do business with his publishing division. His "Non-Store Marketing Report" is an excellent newsletter, 26 weeks for a hundred and thirty-five dollars.

Or you can buy an existing research report in depth on a specific field in mail order, at a fraction of the cost to employ Mac to research a new field. You are sharing the cost with others. It's important information. Yet, Mac doesn't believe that his publishing business should operate with an insufficient margin. The fee is approximately $10 a page for most reports.

There are reports on collectibles, tools, crafts; ready-to-wear, insurance, books; and more are on the way. A typical industry study gives industry size and growth trends. It lists members of the industry. It describes types of product offerings, characteristics, seasonality and more.

It investigates the larger industry participants, offers key operating statistics; estimates sales volume, numbers of customers, average order size, positions of offers and methods of marketing. It analyzes the marketing approaches of several industry leaders.

But Max Sroge's best known publishing enterprise is his U.S. Mail Order Industry Estimates. In it, each year, is a comparison of a panel of mail order houses versus a panel of close to the same number of retail companies. Maxwell Sroge gets known figures released by public companies on their mail order sales. From this, he guestimates sales of private companies in the field which do not release figures. Then he combines the guestimates and the known figures for an overall estimate. Year by year, since Max started and as he continued to do more

research, these estimates have been considered more realistic efforts in the fight for true measurement of mail order sales.

The Sroge staff comes from the biggest mail order companies, from a wide variety of specialties. But Mac is more than a buyer and seller of mail order expertise. He's a one-stop shopping location with ad agency, publishing operation, consulting, personnel divisions. Each is a structured, separate organization. Each has a multiplicity of functions. If you want it, he's got it—or gets it—from brain-storming to telephone marketing to a fulfillment system.

He has charged fees as little as $2,500 for a month's investigation to $192,000 for running a complex operation for two years. He has worked and does work for the giants from General Mills to Armstrong Corp., Gillette to ITT, Bausch & Lomb to Citicorp and 3M Corp. and even the U.S. Government.

He sees the rapidity of change and return to old values . . . more specialized tastes and the fully employed household . . . women's new role, and sharply diminished shopping hours—all speeding mail order growth. "The female work force is growing at four times the rate of the male work force. In recent years, the growth of non-store sales leap-frogged retail sales by two to one." He points out that higher incomes and better education favor mail order. He goes on. "More working women and less time mean more mail order. Mail order taps latent demand of those too busy to shop."

To manufacturers who worry that if they sell by mail order it might hurt their retail sales, he says: "Mail order complements and increases retail distribution. Record and tape sales have gone up 900% since record clubs started. Almost one half billion dollars worth of records and tapes are sold each year by mail, a way of marketing them that didn't exist 25 years ago . . . one-third of all film developed is handled by mail, despite 500,000 retail locations where processing is available." To Mac, the strength of mail order is that it can find and reach direct groups.

"Eddie Bauer (outdoor equipment), H.E. Harris (Stamps), LeeWard (crafts) and Talbots (women's specialty fashions) are all mail order catalog firms owned by General Mills. Each has found the life style interest perfect for it to sell to. But if someone were to take the best of each of these catalogs and group all the selections under one catalog, it would be the biggest bust in history.

"For those who grasp how to segment and compartmentalize, mail order has great opportunity. The growth is unparalleled. Some god is watching over us. That's why there is nothing I find more stimulating than to start a new business for someone; to change the way ads are done and see improved results; to study each new field. There's a chance for newcomers from Fortune 500 to kitchen table entrepreneurs—if they approach mail order correctly. The small mail order entrepreneur will always have an opportunity. There are good career chances.

"My advice to anyone starting out is to be flexible. Don't think direct mail only, or any other form of mail order only. Keep an eye on the new but don't lock on it. Start with the fundamentals. Do as Vince Lombardi says: 'Block, pass and run.' Remember, most people fail from execution, not bad ideas.

"Watch out for your weak points and get people to work with you who are strong in those areas. Generally, creative people are lousy at administration. I'm poor at it but have good executives. Klaus is strong on watching over administration operation. I can plan them.

"What about education? In hiring, I'm not concerned about it. I look for someone bright, with intellect. Preferably, advertising people we hire must have experience. In a trainee, I look for desire and commitment. I set a stiff course for each. I strongly advise those starting out to read everything pertinent. Take a direct marketing course. The Nat Ross NYU course is great. Finish school, and go to college at night if you have to. Work to the maximum now. Forget hours and overtime. Invest in your future with your own after hours work. I did it and it paid off. I encourage each of our new people to look for an assignment in any spare moment—to ask why and learn by doing.

"As success has come, I haven't worked every bit as hard. I do have interests and do take off time with my wife and family. My wife and I went to dude ranches, not fancy ones. We liked the life style. We took the kids. We were not out for form but for a good time, to get a little nature, air, exercise. One day we bought our daughter a horse. Now we have a ranch—Tarryall Ranch—8,500 feet up in Lake George, Colorado, a village of 250 people.

"We have a nice life and a nice family. We have twin sons, 24. One, Mark, is publication manager of our company. Mark is learning fast. The other, David, has created a small gourmet food business. We have a daughter, 26, in hospital adminstration. Mail order has been good to us and can be to you."

There was another time when another man from Chicago was the greatest missionary for another force in American life and culture. He was Albert Lasker, who christened advertising "Salesmanship in print" and made $100,000,000 for himself and far more for others using the new force. Mac reminds me of him.

Chapter 13
Making A Giant In Names And Numbers

With new analysis techniques that can dramatically improve mail order results.

On June 1, 1980, a group of investors...headed by William Howe, President of Metromail...purchased Metromail from Metromedia. Bill Howe has said about Metromail: "It is a little jewel of a company by any of the basic measures of business performance...annual sales growth, return on sales, return on investment." It's much more.

If you successfully test any mail order offer via direct mail and project it, you willl almost surely deal—either directly or indirectly—with one of the three computerized names and numbers giants. Metromail is one of them. This is the story of how it grew, what it does and how it can help you.

Metromail is running neck and neck with R.H. Donnelley and R.L. Polk—to be the largest supplier of direct marketing services to consumer marketing businesses and organizations in the U.S. Metromail also has the largest computer service bureau in direct marketing. Its lettershop capacities are second to none in the world. It has pioneered direct marketing research—with its own marketing research professionals. It numbers among its clients almost every major U.S. company which uses direct marketing.

Metromail provides names and addresses to sell magazine subscriptions, generate leads for insurance company salesmen, make credit card solicitations, obtain new members for record and book clubs and raise funds for charitable organizations. Metromail performs so many different services that no single piece of literature can adequately describe them all, and it can be a real problem to determine how best to describe Metromail's capabilities to a prospect.

Bill Howe puts it this way: "We must learn as much as we can about a client before a presentation. We must develop a "feel" for his business. We must understand his objectives, his requirements, his desires, budget and timetables. Then we can zero in on ways we put our resources to work for him."

Metromail was founded in 1966 by Metromedia, the country's largest independent broadcaster. Metromedia has prominent radio and television stations in major markets across the country. It is a leader in both the outdoor and transit advertising fields. It decided to extend its "Media" services to direct mail marketing, and to start in a big way by acquiring some of the best firms in the field.

In 1966, it bought three leading companies . . . Dickie Raymond, Sampson Hill and O.E. McIntyre. It added Mail Advertising Corporation of America and Cole Publications in 1972 and Marketing Electronics Corporation in 1979. These various companies had been providing a great variety of marketing, list and lettershop services to direct mail users . . . some since the mid-1940's. From them today's Metromail developed, dropping some activities, expanding others, evolving into a direct mail giant.

Bill Howe explains: "Metromail can effectively communicate with more than 68 million of the 82 million households in the country . . . thanks largely to data processing advances which make possible the availability of large numbers and varieties of critical marketing data and new analysis techniques. These provide market segmentation and selection opportunities which can discriminate between good and poor prospects with high degrees of reliability."

Traditionally, mail order companies used lists of known mail order buyers more than mass-compiled names. But the advent of computers made compiled lists more effective for them, particularly magazines. Substantial circulation requirements, sweepstakes offers and personalization opened up compiled lists on a huge scale.

The giant consumer-compiled lists were fully computerized before most mail-order buyer lists. The first computer-personalized mass sweepstakes were very profitable when mailed to such mail order lists as existed. They worked more marginally on compiled lists. But the great volume of names available made lists from mass compilers like Metromail very attractive.

As costs of postage and paper soared higher, marginal lists were dropped by consumer mail order people. Many went back to their earlier principles—avoid compiled lists.

Bill Howe continues: "This led to still another Metromail development, a data marriage of what was known about the buying habits of a name on a buyer list with all that was known about the same name on a compiled list. The computer could compare names endlessly to develop multi-hit lists of those households who made purchases by mail from a number of different companies. Metromail developed a number of significant techniques, all designed to marry the best of its compiled list data resources with mail order information as a means of improving the productivity of profitable lists and making marginal lists profitable. These techniques are: MRCS - Mail Response Checking System; Mail Order Buyers Bank; Data Match; Recycle/STAR File; etc."

As telephone marketing came of age, the right lists and telephone numbers became vital. Metromail had the telephone numbers. A list sent to them could have telephone numbers added, as well as demographics and other individual household data that proved helpful in communicating with the prospect.

Metromail is in the names and numbers business. They have the data banks, the computers, the statisticians, the experience and the know-how. Metromail can serve as the marketing arm of a direct marketer. They have developed much as direct marketing, itself, has—often more in less expected ways, and less in ways first visualized.

A study of the growth of Metromail is important to an understanding of many aspects of the use of direct mail in direct marketing. Its management story is an ideal candidate for a Harvard Business School case study. Its president, Bill Howe, has been a student and follower of trend forecasts and a business riverboat pilot.

Metromail's success has, to a large degree, been due to going with the direct marketing tide—starting and expanding urgently needed services at the right time and stopping or modifying other services whose time had run out in terms of their real potential in the marketplace.

Bill has been running Metromail for eleven years. He worked out projections for growth and profit based on inside experience. He has strong convictions about where Metromail is going, as well as the entire direct marketing field. "In the list marketing area, Metromail is continually committed to improve list counts and coverage, deliverability and overall marketing effectiveness."

Metromail's Computer Marketing Services Division is in Lombard, Illinois. It's a top supplier of merge-purge and rental list fulfillment services, which Bill plans to expand. "We can add a great number of different data pluses to client files as part of their routine processing runs . . . pluses such as address correction services, carrier route and census coding, demographics, telephone numbers, individual characteristics and more. We also can introduce negative screen overlays into a merge-purge program to eliminate poor prospects from a client's mailing lists, whether house or rented.

"Our Metromail lettershops, in four locations, have innovative engineers. They can develop equipment modifications necessary for the most unique mailing packages. We have machine power, manpower and control systems to fulfill basic requirements and adhere to schedules with economy.

"We have great numbers and varieties of products and services to satisfy requirements of magazine publishers, fund

raisers, retailers, banks, consumer goods companies, insurance companies, research organizations and so on."

One target area is the insurance industry, for which Metromail has produced a unique sales-lead getting and handling plan. Every salesman, every sales manager and every general manager or owner of any business which employs salesmen or uses agents should read it. It's called a "Pre-Approach and Follow-Up Prospect System That Works".

This system was developed by Metromail to aid insurance agents in obtaining qualified leads through direct mail and telephone follow-up, and to provide a high conversion rate from lead to sale. The system selects the proper demographic profile of a potential insurance policy holder, whether it be for Life, Health or Casualty.

Bill Howe explains: "Each profile was developed through many mailings with different insurance companies working with Metromail. The profiles are constantly updated. Metromail makes these pre-qualified family counts available through the Insurance Company's Home Office and as part of an Agent's Guide that is distributed to each Agency.

"The agent can select at a zip code level and even a sub-cell level within a zip code. A sub-cell is a small, homogeneous, neighborhood area. An agent can target market his area better than ever before and less expensively for "quality, and not quantity".

This program also supplies its agency area maps of its market (if available) and Family Availability Count Sheets. The zip codes and sub-cells illustrated on these maps coincide with those appearing on the Count Sheets. These sheets better advise where the families selected to mail reside.

Metromail consults and advises on letter selection. "To select names for agents, we maintain a Family Name Bank. We feel, though we have spent many hours developing this pre-qualified list Name Bank, the wrong letter can easily destroy the effort. From experience, we know what type of insurance products can be sold most effectively with our list. Besides letter and copy consulting, we also provide much of the input for developing the Agent's Guide used in prospecting promotion. The letter can be selected by higher management, if desired. Once the agent selects and orders names, the next thing he sees is his replies, plus a telephone print-out that corresponds to each name mailed."

The lettershop operation is performed right in Metromail's main computer facility. Each participating company has supplies of mailing material (letters, reply elements and mailing envelopes) warehoused at this facility. This minimizes time spent between receiving orders, generating the pre-qualified names and mailing. Besides performing the necessary lettershop operation for reor-dering purposes, each month a complete inventory is performed and each company is advised of the outcome.

After the orders are processed, a Prospecting System Count Report advises the Home Office of which agents are using the program, what products/letters they are using, quantities and where they are mailing. "This is a tremendous tool in developing response rates, budgets and extra business," says Bill.

"A main purpose of this program is to keep the agent's time spent developing prospecting programs to a minimum. Metromail can, as described, do much of the back-up work while we supply the agents with pre-qualified leads that have a very high conversion to sales percentage. And that's the name of the game.

"We're great believers in scientific direct marketing by list analysis. We're well along on the development of what we feel will be of breakthrough proportion in terms of our being able to predict higher levels of responsiveness with high levels of reliabilty."

Note: Metromail is located at 901 West Bond Street, Lincoln, Nebraska 68521. Sales offices are in New York City (212) 599-2616; Washington, D.C. (202) 244-2010; Chicago (312) 620-3300; Lincoln (402) 475-4591; Los Angeles (213) 824-0475; Mt. Pleasant, Iowa (319) 385-2284. Headquarters for the Con-sumer Marketing Services Division is at 11 Eisenhower Lane South, Lombard, Illinois 60148. Sales offices are in Chicago (312) 620-3300; and New York City (212) 599-2616.

Mail Order Sampler
Seminar VI

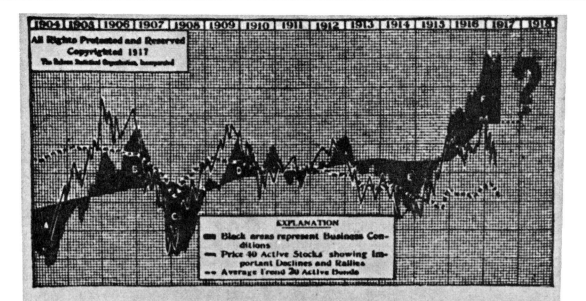

Rumors

send the stock market skidding or skyward in a flash. Babson Service helps you analyze them for what they're worth. Gives you reliable fundamental knowledge for <u>safe investment</u>.

Avoid worry. Cease depending on rumors or luck. Recognize that all action is followed by equal reaction. Work with a definite policy based on fundamental statistics.

Particulars sent free.
Write to Dept. E-22 of

Babson's Statistical Organization
Service Building   Wellesley Hills, Mass.
Largest Organization of its Character in the World

Chapter 1
Direct Marketing Ethics

*Always in mail order there have been
the shady and those with
far higher standards.*

It's probably the easiest business to start in and proved ideal for the fly-by-night. But no mail order business can be sound without repeat business which could only come from satisfaction. Winning trust and holding it means survival.

The bigger mail order became, and later direct marketing, the more the emphasis has been on repeat business. The bigger the companies that have entered direct marketing the more important it has been to avoid risking their reputation.

With each year from 1872 when Montgomery Ward started modern mail order, the emphasis has been more on repeat business. Sears was a bit of an adventurer. But Rosenwald, who became his partner and then bought him out, built Sears Roebuck on customer trust.

Ethics came to mail order because it proved good business. Anyone could go into it and lie and cheat. But to survive, repeat business was necessary. It became important to be honest. There was something more.

The medical profession, with the Hippocratic Oath, developed professional ethics 2,500 years ago. Since then, first the legal profession and then others have developed their own codes of ethics. The closer to a profession any activity is, the more this is so. As an activity gains more acceptance, there is more pride in being associated with it and more of a desire for some minimum code of conduct, if only for an ideal to aim at.

Ethics has come to mail order and direct marketing because it was needed and wanted. Direct marketing is now so universal, it represents virtually all kinds of business. It now starts with the ethics of all business but there are influences to make ethical conduct come to a higher standard in direct marketing, by the same people and firms.

Some people and organizations have particularly contributed. The DMMA, from its first chief officer, Homer Buckley, to the present, has helped. Henry Hoke, Sr. was a strong ethical influence when running the DMMA and later as founder of The Reporter of Direct Mail (now Direct Marketing magazine). "Pete" Hoke, the present publisher, is.

Nat Ross has been the particular conscience of direct marketing. He has influenced for the good a good share of the top people in mail order through the NYU course. He did even more when he founded DMIX, the Direct Marketing Idea Exchange, with its emphasis on ethics written into its constitution.

To my son, Cecil, L.L. Bean is a particular role hero for ethical catalog house behavior. There are many, many others. More and more people in direct marketing are taking pride in it and insisting on their own codes of ethical conduct to live up to. But the concept of direct marketing ethics is not ivory tower.

Many in direct marketing now consider that raising and adhering to standards of self-regulation is essential, that if they don't the government will. The concept is that upgrading direct marketing from within upgrades the perception of direct marketing. The hope is this: The public will then take a more favorable view. Organized consumer groups will have less to criticize. Government and bureaucracy will hold off more regulation.

But to accomplish this requires more than cosmetic changes, more than better public relations. It means actual improvement of ethical practices by those in mail order. Ethical practices include giving honest presentation, fair value, good service and respecting privacy.

The DMMA constitution is explicit. Its objective is to foster high ethical standards. For 20 years the DMMA Ethics Committee has operated. In 1977, the committee was reorganized and enlarged. It made recommendations. Based on them, the DMMA made a new drive for higher ethical standards.

In 1978, the DMMA presented to members its "White Paper" discussing plans for self-regulation by direct marketers. In October 1979, the DMMA issued various Ethical Business Practice Guidelines. These stiffened, brought up-to-date and clarified precisely the self-regulation the DMMA expects from members and others. The DMMA issued more specific guidelines for telephone marketing and advertising acceptance by media.

The Ethics Committee, in turn, has a five member Policy Committee which develops and reviews ethical codes and standards of practice. There is a fifteen-member operating committee whose chairman is responsible for monitoring compliance with the DMMA ethical standards and for reviewing and taking action on specific cases brought before it.

The DMMA Ethics Committee felt that the first step was to clarify understanding of standards by DMMA members, to win adherence and then to influence direct marketers outside the membership to do so. The DMMA would first try to explain, influence and persuade mail order ethical offenders to straighten out and fly right. As a last step it might be necessary to bring in the appropriate government regulatory agency to police serious violators.

In 1978, a staff director of Ethical Practices was hired to work with the committee. He is Jack Cavenaugh. He had worked for The Child Welfare League and The World Health Organization. He had been Director of Development for Columbia University. His wife is with the UN.

"We've just revived and expanded the guidelines. Two committees deal with specific cases at committee meetings ten times a year. I bring an agenda of cases for each meeting. We go over the individual cases to determine if guidelines are being violated.

"The next step is for me to contact the direct marketer involved and explain what we think. We get great cooperation. When we point out what we consider are guideline violations they are usually corrected.

"From my previous background I learned that you don't dictate more ethical behavior. You expose people to alternate choices, different ethical paths. You try to help. You just have to let people decide."

That isn't the end of it. Jack Cavenaugh is out to save mail order sinners, but also society generally from them. To do so, he works as a middleman between any mail order situation he finds in which people can be hurt by unethical practices and government enforcement agencies.

"Essentially, we use the method the Better Business Bureau does. I work with the BBB and the authorities concerned. Today I talked with the Attorney General of the State of Florida, with the BBB for Philadelphia and with the U.S. Postal Inspector for Talahassee, Florida.

"From the DMMA Mail Order Action Line program, we get alert signals. The DMMA publicizes and promotes this hot-line mail order complaint service. As soon as several complaints concern one company, we start watching for more. When complaints build on the company I contact it to find out the trouble. MOAL is a great program and a great help to me.

"I wear three hats. I'm the administrator of the Operating Committee, the administrator of the Policy Committee and the Director of Ethical Practices. I do most of my business on the telephone.

"I've gone to the council of BBB's in Washington and to the Washington Postal Service staff meetings of those concerned with enforcement—the inspectors, the lawyers, the anti-fraud office people. I've visited the New York BBB and the national advertising division of BBB here in New York."

The Ethical Practices Department also functions to influence adherence to privacy standards by members and nonmembers. Routine MOAL complaints are handled by the Consumer Service Department. Any involving serious violations of ethical standards are turned over to the Ethical Practices Department.

In the early 1970's, it was disclosed that for some biggest sweepstakes a substantial amount of prizes was never awarded. It had been perfectly legal. The winning numbers had never been mailed in. The DMMA came out with a "Guide for Self-Regulation of Sweepstakes Promotion" which represented a good deal of soul searching by direct marketers conducting contests. The result has been that, ever since 1974, prevailing practice has been that all prizes have been given. The process of selecting winning numbers continues until the winner is a number actually received.

"Some very professional direct marketers occasionally neglect customer handling, but few do. Some borderline firms seem always in trouble, with constant violations. If a firm is in trouble and seems to want to correct it, we try to help. If it seems incorrigible, we try to get every policing agency possible into the situation.

"The Committee is particularly concerned with mailing offerings which may not be noticed as much by authorities as publication and broadcast advertising. Time is so vital that between committee meetings I proceed on anything that seems warranted. I investigate trouble sources. I collect questionable mailings.

"Our hope is that members can more and more be ethical examples as well as successful direct marketers. We have a member logo identification members are encouraged to use. It's to identify members and not a seal of approval. The Policy Committee objective is to improve the ethics of the field and the image of DMMA projects and programs. It's happening.

"We can do a lot before violations occur. I get a lot of calls from business people about products and promotions they are considering. They will describe what they're thinking about and ask: 'Is it legal? Is it sound? Is it ethical?'

"We get complaints about competitors. We get complaints on customer service from consumers. The vast majority of companies take care of complaints. The first non-delivery complaint from someone about a company MOAL forwards to the company with a request for fast action and usually gets it. When second complaints from the same person about the same company come in, I investigate.

"At this point, if the trouble still continues, I investigate other agencies from the hot-line complaint service of a newspaper to district attorneys in areas where complaints come from and also where companies complained about are located. If others also report trouble, I go back to the company complained about.

"It's easy to work with DMMA members. For membership we seek out more ethical firms. The emphasis on ethics in the DMMA discourages anyone unethical from joining or staying in. Anyone without a basic desire to conduct business ethically is apt to feel out of place."

Sometimes, small struggling mail order firms in desperation use exaggerated misstatements. The wild copy becomes a substitute for capital. When ethically decaffeinated copy pulls 10% of the wilder original, only basic changes in the entire operation can combine ethics and survival . . . such as firing most employees and a brand new start. Yet, anything else builds on sand and tears down mail order. Others become solid citizens. The Little Leather Library, of cheapest material far from leather, led to the Book of the Month Club.

Jack Cavenaugh makes a real effort to help such firms make the adjustment successfully. "Often the major problem is financial, but recognized too late—and the firm goes under. It's to the loss and dishonor of the promoters, the loss of all dealing with them and harms the image of mail order just that much more."

Jack Cavenaugh, the DMMA and the big majority of direct marketers persevere in setting and raising standards for mail order and direct marketing.

Chapter 2

Logistics Of A Lettershop

A trip through one that mails up to 1,000,000 pieces a day . . . what it does and how it started.

He's tall, young looking and has an open, friendly smile. He is Lee Epstein, founder, president and owner of MAILMEN INC., a mailing house in Hauppauge, New York—on Long Island. The company handles only outgoing third class mail, up to 1,000,000 pieces a day.

The MAILMEN building is a new, one-story brickfront, just off the Long Island Expressway. The reception room is small and comfortable, but there's no waiting. We go into the corridor, down to a big executive office, meet Lee, chat briefly and are off on our tour . . . one he has obviously conducted frequently. He's proud of everything; he enjoys his business.

The first impression is of order, meticulous neatness, a place for everything and everything in its place. There are the usual offices for sales and bookkeeping. There's a sizeable office for quality control people. But there's little office space. Most of the 60,000 square feet is production and warehouse space.

Lee explains the logistics. "Sometimes the job is a small test, sometimes a giant mailing—but with the same problems. Clients send instructions. Materials come from different outside sources. Nothing can start until everything for a job comes in. Labels or computer letters come from computer service bureaus. Outside and return envelopes come from envelope manufacturers. Most of the broadsides, fliers, order cards and letters come from printers."

He takes us through a door to a working open floor the

length of the building. There is a long line of inserting machines, each parallel to the other. About half the pieces mailed each day are 8½″ X 11″ pieces in jumbo envelopes. About half are #10, or 6″ X 9″ pieces, in standard size envelopes. In addition, there is high-speed labeling equipment, too.

For each inserting machine there are six feeder hoppers. Each is loaded with literature from broadside and letters to reply envelopes. Each hopper pulls out a piece of literature onto a moving track. At the same time, the machine opens the envelopes, inserts the collated pieces, then seals the flap.

"We pay the average worker about 3 times what we did twenty years ago, but we get more productivity. We expect to bill out $25 per hour for each inserting machine against $10 to $12 an hour, years ago, but the machine is twice as fast. The operator now gets about $5 an hour, including fringe benefits. We can cycle from 2,000 to 4,000 pieces an hour through the machine.

"We try hard to be the best, and put great emphasis on quality control. Once an hour, our quality control people check random envelopes from each machine in the plant. If there's anything wrong . . . something missing, extra item in envelope, any error . . . the machine is stopped. Each sealed envelope turned out in the last hour is opened and checked. Each envelope is then correctly reinserted by hand. The machine is checked. Each inserting compartment is checked. When quality control decides the machine is properly loaded and ready, the switch is turned on and the operation continues."

There is another section for personalized mail. "The pre-addressed continuous forms are delivered to us, either in rolls or in a flat pack. Bursters are used to separate the forms which are then fed into the folding machine for eventual inserting. Each label or computer form is zip coded and is sent to us in zip code sequence. Our sorters separate the finished mail by zip code, and each bundle is either string or rubberband tied, and placed in its unique zip code bag."

Huge mailings are easiest to separate into complete bags, easiest for post office handling, and get fastest post office treatments. Bags have instructions from clients. If a client is running support TV, it's vital that it be delivered in any locality during or as immediately after TV schedules as possible. Postmasters are given a date for release and MAILMEN, a date to release to post offices. They try to cooperate.

Tests that are smallest and include too little mail to deliver a full bag to any zip code are put into mixed zip bags and are apt to be delivered most irregularly by the post office. This makes it very difficult to measure results and predict response. To correct this, sophisticated mailers pay an extra charge to MAILMEN INC. to merge mailings into mass mailings. This means slipping into mail bags of big mailings the few extra pieces from a test for each code center. That's another job for Lee.

To save time and for maximum efficiency, the post office sends their 40-foot trailers to MAILMEN. Lee provides an office for two U.S. Postal Service supervisors. They weigh and check all mail and collect postage just as if at the post office and then supervise loading of U.S. Postal Service trailers. The mail never goes through a local post office but directly to a U.S. Post Office Bulk Mail center for distribution nationally.

A thick canvas mail bag weighs 2 pounds when new. When dirty, it weighs 2½ pounds, adding to the weight of all mail when full. The postal supervisor and Lee's people have to agree on the net weight of the envelopes with all inserts by subtracting the weight of the bag, new or dirty. Each such point is negotiated.

There are two shifts. Lee tried three shifts, but found it a strain with too much overtime of supervisory personnel. Instead of a third shift, in rush time, each shift works two hours overtime. Hours are rearranged to suit.

Plant housekeeping is meticulous. To dispose of waste material, anything that can be, is first separated. Then all waste is bailed for disposal. The entire place is broom clean at all times.

MAILMEN is a busy, growing and successful business. Yet, all I saw had been accomplished in three years from opening shop. But it took Lee's lifetime to get himself in the position to make his success on his own.

"I had average marks in school. I had an above average IQ, but I was lazy. I did what I liked. I had no hobbies, but I did like science in school. Dad had a fruit and vegetable store. I hated it. For the rest of my life I hated penny transactions. That's what potatoes sold for . . . pennies and arguments. I hated it so much, I left home and went to Washington, D.C. where I took a job in the Government Printing Office, as an apprentice. I also took a pre-med course at American University, 9 AM to 12 Noon. I wanted to be a doctor, but I wasn't motivated enough to continue.

"After I returned to New York City, I got a job as purchaser of printing at the Treasury office there. I worked hard, and became Chief of the Printed Materials Division of the War Finance Committee. It was our job to sell bonds to finance World War II.

"When the war ended, I worked for a printing broker for two years, then got a job in the advertising department of I. Miller shoes. From there, I went to work for Bruce Richards, a premium fulfillment house, as production manager. I worked with clients and won the trust of those I worked with. I learned and mastered the problems of handling big mailings, merchandise and shipments. At that time, we did some business with Huber Hoge and more with various Hoge alumni.

"After two years, I left to work for O.E. McIntyre, now known as Metro-Mail. I got the job doing what I had done at Bruce Richards. But working at McIntyre was the difference between night and day. They were big. Their accounts were big. They had the working standards of the big. They were list compilers working from telephone books in all major cities. Mailings were vastly larger than I had ever done. One of their biggest customers was Reader's Digest. The experience changed my life.

"The computer was beginning to make inroads. Ralph Fairbanks was a management consultant to McIntyre for conversion to computer. After two years at McIntyre, I joined Ralph Fairbanks as an industrial engineer. Then I got into a weird venture. It started because one day two engineers and I, between assignments at Fairbanks, got to talking.

"One engineer suggested starting a lettershop. It was a ridiculous idea, without proper capital, equipment, enough customers or business experience. But we did it. Each of us put up a thousand dollars and we rented an automobile showroom in Glen Cove, Long Island. It was 1,200 square feet and that was the beginning of MAILMEN INC., in 1954.

"After we found the location, we bought tables, chairs, Graph-A-Type, Speed-O-Mat and an embossing machine for Address-O-Graph and Speed-O-Mat plates. When I dropped into some of my customer friends from the McIntyre days, first Greystone and Prentice-Hall and then Abercrombie & Fitch gave us work. I got a lot of business but the entire venture proved to be a foolish, rash venture.

"Within three months we were $75,000 in debt. What was the solution? We lived hand-to-mouth. We drew from nothing to $50 a week. Our wives supported us. We got advances. We couldn't pay our withholding taxes (don't ever try that!). By now, we were

in an old garage of 5,000 square feet. Then we had an opportunity.

"Vincent Carosella, of Jetson's (another lettershop), had advanced postage in huge amounts to Toys of the World, which then folded, leaving Jetson's in terrible shape. (Now it's tremendously successful.) Vincent had to raise cash. He offered to sell us his inserting equipment for $16,000. As a result, we could handle substantial additional business from Publishers Clearing House. Harold Mertz, of PCH, loaned us the money and paid us twice a month to help our cash flow situation. Everything went a lot better.

"But we still were underfinanced. The partners still couldn't draw enough money to live. Both my partners eventually withdrew. I owned it all until I got a new partner, who came with his own crew of sorters. We did only machine inserting, and we finally began to show a profit. In 1961, we merged with the Fifth Avenue Lettershop, in New York City. We called the firm FALA-MAILMEN. The partnership didn't work. We sold out to Ted Bates (the top ten advertising agency). Then John Blair bought us from Bates. Blair owned four printing plants, one of which had acquired a mailing house. They wanted to match us with it.

"Blair gave me a three-year contract. I renewed it. I liked Blair, and particularly their president, Jack Fritz. But, gradually, the urge returned to make a try in business really on my own. I realized that I had never been truly happy working either with partners or in a conglomerate structure.

"At the end of my contract, I said good-bye to Jack Fritz and told him what I planned to do. Six key people went with me, with his permission. This time, I thought long and carefully and planned each step of the way. I determined my needs and set about to fulfill them. Every bit of know-how, experience and business friendship was brought to bear on my new venture.

"There were five elements necessary to create my own business. First were the customers. I had enough to be confident of doing a million dollars in sales the first year. Second was a management team. I had put that team together. My plant manager was Bill Vignola. Each member of the team was good, and worked together effectively.

"Third was a building. Charlie Mascioli was a friend of mine. He had built buildings for our company twice before. He had a shell in Hauppauge, Long Island, and decided to gamble on me. Not a penny was required from me. There was nothing down to pay. We knew exactly what we needed in the plant, and Mascioli finished the building to our specifications. The plant was built precisely for a volume mailing operation.

"The fourth requirement was equipment. I had no money, just my reputation. But I had my friends. Half the equipment I got was brand new. Old suppliers asked for no cash down payment. Half the equipment was used. For six months, an old friend had been assembling some of the best used equipment he could find. A top dealer in lettershop equipment, he sold us $200,000 worth of top notch machine equipment for nothing down.

"The fifth requirement was cash. We needed money for payroll, for purchases, for all the expenses of operation. And I wanted enough to be comfortable. First, I went to my friends. We raised $100,000 which was great for starters. But we needed more from a bank. Manufacturer's Hanover Trust turned us down. Our real estate broker helped out with an introduction to Long Island Trust, who gave us a $200,000 line of credit.

"Still, this wasn't the end of it. Before our first day of business, I had rounded up a total of $750,000 in loans or credit. It was great but scary. My wife and I had to co-sign a guarantee for the bank, and we had to put up as collateral our personal assets, accumulated over a lifetime. It was more debt than we had ever dreamed of assuming.

"Our first year was 1977. I had projected to the bank sales of $1,000,000 for the year. We did over $2,000,000. The bank took a look at the statement and told me that for the next year it would increase our line of credit, would return our personal stocks and bonds and ask for no more personal collateral, and would cut the interest rate to one-half of one percent over prime.

"Since then, the business has kept growing. We try always to do a better job. We charge more for it. I come out to the plant only once a week. I have a small office in New York with a secretary. But we're a team. Everyone is highly motivated. I am able to give more incentives than I ever could, as part of a conglomerate.

"I look back now and wonder how it all happened. I had no intention to go into direct mail. So many people helped along the way. Probably the Jetson deal, in 1956, was a key factor. I owe more to my wife than to anything else. Rose has the energy for three businesses. She sets a high standard and so do I. She is General Manager of Sales & Marketing at Time magazine.

"Gradually, in my lifetime, I found a way to use myself, effectively, and also to help others. Twenty-five years ago, I began to work for various charitable causes. I've done more and more since. I try to lead a balanced life. My objective is to spend one-third of my business time on the business, one-third in association activity, and one-third on charities and philanthropies.

"The mailing houses and lettershops have a trade associaton, Mail Advertising Service Assn (MASA). In our association, we try to work with and help with the post office. I head a committee to suggest to the post office efficiencies to save them money. To stay in business, we have to be efficient, and it's necessary for the post office to be efficient as well. Everything affects us. Our customers can only be customers if their mailings make money.

They can only do so if the cost is right. The cost can only be right if everyone concerned is efficient, including the post office. So we try to help.

"I have a hobby of acting as career counsellor. I help place the right person in the right job. To get someone in the right niche, I may call six people in the industry. But often it works.

"We love the city . . . going to the theater and concerts, socializing. We do a lot of entertaining. I do a little exercise. I've lifted many mail bags in my day. But three years ago, Rose got me to go to the Cardiac Fitness Center in the McGraw-Hill Building. I go there three times a week for various exercises. I do it to build up my resistance.

"We've had a good family life. Our daughter, Ellen, is 29 and a teacher on Martha's Vineyard. She's married. Our son, Larry, is 26. He is with CBS as manager of Capital for the CBS-owned TV stations. He ran the radio station (WVBR) in Ithaca when he was an undergraduate at Cornell."

In 1981, volume handled by The Mailmen went up 25% over 1980, to 200,000 pieces from 10 major clients and 20 smaller ones. Lee has found his niche, with his philosophy, hobby, home life, know-how and perfectionish way of doing things. He has achieved an efficiency that has freed him to help others. It's good balance, a fine business and a life we can look up to.

Note: THE MAILMEN, INC., is located at 15 Enter Lane, Hauppauge, NY 11787; (212) 986-4862 (NYC tie-line).

Chapter 3
A Researcher Views Research—For Direct Marketers

What direct marketers are not doing effectively - yet can profitably do.

Tom Ryan—a top researcher trained by Time Inc., feels that way about direct marketing's use of research. "Direct marketers succeed. Book clubs and record clubs are successful. You can't knock success—even without scientific research.

"But in terms of the kinds of research done for marketers of consumer products, direct marketers don't use research to any degree, or even want to. Mostly, they don't do research. Those who have tried it are not wildly enthusiastic. In direct marketing, you've got to get X orders this week. Research benefits can be long-term.

"Direct marketers should use research, both statistical analysis of existing information and getting answers by asking people. Mail order people chiefly have faith only in mail order tests. But testing by direct marketers is not accurate. If you mail 10,000, the number of orders you get is not scientific. The sample received is too small. A split-run in a publication of 100,000 or more circulation is okay. So would be testing a list of 100,000.

"Direct marketers are constantly making judgments built on tests which can range from inadequate to misleading. Research has plenty of drawbacks but can be a valuable supplementary tool. They will find, as owners of national brand store distributed products have, that effective research can increase profits and avoid losses. A few are beginning. Ultimately, as big a percentage of direct marketers as of general marketers will use and believe in research."

Research in marketing started out with the efforts of national magazines to sell more advertising by providing advertisers with more marketing data and by establishing a profile of their readers. Tom Ryan got into it early. He graduated from college in liberal arts, went to law school—and then to Time Inc. in 1940.

For twenty-two years he did research in the advertising department. Time Inc. has been a leader in research. Out of it have graduated some great research authorities, into consulting. Tom Ryan became a consultant in 1962 and has worked for top marketers ever since.

The circulation managers of biggest magazines were the first to turn to research, often first using researchers from their advertising departments. And magazines such as Smithsonian have been first to turn to Tom Ryan for direct marketing research. For readers, Tom gives a little orientation on research.

"There are four or five ways to collect information for a questionnaire. You can mail to a sample. You can telephone to a sample. You can make doorstep interviews personally of individual householders. There's the Focus Group. And there's the Shopping Mall Intercept, just grabbing people.

"Costs of this research have gone up from inflation. Also, there's growing resistance to responding. The percentage of completion is dropping. There is concern now about the reliability and the cost.

"All the methodology was developed in academe. Mail and telephone samples are more expensive and less reliable than formerly. The probability sample, personal household interview survey, can now cost as much as $100 per completed interview. You need 100 interviews. That's $10,000. Clients don't want to pay it. As for the Shopping Mall Intercept, less people want to be intercepted.

"The Focus Group is a small group of people sitting down informally with a trained interviewer. The conversation is casual. The idea is to get natural reactions, although participants are told that they are studied, observed and taped. Focus groups originally came from psychological research.

"The Focus Group is highly controversial. Participants have not always been told the full details of what was happening, when people behind one-way, see-through mirrors were watching. It's been criticized as commercial voyeurism. Professionally, it is thought of less as a true opinion sample and more as a stimulus to bring out copy points.

"For all these reasons, advertising researchers are getting deeper into zip code research. I've done it for my clients. I've done some experimental circulation work for Time and Smithsonian. For Ann Keating, at Smithsonian, we've done some zip code demographic ad testing and for book selling.

"We work with zip codes. Everybody's record is zip code recorded. We've done some work for National Yellow Pages using zip code demography. We constructed a profile of populations in each of 1,800 areas served by individual yellow page directories. A lot of clients won't give the records you need to geo code. To geo code, you need the exact street address. Anyone can buy a computer program for geo coding from the Department of Commerce. All the data comes from the government. You must identify census tracts from your client supplied list of street addresses and estimate data for areas not tracted.

"The 1970 census was the first to give us such detailed data.

In 1972, the census 'Fifth Count' became available. This is a special report. It's only on tape for computer use giving answers on census information by 5-digit zip code.

"We're getting much more from the 1980 census. The 1980 census is still based on the old zip. Assuming it happens, the 9-digit code will break geography into smaller groups. It won't really be in effect fully until 1985 or so. It won't be broken down into useful data until after the 1990 census.

"Magazines have pioneered marketing research and now direct marketing research. Right now, magazines are very profitable and intriguing to work with. The established magazines are on a circulation plateau. There's a cliché now that the future belongs to highly specialized publishers. It seems to be true. For magazines, analyzing their circulation demographically by zip code has proven effective.

"Many magazine publishers and circulation managers have never been convinced it will work on list selection. The cost efficiency is not right for list selection. It can be used for refinement if someone pursues it long enough. Donnelley has 69 million names. If someone could specify by small areas, you could eventually get a 10% improvement. That's the theory.

"It really doesn't give the dimensions for list selection. Mainly, it's a test for the sale of advertising media. For direct marketers, it can be used more as an analytical tool to evaluate the product. But the magazine business is a two-way street to sell subscriptions and promote copy points to do so, but also to sell advertising by evaluation of subscribers."

It seems as though considerable research could be done as to how mail order people could profitably use research. Tom Ryan continues: "A little research is done here and there. For a client we've done a little work on Ted Turner's Super Station analyzing PI orders. The quality came out not so high as upscale magazines but much better than VHF-TV or mass publications.

"Analyzing the quality of orders from each medium—using analytical research—can mean a lot. You're really not selling a unit but, hopefully, a series of purchases. Analysis research all the way is important. But for most direct marketers most analysis ends on the first purchase.

"Yet, bit by bit, direct marketers are beginning to get into research. Magazines, catalog houses, book publishers, are the pioneers. Others will follow. It will be accepted as just as important as product selection, media selection or copy and art creation—and as considerable aid to each."

Note: Thomas E. Ryan, Inc. is located at 1 North Street, Hastings-on-Hudson, NY 10706, (914) 478-0890.

Chapter 4
Computer Modeling For Mail Order Decisions

Robot advisors perform calculations to come up with answers.

Many feel it had a lot to do with the first success of Psychology Today.

CBS used it to help decide whether to acquire certain new magazines. It told the American Association for Advancement of Science that Science 80 should go from bi-monthly to monthly publication. The Kleid Company uses it to advise on list selection for clients.

Each used a robot advisor, a computer model. A small group of circulation and computer experts have created model after model to make more and more kinds of publishing and direct marketing decisions.

Back in 1970, a company called Systems Science and Software in San Diego started to do some interesting work for Psychology Today. Associated in the studies and circulation and marketing reports was Dr. C. Fremont ("Monty") Sprague. Together, they came up with a computer model program.

"And as far as we know, this was the first viable model used by magazines today," says Robert Cohn, Vice President of Policy Development Corp. "It performed calculations to determine the most profitable time to mail, to compare the cash flow effects of faster versus slower rates of growth and to decide on the timing of circulation increases and sales increases."

John Suhler, later president of the CBS Publishing Group, was first circulation director and then publisher of Psychology Today. (John Suhler is the son of Lester Suhler who, as circulation manager of Look magazine, had trained and been a father-figure to a number of today's greatest mail order circulation experts.)

Another member of the Psychology Today organization was Don Goyette. Don had worked with Dr. Monty Sprague on such computer calculated solutions, both for Psychology Today and for Intellectual Digest. In early 1973, Dr. Monty Sprague set up shop on his own as Policy Development Consultants. About a year later, Don Goyette joined him and the name was changed to Policy Development Corp., in which both had ownership.

Computer modeling had been used in the military and by large corporations to explore alternatives in decision making. At Psychology Today and Intellectual Digest, it was used with sufficient effectiveness that other magazines began to turn to it. John Suhler, Monty Sprague and Don Goyette have worked together even after the Psychology Today days. Today, CBS Publications is the biggest client of PDC.

Monty Sprague is president of PDC. Don Goyette is his partner and co-owner. Monty Sprague is an operations research analyst. Don Goyette is a programmer. Bob Cohn joined PDC in 1979. In 1974, Bob had been director of circulation planning for all CBS Magazines. Computer modeling was an important tool. Bob represented the client, CBS Magazines, as far as dealing with PDC on computer modeling for assignments concerned with his responsibilities.

Bob recalls: "As a result of running models, CBS acquired magazines. Also as a result of other models, we could justify heavier direct mail which then paid off. It helped us come up with answers and then sell management that they were the right answers. We have looked at six different game plans on computer, what happens if you change your marketing plans this way or that.

"Computer modeling is quite helpful for acquisition analysis. It enables people to be more thorough. It's very useful for launches, but in slightly different ways. Here you have no statistics, historically, to go on. But you need to determine how much cash you will need and when, for different performances, high versus low. How much money you need depends on the market you're after. Computer programming shows what happens with spending a lot up front, if you invest a lot early in the game. The model then compares it with probable results of spending it later or spending less.

"There are just nine people in PDC; but we are a team. A number of us have worked together for quite a few years, all that time on computer modeling. I like this business a lot. Computer modeling is now generally used and widely believed in. Yet, it is still hard for magazine publishers to make a scientific judgment, even after successful use of computer modeling as to what they would have done without it versus what they did do with it. The equivalent of split-run tests to do so haven't been conducted to the degree they might.

"Take RESPOND, our list analysis system. One could set up an objective test. As yet, no one has. RESPOND enables people to consider hidden costs and back-end costs they might otherwise not. Our publishing model deals in abstracts. It simply assumes what happens if you mail a million names and pull, say a 2½%. It does not get into individual lists. RESPOND is specific. It analyzes the past history of mailers to estimate future advertising cost per order and future percentage of response. It ranks possible lists by their chances to achieve desired response objectives. The two models work in tandem.

"I know of nothing similar to RESPOND. U.S. News was the first to use it. All their list scheduling is done by Kleid. Rose Harper got interested in RESPOND because of her earlier work with computer list analysis way back when Kleid was owned by Dart Industries. Kleid has the exclusive for RESPOND among list brokers. Kleid clients can see a demonstration of RESPOND in the Kleid office and Kleid can use it for them. U.S. News was the first. Now other Kleid clients have used RESPOND. GEO has, and Architectural Digest.

"We work with magazines directly, as well. CBS is our largest client. We have Field & Stream and Mechanix Illustrated. Our smallest circulation client is Art & Auction, with 5,000 circulation. Our largest circulation client is TV Guide, with 20 million. Dick Benson uses us for Contest NewsLetter, for planning. Some magazines still don't use modeling. But most big magazines do.

"Science 83, the new AAAS magazine, is another client. After its initial launch, the magazine's management used the model to analyze when they would increase their circulation (they went to 400,000 after 3 issues and to 650,000 in 1981) and when they would change from bi-monthly to monthly frequency.

"Although these decisions might otherwise have been made intuitively, the model enabled them to pinpoint the revenues and costs that would be involved—and to confirm that they were on the right track with thorough analysis.

"We have small magazine clients and quite a few start-ups. If the model spells out the projected plan, money requirements seem more justified. Savvy magazine, the executive women's magazine, was a start-up client. The editor believed in the concept but could not raise the money to go ahead. By running a model, Savvy management developed a plan to first test and then, step by step, project to larger mailings, assuming first tests came up to the results anticipated by the plan.

"On this basis, investors put up money to proceed. Savvy's actual mail order subscription results proved better than the plan predicted. It was decided to grow faster . . . circulation now is just 200,000 but substantially more than first hoped for at this stage.

"Ogilvy & Mather is a client. They use modeling mostly for their magazine clients. They have an installation. They handle Opera News, Ballet News, some Newsweek business and other magazines. Stone & Adler has just become a brand new client. We've been talking for months. For Stone & Adler, we're modifying the models to work for other mail order products.

"For agencies, there is a little problem that requires a policy decision by them. Should computer modeling be provided as an agency service? The client, if billed, may prefer to have an installation in-house. This may not be good for the agency."

For those who start with a single item . . . in one payment and all cash . . . with no enclosures or follow-up . . . judging success is simple and computer models unnecessary. Mail counts can be entered, total sales kept cumulatively and patterns watched. Future probable carry-over can be guestimated in days. The campaign can be fairly safely projected to other similar media.

But success is sporadic and continued success always dependent on a new big hit. Building a business demands repeat sales. Advertising inflation makes it harder to make money on the first sale. It's more necessary to create future customers. If a customer buys enough later, the initial sale can be marginally profitable, break-even or at a loss. Still, there can be overall profit.

More customers buy when offered credit. Even smaller mail order companies offer to sell via credit cards. Publishers generally bill directly. Making cancellation easy jumps orders. More cancel and return but many more keep and buy the item. It pays off. Selling in series with automatic shipment and option to cancel at any time can be profitable. Bigger companies use their capital to take advantage of these kinds of options.

List rentals become important extra revenue. Package and billing inserts produce extra income at trifling expense. Step up ads and follow-ups offer deluxe models, bigger sizes or longer subscriptions. To get peripheral revenue more variables are added, and more selling steps. An ad solicits an inquiry followed up by one or a series of mailings.

It becomes harder to track all peripheral sales expenses and benefits from the first sale of the first item to a customer. The cost of testing is constantly up. There are forever more variables to test. The cost and the potential benefits of a big projection becomes huge. Making most profitable mail order decisions then requires more statistical work.

This is particularly true of magazine subscriptions through mail order. It proves profitable to spend for a trial subscription more in advertising than the cost of the subscription; to offer a trial subscription at a very special, low price; to take a no-pay credit loss up to 40% of trial subscription received. It's profitable to send those who paid a series of up to nine follow-up mailings to convert to a longer term subscription; to send up to seven mailings to convert an expiring subscription to a renewal; and to do much more.

It now is profitable and necessary to go after subscriptions in many different ways: blow-in cards; gift subscriptions; friend of friend recommendations, in turn followed up; agents; via schools; house ads; 5-way ads; take-ones in supermarket racks; the use of direct mail increased more and more. Space advertising and then TV are now used more. Telephone selling is more used for conversions and renewals. Newsstand sales supplement subscriptions.

Wendell Forbes describes the circulation, editorial and advertising department as three legs of the publishing stool. Each has expenses. Ads and subscriptions (and sometimes other profit centers) contribute income. The publisher must make a plan, as does any business manager. An ongoing publication or a start-up must make up a cash flow and pro-forma statement for his directors and bank.

As regards circulation, the plan requires spelling out in detail the mix of all methods of promotion. All kinds of incoming subscription revenue and all estimated expenditures must be included. Every alternate plan involving a different mix is a different cash flow problem, as well as an estimating one—affecting not just the coming year but a number more to come.

Preparing each such cash flow prediction takes much time, most of which the computer model can save. Since magazines have the most complex variables, computer models can save them most time. The result is that magazine publishers have pioneered the use of computer models by direct marketers.

PDC clients include ABC Leisure Magazines, Americana, the Financial Post, and the Economist, TV Guide Magazine and Black Enterprise, Natural History and Smithsonian. Playboy and Family HandyMan are clients. So is Publishers Clearing House. Architectural Digest and Bon Appetit are. So are the New York Times Company and Newsweek Magazine.

Catalog selling has also become very complex, with many variables. And catalogs are turning to computer modeling. More and more direct marketers are considering using models. "If programming works for a magazine," says Robert Cohn, "it should be just as valuable to product companies in mail order. It's still in its infancy. The big growth and proliferation of applications is still ahead." He cautions:

"The model is a tool. It does the same calculations you do with pen and pad. It does it quicker and faster. Because you feed in the assumed facts, it's simply figuring everything out faster and in more detail. The benefits are entirely dependent on you. But because you can do so much, so fast, and spell out the possible results of alternatives in such detail, you think out problems to depths you would not otherwise do.

"Computer modeling is not a miracle or a guarantee of mail order profit. It's a way of calculating faster. Rose Harper has always believed in preparing pro-forma financial statements for a planned mail order campaign, in making up, beforehand, cash flow projection for the future. Computer modeling is a way to do it faster, easier, and in more detail. It takes the tedium out. It releases executive time for creative work."

Note: For readers of this book, Robert Cohn, Vice President of PDC, has answered the following questions:

Q. *How many computer modeling programs does PDC now have?*
A. At present, we have six basic programs. We're at work on more. We make custom programs all the time. We also adapt the basic programs on a custom basis. Simple adaptations can be made by the user.

Q. *Of your present models, which came first?*
A. The first was our Source/Promotion Evaluation model. It does what Arnold Dumy set out to do in the 1950's for Time magazine, but takes advantage of the improved computer technology since then. More and more circulation managers rely on it.

Q. *What does it do?*
A. This system calculates a number of statistics relating to the long-term profitability of a new business source or individual new business promotion.

Q. *How did other models evolve?*
A. One led to another. First circulation managers, then comptrollers and treasurers and finally publishers got interested. Each wanted models to do something else.

Q. *What came next?*
A. Our Circulation Analysis Model. We call it our "On-Off" model. It forecasts net paid subscriptions, print orders, earned incomes, circulation expenses and subscriptions cash flow.

Q. *What did this lead to?*
A. A model to make it easier to feed in some of the data needed by the Circulation Analysis Model. It was a lot of work to figure the manufacturing and distribution costs needed. These vary constantly. The result was our Manufacturing and Distribution Cost Model.

Q. *How does this work?*
A. This model calculates and prints the magazine's size and configuration as well as paper, printing, binding, freight and postage costs.

Q. *When did PDC develop its financial model?*
A. That came next. It receives information from the Circulation Analysis and Manufacturing and Distribution Cost Models. The user then feeds in the advertising cost per thousand (CPM) per page that management plans to charge. The model then produces projections of income (P&L), cash flow and a balance sheet.

Q. *What came after this?*
A. The EntryPoint Optimizer. This model analyzes postal freight rates and count of magazine subscription lists to determine the most efficient and least expensive way to ship subscription copies.

Q. *Your most recent model is RESPOND. Could you describe it?*
A. Yes, it's a Direct Response Data Storage/Retrieval and Planning Model. It makes it possible for a user to analyze past mail results and plan future mailings faster—in a fraction of the time otherwise required.

Q. *Could you go into how it functions and what it does in more detail?*
A. Yes. The user's first step is to enter data using a computer terminal using simple English statements. The user converses with the system and tells it what is wanted. Incidentally, needed data can be taken directly from fulfillment house operations by way of computer tapes or key-punched cards. After feeding in, the system does the rest.

Q. Can you do this on your own mini-computer or computer?

A. No, all our models are provided by remote computing. This provides the user access to a large, central computer and its sophisticated software. The user needs only a terminal screen hooked up with INFONET, a teleprocessing network. It's a subsidiary of Computer Sciences, Inc. and has access through your telephone almost anywhere in the U.S.

Q. What kind of information does the user enter?

A. As much of its recent direct mail history as possible. You can store as many as 74 variables about previous mailing results. Some of the items stored are: List, maximum names available for each list (universe), merge-purge factor, quantity mailed, control or test, returns by offer, in-the-mail costs, and back-end costs (billing, bad pay copies).

Q. What does RESPOND do with all this data?

A. It calculates all meaningful response/cost ratios used to determine profitability by key and list. These include the response percent of bad pay, cost per order and net revenue per paid copy or order; also mailing cost and billing cost. You then interpret list and test results.

Q. Can you give an example?

A. Suppose a promising test produces a 25% higher response but costs 30% more. You want the volume but at a lower average cost in a roll-out. You analyze on a list-by-list basis and select best lists. You then mail fewer pieces overall, get the number of subscriptions you need but at less cost.

Q. When I want to make my roll-out campaign and know how many orders I'm after, how can RESPOND help me?

A. Tell RESPOND the gross orders you need from your mailing. Ask it to select from all lists you have used based on results versus costs you've given the computer to select what you need. Tell it to first change its calculations on each test by using the lower costs of printing, paper and the cost where your volume mailing will save money per piece. RESPOND then gives you your mailing plan. It details the lists to use to obtain the paid orders you need.

Q. How does it spell this out?

A. It arranges lists in order of descending profitability and shows cumulative order and cost columns.

Q. Conditions constantly change. How do you change the assumption you've already given the computer? If your latest tests show better results; if you increase the price and results fall off; if you have a higher production cost; or a higher advertising cost; or a new offer pulls quite differently. What can you then do to bring RESPOND up-to-date?

A. You can change any or all of these variables singly or all together. RESPOND then gives you a complete revised mailing plan from the best to worst lists. It's complete with projected costs and new nets per order resulting from your changed facts and assumptions.

Q. Is RESPOND based on the advertising cost of securing an income from a trial subscription only or on future commission and renewal as well?

A. The original version of RESPOND is solely concerned with the original Trial subscriptions. Version Two of RESPOND ties in renewal conversion rates to fully evaluate a list's profitability.

Q. Does RESPOND evaluate mailing lists only? Is it for magazines only?

A. RESPOND can be modified to include TV and radio, space and newspaper pre-prints. It has now been modified for use for books and record clubs, continuity series and merchandise catalogs.

Note: Policy Development Corporation has offices at 11722 Sorrento Valley Road, San Diego, CA 92121, (714) 453-3301; and at 400 Madison Avenue, New York, NY 10017, (212) 753-7186.

Chapter 5
Teaching Children To Read Better, Faster

The most rewarding accomplishment of a top direct marketer.

"Theodor Geisel (Dr. Seuss) was the only real genius I've ever met," says Elsworth Howell. Elsworth Howell is one of the mail order greats who made direct marketing possible as it is today. For Grolier Inc., starting with zero sales in mail order, he created over $100,000,000 a year of mail order sales. He sold books, book clubs, sets of books, and every imaginable kind of merchandise. He has a feel and knack that no computer can give.

I asked Elsworth what in his entire career was most exciting. "It was our Dr. Seuss Beginning Readers Program. It was and is great. It taught a lot of children to read better and faster. Theodor Geisel (Dr. Seuss) had a marvelous way with words and drawings. He's 75 now, still going strong and just as well known today. The program was the most exciting thing and greatest contribution I've participated in.

"We tested in 1960 and, in 1961, we went gung-ho. In the early sixties, we used a combination of direct mail, space and working through teachers to hit a peak of a million subscribers. The program is still going strong. It's cyclic, for every new crop of kids."

When Dr. Seuss (Theodor Geisel) and Grolier got together, the impact on the public, educators and the media was like that of "Sesame Street" years later on TV. Dr. Seuss not only was extraordinarily effective in teaching children to read but the extraordinary pulling power of the offer attracted parents who became prospects for Grolier's Book of Knowledge. In time, the family was a prospect for Grolier's Encyclopedia Americana and for its science encyclopedia.

Leaders in mail order think of Elsworth Howell in much the same way as he thinks of Theodor Geisel. People still speak with awe of the variety and scope of merchandise Elsworth Howell sold to book buyers. He was considered more successful at it than almost anyone in publishing. He was said to have a flair for it, a feel for the right offer at the right time with the right presentation.

"I was with Grolier thirty-nine years and two months. I started in 1934, two years before Murphy bought the company. He was Kansas City field manager. All the business was by salesmen then. My first job at Grolier was as assistant editor of the Book of Knowledge. The first mail order started in 1939. The year book had been a positive option. You had to order it each year. Now it was to be sold under negative option and I was given the job.

"We began to sell other books mail order to our yearbook buyers. During the war, books sold by mail order very well and we had paper. After the war, we expanded. We were strictly selling books mail order. Then, sets of books and book clubs and then merchandise. At its height, it made a very tidy profit.

"Merchandise had its day. We did well on our house lists and often on our outside lists. But we made some mistakes. On a camera outfit with an average order close to $200 and sold on credit, we were badly stung when we used outside lists. Later we found merchandise more difficult even to our own lists. We didn't have a good enough margin. It was too close. Overall, books were our real business.

"We started in mail order at Grolier with a captive audience of buyers of encyclopedias. Later, Encyclopedia Britannica, World Book, Collier and other encyclopedia publishers followed our example. In fact, we helped them to get started in mail order. When Jerry Hardy started Time-Life Books, he had a much, much bigger captive audience of Time and Life subscribers. He went outside, a lot further.

"And we had our audience. First, we mailed our own names and then we went outside, first cautiously and then all out. We were quite successful mailing to lists of magazine subscribers. Redbook active subscribers pulled very well when we mailed them. We didn't do as well when we mailed their expired subscription list."

Grolier grew in mail order in a big way under Elsworth Howell. Activity was intense. Testing of items, offers, lists and media constantly increased. Grolier began to be a very heavy publication advertiser. It began to acquire related mail order companies with offers that seemed particularly to fit the Grolier list.

"We had Max Sackheim as an agency. There, we worked with Lester Wunderman and his brother, Irving. When Wunderman, Ricotta & Kline started up, we went with them. Lester continued to service our account. Lester was a good strategist.

"Milton Runyon was running Doubleday mail order. He was and is a hero of mine. I keep in touch with him. John Stevenson and Milo Sutliff owned and ran Greystone Press. Both were brilliant. I think, as mail order managers, we felt we were as good as any agency at copy, ideas and media. But you need an agency. They're out there in the media market place.

"In those days, we operated manually. Now Grolier has its computer operation in Danbury, Connecticut. I'm not familiar with it. But, in lists, we did have selectivity by categories. It all worked out. The business kept growing. It made money.

"Starting in 1965, we began to sell abroad, just in English-speaking countries. It was great for a while. Sales were good in the U.S., too. We had good products. We gave good value and presented our offers conservatively. We never had an FTC problem. Not everything was successful. We folded one division in Chicago, Americana Interstate. But, overall, we built the Grolier mail order volume to $100,000,000 a year.

"We did this originating our own offers and with our own people. I never pirated anyone from a competitor. Instead, we grew them. Bob Clarke, the president of Grolier, started with me. Lew Smith, who was executive vice president of Wunderman, Ricotta & Kline until he joined Book-of-the-Month Club as senior vice president this year, started with me as a copywriter. I trained people."

He certainly did. All through the world of mail order are people trained by Elsworth Howell and by people he trained.

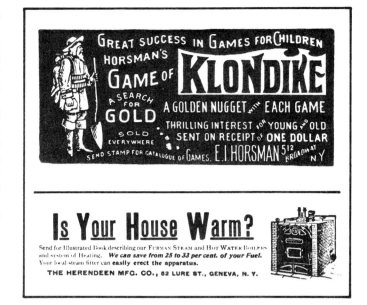

Mike Kelly, a Grolier vice president, went on to Publishers Clearing House. Bob Bull, another vice president, went to Harper & Row. Charles Munoz went to Mattel. Sam Wang became the principal owner of Hy-Aid, a fulfillment house with 300 employees. His partner (now owner of Hy-Aid) was Dick Levinson. Sam was in charge of clerical systems at Grolier. Dick also came from Grolier.

Ed Bakal, who'd been in on the beginnings of the Dr. Seuss Beginning Readers Program went on to run the Marshall Cavendish mail order operation in the U.S. Hank Rossi, executive vice president of Hy-Aid, was credit manager of Grolier. They all vividly remember Elsworth Howell. Everybody in mail order who encountered him did. They talk of him with respect, admiration and affection.

Murray Roman remembers: "Elsworth Howell was the first mail order man I worked with in telephone marketing. We never could make the phones work for Grolier. But Elsworth Howell was fascinated by the possibility and worked with me with great determination. He saw what could be done before all that has happened since in phone marketing."

Those who worked with Elsworth Howell remember him as tough on himself, demanding of others, very able and sometimes impatient. He would go to the point fast in a conversation. He had very definite opinions. Once an experience caused him to form an opinion, he held to it.

He had tight security. He asked for confidentiality and discretion from employees and associates. He was very cautious on giving credit. Every credit manager had to learn that his job was on the line if bad credit went beyond six percent. He ran a tight ship. He wrote advertising copy, himself. "I was a good copywriter and so was Lew Smith. We didn't need freelancers. The agency copywriters did ads.

"I've been in dogs all my life. I'm a judge at dog shows. I'm president of the Dog Fanciers Club. I'm running a dog book business, Howell Book House. I have been disappointed that I could not sell my dog books by mail order, but it doesn't work. Instead, I use reps to sell the book and pet trades."

But don't be surprised if one day you see an ad for the Howell Book House for the Dr. Seuss Beginning Learning Program for dogs.

Chapter 6
The Biggest Combination Of List Businesses

Its restless founder keeps the trade talking, talent coming, the business growing.

It's the Computer Directions Group, and it already includes the biggest combination of list businesses in the world.

The parent company coordinates, plans for and oversees four operating companies: Woodruff-Stevens (list management); Names Unlimited (list brokerage and list consulting); The Computer Direction Group Data Center (list fulfillment); and Data Base Management ("Public" data bases and high technology product development).

Together the subsidiaries offer one efficient, vertical operation in selecting, negotiating rentals of, analyzing results of and projecting profitable use of lists . . . and a lot more—all to sell more profitably by mail order via lists. The entire operation is built around latest computer technology. The restless organizer of it all is Stan Woodruff, out to build the General Motors of lists.

Stan learned about lists by working for a directory publisher. He mastered list selection for direct marketers by first working for and then becoming a partner of a master of lists, Ed Burnett. He saw that direct mail was the form of advertising most used by direct marketers and that right list selection was vital to direct mail success.

Ever since, Stan has concentrated intensely on every possible means of developing more productive list selection by more efficient segmentation. He has used that same intensity, as a list salesman, to successfully promote lists he found productive for clients. He then obtained the exclusive right to manage and deal with clients and other brokers on behalf of the list owner, and organized the first company to do so.

Stan has an IQ of 151, but more significant to his success is his ability to see potential and his relentless drive to go after it. As a disc jockey working his way through the University of Connecticut, he sensed trends . . . what was a hit, what would be, what was fading. His interest in music led him to work first for Audio-Video Products, in 1954 and 1955, and then for Columbia Records.

"Then I worked for Bernie Klein," Stan explains. "He published directories. People wanted to rent names that were in the directories we sold, so Bernie formed the U.S. List Company to fulfill this need." By then, Stan had begun taking night courses. He attended IBM School in the late 50's, studying computer programming long before lists were computerized. In 1958 and 1959, he worked for Howard Mann, of List Corporation of America.

"Following that, I joined Ed Burnett and spent six years with him. While there, I earned a marketing degree from NYU and began to teach for the AMA and at Columbia. I became a partner in Burnett, Appleby and Woodruff. I sold out in 1966."

After selling out, Stan worked for Names Unlimited as executive vice president. Arthur Karl founded Names Unlimited and had been the father of the list business along with Lew Kleid.

"Everybody seems to have worked for Arthur Karl. Even Jack Oldstein, of Dependable, did for a very short time. Marcie Coolidge did before starting on her own (The Coolidge Co.). By now, Arthur Karl was no longer living. I hoped to buy Names Unlimited, but the chance did not then materialize, so I left Names in 1971."

In between, he did consulting for big direct marketers and, having put enough money away, he started his first list management company. "I was a highly paid executive and when the opportunity came, I had the money to live on while the company was developing. I had helped to start the concept of list management in the Sixties. In the Seventies I aided its development. I started up again in list management in 1972. Six months later, Ralph Stevens joined me as a partner and I helped to teach him the list business. He knew the other side of the fence. He had started as a copywriter at Prentice-Hall, and had bought lists by the millions at Famous Artists as Vice President of Advertising. He had been the Vice President of Marketing at Funk & Wagnalls. Ralph was very familiar with the problems facing direct marketers."

Stan continues: "Then, in October 1977, (in an all-stock deal) we merged with Computer Directions Corp., which included Jim Knox, Robin Black and Charles Michel. Jim Knox had worked at Alexander Sales for Manny Piller. Robin had worked for Ed Burnett and at Names Unlimited with me. Charles Michel was a stockholder and formerly one of the original partners in Datatron, Inc., which I had formerly been associated with. They all stayed, offering us a tremendous sales punch." Now Robin Black, Charles Michel, Jim Knox and Ralph Stevens are fellow stockholders in Computer Directions Group, the parent company.

Part of Computer Directions Corp. was CDC Data Center, a computer service bureau. "A service bureau was needed by us in order to offer more storage of lists. Charles Michel was, and is, president of CDC Data Center. He has been pushing new technology and programming abilities in list handling and analysis. One result has been that, in 1978, CDC began to work with Conway Communications Exchange. With the CCE people, we offer computer-to-computer inquiring and ordering, instantaneous order editing, print-outs, order status and shipping status reports. We do not own any of their stock, but we do have a profit sharing arrangement on business we produce.

"Data Base Management is another of our companies. There are two kinds of data bases. One is a public data base for marketing groups of lists by category. Another is a private data base for one's own mailing purposes. List owners throw in their lists for increased and more efficient list rental and usage. We're pioneers in data bases. How we operate Data Base Management is long, involved and somewhat proprietary. It's all part of an effort to use direct mail more efficiently."

Stan Woodruff is constantly endeavoring to make his companies more scientific. That's part of his formula. Another is to make it possible for very able people to make more money with him than if he was not around. He builds up his associates rather than constantly taking the limelight from them. Each company has a strong head and its own executive staff. They are an ambitious crew. Their abilities plus his ideas and drive do it. "I guess I'm the architect around here. I try to be the power that makes things go."

Ralph Stevens is President of Woodruff-Stevens, the original list management company. He introduced mail order-style advertising to persuade list owners to turn over lists to Woodruff-Stevens for management. He then advertises each list with the same mail order aggressiveness. As a master copywriter and a shrewd list marketer, Ralph has done for lists what he did for books, with superb and convincing copy in each ad.

Perhaps the best mail order headline Ralph Stevens ever wrote for Woodruff-Stevens was, "Has Your List Rental Income Increased By These Percentages?" He backed it up with a table of dramatic increases in list rental income and huge totals for accounts cited. A lot of coupons came in from list owners. Many then became clients. Ad after ad written by Ralph promoted advantages of list after list.

When magazines came in strongly, Ralph's ads capitalized on it to promote Woodruff-Stevens as headquarters for magazine list management. Ralph Stevens is an effective speaker and writer. For ZIP Magazine he wrote "Building Your List Bank for More Income from Lists You Own". Every list owner should read it.

Woodruff-Stevens exclusively manages lists for clients including Hanover House, Sakowitz, Starcrest of California, Tax Research Institute, Encyclopaedia Britannica, Grolier Enterprises, Inc., plus many more. It had, by late 1981, 44 employees.

Names Unlimited, under President Robin Black, promotes its list research abilities. The company is over 50 years old. "When the opportunity to buy Names Unlimited came about in 1977, we jumped at the chance," says Stan Woodruff. "Robin Black had worked with me when I was with Ed Burnett. Now, as a result of the Computer Directions deal, we're back together. He is a very capable list marketer. Along with the Computer Directions Group, he is now raising Names Unlimited to its biggest volume ever."

Stan Woodruff is confident of his organization's ability to survive and succeed regardless of economic problems. "A combination of a big postage jump and economic belt-tightening has in the past and may again cause a bad drop in response for quite some time," explains Stan. "But we have a tight operation. We watch costs. We'll come up with new sources of income. We'll survive any bad times to come as we have before. So will mail order. The main problem is to find and train competent people as direct marketing managers."

Stan Woodruff views direct marketing progress this way: "Direct marketers are trying to make direct marketing more of a science. There's more selectivity. There's better control. They mail more totally, but less of each list. They pay three times as much for a list, mail less and get more. The overall cost for orders obtained per thousand mailed has gone down as a percentage of sales." He sees an electronic future in every aspect of list use which will intensify the entire process.

"One existing problem," says Stan, "is that few people yet use all the tools that are available to be more efficient. But the tools are not yet perfect. In 15 years of analyzing zip code areas by coming up with life style clusters of zip codes, it hasn't proved out. Categorically, it hasn't worked. The demographics have been overlayed and they, for the most part, have not worked. We use demographics and psychographics, *but our way*—to supplement our overall analytical methods of selecting lists more scientifically.

"Right now the list industry is undergoing a major change. It's not going to be slow. It is going to be startling. There will be a total revolution in list brokerage in the next five years. List brokers will have to earn their living an entirely new way.

"Winners in this business don't sustain themselves through one good roll of the dice, but through constant innovation and fresh ideas to find the best methods and technology," says Stan. One new advance Stan is proud of is a new computer analysis

program that answers questions to help select lists more scientifically.

It's called SCORE, an acronym for Source Comprehensive On-Line Response Evaluation. It identifies best performing lists and breaks down performance; data gross vs. net; cash vs. credit; return on acquisition investment; best package, offer, list; comparison list by list, control by control, test by test. The idea is to pinpoint how every list is doing against every other list in every possible combination . . . in dollars and in the kind of customers. SCORE evaluates gross-to-net, inquiry-to-sale, orders-to-pieces mailed. SCORE helps analyze results and calculate how to get at lowest selling cost whatever orders are needed.

"There will be a lot more changes and enormous further complications," continues Stan. "There will be more refining of RFM. We're spending $500,000 at our firm in the next several years to make such changes. Just what we're developing is proprietary. But it will be more and more computerized. We're already on line to the major brokers. We're not going to be limited to the list business. We will expand into telecommunications, View Data, Cable TV . . . but when the time comes. We're not pioneers."

Stan has plenty of ideas and more projects all the time. He stimulates his associates, his clients and anyone he talks with. He used to speak more often at trade meetings, and lecture at NYU and elsewhere. "I don't have the time to make many speeches now. I do speak, but only rarely. I write a lot. I'd love to do a book on this business."

Note: In the Help Source Guide are listed reprints of articles, transcriptions and tapes of speeches by Stan Woodruff and his executives with information on how to obtain them.

Computer Directions Group, Inc. is located at 40 East 34th Street, New York, NY 10016; (212) 725-1555.

Chapter 7
The Fast Track To Direct Marketing Success

Time Inc. and Wunderman, Ricotta and Kline were his schools of mail order.

Eight top ten advertising agencies own direct marketing subsidiaries. Of these, George Wiedemann is the youngest president. He had been the youngest senior executive of the biggest direct marketing agency—Wunderman, Ricotta & Kline. Before that, he was the young president of the direct marketing research firm Claritas, Inc.

George Wiedemann came to Claritas from Time Inc. where he started his career, and quickly became the youngest circulation manager in the history of Time magazine. His fast track record is why Grey Advertising Inc. chose him to launch Grey Direct.

It's also why the Direct Mail/Marketing Association selected him to create the most comprehensive direct marketing course available that can be taken at home. Creating a direct marketing advertising agency and a direct marketing course have kept him on a fast track.

George was raised in Kentucky, went to Lawrenceville School and graduated from Trinity College, in Hartford. He has a high IQ, is quick and has many interests. He plays the piano and is into photography. At college, half his courses were economics. Half were fine arts. His marks ranged from B+ to A+. His senior thesis was on Pay TV. Time Inc. recruited him right off the campus in 1966.

He got into Time's management training program. "I valued it. I was highly trained. It was flexible. A trainee floated on the corporate payroll and dipped into departments. The idea was to find what the trainee liked and which department liked the trainee. My first assignment was in corporate R&D. I started my first real job as a writer and promotion man for Time magazine. The first promotion piece I worked on was with Velma Francis, now retired. The first thing I wanted to do was circulation. I felt it was the heart of the business. Bernie Auer was circulation director. I got in the department. Briefly, he was my boss. He then went on to become group vice president. I worked hard for five years. Three of us gradually became tied for number two man to Bob Moore, then circulation director. Then Ralph Davison gave me my first big chance.

"Sometime before, I had done a job for Ralph he liked. Later he moved up to publisher. The job of circulation director became open. Ralph went to Kelso Sutton, the corporate circulation VP, and said, 'I want George Wiedemann for circulation director.' I got the job. But the other two did well, too. One became circulation director of Fortune and the other became circulation director of Sports Illustrated.

"My new job as circulation director was very demanding. I worked like a dog. No facet of the business did not touch it. It was all on a large scale. The volume of domestic circulation income was then $65 million a year. Time was spending $30 million to get it. My job was to get desired circulation quantity and quality at lowest possible cost and to investigate any new way to get it as well as doing existing ways more effectively.

"Lester Wunderman had met my boss. I then brought Wunderman into Time circulation work." It was Wunderman who, with George, built up Time's use of TV for subscription mail order. But the distinctive Time commercials of fast flashing, says George, came first from elsewhere.

"The first WR&K work with Time was support TV. I and they were pioneers. But Time also worked with others. Lester had 85% of Time magazine circulation billing and still does. Bob Fisler used lots of sources, freelancers, small agencies, whatever. Time was very open to possible talent. Via Texas Monthly's Mike Levy, Judith Weiss (of my staff) got in contact with the Richards Group in Dallas, Texas. We flew down and met the president, Stanford Richards. Then the Richards Group did the breakthrough two-minute TV commercial that first paid off for Time.

"Lester did the same formula. WR&K was organized to buy TV everywhere. Richards wasn't. It was their great opportunity but they blew it. Sy Sanders was head of TV buying for WR&K. I learned most about broadcast media from Larry Stoddard, at Y&R. I learned most about TV for direct marketing from Wunderman. Sy Sanders headed up the broadcast department.

"Lester was smart about TV, as he is about everything. WR&K was a heavy user of Simmons, TGI (now merged with Simmons) and all computerized services. He brought in top TV time buying talent. When WR&K uses support TV for a newspaper pre-print, it gets a print-out of viewing habits of Time readers, and selects time accordingly. Wunderman has the same TV research facilities as the big general agencies. Most of the computer runs are for support TV. For straight direct marketing, WR&K goes principally on past mail order results for times and stations considered.

"Time magazine and WR&K are each schools of direct marketing. I learned a great deal from each. At Time, probably Bob Moore taught me the most. He's currently president of Xerox Educational Publishing. Kelso Sutton was business manager and in charge of finance at Time. He taught me the mathematics and calculations I needed to understand the bottom line of direct marketing. Claritas got me deeper into research.

"I never took a direct marketing course or read a purely direct marketing book. But from the beginning at my first job, I studied direct marketing in my own way. I read Claude Hopkins, Jerry Della Femina and David Ogilvy. They all helped. I read Ad Age, Friday Report and Direct Marketing magazine. That helped a lot.

"Incidentally, I'm still learning a lot each time I have to make a speech. I've had to study and research for each. Writing the direct marketing course has been a great teacher. Each client has taught me a lot and launching Grey Direct is the ultimate finishing course.

"One bonus I bring is my research experience. I feel like a pioneer. I've seen what works now, what really pays off, what doesn't and what is still unproven. Some exciting kinds of research for direct marketers are only two years old. There is not much black and white experience of what can return a profit and what can't. Yet I know ways to use research to increase dramatically our clients' direct marketing results.

"We're determined to do a job for each client and study the problems of each as if it were our business. Our first account was Kroy Industries. This is the Kroy Lettering machine right here; I'll show you how it works. It's wonderful. In a recession our best protection would be to get accounts like this. Right away, it saves more than its cost. And it's a hit. We're running with it in the U.S. and overseas."

George has a talent for recruiting and working with talent. He works closely with Iris Shokoff, Senior Vice President Communications Director, and Roy Beauchamp, Senior Vice President Creative Director. All three run the agency in tandem. Combined, they have experience from jobs at WR&K, Rapp & Collins, Time, Life, Sports Illustrated and People. Together they have great strength in magazine circulation. They have considerable successful experience in TV.

"Our intent is to apply for clients the most scientific direct marketing methods that we can use for them. My exposure has been to scientific firms, the biggest ones. Perhaps 20% of bigger direct marketing firms do 80% of the scientific testing and projecting. The other 80% do the rest. Smaller firms are rarely familiar with some of the most effective methods used by some of the biggest and most experienced ones—very profitably.

"Of the first five accounts, three came from Grey. Probably most of the growth of Grey Direct will first come from Grey clients. At each general agency, after a direct marketing subsidiary is launched or acquired, the subsidiary has the chance to convert general marketers to direct marketers.

"General agency and direct marketing discipline can be brought together. A general agency brings more formal methods to a direct marketing agency, and its imprimatur and contacts—client and otherwise. Y&R has brought to WR&K, since acquiring it, huge accounts—like New York Telephone. It brought its contacts in the U.S. and abroad, particularly from its own client list. Perhaps 80% of all WR&K accounts secured since the acquisition came this way."

Interestingly, the agency has been attracting accounts at a considerable degree based on the direct marketing reputation rather than primarily relying on the parent agency's existing accounts.

"At Grey Direct we started, in a modest way, with 6 people, in 1980. But it was a beginning. Each person we bring in is good. We have the strength and backing of a top ten agency, Grey. We have the intimacy and personal attraction of a small start-up agency. I can apply what I've learned from the best teachers in direct marketing."

By January 1982, there were 44 people. George Wiedemann moved cautiously, securing one client at a time. His concern was to get clients that Grey Direct could contribute to and help grow, but not too many. He wanted growth from client success. In both 1980 and 1981 Grey Direct made money. In 1980, Grey Direct secured eleven clients. Almost its entire 1981 billing of over $11 million came from those eleven clients each of which grew from its size the first year.

One account was Times-Mirror Magazines. For it Grey came up with successful TV tests for Outdoor Life, Golf and Homeowners How To . . . and a major projection for Popular Science, after a successful test. In each one, Grey Direct successfully secured subscribers at or below the desired advertising cost.

Other accounts are The New Process Company selling mainly clothing mail order; the Goldhirsch Group to launch Technology Illustrated; National Liberty Marketing to sell insurance; and the U.S. Armed Forces for recruitment. Bristol-Myers authorized a test for a new product.

About half of Grey Direct's business is creating inquiries, for four accounts . . . the Armed Forces, Kroy Industries, Lanier Business Products and Shearson Loeb Rhoades Inc. Grey Direct works for Charter Communications, for Ladies' Home Journal . . . and for ABC Magazine Division, handling Modern Photography.

Most of the accounts are in the development stage. George Wiedemann cautiously estimated that 1982 billings would run twelve to fourteen million dollars. But some expect further growth. By 1982, Grey Direct had subsidiaries in Minneapolis and San Francisco.

"What education do I suggest to prepare for direct marketing? I suspect that a liberal arts education may prepare someone better than a business school. At Time, of Harvard MBA's with considerable talent who went into circulation over the years, perhaps five out of six didn't make it. I think the liberal arts education may keep an open, imaginative mind and aid in innovation."

Note: Grey Direct is located at 777 Third Avenue, New York, NY 10017; (212) 546-1800. You can share with Grey Direct clients the know-how of George Wiedemann by taking (at home) his DMMA direct marketing course. Your company should, if it's going into direct marketing, enroll those specializing in direct marketing. Details are in the chapter on DMMA educational courses and seminars, and in the Help Source Section in this book. It could be a faster track for you.

Chapter 8
The Mail Order Meteor

*He used mail order to build a
$250,000,000 business, starting
from a one-inch ad.*

From a moonlighting venture of a 22-year-old, it grew to join the Fortune 500, by mail order.

As this book goes to press, Edward R. Downe, Jr. is 52. He says he's retired, concerned only with his family, his private life and building his collection of 20th Century American Art.

I watched him multiply his business a hundred times. Now Ed looks back. I asked him to tell you in this book what made it happen. You and I may not be willing or able to do what he did. Ed, himself, might not again. But here's his story.

I never met a mail order man like him or with products like his. Mine were practical. His were exotic. Mine appealed to a wide audience, his to somewhat higher incomes and to special tastes. He was a product innovator. He bought a product untested, on gut feeling, if he felt convinced it was right. It was right so regularly that I always wondered how he chose what. For this book, I asked him. Here is his answer.

"When I was 8 years old, my step-father read to me the stories of G.A. Henty, romantic adventure history-oriented tales of the British Empire. Later, he read 'Beau Geste' to me. I grew up reading history and historic novels at every opportunity. A great deal of what I read concerned India, Africa, Asia—both the Far East and the Near East. I read mostly of the 19th Century . . . the age of Kipling, of the British and of the French Colonial empires. I also read of the Spanish-American War, of World War I, of explorers, sailors, mountain climbers, adventurers and adventures everywhere.

"Years later, most of the mail order products I sold concerned this far off, adventurous, romantic world. One of the best ads I ever did was for old-time British pith helmets I imported from India. I sold British Bobby helmets and capes. I sold butterflies from the Valley of the Moon in Taiwan. I sold an extraordinary number of them.

"I sold historical memorabilia—World War II silk escape maps. The pilots had them in escape kits. There were maps on both sides. They were fabulous, pure silk and in five colors. I was the first to sell Roman coins, by themselves, and in cufflinks. I sold Egyptian scarabs in the mid-fifties when lots of real scarabs were available. I sold Seventh Cavalry insignia. I found in a warehouse American pith helmets issued by the U.S. Army for the Spanish-American War, and sold them.

"Background is major. I was very history-oriented. I collected stamps. It all gave me a sense of the world. It got me into collectibles. All my reading in the martial area affected me. I sold French Army campaign jackets and Australian bush jackets. I was the first to sell tiger and zebra skins. I picked up some remainder books of 'Campfires and Battlegrounds of the Civil War.' I got them from Arnie Hausner at Book Sales, and sold them out. We then bought the plates and did more editions together. I kept selling 'Campfires' profitably for years.

"When I was in college one summer I worked on a farm. I wrote an ad, in 1957, on a model steam engine used in farm work, and sold it successfully in mail order. There has been a relationship between my preferences and experiences and what I successfully sold, but not always.

"Good taste may not be mass taste. I had an expensive experience. I thought blue and white Delft pottery from Holland, which I liked, would sell. I bought $40,000 worth at a good price. It didn't sell. It was too esoteric for the general public. I learned a lot from this."

Ed Downe got into mail order entirely by accident. He had studied at Vanderbilt University with the view of becoming a minister. But after two years, he changed his mind and left. He then worked in Virginia for two country newspapers in 1948 and 1949, and then went to the School of Journalism at the University of Missouri and graduated in 1952. His ambitions were editorial. He got a job in New York working for True magazine in the editorial department.

"I started in the lowest editorial job, the least wanted editorial responsibility at True magazine, writing the mail order shopping column. That's how I got into mail order. Then mail order got me, years later, back into publishing. It was a full cycle. By accident, I went into the job that led to the mail order business and then used mail order to take over, save and revitalize magazines. Mail order was my road to publishing.

"Ken Purdy was editor of True. After I was with True one year, Ken went over to become editor of Argosy. I went with him. I got a raise from $85 a week to $95 a week doing the same job. The same year, I became a mail order moonlighter." He began with one- to two-and-a-half-inch ads and free editorial write-ups. He progressed via a myriad of mail order products and projects to a publishing empire.

"I worked a full day at Argosy. After work, I went to Columbia. I took marketing and business courses. I then went home to my apartment. In the basement, I rented a room for $30 a month. It was 9 feet by 16 feet and had no windows. There I worked from 9:30 p.m. until 3 or 4 a.m. every night. I had as a helper an elderly, stout lady superintendent of the walk-up across the street. She was called 'Briny.' She and I worked, winter and summer, in that windowless room.

"I never slept more than three or four hours. I got up at seven and went straight to the post office, carrying my packages with me. To start out, I always sold small objects, small enough for me to carry a good number of. The Pocket Alarm Watch was one. Another was the TV tube tester. Another was the microscope/telescope combination, the size of a pen. I could take several hundred of them to the post office at a time.

"One of my first really good hits was the Fur-Lined Potty. I bought it first on Delancy Street. I bought enameled pots for 27 cents each. Then I bought Mouton furs for $1 a piece. I sold the potty with the fur for $3.95.

"My first 28-line ad had the headline, 'Hey Fellers, the Real McCoy.' My Esquire ad cost $250 and brought in about $8,000 in sales. It was a major item. Briny and I were putting furs on pots every night. I bought everything for all items. I got the corrugated from Twenty-Eighth Street. I worked seven days a week. In summers, on weekends I got up at 7 a.m., drove my wife and children to Jones Beach and then drove back to New York to work. I worked all day and then drove out to pick them up. It wasn't just time. It was total dedication to business. I gave up smoking, drinking, my social life, practically my health. I worked like an animal.

"Why did I do it? My step-father taught me to live well. To live well, live the good life, you have to have money. That starts you. Once you start, you have to keep going. I once saw a muskrat on a treadmill at a country fair. He had to run at full speed to stay

on. If he stopped, he fell off. That was my situation. I made certain sacrifices. There's no substitute for hard work.

"Hard work is only part of it, however, I had to buy the right items and at the right price . . . and I had to create the right ads. I did it with small space ads. I used large illustrations, beautifully retouched, and carefully selected type. I used very small copy and plenty of white space. I didn't have to describe a button, a butterfly or a pith helmet. My specialty was the out-of-the-ordinary item, the out-of-the-ordinary headline, photograph and ad. I learned when I was a shopping column editor how to select a picture and crop it, making it pop off the page to get attention.

"The next problem was to buy the advertising at the lowest price while getting the most favorable position possible. Developing a house advertising agency saved me 15% of the ad cost. When I decided to sell mail order ads for certain publications, I was paid a commission up to 20%. On an average, together I save 30%."

Ed Downe saved more than all this in advertising cost. He ran every issue in most publications, alternating a variety of items, and got a twelve-time discount. He ran a number of ads in an issue and grouped them for any discount available for volume. When he represented magazines to sell advertising, he was the first to know of distress space available and unsold as the issue was going to press, and bought it at the "disaster rate." It was customary to give shopping column write-ups to advertisers in some relation to numbers and sizes of ads bought. He knew the maximum each magazine might give and often got it. And then there were sometimes "guarantees" when a publication needing ads this month would give make-ups in later issues if results were not good enough.

On July 5, 1957, Ed Downe went into the mail order business full-time, leaving Argosy. This gave him more time to buy, to sell ads, to write copy and produce ads. "My ambition had been to be an editor. Now I was deep in mail order. But that led me to become a sales representative for magazines which led me right back to publishing."

Ed got mad one day because he could not get a salesman to call on him from the American Legion Magazine. He called the publisher and asked him, "If you can't sell an inch ad, how do you expect to sell a page? If you won't call on the small mail order advertisers, you won't get them when they grow. They'll be running in other magazines." The publisher explained that his men had to work on higher priority accounts. It ended up with Ed becoming a sales representative for American Legion, calling on all mail order accounts the regular sales staff did not call on. And soon, Ed was representing one magazine after another. (When Ed sold Downe Communcations in 1975, that division sold mail order advertising for over 35 magazines and earned in excess of $1,000,000 annually.)

Ed found that the commissions made by selling mail order advertisers added up. He became the editor of each shopping column, saving the magazine such costs but getting some write-ups. Soon he hired an editor and a salesman. Now he wasn't sure which helped most, commissions or mail order profits. He began to view it as one pot. Later, he'd say to me, "I always look at it in the round." He began to approach a prospective magazine and sometimes to guarantee an increase in sales to mail order accounts over the previous year to the same accounts. "If I don't sell it, I'll buy it."

He found that for a publication new to mail order, his ads attracted other ads. His ads gave the impression of a number of mail order companies already advertising. This was because he gave such importance from a results standpoint to addresses and names appropriate to the product advertised.

"I felt that the total picture was important—the picture, the product, the ad, the total look, the name offering the merchandise. If it was a war surplus item, I used the name 'Arms and Weapons.' It gave a certain panache, an authenticity. If I had an electronic product, I used the named Lincoln Electronics and The Lincoln Building address. For a typical shopping column item, I used the name Madison House and the 305 Madison Avenue address of the Lincoln Building. For Civil War products, I used Lee Products. I always used easy to spell names, such as Lee, Madison and Prince.

"Luck is a factor. I was a very lucky guy. There was an element of luck, of hard work, coupled with optimism. You can't ever believe you're not going to make it. No matter how bad today is, you must believe that tomorrow will be a better day.

"Another factor is loyalty. My step-father taught it to me. He was a gentleman. In every adventure history book, from Beau Geste on, that I read, loyalty was all important. I was grateful to Raymond Mason, of Charter, for buying my company when I wanted to sell. Out of gratitude and loyalty, when I made a good deal of money, I bought a million shares of Charter Stock, which later sold for twelve times what I paid for it. So, that loyalty made a great deal of money for me. And I consistently was loyal to others in my business life.

"Personal relations are very important. A friend will go out of his way for you. He'll help when you need it. It's an interesting

thing with suppliers. Always conduct your business like a gentleman, and most times it will be reciprocated.

"One time I told Alan Mirkin, of Publisher's Central Bureau: 'Alan, I owe you $30,000. I can't pay you and I need books.' Alan just asked, 'How many books do you need?' He was, and is, a real gentleman.

"Timing of an offer is important. A type of offer that won't work today may work tomorrow and vice versa. I sold high-priced merchandise before anyone. I sold the Minifon Pocket Recorder. It was the first wire recorder, the first with a telephone microphone, the first with a tie-clip microphone. This was in 1957.

"Someone said he could get me in to to see Max Sackheim. I showed him my ad. The ad offered the Minifon for $300 cash, check or money order. There were no credit cards. Max said that no $300 item for cash could work. He felt that far more copy would be required. He said, 'You can't sell it. Forget it.' I was dejected.

"The next week, anyway, I ran my ad in the New York Times, at a cost of $1,800. Over $30,000 of orders came in, all checks. I did $300,000 on Minifon the first year. Max was absolutely right, based on all his experience. But the possibility of selling expensive merchandise had now arrived. And I had stumbled on it. The same offer would have failed a few years before."

All this happened in the eleven years Ed Downe was in the mail order business before I met him. When I did, he was 33. He had had fabulous success and then a $650,000 disaster. He had just finished paying off every cent of it. He was a happy ball of fire. He was on the phone from waking to sleeping, seething with mail order energy. He was innovative, adventurous and ambitious. He was getting ready, to a degree neither of us suspected, for a mail order take-off to tremendous growth.

Gene Schwartz suggested we meet. Gene is a brilliant writer of books and of advertising copy, a Hoge alumnus and a good friend of both of us. One day, Ed and I had lunch. That lunch changed my life and influenced his. I was one of many to be affected by and to affect his success. But at a time crucial to each of us, we helped each other via mail order.

Nothing either of us had done in mail order had been the same. The ads we created, the media we bought, the way we ran our business, our objectives were as different as our mail order experience. But when we worked together, there was a synergy that had surprising consequences.

I was older. I had made many mistakes. I could warn of each. I had done a few things right, some new to him, and I could point them out. I was accustomed to spending a good deal of time on a single project and could do so with him. Ed was so busy that if a tiny ad did so well that he wanted to run a bigger one, he often simply blew it up. The illustration and headline grew bigger. More white space was used. The copy was the same.

I was accustomed to continued testing. Ed rarely had time once the first ad paid out to test again. He just projected. My projections were horizontal, to run a successful ad once, everywhere. His were vertical. He would find a magazine ideal for him, like the old Diner's Club Magazine, predecessor of Signature. He'd run every issue, then more ads in each issue, then for the issue most productive for him, November, he would run as many as ten pages. Ed's items were ideal and at the peak of their pulling power for the pre-Christmas selling season. Mine were seldom Christmas items. For mine, early January was mail order gold.

Ed rarely had a contract with a supplier and very seldom a

written exclusive. He went so fast he was ahead of everyone. Harrison-Hoge had only products it manufactured or had sole import rights on. For each, it had a carefully drawn rights contract. It sold almost entirely via stores products originated by mail order. Ed sold none to stores. We never had a piece of paper between us as to how we operated. I don't recall ever receiving a written order for any merchandise from Ed, ever. He carried his business in his head, made every purchase, signed every check. Years later, he signed each check for Family Weekly and Ladies' Home Journal, for several months after he bought them. (He said it both helped him to learn the business—and save millions of dollars.)

We blended our two methods. It started with me supplying to Ed one product, and a black and white page for it. It was our Adjust-O-Matic Dress Form. Ed ran it in The McFadden Women's Group, where I previously had not paid out. The ad kept running and Ed kept reordering while I protested that it was in the wrong place. But McFadden was happy. The dress form conveyed a homebody image of their circulation. Ed was happy because he had no risk and I did not know.

Next, Ed tried my frog fish lure in Family Weekly. I had a beautiful four-color ad and had previously paid out in Family Weekly, myself. It was the right ad in the right place. The back cover was unsold for Easter Sunday. Ed took it. My headline was, "Frog Murders Bass." Ed's office was, by then, in the Chanin Building at 122 East 42nd Street. From the post office big bags of mail came into the little reception room. This volume of response on a single ad for a single product was new to the office.

For me, all this could not have happened at a better time. They used to say that my imagination was bigger than my pocket book, that I had secretaries for the secretaries, that no messenger boy hired could deliver the first message—he'd be promoted, on the way, to copywriter, media man or product manager. I had overexpanded. I had then gone into partnership with my brilliant alumnus, Malcolm Smith, and his two partners and then worn all three of them out.

One idea I had tied up that business. It was the ten tank display. In a store, I had ten tanks filled with water. Each had a little motor turning a rod that had a wire that pulled a lure that performed in the water.

It was a great show stopper in any store. It built the base of our present successful lure business. But then it tied up money, caused the hiring of electrical engineers and required two-thirds of manufacturing floor space. When supplier delays held up manufacturing of tanks, there were big cancellations of lure orders, lots of inventory and a cash vacuum. My last partner of the three, Dick Davimos, left for Wall Street in the wisest move of his career.

But with Ed, I could have all the ideas in the world—on his overhead. My Prussian wife, Fritzi, made it all possible. In 1958, on a trip to Berlin, Fritzi was assigned to me by the Berlin Absatz Organization, The Chamber of Commerce, to guide me around. She's been doing it ever since. When the partners left, she came in. When I met Ed, I decided it would be easier to make Ed's business grow than mine.

From the moment Fritzi came into the business, we started to make money. The combination of working with Ed and having Fritzi do everything—to buy, fulfill, hire, fire, organize—proved irresistable. Fritzi put "alles in ordnung"—everything in order. Losing money was "verboten". Ed's orders by telephone for four years came up to close to half our volume. His advertising of our products helped our store business grow. Fritzi kept the overhead down at our end.

I drew no money until Dick Davimos, my last partner, got every cent he had invested in the business. This took years; but it all worked. What I did with Ed created the base of Harrison Hoge's net worth. What Fritzi did became an insurance policy of profitable operation ever since. Gradually, young Cecil took over more and more. Today, Fritzi and he (her step-son) are partners.

Ed immediately scheduled "Frog Murders Bass" to run again in Family Weekly. I worried about drop-off and suggested he not do so. Instead, I suggested that Ed run in Parade where he had never run. Ed was off to a buying trip to the Orient but told me to buy Parade for him. I did, and then negotiated one space purchase after another for him—and studied how he bought.

Gradually, I began to realize that, however unwarranted any buy of merchandise or media he made might seem, there was a lot of science to Ed's method. Almost all new items were tested in an editorial write-up, which cost him nothing. Next came a very small test ad in one publication. Usually, it was a twelfth of a page and usually it ran in the same publication that had done well with a write-up. Then he'd run a sixth of a page and then up to a square third or a column.

It was the interlocking aspect of Ed's activities that made them safe. Ed had three partnerships with three different magazine publishing firms for mail order businesses. Ed provided know-how, items, ads, write-ups to run in their publications. They each provided one or two pages of space a month. It was extra revenue for them and profitable, no risk business for Ed.

Ed was a friend to everyone. If any advertising manager, publisher, space salesman or shopping column editor got fired, Ed was there to help. Anyone fired would be asked to lunch. Ed would make an effort to recommend him or her for a job elsewhere. He'd sometimes give a loan, if needed. All this was later remembered at the new job. If any magazine publisher or ad manager was down in ads against last year, he could call Ed, tell him the amount of ads needed to surpass this figure, and often Ed would buy the ads to do it.

Even more than all the money Ed risked was his creative contribution, which again was remarkably complementary to my abilities. Jack Levine was Ed's art director. Jack has great talent. They had started together at Argosy. Ed could get out of Jack untold work, unending revision and constant improvement.

Early in the game, I suggested proposing to Sports Afield for its annual an entire section of fishing item ads. I suggested and helped negotiate the transaction. We ran a 16-page section all on Hoge items and another page with "Frog Murders Bass." At the rate paid, Sports Afield about broke even. Ed took the risk and about broke even. There was no Hoge risk. We made money. Ed was in the hospital with back trouble. I worked almost all night

with Jack for almost a week. But there were pluses for everybody. Ed got the representation of Sports Afield soon after, and Sports Afield got a lot of business over the years. And the trade was most impressed with the Hoge section.

Then I wrote a new full-page ad for the dress form, with a new headline. Jack provided new art for a color page. And Ed edited and revised it all. As a result of running that all over, we shipped for Ed from our warehouse a forty-foot trailer load of dress forms every day. Fritzi got the post office to supply the trailer.

All this went on and on. We ran other lures with full pages in color and Hoge product after product. One Sunday, in 1965, we had the back covers of Parade, Family Weekly and This Week all for Hoge items for Ed. By 1965, 1966 and 1967, we were running in every logical publication.

Meanwhile, I did anything I could to help Ed. And Ed insisted on reciprocating. We were both proud. Each bent over backward to give more than received. Neither wanted any favors. I negotiated buying remnants at a discount, left over space at time of going to press. Ed gave me a royalty on items of his run in such space. I wrote occasional ads for him. One was "How to Avoid Probate." Crown published it. Ed ran the mail order. It became the #1 non-fiction best seller of that year.

Ed was exploding with growth and expanding all the time Hoge ads and purchases of merchandise from Hoge. Whatever I did to help Ed, I was just one spoke to his wheel. Many contributed. As Ed moved on to band wagon growth, more and more wanted to help participate. Each who helped felt particularly important. Few associated with him realized how deeply he was associated with how many others. Somehow, he found time for all. Ed leap-frogged ahead. Three times he multiplied his size by acquiring businesses several times larger than his. Each time, he did it on his own but, more and more, he built a support team to back him up.

The first break-through was Family Weekly, the national supplement. In the fall of 1965, he began to tell me that there was a possibility it would fold, then that he might take it over. In January 1966, he did. But he had in a number of ways prepared for years, not just for this acquisition, but to acquire each magazine which he later did.

The rep business had grown. "As a mail order advertising rep, I knew everybody who later made each take over possible. I knew the accounts. I knew the executives at each magazine I represented. For each magazine I later took over, I was first their mail order advertising representative. I was in the organization of each. I knew who was most able, worked the hardest, contributed the most—and vice versa. I knew the problems. I already had some ideas for the solutions. I had been first in the editorial side. I was in the business side—I was a mail order man. I could operate on the smallest overhead.

"Family Weekly lost three million dollars in 1965. It was projected to lose five million in 1966. Cuneo Printing had taken it over from the original publisher and had offered it for the printing contract to every major magazine publishing company. Each had turned it down. It was scheduled to cease publication on January 16th, when we made the deal in late December 1965."

Ed Downe had found an unusual situation with tremendous leverage potential. Family Weekly had a very favorable contract with the newspapers which distributed it. All advertising revenue went to Family Weekly plus a small payment per thousand. At such a time as Family Weekly should be profitable, ten percent of profits would be distributed as a dividend to the papers. Family Weekly had to deliver as a minimum a 16-page section. On this

basis, if Family Weekly sold at card rates six pages of advertising, it would break even. At an average of five pages, it would lose one million dollars a year. At seven pages, it would make a million dollars a year. Within one month, Ed Downe had Family Weekly in the black.

"Mail order ads saved and resurrected Family Weekly, a publication which was sold for fifty million dollars fifteen years later. And the same pattern repeated itself for McFadden magazines and for the Ladies' Home Journal and every magazine I took over. No ifs, ands or buts . . . mail order saved these publications. Mail order made possible a two-hundred-and-fifty-million-dollar company in the Fortune 500.

"As a rep, I was always low man on the totem pole for each magazine. The biggest, most established prestige mail order accounts were not given to me to call on. But I knew everyone else, the new mail order people, the growing firms, the ambitious ones. And some were just about to get major recognition. I called on them now as I never had before. I turned to everyone I knew. I sold 150 pages the first year for Family Weekly, almost 3 pages an issue, sometimes at midnight. That did it, all with mail order ads.

"One of the things I had been responsible for as a rep was to establish with publications special rates for mail order. To give mail order a standing as a category, I had opened up publications to mail order. Before I represented Family Weekly, outside of book clubs and record clubs, it had taken little mail order. No salesman from American Legion would call on mail order firms. I persuaded American Legion to accept mail order ads and got the representation. At the end, we represented tens of millions of circulations and called on and knew very well the very mail order accounts that would now save Family Weekly.

"A few accounts made a big difference. A very few people by buying a lot of advertising each made the difference. A very few agencies and accounts did it. Family Weekly was a tremendous advertising medium for many accounts and I knew which. The Dutch door, half-page, mini-catalog inserts proved very profitable to the catalog houses using them. Jim Fishel, one of the truly great mail advertising men, bought them for Spencer Gifts. Sunset did and Hanover House and others. They ran almost every week. It was the equivalent of 2 pages of ads an issue.

"I knew which accounts were sound financially and which were shaky. I knew when to give credit and when to be careful. Our credit losses overall were miniscule. I knew the accounts which could give the biggest volume business in mail order at rates profitable to them but sensible to Family Weekly.

"I knew another category of promoter who took someone else's brain work and product and then bought ads at his risk. Dave Geller was by far the best. He did it for Columbia Records and others. Fred Tartar did it for Longine's. I did it for Cecil Hoge's products. These were marketing entrepeneurs. Their pages helped make Family Weekly profitable.

"For most of the traditional book clubs, record clubs and prestige mail order accounts, I used the salesmen from Family Weekly to do contacting. But now they had the story of results for mail order advertisers. Mail order ads attracted more mail order ads."

Ed Downe's mail order advertising sales caused dramatic gains in advertising sold versus a year ago. This created a sudden aura of success, and attracted national advertisers who before had feared for the stability of Family Weekly and held up running. Success bred more success.

It was amazing how few transactions made such a big difference. One day for Ed I brought back a $250,000 order from Malcolm Smith, a Hoge alumnus—for a year's schedule. Gene Schwartz, another Hoge alumnus, ran as much. Some of Malcolm's alumni ran an equally big schedule.

Then there was swap. It was possible to exchange space in Family Weekly with space in other publications and then run Ed's (and my) ads there. More mail order ads for Ed brought in more daily cash flow.

Ed made it his business to work with his salesmen and get to know any of the biggest mail order accounts and direct marketing agencies he had not known before. "I became good friends of Stan Rapp, Lester Wunderman and others."

For Family Weekly to survive from issue to issue, Ed had to sell more mail order ads. He also had to keep national ads coming back. He had to keep for Family Weekly the newspapers which distributed it. He had to get enough credit from Cuneo Printing to keep getting Family Weekly printed.

"Mort Frank had personally signed up most of the papers and personally renegotiated most of the contracts. He was trusted by the newspaper publishers. Without the publishers, we could not continue. I made Mort the publisher of Family Weekly, and he was and is the best. Mort Frank held the hand of each publisher while he fought to survive. When any threatened to cancel, I tried to fly out with Mort to save it.

"I remember the first time I met Mr. Cuneo. He took a liking to me. He extended credit he never had before. I walked into his office. It was enormous. He sat at a huge desk at the very end. On the wall were paintings of each of the last four popes. John Cuneo was in his eighties. He worked until he was ninety-two."

Ed Downe has a bad back. Recurrently, he gets so crippled that he walks like a crab. Instead of stopping, he goes on in torture, making his deals until his back gets better. And this was one of his worse days.

" 'What's wrong, boy?' asked old John Cuneo as he saw me struggle past his office. When he heard about my back, he said, 'Do as I did. Put in a heated pool.' My chances to do that were zero. I had nothing. I had borrowed $250,000 to buy Family Weekly. But he gave me credit. And when he saw that I was making it, he kept on giving me credit."

I worked with Ed Downe and watched him as, like a comet, he streaked across the mail order sky. Then he blasted off through and past the stratosphere into a publishing empire and into areas where others could far more effectively help him than I could. And all the time I worked with him I had more fun than I ever had in my life.

I've flown with him to try to save a Family Weekly newspaper distributing it before it cancelled. I've acquired subsidiaries for him, gotten products for him, met with the largest publishers in Europe for him. My ex-partner, Dick Davimos, brought in the Wall Street firm that first brought Ed public. I introduced Ed to everyone I knew including Ed Miller, who later became president of Downe Communications. I never worked for Ed. I never owned part of his business.

What I got was growth and profit of Harrison Hoge Industries, Inc., which has prospered ever since. To help me build Harrison Hoge, Ed did anything I asked. He helped me acquire a subsidiary. He promoted anything I asked. He gave me volume, lowered our production cost and increased our profit selling to the trade products he advertised. He gave me the mail order purchaser names for our items. He never complained if anything I did for him backfired. One weekend he spent $80,000 of Family Weekly space in a special section just for my products. It bombed. He never said a complaining word.

By 1974, Downe Communications, Inc. was in the top 300 of the Fortune 500. Its magazine subsidiary published 800 million magazines in 1974. It published Family Weekly, Ladies' Home Journal, American Home, Sport and two dozen other magazines.

He used mail order to build his empire. Before he sold out, it owned radio stations and cable systems. It published books. It owned a 300-employee computer center. It had a catalog business, a cosmetic business, a watch business, a pet supply business and more. One subsidiary did nothing but sell mail order ads for magazines and newspapers and made $1,000,000 in profit year after year.

In 1974, the research department of Downe Communications, Inc. made this calculation: Suppose that each copy of each of its magazines published in 1974 were piled one on top of the other in columns; suppose each column was put side by side in front of the Empire State Building; then the columns would stretch completely around the entire square block, would go the heighth of the building, would completely wall in the Empire State Building - and there would still be magazines left over.

It wasn't all easy. Sometimes, when he looked like a meteor, he felt like Eliza crossing the financial ice. He started from scratch and was underfinanced all the way. But he made it, got to the other side, sold out and invested his profits in stocks he knew and understood—mail order and publishing. He tripled his money in a year and bought a million shares of Charter, the company that bought him out. He bought at 4½. It promptly dropped to 3. But then it rose to 50.

Looking back, Ed Downe says, "Mail order is the real true advertising. It is the real true marketing. It shows what is directly attributable to a specific ad. There's a great electric thrill to know you have a successful item. The first count is the big moment. It's tremendous. Then the projection becomes just mechanical.

"Whatever success I've had could only have happened from mail order and in America."

Chapter 9

Helping Creative People Rise In Direct Marketing

*An organization that helps them start,
get better jobs, increase earnings.*

That's the role of the Direct Marketing Creative Guild. Ed McLean and several others started an informal luncheon group called the Direct Mail Writers Club in 1966. Ed is one of the great writers and teachers of direct mail. He travels all over the world giving seminars on it. He needed someone to help the club, and in 1976 he got a dynamo, Andi Emerson.

Andi recalls what first happened. "When I got into it, activities were languishing. It was down to 19 members. In exchange for taking over the presidency, the remaining members gave me a mandate to build a new organization—with a new name, 'The Direct Marketing Writers Guild', a new concept and a new thrust."

Now membership would include only those who wrote for, supervised or bought any medium. The Guild's objective became to raise the professional status of creative people—and to help any creative people to go up the ladder—from the moment they started in direct marketing. In 1980, the Guild went to the next logical step. Andi continues: "We changed the name again, to the Direct Marketing Creative Guild—to include art people as well. We have just put two art directors on the Board of Directors."

Andi and other dedicated members have made the Guild a near necessity for creative people and those who need them. First, she recruited some of the most talented creative people in direct marketing as members. Then she made them work hard for it. For years, Andi was president. Mike Slosberg, then president of Wunderman, Ricotta & Kline, became executive vice president of the Guild, and then president. What new copywriter would not want to meet him and the top creative executives of other biggest direct marketing agencies? Andi recruited the creative stars. The creative starlets followed.

She worked with intensity on something else . . . the WorkLunches. Menus are good, with cocktails before. It's a superb direct marketing course, for a low-cost lunch. The speakers are the best, of the calibre of Tom Collins, Chairman of the Board of Rapp & Collins. Creative people meet each other, learn from leaders, form contacts and friendships. Can job offers be far behind?

Andi sparked the beginnings of the quite high calibre newsletter, The Creative Forum. For it, Andi writes a column. Other top creative people write, edit and lay it out. Members get it free. Non-members can subscribe but might as well join, the subscription cost is so close to the membership fee.

Andi, single-handedly, has raised the professional standing of direct marketing creative people—in a variety of ways. The most dramatic was when John Caples became a director with the title of Member-at-Large, and the Guild organized the John Caples Awards for the most outstanding direct marketing copy and design of the year. Helped by an outstanding group of dedicated experts, she drove to get maximum entrants. They worked to get a panel of prestigious creative people as judges and made a media event out of the annual granting of the awards. Over 600 people came to the 1980 Awards Lunch.

Andi understands the ambitions, trials and tribulations of creative people as they start and climb upward. She started working for a newspaper, then for an advertising agency, then for a printing and mailing house—gaining experience at each step. Then she formed Emerson Associates and became a direct mail consultant, but not for mail order firms.

Gene Schwarz, a Hoge alumnus and great copywriter, whose story I tell elsewhere in this book, was a client of Andi's. "Gene took so much consultant time that within a year I moved my office into his. When I joined him, I knew nothing of mail order. Gene was my instant guru. I was a quick study. He told me, by the hour, tales of his early days in mail order—at Huber Hoge—of the Hoge accounts he worked on, the items he wrote for, the people he worked with.

"Gene's strength was space. I brought direct mail know-how and acquired mail order know-how on direct mail and media. We became partners. And from that time, years ago, I've been applying principals acquired then to experience upon experience since . . . in every facet of direct marketing."

Now Andi is sole owner of her own business, The Emerson Marketing Agency, Inc., a full-fledged advertising agency . . . with a broad experience in all media. It is located at 44 E. 29th Street, New York City. The business is growing and prospering, but she has an addiction—helping creative people in direct marketing.

"People talk to me and ask how to get into direct marketing and ahead in it. I always say to come to our WorkLunches, participate, become part of our organization. I specifically know a number who have done this and climbed up the ladder as a result."

Now membership is snowballing. "We have over 500 members, not just in New York but all over the U.S. and even in half a dozen foreign countries. We have a West Coast chapter and plan to expand in other areas. We are now working on actual writing and designing courses that will teach aspiring writers and artists how to create to the disciplines required of our profession. We emphasize this in our newsletter and at the WorkLunches."

As of March 1982, local and overseas membership was $35, and non-local U.S. membership was $25. For this, you get a great deal. "We put great emphasis on training programs and careers."

Andi is bullish on future direct marketing growth and particularly bullish on chances for women. "Opportunities for women in direct marketing are tremendous. The need is great. There's no discrimination."

After Andi, Mike Slosberg took over vigorously as president. "In general advertising I had belonged to professional organizations. I had been a copywriter. I knew what it meant to a writer or art director to get recognition for creative efforts. In direct marketing the creative people were more anonymous. Often the creative product wasn't exposed. Results were confidential. Now, for the first time, the Guild can give the recognition expected.

"I see the Creative Direct Marketing Guild as a professional organization that can give credit and recognition and for establishing a character and personality for a direct marketing business as well as for results. We're trying for a more professional operation, to help people get it and help young creative people get started."

"Anyone in the creative area of direct marketing is welcome.

We try to orient those beginning. Any young person would gain by joining and attending our working lunches."

In April, 1982 Jim Prendergast became president. For Mike Slosberg it is still a major interest. But Andi nursed it, helped it survive, made its present growth possible and is Honorary Chairman.

Note: The Direct Marketing Creative Guild can be reached at 516 Fifth Avenue, New York, NY 10036, (212) 909-0206. If you're creative and in direct marketing, I suggest you join it.

Chapter 10
The Sweeps

The two sweepstakes that over the years have given the biggest prizes, more prizes, more often, are both for mail order offers.

One is for the Reader's Digest and the other for Publishers Clearing House. For each, increased pulling power proved so dramatic that sweepstakes after sweepstakes have run for many years. More and more big direct marketers rely more and more on sweepstakes to survive and prosper in mail order, and most come to Tom Conlon to run them.

Tom Conlon knows more about sweepstakes to sell anything than anyone on earth. The number of people who have entered sweepstakes run by his company, D.L. Blair, are equivalent to one-quarter of the population of the globe. The prizes given away by Tom's company for clients have come close to $100,000,000. Tom has conducted more sweepstakes for major companies than anyone in the world.

More people go into sweepstakes than vote for president. Many go into one sweeps after another. Dick Cremer, President of Montgomery Ward's promotional mail order subsidiaries, says concerning his biggest campaign: "Without the sweeps, I don't think we could have made it in outside media." For mail order buyers and seller, the sweeps can be an addiction. The habit can go on for life.

Tom specializes in sweepstakes for the biggest companies and estimates that Blair runs "about 65% of major company sweepstakes," although he does not handle Reader's Digest or PCH sweeps. Of the ten largest U.S. magazines, five are Blair clients. Thirty-five of the top Fortune 500 clients are D.L. Blair clients. Blair runs more successful sweepstakes than all other sweepstakes companies combined.

"We supply promotion research, creative development, prize selection and structure and complete fulfillment. We understand the ins and outs and ups and downs in the various laws and regulations governing sweepstakes, contests and lotteries in each state (they may markedly differ). We know how to untangle the federal red tape connected with sweeps. We know how people feel about sweeps, the kind they like, what makes them enter and what makes them buy, too."

Who taught Tom Conlon? How did he start? How can he teach us? If we're in mail order, should we or shouldn't we go into sweeps? And, if so, how? Do sweeps pay off for direct marketers? Are they legal? A nightmare? Do losers get sore?

"Father Taylor taught me at Regis, in Manhattan, where he was head master and I prepped. I went on to St. Peter's. in Jersey City, then to the School of Visual Arts and the Art Students League. To help pay for art school, I became a commercial artist."

He started at the New York Daily News, in the editorial department, as a staff artist. He went on to being advertising manager for a small appliance company, starting in creative and going on to media selection, and then on to Benton & Bowles, one of the biggest advertising agencies.

"By the time I left, I was associate director of promotion. I did the full spectrum, from consumer promotions to trade. It was my first introduction to sweepstakes and contests. Proctor & Gamble are rightly considered the best marketers in the world. At B & B, my main account was P & G. I had three intensive years working for them. Doing so was my best marketing school. I worked with D.L. Blair, who ran the biggest sweeps for biggest companies.

"In 1965, I left B & B to join D.L. Blair. Cy Draddy and Martin Landis had founded it in 1960. The 'D' was for Draddy, the 'L' for Landis. Blair was for the Blair House in front of which they were standing when they named their new venture, in Washington, D.C.

"Cy and Martin had each been contest judges and had worked together for two or three years. The idea for D.L. Blair was to do more than judge, to handle incoming mail and to send out all outgoing mail; to select prizes, to create the contests, the rules and the ideas for them. It was to do it all, to proliferate into anything related.

"The first step was to advance from judging to development of contests and sweepstakes. From the beginning, they depended heavily on strong legal advice. Both spent a great deal of time reviewing or clearing with the government. When I joined D.L. Blair, it was entirely sweeps. Then we added consulting, auditing, research, premiums, promotion testing and fulfillment. I brought tools that worked in package goods, the P & G approach, integrating success and objectives, studying success versus weakness, accomplishments versus objectives.

"We take a hard look, with much historical knowledge. We take past experience and temper it. It's the objective method. The overwhelming majority of D.L. Blair volume has been since I joined them. We feel we know more about sweepstakes than anyone in the world.

"To develop sweepstake approaches, we used a great deal of focus group research, ourselves. I learned this at B & B. It has evolved. We developed formulated methods of analyzing past experience. With the advent of computers, we could do more kinds of more intensive research. We're highly computerized with stored information retrieval. We audit promotions. We have a file of all major sweeps in the country.

"My first direct marketing client was Life magazine. It was a very successful sweepstakes. For me, it was totally different from any previous use of sweepstakes. I became a student of direct marketing. I went through D.L. Blair's research and history for direct marketing accounts. I got in on direct marketing client post mortems and post promotion analysis. I asked a lot of questions. I found that there were some similarities between sweeps for package goods and for direct marketers. Know-how in each helped me help those in the other.

"Sweeps for direct marketers were exciting. Contrasted with package goods where sales results could be sometimes argued about, here you ran sweeps, got orders and compared results at once with sales created without sweeps. Working with direct marketers was even more stimulating because results were absolutely measurable.

"I became senior vice president in 1969. I became president in 1973. I acquired the company as majority stockholder in 1976. Since then, use of sweepstakes has been growing 20% to 25% a year. There's been big growth overall for twenty years. There were some drops in earlier years. Now it's not skyrocketing, but ever increasing."

The twenty-year pattern of growth in sweeps showed big growth in the early 1960's. By 1965, the growth came down. From 1965 to 1968, there was a major decline. There was a build-up from 1968 through 1970. There was a slight plateau in 1970. From 1971, growth continued relatively slowly, about 5% to 10% a year. There was a severe decline after 1974. In 1976, it picked up again.

Are sweepstakes lotteries? "Absolutely not," says Tom. "The FTC once challenged sweepstakes. The government lost. It was the FTC vs. McDonalds, D.L. Blair and D'Arcy, McManus Advertising. It was a landmark case. The FTC claimed deceptive advertising. It was not. The case was thrown out. They leave us alone. Of course, the government quite properly polices honesty and integrity in conducting sweepstakes."

What about prizes offered and never given because the number for such prizes was never presented? "The government did go after companies conducting sweepstakes, on this very thing. Just about every other company in the sweepstakes field signed a cease and desist stipulation on this. We refused. In every Blair sweepstakes, we had always featured in big type, 'Please Be Sure to Claim,' 'Don't Throw Away,' and to emphasize that a number not presented could not win."

But all this caused the public to stay away from sweeps and contests. "That's what has resulted in the uneven growth." D.L. Blair made a survey in the mid-60's and found that 20% of entrants felt that the sweeps or contests had been fixed. After 1971, D.L. Blair took the policy to offer all prizes in a way that each is given away, regardless. "If a number is not presented,

another drawing takes place until the prize is given away." By the mid-70's, 14% of people surveyed still thought sweeps and contests were fixed. At least this was two-thirds of the people who thought so in the sixties. "By now, it's less, as the sweeps image has improved.

"Over the years the sweeps have dominated over games and contests. Of prize promotions, 90% are sweepstakes, 7% are games and 3% are contests. Sweeps will generate ten times the consumer response of any contest which offers the same prize structure.

"Probably 25% to 30% of our clients are direct marketers. You mentioned Dick Cremer, of Signature at Ward, telling you how important sweeps have been for his operation. We started Dick in sweeps. Bob Stone and Jim Kobs have each, in their books, quoted dramatic sales increases and the year-after-year use of sweeps for mail order.

"Sweeps are crucially important to some magazine launches. Advertising Age ran a major story on the successful introduction of New West magazine using contests. Telephone marketing, in connection with sweepstakes, has just started. There are some problems, as yet.

"Our client list is in the Standard Rate and Data Information Agency book. Otherwise, we don't disclose them. About 15% of our business is associated with advertising agencies. We don't work for them so much as share clients with them. Often, working with one client, we develop a relationship with its agency. Sometimes, it leads to another client from the agency. This happened in direct marketing with Wunderman, Ricotta & Kline.

"We, ourselves, never discuss clients or their reputation with sweeps. But it is widely publicized that Playboy, TV Guide, Ladies Home Journal and McCall's use sweeps constantly. Each is a client. Of major general interest magazines, 60% to 70% use sweeps. Some probably never will. Sweeps are highly efficient and cost efficient. Reader's Digest and Publishers Clearing House are two which use TV support heavily. Most others don't. Our research has identified definite value in TV support in that it reinforces credibility by showing winners.

"The use of sweeps is not a quick fix. It's not a replacement for strong creative advertising, a decent product and media support. It's not a panacea when all else fails. It needs a good product, decent creative work, a fair level of media support and a sensible strategy. Success demands meticulous planning and design. But plan and execute knowledgeably and you can get a winner. As a bonus, sweeps do well when the economy is bad. More people enter.

"We have offices in London to service all of the United Kingdom and Europe. We service Canada out of New York. For years, we serviced clients in Asia and Australia from our Australian office. Now we do so from the U.S. Fifteen percent of our clients are outside the U.S. This percentage is growing slightly, and more than that in the United Kingdom.

"We have 320 employees. Not all are in sweepstakes. We have a research division. We do promotion research. This includes attitudinal research and quantitative research. This is largely to get reactions to the sweepstakes, games or contests idea—to test it out or to audit reaction to it later.

"What has been most responsible for our success? Clients trust us implicitly. We will never betray a confidence. Our work for each client is private. Do I like this business? I find it challenging and interesting. We're fortunate in our clients. They're imaginative and stimulating."

Note: D.L. Blair is located at 185 Great Neck Road, Great Neck, NY 11021, (516) 487-9200.

Chapter 11
A Mail Order Fortune

*What way to make it
is fastest, easiest?*

Dick Benson, as Grand Master of Direct Marketing Day in New York, was asked that question. His instant answer was: "Work for a publisher! In all mail order, they spend more. They test more. They know more. You learn more. Then, go out and apply it on your own."

Dick did. He's co-owner of the second biggest newsletter in the world, Contest News-Letter, with 400,000 circulation. At $12 per subscription, it is a $5 million-a-year business. He's one of the most sought after consultants in the world for magazine circulation.

Dick was a key participant in the successful launch of Southern Living, Psychology Today and Smithsonian magazine. "I've done this for over 20 years. My first was Reporter magazine, back in 1949." Time after time, he's taken on a magazine when it was a gleam in the founder's eye and carried it to the launch and on. He worked with the editor, selected the promotion writers, picked the lists to test and, most of all, came up with the deal, the subscription offer.

But he has done far more than be in on the birth of magazine after magazine, big and small. He's applied what he's learned to product after product and is the invaluable consultant for a variety of them.

He learned at his first job in Time magazine circulation. He began to apply what he learned when later he was general manager of Omnibook magazine. He learned and applied more in circulation at Field & Stream. Later, he became part of a team that changed all magazine subscription promotion concepts at American Heritage.

"But it wasn't fast. It wasn't easy. There were curves in the road. It sometimes went down as well as up." Readers note this well. Dick mastered his craft until everything he knew began to pay off.

The turning point in Dick's career was his seven-year stint at American Heritage. Jim Parton, the founder, was the catalyst. "I met Parton sometime before when Bob Strauss helped me get a job as associate editor of World magazine, where Jim was the consultant. It almost immediately folded, and the next day I started with him, in 1954.

"Jim Parton had gone out to raise $200,000. He got a little money from each of the biggest string of millionaires you can imagine. He got Bob Strauss, Jim Sachs, Marshall Field, Ostheimer from Philadelphia, General Stackpole and Roger Philips, of Philips Gas. But, in all, he had only raised $50,000 to start Horizon as a magazine book. I put up a little money. Bruce Catton, the historian, was editor. He put up a little money. We finally had $64,000 for start-up money.

"Jim taught me more than anybody. He was the smartest. He taught me two things above all else: (1) To never lie and always tell the truth in promotion, even if it hurt; (2) after you get a customer, get him or her to come on in to the big tent for a bigger deal and buy an additional item. He brought together a talented team of top creative people.

"He fired us up. He gave us a chance to try our own, new ideas. We invented the brochure. We invented the pictorial envelope, the first spectacular in direct mail. We invented merge-purge. Without computers we eyeballed for duplicates on a regular basis mailings of 7,000,000 at a time.

"The encyclopedia guys and everybody else were getting into the mail for sixty dollars per thousand. We started trying to do that. A year later, we were spending one hundred and ten dollars per thousand and getting a lower advertising cost than we had hoped for, with greater profit. We made the jump from cost per thousand in the mail to cost per order received. We discovered that was all that mattered."

From then on in Dick Benson has been identified with many of the most exciting magazine subscription campaigns ever run. Yet, he does not write copy. He's not a layout man. What is Dick best at? "I'm a promoter. I understand the deal. I do more list work. I'm best at creating the offer, the proposal to make to get the offer. I control the promotion piece. I'm good at what I do.

"For twenty years, I've preached: Always buy from the guy who specializes. Don't do it yourself if you can avoid it. Avoid what you're not good at. I'm lousy at administration. That's why I'm best off as a consultant or in partnership with someone who can administer.

"I stick to what I'm good at. I know direct mail. I know nothing of space. I don't know TV or any promotion but direct mail. I still tell each account that before I become a consultant. Of course, with you, with the old Omnibook (Huber Hoge and Sons was the agency), we did have success with space and broadcast."

Dick has found the perfect lifestyle since he left New York and moved to Florida. He lives forty miles north of Jacksonville. He keeps life simple. He's a very good advisor. "I enjoy being a consultant. I'm not greedy. I work only as much as I want, for whom I want, when I want. I play golf. I work at home. I have no office. Our children are grown. There's just my wife and me.

"About 75% to 80% of my business is with publishers, but I'm doing more for others now. I've worked for Frank Schultz selling grapefruit for seven years. I worked for Ogilvy & Mather for nineteen years. I work for R.L. Polk, for the Robert Jones Agency, for Richard Viguerie, for Fred Simon to sell Omaha Steaks, and for the Interdine Card, in Atlanta.

"I don't work on a commission basis but on a retainer basis. I can work with small clients and on small tests, though I generally insist on bigger tests than my peers to be sure they are big enough to give the client a fair chance.

"One interesting client is the Goodbee Pecan Corp., in Albany, Georgia. It's owned by a family of professional orchard people. They're concerned because new orchards in Texas and elsewhere will soon increase the pecan crop 40%. So, they set up the youngest member of the family in mail order to find new markets. I came in the second year. Walter Weintz started them off. Now, it's building to an important part of their business. This year, we'll do over $1,000,000. This is with no corporate gift business. It's based on finding mail order buyers."

One of Dick's abilities is to select and get the most out of creative people. Dick believes in working with the best writers obtainable. Who are they? "They include Henry Cowen, Bill Jayme, Hank Burnett, Bob Jones, the two Walshes . . . Harry Walsh, in Westport, and Jack Walsh, in New York . . . and Linda Wells. The same ten writers turn out almost half the profitable direct mail in the country."

Dick believes, also, that it is important in any thorough test to test the mailing kits of more than one writer. He insists on testing different writers who don't work together. "You can't run good tests through one copy department. The same copy chief influences and edits all pieces too much. I like to take three different writers for an important test such as a launch.

"I take the three, almost every time, out of the same ten top guys. An unproven writer will still cost $1,500 or more to come up with a complete package. Sure, the best in the country will charge maybe $5,000. Cowen and Jayme will cost more. The $3,500 difference is only small money in the total test, not enough to take a chance. Everything else costs the same. While it's hard on new writers, for $3,500 I can't take a chance."

One reason Dick feels this way is he finds overall costs of testing are now so high. For a launch, he feels $75,000 is now necessary. "I don't believe you can get a yes or a no for a big project for less. You don't want a grey answer. For that, you can mail 150,000 to 200,000 names. I like to test three packages, each from a different offer. I like to make perhaps five other tests varying in price, premium or whatever. I prefer to test up to seventeen lists."

Dick is in other businesses. "Alan Drey and I have a plate company. We sell collector plates for $35 or $40 a plate. We've done well with Historical Times plates. But I also make mistakes. I tried bird plates. Birds bombed. Now, I'm testing another newsletter. I have no idea how it will work out."

His big winner has been Contest News-Letter. "In December 1977, when it was three years old, I bought a half interest in Contest News-Letter. It had 8,000 subscribers. It was a typical kitchen table operation, with an Elliot addressing system." It's still a moonlighting venture. Dick's partners are Carolyn and Roger Tyndall. Carolyn is a housewife. Roger is an air traffic controller. All three are moonlighters.

"Roger writes it. I do all the promotion. Carolyn takes care of correspondence. Contest News-Letter has no peripheral activities. We have no spin-offs. We make no attempt to sell any subscriber anything else. All fulfillment is handled outside. We have one minimum-wage employee (Carolyn's mother).

"For Contest News-Letter, my first mailing was 250,000. Of course, I was able to hedge that by no-risk deals aside from the mailing, such as being on the stampsheets in the Publisher's Clearing House mailings. My contacts got in some safe business that way where we only paid so much a subscription.

"Now, two-and-a-half years later, we have 400,000. But it's still a struggle. We're doing no space and no TV. We've tested each and failed. Probably each can work. But we can only do part of what is potential. We concentrate on what we know will appeal to contestants and we do have the second biggest newsletter circulation in the world."

Note: For readers of this book Dick has answered a few questions.

Q. *How important to your success for clients in mailings has been the development of the web press?*

A. The four-color process web press had begun to be produced around 1957 or 1958. Color could now be used more lavishly and more effectively, and we were the first major publisher to use it. We were also successful with letterpress. But the web press has helped keep costs down while improving quality over the years.

Q. *How effective are computer letters for your clients?*

A. I don't use computer or laser letters too much.

Q. *When is it safest to take risks in mail order?*

A. After tests pay out and confirming tests and projections, I find it possible in certain situations to take much bigger risks. Then my feel for the situation makes risk far less. For

Contest News-Letter, in a co-op insert test, we're testing five million inserts. Yet, it is our first test of inserts.

Q. *Have inserts been successful for you overall?*

A. For my clients I've done a reasonable amount of inserts. They work.

Q. *Have your contacts with your magazine clients resulted in your getting non-risk deals?*

A. I don't get deals for anyone from client magazines. My magazines don't deal.

Q. *How successful have jumbo envelope size mailings been for you?*

A. I've been notably unsuccessful with 9" by 12". I use a number 10 envelope, or 6" by 9".

Q. *When the economy looks bad, do you stop mailing?*

A. I'm a funny guy about the economy. I've read every gloom and doom newsletter and book. But, even at times I believe the economy is in the pits, I truly believe America will overcome. I keep mailing.

Q. *Who is the smartest direct marketer you know?*

A. All my clients are. Rosalie Bruno, of Knapp Publishing, is very smart. Frank Schultz is fantastic.

Q. *How important in pulling power of mailings and ads are strong claims?*

A. I always remember what Jim Parton taught me. For all my clients, we keep claims down. For Contest News-Letter, we don't promise you'll win as a contestant. We just tell you about contests.

Q. *With soaring postage, how have mailings still been able to be productive?*

A. Over the years, postage has shot up, but printing has gone up nowhere near as much. The computer has kept processing costs down. Inserting is by machine. But mainly, it's more scientific list selection and good offers and creative work that overcame inflation.

Q. *But how much longer can constant postage increases keep on, and now jumping paper prices, before direct mail is priced out of the market?*

A. Cost of mailings, including postage, do keep going up but so do the prices we charge for products. But finding the right higher price is not easy. Up to $35 a plate may not get too much resistance and then a $40 price for the same plate drops dead. There are limits you can't push.

Q. *How do you know that you finally have the right price?*

A. One rule I've found over the years is that, once you find the right price for a given year, that further changes of price up or down will pull the same gross dollars. Charge a little more and sell a few less, or vice versa. It's one of the few old rules that still stand up."

Dick Benson likes to mull things over, cogitate a bit and then come to a conclusion. In this book, Carolyn and Roger Tyndall tell of the change he made in their life, the fun of being his partner and the whole story of Contest News-Letter. Frank Schultz tells, as a client, what Dick Benson has meant to him. Thank you, Dick, for your mail order wisdom.

Note: Dick Benson is located at 5 Water Oak, Amelia Island, FL 32034; telephone (904) 261-0121.

Chapter 12
Direct Marketing's Second Revolution

*How Tom Swift and Popular Science
helped propel Ed Nash into it
and mail order success*

It has started, says Ed Nash . . . and will be completed when the skills of general marketing blend more perfectly with those of direct marketing . . . and those of consumer package advertising with the skills of direct response advertising.

In 1982, a great advertising agency . . . Batten, Barton, Durstine & Osborne . . . one with patrician standing and great respect among professionals . . . gave its name to BBD&O Direct . . . and chose Ed Nash as founder. It was a seal of approval of the field, the man and his know-how. His experience is why you should read his book "Direct Marketing: Strategy/Planning/Execution".

Ed Nash is a numbers-crunching, copy-writing idea man who approaches direct marketing as an art and a science. He was born and brought up in New York City in the Bronx . . . boiling with enthusiastic curiosity, imagination and entrepreneurship . . . with the driving desire to make it and the work ethic to do it. His family wanted him to be a doctor. He dreamed of being a scientist. He was selected for a Westinghouse Talent Search award. Science was his favorite subject. He mastered, more than science, the scientific method of thinking. But his entrepreneurship made him apply his scientific ways of doing things to creating money-making ideas.

He always read text books like fiction and any fiction and magazines he could find. He happily, excitedly and enthusiastically absorbed something from everywhere and learned from it all. "Tom Swift taught me that everything was do-able and Popular Science that anything was know-able." Ideas popped into his mind in the most disorderly way. His scientific turn of mind digested, processed and came up with ways to apply them - for profit. He became very good at finding facts and then arranging and deducing from them.

Ed was number two in his class, embarrassed about his high IQ and more interested in making friends and turning ideas into money. His father was a printer and, when he was a child, gave him his own printing press and the love of printing. He wrote what he printed and fell in love with writing, printing and selling what he wrote and printed . . . which he did from the age of eleven. By high school he had been in a half dozen enterprises connected with printing.

He also wrote the school play, for the year book and the school song (still used). At 16, he went to CCNY, still planning to be a scientist, started off with top grades which then plummeted as he found he had no idea what he really wanted to do. After hours he worked as a mimeograph operator for a mailing house but there learned how to operate other machines from inserters to labellers . . . his first hands on direct mail experience.

"At college, I was not challenged, did badly in grades and had taken vocational tests at CCNY and NYU . . . which resulted in a vocational recommendation to try journalism or advertising.

I was surprised. I had never known anyone who made a living writing. So I took a summer job at Friend-Reiss Advertising. After my job I went down to the Post Office and sorted mail."

At Friend-Reiss he was a file clerk and mail boy. He was 17. One account there was Marboro Books, handled by a junior account man, Stan Rapp. "He needed help and asked me to write three and four-line blurbs for each of hundreds of books." Each description was a classified ad of its own, with a key number duplicated in the big coupon below at lower right. Ed had to persuade readers to circle the key numbers of books his copy described. Each of his micro ads had to summarize and synthesize reasons to buy a remainder book (which had not sold previously) so convincing that it would be ordered. "It was a writing discipline. How effectively I wrote affected the results."

The results of better copy could be measured in the coupons. More coupons meant more sales for Marboro, more agency billing and a chance for a raise. Ed Nash had discovered mail order. Since then all he has learned have been refinements. He got so excited about mail order that he dropped out of college. His summer job became a five year stay. He became an account executive for Adam Hats and Marboro Books. He even stopped working for the Post Office.

Ed went to another agency. He wrote bigger mail order ads, soon full pages. They were profitable for clients. Billing went up. He got more raises. "I then made a conscious decision to base my future career entirely on whatever I could contribute to pulling more coupons at lower advertising cost and creating more mail profits."

But he wanted to learn more from those who could teach him most about mail order. He applied for jobs both at Maxwell Sackheim and at Schwab & Beatty, where he landed one.

"The biggest name accounts were there. Vic Schwab read and edited every ad. George Violante was copy chief. The senior writer was Tom Collins. I became a pretty good writer; I still write ads here and there. Vic Schwab's book, 'How to Write a Good Advertisement' was my bible which I read and reread along with John Caples' 'Tested Advertising Methods'." Here too Ed's ads pulled . . . sometimes better than the control ad for famous accounts.

"I was surprised and flattered when I received a recruiting call to become an account executive at another agency. It was then called Smith, Hagel and Snyder. Hagel had left to operate Crowell-Collier which had sold its magazines and had nothing left but the Collier's Encyclopedia business. Hagel had a reputation of being tough to work for. He did have tough standards but was also fair. We got along.

"He offered me a job I took as Advertising Director of Crowell-Collier. It was a new opportunity. As copywriter I couldn't control things. I couldn't influence the offer, item, book selections in a club. It seemed easier on the other side. It was less exciting but I learned a lot. We started selling encyclopedias mail order and to get leads for encyclopedia salesmen. In either case, it was two-step. An ad got the inquiry. Literature or a salesman converted it to a sale. Then we made more sales to our customers. The key was finding products that fitted and presenting them effectively.

"Up to then I had had no back-end experience. Nobody on the agency side did then. On the client side I learned much more, particularly after Crowell-Collier bought La Salle Schools. I went out to Chicago with Warren Smith and Wes Munn to run it. I was 'marketing.' In three years, 'marketing' more than tripled La Salle sales. I brought in Stan Rapp who was at the David Altman agency. La Salle had a separate mail order division. I learned how to run it, at a profit, while helping salesmen increase their end of the business.

"Through Frank Vos who handled the account I was introduced to the Capitol Record Club (owned by Capitol Records). It had started with John Stevenson of Greystone operating it and taking the promotional risk. Capitol Records had taken it back and immediately lost $2,000,000 doing $4,000,000. EMI, the British owner of Capitol Records, didn't understand, like, or want to be in mail order. I was offered the assignment to turn it around, build it up and sell it. I accepted and moved to L.A. where Capitol was located.

"Capitol Records was doing business with Foote Cone & Belding. When the Frank Vos connection didn't work out, it was suggested that I work with Foote Cone. I explained to Lou Scott who headed Foote Cone's West Coast office that this wouldn't work because of their lack of mail order experience. Instead of stonewalling, he agreed with me but said, 'Give me two weeks.' Then he flew all over the country. He had persuaded his management to go after top direct marketing people to hire. He'd ask me who was good. I recommended people, among them Stan Rapp and Tom Collins who up to then had not met each other. At the end of two weeks he called me. Foote Cone had started a mail order subsidiary, Rapp & Collins. Capitol Records became its first account.

"My stay with Capitol Record Club was six years. I was president from 1964 to 1969. I left then to start my own publishing business. The club had grown to $30 million a year. Longines Symphonette had bought it. I had stayed. We planned to expand Capitol Record Club further. But management changed and I wanted to try something on my own. Longines' operated a house agency, so Rapp and Collins lost the account. Its billing dropped from $8 million to $4 million . Foote Cone sold it back to Stan and Tom. They surprised everyone by turning around what seemed like a loser into a winning agency.

"My publishing business was Mass Publishing Inc. It was entrepreneural. I liked diversity and got it. I sat down with all kinds of authors. Some were very bizarre. All were stimulating. I published one book by the head of the homosexual church and another by Rabbi Kahane. I found something interesting in each author. It allowed me to be enthusiastic. I had recorded books on cassettes and sold by mail order. But I like large-scale volume and I got this by selling to stores. I sold psychology books and a lot of others. I started with mail order ads but the retail grew faster. I did $2,000,000 a year wholesale. But it was a bad time for publishers from 1969 to 1973. I had a 26-man staff and the overhead was tough for me. I spent my time talking to people I owed or was collecting from. But I survived. I got away with my shirt and sold out.

"The real estate boom in California helped me. I sold my house, came East and bought 20% of Rapp & Collins. It was a good investment. Rapp & Collins had merged with Stone & Adler and the combination grew rapidly. Doyle Dane & Bernbach wanted to buy it but had a conflict of accounts with Stone & Adler. It ended up buying the Rapp & Collins part of the agency. I did well in the deal . . . but benefitted even more from the association with DD&B. I was executive vice president of Rapp & Collins. Sol Blumenfeld was creative director. He is brilliant.

"At Doyle Dane we had access to their facilities. As we began to handle DD&B clients, we had to learn the DD&B ways of doing things. We had to use our direct marketing skills, blended with what their know-how could add. We had to handle accounts more formally and to meet DD&B standards of operation and procedure. The clients taught us. DD&B did. We all learned from

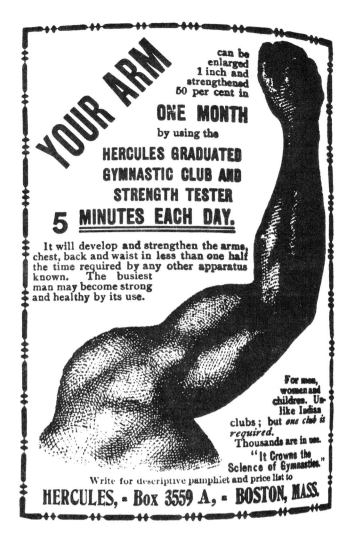

each other. Yet, Rapp & Collins stood on its own feet. For all inter-agency help, we got an inter-company bill. We were still quite self-operative.

"With Rapp & Collins I got deeply into TV. At La Salle and Capitol Record I had been heavily in direct mail. Now I had a full spectrum viewpoint. I had started with space and gone full circle. TV was exciting to me. Consumer Reports was my first TV account. I learned from it. I have no love of one medium over another; all are valuable. I believe in starting with core media and extending into all suitable forms of advertising. So many people use one form of advertising, neglecting others. The majority do, getting further and further from the core, overexpanding in one medium and leaving other core media untouched.

"For many years I had been writing down notes and doing research for a book on direct marketing. When I was a Rapp & Collins client, I wrote a manual to teach what I needed to those working on my account. I think in principles, I abstract ways of doing things. I like to explain things simply in an ad or brochure. I like to write instructions. I read everything that concerns direct marketing and hoard information. I always intended to do a book. For two years I began to think more seriously about it and tell people I was beginning one. Tom Garbett of DD&B had written a book on corporate advertising for McGraw-Hill. He introduced me to them. Three weeks later I had a contract, a deadline, an obligation. I paced myself. I made a good outline and worked out a format. I turned a maid's room into a den. Every night I worked there. Chapters rolled out, with little revision. I finished on schedule."

Ed Nash's book became the selection of three business book clubs and a success for McGraw-Hill. But Ed also sold the book via mail order himself. "It paid off. I did a pre-publication mail order campaign myself. Between an author's discount, a contribution to advertising by McGraw-Hill and a cash discount I had an order margin of about 55%. I ran ads to position the book . . . pages in Advertising Age and DM News, a double spread in Direct Marketing and a mailing to my own list. I gave one free book for ordering five. One out of 15 ordering took the multiple offer.

"The more I've worked in direct marketing the more my ideas have evolved . . . from mail order to the direct marketing revolution that transformed it. Then I saw the outline of a second direct marketing revolution coming . . . one more dramatic than the first. I began to develop very individual ideas how to be part of it, help bring it about and accelerate it. BBD&O gave me the opportunity to do what I dreamed of . . . to help blend more perfectly than yet done (or even contemplated) the best of general agency, and of direct response know-how and facilities.

"Direct marketing is both an art and a science, with some conflict between creative and numbers people. I've had a creative background but a heavy scientific orientation and a scientific approach. This scientific ability and way of thinking gave me a research ability. I feel the inevitability of more scientific direct marketing . . . and particularly of more scientific decision making in direct marketing. Yet I feel a rapport with the art directors and copy people who fear too much of a scientific approach, preferring a more intuitive one.

"Curiosity makes me always want to know more. Some people think because I wrote a book that I must know it all. I still feel I have more to learn than I know. The key is how much to listen, not how much to talk. A client will sometimes tell me the problem and the solution. I'll give back a headline said to me the day before conversationally. I like variety. I'm stimulated by the different problems of each client. If I had a 100 million dollar client who required that I work with no other client, I'd go crazy.

"I'm enthusiastic about BBD&O and they are about direct marketing. We're not building another version of today's direct response agencies. We're part of a new wave. We're developing the new science of direct marketing. I believe that a variety of personalities is needed in such an organization. Brilliant people often have strong personalities. We want to find, develop and keep them. I believe in strong clients. Each client makes us think.

"We have a different way of working between the parent agency and subsidiary and a different set of job descriptions in BBD&O Direct. Every senior is chosen for ability to teach and every junior for ability to learn. I look for young people. There's a direct marketing talent shortage. I'm starting them as project managers. We only take those who are superlatively good, highly motivated and self-disciplined. Some good ones are coming from the Kleid Collegiate Institute of the Direct Mail/Marketing Educational Foundation.

"With us a project manager works on the project from beginning to end, through the creative process . . . getting hands on experience all the way. The department heads personally work on each project while teaching and guiding the project manager as well. Accounts get more from seniors yet often get innovative help from juniors. We're a critical mass. We have highly creative people who provide stimulation. At BBD&O we have permanent

people from the parent agency's research, media and Marketing Sciences Department. It's almost like R&D in psychological selling. BBD&O Direct will be a brand new kind of agency. We're in a unique position. We have two-person teams. All work is checked with the copy director and creative director.

"A top man from a parent agency assigned to its direct marketing subsidiary may have completely inapplicable experience or simply have no direct marketing orientation. At BBD&O we're getting people with experience selected as an ideal fit. Then I work with each. We learn from each other. My BBD&O research man is learning direct marketing. He's excited about it. We've got some exciting research projects. I hope to announce something important within a year, the results of a direct marketing research project not done before.

"I've gone outside the agency. I learned a lot from the client side. I want to select some of my people from it. Only client experience can show as clearly why clients need a job fast. They don't ask for copy by next Tuesday as a whim but to catch the end of a season or for an equally good reason. Some client organizations are very scientific. I've hired people with that kind of experience.

"I love this business. I love handling coupons. I talk about mail order to anyone. I try to help a retailer, anyone in business I meet, however small, to use mail order and direct marketing. Some people have thriving mail order businesses because their daughters went to school with mine and we met.

"I'm enthusiastic, but who wouldn't be . . . to be able to carry on and expand the tradition of John Caples . . . of scientific mail order and now direct marketing . . . with an organization like BBD&O.

LADIES' AND CHILDREN'S SUIT DEPARTMENT.
Spring and Summer Styles.

Every garment quoted by us this season has been selected with great care and for style and finish cannot be surpassed by any other line of *ready made goods on the market.*

5601 Ladies' Ready Made Wrappers, made of new light prints, yoke lined, has wide circular ruffle stitched in around yoke, no exposed edges. Half belt and large sleeves, Watteau back from yoke. Each. $0.75
Per dozen 8.50

Mail Order Sampler
Seminar VII

Chapter 1
The March Of Time-Life Books

*How it grew to number
one and accumulated sales of
over $2 billion.*

In later years, sales of all book operations of Time Inc. became bigger than sales of any Time Inc. magazine. Then they became two-thirds of the sales of all Time Inc. magazines. And, some years, book profits were more than two-thirds of all magazine profits. Sales from inception, overall, of Time-Life Books have passed the two billion dollar mark.

By 1980, the entire book and associated operation of Time Inc. did half a billion dollars a year in sales . . . more than the entire Time Inc. empire did 40 years after its founding. Time Inc. is probably the largest U.S. book publishing company in sales. It's undisputed as number one in mail order sales of books.

Time-Life Books has replaced and surpassed, in sales volume and profits, Life at its height. Life came out every seven days with seven million circulation. One new book title comes out each eight days. Seven million U.S. homes have Time-Life Books.

Now it all seems obvious . . . the mail order opportunity, the remarkable assets of Time Inc. for a special kind of publishing . . . how to tap the picture image of Life and the news image of Time . . . the faith of subscribers in any future Time-Life publishing venture, their admiration for Life and Time photographers and writers—and how exciting content and presentation of books based on this could be.

But at that point in Time Inc., some did not want a book division. Ten years before, Life had published the first Time Inc. proprietary book. In one year, it sold $3,500,000 worth of one title, Life's Picture History of World War II. In the next nine years, Life published and sold by mail order six more books. Joan Throckmorton put together one, The Life Cookbook. The best did $6,500,000 in one year.

Even in 1961, new single volume titles were being introduced which had been underway before the Book Division. But each Time Inc. book had been a one shot. $6,500,000 in sales one year for the best title had been followed by no sales the next. The picture concept, the size of the book, the possible kind of subject matter was taking form. But the enormity of the potential was not realized. This was the situation when Jerry Hardy arrived at Time Inc. in December 1960 . . . from Doubleday where he had been vice president and advertising director.

First decisions were made almost at once—to sell books in series, in continuity programs, with open-end commitments . . . to ship every other month, on approval, with the entire program cancellable at any time. The editorial concept for any series to be published was determined. It would apply the photo journalism of Life to book publishing.

The Book Division would be run very much like one of Time Inc.'s magazines. Jerry Hardy would be publisher, heading the business side. Norman Ross, a former Life correspondent and editor of Life books would head up the editorial department. Advertising would be proven mail order approaches . . . but in character with the image of Time and Life and of the new editorial project.

Each book would be super-size. Each page would be about double that of the average book. Pictorial content would about equal editorial content. Each book would have about 40,000 words, would be less than 200 pages—yet equal content of 350 pages. The subject of each series would be tried and true. There would be no royalties paid. But up-front money would buy the best quality of writing, editing, layout, art and reproduction ever put into such a series.

The first test mailing of The Life World Library was in spring 1960 . . . to Life and Time subscribers. It was a hit. As the first test results were coming in . . . six months after Jerry . . . Joan Manley arrived—in May 1960. Things were getting hectic. The Book Division started with 70 permanent and temporary employees, almost all with Time Inc. editorial experience.

First rollout mailings to subscriber lists were in late summer. The first two volumes (a total of 450,000 books) were shipped in late 1960. By the end of 1961, another 6 volumes were shipped. The series had 460,000 subscribers. Time International had begun sales in Europe and in South America, and even shipped the first volume . . . printed in ten languages.

The success was so great that ultimately 34 volumes were published . . . arriving every other month . . . taking a subscriber almost 6 years to complete a set. Over all the years, 1,500,000 people subscribed. And it's still going.

In July 1961, the second T-L Books series started . . . The Life Nature Library. Three volumes were published in 1961. Between the two series and several single volume titles, 3,400,000 Time-Life Books were sold worldwide. This was the first real year. For all the magazines and divisions of Time, Inc., the entire 1961 increase in sales over 1960 came from the increase of sales of the book division.

By the end of 1961, the division had 140 employees. By 1962, growth was consolidating. The division sold 8,000,000 books, Time International sold 1,000,000 but was not yet in the black in book publications.

In 1962, The Life World Library expanded. The Life Nature Library reached over 460,000 subscribers. Time International jumped its book sales. The Time Reading Program was started and secured 100,000 subscribers. The sales of the Book Division almost doubled . . . to over 6,000,000 books. Time Inc. bought a textbook company, Silver-Burdett.

Early in 1964, Jerry Hardy became the new publisher of Life magazine. Rhett Austell, who was general manager of Time magazine, became the new publisher of Time-Life Books.

Rhett Austell had gone from the Army in World War II to Williams to Harvard Business School to Time Inc. That was 1950. By 1960, he was general manager of Time magazine. He had spent most of those years in circulation and had absorbed the Time philosophy and way of doing things. Rhett recalls: "Each magazine gave extra value for the money and strove for excellence in production and fulfillment as well as in editorial. In books, too, we always tried to give the customer more than he could reasonably expect. On the promotion end, the idea was to be imaginative and innovative, not hard-sell.

"Back in the 1920's, for example, Roy Larsen, then Time's circulation manager, had put a stamp into each letter sent to solicit a subscription. The heading on the letter was 'We'll pay the freight.' In those days a penny stamp could mail a return order card. It was a great success." In the mid-1950-s, Rhett tried his own version of this promotion, tipping a penny on a letter making a 99-cent short-term offer, asking people to send a dollar and "keep the change." Later, he substituted a miniature pencil—to initial the order card.

"Bernie Auer, who was Circulation Director and my boss, and Bob Fisler, Time's Circulation Promotion Director, were both good at coming up with this sort of thing. It was Bernie who got Al Cole of Reader's Digest to run their first rear-cover gatefold with Time's post-paid return card as the 'gate.' As I recall, we got 50,000 subs. McLean Smith, now circulation director of the new monthly LIFE, had a lot of equally good ideas, as did Velma Francis. Both were great writers, too. Al Cole's son, Bob, worked with us then and suggested that we 'upgrade' our invoices by offering longer terms—a year instead of six months, three years instead of one—with modest price concessions. Upgrading worked beautifully in lengthening the average term of subscriptions.

"When I moved over to Time-Life Books, I found the problems similar, but with new angles. The Time Inc. publishing philosophy carried over into Time-Life Books. The separation of the editorial and business sides existed in only slightly modified form.

"For example, a book series, unlike a magazine subscription, was open-ended. The first book, and indeed the sequence of later titles, so influenced the sales success of a series that the publishing side of T-L Books had a big say in these decisions. Even before that, of course, determination of what new series to publish was a publishing decision based on market testing. The editorial department had veto power, but I can only recall its being used once and that was on a single book—a sequel to 'The Best of Life.'

"The number of books in a series was also a publishing decision dependent on order cost and attrition or drop-off in 'take' from one title in a series to the next. But the editors had to be convinced that the subject justified the longer series and that the editorial quality of each book could be maintained.

"Theoretically, an idea for a new series or title could come from Editorial or Publishing or even from outside the organization. Actually, nothing we ever published came from outside. It would be hard to say whether Editorial or Publishing came up with a specific idea; we were, after all, engaged in a joint effort. At first, the idea had been to use editorial material already created by Time and Life. There was hope of many books coming out of the story and picture files. This never really occurred. In fact, for each series, pictures were shot just for it. Each book was usually authored by two people. One was an outside expert on the subject, the other was a journalist. Supplementing their joint effort was a team of artists, copy editors and researchers. The Time-Life News Service, with all its bureaus around the world, was available for additional research and to check or add material, just as it was for a magazine story.

"When I joined the division in 1964, Time-Life Books had its fourth series in the works—The Life History of the United States. I was helped in planning our further expansion because, while the selection of the early series had been Jerry's and the Editor, Norm Ross' decision, the publishing and editorial team they built was a real bunch of professionals. The interaction was so constant and considerable that I'd be hard put to give the credit for specific accomplishments to specific people. We all did it together.

"Jerry believed that when a new man takes over you should leave him alone; and after I took over and he became publisher of LIFE, I scarcely saw him. Joan Manley and Jack McSweeney were of great help in the transition and, more so, each year as we worked together.

"All during the time I was at Time-Life Books, Joan kept developing her abilities and taking on new responsibilities. She'd say, 'I'm just a peddler,' and the fact is she did and does have a real selling instinct. She was very down-to-earth and had a lot of common sense. Always, she knew what would work and what wouldn't. Plus, she was very good with people, at developing them. She dealt fairly with staff, and they had faith in her.

"During my tour at Time-Life Books, we did all our direct mail in-house. We had three or four copywriters and a couple of artists. We used freelancers only on occasion. We had some fine people. Bea Tolleris, who is now retired, was excellent. Paul Stewart was a talented, young direct mail writer. He became one of the stars and is now head of direct mail promotion of Time-Life Books. Bob Yahn was a very able art director. Writers and art directors worked as a team, and they were always aided by editorial researchers to be certain promotion copy accurately reflected editorial content.

"The direct marketing agency we used most was Wunderman, Ricotta & Kline. We valued WR&K for their general mail order expertise, particularly in media buying. We occasionally used them for direct mail, on a fee basis, to write a direct mail piece, to stimulate our own staff. WR&K was loaded with talent. Among others we worked with were Anatole Broyard (he's doing fine book reviews for the Times now), Tim Horan, a very able account man and, later, Peter Rosenwald who'd had his own firm in London in the mid-sixties.

"The minute it was recognized that Time-Life Books had a startingly successful concept, the pressure was on to develop new series. I always worried, in fact, whether we'd have enough new ideas. By far the most fruitful were those series with a logical appeal to Time and Life subscribers—series with words and pictures married in the way subscribers were accustomed to in the magazines. We weren't too concerned with what others did or had done with series or continuity programs.

"Because we were appealing to Time and Life subscribers, outside space was not a big factor in the early years and usually did not pay out for us. Our own lists provided the bulk of volume and profit. Suiting the product to house lists was the key. We tried working with demographic splits of mass lists using census tract data, but we couldn't make it work. Expanding a series to its natural maximum was the safest way to grow. With the more successful series, however, we did gradually begin to look beyond our own lists. It wasn't easy to do so profitably. Some methods worked. Some didn't. It took innovation and group effort—much of it in cooperation with Wunderman—to think of new approaches and to make them work.

"In the '60's, we began to use a proven technique of Lester's—pre-prints in newspapers. They proved profitable, and we used them widely. This gave us a nice boost. Later, they faded, and it's a truism that not many new selling methods ever improved on their initial success levels, although we could transplant them geographically. We regularly had to come up with something new again. For example, around 1966, we started marketing by telephone. Jerry Broidy was in on that at the beginning and is still in charge of Time-Life Books telephone selling. When Walter Rohrer took over from me to head T-L Books he got particuarly interested.

"Also, around 1966, Time Inc. got into mail order records. I asked Francis M. Scott to come over to Time Inc. from Capitol Records. Scotty was particularly knowledgeable about securing rights. He had worked earlier with Hank Luce on special Time Inc./Capitol projects. Jay Gold was in charge of the editorial end—we accompanied each record set with a book—and Wendell Forbes joined us to work as the sales expert with Scott. The record operation was a separate business from T-L Books and never rivalled it in volume or profits.

"In the mid-1960's, foreign mail order sales of T-L Books and T-L Records began to accelerate. In the early 1960's, Time Inc.'s European operations under Walt Rohrer had translated our ads and tried the offers in Europe. When the international book operation became part of Time-Life Books, Walt came back from Paris as Associate Publisher and Jim Mercer, who had been with us in the States earlier, moved to Amsterdam to head up operations. Later, of course, we also moved into the Far East with Ed Schooler and Nick Ingleton in Tokyo. International sales worked out well under the overall direction of John Millington and later Dave Walsh, in New York, and have since grown to rival Time-Life Books' domestic success.

"In 1968, I had become a group vice president of Time with responsibility for all the Company's book operations (including Little, Brown and New York Graphic), and was succeeded as publisher by Walter Rohrer, who, among other qualifications, was a nephew of that great mail-order book entrepreneur, John Stevenson. Later, in 1975, I went on to American Heritage which, at that time, published Americana and Horizon as well as a good list of books rooted primarily in American history."

Walter Rohrer picks up the story: "At the introduction of the book division, I was fortunate, as an advanced production trainee, to be assigned to Jerry's emerging operation for pro-forma formatting and budgeting. I worked on all of this with Bob Foy, the technical pro, whose quality contributions to Time-Life books was a very major element in the company's effort to do things better.

"Jim Menton succeeded me in this capacity when I was sent to Paris to help establish a production operation for Life International and then to Montreal to perform the same function for Time-Canada.

"I rejoined the book operation upon my return to Paris as general manager of the French company responsible for production and distribution operations in Europe. The book operations, at that time, were in their infancy but the potential was obviously great. The big job, beyond finding suitable suppliers for what were to be mass-produced titles, was one of rationalizing in terms of length and scheduling the many language editions to permit co-productions. We dealt with English (spelling), French and German translations under Harmut Belling, a brilliant German expatriot to France, and he relied on the various licensees in the other language areas for the translations. As we were to also produce their editions in Italian, Icelandic, Dutch, Swedish, Norwegian and Finnish, it is a great understatement to say that he was a very busy young man. Somehow, it all worked and Time-Life Books International also was off the ground.

"After a period in New York in the company's production department, I was asked by Charlie Bear to head up the international book operation and I jumped at the opportunity.

"I was very lucky. John Snedaker and Walter Howard had, through trial and error inherent in any start-up operation, laid the ground work for what was to become a very successful operation in Australia and France, and later in Germany, the U.K. and Japan. My job was basically one of stretching out the winners and cutting short the losers. As always was the case at Time Inc., wonderfully competent people contributed greatly at every step.

"After several years, the international division, per se, was eliminated with each profit center—Time International, Life International and the book operations merged with its North American 'parent.' At this juncture, I became Rhett's associate publisher responsible for the international as well as U.S. sales and promotion.

"When Rhett moved up to a group vice-presidency responsible for books, broadcast and records, I coattailed my way to becoming the publisher of the Book Division. On a clear trend upwards, it was not hard to achieve positive results from one year to the next. Inheriting $24,000,000 in gross profits from sales established in prior years in the United States alone, we were able to generate something like $80,000,000 worldwide in 1969, and something in the neighborhood of $10,000,000 in contributions after currently expending $15,000,000 in promotion costs. I am sure these figures have been dwarfed since then.

"During this period, the magazines were having their troubles. Life, feeling the tremendous pressure of television on packaged goods advertising, was losing close to what Time was making. Sports Illustrated was not consistently profitable and Fortune, following capital goods investment, was capricious

"Time-Life Books was probably #2 to Time magazine in profitability but there was pressure on all of us because of Life and the generally soft magazine advertising condition.

"While we in the book division had a relative tiger by the tail and, of course, wanted to take fullest advantage of it, we couldn't make the investments in growth that we wished due to the general corporate condition. An example of this would be the fact that virtually all of our direct mail efforts were restricted to the house list.

"At the time, I thought that we were missing a marvelous opportunity to grow the division and I probably made myself intolerable resisting what I felt to be inordinate conservatism. In hindsight, the temporary and understandable slowdown of those years obviously didn't stunt the growth of the business.

"As a Californian, I guess I felt that I had to get the siren call out of my system and I joined CRM/Boise Cascade in Del Mar, the founders of Psychology Today. As was abundantly clear, Joan Manley was to be the next publisher. I have described her as a Yankee peddler from California, embodying the very best qualities of both. Her success and popularity are deserved and really speak for themselves. While no organization has a monopoly on brains, Time Inc. does possess a unique blend of talent *and* gentility that seems to introduce a multiplier to each quality. Dick Munro and Ralph Davidson, both friends, are perfectly suited to sustain this. It is a superb company and my thirteen years there are a very fond memory."

During 1968, The Time-Life Library of Art was introduced. The Life Library of Photography was launched early in 1970. The Alva Museum Replicas Inc., a subsidiary of The New York Graphic Society, by now had a line of some 1,000 hard-finished reproductions of sculpture works of art and museum jewelry, and sales were increasing substantially. The Seven Arts Society and The Book Find Club had been acquired. The Fortune Book Club for businessmen and the Sports Illustrated Book Club started in 1971.

By now, Time Inc. had minority interest in five foreign book-publishing enterprises. There was Andre Deutsch in England, and Editions Robert Laffont in France, Rowohlt Taschenbuch-Verlag in Germany, and Salvat Club de Ediciones S.A. in Spain. Organizacion Editorial in Mexico handled warehousing and shipping for Time-Life Books. All were prospering with much interchange of Time Inc. book properties.

Little Brown and Company, in Boston, was the largest of the wholly owned book companies and doing very well.

In February 1970, Time-Life Records introduced The Swing Era, the first of a series of book-and-record albums. To promote it, a flexible seven-inch demonstration recording was bound into magazine ads and inserted into mailing pieces. Over 33 million sample recordings were distributed, larger than any record made. By now, Time-Life Records may have distributed well over a hundred million of this one recording. In 1970, Time-Life Records introduced the Beethoven Bicentennial Collection with a 276-page book on Beethoven. In 1973, the Time-Life Records Division was integrated with Time-Life Books under Joan Manley.

The Encyclopedia of Gardening had been launched in 1971. In 1972 came The American Wilderness. In 1973 came The Old West, The Art of Sewing and the global version of the Wilderness books.

During those years, Anatole Broyard, now a book critic for the New York Times, was a copywriter for Wunderman, Ricotta & Kline. He recalls working with Time-Life Books. "Editorially, Time-Life Books did a superb job in nature, science, art pictures and in cookbooks. Management was very able. Joan Manley was terrific, a brilliant woman. She knew when to delegate. Carl Jaeger (now president of Time-Life Books) brought all the talents of a first class football quarterback. He was one, gave that feeling and always referred to himself as the QB. Carl Jaeger was very experienced and he always made shrewd decisions. He could read the opposition's defenses and then find the receiver with the ball.

In 1974, a new recruit came to Time-Life Books, with a different background than most . . . in physics and engineering . . . later as apprentice to David Ogilvy, next the assistant to Dave Margolies, a vice president and mail order deal maker of Columbia House—and then a co-owner of a highly successful business in collectibles which the partners had built up to $6,000,000 a year and sold out to The Franklin Mint. He was Roger Lourie.

Roger was 34 and learning Chinese. He spoke French and German fluently, and Russian less so. He had had a happy year after selling out. He had bought a farm in Connecticut, a co-op apartment in the city and twin Porsches for himself and his wife. They both had spent almost six months in Russia. He had spent a frustrating year trying to buy a company to his satisfaction but had not found one. Now he was ready to work.

For his own company he had worked 80 to 90 hours a week. For Time-Life Books he cut down to 60 or 70. His first job was to get underway the new "Home Repair and Improvement" series, and by January 1975, he did. His second was to launch "The Life Pictorial History of World War II", which was introduced in January 1976. Both were tremendous successes. He recalls:

"1974, 1975 and 1976 were good years for Time-Life Books because of the synergistic accumulation of talent, both on the editorial and publishing sides of TLB. Usually one side is up when the other is down and they compensate, but in the mid-seventies both teams had very heavy hitters in the lineup. It was a time of good games and strong players.

"And so were 1977 and 1978, with one problem." Roger remembers: "In '77 and '78, there was a top harvest of all that had gone before. But for new offers, these were the drought years. There were no major new series, no new hits. Proposed new series failed and there was a paucity of new concepts. Overall, the business hit its highest subscriber numbers because of the successful book and record introductions of the mid-70's; but without new successful products, levelling-off was bound to happen."

"By then, the internal editorial costs of producing a Time-Life Book had risen to between $200,000 and $250,000. For 20 volumes this could mean a $5,000,000 investment. Stonehenge could have a series produced for about 40 percent of this cost," explains Lourie.

"Tree Communications, a free-lance editorial group, had produced 'The Family Creative Workshop' series which did not work, and 'The Encyclopedia of Collectibles' which was, at best, a moderate hit. It contained no prices, to avoid becoming outdated. But collectors wanted to know what was worth what. Then four tests of new book series produced by Stonehenge Press under John Conova's direction were scheduled, with more en route.

Joan Manley took vigorous steps to develop products, prod the editors for new ideas and keep overhead under control. The move to Alexandria helped decrease costs. Roger Lourie was put in charge of a new group whose objective was the development of new products in the non-book area. "In 1977, Manley bought the Book-of-the-Month Club. Then she started Stonehenge Press as a new subsidiary of Time-Life Books. Stonehenge bought editorial products, without going through the expensive Time-Life editorial group.

"As another solution, the Time-Life Books European editors in London produced 'The Great Cities' series. It was an unsuccessful series in the United States, but offered hope in Europe. There were more cities with character there and the titles were more attuned to European interest than American. In the U.S., cities like San Francisco or New Orleans had more of a chance, but the editors were not seriously considering them early on in the publishing sequence. To prove the point, we spent a quick $15,000 for title search to compare the choice of various lead cities in the U.S. San Francisco was the number one choice by a country mile. When the London editorial group finally produced a San Francisco book, it came out too late to dramatically affect the profitability of 'Great Cities.' Additionally, it didn't catch the spirit of San Francisco.

"Moving to Alexandria resulted in substantially less people, as many preferred to stay in New York. This reduced overhead and made the game more fun and the stakes higher for those of us who followed Joan's bold venture. In Alexandria, there was more physical closeness between the editorial side and the business side, which I believe resulted in perhaps more mutual understanding of each other's problems."

In June 1977, Lourie had become manager of new product development and a ranking member of the industry's Committee on Ethical Business Practice, later its imaginative chairman. His TLB operation consisted of the "idea people." "I did everything to motivate my team and instill enthusiasm. I found hungry people and tried to create a 'blossoming' atmosphere. This is typical of Time Inc. and simply a continuation of the philosophy of Henry Luce, who created an atmosphere of comradery and team spirit within the corporate philosophy.

"One result was Time-Life Learning. It utilizes audio-visual equipment and the expertise of Time-Life's editors in a subject matter. What we did was merely create a different outlet for the editorial data that was contained in a Time-Life Book series. Through agreements with schools and colleges, we put on slide and tape seminars of the material in a specific series, such as photography or cooking.

"I left Time-Life Books in 1980, reluctantly but necessarily, because Grolier's offer was too enticing: a very significant increase in salary and the chance to move from operating management to first-line control of decision-making." He is now owner of his own book publishing business, Devin-Adair.

Roger Lourie considers that the quality of people and the methods of management at Time-Life are unsurpassed. "It is refined, thoughtful and participative. That is why Joan Manley gets so much out of her staff. She knows how to motivate with a sophistication that goes beyond mere financial compensation."

"Typical of the meticulousness that is a hallmark of the Books Division is the testing program. To cite a few examples: When Joan stepped up and John McSweeney began to sign the publisher's letter in place of Joan, the signatures were split-run tested. There was no difference, as could be expected. When the Photography series came out, a predominant green color was tested versus a predominant yellow. Yellow, associated by the American public with photography, won by a considerable margin. Both these results could have been expected, but TLB chose the characteristic route of testing to be certain.

"Stan Rapp had the idea, in 1974, of offering 'The High Sierras' as the lead book of the 'American Wilderness' series to those potential buyers living in and near the mountain states. Response was superior to offers using general lead titles. This approach worked best of all in the Northwest with 'The Cascades' and 'High Sierras.' 'The Ozarks' and 'New England Wilds' similarly were successful in their regions. In typical thorough Time-Life fashion, these regional tests took three years to finally prove themselves. Then this approach was extended to the 'Gardening' series: mailings for 'Gardening' highlighted the plants which were most appropriate to the gardener's area.

"Time-Life Records is playing a more important role today than in the past. There is a better overall profit margin and the investment return is usually higher with records than with books. Very important has been the development of the overseas business. It was up to 50% of sales and perhaps 65% profits. The Book of the Month Club in the U.S. and similar national clubs overseas have big potential. But most important still are the two basic Time-Life assets.

"One asset dates back to Henry Luce and Britton Hadden. They said: 'We will hire good people and treat them like gentlemen. We will give worthy employment benefits. We will not rigidly stifle anyone's ideas. We will measure results.' They created in their magazine business the attitudes and manners of their Hotchkiss and Yale backgrounds, and engrained them in the organization by hiring their classmates.

"Much of this attitude has remained through the years and carried over to Time-Life Books. You are allowed personal days off, beyond sick days and vacation, for no specific reason. Unless you constantly overspend, expense accounts are rarely questioned. It is assumed that you will not exceed what is reasonable. This attitude permeates the organization. You are treated with intelligence and sensitivity.

"The other asset is Joan Manley. I am impressed with her decency and her sense of fairness. She is intelligent, alert and straightforward, blunt, ethical and loyal. She is interested in her people, their problems and careers. She gives a good deal of rein and allows people to do their jobs with little second guessing. She helps them select the target and then lets them reach it by themselves."

The overwhelming majority of book sales of Time Inc. have been under Joan Manley's direction. She has assembled the big majority of the team that sells them. To date, Time-Life Books has adapted to every possible medium, to selling all over the world, to use of every possible effective and applicable new technology—and to living with change. In 1980 and 1981, it suffered from the strength of the dollar which reduced foreign earnings translated into dollars and high interest in the U.S. A health series of books was not profitable. Earnings were off, but the basic strength remained. There was a strong future potential

in international markets. The team approach worked well. Joan Manley does not wish to be more prominent than her teammates. But she is in charge . . . responsible for maximum success in good times and survival in bad.

Joan Manley is in the life extension business, the offer replacement business and the offer addition business. It's cost watching, overhead shaving and risk avoidance. It's making stop or go, expand or contract decisions. It's interpreting mail counts and economics forecasts. It's keeping up with the ever-changing science of mail order and applying it. It's using most effectively the wealth of talent available to her. It's the biggest job any woman has in business.

There are a dozen other stories in this book of people who worked for or with Time Inc. Each of these helped me understand better the success of Time-Life Books and its impact on all direct marketing. Most important is the story of Jerry Hardy, who founded it.

Elsewhere in this book is the story of Joan Throckmorton, principal owner of the most successful direct marketing agency owned by a woman; Larry Chait, who owned one of the biggest direct marketing agencies and then became one of the most successful consultants; George Wiedemann, president of Grey Direct, owned by a top twenty general agency; Sandy Clark, head of Clark Direct Marketing, one of the first mail order agencies to provide computer modeling to clients; Tom Ryan, a top consultant in people research and Orlan Gaeddert, the statistical scientist. All came from Time Inc.

There's the story of Wendell Forbes, the great teacher of and consultant in magazine subscription selling; of Leo Yochim, who produced the first commercial computer letters, for Time; of Rose Harper, whose Kleid Company has worked with Time-Life Books since inception and for Time Inc. long before; and of Lester Wunderman's WR&K, which has been the major agency for Time-Life Books for 21 years; and Eva-Tone Soundsheets, which for many years provided the soundsheets with which Time-Life Records sampled The Swing Era and other series.

Time Inc.'s mail order know-how started with the 12,000 subscriptions Roy Larson secured for the launch of Time in 1923. It constantly grew with Time's circulation and in 1930 got the 30,000 subscriptions that launched Fortune. In 1936, it got the over 1,000,000 subscriptions that launched Life. Mail order know-how of Time Inc. pioneered scientific magazine subscription selling. It innovated people research and statistical research, computer modeling and computer letters ... selling subscriptions via telephone marketing and later by TV.

Time Inc. contributed tremendous assets, talent, skills and related experience to the mail order success of Time-Life Books. But the methods of Time-Life Books have since changed the overall operation of Time Inc., and even the concept of magazines to publish. Time Inc. successfully tested and launched Money and Discover magazines, much as if they were new book series of Time-Life Books. And in 1982 Time-Inc.'s mail order know-how was changing the form of Time-Life Books itself, sharply cutting down older operations, revitalizing others, laying the ground work for quite new directions.

Time has taught mail order know-how to many, who have then taught the rest of us. For over 30 spring and fall seasons, executives of Time-Life Books have lectured at the New York University direct marketing course. Jerry Hardy conducted it, before Nat Ross. Joan Manley lectured there. So did John McSweeney, now chairman of the board, and Carl Jaeger, now president. And almost every season since The Direct Marketing Idea Exchange started, a Time-Life executive has talked there. At most Spring and Annual Conferences of the DMMA, Time-Life Books executives talk on latest, more effective direct marketing methods.

Their lectures and talks are on tape and their articles are often available in back issues. Choose your subject: International Mail Order; Efficient Mail Order Fulfillment; New Product Development; New Product Testing; Financial Management in Mail Order; Copy Testing; Producing a TV Commercial; and a lot more. A Time-Life Books executive will teach you, in your home.

In the Help Source Section are details on how to get tapes and reprints of talks, lectures and articles by Time-Life Books and Time Inc. executives and alumni on a wide variety of direct marketing subjects, mostly from Hoke Communications.

Chapter 2
The Stenciler

*A sea captain, who built a
house in 1797, put her into
the mail order business.*

She originally trained for and looked forward to a career as an opera singer. Financial problems at home forced her to give up her music career plans. Then she used another artistic flair—to become a decorator. And then a sea captain—who, in 1797, built a house in East Hampton, Long Island—put her into the mail order business.

It all came about when her first major decorating project, in 1959, was to redecorate the home the captain had built. To do it she researched early American wall designs and, particularly, the early American art of stenciling. She found it widely used in Colonial decorating throughout the entire house.

For the East Hampton house, Adele Bishop copied eleven stencil designs from Early American wall designs she researched. Doing so gave the house authenticity and charm. In decorating the house and using stenciling, Adele Bishop made a discovery. She discovered that the range of stencil design could be greatly enlarged by using transparent plastic.

Adele's partner in the decorating business was Cile Lord. As they did more houses, more and more they built their decorating around stenciling. Their work attracted notice as they became acknowledged authorities on Early American stenciling as an interior decoration art form.

The next step was to start a small mail order business, which Adele Bishop and Cile Lord did. From the beginning, it was a two-step mail order business. Originally, a brochure was offered for 25¢ which offered kits of tools, designs, instruction and selected items.

When John Calloway, Adele's husband, retired in 1970 he began to help. He had been in sales promotion in the New York office of the Los Angeles Times-Mirror Corp., in the magazine publishing division.

They first operated the business from John and Adele's country house deep in the woods of Vermont. John says he's worked harder than he ever did before and that, even now, he's working 70 hours a week. All three "worked like hell" to get the business started, under the name Bishop & Lord. The business is now completely owned by Adele Bishop and John Calloway.

Adele and Cile kept working on their decorating business. Adele spent much time in developing improved methods of stenciling. Cumulative improvements made the kits more desirable. Stenciling, itself, began to be a favorite subject in the women's shelter and craft magazines; and Adele and Cile became authorities. Viking Press contracted with Adele and Cile to do a book on stenciling.

Researching and writing the book was time consuming, but the effort was worth it. "The Art of Decorative Stenciling", 199 pages, had 315 illustrations. Fifty were in color. There were 100 ready-to-trace designs. It was indexed with supply sources and a bibliography. Eight stencil projects were featured, in order of increasing difficulty.

"The Art of Decorative Stenciling" was a big success. The New York Times, The Christian Science Monitor, Early American Life, even Home Furnishings Daily, strongly recommended it. It was called "the definitive book on stenciling." Interest in stenciling was mounting. A number of publications ran articles on stenciling. In 1977, Adele and Cile were featured in eight different magazine articles. Mail orders came in from the articles. The book and its publicity increased their business substantially.

Stenciling had formerly been in vogue during the Art Nouveau and Tiffany era. But now it was being used in many forms for house decorating. By now, it had clearly gained widespread interest as a recognized and basic and popular art skill. It became an "in" craft. Still more editors wanted feature stories.

And in 1977, after seven long, hard working years, the little firm took the big plunge in mail order and dramatically increased its advertising. The firm ran mail order ads in eleven magazines, including Yankee, Early American Crafts, McCall's Needlework Crafts, Good Housekeeping and American Home. The ads offered the book in hard cover, and later in paperback. The ads featured a saving on a combination offer of book and kit which got a good percentage of orders for both. Other kits and items were also featured. The average order jumped. Adele Bishop, Inc. began running in more magazines.

In 1980, after years of doing business from their house, Adele and John established "a real mail order house" in a building in Manchester, Vermont. "We've kept our mail order business as simple as possible," says John. "It's big enough for real necessities. But there is no clutter. There are no useless departments. Our advertising is simple. Basically, we run a simple catalog inquiry ad in major magazines."

Adele's and John's abilities have proven a great combination. Adele's special knowledge and design talent made the business possible. John's retirement added his marketing skills and time to make the business grow. Adele had to give up most of her personal decorating to concentrate on the business.

Adele has been called "the foremost stenciler in America." She is a perfectionist in developing the technique of stenciling. Her concept is to combine with it quality, clarity and simplicity . . . and to make stenciling easier and faster. The mail order business and the book came out of long years in professional stenciling.

Designs were unusual, found by extensive research. Instructions were excellent. Each product, each component of each kit sold by mail order was painfully developed professionally. Even now, forty percent of customers are other professionals while sixty percent are beginners.

Adele keeps coming up with new ideas for stenciling . . . inside and out . . . on walls and floor . . . on textiles and tile . . . and in every room in the house . . . how to stencil doors and draperies . . . armoires and flower pots . . . baskets and bedspreads. She has projects for mailboxes and wastebaskets, shutters and pillows, mantels and placemats. She has some for tinware and woodenware . . . barn siding and book covers . . . old-fashioned bathtubs and beams.

If you prefer, you can stencil her designs on beams, boxes, buckets, book covers, garbage cans, mantels, molding, milk cans, tinware . . . or on trunks, trays, moldings or furniture of all types. The stencils are packaged with complete instructions. There are different kits from simple to complex. There are designs for a wide variety of projects . . . from Early American to Folk Art, Pennsylvania Dutch to Japanese designs, and her new quilt design stencils and Shelburne Museum (VT) stencils.

With each kit, Adele includes a free stenciling course (separately it sells for $3.95) and a sheet of specific instructions for each kit.

Now stencils are printed on Mylar, with indelible inked-on register marks. Adele considers Mylar superior to stencil board, waxed manila paper, architect's linen or acetate. They are larger than most for larger designs. Adele's brushes are 100% China hog bristle. Her Japan paints are packaged in 1-ounce jars in six primary colors, and also in 8-ounce jars in a variety of colors.

Adele Bishop now carries 18 stencil kits totaling 127 designs. The Pennsylvania Dutch and Deluxe Stencil Art are her only 2 precut stencil cuts. Adele feels that the true stenciler should cut his own stencils for a truly original undertaking. Adele has become very excited about fabric painting. She carries two sets (8 colors each) of Stencil Fab® paint and a special fabric paint brush.

Adele Bishop, Inc. now has a four-color catalog, 8½"x11", of 24 pages on heavy stock, done in taste and issued twice a year. Adele Bishop, Inc. currently does over $300,000 a year in mail order business. In addition, there are royalties from Viking Press and Adele still does some professional decorating. But the business is also a source of satisfaction.

John Calloway says: "I can try my own marketing ideas, uncorking creative concepts a conservative employer might not approve. We could get out of New York City and live in the country." It gives Adele the opportunity to develop her own decorative ideas beyond the jobs for individual customers.

What Adele and John really enjoy is travel. Adele's great talent is her flair for design selection. She has always obtained her best ideas from research. She has already been researching museums in London for old stencil designs. Now they want to travel all over the world to research the great museums.

Travel, often necessary in mail order, is one of its more pleasant perks.

Note: Adele Bishop, Inc. is located at Box 557, Manchester, Vermont 05254; phone (802) 362-3537.

Chapter 3
Direct Mail's Greatest Authority

*How a kid entrepreneur, printer
and lettershop owner made it.*

He's one of the most prolific writers of direct mail advertising. He launched and headed the creative graphics division of the biggest printer in the world. He was creative director and vice president of Franklin Mint and launched and headed for them—with overnight success—their first limited edition graphics operation.

He's been an executive editor, is an expert on catalogs and is a direct marketing consultant sought after all over the world. Over thirty years, he collected 20 tons of clippings and printed material about direct mail, mail order and direct marketing, probably the largest single collection of direct mail and catalog samples anywhere. Out of it he distilled a 1,538-page book, the most encyclopedic ever written on direct mail.

His name is Richard S. (or "Dick") Hodgson. He is often considered the ultimate authority in direct mail. His "Direct Mail and Mail Order Handbook" has for years been required reading for top mail order executives. He can help anyone who wants to use direct mail for any purpose. His story will tell you why.

In the depression . . . in the little town of Breckenridge, Minnesota . . . a little kid started a little conglomerate in direct marketing—before it existed. "I was the son of a dentist and I didn't want to work all that hard." When Dick was twelve he began to sell magazines for Curtis Publishing Company. Then his business network began and continued until he found out some things about girls that interested him more—at sixteen . . . and he sold out.

"I started to sell Curtis Publications (The Saturday Evening Post, Ladies' Home Journal and Country Gentleman) when I was eight. I became 'District Agent' for Breckenridge when I was ten. I had ten kids working for me on commission. I got an override.

"We began to deliver handbills for the Breckenridge movie theater. We delivered handbills for a lot of other local merchants, but I liked the Ridge Theater best because they paid us off in theater 'comps' so we could go to the movies free . . . and that was a big plus in getting my 'crew' to give up their other activities and spend their free time delivering handbills.

"Our handbills pulled in attendance for the theater so well it cancelled advertising in the local paper. The newspaper publisher got so mad he got an ordinance passed in Breckenridge against door-to-door distribution of handbills. I got another idea. I put out a weekly mimeographed publication, a daily reminder.

"The 'daily reminder' was called 'The Gateway Examiner.' Along with all of the other work, I wrote most of the ads and designed them. But probably the most important experience I got was selling the ads to the local merchants. I count that experience, along with the experience in selling magazines door-to-door, as probably the most important ingredient in being able to write copy that sells.

"I wrote it and printed it on a mimeograph. I printed ads in it and put printed handbills as inserts inside it. Then my kids went around and sold a lifetime subscription for one cent. All I was

interested in was getting every homeowner in Breckenridge (and Wahpeton, North Dakota, which was just across the Red River) to sign up so I could provide 'paid circulation' to the entire community.

"My 'crew' kept the pennies, but I ended up with a 2,000 name mailing list of names and addresses (which turned out to be the only such mailing list 'in town'). Then I got another idea."

At 14, Dick Hodgson started the Gateway Advertising Service. "I began to do mailings and to write them. I had an Elliot addressing machine, a typewriter and a mimeograph. I became a copywriter for my local advertising. I wrote letters to pull insurance leads for the local insurance agent, to pull new car prospects for the auto dealer and whatever for whomever.

"I don't know if my copy pulled or not. Advertisers kept buying space; but it must have been pretty hard for a soft-hearted merchant to turn down a 12-year-old kid who peddled space at 25¢ a column inch, wrote the copy, designed the ad and gave credit.

"Almost from the age of twelve I started to collect examples of printing. I fell in love with printing, maybe because I had uncles and aunts who were printers. I began to read about direct mail. I became a compulsive clipper of anything that might be useful. I kept it all, even when, at 16, I sold my equipment and business to someone from out of town. And I never lost my love for printing."

Dick graduated from high school in Breckenridge in 1942. Then, instead of accepting a journalism scholarship to Northwestern University, he spent a year at the North Dakota State School of Science. "I took a course called Printing-Journalism. I had enlisted in a special program of the Marines which permitted me to remain in school for a year. So I postponed college. I got a paid job editing the NDSSS newspaper and working as a printer's devil." He kept collecting clippings.

Then he joined the Marines, taking an officers training course. Under Navy Program V-12, he was enrolled in a liberal arts and science course at Gustavus Adolphus College and then in Western Michigan College. "I edited the school newspapers and yearbook at Gustavus Adolphus, worked on the paper and yearbook at Western Michigan and published a special Navy-Marine Yearbook. I got my commission in August 1945.

"After the two colleges, we were given additional training at Parris Island, South Carolina; Camp Lejeune, North Carolina and Quantico, Virginia." Dick then served as a Marine combat correspondent in North China and then became a Marine radio correspondent. "I supplied radio and press coverage of two atomic bomb tests at Bikini and later of two more atomic bomb tests in Nevada." In between, Dick kept reading anything about direct mail and kept clipping.

"In 1947, when I got out of the Marines, I first went to Chicago, where I was an editor of the coin machine section of The Billboard. Here I learned what writing was all about. A great editor, Dick Schreiber, taught me how to edit in my mind as I was writing so the first thing out of the typewriter could go into print. I learned to squirrel away facts about everything.

"One job was to fill two tabloid-size pages weekly with news about popcorn! Popcorn vending machines were big. We had to come up with editorial copy to surround popcorn vending machine ads. There is not much news about popcorn. We created it by tough research and diligent writing.

"I became an associate editor of Tide (an advertising trade magazine) after leaving The Billboard. I covered industrial advertising out of Chicago. I took courses in journalism, publishing and advertising writing at Northwestern University when I was working for The Billboard and Tide. Now my scrap book really began to grow.

"In 1949, I went back to Breckenridge as public relations director of the North Dakota State School of Science. I also had a job as an announcer at KBMW. A linotype instructor died and I took his place. I then gave a course on advertising and journalism. To do so, I clipped anything, anywhere in direct mail and advertising.

"I was recalled to the Marines in 1950. My first assignment was creating 'Recruiting Aids'. I wrote direct mail pieces to get enlistees. I later became Radio-TV Chief for the Marine Corps. I produced and announced seven weekly network radio shows and got involved with network television.

"When I got out of the Marines again in 1952, I was hired by what is now Crain Communications to develop a new magazine, Advertising Requirements . . . the 'Popular Mechanics' of advertising and sales promotion. I worked there with two superbright communicators, G.D. Crain, Jr. and Sid Bernstein. They taught me how to apply principles of communications from one medium to another.

"Advertising Requirements had a section on direct mail. I wrote about big users of direct mail. I joined the DMMA and became active in it and met others in the business. I was active in the founding of the Mail Advertising Club of Chicago (now they call it the 'Chicago Association of Direct Marketing'). Later, I became president of it.

"The group which put the club together included some of direct mail's most brilliant people—Charlie Downes of Abbott Laboratories (one of the all-time greatest), Bob Stone, Roy Rylander, Bob Enlow, Alan Drey, Dick Trenbeth and others. They knew everything about direct mail, and I was like a sponge at every meeting we had, absorbing all of the shop talk.

"I was editor of Advertising Requirements from the beginning . . . and then executive editor of Industrial Marketing. I stayed with Advertising Publications, Inc. for approximately eight years. My collection of clippings became a space problem, including by now lots of articles I had written, myself.

"In January 1960, I joined Andy Andrews in Boston to set up a new mail order publishing company, American Marketing Services, Inc. We syndicated direct mail formats, published a monthly idea service called 'Ad Man's Alley' and published art clip books. I was president of this company. It was an idea business. People came to us with problems. We came up with answers. We created sweepstakes or whatever concept was needed.

"I became, for a short time, an account executive with Andy's advertising agency, American Mail Advertising. It handled very large national companies—but for direct mail only. Later, Andy concentrated on fund raising.

"I kept collecting clippings. Now I was arranging them seriously, writing my comments and whipping them into far better shape. Andy was interested. We started putting together reference materials. I was writing articles and giving speeches. I put out six monographs for Andy, each on an area of direct mail advertising. We came up with the title, wrote them and printed them. We had plans for a continuing series. They attracted the attention of Dartnell who then asked me to create 'The Direct Mail and Mail Order Handbook' . . . and gave me a good contract.

"I had written an article about R.R. Donnelley, the biggest printer in the world—who then offered me a job. I left Andy Andrews to accept it, at a time when business had fallen off for Andy and the move worked out well for both of us. First, I took

six months off to do more extensive research for the Handbook. At Donnelley, I started as advertising and sales promotion manager. Then I set up the Creative Graphics Division and became its director.

"Donnelley did every kind of large printing job. It had every kind of printing equipment. It had catalog expertise. It printed the big Sears, Ward, Speigel and Alden's catalogs down to nursery catalogs like Breck's and Interstate Nurseries. I worked on Breck's then and still work for Breck's as consultant. It was here I got my catalog know-how.

"R.R. Donnelley edited magazines—external house organs—huge circulation ones. A lot of times we created them—submitted the idea, wrote it and published it. I edited the Plymouth Traveler and Adventure Road (for Amoco).

"Donnelley was the only printing company big enough to do its own fullscale R&D. It kept coming up with exciting new technology like automatic jogging. It developed new ink technology. It played a big part in bringing printing into the computer age.

"It used the full range of printing processes—rotogravure and letterpress, offset. It was the largest magazine printer. It printed Look, Life and Time. R.R. Donnelley is huge. It's probably at least five times larger than the next largest printer. Today it does over a billion dollars in sales.

"When I was there the catalogs suddenly got big as a source of business. Donnelley was perfect for me. I loved printing. I was a kid in the candy shop. I liked the creative side. I could use my printing know-how and vastly increase it. I could write. I could meet everyone that mattered in direct mail.

"I wrote more articles and gave more speeches. I attended all the DMMA meetings. I accelerated my clipping. My book had taken 15 years of gestation. After I had taken off six months full-time to work on it, I continued two more years working at my job in the daytime and on my book nights and weekends. In 1964, Dartnell published the first edition.

"Next, in 1972, I joined the Franklin Mint as creative director and vice president. By this time I was buried in clippings. I moved ten tons of files to Pennsylvania. While at home I finished a second edition of The Direct Mail and Mail Order Handbook. Almost immediately I was thrown into a brand new project there. Joe Segel had promised a meeting of stock analysts that within 18 months Franklin would be the largest marketer in the world of limited edition prints. I was assigned the job of organizing and launching the Franklin Mint Gallery of American Art.

"It was the first new venture of Franklin Mint outside of the basic coin and medal business. The average sale of a limited edition offer was $500. We did $1,000,000 to $2,500,000 for an average edition. The field was small but Joe was right. Within 18 months, Franklin was the biggest in it in the world. Now the direction at Franklin, for this division, is to sell framed prints.

"All my past experience proved invaluable. It was exciting working with Joe Segel. He was imaginative, driving and inspiring. It was very satisfying to create a new division from scratch. But he was easing off. He left Franklin before I did. I stayed two and a half years there. I would have liked to stay, but I became even more tempted to leave.

"A lot of things happened. The second edition of The Direct Mail and Mail Order Handbook—a lot more elaborate and bigger than the first—came out. Dartnell promoted it widely, and me. In 1974, the DMMA asked me to fill in at a seminar for Ed Mayer, Jr. I had participated in seminars in the past. Ed Mayer, Jr. and I thought a good deal alike. I felt at home. Ed was a lot sicker than any of us realized. He missed more seminars. At the last minute, I'd get a call. Finally, he couldn't continue and I had to take over.

"At the same time, I was approached by Tom Foster to become a consultant for the Foster & Gallagher catalog business. It was too much work to do unless I went into consulting full-time. There was ample indication of substantial 'consulting income' from other clients. I had royalties and seminar fees. I had no risk. It was irresistable and I regretfully left Franklin, but have never regretted it since.

"I've never promoted my consulting. Requests for service came so regularly I've had to turn down most. I don't have time to handle any more . . . although word of mouth helped by my books and seminars kept getting still more inquiries.

"In the U.S. I do twelve basic seminars a year, with Paul Sampson. In 1976, I did my first catalog seminar. For the DMMA I do two catalog seminars in the U.S. and one in Europe. I do four seminars a year at Dobel in the Black Forest, in Germany. I'm in partnership with Albert Gerardi. He puts on the seminars, promotes them and translates for me into German. We've had 26, so far. In addition, I conduct as many as 10 seminars a year in Europe for various other sponsors including Europe's largest direct marketers. I do some special seminars for the DMMA on other subjects. I do a mini-seminar or participate in panels at DMMA conferences here and abroad.

"In Europe, we get primarily business owners and first level management. In the U.S., attendees vary a lot. We get owners of major companies, lower echelon people, copywriters, managers and new entrepreneurs. In the catalog seminars we go into sophisticated graphics and production. I steer smallest operators, even those with little catalogs, away from it—and into the Basic Seminars. Then they can come back and benefit from the Catalog Seminars."

Dick Hodgson has also written four more full-scale books: "How to Promote Meeting Attendance"; "How to Use a Tape Recorder"; "Direct Mail Showmanship"; and "Direct Mail in the Political Process." "In addition, I've written shorter manuals, including the DMMA's 'How to Work with Mailing Lists'."

But the "Direct Mail and Mail Order Handbook" is the giant. It's extraordinarily encyclopedic, the final pay-off of the biggest direct marketing scrapbook of all time—edited and interpolated by a natural writer, pro editor, prolific promoter and seasoned direct marketer. Sales go on and on, with over 30,000 volumes to date . . . and now at $50. It's even been translated into Japanese.

"Now I'm working on a two-volume set—because in the last edition we had to leave a lot out. There was no room. The set will take me two more years, partly because I'm also writing a 'Catalog Manual' for Dartnell. This will be 400 pages, loose-leaf and really be a seminar in print—as I do the Catalog Seminars in Europe."

Dick Hodgson's consulting business has meanwhile sky-rocketed. He operates under the name Sargeant House—both as a consulting business and to do research for his books and articles. He's constantly buying books, merchandise, subscribing to magazines and newsletters—and taking notes and clippings. "I suspect I have the largest private library of books on direct mail and allied subjects anywhere—over 1,000 volumes. I've even got Mail Order Moonlighting, by Cecil C. Hoge, Sr."

Dick Hodgson has secured clients all over the world: Eastman Kodak, IBM, MacMillan Inc., Garden Way, L'Eggs, Liberty Mutual, The Orvis Company, U.S. News & World

Report, Westinghouse, Rodale Press, GTE-Sylvania and many others.

"I consult, advise and create. About a third of the time, I write copy. Billions of mailing pieces I've written have gone out in the mail. The sales of products from my direct mail copy is over a billion dollars.

"For clients I'm sometimes asked to try to find direct marketing personnel, which is hard. Lack of good people is direct marketing's biggest block. Too many people have a vertical experience lacking breadth. I try to avoid these assignments. I prefer to give management guidelines on selecting, orienting and training good people.

"Sometimes I help select advertising agencies. I'm doing it now for two European clients. It's not easy. The perfect agency for an account usually has a competitive account. Other agencies are often specialized, geared to handle part of the project—but not all of it.

"But to find time to write and finish my books, I'm cutting back on consulting and seminars. I keep reading anything relative to direct marketing. I keep filing. I now have over 20 tons of clippings and samples, probably the biggest collection anywhere.

"I think on a typewriter. I used to write news stories on a linotype machine. I type everything I write. I'm investigating a typewriter with a memory. I use an IBM Electronic 50 for my catalog copy; but it doesn't have enough memory, although it permits use of proportionately spaced type to simplify character counting. But I want one to use in writing my books. The concept is that I'll type and it will come out as typewriter type on my machine. But the memory will convert to book type later for my publisher.

"I also want a system that permits fast copy transmittal. My chief assistant for copywriting is my daughter, Sue Rolfing. She's the best catalog copywriter I've found . . . I didn't train her, it must be in the genes! She lives in Whitefish, Montana, and I'd love to have a system where we could transmit copy back and forth. She's busy raising llamas out there. She can't come back to Pennsylvania when I'm in a copy bind and bail me out like she used to.

"Who's the brightest of the direct marketers? It's a tough question. I'll try to comment, but I'm sure to forget many who should be included.

"Bob Stone is the brightest thinker. Jim Kobs is very bright. Tom Foster is. So is Len Carlson. After launching and then selling Sunset House, he's been a consultant. But he's still a promoter. He owns Lenca, which sells by mail order. He has a mail order business in Japan. He makes financial investments in other new mail order ventures. Bob DeLay is very bright. People don't realize the incredible job he's done at the DMMA, bringing the association from a small group dominated by lettershop operators to the world's foremost direct marketing group, with active participation by all of the leading firms.

"This list is a good start, but then consider:

"Joe Sugarman . . . He's created a whole new approach which has been widely copied. It's great for some things which don't necessarily sell well with conventional approaches. He isn't a direct mail man—his bag is selling off the publication page.

"John Yeck . . . No list of outstanding direct marketers would be complete without John's name. He is a great copywriter, a deep thinker, and is probably the world's most outstanding authority on direct mail for business and industrial selling and lead-getting.

"Alfred Gerardi . . . He's the gentleman with whom I work in Germany and is certainly Europe's leading direct marketer. He has the largest direct marketing agency in Europe (Donnelley & Gerardi) . . . is publisher of Europe's leading direct marketing magazine and Europe's leading direct marketing newsletter. He's created and written some of the most successful of all direct mail pieces anywhere and he's been responsible for helping many successful U.S. mail order businesses get started in Europe.

"Frank Johnson . . . His promotional mailings for American Heritage lead the way for today's higher quality in all forms of mail order promotion.

"Bill Jayme, Hank Burnett and Chris Stagg . . . Three leading west coast copywriters who, between them, probably create over 50% of the most successful publication promotion pieces in use today . . . and their copy techniques have been widely copied by others.

"Dick Benson . . . A brilliant consultant who, for many years, has developed winning techniques for a vast variety of clients.

"Joe Segel . . . High on the list of the brightest in direct marketing. He created the Franklin Mint out of a whole cloth. His genius discovered a whole new market—people who want collections of something but don't want to work at it. The success of the business was strictly a result of his ability to do things nobody else had even thought of before . . . and locate people who could extend his ideas. If Joe hadn't come along, there probably would be no collectibles mail order business today. Nobody in collectibles has even come close to his success with Franklin Mint. He used to say to me, 'Hodgson, I bet that isn't in your book.' Chances are it wasn't . . . and the idea he was proposing was better than anything I'd written about.

"Les Wunderman . . . One of the truly great direct marketing minds still at work.

"John Caples . . . The greatest of the direct mail copywriters of the past 50 years, and still at work today. What a genius!

"Maxwell Sackheim . . . Although retired, nobody should forget his great campaigns which laid so much groundwork for what's done today.

"Harold Schwartz . . . He took Hanover House and spun off a whole host of new catalogs to cover every market segment—the wave of the future.

"Andy Andrews . . . He showed fund raisers how they could apply mail order techniques and raise more funds by mail than they ever raised before by all other methods combined.

"Dick Cremer . . . The job he has done at Montgomery Ward in creating a profitable sideline of selling outside the catalog and stores is already being copied by just about everyone with a general mail order catalog.

"Jerry Hardy . . . His work at Doubleday, Time-Life and for others has played an important role in the development of today's most successful direct marketing techniques.

"Bob Kestnbaum . . . His computer analysis techniques are vital ingredients today in the day-to-day operations of many direct marketing firms.

"Paul Elias . . . the airline seatback catalogs produced by his firm get the widest exposure among businessmen of all 'high ticket' catalogs. They have undoubtedly inspired much of the current wave of upscale gift catalogs. Many think the Horchow Collection is the inspiration for the high ticket wave, but Paul Elias and K-Promotions were there before and certainly got more exposure.

"The list could go on and on, but these are some of the people that come to mind at the moment.

"What is the key ingredient for a beginner to succeed? It's a healthy curiosity—I call it a High Curiosity Quotient . . . what it also takes to become a successful writer or editor. You can be a great word mechanic and never get anywhere. You have to really get deeply interested in the subjects you write about.

"It isn't IQ or courses in school or college. It takes interest in lots of things and ability to put miscellaneous pieces of information together to come up with knowledge. A variety of 'outside' interests is ideal. Someone who spends all of his time on a vertical line of subjects just isn't curious enough to make a good direct marketer.

"A knowledge of what makes business tick is a good idea. Everyone can benefit from training which leads to an MBA—unless they think that's all they need to succeed. Generally, a broad liberal arts training, at least a few business courses and some awareness of the importance of computers in today's business operations is needed.

"Perhaps the best 'first jobs' are either selling or reporting/editing. An understanding of psychology certainly is helpful . . . and you can't live in direct marketing very long unless you understand math.

"I'm concerned about the lack of creativity in direct mail today. I suspect the 'villain' may be direct marketing. Too many of the brightest people have moved away from 'direct mail' into broader direct marketing jobs and the direct response agencies have focused maximum attention on multi-media.

"The world of direct mail is crying out for some truly imaginative new ideas. What we're using successfully today came primarily out of the late 50's and early 60's—sweepstakes, publishers' letters, stamps, tokens, computer personalization. We've refined these and made them more effective . . . but we need many, many new ideas.

"Mail order catalogs have a special dearth of new ideas. I'm amazed at how few catalogers even experiment with new approaches, except to copy what someone else is doing. I've been able to take an idea from an outside-catalogs source, apply it to a catalog and increase response from even a customer file by 35 to 50% without any additional promotional cost. Such increases don't happen every day . . . but few are even trying something different.

"There's also been a love affair with electronics. Lots of talk about cable TV and other gee whiz developments replacing traditional direct mail and catalogs. While the world of electronics offers many new avenues of communication, they won't even begin to replace conventional direct mail or catalogs for several generations.

"What the dreamers fail to recognize is that even the current generation is being taught by a printed word medium—the textbook. People trained to accept the printed word as the primary source of reliable information just aren't likely to swing over to another medium just because it has bells, lights and whistles.

"I went to the Minnesota State Fair in 1938, saw a demonstration of facsimile . . . and heard the boast that this new-fangled device would be in every home in America within two years and would obsolete newspapers. Forty-three years later, how many homes have facsimile sets?

"I hope too many of today's direct mail people don't get carried away with the challenge to create interactive cable TV commercials or videotape catalogs. It may be fun, but someone still has to create the printed things which will do the selling for at least another generation or two . . . and direct mail can't afford to lose any more bright, talented people."

But one man will keep on turning out direct mail winners—Dick Hodgson—as he is now. Somehow, he still spends a lot of time with his wife, Lois, their two daughters, Sue and Lisa . . . and two sons, Steve and Scott. He also managed to become a Lieutenant-Colonel in the Marine Reserve.

Note: Dick Hodgson and Sargeant House are located at 1433 Johnny's Way, Westtown, PA 19395 (215) 399-0962.

Those of us who can't afford his consultation fee can attend his seminars. If not, we can buy his big handbook. If that's too much, we can read it for free in any business library. In the Help Source Section of this book are details on how to get reprints of his articles and tapes of his speeches.

Chapter 4
Tomorrow's Direct Marketing Executives

*A personality profile
as they will become.*

Ray Lewis is publisher and editorial director of ZIP Magazine. He is young, creative and looking at direct marketing with a fresh and different viewpoint. He sees fast-moving change, a tide he feels that ZIP can ride to find its own identity.

And Irvin Borowsky, the entrepreneur president of North American Publishing, is backing Ray in the evolution of ZIP. In the process, ZIP is becoming a more useful magazine for executives in all phases of direct marketing.

ZIP started in 1978—with the concept of covering lists, fulfillment and mail handling in greater depth than any existing magazine. But since then, ZIP has proliferated. Its cover feature article may rotate from one area to another, but each issue runs articles covering marketing, communications, lists, mailing, telephone programs and fulfillment. It's heavy on direct marketing via direct mail. It also touches media and agency activities. "ZIP goes to more people who have anything to do with mass mailing and direct marketing than any other magazine of the field," says Ray. But Ray's preferred targets are his direct marketers of the future . . . the direct marketing generalists.

Ray feels specialists are greatly needed now but that direct marketing technology will soon accelerate its rate of change—so fast and in such unexpected directions that at any time a specialist may find himself or herself obsolete; but generalists with a broad background will be able to adapt. His suggestion to specialists is to broaden out.

Whether Ray's theory is right or wrong, ZIP's in-depth articles are excellent. And Ray is proving a capable journalist, very observant, with a surprising grasp of new technology and one who can help you.

Ray signs his editorial page in ZIP each month next to his photograph, looking like Henry George, sternly admonishing, as though he's been around for a century.

He's not quite that old, but he's no neophyte. He was responsible for circulation promotion for six different publications for ten years before he came to ZIP. He's a very able direct marketing copywriter. He's a dogged, thorough researcher who soaks up information like a sponge and has a photographic memory. And he has made a lot of friends.

Ray was raised in New Orleans, went to school there and then on to Louisiana State University where he was editor of the Reveille daily newspaper. He graduated, went to work for the New Orleans Times-Picayune and, a year later, in 1969, came to New York to conquer the world.

"But instead, I took a 'temporary' position with Geyer-McAllister Publications as editor of Geyer's/Dealer Topics, and then Administrative Management. Larry Lawler was my boss, and vice president of Geyer-McAllister.

"After a couple of years of editing, I applied for the vacant position of Direct Mail Marketing Manager—on a 'tryout' basis. For ten years, I did everything from market research to circulation promotion to ad copy. I helped launch—and wrote the copy for—'Word Processing Report' newsletter and 'Word Processing World' magazine. To launch them, I created the packages and ads, ran the direct mail and placed the space.

"I tried every technique but my mailings bombed—until we had a post-mortem, and decided to research the project again from scratch. We made hundreds of phone calls and visits to people in word processing. We found concern with change which people couldn't keep up with. People felt unsure and over their heads. Some were frightened about job security.

"These people had needed the authentic and impartial information we had about new technology—but needed a compelling reason to spend $69, to actually take action. My new copy conferred on them 'instant authority.' It said, 'We can make you an expert on word processing within your organization.' The new mailing worked and orders came pouring in. This pulled consistently, created a successful new newsletter and then a successful new magazine for Geyer-McAllister—and incidentally hooked me for life on direct marketing. They're still using the same basic copy after all these years!

"Then my boss, Larry Lawler, left to join North American Publishing and work directly for Irvin Borowsky. Together they came up with the idea that created ZIP. Larry had gone to over two hundred advertisers in magazines ranging from Direct Marketing to The Office. He got hundreds of suggestions to broaden the content. They were all over the lot. Work and planning for the magazine started in October 1978. The first working title for the magazine was 'List Management and Mailing Systems'. This was changed to the simpler and more direct 'ZIP' by the publication's launch in May 1979.

"The publication was a monetary success but disappointed many. Advertisers cooled off. Larry Lawler and Irvin Borowsky felt changes were needed. The second issue was postponed.

"Lawler wanted me to come over as editor. By June of 1979, North American made me an offer. But I was loath to get involved. To me the first issue seemed a hodge-podge, mailed to 37,500 people, a strange circulations mix of quite different people with highly varied interests. Irvin Borowsky asked me to make constructive suggestions, rather than criticize. I told him I would want to make it the magazine of marketing and communication for the 30,000 companies that mail the most. I'd help find the people who handle marketing and fulfillment for big mailings. I told him that my basic interest was in marketing and that this would be my editorial priority.

"Irvin Borowsky had faith in the magazine. He gave me my chance. People were eager to advertise. Each saw his portion. The computer guys saw theirs, the list people theirs, and so on. I saw the opportunity to build a new kind of vehicle. I said, 'I'll go for six months, if you will back me.' Irvin said, "yes." I became editor, and off we went.

"My biggest advantage was that I always admit it when I know nothing. I asked a lot of questions, made a lot of new friends and did a lot of work. The magazine had to find itself an audience and an identity. To do so required learning everything almost from scratch about direct marketing. But new developments were popping up on all sides, and I could see the direct marketing field growing by leaps and bounds. To fully understand it, I had to saturate myself in it.

"In all, there were six issues in 1979. 1980 would be the year of decision. Others in direct marketing helped me. Shell Alpert did. He wrote for ZIP and advised me. Jim Atkins helped. He wrote fine articles and made good suggestions. Many people did. We had to make ZIP go. To do so, we had to find an identity, improve editorial and sell advertisers on what we were doing.

"In July 1980, Irvin Borowsky made me publisher as well as editorial director. Now I had the responsibility of delivering the advertising as well as the editorial content. It was a lot more work—and a new type of challenge—but Irvin's confidence and the chance he gave me was worth it. I work with the space salesmen, but I've avoided soliciting space orders myself. To me the most challenging thing in life is creating images and words to move people. I get great satisfaction doing it.

"The problems were the same as at 'Word Processing Report' and 'Word Processing World' magazine. Direct marketing was moving so fast that people had difficulty keeping up. ZIP's job was to dig so deep in its stories and be so current that readers could feel that ZIP was keeping them up with change . . . to the degree that gave them more job security and opportunity.

"In June 1980, the last issue before I was publisher, ZIP had 27 ad pages. By October 1980, ZIP turned the corner and broke into the black. By March 1981, ZIP had 71 ad pages. ZIP was finally going to the right people with the right editorial content.

"We have far more circulation overall than other magazines in the field. We have more complete coverage in each of a number of important areas of direct marketing. In publishing alone, we have 7,200 people (including 2,200 paying subscribers). We are just as complete in telephone marketing. And for these groups we provide deep editorial coverage. We have something for each.

"Editorially, the overall emphasis is on marketing and delivery. But in every issue there's something on the list business and on each important phase of direct marketing. We cover the nuts and bolts, and thoroughly. We develop original articles. We're a how-to magazine. We're pragmatic. We are the only direct marketing book with reader service cards.

"We have authoritative, detailed articles by top people. Seymour and Mary Zoggett wrote our article on subscription renewal techniques. Seymour was circulation manager of Newsweek and Mary of New York Magazine. We've run more articles on telephone marketing than all other publications combined. We have run articles on computers, on testing, on list segmentation. We had the first article anywhere on carrier-route coding, and a major research piece on the nine-digit zip code. We cover package inserts, seminar promotion, specific markets like children and minorities and older people. Right now, I see a big trend toward personalization—so we're doing several major stories on laser letters, ink-jet and word processing."

For such major articles, Ray Lewis personally gets into the research. He wades in. When one or more outside authorities write it, he not only barrages them with questions but he's busy researching the same subject on his own. For articles he writes himself, he restlessly phones, visits, asks, watches and absorbs. Before he starts to write he can spout facts on the subject for hours on end . . . add details about exotic equipment . . . what's good and bad about each make . . . when introduced, limitations, quirks, improvements . . . what it's replacing and what may soon replace it.

Within three short years by summer 1981, he had convinced more and more direct marketers that he was a competent journalist. ZIP, in finding its identity (after some twists and turns) had become a real tool for direct marketers, of growing effectiveness. You can use it.

Ray credits the growing success of ZIP in attracting advertisers to other factors as well . . . to direct marketing growth . . . change . . . hunger for latest know-how . . . and the participation, help and backing of his boss, Irvin Borowsky . . . and to the crew at ZIP. "Like almost all trade publications, we're undermanned. Our people are overworked but they are good

people; and they're getting better and more enthusiastic about direct marketing and ZIP.

"We concentrate on turning out a better magazine. We have no book department. No tapes. We don't promote back issues. To send an article to anyone, we have to photocopy it, for a dollar when asked. But much more important to ZIP readers is any ability we can develop to perceive future direct-marketing developments and needs, and to help direct marketers prepare for change."

His concept is ingenious and shrewd. Specialists in direct marketing run risks of being too weak in other areas and, as a result, may be ruled out for a broader job, be left out if their specialty goes out, or strike out if they run or own businesses but only know a specialty. Big change can only accelerate and multiply the problem.

Ray offers a solution. Become a generalist as well as a specialist. By gaining an overview of many areas boiling with change, be ready for anything. Train from scratch as a generalist or, if a generalist, broaden as you deepen your know-how. His effort is to tailor ZIP to give overviews in depth in such variety as to give greater job security and to help open up new opportunities for today's practitioners.

He feels he has discovered and staked out ZIP's turf . . . not to be completely encyclopedic . . . or in everything . . . or to report fast-breaking news. Instead, he wants ZIP to run the "think pieces" of direct marketing on subjects that are important now— and which will be necessary later. His idea is not just to customize ZIP for readers, but to *help mold readers* into the future direct marketing executives they will need to be able to survive and prosper in the times of turbulent direct marketing change he sees ahead.

Ray Lewis may sometimes steer a bit wide of the mark in trying to further his concept. Like all of us, ZIP may not be all that perfect—every issue, every article. But I find Ray and the concept stimulating. ZIP, I feel, is making a very useful contribution, which I believe will develop and improve.

In the Help Source Section of this book are listed some ZIP articles I particularly recommend for anyone new to direct marketing and rising up in it. Ray will send a copy of any of these articles for a dollar and a copy of ZIP's latest issue free if you are in direct marketing and write on your letterhead.

Note: ZIP editorial and advertising offices are at 545 Madison Avenue, New York, NY 10022; (212) 371-4100. Circulation Offices are at 401 North Broad Street, Philadelphia, PA 19108; (215) 574-9600.

Chapter 5
Making Safer Mail Order Decisions

How one direct marketing agency helps clients do so - using computer modeling.

Clark Direct Marketing, Inc., is a direct marketing advertising agency and a consultant, in New York City. It's a small organization which works mainly for large publishers.

Back in 1975 . . . before most direct marketing agencies and consultants . . . it began to use computer modeling in advising magazine clients. It has used the model to help several magazines get started and to help others find the correct publishing strategy. Expertise in modeling became a big factor in growth.

Junius R. (Sandy) Clark is president. Sandy and Kitty Williams are the people at Clark who work most with the models. Their ability to do so has proved important to clients in making sounder mail order and publishing decisions. Its own modeling helped those clients who did not yet do their own.

"Modeling has become important in working for new clients and in getting new clients," says Sandy. "Perhaps half our clients in the last several years have come in, in part, because of modeling. We encourage clients to deal directly with the computer modeling firms. Many clients for whom we did extensive modeling now do their own. This is the pattern. We're an introductory phase. We'll continue if the client desires. But it's cheaper and better for the client to do his own.

"For three and a half years we did all the circulation marketing for Business Week. We do the same for the Jerusalem Post. On a more limited basis, we work for New York magazine and Metropolitan Home; for Sail, Sporting News and U.S. News and World Report; for Scholastic Magazine on TV and Butterick Publishing. We are working on a special program for a life insurance company. We work on some magazine launches.

"A model is really used to simulate circulation options. It can tell how big circulation should be and how much to spend to make it that big. It also helps in the fine tuning, such as when to raise prices and which sources of business to use. It works particularly well for new publishers for launches.

Sandy Clark has been a believer in computer modeling ever since the early 1960's, when he was at Time Inc. "To make decisions without using all the tools that are available to you is dangerous. Modeling is widely accepted now for magazine circulation, as an aid in decision making. Yet, I'm amazed at how many publishers don't use models . . . and how very few other direct marketers do."

Sandy started in the magazine business while still at Yale. "To earn money at college, I worked for a small magazine and liked it. That helped me get a job with Time Inc.—in the circulation department of Life magazine. My first boss was Wendell Forbes. I worked for him for six years . . . from 1957 to 1963.

"Wendell and Arnold Dumy were the team who, as far as I know, originated source evaluation and the first computer modeling. At Life, they did modeling without today's sophisticated computers. They did the calculations by punch cards. They did it initially to compare list performance over a period of time.

"But as soon as Arnold Dumy and Wendell Forbes completed their first project, about 1962—it changed our thinking. We all began very soon thereafter to use their new computer methods. We jumped the Life renewal series from seven letters to thirteen letters. The extra six letters proved a more valuable source of subscriptions than any outside source. The computer's source evaluation proved it.

"In 1966, I began a six-year job for Time-Life Films, marketing education films to schools and colleges. And there I discovered Roy Fidler." Roy Fidler had been a copywriter at J. Walter Thompson. He then worked for nearly ten years at the New York Times, in promotion. In 1970, he went out on his own. Sandy Clark joined him in 1972 and later became a partner. Roy Fidler's strength was creative. Sandy Clark's background is more the "numbers" side of direct marketing. In 1982, Sandy bought out Roy Fidler, became sole owner of the agency and changed the name from the Fidler Group to Clark Direct Marketing.

"For the first several years, The Fidler Group had served the education field. Mostly, we were concerned with direct mail and telephone marketing. But our know-how was far broader and it was inevitable that we would broaden out. Very likely, it was our starting to work for Cricket magazine, in 1975, that considerably expedited this expansion. While working on Cricket, we did our first modeling."

"Since then, we've taken on consulting for a growing list of magazine publishers. Some clients use us only for creative work. Some want analysis and advice on what they are doing to get circulation. It's about 50/50.

"Today there are 3 basic computer models that magazines can buy or rent. They are Kobak Business Models, Policy Development Corporation and Ladd Publishing Models. Some magazine publishers have their own. Time has one system; so does the Reader's Digest, Newsweek and McGraw-Hill.

Sandy has no special math background. "Working in magazine publishing circulation required—more than math—approaching each problem logically. I could do that. It required learning on the job and hard work. I did both. I have no programming expertise, but I've been trained by Jack Ladd. I enjoy the publishing business and, to be in it, you have to model. Right now, I see applications of computer modeling for book clubs and for mail order.

"I like working with direct marketers, both magazine publishers and others. I like investigating new methods, finding those that work—whether computer marketing, telephone marketing or whatever—and seeing the improved results when clients use them effectively."

Note: Clark Direct Marketing, Inc., is located at 801 Second Avenue, New York, NY 10017; (212) 661-9230.

Chapter 6
The Direct Marketing Days

*How to saturate yourself
in mail order.*

In the U.S., in each of 21 cities from Los Angeles to New York, the Day takes place once a year. Years ago it spread to Canada. Now it's in Europe, Australia and spreading. It's sponsored by the local direct marketing community, usually the local direct marketing club. It can be small, as in Boston, or large, as in Chicago. But everywhere there are strong similarities.

Dates of the Days are staggered. Favorite direct marketing performers can play the circuit. New faces have tryouts, usually at round tables in individual cities. Each Day seeks big names as stars from outside the field.

Each Day is a chance to meet, to mix, to listen, to find out the newest, for newcomers to learn the business, for old pros to brush up on latest changes in techniques and technology. Those who sell to and service direct marketers try to cover most or all of the circuit. But many direct marketers attend a number of Days a year.

At many trade shows and meetings in the U.S., the mood reflects that of the U.S., itself. Japanese and German products and companies seem prominent. The hottest items often turn out to be imported. Old famous names often are discovered to be now the brand names for imports or, all too often, discontinued divisions of conglomerates. The atmosphere is cautious. There's a wary feeling among American manufacturer product personnel still selling U.S.-made products. The overall mood is defensive.

Not so at the Days. Here the mood is exuberant and confident. There is awareness of possible economic downturns or possible special difficulties to come in the field of direct marketing. But there's something else. It's a refreshing throwback to a far earlier day. In this community, America is dominant, expanding, girdling the globe.

There's a sense of inevitable continuing growth. It's a booster community. There's faith. It's a born-again American confidence. It is a revival meeting of the old-time American belief in better times coming, more for all, more shares for the tiny and small trickling down from the big.

Very, very few here have ever seen a depression. For many, direct marketing has changed their lives for the better. Many here benefit from each new direct marketing convert in that, as the field grows, there is more of everything to go around for everyone serving it. Just as in a prairie booster community of a hundred or so years ago, each new convert settler makes the dream a little more of a reality. The confidence of each reinforces that of the other. The Day is a long litany of direct marketing successes.

Direct Marketing Day in New York (and in some other cities) has become a day-and-a-half. Each year more people appear than ever before. They fly in from all over, gathering in the huge grand ballroom for the lunch meeting, streaming into the exhibit areas, overflowing onto the balconies . . . and at most peak times, attending an 8-ring circus of meetings. On the pre-Day, you can roam for four hours through exhibits. The real Day goes on for ten hours, from 7:30 AM to 5:30 PM.

At the New York Day are usually over one hundred direct marketing speakers and panelists. The news each specialist brings is usually good, often overwhelmingly so. The messages are of past success, present expansion and future growth in myriads more ways. The very fact that no one can attend all meetings, hear all speakers, or even a majority of them, seems symbolic of the choice of opportunity available to anyone in or coming to direct marketing. Often conversions from doubters to believers, from luke-warm to true believers, start at the Days.

From marketing classes of colleges for hundreds of miles, over a hundred students come—as invited guests. Professors of marketing attend as well, as guests. Both students and professors are usually interested and curious.

Generally, it all starts with a breakfast panel of three to five experts with a moderator. Each panel member is probably associated with huge mail order compaigns by giants. The atmosphere is informal and friendly. It's an opener warm-up. The moderator sets the mood. Each of the others buttress it. Obstacles, yes, but successful overcomings. The meeting may be on creativity or the future, or another fairly general subject.

Just as it ends, much more is starting in the grand ballroom. The first speaker is introduced, and then takes over—usually optimistically and sometimes as a convert testifying how the power of direct marketing was proven to him or her. The pace is picking up. At each table there are direct marketers, those servicing direct marketers, and guests . . . direct marketers to be. Now this meeting ends.

They stream out and into the lobbies and halls and exhibit areas for a few minutes before the 10 AM meetings. Many stay in the ballroom for the principal meeting of the next session. Meanwhile, in one double public room, Pierre Passavant, beard and all, may be conducting his basic overview mini-seminar. At the same time, in other rooms there are panels and lectures on direct marketing specialties, perhaps in retailing—or in publishing.

At 11:10, things proliferate into more meetings and smaller groups. Now panels and speakers have taken over. One may give a quick picture of the direct marketing advertising agency business. Another may be on catalogs. If so, participants explain the workings and describe the successes of entirely different specialized catalogs, each successful. Ed McLean, looking full of pep, may be off on one of his great lectures on copy and creative misadventure and pitfalls and how to overcome them and come out with mail order winners.

In another room, another panel is examing another problem, such as getting leads for follow-up and successfully converting them into sales. The make-up of any panel usually includes top direct marketing executives of Fortune 500 companies and big consultants in that specialty. There may be a session on international direct marketing, usually with the word that direct marketing know-how is growing all over the world, but that U.S. direct marketing expertise is still on top, and spreading.

In other rooms, other speakers or panels may be covering copy research, TV mail order or the art of adding circulation profitably. A speaker may talk for about ten minutes or so. Almost always, there are questions and answers. Each speaker supplements each other. There is a choice of good sessions with different formats.

Speakers and panelists are selected for contrast as well as message. There are the traditionalists and the futurists and the statesmen seeing more gradual change, progress and improvement. Some are idea people, and promoters. Some are conserva-tive consultants. Some are superb creative people. Others are the MBA's, the numbers men and women.

Each may be a master of a different specialty—of different types of selling, products and services. Each usually has long had opinions reinforced by experience into strong beliefs. They've usually known each other of old. Each has something to say. Occasionally, some see viewpoints of other panelists as obstacles to progress, creativity or profitability. The adversary approach can stimulate.

Now the flow of people is back to the exhibits and then to lunch in the main ballroom. The main speaker is often a big name outside of direct marketing, but first the Direct Marketing Man of the Year is introduced, traditionally by "Pete" Hoke, who also announces some of the DMDNY latest scholarship awards for direct marketing courses. The Man of the Year speaks briefly on direct marketing, usually of its latest progress. The "Big Name" gives the big talk, usually unrelated. The food is good. Agencies and consultants often have clients and prospects at tables. Professors and students mix at some tables with direct marketers and cluster at others. The big lunch is usually finished at 2:30 PM.

Now you can go briefly to the exhibit area. But, at 3 PM the meetings start again. There may be a lecture on the basics of lists, or you may learn about computer fulfillment from the top. A lot more is usually happening, also.

There may be a fund-raising panel with a consultant as moderator . . . a political fund raiser, a specialist who has raised much for charitable causes and the head of solicitation for a leading fund. It's for anyone who wants to raise money for anything. Usually there's a telephone marketing panel with experts and one on the latest in census demographics. There may be one on laser printing and other new, exotic technology. Usually, there are experts on and from the post office discussing latest development, hopes and fears of upcoming postal service and rate changes.

If seven people went with you from your company, you could cover them all. If alone, you could pick which might help you most. Now it's 4 PM. The lectures and panels may now be on lettershop operations or on industrial direct marketing, or on syndication offers. There may be a panel of top copywriters and art directors. Or you may be able to learn about the perils of collecting money from mail order customers. Perhaps there are question-and-answer sessions on cable TV. Usually, there's a panel on the use of inserts and other off-beat media and methods.

Five o'clock, and back to the exhibits. You can keep going until seven, go out for a drink or collapse and head for home. By then, you've picked up literature on computer and laser letters, on supermarket take-one bulletin boards, on home shopping TV program advertising, patented self-forming envelopes from order forms and many, many other goodies. You've met old friends and new ones. You're convinced that mail order is taking over the world and anxious to get deeper into the gold rush.

Most Direct Marketing Days are run by direct marketing clubs. But, in New York, the Day is a separate institution, run by a board of trustees. It doesn't just happen, but takes incessant work. Art Blumenfield, a top computer consultant, describes the procedure.

"Both 'Pete' Hoke and I are on the Board of Direct Marketing Day in New York. It's a lot of work. On the evening of each Direct Marketing Day we begin planning for next year. I spend two or three days a month doing nothing but DMDNY work.

"Every year, we get about 200 volunteers to help put on the 'Day'. We find out who are the real workers and who are the baloney artists. Some have big reputations but prove to be phoney from ground up. On the reverse side, we identify a superb cadre. I've never spoken at DMDNY and never gotten a client from it, but I get a great deal of satisfaction from the good works that we do via DMDNY scholarships and student programs." In May, 1982 DMDNY sponsored a three-day seminar for professors of marketing and provided $20,000 for travel and housing of candidates.

Marketing Days vary from a day-and-a-half to a day, from big to medium to smaller, but the idea everywhere is the same. It's a way to saturate yourself for an intense period in direct marketing. You can pick and choose. You can cover it as a team or alone. You can go with a friend, with others already in the field, or with someone more expert to guide you.

It's best to start with one near enough to avoid travel expense overnight. It's wise to get a program in advance, to do a little advance research, to make up a question list, and to be prepared. But if you want to get a job in mail order, get ahead in it, sell to it, start a division in it, or be an entrepreneur in it, it's a good investment.

Chapter 7
The Making Of A Direct Marketer

How an entire career success evolved and benefited from willingness and ability to work a new way.

He is president of T-L-K Direct, the direct marketing agency subsidiary of Tatham-Laird & Kudner, a quite large U.S. advertising agency. He has been the president of RCA Direct Marketing Inc. From 1979 to 1981, he was Chairman of the Board of the Direct Mail/Marketing Association. In 1980, he was Direct Marketing Man of the Year. He is David Heneberry.

Dave came to RCA Music Service in 1967. In twelve years, he dramatically increased profits. How did he do it? What was his background? What was his education? What expertise did he acquire? How did he apply it? And how can his experience help us to make it?

"My family were farmers. I went to the University of Illinois on an Agriculture scholarship. For two years, I hung in there—until a course in organic chemistry proved I was in the wrong school." So Dave made a hundred-and-eighty-degree turn and majored in journalism, "including Jack Maguire's two-hour-a-week course in mail order and direct mail advertising." It was a small part of a heavy course load Dave took.

Dave was in the top ten percent of his class. He and his twin brother, Donald, now an analyst for the National Security Agency, always had two outside jobs to pay their way.

"We usually worked as waiters, carpenters, or truck drivers. But one job we always did together. We were professional entertainers, close harmony singers. We could dance and talk. We were sort of early Smothers Brothers.

"After college and 2 years Army service, my journalism degree got me my first job as a copywriter trainee at Meredith Publishing Company, in Des Moines, Iowa. My first job was writing copy for subscriptions for Better Homes & Gardens. I was one of a long succession of Midwesterners who trained at Meredith and then went out into the direct marketing world.

"By the time I left, I had become assistant subscription manager. The last week before I left I wrote the first direct mail test piece selling Meredith books by mail order. Before that, Meredith had sold their books only through department stores.

"At college, I carefully avoided math. But at Meredith a subscription writer learned how to figure out if a mailing was profitable and what to expect when a successful test mailing was then sent to more lists. I was confronted with numbers and was surprised to find I could be comfortable working with them. I just needed time to sort them out. Two great guys, still at Meredith, Dick Steen and Jim Narber, gave me lots of time and advice. I was fascinated enough by mail order to work overtime with my numbers. Sometimes, with a noisy old Frieden calculator, I'd be working on mail order math until 2 AM.

"I had worked with straight analytical methods. But just when I came, Meredith was converting from stencil plate to IBM punch cards using data processing machines, the predecessors of modern computers. There were typical growing pains. People at Meredith were nervous about the new methods, particularly older employees.

"I was young and ignorant. I had no resistance to new approaches. I talked to the programmers and systems analysts. I asked and they answered. I was forced to look at calculating with new eyes. I found that the machines made for better reporting. They were a great assist. They could analyze and forecast results much more accurately. From then until now, my entire career has evolved and benefitted from my willingness and ability to work with computer specialists.

"I then got a job working for one of the richest men in the world whose fortune was built first on mail order know-how. He was John MacArthur, owner of Banker's Life & Casualty Insurance Company and a network of associated and ever-growing enterprises. John MacArthur was notoriously indifferent to appearances. When I came to Banker's Life, I was in the advertising department. My first desk at Banker's was laid flat over a sink in the kitchen of an apartment converted into an office. A couple of years later, the Marshall John Advertising Agency was formed as the house agency for all MacArthur activities. I joined it as V.P., Account Supervisor. Tom Brady, a creative director at Marshall John, is now a partner in Kobs & Brady, and still handling Banker's business.

"The important thing I gained at Marshall John was advertising agency experience. I could apply my creative background to several outside clients. It all helped me later, both creatively and in dealing effectively with advertising agencies, when I got back on the client's side.

"Something else helped me at Marshall John and thereafter. I had always been interested in art. At age 12, I took a mail order course in art from Art Instruction, in Minneapolis. Remember their 'Draw Me' ads, still running? It proved to be surprisingly useful to know something about the elements of lettering, graphics, and layout.

"The Marshall John Agency had access to computers at Banker's Life when needed. I added to my experience with computers by listening to the Information Systems Manager, Barth Murphy. (He's now Executive Vice President of Banker's.)

"Julian Haydon, now general manager of R.L. Polk Marketing Services, was then assistant research director at Banker's Life. We worked closely together. He was a strong, relentless logician. He was the first man I knew with the tenacity to work through the details of computer data to improve his decisions. He knew that in a mass of computer detail there could be found facts that, analyzed correctly, could point to a course of action.

"After Marshall John, I spent one-and-a-half years at LaSalle Extension Institute, a division of Crowell-Collier, and moved LaSalle's marketing office to New York.

"I joined RCA Records in 1967. When I came to the RCA Record Club, I found a unique depth of computer-oriented managers. Fulfillment Operations, Customer Service and MIS managers were all experienced programming and systems designers. These were active, live managers. In most organizations, computer people tend to be isolated. They often feel misunderstood and that they may never get the full opportunity to use their know-how and abilities. Often, they're part of the financial department or of a financially-oriented business management.

"But here was an unusual marriage of an overall manager, me, vitally interested in computers and a whole stable of talented department chiefs adept at applying them. We started together with the expectation to use computers to analyze, sift and organize information we needed to improve overall results. I had the authority I needed and great talent to work with.

"We used computers to develop an accurate model of the entire business. This was very important to the RCA Record Club. It was all done inside. We had a large data base of the performance history of every member taken in over the previous five years. We kept building on that base. We did not just look at initial order cost but at lifetime performance. This made for better media selection. We ended up paying more per new enrollment but buying very high quality customers. The average sale per customer doubled. The selling cost for all sales for the life of the customer dropped."

Dave's objective was to go for the bottom line, to improve profitability of each dollar of business done and to then worry about increasing volume. He saw the biggest opportunity to do this in cutting credit losses. "Credit losses were 12½% on record club memberships, which were the overwhelming majority of mail order sales. We reduced this to 6.5% We prescreened for credit acceptability lists to be mailed, using computer techniques. Often, we eliminated 45% to 55% of the names before mailing the list."

Dave also increased business by an expanded network of association with other organizations who marketed by mail order RCA albums, often on an exclusive basis. Sometimes, Dave and RCA came up with mail order offer ideas to create RCA custom albums for others to sell. Often, Dave worked with others on carrying out their ideas.

He put great emphasis on being a good partner to others, and made a great effort to look at each deal from the viewpoint of the RCA trading partner. "Overall, winning trust is necessary for all of us to work together. Organizations like Reader's Digest and Time Inc. have had total integrity in every deal we've entered into. Their word is their bond. Happily, that can be said for most everyone we dealt with."

Dave believes in mail order co-partners for RCA and not just giants. Particularly in TV mail order, he has worked profitably with smaller companies. He's taken some credit losses from some backruptcies of TV mail order entrepreneurs, but surprisingly little.

One effect of Dave's policy is that working with a number of TV mail order operators and doing almost all TV mail order this way, RCA sales via TV mail order have been estimated by outsiders to be twice as high as for arch competitor, CBS Special Products Division. Dave is convinced that his lower margin, low

risk-high volume approach produces maximum profit and least headaches.

It is this combination of computer-assisted business management and pragmatic judgment derived from years of mail order trial and error that T-L-K Direct is counting on from Dave to build clients.

I think Dave Heneberry, because of his mail order expertise, is independent as few top management executives are. His know-how is now a hot commodity. He is open yet discreet, frank yet politic. His security is in his know-how and his judgment.

He mastered his craft. He zeroed in on computers, the most important new tool of his craft. He worked more than most early enough in his career to get a head start, and he is bright. But it is the easy simplicity of his mind and its speed that has paid off most for him.

Chapter 8
The Circulation Fulfillment Business

*How magazine publishers share
expenses of handling subscribers.*

More and more magazines seem to have moved to Marion, Ohio. More magazine subscription coupons have a Marion address. Bills for 200 million copies of magazines came from there in 1980. Why? It's the fulfillment business. In Marion, Ohio, The Fulfillment Corporation of America takes care of it all.

FCA processes millions of transactions a year. It deals with 42 printers, 34 publishers, 700,000 post office employees. If anything goes wrong, the subscriber writes to the publisher at the address instructed . . . Marion, Ohio. If you pay and still get a bill or don't get a magazine or whatever, for more and more publishers you have to write to Marion, Ohio, about it. FCA, who may have nothing to do with the problem, answers.

One reason for this system is that it now costs an average of $6.34, Dartnell Corp. estimates, to write each business letter. The cost to correspond with customers, send bills, collect, deposit and mail renewal letters more and more drives most magazines and mail order companies up the wall. The biggest are in biggest cities where pay of office personnel is highest.

Jack Courtney, President of FCA, recalls: "At first, there were no fulfillment houses. Magazines did their own fulfillment, or magazine printers did fulfillment for publishers. Printers do so today. McCall's was an early example of providing fulfillment services to other publishers. In 1948, two men had an idea that an independent service company could be more efficient and save money for publishers.

"Away from big cities rent and labor costs could be lower. An on-going professional staff to manage such services would permit sharing expensive equipment. These two men visualized use of computers for fulfillment. They had independently tried to develop such a computer in the early 50's which, of course, was too far ahead of its time to be successful. Use of personnel could smooth peaks and valleys (it's tough in everyday practice even with computers).

"Wendell Ward was vice president of Time, Inc., Jack Kinter

was a consultant from Ernst and Ernst. Time, Inc. was working on the installation of unit record punch card equipment for fulfillment. Wendell Ward was spear-heading the project of improving the system. In addition to unit record equipment, Addressograph-Multigraph was developing a machine called Facsimile Printing which would read typed names and address on subscriber record cards and create dickstrip distribution labels. Jack Kinter worked with Wendell Ward on this project. The combination of punch card equipment and facsimile equipment was the key to improve fulfillment in 1948.

"Ward and Kinter conceived the idea of a service company and went into business. The first customer was Newsweek. FCA started in Marion, Ohio. Other than Newsweek, there were two clients. The original location, in 1948, had 16,000 square feet and employed 75 people. Equipment, however, became constantly more sophisticated while requirements became more complicated. In those days subscriber lists were on metal plates, paper plates, even silk plates.

"Wendell Ward stayed with FCA for 22 years. Jack Kinter was here 15 years. Jack Kinter did work at FCA full-time from the beginning and so did Wendell Ward. They did not have serious growth ambitions—they tried to keep it a two man show, but they had bank financing to grow as fast as they could. The company was profitable the first seven years. For the next 15 years, it was touch and go—some red, some black and probably came out a wash. Since then, it has been profitable.

"I worked for McCall's in Dayton as a methods specialist working for the comptroller. I analyzed the fulfillment operation there to determine better methods of work flow. As a result I was promoted to assistant manager of fulfillment. In 1954, I moved directly to FCA.

"The next year, we became part of a public company. The year after that was our first use of computers which enabled us to convert subscriber lists on to magnetic tape. In 1967, another public company acquired the company that owned us and shortly after sold us to American Heritage Publishing, which was at the time our largest customer.

"In 1966 and 1967, we made a really violent change. Basically, all customers were converted to computer fulfillment to meet post office zip code requirements. The cost and upheaval almost broke us up. It was like switching from horses and wagons to trucks. Suddenly, everything was changed all at once. Everything had to be set up on both systems old and new for the conversion. The disturbance was great, but we somehow survived."

In 1969, American Heritage was purchased by McGraw-Hill. While McGraw-Hill has a huge magazine operation, FCA did not become a house operation. Less than 5% of FCA revenues were from products of McGraw-Hill or its subsidiaries. In January 1976, FCA was sold to Engelhard-Hanovia, Inc., another giant firm. Since that time, FCA has seen the greatest growth and profits in its history.

What does a fulfillment company do for a client? Jack Courtney explains: "We perform five basic operations—mail processing and banking, input preparation for computer, the computer processing, mailing or shipment of addressed materials, and corresponding with 8,000,000 subscribers whose accounts we maintain for publishers.

"Each day we receive many bags of mail from the U.S. Postal Service. This mail is presorted by the Post Office by each special address we have for our customers. We receive nine million orders for merchandise or magazines each year, two million payments for the merchandise subscriptions, and two million

changes of address or undeliverable notifications from the post office. Each transaction must be segregated by publication and put under strict accounting control as the mail is opened. The Cage Department opens and organizes the mail. The various types of mail have a numerical and dollar value assigned to them.

"We process up to 17,000 checks per day. This year we are depositing $63,000,000 for our customers using Remittance Processing Equipment. This banking service saves customers banking charges and improves their cash flow. Checks are sorted, enscribed with magnetic ink, and endorsed, and of course, balanced back to the counts that we take when we open the mail. This process establishes the audit trail.

"After banking, millions of transactions are prepared for input into the computer. Our optical scanning equipment reads information from a subscription order or payment form. Each of the staff in the Keystroke area works at a typewriter keyboard with a television display. The unit, called a Cathode Ray Tube (CRT), is connected to our computer. All the transactions above, except those that are scanned, are keystroked—name, address, and subscription statistical information—and deposited in the computer disc storage. The programs are set up so the operator can correct errors that are detected by the computer. At the same time, the computer balances each batch of work to insure that nothing is missed.

"The computer center updates the master subscription list for each magazine. The central processing unit of the computer is the control station and memory that controls the other units attached to the computer, including the Cathode Ray Tube. A disc memory device which is similar to a record player is used to store our master post office file and massive statistical files.

"We have a number of magnetic tape drives which record on tape similar to a stereo tape deck. These tape drives are the basic method used for storage and input of the master subscription files for computer update.

"The A.B. Dick videograph is used to prepare an item called dickstrip. Dickstrip is the name given to the labels that are used to address magazines for distribution. This device prints labels at the rate of 135,000 per hour. As the labels are printed, they are wound on cores which are then shipped to the printing plant and affixed to the publication.

"The top line of the label is a keyline or subscriber code line. This line contains all the information necessary for identification of an account. The computer printer is used to address renewal notices which inform subscribers that their subscription is ending, or bills to collect for credit orders already entered.

"FCA generates about 200 million distribution labels per year, twenty-five million renewal notices, seven million invoices, and one hundred million labels for list rental activity. The magnetic tapes are maintained in the Library with a full-time librarian. We have over thirteen thousand reels of tape. In additon to using paper as a means of communication, we use a telecommunication device which permits us to transmit data to other facilities, via the telephone lines.

"We are mailing in excess of forty-eight million pieces of mail per year. The forms, along with the letters and outgoing and reply envelopes, are put into machines called inserting machines which pick up the individual form, letter and envelopes and assemble them, and at the end of the machine the postage stamp is affixed, or postage is metered onto the envelope.

"FCA spends, on behalf of its customers, four million dollars worth of postage each year. We have a sub-station of the United States Post Office on our premise. We receive excellent cooperation from the Postal Service.

"Here's what happens each time we get a customer complaint. A microfiche (similar to microfilm) copy is made of the subscription records maintained on the computer magnetic tape. This copy can be read by the correspondent to do necessary research and make adjustments as necessary. The correspondent knows where to look for a subscriber record and can tell by the correspondence and the microfiche record what action is necessary. Once corrective action is taken, letters are automatically typed on magnetic typewriters answering the subscriber communication.

"In addition to the magazine and merchandise fulfillment, we operate data base functions.

"The American Heritage previous buyers file contains the names of all purchasers of some 53 American Heritage books. This data base is used to selectively promote for new books as they are developed by American Heritage.

"Today FCA serves 33 publishing firms and 3 non-publishing firms. We perform services for 65 magazine titles which have a total of 8,000,000 subscribers. The largest magazine has 2,600,000. We have some as small as 14,000. It's still not easy to determine the minimum circulation to take on. Each is difficult to price a service charge for. One small publisher may be quite demanding in certain ways. Another may be far simpler to handle. One may only require half a day every two months of Account Management contact work. Another may want us to spend half a day a week. It may take some time to develop working arrangements that are predictable enough to be safe in pricing.

"Usually, the minimum circulation we can profitably service should be 100,000, if only one publication. If several publications, each small, are all from one customer, a minimum 200,000 total is right, with the smallest publication 20,000 to 30,000. But if a good customer has one publication smaller, we've got to help.

"Magazine subscription fulfillment is our largest activity.

Merchandise fulfillment is performed for a few of our customers. Connected with the magazine and merchandise list we perform list rental service, which is the exchange of lists by one publisher to another to promote their publication or sell their products.

"To offer a complete package to our customers, we also offer printing and mailing in connection with the promotion of products or publications. Our printing operation does not print the publication, only letters, forms, envelopes and other similar type materials.

"We maintain an inventory of over five thousand items of stock for our publishers. We stock and ship merchandise for the kind of items publishers feature editorially and offer as a service to readers. We do so generally for a publisher who features two or three items in an issue. It might be eight or ten. We do so as a favor to our clients. We do not stock enough items for a single publication to supply a catalog."

Note: For readers of this book, Jack Courtney has answered the following questions:

Q. *Are fulfillment houses basically computer service bureaus?*

A. Some magazine fulfillment houses were originally computer service bureaus. FCA has always been a total fulfillment house. FCA does not consider itself a computer service bureau.

Q. *Why has the cost of functions performed by a fulfillment house not risen comparably to postage and paper?*

A. Fulfillment houses, using computers and sophisticated computer programs, have kept down costs of magazine fulfillment despite inflation due to substantial labor savings. The high degree of computerization has made the data processing professional and technical staff so expensive that in a shared cost service situation you have a much higher economic advantage than to have all those skills in-house.

Q. *Will in-house fulfillment come back, due to new improved mini-computers and other equipment suitable for in-house processing?*

A. Economically, yes. The mini-computer can put fulfillment back in-house, but probably just as many won't want to get involved. The cost drop will make it feasible, but software and people will be a problem.

Q. *Is FCA concerned with computer research to select lists and make promotion decisions?*

A. Yes, FCA is concerned with incoming subscriptions and all that happens to a subscriber thereafter. FCA is basically not involved in marketing plans for magazines. We do consult on offers in specific promotion plans. FCA does analytical work on order sources, renewal offers, etc., to assist the clients in determining future courses of promotion.

Q. *What do you think of opening mail in the U.S. and banking receipts, of then flying all the mail to a lower labor cost country with all computer processing done there? Will South Africa or India provide the fulfillment houses of the future?*

A. You're late with this question. Work done in other locations has been a competitive problem, a marketing advantage for those who use it, but is becoming less so. We do not foresee the increased use of labor supplies in foreign nations. This is becoming less cost competitive. Domestic operations have more equipment and better management and security.

Q. *What recently developed processing equipment has made the biggest contribution to efficiency?*

A. Equipment making the most dramatic effect—computers, scanners, CRT's and Remittance Processing Devices.

Q. *What type of activities other than for publishing clients are you considering for the future?*

A. Possibly we would consider fund raising, utility or cable television billing, wholesale bank deposit operations, etc., for businesses other than publishing.

Q. *How long does it take FCA to service a complaint?*

A. This question cannot be answered with an average. When you are dealing with many publications there are too many variables regarding first copy service. Computerized methods provide more information and schedules are improved. Postal service is sporadic and probably overall worse than in past times. Complaints require one to five work days after receipt for a reply to put in the mails.

Q. *What role does FCA play and what role the publisher in credit and collections decisions and in improving collections?*

A. The credit manager is the publisher, who operates on statistics furnished from the fulfillment system. Credit restrictions vary and are applied as requested by the publisher with the computer doing the credit evaluation. Slow pay and bad pay are basically controlled by the quality and need for the product. Finding people with a need for the best product is determined by better list selectivity. Thus, picking the best customers improves collections, if the product quality is good enough.

Q. *What does FCA do in the telephone marketing?*

A. We do take subscriptions from telephone switchboards if the publisher has authorized the telephone operation. We do not operate extensive telephone subscription operations ourselves. We will process incoming phone subscription orders.

Q. *How will two-way TV, View Data, electronic fund transfer and other similar instant transmission developments affect FCA?*

A. We have been exploring these points for some time and expect they will occur but not for many years with publications that are published nationally.

Q. *Automation, computerization and other developments in processing equipment keep improving faster and faster. How does this affect FCA?*

A. The pace of change is accelerating. Our public is becoming computer or electronic processing oriented. This leads to a high expectation in terms of product delivery and customer service. A majority of staff becomes more stable, with longer experience. But constant change is not a human desire. It becomes difficult for more experienced people to update and make change.

Q. *Is the fulfillment business a good one for a young man or woman to get into?*

A. Certainly. It is a relatively new business. There are relatively few companies in the business. Extension of fulfillment to industries other than publishing is accelerating. There are good opportunities for females and minorities if they get enough education in basic business and computer sciences.

Note: Fulfillment Corporation of America is located at 205 West Center St., Marion, Ohio 43302; (614) 383-5231.

Chapter 9
The Bloomingdale's Of Catalogs

*That's what Spiegel's
is turning into.*

It's an unprecedented, overwhelming, personality change... more complete, far faster than that of any great catalog or department store. A catalog doing over $400,000,000 annually is changing character and image in only years, what Bloomingdale's did in decades.

Such a dramatic transformation so fast would probably be impossible for Sears, Ward's or Penney's and too dangerous to try if it were. Each is too big, too universally known, too positioned in too many people's minds to do so. It is possible for Spiegel because its size is a small fraction of any of the big three.

It's possible because of Henry Johnson, Chairman of the Board and Chief Executive Officer. It's possible because of a progressive Board of Directors of Spiegel, and because Henry Johnson is a practical man. He's a master of newest mail order methods. He is a realistic futurist of direct marketing.

Henry Johnson has changed the image and appearance of the Spiegel catalog. He has changed the character and calibre of Spiegel merchandise, and Spiegel's entire way of doing business. How he has done so has fascinated top direct marketing management in almost every field.

The new Spiegel catalog is big, nine inches wide and thirteen inches high, and thick—a 650-page personality profile of the customer Spiegel is after. It starts with business separates and ends in bed and is entirely new all the way. Henry Johnson calls it a "department store in print." He says that the covers are shop windows, the sections floors and the pictures displays.

Henry Johnson has now been part of three of the big five catalogs. He's studied department store retailing. He's a bit of a futurist, an economist, a researcher, an analyst. He's a marketer, a superb buyer, a promoter and a down to earth catalog man. He's seen a retailing revolution and a mail order revolution. When he came to Spiegel in 1976, he had a pretty clear idea of where the greatest retailing opportunities lay in the 1980's and 1990's; where for catalog selling; and where Spiegel could best fit into them.

But before he made a move he thoroughly analyzed Spiegel, its history, and every aspect of his theories. Spiegel was founded in 1905. It was the first catalog house to sell on credit.

Spiegel was comfortable like an old shoe. It's clientele was largely ethnic and blue collar. Many Spiegel families raised their children from a Spiegel crib, in Spiegel clothes and furnished their homes from Spiegel, buying it all on Spiegel credit. And many Spiegel families prospered. Children of Spiegel families went beyond blue collar, into professions, middle management and their own businesses.

But many of these second generation Spiegel families were graduating from Spiegel and going on to buy elsewhere, to fill different needs. And Spiegel blue collar families often weren't doing as well and couldn't buy as much or pay as promptly.

Spiegel had generally followed the lead of Sears and Ward. After they went into stores it did. Spiegel opened stores where its catalog customers lived; largely before suburban shopping centers existed; and not in the biggest. Spiegel couldn't give biggest manufacturers the volume Sears and Ward could. It tended to work with smaller ones. It was a struggle to get and give maximum value. In fashion, Spiegel was conservative and stayed with older or middle of the road preferences.

Spiegel turned to imports. To shop for its customer's pocket books it went to Hong Kong, Taiwan, South Korea, the Phillippines—wherever cheapest. Sometimes, quality was irregular and delivery unreliable.

Spiegel seemed locked into catalog order stores in declining neighborhoods; to blue collar customers with inflation squeezed incomes; to small, struggling suppliers in the U.S. and distant, less than reliable suppliers in the Orient. Meanwhile, the costs of labor, rent, taxes, overhead were jumping.

Henry Johnson analyzed retailing, mail order and Spiegel. He used attitude testing to research Spiegel customers, former customers and non-customers. He investigated attitudes towards retail shoppers and mail order shopping. He studied trends. He found that the trend in Spiegel families reflected those in non-Spiegel families.

People weren't making it in one-job families. Blue collar families first made up for inflation by Mother going back to work. But as inflation continued, combined income of two manual or blue collar jobs often did not keep pace. As smart machines took over jobs of manual factory and then office workers, blue collar families had more unemployment.

The families making it fastest were those where both husband and wife had completed most education for most needed specialties. Children of Spiegel families who completed college and professional graduate schools often married spouses who also had. Their lives were dramatically different.

The life styles of these famiies differed from those of their parents. They developed their own tastes and style and fashion preferences, their own hobbies and interests. They had money to shop with but lacked time to shop. They bought by mail order far more, but their own kind of mail order.

The parents had often scrimped and comparison-shopped through life. Much of what they owned was made possible by bargains, sales and discounts. They took off-brands and off-models of top brands. They compromised to get by.

The new successful generation thought differently. They could afford the top brands and designer styles but could not afford the concept of shopping, itself. They needed a trusted source for good value from which, in the shortest possible time with least hassle, they could obtain their needs.

Today the trend has gone beyond two-job families. Many blue collar families have both members not only working but one or both taking on small after hours jobs. But the better educated couples with better jobs had better free lance jobs when they moonlighted and then profitable part-time businesses. The more prosperous new families had less children than their parents and far more personal hobbies and interests.

The key to the success of the better educated two-job family was the woman. She was quite a different woman than her mother, more style-minded, more value-minded and less price bargain-minded. She worked in an office, had a good job and wanted a much better one. Or she was in a profession or owned her own business. She felt safer with national brand and designer name products. She wanted style in clothes she bought. She liked to entertain and little touches to dress up her home. She wanted to share activities with her husband and often had her own activities, as well.

Research showed that for years these were the very customers who were leaving Spiegel but also that young families like these, whether Spiegel customers or not, were often not finding other traditional retail and catalog sources satisfactory. No big general catalog offered the brand names or even the new kinds of items they desired to the extent they wished. Retail mass merchandising by multiplying branches were cutting down on inventory per branch.

Department stores were often dropping name brands rather than be under-priced. Discounters were offering off-models of name brands. Everybody was playing safe featuring the same tired items. The big five general catalogs were all offering mostly all private or lesser known brands. And this at the very time that an entire new market of customers was coming into being, asking only for what they wanted, and far more value than price-oriented.

This new market might not be big enough for Sears, Ward's or Penney's to entirely aim at it, but it was plenty big enough for Spiegel to do so and grow and prosper. And computerized list selection made it possible to segregate, seek out and go after this market as was never before possible.

It became possible because of advances in the science of list analysis and selection. Johnson could use factor analysis to segregate the Spiegel customer list into groups. He could then study in detail the buying habits of the upwardly mobile families he desired and further refine their characteristics. He could study their demographics from credit file and zip code area analysis, where they lived, what they owned, their incomes, savings. He could study their psychographics from their buying record and from different kinds of research, particularly focus interviews— what their interests, likes, dislikes, hobbies, style preferences and hobbies were.

Along with this, Spiegel market specialists studied predictions of the economic future—world and national, for stores and for catalogs, in-store shopping and for mail order . . . from present media and from new media. They studied the trends that were the bases for the predictions.

Their studies indicated constant future lessening of manual jobs and increasing of mental ones. Average time spent per family in shopping would continue to decrease. Preference for non-store shopping would keep growing. Mail order would grow even faster than up to now. In retailing it would be more profitable to go after market segments where spending was freest, by interests rather than just geographically.

Labor and overhead costs of store operation would continue to rise in proportion to retail dollar sales. Catalogs would have an advantage in ratio of personnel to sales but certain kinds of catalog sales requiring less personnel per dollar would be most profitable. Gradually, the crystal ball research and customer analysis research began to show common answers, to indicate how to sell, what to sell, whom to sell to. Spiegel could now create the image of what it wanted its business to be.

Now it was possible to analyze the characteristics in more detail than ever before of that segment of Spiegel customers which most shared them. It was possible to target Spiegel promotion to groups who most shared these characteristics. Most important of all, it was possible to create a new Spiegel catalog featuring the merchandise these selected customers wanted most, to present each item in the way such customers preferred and to do business in every particular in ways these selected customers most favored.

Now the problem was to do so in a way that at one time kept most desirable Spiegel customers from leaving as had happened in the past, to attract new customers like them in big volume, fast—and to keep as much as possible of the other loyal Spiegel customers who accounted for most of Spiegel's volume.

No mail order catalog as large had ever taken as bold a step before. The dollar investment required to put theory into practice was enormous. The merchandise, the styling, the buying methods, the advertising down to each word of copy, the thinking in every particular had to be dramatically changed.

Henry Johnson had quite a transformation assignment, a transmutation and rejuvenation. He had to do it all while continuing daily business. He had to educate every co-worker to what he was doing and win his or her cooperation.

"It starts with a plan. Everyone needs a plan. Some overplan. Others don't plan. Entrepreneurs of the past and of the present still do envision lofty goals. Then the job comes of informing all layers of management of the plan and of selling them on it. Otherwise, plans are academic. And much of what I do is every day to spend hours in selling the basic idea to everyone I'm associated with.

"We explained what we're doing to suppliers. We mailed out in literature our philosophy to resources and banks. We publicized it to the consumer. We used Hill & Knowlton for public relations. We had to start with our own people. Spiegel's had a crummy old warehouse, cheap merchandise, bad credit losses and complaints. The people at each level at Spiegel were accustomed to this. What to do? Where do we go?

"We've changed the company completely. The first thing I did was move our corporate headquarters from that warehouse. But you can't change bricks and mortar and location. We had to move to feel differently about the business.

"Next we closed 200 Speigel catalog order stores. This represented 40% of our sales volume. We expected to lose half of that 40%. We did but through new customer promotion managed to pick up most of the lost sales. We had a far bigger percentage reduction in overhead than in volume. We chose direct ordering which is less labor intensive than through retail order stores.

"From our merchandise selections we eliminated items requiring complicated and costly warehouse handling. We also dropped items and revised services which caused most mistakes and customer complaints. We dropped major lines that were traditional but did not fit the merchandise profile for our target market. Now we could build the new Spiegel.

"We decided on the kind of customer we sought. We would be oriented to a woman who worked in a good job and lived by herself or with a husband. We would be fashion-oriented. This would relate to more than clothes. It would be to the desire to look and feel right in person, in the home, in the car and wherever. Home furnishings would all be designed to be fashion.

"And Spiegel has done it. Spiegel home furnishing is the best. So are domestics, cook and serve. Name brands give security. They're pre-sold. We have hundreds and hundreds of home fashion items, real things. Our patches are real patches, not printed. Our leather is real, not leather-like. We're a genuine shop. Our growth has been excellent since the new Spiegel's has been launched.

"Ready-to-wear is more difficult. Brand suppliers must learn to meet our need for continuity of supply. Sizes, specifications, labeling must be coordinated. Cashmere sweaters must be really so. If we say wool, it must be good wool. We try to live up to our code. We leave out puffery. If the description of a product offered to us seems purely to deceive, we forget it. We only have products we're proud of.

"We have to do copy editing to accomplish all this. We have to reflect our approach in layout and appearance. We have to have more white space. It affects the character of models we photograph. We want beautiful women. We want people not posed. We take most shots with small cameras.

"There is a real opportunity to give the kind of products the new trends cause demand for, to give the kind of quality better outlets featured more formerly, to give the kind of service department stores did but now often can't. And of the five biggest catalogs, Spiegel's is in a unique position to take advantage of it. Ward's, Sears and Penney's sell private label. We're selling name brands.

"We've put in relatively expensive brand name products to emphasize reliability. We emphasize service, our guarantee, unquestioned refunds, taking care of the customer. This is the original philosophy of department stores. But today, the department store often can't get the job done. The problem of service by the department store has changed. The situation of the customer has changed. The customer does not have the time to shop.

"Always before Spiegel's was oriented to do later what the big three did earlier but to sell somewhat lower quality merchandise for somewhat less money. They led. We followed. This is no longer so. Now we're different. We're innovating more, in different ways. Now we're doing something no one has ever done. We're recreating a $400,000,000 business into one entirely different than before. We've been noticed. It's our competitors who first called us the 'Bloomingdale's of Catalogs.'

"We're willing to pioneer a department even if it takes time to start. If products are selected for a group, a fairly large group takes longer to attract. It's the same in a store. You put in a new department first. The customers seek it out gradually, only as they get the habit. A recession stretches the time period required to attract customers to a change in a new type of merchandise.

"One of our objects is a strong position in cook and serve. We want to develop a 'Macy's Cellar' in print—more of a gourmet type department. It's traditional in retailing that if you decide to start a department, it must be big enough to be noticed. To be noticed as having a regular cook-and-serve department you must have fundamental, basic cook-and-serve standard items. One might be a certain kind of strainer gourmets use. How much business you do at once on such items is not as important as establishing the feeling that you have the department and are the place to look for such items. You must gradually develop the business by building a new look.

"The income level has changed. Families have two incomes but less time to spend them. There's an awareness around the whole country, an awareness of new trends. TV has expanded new trends in fashions, cooking, roller skating, whatever. Energy costs have influenced shopping markets. There are new life styles. All this has affected our choice of merchandise, services, presentation and ways of selling.

"We accept credit cards—American Express, VISA and Master Charge. Originally, Spiegel's was most reluctant to get involved. But we see the potential. Offering a choice of buying through a credit card or buying direct increases our charge accounts. If offered a choice between charging on a bank card or being charged direct by Spiegel, 40% will accept and apply for credit direct. We try to solicit charge accounts and accept them from potential customers with the characteristics of those for whom the new Spiegel's is designed. We get the best reorders from our own charge account customers, then from bank cards. We can serve them better directly.

"In Philadelphia, we have a national in-bound, toll-free phone order operation. At Oakbrook, Illinois, we have a sophisticated computer, customer-oriented phone service facility where special, trained operators can access immediately individual customer activities for the past six months. The service specialist can bring up on the computer screen the buying record of the customer she is talking to. We now resolve 80% of customer service requests immediately.

"We're working in many areas. We have greatly improved the covers on our catalogs. When we get established we might do a lot more things. We can't do the number of specialized catalogs that Sears does. But we may later be able to produce segmented catalogs. By that I mean we hope later to vary the catalog by editions according to the buying habits of our customers. Different people would receive different variations of the catalog with pages and sections added or taken out for different groups of customers.

"The computer may make this possible sooner than people realize. In 1981, we started on stream a new sales file, all computerized. We use outside computer programing experts. All this will modernize the way we can use our sales file. There will be more demographics and psychographics.

"We're doing a lot of testing of customers' reactions. We look at customer performance in the broad range. We're also looking at the psychographics of four groups of our customers. We very carefully study what people buy.

"One group is typically upscale. These are women customers who have excellent incomes and good jobs. They range in age from 24 to 54. They live alone or with their husbands. They are fashion-oriented. They use credit intelligently.

"The next group is younger, mid-thirties. They know fashions but their priorities put their spendable income into the home. We call them our Jean group. Both are probably working with combined incomes over $25,000. This is our long-term Spiegel target customer.

"We have another group, our double-knit ladies, who are older, live in an ethnic neighborhood and are more mature. In this group, a typical customer spends more on herself and her home. One reason is that her home is paid for. The children are ready to leave. This group has a good family income of $35,000 to $45,000 but purchases are more utilitarian. This group considers basics more important than fashion. They have the income but feel it's wasteful to put in more fashionable ladies' wear.

"The last group are what we call knob turners. They like gadgets. They buy cookware to hardware to cameras to phone answering devices. They are careful shoppers for brand and price. They use a credit payment plan. They are not much for fashion ready-to-wear but also buy 'Jean' type active wear. They may have the shortest life span of Spiegel customers. We're still learning how to expand their product preferences and motivate them to buy.

"The most productive group in orders received is group one. The second most productive group is group three. They're more mature, less fashionable, have a different taste level but are good customers."

One way to create the new Spiegel has been to create small space ads with style and verve targeted at and in media selected to reach the young working women and upward mobile families Spiegel's seeks. These ads offer the Spiegel sampler catalog, "Discover Spiegel."

"Discover Spiegel", a distinctive catalog designed to attract new customers, is also mailed in volume to selected lists of this same demographic customer group. There are four versions, each tailored demographically and psychographically to the specific groups previously described. They range in size from 60 pages to

84 pages. Outstanding values are offered. It's a sale catalog. Almost every page features sale items. It can only indicate the range and variety of items in the big catalog. It does display the kind of items the new Spiegel features—in taste, style and price. "Discover Spiegel" is a tempter catalog to appeal to the character of customer Spiegel is after.

You can get the big Spiegel catalog by ordering anything in "Discover Spiegel". Or you can get it by paying for it, refundable on your first purchase; or get it by ordering from a friend's big catalog. Both catalogs are put together with extraordinary care and skill. Each is all color on every page. Each has a superb items selection.

Spiegel has spent a fortune in photography. Models selected are just right to uptrend Spiegel customers, yet not too high fashion in sophistication. "We do not feature paint, tires or kitchen cabinets—but instead, food processors, furlined coats, modular furniture and jogging outfits . . . fashion, stylish living, leisure wear."

Spiegel buyers have done a splendid job. The items spell out the personalities and life styles of customers desired. There are phone answering machines and area rugs with the effect of free flowing terra cotta, with plush pile that is like fur. There are swiveling brass globe lamps and sheepskin auto seat covers. There are steak thermometers and European white duck down comforters and mini ice boxes and compact dish washers and laundry washer-dryers.

There's designer everything from Gloria Vanderbilt to Bill Blass, Anne Klein to Geoffrey Beene. There are over 400 famous brand names, usually combined with unusual products. There's Cuisinart and Osterizer and Wamsutta. There's an Emerson swag light with a built-in heater.

There's Kenwood, Soundesign, Lily of France underwear and Karastan rugs. There are Fieldcrest and Martex and Canon towels—big, thick, luxurious . . . and all colors. There's Sony and RCA and Oneida silver and Rosenthal china. There's a Bearcat scanner to monitor (non CB) public service shortwave, and Bialetti's pasta maker from Italy, Char-B-Que indoor grills and Wolverine hiking boots and Revere cookware.

Departments are in depth and there are many departments—a fine one in hi-fi, VTR, TV and radio of 18 pages. The emphasis in fashion is on clothes for office that look good at night. But there's plenty of leisure and glamour fashion clothes. There are 22 pages of gourmet items. There's an 8-page bath bazaar and 13½ pages of slipcovers, 28 pages of curtains. There's a men's shop of 82 pages and 63 pages of bedroom products.

There are 18 pages on women's shoes alone. There's a children's shop of 12 pages and a teenage shop of 27 pages. There are two pages of famous typewriters and 8 of luggage, 2 on calculators.

Henry Johnson has rejuvenated Spiegel, reinvigorated it, given it a youth image, given it charisma. He's imparted a fashion feeling to it. He's making it trusted. He's filled the catalog with famous names. In doing so, he's increased credibility for Spiegel's occasional private brand items.

"It took Bloomingdale's 20 years to change its low class family store to high fashion. I can't do it in three. But competitors

know us as never before. We get good PR from them."
Meanwhile, Spiegel is beginning to analyze dollars and cents
results of its new policies. As inquiries from ads come in,
purchases from catalogs mailed them are tallied. As 'Discover
Spiegel' is mailed out in even greater amounts, sales are toted up
from it as well as conversions to the big Spiegel book. Finally,
overall results and results from old and new Spiegel customers
are being calculated from the new big catalog.

"At present, we're mailing our big catalog to our regular
customers obtained over the years and to our new group of
customers. New customer buying habits are being compared with
those of old, loyal customers. Our new customer group is more
productive. The old group pays well, includes a lot of cash buyers
and buys less.

"We watch what we call 'vital signs' . . . the key indicators
which should go up. Sales per employee must go up. We must sell
more with less people. We have a teamster union for the entire
warehouse catalog business. We had a lot of employees. Labor
cost per employee had kept going up. Productivity per dollar of
labor cost had been going down. Quality control was weak.

"With the new Spiegel we have improved quality of the
products we sell and our service. We have cut the number of
employees in half. Our business is a little bigger. We're very
variable. Any overall sales increase will now be very profitable.
That's going to happen because we're not going to cheapen the
catalog.

"To make the Spiegel transformation through recession has
not been easy. It has taken patience and courage. What has hurt
everyone in retailing is the high cost of money. It's been difficult
for retailers. In 1980, paying 18% to 19% bank interest was an
impossible burden. That was just the beginning. The economy
was bad. Giving credit was risky. It seems that we're verging on
and may have to live through a period of scarcity compared with
the plenty we've always had, of continued recession and depression, of growing special markets and tougher mass markets.

"We're not concerned with it. The retailing business has no
room for pessimists. You need guts. You have a new plan, you
have to hang in there. If the strategy is good, don't change it
dramatically in recessions or booms. In this case, if you develop a
full list of all the demographics and psychographics you're after,
keep going after them.

"Our present selling via the 'Discover Spiegel' campaign is
best for the long run. We will expand our magazine promotion.
We'll keep getting the psychographic and demographic selections
of the potential customers we seek. We'll keep up our image
building.

"We will start item selling in our publication advertising.
Our strength is in our item selection. We shop the world. We
come up with unique items that others do not have or before they
have them."

Meanwhile, the transformation of Spiegel into the Bloomingdale's of catalogs continues.

Henry Johnson is a mail order futurist. He studies every
possible future trend as it may affect mail order and Spiegel. In
the Help Source Section of this book are details how to get a tape
of a fascinating Henry Johnson speech (or reprint of it in
magazine article form) on the future application of electronic
mail order.

Note: Spiegel's sales in 1981 passed $400,000,000 versus
$265,000,000 in 1976 . . . the last year before the transition . . . a
gain of over 50%. For the first quarter of 1982, Spiegel's sales ran
18½% ahead of the same period for 1981.

Chapter 10
Newsletters About Mail Order

*Too many to read . . . some too
good to miss.*

In the fast growing, complex field of direct marketing—with
many specialites—good newsletters can help, but which?

Out of many that have started, here are some to consider,
depending on your situation . . . some edited by people I write
about in this book. One favorite of mine is Friday Report, the
oldest, most continuously published newsletter covering all direct
marketing.

Each week Friday Report extracts brief summaries of key
items from the Hoke Communications entire coverage of direct
marketing world-wide. These include important speeches of top
authorities just taped anywhere . . . anything read by a Hoke
researcher in any trade paper or consumer publication . . . and
interviews by Hoke Sound reporters flagged as important enough
for "Pete" Hoke to consider for Friday Report.

It is oriented particularly, as "Pete" is, to latest developments that may greatly affect the long-term future of direct
marketing . . . changing technology, often featuring experiments
in and possibilities of electronic mail order. There's constant
coverage of latest news of upcoming postal regulations that can
greatly affect direct marketing. For much of what Friday Report
gives a quick summary, fuller in-depth reports are available on
tape within days from Hoke Communications . . . speeches,
lectures, interviews. I find the combined service invaluable.

The Non-Store Marketing Report is oriented, as Maxwell
Sroge, its founder is, to sales, profits, bottom-line results of
biggest direct marketers, new methods of selling. It goes beyond
the umbrella of direct marketing to include coverage of house-to-
house and business-to-business selling by sales forces. But it
predominantly emphasizes direct marketing, and particularly
latest trends, newest profit areas and most recent statistics
concerning direct marketing. It is published every other month.

As described in this book, the Sroge organization has a
statistical research publishing division. This annually reports size
and growth of U.S. mail order sales and makes in-depth
statistical summary reports of fast growing segments of mail
order from time to time. It has the feel of Maxwell Sroge's sense
of entrepreneurship tempered by increasingly thorough, detailed
research and all briskly written by a fine staff. The bigger the
company, the more important it is to read.

The Januz Direct Marketing Letter has a broad constitu-
ency. Some of the biggest direct marketers, and some quite small,
subscribe. Some of the longest established mail order firms do,
and some of the newest. Lauren R. Januz, the publisher, has
personally experienced the trials of a kitchen table entrepreneur
and personally consulted with and written copy for biggest mail
order giants. After gaining experience writing mail order copy, he
set up shop in his home and sold his mail order copy skills . . . by
mail order . . . with ever-increasing success. He then became a
consultant and organized an advertising agency. He published his
newsletter. He sold thousands of books concerning direct
marketing.

Jim Atkins, who first worked for Hoke Communications and has since written many articles for ZIP, founded Telephone Marketing Report. How he did and kept it going with ingenuity instead of money is an exciting mail order story.

Lauren Januz acquired Telephone Marketing Report and publishes it with his accustomed drive. It's for quite big and far smaller direct marketers. It concerns ways to sell more by telephone and to pay less to do it. It covers how to get phone inquiries via each advertising medium, how to convert incoming phone inquiries to sales, and how to trade up incoming phone orders to bigger orders. It reports on outgoing telephone selling to convert coupon inquiries and outgoing cold phone calls and how to select lists for them.

Januz publishes newsletters in two other fields: He operates on two continents. He writes, with solid know-how, both copy and newsletters. For the DMMA Manual, Lauren Januz wrote "15 Basic Rules for Direct Mail Fund Raising".

"Direct Response, the Digest of Direct Marketing", is published by Craig Huey and applies the approach of Board Room Reports to direct marketing. Craig got into direct marketing in 1972, while still at Long Beach University in California, when he was 22. He got interested in political causes which used direct mail. This got him into list brokerage which helped pay for college. He double majored in history and political science. He got teaching credentials for courses on government.

When Craig got into political causes, he shared an office with John Finn, a direct mail consultant in Torrance, California—who became a good friend and a tutor in direct marketing for the causes. Soon Craig was working in Finn's list and creative service business, Infomat. Later, Finn started buying and selling businesses. In 1974, he turned Infomat over to Craig. To successfully run it, Craig became a voracious reader of anything written anywhere that he could find on direct marketing. He started with no money, boot-strapped and has grown very fast.

Craig credits much of his success to the ideas he has gotten in this way, and Direct Response was born because he was speed-scanning so much direct marketing research material for his own

use. It reflects his California, can-do approach. It is widely and ably promoted. He has real ability in the writing of its promotion. It covers a wide swath and is creating its own following. A good recommendation is the continued and increasing success of Craig Huey in direct marketing.

"To grow in direct marketing in lists and in creative work, I have to keep up. The newsletter, itself, has been a means to keep up. To write, I must read. I read 10 to 15 publications a day." Craig is a busy man. He still publishes pamphlets for political causes. He writes for political candidates. "I don't help out a candidate or cause I don't believe in." His inclinations are conservative.

"We are aggressively building in each of four areas in the direct marketing business—both list brokerage and list management, as a creative direct marketing advertising agency and consultant, and with Direct Response. I give readers what helps me—a quick scan selection of any idea-stimulating item we can find anywhere that can affect direct marketing." Craig promotes the Digest as effectively as he does the newsletters of his clients—and makes it as tempting to try it.

Some of the best newsletters about direct marketing concern the selection of lists for direct mail marketers. Rose Harper's Immediate Release (Kleid) is literate, astute and inspirational, with much useful information. Jack Oldstein's List Marketing Letter (Dependable) is like him—friendly, practical, knowledgeable. Issue by issue, it covers more and more. Cumulatively, it's encyclopedic. It's much appreciated.

The newsletters most important to you depend on what you do in direct marketing. If you're using or considering using large-scale telephone marketing, the AIS 800 Report has been highly praised by biggest companies. It covers every facet of inward and outward WATS calls to receiving orders, converting inquiries, calling leads and selecting lists for cold calls.

If you're one of the several thousand newsletter publishers, there are two newsletters for newsletter publishers. Howard Penn Warren's Newsletter Clearing House founded the first one, "The Newsletter on Newsletters". It is competently written, exchanges experience of problems and successes, and fills a real need. It's packed with a wide variety of much needed information. Ray Henry is president of the Newsletter Association of America, which has a strong board of directors, including Howard Penn Warren. The NAA has its own newsletter, along with many other services.

There are a number of newsletters that come with membership in organizations. Two good ones are Copy Cornucopia, from the Direct Marketing Creative Guild, and the newsletter of Women in Direct Marketing. Most such newsletters, like the DMMA's Direct Marketing Journal, are considerably means of communication about club activities and pluses rather than sole reasons to join.

Newsletters which concern the field stop, start, expand, shrink and pause (my own newsletter, The Mail Order Analyst, was temporarily put aside to write this book). In Reference Section VII, starting with page 22, I list newsletters, frequency of publication and subscription rates prior to going to press. I include all reviewed and other specialized ones, as well.

Trial offers vary by newsletters and at different times for the same newsletter. The selection solution is to check each out by reading a sample issue, if available, or at a library at no cost. It's best to subscribe only when you find one or more particularly suited to your situation, and with which you feel happy. But one idea from one issue of one newsletter may change your mail order life.

Chapter 11
Printing Technology vs. Postage Inflation

*What held down printing price
increases while improving quality?*

By the summer of 1981, postage had gone up over 600% in 25 years. Uncle Sam has been the worst inflation offender in direct marketing. Had all costs associated with the mails gone up in proportion, direct mail as an advertising medium might well be dead and buried. But they didn't.

Other stories in this book tell how computers and labor-saving machines have slashed manual costs of getting in the mail—and how creative people and list selection experts produced more orders of higher average sale per thousand mailing pieces sent. But aside from postage, printing and paper are the biggest costs in the mail. Technological advances in printing and associated graphic art services have held down printing price increases—and more than any factor, helped offset postage increases.

Lincoln Graphic Arts is a printer—and an example in fighting direct mail inflation, while improving printing quality. Its four partners have top know-how and rare credentials in direct marketing. Each has worked with direct marketers all his business life.

Lincoln and each partner . . . Norman Eisner, Ed Davidson, Leo Sweedler and Hal Sommers . . . has a special claim to mail order fame. Nat Ross is vice president. Elsewhere in this book you have met or will meet Nat. He has helped many, many people start and rise in direct marketing. Lincoln helped him do it. They funded the hours and back-up people needed.

They're nice people, quality people. They have quality customers—from Mobil Oil to Crown Publishing Co. They are wise in the ways of printing and the mail order use of it. For this book, partners Hal Sommers and Norman Eisner have devoted patience and care to give us some background on changing printing technology and how it has affected mail order and direct marketing.

"We all have dealt with mail order people all our business lives. We all came out of the direct mail lettershop business and went into printing many years ago. Nat Ross originally came with us as a salesman 25 years ago. It was obvious from the beginning that he was a brilliant man. Being a scholar, he took to the theoretical side of direct marketing and today is acknowledged as one of it's leading mentors.

"Since we've been in the printing business, postage has gone up almost twice as fast as inflation. Yet, overall cost in the mail has gone up about the same as inflation. One reason has been that the quantities mailed have increased. Anything mass produced obviously drops in price per unit, particularly printing.

"A major factor is web offset printing. Web means printing from a continuous roll as newspapers do. The web press is not a patented process, nor a great invention suddenly on the scene. It's old and not revolutionary. At first, it had its limitations—only black and white printing on newsprint paper.

"For a long time the quality of color reproduction was not very good, and it was not uniform. Then the process improved, both for black and white . . . and for color. Coated papers began to be used. The efficiency of web improved while quality of reproduction also continued to improve. Now the only difference between the quality of letterpress and web offset is that web still can't produce the gloss of letterpress. The best paper is still best suited for letterpress. However, web offset printing produces excellent, fine quality printing.

"We were not the innovators of web color printing. We got into it 20 years ago—in 1962, about 10 years after it had started . . when we observed that "web" was now capable of producing quality printing.

"The web press could produce color printing at a lower cost because it is capable of using lighter weight paper at less cost. But it had a larger make-ready cost and therefore it was only useful for larger quantities in order to obtain maximum savings. Of course, this favored the big over the small user.

"For a solo mailing, a million was considered necessary to obtain an economic run. But then, as more expensive merchandise and offers were made, often to more specialized audiences, thinking was revised. Color began to be considered so essential that for such quantities perhaps 200,000 would be enough. Tests proved it. Color became more and more essential in catalogs. Color sold higher ticket, better quality items and web could produce color less expensively. But to sell such items quality color printing was also required.

"For the quality of color reproduction to so improve over the last 20 years and to keep cost increases down, a great many things had to happen. New developments were required. It all started gradually—one small advance at a time. Each year, something new came on to improve the end result.

"The press manufacturers developed more advanced machines. The presses became bigger and faster. Our last web offset press we purchased cost us $2,500,000—the only one of its kind in the New York metropolitan area. It's a Harris M-200 and prints up to 8 colors. It can handle 64 digest-size pages in full color or 32 full-size pages in one pass through the press. It can produce 400,000 signatures during the plant's 24-hour shift and folds and perforates simultaneously.

"Presses are more variable. One press can do the work of two. We also have a four-color Miehle web press and a six-color Hantscho. They each have split drives which makes them the equivalent in capacity of four two-color presses and two four-color presses.

"Binding equipment is faster, handles more pages and is more efficient. We have two McCain saddle stitchers and a Sheridan perfect binder. The Sheridan binds spines up to 1¼ inches thick. Equipment can fold more accurately. It was no good just to print faster if the paper tore or the ink splashed, and resulted in more and more spoilage. The mills had to learn to make stronger paper. The ink companies came up with improved inks.

"The industry has improved in countless ways. There have been technological advances in plate making and processing them. They get better and better. Making the coating used to be very technical and took half an hour. Now 3-M has come up with a method to make plates much more economically. One plate now lasts 300,000 to 400,000 impressions. The costs are therefore lower as labor costs are eliminated.

"There have been improvements in color separations using computer scanners. It was experimental twenty years ago. Now it's prevalent. There have been improvements by everyone. They all did this because mail order continued to grow. The market was there and advances were required and achieved. The technology is constantly changing. Now there's a new kind of film to compete with Kodak. It doesn't use silver. New technology is developing constantly, some from Germany and Japan. It's coming up faster and faster. The trade papers and magazines are full of reports about them. It's an effort to keep up and to keep in touch with all these changes. But we do. This business is in a constant state of flux.

"In the printing industry, the skill of the individual is now less important. The equipment is more important. Take the dot etcher. It's not Tiffany quality, but it looks good. It's clean, neat, sharp. It's not perfect. Printing is really not as much an art anymore, but much more a craft. It's more dependent on equipment. But the design of the equipment is still created by people. Organizing the equipment and the use of it by people have greatly improved.

"There's far more efficiency. New York City used to be the printing capital. Printing was the number two industry. It was second only to the garment industry. It was a business of small printing shops. The ALA, the labor union, had 13,000 members in New York City. The New York City printers had the market. Everything was local. They had the business not only for New York City but from all over.

"But it was all very inefficient. Catalogs would be printed in one plant and then trucked to an entirely different bindery plant and then trucked again to a mailing house or to the mail order firm for mailing. And everything done by each plant required hand labor. The set-up of each plant was usually inefficient, with a number of small floors and people going from floor to floor.

"Still, the New York printers had the bulk of the business. To compete, printers in other parts of the country began to become more efficient than those in New York. First, they combined printing and binding and then labeling and mailing in one plant. This avoided all unnecessary trucking and saved labor costs along the way.

"From then on in it was a matter of building bigger plants, or positioning equipment for more efficient use, of substituting equipment for hand labor. All together, it caused a dramatic change. The little printing shops and older plants had difficulty adapting. They couldn't compete. The printing jobs went where the prices were lower. Only the most efficient survived—those who invested in the latest equipment, organized their work force better and combined logical functions.

"When we observed that, we decided to move outside the city to our current plant and therefore realized substantial savings—due to plant efficiencies and lower property costs. We set up our own bindery and mailing departments. Shortly thereafter, we produced the Hammacher-Schlemmer catalog. We were actually mailing the catalogs before all the printing was finished because the binding was completed as they came off the press. In addition, anyone in the country who wishes to deal with our company can buy paper from a mill close to us. Today we compete with printers all over. Purchasers of printing can now print anywhere and mail where they print.

"When web printing came to be utilized, paper costs dropped. The web press uses paper on rolls. Letter press printing required sheet-fed paper. A grade of paper that now costs 45¢ a pound sheet-fed costs 32¢ on rolls. It's a big saving. Some kinds of paper dropped more dramatically when web came in—from 20¢ a pound for sheet-fed paper to 11¢ for web. Then inflation set in. It took years for rising paper costs to bring paper on rolls up to what the same paper had formerly cost sheet-fed.

"For a long time after web came in, the cost of printing—including paper—went down. Then for many years the printing cost—including paper—did not go up. However, since 1975, the cost of paper has advanced very dramatically and the cost of printing very little.

"In 25 years, postage has gone up over 600%. Lists have gone up 300% to 400%. Yet, the printing part of direct mail has not changed nearly as much. For a typical Book-of-the-Month Club package, mailing and handling costs have increased very little.

"Web printing preparation costs are still high. Costs can be as high as $5,000 before printing the first sheet. But these costs are absorbed quickly as volume is produced so that the price per thousand drops sharply for larger mailings.

"From 1975 to 1981, paper increased by 300% while printing—aside from paper—went up 15%. Now paper cost is getting out of sight, particularly for the type of paper required for color printing. Coated paper that used to cost 11¢ a pound is now 36¢ to 37¢. Paper is now 50% to 60% of the overall cost of a printing job whereas it used to be approximately 35% of the total cost.

"Even as prices have sky-rocketed, color printing, particularly catalogs, has increased. But resistance has started to set in. Customers are taking short-cuts. They are cutting numbers of pages and page sizes. They are using lighter paper weights. Some customers are beginning to experiment with newsprint papers and black and white mailings. There's a big emphasis on selectivity of lists, segmentation—to mail less and still try to sell more.

"Nevertheless, the cost of direct mail increases year after year. We just produced 14,000,000 magazine inserts for U.S. Pioneer. We produced 800,000 a day, finished and folded. All of this is possible because of the perfecting of the web offset method. We could never have done it before. Today's printing method is possible due to advanced technology.

"Without this new technology, the printers of today would not be capable of producing the required volume and the mailing houses could not get it into the mail. The old hand tools could never have done it. We used to have sixty people in the day and sixty at night turning out what we do now with machines. In the 1940's, the Book-of-the-Month Club required one person to insert 3,000 pieces of mail. That meant sixty people for each 180,000 pieces a day. Now six inserting machines with six individuals produce that same amount.

"Now we print a million 17″ x 22″ circulars on four-color presses. We used to have to go through the press twice on two-color equipment. To run 170,000 sheets through the press would take six days. At best, we could run 60,000 sheets on one side each day. It would take three days to do one side, six days for both. Then we had to fold it and deliver it in the time required. Today we couldn't function that way. The ability to print in volume has made it possible for the catalog and direct mail pieces of bigger mailers to take advantage of volume cost savings.

"We've seen printing technology continue to improve the quality of direct mail advertising while price, aside from postage, has been kept somewhat in line. It's helped make possible the continuation of catalogs and magazines that are being produced in today's market. We see it in catalogs. 35% of our work is catalogs—for mail order companies and department stores. We see it in magazines which are 40% of our production. We also find it in much higher quality direct mail pieces. That's the balance of our business.

"The use of catalogs and direct mail by direct marketers keeps growing despite all problems, and keeps us growing. But we don't want to be giants. We're unique. We're quite content to have reached our level and we have no current plans to grow much more. We have our own methods. We prefer to buy U.S. equipment. We have an attitude of loyalty to our suppliers, our customers, our people and to direct marketing. We think it pays.

"Nat Ross started his course at NYU 15 years ago. He started the Direct Marketing Idea Exchange over 10 years ago. He works with the DMMA, the Direct Marketing Days and the Direct Marketing Clubs. We back him to the extent of his desire to help people in the industry. And he's helped a lot of them in a great many ways. It's funding something that should be done. Nat has helped the direct marketing industry from which we get much of our business. And that's enough for us."

Note: Lincoln Graphic Arts has a hundred-thousand-square-foot plant at 200 Finn Court, Farmingdale, New York 11735. (516) 293-7600. It has offices at 475 Park Avenue South, New York, New York 10016; (212) 532-4004.

Chapter 12
Safety In Numbers

He's a Harvard MBA Guide,
through the mail order jungle,
for the Fortune 500.

His specialty is how to do more mail order business, at greater profit . . . with least risk and capital tie-up. In his business he has helped clients make millions of dollars of direct marketing sales more safely and more profitably. He does it by analyzing more direct marketing data and statistics than anyone in the world and by emphasizing careful planning. He is Robert Kestnbaum.

He has headed mail order activities for Bell & Howell and been Manager of Direct Marketing for Montgomery Ward. Since then, he has launched and built a direct marketing management consulting firm, R. Kestnbaum and Company. Bob Stone calls him a "super consultant". Kestnbaum clients include the biggest—American Express, IBM and Sears Roebuck. They range from L.L. Bean to the Metropolitan Museum of Art . . . from Lillian Vernon to L'Eggs. They're all over the U.S. and Europe.

The organization's premise is that planning, research, projections and controls lead to mail order success; that virtually no mail order disaster need happen; that most mail order losses need not occur; that sales of profitable items and percentages of profit often can be sharply increased; and that numbers surveillance, day by day and operation by operation, can give constant control.

Bob Kestnbaum strongly believes that mail order success starts with determining whether to go into mail order at all; what field to enter; what products to select, what offers to make; what appeals to use; what media and lists to select, when to start, stop, expand, contract.

Bob Kestnbaum helps giants, but he says: "Good management can be implemented by even the smallest companies. You do not need a giant computer or a large staff. You do need to plan, monitor and control the key elements of your business . . . those that are at the very core of its success.

"The manager of the smallest business can start with accurate counting . . . if not of all transactions, then of samples.

Much can be developed using manual counts or reports summarizing information from various sources. The next step is simple calculating, spotting trends . . . and estimating final out-comes. But every direct marketing business should have a computer. Complex information can be processed and reports can be greatly facilitated. Today, even the smallest company can afford some kind of computer system, which can be purchased today for less than $50,000."

Bob Kestnbaum was born and brought up in Chicago. He got an AB degree from the University of Chicago, then an AB from Harvard and then an MBA also from Harvard. He spent three-and-a-half years in the Navy and left the Navy in 1958 for his first job . . . at Bell & Howell, working for Maxwell Sroge. The story of Mac Sroge and of how the Bell & Howell home movie camera and projector kit changed mail order history forever is told elsewhere in this book. Bob came just before this was getting under way. Initially, he was the administrator and coordinator. Two years later, Bell & Howell formed its own mail order subsidiary, Robert Maxwell . . . using Bob and Mac's first names.

"Mac set up the deals, found the items and created mailing pieces," explains Bob. "I was the principal salesman and administrator. Later, Mac went on to Wunderman, Ricotta & Kline and then started his own business."

After Maxwell Sroge left, Bob Kestnbaum ran Robert Maxwell, gaining additional mail order experience. He liked to analyze each correct and misstep. He kept searching for data to make sounder decisions. He set up checks, safeguards and controls and at each step he reported to top management what was going on. He explained to senior executives the objectives and results, tests and projections, and how analysis was derived.

"In 1966, I tried to get Montgomery Ward to sell movie outfits. To interest them I wrote a plan outlining how to set up a department to make solo mailings to their list and to use inserts in their bills. They called me and said they did not want to sell movie outfits but offered me a job to set up such a department. I said no. Later they made another, more tempting offer, which I accepted. I became Direct Mail Manager.

"After Wards, I became a direct marketing consultant. Among my first clients were cameras and Quaker Oats. While doing this, other companies asked for help in going into direct marketing. Over the years more companies have sought us out. We have never solicited business in 14 years. All our clients have come by word of mouth and referral.

"One big advance in direct marketing occurred when two fellows from Hewlett-Packard came to my office to talk about a new handheld, electronic calculator for engineers. No one had sold anything like it before. It would sell for $395. Bill Hewlett wanted to sell it by mail order. I was sure the product could be sold by mail. This was in August 1971. Hewlett-Packard started the project with a few people and it grew to become a separate division. Calculators were first sold by mail; then college bookstores were solicited to carry HP products; then distribution was expanded to retail, department and specialty stores.

"I helped design some cosmetic aspects of the product. It was going to be a drab brown. I explained that a high quality, expensive item should be more attractive and urged a black design with a chrome stripe. We tailored it to be a viable mail order product.

"From the beginning, our company planned every mail order step and every Hewlett-Packard mailing. We developed a better way of structuring list selection to be sure that all viable market segments were explored. We specified the data to be retained on the customer mailing list. We developed management reports. We analyzed confidence levels. We projected the most probable profit of a given plan. We compared different profit objectives. We ordered all lists as long as their mail order continued.

"Meanwhile, in 1971, American Express started with us. At that time, Stan Fenvessy and I formed Fenvessy & Kestnbaum. Stan is an expert in operations, administration and physical facilities. My expertise is in planning, financial analysis and marketing. The combination of our capabilities provides a full-service organization.

"American Express was the first project that Fenvessy & Kestnbaum worked on as a joint activity. We worked together very well and have done so many times since. If Stanley works for a company, he may bring us in and vice versa. We're always in touch. We use each other's offices and are a good team. We have been effective in helping American Express and other companies to build a large mail order merchandise business.

"We have done a great deal of work to segment the American Express list. Some information learned in this effort has revolutionized the company's thinking. Major changes were made in specification of names selected for upcoming mailings. Results were then much higher than achieved with the original methods to select names. But we did not accept this as final. We continue to refine the methods used. The process is perpetual."

To Bob Kestnbaum, many of the risks and losses in direct marketing are unnecessary. "Some of the most serious hazards facing a relatively small business arise from the reluctance of owners and managers to *anticipate* events . . . inability to recognize whether events are following their *anticipated trend* . . . and failure to make better use of information. Only a handful of sophisticated companies do, themselves, what we do. A surprising number of accomplished direct marketers retain some theories or techniques that are quite disadvantageous. But when shown a new way, they accept it readily.

"Marketing planning and analysis is the foundation for *anticipating* events, tracking their progress and *maintaining* financial control. Data, by itself, tells no story. It must be grouped and categorized. Flexibility and imagination in arranging information within data bases can provide the means for control and evaluation of any direct marketing business.

"Direct marketers have a unique capability to measure response, analyze it and predict from early response what final results will be. Patterns can be developed for each step in a program from receiving inquiries to converting them, receiving payments and returned goods, by season, type of media, individual medium or whatever.

"Every stage is measurable as to how much money was spent, how many people were reached, and how many responded, and what sales were produced. One of the most appealing aspects of direct marketing is the sense of precision that results from the ability to test with limited risk, to launch programs in small quantities and to expand carefully based on prior results.

"Catalogs or brochures are salesmen. Advertisements and mailings are selling costs comparable to discounts to dealers or to salaries and commissions paid to salesmen in other marketing channels. The costs for advertisements and mailings are known first. The results and, therefore, profit or loss are known later. Sales commissions and discounts are known in advance and are generally fixed.

"In direct marketing, selling costs are variable and become known when results are tabulated and compared to advertising costs. Direct marketers are more interested in advertising costs per order than in cost per thousand or absolute advertising costs.

In direct marketing, selling costs vary dramatically for different products, presentation, media and times. Each type of medium and format attracts somewhat different kinds of people, requiring separate calculations of costs and profitability.

"You can also identify the external events which may influence costs and results. You can forecast, or at least track, these events, modifying the operation of your business as necessary to reduce loss and increase profit. But to do so takes constant study and evaluation.

"Costs of everything from product to shipping, labor, processing and overhead . . . to printing, postage and media . . . must be known at all times. They often rise rapidly. Any figure can be outdated quickly. Some costs vary dramatically in quantity versus short runs. All costs must be constantly recalculated, particularly for each new product and new campaign. Careful projections of costs and anticipated results and profits should be made before each test and projection. A surprising number of experienced direct marketers fail to do so early enough to adjust their offerings or promotion plans. Yet the numbers can suggest what to do."

For Bob, success in direct marketing requires ever-improved application of numbers science and ever more painstaking thoroughness. "In our business, there is plenty of detail. Launching a direct marketing campaign requires attention to immense detail. Even in its test phases, it's very complex. But you can't get lost in the forest. You must see the top of the mountain.

"We analyze each business we look at. We work with the company to set objectives for sales, profit on sales, ROI (Return on Investment) and absolute profit. We assess company objectives. We're extremely thorough. We dig deeply. We try to be practical and not to operate in an ivory tower. We try to innovate, to step back and conceptualize. We build a plan and work out the consequences far into the future, after making assumptions and predictions. We compare alternate plans with a lot of help from the computer. We recommend what we find to be the winning plan. When a program is implemented, then we follow through to be sure it happens according to plan.

"Planning figures indicate what you want to happen. Budgeting figures describe what you expect to happen. Forecasting data tells you what probably will happen. Reports can describe and compare plans, budgets and forecasts. Figures so used provide management control and evaluation."

Bob Kestnbaum has strong opinions on the use of numbers science in list segmentation. "Sears Roebuck was working with the first forms of segmentation at the turn of the century. But until the 1930's, Sears, Wards, Aldens and Spiegel essentially distributed catalogs to any customer who had purchased a specified amount within a designated time period. In the depression, this was considered too wasteful. A more analytical approach was adopted—but without computers, a very simple one. It was the first RFM formula, a method to determine to whom and how often to send catalogs.

"Catalogs were coded and results tabulated on the basis of various combinations of recency, frequency and monetary value of the order. In general, a two-order customer seemed worth twice a one-order customer. A customer who bought within the latest twelve months was worth twice a buyer who last bought 12 to 24 months ago. Those who last ordered 24 to 30 months prior to mailing were worth only 75% as much as those who purchased 12 to 24 months before. Frequency (single versus multiple orders) in the four seasons before was weighted 50%. Recency of the last order was weighted 35%. Monetary value of orders was weighted 15%.

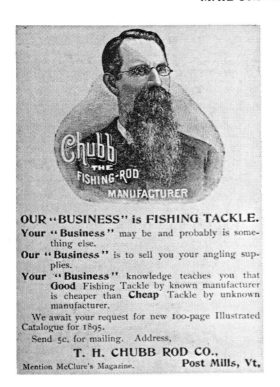

"Using this rough method, the mailing of fewer catalogs produced sales at far lower selling cost. The man who popularized RFM was George Cullinan when he was at Aldens. Specialized mail order companies began adopting similar techniques. They placed recency first on the list. For many direct marketing people, segmentation has never progressed beyond the RFM stage.

"Our position is that segmentation based solely on RFM is dead. Today's techniques and technology permit a much more exciting approach. Computers allow us to process and store more information about customers. Computers make possible a dramatic expansion in techniques of analysis. We understand much more about human behavior and the factors that predict it. Now we can do a good job of predicting the performance of groups of people . . . according to the *likelihood, amount* and *type* of further purchase.

"We can evaluate 30, 50, even 100 variables for a list segmentation model. We use regression analysis or other appropriate techniques. It is vital to understand what products people have bought and will buy. If you group and characterize customers properly, it's surprising how much more effectively they can be served and sold.

"A large catalog firm in Europe has kept track of purchases by mail of many types of products. It has compared bargain appeal versus full price offers and kept track of the purchase of low versus higher-priced products. It used a cluster analysis technique. It then calculated the *probable frequency* of each customer's purchases next season and the *probable time* of *those purchases*. The most appropriate catalogs are then sent to customers in time for probable purchase decisions.

"We have tried consistently to be at the cutting edge of new analytical and financial control methods in direct marketing. We're always looking for new kinds of information. The more available, the more we can analyze and look at creatively, and the better job we can do."

Magazine publishers pioneered computer modeling in direct marketing. Bob Kestnbaum has been pioneering computer modeling for direct marketers outside of the magazine publishing field. At R. Kestnbaum and Company, new and different uses of computer modeling are constantly being developed.

"For example, a catalog company has a series of choices. It can grow its business by mailing more catalogs to more people, by adding more products to its line, or by developing more catalogs or more media and increasing frequency of contact. It can spend money on these in many combinations and amounts. Computer modeling can help make the best choices.

"Computer models can show the results of different business devlopment alternatives in terms of net present value or the discounted value of all future cash flows. This lets us compare alternate strategies. It's possible to determine whether the extra risk associated with a bigger campaign is warranted.

"Once the plan is selected, a projective model can be developed to detail a future campaign and monitor its progress. As a campaign is run, sales, costs and profits can be compared at each step to those anticipated. It can be done for an existing or entirely new business. We can learn when monthly sales should peak, when monthly profits should begin and when, on a cumulative basis, the programs should break into the black. A computer control report can display at a glance the current status of each campaign and the component mailings and advertisements. It can display actual results to date and *project* the program to a *final outcome.*

"Helped by this, managers can take timely action—wherever warranted. The model can be adjusted as the campaign is changed. Business development and growth can be optimized. If new categories of merchandise or services are introduced, predictive models for these can be developed."

R. Kestnbaum and Company has developed special models for catalogs, continuity programs and other different kinds of direct marketing decisions.

"We have produced a computer model that employs some 29 types of variables to calculate the lifetime value of a buyer—recognizing that profits earned in the future are worth less than those that are earned today. With other models we can develop a merchandise plan by product and lifestyle category. We can predict business expectations by product category and make weekly updated projections. For some clients we keep sample customer data on our computer which incorporates performance history of each product and merchandise category. We can develop different strategies and work through in detail what the repercussions of each strategy would be. We can also perform a financial analysis of proposed direct marketing programs.

"Our strength lies in four things—long-range planning, business development strategy, financial planning and statistical analysis. When launching new business cash flows, we estimate for five years for each of a number of alternative plans together with personnel and facilities requirements."

"Kestnbaum plans, reports and manuals are MBA primers of complex direct marketing operations. These and transcripts of his speeches and reports of his articles comprise a how-to direct marketing science book uniquely different . . . a Fortune 500 direct marketing how-to kit and a detailed regimen.

There are forms and charts, worksheets and reports, and descriptions of computer models to keep you on track. Any failure of the number of inquiries, orders or payments to arrive as planned or within a grace period triggers a demand for management action.

But Bob Kestnbaum cautions: "Be practical. Avoid too many, too long and too frequent reports. Determine for your

DOTY'S
CLOTHES WASHER,
THE MOST POPULAR, BEST, AND
Cheapest Washing Machine
EVER INVENTED.

It is easy to operate, sitting or standing; takes but little room; injures no garments; finishes its work in from two to four minutes; is durable, convenient, and the only Washing Machine ever known that is **LIKED THE BETTER, THE LONGER IT IS USED.**

Recommended as the **Very Best** by Solon Robinson, Orange Judd, Prof. Youmans, and many other prominent men.

At the Great Fair of the American Institute. Oct., 1865, where all the principal Washers in the country were ably represented, it was awarded the FIRST PREMIUM.

On receipt of **$20** from places where no one is selling, we will send the **Washer** and the famous **Universal Clothes Wringer,** (and pay the freight if within 200 miles of New York.) The Washer alone will be sent for **$12.** Wholesale Terms Circular sent free. Exclusive right of sale given to the first responsible applicant from each town.   **R. C. BROWING, General Agent, 32 Courtlandt-st., N. Y.**
(Opposite Merchants Hotel.)

---

business the lifestream factors and focus on them. Most good management reports are only one or two pages long.

"All projections made in direct marketing are governed by their underlying variables and are subject to some statistical variance. The confidence level of projections can be estimated. Before undertaking major programs, whatever the strategy, adequate projections should be made and the downside risk should be assessed. The progress of each campaign should be carefully tracked. After each campaign, final results should be evaluated thoroughly and accurately.

"Doing this for clients got us into analysis of product choice, offers and approaches and into a study of results from each medium. In direct mail, what started out as a thorough report of the effectiveness of each list used led to consideration of the most effective way to select lists. Clients asked us to analyze the choice of new lists and of most effective ways to segment customer lists.

"The first requirement of success is to offer a desirable product or service. One of the prime factors in direct marketing failure is the lack of a strong offering. We don't encourage me-too items. Instead, we hope our clients will develop products or services that are unique, have clear character and are responsive to special needs. Great businesses stand for something special. It is important to create a unique position for each business."

Bob has written an outline of the art of two-step mail order . . . getting an inquiry and following it up by mail. His suggestions are quite practical for very small companies as well as the largest.

"Very often, it's more profitable to produce inquiries at relatively low cost and to convert them to sales through follow-up mailings or by salesman. The largest investment is that of obtaining the leads which then become a very special and expensive list. It's important to get maximum return on this investment. Follow-up mailings should almost always be used even if salesmen calls are made.

"The response to a series of follow-up mailings frequently fits a pattern in which each mailing produces about 40% to 50% of the response rate of the preceeding mailing. For low-cost items without much repeat sales, the conversion series must be shorter. For business and industrial products and services where a single order may lead to sales of many thousands of dollars, companies can afford to make more follow-up mailings. The profitability of each effort in a follow-up series should be determined. Additional conversion efforts should be made until the last in the series is no longer profitable.

"It's not unusual for business and industrial inquiry lists to be worth anywhere from $10 per name to hundreds of dollars per name in future profit, making them the most valuable type of list in existence. Business organizations should plan their activities carefully to use these lists well in order to realize full revenue potential.

"The interplay between producing and converting inquiries should be continuously studied and refined. Changes in offer, appeal or format of advertisement or mailing can lower or increase the cost per inquiry, and also affect the rate of conversion into orders. Each change in method of developing inquiries and each variation in the conversion series should be tracked and evaluated separately. Through experimentation and accurate record keeping, the process can be refined and fine tuned, sales costs lowered, and volume increased.

"This can be done with mathematical precision. Yet our experience indicates that few companies using direct mail to develop inquiries are able to execute sufficient control and supervision over the process to be able to develop figures as precisely as desired. This is particularly true where salesmen are used to follow-up and the final sale may occur months later."

Bob's organization has studied various phases of a wide variety of direct marketing methods . . . and particularly overall strategy and bottom-line results of different approaches. "In many respects, ROI (return on investment) is the best measure of success. Direct marketing campaigns typically show a high ROI. There is a time value of money. Money earned today is more valuable than money earned in the future. It can be reinvested to earn more money. Pernicious inflation cheapens future dollars earned. But by timing advertising expenditures, you can reinvest even moderate profits several times a year into new campaigns—and produce high ROI."

From first clients he learned the importance of bringing each to a clearer definition of volume and profit objectives, before proceeding. "It is vital to establish in advance what will be the standard for measuring success. Then you can make decisions and avoid misunderstandings. This is so for Fortune 500 companies as well as smaller firms." Bob Kestnbaum emphasizes avoidance of false starts, of unproductive approaches, of unnecessary development costs. He's quiet, cautious and confident.

"We have had some client failures, and one business created from scratch that could not be expanded beyond a smaller scale than desired. We work for about forty clients currently. Some sell consumers, and some other businesses. Some sell products one at a time and some use catalogs. Whether they sell products or services, our clients cover the spectrum. Many times we've been brought into situations where decisions had to be made to stop or continue. In a few, we have advised closing down the project. Sometimes, we're hired to help make a success more succesful and sometimes to launch a brand new direct marketing activity."

Bob Kestnbaum has a unique ability to relate MBA expertise in general marketing to direct marketers. He makes direct marketing considerably more understandable to them. He is reassuring to them, and so is the entire Kestnbaum organization.

"Currently, our organization has twenty people including nine consultants. We have an outstanding group. All but one of our consultants have MBA's, most from the University of Chicago. Most had a few years' experience in business. They all learned direct marketing in our firm. Business school graduates are analytically oriented. In addition, we have a corps of business analysts, a support staff, and a computer department, all of whom are vital to our success.

"We look for certain attributes in hiring everyone for our firm. We emphasize personal integrity, willingness to deal with detail and a grasp of numbers. We like people who learn quickly and who are flexible in their thinking. We emphasize training and personal improvement. One consultant is Jules Silbert, who had as president of the mail order division of Lane Bryant, built it into one of the largest mail order enterpises in the U.S."

Kate Kestnbaum, the ninth consultant, has no MBA. She has a KBA. "Kate is a Wellesley graduate. We were engaged for five years. We did everything together. We studied together. We worked together at home using a partner's desk. She was active and very effective in a number of community organizations.

"About 1974, Kate was undertaking a volunteer task to raise money for a community organization using direct mail. I gave her an office with us and helped her. In the process, she became very knowledgeable. Then I urged her to join us.

"Usually, two consultants work on each project. I have primary responsibility for some clients and try to work with every consultant on at least one or two projects. There is great emphasis in our shop on continual improvement of skills and productivity. We try to be creative, not by writing or designing ads, but by developing some very exciting, innovative concepts.

"Follow through is a very important part of the success we have had. We are usually retained to implement what we have recommended. I doubt that as many as half a dozen client relationships have been short-term. Most last for years, many for more than five or six years. Yet, all client agreements permit cancellation by either party on ninety-day notice.

"R. Kestnbaum and Company is complementary to and not competitive with advertising agencies. We share clients with many agencies and work closely with them. We've written creative strategies and copy platforms when we are more familiar with the product, the company and the market than the agency is, but we're not interested in being in the agency business. Our role is to help management and its ad agency to develop an overall plan and to help see that a project develops according to plan.

"Our business has been a lot of fun. Everyday I learn something new. It never stops. We're all learning. One-third of the work we do each year has never been done before. We are not satisfied with doing the same work the same way. Different techniques and concepts are always developing. We constantly study anything that affects planning, analysis, and management of direct marketing ventures."

In 1973, in a published interview with Bob Stone in Advertising Age, Bob Kestnbaum asked: "Why doesn't IBM offer follow-up items by mail order to IBM office products customers?" Four years later, IBM employed Bob to answer the question, Should we be using direct marketing? "We developed a plan for IBM to start a supply business via mail order. IBM accepted it and formed IBM Direct. Today it is a substantial mail order business. IBM Direct was launched selling supplies. Now it sells typewriters and other products by mail and telephone. Today, IBM is using direct marketing in many divisions. We work for several of them. Elsewhere in this book I tell the story of IBM Direct for which R. Kestnbaum and Company is a consultant, and for which the original marketing plan was created by Bob Kestnbaum.

"We're always driving ahead. We're looking for new ways to make better direct marketing decisions. The search for new ways to improve results is never-ending. And new, more effective methods keep evolving at an accelerating pace. We are excited about direct marketing's future.

"The opportunities in direct marketing are spectacular. The range of merchandise and services that can be sold by direct marketing appear almost unlimited. In this decade, many department stores will become true direct marketers. Businesses of all types are beginning to realize that they should consider direct marketing as part of their plans to sell virtually any kind of product. Business-to-business mail order is still a frontier. Direct marketing is being integrated into the total marketing mix. Big companies will do well but there will be ample specialized opportunities for smaller firms."

If you're in or thinking of going into direct marketing, Bob Kestnbaum has some words of caution. "Be alert to shifts in the economy and in people's attitudes, in buying patterns and in direct marketing techniques." He also has a few questions to ask you: "What alternatives do you have to choose from to make your own business grow? How can you evaluate them? How well do you anticipate events? How well do you plan for the next campaign, the next year, the next five years? How well do you track actual results against your plan so that you can take action if the two diverge?"

For the marketing management personnel of clients and for each associate, Bob has made R. Kestnbaum and Company into an advanced Harvard Business School of direct marketing. You can attend in your home. Tapes of Kestnbaum lectures and talks and reprints of his articles are available through Direct Marketing magazine and listed in the Help Source Section of this book.

Note: R. Kestnbaum and Company is located at 221 North LaSalle Street, Chicago, Illinois 60601; (312) 782-1351.

Mail Order Sampler
Seminar VIII

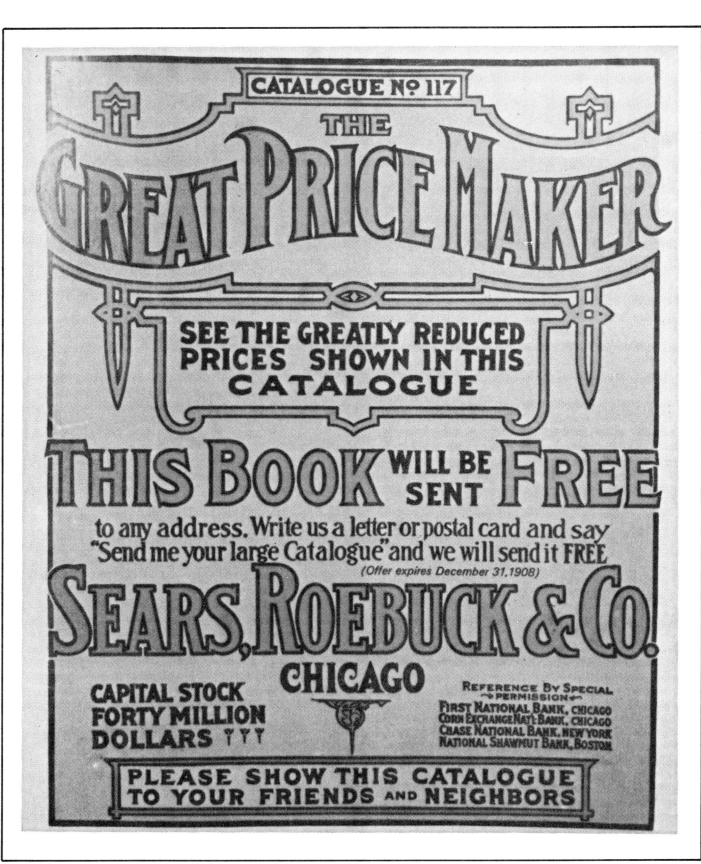

Chapter 1
The Direct Marketing Seminars

Some recommendations and background.

In college a seminar is a group of advanced students, usually twenty or so, who study a subject under a professor. It's more informal than a class. There's more give and take. The teacher can more easily detect a student's difficulties.

Each student does original research. Each exchanges results with the others. There's synergy, an impact of mind on mind that stimulates more than a more formal class. At first, seminars supplemented lectures but proved so effective in teaching as to replace them.

From the University the seminar spread to the professions, then to industry. In almost every field it has become the preferred method to keep up with change. Wherever change has come faster and more constantly, seminars have been more in demand, particularly in direct marketing.

A business seminar is a briefing. It's a conference, a meeting of executives. It can be basic or advanced, an overview of a broad field or in great detail on a segment of a field. It can be a first orientation of a brand new area or an update of a developing one.

A seminar can be for a week, a day or anything in between. Most are three or four days. Some of these are several one-day seminars, one after another—each on a related subject. A seminar is intensive. In any all day seminar, the group eats together. For a several day seminar most attendees travel to stay at the motel or hotel where it's held. If so, the group usually meets informally for all other meals, in two's and three's. Usually, each attendee gets a workbook with supporting written material, and often extra pamphlets. Each attendee takes notes. It's concentrated hard work.

But it can be fascinating. Some attendees continue the discussion together at breakfast, at dinner, often until late in the evening long after the day's seminar is over. It's a place to meet and get to know people in the field. Often one can help the other in business. Often friendships start that continue. The conductor of the seminar often gets deep into discussions of an attendee's business. This, too, can lead to further personal meetings.

In this book is a story on Ed Burnett. His seminars on list selection are excellent and thorough. Ed is particularly strong on business-to-business direct marketing. Usually, the Burnett seminars are put on by his own company, Ed Burnett Associates, and most frequently in New York City. One advantage is that you can get them on tape for a fraction of attendance cost. Full details are listed in the Help Source Section in back of this book.

When available, the Ed McLean seminars are excellent. They are on direct mail both on copy and on the mathematics of figuring costs. He is particularly strong on magazine and newsletter circulation, and particularly on renewals. Some years, he's doing seminars outside of the U.S., but usually full information is available through Hoke Communications.

A Jim Kobs seminar is always good. His particular strength is on building offers. A story on him is in this book. He usually does several for Advertising Age in the Chicago area and has done some for Temple University, in Philadelphia. Details are in the Help Source Section in back of this book.

Specialized associations and publications from time to time have seminars on special areas of direct marketing. The Association of American Publishers, through its Direct Marketing/Book Club Divisions, has excellent seminars on selling books mail order. Folio magazine has some on magazine subscription marketing. The Association of Newsletter publishers has some on marketing newsletters.

Occasionally, a seminar occuring in just one city will be valuable. Once each year at the University of Missouri, Martin Baier, Bob Stone and Bill Steinhardt (a Hoge alumnus) have a seminar on various aspects of direct marketing.

Rene Gnam travels a good deal offering seminars on direct mail. Rene is very strong on magazine subscription marketing and does an excellent job. Shell Alpert does seminars every year on various areas of direct marketing, particularly direct mail. He is often sponsored by Rodale Publications. Details on all of the above are in the Help Source Section of this book.

Running seminars has become a bigger and bigger business. A trade magazine finds seminars a profitable new division. Associations, particularly, are deep into them. Anyone can start one. The best ones are usually marriages between top experts in a field who have a flair for teaching and professional educators. Not surprisingly, in any field where there is a sudden need for seminars there is later a shakeout and the fittest survive.

The most outstanding seminars on direct marketing are run by the Direct Mail/Marketing Association. One of the primary functions of the DMMA is education. It is better geared to operate seminars and has more top leaders in the field available than anyone.

The DMMA is not a luxury club. There are no high-ceilinged, big lounge rooms with deep, leather-cushioned chairs and sofas. The DMMA has chosen to concentrate on education programs. Largely, it is an on-the-job-training mutual association, an information exchange, a joint investigation of opportunities and problems.

DMMA education is not a Harvard Business School. Instead, the arts, the crafts, the technology—above all, the changes and methods of all the varied forms of mail order and direct marketing—are taught. The ways of attending are varied. It's an endless, ever-growing, travelling road show—brought to you.

For years the backbone of DMMA teaching talent has been Dick Hodgson and Paul Sampson, each of whom have rare talent. Each has been personally very successful in direct marketing. Each has been Chairman of the Board of the DMMA.

In a typical year, Paul Sampson and Dick Hodgson will criss-cross the country with the Basic Direct Mail/Marketing Institute, for as many as twelve sessions. The Institutes are four days, Monday through Thursday. In between, Dick Hodgson will put on sessions of the Catalog Institute and Paul Sampson has "Introduction to Direct Mail Marketing", both in still more cities. I tell Dick Hodgson's story in this book.

Another top authority who conducts DMMA seminars is Pierre Passavant, who came from Xerox, and whose story is also in this book. He is superb on copy, creating ads and mailings. He is up to the second on methods, strong on media and mail order math, and a natural showman and teacher. In an average year, Pierre has 18 programs of three days each. His seminars are on lists, copy and art, and mail order math and finance. Each year he may conduct his seminars several times in New York, Chicago and Los Angeles—and once a year in other cities.

These are the seminars to start people off in the business. These are interspersed with others more advanced and more specialized. Pierre has the "Direct Marketing Copywriters' Workshop".

The DMMA is more and more going far beyond these seminars. The trend is to specifics, to learn specialized ways to do things. There are more seminars for narrower needs. Once the basics are learned, the newer concept is to go to the specialist more than to the general practitioner. Attendance is well over 2,000 in the U.S. and almost 500 in Europe.

It may be a seminar by Stan Fenvessy (whose story is in this book) on "Mastering Physical Fulfillment". It may be on fund raising or on one field like "Direct Marketing for Banks" or for associations. It may be for chief executive officers only or on "Outbound Telephone Marketing" only. A new one is on computers in direct marketing.

It may be in a suburb like Oakbrook, outside of Chicago, or White Plains, outside of New York, or Arlington, Virginia, outside of Washington D.C. More likely, it's in the center of a major city from Dallas to Kansas City, in Atlanta or Boston. Again and again, seminars are in the biggest centers—New York. Chicago and Los Angeles. Sooner or later, the DMMA seminars you need should be in a place practical for you to go to.

More and more, the emphasis has been on flexibility and specialization. Anyone can attend for one day for a specialized segment. The average attendee takes 1.6 days. There is a strongly felt need to keep up, to constantly update knowledge of mail order and direct marketing and to learn with leaders.

This is not new. First the DMMA taught effective use of direct mail, then mail order via direct mail and then using all media. Now it teaches latest technology in more and more specialized ways. It teaches more and more aspects of direct marketing from the creative to financial. Now there has been a surge in the number and variety of seminars offered, forced by necessity. The situation came about because of a need to update the know-how of people in the business and to train those entering into it.

The need came from ever-accelerating growth and change. The fraternity and sorority of those who made it big with their mail order know-how wanted their companies to grow further as fast as potential allowed. They found that they could only do so by hiring capable assistants and providing them with training in latest direct marketing know-how required for each of a number of jobs.

In the mid-1970's, change and growth had come so fast that DMMA members felt its educational efforts had to be expanded and proliferated to keep up. A study was made, report submitted and much of what has been done in DMMA education since has been the result.

The report emphasized the new conditions in mail order. Computerized lists, laser printing, changing life styles, alternate delivery, electronic communications have all contributed to changes in the methods and techniques of direct marketing. Providing an up-to-date education on the many such changes was the primary recommendation.

The decision was made to hire an educational professional to organize, back up and carry through a far broader educational program. In January 1978, Dante Zacavish was hired as vice-president of the DMMA, responsible for all educational programs, seminars and institutes of the DMMA.

Dante was a remarkable choice—an able educator and a self-made mail order entrepreneur with a personal knowledge of what education can do for upward mobility. Dante came from the school system in Wilton, Connecticut. Donna Hanna, a program manager, has also worked for a school system, but in personnel and only for a year.

Dante succeeded in the education field through self education, and as a mail order moonlighter selling educational products to schools. He has a non-ivory tower viewpoint and an interest in the small and the tiny as well as the medium and big. He can identify with the business owner and management and with the careerist.

The drive of Dante, added to that of Bob DeLay and the push of the DMMA directors, has proliferated the number of courses, varied their kinds and targeted them to fields where need is and jobs are. "We started by mailing an educational needs assessment and educational progress survey to 1,865 voting Association members. We listened to direct marketing professionals. We interviewed leaders."

To find out further what courses were most needed, Dante got out into the field. He met with members. He investigated where jobs needed to be filled and where more training was required. He got the viewpoint of employers who wanted to fill jobs and of those who wanted to advance in jobs. He researched attendance of present seminars.

"At each seminar we provided an evaluation form. We asked 1,000 attendees what in a seminar was most helpful. At the end of each term we asked the question: 'Are there other courses you'd like to take, and if so, which?' 60% to 70% filled out the questionnaire.

"All this gave us a list of needs, a blueprint for new educational programs. The research revealed that specialized how-to programs were top priority."

Using these methods, the DMMA has added more and more special programs and specialists to conduct them. Two who have been highly praised are Wendell Forbes, with his "School for Magazine Marketing", and Elliott Abrams and his seminar, "How to Work Effectively with Your Mailing House to Save Money". There have been new seminars for telephone marketing, advanced copy—for special fields . . . for banks, for politicians, for whatever need.

Step by step, the DMMA education program has developed. Now in speeches, round tables, councils, conferences, trade meetings, seminars and workshops it teaches all over the U.S. and most recently over the world.

Dante keeps checking how much valued each seminar is. Questionnaires given each attendee ask whether he or she has benefited. Attendees overwhelmingly approve. For Passavant courses, 94% to 98% approve. For any course, approval tends to go up and then plateau. "Sometimes there is great need for a certain seminar. We fill it. Demand slacks off. We cut back. Now we're into continuing programs.

"We run shorter workshop sessions. We've had a Mail Order Financial Planning and Analysis Workshop, a Multi-Media Workshop and a Creative Workshop. Still more mini-seminar samplers are put on at DMMA Annual and Spring Conferences, List day and other DMMA events, also at important Direct Marketing Days. Each is a one or two-hour digest of an all day or several day seminar." Most DMMA minis are conducted by Paul Sampson, Dick Hodgson and Pierre Passavant.

A new seminar idea comes from anywhere. Wherever direct marketers gather, Dante goes and listens. "I listen to anyone. I talk to direct marketers anywhere, on an informal basis, one-to-one. At the last conference I talked to 18 or 20 people about what needs are important. When I hear of a need over and over, I ask others about it. I pick up talk from members. Often council members come in with suggestions.

"Parts of a seminar may be so popular that expanding to a seminar in that interest is indicated. If, in any way, enough informal interest is generated, we send a Needs Assessment Query on it to appropriate members. Then, if needed, we have to search for the talent and know-how to teach it effectively. Or, if we find an expert teacher in an area of direct marketing, we investigate the need for that know-how.

"I like developing new seminar programs. It's great to get an idea for one, look at it upside and downside, be realistic. There are exciting opportunities for seminars."

Dante got interested in developing special seminars specifically designed for and with a trade association. "I felt we should cooperate with other associations and groups in developing such programs—wherever it contributed to the needs of enough DMMA members. It's part of a long-range plan. We're working with Paul Le Blanc, of Saks Fifth Avenue, on the project. We will continue to work with others.

"We've done this with the British Direct Marketing Association, the BDMA. We did it in France with the UNPD, the French equivalent association. We did it with the Finns, the Norwegians, the Japanese, the Dutch, in New Zealand and Australia, with the Canadians and the South Africans. Paul Sampson was in South Africa doing workshops there. Mail order is growing there."

Non-members may attend DMMA seminars, but at a higher fee. If you are going to attend several, your membership may cost you nothing. The difference in attendance fees can pay for it. This is particularly so for companies with several executives to send to seminars.

For big company members Dante will put on a seminar just for them, or create one for them, or put on "think tank" sessions with Stan Rapp and Liz Forest, or even a one-time consulting session with authorities bearing down on company problems, or supply a mail order course on direct marketing to indoctrinate personnel.

"Our professional development program in direct marketing is new," says Dante. "It's an independent program of home study. It includes a final examination. We give a continuing education credit through the National University Study program which costs about $400." George Wiedemann, President of Grey Direct, wrote it.

Dante thinks of the small, too. "The DMMA has a responsibility to the entire mail order and direct marketing field, to the big and to the little. Everyone in the business has a cooperative right to grow together. One of my jobs is to nurture seeds. Small mail order people are creative people. They are not engineers. They need practical help. We seek them out.

"Some people say that the small guy can't afford a seminar. We don't think that way. My job is to develop an economic vehicle, a seminar the small guy can afford." Tapes of mini-seminars are made by "Pete" Hoke. They are available for $9 to $18 to anyone through Direct Marketing Magazine. Some I recommend are listed in back of this book.

"I'm thinking of doing a seminar, naturally, at the Holiday Inn at one hundred locations. The fee would be about $50 or $60. Holiday Inn curently has satellite transmission with live interactive telephone. My idea is to put on a seminar from one location, headed by Pierre Passavant. A para-professional would be stationed at each other location.

"It's a program concept for which I have the format. We are discussing the use of a program outline that would stimulate questions which would be relayed to and then answered by Pierre Passavant. John Yeck would be responsible for the questionnaire, and the Institutes would be handled by Yeck Brothers."

Dante favors this type of seminar over video tapes, video discs or the DMMA becoming an information provider for some form of Viewdata—perhaps being a teaching machine of direct marketing by telephone over your TV screen.

"I like what I'm doing now. I don't teach. I'm a professional educator, a manager and an administrator. The talents are great. They're an open group. They show what they know. They're quality people and know what they are doing. Pierre, Paul and Dick are wonderful to work with. Stan Fenvessy and Elliott Abrams are great people and great teachers. Wendell Forbes is and so are the others. They contribute. They're great on meeting commitments.

"I love mail order and direct marketing. I'm enthused about the opportunities for this—getting started in it, particularly for women. There are, in services and all, at least a million jobs created by direct marketing."

Who gets most from the seminars? "I think that some who have been in the business for six or seven months do well. They have been somewhat immersed in the business; and if they are bright and good listeners, they learn quickly. The more past education they have had, the more they get out of the seminars.

"People who know how to sift learn faster. People who come cold with no experience and insufficient past education can become almost schizophrenic. I don't assess their backgrounds or ask how many years they've been in the business. They have to be self-starters. They have to put in long hours everyday of a course. They should have some understanding of numbers and of finance. Otherwise, they get buried in detail and confused.

"I get great satisfaction at seeing the growth of people taking the seminars. Even in a three or four-hour presentation we open up people's minds. In one to several days, we help them form concepts. Sometimes they get a new approach to their careers and businesses."

Members help each other learn. The big teach the small, the veterans, the newcomers. The specialists teach the generalists and experts in other specialties. "How did all this start? Somewhere along the line the feeling of the DMMA developed that the people in the industry were its most valuable product."

Dante has a wider understanding than most of the problems of the owner, manager, employee and small entrepreneur—of hiring and developing people ... of getting jobs and advancing ... of smallest start-ups. He is a sophisticated educator. He's at home with change. He can quickly grasp changing technology. He's attuned to big business needs. But he has personally known what it is to be tiny, to make mistakes from lack of knowledge, to grow and succeed by overcoming. He can help you as he has helped others and as others at the DMMA can, also.

If you have or want a career with the big, leaders of the big help train you. If you are big, they can help train your people. If you are small or tiny, you can learn how the big made it, sometimes from a tiny start. In the reference section in back of the book I list current DMMA seminars. But they constantly change. There's a continual flow of new ones. Better check the DMMA office at 6 East 43rd Street, New York, NY 10017; (212) 689-4977.

Chapter 2
IBM's Mail Order Sales Reps

*Much of IBM Direct's mail order operation
is surprisingly simple, pragmatic and
applicable to smaller companies.*

How did IBM conquer the world in computers—and sell more business equipment to more businesses than any other company?

Its formula has been to often be the first with a dramatic new product; to innovate; to provide in-depth service first; then to keep improving it; to treasure customers and its own reputation.

Only with this backing and approach does IBM feel that sales reps can play a role. But more than anything IBM is a company of sales people. IBM seeks to recruit the more intelligent, more stable sales people to guide, support and motivate them more; to strictly control what the sales force promises customers.

IBM's effort has been to analyze potential and project anticipated sales; to plan; organize in detail; set quotas of sales and expenses; to compare constantly the anticipated with the actual; to execute as planned to the maximum by assigning accountable responsibility.

IBM's Direct is a direct marketing arm of IBM, first launched by and for IBM's Office Product Division. It has expanded rapidly. It is serving as a model for IBM direct marketing in other countries. It is working with other IBM divisions. It will become an important marketing factor for IBM's future.

IBM Direct uses a good deal of sophisticated direct marketing techniques and technology. But much about its mail order operation is surprisingly simple, pragmatic and applicable to smaller companies. If the smallest firm is proud of its products and reputation, values its sales force and wishes to direct market accordingly to companies, IBM Direct's experience can be a useful example . . . whatever it sells and even if through commission reps.

No outside direct marketer has been hired to run IBM Direct. No direct marketing trained executives from outside work there full-time. No mystery is made of mail order. Fashionable direct-marketing words are rarely used. Direct Response Marketing, of which IBM Direct is a part, is managed by J. Bousa III. Working for Bousa is J.J. (Jerry) Coyne who has been with IBM Direct since its inception in 1976. IBM Direct has used several consultants to help it grow, including Bob Kestnbaum (R. Kestnbaum & Co.) of Chicago and Bob Chapman (Chapman Direct Marketing) in New York. But Jerry relies heavily on the way IBM salesmen and sales managers have always operated. Jerry explains it this way:

"I grew up in IBM with typewriter sales reps. I've traded on my experience selling face to face. I know the products we sell and the customers and prospects we sell to. IBM's primary reliance has always been on service and on salesmen. IBM Direct is an extension and support to IBM customer service—and the IBM sales force. Selling through the mail captures some techniques we used as salesmen.

"Take format testing. We experimented with a sales presentation. We sold differently on different sales calls. When we found a way that closed more sales and more quickly, we stayed with that way. Format testing in direct mail is the same.

"Each mailing piece and each ad for IBM Direct reflects what we learned as IBM sales reps—and what we keep learning from IBM sales reps. What we say in the mailing piece reflects the sales calls representatives currently make. When we sell more complex equipment we try to anticipate the questions in the minds of the prospects reading our piece. We can then answer in the mailing piece, just as a sales rep would, questions most likely to be raised—such as: Why is an electronic typewriter better than an electric typewriter? Can this copier produce reduced-size copies?

"We work with sales people to determine which products to sell and the selling points we should get across for each. We take pride in being, thinking like, and working with the sales force. I think of each piece of paper as a sales rep making a mail sales call to point out benefits of IBM products . . . a call even in a remote area, or to any firm, however small.

"The job of a sales rep is to sell . . . to create and keep customers. Each mailing piece is intended to be a script of what that sales rep might say. But I continue to rely on our sales force for ultimate customer satisfaction. If the customer is unhappy, the sales rep will call, find out the problem and correct it.

"We're a marketing channel, complementary to the sales force—and we're synergistic. It's a challenge to integrate with a successful sales force, to help and not hinder it.

"We think that direct marketing is analogous to other forms of marketing that IBM people are expert in. That's why we've chosen IBM employees for IBM Direct, rather than going outside. Certain things about the way IBM operates might not seem as vital to an outside direct marketer. We've found it more desirable to teach IBM people direct marketing. This comes from IBM history and how and why IBM went into mail order.

"By the 1970's the cost of a sales call had risen sharply . . . to the point that small reorders for suppliers such as typewriter ribbons were costlier to handle through sales reps. Our management wanted to test alternative ways of selling these supplies."

Jerry Coyne had started as an IBM trainee in 1960, after graduate work in education, a degree in philosophy and two years of teaching history and economics. He has sold typewriters and copiers to businesses of every kind including the State Department and later to the Department of Defense in Washington, D.C. He has managed Office Products Division (OPD) branch offices, been an OPD district manager and on headquarters staff, marketing copiers. "Then I got an invitation from Bill Sutherland who headed up the Market Channel Development to join him in launching IBM Direct.

"In late 1976, Bob Kestnbaum was contacted and retained as a direct marketing consultant for IBM. With his assistance a business case was presented to upper management, with a financial proposal. It involved many of his concepts. The name, IBM Direct, was suggested and general management gave approval for a pilot test.

"We selected certain criteria in planning IBM Direct. From the first, we decided that at IBM Direct we'd sell each product with an explicit guarantee. IBM has been successful because the rep always has indicated that if a customer is dissatisfied, IBM will do what is needed to give satisfaction and even take the product back if necessary. We do the same at IBM Direct. The rule here is that we must satisfy the customer. We felt that we could be successful because of the IBM reputation. Each mailing piece reflects the way that IBM is known. We're trading on IBM's good name, and we protect the name. There are no wild claims.

"Our first objective has been to create and maintain customer satisfaction with anything IBM Direct sold. We make a great effort to ship promptly. We fill orders for supplies within 24 hours. For hardware, there's credit checking which takes a little more time."

IBM Direct started largely with the bread-and-butter supply items of the Office Products Division. These were the basic supplies needed most often by customers. "The first tests were to help IBM Direct zero in on the most practical and profitable objectives.

"In mid-1977, we tested two different flyers. One flyer included 200 IBM supplies. The other included the 40 most popular. We measured results. These and subsequent mailings determined and confirmed which items to include and which to drop. We found where our revenues came from. Our efforts began by selling supplies. Gradually, we began to sell equipment. As mailings increased and brought more familiarity with IBM Direct, we kept adding more."

By 1981, IBM Direct had worked out an unusual mix in its catalog. It sold basic supplies but also some equipment . . . and it displayed, described and got leads for more sophisticated equipment. The leads went to the sales force.

"We feel that we can sell certain products without the assistance of face-to-face sales representatives. I call them commodity-like because they are known and accepted enough to be sold by mail. We've determined these by elimination. We feel that the IBM electric typewriter is fairly well known, that it's almost commodity-like. Consequently, we're selling the Selectric III. I was not surprised when we successfully sold these products at over $1,000 each by mail order. Then targets of $2,000 seemed reasonable to test. I don't know yet if many products in that price range are enough of a commodity to be sold by mail order. However, I do believe that price alone is not the indicator of what can or cannot be sold by mail.

"We're testing sale of the IBM Executive Copier 102 for around $3,000. I believe face-to-face selling is required for concept products such as the IBM Displaywriter. It's new and, we believe, the latest in word processors. This kind of IBM office equipment may, at first, require more explanation and demonstration than our direct mail can cost-efficiently get across. We also believe that as a product's cost increases, the customer expects the courtesy and needs the reassurance of a representative."

The IBM catalog sells typewriter ribbons, tapes and cartridges . . . magnetic cards . . . copier supplies, a wide variety of elements for typewriters . . . and computer terminal tables in addition to electric typewriters, electronic typewriters, copiers and portable dictation equipment.

Copy emphasizes convenience, quality and the IBM name. Copy is factual and businesslike. The layout is crisp, clean, uncrowded and quiet. Color is used not to excite or dramatize or tempt, but to subdue and restrain. Description of each item is tight, informative and educational. It tells precisely and carefully what to use with what. It's easily understandable.

A volume discount can offer savings up to 25% for certain accessory items. At times, free offers are made as alternatives. For example, a purchaser may get free correctable film ribbons and lift-off tapes by buying two dozen and getting one dozen free—also a supplies price protection contract for a year is available.

The discounts, price protection and convenience effectively

compete with other sources which advertise similar supplies. A separate order card each is used for the IBM Selectric III and for the IMB Executive Recorder . . . "The smallest dictation unit ever offered by IBM". The IBM Displaywriter is pictured, described and an inquiry for it solicited—for sales reps to follow up. An IBM Series III Copier is pictured on the center spread and inquiries solicited.

The constant thrust of the catalog, but never overdone, is the request to phone in. IBM Direct takes phone orders or inquiries any business day from 8:30 AM to 8:00 PM. A toll-free 800 number is featured. A sticker with the phone number and the suggestion to affix it to your telephone is included. A phone order or inquiry currently is urged with more emphasis than to mail in. More orders come by phone than by mail. Each year, several hundred thousand phone orders and inquiries come into IBM's phone handling headquarters in Dayton, New Jersey. Many order, some inquire. Sales are being made and leads for much bigger sales generated at the same time.

To launch IBM Direct has been a major effort aided by top consultants. "Bob Kestnbaum has assisted us internally and Bob Chapman creatively. I've watched other direct marketers. I've taken courses, gone to trade meetings and attended seminars. But the vast majority of direct marketers are in non-business fields. We're in industrial direct mail. Often, we don't find what others do with consumer low-ticket items to be applicable to our problems. And speeches, articles and seminars on direct marketing seem to rarely discuss integrating mail order and lead getting with and for sales force activities.

"We find that the experience of IBM and our own experience since starting IBM Direct to be far more applicable. The Office Products Division is one of several divisions of IBM and IBM Direct is gradually working with other divisions. In addition to using direct response marketing for sales, the Office Products Division has had an ongoing program to get leads for sales reps. Other divisions also have used direct mail for lead getting. And while these lead-getting campaigns were always measured, I believe that they are done even more scientifically now.

"Purchase orders from companies have always, to some degree, come by mail . . . for a wide variety of IBM products . . . particularly for supplies and from remote locations for hardware. Ordinary IBM procedure, before IBM Direct, had dictated that each order be confirmed by a salesman. Setting up IBM Direct changed the procedure and began actively to solicit mail orders.

"Originally, IBM Direct's function was to sell by mail. Then it began to plan lead gathering and the integration of leads and mail order and telephone. Office Products Division uses media for advertising for leads. Concerning lead gathering, IBM Direct commits to produce for representatives so many leads for so many dollars. The leads must be of sufficient quality so that closures have the desired expense-to-revenue ratio. The integration between lead mail and sales mail is close. Success for either depends on how people respond."

The training and experience of an IBM salesman made the transition to mail order selling quite natural. Jerry Coyne points out: "IBM knew which offers pulled in more sales inquiries. IBM salesmen, as well as IBM management, knew which offers were most effective in closing a sale. We sell a lot of IBM typewriters to current owners of IBM typewriters. Owners sometimes trade in IBM typewriters in much the same way as they trade in cars. A trade-in offer is a strong offer. We've found that the trade-in offers and other offers, that have always helped salesmen sell, work in mail order as well.

"Take segmentation and list selection. We've benefited from

Bob Kestnbaum and Bob Chapman. We've become oriented to recommendations of seasonality and selectivity. But aided by this, we select lists of people to sell mail order to the same way that salesmen use selected prospects to call on. The newest IBM sales rep learns quickly which accounts are the best prospects or the accounts with installed inventory. A similar kind of selectivity works just as well in direct mail.

"We are proud of the development of our ability to maintain and manage lists both of our customers and prospects. We started mailing to our own customers at the Office Products Division. We mailed our first outside lists in any numbers in 1979. We've found the relative value of non-customer names to new customers. We now have some history comparing them. We're always testing and experimenting.

"For example, we just tested two catalogs with virtually the same content. One with a beige cover had a more bold approach in picturing the bigger product items. The other catalog with a yellow cover was more subdued in picturing them. This catalog, however, emphasized the telephone on the cover. We sent these catalogs to matched panels of established customers and people who had not done business with IBM Direct before. The result was varied. The telephone cover and more played down catalog did better with those who had not yet bought from IBM Direct. Both catalogs were prepared for IBM by Chapman Direct Marketing. Our next catalog will be a combination of these two catalogs, yellow outside and beige inside. The phone number will be emphasized on the cover. The bold approach for bigger items will be inside.

"We have the capability of planning and measurement. Bob Kestnbaum performs a role in helping to structure tests and in confirming analysis, helping determine if the test and the analysis of results are valid. As we get more experience, we are growing our own facility to do this in-house in the future. But as we keep moving into new operations, I expect we'll continue to need outside expertise to help us set up and operate.

"We look for new operations in direct marketing to business. A major motivation in launching IBM Direct was to create an additional sales channel—to develop a closer and more frequent contact with customers . . . to give quicker and better service to more people."

IBM Direct has moved beyond the catalog, based on performance of products within the catalog. It's running solo mailings as well. Color stock is varied within the envelope instead of adding colors. A solo may be on simplest supplies only or on one product only, with accessories. One is on the IBM Electronic Typewriter 75. Here more color is used, but with considerable restraint. It's predominantly a black and white piece, for a plain, business-like presentation. The Chapman agency uses all its expertise to keep the direct mail in character with IBM character, a simple one-to-one sales rep's approach.

"While the agency is primarily responsible for creating our direct mail, we're also providing input for copy. We work through the Office Products Division Advertising Department. In this department we don't have a full-time direct marketing copywriter. We do have advertising-trained people. We see that it reflects what our sales reps would say."

IBM does not give out sales figures for IBM Direct and avoids indications of how much it sells of what. Jerry says: "Our growth is very satisfactory, and we're expanding. All of us are very proud of that. More IBM divisions, offices and subsidiaries have gone into direct marketing, here and overseas. IBM in Canada is direct marketing on a very large scale. IBM's operation in the United Kingdom is underway with direct marketing. The IBM Direct operation here has been a model for both.

"There's much in direct marketing that we have not yet done. For example, we have an inkjet capability and we have not yet used personalized letters. We are now considering them. We've primarily relied on mail rather than media, although we're beginning to use media more. In 1979, we tested media to sell the Executive Recorder—in conjunction with our mail. We will continue testing space. We're also going to expand our test of telemarketing—to cold names, names we've mailed to and to accounts. We haven't got all the answers, but we're getting more all the time.

"We are modeling with computers. We have a five-year plan. We sell $1,000 and up typewriters. We're developing new methods.

"A key measurement of success at IBM for a marketing rep, a department and for IBM Direct is expense to revenue. Direct response is measurable and it can constantly be tested to see if it can be made more cost efficient. That's what I like about it. I like the challenges of being on a revenue quota and an expense target for IBM Direct . . . of working with IBM reps to do more for them . . . of finding new ways to give better service, by mail, to IBM customers.

"I believe an increase in business-to-business selling through direct response is inevitable. This is because of the rising costs of face-to-face selling combined with the growing acceptance of doing business through direct response. I don't think company size is a criterion for use of direct response. Rather, I believe any company with a good product, good reputation for service and a logical approach to using mail, phone and media can succeed with direct response marketing.

"I think a marketing background is very helpful in working in direct response marketing. However, this technique depends on successful structuring and analysis of marketing test program. Consequently, a basic understanding of statistics is also quite helpful.

"College students can begin now to learn about direct response marketing simply by reading the catalogs and other direct mail that comes into their homes. What do they dislike? What appeals to them? This type of analysis can be a valuable primer for the field of direct response marketing."

IBM Direct is an example that a salesman-oriented company can feel quite at home in, and be in command of its own, direct marketing. It may very well indicate that medium and even quite small businesses—as well as IBM—need not be overawed by direct marketing expertise . . . but simply consult with and use it, along with common sense.

Chapter 3
How To Use Statistics In Direct Marketing

—to set up tests more scientifically, judge results more accurately and project more profitably.

That is the specialty of Professor Robert C. Blattberg, who teaches statistics and marketing at the Graduate School of Business of the University of Chicago. He is writing a book on marketing which will cover direct marketing, and has written a very thorough article, "Decision Rules and Sample Size Selection for Direct Mail Testing", for the Direct Mail/Marketing Association Manual. It's in the section on "Testing, Analysis, Economics".

Professor Blattberg is an authority on setting up mail order tests more scientifically in order to project test results more accurately. He says, "The 1980's are seeing more sophisticated use of data by direct marketers not only to analyze results but to improve their methodology."

Good test designs are vital in direct mail testing. Tests can be carefully designed regarding what is being tested and where and how it is being tested. "One of the advantages of mail order marketing is the ability to use the actual sales response to test almost every aspect of a firm's strategy." However, it is also possible to design a poor test. If this is done, wrong decisions can be made resulting in lost profits to the firm. Sometimes, a lot of money is lost from a lack of statistical know-how.

"My expertise in direct mail testing is statistical. I help devise tests and then assist management in judging the results. Direct marketers, big and small, are just beginning to get into statistical analysis in more depth. They're realizing that since this business is built on testing, they must be able to set up tests that can give the statistical information most completely at least cost. Some don't understand testing. They don't take the right sample. They test one variable at a time while a statistician can design an experiment that can accurately test two variables at a time and save testing money."

"Some still use crude methods. For example, they project sales levels from list tests without worrying about the natural attenuation to the mean. Statisticians can refine the techniques and make the projections safer.

"Some don't build confidence levels correctly. They may figure on a percentage basis of comparison (1.8% versus 2.4%, or whatever) but not consider average order variance. They may not project future counts accurately. I've developed a projection system to do so. But statisticians and direct marketers feel comfortable together. And they will be working more and more together in the future.

"The language of statisticians can frighten new direct marketers but needn't. Many don't know what the words 'confidence level' mean. Yet, they merely refer to how sure you can be that the test figures are a representative sample - and indicate reasonably well what you can expect future results to be -if you project, with all factors the same. Of course, they never can be exactly the same, which makes mail order an art as well as a science. But statisticians help.

"The term, 'decision rule,' merely means how to decide the winner in a test. You set the confidence level and determine the statistic to use to make a decision, apply the decision rule and them make a decision. Each decision is always a compromise. The statistician just helps you make a better compromise and sounder, safer, and more profitable decisions . . . to test enough names and no more."

In Bob's article in the DMMA Manual, he spells out the statistical procedures to determine sample size and make decisions from direct mail tests. He gets into the math. At the end of the article he supplies mathematical tables to make it easier to select the right sample size and to use decision rules. He's teaching you a bit of the laws of probability - and of greater mail order profitability.

"Mail order people live in an imperfect statistical world. Statisticians like a confidence level to be 90% and even up to 95%. Practical mail order people are more content with 80% to 85%. This means that four out of five times the right decision will be made, at a considerably lower cost of testing. Yet, these statistical guidelines - considered satisfactory by most direct marketers - seem very crude rules of thumb to professional statisticians."

Bob got into working with direct marketers in a funny way. He was called in to be an expert witness for Baldwin-Cooke of Morton Grove, Illinois—in a law suit for infringement of copyrights by Keith Clarke of New York City. Both are publishers of diaries.

Bob testified as to the amount of customers lost versus gained as well as to the amount of residual losses from probable later sales to the lost customer. The diary business involves multiple sales and year-after-year purchases by many customers. Often a first time purchaser of one or a few diaries will later increase the multiples and buy year after year.

Tom Nichols, owner of Baldwin-Cooke, made all his records available to Bob Blattberg. "Tom Nichols was a very impressive man. He had no formal statistical training yet kept a very tight

Underwear for Fat Men.
No. 16R5044 Men's Extra Size French Balbriggan Undershirts. Fine gauge, soft silky finish, made from finest Egyptian yarn. Fancy collarette neck, pearl buttons and ribbed cuffs. Full size and large. Sizes, 44 to 52 chest measure. Retail value, $1.00. Ecru color.
  Price, each.................$0.79
  Per dozen................. 9.48
No. 16R5045 Men's Extra Size French Balbriggan Drawers to match above. Sizes, 44 to 52 waist measure.
  Price, per pair............$0.79
  Per dozen................. 9.48
If by mail, postage extra, each,
10 cents.

statistical control. He knew his business. He kept exceptionally efficient records and knew what a customer was worth to him. I used a statistical technique called a Narkov chain to indicate how reorders normally occurred, and how much later sales and profit an average first order led to. It was all based on applying Baldwin-Cooke's past records to predict the future value of a customer. Baldwin-Cooke won the case and in the process I got a feel for mail order."

Bob graduated from Northwestern University, majoring in mathematics. He got an MBA and Ph.D. in Industrial Administration from Carnegie-Mellon, in Pittsburgh. He took one course in marketing. His thesis was on econometrics. Bob has taught for eleven years at the University of Chicago Graduate School of Business.

Bob met students at the University of Chicago who were in direct marketing. One of them, Joe Malone, later at Time-Life Books, called him in to do some regression analysis of lists. Gordon Grossman, a consultant for Time-Life Books, had set up the project but wanted a statistician to carry it forward. Since then, Bob has done similar regression analysis work for other direct marketers.

"I usually use SPSS. It was developed at the University of Chicago to analyze social sciences. Norman Nie and Tex Hull created it. It was first used experimentally about fifteen years ago and more generally from about 1970. In 1975, Norman Nie and Tex Hull set up their own consulting business based on it. They've done phenomenally well. SAS is a good multivariate system developed by the University of North Carolina, but I prefer SPSS.

Bob has been working with direct marketers for five years. "I work mostly for large direct marketers but there's a lot of potential for smaller direct marketers to improve profits by statistical analysis. Large firms such as Time, Inc. compare selection of lists using regression analysis against control lists. They know it works." Most of Bob's clients are consumer product general marketers, and he gets his clients by referral. "Someone gives my name as an expert."

He's done some work for Bob Kestnbaum on analyzing variance of tests. For Len Quenan, Research Director of R.L. Polk, Bob worked out a method similar to regression analysis but one Bob felt is superior. "Len Quenan is very bright and excellent to work with. The method we used was a statistical procedure called log linear modelling."

The Blattberg family combines art with science. Bob's consulting business makes him an entrepreneur in the science of using statistics. His wife, Barbara, has an art gallery. Both do well.

Note: Professor Blattberg is located at 230 East Delaware Place, Chicago, IL 60611; telephone (312) 943-5141.

Chapter 4
Classic Mail Order Copy

*"From Immigrant Boy to Millionaire
Copywriter . . . Across the Decades"*

That's his title for this story. He created mailings and ads for biggest publishers. His copy sold more how-to books than ever before in history. He created the first mailings for the first continuity book programs in America.

He was my professor of copy, my day in and day out tutor, and for one after another of my employees. If you ever write a word of copy, he can help you. If you're interested in a creative career in direct marketing, the story of his career can help. For anyone interested in any way in today's direct marketing, Fred Breismeister's story can help explain its origin.

"I was born near the 'Unter Den Linden Strasse' in Berlin. My dad met my mother in Lisbon, Portugal, where she was governess for the Magellan children (yes, descendants of the world circumnavigator). My eldest brother was born on 86th Street in New York, another in Magdeburg, Germany, and my sister in Romania.

"My father and eldest brother were two of the finest cartographers in the world. My brother Bill's 'Equal-Area Projection' is much used on world maps. He prepared the maps used by the U.S. Commission to help settle boundaries after World War II. He prepared the Antarctica Maps for Admiral Byrd who named a mountain peak there after Bill.

"I went to P.S. 34 in the Bronx, got interested in writing by the third grade and was raised on Jack London, Joseph Conrad, Charles Dana, etc. I dreamed of shipping off to sail the oceans of the world. But I didn't. Instead, I went on to Evander Childs High School in the Bronx."

One high school course, in shorthand, got Fred his first job as a stenographer for a magazine—where he learned advertising make-up. He decided, after starting business courses at night, to break into advertising copywriting. It took him eight years, getting preparatory experience in a variety of jobs by day and taking one course after another at night. He began to clip and collect ads and to study and analyze which were effective and why. This combination of preparatory experience, related courses and personal study and observation of actual advertising gave him a head start when he finally got his first copywriting job.

"For about eight years, while taking night courses, I shifted from one advertising job to another, hoping to find one that would lead to copywriting . . . The Advertising Make-up Department of the old Leslie-Judge Publishing Co.; Hanff-Metzger, McCann-Erickson, Doremus & Morse, the Advertising Department of Ward Baking Corp., and Butterick Publishing. A copywriting job continued to elude me. It was a bit frustrating; but my spirit and faith in myself never faltered.

"At Butterick I wrote a book of form paragraphs, and thus kept several typists busy answering correspondence from subscription workers. I went beyond my job to prepare ads to get subscription workers, and printed folders to inspire them to become active producers. After that, I put in three months at the Waterbury Republican-American preparing ads for local merchants.

"For those same eight years, at night, I took all kinds of courses in copywriting, production, selling and marketing ... at Columbia University, the 23rd Street YMCA, the New York Advertising Club and New York University. My most instructive and inspiring teacher was Professor Hotchkiss, Dean of the Marketing School at New York University. For the first years I took two nights of advertising courses and two nights of art at Mechanics Institute.

"But four nights were too much. For anyone, three nights a week of university courses are plenty. Any more are too much of a sacrifice. Some time is necessary to enjoy life—to keep from becoming a bookworm, and from going stale. I cut my courses to two (and at the most three) nights a week. I wasn't after a degree but learning how to make a living in advertising. I recommend that others under similar circumstances do the same.

"If I had to break into direct mail advertising writing again, I believe I'd do it more quickly by offering to write a complete direct mail effort for a mail order offer ... for free if it didn't outpull whatever copy my prospective employer was currently using. Otherwise, employers demand experience which only a copy job can give.

"Finally, I got my copy job. I showed my sparse samples plus my books of ads prepared at Columbia and New York Universities to good Dan Henderson in the Hearst Magazine Division. He took a chance on hiring me as 'Ann Orr', doing all the response letters and new subscriptions mailings for Good Housekeeping Magazine."

All Fred's experience and all his courses began to pay off very quickly, and then for the rest of his life. "I had used my shorthand only briefly in my first job, but I found it a wonderful aid throughout my business life. Of course, I took notes at university classes. Later, I did this at business conferences. But my shorthand's greatest help was in enabling me to write ads and selling letters as fast as the ideas came, then correcting my shorthand notes and being able to dictate virtually finished copy. It was a great boon. If anyone will pick up this skill, it will pay off lifelong."

By this time, Fred had strong opinions on what would pull most effectively in a mailing based on all he had read and observed. "I concluded that selling person-to-person or by direct mail employed the same principles: attract attention; arouse interest; create desire; effect a sale. I planned all my ads and mailings this way.

"My art and layout training was a tremendous help. I visualized an entire ad, or all components of a mailing, and thus could give each part the proper space and emphasis to accomplish the one function of the above four that it should. Making rough (but close to finished) layouts and specking type faces and sizes saved time and friction between copywriters and art department. It also assured a much better, more finished and more succesful ad or mailing. It avoided miniscule, hard-to-read type sizes. Years later I tried to train my copywriters to work by these principles. I let them know that the responsibility for the finished ad or mailing was their's—not that of the Art or Production Departments."

"My family being professional, non-business oriented, I had to learn the hard way—that is, by dint of study, and seeing what was pulling most successfully. You can profit immensely by examining mailings and ads that you know are money-makers, and analyzing how they employ the above four principles."

Fred Breismeister's methods worked well for Hearst. "I well remember the thrill of putting the first four million mailing (costing over $130,000) into the mails, and that wonderful feeling of seeing it pull its head off. And when my renewal efforts outpulled the old series, I was asked to show Cosmopolitan, Harper's Bazaar, Motor Boating and other Hearst magaziners how they should do it."

The copy approaches, so successful for Hearst then, are now even more productive thanks to laser letters, contests, segmentation and all the rest. Here is Fred Breismeister's recipe to increase results from a magazine subscription renewal series (it works as well for newsletters):

"1. Have all renewal efforts reflect confidence that the subscriber wants the magazine, that is: don't go begging for the renewal. Instead, politely render the service of making renewing easy and convenient. Your renewal series should reflect your most skillful letter writing.

"2. Start your renewal series as early as you can. For example, on two and three year subscriptions, I found that I got maximum results starting the series six months before expiration.

"3. If you're billing for short-term subscriptions (six months or less), go after conversion to longer term right with your first bill.

"4. Naturally, continue the series as long after expiration as results warrant; that is: as long as you are getting your renewal subscription at less than the cost of getting a new subscription by mail.

"5. The preceding has to be governed by circulation guarantees and the publisher's policy on the total circulation that he finds most profitable to maintain. The renewal series and new subscription mailing are effective ways to keep circulation at the most profitable level for the publisher.

"6. Work every type of subscription for maximum profit. For instance, at Hearst I found that two or three payment agent-produced subscriptions were good for only a single mailing. After that, mailings to outside names produced better subscribers at lower cost.

"7. Similarly, the results obtained from every source of expiration should be carefully analyzed—and your renewal series shortened or lengthened, according to the cost of getting renewals from each type of subscriber."

At Hearst, Fred was developing his methods further, while enjoying life more. "I was the fair-haired boy there. By then, I was driving a snazzy convertible, sailing a 40-foot sloop, keeping company with a free-spending redhead and asking for a $50 a week raise. When I was offered $30, like a dope, I left Hearst ... out of the frying pan, into the fire.

"I prepared to start a financial magazine for a queer duck in Wall Street, but after a few months my financial genius of a boss held up my paycheck. My lawyer got a settlement. Then, after coming out tops in a stiff copywriting test given me by Eastman-Kodak in Rochester, I turned down their job—which I later regretted.

"Instead, I took on doing circulation work for the magazines of Doubleday-Doran. I worked for Mr. Eaton, Vice President, and for Mr. Charley Roe, his assistant. That was pleasant ... living in Kew Gardens, driving out through lush farmland, working in an office set in the midst of rose gardens. It was 1929. From office boys to elevator operators, almost everyone was playing the Stock Market and making killings. Prosperity was booming right through the roof!

"Milo Sutliff was doing great things with the Doubleday Book Clubs . . . The Literary Guild, The Dollar Book Club, the Crime Book Club, etc. but things were different in the Doubleday Magazine Division. Old Doc Eaton bought American Home from Doubleday-Doran and took it to New York and then, with his wife, built it to a money-making success.

"These events left only World's Work and Radio Broadcast in the Doubleday Division. The days of such magazines as World's Work and Review of Reviews were numbered. The stage was set for the more lively newcomers, such as Time, Life and Newsweek. Charley Roe and I saw 'the handwriting on the wall'.

"Mr. McKinnon, of Pictorial Review fame, started a new publishing company with 'Movie Magazine', 'Amazing Stories' and 'Plain Talk'. He persuaded Charley Roe to join him. Charley enticed me to do the direct mail circulation work. Everything went swimmingly. Circulations leaped skywards.

"Then the bottom fell out! The Stock Market crashed! Ruined millionaires jumped from skyscraper windows. The huge circulation we had built became an albatross around the neck of Mr. McKinnon. The offsetting advertising revenue all but evaporated. Charley and I had helped speed Mr. McKinnon's Company into oblivion.

"I took a half-time job with Parent's Magazine. Charley and I formed a partnership to sell short-term, one-dollar subscriptions for about fifty magazines, by *direct mail*. It was a tiny forerunner of Publishers Clearing House. We were allowed to keep all the dollars that came in. And they did come in! Incidentally, we used sheets of stamps similar to those of Publishers Clearing House. We didn't realize we had the makings of a huge business because in the depression, without capital, it was tough to survive.

"Charley Roe suddenly died. His passing left me at a low ebb, without the heart to follow through without him. My Dad wanted to see my older brother, Rud, in Los Angeles and we drove out. In warm, sunny L.A., playing tennis occasionally, I didn't feel the Depression so badly.

"But when I got back East the Depression was everywhere. Lines of people were waiting for soup hand-outs. Capable, brainy men were on street corners selling apples for 5¢ each. Long lines were applying for welfare doles. No new building was going on. Business seemed at a standstill. The cold of autumn was turning into the colder winter. The gray skies reflected the grey mood of the people. It was frustrating, demoralizing.

"I just couldn't take it. I escaped by economical bus to Miami Beach, where I swam and played around. Then came reality . . . a telegram, a job! I'd be Director of Advertising Promotion for the Hearst Business Magazines! The salary was *less than half* the salary I had refused just three short years before.

"But these were big 1931 dollars. After no pay at all, any salary looks mighty big. I went North. Herb Mayes was editor of American Druggist. He later became the big man at McCall's. Herb told me that direct mail couldn't sell subscriptions to American Druggist. But mine did. I even bested him badly later in a letter writing contest. Mine won. Then I found another challenge."

The Depression forced the development of new, innovative ways of selling via mail order. Some of these methods started in England and were brought here and then modified. Fred Breismeister became part of this process when he began to work with John Stevenson. "I first met that young genius, John Stevenson, at the New York Post. I was immediately captivated by his well modulated English accent and suave manner. John hired me primarily to prepare the newspaper ads and related mailings for the Rand McNally Unabridged World Atlas for a New York Post circulation building campaign.

"Such book-selling campaigns were operated in about the same manner as similar campaigns in England, in which the reader saved from 20 to 50 odd book coupons which were published daily. These coupons entitled a reader to buy a book at a very low price. At the time I joined it, the New York Post was already well along with similar campaigns selling, volume by volume, sets of Mark Twain and Charles Dickens.

"The Post had a syndication department to furnish other newspapers the promotions which worked for the Post. Once the campaigns were proved successful running in the Post they were simply matted and sold to other newspapers throughout the U.S.

"Although the New York Post had only 250,000 circulation, my Atlas campaign sold over 300,000 Atlases, even though it required a record high number of daily coupons to be saved from the Post. One Atlas ad run in the New York News helped accomplish that amazing feat.

"The key to profit for the Post was the deluxe edition step-up. While waiting for Atlases to be printed and bound by Rand McNally, we gave all regular edition buyers the privilege of switching to a super Deluxe Edition for only $2.00 more per copy. This Deluxe Edition cost the Book Division less than 20¢ more! This Deluxe switch turned out to be a fairly common practice among mail order publishers to increase profits.

"One book campaign merged into the next. Before the Atlas campaign had run its course, we were started on a children's set called 'The Wonderland of Knowledge'.

"When the Post was sold and the series ended, John Stevenson and I went to the office of William Randolph Hearst, Jr., and I marvelled as smooth-talking John sold Bill Hearst a book-selling, circulation-building campaign for the Journal-American. That kept us hopping, grinding out full-page newspaper ads—sometimes spreads—generally just in time to make the lobster shift.

"You have to produce profits to stay in mail order. But once you do, employers come looking for you. Leonard Davidow operated the Consolidated Book Company in Chicago, and among other things, ran the Family Weekly Sunday Newspaper Magazine supplement for Mr. Cuneo of Cuneo Press. Somehow he had heard of me and invited me to come to Chicago to prepare a book-selling, circulation-building campaign for his 'University of Knowledge' 20-volume set.

"But hardly had we launched this with the usual type of coupon-saving campaign in Springfield, Illinois, than John Crawley of Wm. H. Wise and Company enticed me back to New York, in 1938. I loved Chicago but liked his offer better. So I packed my Lincoln-Zephyr and, with a howling snow blizzard most of the way and 18-wheelers skidding off the highways, I got back in time for Thanksgiving dinner."

In my story in this book on John Crawley, I tell of Fred's accomplishments at Wm. H. Wise and quote him in detail as he recalls it all. It was at Wise that I met Fred Breismeister, when Huber Hoge handled the Wise broadcast advertising. Fred was in charge of all broadcast advertising as well as all direct mail.

Usually, two or three copywriters were working for Fred, almost always starting off as beginners with little previous mail order experience. The idea was simple. The trainee would learn to write the words Fred would have written if he had had the time to write them. He used the same system with me and with every Hoge writer-trainee.

Fred appeared mild and quiet but was thorough. He expected careful, painstaking work. Initial copy of trainees seldom was. The trainee's copy might leave out vital points, be lazily written, confused or overwritten. But it got Fred's full attention. He'd walk to the file, get out proven mailing pieces and pencil in paraphrases. A phone call might interrupt; John Crawley might come in. If so, Fred would often praise something the trainee had done. He'd give no hint the copy was lacking.

Fred has a special enmity for lazy, unnecessary, vague and general words. He sought specific, colorful, descriptive, action words. He was a patient detective investigating end benefits in utmost detail. His trainees had to construct from scratch to his specifications. Our radio trainees had to select from his wonderful mailing pieces key words and convert print words to spoken ones. Always the radio copy that emerged after Fred's revisions was overlong. Now came the most important task, cutting copy. In the end, the copy was tight. The lazy words had been eliminated and the right words put in.

Fred was bitterly opposed to lazy cutting. Rarely was it permissable to cut a paragraph, sentence or group of words. Instead, trainees learned to cut individual words, to make each paragraph, sentence and group of words slightly shorter. The necessity of each article and connecting word was considered. A shorter word would be substituted for a longer one. With the aid of his assistants, Fred produced an unending flow of effective copy. What a job he did!

He taught me more than anyone about cataloguing what a book contains or a product can do. For the doctor book, extra diseases mentioned could mean extra sales to those intensely interested—so can appropriate cataloguing for any item. In his own way, he was infinitely patient. Fred trained the Huber Hoge trainees. As fast as I hired one I'd send him or her to Fred. Six months or a year later, the trainee would emerge battered, but a writer.

Jerry Kenny, who worked for Fred at Wise, went on to head up mail order book sales for Hearst. Al Goldman, who started at Huber Hoge and for it trained under Fred later became creative head of Benton & Bowles. And many others learned and benefited from Fred, as well.

Fred helped me in many ways. At a lunch, dinner or meeting with him, I would spout ideas as I did with anyone. But with those I talked of to others, I only occasionally proceeded. But Fred always had a pencil with him. He could take shorthand as fast as I could talk. He'd write down any idea I threw out, however wild. Then he'd telephone me and ask me to name a deadline when I would submit a detailed draft. The work was tough but the results rewarding.

Fred took the responsibility of dealing with me for all radio and later TV advertising. We worked as a team. It gradually developed that I would propose, he would authorize it and then make it happen, using my employees as if his own. He trained a long succession of Hoge copywriters.

Fred continues: "I hadn't been with John Crawley too many years when John Stevenson launched the Fiction Book Club. With other projects in mind, he invited me to become a one-third partner. I probably would have accepted if I were single, but did not because my wife and I had two sturdy boys we dearly loved. We knew we could give them a college education and a good start in life and felt we couldn't gamble on their futures."

Fred was earning bonuses at Wise based on business he created. Some years they were big and he put the money into real estate when it was low. Soon copy skill, turned into bonus and then into increasing value real estate, made him independent. "I

expected to stay with John Crawley for the rest of my life." But unexpected difficulties at Wise (told in my story on John Crawley) resulted in Fred's leaving. After doing some consulting, Fred accepted an offer to come with John Stevenson.

"Greystone had continuities before I joined them in 1954, such as: Music Treasures of the World; Art Treasures of the World (portfolios); Children's Record Guild; and, I believe, 'Living Language Courses'. I worked on all of these projects but originated the advertising for none of them.

"I did the original mailings on Encyclopedia of Photography, the 48-volume World and its Peoples, Shakespeare Plays in Text and Recordings by the Old Vic Player, etc. I also revised mailings for Music Treasures of the World, The Art Portfolios, Children's Record Guild, etc.

"I did develop the entire mailings for the continuity program libraries ... The New Illustrated Encyclopedia of Gardening ... The Encyclopedia of Animal Life ... Encyclopedia of Photography ... The Practical Handyman's Encyclopedia ... Art of the World ... The World and Its People and others.

"I did very close to finished layouts of circulars, letters, order forms and envelopes, specked the type and supervised preparation of finished art ready for camera. Robert Rotter, whom I had used at Wise, at first did much of the finished mechanicals. Then I used other artists, mostly free lance. The Practical Handyman's Encyclopedia was Greystone's biggest money-maker in libraries. I brought it to John Stevenson lock, stock and barrel, and he rewarded me by giving my wife and me a trip to Europe on the Sun Deck of The France."

Fred Breismeister stayed with John Stevenson until it was time to retire. But I introduced Fred to Ed Downe and, instead of retiring, he became president of Downe's book publishing subsidiary. For Ed he sold 9,000,000 volumes of a paperback series, "The World's 100 Greatest Books". He built up a major equity in Downe Stock based on stock options given executives. So again, copy skills were building capital for him.

Fred enjoyed working with Ed Downe as he had working with John Crawley and John Stevenson. "John Stevenson, Milo Sutliff and John Crawley were all beautiful people to work with. I enjoyed making money for all of them, and wanted nothing more than to see them get richer with help from me; because that enhanced my reputation, made me more valuable, and built up the demand for my services.

"I enjoyed working at Wise, particularly, because at Wise I was pretty much the kingpin and everybody liked me. Ed Downe was a super salesman, always optimistic. I loved working with him, and only wish I could have done more for him."

For readers of this book, Fred Breismeister has summed up some quick but very valuable points in producing effective mailings that sell.

"THE ENVELOPE - You MUST have it opened. They say that 50% of all mailings never get a chance to do their selling job because their envelopes are never opened. So it's very important to learn this first lesson first—especially with the high postage rates we have today. Study the envelope of mailings you receive from knowledgeable mailers such as Time-Life Books. Note how every one gets the favorable attention of recipients by boldly bringing his or her attention to how he or she will benefit.

"Every part of every piece of a mailing must do that ... *show how your book or product will benefit and profit the recipient*.

"The SELLING LETTER - How short should it be? How long should it be? The letter should be as short as possible to do the most effective selling job under the circumstances where it is being used. For instance. I have written many very successful

ONE PARAGRAPH selling letters that were used very early in magazines renewal series.

"On the other hand, I have written many most profitable FOUR-PAGE selling letters. I have been asked by copywriters I have trained, 'How long can selling letters be?' My answer has always been: 'As long as you are improving your chances of making a sale, you are O.K. As soon as you write a single sentence, a single word that doesn't improve your sales-making effectiveness, your letter is too long. Do not write flowery language, eloquently, or display your big vocabulary. Just show your reader how he will benefit so he'll mail in that order card.

"Yes, everyone uses too many words in writing letters and circulars. It takes time and work to tighten copy. Time and again, I've sent back copy with the comment, 'Say it all with one-third less words'. I know! I have been tightening my own copy all my life. Try it. You'll be surprised.

"THE SELLING CIRCULAR - Who needs all those pictures, drawings, captions, headlines, subheads and copy? Look at the circulars in the mail from top direct marketers. Note how each follows the four basic principles of making a sale: 1) Attracts attention; 2) Arouses interest; 3) Creates desire, and 4) Effects the sale.

"Notice how the first section of the 11" by 16" circular definitely ATTRACTS THE FAVORABLE ATTENTION of the recipient by immediately showing a big benefit for him or her.

"Look at the next 11" by 16" section of the circular as you open it up. Note how it AROUSES INTEREST with plenty of display type and its copy in large size type, easily read.

"Now open the circular up all the way and see the 16" by 22" inside of the circular. Here are the nuts and bolts. It does the job, in words and attractive pictures, of CREATING DESIRE by showing and telling all the beautiful end-product benefits the reader will get. And, at the bottom, it EFFECTS THE SALE.

Who reads all those hundreds of words? My answer is 'No one'. The direct mail buyer skips from here to there. The important thing is that no matter where eyes light and reading starts, there is effective selling copy that convinces him or her that these books or this product will give much that will benefit with pleasure and profit.

"Sometimes a recipient will barely glance at a mailing before convinced to mail in the order card. Another recipient might peruse it very thoroughly to become satisfied that the product being sold benefits him or her in many ways. Such a reader may want to read about certain ways the product benefits in great detail but not others.

"Other readers range all the way between these two extremes. The important thing is that they all see and read enough to convince themselves of the benefits they will get and convince themselves to *mail in that order card!* Nobody reads all that's there, but it's all there to convince the most skeptical. And the order cards rolling in by the thousands show that it does the job.

"What are my happiest mail order memories? The thrills of bringing home the big winners! There was nothing like the first multi-million subscription mailing on Good Housekeeping . . . except boosting to all time highs the renewal records of Good Housekeeping subscribers.

"But then bringing in each big success at Wise & Company was a great thrill: The Popular Educator, both as a magazine and as a 10-volume set; The Home Handyman's Guide; 100 World's famous Paintings; Your Dream Home and How to Build it for $3500 or Less; The Pictorial History of World War II and building it to a 10-volume set. And it was always a thrill to get each winner whomever I was associated with.

"If I had it to do over again, how would I do it differently? I'd break into it much more quickly, and probably as a partner or in my own business. Looking back, I believe I would have enjoyed greater financial success and lived a more pleasant life, if I had gone with Eastman Kodak. But with any shortcomings in any association I've had, as I said, we had our thrills when we booted home the winners.

"Of course, I enjoy retirement very much: sailing, tennis, fishing, gardening, wintering in Florida. But one can even become slightly satiated with Paradise. I notice among fellow members of our Senior Men's Association that the more contented ones do part-time consulting, etc. I sometimes miss some of the excitement, activity and pleasant contacts. I advise all retirees not to retire completely—just two-thirds!"

And I advise anyone who ever writes a word of mail order copy to re-read this chapter, copy Fred, and consider well his copy advice.

Chapter 5
The Rich List Mail Order Business

*"The very rich are not
like you and me."*
—F. Scott Fitzgerald

Harvey A. Rabinowitz agrees. "They buy more. They have the liquid capital to take a flyer. About 5% of the U.S. population has about 75% of the disposable income (after necessities and quasi-necessities). Overwhelmingly, they invest more. They provide the majority of venture capital for risk situations."

Harvey Rabinowitz and his wife, Geri, are in the rich list mail order business. They own W.S. Ponton, "the investor list people", and the oldest list compiling business in the U.S. It was founded in 1885. O'Henry, between writing "The Gift of the Magi" and other stories, sometimes addressed envelopes for Ponton—for two dollars a day.

In 1967, Ponton was on the verge of bankruptcy and was only saved by being taken over. "We really took the name, and started from scratch," says Harvey. "We did everything differently. We threw out the old Ponton lists and started with our own new ones, putting over a quarter of a million dollars into compilation.

"We had no previous experience in the list business. But in analyzing the records of Ponton, we found that W.S. Ponton had gotten into difficulty because of giving generous credit to big respected companies like Penn Central and Four Seasons Nursing Homes, which later went bankrupt. We changed the policy.

"We literally collect in advance from every customer, on every rental, with no exceptions . . . from the most giant company, the most respected list broker, or whomever.

"Looking through the Ponton company records, we found that it had had other problems with customers. Renters of lists had sometimes attempted to tie payment for rentals to results. Apparently, these people would rent lists and then determine which lists did not show a profit and sometimes not pay for such lists or chisel when the bill came. We didn't want to wait for our money, have arguments about money, or to not be paid. We didn't want to send bills and worry about receivables."

BUCKEYE MOWER.
WITH FOLDING BAR.
AULTMAN & MILLER'S PATENT.

The subscriber takes pleasure in calling the attention of FARMERS to the "BUCKEYE," the most complete and successful Mower ever introduced; combining, in the simplest form, all the qualities necessary to a perfect Mower. I's frame is supported on two driving wheels, either of which is independent of the other. The CUTTER BAR is attached to the frame by a DOUBLE HINGE JOINT, which allows either end, or the whole, to rise or fall, to conform to inequalities of the land. By means of a lever the Cutters can be raised to pass obstructions or over cut grass—in mowing can turn either to right or left—always throws itself out of gear in backing, and backs with the ease of a cart; is light draft, free from side draft; has no weight on the horse's neck; is safe for the driver; almost noiseless in its operat'n; works well on any land—side hills or salt meadows; and in any grass, whether lodged or standing, at a slow walk of either horses or oxen.

WHEN NOT IN USE, THE CUTTERS CAN BE INSTANTLY FOLDED OVER THE FRONT OF THE FRAME, AND THE MOWER THEN DRIVEN ANY DISTANCE ON THE ROAD. THIS FEATURE BELONGS, EXCLUSIVELY, TO THE BUCKEYE MOWER.

Since its first public exhibition, at the Great National Trial of Harvesting Machines, at Syracuse, N. Y., July, 1857, at which it received the HIGHEST AWARD, THE FIRST PREMIUM GRAND GOLD MEDAL AND DIPLOMA, AS THE BEST MOWER, IN COMPETITION WITH MANNY'S, KETCHUM'S, HALLENBECK'S, ALLEN'S BURRALL'S, KIRBY'S, HEATH'S, and several others, its principles have been fully tested by more than One Thousand Farmers, and, without an exception, has received their unanimous approval. During the past season, numerous First Premiums were awarded to the "BUCKEYE," including the New-York and Connecticut State Agricultural Societies.

Every Machine is built of the best material, and in a workmanlike manner.

It is warranted to cut and spread from ten to fifteen acres of grass per day, with a span of horses and a driver, as well as is done by the best mowers with a scythe.

The demand the past season was far beyond our ability to supply, and we trust orders will be forwarded early, to prevent disappointment. ☞ Circulars, with full description, forwarded on application.   JOHN P. ADRIANCE,
Manufacturer and Proprietor,
No. 165 Greenwich-st., New-York.

Since then, the born again W.S. Ponton has won a reputation as an unorthodox business that, while small, is successful and growing based on its own highly individual way of doing business. "We do it our way. We don't release magnetic tape. Nothing goes out. We did at first. But a California firm stole names. We sued and won. But we don't want aggravation. We deal with brokers but usually for 15% instead of 20%. We do give 20% for volume.

"W.S. Ponton had too loose an operation and sometimes too much overhead in relation to sales. We had our own ideas on the kind of names to handle, the terms to sell on and how to operate. We started up again in a tiny way, by mail order. We advertise our lists by mail and get orders with money by mail. It works." The new W.S. Ponton has no desire to be the biggest in the list business, or anywhere near it, or even to grow larger than this year's volume, estimated at over $500,000.

"This business is in our home, in remodeled ground floor offices. We use a computer service bureau. We have seven full-time and five part-time employees. My wife, Geri, is fully in charge. I spend half time. The first year we started in business, our gross sales volume was $12,000. But we did it our way. Last year, we did $390,000. Now that we're passing $500,000 this year, we want to stop growing. We won't expand. We won't take over other list companies. We're bursting at the seams.

"We specialize in investor lists. It's a big field. Nobody else has these lists. These lists came from our own sources plus investment firms. Our family is in the investment business. We market their lists. We have a clipping service. We recompile every two months. We guarantee our business lists 95% for deliverability and our consumer lists 90%. We refund the minimum third class postage. 70% of our lists are consumer and 30% are business. 65% to 70% of our customers repeat. Our names are practically all compiled by us but we do some brokerage.

"Some curse us. Some praise us. We lose business. We've walked away from business. We just turned down a 400,000 order from a stock broker. But this is the way we operate. We're the fastest pay in the industry whenever we buy anything. We're glad to take this task. We pay royalties. Most people conform to our ways. If anything is our fault, we give money back when warranted. I gave a full refund last week because it was justified."

Others in the list business seem to admire more than criticize the Rabinowitz approach. The Direct Marketing News and ZIP magazine have done stories on the new W.S. Ponton. Maybe W.S. Ponton will start a trend. "In the list business, I think you will find that more and more people will ask for cash. We don't have to check receivables. We don't have to argue. If I buy anything, I have to pay for it without quibbling. If anyone rents names, it should be the same way. We have lists we can do this with. We advise anyone if it's not acceptable to rent other lists."

Harvey graduated from the University of Pittsburgh in 1953. He was basketball manager and year book business manager. He went to the Dickenson law school. He had a very high IQ. As soon as he got into his family business, on leaving law school, he had very strong opinions. And his family agreed with him. "We were in wholesale, mostly dry goods. We were giving much too much credit. We didn't like being in the banking business. We got out.

"I worked for the Commercial Credit Bureau in their computer operation for ten months. I was credit manager and controller for a car stereo wholesaler. I'm an accountant. I work as an accountant in my family investment business. I'm not a registered representative. My brother-in-law is. I don't buy and sell and cannot and will not. I have an accounting and psychology background. I'm not a CPA. I hire one, I spend half the time in the investment business and half on Ponton."

W.S. Ponton is a manufacturing business. Two girls do the manufacturing. They scan newspapers from every section of the country and many publications of all kinds looking for rich people in the news. Ponton buys lists of defunct brokerage businesses. It looks for and acquires names of any and all kinds of rich people and then puts them through the computer. It compares them against telephone and other address directories, and also against a current "nixie" file.

Ponton has names of many kinds of rich people. "What they all have in common is that they invest." Ponton has 1,721,000 total investors on its master mailing list, by type of investment. What is your pleasure? Wealthy Arab gamblers or Jewish heavy investors? Would you like gold or silver bullion buyers, or diamond buyers? How about 9,000 multi-millionaires, 60,000 millionaires or 140,000 almost-millionaires (net worth of generally $750,000 or more)?

Ponton is the investor list department store. It has 90,000 gamblers (most take junkets to Las Vegas, Atlantic City, London or the Bahamas). How about Krugerand buyers? Hard currency buyers? Or cattle and new movie investors? Perhaps you'd prefer Swiss Franc insurance annuity buyers or members of very exclusive country clubs who invest in stocks, bonds, commodities or land. Your choices can go on and on. There are Jewish philanthropists and investors who are known art lovers, collectors and contributors. Would you like women who invest in stocks, bonds, commodities or land, or multiple large donors to charities—or buyers and sellers of puts and calls.

How about pure commodity future buyers, limited partnership investors or just people with large deposits in savings accounts. Ponton has them all and more, more, more rich people.

"We like our business. We may work up to two AM. But our people leave at five PM. And usually we do. We don't take our problems upstairs. We like selling for cash. We don't have write-offs. Our profit is nice. If volume dropped from $500,000 to $300,000, we could still go to Palm Beach. We're very lucky. We go our way, We don't even belong to the DMMA.

"I've no interest in going into any mail order business, selling a product myself. Do I have any advice for anyone wanting to go into mail order? Don't! For the little guy, misleading ads and mailings for get-rich-quick books give false hopes of easy, quick, big profits in mail order. Only those who advertise to the ignorant get rich quick.

"People come to us. They've read this kind of book. Often they're bright people. They should know better. They can't make it. A one shot will fail. Charities have pulled 8% to 14% on our lists. They're strong lists but only for offers suited to them and only for people who have a way of following up customers and continuing to sell more to them.

"On any list, "nixies" are an on-going problem. People move faster than lists are updated. Only start in mail order with large capital, with long staying power, and only if you're after an annuity. Repeat sales are the only way to survive. Don't expect much from books that promise to tell you how. Please make sure you know the risks before you start.

"Anytime, any year, any month, the economy may get worse. Be careful. But the mail order business is growing, growing, and growing. Our business increases. We thank the day I stumbled onto Ponton."

Note: W.S. Ponton of Pittsburgh, Inc. is located at 1414 Hawthorne Street, Pittsburgh, PA 15201 (412) 782-2360.

Chapter 6
Mail Order Cum Laude

*She made it in book clubs,
tells how they operate and
gives some career advice.*

On April 1, 1981, she graduated from book clubs to become president of Dell Publishing . . . a Doubleday subsidiary. On October 1, 1981, she graduated from Doubleday to become president of Publishers Clearing House.

Robin Smith was one of the first fifteen women graduates of Harvard Business School. Rising from a trainee start, she became general manager of all Doubleday U.S. book clubs. She participated in the overseeing of dozens more Doubleday, or partially Doubelday-owned, book clubs overseas. While she was responsible for the advertising, the Literary Guild doubled its membership and currently has about a million and a half members. The Doubleday Book Club, which had been declining, surged back to over a million members.

But Robin thinks that circumstances helped her greatly; that it's not unusual for women to succeed in publishing; that it's part of Nelson Doubleday's style to develop, train and advance people rapidly; and finally, that mail order is ideally suited to measure career performance, for any employer.

"That's what is very attractive to women about mail order. It's quantitative. Accomplishment can be traced. Anyone, man or woman, can have an idea, write an ad, recommend a media selection. The mail count shows the contribution. There are more women mail order executives in Doubleday now. Marcia Schmidt is in charge of the Doubleday Book club. Sally Reich is working on the Literary Guild." (She's graduated too, to her own business.)

Robin grew up in suburban Philadelphia where she graduated from the Baldwin School. At Baldwin she was circulation manager of the newspaper and editor of her class yearbook— relevant experience for a future mail order publisher. Next was Wellesley, following in the footsteps of her mother and grandmother. There she graduated as a Wellesley scholar with a major in French literature, after a junior year in Paris. She entered a Harvard-Radcliffe program of seventy women students to take courses at Harvard Business School . . . and at the end of the year, with seven other women, transferred to Harvard Business School (women were not admitted directly into the Harvard MBA program). She took mostly marketing, advertising, retailing, accounting—basic courses.

After graduating, Robin married and moved to Los Angeles. Her husband, who worked for Xerox, had been transferred there. Robin got a research job at the Carnation Milk Company. She went on to BBD&O Advertising Agency, in media and research.

Robin's husband was transferred to New York and she followed with her daughter. "BBD&O offered me an account executive job in their New York office, handling Campbell Soup. The woman who had had the job for three years was leaving. It made me wonder how far a woman could go there.

"A friend at Doubleday, who was secretary to Nelson Doubleday, told me that Doubleday wanted some new MBA's— that there was a lack of middle management and an opportunity for advancement. She explained that Doubleday's largest business consisted of its book clubs with memberships sold by mail order.

"I had no idea of mail order and was quite unfamiliar with book clubs from a business standpoint, but publishing appealed to me. Publishing had always had high-powered women in it and seemed to me more varied and stimulating than a product business. My friend got me an appointment with Nelson Doubleday. He seemed open to the idea of women executives, willing to judge on accomplishment, and sent me over to the Doubleday research department. After an interview, I was offered a job and accepted it.

"There were only five of us in research—and all young . . . even the department boss, Dave Shepard, who is now a consultant. We did some internal research for different departments. Mostly, we were looking at acquisitions.

"It was heady stuff looking at companies. There were a lot of federal funds for education. Publishers were expanding. It was the second half of the go-go sixties. Doubleday had already purchased the Trigg-Vaughan TV and radio stations and Laidlaw Brothers, a prominant elementary/high school text publisher. We'd look at other possibilities. But usually we'd investigate, find out some bad reports and recommend against acquiring. Finally, Doubleday set up its own multi-media company."

In less than a year, Robin took over the research department. "I reported to Nelson, then to Walter Freese, a group vice president. I had some contact with the clubs. For them we did anonymous research. We stood outside book stores and asked questions. I liked publishing. It was unbusiness-like and fascinating. The 'product' was always changing.

"I worked very hard but it was some time before I pictured myself as getting up to a top job. Doubleday didn't go out of the way to create opportunity for women, but it left the door open for women to rise. Yet, probably no one at Doubleday pictured women in top mail order jobs, although they had pretty good jobs as editors.

"Once it was proposed that I be made assistant advertising manager. Ed Fitzgerald, who then headed the book club, was said to be against it because he felt it would be a blind alley for me, that they'd never make a woman advertising manager.

"Nevertheless, my first club job was advertising manager— just me and an assistant. Largely, I was concerned with space media, magazines and newspapers. I dealt with the agencies: Frank Vos; Rapp & Collins; Wunderman, Ricotta & Kline; and David Altman.

"Whatever career success I've had has come partly from luck and timing. Partly, my chance came because Doubleday was just starting the product management system. At that time, we had 28 clubs with one advertising manager for space, and one for direct mail. The club magazines were directed by someone else. Coordination of approach was poor. As an experiment, I was given the Literary Guild to run.

"At Doubleday there were a lot of shibboleths. We were taught that there were months when it was death to advertise, in April, May and November. It was policy never to run the Dollar Book Club in the same medium as the Literary Guild. As Doubleday did more advertising for its clubs, these strictures were difficult. There wasn't enough available space in the right months and without conflicts.

"I probably had a certain fearlessness. We began to disregard the old rules. We found that the traditional months were best. But we still made money in the previously forbidden months. We had less competition then.

"The timing was right. In 1972, everybody was riding high and everything was working. The added months and schedules, while not as profitable, were profitable enough. I was rushing hard trying to get the agencies to try new things. We tried TV and had a couple of successes. We were the first book marketer, I think, to try a large, general agency for book clubs. That was SSC&B. We bought TV time very cheaply, very advantageously. TV did not keep paying out, but then it was additional and profitable business. It was selling people on books. I doubled the print budget. The next year was the most profitable year for the clubs until recently, and by a wide margin. I got some of the credit.

"My responsibilities still were mainly the growth of the Guild, but I began to get into other Doubleday book clubs. The old Doubleday Bargain Book Club was declining. It looked like it would lose money in a few years. We analyzed the trend. We looked at patterns of book selections. They were heavily Gothic and Romance. The advertising was overwhelmingly bargain directed. It emphasized the wide choice of books and how cheap they were. We completely reoriented the appeal, played down the bargain and played up the romance. The change was very successful.

"Then I became concerned with new clubs, ideas for them and safe development of them. I kept working hard to keep achieving growth in all kinds of conditions, and in new directions. Not everything has worked. For example, in 1969, the Michael Field cooking program seemed to start with great potential. Yet, when Michael Field died it proved too difficult to continue the project.

"One area I got into was analyzing the clubs, one by one, for future profit potential—where best to put effort, risk and capital for best return on investment. We found that for Doubleday the economics were not right for most specialized programs and clubs, particularly the non-reading specialty clubs in entertainment and hobbies.

"We also found that time-dated media had, to some extent, replaced books. The Better Homes & Gardens annuals and those of others had become more elaborate. They offered a lot more than, for instance, a Doubleday Decorating program could. There were a lot of special interest magazines with such annuals. We reduced the number of clubs from 28 to 10, pushed the big membership reading clubs for far more overall volume and profit.

"The media costs to acquire members in the specialized clubs and programs often became too high for us. We didn't own magazines. Perhaps these specialized clubs have to be satellites or have little overhead. Our ability was in high volume, low ticket clubs. We used to think that 100,000 members were required as a minimum. Newsletters are attractive but often have to be run out of your garage to make money. Small, specialized clubs and programs may be practical for smaller companies and entrepreneurs who can operate with less overhead.

"In England, Doubleday proliferated into more specialized clubs. They don't have as much mass media there, and tastes are different. You could successfully run a book club there on something quite specialized, like railroads. They're very big on old treasures and ancient history. They read more. There, clubs can provide benefits not possible in the U.S. That's because England is so compact. A club can organize a day at the museum or at theaters. It can be much more of a club. Also, there is no discounting in retail stores.

"By and large, we stuck to what we did best. This can mean getting in a rut. It is sometimes discouraging that no record clubs have succeeded with book clubs and no book clubs in records. We did no insurance. We did some collectibles, and developed a rather large and profitable merchandise operation. In the main, however, it seemed that we couldn't cross over. The theory appeals to me that certain companies do well with dominant market shares but not when they go into a field where this is unlikely because others are already so entrenched.

"New products are extremely important. We attempted to stimulate all concerned in the creative process. To come up with new products, we called on all the help we could get. Doubleday has a whole new products department. Here the danger is becoming a bureaucracy. There were no bounties for coming up with a new product idea that is accepted, but we all knew the importance it has when our effectiveness was judged. The agencies came up with some club ideas. Frank Vos did with the Military Book Club. Ideas came from anywhere within the company. Stan Rapp helped us in organizing inside brainstorming sessions."

Note: For readers of this book Robin Smith has answered the following questions I have asked.

Q. *How important have you found the computerization of book club operations to growth and success?*

A.   The business wouldn't be here today without them. Doubleday has three and a half million active accounts. Without the computers it couldn't keep track of all the transactions. Its back-end knowledge would be much weaker. It wouldn't know anywhere near as much about where our business comes from. It would have to cut out a lot of activities.

Q. *In what way does Doubleday use computers?*

A.   Doubleday's fulfillment system had been computerized by the time I got there. Since then, it has been modified to provide a marketing system. Its use has been critical for Doubleday. When I left we were in the midst of a massive redesign to a data base, marketing-oriented computer system.

Q. *Has computer modeling been important to Doubleday?*

A.   Yes. We did our own. We did a fair amount from simple modeling to more sophisticated. We used modeling for new products, for our five-year plans, for credit. It was terribly valuable.

Q. *How effective have you found zip code area demographic research in list selection for direct mail?*

A.   We did some demographic research but it was not decisive. A number of years ago, we did a segmentation study of members of the Literary Guild. We used factor analysis. We did surveys of members and of neighbors. Through factor analysis, we uncovered a number of segments, too many, in which nothing differentiated members and neighbors but interest in reading.

Q. *Has people research, asking questions, been practical in making mail order decisions?*

A.   We did a lot. We supplemented testing with research. We did a lot with focus groups. They were helpful for ideas creatively, to come up with appeals—both in graphics and copy.

Q. *How did you use focus groups in making decisions?*

A.   We held sessions with current members to find out their perceptions of the clubs. We did it often before launching a club to find out if people like the idea and would consider joining. It was not quantifiable, but it could provide hypotheses. It could also cause confusion. It was often more helpful in warning than in

pointing the way. I liked to go to sessions. In some cases when we got bad vibes in focus group research, we did not go ahead with projects.

Q. *How consistently reliable is research in making decisions?*

A.   It varies by type and situation. Research doesn't always work. We tried TV research. We used Scherwin and other techniques. A number of commercials were shown, then tested in a laboratory setting. Unfortunately, there was no correspondence between the research and the mail order tests later. The commercials research said were best were worst, and vice versa.

Q.   How did you analyze and consider all the possible new club and other mail order project ideas that you came up with?

A.   We had systems for screening ideas, calculating the risk vs. the reward and cost of entry. We had a check list. I got interested in this a long time ago. The method works well. But our new product record was still not all that great.

Q. *Did you go systematically after acquistions of mail order publishers and product businesses?*

A.   We didn't acquire much. Sometimes, I think that there is not much in a mail order company to sell. But acquiring people is something else. Our merchandise business started with graphics. We hired Bernie Schwartz from the Collectors Guild, at first for graphics only. At first, I was against it. I don't like to fire people, and I worried about bringing in a specialist for a field that might not continue. But it worked out. The graphics were successful and led to merchandise. Bernie was and is responsible for it.

Q. *Does Doubleday still do as much as possible in-house?*

A.   Doubleday still does most direct mail creative work in-house, and all fulfillment operations in-house. It still prints almost all its book club selections in its own plants. It does mail direct mail mainly from outside lettershops. It maintains its own lists. The trend continues, overwhelmingly, to do everything possible in-house.

Q. *How big an in-house creative staff does Doubleday have?*

A.   In Garden City, we had fifty creative people, most of them in direct mail. A good combination is the creative impetus of different agencies and control by inside creative people in a tight schedule. Of course, they can get stale.

Q. *What did you do then?*

A.   Once we decided that the Guild Magazine was not "up to snuff". We hired Push-Pin Studios and SSC&B to try new formats. Push-Pin was very creative but came up with a big newspaper. SSC&B made a very credible contribution. But our own creative service did the best job.

Q. *Did you use outside free lancers to create mailing pieces for important tests? What about use of your agencies for such tests?*

A.   We used free lancers and agencies on fee to turn out direct mail, but overwhelmingly, in-house talent.

Q. *For a test did you create several mailing pieces? If so, did you select one to test or test each?*

A.   Usually, we created several packages to test against the control package.

Q. *With your in-house staff, which came first, copy or layout—or was it a team effort from the start?*

A. In creating advertising, copywriter and art director work together pretty much from the beginning. Research is important in the process.

Q. *In new product launches, did you rule out many products without actual testing, by your screening methods? How did you decide whether to actually test?*

A. We could screen a lot or test a lot—maybe go out and test three or four new products, each with several approaches, and hope that something will work. We tried to narrow the testing, as it has become almost prohibitively expensive.

Q. *Did you personally keep testing moving?*

A. I did try to push things ahead, get started on tests and get answers.

Q. *How did you decide whether to go after a number of smaller but profitable projects versus less but bigger ones?*

A. In launching new products and developing new methods, we had to avoid small-time, limited successes and concentrate on several big ones.

Q. *If one product promised more profit per dollar but was somewhat more limited, where did you draw the line?*

A. We analyzed carefully such situations. When I left, we were working on a management-by-objectives method with our people, coupled with a strategic planning process. As far as I know, we were the first in mail order to do this.

Q. *If you tested and failed, did you forget it? Or sometimes, after a post-mortem, did you decide to try again? How did you decide?*

A. I liked a "bust" best, if a test failed. Then we just stopped. If it was close, we could get seduced into trying again when sometimes we shouldn't. We didn't often fail, come up with a new approach, and then succeed. What can be a real trap is to come up with good order costs and to proceed before knowing what will later happen. It's easy to figure an arbitrary member life long enough to be profitable. It's tempting to hope for better than average back-end. But after every test, we always had a post-mortem. Sometimes, we came up with something.

Q. *Can improving back-end follow-up often increase overall gross profit enough to turn failure to success?*

A. We didn't find that back-end follow-up to extract maximum profit from the customer was the key. It's often very difficult to improve this. There's more leverage in improving the original order cost. We had to keep balancing off the offer, the commitment, how to sell in order to achieve a lower membership acquisition cost and not get worse results in the back-end, in member life and average dollar purchases by member.

Q. *What was Doubleday doing to experiment with new forms of TV, cable and two-way TV?*

A. We tried to broaden our market. One reason we tried TV for clubs was the limited print and direct mail media universe. But TV recruiting results are extremely variable. Perhaps average TV circulation is too low-grade. We did nothing in cable, which might have better demographics.

Q. *How effective was telephone marketing for Doubleday?*

A. We did not have too good success. We were interested in trying more. We felt we probably needed to do it ourselves for control rather than to use outside services. Time-Life does a lot of telephone marketing.

Q. *How effective has support TV been for Doubleday to back up a big mailing, space campaign or both?*

A. When we tried it, we probably didn't have the use for it. It failed. It would have been great for pre-prints, when we were using them heavily. Book-of-the-Month Club claims that support TV works for them.

Q. *How has new technology in processing mail affected Doubleday most?*

A. We cut down phenomenally on people in more manual jobs. In Garden City, in ten years we cut down from 1,400 people to 700 while, during that same time, the business more than doubled. It was a part of changing methods.

Q. *How did all this happen?*

A. The biggest difference was more and more use of computers. We reduced personnel partly with more computer use, a lot with more automated processing, partly with OCR (Optical Character Reading), and partly with the Wofac System. Word processing and other technology keeps making it possible to get more work done by less people. We lost by attrition. We kept the best people and gained further in more productivity per person.

Q. *What other changes are important?*

A. Greater selectivity is very important. There has been an enormous improvement, however, in finer and finer tuning in selctivity of lists and media. New, more selective media have helped. But you can't segment potential book club members just on income. Faster web presses have helped in direct mail. For books Doubleday has its Orange Plant, the fastest book presses in the country.

Q. *What changes have been negative?*

A. Book rates in the mail have quadrupled in ten years. This has hurt a great deal. We had to develop a lot more sophistication to overcome all this. There's government regulation and consumer pressure. We constantly worked to improve our own self-regulation and our customer service.

Q. *What does the future hold? Cable? Video disc publishing? Video disc clubs? Video sheets via direct mail? Electronic publishing?*

A. Doubleday sees changes in the future. It's interested in new media and new kinds of publishing. We did not make experiments in cable TV, but we planned to do so . We did not plan on going into video disc production. We were interested in the possibility of video disc clubs at the right time. We didn't investigate video sheets as a solo mailing. Electronic publishing as a possibility was not a high priority.

Q. *Who are some of the finest and most stimulating people you've worked with in mail order?*

A. Harold Schwartz, of Hanover House, is very imaginative. Jerry Hardy is very able. Stan Rapp is full of ideas and so is Lester Wunderman and Frank Vos. Nat Ross, Rose Harper and a lot of others in direct marketing are fine people and stimulating to work with.

Q. *What are your abilities which have helped you most in your career?*

A. Probably some have been creative and some business. Some strengths are probably being able to size up situations, decide priorities, get more out of information, risk taking, organizing and planning. I'm pretty good at evaluating people, seeing that they get experience and promotion opportunities.

Q. *For mail order management positions do you look for college graduates, MBA's, just smart people or only those with experience?*

A. Doubleday is very big on MBA's for marketing and financial jobs. But several of its top people are not MBA's. We did hire people with prior experience and smart beginners. A lot came to us in the middle of graduate school night courses and finished while they were with us.

Q. *Is it better to start with a small or large company?*

A. Some argue that starting out in a small company is best. This can be countered by the possibility of insufficient or even wrong training and the creation of habits hard to change later. In a large company that does direct marketing well, people share their know-how. For example, I never heard of someone in media who couldn't go to the financial people and ask questions.

Q. *Is there still a good deal of competition for highest quality MBA's?*

A. Yes. Most MBA's starting out are most attracted to consumer products and consider experience with them more valuable than in mail order.

Q. *Did you look for MBA's with special training?*

A. We liked a broad-based educational background. But today, being an MBA is less and less of a qualifier. It doesn't guarantee someone special now that there are more MBA's than there were.

Q. *Was it hard to get beginners of the calibre you wanted?*

A. Yes. We tried to get the top of the class from top graduate schools. We favored brighter people with more education.

Q. *How do salaries in direct marketing today compare to those in equivalent jobs?*

A. Direct marketing is growing as a form of marketing. I think salaries in it are excellent compared with those in other kinds of marketing.

Q. *How should talented beginners select a company to go with?*

A. I tell them to look at the driving force behind each company. Is it sales? I mean personal selling and managing salesmen. If so, it will be a heavy battle for an MBA with an analytical and business management orientation. Is it finance? If so, marketing planning may not be recognized to the full. Look for a company where the driving force will favor the kind of skills you have.

Q. *Did you have top executives who have made it in mail order with no college degree?*

A. Yes; some have started in minimal jobs out at Garden City or in other plants.

Q. *What steps does Doubleday take to trade up people from bottom manual jobs that are disappearing to mail order management jobs?*

A. Doubleday tries hard. All its job openings are posted, for instance. It considers for a job people with talent who started at the bottom and who have less than its educational requirements, if their talent warrants.

Q. *What kind of trainee program does Doubleday have?*

A. It doesn't have one. It does move promising people into a progression of jobs. Usually, the MBA's go into financial analysis, into product management, and media. Most non-

MBA's go into services or a lower level assistant job elsewhere. We liked to move promising people into media, then to product management and then to financial analysis or into services, switching them around.

Q. *What did you do to orient and update your people on various facets of direct marketing , particularly latest developments?*

A. Doubleday spends a lot on this. It now has a large number of marketing people taking some outside courses or seminars at Doubleday's expense. Some attend the Nat Ross NYU course. Others go to the DMMA three-day programs. If someone is great in marketing but weak in financial analysis, it will send him or her to a financial seminar. It sends them to public speaking courses, writing courses, management courses, etc.

Q. *What books do you recommend for those starting out in direct marketing?*

A. I like the Drucker books; I like Bob Stone's book and the Levitt books—particularly "Marketing Myopia".

Q. *What progress has been made in getting blacks into the mail order management operations of Doubleday?*

A. We recruited in the black universities and graduate schools to attract talented blacks with and without MBA's. The most talented get a lot of offers from large corporations and do not generally choose mail order. It's hard to find minority candidates. We had a couple, but would have liked more. Doubleday is participating in the DMMA minority summer internship program.

Q. *Do you advise young people generally who are starting out to consider direct marketing?*

A. Absolutely.

Q. *What qualifications are needed?*

A. For best chances they should be somewhat entrepreneurial, analytical with a turn of mind for the concrete. It's not for the back slappers, the personality people who want to use their charisma. Extraverts do succeed in it. But introverts can make it.

Q. *What are the chances for women today in direct marketing?*

A. It's a wonderful career path and very good for the very bright who are not necessarily outgoing.

Q. *Can a woman today succeed as easily as a man?*

A. Lots of women feel that they're not getting the breaks. They have a real desire to succeed based on solid, proven accomplishment rather than connections. Women starting out today are more ambitious, more determined to get equal opportunity, particularly in direct marketing.

Q. *Women have made it at Doubleday. What is being done to get more of them?*

A. In mail order, most top positions are still not held by women. But Doubleday makes a big effort to get them. It hires two women MBA's for one man MBA.

Q. *Are women executives today more relaxed and under less pressure?*

A. In some ways they are. In other ways, I think they are not. They feel more confident, less insecure, get along better with each other and with men in business. But career and home is probably more of a strain.

Q. *How has your career affected your home life and your daughter's upbringing?*

A. My child is sixteen. She's very well adjusted, although I'm divorced and work at a hard pace. At first, it was terrible and still is very hard to do everything. We live in Manhattan. A lot of women with these strains, I fear for. Some have built-in disappointment. Trying to do both home and job is draining. I haven't had the time for all the activities I'd like.

Q. *Is mail order too dangerous for the small entrepreneurs?*

A. Yes, if a beginner has no knowledge or help and is putting in money substantial to him or her. If the investment is small and the loss can be afforded, then the testing is learning, and it can be a good move.

Note: Robin Smith was the recipient of the tenth anniversary award of the Direct Marketing Idea Exchange. She has lectured and talked on careers in direct marketing at New York University and elsewhere. A tape can be obtained from Hoke Communications. Details are in the Help Source Section of this book. With a talented tutor as nice as Robin, you talented readers can pursue a mail order career cum laude, too.

Chapter 7
Mail Order's Mini-Insert World

Its start, growth and marriage brokers; how to use it profitably.

It started as a mini-medium. It has grown bigger than ever suspected. Most now feel its biggest growth has just begun. It has nothing to do with the big inserts . . . the pre-print sections, the big free-standing inserts on post card and stock . . . the full pages with post card attached . . . in newspapers and magazines.

Leonard E. Holland was the father of it. He had been sales promotion manager of the L & C Home Catalog. After that he was direct mail manager for the Popular Club Plan Catalog. In 1959, he started in business for himself . . . with a new idea.

Len had found at both the catalog houses he had been with that the most profitable form of advertising was a package insert in the catalog house's own package. But it required the right offer appropriate for the package. Len's idea was to arrange marriages between someone with a mail order offer and a quite different firm shipping a mail order product.

Len had a theory that if a certian offer was highly profitable when enclosed with a certain product, it would be successful when enclosed with similar products shipped by other firms. He was convinced that doing so could be desirable to both the shipper and the firm making the offer.

Len proposed the idea to the Columbia Record Club and to Damar, a catalog house quite active at that time. It worked. Dave

Margolies, who owned Damar, got money. Columbia got orders at very low selling cost, and Len got a list broker's commission. Len had not only started a business, he had started a new advertising medium. For two to three years, Len had the field all to himself, and the field proliferated.

In 1962, Len started his first co-op mailing, getting a number of direct advertisers to share the same envelope, often using the same material as for the package insert. In 1963, Len started his first billing enclosure program. From the beginning, he had started as a list broker, as well.

In the early years, Len was like a real estate broker getting listings. His main problem was to get sources . . . shippers of mail order items who would accept package inserts. Billing inserts were tougher. With credit cards, less offers were made on open billing. Then there was the problem of just how many inserts would be productive in a package, with a bill or as part of a co-op package. Also, Len had to find out who could profitably use package inserts, billing inserts or co-op mailings. Another factor was comparing the results of inserts shipped by mail versus with items sold through stores.

Package inserts proved to do the biggest job. Len estimates that almost 80% of users of all three media represent package inserts only, that about 15% represent billing enclosures and 5% represent co-op mailings.

It seemed that more and more mail order customers, even for high ticket merchandise, bought for cash. Most who bought on credit did so via credit cards. Only a small minority of transactions were directly billed to the mail order customer. It wasn't easy to get an offer for big coverage with billing inserts, since for best results only one or two inserts could be enclosed with each bill.

There was a lot to learn for everybody. Co-op mailings had to charge postage, envelope, label and mailing costs, while package inserts did not. The answer was to put more inserts in a co-op envelope. This cut results.

For a while, there was a flood of co-op mailings but most did not succeed, both for participants and the promoter. Mail order firms organizing a co-op did very well if they could get six or seven enclosures to pay them and include their own pieces, as well, for a free ride. So a co-op was tempting to organize. But overcrowded co-ops did not pay out. Users dropped out. All the co-op distributors of huge consumer mailings except R.H. Donnelly gave up. In 1981, John Blair started again.

Whether package inserts, billing inserts or co-op mailings, too many participants killed response. In the end, package inserts seemed to work best with three participants, sometimes with four, and rarely with more. With bills, one insert had the best chance, sometimes two and rarely more. With co-op mailings, the promoters liked a dozen or more; the participants liked six or less.

Inserts in store packages were far less productive, but worked if the cost per thousand was very low and the offer insert very related. Also, offers with a time limit such as magazine subscriptions, had a problem. Store packages often stayed in stores long after the time limit. In mail order packages and bills, how close the offer enclosed was related to the item shipped or billed had a lot to do with success or failure.

Only a few co-op mailings out of all started survived, but these are succeeding. The biggest is Carol Wright of Donnelley Marketing. Couponing later became far more popular and made Donnelley's Carol Wright program enormously successful. It also got envelopes open and made Carol Wright great for mail order insert users. But the total number of smaller yet sizeable co-op distributors dropped to about twenty. Then mailers began coming back to co-ops, cautiously. Distributors began starting up again, carefully.

Len remembers: "At first, there was a lot of resistance from sources in those early days. Our growth was decided by how many shippers we could persuade to accept inserts. Then we got the sources and my problem was the competition from others in the field."

The growth of the field again required new sources . . . more packages, bills and co-op mailings to offer advertisers. Then everything began to explode. Co-op mailings were organized by mail order companies, a lot of them. Leon Henry went into the brokerage business similarly to Len. Then, more and more, others did the same. The bigger list brokers began to do so.

"It was first thought by many of us," says Len, "that inserts would be a medium for small mail order firms, for those who could no longer make solo mailings pay out. Instead, it's another form of direct mail primarily for sophisticated marketers who already use solos. We sell mostly to big people. We discourage one-shots from small people. We discourage low ticket items except to get names for a catalog, a continual follow-up by mail. We discourage a newcomer with a $9.95 item, while Ambassador Leather may make it with a $4.95 item. They have a catalog and lots of following and can make it work."

Today there are more and more specialists in mini-insert mail order. Most large list brokers have a department. Dave Florence, of Direct Media, says that the mini-inserts in packages and bills and co-op insert programs represent 10% of Direct Media list rental income. And it's growing for brokers faster than the overall list brokerage business.

Dependable Lists got into inserts early. Walter Karl every year publishes a package insert directory. Abelow Response does nothing but broker inserts. Rubin Response, in Chicago, is putting great effort into it, with great success. The Wessel Co. of Elk Grove Village, Illinois, is a printer, one of whose specialties is insert printing. It prints over a billion inserts a year, specializing in four-color lithography . . . mostly 3 or 4 panel inserts folding to 6⅛" by 3½".

The man who speaks most for and crusades most for inserts is Leon Henry. In 1969, Leon went into the business of brokering package inserts, billing inserts, and co-op mailings. "I started in a modest way," says Leon. For nine years before, Leon operated The Home Business Report, a newsletter for moonlighters. Leon graduated from the Wharton School at the University of Pennsylvania, and then got a Master's degree from the Columbia School of Business. He has always been an entrepreneur. He wrote one book called "How to Make Twice As Much in Half the Time".

His insert business has grown constantly. "I've had no down years," says Leon. "Different users have burgeoned one year, then another. In 1977, magazines offering subscriptions began to use inserts in a big way. Every year, inserts became a favorite medium for some new group. And 75% percent of those who start with us each year stay in. We've built a small base, a steady core that has kept growing. With every postage increase, our business jumps.

"We're beginning to diversify. We do a list brokerage, as well. We're still not big, even in inserts. We were at the bottom of the top five in the field. Now we're in the middle. Walter Karl is big. Unimail was but is now out of it. Larry Tucker has been growing fast. Bill Stroh is quite substantial in volume. Dave Palgon has kept growing with Media Masters, and Leonard Holland started it all."

Leon has experimented with a wide variety of inserts. For a while, he tried inserts in grocery bags in supermarkets, but they did not pull. Leon uncovered other areas that worked very well, though. "Acknowledgements are like statement stuffers, but few are available. Door-to-door distribution is cheaper than anything else but often less reliable on distribution. Inserts with packages of samples are often very good. Catalog bind-ins are becoming a phenomenon. Inserts that go with someone else's circular are ride-alongs, and often very strong—and in big volume.

"Years ago, there were quite a few mailers. There was a lot of misuse and inadequate testing. Then many who had failed came back. They tested inserts more scientifically and thoroughly, with more patience. The right marriage of product and insert distributors began to work more.

"We still have problems in inserts. One is dependability in inserting by mail order shippers and manufacturers. Another is rising costs of inserts to advertisers. These costs keep going up but remain a fraction of the cost of solo mailings. But we work hard to make inserting more dependable and to keep costs in the mail a bargain compared with other mail order advertising, particularly solos.

"My job is to expedite these opportunities—to marry mail order companies to use each other's packages as media. I've been in alternate media for 25 years. We have a 16-person staff and our own word processor. We represent 1,500 insert programs. We help clients and ourselves. Distributors earn more. Advertisers save. We keep searching for unique distributions."

Leon sells the small and the big. "We'll take a test of 5,000 to 10,000 or an order of 5,000,000 inserts. We advise new insert users not to create an insert specifically for the medium—one which is untested copy. Instead, we recommend starting with an insert piece that had been pre-tested in some other medium. A number of tests should be made at once or over a period, not just one. We recommend using 10,000 pieces for each one step test and 25,000 pieces to pull inquiries for a two-step test.

"There are at least 500 million inserts distributed annually. There are 2,000 distribution outlets, of them at least 50 'programs' with one million or more potential annual circulation are distributed. Yet, we estimate that there are still no more than 500 to 700 advertisers."

Leon Henry is a walking chamber of commerce for inserts, a walking glossary of its terms. He constantly tells the insert story and preaches the word. He is the auctioneer of its opportunities to get protection rights for a field. From San Diego to London, he speaks at direct marketing gatherings. He lectures at universities. He sends his flyer, "Enclosures Are In", free to anyone in direct marketing and even a free subscription to his excellent newsletter of inserts, "Media Interaction".

"Inserts are now poised for really giant growth. The parts of the puzzle are falling into place. As postage increases have accelerated more and more—far faster than inflation—more and more mail order people are turning to inserts. The need to reduce postage has become imperative. Mailers consider any alternative that will produce orders at equal cost. Sales representative firms have come into inserts who are responsible and capable.

"The race is on to test results and project before competitors do. Today it's difficult to open up a mail order package without an RCA Record Club and a Nashua Photo insert in it. Open a package from L.L. Bean, or whatever, and you'll likely find an insert from Time magazine. In field after field, firms with foresight have moved into inserts—the little medium with the big future.

"We now represent nearly every major mail order gift house which accepts advertising in packages. We have a new project in the works to print our own inserts. We've developed a new multi-concept called 'Priority Post' which is distributed in bank statements of major banks."

Note: In the Help Source Section in this book, addresses and phone numbers of Leonard E. Holland, Leon Henry and other brokers specializing in inserts are listed. Also, details are given how to get reprints of articles and tapes of speeches of Leon Henry, as well as those from ZIP Magazine, the DMMA Manual and by others in the field.

Chapter 8
The Most Prolific Copywriter I've Met

How he started and developed.

Out of the West . . . strong, tall and handsome . . . with a smile that lit up our entire office . . . came an extraordinary writing talent, Gene Schwartz.

His copy has sold the widest variety of products by mail order, including well over ten million books. He has written more ads, mailings and commercials on single volume books than any copywriter I know. His collection of modern art comes from his copywriting skill.

Gene Schwartz came from Montana, joined Huber Hoge and Sons at 21 as a messenger—and within weeks of being hired, was writing his first copy. Within a year, he was writing winners for our clients and has written them for many clients ever since, at an accelerating pace. Gene's copy has launched hundreds of products, dozens of businesses and sold books for a big share of leading publishers of how-to books. He became an author. His wife, Barbara, became a famous decorator.

To write about Gene brings back memories of when he arrived. Millie Klock, our office manager, took to him as a mother. Sherman Lurie, our creative head, took a fatherly interest. Gene started with us, went elsewhere, came back and then went on and on elsewhere. In my book, "Mail Order Moonlighting", I tell in detail half a dozen anonymous anecdotes about Gene.

He wrote hundreds of commercials for Huber Hoge and Sons and did much research in preparing them. He sought out library books for research for style or association. He read them incessantly, even on the subway. He carried them along on his dates with Barbara, his wife to be, courting her. He'd write at night, on weekends, anytime, anywhere. He was imaginative and full of ideas.

For Huber Hoge he wrote a radio commercial that started with, "Did you ever see a robin step up behind another robin— and kick its legs from under it?" He had researched that this happens. It sold tens of thousands of Audubon Bird Books. Huber Hoge was then running some of the first TV commercials to sell books by mail order. For Doubleday we sold one out of 14 TV set owners the Jon Gnagy "You Can Draw" book. Gene wrote commercials for it and for "The Kajar Magic Book" and then "The Commander Rigby Jet Plane Book". To sell books, each demonstrated. Jon Gnagy drew pictures, Kajar did tricks and

Commander Rigby hurled planes around the room. Gene got deeply into TV production.

For Doubleday, Simon & Schuster and others, we sold memory books via radio and then TV, with Gene's copy. In fact, Gene never stopped selling memory books. Later, he bought memory books from Frederick Fell, Inc . . . first for his own company and then in partnership with Fred Fell, himself. Fred says that those efforts sold over a million memory books.

At Huber Hoge, Gene's copy sold books of Doubleday, Wm. Wise, Prentice Hall and other publishers. Long after his years at Huber Hoge, Gene bought books from Prentice Hall, and sold with his copy so many that George Costello asked him to write a book on how to write advertising. Gene did, "Breakthrough Advertising", which Prentice Hall published. I recommend you try to get it from a business library.

While at Huber Hoge, Gene began to write very effective space ads. In one weekend, from a confirming test using four newspapers, Gene's ad pulled $150,000 in sales for a car repair book—and made $30,000 from one paper.

Gene set up an after-hours school and taught mail order copy to the new copy trainees as we took them on. By the time he was 25, we had started a business together and he had made $60,000 on his share of the profits. By now, Gene would come in the morning with a full page ad he had written the night before. But two or three days later, he'd come in with a complete rewrite, entirely new copy from beginning to end.

He could paraphrase an ad with great speed and sometimes did it almost for fun. From the book, "The 100 Greatest Ads", he took the great ad by Jim Mathes, written 30 years before . . . "Down from Canada come tales of a sparkling new beverage." This had launched Canada Dry in stores. Gene paraphrased it to sell by mail order a new plant, Lythrum, developed in Canada. We ran it with tremendous success.

Gene wrote for me in field after field and product after product—both for products we were partners in and for clients . . . for anything I asked . . . and years later, long after he left. He wrote for cosmetics, fertilizer, toys, books, whatever. He wrote one ad which sold over 2,000,000 fishing lures for me. It provided capital when it was important. There even came a time when I drew no money from my business and free lanced for Gene. It was Gene who told me of Ed Downe, which led to my association with him.

Gene was the first to sell cassette how-to tapes in tremendous volume. "Automated Learning", with his copy, multiplied sales and continues to this day. Gene's copy for book after book for Frederick Fell made it a substantial company. It's now part of a public company. Gene has written more ads than he can remember.

"I never keep copies of ads or direct mail pieces. I've written copy for over a hundred companies. I like writing mail order copy. I like writing how-to books, too. The book I enjoyed writing most was 'How to Double Your Child's Grades in School'. It sold about 350,000 hard-cover copies in the United States and about 250,000 in foreign languages. It still continues to sell as a Barnes & Noble paperback."

Gene wrote it when his son, Michael, was nine. "I wrote it for him and began to work with him when he was in the second grade. The book had led to my helping Michael when he was at Horace Mann. He was very interested in certain subjects. We worked together in physics and math. Now he has to explain to me what he has studied. He's beyond me.

"Michael is 22 now. In June 1980, he graduated from the Wharton School of Business. He has a job as an arbitrager for

Drexel Beckman. He's already been promoted three times and is being promoted for the fourth time as a specialist. He is now, at 22, the youngest floor specialist in the New York Stock Exchange, trading Caesar's World. Drexel Beckman considers that he has the finest math mind of any trainee they've ever taken on.

"I've been in over a dozen businesses. I think I've enjoyed most of all selling 'How to Double Your Child's Grades in School' and the cosmetic business I have with Oleda Baker. This came about because her book, 'The Model's Way to Health, Slenderness and Beauty' did not sell when first published by Prentice-Hall.

"I bought the mail order rights to the book first with Ed Downe, and later from him. I wrote an ad that featured her in a mini-dress, and innovated the headline . . . 'Why models stay young till 60'. I also introduced the idea of putting her exact age . . . year, month and day . . . in every ad—which is still being done. My ad sold 60,000 books. She then called me up to see what kind of a weird creature had done all this when no one else could before. We met and went into the cosmetic business together."

Gene has blended Oleda's face, her hair, her figure with his offers, his headlines, his copy. The result documents hope, aided by unretouched photograph after photograph of Oleda. From labels to ads for cosmetic product after product, Gene displays Oleda. He proposes to any woman that she try Oleda's way, with Oleda's cosmetics. What a wonderful name, exotic—yet the Kodak of cosmetics.

Then Gene Schwartz . . . at 51, and looking in magnificent condition . . . suffered a massive stroke. The doctors fought for his life, and won . . . but gave him very little chance of ever using his right arm again. Gene says of his experience: "My stroke almost killed me. But when I lived, I felt I had a right to live as I wanted. And I have. My stroke liberated me.

"My stroke was an interruption. It took me three months to get out of the hospital. I had lost the use of my hands for typing. Within three days of returning from the hospital, I started dictating my own copy. The first day I did, I dictated 18 pages. It was bad. But nobody told me. It got better and kept getting better."

Gene began to vary his writing and his activities more than ever before. He wrote a novel which was published in 1981 with a 250,000 soft cover printing. "I like writing books better, I like writing novels. I can become a story director, work with characters, work out their problems and live them out. As far as the work of writing copy or a book is involved, each is about the same."

He reactivated interests he had never gotten around to before. "In 1973, I had written and put away a book of metaphysical poetry. After my stroke, I opened a drawer, saw my poetry and read it. I liked it and decided to try to get it published. I wasn't sure anyone would publish it all until Strawberry Press volunteered. Another book I just finished and am very happy with is called 'Small Gifts of God'. It's the story of my stroke, fictionalized.

"I retired from my own mail order after my stroke, thinking that over 25 years in this business was adequate. However, within two months of arriving home from the hospital, I found myself right back in it again. It's the most exciting activity I've ever known, which I think I'll do to some degree as long as I live."

Gene keeps his mail order business simple with least overhead and risk. "We use space advertising and special inserts. All fulfillment is done out of house. There's no office, staff or any employees. I do it with a telephone and a calculator." From 2 to 4 PM each day, he operates his own book publishing business, Instant Improvement, Inc. "In the last six months, we've sold close to 70,000 copies of 'Internal Exercises' at $13 each, mostly by direct mail."

Gene is also doing something I've never seen done before, selling by mail order poetry—his own. It's called 'The Sound of One Mind Thinking". Gene calls it "a simple book of discoveries about the metaphysical world" and calls the 41 poems in it— never labelled as poems—"puzzles for the soul".

He continues to work as a consultant to Marty Edelston, publisher of Board Room Reports (220,000 circulation) and Boardroom Books. "When I had my first meeeting with Martin Edelston, we agreed that my fee would be $2,500 down. Then, in the conversation, Marty mentioned that he had, I believe, about $3,500 left in business capital at that time—before the fee. Yet, he insisted that I go ahead.

"I was so embarrassed that I went right home from the meeting and wrote the ad, 'Read 300 magazines in Thirty Minutes'. This was the launch piece for Board Room Reports. For the second fee, I took stock in the corporation (which I later sold back to Marty). The business is now well over fifteen million, and quite profitable. I now serve as a consultant to Marty, for a much larger monthly fee—and write no copy. We just have lunch or dinner once a month.

"Rodale Press is a client for Prevention subscriptions and Rodale health books. I've written copy for them for 7½ years. One piece I wrote for Prevention, in January 1981, became the control piece for Prevention. Nothing since has pulled subscriptions more profitably than it has. I wrote the ad for 'The Book of Natural Health' which has sold 275,000 copies . . . and successful ads for many other Rodale health books.

"Rodale pays me my highest fee . . . a page down for each ad, and another page if the ad is successful (which I use for my products). So far, I have been successful with every ad I've written for them, except one. I use a rather rapid writing system now, for all my ads. In January 1981, I earned four pages from them for two ads . . . for what my time logs told me was four hours of writing time.

"Since Prevention's paid rate was then $13,200, that gave me a figure of $13,200 an hour as a writing fee. This gives me the time and freedom to go on to my scientific and philosophic reading, my art collection and my esoteric attempt at fiction."

All this is within 18 months of Gene's stroke. He can type now with the right hand he had so little chance of ever using again. And to keep up his prolific production of copy for his clients and his own business, he dictates.

"For ten years before I've dictated correspondence. I have an excellent memory. I can see in my mind as though typed on the page whatever I've just said. I can, therefore, correct as I dictate. Ninety percent of what is transcribed becomes part of my finished draft."

Top mail order copywriters marvel at how fast and prolific he is . . . and how many ads of his have been run repeatedly for so long. His ads and headlines have been lifted bodily and run all over the world for mail order advertisers of similar products. For Huber Hoge he wrote an ad in 1951 for night driving glasses. As late as 1981, another manufacturer ran the ad almost word for word. His headlines, particularly, have been used for decades.

Thirty years ago, he wrote an ad for Huber Hoge with the headline, "Why Haven't TV Owners Been Told These Facts?"... for a TV repair book. The headline has been used again and again, ever since. In 1981, we, ourselves, used it for a fishing lure ad, "Why Haven't Fishermen Been Told These Facts?"

Meanwhile, Gene has progressed. "I'm in a new mail order phase. It's fun to play with new techniques."

Here is Gene's advice to anyone starting out as a direct marketing copywriter:

"First: Buy teachers with your time instead of going for the highest salary. I had Cecil Hoge, Sherman Lurie and Hank Hoffman, to mention only the three premier examples.

"I remember one evening when Hank came into a room where three of the young Hoge copywriters were talking. He joined the conversation and then began to give some examples of how he created his own unique and overwhelmingly convincing style. The other two left, because they had dates. I remember thinking they were insane to trade that kind of money-making knowledge, even if for a date with Marilyn Monroe!

"Secondly, read everything. Don't specialize. You never know when a stray fact will lead to a great headline, that in turn leads to a small fortune for you and/or your employers.

"Finally, if you want to write literature, start a novel. There, your style can be displayed. In mail order, your words should be, as I've repeatedly said, like the windows in a storefront. The reader should be able to see right through them and see the product."

Gene's wife, Barbara, keeps up with Gene's pace in her profession. "Barbara continues to be more and more successful in her decorating business. In today's New York Times, the entire front page of the Home section and a follow-up story inside is on her latest designing job."

And Gene continues to be Gene. By the time you are reading this book, Gene will have written another book and still more mail order hits and added still more to his modern art collection and creative experience.

Chapter 9
Direct Marketing's Laser Age

*Personalized letters at
twenty miles an hour.*

Printronic Corporation of America is a pioneer in it . . . with an unusual 30,000 square foot plant in an unusual place, the 25th floor of 10 Columbus Circle, in New York City.

Here, laser-printed words pour out of computers faster than ever printed by any non-laser method, in the history of the world. Here are the Sperry Univacs that can laser-print the Bible in a minute . . . and "Gone With the Wind" in half a minute . . . and can, at the same time, print each page in a different language . . . and personalize each paragraph. Here is a lot more sophisticated computer equipment . . . from an IPL Computer to a Memorex disk drive . . . all working for direct marketers.

Leo Yochim and Susan Keenan are the founders of Printronic Corp. Leo describes their business: "About half of it is producing personalized letters, either electronic laser or computer printed. Most of the rest is eliminating duplicate names between lists."

Printronic Corp. has been growing fast, because of these factors: The remarkable development of the computer; direct marketing's unique ability to benefit from it and the acceleration of growth of direct marketing; the greater pulling power for direct marketers of a computer and then a laser-personalized letter, and its ever decreasing cost to produce; the growing need of direct marketers to eliminate duplicate names, and Leo Yochim's ability to come up with a better way to do so . . . by computer.

"The public still does not recognize what a computer letter is. It's addressed and typewritten individually and personally. It can refer in body copy to the names of and facts individual to each person to whom it is sent. The average person receiving one regards it as more personal—and opens it up more often, reads it more carefully and responds more frequently to it than to printed direct mail advertising.

"A personalized laser or computer letter produces orders or inquiries in much bigger volume and at more profitable advertising cost per ad or inquiry—compared with the same offer made to the same people with conventionally printed direct mail pieces. Computer elimination of duplicate names is more and more necessary, and can be done better and is at lower cost. So is producing labels and many things you can do with lists via computers."

How did Leo get into computers? Via the United States Marines—which, as soon as he joined, assigned him to work on electric accounting machines, the predecessors of computers— and then to take the IBM course in repairing tabulating equipment. This was during the Korean War. His first post-war job was with a firm of consulting actuaries and involved probability studies.

"In 1950, a computer could print at the speed of 100 lines a minute. Computer letters began when the first business computers were installed in 1952, but in a very limited way. This was impact printing, hitting individual characters much the same as a typewriter. In 1953, Leo took a second IBM course, this time in computer programming." For the next 10 years few computer letters were produced. Only capital letters and little punctuation could be used. They looked like telegrams. Computers did produce bills, invoices and statements.

All this time Leo was acquiring a needed skill, and began to leapfrog. He worked for Burroughs and then for G.E. Next he was hired by CBS, as Manager of Systems and Procedures. He went on to Price Waterhouse as a computer installation consultant, for their clients.

Meanwhile, in 1960, the Post Office announced it would later start, nationwide, a zip code system. This meant mail order firms had to plan to computerize, in time—or maybe go broke. Leo's talents and experience were needed. "In 1963, the IBM 1401 computer began to print in upper and lower case. The speed was 600 lines a minute. Before then, computer letters had been short, memo-like messages in capital letters—an extension of the ability to print labels, invoices and statements.

"Billy Graham and Oral Roberts were the first users of wider, fuller size computer letters. From a friend I learned that Billy Graham had asked IBM for a computer train to enable the computer to print in upper and lower case and that, although a custom job, the cost would be $5,000. I got interested in applying my know-how to computer letters . . . on my own . . . as a moonlighter.

"At the end of 1963, I ordered one, myself. Delivery took six months. I installed it at a service bureau in downtown Manhattan. Then I persuaded TIME to test it. For TIME, on July 4, 1964, I printed the first practical commercial letter on computer. This computer letter, plus a business reply envelope and outside envelope in two colors, cost twice as much to mail as TIME's standard piece. The standard then cost $65 in the mail. The computer letter was $130 in the mail versus $260 per thousand in 1981.

"Putney Westerfield was circulation manager of Time Inc. He authorized the letter, also signed it, and mailed it . . . splitting it against a control. The test had been a mailing to the membership list of the American Medical Association (AMA). The AMA knew the college and the specialty of each doctor. The letter went like this: 'Ever since you graduated from Harvard you've specialized in pediatrics. That's why you're good at it. That's the way TIME is in news.'

"When it pulled four times the response of the control, Putney retested it. The re-test confirmed. The projection to the full AMA membership (287,000 names) held up. But we couldn't get any more names. Only the AMA names were on magnetic tape—which the use of computer letters required.

"Computer letters were profitable to use from the first. But there were many obstacles to their use. Mainly, there were few mail order buyer lists on magnetic tape. Only when this occurred and when certain technical problems were overcome could a big volume computer letter business prosper. I had raised money and was now a minority partner in a business which was not making money. I resigned, turning it over to my associates and left to make a new start.

"For a year I sold computer printers. One customer was St. John's Associates Letter Shop. In the mid-1960's, I went to work for them as a salesman. Susan Keenan was production manager and had had a great deal of experience, some of it with computers. Susan and I left St. John's and later started Printronic. I first began to sell computer letter programs.

"By now, conditions were much more ripe for computer letters. Reader's Digest started in the late 1960's, in a big way for those days. The problem then was limited capacity to produce computer letters. People were finding them tremendously productive but were finding difficulties getting them produced. Alan Cartoun, at Longine's Symphonettes—in 1968—wanted to mail a million computer letters but did not know where to get the job done.

"I said I'd do it, and got the order . . . for a million letters. But I had no money and no place to do it. At that point, Printronic was really a printing broker. But I knew that Longine's own computer could do the job. No one at Longine's knew how to use it to produce the letters. I did. Alan Cartoun was very astute and we made a deal. My contribution was to create the program for the letters, write the letters and help select the names. I gave them my creative ideas. Only names then on magnetic tape could be used. I knew which lists were on magnetic tape.

"Essentially, Longine's used my know-how, put up money as needed for the campaign and allowed me to use their computer from Friday at 5 PM to Monday at 9 AM for my other clients. My first big successful campaign for Longine's was with R.L. Polk compiled names. For each name and address Polk had the name of wife, children and whether owner occupied. I selected 300,000 of these names and wrote the letter copy. The mailing was a fantastic hit. To project I ordered—as a consultant—seven million names from Polk. The projection paid off, too.

"We began to do computer letters for RCA. We opened an office at 30 East 60th Street, in New York. The first year in business, Printronic billed $50,000. The next year we did $100,000, and then $300,000. Reader's Digest, Time Inc., the insurance companies and Fingerhut became our clients.

"I had started my seminars in 1968 or 1969 with the DMMA. Over three years we had close to 700 students. My share of the income helped launch our business. Later, a good deal of our business came from former students. Then, as the business grew, we had no time for seminars . . . until recently, when we had added enough staff.

"By 1969, computers could print 1100 lines a minute. Computers had made it possible to merge any two lists and purge out duplication between the two. But the first methods to do so were imperfect. In 1969, I developed my own duplicate elimination program.

"In 1969, 1970, and 1971, our bread and butter account was still Longine's. At first, our staff was just Susan and me. Then we hired a programmer and an operator. About 1972 or 1973, we took over an IBM 360-30 computer installation at St. John's. There was nothing down, but it cost $200,000 a year. We got the programs for it, as well.

"In 1973, Mead Digital Systems introduced the electronic letter. It used ink jet printing to spray ink, shooting droplets on continuous forms . . . the first non-impact printing. In 1975, IBM brought out the laser beam printer. It was non-impact. It used the electrophotographic process and printed 20,000 (or more) lines a minute.

"In 1974, we took 10,000 square feet at 655 Madison Avenue. We shared space with Norman Suslock. We shared the computer cost and the rent. Norman stayed for one year and then left for Connecticut. Within two or three months we used all the computer time. By now, more and more lists were on magnetic tape. Printing labels by computer was more and more done, and began to be done by laser. By 1975, we were doing laser printing. And our Dupe Elim program was booming as well as computer letters.

"Our program is the best in the business. With the Printronic method, you don't have to sort by account number or zip code sequence. You can sort five million names alphabetically in an hour. As a result, we've had a big success in duplicate identification. I've sold our program to forty of the biggest . . . to R.H. Donnelley, Hearst, R.L. Polk, Spiegel, Kiplinger, Sloan Kettering and many more.

"By 1977, impact printing by computer had speeded up to over 2,000 lines a minute. But production of electronic letters, labels and printing by laser had become ten times faster. And on booklet-type presentations, twice as much personalization was available.

"On January 1, 1980, we moved to 10 Columbus Circle, tripling our floor space. In early summer 1980, Sperry-Univac brought out its 0777 computer laser printer. By September, one of the first twenty was installed at our plant. We now have three. We use each primarily to produce laser letters and labels. Each can do 500,000 labels an hour. The computer can run 12 jobs at a time and prints 22,000 lines a minute.

"I've watched this technology grow and constantly do a better job, faster and for less money. We now print at 22,000 lines a minute—equal to 44,000 lines of book type a minute . . . fast enough to print a 1,466-page book in a minute . . . and a 733-page book in half a minute. By 1981, we could completely type and personalize 20,000 computer letters an hour for $8 or $9 a thousand, a fraction of what it formerly cost.

"Twenty years ago, we could produce 2,000 labels an hour by computer—at $15 per thousand. Now we produce 500,000 labels an hour at 75¢ per thousand. When they first came out, magnetic tapes could store 10,000 names. Now we have 1,000,000 names on one tape and 2,500,000 names on one disk.

"For clients we create computer programs to type and personalize electronic letters to send to their names. The clients forward to us tapes containing name and address individual data needed to personalize each letter. For each client's individual job we program one of our computers to read each tape as it is run through it, and instantly to laser-type each letter . . . with whatever personalization the data on this tape calls for. For clients we have here computer tapes of as few as 2,000 names, and as many as 15,000,000.

"We have a thousand list rental tapes on hand. No two are the same. We keep each an average of two months. This is long enough to check that everything went well, that there were no problems or undue mistakes. If there are, we check the tape, run some letters, find the mistakes and correct them. If a mistake is ours, we make it up to the client, but we don't usually make mistakes.

"We have over $1,000,000 worth of computer programs on Memorex Disk. We have over 3,000 programs to convert outside rental tapes to computer and laser letters. In our files are the names of 50 million people who have moved in the last five years. For 35 million of them we have new addresses. The other 15 million names are of people whose present addresses we don't know. These are nixies. We can check anybody's list, update the addresses of people on it or identify them as nixies. We do it by running both their lists and these 50 million names through our computer and comparing them. We have a Memorex Disk Drive 3652. It's the machine with which we operate our Dupe Elim program. It has room for over one billion, two hundred million characters of information. It contains 5 million names and addresses. To search all 5 million, we don't need a match code or account number. The Memorex can pull out any one of 5,000,000 names and addresses and display it on the terminal screen . . . within 1/10th to 1/100th of a second."

Printronic's most sophisticated computer units are the Sperry-Univac 0777's. A special computer program inserted

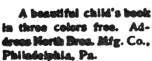

inside each 0777 for each job instructs it to execute in sequence one step after another and to perform different operations concurrently, all at tremendous speed. The program inside one may be ordering it to perform each needed step to print each character of each label and to go on from label to label . . . and inside the other be orders to personalize one letter after another with individual name, address and references to personal facts in the text, different for each letter.

Inside the 0777, a rotating multi-faceted mirror is sweeping six laser beams simultaneously across the surface of a continuously rotating photo conductor drum. The surface of the drum is being constantly electrostatically charged. Another device is causing each laser beam to form an electrostatic "image" on the drum. Each image is being toned by ink-like particles. Each image is being transferred from the drum to continuously moving paper and melted into the fiber of the paper, forming a permanent image. A seventh laser beam is timing the entire operation.

The paper is being transported inside by a constantly moving ten-foot tractor belt which brings the labels or letters up to the top of the 0777 and out, completed. Five abreast, labels flow out at twenty miles an hour. Completely personalized laser letters come out at the same speed. The 0777's are working for Printronic at the same pace 24 hours a day. Time is required to start, stop, adjust, change jobs, service and maintain. But some users get over

three million feet of paper laser-printed each month by one 0777, That's over 550 *miles* of paper a month, over 6600 miles a year.

For small tests, Printronic has still other Documation computer printers, far slower but still unimaginably fast to most of us—yesterday's computer miracles. "We keep upgrading. We replace older, slower machines with newer, faster ones. The turnover and improvement never ends.

"We mail twenty million pieces a month and process 100 to 200 reels of list tapes a day. We have a lot of clients, including big ones. But we don't want any big one to become too big a share of our business. In 1980, our biggest account was 12% of our business. That's healthy and growth is accelerating. But it's balanced growth. We get new customers 90% by recommendation. At one magazine, the last four circulation managers, when they went on to new jobs in circulation at other magazines, became our clients there. This is typical.

"People do business with us because they trust us, because we're cost efficient and because we're always working on new developments to improve results or save money. We keep improving whatever we do. We use latest equipment. We have a machine that glues, die cuts, folds and ties, making a self mailer.

"We've got something new, unique. The name, street and zip lines all have upper and lower type with proper punctuation and all spelled out. There are no abbreviations. It's our colored Cheshire label. It looks like a clipped coupon, in color. Just using it has jumped mail response 20% to 40%.

"We're constantly into new developments. In a year or two, laser printers will print a bar code on the label. Pieces will be automatically sorted, sent to the post office and automatically sorted again. The local postman will be the first to touch the mail. This will further reduce costs.

"In 6 months, there will be terminal cassettes of different types. There are 50 manufacturers of terminals. IBM, IT&T or any terminal can hitch up with our terminal. Then you can just dial us. We're working on programs for computer letters to be used for two-step. Your girl can sit in front of a terminal in your office hooked up by telephone to our computer. She can take all inquiries you received each day for your products and type each address, together with certain keys indicating data about the person inquiring, on the terminal.

"Our computer will immediately type out a personal letter based on the data fed in. At the same time, the name and address will go into the file we'll maintain of your inquiries. Each day we'll mail for you all the computer letters we've done for you. The inquirer gets a same day answer—including sales literature, order blank and return envelopes.

"We do a lot of business with fund raisers. Laser-printed, personalized fund raising letters are remarkably effective. Often a letter thanks a past donor for the latest gift and specifies the date given. It may also suggest a small, medium and larger amount to give for a need it describes. If so, varying the amounts requested for each person written to has been found effective, with the smallest amount requested no smaller than the biggest gift the donor previously made. Just putting in each letter the date of the last contribution has doubled the response.

"It's what you put in a laser or computer letter that sells. When I started out in computer letters, few copywriters understood what a computer could and couldn't do and how to make a computer letter do all it could. To sell computer letters, I became creative. I became a copywriter.

"A number of people helped me. Dick Crohn was a consultant, copywriter and marketing man—and a giant help to me. Way back in 1964, he introduced me to Larry Chait. Ed

Mayer, Jr. worked for Chait. They were very kind and helpful. They made me understand direct marketing far better. I learned and kept improving. I've always been a good communicator and became a good teacher of the effective use of computer letters and of computers in direct marketing more generally. We have a very able, full-time art director—John Day, and work creatively with clients when asked. We have a good crew."

Printronic has a reputation of helping clients . . . creatively, by know-how and by being meticulous. "Our business is now growing very rapidly, both in computer letters and in duplicate elimination. To keep up with it we are open 24 hours a day . . . seven days a week." Leo and Susan have created a remarkable team feeling. Employees work hard and try hard to be meticulous. Leo and Susan go out of their way to watch out for each.

"We have about 50 people. When we moved here we asked them what they wanted most. It was a gym. We put in a small one with a good deal of exercise equipment, and even an adjoining shower. We asked them what they wanted most after that. It was a restaurant. We put in a complete kitchen with stove, refrigerator, kitchen cabinet, everything. We have adjacent dining space with circular tables surrounded by chairs. Anyone of us can come, cook anything and eat. It's also a sort of club room. We have a lending library, and even a cents-off coupon exchange."

Many direct marketers are grateful to Leo Yochim for the cheerful, kindly way he has helped them learn how to use computer and now laser letters to greater profit . . . and then kept them up-to-date with latest developments, whether personalized letters, duplication elimination and other ways to use computers to save or improve results per dollar spent.

"We have a schoolroom with blackboard, chairs and desks and even a podium. We hold seminars. I love to teach." Printronic is an unusual organization, and Leo Yochim and Susan Keenan are unusual people. The atmosphere is friendly, relaxed, but very efficient. They are proud of their business and serious about their work, and also perfectionists. They are thorough pros and have pioneered a great deal. Leo has always avoided too much personalization but came up with unusual ways to personalize . . . such as referring to neighbors by name on the same street.

Leo looks to future growth even more exciting than up to now. "Direct marketing keeps growing faster and laser and computer letters keep becoming more profitable to direct marketers. There's great opportunity as a result. Young people have a big potential in direct marketing, if they have what is needed. The most important traits we value are imagination, common sense and the self-discipline to work hard enough to take advantage of an opportunity. We try to select young people with these traits. We then train them internally."

Leo has frequently lectured at New York University's direct marketing course, and spoken at direct marketing clubs, Days and conferences in the U.S. and abroad. For the Direct Mail/Marketing Association, Leo Yochim has written a clear, concise and thorough history of computer/electronic letters and analysis of capabilities and requirements. It covers in depth many aspects of impact printing (computer letters) and non-impact printing (electronic letters). It includes do's and don't's concerning writing for computer letters.

How to get tapes of lectures and copies of articles by Leo Yochim is explained in detail in the Help Source Section in this book.

Note: Printronic Corporation of America is located at 10 Columbus Circle, New York, NY 10019; telephone (212) 247-8800.

Chapter 10
David Ogilvy's Lifelong Love Affair

. . . with mail order

How it helped his clients sell just about anything better - and him to become world-famous.

More than any other factor, the lessons of the mail order method built his agency to over $2 billion in billings . . . a global network of 115 offices . . . and over 6,000 employees . . . the second largest agency in U.S. billing . . . including as a subsidiary the world's second largest direct marketing agency.

Fortune magazine called him a genius, as do many of his clients. Every ad and commercial created for the agency he founded bears his hallmark. He wrote the most widely sold book on advertising. Mail order is only part of the recipe of this Scotsman, who studied as a chef in Paris. He is David Ogilvy, founder of Ogilvy & Mather International.

Some Ogilvy ads are legends. Some are classics. Most are brand new, but with the Ogilvy style. You cannot watch TV or read publications without encountering them. Each is based on considerable research (his specialty). It socially reassures as it sells, and is remarkably effective for clients.

What has mail order to do with his ads and commercials for TWA, Shell, the British Travel Authority and some 1,600 other clients of his agencies?

"Direct response was my first love. And later, my secret weapon," says David Ogilvy. How he developed, honed and perfected this weapon is told in this story and interview with him.

If you're thinking about going into advertising, heed his advice. "Everyone should start his advertising career in direct marketing, to get his feet on the ground. Creative, media and account people should all be trained in direct response." If you are in advertising or use it, to any degree and in any form—if you're in mail order, whether as a moonlighter or in the Fortune 500, he can help you.

To emulate David Ogilvy, be born with brains, to social privilege, in Surrey, England. Have ancestors and relatives who have been high in government, the military, Parliament and the literary world. Desire attention from infancy. Have an ungovernable curiosity. Be noticed . . . by driving grown-ups wild, asking innumerable questions, from the time you can talk.

Develop an early yen for money. "I did at the age of five. Needed it for candy." Be exposed to witty, literate conversation. Develop a vocabulary. Read books, but only what you like. Start to write—anything, early.

"I have written well since I was a boy. I became passionately interested in the U.S.A. at age eight when I read Huck Finn; later I devoured Sinclair Lewis, and then Willa Cather. At age nine, I went to St. Cyprian's an English boarding school, and at thirteen, to a Scottish boarding school.

"I wasn't a scholar. I was a duffer at games. I was a rebel and a misfit. In short, a dud. I was a duffer at Latin and Greek which were compulsory. Education bored me. But I got high marks in

History and English. I was president of the Debating Society at school and acted in theatricals. I went on to Oxford for two years, failed every examination, then quit—and at twenty, became a chef in Paris."

David's big brother, Francis Ogilvy, was a classical scholar. He was a copywriter in a prestigious London advertising agency—to earn a living. To bring David back out of the kitchen, Francis came up with what proved to be an inspiration. He induced younger brother David to sell stoves house to house.

It appealed to David. He would shock the family by making cold calls at the servant's entrances of the biggest country houses in England. Besides, the stove was a product he believed in. It was invented by a scientist, a Nobel prize-winner. It burned coke and was more economical and more heat-efficient. David judged it as a chef. He cooked on it.

"I first learned that I could persuade when I started selling Aga Cookers door-to-door at age 23." To gain access to any house required his skill as an actor. Once inside he performed for a captive audience. He could debate the competition, win the applause of an order, and praise from his boss, for getting it. He could change his act with every call and make money while having fun.

David cooked on Agas for customers, demonstrated at shows, and secured favorable publicity from schools and hospitals. He out-sold other Aga salesmen, because no other Aga salesman had been a chef, or a debater, or an actor, or a writer or worked so hard. Inevitably, Aga management asked him to show the other salesmen how. For them, in 1935, he produced what years later Fortune magazine called the best sales manual ever written. Were you to read it today, you would have great difficulty to avoid ordering an Aga.

The manual (The Theory and Practice of Selling the Aga Cooker) made him an advertising man. "I got incurably interested in advertising when I was 24; since then it has been my life." Much of all he has believed in since, he put in that manual . . . in about 11,500 words—with no pictures. Since then he developed an uncanny picture sense for ads, but never lost his faith in long copy. Any mail order copywriter reading that manual can only feel awe.

No selling argument is left unsaid. Each feature's advantage is explained. No objection is not answered (as in a rebuttal of a debate). No selling situation and what to do about it is not gone into. The salesman is instructed how to dress; how to research a prospect; how to select the appeal most suited to the prospect; how to get in; what to say; when to listen; how to get the cook on your side; how to ask for and get the order; even when to leave.

It's written with wit, is fun to read and hard to put down; and makes a religion of the product. It has the excitement of a miracle-science article in Reader's Digest. No cook book has equal appetite appeal. The endless variety of mouthwatering viands described by this chef with an irresistible way with words makes any reader hunger.

Even before he has whipped up desire to a high pitch, he has rationalized the Aga's purchase as a high-yield investment that pays for itself in savings, and then returns an annual dividend. He has taken the Rolls Royce of stoves and made it pay for itself; and then offered it on credit, on time payments—thus widening the universe of prospects.

The manual changed and enlarged the Aga Cooker business, proved indisputably the advertising ability of David Ogilvy and got him a job, at 25, with Mather & Crowther, the advertising agency for which Francis Ogilvy worked. To advertise anything, David turned his ungovernable curiosity on every facet of the product or service—and its customers. He studied relevant

advertising as originated in the U.S.A. He studied its most measurable form, mail order advertising, as done in the U.S.

"I started by taking a correspondence course in direct mail. I bought it out of my own pocket from the Dartnell Corporation in faraway Chicago. One day a prospective client dropped into the agency. As his advertising budget was only $500, he was fobbed off on me. The man had bought a country house and was about to open it as a hotel. He needed customers-in a hurry. I took his $500 and spent it on sending out postcards to people living near his hotel. I wrote the copy on that postcard—about a hundred words. Six weeks later, my first client opened his hotel. Full house, sold out. I had tasted blood.

"At Mather & Crowther, I developed the habit of hard work, even more when my salary was doubled. I became Research Director. A Chicago clipping service kept me supplied with every new advertising campaign that broke in the U.S."

To master American advertising methods, he came to America. There, he worked in a venture backed by Raymond Rubicam, then the most successful advertising man in America, and for George Gallup, the greatest advertising researcher of the time. He picked the brains of anyone he could meet who was creative, innovative and successful—in advertising or among advertisers.

Raymond Rubicam was at the top of his advertising fame, almost worshipped by the young talent coming in. George Gallup had correctly predicted that Roosevelt would defeat Landon in 1936—the opposite of the up-to-then prestigious Literary Digest poll. Now he was applying his polling talents to advertising. For Gallup, Ogilvy applied them to the movies—until he could predict the income of a movie before it was made within 10% of accuracy.

Tutored by Raymond Rubicam and George Gallup, he continued his studies of advertising and read every book on advertising ever written. "From Gallup I learned factor analysis. But it was Claude Hopkins' 'Scientific Advertising' which formed me as an advertising man.

"I also came under the influence of John Caples. He is that very rare bird—a highly creative writer and an indomitable analyst of results. His book, 'Tested Advertising Methods', has been my bible for 40 years."

Both Hopkins and Caples preached that the mail order method, applied to almost every kind of advertising, could improve it. Test advertising could be measured and traced to individual ads; and lessons learned applied to unmeasured advertising. Ogilvy found confirmation from all he had learned selling house to house. Had not Albert Lasker built the most profitable agency of its day, Lord & Thomas, on the mail order know-how of Claude Hopkins?

Young Rosser Reeves was applying the same principles to consumer copy for store-sold products. Later his "Build Healthy Bodies 12 Ways" built the Wonder Bread business. Frank Hummert applied these principles to radio advertising, promoting premium offers as if mail order items and intertwining them with soap opera plots. David learned from Reeves and Hummert.

In early 1939, he returned to England to report to Mather & Crowther what he learned. "I was 27, and had yet to write my first advertisement." Sir Francis Meynell was then creative director and a typographer and poet as well. David proceeded, in a talk before the entire agency staff, to preach the word from America— the use of the mail order method to improve almost any kind of advertising. He gave them a good deal of Claude Hopkins, of John Caples—and of David Ogilvy. He quoted Starch Readership surveys comparing readership with pulling power. He gave them Gallup to prove that many conventional notions of advertising folk were indisputably wrong.

His summary was advice to combine scientific advertising research with scientific mail order methods. The transcript of his talk is now in the Archives of the Advertising Trust, in London. After World War II, it became the basis of the agency he formed, the basic presentation he made to each client, the training he gave each recruit, the gospel he preaches today.

During World War II, David was on the staff of Sir William Stephenson (Intrepid), and later Second Secretary in the Washington Embassy. Shortly after World War II, on his farm in the Amish country, he almost went into the mail order business— selling cheese. "I got to the stage of preparing art work and literature." Instead, he started Ogilvy & Mather, and used direct response methods to get his first clients.

That was in 1948. Mather & Crowther backed him, as did S.H. Benson & Company. Together they invested $100,000 in the new agency (then called Hewett, Ogilvy, Benson & Mather). Later David had the pleasure of seeing Ogilvy & Mather buy out his old employer.

Anderson F. (Andy) Hewett came in as president and invested $25,000 at first, and later more. David put in $6,000 and was vice-president. Andy had been at J. Walter Thompson, McCann-Erickson and J. Sterling Getchell. They felt the same about the importance of research. Both admired Young & Rubicam, the mail order method and long copy. They made a great effort to attract top talent, and paid some people more than themselves.

"When we started Ogilvy & Mather in New York, nobody had heard of us. But we were airborn within a few months and grew at record speed—so fast we repeatedly had to turn down new accounts. How did we achieve this meteoric growth? By using my secret weapon—Direct Mail. Every four weeks I sent personalized mailings to the manufacturers who were our prospects. I was amazed to discover how many of our new clients had been attracted to Ogilvy & Mather by these mailings. That was how we grew."

The first account was Guinness Stout. Then two accounts came in almost simultaneously—Sun Oil and Helena Rubinstein. Then came one account after another. In 1950, 1951, and 1952, out of the fifty best ads selected by a panel of advertising people, ten were produced by the new agency. More important, sales of clients jumped dramatically.

"During the first year of Ogilvy & Mather, I was the Research Director. Then I started having ideas for advertisements." His ads combined what he had learned from Hopkins and Caples with techniques to get high readership learned from Gallup. He had the high ethics of Raymond Rubicam in copy— but the style was pure Ogilvy.

Helena Rubinstein said: "The advertising has been the most outstanding that I have ever seen done in the cosmetic industry." For Rubinstein the winning headline was "How Women Over 35 Can Look Younger". But for Madame Rubinstein he created great snob ads with beautiful women in settings such as an English Hunt in the midst of dogs, style and glamour, and the headline, "Command Performance".

Ogilvy ads almost dominated The New Yorker, while his Life magazine editorial ads jumped readership for advertiser after advertiser. For British Travel, readership multiplied six times over the same size ad run a year earlier through another agency. The agency sent a Connecticut couple, Bree and Peggy Walden, to tour Britain. An entire series of editorial size ads was built on their trip.

Associates found Ogilvy to be brilliant, meticulous, a perfectionist—tough on others, more so on himself. Often he'd hold up an ad long after deadline, while perfecting it. What he did not know, he quickly learned. He studied ads that worked. He put in lots of research, more elbow grease. He was considered by all to be a hard worker. He loved to set up a picture. As Alfred Hitchcock did in movies, he'd put himself in the advertisement, for a while quite frequently.

The agency's success came from the sales success of the ads. After a year as a client, sales of Sunoco Dynalube Motor Oil went up 40%. The agency employed direct marketing, before it was invented, by using the mail order method in the mainstream of big company marketing.

For the Chase Bank, HOB&M ran Getchell type ads that were all type, each with a coupon—and increased loan applications 49%. For Palm Beach clothes in Life magazine, HOB&M pulled 15 times as many coupons for the same size ads as run the year before in Life through a different agency. The difference was an editorial style ad, "The Suit Revolution", done with flair and power. For British Travel, HOB&M used coupons.

Good Luck Margarine was David's first mass success, with long reason-why copy. It succeeded. So did ads for Dove Soap. The agency had a way of making mass class and class mass.

From a token budget Ogilvy created a highly successful business . . . when he put the eyepatch on Baron George Wrangel, who was the model for his ad, "The Man in the Hathaway Shirt". He considered the best headline he ever wrote was for Rolls Royce: "At 60 miles an hour the loudest noise comes from the electric clock." If you couldn't buy a Rolls, you could have a glass of Schweppes, and feel almost as rich.

Then he moved into direct marketing, measured persuasion. "I started a Direct Response Division in the New York office of Ogilvy & Mather—long before competitors. Today we have Direct Response Divisions in New York, Frankfurt, Paris, Singapore, Melbourne, Sao Paulo and London." It's mail order with the Ogilvy touch.

"We sent out a five-page letter that sold 716 Mercedes Benz in six weeks. We used Direct Mail to sell $750,000 Cessna executive jets. We delivered mysterious cartons to the office of prospects. When they opened the carton, they found a live homing pigeon, with a note saying: 'If you would like a test flight in a Cessna Citation Jet, release me.' A lot did, with the name of the prospect strapped to their legs. We sold aircraft—and an old medium was reborn . . . carrier pigeons."

In 1971, American Express began direct mail solicitation for card members, guided by Ogilvy, with constant testing. In six years, while costs in the mail went up 11.6%, it became possible to acquire members for 28% less.

Sears was enormously sophisticated in mail order . . . like targeting credit solicitations to special segments. One mailing got response from 28% of pregnant mothers mailed to open accounts.

From scratch, Shell Oil built a 40 million-dollar-a-year mail order business, because Ogilvy's mail order people saw the possibilities of the Shell Gas Card list for merchandise sales.

More dollars of mail order products are sold via direct mail than by any other medium. Four-fifths of Ogilvy & Mather's Direct Response billing was in direct mail. Direct mail was also an outlet for the most varied, largest copy possibilities of any media. Why not acquire more specialized know-how in direct mail than competition, and combine this with Ogilvy strengths in space and TV?

In 1974, Ogilvy & Mather bought Hodes-Daniel, a creative lettershop and printer specializing in direct mail. With it came Jerry Pickholz, now President of Ogilvy & Mather Direct. Jerry is an accountant, a CPA and a very able direct marketer who had joined Hodes-Daniel in 1960. "I was controller. I installed the cost-accounting system. That got me with the business."

Hodes-Daniel had worked for small credit companies which were acquired by big ones—for whom Hodes-Daniel then worked. These included Citibank, Bankers Trust, Continental Bank of Illinois. Hodes-Daniel began to work for them on credit card acquisition. To place media advertising, it set up an advertising agency.

The direct response part of Hodes-Daniel joined with the Ogilvy & Mather Direct Response Division. Some other parts went with appropriate divisions. The lettershop and data processing were sold. Three years later, Jerry Pickholz became president of Ogilvy & Mather Direct Response—the new combined unit.

How Hodes-Daniel was acquired, absorbed and transformed into the Ogilvy & Mather image is an indication of how the entire 105 office network has been formed. David Ogilvy had planned it.

He had always enjoyed the hunt for new clients. He made himself a brand name with more recognition than anyone else in the advertising agency business. And he kept recruiting people who had a similar creative flair, until it seemed that he had found the fountain of perpetual creative youth.

The calibre of his recruits made it possible. Roger Lourie recalls how he got into mail order by working for David Ogilvy. Later, Roger built up his own mail order business, headed new product development at Time-Life Books and became vice-president of a divison of the Mead Corp. "At Ogilvy & Mather I was a young trainee, and account executive for Maxim and other accounts. As a trainee's privilege, I could work on special projects for Mr. Ogilvy. These were after hours, on my own time and unrelated to my work.

"Mr. Ogilvy knew that I had a scientific background. I was a graduate of M.I.T. One project Mr. Ogilvy asked me to undertake was on communications in the future via satellite, to the home. This was in the early 1960's. I worked six months on the report. It was quite extensive, 200 pages or so. The title was 'Communication: From the Satellite directly into the home'.

"Unbeknownst to me, Mr. Ogilvy submitted my report to CBS, saying: 'We have innovative young people at Ogilvy & Mather. This will show you the kind of thinking we develop among them.' The result was that Goddard Lieberson, President of Columbia Records, offered me a job learning the mail order business at the Columbia Record & Tape Club. David Ogilvy advised me to take the job because he felt that mail order would be bigger and bigger in the future."

The effect of such treatment made Ogilvy & Mather highly desired to work for. David Ogilvy is a father figure. It's not unusual to discuss an employee's career prospects from his or her viewpoint, and to attempt to further them. There is high staff morale.

Hodes-Daniel was bought from a conglomerate. But the staff was given part of the pie with attractive incentives. Each staff member was oriented individually to the Ogilvy & Mather way.

Where accounts are shared with the direct agency, direct marketing advertising is kept in character with the general campaign. The writers at the parent agency send over a positioning statement. Work done is then sent back to Ogilvy & Mather who may make editing suggestions. The idea is to create direct marketing advertising which in its way has the Ogilvy & Mather elegance of style.

Ogilvy & Mather Direct participates in most new business solicitations, but makes its own presentations to direct response prospects. It works with other offices in the network which seek help in direct response. By 1980, overseas direct response billing was 36% of U.S. billing—and growing faster.

In 1981, Ogilvy & Mather Direct handled the equivalent of $100 million in billing. In January 1982, it acquired A. Eicoff & Company, a deal made the previous November. Eicoff handled over $50 million more, mostly TV. Ogilvy & Mather, Inc., had shared two clients with Eicoff, Avon and Mattel.

One new account for Ogilvy & Mather Direct Response, in 1981, was Vermont Castings, selling stoves by mail order. Neil Fox, Marketing Director, explains why. "I was looking for an agency with direct marketing expertise but not inbred, not ignorant of general marketing strategy.

"My desire was to get the strategic, creative thinking of a general agency and the technical know-how of a mail order agency. At O & M, a strong Ogilvy philosophy permeates the place. It really does exist. There's a sense of professionalism. Ogilvy is a symbol of a certain school. They have done really outstanding work for American Express. We hope that for us we'll get the best of two worlds, general marketing philosophy and direct response technology."

At first, David Ogilvy wanted creative people whom *he* could lead. Then he wanted leaders who lead better than he could. To do this he resigned as chief executive officer and became, instead, a creative consultant to his own business. The business grew as never before.

Today, more than ever, he believes in the mail order method. "For 45 years I have kept my eyes riveted on what mail order advertisers do in their ads. From this observation I have crystallized some general premises which can be applied to all kinds of advertising.

"Whenever I look at an advertisement, I can tell at a glance whether the writer has had any Direct Response experience. Nobody should be allowed to create advertising for print or broadcast until he has served his apprenticeship in direct response. That experience will keep his feet on the ground for the rest of his life.

"The Direct Response business has exploded, and is going to go on exploding. For 40 years, I have been a voice crying in the wilderness, trying to get my fellow advertising practitioners to take direct response seriously. Today, my first love is coming into its own. Those in it face a golden future."

When David Ogilvy was twenty-four, he put these words on the cover of his Aga Stove manual: "The perfect Aga salesman combines the tenacity of the bulldog with the manners of the spaniel." David still does. He is an Elizabethan adventurer who can go for the jugular and write a sonnet.

Scott M. Black, a leading money manager, said in 1982, "In my opinion Ogilvy & Mather is the best-managed publicly owned agency . . . in creativity, research and placement." It was the only advertising agency included by Smith Barney, Harris Upham & Company in its January 1982, list of "Special Situations and Smaller Growth Stocks".

To succeed in mail order or advertising, read "Confessions of an Advertising Man", by David Ogilvy. In the Help Source Guide in this book are listed speeches and articles by David Ogilvy and those by his executives which pertain to direct marketing, particularly those by Jerry Pickholz, President of Ogilvy & Mather Direct Response, 675 Third Avenue, New York, NY 10017; (212) 986-6900; also instructions on how to get them.

Mail Order Sampler
Seminar IX

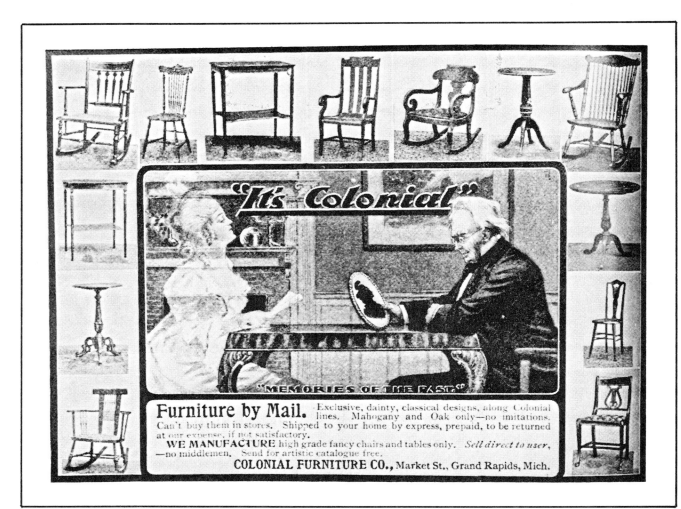

Chapter 1
Direct Marketing's Most Misunderstood Concept

*"It makes or breaks
pulling power of ads."*

"It's the offer," says Jim Kobs. To Jim, only the creation or choice of a product precedes it. The offer is the base of the strategy, the foundation of the copy appeal. It's what mail order is all about.

Jim should know. He's the co-founder of Kobs & Brady, which some say is today's fastest growing direct marketing advertising agency. He's the author of the much praised and fast selling "Profitable Direct Marketing," which I review in this book.

Jim Kobs has based much of his career on coming up with more effective offers, improving offers and presenting them differently. The importance of the offer hit him as soon as he started in mail order advertising. As a copy writer, he would start his selling efforts by selling his boss or client to use the offer alternatives he came up with.

And often the Jim Kobs offer changes had dramatic results in split-run tests. Often Jim's ad and offer won. Jim speaks quietly. But he's intense, confident and competitive—and persuasive. For years he has preached the gospel to his clients and his employees about the power of offer improvements. He has written articles about it, given speeches on it and lectured at universities concerning it. His "99 Proven Direct Response Offers" (on one page) is a classic reprinted many times.

He's purposeful, driving and basic. Just as he emphasizes the offer he reduces all direct marketing to fundamentals. He avoids gobbly gook. He makes mail order simple for non-mail order executives of big business. He talks well with treasurers. "Most financial experts like to work with direct marketers. They like gradual projections based on results. They quickly see testing as something like R & D that you never stop."

Jim graduated from the University of Illinois where he took Jack Maguire's direct mail course. His first job was at the Rylander Company, a Chicago lettershop with creative services—where his boss was Jack Thompson.

He went on to be creative head at Stone & Adler. There he progressed to account supervisor, then general manager and, finally, executive vice president before he opened, with Tom Brady as a partner, Kobs & Brady Advertising. Since then, Kobs & Brady has grown faster and faster.

"When Bankers Life & Casualty terminated Marshall John, their house agency, I went into partnership with Tom Brady. We took over the best personnel of Marshall John. When we started, Bankers Life & Casualty was one hundred percent of the billing. It's now twenty percent.

"We had a chance to start in business without risk because we had one big account. Bankers was getting out of a number of house facilities. They wanted to get out of Marshall John. They asked us what it would take. We said a new agency would be needed completely divorced from any house agency connection.

"Essentially, Tom brought the Bankers Life account and I brought the Encyclopaedia Britannica account, which I had worked on at Stone & Adler. When we started, we added Shopsmith, Stouffer Foods, and Michigan Bell. These were all accounts taken on a full service basis.

"We opened in April of 1978. In the last half of 1978, we worked for other people on a project basis. We added La Salle Extension University, Signature Financial Marketing, and Demco. Here we took on an assignment. The accounts got to know us. Each later found its own level. For Signature Financial Marketing, we now handle Ward's Wide World of Travel and various other clubs. We value all these original accounts very highly.

"In each case the single project was not so much a test of the product as a test of us. Last year, the game plan was to build from those projects. We got all the La Salle business. We built up the Bell system accounts and have now worked with sixteen out of nineteen Bell operating companies, many are full service. This year, we have only two new accounts. We have Xerox. We're helping them sell equipment by mail, plus aftermarket supply products, and to build store traffic. We're doing consulting for G.E."

In 1981, Kobs & Brady billing was the equivalent of twenty-two million dollars a year, up comfortably from 1980. It had added Helene Curtis, Littleton Stamp & Coin and Honeywell. "We're probably the largest indpendent agency in direct marketing," says Jim, "certainly in Chicago. I don't know any agency in direct marketing, not owned by a top general agency, that is as big.

"Direct mail is a little less than half our billing. Space is about forty percent. We're doing some TV. We only accept an account with potential for growth, one that is compatible to present accounts, and one that is financially sound. Our operations have been profitable from the first year. So far, we've turned down more accounts than we've accepted. We're selective.

"We bill our accounts as lawyers, accountants, and other professional people do, on an hourly basis. We try to average out at the equivalent income of 15% of media bought. To estimate annual billing, we capitalize gross income by multiplying it 6.67 times. I think some New York direct marketing agencies are still more on the straight commission basis. Others have been getting into the fee basis. More and more agencies are."

Jim was only 39 when he and Tom Brady launched Kobs & Brady. He had already been president of the Chicago Association of Direct Marketing. Jim and Tom are ambitious. They believe that growth will come first internally, that the key to growth is performance and that future growth will accelerate to the degree they can build the organization soundly.

"We're more concerned with building an organization than with billing. Our first objective is to make conditions right to draw and keep top talent. So far, we haven't had one key person leave. To get people, we run ads. We use personnel agencies. But a lot of people come to us on their own.

"We have a lot of good pros, a good team. Bill Gregory, our creative director, was creative director of Stone & Adler. Some of our people came from Marshall John, some from Maxwell Sroge, and some from Eastern agencies. We're very busy growing. It's too early for a five-year plan. We have no target for growth aiming at comparing with Stone & Adler or Wunderman." But Jim Kobs is a competitor for Kobs & Brady and for his book, "Profitable Direct Marketing," which already is having an effect on Kobs & Brady growth. Jim wants each to be number 1.

"The first part of my book is slanted to someone just starting out. It's very basic. It goes fully into testing, the test matrix and how to expand a test, but not into more than needed at that stage.

For the same reason, I have one multi-media chapter. I compare all media in one overview.

"I go into RFM. I go into how to apply the point system. I go into establishing the value of a customer. The newsletter 'Blood & Guts' did the best comparative review of my book than any other."

The advertising for "Profitable Direct Marketing" by Kobs & Brady is a lesson in mail order. Tom Brady wrote the letter on the back of "99 Proven Direct Response Offers," which you get free just for reading the direct mail. Jim has not neglected the offer and double-size order card which is a masterpiece. Rance Crain, President of Crain Communications, signs the main letter. The black and white 8" by 11" workhorse piece is simple, direct and convincing. Kobs & Brady is not leaving the success of this book to chance. In my review, I recommend it strongly.

For years, Jim has lectured on direct marketing at Roosevelt University, in Chicago, and at New York University. He has done seminars for Advertising Age, for the DMMA and various direct marketing clubs. "I keep up this work because it's good for the field. I still give a dozen or so speeches a year. I still lecture at Roosevelt University and at the University of Wisconsin. I still talk at some Direct Marketing Days. I give a lecture or so a year to marketing students. I do seminars at the University of Illinois."

Note: For readers of this book, Jim Kobs has answered a number of questions.

Q. *How important do you consider research and computer modeling for direct marketing?*

A. It's getting to be very important. We have no research director but work with several research organizations. We use research a good deal to monitor recommendations.

Q. *Is computerized media buying becoming essential for direct marketing?*

A. Media buying is now much more sophisticated. We use all the tools. For Bankers Life & Casualty, there's an identifiable age for the prime market. We get computer print outs of customer characteristics and compare with that of each media buy. We also look at past results.

Q. *How effective is life style zip code marketing in list selection?*

A. Whether it be life style zip code marketing or the basic concept of computer selected zip code areas by past ordering patterns, or whatever research method, too many people want easy solutions. They want simplistic answers. List selectivity pays off, but requires hard work to study and analyze results.

Q. *As direct marketing is used more universally by biggest companies with more of them having New York headquarters, does this favor a New York direct marketing agency over a Chicago one?*

A. We have clients from coast to coast. Wunderman has been very successful. Probably a New York location has helped. There's no advantage in media, production or talent availability, but there is an advantage due to the attitude of New Yorkers. The Hundred Million Club, in New York, for instance, almost never has a guest speaker from out of town. The Chicago Association of Direct Marketing constantly has out of town guest speakers. Chicago is less provincial, and it has tremendous advantages for direct marketing.

Essentially, big billing from direct marketers in New York comes heavily from books and records. In Chicago, there's great strength in catalogs, and in business and industrial direct mail. In New York, agencies are less active in direct mail. Of the biggest New York agencies, many did not even do direct mail until recently.

Q. *What are the opportunities for young people interested in direct marketing advertising as a field to go into?*

A. For young people who are ambitious, direct marketing is an excellent career. You can get ahead faster. It's a specialty. There's less competition. It's a field that's growing fast. You get turned on by the measurability, by ads that pay their way, by the proliferation of the field into other media. Direct mail is not glamorous. Space is more so, TV spots much more so.

Q. *How important is a high IQ?*

A. It helps but I'm sure that basic intelligence and self-discipline is enough.

Q. *What educational prepration do you recommend for direct marketing?*

A. For those in college interested in direct marketing, I suggest taking courses in advertising and in journalism. More and more advertising courses now give some attention to direct marketing. It's beginning to get included in the business departments in marketing and other courses. Math helps; be sure to take enough math to be familiar and comfortable with it.

Note: In the Help Source Section, I tell how to get a copy of Jim's classic article, "The Most Misunderstood Concept in Direct Marketing," or a copy of "99 Proven Direct Response Offers" and of his book, "Profitable Direct Marketing." Thank you, Jim for helping us.

Chapter 2
The Direct Marketing Prophet

The Kansas City Star calls him
"The Father of Zip Code Marketing".

In a classic article in the Harvard Business Review he predicted with clarity and in detail the tremendous impact and enormous money-making potential for mail order of the use of ZIP Codes, long before most others grasped it.

For twenty years, using more and more scientific methods, Martin Baier has been direct marketing insurance for Old American Insurance Company. Bob Stone in his great book, "Successful Direct Marketing", tells in fascinating detail just how Martin Baier selects from lists names in ZIP Code areas with life-style characteristics more prone to buy specific products and services.

He is senior vice president and marketing director of Old American Insurance Company. As a right arm to president Joe McGee, Jr., he has helped pioneer the development of a house list of 22 million names—almost everyone in the U.S. particularly suited to the insurance policies Old American sells. During this same period, using sophisticated direct marketing methods, sales have gone up six times—by mail order and through agents, both distribution systems using aggressive direct marketing techniques.

He heads a committee of the Direct Mail/Marketing

Association to deal with the U.S. Census Bureau to get maximum data about the burgeoning growth of direct marketing. He conducts panels, give speeches and lectures on the elements of the marketing concept, marketing research, ZIP Code selection by the "Life-Style" method to improve mail order results and decision-making by more scientific direct marketing.

Martin was born and raised in Kansas City. His first job was for a motion-picture trade magazine, in 1938, wrapping magazines for mailing. Soon he was writing mail order copy for subscription mailings. Boxoffice was also his introduction to his wife, Dorothy, who was his boss's secretary.

He had intended to go to the University of Missouri School of Journalism. But Ben Shylyen, Boxoffice publisher, said to Martin, "You already know how to write. I'll give you a full-time job with flexible hours to suit your classes. Work your way through college and go for a Business degree." Martin did, got a B average, and learned to set type in the magazine's print shop. Martin graduated from the University of Missouri in 1943 and went into the U.S. Navy as a supply officer. In 1946, he came back to Boxoffice and became circulation manager.

In 1948, he got a new job, with the Tension Envelope Corporation, as advertising manager. Now Martin could learn a lot more about direct mail. He read the "Reporter of Direct Mail", published by Henry Hoke, Sr. He joined the Direct Mail/Marketing Association. Through it, he met Henry Hoke, Sr., Ed Mayer, Homer Buckley, Fred Gymer and lots of other direct mail pioneers.

He met another young man in the business of selling through the mail. It was Bob Stone, in 1948. They exchanged what know-how they had. Both were serious students of the business but Bob had been at it several years longer. "Bob has taught me more than anyone else. We've been close friends for over 30 years. At times, when we were in business together, we practically lived together."

Martin began his life-long concern with adding more and more self education which could help in his career, sharing information, mixing with others coming up, learning from those further along. He began to speak to groups as well, on the more effective use of direct mail. His first important speech was before the Hundred Million Club in New York. He began to learn a good deal from Tension Envelope customers. One was M.P. Brown, who had started as a moonlighter in mail order —with his wife—from their home in Fort Worth, Texas.

M.P. Brown sold business services to business firms. His first success was a series of collection stickers sold by mail order. Bob Stone was with the National Research Bureau. One day, Bob called Martin to say the N.R.B. was considering buying M.P. Brown, Inc. and would do so if Martin would come with the company and work with Bob. In 1954, Martin went from Tension Envelope Corp. to M.P. Brown, Inc., which then moved to Burlington, Iowa.

The owner of National Research Bureau was Bill Wood. N.R.B. also sold business services to business firms. They sold employee relations racks of booklets and a lot of different syndicated newsletters. They also had a large ad clip service. For National Research Bureau, Bob Stone sold individual booklets by direct mail through its Direct Mail Division. Both companies sold imprinted specialties like Football and Baseball Handbooks. It was a great combination.

"From here on in, we became a team. Bob and I became part owners of M.P. Brown, Inc. I was vice president and general manager of M.P. Brown, Inc. Bob had a comparable job, in addition, at National Research Bureau. Together, and with Bill Wood, we built up both companies.

"M.P. Brown had been doing about $400,000 a year before National Research Bureau bought it. In seven years, we built it to between $1,500,000 to $2,000,000. National Research Bureau did about the same. We placed everything we earned back into the business and drew out relatively little.

"Incidentally, M.P. Brown, Inc. had an important by-product. It compiled a big list of business names but had no time to promote the list. We called Leo Gans to Burlington, Iowa. He set up one of the first computerized business lists with the M.P. Brown names. This became the beginning of today's National Business Lists, still owned by Leo.

"In 1960, I left M.P. Brown, Inc. to join Old American Insurance Co . . . and return to Kansas City. Soon after, Bob Stone left National Research Bureau, too, and went on to start a Businessman's Record Club, then to be a consultant, and finally to start Stone & Adler.

"Joe McGee, Jr., was president of Old American when I joined the firm in 1960, but was already an old friend. Joe's father and two of his uncles had, in 1939, started Old American with two unique attributes: selling by mail and offering insurance products to senior citizens, a market segment largely ignored by the traditional insurers."

Martin and his boss, Joe McGee, Jr., were particularly interested in applying to selling insurance the latest scientific methods of list selection in customer lists, house-compiled lists and outside buyer and compiled lists. Even before ZIP Codes, Old American had worked to develop buyer profiles of its policy holders. Martin and Joe had been interested in the RFM and other methods to select prospects to mail who were most probable to become customers. Both became fascinated in working to use computers to apply probability theory to mail order, particularly in list selection.

They both felt that mastery of new, more sophisticated mail order marketing was an important key to Old American's growth. Martin decided to go back to the University, at night, to study the latest marketing methods, looking for applications to mail order. In 1965, 22 years after he had graduated from the University of Missouri, Martin went back. It took him five years to earn an M.A. degree in Economics.

The course was heavily oriented to Institutional Economics. It emphasized the importance of economics in society. Martin studied micro- and macroeconomics. His courses included statistics and probability theory. He got into regression analysis. He studied the writings of Thorstein Veblen, John Galbraith, John Maynard Keynes, Clarence Ayers, Peter Drucker and others.

He did this while applying what he learned. He took on more and more in his job. He was studying at work—how many pieces to mail for a test, how to determine confidence levels for a test and decide whether to trust the test results. Joe McGee, Jr. was a tremendous believer in education and backed Martin all the way. Martin did well. "I got 3.7 on a scale of 4.0. All A's except for two B's!"

To compile his graduate work, he had to do a thesis. His was on the promise of ZIP Code marketing. ZIP Codes were just coming in. Many feared ZIP Codes would ruin mail order due to the extra overhead they would cause. Martin's thesis was thorough, careful and documented with a wide array of facts, including ZIP Code marketing test results from Old American's use of ZIP Code data.

All the time Martin had kept up his contact with the DMMA which has always been important to him. Joe McGee, Jr. had been president of the DMMA in 1955. That's how Martin and he met, which led to Martin joining Old American. In 33 years,

Martin has missed the DMMA Annual Conference only once. He is active in the Direct Marketing Insurance Council of the DMMA. The DMMA has helped and still helps. At each annual conference, he attends as many educational meetings and seminars as he can fit in. Over the years, the contacts have helped in many ways.

He also attended first the Direct Mail Days and later the Direct Marketing Days in important cities. In May of 1966, at Direct Marketing Day in New York, a debate on whether ZIP Codes were good or bad for direct marketing took place—before 2,000 direct marketers. Martin was given the pro position. Essentially, he presented his thesis.

Ernie Frawley, from the Harvard Business Review, was in the audience and heard Martin's presentation. Afterward, he spoke to Martin and said the concept might be developed into a Harvard Business Review article. Edward C. Bursk was then editor of the Harvard Business Review. He liked the piece. It was run as an article in the January-February/1967 issue, to coincide with the advent of compulsory use of ZIP Codes by direct mailers.

Meanwhile, Old American was applying more and more of Martin's ideas. Old American specialized in selling insurance to older people. Martin got more and more interested in scientific decision-making and the use of computer technology. Professors from the University were interested in the experiments in ZIP Code marketing planned by Old American. Martin organized a task force of students and professors to help in the project. In 1970, Steve McDaniel, who received an MBA from the University of Missouri-Kansas City, joined Old American. Now he is Director of Direct Marketing Operations, reporting to Martin. In 1969, Martin began to teach marketing courses in the School of Administration at the University of Missouri . . . and still does, one three-hour course each semester.

Old American had, before Martin, gotten early into the compiling of mailing lists of older people. Now it was building a huge compiled list just as R.L. Polk had done for auto registrations and Metromail had done for telephone directories. When ZIP Codes became mandatory, suddenly every buyer list and compiled list could contribute to building up a personality inventory by ZIP Code area. Huge lists like Old American's suddenly could contribute invaluable information. And each list was forced to do so. The big compiled lists were on computer first. Mailers who had never used them before began to test them.

The idea of segmenting these huge compiled lists seemed to promise profitable use of big portions, even if the entire list wouldn't work. To do so better, Martin had started using cluster analysis in the mid-1970's. He had already pioneered the use of factor analysis and regression analysis in direct marketing. All this he had first learned in his graduate economic courses. Steve McDaniel became a vital part of the model's development. So did several professors at UMKC: Merlin Spencer, Richard Hamilton, Bob Brazelton.

Very likely Martin's efforts at Old American were the first life style market segmentation breakdown of ZIP Codes. The least squares method of regression analysis had been used in numerical analysis for a long time. Martin believes Old American was the first direct marketer to use it. Martin was the pioneer.

Essentially, Martin treated all the ZIP Code area data as the personality inventory of the ZIP Code area. Using factor analysis, he came up with a biographical profile of the area. He applied psychographic measurement techniques. The Life-Style Market Segmentation concept came from the social sciences, with economics at its core.

Old American's first interest in ZIP Code data was to select those ZIP Code areas with life styles most similar to those of holders of various Old American insurance policies. But such a wealth of data was available on so broad a base that Martin saw it could be invaluable to others. Offering Life-Style Market Segmentation to others on a service fee basis provided a way to share the expense of developing future data and to amortize Old American's original investment to develop the model and the data. It also quickly proved a way to expand the rental of Old American lists. In the case of the house-compiled list, rentals to others could generate more revenue. The strategy worked perfectly.

Soon after the Harvard Business Review article, a big effort took place to get the Census Bureau to make its 1970 figures available by ZIP Codes. "John Daly, then of the DMMA, was in on it. Bill Fay, chief of the Census Bureau's Geography Division, favored it. Dick Johnes, of the Post Office Department, saw its potential. Postmaster General Lawrence O'Brien went to bat for it. He said he wanted to push anything that got the use of the ZIP Code into the mainstream of business life. The Census Bureau accepted the challenge."

Meanwhile, back in 1969, the Internal Revenue Service published its 1966 "Statistics of Income" series, broken down by ZIP Code. "Vito Natrella at IRS was responsible for this. Yuan Liang, with Metro-Mail, conceived the idea for ZIP-O-DATA, now published annually. More and more people in direct marketing got interested." Donnelly Marketing and Metro-Mail, started working with ZIP Code area geographics, demographics and psychographics in the early 1970's.

By the 1980 census, Martin Baier's work with census data was more and more recognized all over the world. His expertise is acknowledged. His specialty is getting valuable marketing information out of the compiled answers to seemingly obscure questions.

"Whether a person occupies his own apartment or house or rents in someone else's house can tell you a great deal about his or her life style. But, in marketing a product, look beyond some of the census data such as household or family income. Income is a good indicator of a person's *ability* to buy. It's not necessarily a good indicator of whether people *will* buy.

"Occupation, education, age, ethnic background and marital status will tell marketers more about what that person is liable to buy with his income. A lawyer is likely to have a much different taste in magazines, for instance, than a plumber—even when both have identical income levels.

"ZIP Code marketing is based on the generally accepted theory that people with similar life styles are prone to buy similar types of products—even if their income differs. Old American has combined this theory with computer technology, sophisticated analytical techniques and statistical procedures in order to develop a totally unique system. We have tested and we continue to refine the system with our own mailings. We also do a fair amount of analytical consulting with other major direct mailers.

"We've often seen response increased 50% or more this way. We've been able to mail lists, with ZIP Code selections, that we couldn't mail before. Sometimes we can mail an entire file once and then remail half the file a second time using Life-Style Market Segmentation."

Old American currently sells a variety of personal insurance products. It sells life, accident and hospitalization coverages. "But because of the segmentation of our lists and our life-style marketing techniques, we're now intrigued with offering other non-insurance products to our large mailing lists. We're going to be testing some such products. And the data we'll be getting in ZIP Code areas may allow us to try merchandise again and without competing with other users of our lists. We think, using our new information, that we'll have a chance."

The idea is to select ZIP Code areas with a bigger percentage of those people prone to buy your products. Direct marketers have ranged from being intrigued to dubious about the effectiveness of ZIP Code marketing. But more and more feel that direct marketing is on the verge of tremendous break-throughs in the art of scientific list selection using techniques such as those involved in ZIP Code marketing to a more advanced stage. And Martin Baier's contribution to the entire science of the use of research data is more and more acknowledged.

Martin has done every job in direct marketing. He's a researcher. He's a product developer. He's a media buyer. He's strong in copy. Perhaps his greatest strength is list selection. He's a pro. Martin writes on a very complex and technical subject with great simplicity, clarity and in an orderly, 1-2-3 way.

He's one of the greatest teachers in the U.S. of direct marketing. In the past eleven years, he has taught four different courses at the University of Missouri-Kansas City. One is "Elements of the Marketing Concept". Martin says it's the "core" course in marketing. Another course is "Marketing Research". Another is "Marketing Channel Systems" in which there is emphasis on direct marketing as a channel. All three are credit courses. He also conducts Continuing Education Courses on Direct Marketing. Bob Stone has often lectured at these. Bill Steinhardt (a Hoge alumnus) has lectured on copy. One time Martin organized a course on Saturday mornings with two guest lecturers each week, all in Direct Marketing, in Kansas City. Martin's graduates have gone on to careers in numerous fields, many in direct marketing.

Patricia McCarthy, one of his recent students (while working as an international flight attendant for Trans-World Airlines), wrote such an impressive thesis on two-way TV, that it was printed in full in *Direct Marketing* magazine.

He's a fine friend to many in direct marketing. One close friend to Martin is Max Ross. For years, Max worked for Old American, until he left in 1967 to become a free lance direct marketing consultant. Max, Martin and Bob Stone have been a close triumvirate for more than 30 years.

Of all Martin Baier's teaching contributions the most important is his book on direct marketing. "Pete" Hoke calls it "the first real college text book on direct marketing". McGraw Hill is publishing it under the title—Elements Of Direct Marketing—. Read it.

Meanwhile, Martin is kindly answering the following questions I've asked for readers of this book.

Q. *How does Old American buy lists, on a gross or net basis after merge/purge?*
A. When merge-purge is used, Old American buys lists on a net basis.

Q. *Does Old American manage its own list?*
A. MDC (Market Development Corp.) manages our list.

Q. *Do you rely mainly on one broker or several?*
A. We use many list brokers over the country, most in New York City. We find certain brokers are so close to and know so well certain lists that matching our know-how and theirs helps us greatly to use those lists profitably.

Q. *Do you swap or barter your own lists for other lists or media?*

A. We don't do much swapping, except with competitors' lists.

Q. *How much of Old American's mailing volume is to outside lists versus to house and buyer lists?*
A. About one-third of our mailing volume is to outside lists.

Q. *Do you compile lists on your own, with others or rely on others?*
A. We're constantly compiling lists. We occasionally share costs with others who need the same compiled list.

Q. *Have computerization and creation of data banks increased the dollar rentals of compiled lists versus buyer lists?*
A. The usage of compiled lists in dollar rentals may have been 10% to 15% of all list rental dollars before computerization of lists generally. This has probably gone up to 30% to 35% in 1980.

Q. *How often do you mail your customer list versus your compiled house list?*
A. We have a customer list of 500,000 which we mail six times a year. We have a large compiled house list which we mail at least once a year. Often we mail it selectively a second time.

Q. *How many names do you mail for a test?*

A. We try hard to keep to scientific minimums, derived from probability tables. For example, a certain offer may require only two orders a thousand to just break-even. A 10,000 test, thus, would result in only 20 orders, an impossible number from which to predict results from follow-up mailings.

Q. *How scientific are direct marketers today?*

A. We're probably about 75% scientific in our own use of direct marketing at Old American. Direct marketers often talk a good game about how scientific they are, but it's surprising how few use the scientific tools they could do to the degree they could when practical and profitable to do so. Sometimes, I think that at least half of all direct marketing effort is still very unscientific.

Thank you, Martin Baier.

Chapter 3
The Mail Order Systems Man

*How to handle
mail order customers.*

He is the most sought after mail order consultant in the world—in his specialty . . . reducing and eliminating customer complaints, speeding delivery and cutting fulfillment costs.

His systems are used by big catalogs, huge circulation magazines, Fortune 500 companies to launch mail order divisions and even the U.S. government.

Stanley J. Fenvessy, who is an attorney and Certified Management Consultant, has reorganized the order procedures, customer handling and shipping methods of big companies in a wide variety of situations. Some have called him in to a fulfillment disaster. Others asked him to help them provide faster fulfillment than ever before achieved in a specific field. And he did.

Some of his methods are so simple and basic they can apply to anyone starting out, with smallest volume and least equipment. Whatever is involved after the order comes, he takes the mystery out and advises what to do for each size of business—smallest, growing fast and biggest.

You can be a client or, if you can't afford it, attend a seminar, or read his book (free in a library) or get a free copy of one of his articles in the DM News or elsewhere. Articles are often based on answers to questions about specific problems. For readers of this book Stanley Fenvessy tells what he does and how it all came about.

He was born, brought up and attended high school in Rochester, New York . . . graduating as the Standard Bearer (valedictorian). In 1940, he graduated from the Wharton School of the University of Pennsylvania with honors . . . in the top ten to fifteen of his class. He majored in accounting and law.

His first job was in the Classified Advertising Department of the Washington Post, writing real estate ads and obituaries—for a year and a half. He wanted to become a tax attorney. He got a

job with a firm of lawyers and accountants and went to Georgetown Law School from 5 to 7 PM. Soon after, he joined the Navy.

"College people were then being recruited for a special Navy operation. I was interviewed. It was secret work. I was told to enlist as an ordinary yeoman in the Navy. Then I was assigned to Naval Intelligence, in a department cracking codes . . . a kind of work now done by the National Security Agency.

"Everyday, I came in civilian clothes. I was an enlisted man processing paper—from intercept stations all over the world which intercepted every enemy and allied message. All were processed, decoded, crypt-analyzed and sent to the fleet. Eventually, I became an officer running the paper processing operation. The process was sort of like the mail order business.

"There were physicists, mathematicians and engineers there who designed special equipment to process communications and to break codes. The machinery was built on a top secret basis, and sent in sealed box cars (with an enlisted man and officer inside) to the Navy Yard in Washington. Then the equipment would go to suburban Washington, near Bethesda. After the war, the group that designed this equipment set up Engineering Research Associates, which was then acquired by Remington Rand and renamed Univac.

"In August 1945, when I was going on leave to visit my in-laws in Chicago, I heard on the radio of the surrender of Japan. I thought I'd better look for a job that could use my skills. In Intelligence, I had had experience with data processing equipment (predecessor of the computer). I was trained as a lawyer and accountant.

"My father-in-law had contacts with and introduced me to several of the big mail order catalog companies. I said to each: 'I don't know anything of your business, but it seems complex with many transactions. This is my background. I think I can help.' Speigel and Aldens gave me offers. I took the job at Aldens. The Service had set my whole career.

"George Cullinan was vice president of advertising and marketing at Aldens, in charge of producing and circulating the catalog. In the 1930's, he had developed RFM (Recency, Frequency, Monetary), the formula to determine which customers to send catalogs to. By the time I came, the RFM formula was accepted as a way to get almost as much business but only mailing half as many catalogs. It was, by then, used by Sears and Ward as well as Aldens. George Cullinan taught me a lot. He died in the early 1960's.

"My starting job was as a methods engineer. There were no punch cards then. Only 20% of orders were manually tabulated for sales analysis. It was too expensive to analyze and tabulate all orders. I developed the first applications of punch card data processing in the mail order industry. One was to key and summarize marketing data on 100% of orders. This made analysis far more accurate. All catalog houses then had Address-O-Graph or Elliot plates. They kept records on stencils. I developed the first customer records on tab cards in 1946.

"Later, I became fashion merchandise controller with 30 people under me. To estimate demand for new items we'd check first mail counts and mark up our catalog with the dollar sales. We'd compare with results of last year's catalog for the same number of mail days after mailing. We'd assume that a new item would project in sales similarly, for final sales versus those already received. Before that, we had ordered a bare minimum. Now we'd reorder.

"This was the only safe way. It could only be done after the catalog was out. We tried every other way. We showed people advance copies of catalogs. We showed them photographs or the actual merchandise. We interviewed people to research new items. Nothing worked to estimate demand except counting first orders and projecting from them."

After five years with Aldens, Stan Fenvessy spent five years with a prestigious management engineering firm doing systems work. Then he had another five years with a conglomerate of mail order businesses. He worked with Meshulam Riklis, who controlled it.

Stan reorganized order handling for one of its companies— L. & C. Mayers, a wholesale catalog house in New York . . . and became head of the group including Spors in Minneapolis and Temple Company in Philadelphia. "In those days, catalog houses used customer orders to pick from. But we installed an extensive punch card unit record system. We keyed incoming orders and printed out, picking documents and labels."

Stan Fenvessy's last job was Administrative Vice President of Ethan Allan Furniture where he spent five more years. Then he bought a share of a consulting company. "I had never done any selling. But I discovered I had the ability to sell . . . and then started my own consulting business.

"We had received a call from the Curtis Publishing Company when Joe Culligan had been brought in to run it in 1965. My partner was away and I went in to see him. I have never seen a more fruitful operation for cost reduction. Curtis had 25 million names. Although they had data processing, they had a huge staff for fulfillment and a lot of delays and complaints. Just to deposit tens of thousands of checks for $2.98, $3.98 and many other small amounts required very big overhead.

"We got a tape of the checks and analyzed them. 85% were 8 to 10 common amounts. We got the idea of sorting these numbers into groups of 100. We could do it in batches of these dollar amounts. One hundred $2.98 orders required one entry of $298.00, and so forth. We cut the staff by over 50 people. Our systems proposals saved Curtis over half a million dollars, immediately. It was an illustration of neglect of back operation. They could have done what our firm suggested 25 years before.

"After working for Curtis, I got a call from Ed Davis, of Newsweek. He said, 'I get complaints. Editors and publishers get them. Go to Dayton, Ohio. Stop the complaints. You'll tell me they're just a symptom, but stop them.' It was Newsweek's own operation. Things were in a problem state. There was a very difficult personnel situation we could not remedy. We organized complaint handling. We listed all problems. We moved the operation from Dayton to New Jersey, and Newsweek set up with new people and new attitudes. As a result, complaints stopped as billing and complaint handling rapidly improved. It saved substantial money."

Fenvessy Associates had started in 1965. Mail order had grown into direct marketing. Magazines were hitting peak circulations. Competition with TV was hurting. Efficiency in handling mail order subscriptions was a must. "Our initial engagements were working with magazines which were becoming computerized. We worked for Look. Mike Cowles had gone to Wall Street to raise money. The investment bankers said: 'You're the only major magazine not using data processing. How can you expect to raise money if you're not up-to-date?' Mike asked Lester Suhler, his vice president in charge of circulation, why Look was not computerized. Lester said: 'We're fine', but hired me to analyze whether to go computer. I found that at that time, Look did a better job as it was—without a computer. I advised, at that state of the art, to wait." Stan Fenvessy is an expert in mail order processing technology who often recommends simplest, least sophisticated methods—where warranted.

"My first mail order customer was Consumer Reports. They were getting letters saying 'Study your own subscription service'. They had 40,000 unanswered letters. I took them from backward to more advanced . . . from manual to punch cards. I worked with them for a number of years. Now their fulfillment operation is closed down and they use a fulfillment house.

"When I first met Lillian Katz, the Lillian Vernon volume was about $6 million dollars a year. The business was very seasonal. There were thirty employees. For her situation, instead of putting in a computer, I recommended the use of a computer service bureau. Typists simply type orders onto sheets that can be read by the optical scanner of the service bureaus. Now Lillian does over $30 million and still uses the same system and service bureau.

"We've worked with Leon Gorman at L.L. Bean during a period when Bean went from an annual volume of $10 million to $125 million. Leon Gorman's brilliance is the emphasis he put on service—before expanding. Service permeates the place. L.L. Bean's most important characteristic is loyalty to the customer. Leon appreciates the importance of the customer. The result is that L.L. Bean has a terrific reputation for customer service.

"Leon Gorman used the system we developed when he did $10 million to $15 million a year to then do ten times as big a business—just by increasing the scale of the system. He did it without overmanning. He had teams and team leaders. He could add to a team or take a team member to become a team leader and form another team. Finding these formulas and systems and developing team leaders meant he could take on the volume when it came. When sales exploded, he had people there.

"For L.L. Bean one decision was how to handle phone orders. Could Bean do it? Should we get a contractor? The decision was that Bean should do it all. There was no 800 number to take orders. Initially, Bean had nine people answering the telephone. Now, at the peak period, Bean has 178 people on telephone answering and selling. Leon Gorman could have used an outside telephone answering service. He felt the considerable extra difficulty of developing L.L. Bean's own telephone marketing staff, which gave extra and more personal L.L. Bean service, was necessary. We're now making a study of the possible introduction of an 800 number.

"He also gave much care to corresponding with customers. At one time, orders were not solicited on credit, but under certain circumstances orders were shipped on open account. I suggested forgetting credit and switching to credit card. Billing directly is more expensive for a specialized mail order catalog than credit card handling cost. So is setting up its own credit card.

"The big three general catalogs have enough volume to set

up their own credit and credit cards. A book club or a publication can. A magazine billing operation is the offspring of setting up the account when the magazine gets the name. It just instructs paid or not paid. If not paid, the computer bills. If through an agent, it pays a commission. It's automatic. It suits the approval selling of subscriptions. It's less desirable for a specialized catalog, even a big one like Bean."

Fenvessy Associates, together with its Chicago affiliate Fenvessy & Kestnbaum, now has over 23 people. The New York office covers mail order administration from data processing to cost reduction and controls, from materials handling equipment and facilities to systems and procedures to fulfillment. Its clients have ranged from IBM to McGraw-Hill, to CBS Publications, from the Metropolitan Museum of Art to the American Association of Retired Persons, Citibank to L'eggs.

"Our business is extremely oriented towards improving service, to ship orders faster and handle complaints faster. When an operation is giving good service, it is also economical. Less people are needed for customer handling.

"Probably 40% of our work is related to mail order and publishing. The other 60% is mostly trading on our mail order know-how. A lot of our work is in analyzing for clients what equipment is needed and how to use it most effectively to systemitize. This had been particularly so since the beginning of computers. We computerized the sex life of the cows at the King Ranch, developing breeding records. We simplified the paperwork of the Carrier field sales force who sell air conditioning. We designed office-of-the-future systems for the new headquarters buildings of AT&T, American Airlines, General Foods and many others.

"We put Armstrong World mail order business on computer. We analyzed the situation. Armstrong World was operated as a magazine and got subscriptions. The order processing fulfillment was run by Ambassador Leather on contract and Ambassador wanted out. We got a system 34 that Armstrong owned but was not using. We got a package program that has worked quite well.

"We don't always advise that clients mechanize. I advised Williams-Sonoma to use word processing in their general office but not for mail order. Basically, a business needs to do $4 million to $5 million before it computerizes. Bedford Fair in Mt. Kisco, New York, is a ladies' dress mail order catalog house doing over $5 million a year. We put them on a mail order computer program package and system 34. Often, going on computer can help a lot and sometimes give unexpected benefits. We used to put computer beginners with service bureaus. Today there are excellent package computer programs for mini computers that can bring data processing right into the office of a small direct marketing company."

In 1973, the Norman Vincent Peale Foundation for Christian Living had 500,000 names on metal plates and were going to put up a building for them. "For them we put the names on computer and used microfiche records. No building was necessary—until tremendously successful mailings greatly enlarged the volume."

"Computers out of control can cause mail order disasters. I have heard that at the Diner's Club, tapes that had extensive billing were lost. People were never billed. Other businesses have lost tapes of parts of subscription records. The greatest calamity was Kaleidoscope, the luxury and fashion catalog. Sue Edmondson, the founder, picked goods and her husband ran the business. When they had personal problems and divorced, he left—while Kaleidoscope was in transition from one computer system to

another. She never replaced him. Just before the end, she called me. 'I can't get the orders out of the computer.' It ended in bankruptcy, unpaid creditors and unshipped customers.

"A business must ship promptly and handle correspondence and complaints promptly. Otherwise, a business can't grow. And if the condition isn't corrected, it can rapidly get worse and destroy the business. You must take care of customers. It's the only way to survive and it's only right.

"One of the very biggest mail order operators in the world is Uncle Sam. The Superintendent of Documents offers 25,000 different publications. It also sells 438 different subscriptions by mail order. It does over $70 million a year. But each transaction is small, many less than $2.00, only in huge volume. One of its services is an operation in Pueblo, Colorado. People write and send in money to Pueblo for all publications offered by the federal government.

"When we were called in, service was in very bad shape. Shipping orders was three or four months behind. People would write to the White House, to their Senator, to any branch of the government complaining about the service. The number one government image of bad service was the Post Office. The number two was the Superintendent of Documents. Now we can do it all in a day or two, and with one-third less people. People get promptly the booklets they send for. Congressmen and the government are not annoyed by complaints as before.

"Mail order management engineering is a systems business in every way. Analyzing the work, organizing it, automating it, measuring it and assigning quotas and giving incentives all help do more. An incentive system is the ultimate. An incentive system is self-supervisory. It saves supervision expense. Productivity can increase 40% to 50% with incentives. A company has to have 200 people or so before it works. It requires a number of people working continuously on an individual operation. A group incentive can be used in a whole mail room. An individual incentive can be used in keying, in picking, in packing and in answering correspondence. An incentive system can only work if the company has enough employees. The business should not be too seasonal. People need to be trained and shown how to benefit more by mastering the job more. Incentives don't work for temporary, untrained and uninterested people. Employees need to stay long enough to know their work, to improve speed and to realize that they can be good enough and fast enough to get a bonus.

"There's 40% lost time in most clerical and production operations. The first step is a measurement system—simply to measure what is a reasonable productivity for a given job. Just doing this and telling people what is expected can sometimes reduce the 40% wasted time to 25%. Measurement means, 'I'll give you an hour's work. Sign out on this sheet. In this hour you should do this.' Measurement picks up a lot. But if there are too few employees, a staff of engineers can't even measure a reasonable productivity. When practical, it's a great help.

"But giving a bonus may achieve 125% of the productivity for a job which a measurement system has rated at 100%. After people realize how they can personally benefit, they may suddenly do things faster than they thought they could.

"Dedication of the people in the company is very important. This can come from attitude, morale, organization, feelings about management, successful team spirit, location and other factors. The firms which ship fastest and most efficiently have the best leadership and most dedicated people. Management is usually more personal.

"Often the small town is the place for the best labor and the most dedicated people. They come in at 7 AM. They're loyal people. Of course, there are good people in cities, but attitudes are better sometimes just out of the city. We moved John Wiley, the book publishers, to New Jersey. They told me: 'You estimated that we would cut our staff from 36 people down to 29 people. We've been able to cut down to 19 people.' Out of Manhattan, there were new attitudes.

"One of the most impressive mail order operations is Hanover House. Harold Schwartz, who runs it, is an accountant. He's very good. It's a very successful operation in a country environment. Harold is a master of incentive systems. He has 85% of his people on incentives.

"Harold Schwartz asked me to visit his operation and give him my personal evaluation. I said, 'The way you oversee half your business is perfect. To make changes in the way you handle the other half would not give enough improvement to justify the cost of our services." Later, Harold brought us back to study his incentive system.

"Relatively few mail order businesses use an incentive, only big mail order houses. Harold does it at Hanover House and does $70 million a year. Sears, Ward & Penny do it, and medium size businesses like Foster & Gallagher and Popular Club Plan use incentives.

"The use of incentives may not always be practical but, by whatever method, the customer must be satisfied. It's not only right to do this, it's good business. You must back up your business with good service. My theory is that the whole back-end should be related to giving superior service, faster service and at lower cost. You can't afford not to. Those people who put in their catalogs 'Expect delivery in 4 to 6 weeks' suffer from it. To those who use heavily outside vendors for drop shipping, I preach that they must have their own inventory. When the customer orders, he expects the product promptly. The goal should be two weeks from when the customer mails the order to receipt of the package. All good operations do this.

"Stuart McGuire (a Fenvessy client) gets 15,000 orders a day. 87% of orders received today are shipped tomorrow. General Nutrition (another Fenvessy client) does close to $50 million a year and competes directly with drug stores. It sells vitamins and health foods. 75% of orders it receives are shipped the same day. Every hour, orders come out of the computer and are rushed to the shipping floor.

"And being more efficient uses less people, less space and less money. For Michigan Bulb, we saved them putting up a new building. We said: 'We can make this building work.' We were able to handle a markedly bigger amount of business for less cost.

"People sometimes ask about our association with Bob Kestnbaum. R. Kestnbaum and Company is owned by Bob Kestnbaum, operated out of Chicago and is concerned with direct marketing. Fenvessy & Kestnbaum is a jointly owned company operated by myself and Bob for someone who wants a total service, a start-up, for instance. We've worked for IBM, Armstrong, Moore Business Forms, Hewlett Packard and for over 30 clients together. Fenvessy & Kestnbaum allows Bob and me to meet with a client and offer a total service.

"Or either of us can work separately for a client on our specialties. The client can decide. Lillian Katz may want one area and the Metropolitan Museum of Art another. We can consult on general management, on lists, on total organizations and on acquisitions.

"When Maurice Segal was the president of American Express Credit Card (now he's at Zayre), he figured there was a future in mail order and called us in to analyze it for American Express.

"Fenvessy & Kestnbaum did a feasibility study of what to do, what to sell and how to go about it. We've been with them ever since. Although Bob and I knew that the higher the income, the less probability there was of buying by mail order, we felt that if there ever was a chance to sell high ticket items to high income people, this was it. We aimed high and advised concentrating on high ticket products, higher than sold before by mail order. It worked.

"One interesting point . . . from the beginning, American Express used an outside computer service. American Express does over $100 million a year. It still uses a service bureau but has now bought it.

"Who have been the most interesting people I've met in mail order? George Cullinan was. Maurice Segal, formerly of American Express Credit, is. Leon Gorman, president of L.L. Bean, is very impressive. David Shakarian is. He started in mail order vitamins and now controls General Nutrition which, in addition to its mail order, operates 800 stores. Richard Viguerie, the mail order political fund raiser, is probably the most dynamic of my clients.

"Garden Way is a fascinating mail order operation. The Troy Built Division of Garden Way sells 80,000 to 100,000 roto tillers a year at an average of $800 each. It's now a college case history. Yet, people said it would never work.

"Mail order is always fascinating. There's always something new. In England, the Subscription Manager of Which magazine told me of what I believe will be a trend. They get authorization from the subscriber to deduct directly from the subscriber's bank account, the renewal subscription cost . . . automatically as it falls due. It operates like a book club, a sort of negative option. The cost of renewals is eliminated.

"What do I advise someone starting out who is small and with limited money? Share costs where you can. Do it for list maintenance, for systems and operations. My hope is that soon you can do it to fulfill. At the present time for magazine fulfillment operations, almost everyone uses a contractor, like Charter in Des Moines and Neodata in Boulder. This has not yet taken place generally in the mail order business. Yet, there is a need and a demand for service organizations to warehouse and fulfill mail order merchandise.

"For L'Oreal Cosmetics, who is coming over from Europe, we have a contractor for processing and another for fulfillment. Someone will soon do it in total. People are now forced to struggle in the early stages. It's a big leap to set up a mail order operation. Mail order merchandise fulfillment service is not yet available in major proportions. But plenty of people want the service. It will come soon, in about two years.

"When anyone starting out does fulfillment, it's important to remember that there are always opportunities to save. In a small operation, saving every penny can mean survival. And the bigger the organization, the easier it is to spot opportunities to save in mail order operations. Above all, keep your customers (and keep them happy)."

Elsewhere in this book I review Stanley J. Fenvessy's book. I strongly recommend it. A Fenvessy Seminar is the best you'll find on mail order systemization. You can read a page or more of Fenvessy's detailed fulfillment know-how each issue in DM News. Tapes of Fenvessy talks and lectures and reprints of articles are available from Hoke Communications. Full details are in the Help Source Guide in this book.

Note: Fenvessy Associates, Inc. is located at 745 Fifth Avenue, New York, New York 10151 (212) 751-3707.

$1.00   **THE GREATEST VALUE IN A WHITE LINEN UNITED STATES NAVY SAILOR SUIT.**

Material, fine white linen. The little blouse is made exactly like the summer uniform of the United States navy. Light blue sailor collar of splendid washable rep, trimmed with three rows of white tape. Cuffs and shield are also made of blue rep. Silk embroidered anchor in front. Fly front, outside breast pocket, white linen four-in-hand tie. Full cut bloomer pants, with side pockets and elastic at bottom. State age.

No. 40K4420 Price for sailor blouse with bloomer pants, sizes, 3 to 10 years only...**$1.00** If by mail, postage extra, 19 cents.

Chapter 4
Selling Books By Mail Order

Syndicating mail order offers to others.

Publishers from all over North America retain him for mail order and book club consultation, planning, and new business development. He does it all from 3767 Prairie Dunes Drive, Sarasota, Florida 33581 (813) 921-3359.

Andrew E. Svenson, Jr. is president of Andrew Svenson Company, Inc., and very happy with his balmy Florida location. "My wife Barbara and I were living in Des Moines, Iowa, when we first visited here during the winter. It was fifteen degrees below zero when we left Des Moines; it was eighty degrees here. It was an easy decision to make. We moved here in 1979, and I've been commuting to see my clients ever since then."

His clients are in New York, Chicago, Los Angeles, and Toronto. They have included some of the best known names n the business—American Heritage, Columbia House, Doubleday, Hearst, Publishers Clearing House, Scholastic, Time-Life Books, World Book Encyclopedia, and others. Smaller publishers also have sought his advice on selling books by mail, the specialty in which he has become an acknowledged expert.

"When I work for a company as their marketing consultant, I become an active member of the marketing and management team. Sometimes that role is as the president's or the marketing director's advisor on long-term planning and development. In other cases, it involves responsibility for directing the current mail order marketing effort. In those instances, it's very much a hands-on, shirt-sleeve working relationship with the staff and advertising agencies. Most of our consulting work is done with publishers of books. But we also get into magazine and newspaper circulation and catalog sales, too."

One specialty Andy has is book syndication and co-ventures. He helps create the format, offer and advertising for a mail order property of one publisher, then matches it to the product needs and resources of another. He seems to know practically everybody in the industry, and he regularly arranges these joint promotions. Another area of concentration is setting up or reorganizing mail order departments for book and magazine publishers.

Andy Svenson became a marketing consultant at age **39,** after 17 intensive years of publishing and mail order experience. But he was born into the editorial side of publishing. "I grew up in a publishing atmosphere. My father was an author. For 25 years, he wrote the Hardy Boys and other mystery series for youngsters.

"My father had been a newspaperman for the Star Ledger and Newark Evening News, in New Jersey. A reporter there became a close friend. His name was Howard R. Garis, and he moonlighted as the author of the Uncle Wiggily stories. He urged my father to get into writing juvenile fiction and introduced him to the Stratemeyer Syndicate, the producers of most of the famous book series, including Nancy Drew and the Bobbsey Twins. In 1948, he joined Stratemeyer and began writing the Hardy Boys. Later, he became a partner and owner of the business."

With this background, Andy naturally gravitated toward writing and publishing. He majored in journalism at Lehigh University where, coincidentally, he was a classmate and friend of two other young men destined for success in direct marketing and publishing—John Canova, now publisher of Time-Life's Stonehenge Press, and Robert Teufel, president of Rodale Press, publisher of Organic Gardening and Prevention magazines.

Andy's first job in publishing after college was as a reporter for the Bethlehem (Pa.) Globe-Times, a small daily newspaper with a reputation for exposing local political shenanigans. Within a year, an investigation started by Andy had resulted in the conviction of an elected official on criminal charges involving a shooting and an attempted police cover-up. The 21-year-old reporter's scoop was written up in Editor & Publisher, the magazine of the newspaper industry.

"The newspaper work was exciting, but I wanted to get into the marketing and business side of publishing." He went to New York and found a job with Doubleday & Company, Inc., the publishers and book club operators.

"With my journalism background, I figured that I would get into advertising at Doubleday, but nothing was available. I started instead in trade sales. It wasn't until the director of advertising decided to reactiviate the trade mail order department in 1962 that I got the chance.

"There had been some trade mail order activity at Doubleday under Jerry Hardy, who left in 1959 to start up Time-Life Books. It had been quiet in that area after he left, and no one in the publishing division at that time knew much about mail order. But they remembered my interest in advertising and asked me if I wanted to become the mail order manager. It meant a $1,000 raise to $7,000 a year, and I jumped at it. That's how I got into the mail order business. I'm fortunate the real pros in the Doubleday book club division—Jack Cassidy, Bill Tynan, and others—were so patient and helpful in teaching me the basics."

Andy later went on to become sales and advertising manager of Cornell University Press, where he put both his trade sales and mail order experience to work. Then in 1966 he was named special projects director of Xerox Education Publications and its Weekly Reader Childrens Book Club division in Middletown, Connecticut.

"The Weekly Reader opportunity was a major one. The company had just been acquired by Xerox and was set for some ambitious growth. The summer Weekly Reader list of four million children at their home addresses was the prime one, and we began to develop one-shot books and continuity offers to supplement the book club sales."

One supplier of book series for the new Weekly Reader program was the Better Homes and Gardens book division of Meredith Corporation. Andy was soon invited to do the same kind of business development for Meredith as director of mail order marketing in New York.

"The situation at Better Homes and Gardens was a lot like the one at Weekly Reader," Andy recalls. "The elements common to virtually all successful mail order publishing operations are a major list resource, a well-defined editorial franchise, and a name that has credibility and authority with the public. These two companies have it. So do such publishers as Time-Life, Readers Digest, National Geographic, Smithsonian and Southern Living. And look at the great mail order book programs they have."

The Better Homes and Gardens mail order programs flourished. "We had a lot of things going for us in the late 1960's: good products, some tremendously successful sweepstakes promotions, high responses and low costs by today's standards.

We were successful, but let's face it, we weren't *nearly* as sophisticated in running our businesses as we are today. It's interesting to speculate on what might have been done if we had known then what we know today!"

But "like most mail order people", Andy had a desire to go into business for himself. And the business niche he saw ready for an entrepreneur to exploit was in the syndication sale of mail order books to other publishers. He announced his new business on Independence Day, 1971. He was 32 years old, $10,000 in debt to the bank for the money he borrowed to finance the venture, and "reasonably scared" by both the realities and unknowns of the new business.

"I became an independent sales rep dealing with syndicated book promotions—one-shots and continuities that could be promoted as solos or through inserts. I represented all the major publishers and began to acquire exclusive syndication rights myself to certain other books and sets. We created and printed the promotions for our own titles, warehoused and drop-shipped books for the mailers, and performed the entire syndication sales function."

The opportunity to run a major, diversified marketing operation still intrigued him, however. In 1973, Better Homes and Gardens asked Andy to return as divisional director of marketing. When the company offered to buy an interest in his syndicated products, an agreement was reached and he returned to Meredith, this time to be headquartered in Des Moines.

"Under the new set-up, I had responsibility for the retail trade, mail order, book club and syndication profit centers as well as our Canadian subsidiary. It became a $55 million sales operation, more than doubling in size during my five years there."

What lured Andy back once again into the role of the mail order entrepreneur, this time as a consultant?

"I felt it was time to make some long-range career decisions. Was my place to be in a large corporation or would I have more satisfaction working for myself? Having been in my own business before, I was confident I could do it again. I decided to get into consulting, full time, long term."

He set up his consulting venture in 1978 and in a short time had many of the country's leading publishers as clients.

"I'm dealing with many different projects and situations at once now—each stimulating and enlightening in its own way. A good number of the marketing problems, of course, are ones I've faced before myself or with other clients. So the best answers and proven approaches are often known. Still, it is a continual educational process. We're learning more and discovering new things everyday."

All this keeps Andy very busy. He works hard, and he's enthusiastic about what he does. "It's exciting to be involved in direct marketing, especially now. The progress we've made in the past 20 years probably will look insignificant compared to growth we'll see in the 1980's."

Note: Andy Svenson has answered the following questions for readers.

Q. *How important has been list selectivity in the mail order success of your clients?*

A. There have been some dramatic increases in response as a result of careful segmentation, and it's becoming more refined and productive. Products that might never have gotten off the ground otherwise are turning good profits. Rising costs will continue to demand that we "fine tune" the ways we operate our businesses.

Q. *When did you first recognize the importance of statistical and market research?*

A. In the late 1960's, when I was in charge of mail order at Meredith. We had a strong research department and we used outside research consultants.

Q. *How important was it?*

A. Very important, even if the research simply verified what we already assumed, the old truths. The impact of recency, frequency, and purchase size on responsiveness, for example. Later, when we got into more sophisticated regression analysis, we uncovered additional, large segments of our house lists that we could promote.

Q. *At Meredith, when you grew so fast, how did you recruit and train direct marketing people?*

A. Finding good people is always a challenge. At Meredith, we didn't have a formal training program, but we had a lot of smart young men and women. When I needed to fill a junior spot, I looked around the company for someone brighter than the others and interested in direct marketing. That was more important than specific mail order experience. If a person is enthusiastic and capable, the basics of the business can be taught easily. You've got to find people who *like* the mail order business, who really *enjoy* what they're doing. That's crucial to success in any area. And management must be open and receptive to their ideas. Suggestions on how to do things in new and different ways should be sought out and encouraged. It's a two-way street; the best managers actively participate in the whole business process with their staff members. They're not merely supervisors, but creative partners bringing out the full potential of their people.

Q. *How do you view women in direct marketing?*

A. With a lot of respect. Many of the top direct marketing managers today are women who have finally received the recognition they deserve as first-rate professionals. There are a few women who were real trail blazers—Joan Manley and Rose Harper, for example. And so many others who are near or at the top of their organizations—Marilyn Black, Patsy Bogle, Jeramy Lanigan, Helen Sevier, and Robin Smith to name a few.

Q. *Beyond the top managers, is there a talent shortage in the direct marketing industry?*

A. We can always use more talented people. The rapid growth of the industry risks the chance of diluting the quality of its managers. The work being done by the DMMA Educational Foundation in encouraging student interest and study in direct marketing is very important. We need more of that.

Q. *Is it hard to find top talent outside of New York and Chicago, the direct marketing centers?*

A. Not really. It's just that the concentration of companies and service agencies in those areas gives the impression that it's all happening there. In fact, I think the caliber of talent across the country is remarkably good and consistent. The industry is small enough and the exchange of ideas is free enough to allow anyone who's interested to stay on top of new developments. And more and more smaller companies are luring away the "big city" managers with comparable salaries and a more attractive life style. With the annual executive job change in direct marketing estimated at around 20%, the experienced people are well distributed, and that's a healthy situation for the industry.

Chapter 5
How To Benefit From Post Office Decisions

One gave mail order its big opportunity; and enabled two brothers to succeed.

Any post office regulation can vastly change mail order overnight. Coping with it can seem difficult, perhaps ruinous. Sometimes coping has required new ways and new technology, but has created new opportunities. Let's examine how the founders of one not huge but fast-growing list management company saw their chance and made it happen.

George-Mann Associates was formed in 1966 by the brothers George and Manny Sharoff. It was started in the days when the post office first introduced the ZIP Code system which required all mailing lists to include a zip code in their addresses. The old addressing systems did not lend themselves to adding ZIP Codes economically, nor to the newly developing computer systems which were just coming into the industry and could economically match the zip codes to the addresses. George Sharoff recalls:

"Manny and I were both working for Shore Direct Mail at the time, a mailing house that was gradually positioning itself to incorporate the new computer addressing system into their operation. Thus, when many list owners expressed a great reluctance to undertake the cost of converting their mailing lists, we saw the opportunity to form our own company to underwrite the costs. After each conversion was complete, we would market each list throughout the industry and share in the rental income with the list owners. The cost for underwriting the conversion of the lists was repaid from the first rental income that each list produced.

"We called the company George Mann Associates, Inc. It was a list management company. Various list brokers were already engaged in converting mailing lists as a by-product of their brokerage work which had fallen off due to the lack of lists that had zip codes. But George-Mann was the first list management company that dealt exclusively with converting and marketing mailing lists. We had only high hopes, a new concept called list management and very little capital when we embarked on our venture.

"Through the years we had developed enough good will so that several computer firms gave us a line of credit much greater than most new firms would normally receive. Even then, the cost of converting each list was considerable, and though rentals were being generated, the initial costs threatened to engulf our tiny company. To further complicate matters, many list brokers were suspicious of this fledgling company that called itself a list management company and inserted itself between them and the list owners. It therefore became imperative that the list brokers receive reasonable assurance that they would not be circumvented when orders were being placed by the mailers.

"To assure the list brokers that we represented no threat to them, all list rental orders were accepted only through list brokerage offices. A national sales program was developed that advertised this policy. Thus, a solid working arrangement between the list brokers and list managers was forged which is still followed to this day. All George-Mann contracts are written to include a list brokers commission. This very same policy is being followed by all list management companies throughout the industry. Today, list management is a recognized part of the direct mail scene. Many list brokerage offices also have management companies as an added but separate service for their clients.

"We take great pride that we contributed in developing the list manager's roll as an integral part of the direct mail industry, and that our company was in business almost 2 years before most major management firms entered the field.

"Today the list manager's roll is clearly defined. Whereas the list broker works with the mailers selecting lists from all industry sources, list managers only promote the lists that are under their management. They must learn how each list was generated, determine the type of individual that is on the list, and all other pertinent information necessary to prepare an attractive and informative promotion. The promotion must first acquaint the list brokers of the availability of the list, emphasize its positive features and pump them up to recommend it whenever possible. Then a second promotion must be prepared to acquaint the mailers with the list and motivate them to test it. Thus, both the mailers and brokers know about the list and are constantly prodded to use it.

"List managers must be highly skilled professionals who know their market and how best to reach it. They must use direct mail, space ads in all the industry media, phone calls and personal visits to each list brokerage office, and any other means that will generate a rental. For only through a full-time national sales program can maximum rental activity be achieved. We are pleased that we pioneered many of the promotional programs that have now become standard industry practice.

"The forces that led to the success of our venture were many, but above all, the help and kindness of many individuals whom we had both worked with prior to their starting their business was paramount. As an example:

"After discharge from the Army, I held several positions, none of which particularly interested or motivated me, until I received a call from a boyhood friend, Chester Carity. Chester told me of a new mail order business that he was helping to start for the Huber Hoge Agency, and since I had briefly worked for Alden's Inc., he thought I might fit in. This phone call was to change my life.

"The Huber Hoge Agency was pioneering a relatively new type of mail order sales. They searched out new and interesting products which they could sell directly to the public through major advertising programs. Some of the products that they were first to introduce and sell directly to the public included: chemical fertilizer for the lawn, plastic storm windows and many other products that today are staples in many homes throughout the country.

"In those days, the Hoge agency had assembled the finest staff of copywriters, product managers, account executives, and time and space buyers that could be found in any direct mail agency. The experience I gained working with these bright and innovative people served me throughout my career. I worked for Aberdeen Corp., a subsidiary of the Hoge agency, and was constantly in contact with the Hoge people.

"At the Hoge agency everyone was involved in every promotion from the office boys to the top executives. The excitement and vitality that went into each promotion was infectious. I remember speaking with one of the office boys, who in his excitement told me: 'Some day we will be able to elect a new President of the United States' This prophecy was not too far off the mark. For today, presidential hopefuls all hire a top notch direct mail agency to raise money for their campaigns. And George-Mann supplies many of the lists that they use.

"Years after I left the Hoge organization, the people I met and worked with were constantly crossing and recrossing my path. Many made significant contributions to the growth and success of George-Mann . . . like Malcolm Smith, who was an account executive at the agency, and today is one of the largest list owners in George-Mann's portfolio of lists . . . like Chester Carity, my boss at Aberdeen, who later formed his own mail order company along with Hank Hoffman, probably one of the greatest mail-order copywriters of all time . . . and like several other Hoge alumni. They hired me to handle their fulfillment operation. This led to several more years of broad product promotion and fulfillment experience. Several years later, I joined Shore Direct Mail where I sold printing and mailing work and ultimately computer conversion of mailing lists.

"Manny's early background, on the other hand, was much different than mine. When he was discharged from the Army, he and another young man formed their own music group. They played many of the top night clubs around the country. They also wrote some music which was published, and Manny became a member of ASCAP.

"In 1950, they were booked for an 8-week engagement in the lounge of the newly built Desert Inn, in Las Vegas, and they stayed 8 years. This was followed by 7 years at the Hacienda Hotel, also in Las Vegas. When this engagement ended, the music world was changing (rock and roll music came in) and Manny decided to bring his family back East and start a new career.

"He joined Dependable Mailing lists as an account executive where he received his list rental experience. Interestingly enough, many years earlier when I worked for the Hoge agency, at the suggestion of my boss, Chester Carity, I had recruited Jack Oldstein to work for them. Jack later formed Dependable Mailing Lists.

"Manny ultimately left Dependable and joined me where we both worked for Shore Direct Mail. When a number of their clients expressed a reluctance to convert their mailings lists due to

the high cost of conversion to computer, we saw the opportunity to form a company expressly for this purpose and formed George-Mann Associates, Inc.

"If there is any advice that Manny and I can offer anyone who might want to go into their own business . . . it is that they learn their trade well first, and do the very best they can for whomever they work for. Developing a personal reputation in the field for good quality work is most important. For what your peers think of you can play a significant part in these plans.

"The direct mail and communication fields are changing greatly with opportunities opening for all types of communication services. Learn your trade well! Be reliable! Develop a solid reputation not necessarily for brilliance but for quality work and dependability! And you will be amazed how many people in the industry who have come to know you will help you form your own company."

Note: George-Mann Associates is located at 403 Mercer Street, P.O. Box 930, Hightstown, NJ 08520; (609) 443-1330.

Chapter 6
Learning At No Cost

Classic mail order; today's direct marketing background; specific help.

No way can teach you so much so fast for nothing. Few people written about in this book have not been helped this way. Some feel a single book changed every previous idea about mail order—and future life. At any business library you can read most books I recommend here, and some may be at your neighborhood library—in each case, free to read. Any book you need to refer to frequently, you may then consider buying.

I strongly recommend *The Americans—The Democratic Experience* by Daniel Boorstin. In it is the story of mail order's beginning and growth told by a sociologist and historian. Boorstin sees advertising, marketing, market research and statistics as powerful social forces. He tells how each started and developed.

He tells the story of Americans who didn't just make things better but promoted them better; of immigrants who tried in America successfully what had been paying off in Europe; of the development of standardized manufacturing, of quality control, of expanding sales potentials—from the neighborhood to the region to the state to the U.S. to the world.

In this fine book (in pocketbook, a set of three) is an American pre-history of mail order. There's the story of earliest, more affluent settlers mailing their orders to England for much of what they had in their homes; of mountain communities, a century later, sending written mail orders for goods from cradles to pianos, along with pack trains of mules to bring ordered goods back.

Boorstin's fine book gives us perspective. It allows us to view mail order and then direct marketing as an inevitable development as American as apple pie, and to understand better how people make money in it.

After Boorstin, here are some other great books vital to read: *Scientific Advertising* by Claude Hopkins. I read it almost fifty years ago. The words still apply, prepare you to understand direct marketing today, and electrify. In mail order, "false theories melt away like snowflakes in the sun . . . every mistake is conspicuous . . . every feature, every word and picture teaches advertising at its best." If you have a glimmer of interest in mail order or advertising, read this book. David Ogilvy says, "It formed me as an advertising man." Crain Books.

Tested Advertising Methods by John Caples. He came into mail order advertising as if a scholar, studied it, mastered and then applied it to biggest companies. He kept more split-run comparisons over more years of more dollars than any one before. John Caples is a master teacher. He explains with total simplicity and clarity. He was the first direct marketer, applying mail order methods to mainstream advertising. His specialty is headline research. Prentice-Hall.

My First 65 Years in Advertising by Maxwell Sackheim, is a great panorama of mail order. Maxwell Sackheim's book is like himself—unprepossessing, promising nothing, with each word a gem. He's the dean of mail order, the man who all his life helped others get rich in mail order. He teaches with stories and ads reproduced, by indirection. It's friendly, folksy, fun and easy to read. He tells how it all began, developed, grew . . . the great ads he wrote, the businesses he started, the people he trained. Insist on reading it. Tab Books.

The Fact Book on Direct Response Marketing compiled by the DMMA. Statistics and figures, estimates and guestimates, graphs and surveys, facts and analysis. Each year it's researched, assembled, edited and published by the Direct Mail/Marketing Association. Each year it's better, more accurate, more of a "world almanac of mail order" and more necessary to own.

It's all there: the guidelines on the key laws and regulations of the postal service, on the FTC and on sweepstakes, on media acceptance, both space and broadcast, on telephone marketing; the most asked questions on the merchandise shipping rules—and the answers. There's a brief history of direct marketing and fast updates and definitions of latest technology changes.

In the Fact Book are year-by-year comparisons of postal rates for almost twenty years, by classification. It also includes the latest bad debt trends, newest consumer attitudes. There's a glossary and a bibliography of recommended books. DMMA.

The Direct Mail and Mail Order Handbook by Richard S. Hodgson. This is the encyclopedic, comprehensive classic on the use of direct mail for mail order, direct marketing, or whatever. Mail order sales created by direct mail are many times those from publication and broadcast advertising combined. Whatever other mail order media you start with, you'll end up using direct mail in some form. The first step is to study this 1,555-page book.

Whether you need to create the copy and layout, select the lists, produce and get out the mailing or spend the money, read it. It covers every kind of direct mail for virtually every kind of user. It goes into nearly every aspect—and quotes almost every top authority. Just to list the subjects it covers would add another chapter to this book.

You can get Dick Hodgson's advice free by reading his book at a business library. You can own his book for a small fraction of attending one of his seminars and for a tiny fraction of the consultant fee biggest firms pay him. Dartnell.

Successful Direct Marketing Methods by Robert Stone. Professor Nat Ross, who conducts the great New York University direct marketing course, calls it "*our* book, *the* book of direct marketing". It's an extraordinary encyclopedia of mail order science. Bob Stone describes a phenomenon. He describes an explosion. He gives the Fortune 500 a direct marketing how-to book. I know of no single book in the business field that has received the wide-eyed praise of so many top experts.

It's structured like a text book. It's laid out with an art

director's use of white space and just the right balance of pictures and words. It's a complete course for the advanced student. It's concise and does not ramble. As in a good ad, each word works.

Whether you're a retailer, manufacturer, wholesaler or service, your field of interest is covered. Actual ads, letters, circulars and commercials are shown and results given. Advantages of one method are listed and weighed against disadvantages, then compared with those of another method. Often, "the best of two worlds" compromise method is then suggested.

Bob's book is for the serious and determined, the purposeful and self-disciplined. You must pay attention to teacher all the way. It's a book to be lived with, struggled with and fought with. Bob is a challenge. To clarify, Bob carefully defines everything and supplies a glossary for reference. Even with this help the most difficult parts are beyond many beginners.

It's an ideal book to be used by those starting a career in sophisticated mail order and direct marketing and for the executives of any substantial business going into the field. Interspersed with actual experience, it becomes more and more understandable and helpful. There are many ways for smallest beginners to start in simplest forms of mail order. But to go into bigger volume and then into the stratosphere, Bob's book is a must.

He never stops preaching that repeat business is the key to profits . . . that, of the thousands who buy, the hundreds who repeat are the foundation of any future . . . that the most precious asset of any direct marketing operation is the customer list. His

section on how to build a catalog is one of his most exciting and helpful to the smallest, most specialized catalog operator.

Bob takes you step by step. He gently and clearly explains. He gets you involved with the self quizzes. For every difficult page with its complex words, there are dozens of easier ones with simpler words. He uses graphs and charts which quickly clarify involved concepts. But it is the endless variety of case histories and continual quotes from other authorities (each a specialist) which make his book so invaluable.

The bigger and more sophisticated you are the more you can get. This is Bob's book for big boys in the business, and many who are smaller. It's all there . . . preprints to TV, telephone marketing to contests, computerized personalization to magazine inserts.

In every general statement, he qualifies that it is usually the case. He is as careful as a prescribing doctor. Only your situation can determine how valid any part of his advice is for you. Word by word, page by page, he leads you to think, deduce and decide for yourself.

It's not a book you need to start in business with an inch or classified ad, but it is a must if you then succeed. It's for pros and for those who want to seriously train to become pros. It's specified as a text book in more marketing courses than any book on direct marketing or mail order. It's in most business libraries. You can sample it and when you're seriously in direct marketing, buy it. You will refer to it continually thereafter. Crain Books.

Direct Marketing Market Place. It is the directory of the direct marketing industry. I keep two on hand, one at the office and one at home. It's the most encyclopedic listing yet of direct marketers and services, from computers to creative. It's by classifications and over 300 pages. There's a wonderful cross-index in the back, by company and individual. It lists the address and phone number for each, as well as classification reference to obtain more information. Anyone in this business needs it. Hilary House Publishers, Inc.

The Great Brain Robbery. It comes from the smash hit programs of its bright co-authors on entrepreneurship, showmanship and brainstorming. Bob Considine is a super salesman and Murray Raphel a super retailer. This book is not on mail order or direct marketing. It's a mixed bag of 500 promotional ideas. Many are unusual, some off-beat, some amusing and others tried and true. It may give you ideas on product selection, provide a twist to improve an offer, prod you into new copy approaches, etc. Because so little concerns mail order, I suggest you sample it in a business library before buying. Self-published. Details in the Help Source Guide.

The Handbook of International Direct Marketing. A sound book for sophisticated direct marketers starting in any country and planning to project internationally. World mail order races ahead. Technology outmodes, but much of what the pioneer contributors write on is classic, essential know-how told clearly, concisely and often with anecdotes. Jack Gellman's chapter (on magazine, book and record promotions) is alone worth the price. He tells how 200,000 gorgeous color brochures were destroyed in Germany because of several legally uncleared words; of the tattered 5-year-old telephone directory in Addis Addaba that proved a small promotional goldmine, and on and on. Thorough, complete. Excellent. McGraw-Hill.

Profitable Direct marketing. It's Jim Kobs' book, very good and very easy to read. Jim has helped a lot of people and can help you. His creativity pours out of his book. He uses simple words. It's fast moving, to the point and easy to grasp.

Jim sticks to subjects he's thoroughly familiar with. He explains and defines simply. This is a great book. Every page and word is must reading for anyone considering the field. What is

This is the General Manager's Residence of the wonderful R. A. Long farm, Longview, Mo. The buildings, all designed by Architect Henry S Holt, Kansas City, Mo., have roofs of Imperial French Tile.

A Terra Cotta TILE ROOF

is acknowledged by most of the leading architects to have every point of superiority in its favor: architectural beauty, perfect protection from fire, leaks, moisture and weather changes wonderful durability without repairs, and therefore eventual economy.

Consult your architect and write for illustrated booklet, "The Roof Beautiful," printed in colors. It contains views of many beautiful homes with roofs of Terra Cotta Tiles, and is sent free upon request.

LUDOWICI-CELADON CO.   Manufacturers of Terra Cotta Roofing Tiles
General Offices: 1109-1119 Monroe Building   CHICAGO, ILL.

what is all made clear. Direct mail is an advertising medium. Mail order is a way of doing business, direct response is an advertising technique, and direct marketing is all three. And it's all the tidal wave of the 80's.

The first 120 pages comprise Jim's plan to consider and, step by step, go into direct marketing. Pages 121 to 284 cover eleven case histories with an average of about fifteen pages each. For each, Jim tells a great story based on hard facts he quotes. There's drama in each one, the facts, the ads and mailings, the results. Case histories are varied.

There's Hewlett-Packard for big ticket business mail order; Sunset House for one contest after another; Haband for blue collar bargains; Lanier Business Products for leads for salesmen; and A.B. Dick for converting small accounts from salesmen to phone and direct mail follow-up. Some of the companies written about in my book are in his but with stories told quite differently—with emphasis on advertising strategy decisions made at each phase.

Jim is talking directly to you all the way. He suggests self-examination of any would-be direct marketer. What resources do you start with? Mailing list? Warranty cards? Retail package inserts? What are your big opportunity areas? Alternate distribution? Smaller Accounts? Specialized products?

Do you need leads for salesmen? How about product testing? What about after markets sales? Do you want to improve the performance of your regular advertising? Jim shows how to do each.

Worried about selling via mail order and upsetting stores you normally sell to? Jim cites the case of Polaroid which jumped store sales (as free extra) when the same products were sold in stores and by mail. He cites studies of insurance companies where agent sales jumped for people who were mailed offers to buy insurance directly from the company. He cites the book business with book store sales going up roughly in proportion to book club sales increases.

There are plenty of facts important for the smallest mail order operator to know. For an identical mailing it's not unusual

for a customer list to pull three to six times that of an outside list. A Fortune 500 company tested two ways the identical ad, under their own name and under a new name. Their name pulled 91% better.

A bill-me offer will usually do about twice as well as the same item sold for cash—for lower-priced items, less so. A 25-cent package of seeds as a bonus with the first volume of a gardening encyclopedia has upped results 42%. On a fifty dollar business product, a premium costing less than a dollar improved results 20%.

Jim points out that a two-time buyer is much more likely to keep buying. One firm sells a gift item more of which can be used each year: Out of 100 customers, 49 will buy again the following year. Of those who place a second order, 68% will buy again the third year and 76% of these will also buy the fourth year. Once a buying pattern is established, customer loyalty and repeat purchases remain high.

Jim explains the use of probability tables in estimating future results and does so simply and well. By working on a slightly less accurate probability prediction, you can make a far smaller test and still have a very small percentage of possible error.

Jim is particularly interested in mail order products . . . how to find, develop and improve them. He is very creative at it and keeps coming up with ideas like starting a second direct marketing business to sell the same products under a separate name to a special field.

His book is loaded with nuggets: Concentrate on best segments of a list. It's not unusual for better segments to pull six to ten times that of poorer segments. Canada, Belgium, Denmark, West Germany, Great Britain, Ireland, Holland and Australia are most like the U.S. market and are the simplest areas to export your successful U.S. offer to. A newspaper insert test of a low-priced women's product pulled 40% to 50% better in markets with circulation of 500,000 or less, compared with larger markets. A good direct mail test is 50,000 pieces.

If you ask for inquiries, keep testing more follow-ups in series of three, four and five. Twenty percent of a firm's customers account for 80% of sales. Segregate these customers and maximize follow-up to them. Develop customized products for specialized markets. Try for multiple unit sales. Promote list rental income. Start a catalog. Look beyond 12 months.

The more you read of Jim's book, the more treasure you find.

For a full page and bind-in card in a magazine, costs can be up to three times higher and results four times greater. Telephone marketing is difficult when calling cold prospects but effective on previous customers or following up inquiries or people who have not renewed subscriptions. A negative appeal is often stronger than a positive one to help people avoid something.

Most marketers don't believe you should expand a test more than five to ten times the quantity originally tested. The life cycle of a mail order product is usually three years, but sometimes comes back years later. Simple changes in offers in the coupon have improved results 25% to 50% to even 100%. Giveaways jump orders, and some giveaways pull two or three times better than others.

Avoid "trivia testing" but do retest important elements of your ad or mailings regularly. Most direct marketers don't test enough and don't study and analyze test results enough.

I urgently suggest that you read "Profitable Direct Marketing". If you can't afford it, please go to a business library. Crain Books.

The Direct Mail/Marketing Manual. It's the living, growing book of all forms of mail order and direct marketing. Close to 70 authorities in every area of the field write it. Every medium, virtually every facet of direct marketing, is covered. Updating never stops. It's loose-leaf. Pages never stop coming. Each is punched and slips into the ring binder provided. New binders come each year.

It can't be bought but is free to members of the Direct Mail/Marketing Association. Extra copies can be bought by members for $100 each. It's often used by biggest direct marketers to train new middle management executives and update others. It's separated into ten sections. They are: I) General, Planning Strategy; II) Lists and Media; III) Creative; IV) Production; V) Fulfillment and Operations; VI) Testing, Analysis, Economics; VII) Ethical, Legal, Regulatory; VIII) International; IX) DMMA Reference (for members), and X) Index.

Each section contains from six to sixteen manual releases. Each release is two to six pages. It may be written for the manual only or be edited from an article or transcription of a speech. Each is an overview yet in far more detail than in The Fact Book. Often, the authority is one of the several best specialists in the world on that subject.

The end result is information you need, much of which you can't get elsewhere. I recommend that you study the Manual if you work for a DMMA member. It is not available in libraries or anywhere else. A non-member can buy an individual section, but only one—ever. If you are looking for a job in the field or starting in mail order in a tiny way, you'll have to do without it to start. If you manage or own a firm in mail order or direct marketing or are seriously planning to start one, join the DMMA and get the Manual. Other benefits of joining are thoroughly explained elsewhere in this book. DMMA.

Keep Your Customers! (and keep them happy) How to turn complaints into compliments. This is Stanley J. Fenvessy's book which any manager of a mail order business should read. Most of what he advises requires virtually no outlay for technology, yet is the heart of procedures big companies pay him big fees to set up for them. Some of his advice can apply to the smallest venture and much of it to small companies. It's invaluable for any company or division growing big fast. It's specific, simple and necessary for efficient customer handling, once the mail order is received. It's at most business libraries and is available from the Direct Mail/Marketing Association, Publications Department. Details in Help Source Section.

How you too can MAKE AT LEAST $1 MILLION (and probably much more) IN THE MAIL ORDER BUSINESS by Gerardo Joffe. This is a blueprint book. It tells you exactly what to do to make the money on the basis of "I did and you can, too." I dislike the title. I'm, against blueprint books. To me, the blueprint is like a plan to win the last war. But its author is· exceptionally bright and writes extraordinarily well. Joffe's book is remarkably helpful. He uses plain, simple, brass tack words. He tells how he started, built and sold two mail order businesses, one for a million dollars.

How to Start and Operate a Mail Order Business by Professor Julian L. Simon. This is a practical, sound book. Its author was first a successful, small mail order entrepreneur who built a business from a classified ad and sold it at a good profit. He's written three other text books on economics, advertising and social science. This one is a thorough text book for the quite small to medium mail order business. It's specific, ABC and 1-2-3. Prentice-Hall.

How To Build Your Business By Telephone by Murray Roman. It is an important direct marketing book. In the book you are now reading, my chapter on "The Roman Empire" tells his story in detail. Murray Roman works for giants, making over 15 million phone calls a year for his clients. He's amazing and his help can be vital to you. He is just finishing a new book which includes a vast number of case histories and covers newest techniques and technology. Murray Roman created telephone marketing as it is done today. He has fascinated the Fortune 500, mesmerized business graduate school professors and hypnotized presidents of the largest direct marketing agencies. He has started with tests of 200 to 500 phone calls and gone on to as many as twenty million (for the Ford Motor Company). Many people I write about in this book work with him. Read this (or his soon-to-be-published) book. Prentice-Hall.

The Law and Direct Marketing. It's a needed tool for the lawyers of direct marketers. It's a necessary guide for owners and managers of mail order businesses, as well as creative people, consultants and agencies. It includes an overview of legislation concerning direct marketing. It quotes from and summarizes specific laws, state by state. It combines this with considerable coverage and interpretation of federal laws and regulations that concern direct marketing.

Also included are: an overview of the FTC 30-day rule on delayed delivery of mail order merchandise; the answers to most commonly asked questions about the "mail order merchandise" rule; quotations from the FTC advisory opinion allowing mail order testing of products not yet manufactured or obtained—including the very strict guidelines for doing so.

Also, there are: summaries of FTC regulations on truth in lending, Regulation 2, in full disclosure of cost of credit to mail order customers; an overview of FTC rulings and guidelines on price reduction ads; price comparison; use of the word "free"; use of the word "new"; the applications of such rules to wording in headlines, body and coupon; guidelines to wording and terms of

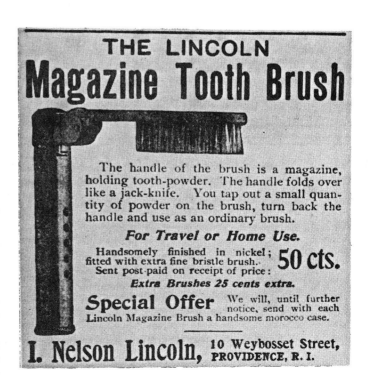

warranties; DMMA guidelines to self-regulation of sweepstakes promotion. It's in loose-leaf form with a ring binder provided.

If you're a small start-up mail order entrepreneur, read it in a business library. If your company is prospering and in mail order for keeps, buy it. DMMA.

Confessions of an Advertising Man by David Ogilvy. The most fun-to-read book on advertising (and most widely sold). The most famous man in advertising surprises, amuses, fascinates and gives do's and dont's. He cites the often startling differences in readership or response changing an advertisement has caused. Important for anyone in advertising, media or mail order. In most libraries. Atheneum.

How to Advertise - A professional guide for the advertiser. What works, what doesn't. And why. By Kenneth Roman and Jane Maas. Two senior Ogilvy & Mather executives synthesize the Ogilvy method. A little gem of an overview. Simple, quick, clear. Just touches direct marketing, but can orient any trainee or moonlighter in advertising. The needed primer for any executive not trained in advertising but concerned with it when spending $50,000 or more with an agency. The more spent, the more it is needed. Pointers on the research, the creative approach, the production steps, the media selection needed—for TV, print and direct mail. Sound tips how to judge better the effectiveness of copy when you first read, view or hear it. From testing to how to sell to kids; from how to look at a media plan to picture as well as truth in advertising; how to be a better client and how to select an advertising agency; case histories; even explains the jargon; Good. St. Martins Press.

Mail order is not a business but a way of doing business. To start a small mail order business it's necessary to first learn the fundamentals of managing any business. Whatever the product or service you or your boss sells, it is necessary to learn the history, changing methods and special problems of the field however sold.

All this can be done with books. There is a wonderfully practical book for small start-up business called Small Time Operator. It's written by an accountant and tells step-by-step what you need to do to launch a small enterprise. It's recommended by the Small Business Administration, by the Bank of America and by me. It's published by Bell Springs Publishing Company.

For decades the books of Peter Drucker have helped bright young management trainees make career break-throughs. He is the father of business management as taught today. He has opened the eyes of bosses of biggest companies. Among those written about in this book he has particularly influenced Lester Wunderman, Robin Smith and Ed Burnett. Whether you work for a big or medium sized company or a small venture, I urge that you read him. Start with his latest book, "Managing in Turbulent Times", Harper - and work your way backwards through his many and wonderful titles.

In the smallest, simplest business whatever you read about bookkeeping will help. In complex management mastering accounting will help. In either, what you learn about computer programming and systems may mean survival.

In whatever field you'll find books to give you background, knowledge of change and clues to its future . . . books about producing, selling and fulfilling just that kind of product or service. These we can't list in the Help Source Section. Your reference librarian can help.

We do list all books reviewed here, with information where to get them. We give microreviews of more books including more specialized ones. In one business lifetime, however hard you work, you can only acquire limited experience. Reading case histories of others with similar problems can multiply your experience and be a vital part of continued business self-education. Borrow first, but later buy books you need to keep.

Chapter 7
How A Retailer Can Create A Mail Order Profit Center

Brooks Brothers shows how

Brooks Brothers is the largest retailer of better made clothing, the most famous and reputedly the most profitable.

One hundred and sixty-three years after its founding, in 1818, almost a century after receipt of its first mail orders and over 80 years after it began to issue regular catalogs that are still on record—an enlightened management made a commitment to direct marketing, a quite different way:

The commitment, in early 1979, was to organize mail order sales of Brooks Brothers as a business within a business. It would be a quasi-autonomous profit center within a traditional retail environment. It would have separate responsibility from promotion creation to fulfillment. It would sell with catalogs, space ads, bill enclosures, direct mail pieces and whatever media it determined. It would select from goods currently stocked. It would create and develop its own promotions.

By summer 1981 (two years later), profitable mail orders were pouring in, with unlimited growth in sight. As a bonus the mail order advertising was sending entirely new customers to Brooks Brothers retail stores, was proving a unique test medium for items which then sold well in the stores and was providing useful information as to where it might be most profitable to launch new Brooks Brothers stores.

For the smallest, most specialized retailer and the largest, most general one, Brooks Brothers was providing invaluable clues to a mail order puzzle—why retailers so seldom benefit from the mail order sales that seem so logical to get. Retailers are growing faster in telephone and mail order sales than in walk-in business. More and more retailers are going after mail order business, but nowhere near as successfully as many direct marketing authorities feel is possible.

The sudden mail order success of Brooks Brothers came about because of an unusual history, its avant guarde management, some computer problems, and the quite different background of the man hired in 1979 as Vice President of Direct Marketing.

Its president, Frank T. Reilly, is an innovator who chose direct marketing as a medium to extend the tradition of Brooks Brothers in a quite unique and different way. He chose Alfred M. Schmidt, Jr., to head the new direct marketing operation.

Al Schmidt had never worked for Brooks, had no experience in retailing and knew nothing of men's wear. He had started with the ideas of an entrepreneur—in a niche business, in the shrinking universe of knitted wear for nuns. As population soared, the numbers of nuns diminished. Of those that remained, many changed their habits of buying habits, and many of them later gave up wearing habits much of the time. It was his father's business.

When nuns bought in religious stores, Al sold them. When they began to buy in department stores, Al sold department stores. When their purchases fell off, Al sold the knitted shrugs and knitted slippers the nuns liked ... to hospital gift stores, retail stores and then to mail order catalogs. He called on heads of mail order catalogs and fell in love with the mail order business. He studied at night, got a real estate license, moonlighted as an investor in office buildings in the suburbs, bought country land and subdivided, built on it and sold, profited and bought, in 1971, a mail order business—New Hampton General Store.

The New Hampton General Store was located in a 200-year-old building in Hampton, New Jersey. The catalog featured general merchandise with an old-fashioned flavor delivered with old-fashioned customer service and dependability. Al started by studying its history, its customers, their complaints and making his analysis of its chances to grow.

"My conclusion was that nine-tenths of the secret of success of a mail order business was customer service. To concentrate on it meant learning to do everything myself. I opened mail, looked at orders, edited them, picked orders, punched them, swept floors and did anything that had to be done. My next step was to install an IBM Model 10 System 3 Computer and computerize. To do this, I learned programming and developed a good knowledge of what computer hardware can do.

"Periodically, I rented computer time from Zale Jewelers to update my master file. I took magnetic tapes to New York City and used inexpensive weekend time. As part of the procedure, I ran my labels and put my mailing list on four-part paper. Then I'd rip apart pre-printed labels for mailing and list rental use. I had accumulated mail order know-how bit by bit—first selling knitwear by mail order to stores; then meeting managers of mail order catalogs when I sold them items. Now I learned a great deal very fast by trial and error."

Al had graduated cum laude from Blair Academy, a prep school in Blairstown, New Jersey, and with Senior Honors from Dartmouth, majoring in economics. He had studied real estate and now he studied the mail order catalog business as intently. "I did not attend many seminars. I read about the psychology of direct marketing. As a member of the New England Mail Order Association, I interfaced with many of my peers in the business. The meetings were always helpful and informative, and I was very fortunate to meet and make many friends who knew the mail order business well.

"Of all people in direct marketing I met, to me, the dean was Bill Knoles of The Stitchery. He had and still has more know-how in his little finger than heads of many more sizeable mail order businesses.

"By 1977, the New Hampton General Store catalog distribution had grown to eight million a year and I sold out to Hanover House. As part of the sale, I took a one-and-a-half year employment contract as a Vice President of Leavitt Advertising. When I got there I discovered that New Hampton General Store had more functions, such as purchase orders, on data processing than Hanover House. However, Hanover House proved to be the ultimate graduate course in Direct Marketing.

"For them I managed the New Hampton General Store Division and started another catalog, 'Pennsylvania Station'. We designed it for a special market of well-to-do working females. We tried to define and fill this special population segment's needs. It featured apparel and anything foldable from closet accessories

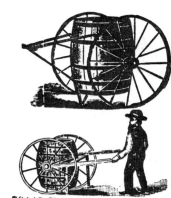

Barrel Carts, for use in the garden and for feeding purposes; can be attached to any good sound barrel; one cart required for each barrel used.
Height of wheels, 3 ft. axle stubs bolted direct to barrel. Wood or iron frame. Wood wheels and frame probably strongest. Weight, 65 lbs.
70448 Barrel Cart, steel wheels.
Price.............$3.25

70449 Barrel Cart, wood wheels. · Price $3.25

to living room furniture suitable for apartment living. We had the first catalog to include a phonograph record describing the catalog contents. It was done on Eva Tone flexible discs and bound-in."

"Harold Schwartz, President of Hanover House, put emphasis on increasing the average order, increasing labor productivity and leveling out yearly peaks and valleys by issuing a variety of specialized catalogs right for different seasons. This, in turn, made possible a larger base staff who could be trained well enough to cause a real increase in productivity. Lana Lobell was strong in June and July, Hanover House before Christmas and Lakeland Divisions in spring and fall. All the catalogs had big mailings the day after Christmas. The result was a more even year-round business that could better support the overhead that a large computer operation demanded.

"My contract went to December 31, 1979. During the last six months of that contract, Brooks Brothers was having some problems in order fulfillment - after putting a new system on computer. Frank T. Reilly, President of Brooks Brothers, asked if I would take a look at the problem on a Saturday morning.

"At that time, Brooks Brothers had been faithfully mailing 300,000 customers a catalog 3 times a year to people who had bought within the last five years, with no analysis of results. The catalog was intended to be a 'store index'. Any results were always justified by 'generation of floor traffic'. The catalog was part of the overall advertising program."

The parent company of Brooks Brothers is Garfinckel, Brooks Brothers, Miller & Rhoads, Inc. Owned by it are the stores of Brooks Brothers (28 by the end of 1981, one store and two shops in Japan)... the Miller & Rhoads department stores of Richmond, Virginia ... Garfinckel's of Washington, D.C. ... Miller's of Chattanooga ... Harzfeld's of Kansas City ... Catherine's, with 120 stores for extra large women ... and Ann Taylor, a chain of 30 young women's specialty shops. The parent company of all this is ASC stores, a subsidiary of Allied Stores.

"Brooks Brothers is operated from New York. It had asked the corporate data center in Richmond for a method of data processing to handle mail orders. Richmond came up with a system to perform on computer each step of the old manual system. I could see that the problem was not in computer expertise. It was in lack of familiarity with the most efficient way to run mail order fulfillment. Brooks Brothers management knew its customers and its business inside and out. But mail order fulfillment, mail order marketing, response tracking anlysis and computerizing them were quite different problems.

Spray Pump--The Advance.

70446 Outfit consisting of pump (barrel not included); 6 feet of hose fitted with couplings and brass spray nozzle. Price......$11.90 This pump can be attached to any good, sound barrel and the barrel hung on either of our barrel carts and used or spraying plants, shrubbery, vines and trees, washing buggies, watering gardens, lawns, etc   It has an agitator which commences as soon as the pump-handle is worked, preventing the settling of any mixture with which the water is charged

"After hours, at Hanover House, I wrote recommendations. I pointed out ways to build a viable Brooks Brothers fulfillment system. Brooks Brothers meanwhile went back to manual fulfillment. I continued at my duties at Hanover House. After my contract ended, Frank Reilly asked me to take over the mail order operations at Brooks Brothers. In March 1979, I did.

"The Executive Board of Brooks Brothers is an unusual and very enlightened group. Frank Reilly is an unusually foresighted executive. In our first negotiations, I was very stimulated by them, and they gave me all the backing I could have asked. The mail order business would be on its own. This would need a manager with a full administrative overview and direct marketing expertise. They were taking the risk of putting in an outsider who had mail order know-how but would have to develop as close a knowledge of Brooks Brothers history and of its customers as they had.

"It took me six months to get rudimentary data processing organized. My big emphasis was on customer service." In the Brooks Brothers library were catalogs issued from 1900 on, from which Al learned much of the history of Brooks Brothers. He asked employees questions and watched Brooks Brothers customers select clothes and tailors working with customers.

There are those who say that time stands still in the fitting rooms of Brooks Brothers, that its clothes and its advertising seem impervious to change. Al learned quite differently. Brooks Brothers has done much that has been innovative. Its talent has been to innovate but never leave its traditions.

"Brooks Brothers was the first retailer of ready-made clothing. In fact, Abraham Lincoln was shot in a Brooks Brothers suit. Brooks introduced the use of Indian Madras, English Foulard neckwear, button down collar shirts, Harris tweed for sportswear, shetland sweaters, camel hair polo coats and lightweight summer suits.

"Brooks Brothers catered to the very elegant life styles of the better class, of the established families. It assisted the Nouveau Riche to fit in. Brooks Brothers catalogs were educational, for this purpose. The 1919 catalog contained many interesting items. . . shooting outfits, polo gear and hunting coats, jockey's silks, puttees, automobile clothing and sundries, military uniforms and livery . . . servants' outfits, including an overcoat of black dog fur.

"Brooks Brothers began to produce a number of small lifestyle booklets early in this century. Each was about two inches by four inches. They dealt with such topics as the necessary items for a golf weekend . . . the golf clubs needed from mashie to putter

and what to wear from knickers to golf hat. There were other booklets—what you need for a motoring weekend—goggles, duster, strap-down trunk for the rear of the auto—and, of course, a bear rug. Another listed the necessities for an ocean voyage. One instructed how to tie a proper cravat."

Brooks Brothers has always had a high level of exclusivity. There is a slight but perceptible curve to the collar of a Brooks Brothers buttoned down shirt, which no others have. The slope of the shoulders, the drape and cut of a Brooks Brothers suit is different enough in its quiet way to be quite recognizable. Head waiters see it, legend says, and give a better table . . . bankers more credit . . . while sales prospects, of the better sort, more trustingly sign on the dotted line.

"Our basic thrust was to continue to do what the Brooks Brothers mail order catalog has attempted for over 80 years. But we would do it in a technical environment. We'd use the latest, most advanced data-processing techniques, telephone order receipt procedures and order fulfillment methods. But, we would not forget that we were merchants first. And we would examine and avoid the missteps that, with all advantages, retailers have so often made in mail order."

Of all businesses, retailing has seemed more applicable to mail order than any other. Mail order is a form of retailing. Store management has a finger on the pulse of the consumer. The cash register daily rings up what sells and shows what does not. A store buyer observes what sells everywhere, knows what to pay for items, where to get them, which to sell, when to sell them . . . and how to watch pennies and keep overhead down . . . how to promote and give inducements, showmanship; how to be newsworthy; how to attract people; how to advertise and keep in character.

There are 1,500,000 retail stores in the U.S. Quite a few successful mail order businesses started with a retail store, but very few stores have had great success via mail order. Even before World War I, R.H. Macy lost millions of dollars attempting to compete with Sears Roebuck with a Macy catalog . . . and gave up.

The more Al studied this the more he asked himself questions. Why, with such advantages, don't retailers do far more business far more profitably via mail order, and why do so many do so little in it? Why hadn't Brooks Brothers, after 163 years of such advantages, not done more, far more mail order, with known and definite profits? Why particularly when it had received its first mail order almost a century before?

"Retailers have been slow to adopt direct marketing techniques. There is a conflict between retail mentality and direct marketing discipline. Very few direct marketing environments have the merchandising staffs to compete with retailers. Very few, if any, retailers have a staff that can be redirected to direct marketing.

"The direct marketing management pool is small and technological. Expertise is segmented and overall know-how often unavailable. Very few executives are available with an administrative overview to lead a direct marketing division. There is an organizational split of advertising, merchandising and operation. The retail structure prevents a coordination of these activities. Most executives have a lack of understanding of the importance of fulfillment, and tend to put the greatest efforts in the promotion creation area.

"There is a conflict of seasons between mail order and retail operations. To the department stores the day after Christmas is an off price period culminating in inventory. Everybody is tired from the Christmas rush. To the direct marketer, the day after

Christmas begins the second best sales period of the year, at full price. The initial reaction at Brooks Brothers when I wanted to mail a catalog the day after Christmas was one of great surprise.

"Retailers often have little understanding of the characteristics of mail order items. Often, initially, they consider direct mail unimportant. They seldom realize the necessity for additional direct marketing merchandise staff. A big pitfall is vendor contribution to advertising. There is nothing wrong per se in accepting vendor contribution, but too often the vendor wants to control the items to be promoted and the nature of the promotion. This can lead to the promotion of items which don't have direct mail sales appeal . . . it can hurt the development of unique store image. Total freedom and control of what to advertise, at what price, when, and in what way is necessary.

"Many retailers wish to run their catalog as a store index, to display all important department items regardless of their mail order selling appeal. Most retailers want the promotion to show every wrinkle of every garment and many have little understanding of the power of life style promotion. They usually have little understanding of the importance of list expertise or the importance of the growth of a master file of names.

"The general direction of accountancy differs between retailing and mail order. Direct marketing lends itself to accountancy on a promotion basis, rather than a monthly P/L basis. There are no open-to-buy restrictions in a direct marketing environment. Results are judged by promotion cost ratios to sales. Catalog request ads mean a deferral of profit for growth of the master file. These problems were attacked in the shaping of the Brooks Brothers direct marketing policy.

"A catalog mailing or any advertising for a Brooks mail order operation causes recipients to come into Brooks Brothers Stores and buy. One major consideration in setting up Brooks Brothers direct marketing was, 'Should my division seek credit for these sales?' If direct marketing accepted a promotion cost credit, the buyers would be justified in insisting that the best department items be featured even if they had a poor catalog sale history or lacked mail order characterisitics.

"What I wanted instead was the commitment the Executive Board had given me of a quasi-independent direct marketing operation. Success in direct marketing can only come when top management makes such a commitment. This is the single most important element. And Brooks Brothers supported me and gave me the money needed to do the job.

"In March 1979, I first looked at the mailing files. Brooks was mailing 3 times a year to 300,000 buyers who had made purchases four years before. There were some product codes in the files. I took the files to MAGI, a list maintenance company. We defined 60,000 people who had bought by mail once in the previous five years. Today we have over 225,000 mail order buyers of 24 months recency, and the file is totally segmented on a Recency, Frequency, Dollar Value Basis, as well as full product identification information.

"We began to use rented files. At one point, rented names amounted to 70% of catalogs mailed. Now we are using an even balance of house and rented names. Our largest mailings are approximately 2,000,000 names from all lists. Annual circulation in 1981 will be 10,000,000. We mail a women's catalog 3 times a year and Brooksgate twice a year. We mail three standard catalogs a year. In January 1981, we mailed a pilot catalog for our Brooksgate line . . . our young men's department. We mailed a half a million. Store business went up 70% in that department. I was delighted for the stores to get this business . . . even if mail order got no credit for it.

"I did an exhaustive study of files of rental names used. On rental lists of over 50,000 names, we segmented all sectional centers within a hundred miles of any Brooks store and compared keyed results with those names located in the balance of the United States. The catalog pulled a 50% higher response outside of the hundred mile trading areas around Brooks Stores. This meant that our expansion potential was unlimited. In Dubuque, or anywhere, our appeal was hitting consumer sensitivity. This proved that the Direct Marketing Division had huge potential growth.

"Brooks Brothers now has the most sophisticated, up-to-date data processing. We have great programmers in our Corporate Data Center, in Richmond. We now have 25,000 square feet for our fulfillment center including clerical, data entry, warehousing and merchandise interface. We are on-line to our Richmond IBM 370 Computer. Our average order is now $80. For women's wear, it's over $100. We expect this will rise steadily. We have found that we really can sell $300 suits by mail. . . something that no one else has been able to do.

"We've set up a fulfillment center that is completely flexible. Our people are cross trained. We have many office people trained in data processing. We just instituted a discipline, Short Interval Scheduling. We set up goals of accomplishment of one hour's work. Each employee is given one hour's work at a time based on pre-established goals for the task. At the end of the day we make up an efficiency rating for each employee. We close out SIS at noontime and at 4:30 PM. We establish how many hours of labor

are available to accomplish the existing workload. We may only have 8 hours of labor available for the 14 hours of work with a shortfall of 6 hours. If the shortfall persists or increases, a management decision must be made for overtime or a staff increase. It's a great tool for individual and management efficiencies.

"All space ads are now two-step, offering catalogs. Merchandise offers in space ads haven't done well for us. Before I came, space ads to distribute catalogs or sell merchandise were basically not run. We now use a large amount of space using various ad sizes, with a comprehensive program of catalog request ads.

"Until July, we had an 800 number in Reno with telecommunication to our Raritan fulfillment center. We've now moved the 800 number in-house to our New Jersey fulfillment center. We have not planned outgoing telephone marketing as yet. It seems out of character with Brooks Brothers.

"The catalog operation is having very good growth. Compared to a typical Brooks Brothers Store, direct marketing has the fastest growth rate. Of course, we won't continue to grow at the same percentage rate.

"When the new mail order data processing system began, it was called the Al Schmidt System. When it succeeded it was called the Brooks Brothers System, and now that it is being used for Garfinckel's, it is called the Corporate System. Next year it will be used for Ann Taylor, then probably for Miller & Rhoads. I have consulted with Ann Taylor, Garfinckel and with Catherine's. One of our biggest problems is finding personnel who have at least a quasi-direct marketing background.

"We're interfacing market data with our new-store study group. Direct marketing acts as a probe to determine customer acceptance in areas where we are considering new stores. Our mail order lists of customers can form a new core of Brooks customers in those areas.

"We have looked at other countries. A lot of Brooks Brothers merchandise comes from England. It's not sensible to sell there. Canada and Mexico are more logical. There are so many expansion possibilities. We produce catalogs without prices for Japan, for in-store use.

"I have seen the difficulties of running a mail order business within a store, and on its own. Today the small catalog with a low average sale has a struggle. Many small mail order companies only run at a profit the last 4 months of the year. It is extremely difficult to maintain basic staffs, data processing systems all year for 4 months profitability. Now these small companies have to cope with union activity, with year round overhead. They must have expertise at every level. They must create other catalog images to achieve a year round balanced volume.

"A start-up catalog today has a considerable investment. It needs the power of a trusted name to get it off to a good start. Often a retailer has built up trust in a name over generations as

has Brooks Brothers. When mail order expertise is added and the mail order division follows the traditions of the store, a retailer has a big advantage in launching a mail order division compared with a new mail order company.

"I value experience in fulfillment of a catalog operation, knowledge of needed computer programming and computer programs, list segmentation, of media and of every phase of direct marketing. I believe in a marriage of mail order skills with the resources and credibility of a fine retailer. With it, I believe there will be more and more success of retailers in mail order - as we have had at Brooks Brothers."

Chapter 8

Starting In Direct Marketing

Applying a skill to learn more and advance more . . .

She's young, talented and black . . . and direct mail manager of a small cosmetic company. Her name is Barbara Lewis and she loves mail order and her job. "It's a great opportunity - I'm very excited." It's her second job in direct marketing.

Barbara Lewis, at twenty-six, came from Harlem via the United Church of Christ to the heart of the mail order world. She studied for education but converted to mail order. She got started and then ahead in mail order by dreaming, working and planning; by seizing an opportunity she saw in her first mail order job. To do that job she had to become immersed in mail order and direct marketing.

Barbara went to public school in Harlem. Her early world was black. "My first integrated experience was in high school in the Bronx." Barbara competed and did well. She got above average school marks.

For freshman and sophomore years, she attended Baruch College, City University of New York. "It was slowly changing to a liberal arts curriculum. It was a disappointment in terms of having a college experience." Barbara went on to Virginia State College, Petersburg, Virginia. "It was a very nice place. I experienced a lot more than the academics - and isn't that a part of college too?" She majored in education.

At high school, she enrolled in the Youth Services program. "After school, we worked for three hours each day on community related projects. It was good training." At college, she had jobs on campus. "I was clerk-typist and later I was dormitory counselor. The typist job kept my skills sharp and the counselor job enhanced my human relations ability."

Barbara came back to New York to a recession and teaching depression. "There were no teaching jobs. I got a job in a day care center, part time, and then a job as a secretary at the United Church of Christ.

"I didn't work in the church but in the operational end. The church had an Office of Communications department funded to conduct television workshops throughout the country. These workshops were to educate citizens about their broadcasting rights. It was a busy office. I became a project manager. We did consumer activist work. I worked with radio and TV stations. I never got on the air myself. It was mostly contact. I was good at it.

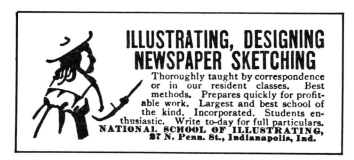

I stayed for four and a half years and then decided to make a move.

"I went to an employment agency in September 1977. I said, I've got several skills. I want to use them where I can earn more, learn more and advance more. The agency sent me to the Direct Mail/Marketing Association to be interviewed. I was hired for Information Central to research and answer questions. My initial job was to educate myself into direct marketing. I had the self-motivation and the resources available to me. I liked to read and I liked my job."

One of the perks of her job was that she could take courses on direct marketing, attend seminars on it, read books, newsletters, and magazines about it. She was surrounded by know-how. And more became available to her every day. Often she travelled expenses-paid to where she could learn more.

She took the Nat Ross NYU Direct Marketing course for three consecutive semesters, in 1977 and 1978. In 1978 and 1981 she attended the Annual Conference of the DMMA. She attended catalog seminars, lettershop seminars and those of Pierre Passavant on copy, on lists and on finance.

All day she researched mail order, talked about it, answered questions about it. She got deeper into more aspects of it than most people twice her age who are in it. She became like an ever hungry guest at an endless feast, eating up mail order know-how as fast as served.

"I became a member of the Hundred Million Club. I went to many of the monthly lunches and read newsletters. I attended and still do the Women's Direct Response Group monthly luncheons. It's a marvelous group. Forty or fifty of us meet at lunch to discuss aspects of direct marketing and hear a guest speaker. I have read Stone's book, Hodgson's book, Jim Kob's book, Joffe's book and your book. I read regularly Friday Report, Direct Marketing Magazine and the Postal Newsletters."

Her job was to listen to people who asked questions about direct marketing, dig out information and pass on answers. She acted as an investigative reporter on a project. She researched and wrote.

"I got satisfaction from knowing I helped people. People would call up and say they want to go into mail order. They knew nothing and could lose a lot of money. I warned them to be careful. They thanked me for being honest. I liked the researching, investigating and writing. I enjoyed mail order, PR and meeting people. It was very exciting—particularly the special projects—the Monographs we've been creating on Direct Response, print, new electronic media.

"I was building a career in direct marketing. I felt that one day I'd create items to sell as mail order products. I felt I had good ideas, that one day my chance would come." Meanwhile, Barbara progressed and became Manager of Information Central. Then her chance did come. "After four and a half years I sadly left the DMMA. It was time to get more direct marketing 'hands on

experience' and to solidify the training and knowledge I gained at the DMMA.

"What advice do I have for someone wanting to start a career in direct marketing? Read all you can on the subject. Get on mailing lists. Become a mail order buyer. Buy to learn how to sell. Are young blacks aware of direct marketing? As junk mail, yes; as a career opportunity, no. But those I talk to catch my excitement. At least they are interested in listening. I have a boy friend, a school teacher. He thinks I'm brilliant."

And, Barbara, I do too.

Chapter 9
Mail Order Mergers

*Buying and selling
direct marketing businesses -
advantageously.*

Mail order mergers never stop. They get bigger and more frequent as mail order companies grow faster, jump earnings and become more attractive to acquire. Merger brokers are getting into mail order.

Figi's is a gourmet catalog so delectable it has been bought three times by Fortune 500 companies—first by W.R. Grace, then by Metromedia . . . then by American Can (for over three times the price Grace paid). American Can bought Fingerhut in Minneapolis, a big mail order firm, for $134 million, in January 1979. Then, in October 1980, it bought into Franklin Mint. But in March 1981, Warner Communications bought all of Franklin Mint for $200 million.

Starting a mail order business, building it and selling it has become an effective way to tuck away a fortune. Some have done it more than once. Buying a mail order business has become the "in thing" to do for a Fortune 500 company. The trend started in the 1960's, warmed up in the 1970's and accelerated in the 1980's.

General Mills bought five mail order companies in five years up to 1974, paying close to $50,000,000 for them. Quaker Oats bought three . . . Herrschner (patterns and needlecraft), Brookstone, a catalog house selling tools, and Bank Street Clothiers which, in 1981, did $40 million. Quaker has said it plans to buy more. And, of course, after Container Corp. of America merged with Montgomery Ward, Mobil bought it all. Then it bought W.H. Hall which prints catalogs, including Ward's.

More and bigger companies are acquiring mail order firms. Pitney Bowes, in 1979, bought the Drawing Board for $22.6 million in stock which went to over $26 million by the closing. This was a good mix with Grayarc, the business catalog house which Dictaphone Corp. bought—before being, in turn, bought by Pitney Bowes. Reeves Communications bought the Sam Josephowitz world-wide combine (Musexport doing $202 million a year) for $70 million in cash and securities.

American Express acquired, in 1981, Mitchell Beazley Ltd., a mail order how-to book publisher in London just getting involved in video publishing. American Express, in 1980, bought Office Electronics, a big computerized mail order fulfillment house. Meanwhile, most of the top twenty general advertising agencies acquired direct marketing advertising agencies. By spring 1982, 17 out of the top 20 had one. Young & Rubicam, the

biggest, acquired four. Compton Advertising, Inc. acquired three.

Few growing mail order firms do not get calls from prospective buyers of the company. The Direct Mail Marketing Association got so many calls that in 1981 DMMA Information Central (its question-answering service for members) began to pass along in confidence to members inquiries about buying and selling. Business brokers and merger consultants found that a hot item to offer a client was a mail order company.

Merger consultants work with large companies, usually Fortune 500, and with large private investors to acquire mail order firms. They often work with very strong venture companies. It may be with clients to sell businesses. The Fortune 500 are not interested in mail order companies that make less than $300,000 after tax. They want those with a consistent record, none with troubles.

In 1980, the Miles Kimball catalog was sold. Alberta Kimball and Ted Lehye have always kept sales figures confidential. But "Pete" Hoke has quoted trade estimates of Miles Kimball sales for 1979 to have been about $35 million, and pre-tax profits to have been $3,000,000 or so. The sales price was 34.5 million. The purchaser was Harlequin, the paperback book house. Harlequin is owned by Torstar, which also owns the Toronto Star. Harlequin has a big mail order business as well as trade sales. In the purchase deal, Ted stayed on as president with a five-year contract. Mrs. Kimball and other Miles Kimball executives also were given contracts to stay on.

Not all mail order companies acquired fit the acquiring firms. Some are sold later. Burpee Seeds was bought by General Foods but is now owned by IT&T. Parker Pen bought Norm Thompson, the outdoor clothing catalog house, and operated it profitably for years as it grew. But Parker sales were 95% in writing instruments and it therefore sold Norm Thompson. CBS bought National Needlecraft and made excellent money from it for years . . . but when Needlecraft sales fell off, CBS decided to concentrate on records and sold it.

In April 1979, John Kluge, Chairman of the Board of Metromail, became interested in selling the company. He wanted to do so in a way that would give an ownership opportunity to Bill Howe, Metromail's president, and maximum opportunity for those in the organization. The solution was to bring in one of the leading venture capital companies. A deal was structured to retain management and bring them into ownership.

The Metromail deal was really selling three companies. One was Metromail Corp. and its list compiling business. Another was Cole Publications and its 150 metropolitan street directories, another operating unit. The third was Marketing Electronics, a top computer service bureau for mail order firms. On June 1, 1980, Metromail was purchased by a group of investors headed by Welsh, Carson, Anderson & Stone. Bill Howe, president of Metromail, Inc., became a major owner of the acquiring companies—with 233,000 out of 2.6 million shares.

There's a growing feeling among major corporations that direct marketing will be more of a growing force. There are large numbers of privately held mail order companies. No one of them is a major factor. More and more big companies are making commitments to get into mail order.

Here's what one mail order merger consultant told me: "Some Fortune 500 companies have made mail order acquisitions but then failed to run them in a way that resulted in continued profitable operations. They had no strategic commitment. An acquiring company must want to be in mail order. After the acquisition, it must get into management. It must be patient and stick with it. There must be no deviation from a firm policy to help the company acquired to continue to develop . . . with money and with management.

"Big companies that succeed in their mail order acquisitions look for specialty niche situations, and have a continuing commitment. Take Quaker Oats. They bought and then built Herrschners to a larger level, very successfully. Quaker Oats' management understands what it takes to make it with an acquired mail order company.

"What are the qualifications for an acquiring client company? Have they the financial resources to make the deal? Sellers prefer buyers with quick assets of $40 million or more. Have they made an acquisition in the past? Sellers like to avoid window shoppers. Is the chief executive officer of the acquiring company involved? Does he really want his company to go into mail order—and to stay in it? If so, it's possible to make the deal faster.

"Today, manufacturing companies most desirable for acquisition sell for seven or eight times after tax earnings. This runs to one-and-a-half times book value. But a quality mail order situation will get twelve-and-a-half or more times pre-tax earnings. Usually, this runs three to five times book value. This was the pattern in the purchase of Fingerhut by American Can and of Daytimers, by Beatrice Foods.

"Yet the buyer is usually able to buy a mail order company entirely for assets without assigning money for good will. The computer system is capitalized on a use life of ten years and written off over this period. This includes the value of the customer names. If so, Uncle Sam participates as partner. There is no definite tax ruling on this. The tax counsel of the buyer and of the seller confer."

And so, on and on the mergers go. One big German mail order firm, Otto-Versand, bought Spiegel, doing almost half a billion dollars. Another huge German mail order house, Quelle, was buying Aldens as we went to press. S.C.J. Investment Company of Racine, Wisconsin, bought Wisconsin Cheesemakers Guild Ltd., a catalog house. Bradford Exchange bought Hammacher-Schlemmer to build its mail order catalogs while using its retail location as a showroom. Every day, it seems, new and bigger deals are announced.

Chapter 10
The Direct Marketing Laws

*Mail order sin started
shortly after mail order.*

The original mail order sin was simple—to advertise, keep the money received and not ship. But as mail order flourished, so did mail order crime and sin . . . in as many different ways as varieties of mail order.

But the overwhelming majority of people who ordered and sent in money did get their merchandise. Losses due to fraud were always tiny compared with mail order sales. The percentage has diminished with the years until it is an infinitesimal percentage of all mail order sales.

Further, the vast majority of all losses of monies sent to mail order firms came from bankruptcies, mostly of firms which intended to ship but folded before they could.

Every action causes a reaction. As fast as developments in mail order made possible new forms of sin (which then occurred), specific laws were passed and specific government agencies authorized to enforce them.

When C.O.D. came in, the sinners started to ship unordered merchandise. When credit came in, they shipped something unordered, with a bill. A hundred years ago, the type of mail order crime was more horrendous, selling cancer cures and other patent medicines.

Each new medium created new forms of sin. When radio first became big, Doc Brinkley (a Kansas cancer cure specialist) was legally driven out of his state because of his wild claims via radio advertising. He moved to Mexico and started XENT, a Mexican border station of 100,000 watts. You could hear it loud and clear in New York—late at night. It was a 24-hour medicine show of mail order offers.

The telephone led to the sale of stock, real estate and whatever by boiler room batteries of confidence men. TV liberated the pitch men to new worlds to conquer. Each new kind of business had new possibilities. In the 1930's, accident insurance companies in states with little or no requirements for formation of an insurance company ran mail order ads all over the country. Policies were cheap and claim settlement for some companies a rarity.

The mills of the government gods grind slowly, yet they grind exceeding small. And, in time, laws were passed to correct each abuse and government agencies set up to enforce them. At first, enforcement in many areas seemed a slap on the wrist. Pinpointing responsibility was a problem. But, gradually, machinery was built up in a variety of government agencies to go after anyone concerned. Penalties toughened.

More and more laws passed. More and more government agencies and personnel were put on the trail of mail order offenders. First the Federal government, then State governments and finally county and municipal governments passed their laws and put their sleuths to work. Being against mail order sin was often an assist to a career. Legislators found that introducing new laws could score political points at election time.

All this time, every kind of mail order abuse added together was becoming a smaller and smaller percentage of all mail order

and then direct marketing sales. But exposure was increasing. And the more universal direct marketing became, the more irritating the pettiest of abuses became.

Again and again, ways of doing business that before were legal became illegal. Sweepstakes, contests, the word "Free", price comparison, claims of every sort began to have specific legal do's and don't's. The FTC began to develop guide lines for what to say and what to do, business by business.

At first, the government went after most flagrant cases of the fly-by-night variety. Now the FTC, for example, goes after the small and the big, the beginners and the long established, the companies and the individuals, and anyone or any firm connected with each offense. At first, the flamboyant cases of the small were most publicized and the slips of the giants were handled with more discretion. Then the FTC began to use publicity, itself, as a means of discouraging offenders, whatever their size.

The FTC starts with an investigation. It usually offers the first offender (if the FTC feels it warranted) the option of signing a consent order. The offending firm can state that it doesn't admit having done anything wrong but it agrees to not do it anymore, very specifically spelled out. Then if it violates the order, the FTC goes for maximum penalties. At each step, the FTC may send out releases to newspapers nationally on what it is doing.

Reputable companies may feel strongly that they, and not the FTC, are in the right and be fighting the case legally. Still the publicity streams out as well as where admission of an offense is made. Haband, Inc., the mail order men's wear firm, agreed to pay $30,000 in civil penalties to settle one suit. The problem was delayed delivery and failure to notify customers that they could cancel orders and receive refunds instead of waiting for delivery, and failure to supply a postage paid card and an envelope to aid customers in exercising refund privileges. For a hundred years before a recently passed law there would have been no legal offense. Haband has an excellent reputation for value and promptness of shipping.

A federal judge imposed a $1,750,000 civil penalty on Reader's Digest (in 1982 the Supreme Court upheld it). This was apparently the result of a failure to check the files of several years prior concerning an FTC consent order signed by Reader's Digest. Turn-over of personnel can make adherence to each detail difficult. In this case "travel checks" and "cash convertible bonds" were used to dramatize a price saving for a subscription. The check or bond was made out to the individual mailed but

only payable if the subscription order form was filled out, signed and mailed in. The technique had been often used by leading magazines.

The Book-of-the-Month Club was fined $80,000 by the FTC for a violation of the law against cashing checks received before delivery. The Book-of-the-Month Club is one of the top aristocracy of most reputable mail order firms. Apparently, it was a personnel control problem.

The general effect of such laws, regulations and enforcement has been to tighten up the standards of all mail order companies. Particularly welcome to almost all direct marketers is a crackdown on offenders who seriously harm the public perception of mail order as a whole.

The "GR Valve" is a small plastic device inserted into the hose between the PCV valve and the carburetor of an automobile. Its ads stated that it saved gas by adding air to the fuel mixture. The savings promised were qualified by the words "can" and "up to."

The headlines states, "Now! Transform Air into Fuel and Increase Your Mileage up to 28%." Subheads had such statements as "Guaranteed Gas Savings! Save up to 25¢ a gallon . . . up to two full gallons every 60 miles you drive!!"

The FTC accepted consent agreements with American Consumer (which later went bankrupt) the mail order firm that sold the valve to consumers, with the wholesale distributor of the valve which sold it to American Consumer, with another firm that sold the valve by direct mail soliciting mail orders and through retail stores, with a former astronaut who endorsed the valve in the mail order ads and received commissions and with the advertising agency which prepared TV advertising for one of the mail order companies. Officers of the distributors of the mail order companies were also named in the complaints.

This seems an obvious case of a gadget that promised and

"Just where in his desk does Argyle keep COMPANY papers?"

STRICTLY BUSINESS by Dale McFeatters.
Copyright Publishers Syndicate. Courtesy of Field Newspaper Syndicate.

didn't deliver. But suppose you invent a gas saving device for automobiles. You try it and notice that you use less gas. Others try it and report specific, substantial savings to you. The FTC has a suggestion. "If you make any gas saving claims, they should be based on the Environmental Protection Agencies 'dyanometer' tests." Personal testimonials are probably not enough (since variables are not controlled in actual driving as they are in tests).

Today postal inspectors decide which mail order products are mailable under the postal regulations. There are federal laws on frauds, swindles, lotteries, pyramid sales and obscenity, and postal inspectors to interpret them. There are FTC guidelines for each of many individual fields such as advertising binoculars, ladies' handbags, jewelry, wigs, etc.

Different states have different mail order merchandise and consumer protection laws, advertising restrictions, sales and use taxes, municipal ordinances and private restrictions. They may concern unsolicited merchandise, trade names, unfair and deceptive trade practices, etc. In some cases, the FTC "home solicitation" rule pre-empts state law.

Direct marketing laws and rulings can be confusing and even contradictory. A major out-of-state mail order firm was compelled to collect sales taxes even though all its sales in that state were made and delivered through the mail.

It is probable that big fines and penalties for some top direct marketers have only been occasioned because someone didn't know, wasn't told or didn't check. It may simply have been someone in middle management making a direct marketing decision without realizing its legal implications. It could be simply approving a proposal or copy of a consultant or agency.

Top management can be entirely unaware of such action or inaction until too late. A lawyer may never have been consulted. Few lawyers have easily at hand latest federal rules and guidelines. Until recently, a compilation of state laws concerning direct marketing did not exist.

A way of doing business, describing a product, or wording a coupon may have been done by reputable companies and been accepted as normal practice for years. Yet, at any time, new laws worded or interpreted or both by those unfamiliar with direct marketing can make the same practice illegal.

It may be included in new laws or regulations of various kinds: "Unfair methods of competition"; "Unfair or deceptive acts or practices"; "Unconscionable consumer sales practices"; "Itemized specific practices listed with broader language to reach practices not listed"; "Fraud".

It may be state taxation of mail order sales (which is in constant flux, with great diversity and myriad requirements). It may be state rules for disclosure of terms, for negative option.

Today the Government is deep into the direct marketing business. The post office sells mint issues of stamps to collectors. The Army, Navy and Air Force use direct marketing to get inquiries and then close them, signing on the dotted line as recruits. Dozens of government departments sell books by mail order.

It has been pointed out that in many instances the Government may be violating its own direct marketing laws, subjecting its own employees to possible fines and worse. So far, nothing has happened on this. But maybe the FTC will shut down the Post Office or vice versa. Possibilities are exciting.

Every legislator uses direct marketing to get elected. When I was on the Mutual Broadcasting System answering questions on mail order, I shared the microphone with a leading authority on political direct marketing. One question phoned in was, "I contributed money to a legislator's campaign. I later learned that there was an overage which after the campaign was used to help elect other candidates I had no interest in. Why was this done?" I let him answer that one. I'm sure that the politicians meant nothing wrong, but direct marketing laws they legislate will also apply to them.

There are FTC guidelines for self-regulations by advertisers, by advertising agencies and by media. Today advertisers, advertising agencies and media have liabilities. The FTC can demand corrective advertising. It can order an advertiser to scrap a campaign that cost tens of thousands of dollars to create. There are working guidelines for the use of testimonials, endorsements and pictorial representation.

The FTC states: "Advertising agencies should take extra care to see that claims are supported. The FTC staff suggests that they first make a list of all claims in an ad—direct and implied—and that they supply the advertiser with that list before the ad runs. Support for each claim should be on hand before the ad runs.

The FTC states: "Mail order companies run a serious risk of violating the law if they rely only on the manufacturer's endorsement about a product. To be safe the mail order company should make its own verification."

Privacy laws and regulations now are moving into list rentals. 10 states now prohibit rental of the auto license list. Some states prohibit the sale or rental of a list compiled by state officials. In Minnesota a fund-raising law prohibits a non-profit organization from the sale, exchange or rental of donor or membership lists. More than 30 potentially damaging bills were before the states when this book went to press.

All this can be confusing. Of 50,000 questions asked the DMMA about mail order and direct marketing, the most repeated questions were regarding how to obey the law. The DMMA has a superb manual for direct marketers, in loose-leaf sections—available individually. The section on legal, governmental and ethical aspects of direct marketing is the number one section asked for.

In the DMMA Manual, one section of nine releases is a compilation of information on all major FTC regulations affecting direct marketers, USPS regulations and guidelines, sales and USC taxes, the Privacy Issue and Ethical Business Practice Guidelines.

Release #710.1 is on FTC Credit regulations affecting direct marketers, the Truth in Lending Act, Regulation Z.

A release in October 1979 covered the Unfair and Deceptive Advertising Act. This covers deceptive pricing, retail price comparisons, advertising, retail prices which have been established or suggested by manufacturers; bargain offers based upon the purchase of other merchandise; miscellaneous price comparisons; savings claims based on comparison with equivalent merchandise; bait and switch ads; free samples; use of the word "New"; use of the word "Free"; late delivery refund; negative option plans; guarantees; use of endorsements; dry testing (without merchandise and then sending delay letters).

There are postal service guidelines, rules on interstate taxation, on sales and use taxes for direct marketers varying by states and even by counties. One release (160.6) by Richard Barton explains "The Federal Regulatory Process".

The DMMA has devoted great effort to explain FTC regulations. It even got Dick Cremer of Montgomery Ward to interpret the Regulation Z credit regulations. It went into other FTC credit regulations. Its Releases 710.2 and 710.3 cover "FTC Regulations, Rules and Guides Affecting Direct Marketers".

The DMMA provides information that if obtained from

LEGGETT'S PARIS GREEN OR DRY POWDER GUN.

For Orchard, Vineyard, Garden or Potato Field. Distributes Paris Green, Sulphur, "Fungiroid," (a powdered Bordeaux Mixture) or any dry powder. THOUSANDS IN USE Illustrated Circular on application.

A Wonderful Invention Light, Swift, Easy, Safe, Strong and Cheap.

70441 Supplied with necessary tubes, nozzles, neck and body straps for dusting trees, shrubs, vines or plants; will apply paris green, hellebore or any dry powder quicker, easier and cheaper than by other methods; weight when in use, 5 lbs., boxed for shipment, 20 lbs.; circulars mailed. Price......$7.50

accountants and lawyers specializing in FTC work would be most expensive. Although no substitute for a lawyer, I consider it an aid and supplement to one.

Many mail order firms try to get advice from the post office or FTC by submitting plans and advertising before running any new campaign. Government people are quite shy about approving anything in writing.

The Government people are usually careful to say that reactions by them are not based on thorough investigation and, if evidence should come up in the future that any statement of copy was fraudulent, they will still feel free to prosecute.

However, submission of advertising in advance would be taken by any jury and most judges as an effort to do business within the law. Many firms submit copy, take verbal suggestions for changes make the changes and confirm it all in a letter to the Government Agency talked to.

Direct marketers feel at the mercy of Government which may arbitrarily at any time change the rules of the game. They worry that third class mail may disappear, that legislation banning telephone marketing will be introduced, that the rental of lists might be forbidden.

This makes government relations by direct marketers very important. The DMMA has a Washington office to do this. The job starts by finding out exactly what the Government—federal, state or local—wants direct marketers to do and then explaining it to them.

To do so starts with knowing what the legislators, committees and chairmen who created the laws wanted them to accomplish. This means monitoring working sessions that develop such legislation.

Interpretation of the law varies by government personnel, officials and agency heads as well as by administration and political climate. This means constant contact. The courts may

issue decisions on the legality of a law or its interpretation. Much watching of the legal process is required.

All this requires that the Government Affairs Department of the Direct Mail/Marketing Association, headed by Jonah Gitlitz, Senior Vice President, work closely with DMMA legal council to get legal opinions and reactions. Dana "Todd" Ackerly is the DMMA's Washington counsel. He is solely concerned with postal rate classification. Gil Weil in New York, of Weil, Gutman & Davis, and Bob Sherman are the DMMA's outside general counsel. The Government Relations Department works with Gil Weil on non-postal government matters such as FTC regulations, privacy legislation and other matters. They work together as a team.

Intent, actions and interpretation by government and courts depends on perception of direct marketing by them. The first step is to find out that perception by knowing those concerned and getting their views first hand.

The next step is to pass these views along to direct marketers. Objective analysis may uncover where unfavorable perception is warranted. Changed action by direct marketers can then change perceptions.

Just informing those in Government what direct marketing really is can change unfavorable perceptions. Convincing government that direct marketers have ideals and wish to upgrade standards can also do so. So can showing government that direct marketers can and will self-regulate.

Creating and interpreting laws do not happen in a vacuum. Sweeping trends such as the rise of direct marketing affects everyone. Unfavorable reaction can be a small minority but vocal, organized and powerful in politics and the media beyond its numbers.

Changing the perception of critics of direct marketing can quickly change the perception of government. Actions by direct marketers to self-regulate can do so. So can informing critics of such actions. This means identifying critics, getting their views and attempting to alter them by action and information. For the DMMA the Government Affairs Department works with the government to gain maximum cooperation.

The key to DMMA goverment policy is to uncover, face up to and correct direct marketing shortcomings criticized or not . . . to inform public and government of what it's doing . . . to help

government by self-regulation . . . to furnish deeds before words. . . to take aggressive, realistic and not cosmetic steps to correct when needed.

Many government legislators and administrators prefer to encourage self-regulation rather than to rely on government action. The DMMA tries to work constructively and openly with government to agree on what direct marketers are expected to do to fulfill the letter and spirit of laws and regulations that concern them.

The Government Affairs Department deals with government on the national, state and local level. A good deal of contact is by telephone, but the bulk of it is through the mail. Four major mailings a year are made to key people at government agencies by the DMMA.

First the DMMA monitors federal and state government for regulatory and legislative activity that concerns direct marketing. Then it develops the strategy needed. It makes every effort to work with the government agencies or legislators early enough in the game to help affect the final shape of the proposed laws or regulations.

Once the government has acted it's rare to modify laws or regulations. Each situation is different. For telephone marketing the DMMA gets a telephone law specialist.

Several years back, the FTC proposed a late delivery rule. Many DMMA members wanted no regulation at all. They wanted to fight it. The DMMA proposed a compromise to meet reality. On the one hand, it had to convince the FTC to modify the rule. On the other, it had to convince members to cooperate. The further away from each other the FTC and mail order people are the more difficult it is for either to have a perception of the activities of the other and of the need to work together.

The DMMA believes in cooperation, in showing the government that direct marketers have ideals, want to self-police and will, and then in proving it to them. It believes that, when there is a reasonable reason for government regulations, responsible direct marketers can work for a fair and equitable law or rule much more effectively than in fighting it.

It conducts a "Freedom to Mail" campaign for self-policing rather than government regulation. It considers the cornerstone of "Freedom to Mail" to be the disclosure by mailers to customers that their names are rented. The DMMA keeps after mailers to do so. It sponsors the Mail Preference Services. It helps those who desire to have their names taken off mailing lists. It keeps expanding the Mail Order Action Line, a phone and mail service it operates for consumers to expedite handling of complaints. It keeps coming up with self-regulating and other steps to improve member dealings with customers and the public.

The DMMA seems to have won considerable confidence from the Post Office and the Postal Rate Commission concerning DMMA supplied data at rate change time. This helps the DMMA work on behalf of fair postal rates for direct marketers. In 1974, DMMA officers testified three or four times before Congressional committees, and one time in 1980.

Very likely, it will be far simpler for direct marketers to live and work with the government then it may sometimes seem. Albert Kramer, Director of The Bureau of Consumer Protection, says that both the FTC and direct marketers have the same objectives, to flush out the bad apples.

He points out the particular need for honesty, accuracy and reliability in direct marketing ads. He feels that the solution is adequate self-regulation. He believes that if it's done, the role of the FTC in direct marketing will be small in the future. So I tend to agree with Albert Kramer, but I do suggest that all in direct marketing make a special effort to be informed on most basic government laws and regulations concerning direct marketing.

A tape of a speech on this subject by Albert Kramer is available. Full copies of FTC regulations on any aspect of mail order and direct marketing (such as credit regulations) can be obtained. Interpretive summaries of the Council of Better Business Bureaus on FTC rules are available. So is a copy of the FTC News, the FTC newsletter and material from the post office of its regulations. How to get each is listed in the Help Source Section in back of this book.

One invaluable source is DMMA's "The Law & Direct Marketing", with the laws of each state and most municipalities, and state by state—and federal laws. It is reviewed in this book.

Note: If you sell abroad, realize that each country has its own laws on direct marketing, often quite different. In West Germany, advertising mail can not be sent unless the potential recipient has first requested that his or her name be included on mailing lists. Other countries have equally surprising laws which you had best familiarize yourself with before you start.

Chapter 11
The Biggest Direct Marketing Agency

How it became the fastest growing part of the biggest general advertising agency.

Wunderman, Ricotta & Kline is biggest. It's a very highly respected and much talked about agency. Direct marketing as known today started with its founding.

You may never work for it, sell to it or become a WR&K client. But if you're in mail order it can help you. Because it innovates and pioneers ways to sell more profitably via mail order. It had much to do with the revolution in methods that transformed the then small mail order field into today's huge direct marketing one.

Its merger with Young & Rubicam, the biggest general advertising agency, started many of the top ten general agencies to acquire or start direct marketing subsidiaries . . . and a second direct marketing revolution. The most proven mail order methods are merging into the most effective general advertising methods and neither will ever be the same. Some think a hybrid is being created more effective than any previous advertising.

A direct response agency can only grow if the advertising it creates for its clients succeeds. Its billing consists largely of projection of successful tests it has prepared. Unprofitable campaigns often mean lost accounts. Even a superb salesman can scarcely replace account losses due to result failure.

WR&K has created more successful tests than others. It has projected successes further and into more media. It has kept accounts longer. Becoming its client is joining a club, one with an exclusive membership for each classification and with almost all classifications filled. To secure a client or become one, it's often necessary to create a new classification, actually create a new way to direct market.

WR&K is a new idea place. It has a strong team led by and responsive to an unusual man, Lester Wunderman . . . founder and chairman. From the first, innovation combined with practicality. There was, and is, a no-nonsense approach to advertising. The starting group were young. They had had good jobs but wanted to be in a new environment. There was an attitude. They would not toady. They wanted to be judged by results. Then, as now, Lester Wunderman was the leader. He could persuade and win over others whether recruiting talent, soliciting accounts or stimulating staff to do more and, to his marketing viewpoint.

Anatole Broyard is now one of the country's top book reviewers for the New York Times and the author of two books. But from late 1963 until April 1971, he first wrote copy and later supervised other copywriters as well for WR&K. "I had first written mail order copy at a small agency for its only mail order account and then did free lance for others. I enjoyed writing mail order copy and seeing the results. I liked it much more at WR&K because the testing and projecting were done so scientifically."

"I was solely concerned with copy. Lew Smith was my first boss and a very good copy chief. Bill Calhoun was art director. Bill Keisler was creative head. He was so genuinely nice he made creative people go all out to produce."

"But Lester Wunderman was the resident genius. He was endlessly interesting, charismatic, and the best salesman. He loved to play to an audience. He was the best businessman. Lester set most policy. WR&K was a good place to work. I wrote copy for the Literary Guild. Later WR&K began to handle the Book-of-the-Month Club and I wrote for it. WR&K quadrupled results with its first ads. Then I worked on Time-Life Books, and also on Psychology Today."

"I found Wunderman, Ricotta & Kline intellectually stimulating with tremendously talented and fine people. People there were equal to and sometimes superior to those in the literary world. Lester collected primitive sculpture and Irving's hobby was chamber music. Both were very original people and accessible. The doors to Lester and Irving Wunderman's offices were always open and anyone could propose ideas.

"I could, on my own time, write book reviews. Several appeared on the front page of the New York Herald Tribune and The New York Times Book Section. This led to my present job. Otherwise, I'd be there now. I was happy and content."

Lester had joined in 1948, and became increasingly important in the Max Sackheim Advertising Agency. The managers of mail order businesses were quick to see that Lester Wunderman could contribute considerably to their businesses. Some of the brightest upcoming talents were stimulated by his thinking. For this book, some of each recall their first reactions to Lester.

Milton Runyon was executive vice president of Doubleday, in charge of mail order. He remembers Lester as important in the Max Sackheim Agency, a good businessman, sound in mail order, with brilliant ideas. John Stevenson then assisted Milo Sutliff and later launched the first continuity hard cover book programs. "Lester was, from the beginning, very capable in mail order. Later, I did business with WR&K with some of my own offers. I used to meet with Lester every Wednesday afternoon."

After John Stevenson had left Doubleday to found his own book business, Jerry Hardy was the man the Max Sackheim Agency had contacted. Jerry was a rising star at Doubleday. Jerry, who later founded Time-Life Books, says: "The best indication of my opinion of Lester Wunderman and of WR&K was that when they were just starting, I almost joined them. I've done business with Lester at Doubleday, at Time-Life Books and at The Dreyfus Corp."

Elsworth Howell, of Grolier, first worked with Lester in the Max Sackheim days. "Lester was a good strategist," recalls Elsworth. More than that, Lester was a planner and a marketer. He could observe a small, unexpected success in a new area, see the widest possible potential expansion and persuade others to join in as he drove through its projection. He had a flair, instinct, feel for deducing the proper next step. He planned strategy, carefully and thoroughly.

WR&K started with certain principles. Copy and media would be important but strategy and planning even more so. The partners signed a no-nepotism agreement. They agreed to bring others into the ownership when talent warranted; to attract by sharing. Lester Wunderman was the planner, the marketer, the mail order strategist and the driving force of a close team. They were pros and confident. The atmosphere, as success came, attracted others.

Clients came quickly. First, Jackson & Perkins, Columbia Records and Grolier did. Later, Doubleday did. Famous Artists did. A year after Jerry Hardy founded Time-Life Books, it did. And once accounts came, they usually grew quickly.

In mail order, as in direct marketing now, every method, every tool, every medium, every ad and product tends to wear out. Mail order people have always needed to come up with new ways of doing things more productive than the old. This ability became a hallmark. And when Lester stimulated WR&K to develop a new method, he persuaded clients, and often media to try it.

To Lester the insert was a natural and logical marketing development. All ads had a reply vehicle. The coupon developed. Some mail order advertisers tried a coupon the size of a post card and made it a paper post card. Then someone in the Post Office objected. That led to the first cardboard post card with a page ad. These began to proliferate. Lester and later WR&K played a part in these developments. Now, Lester adapted it further by using a post card stock, multi-page insert broadside—with a post card as part of it instead of the coupon.

Lester's clients had huge success with his adaptations. Probably the biggest and most dramatic success was for The Columbia Record Club, with a four-page insert in TV Guide. The center-spread insert position in TV Guide became the most

fought for media buy in mail order and then direct marketing. For years WR&K clients dominated it.

He had discovered a new medium, a hybrid combination of direct mail and of publication advertising . . . a medium with unprecedented reach and power. But to utilize that medium, he had to persuade publications to be willing to bind in such inserts and mail order advertisers to use them. It was chicken and egg. One advertiser alone was not worth the trouble for media to make such sweeping changes. One publication like TV Guide was not enough to convert the needed advertisers.

Lester was the missionary who, more than any other man, got publications to allow inserts, and advertisers to use them. In so doing, he built up major magazine billing while creating sales for clients that otherwise would not have existed.

WR&K came up with an arsenal of hybrid media for clients to select from. Many others jumped in and sometimes contributed new variations. Innovative media did. But more than others, Lester studied the new hybrid media for ways to use them more effectively. And often, WR&K came up with improved ways before others.

Often, the agency proposed the concept of a new hybrid form to a publication and even an advertising rate for it. Gradually, WR&K assembled more information about what each kind of insert cost to produce, what it produced in response and what advertisers could afford to buy it at and media to sell it at . . . including what outside printing cost should be reasonable. It had more records of results from hybrid media and knew more how to use them effectively. This helped agency clients and also to get new clients . . . if not now, later.

An early success, and in class media, was American Heritage Books. Dick Benson had been at American Heritage and contributed a lot of its success in direct mail. His consulting firm, Benson, Stagg & Archer—which he later started—became quite big and successful. Then, because of different ventures that did badly, Benson, Stagg & Archer closed. Lester saw an opportunity to help clients, Dick Benson and WR&K. The result was a WR&K subsidiary, in which Dick Benson shared, to consult on and create direct mail. This was unusual because direct mail had always been done by the printers, brokers and mailing houses. The advertisers had dealt directly with them.

The Benson connection lasted two years but, thereafter, direct mail continued to become part of the overall marketing plans of WR&K. For more and more clients, the agency got into direct mail as another marketing form. It developed direct mail creative people of its own. It worked closely with Rose Harper, of the Kleid Company, on list selection.

One large client WR&K succeeded with in its early years was Bell & Howell, particularly in direct mail. Maxwell Sroge had been with Bell & Howell when the first test of their camera and projector offer was made in Chicago. He had persuaded the syndicator to launch it. Mac came with WR&K for a short time as account executive for Bell & Howell. WR&K put them into space successfully. WR&K also did a lot of direct mail for them.

Harry Kline retired only a few years after Wunderman, Ricotta & Kline's founding. Ed Ricotta retired several years later.

But from the start until now, Lester Wunderman has been planning, guiding, leading and creating much of WR&K's growth. The agency grew, proliferated, changed in form and scope with Lester always in the forefront. He seems just to be getting his second wind.

After the successful start in the U.S., WR&K expanded into Canada . . . the first major U.S. direct marketing agency to do so—and with considerable success. It was the first step of world expansion. Peter Rosenwald, who had been a consultant to Doubleday for international sales, joined WR&K. Then, with Peter's help, Lester set up co-ventures with agencies in England and then in France.

Meanwhile, the agency grew faster than ever in the U.S. More than accounts, Lester valued the assembly of top talent. He valued creative work . . . but as part of and a stage in something far more comprehensive. The effect of his planning and product and client queries was to give far more ammunition to the creative people . . . to provide an environment that attracted the best of creative people and got the best out of them. Lester Wunderman won their confidence, influenced them and guided them. He could excite their imagination.

He could do this with clients, prospects, even competitors. When the top ten general advertising agencies started to shop for acquisitions of direct marketing agencies, WR&K became the most desired plum. The marriage of Young & Rubicam, the biggest general agency, and WR&K, the biggest direct marketing agency, became the inevitable result.

More than an acquisition, the merger has proved to be an inspired alliance . . . made with perfect timing to gain fullest benefit for each. Ever since the merger, outside of internal growth, WR&K's biggest source of new business has been from Y&R clients.

The cause was the explosion of direct marketing and of Fortune 500 companies using it. Before, Y&R did not have the facilities for them and WR&K was unfamiliar to many of them. WR&K told its story to Y&R clients, got test authorizations, made them pay out and projected them. It was only possible because of the standing of Y&R and the direct marketing capability of WR&K . . . which was created years before the merger.

Growth of the agency after the Y&R merger dwarfed anything before. In the U.S., WR&K acquired General Foods, General Cigar, Proctor & Gamble, Merrill Lynch and Johnson & Johnson. In England and France, the co-venture partner agencies were fully acquired. Thereafter, WR&K set up its own offices or acquired agencies in leading world cities. One reason for overseas success was that WR&K was so successful in the U.S. for world companies. Time-Life Books began to work with WR&K in country after country. One by one, Y&R introduced WR&K to its accounts—in the U.S. and all over the world—to the profit of each.

But while all this was happening, WR&K's original accounts grew and grew. CBS-Columbia House and Time-Life Books grew to be the two biggest accounts in direct marketing. CBS-Columbia finally billed 30 million dollars a year. Lester and WR&K never stopped developing new methods, new media, new expertise to bring to each client.

Wunderman, Ricotta & Kline has more facilities than any competitor. It has offices all over the world. It has so many accounts there is virtually one in every logical category. It has more Fortune 500 accounts and more mainstream marketing accounts using direct marketing methods.

Yet, WR&K has more longevity with the most traditional of mail order accounts . . . and is more entrenched with them than ever before. The majority of its growth has always been internal . . . by creating growth, account by account . . . by stimulating use of new media for accounts overall. With the merger WR&K print media activities grew. Then direct mail billing took a big jump as Y&R brought in a parade of clients for guidance in it.

Its TV growth had been so fast and so huge that super-imposed on its organization which had won its spurs in traditional mail order media was another, younger organization of electronic media experts. First, WR&K established expertise in TV support advertising to increase orders from ads and mailings. It did so for Time-Life Books Inc., for whom it had handled space from the early 1960's, but never TV. But, in 1980, it started to test and, in 1981, to project TV mail order advertising for T-L Books, with great success. Then, Lester introduced WR&K's new capability in TV to each logical account new to it.

WR&K has more employees in the U.S. than any other direct marketing agency and almost as many outside the U.S. There are offices in Sydney, Australia, and Copenhagen, Denmark . . . in Montreal and Toronto . . . in London and Paris, in Amsterdam and Barcelona. And with Y&R, it shares offices in Brussels and Sao Paulo . . . in Milan and Oslo and Helsinki.

Of Y&R's network of 14 specialized agencies, it became the second biggest, and for years, the most profitable per million billing. For years after the merger it was the fastest growing part of Y&R's overall business. It is the thirty-first agency in size of all general agencies.

Talent speeded WR&K growth. Growth attracted more talent. Some moved on. The chairman of the board of one competitor is a WR&K alumnus. So is the president of another. Both are owned by top-twenty general agencies. The president of one of the largest independently owned direct marketing agencies is an alumnus. Other alumni are the backbone of direct marketing management of a constantly growing number of firms.

The cachet of having worked for WR&K has been enough for anyone with the briefest of tenures to get a job in direct marketing almost anywhere on the globe—or to become a consultant. Those who stay longer often go to the top wherever they later work. Many of WR&K's best people of many years past have stayed, and often done best of all. A tremendous team remains—constantly added to as growth is required. Lester is known as a good hirer who staffs talent in depth.

Talent is constantly developed from within and brought in from outside. Talent can make good anywhere in the world in a WR&K office and move into bigger things on another continent. More and more Y&R people have been taken into WR&K—and praised as good. Top leaders in direct marketing, when offered a chance to join, often came.

Among this talent, Lester keeps the peace . . . between the far-flung offices and WR&K top brass, WR&K top management and that of Y&R . . . between clients and agency . . . between controllers and creative people. He and Ed Ney, Chairman of the Board of Young & Rubicam, keep an eye on volume and profit, growth and stability . . . the exciting future and this year's bottom line.

More effective and unusual than that of any competitor is Lester's brand of public relations. Others state the size and growth of direct marketing with precise but unproven figures. Lester does not. He is constantly referred to yet avoids overexposure. He does not oversell the future. The impression is of an agency preferring to be judged by results.

Stories, articles and interviews rotate from one department and key executive to another. There are tactics stories—how to

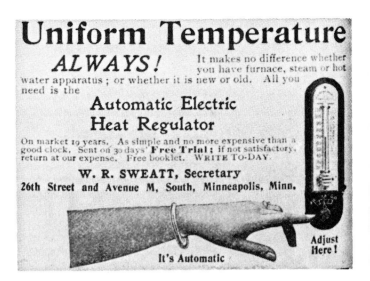
do it and how it was done. Each adds to the feeling of vitality and variety of WR&K talent. When executives talk, each time the subject is on developments important to anyone in the field. They have given dozens of lectures at New York University. Collectively, the tapes of these speeches and occasionally ones by Lester are a splendid direct marketing course. They are obtainable from Hoke Communications. Details are in the Help Source Section of this book.

The explosion of direct marketing made WR&K possible. Very likely, Lester Wunderman made that explosion bigger. The agency's performance made its own tremendous growth possible. Lester made both the performance and the growth happen. The Y&R marriage speeded it along. And I think Lester's speeches accelerated growth still more. He does not speak often, but he prepares a speech with great care. However successful a speech, he's apt to polish it and hone it, should he ever use it for a different audience—usually with even more effective quotes.

Often, he quotes from what stimulated him to help stimulate others. A quote can set a mood or make a point. One speech may include T.S. Elliot, George Orwell and Hayakawa, Gertrude Stein and Alvin Toffler. Peter Drucker is usually present. It may refer to The Age of Discontinuity or The Age of Uncertainty. But each quote strengthens the structure of the speech. Each sentence is a building block for the case Lester is building.

The presentation makes a Lester Wunderman speech the "piece de résistance" wherever delivered. He can persuade, whether one to one, in a small meeting or to thousands. But to large groups he adds what he has studied of the theater and in public speaking. He may start or close with poetry, perhaps sung or with music as background. He opens quietly. He's polished. Throughout, he times each sentence effectively. To hear a Lester Wunderman speech is an experience that can mesmerize, but always convinces.

The impact on associates, newest staff, clients, anyone in or new to direct marketing, is always electric. There are three of his speeches I particularly recommend that you hear. Each is on tape and available from Hoke Communications. Details on how to get them are in the Help Source Section in this book.

One was presented in 1968—"The Seven Steps to Planning the Marketing Program". It contains the original concepts on which WR&K was founded. Then there's the "Our Tools Are Getting Rusty" speech given in 1975. In it, Lester listed one seemingly insurmountable problem after another of outmoded methods. Yet, for each, almost as an aside, he dropped a word of a WR&K solution. The effect was that sophistication and innovation was needed to avoid direct marketing disaster and left the listener with the conviction that WR&K had plenty of both.

To me, his greatest speech was delivered in London, in 1980—a refinement and expansion and perfection of a great speech he had given in 1979 in the U.S. It is "The Frontiers of Direct Marketing from Jamestown to the Year 2000". Please listen to this tape. It's got everything and teaches more about direct marketing than any one lecture ever given.

Lester Wunderman personifies the latest, changing, most scientific direct marketing. He is an analyst of change and of opportunity. He's had more to do with the success of mail order of more Fortune 500 companies than any other man. The use of direct marketing methods in mainstream marketing of biggest companies is his specialty.

Lester Wunderman has taught not just his employees and clients but the entire field the importance of strategy, planning and marketing, overall. He has some of the qualities of Peter Drucker. He might have been at Harvard Business School and written books on business science.

He can help anyone new to or in direct marketing to use it more effectively. Just read or listen to what he says. I particularly recommend that you send for reprints or tapes of the talks by his executives and him that seem most pertinent to your situation. Refer to the Help Source Section for details.

Chapter 12
Mail Order Fun

How to make money unscientifically

All his professional life, Joseph A. Ecclesine has been highly successful creating promotions for biggest companies. But, after hours, he had mail order fun, and still does. He's retired now and operates from the new "Global Headquarters" of The Wry Idea Company, Box 22408, San Diego, California 92122... his home.

Twenty-five years ago, as a creative outlet, Joe founded The Wry Idea Company... moonlighting from his home which was in Rye, New York. A free write-up in House Beautiful Magazine launched Joe's first mail order product, "The All Purpose Greeting Card". The user needed only to check off any one of more than 60 sentiments on each card, from "Get Well" to "Happy Birthday". Joe was surprised when response was enough to force him into production.

Ever since, Joe has persisted in coming up with impractical product ideas and testing them. And The Wry Idea Company has persisted in making money. In seeking new items, Joe carefully avoids method, organization and system. Instead, they are the products of an impish and sometimes fevered imagination.

When Joe discovered the village of Shady, New York, he immediately got a post office box. This gave birth to Shady Enterprises, Joe Ecclesine, prop. of P.O. Box 25, Shady, New York. "I used it to sell genuinely worthless stock and similar fancies... including membership on our Board of Directors, be-ribboned and framed."

Joe developed new items not for profit, but for fun... yet with a good batting average. Some have kept up modest success from inception. Joe has a flair for such items as his dashboard mini-plaques... "God Bless This Car", "God Bless This Boat" and "Thank You For Not Smoking".

In a joint venture with a kindred spirit, Joe introduced the "Presentation Series of GOLDEN SCREWS. Authentic reproductions from The Screwmaker's Hall of Fame". These included "the Square Screw, the 90-Degree Screw, the Inverted-U Screw and the Zig-Zag Screw". Each was illustrated with an engineers drawing and described with the gravity of a Franklin Mint offer.

Selling words few people understood made good sense to Joe. Joe created a motto. "Eschew Obfuscation". He put it on a masonite plaque. He advertised it in Saturday Review with a classified ad (which immediately succeeded). It produced ample orders at $2.50 each. Joe expanded, first with more classified ads and then with inch ads.

Reproducing and selling two words would seem like a simple business. But Joe overcame all this. Joe kept changing his plaque. He made one in formica and sold it for five dollars. Soon Joe had three plaques... "regular, deluxe and grandiose".

Demand forced expanding beyond plaques. Customers wanted "Eschew Obfuscation" in other applications. Over the years, Joe had "done everything but a needlepoint kit". Joe went into an "Eschew Obfuscation" catalog, which added a wide variety of fun products. Joe built up his catalog for 20 years, from 1955 to 1975. For it, Joe did his own layouts and mechanicals.

Joe now offers a basic wall plaque in masonite... "for placement where obfuscation is likely to occur." It's 8 1/2" by 3 2/3". It has gold lettering, an easel and a hanger (made of silver antique metal). There's an emerald green border.

Joe sells "Eschew" T-shirts. As Joe explains, "They make ideal attire for bishops' synods and for divorce hearings." He sells "Eschew" letter seals. "Affix alongside cogent paragraphs in your letters." Joe suggests. He also sells "Eschew" bumper stickers... "The very first selection of The Bumper-Sticker-of-the-Month Club." Joe sells "Eschew" tote bags, too, to carry all those "Eschew Obfuscation" items in. It's all fun.

Joe has made money despite a severe lack of the trading instinct. Projecting any success never interested Joe as much as the next off-beat idea. "I was a compulsive manufacturer. I bought dear and sold cheap. As soon as I got *volume* orders as a premium, for gifts or from stores, I was in trouble. One stationery store filled a window full of my items and sold 40 in a day. But I had no margin."

Joe has just completed what he considers the peak accomplishment of his career, his grand opus, his book... "How Not to Make a Million Dollars in Mail Order"... written in considerable detail. He is modest because mail order was the bulk of Joe's business and always made money for Joe. It still does. "My ad budget is less than $1,000 a year." Joe's classified and one-inch ads pull at low selling cost. He keeps getting repeat and recommendation business. It's been a very small enterprise.

However, The Wry Idea Company has consistently made money. It gave just enough extra income, security and confidence to make it possible for Joe to free lance. "For twenty years, I made more money than on a salary." Joe got good pay from giant companies like Newsweek, Continental Cars, CBS, NBC and American Express. All this time, his own mail order was profitable fun.

"Mail order has been a side venture for me most of my business life. I'm an addict. More recently, it's been a retirement supplement." Several years ago, he had a heart attack 'from cigarette smoking'. He cut down the free lance work and streamlined the mail order business. "I devote four to five hours a week to it now a few months of the year." It's still profitable fun. For a retiree not in perfect health, that's the bottom line.

Chapter 13
The Mail Order Future

*Its seeds start problems of survival
and possibilities of success for you.*

By spring, 1982, direct marketing was huge, with predictions of far more enormous future growth. A science fiction future seemed to be getting under way. But, there was concern. Previously successful methods seemed to be rushing to obsolescence, speeded by accelerated inflation of selling costs in every medium.

The problem was to keep making money with present methods; to prepare to shift to new areas; but not to live in the future too soon, before it was profitable. The new technology was dropping in cost while improving in quality. This showed on a graph by a line which constantly curved downward. Another line representing the constantly rising costs of present methods curved upward. One day the two lines would meet and kiss, in a classic "kissing curve".

It would be the fade-out kiss for most direct marketing as we knew it. A new communications revolution would make mail order methods as universal as computers, while driving out of business direct marketers who did not join the new wave. Mail order had vastly proliferated into direct marketing. Now both were expanding into a far more universal marketing. It would be used by largest and smallest companies.

The mail order future had already happened on a test scale.. . living catalogs with 54,000 pictures on a video disc, instant electronic mail, and push-button mail order on two-way TV. There already existed instant electronic money transfer and instant credit card payment, instant delivery of video newsletters, instant instructions, instant custom news and instant games. It was now possible to have instant inquiry and order counts and instant projections of what future instant sales should total.

But full-scale use, practicality and profitability was something else. There would be a kissing curve for each of many developments, at different times. For some it might never come. Yet, an overall electronic communications revolution was underway.

The French call it "Telematique". Harvard Professor Anthony Ottinger calls it 'Compunications". Harvard Professor Daniel Bell calls it "The fourth revolution in social interchange". First speech, then writing, then printing changed our world. Now comes telecommunications to dwarf all change, to date. It is segmentation come to TV . . . in constantly proliferating variety.. . created by the merging of telephone, computers and TV, into a single yet different system.

Professor Bell calls it the replacement of paper economy by an electronic one . . . culminating in "The Information Society". Stanley Marcus sees it as replacing selling floors and catalogs . . . a greater use of direct marketing techniques and far more mail order from the home. "The smarter retailers will probably get into the mail order business."

One dream is to produce entire video disc magazines and newspapers on inexpensive metal foil with video news and features and video demonstration ads. Another is to store entire electronic libraries on computer and print out books only on special order on a home facsimile printer. Another is the home ticker tape for fast-breaking news, hand-tailored to each subscriber.

How much of this will really happen? We don't know. But never in marketing history have such great investments and speculations been made on future expectations. For the new communication technology intertwined with direct marketing, the stakes are huge—for companies, entire industries, even governments. RCA hopes to restore NBC's fortunes with it. Ma Bell plans to dwarf all past growth with it. Xerox and IBM hope to win the decisive victory over each in it.

The electronic mail order future can best be visualized by examining the seeds and start of some of its new forms. Cable TV started for communities just beyond a TV coverage area. A community antenna would be set up . . . higher, more sophisticated and more expensive than individual homes could afford. The TV signal was picked up. It was then relayed to individual homes by cable. A local entrepreneur organized it. Then an entrepreneur got an idea. Why not make slides and tape the audio for a commercial for the local drug store . . . and telecast it? Why not run a taped TV show? Why not be a TV station? These ideas came and were carried out one at a time.

Community cable antennas began to be businesses, to cluster into systems, to have associations. Ted Turner's "Superstation" showed the big time potential of cable—first sending signals by radio relay. Then space age TV began.

In 1945, Arthur Clarke, later author of "2001: A Space Oddysey", described future space satellites circling the equator and broadcasting radio and TV to the world. Now there's a space satellite traffic jam over the equator. A satellite can carry up to 24 transponders. One transponder can service one satellite network.

Canada began installing miniature earth stations . . . fourfoot receiving disk antennas . . . on the roofs of homes in remote areas—to receive programs via satellite. Comsat, RCA, CBS, Western Union International and nine smaller companies filed applications with the FCC to beam from satellites directly to homes—using even smaller disk antennas, 2½ to 3 feet in diameter.

With cable came even faster growing pay cable, for special programs including big star, recent movies and big sports events, but for a cost of so much a month. A scrambled signal was telecast and each pay TV subscribing home was provided with an unscrambler, a decoder. Many felt that pay cable would later add commercials.

UHF-TV had always been a tough business. Now it began to make money, generally by diversification. Black UHF-TV stations, sports UHF-TV stations, religious UHF-TV and many varieties began to prosper, each a market for specialized mail order. Then pay TV companies began to lease time on UHF-TV stations to telecast its "scrambled" pictures. In some cases even UHF stations which had gone off the air, now with the new revenue, could go back on.

Another development was QUBE, the innovation of Warner Cable (a subsidiary of Warner Communications). It was two-way TV and first tried in Columbus, Ohio. The potential and capital requirements of QUBE proved enormous. Warner Communications sold 50% of Warner Cable (for $175 million) to American Express, resulting in Warner-Amex Cable. On QUBE it was possible to be billed for each pay TV movie tuned in . . . as if for a long distance telephone call.

QUBE expanded on cable systems . . . in Cincinnatti, in Houston, in Pittsburgh, and then more cities. The idea is to involve the subscriber in services offered, each charged as if calling the telephone company for a weather report. QUBE uses a cable, not a telephone line. QUBE also sells services by direct marketing.

A popular QUBE service has been home protection with

burglary and fire alarms hooked up from your home to a central surveillance office—also an adaptation as a sort of media alert system for patients with chronic illnesses. Games are offered, as well as books, records and tapes, insurance and shopping services. Some are sold directly over TV, some by two-step via two-way TV. You just push a button to buy or inquire.

All this has led to QUBE using more and more channels to offer in more variety more ways to spend money. In 1981, Warner Amex Cable Communications brought out its QUBE III home console to accomodate up to 110 program channels for home service, data information and video entertainment with narrow cast channels and 12 interactive response buttons.

More cities demanded that cable systems convert to two-way TV. Manufacturing the black box for it became big business To set up QUBE in a single city is said to require 50 to 100 million dollars. Profitability, of course, depends on whether enough people respond enough to services offered by a variation of the mail order method.

Another TV development, narrow casting, makes possible mini-TV stations that fit snugly between two big city stations, the coverage areas of which do not touch. Each narrow casting station can be built for a small fraction of the cost of a major station. The FCC has opened the door to set up 4,000 new VHF and UHF narrow casting stations with coverage areas of from 5 to 40 miles.

Words, numbers, letters, symbols and graphs on cathode ray terminals came with computers. Then central computers sent them by telephone or cable to terminals and other computers elsewhere. Computer banks brought data, news and information services by phone, wire, cable or broadcast into offices and homes. TV and computer and telephone began to be used together to do so.

It was first experimented with in a very tiny way in the U.S. But the British pioneered instant marketing of data services, electronically—and direct marketing of far more goods and services by electronic two-step. Gradually, they developed entirely new electronic variations of the mail order method. The direct marketers were "providers". One concept is to put encyclopedic information on computer and make the TV set a vending machine.

The viewer can tap keys on a typewriter-style keyboard to communicate with the provider and indicate the kind of information desired on gardening, or whatever. A menu of kinds of garden information appears on the screen. With several more taps, the viewer zeroes in on the instructions to plant climbing roses for the area. All the how-to books on earth could become available this way.

The same principal applies to making reservations to go to the theater, on a cruise or to rent a house. In each case, there's a direct marketing dialogue between viewer and advertiser. It's living classified, via two-way TV, the people's direct marketing place. Classified is one-third of the revenue, the most profitable advertising per dollar and the financial backbone of U.S. newspapers.

The system can also turn your TV set into a computer and supply the use of a great variety of programs. It can help keep books for a home business, be a teaching machine, or become an arcade of electronic games. In the future, it can do almost endlessly more. The viewer can be charged for any of a variety of services as used, exactly as if making a long distance call.

Prestel is the system created by the British Post Office. It soon developed that people did respond when offered a chance to buy certain kinds of services. Sometimes a buying decision can be made by pushbutton or a request can be made by the viewer for

personal, phone or mail follow-up. Prestel has now been tested in
Switzerland, Germany, Holland, Australia, Hong Kong and the
USA. Prestel data is sent on standard telephone lines. The generic
term for this is Video Data. By 1982, worldwide Video Data was
rapidly becoming a reality.

The French Post Office started later than the British, but
with a very ambitious program. It first tested its electronic phone
book, "Tele-Tel", in a tiny way, then a bigger test and then
planned its 1982 expansion to 270,000 terminals and by 1992 to
30 million. By then, instead of the enormous cost of printing
phone books, it hoped for a new profit center. In December,
1981, first tests of the French "Tele-Tel" system began in several
U.S. cities. "Tele-Tel" also offered applications for banking
service, travel services, restaurant and travel reservations and
"tele-shopping". La Redoute, largest mail order catalog in
France, joined in experiments. Subscribers could be billed for
each phone information request, an instant direct marketing
business. Further, for terminal production, cost would drop so
low a huge export business was expected. Sales of 24 million
terminals to the U.S. alone were anticipated.

Meanwhile, the Canadian Government joined the Video
Data competition with its own version, Telidon, which has been
praised as having outstanding graphics.

Two of Canada's largest publishing and communications
companies have created Infomart a big developer of videotext
and teletex software and applications. In an Infomart test in
Canada of videotex, the Hudson Bay Company sold books,
records, toys, name brand clothes and much more with good
results. In 1981, Infomart's U.S. subsidiary, Videotex Systems,
provided a teletex service offering instant market crop data and
other video data information to farmers. Other governments
began to see that video data could make nationally owned postal,
phone and telegraph systems more profitable, with new services
and products sold by instant direct marketing. By 1982, over 80
Videotex experiments were in progress around the world. U.S.
companies alone had committed over $100 million to videotex
development.

In the U.S., the Post Office was also getting interested in the
new electronic communications—along with the newspapers, the
movie companies, the broadcasting industry, the magazine
publishers, the telephone industry, the computer manufacturers,
and much of the Fortune 500. The U.S. had started electronic
communications. It was ahead in most forms and set out to catch
up on video data as well.

Some in electronic communication still hoped to take over
the majority of the mail business from the Post Office . . . as UPS
had taken over from Parcel Post. Lettershops nationwide began
to band together to organize their own electronic mail for
regional post office delivery.

The computer led to computer data banks on subject after
subject. Computers that could communicate with each other led
to computer data networks which led to services to be sold by the
mail order method—only instantly. Soon, almost all big companies could send electronic mail to each other by various means,
including elaborate computer networks.

Ma Bell had created a fiber-optic telephone system with
capacity for several times the numbers of TV, radio and voice
signals carried by cable and broadcast in the U.S. it could
completely supplant broadcasting and supply directly to the
home computer, newspapers and magazines. In 1982, in an
historic settlement with the Anti-Trust Department, it agreed to
give up ownership of all 24 of its local telephone companies. In

return, it received a go-ahead to set up a separate unregulated
subsidiary to compete in electronic communications.

Time, Inc., was considering a hybrid teletext combining a
service by satellite to cable TV systems with the use of telephone
wires. A subsidiary of Tymshare, Inc. was operating multipoint
distribution systems to transmit pay TV signals through the air
which could also be used to transmit information or computer-
aided instruction for home use.

By 1982, over three times as many messages were transmitted electronically in the U.S. as by hand. By 1982, it cost twice
as much to mail a first-class letter as to make a local phone call in
many cities. Mail costs could only go up . . . while electronic costs
could only go down, relatively.

Giant companies began staking out claims in the communications direct marketing future . . . acquiring, going into joint
ventures with some, battling it out with others. Wall Street saw a
coming profit burst-out for communications firms in the right
situations. Satellite married cable, computers married TV. The
Post Office started keeping company with Western Union . . .
RCA . . . and Lord knows whom. By spring 1982, the Telephone
Company, banks, retailers, newspapers and cable TV stations

were angling for position to supply home computers or specially adapted TV sets with news, classified ads, stock quotes, theater listings . . . banking services and shopping for merchandise.

Predictions of the electronic mail order future go beyond what has been so far experimented with. "TV, as we know it today, will be a museum piece by 1985," says Alvin Toffler. Mort Goldstrom, of Viewtron Corp., predicts that by 1990 video information systems will account for $250 billion in retail sales (almost all by instant direct marketing) and $2 billion in advertising sales.

Electronic transfer will revolutionize mail order," says Stanley Marcus. "By 1986, every house will have a home entertainment room. It won't be uncommon for a family to spend $200 to $300 a month to buy services from entertainment to information to education," says Michael Dann, Consultant to ABC Video Enterprises.

Others say: Laser projection big picture TV, as good as movies—with four times the detail of today's TV and able to handle more words, bigger and more clearly (ideal for instant direct marketing) will be here before 1990.

Twenty million TV homes could have some form of teletex service broadcast to them and as many as 12 million could have some form of videotex via telephone wire or cable by 1990. Newspapers will drop reference sections such as stock market information. It will be instantly direct-marketed—often by newspapers . . . electronically. A new, international cable TV system will provide shopping at home . . . with products shipped to you from countries all over the world.

Advanced "hybrid" systems will come into existence in the mid-1980's and allow users to simply key in numbers on their TV keypad, which will be connected to an auto-dialer and phone line without interfering with normal telephone conversations. "Hybrid" systems will be a way for the major broadcasters—CBS, ABC and NBC—to provide teletext and teleshopping services to the roughly 50 million households which will not be wired for cable by 1990.

The mail order method will affect every medium. There's a fermentation of electronic and other application ideas among imaginative leaders in media and direct marketing. This new world seems hybrid everything with applications everywhere. It's yesterday's mail order and today's direct marketing transformed into tomorrow's instant measured marketing. When General Motors buys 7,000 video disc machines for dealers to close sales, it's the forerunner of countless dealers in anything, anywhere doing the same. It's instant direct marketing.

Video-disc catalog galleries with an array of machines can offer a choice of specialized catalogs . . . and offer more stock than the world's biggest store . . . for instant sale and later delivery.

Airports will be lined with data vending machines. Each will print out information on whatever subject . . . instantly charged to a credit card inserted. Other video disc machines in the airport will demonstrate any product. Insertion of credit card and pushing buttons will at once electronically transmit orders to ship and bill to the card holder.

The cost of producing and mailing a Sears Roebuck catalog is jumping upward and will continue to rise with inflation. In 1981, Sears put the entire contents of its 236-page summer catalog on video disc, a living catalog which included the modeling of sportswear and instructions on how to operate a sail plane. There were videotape sequences, stills, diagrams and text—and full color. Sears distributed 20,000 video-disc catalogs

in test markets where no print catalogs were offered—in nine Sears stores, and to 1,000 homes of which one-third were Sears customers. Results were secret, and if successful, projection could only come when sufficient homes have compatible video-disc players.

But Henry Johnson, Chairman of the Board of Spiegel, said that cost of production and distribution of video-disc catalogs could be less than the over one pound main catalogs of the big catalog houses. Mac Sroge says that by 1990, one out of three catalogs will be on video disc.

Dick Evans says that his company, EvaTone, will be able to put smaller catalogs and mailing pieces on light, flexible plastic video discs similar to the discs EvaTone has made over one billion of, to record everything from Time-Life sample recordings to Ronald Reagan campaign promotions.

The effectiveness and profitability of the video-disc catalog was still conjecture as it was for many intriguing new possibilities. Magazines tailored by computer and put together page by page, on computer-driven collating equipment were being tested. This could also mean custom catalogs according to customer lifestyle preferences. Some new developments would work. Others would not. But the continuing segmentation of communication and some kind of profitable use of it would accelerate. It is a revolution.

In all its forms, the throbbing pulse of instant direct marketing will be the barometer of business . . . infinitely more than mail order and direct marketing ever were. Just as the strategy, technique and methods of mail order created direct marketing, they will be the foundation of instant direct marketing and all world business.

The paper mills, the printing plants, the U.S. Postal Service, newspapers, magazines and TV stations will all have to join the revolution . . . or see themselves priced out of direct marketing, and then the business. Its ongoing growth can no more be resisted than, at previous times, the move to the suburbs, the shopping malls, air travel, computers or advertising itself. And its methods will be universally used.

Some say instant direct marketing will be dominated by giants. Others say its endless flexibility and opportunity will be too fast and varied for the big . . . and that leaner, stripped down, smaller ventures will take over from corporate dinosaurs. Alvin Toffler says that the U.S. will see an electronic version of cottage industries, with the entire family participating. My feeling is that amid the most sophisticated and complex applications of the mail order method, there will be simplest nooks and crannies for smallest entrepreneurs . . . and that for big and small it will be mail order's coming golden age. The technology and tactics of mail order keep changing but the strategy remains the same. It's still the art of zeroing in by trial and error and analysis.

Many shrewdest direct marketers still advise putting most effort into making money in mail order today with methods that are working today. Stan Rapp has one of the most creative minds in direct marketing and is chairman of the board of Rapp & Collins, an outstanding direct marketing agency. He is very future-minded but warns: "Don't be a futurholic."

By spring 1982, RCA had lost $183 million launching its video discs. Retailers had sold in 1981 only a third of the RCA disc players RCA expected. Japan's Pioneer Electronics is huge. It has a long record of success and the reputation of an aristocrat. It has always been determined to be ahead with the best. The quality of its video discs and video disc players has been widely praised.

But through 1982, sales were disappointing. Meanwhile, Pioneer had poured money into the project while others made big profits from video cassette recorders and tapes. Yet buyers of RCA video disc players had bought 30 discs each on average, three times as many as expected. RCA and Pioneer slashed player prices and went ahead.

Some experts stated that two-way electronic shopping might have a bright future but that by 1982 it was still minuscule in total sales . . . growing very slowly, with lots of bloody noses. Ted Turner has said that the rapid growth of cable could make newspapers as we know them disappear by 1990. Other experts predict that printed media will coexist with electronic for decades. International Resources Development Inc., predicts that during the 1980's "more than 90% of readers will continue with paper papers and use the electronic newspaper for greater depth information".

The U.S. General Accounting Office expects that electronic mail will be so universal by the 1990's as to cut post office personnel two-thirds. But when on January 4, 1982, the U.S. Postal Service started its electronic service, public response was dismal. At least 20 million letters or 385,000 a week had been estimated. The first ten weeks the average was 6,650 a week. Experts called it a surprising failure. Some said that too many rules and regulations had made it impractical for most users. The future was starting slowly yet still seemed inevitable.

"Pete" Hoke studies the mail order future constantly. He warns that some who had used the Cable TV Demonstration shopping shows have had miserable results. But he says: "It's not too early to consider if, how and when you fit into the information society . . . and to be thinking of yourself as an *information provider* to your customers and prospects."

My advice is: Be careful. Keep up with change. Work for a company that does. Use your common sense and thorough research. If experience then indicates that you don't belong in mail order, get out of it. If you are suited to mail order, my guess is that you'll be rather happy with The Mail Order Future.

Note: A quick glance over the following preparations for the mail order future may be of interest.

In June 1980, Ted Turner started his 24-hour Cable News Network . . . broadcast by satellite. In January 1982, he started a second cable news network. In March 1982, Westinghouse and ABC-TV jointly started two other TV cable news networks. Getty Oil, in 1980, launched its Entertainment and Sports Network. ESPN broadcasts 8,000 hours of sports a year by satellite via cable . . . 24 hours a day . . . including water polo, fencing and softball . . . for sports junkies.

By spring 1982, cable networks were being formed for many special interests. There was one for blacks, one for Spanish-Americans. There was one for senior citizens and one for Italian-Americans. Irish TV started on cable. There was a cable TV coupon distribution network and a 24-hour disco network. There was a business channel and a financial channel.

WFMT, Chicago—a classical music station—became the first radio "super station" on cable . . . was so desired, that many subscribed to cable TV just to get it. Businessmen's associations and unions began starting their own networks and planning more. A variety of religious cable TV networks started. There was an all-sports channel in New York City and another in Chicago—with just local sports.

Everybody wanted in. Westinghouse bought Teleprompter (for $646 million), a giant cable network, which also owned 50% of Showtime Entertainment, the second largest supplier of shows

to cable systems. Xerox acquired Western Union International. The New York Times purchased one of the largest cable systems in the country and organized a division to furnish programming to cable stations. The Hearst Corporation formed Hearst Cable to acquire cable systems.

In 1981, supplying video services became the biggest source of income for Time Inc. It owned Home Box Office, with seven million subscribers, the biggest pay TV system . . . and also American TV and Communications, the nation's largest operator of cable systems.

Between 1975 and 1982, the number of homes subscribing to basic cable, a signal-enhancing utility-like service, has increased 200%, to 21 million. Revenues more than doubled to $2 billion. Since 1977, the number of pay cable subscribers has increased by more than 16-fold and pay cable revenues multiplied 14 times to $1.2 billion in 1981. In 1981, RCA auctioned off for $90 million its satellite which it later launched (in January 1982).

In November 1981, the first national survey rated the popularity of pay and non-pay cable TV shows. Four of the cable movies that week got ratings of 30% or more of pay-cable homes. Cable TV attracted good audiences not only when movies were telecast, but all day and all night long.

By spring 1982, one out of three American homes were wired for cable. By 1983, cable is expected to pass 50 million homes, and some experts predicted 45% of American homes would have cable by 1985. A study, New Opportunities in Satellite/Cable TV Networks, predicted 100 basic cable networks by 1990 with revenues of $1.6 billion, one quarter of it to "super stations". An Ogilvy & Mather 1981 study predicted that by 1990 the standard TV networks will lose a third of the audience to cable TV.

But developments underway could increase such predictions. AT&T began discussing a joint venture "hybrid" system with cable systems . . . to transmit information by cable to the home from the central computer . . . and transmit back by telephone to the computer requests for information or responses to questions. This would be crucial for home video shopping. Hybrid systems were under development by CBS and AT&T to allow home viewers to place "teleshopping" orders by sending signals over their telephone. And more is happening to affect this.

AT&T made video data home tests in Albany, New York, and in Austin, Texas, as well as in Coral Gables, Florida, in cooperation with Knight-Ridder newspapers. By mid 1981, Ma Bell had spent over $20 million testing its Electronic Information Service, a computerized home retrieval system. By then AT&T had adopted videotex and teletex standards compatible with Canada's Telestar System. In 1980, AT&T's Dial-It service received 299 million calls in New York City alone. By 1982, it was launching and planning a myriad of Dial-It information services from sports to horoscopes—all marketed with an instant variety of the mail order method.

Bell Canada, in 1981, started a 2-year test of electronic yellow pages in Toronto, Montreal and Quebec using Telidon technology. Bell Canada and the Canadian Government tested VISTA which offered services on two-way TV, in one of the largest experiments in the world.

Burroughs was working on an intelligent telephone with a built-in printer, some type of display, magnetic memory and facsimile reader. General Telephone and Electronic Corp., the second largest telephone company, became the exclusve U.S. licensee for the British Post Office's Prestel system and began to sublicense it. GTE acquired Telenet which operated, for 500 corporate clients, a network to allow computers and computer terminals to communicate with each other, using a special technology. Telenet could do so regardless of varying speeds, software, protocols or formats—for terminals of all major makes. Telenet began to layer on top of its basic network service many applications from electronic mail to financial services to travel information and reservation services. Telenet launched "Telemail" to provide person-to-person communications by a variety of data terminals and word-processing equipment at about 40¢ to 80¢ a message.

GTE began to offer another service, Infovision, to the Washington Post and other newspapers on a franchised basis. A local newspaper can become an electronic yellow pages publisher. A GTE subsidiary, Jerrold Electronics, originated "Playcable", the electronic games service to cable subscribers.

Databank services became attractive to big companies. The Reader's Digest bought an 80% interest in The Source, whose founder called it the "information utility". It's a computer network that provided UPI news, stock market information, a restaurant guide, games and many other data programs to anybody with a terminal, usually a home computer.

Subscribers can send electronic mail to each other. They can "chat" via computer. Offers by direct mail or advertisements may be sent electronically, directly to the recipient, by computer. There's also "The Money Saver" computerized and comparative shopping service. Users are given a 20% to 30% discount on major appliances, TV sets, stereo and hi-fi equipment, cameras, furniture, watches, crystal, calculators, tires and power tools. The user orders by typing the make and model number desired in the computer terminal.

Comp-U-Card members have access to its computerized data bank. By presenting specifications, they get price quotations and delivery charges on more than 30,000 items. All models are current. Prices offer savings of 20 to 40 percent. Comp-U-Card receives a commission of 3 - 5%. It receives tens of thousand of phone calls a month.

In 1981, The Times-Mirror Satellite Programming Company (owned by the L.A. Times holding company) formed a joint venture with Comp-U-Card for a televised home shopping service. Warner Amex, in cooperation with Comp-U-Card, offers an electronic shopping service using in-house terminals via QUBE subscribers. By summer 1981, other electronic and cable services were in operation and being formed.

Comp-U-Serve is owned by H. & R. Block. A subscriber can call up news, financial information, computer games and even recipes. Thirteen newspapers with Comp-U-Serve are offering electronic editions to customers . . . including information on more than 32,000 stocks. Comp-U-Serve plans to add commodity news, energy information, entertainment reviews, sports standing and additional video games. Comp-U-Serve Inc.'s Micronet Service is aimed at the computer hobbyist. Customers can get data on travel, data and commodities.

Another company, Cable Text, offered highly specialized information services, much like a trade or professional magazine or newsletter, by satellite. It did so over 800 channels . . . via over 3,000 satellite disc earth stations to cable systems.

In spring 1982, Newsnet started transmitting (for a premium extra charge) 100 newsletters . . . to personal computers of subscribers. Soon they could be ordered, called up to the terminal, and billed electronically. The huge potential was indicated when an expensive daily newsletter, Platt's Oil Gram News began a Telex edition . . . for $2,900 annually, plus wire costs, a total of over $10,000 in some parts of Asia. Units of

McGraw-Hill Inc. and the Mead Corp., in 1981, began creating an electronic version of McGraw-Hill's 31 magazines from Business Week to Aviation Week and Space Technology to Chemical Week. The Wall Street Journal and Barron's in 1981, began to offer news, stock quotes, stock research and information to cable TV subscribers through a data retrieval network.

In 1980, Mead Corp. launched its Nexis news archives. It includes the Associated Press, UP, IP and Reuters; the Washington Post; the BBC summary of broadcasts; Newsweek; The Economist; U.S. News & World Report; and Dun's Review. McGraw-Hill bought Data Resources, Inc. Boeing, Chase Manhattan, Citicorp, Control Data and GE all went into computerized data banks. Dow Jones paid over 30 times earnings for National CSS, a computer services firm . . . to help sell on-line information Dow Jones already distributed by mail. CBS prepared electronic publishing experiments.

Tandy Corp.'s Radio Shack, Comp-U-Serve, a bank and United American Service Corp. started a joint venture to offer banking services, bookkeeping services and a "shopping list" of information via a Radio Shack TRS 80 color computer in each home. The Washington Post, Gannett Corp., Times-Mirror, The Dallas Morning News, all got into videotex experiments. AP News began working with QUBE. So did the Columbus Dispatch and the Norfolk (VA) Pilot and Ledger.

American Elsevier Publishers is Dutch owned. A subsidiary is Dutton, the book publisher. American Elsevier began putting a million pages of information into its data bank every year. Subscribers could get information on microfiche displayed on the terminal screen or as printed hard copy. The microfiche could be converted into a print out. A computer index for it all was available.

"The Computer Cookbook" is actually a listing of computer accessories and services for owners of personal computers. Bill Bates self-published it in 1979. His first mail order ad in computer magazines was a hit—selling a loose-leaf binder edition. Then he published it electronically. He says: "Every cost of traditional publishing is going up while costs of computers, word processors, satellite transmission and silicone chips are going down."

Other paperless books are being transmitted electronically without paper, printing or bindings. Book publishers began checking out back lists for material to put on video discs, in data banks, on microfiche and to furnish to computers and cable systems. Big publishers of non-fiction, particularly in educational and technical material, began to think about starting divisions or buying companies in electronic communications.

Houghton Mifflin scheduled for 1982 marketing a video disc called "How to View The Birds" to go along with its best-selling book, Roger Tony Peterson's "Field Guide To The Birds". In November 1981, an American Express publishing subsidiary announced a joint venture with Thorn EMI video programs to produce and distribute video books for cable, home video and TV.

Computer software publishing began to grow fast. It brought out simple strategic games like checkers and programs that allowed users to make budget forecasts and a lot more. Daniel Fylstra started with a ¼ page mail order ad in BYTE magazine. He offered programs for economics, chess and electronic watches on a TV screen. Then, with Peter Jennings, who had invented a program for chess, he introduced Micro-Chess which, in two years, grossed over $2 million.

The Gamemaster Corp. offered computer games people could play together . . . from their respective homes by interactive phone connection to Gamemaster's computer. Soon one player might be a computer. Some experts think that future video games will use video discs to give realistic scenery. Lasers can lock into any of the 54,000 frames in a disc and allow the scenes to be played in any order the viewer . . . or a computer . . . choose.

The Chilton Publishing Company, in 1981, began producing series of how-to-do-it programs on auto repair and other subjects for TV, cable, video tape and video disc. The same year two Hollywood firms, Home Theater and Video Associates, teamed up to publish a 250-volume home library of how-to subjects for videotape and video disc—from tennis to decorating. The first 30 cassettes were finished and the other 220 in various stages of development.

MIT has made a bicycle repair video disc with slow motion pictures, diagrams and drawings. Viewers may choose alternate ways to study and learn specific repair problems. Videofashion Quarterly is a new fashion magazine, a 90-minute videotape cassette featuring highlights of fashion shows in Rome and around the globe.

ABC went into a performing arts cable network with Warner-Amex . . . a joint venture for cable Sport Spectaculars with Getty Oil . . . a cable network of women's programming with Hearst . . . and a cable news network with Westinghouse Group W. ABC joined forces with the Shubert Organization and with Robert Altman to restage Broadway, Off-Broadway and regional productions for video distribution.

In January 1982, NBC with Rockefeller Center launched The Entertainment channel. MCA, Inc., bought the USA network, supplying sports and entertainment programming to over nine million cable viewers, from Time, Inc., and Paramount Pictures Corp. and then went into a cable joint venture with them. Charter Publishing set up a cable program division based on material from the Ladies Home Journal and Redbook.

Family Circle, owned by the New York Times, entered into a joint venture to supply material from its women's special publications for 65 half-hour cable shows. In 1982, Walt Disney Productions and Group W Satellite Communications organized a $100 million joint venture, the Disney Channel to begin broadcasting 16 hours a day of children's programs in 1983.

The American Teleshopping Network presented 60 items from the Neiman-Marcus catalog. The Shopping Channel became a video extension of Comp-U-Card. A Viewtron test for Knight newspaper and AT&T enabled viewers to summon a catalog text and pictures on a specially adjusted TV set. Satellite Syndicated Systems in Tulsa, Oklahoma, developed its TV Shopping Show.

American National Communications, Inc., joined with the Consumers Distributing Catalog in one test. A four-color catalog with 260 items in 72 pages was mailed to subscribers. Then the same items were demonstrated via TV. "Show Scan" is a method of "moving" the printed page on to the TV screen at very low cost. Southern Satellite Systems tested a show-scan catalog, a 30-minute program appearing 24 hours a day in three markets.

By January 1982, over 100 national advertisers had participated in the "Home Shopping Show" broadcast to over 530 cable systems by the Modern Satellite Network on cable TV. The first video store via cable . . . The Cable Store . . . opened in 1981 in Dallas, Texas, and carried items from seven to one thousand dollars. In November 1981, The Video Shopper went on cable TV using demonstrations on TV combined with a 48 page catalog as though a catalog showroom with Consumers Distributing.

Warner Amex Satellite Company announced that it was planning a home shopping channel. Cable companies started taking advertising inserts in their bills, making it possible to direct market an item via the bills and on cable to the same subscribers. The telephone companies began to race to cable TV companies with plans to introduce the new shopping services.

In March 1981, Cableshop was launched by J. Walter Thompson, second largest advertising agency. Cableshop went on the air in Peabody, Massachussets with four channels. One listed all commercials to be shown, which were three to seven phone in, give the key number of a demonstration commercial and have it telecast on one of the channels. By the time you are reading these words, some of these ventures will have been cancelled, aborted at the start, or later dropped. But many more will have more than replaced them. To survive, new electronic media must be profitable for direct response advertisers who may provide much of the income . . . which may be a mail order opportunity.

The Help Source Guide
And Index

The Help Source Guide

Imagine Harry and Me advertising our PEARS in Fortune!

OUT HERE on the ranch we don't pretend to know much about advertising, and maybe we're foolish spending the price of a tractor for this space; but my brother and I got an idea the other night, and we believe you folks who read Fortune are the kind of folks who'd like to know about it. So here's our story:

We have a beautiful orchard out here in the Rogue River Valley in Oregon, where the soil and the rain and the sun grow the finest pears in the world. We grow a good many varieties; but years ago we decided to specialize on Royal Riviera Pears, a rare, delicious variety originally imported from France, and borne commercially only by 20-year-old trees. And do you know where we sold our first crop—and the greater part of every crop since?

In Paris and London, where the finest hotels and restaurants know them to be the choicest delicacy they can serve to discriminating guests. And they serve them at about 75 cents each! Our Royal Riviera Pears went to other distinguished tables too—to the Czar of Russia and to the kings and queens and first families of Europe. We got a great kick out of wrapping big, luscious, blushing Royal Riviera Pears in tissue and knowing they were going to be served on golden plates and eaten with golden spoons.

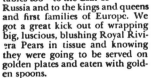

America's Rarest Fruit— Shall We Ship It Abroad?

But I'm getting away from my story. The idea that kept coming to Harry and me was this: Why must all this fruit go to Europe? Aren't there people right here in America who would appreciate such rare delicacies just as much as royalty? Wouldn't our first families like to know about these luscious, golden pears, rare as orchids, bursting with juice, and so big you eat them with a spoon? Wouldn't folks here at home like to give boxes of these rare pears to friends at Thanksgiving and Christmas?

So we made an experiment. We packed a few special boxes of these Royal Riviera Pears and took them down to some business friends in San Francisco. You should have seen their faces when they took their first taste of a Royal Riviera. They didn't know such fruit grew anywhere on earth.

Well, a banker wanted not only a box for home, but 50 boxes to be sent to business friends to arrive just before Christmas. A newspaper publisher wanted 40 for the same purpose, and a manufacturer asked for 25. And that gave us another idea. We sent 11 sample boxes to important executives in New York, and back came orders for 489 Christmas boxes for *their* friends.

A New Christmas Gift Idea

That seemed to indicate there were plenty of men looking for something new as a Christmas remembrance for friends who "have everything." The next year, orders came in for several thousand boxes of these rare pears, and you never read such letters as we got afterward—not only from the men who had *sent* the pears and made such a hit, but from folks who *received* them and wanted to know if they could buy more.

Well, that's how Harry and I got the idea that there must be *enough* discriminating people right here in the U. S. A. who'd like to do the same thing.

So we talked it over the other night and said, "Let's put an ad in Fortune—and see." We got a shock when we found what it would cost us to do it, but here we are—and *you* are going to be the judge.

Right now as I write this, it is late September, and out here in this beautiful valley our Royal Riviera Pears are hanging like great pendants from those 40-year-old trees. We'll have to watch them like new babies from now until picking time—not a leaf must touch them toward the last—trained men will pick them gently with gloved hands and lay them carefully in padded trays. They'll be individually wrapped in tissue, nestled in cushion packing, and sent in handsome gift boxes lithographed in colors, to reach you—or your friends—firm and beautiful, ready to ripen in *your* home to their full delicious flavor.

I envy you *your* first taste of a Royal Riviera—every spoonful dripping with sweet liquid sunshine. And you can just bet that every one who receives a box is going to have the surprise of his life.

We hope that right now you'll make up your list of business and social friends and let us send them each a box with your compliments. We'll put in an attractive gift card with your name written on it, and

we'll deliver anywhere in the United States proper, wherever there is an express office, express prepaid, to arrive on the date you name. And don't forget to include a box for yourself! A "Medium Family" box (10 pounds) is only $1.85. A "Large Family" box (double the quantity) is $2.95. At these low prices these pears cost a mere fraction of what you would pay for them in fine restaurants and hotels. And here's how sure we are you'll be delighted. If, after eating your first Royal Riviera, you and your friends don't say these are the finest pears you ever tasted, just return the balance at our expense and your money will come back in a hurry. Harry and I have agreed you are to be the final judge—*and we mean it*.

Just one more thing—there are far more folks reading Fortune than there will be boxes of Royal Riviera Pears this year. So, if you want to be sure to get some, we hope you'll send your order right along. We are putting a coupon down below, but a letter is just as good. Only, if you write, please say you saw this in Fortune.

HARRY and DAVID
Bear Creek Orchards, Medford, Oregon.

Bear Creek Orchards, Box 1201, Medford, Oregon.
Send Royal Riviera Pears to the list attached, all express charges prepaid, to arrive (date)........... Enclose a gift card bearing the following name

.... "Medium Family" boxes (10 pounds) at $1.85 each.
.... "Large Family" boxes (double quantity) at $2.95 each.

I enclose check (or money order) for $ ....

Name..
(YOUR name here—please PRINT plainly)

Street...

City............................ State...............

Prices outside } Honolulu, $2.25 and $3.20. Winnipeg, $2.40 and $3.65. Montreal, $2.70 and $4.05.
U.S.A. proper } Vancouver, $2.00 and $3.10. Toronto, $2.65 and $3.95. Quebec, $2.80 and $4.15.

The Custom Direct Marketing Course

*Where to get specific help
that goes far beyond this book . . .
for your exact situation*

For the very big, very tiny and those in between, there is a great deal of specific help available; for different kinds of mail order products and services; for virtually every phase of starting and conducting a mail order business; for the widest scope of situations and each stage of growth.

It has taken me and a small staff four years to find, list and describe what follows. Included is material suited for beginners, for the sophisticated . . . for moonlighters or established companies . . . to help in a career or a business . . . in the mail order business or to sell to or service those in mail order.

Experience is multiplied by the know-how of others. But it's important to avoid being swamped by material available. Therefore, I usually describe enough so that you can select only help practical and applicable to you. For the tiny I emphasize material that is free, costs least or can be borrowed from a library. For the big I emphasize help geared for them . . . at whatever cost, but suggest ways to save cost.

My suggestion is that newcomers familiarize themselves gradually with mail order. I point out first help for those considering a career and for anyone starting a tiny mail order business, and more sophisticated help to larger firms starting in a bigger way. As you start and succeed, more and more will apply. No one needs all the material or ever will. But those who use the most applicable will rise the fastest.

Even a small company with several people desiring self-education in mail order can use a considerable amount of help. One person can become company librarian and gradually assemble material for others and form a training program for beginners. Material can be rotated. Those people learning specialties in mail order can each get appropriate help. This system is helping our company grow and can help others.

Let's start with free help. Many have agreed to help readers of this book with material not generally available. And most who need information don't realize how much is available that is free. For instance, publishers of various newsletters are offering sample issues. These newsletters are very useful to those in mail order. The regular prices of the free copies add up to a number of times the cost of this book.

The caliber of what is available is often surprisingly good. Some free material is quite sophisticated, although most is simple and ideal for beginners.

Reference Section I
Free How-to Help

There's a lot of it available . . . from government, institutions, businesses . . . consultants and advertising agencies, publications . . . enough to keep you busy reading for some time.

There are pamphlets and issues of newsletters and magazines, and sometimes subscriptions. From those available I've selected and described well over a hundred amounting to several thousand pages. Some represent hundreds of dollars at normal prices. Yet the cost to produce these is only a small minority of the cost to print and mail to you, at no cost, all the material made available through this book.

There's a great deal of free government information helpful to any new tiny to small mail order business, and some from institutions. Businesses and trade associations tend to offer material helpful to start careers, progress in them . . . and for medium and larger businesses to start and build mail order divisions. I intermix descriptions of help from each.

Let's start with government help. I've looked through many hundreds of pages of government catalogs listing thousands of government publications, some entirely free and some at very little cost, which I'll describe later. I've selected some of each, helpful to mail order people. Let's begin with those of the Small Business Administration.

Management Aids,
Small Marketers Aids,
Small Business Bibliographies

These are published by the SBA to help small businesses start and grow. I have selected 40 of them. If you are in or starting a quite small mail order business, how would you like a brief overview of each of many general business problems involved? How would you like different authorities, each specializing in certain problems, to give you some quick, short answers to questions you may have on any of these problems?

Picture a faculty of over fifty professors to brief you on the essence of each problem. Imagine them from the graduate business schools of colleges and universities as well as those conducting business courses at these institutions . . . forced to explain with short, simple words . . . to avoid long and technical ones . . . to teach so that we can clearly understand - even if we didn't complete college or finish school, and even if we weren't at the top of the class.

The Small Business Administration has done all this. They publish short pamphlets which are free and longer booklets at nominal cost, on a wide variety of business subjects. I've selected those I consider useful for small mail order ventures. The authorities who researched and wrote the material for these booklets comprise a faculty of over 50 to help you.

Each booklet is brief, general and geared to the quite small. For those with sophisticated backgrounds, advanced education, and substantial experience, the value of these pamphlets and booklets is reduced. But for those less experienced, the pamphlets and nominal price booklets often are helpful. Together they comprise the equivalent of a substantial book useful for mail order moonlighters starting out. The following free booklets may interest you.

Thinking About Going Into Business?
33 questions most often asked are answered; useful for the very small. MA 2.025

Checklist for Going Into Business
Practical, common-sense; first steps covered. MA 2.016

Incorporating a Small Business
Spells out the details how to do it. MA 6.003

Learning About Your Market
Simple do-it-yourself research suggestions. MA 4.019

Finding a New Product for Your Company
Asks you 3 questions about products you might consider. Your answers help guide you. Suggests sources, books to help. Can prod your thinking. MA 2.006

Handicrafts

There are many booklets on specific kinds of businesses, including handicrafts. Many successful mail order businesses started from a craft hobby. Here's a bibliography of books on a variety of crafts as a business (perhaps including several on your hobby). Warning! In recent years crafts have often not done as well in mail order as they did earlier. SBB 1.

Marketing Checklist
It's for small retailers but equally useful for small mail order firms. You're asked to check yes or no to 156 questions. You can answer fairly quickly, but must think as you do. By the time you're finished, you'll have some idea how to better organize (or reorganize) your business. MA 4.012

Pricing Checklist
For small retailers but helpful to small mail order firms. Caution! Margin for retailer is usually far smaller. MA 4.013

Simple Break-Even Analysis
It's for small stores, but useful for new, small mail order firm. MA 1.019

Planning and Goal Setting for Small Business
An overview of the famous "Management by Objectives" plan, adapted to the smallest business. MA 2.010

Checklist for Profit Watching
Important for the tiniest firm to help judge overall financial results for a period. MA 1.018

Analyze Your Records to Reduce Costs
Important for tiny ventures in first years. MA 1.011

Preventing Embezzlement
Practical advice. MA 3.009

Sound Cash Management and Borrowing
Good to read the day you start a tiny mail order business. That's when going broke starts if on the wrong financial foot. MA 1.016

Steps in Meeting Your Tax Obligations
Not taking them is why many small mail order firms go bankrupt. This booklet was written for small retailers, but is equally important for anyone starting a small mail order venture. MA 1.013.

The ABC's of Borrowing
What you have to do to qualify for a business loan. MA 1.001

Delegating Work and Responsibility
Important when a small successful mail order business starts to expand. MA 3.001

Data Processing for Small Business
Helpful bibliography suggestion! Show to your reference librarian and ask for latest similar books. SBB 80

Others of the 40 booklets I suggest you consider are the following:

Management Aids (MA's)

A Venture Capital Primer for Small Business	MA 1.009
Attacking Business Decision Problems with Breakeven Analysis	MA 1.008
Basic Budgets for Profit Planning	MA 1.004
Business Plan for Small Manufacturers	MA 2.007
Can You Make Money With Your Idea or Invention?	MA 2.013
Can You Use a Mini-Computer?	MA 2.015
Introduction to Patents	MA 6.005
Management Checklist for a Family Business	MA 3.002
Pointers on Using Temporary Help Service	MA 5.004
Problems in Managing a Family-Owned Business	MA 2.004
Selecting the Legal Structure for Your Business	MA 6.004
Techniques of Time Management	MA 3.003
What is the Best Selling Price?	MA 1.002

Small Marketer's Aids (SMA's)

Keeping Records in Small Business	MA 1.017

Small Business Bibliographies

Home Businesses	SBB 2
Marketing Research Procedures	SBB 9
Inventory Management	SBB 75
National Directory for Use in Marketing	SBB 13
Financial Management	SBB 87
Selling by Mail Order	SBB 3
New Product Development	SBB 90

There are many other free booklets and many longer specialized booklets available for very little cost. Some on new subjects are constantly being researched, written and published. Some are being updated. Remember, individual pamphlets and booklets may be out of stock. Some are occasionally dropped when out of date.

To get any of the free booklets described, the latest list available and the latest price list of for sale SBA publications, write to: *U.S. Small Business Administration, P.O. Box 15434, Fort Worth, Texas 76119.*

If you want to investigate government help other than information, the following may interest you:

Directory of State Small Business Programs
This 52-page book is published by the U.S. Small Business Administration and lists aid and loan programs of small agencies of each state which operates such programs, including those for minorities and women. Before you apply for a loan, caution! Successes in mail order as a result of such borrowing are very few. Cases of a lifetime debt far outnumber them. For book write: *Office of Advocacy, U.S. Small Business Administration, 1441 "L" Street, N.W. Washington, D.C. 20416; (202) 655-4000.*

My advice is: Risk money you can afford to lose when starting a mail order business or get a risk-taking partner, but don't risk borrowed money. Borrow to project success. Start to acquire know-how to reduce starting risk. Take all know-how help with a grain of salt. Add common sense.

The government provides know-how help to new entrepreneurs because new small and growing businesses traditionally provide increased employment. Others offer help for other reasons: To sell still more know-how; to gain new customers and help customers grow; to gain good will from future customers; to increase the pool of talent to hire from; or because they like to; or want to repay for help received when they started out.

My effort is to describe the help so that readers can be selective in sending for it, saving time for themselves and expense for those supplying booklets. Sending for information quite unnecessary or impractical for the situation helps no-one. Do me a favor and be selective!

If you consider starting a mail order business, the following may be helpful:

Checklist for Starting A Successful Business
48 pages; by Joseph Mancuso. Write to: *The Center for Entrepreneurial Management, 83 Spring Street, New York, NY 10012; (212) 925-7304.*

Entrepreneurship Aptitude Test
A simple 16-question test to point out strengths and weaknesses that can contribute to success or failure in a new business enterprise; developed by a non-profit organization. Write: *The Entrepreneurship Institute, 3592 Corporate Drive, Suite 100, Columbus, OH 43229; (614) 895-1153.*

Here's some advice for the small, and some for the big, starting a mail order venture.

Sales by Mailmanship
A very brief overview for mail order beginners from home; selecting items, selecting an advertising agency; preparing a shopping column ad. Write: *House & Garden Magazine, Shopping Around Dept., 350 Madison Avenue, New York, NY 10017; (212) 880-8800.*

How to Select A New Direct Marketing Venture
Written for sophisticated, larger firms, not moonlighters, by Frank Vos, founder of a top direct response advertising agency. The Frank Vos Co., Inc., 475 Park Avenue South, NYC, NY 10016; (212) 684-7600.

Your Corporation's Good Name
Possible perils, problems, surprises in choosing and clearing the name of your corporation or subsidiary. Very useful. Write: *CT Corporation System, 1633 Broadway, NYC, NY 10019; (212) 664-1666.*

If you want to patent an invention or register a trademark, there's free government information to help you. Here are booklets from the Patent and Trademark Office.

Questions and Answers about Trademarks
What a trademark is, what it does, how to establish trademark rights; who may own one, how to file, how to search already registered marks; assignments, foreign applications.

Questions and Answers about Patents
What a patent is, how long it lasts, extension; what can be patented, "patent pending" and "patent applied for"; how to apply, prepare application, models; confidentiality of applications; when to apply, effect of previous publicizing in print; joint invention, employer application, transfer of rights; patent search, reviewing existing patents; infringement, patent protection in foreign countries.

"Disclosure Document Program" of U.S. Patent and Trademark Office
A service for inventors. How to provide evidence of conception of an invention.

For any or all of the above, write: *U.S. Department of Commerce, Patent and Trademark Office, Washington, D.C. 20231.*

If you're interested in a career (or already work) in direct marketing, what others earn in it may concern you.

National Salary Guide
A head hunter's survey of what direct marketing jobs pay; includes ranges for 18 specialties, from creative to marketing fulfillment. Write: *Crandall Associates, Inc., 501 Fifth Avenue, NYC, NY 10017; (212) 687-2550.*

If your company has salesmen and wants to use direct marketing methods to get more out of them, this leaflet may help:

How To Improve Sales Force Productivity
How to use direct mail to search for and find qualified, interested prospects more easily at lower cost and more effectively than a salesperson can; how to up the quality of returns, how to increase quantity. Write: *Yeck Brothers Company, 2222 Arbor Boulevard, Dayton, OH 45401; (513) 294-4220*

If your company considers going into mail order, the first step is to research people's attitudes toward mail order, who buys what by mail, when and why. The following might help:

Parade Mail Order Survey
In six cities 2,000 subscribers to Sunday newspapers carrying *Parade* Magazine were surveyed. They were asked how many bought by mail; average frequency, most spent for a single purchase; how many bought from catalogs . . . magazines . . . Sunday newspaper magazines; frequency of mail purchase via Parade.

Customers were asked why they bought; what in the ads read convinced them to send in a coupon. Factors considered very important were ranked by men and women. Kinds of products they were most interested in buying by mail were ranked . . . by age groups . . . by men and by women . . . by education . . . by income. Readers ranked the kinds of books they were most interested in buying by mail. Those disappointed in mail order purchases ranked principal reasons why.

It is important to mail order people from moonlighter to Fortune 500 . . . from executive trainees to top officers . . . in companies and advertising agencies. Write: *A. R. Pironti, Parade Publications Inc., 750 Third Avenue, NYC, NY 10017; (212) 573-7000.*

Information From Better Homes and Gardens Consumer Panel
The panel was asked detailed questions about mail order buying. Answers received and preferences determined concern the following: Percentage who bought by mail from catalogs; repeated from same catalog; reasons they liked to buy by mail, ranked; the reasons (ranked) they bought specific items from specific ads. Quite interesting is the percentage which preferred to buy from a firm with a post office box number vs. from one with a street address; also the percentage which preferred that shipping charges be stated separately vs. all-in-one price; the percentage which preferred to tear out a pre-printed post card bound into a magazine vs. cutting out and filling out a coupon . . . vs. calling a toll-free 800 phone number . . . vs. using a postage-paid return envelope; and which of eight kinds of books on home improvement they'd be most likely to buy, by percentage . . . ranked.

This is all a small part of the panel's answers, useful to anyone in mail order. Write: *Better Homes and Gardens, Locust at 17th Street, Des Moines, IA 50336; (515) 284-3000.*

These two studies are excellent. Other fine research reports are continually made by publications, broadcasters, associations and business firms and obtainable without charge.

A newsletter which can give you a feel for mail order customer reactions is the following:

Direct Line Report
Special issue! What mail order buffs who read Direct Magazine think, buy, look for; why they buy by mail; their complaints, attitudes; reactions to claims. For sample issue write: *Direct Line Report, 60 East 42nd Street, Room 1825, NYC, NY 10165; (212) 883-1995.*

Once you go into the mail order business, matters concern you that did not before, such as people moving.

Population Mobility: Its Impact on Direct Response Marketing
If you mail or consider mailing to any list, this booklet is important to read. Write: *Market Compilation and Research Bureau, Inc., 11633 Victory Boulevard, N. Hollywood, CA 91609; (213) 877-5384.*

Sometimes a very useful free summary is taken from a detailed study, available at a charge, often a big one. The following summary is helpful for anyone considering or already in a catalog business:

The Future of Catalogs
Marketing and production; free highlights of $7,500 study which is based on telephone and face to face contacts and mail survey of catalog users. Physical characteristics of 1,600 actual sample catalogs collected have been tallied. *Printing Industries of America, Inc., 1730 North Lynn Street, Arlington, VA 22209; (703) 841-8168.*

Today there's increasing opportunity in specialized mail order products to specialized groups. There's a great deal of research on segmentation of lists to reach those especially desirable to sell a specific product or service. One form of fascinating research is on segmentation to reach different ethnic groups. If you have an ethnic product or service, this can help.

All Americans
They have a dual heritage, each belongs to a separate ethnic group. Booklet gives historical coverage of the evolution of family names; explains how ethnically segmented marketing to a narrow universe can help make offers more responsive; cites successes doing so; how it helps politicians, political parties, schools and clubs to promote more effectively; benefits cultural events, lecture tours, membership drives, religious organizations and travel promotions . . . and maybe can help you.

Excellent, highly interesting. Write: *Consumers Marketing Research Inc., 600 Huyler Street, South Hackensack, NJ 07606; (201) 440-8900 and (212) 697-1257.*

An invaluable source of research data to largest and most sophisticated direct marketers is the Bureau of Census. Shortly I'll describe and list some of its for sale material. But the following are free:

Census, Surveys, Measuring America
A brief overview of programs; 12 pages. Write: *Customer Services DUSD, Bureau of the Census, Washington, D.C. 20233; (301) 763-4100.*

Catalog of Training Activities
Bureau of the Census, 1981. Dates, location, details and application blanks for Bureau-sponsored data user workshops, seminars and courses. Write: *Customer Services DUSD, Bureau of the Census, Washington, D.C. 20233; (301) 763-4100.*

Telephone Contacts-for Data-Users
4 pages listing names and telephone numbers of subject specialists of the Census Bureau in the demographic and economic field. Write: *Customer Services DUSD, Bureau of the Census, Washington, D.C. 20233; (301) 763-4100.*

National Clearinghouse for Census Data Services
A referral service for data users; address book of organizations offering specialized assistance in obtaining and using statistical data and related products prepared by the Census Bureau: Lists, names, addresses, phone numbers of data user services, officers in Census Bureau regional offices; also lists, training programs, seminars, and conferences in accessing and/or using census data; for the sophisticated mail order user of census data. Write: *Customer Services DUSD, Bureau of the Census, Washington, D.C. 20233; (301) 763-4100.*

Many countries have trade offices in New York, Chicago or Los Angeles. Most have consulates in one or more key U.S. cities. The consulates can refer you to trade offices which often have useful printed material at no cost . . . lists and descriptions of trade fairs, notices of exhibitions in the U.S. or products from their countries, addresses of publications describing items. Some publish pamphlets, catalogs, magazines or newsletters describing products. The following are several excellent publications. There are many others, simpler and briefer in most cases, but quite useful, and free post-paid.

Asian Sources
An issue of this big glossy monthly magazine is close to 300 pages. Different issues feature different fields of products primarily from Hong Kong, Taiwan and Korea. Issues may feature toys and sporting goods, gifts and home products, electric kitchen appliances and notions, other fields. For free sample issue write: *Subscription Department, Trade Media Ltd., P.O. Box 1786, Kowloon Central, Hong Kong.*

China Sources
Over 40 pages, many in color; monthly magazine showing the gamut of goods available from Mainland China. Embroidery, leather suitcases, wool blankets, calculators, leather footware, carpets, silk ties, stuffed toy animals, towels, clothing luggage and more. For sample copy write: *China Sources, P.O. Box 4436, Kowloon Central, Hong Kong. 5-795-2733.*

Hong Kong Enterprise
Monthly catalog magazine of toys, housewares, gifts, technical products; full color product pictures; descriptions. Write: *Hong Kong Trade Development Council, 548 5th Avenue, NYC, NY 10036; (212) 582-6610.*

Hong Kong Toys
Annual toy magazine; write: *Hong Kong Trade Development Council, 548 Fifth Avenue, NYC, NY 10036; (212) 582-6610.*

Taiwan's Trade Winds
A jumbo-sized business journal. In a typical issue there are over 300 ads which describe over a thousand items. Articles report on new products, expanding companies, new fields of products, much more.

It features sporting goods and toys, housewares and costume jewelry; stationery and furniture, leather and plastic items, luggage, ceramics, notions. Items are simple and low cost. You can get a good idea of what Taiwan makes best and whether a specific product you design in the U.S. can be made there. Quality is improving. Manufacturers can make entire products or components. To get occasional issues free, write on your business stationery to: *Taiwan's Trade Winds, P.O. Box 7-179, Taipei, Taiwan, R.O.C. (02) 3932718.*

If you import products you need to know before you buy the landed cost in the U.S. Information is available from shipping companies on boat, plane, truck and rail costs . . . and from forwarding agents and custom brokers on their charges. Later I'll list books and magazines to help. But for free information on customs the U.S. Government will help.

The smallest mail order business which imports anything directly needs to be familiar with how to deal with the U.S. Customs Service, as does the smallest business elsewhere in the world exporting to a mail order firm in the U.S. Here are two publications I suggest you read:

United States Import Requirements
How to file a customs entry, in-bond shipments, warehouse entries; special customs invoices, bills of lading, machines; restricted merchandise, prohibited imports; U.S. Government Printing Office 0-775-520. Write: *Bureau of Customs, Washington, D.C. 20226.*

Customs Rulings on Imports
This 14-paragraph fact sheet explains classifications, how to obtain a ruling. GPO-960-357. Write: *U.S. Customs Service, Dept. of Treasury, Washington, D.C. 20229.*

The IRS wants to help you, too. I suggest small mail order firms consider:

Tax Guide for Small Business
Write: *Internal Revenue Service, P.O. Box 25866, Richmond, VA 23260;* telephone: Publications Division (202) 488-3100.

After investigating items, you'll want to research service sources. Biggest companies as well as smallest entrepreneurs want to avoid staff expenses to start. Lettershops, computer service bureaus and fulfillment houses simplify going into mail order and cut down overhead risk. Knowing whom to turn to becomes important. You seek services which work effectively for others in mail order. Just glancing through Direct Marketing, ZIP and DM News will find advertisements and editorial mention of many. The following are booklets which can help, particularly medium to larger firms.

Source Guide
"Classified Source Guide" reprinted in booklet form. *ZIP Magazine, 545 Madison Avenue, New York, NY 10022; (212) 371-4100.*

MASA Membership Directory
A purchasing guide to mail advertising services; the membership roster of the Mail Advertising Service Associations, MASA. Members are lettershops, usually the best in each area, performing any of these many functions: Addressing, list maintainance, labelling; art and copy, data processing, computer letters; machine inserting; offset printing; list compiling and brokerage; packaging and shipping; secretarial and phone answering.

For each lettershop listed, its sales volume, the names of its principle officers and even the year it joined MASA is shown. Keyed letters indicate which service it performs. Very useful as soon as you mail your first list. Write: *MASA, 7315 Wisconsin Avenue, Suite 818E, Washington, D.C. 20014; (301) 654-7030.*

Post Office Directives/Titles, Publication Number, and Last Date of Issue
The U.S. Postal Service has many publications helpful for those in mail order. Most numerous are free pamphlets called "Directives". My favorite "Directive," and vital to all postmen, is one on how to avoid and what to do about dog bites. I've tried to select some of equivalent importance to anyone in mail order concerned with the Post Office. They are listed as follows:

A "Bottom Line" Estimate of Your Presort Savings. Pb 231. 6/81.

Addressing for Optical Character Recognition. Nt 165. 6/81.

Business Reply Mail, Regulations, Applications, Annual Renewal. Pb 115. 1/81.

Central Mail Delivery. Nt 69. 8/81.

Computer Programming for Presort. Pb 232. 6/81.

Domestic Postage Rates, Fees, and Information. Nt 59. 11/81.

First-Class, Third-Class, and Fourth-Class Bulk Mailings. Pb 113. 12/81.

How to Order Stamped Envelopes. Nt 18. 1/82.

Information Guide on Presorted First-Class Mail. Pb 61. 6/81.

International Postage Rates and Fees. Pb 51. 3/81.

Mailer's Guide: Update of 1980 Issue. '82.

Managing Mail Preparation. Pb 72. 8/80.

Metered Better, Treated Better. Nt 125. 10/81.

Modern Mailroom Practices. Pb 62. 2/81.

Packaging for Mailing. Pb 2. 5/78.

Packaging Pointers. 227. 10/78.

Plant Quarantines. 14. 4/81.

Postal Inspectors Protect Consumers. Pb 250. 1/80.

Presort First-Class Mail. Pb 230. 6/81.

Presort First-Class Mail Case History (Georgia State Bank). Pb 249C. 1/81.

Saving Dollars Through Plant Loading. Nt 27. 5/71.

What are the New Letter Mail Dimensional Standards. Pb 84. 5/79.

ZIP + 4: Sample Computer Tapes (Program Instructions for Customers). Pb 261. 3/81.

The Expanded ZIP Code. Nt 166. 9/80.

ZIP + 4: The Expanded ZIP Code. Nt 185. 3/81.

ZIP + 4: What's in it for Business and Government. Nt 186. 4/81.

ZIP + 4: Facts Consumers Should Know. Nt 187. 3/81.

Request copies of *free directives* from your local postmaster. If not in stock, ask him to send for it. Only if local request is negative, write to:

U. S. POSTAL SERVICE
Documents Control Division
Attention: Ms. Boudreau, Room 5330
475 L'Enfant Plaza S.W.
Washington, D.C. 20260
Telephone: 202-245-5550

Booklets constantly come out with advice to operate a mail order business, some for the small and some for the big and in between. The following are helpful. Many more are available.

99 Direct Response Offers That Can Improve Results
7-page reprint of article in Direct Marketing Magazine. Write: *James Kobs, President, Kobs & Brady Advertising Inc., 625 North Michigan Avenue, Chicago, IL 60611; (312) 944-3500.*

Profit Management in Direct Marketing
Media selection, control, house list segmentation; financial management, entire business plans. Write: *Al Migliaro Sr., 15A-1919 Sandy Hill Rd., Norristown, PA 19401; (215) 275-3829.*

Profitable Response

Guy Yolton; a top direct marketing consultant who teaches direct marketing to attendees of the DMMA Basic Seminars, gives a mini-seminar in booklet form for use of direct marketers. This little booklet has helped Yolton clients, helped Yolton get clients and can help you. Write: *Guy L. Yolton Advertising, Inc., 6073 Arlington Blvd., Falls Church, VA 22044; (703) 237-8550.*

Great Expectations

How to calculate potential mail order profit; order margin analysis form included; useful. Write: *Shell Alpert Direct Marketing, 444 Lakeview Court, Langhorne, PA 19047; (215) 752-3433.*

Do's and Don'ts for Direct Marketers

29 tips. *Saxton Communications Group, Ltd., 605 Third Avenue, NYC, NY 10158; (212) 953-1300.*

Response Strategies

10 issues of Consultant Shell Alpert's column in ZIP magazine; in question and answer form. Write: *Shell Alpert Direct Marketing, 444 Lakeview Court, Langhorne, PA 19047; (215) 752-3433.*

Catalog Advisor

An excellent help to the new and small in mail order considering or starting a catalog business. It takes up: advantageous catalog sizes; self-cover vs. separate cover; gives 22 copy and production tips; tells how to prepare camera-ready copy, prepare your catalog yourself; how to work with photographers; outlines job procedures, explains paper stock and weights; gives do's and don'ts; details 12 printing factors which must affect the printing time table. Write: *Vividize Inc., 23 Campbell Drive, Dix Hills, NY 11746* or: *4446 E. Cortez, Phoenix, AZ 85028. 1-800-645-5522; in NYS 212-895-5122.*

The Catalog Marketer

For the medium to large firm; creating, producing and mailing profitable catalogs. A tight, well written newsletter: News, creative ideas, new items; production and list selection suggestions, decision making analysis; questions and answers; how-to tips. For sample issue write: *The Catalog Marketer, Maxwell Sroge Publishing Inc., 731 N. Cascade Avenue, Colorado Springs, CO 80903; (303) 633-5556.*

Shortly I'll list in my sections on low-cost booklets and on articles and tapes considerable information on creating effective mail order advertising as well as guidelines on ethics or government rules and regulations concerning mail order copy. But larger mail order advertisers will find it particularly useful to get information from the Federal Trade Commission. For them the following is recommended although perhaps involving too much detail for smaller ventures to study.

FTC News Summary

Keeps you in touch with FTC regulatory activity. It can quickly clarify for anyone in mail order much about the interpretation, regulations and penalties for infractions of laws and regulations which concern direct marketing. Free subscription: Federal Trade Commission, Publications, Washington, D.C. 20580; (202) 523-3598.

FTC Regulations

Full copy. U.S. Code of Federal Regulations, Title 16 - Commercial Practices - Chapter I and II: Office of the Federal Register, National Archives of Records, General Service Administration, U.S. Government Printing Office, Washington, D.C. 20036.

Postal Inspection Service—Law Enforcement Report— Quarterly Post Office Report

What the Post Office does to mail order offenders; what it views as violation of Post Office fraud laws and regulations. For free subscription write: *Chief Postal Inspector, U.S. Postal Inspection Service, Washington, D.C. 20260,*—on business letterhead; identify potential business use of report.

The smallest mail order entrepreneur should know the laws and regulations that affect the tiniest ads and transactions. Shortly I'll suggest articles and tapes to help. The following booklet explains what the mail order consumer is generally considered entitled to in buying.

Shopping by Mail

Protection for the buyer in mail order transactions (3 pages). Write: *Consumer Information Center, Pueblo, CO 81009.*

Two booklets concerning copy writing are:

Copywriter and Designer Checklist

For a copy, write: *Pierre Passavant, P.O. Box 1206, Middletown CT 06457.*

Direct Response Marketing

A brief booklet and ten-point checklist to aid in creating direct mail copy, by a Hoge Alumnus and president of the Direct Marketing Club of Kansas City, William Steinhardt. Write to: *Steinhardt Direct, P.O. Box 7046, Shawnee Mission, KS 66207; (913) 648-2911.*

Mail order people dream of paying for advertising in top media on a per inquiry or per sale basis. Here's such an opportunity.

Parade Information Center

Free Letter, Parade Information Center editorial page, list of newspapers carrying Parade Sunday Magazine (over 20 million circulation) and application for listing of your catalog, descriptive brochure or booklet or product description. You pay per inquiry or per order. Caution! You get bingo card computer inquiries, as many as over 20,000 for one free booklet. Small ventures with no experience in how such inquiries will convert to sales are advised to use copy for an outright sale. Response is usually in the hundreds but with sure profit per order. Write: *Kathleen Ryan, Manager Direct Marketing Services, Parade Publications Inc., 750 Third Avenue, NYC, NY 10017.*

Shortly I'll describe information available (paid) on media selection. Most publications will send you free a media kit with a sample issue, circulation and rate information, often research as to the kind of readers reached, and sometimes mail order success stories of advertisers.

Almost every list company will send you, at no cost, a catalog of lists with list rental costs, characteristics and sometimes success stories of use by mail order firms. Included in some catalogs is a great deal of information on list selection, direct mail use and receiving rental income from your own lists. The following report can help.

Survey of Mailers

Conducted by Harvey Research Organization for SRDS. The study involved 38 brokers and advertising agencies and 69 list users. It concerns the extent of list testing, criteria for list selection, seasonality of testing programs; the nature of the relationships between the mailer, the list broker and the list manager in test list selection; criteria for retesting marginally successful tests. For copy of complete study report write: *Standard Rate and Data Service, Inc., Promotion Department, 5201 Old Orchard Road, Skokie, IL 60077; (312) 470-3100.*

The following are excellent:

Scriptomatic Guide to Better Direct Mail
Planning, list compilations and rental, design and printing of direct mail; addressing and mailing systems. Write: *Scriptomatic, Inc., 2030 Upland Way, Philadelphia, PA 19131; (215) 878-9600.*

Dun's Direct Mail Marketing Guide
18 different ways to use direct mail; 8-point professional checklist to follow in developing successful direct mail campaigns; how to select lists, analyze customer accounts; creative advice. *Dun's Marketing Services, Three Century Drive, Parsippany, NY 07054; (800) 526-0665; in New Jersey (800) 452-9772.*

Direct Mail Tips
Four useful flash reports: "The 10 Commandments of Printing Economy"; "Computer Personalization for Smaller Users"; "Common Printing Terms"; "Postal Rules through the Years". For all four write: *Federal Letter Co., 1910 Walnut Street, P.O. Box 1667, Kansas City, MO 64141; (816) 421-5164.*

The following excellent newsletters will send sample issues:

Immediate Release
The superb newsletter by the intellectual of lists, Rose Harper; every issue informs, teaches, delights anyone using direct mail. For free issue write: *The Kleid Co., 200 Park Avenue, New York, NY 10166; (212) 599-4140.* An outstanding issue is April 1982 ... Seasonality Study/Update #6 ... telling when to mail.

How to Use Mailing List Selections
Very useful for all sizes of mail order firms using direct mail. Prepared by one of the biggest. Simple, clear, important. Write: *Doubleday Mailing Lists, 501 Franklin Avenue, Garden City, NY 11530; (516) 294-4065.*

List Insights
Newsletter—deals with list analysis, qualification of prospects, tape layout formula, list testing, dummy names, etc. Receive sample issue by writing on your company letterhead to: *Ted Malek, President, Prescott Lists, 17 East 26th Street, NYC, NY 10010; (212) 684-7000.*

Non-Store Marketing Report
Maxwell Sroge pioneered Fortune 500 mail order ... publishes studies in depth on different mail order fields and yearly growth estimates. The research is drawn on in this twice weekly newsletter for the big, but useful to any. Well written. For sample issue write: *Maxwell Sroge Publishing Inc., 731 North Cascade Avenue, Colorado Springs, CO 80903; (303) 633-5556.*

Dependable's List Marketing Letter
Special issue! List brokers/list managers/compilers; who does what for you? And which do you need—and when? If you select names from various lists and merge/purge to eliminate duplicates, should you pay for all names rented, those you use after eliminating duplicates, or how many? When certain technological innovations and computer applications can save money and when they cost more than they're worth; when and how best to save money exchanging lists; some cautions. For sample issue contact: *Dependable Lists Inc., 257 Park Avenue South, NYC, NY 10010; (212) 677-6760.*

In Seminar II, Chapter 11 is the story of **DM News** which will send anyone a sample issue who writes on their business letterhead or encloses a business card, to: *DM NEWS, 19 West 21st Street, New York, NY 10010; (212) 741-2095.*

Why Mail Promotion Works When Selling to Business
Cites readership studies, results of an IBM survey, results of an NCR survey; explains simply how direct mail can be used by business firms. Write to: *Yeck Brothers Company, 2222 Arbor Blvd., Dayton, OH 45439; (513) 294-4000.*

Bulk Mail Postage Table
For the giants. Shows latest postage costs for mail drops between one and ten million pieces. Designed to project postage-check budget and plan the amount to be deposited for third-class permit accounts: *MCRB, 11633 Victory Boulevard, North Hollywood, CA 91609; (213) 877-5384.*

Business Mail is Different
ABC's how to assist in process of selling by sales person, distributor, dealer. *Yeck Brothers Inc., 2222 Arbor Blvd., Dayton, OH 45439; (513) 294-4000.*

When Should We Mail
Outlines the best months to mail offers; business, industrial, financial; entertainment, education, fund raising; other types. Also a guide for judging response rates by month. *Dufford Marketing, 707 Wilshire Blvd., Suite 3800, Los Angeles, CA 90017; (213) 621-1400.*

Instant Direct Mail Data
On one 8½" x 11" page: Estimated Third Class pre-sort discounts for 100,000 and up mailings; how to calculate them; useful estimator. On other side, approximate household count by state/SCF. *Wiland & Associates Inc., 1101 International Parkway, Fredericksburg, VA 22401.*

Syndicated Mailings
How to use them for your mailing list (for owners of larger lists); brochure explains what syndication is; advantages for list owner, syndicator; how merchandise is handled; typical syndication items; how to get started. Second brochure defines "Free Ride" inserts, who can use them, cost comparative results vs. solo mailings. Write: *Spectra Marketing, 600 Third Avenue, NYC, NY 10016; (212) 986-4220.*

Computing Probabilities
How to estimate future mail counts from results to date. Write: *Alan Drey Co., Inc., 333 North Michigan Avenue, Chicago, IL 60601; (312) 346-7453.*

Third Class Deliverability Study
By Doubleday Publishing Company: Report shows that the Postal Service was wrong on 82% of the mail it returned as "Undeliverable." Doubleday remailed 1948 "Undeliverable" first class. Only 18% proved undeliverable. For copy write: *Jon Mulford, Director of Postal and Regulatory Affairs, Doubleday & Co., Inc., 501 Franklin Avenue, Garden City, NY 11530.*

Mail Order in Japan
The April 15, 1981 DM News has an excellent abstract of a 256-page report, "Market Analysis of the Japanese Direct Response Industry." Estimate of mail order sales in Japan are shown by years, broken down into six classifications. The report covers customer attitudes, response rates, credit selling, newspaper characteristics. For reprint, list of topics researched and more information on study, write or phone: *Japan-America Direct Response Group, 201 East 28th Street, NYC, NY 10016; (212) 683-2754.*

Use of Checks in Direct Mail Solicitation
Bulletin #80.4. *Shell Alpert Direct Marketing, 444 Lakeview Court, Langhorne, PA 19047; (215) 752-3433.*

Virgil D. Angerman is one of the most respected direct mail consultants in the U.S. (and has a world-wide reputation). For Boise Cascade Envelope Division he has written seven much praised bulletins (from 1 to 8 pages each). To obtain, write on business letterhead or enclose a business card. *Boise Cascade Envelope Division, 313 Rohlwing Road, Addison, IL 60101.* The bulletins are:

Bulletin No. 9-B—The Mathematics of
    Planning Profitable Mailings
Bulletin No. 18—101 Suggested Headings for
    Reply Forms
Bulletin No. 20—10 "Sales Calls" You can
    Make by Mail
Bulletin No. 22—What to Say Instead of
    "Place Stamp Here"
Bulletin No. 23—32 Copy Ideas for
    Reminder Messages
Bulletin No. 24—How to Put the Free
    Space on Business Reply Envelope to
    Profitable Use
Bulletin No. 26—How to Plan a Package
    Insert and Use it Effectively

New Envelope News
A jumbo picture-tabloid newsletter that comes in a jumbo envelope. Each issue shows more kinds of envelopes, cites case histories, quotes savings, benefits, added results of their use by specific firms. An easy to read education in envelopes; selecting them, buying them, selling with them, using inside and out for copy and art. To subscribe free, write: *New Envelope News, Tension Envelope Corporation, 819 E. 19th Street, Suite 353, Kansas City, MO 64108; (816) 471-3800.*

Enclosures Are In
A specialist in them for over 20 years reports on the effectiveness of package inserts, statement stuffers, co-op mailage and how to test them. Write: *Leon Henry Inc., 455 Central Avenue, Scarsdale, NY 10583; (914) 723-3176.*

The Development Chronicle Newsletter
Special issue on power of personalization; when most effective; anatomy of a personalized letter; copy suggestion tips; changes, personalization check list; do's and don'ts; data processing tips to increase results; basic categories of personalization; case history comparisons of personalized vs. printed letters. Thorough, useful; excellent for fund raiser and general direct marketer. Write: *NLT Computer Corp., National Life Center, Nashville, TN 37250; (615) 256-7600.*

Media Interaction
For marketing and advertising executives; case histories of mailers, problems of insert users, studies of insert distributing programs. *Leon Henry, Inc., 455 Central Avenue, Scarsdale, NY 10583; (914) 723-3176.*

What Can A Mailer Use Besides Direct Mail?
The story on package inserts statements (stuffers), co-op mailings. Write: *Leon Henry, 455 Central Avenue, Scarsdale, NY 10583; (914) 723-3176.*

How Much is Your House List Really Worth?
A new appraisal method by Shell Alpert in ZIP magazine. For reprint, write: *Shell Alpert, 444 Lakeview Court, Langhorne, IA 19047; (215) 752-3433.*

Mailing List Management Questions Answered
The 15 most frequently asked. Just two pages but helpful. Write to: *Market Compilation and Research Bureau Inc., 11633 Victory Boulevard, North Hollywood, CA 91609; (213) 877-5384.*

After creating copy and layout for a mail order ad or direct mail piece, it must be produced. Doing so with quality reproduction at moderate cost is the concern of any entrepreneur or top executive in mail order. For the moonlighter, presentation must be simple and low-cost. For the biggest and most sophisticated production, cost and technique is a problem. Poorly done or overcostly, it can lose an account for an advertising agency and money for a mail order firm. The following information may help you in this regard.

What it Costs to Produce and Print an Advertisement
For the latest annual survey attach your business card and write: *Trout and Ries Advertising, 1212 Avenue of the Americas, New York, NY 10036; (212) 869-8888*

U & LC International Journal of Typographics
Splendid! Fascinating! Typeface selecton for each element of every mail order ad and mailing greatly influences reader reaction. It sets and affects the mood. In over 80 pages an issue, you're shown how. The classic typefaces, the new typefaces, the great type designers; the origin of typography, its history and variety; the skill and art of typeface selection; how to get a feeling for it; important for anyone concerned with the appearance and results of mail order advertising. For free subscription, write: *U & LC, 216 East 45th Street, New York, NY 10017.*

Blair Graphics Report
Four page newsletter; quite helpful, informative, educational on processes to anyone in printing production. A typical issue takes up one subject such as color reproduction. Well written; clear; illustrated. For no-charge subscription write *Adair Brown, The Blair Graphics Company, 9 West 57th Street, New York, NY 10019; (212) 838-9191.*

Technically Speaking
A six-page brochure; describes a web offset operation that has custom-built all finishing operations into its running press . . . from a roll of paper to a finished product . . . with no secondary operations. The finished product can include a variable data image with letter personalization and addresses, die-cutting (windows); perforations; scented scratch-off inks; hi-color process printing. Write: *Webcraft, Box 185, Route One and Adams Station, North Brunswick, NJ 08902; (201) 297-5100.*

10 Do's and Don'ts for
On-Time Less Costly Mailings
By Lee Epstein. Write: *The Mailmen, Inc., 342 Madison Avenue, NYC, NY 10017; (212) 986-4862.*

The Color Explosion
Top magazine designer, John Peter, tells the exciting, fascinating story, the history of color in printed communication. From color photographs to color printing to web offset process to computer scanners; the effect of color. How the magazine art directors view and use color. Write: *Spectrum Inc., 3940 West 32nd Avenue, Denver, CO 80212; (800) 525-8149 (Toll-free).*

A Color Separation Primer
How laser beams of light make color separations; the advantage of the process and its possible future; brief, clear; by Helen Eckstine who trained as a journalist, got a master's degree in psychology and co-founded Spectrum Inc.—a top color separation

firm using only color technology. Write: *Spectrum Inc., 3940 West 32nd Avenue, Denver, CO 80212; (800) 525-8149. Toll free.*

50 Questions That Will Save You Time and Money
Helps you understand color separations; covers basics of electronic dot generation system; standard primer; covers retouching, original art, prescreened copies; fine resolution and ganging; the best way to indicate size, cropping, proper screen ruling and more. Write: *Spectrum Inc., 3940 West 32nd Avenue, Denver, CO 80212; (303) 458-8660. Toll-free: 800-525-8149.*

Laser Tone News
A splendid newsletter! From issue #1, it becomes a continuing production course, featuring the use of laser color separations. Important to anyone in large companies concerned with color advertising; a must for art and production people in agencies and advertising departments; useful to small enterprises considering any color advertising.

The Laser Tone News first explains how to view transparencies, reflection copy and proofs correctly; what films to use; mounting of proofs for viewing; problems of color perception by different people. It tells how to judge color, what is most difficult to correct; how to best give color correction instructions to color transparency firms; how to prepare copy for color printing. Stripping and positioning negatives to produce film or plates for the final printed piece is thoroughly explained. The words are simple; nothing frightens, illustrations clarify. The entire process is laid out. Reflection art work, direct scanning and airbrushing are covered.

One issue instructs how to design, layout and proportion copy; how to use an electric calculator for sizing. Another describes what may be possible to do when color copy separations or press sheets (when viewed correctly) are seen to have flaws. It includes a trouble shooting guide with possible solutions for different problems.

Two issues summarize developments of a hundred years from first color plate to laser separatives. They then take you through each phase of latest laser scanning to produce separations. Diagrams and drawings show how it is done. Each issue makes you want to read the next. Write: *Spectrum Inc., 3940 West 32nd Avenue, Denver, CO 80212; (303) 525-8149.*

There are booklets on many aspects of mail order. Here are just a few of the excellent ones available:

How to Turn More of Your Telephone Inquiries into Sales
How to do it; 11 pages. *Reuben H. Donnelley, 825 Third Avenue, New York, NY 10022; (212) 972-8266.*

Phone Selling—Personal and Recorded
Smith/Hemmings/Gosden Direct Marketing Agency, 3360 Flair Drive, El Monte, CA 91731; (213) 571-6600.

AIS 800 Report
Special Issue! How to design a direct mail piece to get optimum use of 800 number: changing offer, personalizing, urgency; use of artwork, positioning and size of type to feature 800 number; 800 number in space ads, how Zerox does it; making the TV commercial part of the phone call; case histories, applications; upselling; renewing; training telephone representatives; equipment; sharing lines. A wonderful newsletter. Write for sample: *AIS, Inc., 353 Lexington Avenue, NYC, NY 10016; (212) 683-9070.*

Outgoing Telephone Marketing
How to test a direct response offer by telephone . . . for $1250, making 500 phone calls. How one test gave answer on which premium to use, what price to use, and which of other offer variations to project . . . in a week's time. Analysis took one day. One offer fell flat. The script was changed and new tests made the next day. Phone feedback gave new ideas for prompt script revision and improvement. List analysis took place as calls were made. For more details, send for "14 Facts About Outgoing Telephone Marketing." *Edward Blank Associates, 71 West 23rd Street, NYC, NY 10010; (212) 741-8133.*

International Direct Marketing Letter
Bi-monthly newsletter covers methods to promote products, services worldwide via mail order. For sample copy write: *IDM Letters, 8716 Plymouth Street, Suite 2, Silver Springs, MD 20901; (301) 588-3959.*

Gardening by Mail: Where to Buy it
It lists over 300 different plants and seeds in alphabetical order with catalogs that offer them. Self-addressed, stamped, business size envelope with two (2) 20¢ stamps must be sent to: *Mail Order Association of Nurserymen, Inc., 210 Cartwright Boulevard, Massapequa Park, NY 11762.*

Direct Mail Fund Raising
Facts, myths, frustrations, correct techniques, erroneous assumptions, pitfalls; essential steps, warning signs of costly mistakes. Consultant Carol Enters advises; reprint, Fund Raising Management. Write: *Carol Enters List Co., (CELCO), 381 Park Avenue South, NYC, NY 10016; (212) 684-1881.*

Your Direct Mail Annual Appeal
How to start and manage it; 16 pages; essentials for fund raisers step-by-step and thorough checklist. *Epsilon Data Management, Inc., 24 New England Executive Park, Burlington, MA 01803; (800) 225-1919; in Massachusetts 617-273-0250.*

Donors and Dollars
Direct mail in fund raising; economics; percentage of donors expected to be returned year by year over 10 years; increase in gifts with and without upgrading; how to increase gifts; different fund raising applications; cautions, sound advice. *Epsilon Data Management, Inc., 24 New England Executive Park, Burlington, MA 01803; (800) 225-1919; in Massachusetts 617-273-0250.*

The Epsilon Letter
Special issue! Super personalization; very personal copy me to you using individual file data; easy, natural, friendly feeling; copy writing; eye-catching ways to personalize; names to concentrate on; the computer personalization process; ink jet or laser. Valuable; Volume 6, Number 3; September/October 1981. For sample copy write: *Epsilon Data Management, Inc., One New England Executive Park, Burlington, MA 01803; (800) 225-1919, in Massachusetts 617-273-0250.*

The Harvest Concept
Fund raising guidelines; areas of change; ways to increase donor response; *NLT Computer Services Corp., National Life Center, Nashville, TN 37250; (615) 256-7600; (800) 251-3384.*

Video-Print
View Data will bypass cable TV systems, reports Video-Print newsletter (on home information systems). For issue with analysis, write: *Video-Print, International Resource Development Inc., 30 High Street, Norwalk, CT 06851; (203) 866-6914.*

Books for Direct Marketers (booklet)
Catalogs, describes currently available books related to direct marketing. Subjects covered include direct mail, mailing lists, direct marketing law, telephone marketing, international direct marketing. Avilable without charge from *Publications Division, DMMA, 6 East 43rd St., New York, NY 10017; 212/689-4977.*

New, free booklets and brochures are constantly brought out, often quite valuable, some if you're small and some if you're big. Often these are mentioned in advertisements and editorial notes in Direct Marketing magazine, ZIP magazine or DM News . . . with information where to send for them. To find out how to get these magazines, read page 443 of Reference Section VII.

Reference Section II
Low Cost How-to Information

Booklets and Brochures
to help you succeed as an entrepreneur
in a career in mail order

There are more all the time. Most help the small and some the big firms. Let's start with some from the government. The Small Business Administration has many publications for sale at nominal prices. Consider the following 12 which I have selected. Each is in considerably more detail than the free booklets the SBA offers. Each is written by one or more established authorities, in simple language for smaller ventures.

Starting and Managing a Small Business of Your Own
Spells out essentials necessary to know in starting the smallest business and about which small mail order moonlighters often are unfamiliar. Useful. 045-000-00123-7. 95 pages. $3.75.

Decision Points in Developing New Products
Provides a path from idea to marketing plan for a small manufacturer that wants to expand or develop a business around a new product, process or invention. 045-000-00146-6. 64 pages. $1.50.

Buying and Selling A Small Business
Sources of information; using financial statements, analyzing market position; the buy-sell transaction, process and decision. 045-000-00164-4. 122 pages. $3.50

Managing for Profits
Marketing, production, credit; other aspects; for any small business. A good deal is helpful to the little mail order venture. 045-000-00005-2. 155 pages. $2.75.

Guides for Profit Planning
How to compute and use break-even point; level of gross profit; rate of return on investment. It helps make business decisions yet is written so simply that no specialized training in accounting or economics is needed. 045-000-00137-7. 59 pages. $2.50.

Financial Control by Time-Absorption Analysis
Biggest mail order losses often come after initial success . . . during expansion and due to lack of financial control. This technique for all kinds of businesses can help. 045-000-00134-2. 138 pages. $2.75.

Strengthening Small Business Management
How to apply to a small firm the principles which are profitably used by large ones. 045-000-00114-8. 155 pages. $4.00.

Handbook of Small Business Finance
Covers points often missed by small mail order entrepreneurs. 045-000-00139-3. 63 pages. $3.00.

Ratio Analysis for Small Business
How to judge profitability and soundness of firm from a financial statement. 045-000-00150-4. 65 pages. $2.20.

Cost Accounting for Small Manufacturers
Important if you manufacture any of your own mail order items. 045-000-00162-8. 180 pages. $4.25.

Export Marketing for Smaller Firms
A successful mail order item in the U.S., may sell successfully in other parts of the world. This manual for owner-managers of smaller firms can help. 045-000-00158-0. 84 pages. $2.20.

Small Business Goes to College
Describes courses on small business management and entrepreneurship given by over 200 colleges and universities. 045-000-00159-8. 82 pages. $3.25.

As this book goes to press, the above prices are in effect and there are no charges for postage and handling. Please remembr that prices rise with inflation. Each year some titles are dropped, old titles republished and new titles added. To order or for latest information, write: *Superintendent of Documents, U.S. Government Printing Office, Washington, D.C. 20402.*

The U.S. Postal Service has various publications at modest prices useful and essential for mail order firms. Starting ventures should consider:

National Zip Code Directory and Directory of Post Office
Latest issue. Important for smallest starting moonlighter. List of Post Office branches and postal stations by state, country, and alphabetically by name. $9.00.

USPS International Mail Regulations
Important if you mail to names outside the U.S. #42. $10.00.

International Express Mail
Pb 45. $.50.

Acceptance of Hazardous, Restricted or Perishable Matter
Pb 52. $ .50.

Mail Classification
HB DM-101. $.50.

Managing Mail
1971, reprinted 1978. 94 pages, illustrated. $5.00.

Marking of Country of Origin on U.S. Imports
13 pages of precise information; forms of marking; special marking of combined articles; of containers; special statutory marking; special marking on certain articles; those not requiring marking. Published by U.S. Customs Service; Stock # 048-002-0051-0. $.40.

Order any of the above from *Superintendent of Documents, U.S. Government Printing Office, Washington, D.C. 20402; (202) 783-3238.*

The U.S. Patent and Trademark Office also can help, if you wish to patent or trademark an item:

General Information Concerning Patents
More detailed than free booklet; non-technical, very detailed from application to granting. $.95.

General Information Concerning Trademarks
Same as for patents. $.95.

Patents and Inventions: An Informal Aid for Inventors
Guidelines and information about where and how to obtain a patent. U304-00511. $1.30.

Order any of the above from: *U.S. Department of Commerce, Patent and Trademark Office, Washington, D.C. 20231.*

One of the biggest banks, Bank of America, has an entire publishing division to help the smallest businesses start and grow. It publishes business management manuals authored by excellent authorities on varied subjects. I've selected five that are important to small mail order enterprises. Each manual is available by mail for $2 postpaid.

Steps to Starting a Business
Excellent step-by-step, beginning primer for any small enterprise, including mail order. Volume 14, #7.

Avoiding Management Pitfalls
Many go broke in mail order simply because they didn't know and have never been told how to avoid them. Worthwhile. Volume 15, #6.

Financing Small Business
Unanticipated cash demands, not planning for needs, not knowing how and where to borrow has often caused mail order businesses to fail—while expanding. Read this book. Volume 14, #10.

Understanding Financial Statements
Bank officers know how to get vital information about a business from its statement, in minutes. Few small businessmen do. This shows quite simply how to get a great deal from your own statement and that of others; also to undertand far better the kind of statement banks will loan money on. Volume 14, #6.

The Handicrafts Business
Many successful moonlighters started their mail order businesses from their hobbies. If yours is handicrafts, this book is a good overview. Volume 14, #9.

Bank of America has published other excellent manuals (including "Mail Order Enterprises") which in early 1982 were out of print. Each year new manuals are published and some out of print are updated and re-issued. To order any of the above or get information about newly reprinted or published ones, send check or money order payable to Bank of America to: *Small Business Reporter, Bank of America, Department 3401, P. O. Box 37000, San Francisco, CA 94137; Telephone: 415-622-2491.*

Many quite helpful inexpensive booklets are offered by media, services, consultants, book publishers, and other organizations. Here are a very few typical of those available.

How to Start a Successful Mail Order Business
Excellent for new small, beginning mail order businesses; published by House Beautiful Magazine, to help its shopping column advertisers. $1. *House Beautiful, 1700 Broadway, New York, NY 10019; (212) 903-5126.*

Introduction to Direct Marketing
Fundamentals, references; by Chaman L. Jain & Al Migliaro; published by AMA Communications. $7.50 AMA members, $10.00 non-members; Write: *AMACOM, 135 W 50th Street, New York, NY 10020; (212) 586-8100.*

Direct Marketing
A reference booklet of material concerning direct marketing, reprinted Advertising Age; paper. $4.95; *Crain Books, 740 Rush Street, Chicago, IL 60611; (312) 649-5250.*

National Survey of Consumers' Attitudes/Direct Mail Advertising
Robert Hansen/MASA, International Volume I, 32 pages: $7.50. Volume II, 109 pages: $12.50; *MASA (Mail Advertising Service Association International), 7315 Wisconsin Ave., 818-E, Bethesda, MD 20814; (301) 654-7030.*

66 Suggestions about Saving Money on Postage
How to increase speed of postal service; ways to reduce weight of envelope; how commercial mailing services can save time; specifications of items to avoid surcharges. $5. *Daly Associates, Inc., 702 World Center Building, Washington, D.C. 20006; (202) 659-2925.*

Domestic Direct Response Supplies Register
List Companies	**$5.00**
Direct Marketing Agencies	**$7.50**
Direct Marketing Consultants	**$5.00**
Direct Marketing Lettershops and Printers	**$5.00**

The biggest of each are DMMA members and listed in the above with names, addresses, phone numbers and whom to contact. Useful for bigger direct marketers who need the best (and sometimes expensive) help. *The Direct Mail/Marketing Association, 6 East 43rd Street, New York, NY 10017; (212) 689-4977.*

Classified Advertising Means Business
How to write your first classified ad, what to say: Claims, headings, use of capitals; choice of words, which to avoid; how to simplify, save works; keying, timing, repeating; follow-up via brochure or catalog, correspondence; postal system; FTC; dealing with magazines, selecting advertising agency. $2.50. *Classified Ad Dept., Rodale Press, Inc., 33 E Minor Street, Emmaus, PA 18049.*

How to Write a Classified Ad that Pulls
What to say. $1.75. *Davis Publications Inc., 380 Lexington Avenue, NYC, NY 10017; (212) 557-9100.*

Great Catalog Guide
Over 600 catalogs listed by 27 classifications. Name, address, catalog price for free. $1. *DMMA, 6 East 43rd Street, NYC, NY 10017; (212) 689-4977.*

100 Best Headlines Ever Written
Selected by Murray Raphel; comes with annual direct mail package of creative ideas. $3. *Murray Raphel Advertising, 1012 Atlantic Avenue, Atlantic City, NJ 08401; (609) 348-6646.*

90 Test-Worthy Envelope Ideas for Direct Response
$4.95. *Transo Envelope Company, 3542 North Kimball Avenue, Chicago, IL 60618; (312) 267-9200.*

The Dependable List Company* publishes a set of six mini-books. I call them "The Little Library of List Know-How." Each is a brief overview of an area. They are practical, understandable and perfect for anyone starting out.

The Dollars and Sense of Direct Mail
Mail marketing guide; practical concepts of math and finance by Pierre Passavant*; developing a campaign profit and loss worksheet . . . for a one-shot promotion, for a two-step

promotion; for "club" promotion; for catalog promotion; contribution to promotion and profit: basic formula for mail order math; determining life value of a customer; much more. Excellent.

Psychographics: Life-Style of a Mail Order Buyer

How to find people whose tastes match your product . . . enough to reduce other purchases to buy it; how to predict which mail order buyers, of what, are most apt to buy what other products; how a data record on computer of charge accounts opened, gifts made, courses taken . . . helps determine who will buy your item; how Ward and Sears tailor list selection to fit the offer, psychographically—and how you can.

How to Test a Mailing List

Why and what to test? How much to spend; what to look for. How much to test at one time . . . what to include in every test; how many names and how many from each list should you test . . . for different price ranges; how to judge test results; how much difference in test results is significant; factors which influence response; how to decide whether to stop, project . . . or re-test.

How to Profit from Co-Ops, Inserts and Specialized Response Media

Advantages, requirements of each; programs to select . . . for male oriented items, female . . . for gifts; general merchandise; in the health field; to reach old people; package vs. billing inserts; newspaper inserts; co-op mailings; special interest: professional, business and industrial fields. Some cost comparisons with solo mailings.

How to Computerize Your Mailing List

Should you or shouldn't you? The many advantages . . . and when it's usually not recommended; when you have to; what computerizing can and can't do; essentials, options, layouts, decisions; eliminating duplicates; how to maintain; clean your list . . . use it as a research tool, make it a profit center.

Peripheral Thinking: Beyond the Bull's Eye

How to think in more depth about list selection . . . after you've tested and succeeded and projected . . . after you've creamed your most predictable potential; how to use compiled lists . . . business, professional, consumer; how to custom compile your own; ways to find and develop plus profit lists . . . experiment with least risk and best chance . . . develop profitable, peripheral volume bigger than all lists used up until then; mind prodding.

For each mini-book desired send $1 to *Dependable Lists, Inc., 257 Park Avenue South, New York, NY 10010. (212) 677-6760.*

Here's some advice for the small, and some for the big, starting a mail order venture:

Guide to Start Your Own Mail Order Business

Send self-addressed business size envelope and 35¢ for handling to: *Tops in the Shops Department, Redbook Magazine, 230 Park Avenue, NYC, NY 10017.*

Reach More Prospects for Less Money

Gerald Reisberg, V.P. of Dun's Marketing Seminar, takes the business mailer step by step through a 15,000 piece mailing program. Useful for new direct marketers to industry. $1.50. Write: *D & B Reports, 99 Church Street, New York, NY 10007; (212) 285-7679.*

How to Prepare Your Own Camera-Ready Copy for Offset Printing

Very useful for newcomers to mail order in smaller ventures. Send 50¢ to: *Sagamore Graphics, Inc., 68 West Main Street, Oyster Bay, NY 11771; (516) 922-6491.*

Standard Industrial Classification Manual, Revised 1982

Revised periodically; valuable to anyone selling to business by mail order; defines industry with a four digit code; contains the titles and descriptions of industries, numerical and alphabetical indexes of manufacturing and non-manufacturing industries. $15.00. Write: *Superintendent of Documents, U.S. Government Printing Office, Washington, D.C. 20402.*

The Department of the Census is an invaluable source for market research and, increasingly so, in mail order. The following booklets are available at very low cost:

Factfinder for the Nation

Topical brochure issued irregularly. Each describes the range of census material available on a given subject and suggests uses. I recommend that mail order people send for any of the following (at 25¢ each) which may be applicable.

1. Statistics on Race and Ethnicity
2. Availability of Census Records about Individuals
5. Reference Sources
6. Housing Statistics
7. Population Statistics
8. Geographic Tools
10. Retail Trade Statistics
11. Wholesale Trade Statistics
14. Foreign Trade Statistics
15. Statistics on Manufactures
18. Census Bureau Programs and Products
19. Enterprise Statistics
21. International Programs

Write: *Customer Services (DUSD), Bureau of The Census, Washington, D.C. 20233;* or phone *Publications, Census Bureau (202) 763-4100.*

Here is a booklet every new direct market firm should read;

Common Sense of Everyday Ethics

36 pages. $1.00. Write: *Ivan Hill, The Ethics Resource Center, 1730 Rhode Island Avenue N.W., Washington, D.C. 20036; (202) 223-3411.*

The following reports are based on the 1980 Census. To order, write: *Superintendent of Documents, U.S. Government Printing Office, Washington, D.C. 20402; (202) 783-3238.*

Block Statistics

Issued 1982; population and housing unit totals and characteristics for individual blocks in urbanized areas; for selected blocks adjacent to urbanized areas, for blocks in places of 10,000 or more inhabitants, some other areas. Consists of 375 sets of microfiche (non-printed reports); includes a report for each SMSA (Standard Metropolitan Statistical Area) showing blocked areas for each; for each state and for Puerto Rico, showing blocked areas outside SMSA's. A U.S. summary is index; series PHC80-1. Copies available for cost of reproduction as each set of tables is completed.

Census Tracts

To be issued late 1982 or 1983; analyzes population statistics; general characteristics; age, race, sex, marital status, social, economic, housing; also analyzes manufacturing statistics; by states. Approx. $3 to $6 for each. Series PHC80-2.

Measuring Markets: A Guide to the Use of Federal and State Statistical Data

Describes usefulness of government data in market research. 101 pages; $3.75. GPO No. 003-009-00326-1; prepared by Bureau of Industrial Economics.

Summary Characteristics for Governmental Units and Standard Metropolitan Statistical Areas
To be issued late 1982; statistics on total population and on complete count and sample population characteristics such as age, race, education, ability to speak English, labor force and income; also on total housing units and housing characteristics such as value, age of structure, and rent; by states, SMSA's, counties, county division governments; report for each state, D.C. and Puerto Rico. Series PHC80-3. Copies available for cost of reproduction as each set of tables is completed.

It's surprising how much additional information is constantly made available in the form of low-cost booklets, often from the same sources. Keep checking Direct Marketing magazine, DM News and ZIP for mention of them. Now let's go on to another source of information quite valuable to anyone in mail order: some books you can borrow or buy.

Reference Section III
Books

Here are listed and described 116 books helpful in direct marketing. The 18 of these which I review in Seminar IX, Chapter 6, are marked with an asterisk. Some books are helpful for the tiny, some for the huge, some for the in-between and some for everybody (almost all borrowable).

Small or big . . . whether you want to service, sell to, or be in the mail order business . . . before you start, do me this favor: research the field of direct marketing. Read some of the excellent books on it. The first that I recommend is:

*The Americans: The Democratic Experience** A social-economic history. In it is explained what led to mail order becoming part of our culture. By Daniel Boorstin; in cloth, $20, *Random House;* in paper, $5.95, *Vintage Books;* both publishers are at *201 East 50th Street, New York, NY 10022. (212) 751-2600.*

To research the field, the following are often the first referred to by biggest companies:

The Fact Book on Direct Response Marketing*
Jumbo book; bigger with each edition; for pros, beginners . . . big, small; $39.95. 1982, *Direct Mail/Marketing Association, 6 East 43rd Street, New York, NY 10017. (212) 689-4977.*

Direct Marketing Market Place*
$40.00; *Hilary House Publishers, Inc., 1033 Channel Drive, Hewlett Harbor, NY 11557. (516) 295-2376.*

Direct Response: The Consumer Mail Order Business
An assessment of the present and future. $300; by *Probe;* a research unit of *Arthur D. Little Resources, Acorn Park, Cambridge, MA 02140. (617) 864-5770.*

1982 United States Mail Order Industry Plus Quarterly Financial Update*
Total volume, breakdown by category, much additional data; published annually; $65; *Maxwell Sroge Publishing, Inc., 731 North Cascade Avenue, Colorado Springs, CO 80903. (303) 633-5556.*

DMMA Direct Mail/Marketing Manual*
Published by *Direct Mail/Marketing Association, Inc., 6 East 43rd Street, New York, NY 10017. (212) 689-4977.* The following sections are available to non-members.

General Planning and Strategy	$35
Lists & Media	$35
Creative	$75
Production	$35
Fulfillment and Operations	$35
Testing, Analysis and Economics	$35
Legal, Ethical and Regulatory	$35.

Inside the Leading Mail Order Houses
The top 200; the new growth companies; who owns and runs each and how each markets; a summary of each business; the company history, facilities; actual or estimated volume, profits; number of catalogs mailed; average order; size of customer list; $65; *Maxwell Sroge Publishing, 731 North Cascade, Colorado Springs, CO 80903.*

Other Sroge Publications*
Depth-in-Industry Studies; *Maxwell Sroge Publishing, Inc., 731 North Cascade Avenue, Colorado Springs, CO 80903. (303) 633-5556.*

1982 Books by Mail—2 Volumes	*$1,500*
Food by Mail—2 Volumes	*$1,500*
Collectibles by Mail	*$1,075*
Crafts by Mail	*$1,075*
Ready-To-Wear by Mail—3 Volumes	*$1,950*
Sporting Goods by Mail	*$1,075.*

The following is a study that can be applied by top executives and substantial companies but is fascinating to anyone employed in mail order.

Direct Marketing Compensation
An $85,000 study; job description, compensation (30 positions in marketing; finance, creative, media), operations. $425; *Direct Mail/Marketing Association, 6 East 43rd Street, New York, NY 10017. (212) 689-4977.*

Let's consider books useful to the small beginner entrepreneur. We'll include some helpful to larger firms. Many small mail order people who succeed start with a proprietary product or concept . . . something not done by others. Inventing a product is one way, although few have the ability. Even then carrying a simple invention from idea to product is a painful experience, time consuming, and extremely hazardous. But one inventor who has succeeded has written an excellent book useful for the inventive mail order beginner.

Inventing for Fun and Profit
Robert Lay Hallock, owner of 30 patents, explains. Paper $1.98; #53312X; cloth $6.95; #53311; *Crown Publishers, 34 Englehard Avenue, Avenel, NJ 07001. (201) 382-7600.*

Often inventing a small mail order product starts with a hobby or skill. A few years ago, craft hobbies were big in mail order although far less so now. Still, many start and succeed in this way. The following books may help give you some background.

The Mail Order Crafts Catalog
Margaret Boyd; lists and describes a wide variety of crafts. You may find one that fits your skills. $7.95; *Chilton Book Company, Radnor, PA 19089.*

The Craft Business Encyclopedia
Michael Scott; how to create a business from your hobby; opportunities, pitfalls, do's and don'ts; $3.95 paper; *Harcourt, Brace, Jovanovich, 757 Third Avenue, New York, NY 10017. (212) 888-4444.*

Self-publishing a book or starting a newsletter is another way to develop a product you own and others don't. Most who try to do so fail but constantly some succeed. If you have some how-to expertise and write well, the following may be useful.

The Encyclopedia of Self-Publishing
A good deal of this book advises how to sell the trade, but it's also quite helpful if you start by mail order. $32. *B. Klein Publications, P.O. Box 8503, Coral Springs, FL 33065. (305) 752-1708.*

Newsletter Year Book Directory
United States and Canadian Newsletters. Lists more than 2,000; describes contents, frequency, circulation; $35, 200 pages. *B. Klein Publications, P.O. Box 8503, Coral Springs, FL 33065. (305) 752-1708.*

A Practical Guide to Newsletter Editing and Design
L.H. Wales; $4.50 paper. *Iowa State University Press, 2121 South State Avenue, Ames, IA 50010. (515) 294-5280.*

If inventing or writing is not for you, consider this. Do you collect anything? For a while, collectibles became bigger than crafts in mail order but then also subsided. But tremendous numbers of people start and succeed this way still. In this book in Seminar I, Chapter 6, "Making a Mint in Mail Order" and Seminar II, Chapter 7, "Mail Order Collectomania," I tell how big and small have succeeded. To get an idea of the scope I suggest that you read the following:

The Time-Life Encyclopedia of Collectibles
Each volume covers a variety of fields. Read the areas covering your interests. $14.00 a volume. *Time-Life Books, 777 Duke Street, Alexandria, VA 22314; (703) 960-5000.*

If you don't invent, write or collect, team up with someone who does. If not seek a product or products from a source. This is difficult because of lack of profit margin available. It's more difficult for single products. It's easier for a group of products preferably built around a concept for a simple but unique specialized catalog.

To find products, look everywhere . . . in stores, catalogs, publications and at shows. In Section VII, I list and describe some U.S. trade shows you should consider attending. But if you travel abroad, you may find a product not yet in the U.S. You may be able to bring in a small amount with an option contract to bring in much more, on a sole rights basis and at a price lower in relation to selling price.

Trade Show and Convention Guide
Lists over 4500 Conventions and Trade Shows in the U.S., Canada, and many foreign countries. $55. *Tradeshow Convention Guide, Box 24970, Nashville, TN 37202.*

The following book may be useful if you do or could travel outside the U.S.

Exhibitions 'Round the World
A compilation of the major trade fairs of the world arranged, geographically and by production category. Airmail $20. Published by *Trade Winds, P.O. Box 7-170, Taipei, Taiwan, R.O.C.*

Many try to raise money to start a mail order business, with a product, an idea or none. Few get money and most of these regret getting it. But the tiniest success attracts money partners . . . and often enables you to get along without it. Caution! Mail order ideas have been stolen while looked at. But for sound mail order projects, carefully planned and preferably successfully tested, money is continually raised. For this purpose, consider the following books:

Guide to Venture Capital Sources
By Stanley E. Pratt; lists 604 venture capital companies and 164 small company underwriters; by state, backgound of each, whom to contact; $75.00, 6th Edition, 1982. *Capital Publishing Corporation, 2 Laurel Avenue, Wellesley Hills, MA 02181; (617) 235-5405.*

Handbook of Business Finance and Capital Sources
By Dileep Rao, PH.D; comprehensive listing of available private and public sources of capital. Plain words; narrative text; thorough checklist of what financial institutions look for; descriptions of nearly every method of financing business operations; more than a thousand sources; in every state; includes tables, lists and diagrams. 470 pages; $75, 1982 Edition; *Inter Finance Corporation, 305 Foshay Tower, Minneapolis, MN 55402. (612) 338-8185.*

Many new sophisticated mail order ventures require substantial capital. But many small ones constantly start with little to almost no capital, and some succeed. Biggest companies are often better off to start small in mail order, with small tests and small staffs. Little people are foolish to risk their savings or those of others and are advised to substitute imagination, persuasion, work, time and frugality. This has often worked. Research and competent advice can usually help considerably. Some self-help books for the small to larger that may interest you are:

Copyright It Yourself
How to do it; the new copyright law; forms; E.G. Hirsch, $15. *Whitehall Company, 1200 S. Willis Avenue, Wheeling, IL 60090. (312) 541-9290.*

How to Be Your Own Advertising Agency
Bert Holtje; $17.95. *McGraw-Hill Book Company, Princeton Road, Hightstown, NJ 08520. (609) 448-1700.*

Do-It-Yourself Marketing Research
Author George Edward Breen has a BA from Yale, an MBA from Harvard Business School, a PH.D. from NYU. He's been a top marketing research director. He tells how non-research specialists, with only math learned in school and required clerical time, can find out whether prospective customers really want the product or service about to be offered. He explains research interviews, group interviews; telephone interviews; research analysis; when to use and how to choose a research firm. $24.95; *McGraw-Hill Book Company, Princeton Road, Hightstown, NJ. (609) 448-1700.*

How to Advertise Yourself
By Maxwell Sackheim; how to use mail order techniques to promote your career; $5.95. *Macmillan Publishing Company, Inc., 866 Third Avenue, New York, NY 10022.*

How to Handle Your Own Public Relations
Herschell Gordon Lewis; $19.95. *Mason National Publications, 3601 Park Center Boulevard, Suite 117, Minneapolis, MN 55416.*

The Publicity Manual
Kate Kelly; how to get free publicity without hiring a professional; how to write and use press release and press kits; give interviews. Lists media directories; clipping services, public relations firms. $29.95; *Visibility Enterprises, 11 West 81st Street, New York, NY 10024. (212) 787-9239.*

For mail order expertise the ideal is to have competent advisers. Few of them however, whether advertising agents or specialized consultants, can make a profit guiding the tiniest. But there are helpful books. I'll try to help you find the right ones. Read them thoroughly and be sure you understand them.

If you are new to business and wish to start in a tiny way, consider these two books:

Small Time Operator*
How to start your own business, keep your books, pay your taxes and stay out of trouble. Sensible, practical how-to book for small businesses starting out. Tax laws, SBA loan rates, book reviews. Recommended; Bernard Kamoroff; 192 pages. Paperback, $7.95. *Bell Springs Publishing, Box 640, Laytonville, CA 95454; (707) 984-6746.*

Mail Order Moonlighting
Cecil C. Hoge, Sr.; $7.95 at stores, in libraries. *Ten Speed Press, 900 Modoc, Berkeley, CA 94707.*

Whether you are small or large, an economist now famous for books on the future may help you succeed in mail order in the present. He did in mail order, starting with a tiny venture, and wrote the following book:

How to Start and Operate a Mail Order Business*
Julian L. Simon; thorough, sound, practical; $21.95. *McGraw-Hill Book Co., Princeton Road, Hightstown, NJ 08520. (609) 448-1700.*

Many are interested in mail order, not to go into it but simply to sell products or services to those in it. If so, a step might be to look over these two books:

Directory of Mail Order Catalogs
Like to sell your product or service to catalog marketers? Listed are names and addresses of 4,000 catalog firms: manager, production category, frequency of issue, size, list. $95; *Grey House Publishing, 360 Park Avenue South, New York, NY 10010. (212) 684-6485.*

Mail Order Business Directory
Contains the names of over 6,000 mail order catalog houses; 500 largest firms indicated. Over 430 pages; $55; 1982. *B. Klein Publications, P.O. Box 8503, Coral Springs, FL 33065. (305) 752-1708.*

Small or big must give names to their products and companies. They sometimes register copyrights or apply for patents. They may need to import and must deal with the Post Office. These books can be helpful for reference.

The Trademark Register of the U.S., 1881-Present
Over 450,000 currently registered trademarks in use today; 1184 pages. Federal regulations on patents, trademarks, copyrights; paper, $107. *The Trademark Register, 454 Washington Building, Washington, D.C. 20005.*

The Custom House Guide
Latest revisions of U.S. Tariff Schedules alphabetically. Import index of over 36,000 commodities. An encyclopedia of customs regulations, procedures, problems and structure. $134 (N.Y. and PA include state tax). *The Custom House Guide, North American Publishing, 401 North Broad Street, Philadelphia, PA 19108. (215) 574-9600.*

Guide to U.S. Postal Zones
Identifies any U.S. postal zone to determine postal charges. Includes over 900 official postal zone charts. $40. *A. R. Venezian, Inc., 10-64 Jackson Avenue, Long Island City, NY 11101.*

Mailer's Guide to Postal Regulations
Written and published by *Metro Information Services, Inc., P.O. Box 1550, New Rochelle, NY 10802. A subscription service. Guide plus one year subscription to instant update service; $66.50. Rules for preparation of first, third and fourth class mail. Changes in postal rules and rates for one year included. Send to above address or phone (914) 632-7293.*

Zip/Area Code Directory
Matches up postal zip codes with telephone systems, area codes. $2.95; *Pilot Books, 347 Fifth Avenue, New York, NY 10016. (212) 685-0736.*

Zip Code Sales Information Guide
Contains 450 five-digit zip code market area maps with corresponding family income and population; $90. *Data Publications, 24 East Wesley Street, South Hackensack, NJ 07666. (201) 343-7271.*

International Postal Handbook
Rates, regulations, restrictions and advantages of all classes of outgoing and incoming mail for every country in the world; $12.50. *New Harbinger Publications, 624 43rd Street, Richmond, CA 94805.*

Below are listed and described some of the essential books of recent years on direct marketing. Almost all are written by advertising and promotion experts and emphasize these aspects. Large companies use these books to train staff. On-the-way-up executives find them career books. Owners and managers use them for orientation. Good for the small too.

Successful Direct Marketing Methods*
Bob Stone; $24.95. *Crain Communications, Inc., 740 Rush Street, Chicago, IL 60611. (312) 649-5215.*

Profitable Direct Marketing*
Jim Kobs; $22.95. *Crain Communications, Inc., 740 Rush Street, Chicago, IL 60611. (312) 649-5215.*

Direct Marketing: "Strategy, Planning, Execution"*
Edward L. Nash; designing products; creating basic marketing plan; planning offer to planning layout; direct mail copy; evaluating results; highly praised. $24.95. *McGraw-Hill Book Co., Princeton Road, Hightstown, NJ 08520. (609) 448-1700.*

Direct Mail and Mail Order Handbook*
Richard Hodgson; $52.50. *The Dartnell Corp., 4660 Ravenswood Avenue, Chicago, IL 60640. (312) 561-4000.*

Direct Mail Advertising & Selling
A galaxy of top experts each explain their specialties. Every retailer interested in mail order sales should read it. $19.95; National Retail Merchants Association, 100 West 31st Street, New York, NY 10001. (212) 244-8780.

Response Television: Combat Advertising of the 1980's
John Witek; hard cover; $19.95. *Crain Communications, Inc., 740 Rush Street, Chicago, IL 60611. (312) 649-5215.*

Mail order is advertising oriented. Many great advertising people have been masters of mail order. Many have studied it,

Virtually all have been fascinated by it. And many have taught much to masters of mail order, and can to you. The following are books by advertising greats I suggest you read.

Scientific Advertising*/My Life in Advertising
David Ogilvy says that the author of these books, Claude Hopkins, "formed me as an advertising man". These books have mesmerized many. Crain Communications thought so much of them they brought out a two in one edition, a real bargain at $9.95. May be out of print. Check your library. *Crain Communication, Inc., 740 Rush Street, Chicago, IL 60611. (312) 649-5215.*

A Technique for Producing Ideas
James Webb Young; hard cover; $4.95; *Crain Books, Inc., 740 Rush Street, Chicago, IL 60611. (312) 649-5215.*

Motivating Human Behavior
Psychologist Ernest Dichter applies psychology to selling, advertising, marketing; persuasion of associates, employees; changing attitudes, behavior. $31.; *McGraw-Hill Book Company, Princeton Road, Hightstown, NJ 08520. (609) 448-1700.*

Reality in Advertising
A classic by Rosser Reeves; $10.; *Alfred A. Knopf, Inc., 201 East 52nd Street, New York, NY 10022. (212) 751-2600.*

Confessions of an Advertising Man*
David Ogilvy; $5.95; *Scribners Atheneum, 597 5th Avenue, New York, NY 10017. (212) 486-2700.*

One book I suggest you read is:

Risk-Free Advertising
Victor Wademan tells how to come close to it. A scientific advertising approach; $18.95. *Order Dept. John Wiley & Sons Inc., 1 Wiley Drive, Somerset, NJ 08873; (201) 469-4400.* Going out of print, but check your local business library.

Everyone in an executive capacity in mail order, before approving advertising or writing it, should be aware of the laws, regulations and government administrative guidelines that concern mail order copy. The smallest entrepreneurs should read the free information available and recommended in Reference Section I of this book as well as Seminar IX, Chapter 6. Medium and larger firms should own the following:

The Law and Direct Marketing*
$150; *Direct Mail/Marketing Association, 6 East 43rd Street, New York, NY 10017. (212) 689-4977.*

The Law of Advertising
George and Peter Rosdon. 2 Volumes, $100; *Matthew Bender & Co., Inc., 235 East 45th Street, New York, NY 10017. (212) 226-5700.*

Now you can more safely work with your creative people... whether agency, free lance, staff or yourself. An excellent book on how to deal with your agency, and not just on copy, is the following:

How to Advertise*
Kenneth Roman/Jane Maas; A professional guide for the advertiser. What works, what doesn't and why. $9.95, 1982 Edition. *St. Martin's Press, 175 Fifth Avenue, New York, NY 10010. (212) 674-5151.*

For any mail order enterprise, small or big, there will be at times a need for free lance copy. The following is useful particularly for medium and larger firms.

How to Work With A Direct Response Freelancer
Also advantages and disadvantages of using staff, agencies, or

consultant for marketing, copy and creative work. $8. *George Duncan, 29 Concord Avenue, Cambridge, MA 02138. (617) 547-5638.*

The biggest direct marketer often has the problem of training beginning mail order copywriters from scratch. The smallest must train themselves. Below are listed and described some of the great classic books on mail order advertising and persuasion which have helped many of today's top direct marketers.

Tested Advertising Methods*
John Caples, $5.95 paper, $14.95 hardback; *Prentice Hall, Englewood Cliffs, NJ 07632. (201) 592-2000.*

My First 65 Years in Advertising*
Maxwell Sackheim; $9.95; hard cover. $5.95 paperback; *Tab Books, Blue Ridge Summit, PA 17214. (717) 794-2191.*

How to Write a Good Advertisement*
Victor Schwab; A classic; out of print, but try your local business library.

Robert Collier Letter Book
Another classic; out of print, but try your local business library.

If you are not a professional copywriter and must write mail order copy for ads, catalogs or direct mail, the following specialized monographs and books are short, basic and useful.

How To Write Powerful & Effective Small Space Ads (Monograph)
(#7680), Stephen Nevard. How to construct small catalog ads that get big attention. $8. *Direct Mail/Marketing Association, 6 East 43rd Street, New York, NY. 10017. (212) 689-4977.*

Direct Response Print Space (Monograph)
Space specialists tells how to create mail order ads: How to create believeability, motivation, headlines and how best used, 26 appeals, 7 methods to generate interest and create desire; good graphics; how copy and offers work best together; gives samples of ads that work. $24.95. *Direct Mail/Marketing Association, 6 East 43rd Street, New York, NY. 10017. (212) 689-4977.*

How To Write Successful Direct Mail Letter Copy
Maxwell Ross, $10; *Direct Mail/Marketing Association, 6 East 43rd Street, New York, NY. 10017. (212) 689-4977.*

Catalog Copy—The Long and Short of It
(#7679), Jane Corcillo. Make your copy make the sale. How-to's of this specialized writer's craft; $8. *Direct Mail/Marketing Association, 6 East 43rd Street, New York, NY. 10017. (212) 689-4977.*

Better Brochures, Catalogs and Mailing Pieces
Practical ways to create them, by Jane Maas. $9.95. *St. Martin's Press, 175 Fifth Avenue, New York, NY 10010. (212) 674-5151.*

500+ Ways to Increase Your Direct Mail Response
24 pages; $25. *Januz Marketing Communications Inc., P. O. Box 1000, Lake Forest, IL 60045. (312) 295-6550.*

Using Direct Mail to Increase Sales and Profits
For clients Ed McLean sold over $500 million in products and services in 17 years, mostly by direct mail; he has taught thousands direct marketing in seminars; he has put his know-how into the book: Direct Mail Strategies: For sales and marketing executives; $59.95. He has written two other excellent books: The Basics of Copy, $15, and The Basics of Testing, $15. All these are available from *Ed McLean, Thistle Hill, Ghent, NY 12075. (518) 392-9788.*

Advertising Writing
W. Keith Hafer and Gordon E. White; $22.95. *West Publishing*

Co., 50 West Kellogg Blvd., P. O. Box 3526, St. Paul, MN 55165; (612) 228-2500.

Every direct marketing manager and entrepreneur needs to understand thoroughly the art of media decisions. In selecting media the following will be useful:

Media Planning: A Quick and Easy Guide
Jim Surmanek; $9.95; *Crain Communications, Inc., 740 Rush Street, Chicago, IL 60611. (312) 649-5215.*

Advertising Media
Donald W. Jugenheimer and Peter Turk; 230 pages; hardbound; $29.95. Step-by-step analysis of media planning process from start to finish. *Grid Publishing Inc., 2950 No. High Street, Box 14466, Columbus, OH 43214. (614) 261-6565.*

Direct Response Broadcast and New Electronic Media (Monograph)
Experts tell how to make broadcasts pay; explain terminology, planning, budgeting, media buying, writing copy; cable and TV video text systems; broadcast production. $24.95; *Direct Mail/ Marketing Association, 6 East 43rd Street, New York, N.Y. 10017. (212) 689-4977.*

The following media directories are important:

Ayer Directory of Publications
Personnel, advertising rates and circulation of more than 22,000 publications; newspapers, dailies and weeklies; magazines: consumer, business, technical; professional, trade; $66; *Ayer Press, One Bala Avenue, Bala Cynwyd, PA 19004. (215) 664-6203.*

Media Cost Guide
Rates and coverage: newspapers, TV, Cable TV, radio, magazines. Approximately TV Guide dimensions; 150 pages; quarterly; $25 per issue; $60 yearly subscription. *Media List Guide, 75 East 55th Street, New York, NY 10022. (212) 751-2671.*

The Media Library
Six market-by-market media planning guides for newspapers, consumer magazines, radio, television, business publications and out-of-home. Highly praised. $162; Encyclomedia, 342 Madison Avenue, New York, NY 10017. (212) 953-1888.

Standard Rate and Data (Price Including Postage)
    Spot Radio and Data, $123.
    Spot Radio Small Markets Edition, $39.
    Spot Television Rates and Data, $110.
    Network Rates and Data, $110.
    Consumer Magazines and Farms Publication Data, $106.
    Business Publications Rates and Data, $125.
    Canadian Advertising Rates and Data, $114.
    Print Media Production Data, $68.
    Direct Mail List Rates and Data, $92.

Published by *Standard Rate and Data Service, Inc., 5201 Old Orchard Road, Skokie, IL 60077.*

The following will be important in selecting outside lists, working your own list and using telephone marketing in conjunction with media and direct mail:

How To Work with Mailing Lists (Monograph)
Richard Hodgson; $12; *Direct Mail/ Marketing Association, 6 East 43rd Street, New York, N.Y. 10017. (212) 689-4977.*

The Buddy Pitch—How To Make It Work
(#7678), Jess Clarke. Make your list grow *and* yield more sales. Build good will while you build profit. $8; *Direct Mail/ Marketing Association, 6 East 43rd Street, New York, N.Y. 10017. (212) 689-4977.*

Telephone Marketing*
Murray Roman; $32.95; *McGraw-Hill Book Company, Princeton Road, Hightstown, NJ 08520. (609) 448-1700.*

Telephone Marketing (Monograph)
Compilation of reports by 10 leading authorities; detailed use in consumer sales, repeat sales, lead generation, fund raising; renewing, billing, upgrading; book promotion; business-to-business selling; prospect screening; pre-sales appointments; how to and when to use WATS lines; legal aspects. $24.95; *Direct Mail/ Marketing Association, 6 East 43rd Street, New York, N.Y. 10017. (212) 689-4977.*

Using 800 Numbers Properly
(#7681), Allan Caplan. How to multiply sales and get your money's worth with 800 telephone service. Pamphlet, $8; *Direct Mail/ Marketing Association, 6 East 43rd Street, New York, N.Y. 10017. (212) 689-4977.*

The smallest moonlighter is concerned with producing an ad or mailing after copy and layout are prepared. For larger more sophisticated direct marketers, it's more important. A career in advertising requires knowledge of it. The following are some books a beginner can learn from and the more experienced sometimes benefit as well.

Preparing Art and Camera Copy for Printing
Henry C. Latimer; Steps, procedures, process at each stage explained and illustrated. 192 pages, 285 illustrations, $31; *McGraw-Hill Book Company, Princeton Road, Hightstown, NJ 08520. (609) 448-1700.*

Complete Guide to Paste Up
Walter B. Graham; paperback, $16; *Modern Litho Printing, P. O. Box 369, Omaha, NE 68101.*

Dover Pictorial Archive Book Catalog
World's largest collection of copyright free-art; over 100,000 designs in over 250 books, mainly at $4 to $5. *Dover Publications, Inc., 180 Varick Street, New York, NY 10014.*

Important in advertising production is a knowledge of type selection. The following can help those starting out.

Type and Typefaces
J. Ben Lieberman; $14.95 hardbound; $9.95 paper; *Myriade Press Inc., 7 Stony Run, New Rochelle, NY 10804; (914) 235-8470.*

Designing with Type
James Craig. $15.95; *Watson Guptil Publications, Inc., 1659 Oak Street, Lakewood, NJ 08701. (201) 363-4511.*

Photo Typesetting
A Design Manual by James Craig. $22.50 *Watson Guptil Publications, Inc., 1659 Oak Street, Lakewood, NJ 08701. (201) 363-4511.*

Computer Age Copyfitting
Leslie Rasberry tells how to copy fit with a simple pocket calculator and an inch-pica ruler. Hot or cold type, large or small layout. $8.95; *Art Direction Book Co., 10 East 39th Street, New York, NY 10016; (212) 889-6500.*

For larger companies and advertising agencies the following are often used to train and upgrade advertising production people and for reference.

Graphics Master #2
Print production workbook; $47.50, 113 pages. Highly recommended. *Dean Lem Associates, Inc., P. O. Box 25920, Los Angeles, CA 90025. (213) 478-0092.*

Graphic Arts Encyclopedia
George A. Stevenson; in 492 pages, with over 3,000 illustrations, answers questions about publications and orients beginners. It's useful for all concerned with producing advertising for direct mail. $34.95; *McGraw-Hill Book Company, Princeton Road, Hightstown, NJ 08520. (609) 448-1700.*

Printing and Promotion Handbook
Daniel Melcher and Nancy Larrick; 1976, $34.95; *McGraw-Hill Book Company, Princeton Road, Hightstown, NJ 08520. (609) 448-1700.*

Possible costly misunderstandings with printers might be avoided by reading the following:

Trade Customs & Printing Contracts
Advice to printers that involves you if you ever buy printing. Their rights and yours as viewed by their association and its lawyers. How long do quotes stand? Cancellation of verbal or written order; ownership of sketches, copy, dummy proposed by printer; of art work, plates, negatives, positives supplied by printer.

Extra charges based on condition of copy, alterations; who pays for errors in different situations; press proof charges; variation of quality between color proofs and printed job; payment of overruns; credit for underruns; damage to work in progress; storage and delivery charges; production schedules; additional costs when customer furnishes materials with wrong specifications; terms; indemnification.

A trade custom not printed in a contract may not be legally enforceable. Your printer may not interpret any individual part according to trade customs. You and your printer can agree to anything regardless. But knowing what printers often expect is vital. Read this booklet. Specify with your printer your mutual understanding. On a big printing order show this booklet to your lawyer, then make legal contract with printer (simple if possible) to avoid later possible dispute. $19.95. *Printing Industries of America, Inc., 1730 North Lynn Street, Arlington, VA 22209; (703) 841-8139.*

For big companies and agencies the following may be useful:

The Creative Black Book
Lists over 23,000 suppliers for graphic arts, advertising, promotion publications, films, etc. International; $45, 1982. *Friendly Publications, Inc., 401 Park Avenue South, New York, NY 10016. (212) 684-4255.*

The fastest growth mail order medium is TV, which makes the following book important.

How to Produce an Effective TV Commercial
Hooper White; practical comprehensive; covers essential steps; choosing production company; negotiating; editing decisions; new technology; 302 pages; hard cover, $25.95. *Crain Communications, Inc., 740 Rush Street, Chicago, IL 60611. (312) 649-5215.*

After you get all those orders and inquiries the following books become important:

Fulfillment Operations in Direct Marketing (Monograph)
An introduction: collaboration of FMA, DMMA and 29 experts. What to avoid in your order form that will cause fulfillment problems; how and where to open mail, equipment, procedures, work flow; personnel; handling; sorting; cashiering; batching; depositing; mail opening machines, optional scanning equipment, document procedures; security; credit and collection. $24.95; *Direct Mail/Marketing Association, 6 East 43rd Street, New York, NY. 10017. (212) 689-4977.*

Keep Your Customers (And Keep Them Happy)*
Stanley J. Fenvessy. Ask for it in your library.

A Common Sense Approach
Ray Vitullo; A system to screen and process, record and track inquiries; study and analyze performance of ads. 53 pages; $25; *Raymond and Nicholas Advertising, 330 Mountain Avenue, North Plainfield, NJ 07060. (201) 754-6400.*

More and more the emphasis is to treat direct marketing as an area of overall marketing and to apply all the skills of general marketing to it. For this, the following books are recommended:

Fundamentals of Marketing
William J. Stanton; University of Colorado; $19.95; *McGraw-Hill Book Company, Princeton Road, Hightstown, NJ 08520. (609) 448-1700.*

Marketing Management
Philip Kotler; 1980 edition, hard cover $26. *Prentice Hall Inc., Englewood Cliffs, NJ 07632; (201) 592-2000.*

Adventures of a Bystander; $12.95 hardbound, $4.95 paperback.
Age of Discontinuity; $13.95 for hardbound; 15.95 for paperback,
Concept of the Corporation; $11.95
The Effective Executive; $12.00
Management, Tasks, Responsibilities, Practices; $23.95
Managing for Results; $12.50
Managing in Turbulent Times; $10.95
The Practice of Management; $16.95 for hardbound; $4.50 for paperback.
Technology, Management and Society; $3.95 paperback only.
Peter Drucker; *Harper & Row Publications, Inc., 10 East 53rd Street, New York, NY 10022. (212) 593-7000.*

Success in the U.S. leads to mail order expansion overseas. To do so, the following can be helpful.

Handbook of International Direct Marketing*
John Dillon; $44.95; *McGraw-Hill Book Company, Princeton Road, Hightstown, NJ 08520. (609) 448-1700.*

Foreign Commerce Handbook
Guide to organizations that are helpful in international trade; describes in alphabetical order 100 key subjects. #6244, $10. *U.S. Chamber of Commerce, Special Publications Dept., 1615 "H" Street NW, Washington, DC 20062. (202) 659-5602.*

International Direct Marketing Service Directory
Over 270 names of direct response suppliers on 6 continents and in 25 countries: creative agencies, printers, lettershops, list brokers, EDP bureaus and fulfillment services with telephone numbers; $12.95; *Information Center, Direct Mail/Marketing Association, 6 East 43rd Street, New York, NY. 10017. (212) 689-4977.*

The future of mail order will be electronic, say many. If so, the following books are particularly useful to those interested.

Guide to Electronic Publishing
For book, magazine and newspaper publishers and those starting from scratch. Co-authors Frances Spigai and Peter Sommer explain the opportunities and pitfalls. Covers on line and newsdata systems; $95. *Knowledge Industry Publications, Inc., 701 Westchester Avenue, White Plains, NY 10604. (914) 328-9157.*

Video Discs: The Technology, the Applications and the Future
$29.95; *Knowledge Industry Publications, Inc., 701 Westchester Avenue, White Plains, NY 10604. (914) 328-9157.*

Videotext: The Coming Revolution in Home/Office Information Retrieval
Edited by Efrem Sigel; $24.95. *Knowledge Industry Publications, Inc., 701 Westchester Avenue, White Plains, NY 10604. (914) 328-9157.*

Future Development in Telecommunications
James Martin; 668 pages, $37. *Prentice-Hall, Inc., Englewood Cliffs, NJ 07632. (201) 592-2000.*

A valuable source for latest books on mail order, geared usually for substantial firms, is the book catalog of the DMMA.

Books for Direct Marketers
The DMMA's selection of direct marketing publications for the professional. Each issue adds more excellent ones. Books, newsletters, magazines; all available from this one source: *Direct Mail/Marketing Association, 6 East 43rd Street, New York, NY. 10017. (212) 689-4977.*

Great Book of Catalogs
A classified directory of over 2,000 U.S. Mail order catalogs. 176 pages, $9.95. *Steve and Betsy Pinkerton, Pinkerton Marketing, Inc., 135 Oak Terrace, Lake Bluff, IL 60044.*

Inside the Leading Mail Order Houses
The top 200; the new growth companies; who owns and runs each and how each markets; a summary of each business; the company history, facilities; actual or estimated volume, profits; number of catalogs mailed; average order; size of customer list; $65. *Maxwell Sroge Publishing, 731 North Cascade, Colorado Springs, CO 80903.*

Reference Section IV
Continuous, Custom Direct Marketing Course

Advice from top authorities in specific areas . . . specialized guidance to help develop your business and career.

Many whom you've met in previous pages have written or spoken in more detail on subjects you may be interested in. I list some of this material with brief description and tell how to get it, in the following pages.

Many others can help you with their experience and advice. Described here is how-to-help from the huge selection available . . . of talks and speeches, lectures and panels of experts . . . and of interviews and articles and stories and reports . . . concerning a wide variety of aspects of direct marketing. There is so much useful help that this section is just a sampler of what is available . . . and there is more all the time.

This help is sometimes given by a chief executive officer, a founder, an important Fortune 500 executive or a controlling owner of an important service organization. Much of it is by executives not available as consultants. Some of it is by the most expensive specialized consultants . . . helping for no pay. Included is help by those who have succeeded in specialized ways, sometimes on a small scale.

There is help to start at a bottom job, to rise, and for top executives to keep up and expand horizons; for biggest companies to open a mail order division or expand one; for smallest moonlighters to start part-time at home; and for entrepreneurs in between. This custom coaching and tutoring covers the widest variety of subjects concerning mail order.

Sometimes material is taken from a session of a university course, a mini-seminar or a key part of an association meeting, a direct marketing club meeting, a Direct Marketing Day. Sometimes it's an interview, news story or special report or issue of a publication. In some cases, it's from a program or special issue an organization or magazine may have taken up to a year to prepare.

Leaders and experts pass the word on subjects each knows best, often in surprisingly forthcoming detail. None gives a blueprint for sure success. Many provide specific do's and don'ts. You may get exposure to concepts, tactics, strategies and techniques new to you . . . or in more detail than before. Knowing more about what is working and what is failing can help make better decisions and improve performance. Anything an expert says or writes may stimulate your mind and prod and jog your thinking into an application to your own activities.

Sometimes basics and fundamentals are covered, and other times sophisticated methods. I'll indicate which. You can select guidelines which apply most to you. Advice is often quite candid with specific warnings important to know. There is hard-earned information which successful direct marketers pool with each other. Often analysis and discussion are quite thorough concerning a special area with detailed suggestions how to start and organize . . . to execute and operate.

Beginners at big companies are oriented. Smaller company owners and managers learn the principles, practices and methods successful for the big. Even the tiny can often find useful tips, mind-tickling and idea-stirring stimulation, and solid background facts needed and before perhaps not known. From the moment you consider a mail order career or business . . . to your successful retirement or selling out . . . at each stage sound advice is available.

From the wealth of publications, articles and taped talks available I've selected several hundred I've felt representative of those most useful. I describe each help source, sometimes with a line or two, sometimes with a sampling of the advice contained. You can research a product field, a way of selling, a consultant or organization. You can select as tutors and coaches from the successful in any of most mail order activities.

How would you like a course in mail order taught you by the executives (past and present) of a company that has successfully made over two billion dollars of mail order sales . . . a course that has never been taught before assembled in this way . . . but which you can take personally?

You can assemble such a course taught you by the executives of Time-Life Books. Or you can put together a course of even broader scope taught you by various executives of the entire Time Inc. Corporation. You can have a course taught you by the executives of Wunderman, Ricotta & Kline, the largest direct marketing advertising agency, including superb lectures by the founder, Lester Wunderman. Or you could make up your own course taught you by executives of various organizations.

It can be in printed form, on tape or both. The printed material is from articles from publications found in many business and college libraries. Copies of the articles or back issues containing them are available from the magazine publisher at low cost.

The use of tapes can be helpful and timesaving, especially for those who commute by car. Companies can rotate tapes among employees. The cost of giving the entire New York University Direct Marketing Course to each new trainee can be nominal. Tapes of the really great speeches, such as Lester Wunderman's, have an excitement and charisma that print does not convey. My hope is that business libraries will begin to make the tapes described available.

A big share comes from Hoke Communications, Inc. Another huge share comes from the Direct Mail Marketing Association, but mostly for members . . . so much so to make membership a bargain. In recent years, ZIP magazine has become a source of major research articles on key developments; from insert programs to laser letters. DM News has contributed special sections in every issue on entire fields—from TV direct marketing to printers specializing in direct marketing. In this section, I refer also to other sources, including chapters of this book.

Please note that the mailing address of each of the above is not repeated under individual listings of research material listed in this section. Instead refer to Section VII, page 443, for these addresses. The addresses of less frequently referred to research sources are given under each listing in the Help Source Section.

Every article described I read. Many tapes are by those I interviewed in this book. Many are by others whose work I am familiar with and have studied or listened to. But in writing this section I, in many ways, drew on material written by the magazines listed, particularly "Pete" Hoke's longer reviews of tapes in Friday Report and his staff's shorter ones in "Ideas in Sound."

Those types of articles and speeches that primarily explain current state of the art technology, or predict the future, age rapidly. Those types which concern creative approaches and case histories rarely age—and I recommend them accordingly.

Rather than an alphabetical indexing I've tried to aid you to

select your own custom course by arranging references according to your mail order situation. Let's start.

Beginning

Now let's consider how to locate how-to information which might help to get a beginning job in direct marketing or, perhaps, to start a quite small mail order business, possibly even part time—from home. There are simple ways to do either. Remember, much of this book and most of the help sources listed are to help expand success—acorns to become oaks—the big to become bigger and more profitable . . . and often in complex ways.

Yet beginners need not be confused or overwhelmed by the size, sophistication and technological changes of direct marketing. The newest, and certainly the small to tiny, can at first ignore much of all so laboriously assembled here . . . but which may help mightily later. But let's do first things first! Consider referring to the following:

Getting a Job in Mail Order*
How best to do it—without experience . . . when beginners are turned away. Seminar I, Chapter 5, this book.

Helping Direct Marketing Beginners*
Freeman Gosden, Jr., President of Smith-Hemmings-Gosden of El Monte, California, not only runs a top direct marketing agency. His major hobby is educating, talking to and helping young people to get started in, and succeed in, direct marketing. Seminar III, Chapter 13, this book.

Starting in Direct Marketing*
Apply a skill to learn more, advance more and make more in career and your own business. See Seminar IX, Chapter 8, this book.

A Mail Order Fortune*
What way to make it is fastest and easiest? That was the question asked a prestigious panel at Direct Marketing Day in New York. Read how top consultant Dick Benson answered it. Seminar VI, Chapter 11, this book.

Your Best Mail Order Opportunity*
Most perfect for traits, interest, training and experience; for situation, lifestyle and pace. See Overview, Chapter 2, this book.

The Mail Order Underground*
How most businesses start . . . with classified ads . . . sometimes for the price of dinner, even breakfat. See Overview, Chapter 14, this book.

Retirement Mail Order*
Why more retirees are going into it, and have; some cautions. Seminar V, Chapter 3, this book.

Mail Order Fun*
How to make money unscientifically. Seminar IX, Chapter 12, this book.

Success in Mail Order—West Coast Conference DM—9/27 -28/79
Freeman Gosden, Jr. tells how. On tape, Hoke; Part I: # 19-0404 - LA - $16; Part II: # 19-0412 - LA $16.

Mail Order Success from scratch
It's still possible but it's tougher to start a mail order business today than it used to be, says Peggy Ryan. She is Director of Mail Order for House Beautiful Magazine, 717 Fifth Avenue, New York, NY (10022).

One or two items are not enough. You need extra products to offer to new customers. Over 25 years, Peggy has sold close to 10,000 pages of mail order ads. She averages 363 pages a year, mostly of small ads. She has seen thousands of mail order firms start mostly from moonlighting; many grow and prosper and many come and go.

New mail order people come in all shapes and sizes . . . from ambitious young people to bored, retired senior citizens. A new business with the best chance of success is one that zeroes in on a specific merchandise category and makes it its own. Peggy cites Yield House Furniture kits and The Stitchery (needleworks kits) as examples.

The most important first step is research. Learn the mail order marketplace. See how a catalog is put together. Understand how orders are fulfilled. Then seek advice. On tape, Hoke; # 10-0530 - LK - $10. Important for small to medium beginners. Also article in DM magazine; April 1981, Volume 43, # 12

Suppose instead of starting your own business you've got your entry job in direct marketing and now want advancement. You wonder what the next step is. The fastest career advancement often means working for the winning companies. They seek career winners to work for them. Competition for jobs and for advancement is greater. Here is a summary of help sources to aid you to determine their requirements, to aim higher, be more qualified, then learn more and faster . . . to have a better chance in the race to rise.

Read also of special advice for creative people, of fast career success, of specialized mail order career success - even in a museum, of the use of specialized ways of working, of career success for women.

Mail Order Cum Laude
Robin Smith went to Wellesley, was one of the first 18 women to go to Harvard Business School, went on to become president of 10 Doubleday Book Clubs, then of Dell Publishing, then of Publishers Clearing House. Her mail order career story and some good career advice from her. Seminar VIII, Chapter 6, this book.

The Job Market—NYU, 3/7/78
How to shape your career. Prominent direct marketers' careers examined. Robin Smith on tape, Hoke; # 18-0002-NY - $10.

Getting a Better Job in Direct Marketing*
"How to Reach Your $50,000 Goal" is the title of a speech by Karen Gillick. She helps people in direct marketing to do it . . . together with her partner, Suzanne Ridenour, in Gillick-Ridenour Associates. Her story, some tips to get into and up in direct marketing. Seminar III, Chapter 11, this book.

Stimulating Direct Marketing Careers*
Nat Ross is founder of the Direct Marketing Idea Exchange and, for 15 years, has conducted the New York University Direct Marketing Course. How he has helped many become leaders in direct marketing and perhaps can help you. Seminar III, Chapter 4, this book.

Success as a Direct Mail Manager—DM Conf., LA, 1/23-24/78
Freeman Gosden, Jr.'s ten success rules; a checklist of what to be aware of; a dozen tips on how to learn from the competition; much more. On tape, Hoke; # 18-0061 - LA $8.

Direct Marketing Personnel Trends—100 Million Club, 1/10/80
Experienced direct marketing personnel are in short supply, says consultant Richard Benson. He goes on to say that companies operate with too few people, without training programs, and then steal experienced personnel from each other. He explains how the results can be great opportunities for those wth experience. On tape, Hoke; #10-0129 - HM - $7.

The Mail Order Recruiter*
Hal Crandall; how he pre-selects his candidates. His career advice to anyone in considering direct marketing. Seminar II, Chapter 6, this book.

Direct Marketing Job Myths
When job hunting or hiring, many lose by not questioning myths, says consultant Hal Crandall. Some myths are: 1) It's hard to get a job after 40; 2) You must exaggerate past earnings; 3) It's fatal to be unemployed when job hunting. Yet, biggest opportunities come to those over 40, with a record. Exaggerating earnings can easily be checked and *lose* a job. When unemployed, you have the advantage that you can start at once. Much more. DM magazine; October 1979, Volume 42, # 6.

Fired Direct Marketers Tell Why
Job consultant Crandall tells why their traumas sometimes caused later success; how they then capitalized on past mistakes . . . and turned adversity to future benefit. DM magazine; September 1980, Volume 43, # 5.

How to Get a Job
Hal Crandall explains how flexibility can help; how long to stay in one direct marketing job; how to price yourself salary-wise; critical factors; interview problems; advice from top executives in field. Excellent. DM News; April 15, 1980.

Direct Response Techniques Can Be the Key to Your Career
Caroline Zimmerman is an authority on direct marketing and author of books on career advancement. She also heads her own advertising agency. She says: Use direct response for your career. Write reports, strategy statements, new business proposals, with reader in mind. Translate product/service features into "reader benefits" in all communications, just like advertising. On tape, Hoke; # 11-0207 - JP - $12.

How to Get a Copywriting Job—DMCG, 4/4/78
A panel of creative heads from agencies and advertisers describe whom they hire, how they hire, why they consider candidates and why they rule them out . . . from sloppy, misspelled resumes to claiming credit for work never performed or overpriced, self-proclaimed experts. Very useful. On tape, Hoke; # 19-0164 - DW - $8.

Helping Creative People Rise in Direct Marketing*
The Direct Marketing Guild bands together those who create direct marketing advertising. How it helps beginners break in, rise and succeed. Seminar VI, Chapter 9, this book.

The Fast Track to Direct Marketing Success*
How George Wiedemann became one of the youngest circulation managers of Time Magazine, the youngest senior vice president of the biggest direct marketing agency and the founding president of Grey Direct . . . the direct marketing subsidiary of Grey Advertising . . . a top ten general agency . . . and its almost instant success. Seminar VI, Chapter 7, this book.

Making a Career in Museum Mail Order*
How Paul Jones started from the bottom in Gimbel's department store, got into direct mail; how he went into the lettershop field, rose through the ranks . . . a black man in a white mail order world . . . how he joined the Metropolitan Museum of Art and became Director of Direct Marketing. Seminar V, Chapter 11, this book.

The Making of a Direct Marketer*
David Heneberry is president of TLK Advertising, the direct marketing subsidiary of Tatham-Laird & Kudner, a top-ten general agency. He is former president of RCA Direct Marketing. How his entire career success evolved and benefitted from willingness and ability to work a new way. Seminar VII, Chapter 7, this book.

Women in Direct Marketing*
Their present opportunities; what their own organization, The Women's Direct Marketing Group, is doing about their future; how it helps women get started, then rise in direct marketing. Seminar V, Chapter 5, this book.

Winning Women in Direct Marketing—DMMA Conference, 10/27/80
Eileen Rhudy-Sonheim, VP of Market Compilation & Research Bureau; Jo-Von Tucker, The Photographers, Inc.; Rosalie Bruno, Knapp Communications Corp.; Helen Sevier, Bass Angler's Sportsman Society; how each made it; on tape, Hoke; # 10-0555 - DM - $15.

Making a Career as a Woman Direct Marketing Consultant
How Betty Anne Noakes learned direct marketing in Canada (at the Reader's Digest), went to New York, succeeded in direct marketing; how she joined the then biggest direct mail consulting firm . . . then started on her own . . . and made it. Some sound advice for anyone using direct mail and for those starting careers. Seminar IV, Chapter 6, this book.

Mail Order Research

It's still in its infancy. Old timers are often most reluctant to use it . . . and upcoming young executives most eager. It's constantly being used in new ways. Fortune 500 companies in mail order are partial to it. There are plenty of speeches, talks and articles on it, available on tape or in print. I'll describe some.

Why Market Research is Important—International DM Conference, 2/24-27/81
Research Consultant Robert Kaden explains: Good research can cut costs and increase efficiency of mail order campaigns. Kaden discusses mail order applications of research in pre-testing, post-testing, theory, pratical case studies, problem solving. On tape, Hoke; # 11-0076 - DM - $$22.00 (2 tapes).

People Research*
Robert J. Kaden, President of Goldring & Co., a leading research firm, tells how to use it to sell more in mail order. Seminar III, Chapter 7, this book.

Finding the Gold*
A direct marketing statistical scientist, Orlan Gaeddert, describes his job and how statistical research pays off in mail order. Seminar V, Chapter 9, this book.

How to Use Statistics in Direct Marketing*
Consultant and Professor Robert C. Blattberg details. Seminar VIII, Chapter 3, this book.

Using a Statistical Approach
Direct mail is a statistical business, says Orlan Gaeddert. When mailing campaign numbers are properly analyzed, they often reveal patterns to use as a successful marketing tool. A statistician helps by constructing a simulated model to approximate the outcome of a proposed campaign. Still valid. Worthwhile. DM magazine; May 1974, Volume 37, #1.

Focus Groups
Gene Telser, consultant, explains what they are and what they can do, how extremely useful they can be if understood and used properly; what to do in forming a group, knowing what questions you want answered and what kind of people you want answers from. DM magazine; June 1980, Volume 43, #2.

Consumer Reaction to Direct Mail—DM West Coast Conference
Dan Kubic, VP of Televisa in Los Angeles, and Win Barnes, President of Kross, Inc., in San Fernando, California, explain

how a focus group works and what it can tell you to help make your direct mail more effective. On tape, Hoke; # 19-0409 - LA -$8.

Research When Introducing New Products
Roger Lourie, former director of New Product Development Group, Time-Life Books, explains its use—to define and develop the logical extension opportunities of your company's basic business. How best to introduce new products. DM magazine; December 1977, Volume 40, #8.

Research Techniques To Increase Response—DMMA, Paris, 2/24 - 27/81
Robert Kaden cites case histories to show you how to apply them; how to supplement information gained from mail order tests. On tape, Hoke; # 11-0087 - DM - $22 (2 tapes).

Promise Testing LIDMA, March, 1980
A very thorough report of an important speech by Jerome Pickholz . . . on a research technique that Ogilvy & Mather Direct Response Inc. (of which he is president), has found most effective. He says, "All ads promise . . . but great ads promise the single most important benefit or difference the product or service has to offer." He then shows how to isolate that promise "before the first piece of mail is dropped." DM News; April 15, 1980.

The Importance of Color in Advertising—DMMA Manual
Kurt Vahle explains the dramatic and psychological effects, tradition about color, attraction vs. visibility, reactions to colors. Release 4050; reissued February 1978.

The Impact of Changing Demographics—NYU, 1/20/82
The 1980 census showed major shifts: Working women; lifestyles; age distribution; geographics; Peter K. Francese gives insights into effects of these changes on direct marketing. On tape, Hoke; # 12-0001 - NY - $10.

The Use of Surveys in Direct Marketing Research
Six basic ways research can improve mail order profits; advantages, disadvantages of mail surveys; how to construct, conduct and follow-up a mail survey for most effective response; analysis of findings; DMMA Manual.

Survey of Durable Goods Companies
Conducted by the Business/Industrial Council of the DMMA. 44% of respondents considered direct mail important to their marketing sampling of 735 companies. An excellent summary of this report is in the DM News, November 15, 1981.

Perceptions, Behavior & Attitudes.
Of American Express cardholders regarding direct mail; report by National Analysts, a division of Booz-Allen & Hamilton for American Express Company in cooperation with the Direct Mail Marketing Association; their unaided vs. aided awareness of offers received; kinds most likely to cause positive reaction and why; negative reactions.

Response to offers vs. attitudes; kinds of offers most likely to have been responded to by cardmembers vs. potential card members; percentage of cardmembers who responded to each of various kinds of American Express offers; what percentage tend to like buying through the mails; tend to feel they get too many offers; characteristics of card members who responded to American Express mail offers.

An important study but not publicly available; American Express and the DMMA have kindly agreed to make it available to readers of this book for examination at the library of the DMMA, 6 East 43rd Street, NYC. Phone for appointment (212) 689-4977. Non-members by appointment Wednesdays only.

Finding and Developing Products

Some mail order firms are far better at it than others. Some mail order people have an exceptional knack at it. Small or large, no mail order business can attain maximum growth without the ability to do it. None can even start without a product.

It's not easy. There's no simple secret. Yet some people consistently do it very well. In this book I tell the stories of entrepreneurs with a knack for it. One is about Ed Stern* who found safe, sound success . . . developing one new product after another. Ed Stern is the owner of one publishing company . . . an executive of a second . . . and receives royalties from a third . . . all due to his flair for developing products. Seminar III, Chapter 6, this book.

How to Create a Product For Mail Order Success

In DM magazine he tells how to create a product for mail order success and how he did it. Ed Stern became interested in the side effects of prescription drugs due to a personal experience. He converted his interest to a mail order success for his then employer, Grosset & Dunlop, Inc. It wasn't easy. He researched the market, determined the need, wrote the book. Then he tested cautiously for G & D and came up with a hit (sales are now over 650,000 copies). He still gets royalties. DM magazine; June 1977, Volume 40, #2; also on tape, Hoke; # 17-0179 - AJ - $8.

In August 1981, Ed gave a talk at the 100 Million Club in New York City. He told more; how a small entrepreneur can find a successful product to sell and avoid product failure. It's on tape, Hoke; # 11-0531 - HM - $10.

There is more how-to information which might help you whatever kind of product or service you wish to sell by mail order. Here are descriptions of several talks and articles I recommend.

Survival of the Smartest

It's from new products. Tomorrow's survival is today's new idea. The business which doesn't plan its future often finds no future. Roger Lourie, former manager New Product Development Group, Time-Life Books, details. DM magazine; March 1980, Volume 42, #11.

Development and Merchandising—DM & MO Symposium, 4/26-28/78

Roy Abrams teaches how to create and sell a product; explains techniques to develop products, then merchandise to specific market segments, with case studies. On tape, Hoke; #18-0201 - 1D - $6.

New Product Development—NYU, 11/14/78

Experts tell what it takes to create an effective new product development program; how to generate ideas; come up with new concepts, evaluate them; the critical factors in marketing a product . . . timing, financing, costs. On tape, Hoke; #18-0307 -NY - $12.

Now you have a job or business in direct marketing and are beginning to succeed at it. You particularly want to get more know-how in advertising, both creative and in media, and in overall marketing. Let's start with creative . . . first things first.

The Offer

Direct Marketing's Most Misunderstood Concept

"It makes or breaks pulling power of ads," says Jim Kobs, President of Kobs & Brady. How Jim Kobs' expertise in offers helped his clients, helped him and his partner build a tremendously successful advertising agency and can help you. Seminar IX, Chapter 1, this book.

99 Direct Response Offers That Can Improve Results

Jim Kobs' check list of tested, successful propositions to improve results of a mail order ad. DM magazine; October 1975, Volume 38, #6.

Mail Order Guarantees—DMMA Manual

Dick Hodgson shows and explains guarantees used by mail order advertisers: Sears Roebuck, Encyclopedia Britannica, Publishers Clearing House, others. Release 2104, September 1978.

Writing Successful Ad Headlines—DMCG, 2/6/80

One of my bigger mistakes over 25 years ago was not hiring Tom Collins. He became co-founder of Rapp & Collins . . . a great creative writer for a great creative direct marketing agency. He says: Ad headlines should appeal to the "cave man values" of prospects. Benefits include survival, freedom, comfort, escape . . . get to know your prospect before writing . . . people are too busy for subtle headlines that hope to arouse curiosity. If the benefits to the prospects are carefully delineated, the headline will write itself. Push product advantages . . . why it's better, bigger or faster. On tape, Hoke; # 10-0044 - DW - $10.

How to Write Successful Closing Copy—DMMA Manual

Consultant Maxwell Ross cites specific examples of good closing copy . . . limited offer, guarantee, no obligation, send no money, installment . . . the P.S. close . . . how to do each. Release 6306, February 1978.

Your Order Card

More creative use to generate improved response. ZIP magazine; June 1982.

Recipe for Writing Great Copy—DM Creative Guide, 5/7/80

Three copy authorities . . . Leonard Reiss, President of Schwab & Beatty . . . Frank Johnson, Consultant . . . and Irving Wunderman, Sr., V.P. of WR&K, give it as "five parts strategy, one part poetry"; 75% of what makes an ad or direct mail piece work is the soundness of the strategy used as a base . . . knowing what to say is more important than how you say it . . . good advertising consists of making a believable promise to the right audience . . . copy doesn't have to be eloquent. It can be colloquial, but must be grammatically correct . . . make copy interesting. The public does not consist of creative people but does determine the rules of advertising; the five elements outlined. On tape, Hoke; #10-0292 - DW - $10.

Seven Deadly Mail Order Mistakes—DMMA Manual

Pioneer expert Maxwell Sackheim's classic don't's in writing copy. Release 210.1; April 1977, written decades earlier.

Classic Mail Order Copy*

Fred Breismeister has sold books, clubs, continuity programs, sets and magazines for Doubleday, Hearst and others. He has written more how-to mail order copy than anyone I know. He wrote the copy for the first continuity programs in the U.S. He taught me much, trained members of Hoge alumni and gave valuable creative advice while telling his story, "From Immigrant Boy to Millionaire Copywriter . . . across the decades". Seminar VIII, Chapter 4, this book.

The Editing Process—DMMA Manual

Guy Yolton, founder of his own Washington D.C. advertising agency, says it is paramount to writing good copy. He cites seven major areas to edit carefully for effectiveness: 1) for warm-up; 2) for stoppers; 3) "author's pride"; 4) asking for order; 5) for reason why; 6) for the market, and 7) to stretch benefits. Release 6307; issued May 1976.

Direct Response Graphics—DMMA Manual
Fundamentals for the Art Director. Victor Zolfo, V.P., Throckmorton-Zolfo. Release 330.1, May 1979.

Art and Design—London DM Day, 10/12/78
Time-Life Books creative executives explain effective use in designing a direct mail package; how the package is created; what dictates its size; when does art control copy? On tape, Hoke; #18-0462 - BD - $8.

Breakthroughs in Copy and Graphics—NYU, 10/9/78
Irving Wunderman and Bill Keisler, two great R&K ad creators, examine today's foremost creative teams to learn how they apply rules and break them; how to find real problems advertising must solve; arrive at approaches worth testing; lessons to learn from successful and failed ads; how to develop a critic's view of your own work. On tape, Hoke; #18-0303 - NY - $12.

Copy and Design in Promotion—NYU, 3/10/81
Spencer Lambert, T-L Books alumnus, outlines the creative problem-solving approach: The creative staff must expand its role to the entire promotional process . . . to fulfill objectives and beat controls. Specific objectives are necessary. Position the product against competition; spell out its unique aspects. Emphasize the advantages of price, product and offer.

Lambert outlines necessary creative decisions: If the concept is not different from an idea someone else is successful with, don't test; but if you go ahead, test big. Putting together a mailing piece or space ad takes teamwork. The creative staff must be in the total marketing program . . . even suggest out of its area, for instance price policy. In reverse, if a list person has a copy idea, the creative staff must listen.

Lambert says that the function of the envelope is not solely to get people to open it. The envelope is your store window, welcoming your customer. The brochure is the store itself; order commands to "order now" really work. Specification boxes with details are important.

Creative people must watch market place trends. He cites Time-Life Books experience. Featuring King Tut in advertising the "History of Man" series . . . during the King Tut craze . . . was very successful. Inflation created the trends that make the Time-Life series successful on "How To-Fix-It" for the home. On tape, Hoke; #11-0003 - NY - $15.

Copy Art and Creativity—NYU, 10/30/79
Don Kanter, Copy Chief of Stone & Adler, establishes their functions and objectives . . . explores the basis of creativity. On tape, Hoke; #19-0309 - NY - $12.

Copy, Art, Graphics—NYU
Dick Jordan and Vic Zolfo give a step-by-step guide to create each effective selling element. On tape, Hoke; #18-0003 - NY -$10.

Managing successful Creative Interaction—DMMA Manual
Its five basic steps. Release 330.1; May 1979.

Understanding Creative Types
Consultant Wendell Forbes explains: The care, feeding and appreciation of those who write copy and make layout . . . needed if they are to make maximum money for you. Valuable. Folio Magazine; February 1977.

"Creatives" vs. "The Organization"—DMMA Conference, 3/10-13/81
Should "creatives" conform? Should the "organization" compromise? Or should it confront? Pierre Passavant, at his best, gives straightforward ideas to help artists/writers and managers/administrators work together at their best. On tape, Hoke;

#11-0180 - DM - $10. Also see Passavant's excellent, similar article, "Management vs. Creative: The Art of Compromise"; DM magazine; June 1980, Volume 43, #2.

Effective Direct Response Typography
Copy authority Don Hauptman gives "how-to guidelines on graphics" to help insure that your strong copy gets the strong design it deserves. DM magazine; December 1979, Volume 42, #8.

How to Tell What's Wrong and Right About Creative Work— NYU Advanced, 7/20/81
Tom Collins explains and teaches: How to recognize and use priceless essentials of creative planning and evaluation; make your ads visualize and attract the true prospect, reflect the most appropriate ultimate benefit, and lead the reader by the hand from mild interest all the way up the staircase to the response decision. On tape, Hoke; #11-0417 - NY - $25.

Should You Write Copy by Formula?—DMMA Manual
Properly used, yes. Well-known copy formulae are cited and described. Some are known by their initials: A-I-D-A, D-D-P-C and P-P-P-P. There are Frank Egner's nine points, Jack Lacy's five points and Robert Stone's seven points. Release 6301; reissued November 1976.

Style and Substance in Direct Marketing—DMIX, 5/10/78
"They can't be separated," says George Lois, one of the greatest creators of general advertising. "Direct response is not all technical savvy, lists, media, die-cut inserts, premium offers and mumbo jumbo of details that obscure product advertising." Lois pleads for genuinely talented art directors, more class, elegance in direct response ads. Important. On tape, Hoke; #18-0233 - IX -$8.

25 Ways to Improve Your Inquiry Response Rate—DMMA Manual
Expert Herbert G. Ahrend's checklist to make your inquiry-getting more profitable is divided into universally applicable suggestions: Ideas which apply only to space ads, ideas for direct mail and methods of qualifying (or limiting) inquiries. Release 815.1; issued April 1978.

Bad Copy's Major Sins—New England DMA, 11/5/81
Two of them are lack of clarity and dullness, says John Tighe. Long paragraphs, sentences, drag down copy pace. Keep copy moving, he advises. Brevity, proper use of white space, short lines, make for good copy structure. Use teasers on envelope to appeal to reader's emotions. On tape, Hoke; #11-0746 - PB - $10.

How to Recharge Creative Batteries—New England Association of DM, 3/12/80
Stan Rapp is President of Rapp & Collins, a superb idea man and noted for his ability to get others to come up with creative answers they thought they couldn't. He says: "Get the creative juices flowing with the positive, motivational 'I wish' formula . . . It makes use of outrageously and seemingly unrealistic ideas to stimulate solutions to marketing problems."

"First get the situation clearly fixed in your mind, then do some 'lateral thinking'. Allow your thoughts to travel to the fantasy part of the brain—where the bulk of ideas come from. Then work on and gradually form the idea into a realistic one. Creativity is part of us all. Everyone has the ability to recharge these creative batteries." On tape, Hoke; #10-0137 - NE - $10.

Seven New Ways to Be Creative—100 Million Club, 5/10/79
Expert Caroline Zimmerman says creative rules must be broken to succeed in direct mail. The key to success is knowing when and how. She cites examples. She gives seven new ways you can be creative. On tape, Hoke; #19-0264 - HM - $8.

The Most Prolific Copywriter I've Met*
How Gene Schwartz started at Huber Hoge; how his copy later launched "The Boardroom" newsletter . . . sells books for Rodale Press . . . some of his advice on copywriting. Seminar VIII, Chapter 8, this book.

Direct Marketing's Unsung Heroes
How editors, marketing people, presidents and publishers all have a hand in producing truly excellent direct mail pieces . . . by Christopher Stagg; DM magazine; February 1981, Volume 43, #10.

Translating Mail Order Success From One Medium to Another— Washington DM Club, 1977
Barry Blau, formerly chief, Ogilvy and Mather Direct . . . and long before a Hoge alumnus . . . says: "A great sales pitch in one medium is almost always translatable into another. A good 'copy surgeon' can take a TV spot from a print ad and create a pure, hard, crystallized sales message." Barry shares experiences and lessons learned. On tape, Hoke; #17-0496 - WM - $6. Also in DM magazine; September 1978, Volume 41, #5.

How to Tap Emotional "Trigger"
George Duncan, top consultant in copy and promotion, explains the emotional nature of direct mail and the role emotions play in making decisions. On tape, Hoke; #10-0593 - PB - $7.

David Ogilvy On Advertising—100 Million Club, 1/14/82
Taped from a film presentation. What to test, how to create effective direct response ads. Hoke; #12-0053 - HM - $12.

The Basics of Direct Marketing—DM Day NYC, 3/29/79
A Pierre Passavant mini-seminar. covers copy, art; how to get maximum response; gives intensive review of elements necessary to make advertising successful, profitable. On tape, Hoke; #19-0134 - ND - $8.

How to Get Response
How to pull inquiries and orders: Pierre Passavant covers copy, art; business promotion, consumer; positioning your company; studying the product; gives 10 major elements of method to develop "best offer". He discusses in detail personalized promotion (computers, ink jet, laser); he tells how to use art to increase readership and response; how to use premiums; what creative tests to make and how; he covers promotion after the order comes in (resale, inserts, referrals). Good. On tape, Hoke; #11-0459 - PP - $24.

Eagles and Turkeys—San Diego DMD, February 1980
Some packages fly, some don't. Hank Burnett explains why, and gives some of the real tricks of the direct mail copywriting trade. On tape, Hoke; #10-0048 - SD - $12.

The Essentials of Direct Mail—San Diego DMD, February 1980
A mini-institute by top writer and consultant Chris Stagg, who has written winning subscription copy for leading magazines . . . has been a consultant, a top creative director, founded and headed the DMMA Creative Council and has been president of the biggest direct mail consultant firm at the time and of the Direct Marketing Creative Guild. He's a great teacher and on tape, Hoke; #10-0047 - SD - $10.

Writing Winning Direct Mail Copy—LIDMA, 9/19/79
Consultant Lawrence Chait advises: Spend 80% of your time searching, investigating and planning and 20% creating the direct mail package. Chait traces the necessary steps to assemble evidence before writing; cites examples well done; advises concentration on selling inactive customers; gives 10-point copywriting plan which exemplifies his 80-20 rule. On tape, Hoke; #19-0395 - LI - $8.

Copy Fundamentals for Direct Mail Letters—DMMA Manual
Top direct mail letter writer Maxwell Ross gives his method. Release 310.2, May 1979.

101 Suggested Headings for Reply Cards—DMMA Manual
Virgil D. Angerman gives headings for reply forms which offer benefits, make promises, create action . . . and are designed to pull inquiries or orders. Release 6308; reissued January 1978.

Envelope Copy—NYU, Nov. 28, 1978
The envelope has one momenet to generate interest or the letter joins the trash, says Consultant Wendell Forbes. He suggests ways to get yours opened. On tape, Hoke; #18-0309 - NY - $12.

Get Your Envelope Opened
By John Tighe. How top pro's create "envelope openers". Important article. DM Magazine; December 1980, Volume 43, #8.

Innovative Envelope Formats
ZIP magazine; May 1982.

Envelopes in Second Class Publications
A review of USPS regulations. ZIP magazine; February 1982.

There is a great deal of expertise available on the creation of most effective business and industrial direct response advertising, particularly via two-step . . . getting an inquiry and then following up with direct mail, salesmen or both. The following are representative of the very many talks on tape and articles in print available.

Increasing Business Sales Leads From Your Space Advertising— ZIP, November 1980
Rene Gnam spells out how to get and close them in greater quantity, yet better quality, at lower cost.

More Effective Industrial Direct Mail
Consultant Herbert Ahrend analyzes industrial marketers who are succeeding . . . and failing . . . in direct marketing, and why. DM magazine; August 1981, Volume 44, #4.

How to Write Industrial Copy that Pulls
Herbert Ahrend details formulas to improve copy. DM magazine; October 1974, Volume 37, #6.

Using Follow-Up Sales Letters to Continue Your Sales Calls
Top pro Sig Rosenblum explains how; DM magazine; March 1978, Volume 40, #11.

Techniques to Convert Leads to Sales
Sig Rosenblum tells how to create pieces to maneuver your salesmen into a selling situation; get ripe, ready-to-buy prospects who can be "corraled, cultivated and clinched". DM magazine; october 1977, volume 40, #6.

The Mass—Produced Business Letter
ZIP magazine; June 1982.

Increased Personalization—LIDMA, 6/18/80
Ray Lewis, Editor-Publisher of ZIP magazine, says it's the most important part of direct mail for the near future, made possible by computer and laser technology. More personalization costs more, but increased response makes the investment worthwhile. Letters must appear individually typed and be signed by important organization officials. Details and spelling must be right. As we all know more about prospects and customers, personalization possibilities will be greater. On tape, Hoke; #10-0411 - LI - $10.

Personalized Mass Mail
Its growing importance. ZIP magazine; February 1982.

Ink-Jet for Personalization
A.B. Dick, Jetson's, National Pre-Sort, Webcraft, UARCO and others; ZIP magazine; April 1982.

Creative Checklist for Direct Mail—DMMA Manual
Simple and point-by-point . . . 28 points to help channel thinking, focus on effectiveness, evaluate creativity of direct mail pieces. Release 6201; reissued February 1978.

The 10 Most Common Pitfalls in Direct Mail Testing
Consultant Milton Pierce explains. ZIP magazine; April 1980.

Following Up
on responses and sales leads. ZIP magazine; April 1982.

Selecting Lists and Media

Let's start with list selection. It seems simple but is getting more complex and can be confusing to those starting it. Wrong list selection can defeat a good product, offer and presentation.

Fortunately, some of those with most list selection know-how give it freely to others and are excellent in writing, eloquent in speaking, and effective teachers. On the following pages I briefly describe speeches, talks and articles available on tape and in print, all just a sampling of far more available.

What to Expect When You Do Business with a List Broker?
Fred E. Allen, president of his own list brokerage firm in Dallas, Texas, explains the process; how the broker can help your mailing reach the right people at the right times. On tape, Hoke; #18-0156 - HU - $8. Also in DM magazine; June 1978, Volume 41, #2.

How to Select Names for Lists—DMMA Manual
How to make a test selection truly representative of the whole list, or that part to be used; how to evaluate various kinds of list selections. Expert Angelo Venezian explains it fully. Release 8141; October 1979.

Making Right List Decisions—DMMA Conference, 10/22/79
Ralph Stevens is president of Woodruff-Stevens Associates, the list management subsidiary of Computer Directions Group, Inc. He started as a copywriter for Prentice Hall and is a very good one. He bought tens of millions of names as advertising director of Famous Artists. He's uniquely able to give advice on renting names. He explains testing, seasonality, segmentation, how to avoid costly mistakes. On tape, Hoke; #10-0457 - NY - $12.

List Success Strategy*
How Rose Harper used accounting experience to select lists more successfully for clients; how her numbers know-how helped her acquire the Kleid Company after over twenty years working for it . . . and then to more than triple its size. Sound advice from her to anyone in mail order. Seminar I, Chapter 3, this book.

Correct Analysis of Mailing Lists—DMMA Manual
It's the key to successful mail order, says Rose Harper. How to systematically analyze list performance. Nine charts included show list history mailing record, allowed order cost and analysis of cost usage by category response; also analysis by duplication factor, dollar income, name and more; concentrates on list keying, customer information and grouping. Six pages, Release 5308; Appendix II, April 1979.

Advice from a List Maestro*
List consultant, broker and manager Ed Burnett . . . who has helped clients select over a billion names . . . sums up and synthesizes his selection know-how. Seminar III, Chapter 9, this book.

Effective List Marketing
Ed Burnett's master course in the use of lists and the selection factors; demographics, psychographics; how to work with list brokers, managers and compilers . . . with consultants, computer houses and lettershops; how to make them work for you.

He tells how to test copy, package and offer . . . advises on timing and market selection; explains how to read test results and make list continuations; how to test more while spending less; how to use 5th digit zip selection to improve test results; how to code lists and track response. He explains the nixie factor; how to determine the right lists to reach prime markets . . . and to find peripheral markets. He compares the effectiveness of individual vs. title addressing.

Ed Burnett tells how to get the most from your customer list. He explains the advantages of rifle shot vs. shotgun list selection. He tells how to coordinate direct mail with your sales force; explains zip code analysis, decoys, how to keep computer costs down; how many mailings to send to the same list; how to use direct mail to get repeat orders and multiple sales. He discusses co-ops and package inserts. He includes warnings. On tape, Hoke; #17-0353 - EB - 4 cassettes, 5½ hours; $40.

Damaging Misconceptions About Direct Mail—100 Million Club, 7/13/78
Ed Burnett examines them one by one . . . in the order that each can harm most a mail order newcomer . . . clarifies each and recommends what to do. On tape, Hoke; #18-0353 - HM - $8.

How to Mail the Fortune 1,000 For Greatest Profit
Ed Burnett explains: Fortune 1,000 companies, branch plants, subsidiaries, divisions employ millions. Over 100,000 executives make buying decisions and comprise the perfect business and industrial list; how to reach them. DM magazine, March 1976, Volume 38, #10.

How to Improve Your Method of Selecting a Business List
Ed Burnett explains the tricky business . . . how list compilers utilize word-processing technology to create more specialized lists selected from broader lists . . . the groups within categories to choose from; how to make the right choice . . . which can determine profit or loss. A thorough, detailed analysis. DM magazine; Part I, March 1978, Volume 40, #11; Part II, April 1978, Volume 40, #12.

When Is Best Time to Mail?—DMMA Manual
Rose Harper outlines changing seasonal patterns for nine different business categories with chart, developed by Kleid Company. Release 2107; Appendix VI, October 1979.

Seasonality Studies Reveal Productive Mailing Periods
The best time to mail depends whether you're mailing to an outside list or to a house list; whether to a business or consumer; whether your product reflects a seasonal interest or activity. Feature story in ZIP magazine, September 1981, Volume 4, #7.

List Segmentation and Projective Models—DMMA Manual
Top experts briefly review past developments and applications of segmentation techniques. Describes two basic ways to use segmentation in direct mail; gives five basic steps. All ten principles. Release 620.1, October 1979.

The History and Evolution of Segmentation—DMIX, 5/9/79
Consultant Robert Kestnbaum's classic analysis: How the science of classifying customers for most profitable mailing started with Sears before World War I, through necessity advanced greatly in the Depression; its still primitive state before computers and dramatic post-computer development; its exciting future to help mail less and sell more. On tape, Hoke; #19-0252 - IX - $8.

Demographics
Their growing importance in the mailing industry. ZIP magazine; March 1982.

The Direct Marketing Prophet*
The Kansas City Star calls Martin Baier "the father of Zip Code

Marketing." He is VP and Director of Sales for Old American Insurance Company in Kansas City. He teaches direct marketing at the University of Missouri, and is the author of an authoritative text book on direct marketing. His career, success and advice. Seminar IX, Chapter 2, this book.

Using Sampling Procedures to Postal ZIP Coded Files

C. Richard Cryer cites special selection techniques using judgment, systematic and random sampling and based on the five-digit ZIP code. DM magazine; April 1977, Volume 39, #12.

Mining Gold From Your House List—NYU List Course, 10/15/80

Evelyn Deitz, of CBS Columbia House, and Gordon Grossman, Consultant, tell how: Segmentation of lists . . . to produce better results from existing products and services; development of new products ideal for known interests of customers; how to isolate sub-segments of house lists which are most productive for your own offers, and for outside users of your lists. On tape, Hoke; #10-0459 - NY - $12.

The Role of the List Broker—DMMA Manual

List broker Florence Wolf discusses the list broker's services in building and developing direct mail programs for direct marketers . . . in research, planning, serving as the creative agency's partner, evaluating results and finding new markets. Release 5202; January 1977; "Lists and Media" Section.

How, When, Where of Compiled Lists—NYU 11/21/79

Experts Holt Ardrey and Norman Sturm explain how business and consumer lists are compiled; how they're selected, segmented, used successfully; how to select for maximum response at lowest cost. On tape, Hoke; #19-0341 - NY - $10.

Everything You Ever Wanted to Know About Lists—Pacific Symposium, Sydney, 6/17-19/80

Murray Miller, President of American Express Direct Response, tells it all. He knows. On tape, Hoke; #10-0427 - PP - $10.

Back End Analysis

Your most important prospect, your current customer; ZIP Magazine; June 1982.

New Data Banks

They offer flexibility and savings. State of the art; the firms which offer them; the co-operative banks; the mini-banks; the biggest data bank of all; the private banks; how they make it possible to use lists not profitable before; build larger lists for small mailers, better lists for big mailers; create just right custom lists; find new prospects who match a firm's established customer profile; combine response and compiled lists. An excellent overview article. January 1982, ZIP magazine, 401 North Broad Street, Philadelphia, PA 19108.

Public Access—Data Banks

Describes in detail those of Donnelley, NBL, Metromail, Polk, Demographic Systems, MDR, The Executive and Business Banks at Direct Media, M/D/A, Roman, Data Base Management, JAMI, College Marketing Group. ZIP magazine; February 1982,

Data-Base Technology

Taking advantage of it; by Stan Woodruff. ZIP magazine; July/August 1981.

Computer Matching of Lists

How to Make the Most of Your Merge-Purge Program

Leo Yochim, President of Printronic Corp., New York City, and leading authority on computer matching, tells how. DM magazine; April 1979, Volume 41, #12.

List Consultant and Copywriter Partnership

It must emerge, says Rose Harper. What list experts know about individual lists can help create the most effective copy approach to the list. DM magazine; March 1979, Volume 41, #11.

Merge/Purge

Getting the most from your next one. ZIP magazine; March 1982.

The First Thorough Look at Non-Household Mail Flow

Ed Burnett examines USPS "Non-Household Mailstream Report." DM magazine; April 1981, Volume 43, #12.

Pre-Sort Discount Programs

How they're paying off for mailers; ZIP magazine; May 1982.

Media

Many consider media selection far simpler than list selection. Magazines particulary are often specialized, already segmented. But first mass publishers of magazines and newspapers and then more specialized ones began to offer choices . . . and then more choices, allowing the advertiser to segment circulation in more and different ways. This accommodation has been invaluable to mail order advertisers but made media decisions more difficult as they became more important.

The selection, training and care of a media buyer became more important to the direct response agency, and to its clients. Media know-how became more important to any owner or top general executive in mail order and to many specialized ones. The advent of the use of multi-media accelerated the process. Direct marketers now usually use more kinds of media, and sometimes to help each other; for example, TV to support and make more effective space or direct mail advertising.

Top authorities in media buying have given many fine lectures and talks and written excellent articles which explain the process and, in some ways, sample the know-how. Some of these I review.

Direct Response Media—DMMA Manual

Gordon Grossman clearly and succinctly gives an overview. Excellent. Release 130.1, issued April 1979.

How To Buy Media—NYU, 4/7/81

Timothy Sharpe, Sr. VP of McCann Erickson Direct Response, and Iris Shokoff, Sr. VP of Grey Direct, explain: Sharpe says that TV is glamorous. Its potential is staggering, reaches 98% of U.S. households which spend an average time of six hours and 12 minutes daily watching it. TV is the main source of news and most authoritative one for most adults.

The three main ways direct marketers use TV are one-shot selling, getting leads, and as a support medium. One-shot selling contains the whole message and offer in one commercial. It stands on its own and usually needs 120 seconds. To get leads via TV is a two-step process. TV gets the lead. Direct mail follow-up converts. As short as a 30-second commercial has sometimes worked. As support, TV is the means to increase returns obtained by space, direct mail or both. If your primary medium reaches about 25% of homes in the area, TV support will probably pay for itself.

A simple commercial on a simple set can be put together for $9,000 to $10,000. The message should be clear, direct. The offer should be complete and as understandable as possible. The tag (phone number, address, or both) is crucial. In a 60-second commercial, the tag should last 15 seconds of the commercial. In a 120-second commercial, the tag should last 25-30 seconds. The best results are when the tag is localized.

Media tools are needed to create a media plan, says Iris Shokoff. These include Standard Rate and Data, Publishers Information Bureau sheets and snydicated research which Standard Rate and Data contains on magazines; closing dates, circulation, rates, actual size of magazines; Publishers Information Bureau sheets offer a wealth of information about major corporations. They also give information concerning the seasonality of product. With syndicated research it is possible to determine profiles for various magazines.

Shokoff outlined a program Rapp & Collins did a few years ago for Architectural Digest. It found a reader profile: 60% female, 42 median age, well educated. Then Rapp & Collins researched the psychographic profile: Affluent lifestyle, high self-esteem, upwardly mobile. The next step was to check up on the media the competition used. The research was analyzed; tests and then projections were made. On tape, Hoke; # 11-0007 - NY -$15.

Print Advertising: How to Buy It From One Who Sells It—NYU
One of the best lectures made on the subject; by Florence Simon-Peloquin, Director of Direct Marketing of Woman's Day and one of the smartest women in mail order media; a classic; the characteristics of space advertising; what media suits what mail order product, by categories of merchandise and publication; covers buying, position, best months, evaluation of results, use of insert publication; gives do's and don't's. DM magazine; May 1975, Volume 37, # 11. Also on tape, Hoke; later speech on same subject CADM, Chicago, 3/16/77; # 17-0110 - CD - $8.

Direct Response Space Advertising
A special feature section on the use of magazines and response advertising by direct marketers. DM News, September 15, 1980.

Print Advertising in Mail Order
David Geller gives the do's and don't's of buying print space in magazines; how and when to buy efficiently. On tape, Hoke: # 17-0008 - NY - $10.

How to Sell Mail Order Ads*
David Geller has sold more mail order ads than anyone in the world. How he did; his unusual career; how he often gambles on the results of ads he sells, backs entrepreneurs, finances businesses; why so many who succeed in mail order buy ads from him; how he may help you. Seminar IV, Chapter 4, this book.

Reaching the New Rural Buyer
Income or lifestyle improved for older and younger families; ZIP magazine; February 1982.

How To Sell Via Mail Order on TV
Malcolm Smith has sold over 10 million records and tapes via TV mail order and made millions of sales of products via mail order. He is a Hoge alumnus. He explains his simple, effective and unusual methods, advises what to do, and warns what not to do in testing and projecting a mail order item on TV. Seminar V, Chapter 10, this book.

Broadcast Techniques—Hundred Million Club, 4/16/81
Martin Grossman, VP and General Manager of Eicoff & Lennard (NY office), explains: The principles behind TV techniques used by direct marketers are no different than the basic principles of print and direct mail. TV is a part of direct marketing. The disciplines must be the same. Testing is essential. But to save dollars, testing must be planned carefully before shooting the commercial begins. The time to test price and creative elements is when the writer sits down to write . . . not in the studio. Three techniques are used in TV: Direct sale, generation of leads and TV support. Production costs can range from $15,000 to $150,000. Avon commercials ask for leads,

Playboy magazine for subscription orders. The AAA auto club uses TV as support for a direct mail piece.

There is no price limit to TV offers today. TV formerly was associated with record offers. $9.95 was considered the limit, then $15.95 and then $19.95. There's no limit now. Many companies now find TV an indispensable tool. Before jumping into TV, consider overall company needs, image needs, bottom line needs. TV has its rightful place beside print and direct mail. And before projecting the final campaign, the offer, creative approach and price should all be tested. On tape, Hoke; #11-0236 - HM - $7.

The Cable Opportunity
Mike Slosberg, Exec VP, Marsteller Inc., notes specific advantages of cable for direct marketers. DM magazine; July 1981; Volume 44, #3.

Cable TV Direct Marketing*
How Ted Turner opened a new horizon for mail order TV—with his Atlanta "SuperStation" and the Cable News Network. Seminar III, Chapter 5, this book.

The Super Station, The Cable TV Network and Direct Marketing
Ted Turner tells the vital part that mail order has played in the building of his empire. On tape, Hoke; #11-0655 - DM - $10.

Progress Report on Interactive Video
DM News special Feature Section, March 15, 1982.

Radio Support Came First*
Consultant Gordon Grossman tells the story . . . and how TV support began, its early success for Reader's Digest. Seminar IV, Chapter 2, Page 159, this book.

TV Support Comes of Age
Timothy Sharpe, of Schwab & Beatty, cites massive use of TV to support huge mail drops . . . for inserts in newspapers and magazines; by Reader's Digest, RCA, Columbia, Time, National Liberty. The key to TV use is the percentage of the market being reached by space, direct mail or both. It should not be less than 25% and preferably more like 50%. Sharpe points to Columbia's use of an involvement/measurement device. A blank, unexplained yellow box in print media is referred to in TV commercials. The TV commercial tells the consumer that the yellow box is worth an extra free record by simply writing a record number in. Orders with the yellow box filled in are then known to be from TV. On tape, Hoke; #18-0035 - NU - $6.

TV Support—DMMA Conference, 10/13/76
How to use it for your mail campaign. Vicky Swackenberg, Business Manager, Time Inc., shows how it works for some but is unproductive for others; how to use TV support for a direct mail or print program, or for both. DM magazine; March 1977, Volume 39, #11 (based discussions DMMA Annual Conference, Atlanta, GA, 10/13/76).

Combined TV And Mail Often Effective
Its value depends on the mailing density in the TV market, says Francis G. Ronnenberg, Circulation Director, Reader's Digest. The household penetration should be pretty high for additions of TV support to be successful and profitable. DM magazine; March 1977, Volume 39, #11.

The Multi-Media Umbrella—NYU, 4/3/79
Roy Abrams (now VP of Margrace Corp.), outlines multi-media marketing and planning; its synergism and interdependence, multi-media analysis, market segmentation. On tape, Hoke; # 19-0006 - NY - $12.

TV Support Changing Face of Advertising—CADM, Chicago, 3/14/79
Al Eicoff, pioneer of TV mail order, outlines TV mail order

advertising history from 1948 and its newest development, TV support. Eicoff says: "Today, TV support advertising is a science producing results beyond the wildest expectations of advertisers. It began haphazardly. It was born of the need of insurance and record clubs for a written commitment. This forced the use of newspapers and direct mail and led to the TV support idea. On tape, Hoke; # 19-0111 - CM - $8.

The Telephone Marketing Medium

It's the only universal, two-way direct marketing medium. It's particularly effective and profitable when used to increase the results of other media. These media cost the same, whether telephone marketing is added or not. As media cost increases, the added use of telephone marketing follow-up may become the difference between profit and loss.

There is available ample and excellent orientation on how to use telephone marketing. Talks, speeches and articles on it are available to you. The following are only a few of the many excellent ones.

Pioneering Phone Selling for the Fortune 500
Murray Roman tells how it began and grew. Seminar III, Chapter 10, this book.

The Essentials of Phone Marketing
Norton Dunn is Marketing Director of the Telemarketing Division of R. H. Donnelley Corp. He tells how to use telephone marketing, find people to do it and motivate them; how to combine the telephone with use of other media, create an effective phone message; and how to react to the person phoned; how to ugrade telephone orders; how to use profitably outgoing and incoming WATS phone services. Interview 1980; #10-0505 - LK -$10.

The Most Direct Response Medium—DMMA Manual
Ernan Roman, V.P., Campaign Communications Institute, covers telephone marketing in depth; Release 250.1; April 1979.

Telephone Marketing's Unique Benefits—DM Club Philadelphia, 2/18/81
They include immediacy, flexibility and "personal touch". Turnaround of order five to fifteen days faster than direct mail promotes customer satisfaction. Telephone marketing allows faster cash flow, instant tracking of results.

"It's much easier to upgrade customers by phone than via other media," says Andrew Thompson, Vice President, American Tele-Marketing Inc. In one campaign, 56% of TV Guide subscribers contacted by phone were upgraded. Personnel making or taking calls should be courteous, have pleasant voices and work no more than a five-hour shift. A well-organized order form with check boxes eliminates unnecessary writing.

In a typical week in the Wall Street Journal, 38% of all space ads included an 800 number. 20% to 30% of those calling an 800 number have questions regarding the offer and product. These potential customers are lost in space ads and direct mail campaigns without an 800 number. On tape, Hoke; #11-0161 -PC - $10.

How Can Telephone Marketing Help You?
Murray Roman, President of Campaign Communications, Inc., explains: Today's successful telephone operations must be controlled by a rigidly controlled production line approach in which every element is geared to achieving projectable cost-effective goals. DM magazine; August 1975; Volume 38, #4.

DM News reports on the growth story of Campaign Communications, Inc. (CCI), Issue of 3/15/80.

Telephone Marketing's Growing Popularity
Skyrocketing cost of personal sales calls largely causes it, says Murray Roman. A phone call is 2% of the cost of a personal sales call. Controlled telephone marketing, using a tested script and good communications, is as predictable as direct mail, he says, and is more quickly measurable. Careful selection of list and communicators can be as essential to success in a telephone campaign as a quality offer and message. You must reach the right people. Preceding calls with direct mail can increase response up to five times, he claims. Careful targeting of calls or prior relationship with the person being called also improves results. Magazine subscribers, for example, are usually happy to receive a call warning that a subscription is expiring. Random "cold calls" are unprofitable, he emphasized. On tape, Hoke: # 10-0168 - LK - $10.

Profit, Pain and Change
The DMMA states that telephone marketing accounts for the highest dollar volume in direct marketing . . . of any medium. It became so heavily used that restrictive legislation potential became very real. Then WATS rates leaped. A special section in DM News . . . July 15, 1980 . . . reports that despite this telephone marketing properly used is profitable.

Telephone Success, Dangers, Mistakes
One view is that telephone marketing can not only generate a better qualified response but can also be more cost effective than other media or even a sales force in the field. Another is that telephone marketing, by itself, cannot do a proper job; that it must be preceded by some kind of preparatory campaign or contact; that otherwise, it can be a trap, but that the combination of telephone marketing with direct mail can increase overall response two-and-a-half to seven-and-a-half times. Both views and much more in the special feature section on direct marketing in DM News; November 15, 1981.

Selecting Lists for Telephone Marketing
A feature article ZIP magazine; July/August 1981.

Telephone/TV Combination
A feature article, ZIP magazine; September 1981.

The Hybrid Media

Combining media in unique ways has always been possible and sometimes done. But over 30 years ago, it began to be used effectively in mail order. Lester Wunderman was a particularly imaginative pioneer, as he has been in most direct marketing developments.

Bound postcards have become magazines of direct mail and cooperative catalogs. Mini-inserts have put the equivalent of a number of space ads into envelopes. Pre-print sections have put the equivalent of solo mailings into newspapers. Insert pages on postcard stock have become the equivalent of super sized double postcards, with return card to be torn off by the sender and postage paid by the advertiser.

New variations never cease. Free standing inserts in newspapers may be bought by geographical areas selectively. Take-ones in supermarkets are used as in newspapers. Broadcast messages are put on flexible records and bound into magazines or enclosed in envelopes and mailed. Hybrid media often combine advantages and lessen disadvantages of single media. They range from least to most expensive media buys. The more the proliferation the more know-how is needed for effective selection, as specific variations are highly suited to one and poorly suited to another mail order situation.

There are specialists in each form of hybrid media. Many

have given talks and speeches and written articles available on tape and in print to you. Below are mini-reviews of some excellent ones, and there are many others.

Mini-Inserts*

How they started and grew . . . became a substantial mail order medium; the story of several leading mini-insert brokers; how mail order firms profitably use them. Seminar VIII, Chapter 7, this book.

Everything You Wanted to Know About Inserts

Leon Henry, the insert man, tells you: co-ops, package inserts, billing inserts; do's and don'ts; how to succeed with them; DM magazine; October 1980, Volume 43, #6.

Making Co-Ops Work For You

It depends on how they're used, says Philip N. Dresden, President of R. H. Donnelley Corp.; a classic explanation of how to make a co-op package insert or billing stuffer medium more efficient. "They're at their best creating an inquiry or a first-time sale for profitable follow-up." DM magazine; April 1976, Volume 38, # 11.

Packages And Mailing Inserts—Donnelley's Carol Wright

How its cents off coupon triggered retail grocery sales, provided a highly effective mail order medium and erected a profitable mail order business for Donnelley Marketing by John C. Holt, VP, R. H. Donnelley, and former president of Donnelley Marketing. DM magazine; May 1980, Volume 43, # 1.

Will Mini-Insert Use Decline

In a July 15, 1981 story, DM News reported that enclosures in bills from oil companies, banks and sometimes airlines may not be as productive as originally thought . . . and quotes top executives who indicate lower response. Read it.

Developing Print Media for Direct Marketers*

From catalogs to solo mailings and particularly hybrid media . . . insert sections in newspaper. The story of John Blair . . . the Blair Graphics Companies . . . Blair Marketing and Bob Hemm, its president.

Blair Marketing, Inc., distributes nationally co-op preprint ad sections to newspapers and delivers more circulation than any similar section and more than almost all magazines. Hemm tells its start, how mail order people use it profitably, test at least cost. Seminar IV, Chapter 9, this book.

Blair Marketing's Hybrid Media

Explains how pre-prints work. Blair pre-prints are distributed 20 times a year to 101 major newspapers with 30 million total circulation. Space in sections is available on a remnant basis for slightly over half price. Blair also runs "Sunday Extra," a mini-insert program in a 6" x 9" envelope distributed in newspapers in smaller markets. Mail order people have done well. Interview Donald Hubert Jr., V.P. Finance; on tape, Hoke; #10-0495 - LK -$10.

Advantages of Pre-Print Insert Sections—LIDMA, 1/17/79

Robert Hemm, President of John Blair Marketing, explains: Experimenting with newspaper inserts is low cost; there are tremendous options. Flexibility allows a choice of 89 markets . . . with copy by market, sectionalized copy, split testing, full color. On tape, Hoke; #19-0033 - LI - $8.

Unusual Success with Unusual Media*

What is the most distributed disk in the world? No! It's not Elvis, the Beatles or Slim Whitman. Find out in Seminar IV, Chapter 7, "Sound Mail Order." The story of Eva-Tone Sound Sheets . . . flexible plastic records bound into magazines and slipped in envelopes . . . and how they sell via mail order.

Production and Printing

The less known about either . . . by anyone in mail order concerned with them . . . the greater can be the problems. Test costs of ads can leap. Direct mail costs in the mail can rise over estimates. Closing dates of ads can be missed. Background of black and white pictures can become mud. Color reproduction can sicken. Advertising can repel. Orders can be lost for clients and accounts for agencies, and advertising which should succeed fail.

Ignorance is no excuse when expertise in either is available on tape or in print for any non-specialist. I describe some as follows.

The Basics of Production—DM Day, NY

Elliot Abrams is an expert printer and lettershop owner (Tyme Letter Service). He is thorough and business-like with a common-sense approach. He explains exactly what to do (and what not to do) in producing printed material for advertising . . . of quality, at a reasonable cost, and in ample time. On tape, Hoke; # 10-0202 -ND - $10.

40 Ways to Cut Direct Mail Production Cost—DMMA Manual

Dick Hodgson lists cost-cutting factors grouped in basic production categories; planning, art work, photography, typography, plate making, printing, finishing, paper, envelopes, other items. 4 pages, Release 4002; Appendix IV, February 1978.

Production Reverse Timetable—DMMA Manual

Consultant Maxwell Ross gives his method to meet deadlines of producing advertising. Release 400 S, February 1978.

Working With Your Printer

How to select dependable, affordable printers; how best to consult with them on sizes, paper, color, folding, as you develop your pieces; avoid pieces that cost too much to produce or cannot fit on ordinary presses or waste paper and press time. In depth, ZIP magazine; 6½ pages, November/Decembr 1980.

The Revolution in Printing Techniques

Newest innovations, electronic, digital, preparation; systems designation; to go from photographing art to printing press without film. How computer graphic techniques are used for all proofing, manipulation, editing, storage and transfer of full color pages for reproduction. Experts each explain their specialities. On tape, Hoke; # 11-0645 - DM - $15.

Direct Marketing's Laser Printing Age*

Personalized letters at 20 miles an hour . . . printing 500,000 labels an hour . . . Leo Yochim tells how computer printing and then laser printing started and grew. Some advice how to use it for mail order. Seminar VIII, Chapter 9, this book.

Advances in Ink Jet Printing

Norman Stern, Marketing Manager of Mead Digital Systems, describes new ink jet systems . . . with speed increases, sharpened resolution. Some units address letters; others attached to web presses put variable messages on direct mail pieces as printed. Mead's System is based on gang multiple jets per print line; capable of infinite variety of fonts and sizes. On tape, Hoke; #11-0545 - MA - $10.

Individualization and the New Technology

Richard Mattern of IBM reports on the 3800 . . . its many new features, ability to print anything . . . the creative use of the new technology developed for direct marketers. DM magazine; February 1980, Volume 42, #10.

Computer/Electric Letters—DMMA Manual

"Specifics for Direct Mailing." Authority Leo Yochim outlines. Release 4202; May 1979. Clear, thorough, excellent.

Testing

Almost every mail order business and product starts with it. Most mail order firms do too little of it. Some do too much. Some test what is not necessary and not always what is necessary. Some set up tests inadequately. Some interpret test results incorrectly. Most smart mail order people feel that most people in mail order can lower advertising cost per order and make bigger volume possible . . . by more effective testing.

The following are my descriptions of talks, speeches and articles on testing in direct marketing, available to you on tape and in print.

What Tests Teach*
Gordon Grossman is a direct marketing consultant and former Direct Marketing Director of Reader's Digest. His knowledge of tens of thousands of tests made by the Digest and others is one advantage of using him. His career; the easiest, safest, most profitable step he suggests first; more advice. Seminar IV, Chapter 2.

The Importance of Testing—LIDMA, 3/2/81
Jerome Pickholz, President of Ogilvy & Mather Direct Response, discusses testing in the mail and promise testing, a survey technique. The advantages of promise testing, he explains, include lower cost than either testing in the mail or research with focus groups, and lack of bias often found in focus group situations. Promise test procedure involves having consumers rank advertising claims in order of importance and uniqueness. The few which rank the best are then tested by mail, he notes. Promise testing should not be accepted with blind faith, he adds.

Mail testing is more appropriate for variations in format, copy, premiums and involvement devices. Don't test variables that will probably produce differences too small to be statistically significant. These include different paper stocks, color variations and small copy changes within the same format. The only exception to his rule is when small differences can affect the cost of the program.

Be sure that tests are made using a representative sample. As the response rate drops, he explains, the sample size needed to obtain a valid test increases. Other variables that can affect test validity are: season, change in competitive environment and time lag between test and rollout. You can never have 100% accuracy in tests, he concludes. But careful testing can produce 80% - 90% probability that test results will prove true. On tape, Hoke; # 10-0139 - LI - $12.

Finding Markets, Media, Results
"Testing paves the way," says Bob Cherins, now partner in McCaffrey & McCall Direct. He discusses the definition, location and potential of a market, along with effective media selection to target that market. DM magazine; January 1979, Volume 41, #9.

Product Pretesting—M.O. Symposium, Montreaux, 4/25-27/79
Gordon Grossman explains: The principles, procedures, techniques of pre-testing . . . with examples. On tape, Hoke; # 19-0184 - ID - $6. Also DM magazine; July 1979, Volume 42, #3.

7 Basic Ground Rules of Testing—DMMA Manual
Expert Jim Kobs suggests major areas to test in products, pricing, formats, copy. Release 8102; Appendix VI, February 1978.

Testing: An Overview
Consultant Betty Anne Noakes quietly, sensibly and thoroughly covers what it can and cannot do; how to use and not misuse it. A DMMA Circulation Council transcript of speech at "Insider's Luncheon".

Profitable Copy Testing—DMMA Manual
Gordon Grossman tells how to do it. Release 8110; September 1978.

Test Results—DM Day, New England, 5/21 - 22/81
Which ad pulled best—and why? Which package rang the bell? Stan Rice, VP of United Business Service, explains, analyzes and draws conclusions. What future do's and don't's are indicated. On tape, Hoke; # 11-0396 - NE - $10.

Probability Estimates—DMMA Manual
A scientific approach to minimize risk in direct mail testing, by John McNichols. Probabilities can go a long way in providing a useful tool to decide the size of a test mailing, degree of confidence and limit of error. Two probability tables are included—one for 95% confidence level and the other for 99% confidence level. Release 8103; to be read in conjunction with Release # 610.1.

12 Rules for Direct Mail Testing—DMMA Manual
Consultant Richard Hodgson thoroughly discusses and gives reactions for each. Sound. Release 8101; Appendix VI, October 1979.

How to Determine Your Winners and Losers—DMMA Conference, 10/26/80
Richard Hodgson, consultant, tells in detail—and what to do about it. On tape, Hoke; # 10-0584 - DM - $10.

How to Make Zip Work For You on Tests—DMMA Manual
Ed Burnett outlines the use of "Nth" name selection and last digit zip selection. Charts included give last digit zip analysis. Relase 814.0; Appendix VI, 4 pages, September 1977.

When Two Factors Affect Response
C. Richard Cryer, VP of Scholastic Magazines, explains: The interaction of both is often more important in a direct mail promotion than the main effect of either; some practical techniques to obtain a more complete picture of what is happening. DM magazine; January 1977, Volume 39, #9.

Decision Rules to Direct Mail Testing—DMMA Manual
Professor Robert Blattberg makes them clear: How many names to mail for test adequate to make safe decisions for projecting; explains the tables given to facilitate sample size selection; gives examples to help you understand procedures and tables' use. Release 610.1; October 1979.

The Mathematics of Testing—Chicago Assoc. of DM, 4/21-22/81
Professor Robert Blattberg explains: How to apply the statistical rules that help insure test results that you can count on . . . when you make decisions for further projections. On tape, Hoke; # 11-0253 - CM - $10.

Fund Raising

Let's assume you'd like to raise some money for an organization you belong to or consider a career in fund raising using direct marketing methods. If so, the following speeches and articles could be of use to you.

How to Raise A Billion Dollars*
The story of Francis Andrews, President of American Fund Raising Service, Inc., and how he revolutionized fund raising . . . cutting the cost of raising money to a fraction of previous cost and raising unprecedented amounts for many worthy causes . . . all by direct marketing. See Seminar V, Chapter 6, this book.

12 Key Steps to Direct Mail Fund Raising—DMMA International, 2/28-3/3-78
Detailed how-to from a master, Francis Andrews. On tape, Hoke; # 18-0133 - DM - $6.

Charitable Fund Raising

A special featue section in the August 1981, DM News.

Similarity of Fund Raising Art—Direct Marketing World, LIDMA, 5/21/80

Jane Biral of United Negro Fund explains; she outlines cost saving efforts and merge-purge efforts, including latest applications; ways of designing mailings for special groups; sophisticated analysis of technology that created merge-purge systems. On tape, Hoke; # 10-0340 - LI $10.

Computers and Fund Raising—DM Day Houston, 5/17-20/79

Richard Viguerie, President of the Viguerie Corporation, is the great political fund raiser whose success for clients has been greatly based on his skillful use of computerized lists. He explains how fund raisers can use computers to raise more money at less cost. On tape, Hoke; # 19-0272 - MA - $8.

Fund Raising Know-How—DM Assoc. New England, 4/28/80

Richard Viguerie tells details how fund raising is done and can be done better. On tape, Hoke: # 10-0279 - NE - $10.

Computerizing and Maintaining Your Mailing List—DMMA Manual

Consultant Arthur Blumenfield tells whether, when and how to do it. Release 200.2; April 1979.

How to Buy a Computer—St. Louis DMC, 11/7/79

Blumenfield advises when to consider buying; how to find out what you need; how to select hardware; how to investigate software; when to consider "canned software;" how to proceed; whom to see first. On tape, Hoke; # 11-0270 - ID - $7.

Egg Head Mail Order*

How MAGI (the Mathematical Science Group, Inc.) started as physicists and mathematicians in nuclear science . . . using computers but found computer applications to mail order list maintenance and list selection. Its success for clients; its advanced methods. Seminar II, Chapter 3, this book.

Safer Mail Order Decisions*

How one direct marketing agency, Clark Direct Marketing, helps clients to make them use computer modeling. Seminar VII, Chapter 5, this book.

Mail Order's Long-Term Tool

You must use computer models as a context to understand a company, its people, capabilities and goals . . . , says top marketing consultant Bob Kestnbaum. They are tools to assist thinking. He discusses some he's used. Models can look at past purchases of customers and then indicate possible future purchases. Modeling helps a company determine its future course. Interview on tape, Hoke; # 19-0551 - LK - $8.

Modeling and Systems for Target Marketing—NYU, 1/20/82

Robert Cohn, VP of PDC, and Ernest Clevenger, VP Plus Media, Inc. describe how management techniques and computer models provide tools for direct marketers to evaluate alternative marketing plans and target in on most profitable strategies. Forecasting earned income, cash flow, goals, price levels are crucial ingredients in determining product growth. On tape, Hoke; # 12-0013 - NY - $10.

Automation and Computerization of Envelope Inserts*

John M. Jenks, President of the Philipsburg Division of Bell & Howell, Inc. tells how it developed the intelligent mail order machine; how it slashed costs and made possible unprecedented segmentation for billing and co-op direct mail inserts. Seminar II, Chapter 10, this book.

Catalog Marketing's Transformation

Herb Engel, VP, R. R. Donnelley & Sons, predicts how electronic technology will eliminate many of the present heartaches of putting a catalog together.

An art director will snap a shot. The output will be color separations in digital form on stored tape or disc. Data will be transferred to a sophisticated color TV console used to up the page. The console operator will be able to control operations now done by hand. Images will be called up and merged with others already in the console.

Color corrections will be accomplished either locally or globally. Satellites already transmit data to earth stations and take one to three minutes to transmit an 8″ by 10″, four-color page . . . containing 70 million to 200 million bits of information . . . to anywhere in the world.

For binding catalogs, pre-printed labels are becoming defunct. Computer-controlled, ink jet printers can address catalog covers and order forms as the catalog is bound. New customers and address changes can be added to computer tape as late as 8 working days before the binding process. Catalogs will become more personalized. Readers will be directed to certain parts of the catalog with a personalized note pertaining to their wants and needs. The personalized message will be highly motivating, based on each reader's interests and buying habits. On tape, Hoke; # 10-0476 - CM - $10.

Computers and Mail Order

The use of computers is becoming universal and helping to make universal the use of the mail order method. Basic computer know-how as it applies to mail order is becoming a must for direct marketers.

Orientation on computers, from overview to considerable specialized knowhow important in mail order, is constantly being updated. Speeches, talks and articles are available to you on tape and in print. Some of them I will now describe.

Current Computer Applications

Special featues sections in DM News; July 15, 1981, and July 15, 1982. Based on interviews with direct marketing computer authorities; potentials, problems, developments.

Direct Marketing's Marriage to Computers*

Computer consultant Arthur Blumenfield tells how it happened; when to use a computer . . . in house, outside or not at all. Seminar I, Chapter 8, this book.

Minicourse on Minicomputers—LIDMA Workshop

Four hours of instructive information: Art Blumenfield on applications, Tony Caputo on options and specifications, Vincent Des Champs on Financing; Stan Woodruff gives case history of Computer Directions Group use. On 4 tapes, Hoke; # 18-0446 through # 18-0449 - $29.95.

Ways to Jump Results

One way to do it with the same lists, media and advertising is snydication. Results sometimes double or more. The following stories explain.

How Syndication Works—WDRG, 1/22/80

Kip Monroe, President of Mutual Marketing Associates, a leading syndicator, explains: Syndicators offer products to various companies' customers . . . including banks, catalogs, and credit card companies. The syndicator usually does all the work . . . art, copy, printing, testing, fulfillment, handling customer correspondence and complaints. Syndicators can stimulate sales surprisingly from inactive as well as active customer lists. On tape, Hoke; # 10-0045 - WD - $10.

Third-Party Sponsorship of Proven Offers*
Andrew Svenson has been responsible for selling over $60,000,000 worth of books a year for Meredith Publishing. He has set up mail order book departments for book and magazine publishers. His specialty is arranging marriages between publishers . . . selling the book of one to the customers of another, under its sponsorship. How he does it. Seminar IX, Chapter 4, this book.

Reverse Syndication
Third-party sponsorship offered; Aldens, the general catalog firm, aggressively markets it. Aldens provides its customer list, endorsement and credit system to products acceptable. Detailed story in DM News; February 15, 1981.

The use of credit cards is another way. More people buy. The average order is higher. Credit cards made it possible for firms of any size to sell big ticket items. They made big-scale telephone marketing possible. Incoming phone orders giving credit card numbers can be traded up as accessories are suggested.

Spencer Nilson is editor-publisher of the Nilson Report (on credit cards, debit cards, bank cards). He is the acknowledged authority on credit card use. One excellent speech he has given explains the credit card as an effective mail order tool: how credit card options used in sales promotion can increase sales 30% and reduce losses with virtually no added expense; how it works by product and service. On tape, Hoke; # 10-0234 - ID - $7. Another discusses the immediate future and new applications of credit cards. On tape, Hoke; # 10-0251 - ID - $7; also brainstorming session; Spencer Nilsonon on the credit card story, on tape, Hoke; # 10-0218 - ID - $22. Or article based on all three in DM magazine; July 1980, Volume 43, # 3.

Another way is the use of sales promotional techniques. Thomas Conlon is president of D. L. Blair*, the biggest firm running sweepstakes for advertisers. He tells the sweeps story; Seminar VI, Chapter 10 this book. Also in the DMMA Manual, he spells out the use of various promotional methods, of premiums, sweepstakes and sampling; of coupons, contests, cash refunds and price promotions. Valuable. Release 230.1; April 1979.

Mail Order Math

The smallest moonlighter must grasp it before starting. The biggest company must indoctrinate its managers in it before starting a mail order division. It must be constantly updated to latest changes of costs concerning it. Every direct marketing specialist should have an overview of it.

It's fundamental to mail order. Some of those with the smartest brains in mail order have explained it and clarified it in speeches, talks and articles available to you. I describe some of these as follows:

Direct Marketing Economics and Budgeting—DMMA Manual
Pierre Passavant explains basic profit and loss statement analysis in direct marketing promotion. He demonstrates the linkage between the cost per thousand (CPM) of advertising space ads bought and the cost per order (CPO) of orders received from the ads. He discusses response rates for both one-step and two-step efforts. He covers break-even calculations, back-end analysis and return-on-promotion investment analysis. Release 600.1; October 1979.

Financial Management—NYU, 3/27-79
It's the bottom line; John Canova is VP of Stonehenge Press, a Time-Life Books subsidiary. He tells how statistics and operative data are used to measure activity and to make marketing decisions; it's critical to the survival and success of all businesses; how to apply profit-oriented guidelines to marketing plans. On tape, Hoke; # 19-0005 - NY - $12.

Financial Analysis in Decision Making—NYU, 7/23/81
John Canova outlines financial planning, pricing and cash flow He reviews classical financial principles as they apply to mail order sales; determining maximum allowable cost per order; how this applies to media decisions, budget, profit management. On tape, Hoke; # 11-0420 - NY - $25.

Mail Order Profit—NYU, 10/16/79
It's the name of the game, says John McSweeney. After advertising strategy, testing, psychographics, demographics, list segmentation, creative breakthrought . . . profit remains a necessity. How to keep this in focus; on tape, Hoke; # 19-0308 -NY - $12.

Financial Planning Analysis
Robert Kestnbaum, top consultant, outlines what it is, how it fits into total direct marketing planning. Gives a simple, quick way to evaluate profitability . . . then a more sophisticated way. DM magazine; October 1978, Volume 41, #6.

Control and Budget Reports—DMMA Manual
George Larie, VP Doubleday Book Club Division, explains their importance, outlines how to prepare and use them. Manual Release 510.1; October 1979.

Marketing Strategy

It should start from the moment every mail order business is conceived. Without it mail order is small-time, day-to-day, limited and dangerous. The most successful direct marketers are the most able strategists. Many have told and written how they develop mail order strategy . . . and you can too. Much of this is on tape and in print and available for you. Some of it I describe here.

The Seven Step Marketing Program
Lester Wunderman's great 1969 speech that gave the strategy that helped create, build and expand businesses of clients . . . and make Wunderman, Ricotta & Kline the world's largest direct marketing ad agency. The program is as sound as ever. In article form. DM magazine; March 1969, Volume 31, #1.

Successful Mail Order Advertising
A 28-point checklist by Lester Wunderman. Classic advice as sound today as when taped by Hoke in 1969. #69 - PHD - 3C; $6.

From Ideas to Results—DMMA Manual
Lester Wunderman tells what it takes. Release 1104; June 1976.

Direct Marketing Concepts for General Advertisers—Seminar Sponsored by DMMA
Accountable advertising applied to national campaigns; capitalizing on national dominance in a field to launch a specialized mail order business. Lester Wunderman gives examples of success in each. On tape, Hoke; # 11-0197 - ND - $10.

The Culmination of All Direct Marketing "Arts"—Hundred Million Club, 8/14/80
That's direct marketing strategy, says Ed Nash, Executive VP of Rapp & Collins, Inc. He outlines the steps necessary to plan it: Know the product or service inside out. Describing the product can be the most difficult step. Know your audience. The public tells you what they want. You don't tell them. The consumer is lazy, doesn't want to think, is often unpredictable, very distrustful . . . individual, not a statistic. Create offers with these factors in mind. Know your total marketing environment of every factor that can influence marketing strategy. This includes

competition, media, distribution, government regulations, economic trends. On tape, Hoke; # 10-0477 - HM - $10.

What General Marketing Can Teach Direct Marketing*
Dr. Philip Kotler is the author of the most widely sold text book used in post graduate business courses and a top professor of marketing. He suggests methods to attain more of full potential, take fewer unnecessary risks, perhaps work less hard. Seminar IV, Chapter 5, this book.

A Marketing Authority's Message to Direct Marketers*—DMMA International Conference, 2/26-29/80
"How long will direct marketers ignore marketing?" used in Seminar IV, Chapter 5, was taken from the title of this speech in London by Professor Philip Kotler. The speech covers the subject in more detail. On tape, Hoke; # 10-0084 - DM - $10.

Close-Up on Marketing Strategies—DMMA Conference, 2/26 - 29/80
An all-day seminar workshop with Professor Philip Kotler and Harold Martin. On tape, Hoke; # 10-0092 - DM - $40.

Direct Marketing: The Unknown Giant—DMMA Manual
The treatise that made more big company newcomers to direct marketing realize direct marketing potential than any single speech, column or article. Makes clear what it is and its power. Cites applications, some bases of catalog marketing, use of syndication as way of two different marketers working together. Release 1501, April 1979. Bob Stone.

"No Secrets to Success"—DM Club, Washington, D.C.
—says direct marketing authority, Joan Throckmorton. "Failure is no mystery . . . outside forces can impede success . . . but with professional experience, sensible tests, thorough analysis, cautious projections, there is no reason to fail." On tape, Hoke; #11-0042 -WM - $10.

Hazards for a Growing Company—DMMA Conference, 10/28/80
Experts Robert Kestnbaum and Pierre Passavant advise senior officers and managers of firms with sales of $3,000,000 to $30,000,000 and growing fast via direct marketing. A crash course of planning and analysis to avoid potential problems; how to attain control by financial planning, market and product development; managerial methods to help survive and succeed. On tape, Hoke; #10-0561 - DM - $15.

What Makes a Mail Order Business Successful—DM Day, Detroit, 5/3-4/81
Maxwell Sroge, who has launched one Fortune 500 company after another into mail order, says "execution is the name of the game", and spells out how to do it. On tape, Hoke; #11-0219 - DD - $10.

Marketing Strategy and the Multi-Media Concept—NYU, 11/29/80
George Wiedemann, President of Grey Direct, explains: Define competition; target audience; create message, offer action strategy and rationale. Cites benefits of full media use to execute strategy. On tape, Hoke; # 10-0005 - NY - $12.

Taking Advantage of Change—by Mail Order*
The story of consultant Lawrence G. Chait, who has done it for some of the biggest companies in the world. Seminar III, Chapter 8, this book.

Direct Marketing as a Scientific Process of Business Growth and Profitability—NYU, 9/26/78
Chait explains 30 years of changing direct marketing experience: Applying computerization, lifestyle analysis and buying the characteristics of a consumer list; media independent marketing; the increase in interactive communication technologies; how all

this created a new phenomenon, our distributive economy; how professional direct marketing people became scientists of advertising and selling. On tape, Hoke; # 18-0301 - NY - $12.

Keep Up With Change—LIDMA, 11/19/80
Unless executives do, they can't fully take advantage of marketing opportunities, says Lawrence Chait. He explains how best to keep an eye on enormous communication changes and shifting attitudes; lists 15 elements of strategic planning in direct marketing. On tape, Hoke; # 10-0603 - LI - $10.

Safety in Numbers*
The story of marketing consultant Robert Kestnbaum . . . a Harvard MBA guide . . . through the mail order jungle . . . for the Fortune 500. Seminar VII, Chapter 12, this book.

Direct Marketing Vs. General Marketing—NYU, 4/28/81
Mike Slosberg, VP of Marsteller A.A., says: Direct marketing was the original form . . . selling began as direct marketing . . . the marketer supplied his goods directly to the buyer . . . general marketing and general advertising began with more complex distribution . . . dealers, wholesalers, sales representatives between seller and buyer.

Slosberg compares: Direct response and general advertising differ widely, yet there are great areas of similarity; some techniques of general advertising can improve, increase impact and effectiveness of direct response advertising. Strategy disciplines of general advertising can help direct marketers. On tape, Hoke; # 11-0010 - NY - $15.

Mail Order Mergers*
Buying and selling direct marketing businesses—advantageously. See Seminar IX, Chapter 9, this book.

Mail Order Housekeeping

A mail order business undertakes, by its existence, to ship what it offers, promptly . . . to refund money when requested, promptly . . . to answer customer complaints and correspondence concerning service, promptly.

Quick success and sudden growth can create instant chaos in shipping, refunding and customer correspondence. This can destroy customer good will and cut off media which then refuse to sell the firm advertising. It can result in government prosecution for legal infractions. It can lose a lot of money and maybe put the mail order company out of business.

There is no sure blueprint to make a mail order fortune. There are excellent blueprints for every aspect of mail order housekeeping. Exactly what to do is spelled out in talks, lectures and articles described here. And there are many more excellent ones. There is housekeeping advice for different kinds of mail order businesses, of different sizes and at different stages in growth.

Fulfilling the Promise—NYU, 7/23/81
Stanley Fenvessy explains the vital importance of fulfillment and customer service; takes you through the "back end" of the direct marketing business; details its organization . . . order processing, fulfilling, complaint handling . . . every phase of servicing customers quickly. Satisfactorily and economically. An advanced seminar on tape, Hoke; #11-0421 - NY - $25.

Mastering Customer Service—DMMA Conference, 10/29/80
Stanley Fenvessy explains how to organize, establish priorities, simplify . . . mechanize and standardize customer handling . . . use latest techniques where suited . . . all the while improving service. On tape, Hoke; #10-0567 - DM - $15.

Questions and Answers on Fulfillment
Featured in every issue since inception of DM News; a splendid series; detailed and practical. Read them all. Stanley Fenvessy.

Organizing Mail Order*
Stanley Fenvessy tells of his career and cites many examples of improving fulfillment. Seminar IX, Chapter 3, this book.

Credit, Fulfillment, Cutomer Service—FMA Meeting, 6/10/80
Walter Stevens, Assistant Director Consumer Affairs, Time-Life Books, spells out what is required: Process orders quickly and accurately; design order form properly and explain clearly offers and terms. The form becomes a legal document. If you use an outside "800" number service, get involved with the form and script used. Be sure that the service transmits orders quickly. Clock operators. Are they courteous? On tape, Hoke; #10-0403 -WF - $10.

Credit, Fulfillment and Customer Service—NYU, 5/3/77
Carol Flaumenhaft, Director of Consumer Affairs, Time-Life Books, explains the importance of well organized operation, in-house and from outside company . . . and how to achieve it. DM Magazine, June 1977, Volume 40, #2.

From Receipt of Order to Shipment in 8 to 32 Hours—DMMA Conference, 10/29/80
Top executives of four of top U.S. mail order firms tell how: The standards, techniques, reports that make it an achievable, every day standard; on tape, Hoke; #10-0562 - DM - $15.

Cost Efficient Customer Service—DMMA Manual
Joseph J. Kelleher, Vice President of Publishers Clearing House, tells in detail how to achieve it. Release 5202; October 1979.

Preventing and Handling Customer Problems—FMA, 1/23/80
Thomas Lagan, Subscription Manager of Publishers Clearing House, tells how PCH deals with customers for fastest attention; how it works with publishers. On tape, Hoke; #10-0043 - WF -$10.

Delivering and Fulfilling—DMDNY, 4/9-10/80
A panel of computer fulfillment authorities from Neodata Services, RCA Direct Marketing and CBS Columbia House, moderated by Murray Miller, President, American Express Direct Response. On tape, Hoke; #10-0196 - ND - $10.

On-Line Fulfillment System—FFA, 2/18/81
How it works for Time-Life Books. Carol Flaumenhaft, Panel Director of Consumer Affairs, explains. The system allows daily processing of orders, payments and book returns. Book orders are filled in 48 hours. Other benefits are: prevention of duplicate orders, elimination of prior bad debtors; maintenance of customer records; easier handling of customer complaints. The conversion from the previous manual system reduced staff 50 percent and cut delivery time from five down to three weeks while it halved complaints. On tape, Hoke; #11-0163 - FM - $10.

Choosing a Mailing House
Joel Weiss spells out the basic ways for sensible selection. DM magazine; May 1980, Volume 43, #1.

Catalog Fulfillment Changing Course
The effect on fulfillment of the evolution of catalog mail order marketing from a low-ticket to a high-ticket business; how it decreases some costs and increases others in processing and handling orders; bright and dark aspects. Stanley Fenvessy tells it in DM News, February 15, 1981.

The Circulation Fulfillment Business*
The story of Fulfillment Corporation of America. How an executive from Time Inc. and consultant to Time started it; its growing pains and computerization; how it works with its

magazine publisher clients; President Jack Courtney's advice to direct marketers. Seminar VII, Chapter 8, this book.

How to Collect Money—NBCA, 5/13/81
Hillel Felder, Manager of Circulation Marketing of McGraw-Hill Publications.

Be sure that subscribers know that the invoice is a bill and not a renewal form. Don't hide the facts. Use large, bold type. An invoice is not a place for cute teaser copy or pretty pictures. Clearly tell how much the subscriber owes. Put the amount in a big black box. Tell exactly how to pay. If the subscriber has any question about an invoice, the response rate will decrease.

Often individuals subscribe, but the company pays. This creates problems at two ends. Many accounting departments hold invoices 30 to 50 days. They don't always return the invoice copy. State clearly on invoice that an invoice copy must be sent back.

Analyze renewals. Go after the sources. Keep collection statistics by bill numbers. Use the same procedure for foreign orders as for domestic ones. In-house operation improves collection. People sending cash with order renew better. Try upgrading the offer. Stuffers also increase income. Test different subscription prices. The freshness of the mailing is important. The bill should get there fast. On tape, Hoke; #11-0349 - BC - $10.

Your Collection Series—DMMA Manual
"It's the moment of truth," expert Robert Redmond explains. A sale cannot be considered complete until payment has been received; good collection letters must not incur customer resentment . . . and still collect; how to create them; Release 2109.

Fulfillment Company Functions
What they do; how to get most efficient service from them; keep offer simple and order form easy to fill out, with room for requested information. Conduct shipping test to see that packaging is adequate. Set up method for handling return merchandise. State expected delivery time; include expiration date in ad. On tape, Hoke; #12-0056 - MW - $10.

Preparing Your Fulfillment Work for the Computer-Input Process
By Sandy Grossman; ZIP magazine; April 1982.

UPS now ships the majority of mail order packages. Periodically there is consideration of alternatives to the post office for distribution of direct mail. Alternates are continually tested as a hedge and warning against postal rate increases. The following tape and article may concern this.

Advantages of Non-Postal Distribution—Phoenix DM Club, 10/20/81
Gary C. Van Wie, President of United Advertising Distributors, cites them: 1) greater control over delivery date; 2) higher readership; 3) better target marketing and market saturation; 4) lower cost (no permits, no list, no adressing); 5) still a novelty form of delivery; 6) message not overshadowed; 7) results are comparable. On tape, Hoke; # 11-0731 - PD - $10.

Private Delivery—Alive and Growing—DMMA Manual
Coleman W. Hoyt, VP, Reader's Digest, reports on its status and practicality if postal rates become uneconomical. Release 460.1.

Ethics, Regulations and Laws

More and more people, proud of their business, work to raise the ethics and standards of direct marketing.

This leads to self-regulation which is simpler and more desirable than the regulations of bureaus and laws applying to direct marketers which can be cumbersome, costly and time-consuming. Direct marketers who do not self-regulate and ignore regulations and laws take serious risks.

Bigger direct marketers turn increasingly for advice to legal specialists thoroughly versed in the regulations and laws applying to direct marketers. But most violations are entirely unintentional and caused by employees unaware of details of regulations and laws. There are available to you tapes and articles which give specific legal do's and don'ts. Some are described here. There are other excellent ones.

The Rising Standards of Mail Order*
Some background; the DMMA's role in raising them; Seminar VI, Chapter 1, this book.

Guidelines for Print Ads
As adopted by the Ethics Comittee of the DMMA. Part of its continuing effort to raise standards. DM magazine; February 1977, Volume 39, #10.

The Direct Marketing Laws*
Why they exist; possibilities of unknowing infractions, of more laws; what leading direct marketers are doing to better insure that pertinent direct marketing laws and rulings are known and obeyed . . . and to self-police and make unnecessary additional future regulations. Seminar IX, Chapter 10, this book.

Federal and State Crackdown—NYU
Consultant Pierre Passavant warns that promotions must be accurate, not violate regulations . . . that penalties are severe, costly. He spells out what to do to obey the law and sell profitably by mail order. DM magazine; October 1977, Volume 40, #6.

Crimes You May be Committing—New School, NYC, 2/17/81
Explains the practical application of laws to your mailing; how federal, state, local regulations affect every piece of mail you distribute. On tape, Hoke; # 11-0159 - DS - $10.

The Legal Audit—DM Day, Minneapolis, 5/14/80
Sheldon Halpern, partner in Robins, Davis and Lyons, a Minneapolis law firm, explains how to shorten the odds of the increasingly complex legal environment; how laws impact every aspect from how the offer is made to how the order is fulfilled; an in-depth review of salient legal problems in direct marketing. On tape, Hoke; # 10-0302 - MN - $10. Also in article form, DM magazine; November 1980, Volume 43, #7.

Guidelines for Ethical Business Practice—DMMA Manual
For all direct response marketers, DMMA.

Special Marketing Opportunities

They are increasing fast while broad, mass-market mail order becomes more difficult. The case histories in Reference Section V indicate how varied the opportunities are. There is much expertise available on specific fields of such opportunities. Your background, experience, abilities and preferences all affect the opportunities for career and business best for you, as described in Overview, Chapter 2, this book.

To give just an indication of the information available on special interest fields, here are descriptions of several available.

Retail Direct Marketing
DM News; Special Feature Section, December 15, 1982.

Financial Direct Marketing
DM News; Special Feature Section, May 15, 1982.

Direct Response Travel Advertising
DM News; Special feature Section, February 15, 1982.

The $200 Billion Black and Hispanic Market
Minority Mail Order: The reality and potential of the expanding minorities market; most relevant products and services; special problems; successes and failures. Experts report. On tape, Hoke; # 11-0651 - DM - $15.

International Direct Marketing

Mail order is a world phenomenom. The average income, efficiency of the post office, availability of media and government regulations in each country greatly affect its degree of success. Some offers succeed in one country and not in another; but more and more items can be successfully sold in one country and successfully tested and projected in others—often in many others.

The more any mail order firm succeeds in the U.S. the more logical it is to extend that success to other countries to the maximum possible. It's possible to sell to direct marketers in other countries, to form joint ventures with them or to set up a mail order operation in key countries.

But doing so is greatly aided by maximum know-how of international direct marketing. Lack of knowledge can be expensive. Much information is available on tape and in print. Here are descriptions of some speeches, talks and articles that can help.

Opportunities and Problems—NYU, 5/9/78
For some American companies like Time-Life Books, international mail order has been notably successful, says Peter Rosenwald, President of Reeves International. Others have utterly failed; the factors creating opportunities and problems. On tape, Hoke; # 18-0011 - NY - $10.

International Direct Mail
It's difficult but rewarding, says Robert F. Roth. It's a heavy burden to organize and implement a direct mail program internationally . . . but it has high impact. DM magazine; January 1981, Volume 43, # 9.

International Direct Marketing: DMMA Report of Status by Countries—DMMA Manual
Canada: Release 800.1, October 1979.

United Kingdom, Ireland: Release 800.2, October 1979.

West Germany, Australia, Switzerland: Release 800.3, October 1979.

France, Spain, Italy, Israel: Release 800.4, October 1979.

Norway, Sweden, Finland, Netherlands: Release 800.5, October 1979.

Australia, New Zealand, South Africa, Japan, Hong Kong: Release 800.6, October 1979.

Mexico, Brazil: Release 800.7, October 1979.

Regulatory Statistics Affecting International Direct Marketing—DMMA Manual
Compiled by Information Central: Release 800.8, October 1979.

Statistics and Information—DMMA Manual
DMMA estimates of direct marketing advertising and sales for 18 countries by years, over three-year period; source DMMA and International Advertising Association, 1980 survey. Advertising estimates are broken down by media. Sales are also ranked by categories of products and services. Consumer attitudes and major trends affecting direct marketing are commented on . . . all this by countries. Release 800.9; July 1981.

Japanese Mail Order Gaining at Double Retail Rate
. . . says Kaoru Ogimi, President of the Japan Direct Mail Association and President of Reader's Digest of Japan, Ltd. He

describes problems and opportunities. On tape, Hoke; # 10-0622 -JP - $10.

Japan's Untapped Mail Order Market

Japanese firms have only begun trying large-scale direct marketing since 1975, says Kazuko Rudy, Mail Order Marketing Manager, Time-Life Books, Tokyo. Japan is still 10 to 15 years behind the U.S. but Japanese consumers are accepting direct marketing, she says.

Larry Schenker of the Japan-American Direct Response Group, 201 East 28th Street, New York City, NY 10016, describes how Time Inc., Franklin Mint, Reader's Digest, Encyclopaedia Brittanica and other U.S. firms are using direct marketing in Japan. On tape, Hoke; # 10-0610 - LK - $10.

UK Direct Marketing

How it differs from U.S. Andrew J. Byrne examines the state of direct marketing in Great Britain. "Enclosures drew fantastic response in recent UK tests, but various market conditions made it almost impossible to rent good mailing lists." DM magazine; August 1980, Volume 43, #4.

Brazilian Mail Order

Vincente P. Salvi is Direct Marketing Director, Monde Latina, Ltd., Rio de Janeiro. Sek Seklemian is a retail consultant and advertising columnist in Brazil. They report that mail order merchandising is an emerging growth industry in Brazil.

Since 1970, over a hundred mail order firms have started. They sell everything imaginable by mail. Retail stores, in country areas where newspapers are weak, direct market by mail.

Salvi runs the mail order merchandise division of a large Italian publisher in Brazil. Sales of books, housewares, watches and other offers by mail order have increased dramatically. Tests offering fashion merchandise have been successful.

Brazilian mail order is still difficult but postal service is improving. 90% of orders are C.O.D. which the buyer must pick up at the post office . . . when notified. The post office then transmits the cash to the vendor. Delivery via post office takes 90 days. Private delivery to deliver, pick-up, transmit funds quickly is being set up. Interview in DM magazine; May 1981, Volume 44, # 1. Also on tape, Hoke; # 10-0611 - PH - $8.

French Mail Order—DMMA Conference, 3/10-13/81

Bruno Manuel, Director Nucleus et Manuel Direct Marketing, examines it: how the French adapt American successes; how Americans adopt French mail order classics; how same products develop a double nationality. On tape, Hoke; # 11-0170 - DM -$10.

Mail Order Change

It is ever faster, more sweeping and more important to keep up with for anyone in direct marketing. Change is so rapid that on no other subject do talks, lectures and articles become so obsolete so fast.

To update changes, there's a constant stream of new talks, lectures and articles on change. To keep up with them is as important for direct marketers as for surgeons and doctors to keep up with the literature of their professions or lawyers to keep up with latest legal precedents in their specialties.

Any of them recommended here may be outdated by the time you read this book. Therefore, I describe very few, more to indicate what to seek as later ones become available.

The Mail Order Future*

Its seeds, start, problems of survival and possibilities of success for you. Seminar IX, Chapter 13, this book.

The Future of Direct Marketing—New School, NYC, 2/17/81

How it looks, Jerry Reitman, VP, Ogilvy & Mather Direct. On tape, Hoke; # 11-0001 - NY - $15.

Teleprinting and Telecommunications—NYU, Advanced Seminar, 7/22/81

Computer hardware systems potential—soon; provisions to capture orders automatically from CRT's, TV response devices, telephones.

Expert Leo Yochim details new hardware, improved software. He analyzes cost efficiency, applications to various direct marketing modules. On tape, Hoke; # 11-0419 - NY - $25.

Tomorrow's Electronic List World—NYU, 1/20/82

Top consultant Lawrence Chait tells how to prepare truly for it . . . and why it will be a boon for direct marketers. On tape, Hoke; # 12-0014 - NY - $10.

The Direct Marketer's Role in the Electronic Revolution—DM Club, Phoenix, 1/20/81

"Pete" Hoke says: "Direct Marketers must begin thinking of themselves as information providers in the emerging computer communication technology. They must pay attention to the links now being forged into a chain, linking data bases to home and business terminals. The major mergers in publishing, broadcasting and mail order are signals of the rush to take dominant positions in retrievable data bases. On tape, Hoke; # 11-0045 - PD - $10.

The Mail Order Scientists*

They research, advise and plan . . . predict, compare . . . signal to stop or go, speed or slow . . . make mail order bigger, safer, more universal. See "Overview," Chapter 9, this book.

Direct Marketing: State of the Art

First annual study completed Spring, 1982; statistically analytical update; prepared by Marketing Research Consultant Arnold Fishman, Marketing Logistics, Deerfield, IL 60015. Responses by blue ribbon panel to questions about future growth, technology, change. 70 page report in Direct Marketing Magazine, July, 1982.

Electronic Mail Order

Special issue, March 15, 1982; DM News: excellent overview. Two good articles are: one on video-tex, teletext, view data, clarifying and explaining in detail; another on the superstations with a view of advantages and limitations of the three biggest . . . now and in the future . . . the first by the media department of Ogilvy & Mather and the second by that of N.W. Ayer, top advertising agencies.

The Cable Revolution

"Pete" Hoke gives insights on new direct response medium . San Diego Direct Marketing Conference, February, 1982. On tape, Hoke; # 12-0071 - SD - $12.

New Technologies

How to lift response through computerized direct mail; Leo Yochim. On tape, Hoke; # 12-0062 - $12.

Viewdata and Direct Marketing

A taped client meeting for sponsors of the joint Link/Hoke Communications Viewdata Study. Each sponsor is paying $4,000 for the final four-volume report which describes Viewdata Technology and the current activities and future plans of its participants.

The taped meeting is a preliminary progress report. It covers electronic shopping and gives an overview of electronic communication and its development worldwide. It includes key points and analysis of Viewdata as a new electronic shopping vehicle. It covers Prestel (English name for Viewdata) international market trial; cable catalog channels as potential complements to Viewdata. It discusses the two-way service for shopping, banking, information, entertainment and security offered by Compu-Serv Corp.

Anthony Book, Manager of Development Projects for American Express, explains the scope of Prestel in the United Kingdom. Prestel's markets and analyzes the use by American Express of the Prestel System to sell goods and services. Roy Bright, Director General of Marketing of Telematique, France, discusses the electronic communication explosion in Europe; the growth of the Prestel and Teletel Viewdata systems; the advantages and disadvantages of various systems; the problems foreseen for the future of American Viewdata Systems.

The entire meeting taped by Hoke; # 10-0394 - LH - $50.

Computerworld Extra
Great special issue of a great publication; helpful background to understand scope of application of computers to direct marketing; orients and updates; history, latest developments, predictions; computer networks; earth station, satellites; viewdata, teletext. I recommend you send for the September 17, 1980 issue, the March 18, 1981 issue. Each is over 120 jumbo pages. $7.50 each. Circulation Department, Computerworld Extra, 375 Cochituate Road, Framingham, MA 01701. (601) 879-0700.

So far, in this section I've referred to articles and taped talks on general subjects helpful to a wide variety of mail order businesses. But there are many which concern specific kinds of mail order businesses only. It is possible to create for yourself entire courses which each concern just one kind of direct marketing firm.

You want to start a catalog . . . succeed with one you own or manage—get a job to sell to one—and simply understand how the catalog business works. But you really want to get a thorough background. Or perhaps you're interested in a certain type of catalog. You refer to the catalog case histories in Reference Section V. You also want a lot of how-to information from many angles. Refer to the following. Check the reference sources for more and more up-to-date information. Try to get all you can at a business library . . . before you start spending money.

Inside the General Catalog—International DMMA, 2/20-27/81
Some of the world's top catalog executives . . . from Simpson-Sears, Canada . . . Sears Roebuck, USA, A/S Direct Norway . . . and Quelle, West Germany, examine many aspects: promotions and advertising, operations and new merchandise. On tape, Hoke; # 11-0074 - DM - $22 (2 tapes).

Specialty Catalogs—NYU, 3/3/81
Bill Henry, of L. L. Bean, advises: Be expert in your product lines; reflect this in your catalogs; really know and have all information on your products; test products and learn uses, how they are made; don't have just one item of a type, have some depth in a specialty. Have stable lines; develop customers who will be with you a long time.

Study customer file based on frequency, recency and monetary value of orders; determine which product lines are selling best, which lines have biggest profit margin, what trends are. Learn which media are working for what products; research who new customers are . . . men vs. women, how this is changing; familiarity of new customers with your firm.

Create an image of authority in your selling area; know what you sell; position your firm competitively in the right niche; offer unique products and good value; have a management approach; know what customers want; emphasize fast, accurate fulfillment;

deliver when needed, a short time after people order; hire good people; make up integrated annual plan; look at least one year into the future. Above all, realize the importance of customer service and customer relations. On tape, Hoke; # 11-0002 - NY -$15. Invaluable.

Catalogs, Merchandise, Markets—NYU, 10/7/80
Top catalog consultant, Roy Hedberg, examines what specialty mail order is and involves; the difference between Wards, Sears, Penney, Spiegel and Aldens; explains what creativity, merchandising, promotion area abilities are needed; the use and rental of the house list. Thorough; on tape, Hoke; # 10-0344 - NY - $15.

The Catalog Mail Order Business
DM News covers the catalog business in depth in its February 15, 1981, issue.

The Fundamental Elements of Successful Cataloging
Chapter 25 of Julian L. Simon's book, "How to Start and Operate a Mail Order Business"; DM magazine, October 1980, Volume 43, #6.

Concepts, Execution, Analysis—Midwest DM Days, 3/4-5/80
Step-by-step guide to catalog effectiveness from initial planning to final result and evaluation. A panel of executives from three companies; on tape, Hoke; # 10-0117 - CM - $10.

Creation of a Catalog—DMMA Conference, 10/25-28/81
In one day! This taping of an all-day workshop is innovative, instructive, comprehensive. The audience helps create a catalog. Outstanding experts pose problems and give guidance. The audience examines alternatives and possible compromises . . . tries to improve solutions. DMMA Library, 6 Eat 43rd Street, NYC; (212) 689-4977. Non-members by appointment Wednesdays only.

The Catalog Panel—Conference DMCSC, 1/23-24/78
Prestigious catalog experts discuss in depth the most vitally important checkpoints; readership, responsiveness and retention . . . mailing strategy, copywriting and design techniques; also mail order handling, answering requests, incentive offers and phone orders; much more; individual questions answered. On tape, Hoke; # 18-00048- LA - $10.

Catalogs, Merchandise, Markets—NYU, 4/10/79
What makes a catalog profitable? How do changing markets affect your customers? What are the markets of the future? How to avoid mistakes in catalog preparation and distribution . . . by controlling costs of products, printing, paper and mailing lists. Harold Schwartz, president, Hanover House Industries, Inc., Hanover, PA. On tape, Hoke; # 19-0007 - NY - $12.

Trends, Opportunities, Dangers
Harold L. Schwartz multiplied the success of Hanover House Industries, Inc., of which he is president. He proliferated its specialized catalogs as he propelled volume past $100,000,000 annually.

He says: Catalogs will move faster from low to high-ticket items. The low-ticket catalog is doomed as costs keep rising. Big catalogs will more and more split into smaller units . . . and only distributed at a charge or with the requirement of an order being a must.

More in-store retailers will move into catalogs as high borrowing costs make expenditures to construct retail stores sky high. A different mentality is needed for stores than for mail order. More quality retailers will enter the field and force out the old. The combination of telephone marketing and credit cards has significant impact.

Mail order is now a narrow market. The "Mom and Pop

Store" type of catalogs face dangers. A minimum of $500,000 capital is needed. It's easy to lose $200,000 in a short time. The near future will be "much tougher" for catalog marketers; many will fail. Survivors will have big increases in profits. Important, DM News; February 15, 1981.

Strategic Planning and Decision Making—NYU, 7/21/81

Harold Schwartz, President, Hanover House Industries, Inc., advises on making decisions you won't regret; explains the economic base of mail order markets; market definition, consumer research, analysis and planning; determining critical issues by computer modeling and by testing programs; drawing conclusions from data; creating marketing strategy; translating planning decisions into realities; he cites case studies. On tape, Hoke; # 11-0418 - NY - $25.

Analyzing Your Catalog—DMMA Manual

The DMMA tells how to take apart your catalog like a financial analyst . . . often to find the key to greater profits. A financial analysis chart is included, with suggested mathematical computation. Four pages, illustrated; Appendix VI, October 1979. Also read newer release 630.1.

Catalog Profits

They don't come accidentally, but from sound management. Joseph Dunn, President of Yield House, analyzes just what good catalog management is . . . step by step. DM magazine, March 1980; Volume 42, #11.

Selecting Catalog Products—International DM Symposium

Leading consultant Leonard Carlson details some of the best selling mail order items from a number of countries over 20 years. On tape, Hoke; # 11-0282 - ID - $7.

Merchandise, Marketing and Costs—DMMA, 10/27/80

Harold Schwartz, President of Hanover House Industries, Inc., Robert Edmund, of Edmund Scientific, and Alfred Schmidt, Jr., Vice President, Direct Marketing, of Brooks Brothers, discuss successful approaches for quite different kinds of catalogs. On tape, Hoke; # 10-0544 - DM - $12.

How to Think about Catalogs and Retailing

One of America's great merchants, Stanley Marcus, says bigness may not be best, that smartest retailers will turn to direct marketing; gives much wisdom, fascinating anecdotes of Neiman-Marcus; tells the two most important ingredients for retail success; discusses the possible future of direct marketing retailing via electronic media for instant selling. DM magazine; May 1979, Volume 42, # 1. Also on tape from speech at Houston DM Day, Hoke; #19-0087 - $10.

Keys to Successful Catalog Operation

Erv Magram explains the mixture of components of successful catalogs, merchandise selection, how space is allocated, repeating "hit" items, and page size of catalog, and far more. DM magazine; September 1981, Volume 44, #5.

The Age of Catalog Specialization

How to narrow horizons and pinpoint audience; how to attain the right margin; how to select merchandise; what items to feature in ads; Lillian Katz, President of Lillian Vernon, Inc., talks. On tape, Hoke; # 18-0358 - DW - $8.

Catalogs—Creative—CADM, 2/13/80

Your catalog must be special, unique, must have a definite point of view, says Jo Von Tucker, V.P. of The Photographer, Inc. Your image should start with the cover and continue throughout the catalog. Make presentation dramatic. Capture customer attention; make it easy to shop in your catalog. On tape, Hoke; #10-0081 -CM - $10.

Catalog Promotion Methods—DMCG 3/5/80

Bill Henry, VP of L. L. Bean, and Harold Schwartz explain: New customers are obtained at less cost through space, says Henry. The L. L. Bean computer designed its marketing strategy. It recommended use of small space as as much as possible . . . close to month of catalog issue. Harold Schwartz says: "Loser items can be winners, with new positioning. He cites examples. On tape, Hoke; # 10-0133 - DW - $10.

Print Production—DMMA, 10/26/80

The special problems and requirements of catalogs; ways of saving money; what to avoid; Adola Cooper, Bloom Advertising Agency, Max Dunlevy, Lehigh Press. On tape, Hoke; # 10-0583 -DM - $10.

How to Determine Your Winners and Losers—DMMA, 10/26/80

Top catalog authority Dick Hodgson explains . . . and what to do about it; on tape, Hoke; # 10-0584 - DM - $10.

Selectronic Catalogs: The Wave of the Future

Two insiders look at the future of cataloging. With all costs rising at unprecedented rates, it is essential that catalogs become more personal, without wasting paper, ink, postage; that catalogs be customized and printed for the needs and desires of those mailed. David Saxman, Leon Packman; DM magazine; July 1979, Volume 42, # 3.

Let's assume you want to get a brief overview of the automatic shipment club business. First you might consider a quick overview of several speeches and articles as listed below. Then you might check the case histories available of various clubs, as referred to in Reference Section V.

Book and Record Club Direct Marketing

Special Feature Section, DM News; April 15, 1981, Important. An incisive analysis by Lester Wunderman; Excellent article by top club executives; changes, fragmentation; developments.

Everything You've Always Wanted to Know About Book Clubs

Leonard Malleck, President of Outdoor Life and Popular Science book clubs, gives an A to Z overview; particularly interesting to magazine publishers considering a book club. DM magazine; March 1979, Volume 41, #11.

The Problems of a Book Club Manager

The importance of good book fulfillment, and knowing what it costs. Its aid in controlling bad debt write-offs. Ralph Raughley, book club consultant, explains. DM magazine; June 1977, Volume 40, #2.

Book Clubs for Segmented Tastes

A top book club expert, L. William Black, analyzes them and why, out of 164 mail-order book clubs, most appeal to a highly specialized market. DM magazine; June 1978, Volume 41, #2.

Suppose you were interested in magazines . . . either to work for one, sell subscriptions for one, sell to one or start one . . . or possibly in newsletters. Problems, opportunities and marketing methods are often similar for either. Let's assume you want to research magazines in more depth and newsletters more briefly. If so you might check the case histories in Reference Section V and then the following descriptions of how-to speeches and articles. You could then go to the sources listed and ask for more up-to-date material. You could probably get it in far greater variety, particularly if you ask each source for suggestions where else to check. Try to get material from your business library . . . for no cost. Let's start with magazines and then go on with newsletters.

Selling Subscriptions by Mail Order*

Wendell Forbes is a top consultant to publishers and a master teacher. Among those who trained under him at Time Inc. are top executives throughout the direct marketing world. His story and much valuable advice by him is in Seminar IV, Chapter 11, of this book.

Subscription Marketing

Special feature section; news of tests; case histories of success; how to upgrade length of subscription; use of TV; introductory offer. Good job! DM News, 19 West 21st Street, NYC, NY 10010; (212) 741-2095.

Raising Money for Publishing Projects

James Kobak tells how. Folio Magazine; December 1976.

Fundamentals of Circulation Promotion—NYU, 11/29/77

It starts by defining the terminology; explains the importance of each kind of subscription; discusses how it is obtained; covers newsstand sales; examines measurement of current profitability; explains how to plan future growth more safely, particularly using computer modeling; takes you step-by-step through the process of securing subscriptions . . . from first solicitation to maintenance through renewals; spells out how to test; select lists and media; analyze results; then how to project and refine successful tests and establish longevity. Dan Capell and Eliot Schein. On tape, Hoke: # 17-0350 - NY- $10.

The Rules of the Circulation Game

An important article for anyone in the magazine or newsletter business who is concerned with getting subscriptions; by consultant Wendell Forbes; Folio Magazine; August 1975.

Subscription Marketing by Publishers

DM News Special Feature Section, January 15, 1982.

Some Timely Criticisms of Subscription Methods

Consultant Dick Benson advises: Simplicity is the fundamental principle of direct mail and cannot be over-emphasized. A company should decide what business it is in and concentrate its talent in that area. DM magazine; August 1979, Volume 42, #4.

Direct Marketing Circulation Strategy—Canadian DM Conference, 5/25-28/80

Intriguing insight from Wendell Forbes, a "Best in the Business" expert whose Dickensian charm covers a steel-trap mind. On tape, Hoke: # 10-0327 - DC - $15.

Circulation Management of Business Publications—NBCA, 3/11/81

Harriet Matyska, Circulation Director of United Business Publications, advises: Get involved . . . get enthusiastic about all segments of your publications; know your editorial product; have rapport with ad director, production director, editors, publisher. To plan better strategy with publisher, understand what is happening in each department. Try consumer magazine tactics such as co-op mailings, telephone marketing to offset postage increases. On tape, Hoke: # 11-0192 - BC - $10.

Free Circulation to Paid

How to convert it successfully, as only a few magazines have actually done. By William F. Fahy, Jr., DM magazine; May 1979, Volume 42, #1.

New Income Producing Opportunities For Special Interest Magazines—NBCA, 5/14/80

"Publishers are in the information business," says William M. Stocker, Jr., of McGraw-Hill Publications. "Print is only one medium." He describes in detail the development of other information services; seminars, trade shows and newsletters . . . computer data bases, reprints and books . . . all sold by direct

marketing; describes the proper market research, testing and auditing of results necessary before launching each new product and service; discusses introduction of new information products for which capital investment is relatively low and which can help smooth peaks and valleys and add revenue. On tape, Hoke: # 10-0299 - BC - $10.

Source Evaluation

By tracing all conversions from trial subscriptions and renewals for a term of years, later it's possible to compare the long-term value of subscriptions from one source vs. another. Wendell Forbes explains. Folio Magazine, November 1977.

Customized Magazines—100 Million Club, 11/9/80

Customized, special interest magazines will soon come into their own, says Joseph J. Hanson, Publisher of Folio Magazine (the superb magazine for magazine publishers). With computer-controlled bindery selectivity, special interest sections will customize the magazine for the reader's needs and wants. Readers will be able to buy editorial options, as for cars. Gardening, business and New York entertainment sections can be added . . . by computer. Hanson discusses the present new ability of magazines to compete with TV, by segmentation and the future ahead. On tape, Hoke: # 10-0531 - HM - $10.

Newsletter Promoting Strategy and Techniques—NAA Conference, 6/22-24/80

Consultant Rene Gnam details; On tape, Hoke: # 10-0433 - NL -$24.

The Future of Newsletters—NAA, 5/22-23/78

Gordon Jones, President, McGraw-Hill Publications Company, discusses it, and explains why the publishing giant is very much committed to the newsletter field. On tape, Hoke: # 18-0259 - NL - $8.

Operations of the Big and Options of the Small—Cleveland DMA, 6/13/80

Kiplinger Washington Editors Inc. is the biggest publisher of newsletters. It originated them on a big scale. Bill Armstead, of Kiplinger, discusses steps from sorting incoming mail to list maintenance . . . policy decisions critical to a smooth system— advanced renewals, whether to extend the term or refund money—whether and, if so, when to send grace copies.

Shirley Mackey is President of Publican, Inc. of Greenbelt, Maryland. She discusses the choice between using a computer service bureau, a time-sharing computer service, or in-house fulfillment on your own computer. Software is critical. You must be able to accomplish your needs and produce reports. Both are on tape, Hoke: #10-0404 - WF $12.

Reference Section V
The Case History Sampler

To help orient you to a field
. . . prepare for a job choice . . .
. . . multiply your experience.

Case histories in the Help Source Guide and Index are divided into classifications, each arranged alphabetically. These classifications are my own, arbitrary and as follows:

Catalogs—general . . . catalogs—specialized; two-step mail order for non-catalog firms; continuing mail order sales . . . in which I have included clubs, continuity programs and magazine subscriptions plus something else. I call this the Offer Stream and refer to making one offer after another to the same customers. The offer often is related to the kind of products or services formerly purchased by the customer.

Just as mail order is a method of selling, each of these classifications is a way of selling by mail order. Some firms in mail order use one of these ways only. Some use more than one and some all. Most use one way predominantly. Case histories listed in the Help Source Guide and Index are classified according to the way of selling which each currently uses . . . predominantly or solely.

Mortality is high for firms selling by mail order one item only in one step, without follow-up to solicit further purchases. Therefore, I have not included in this section single item success stories except as part of one of the classifications listed.

A case history may describe a method, field or a product that does not concern you at this time. Yet it may stimulate you to direct market in ways you have not yet considered.

Much of the methods used to sell magazine subscriptions by mail order apply to newsletters. There are also applications for selling insurance by mail order . . . converting a short-term trial policy for a longer one, renewing those whose policies are expiring and mailing to those whose policies expired earlier. A lot learned in selling magazine subscriptions is helpful to the promotion of book clubs, continuity programs and sets of encyclopedias by mail order. In Seminar VI, Chapter 11, of this book I tell how Dick Benson applied some of his successful methods for publishers to profitably sell grapefruit, peanuts and merchandise.

Two-step is often used to start small specialized catalogs and is often continued long after mailings of catalogs to outside lists supply most volume. For catalogs the use of two-step mail order is similar to that of firms who follow up with brochures. The difference between a quite small catalog and a brochure featuring a number of items may be hard to define. A catalog of many items may originate as a brochure. A solo mailing to outside names may originate from a follow-up to those inquiring in two-step mail order. Leads can be secured for and closed by salesmen in the same way so that any firm employing salesmen and needing inquiries can learn from two-step mail order.

Clubs, continuity programs and magazines are forms of automatic shipment authorized by the customer. Each can teach many in other forms of mail order a great deal about creating loyal customers who keep buying.

The Offer Stream method can be used to follow up any

satisfied mail order buyer. the only requisites are that the products or services originally offered be of sufficient quality, and that the offers made thereafter are sufficiently suited to the customers mailed, judged by analysis of previous purchases and various ways of assuming lifestyle, income and other pertinent data. Offers may be made to catalog customer . . . to clubs, continuity programs, magazine subscribers . . . or to previous purchasers of a previous item.

The result is that a case history of success in mail order can offer lessons of applications to a remarkably wide range of other mail order situations. Few in mail order do not try to learn something of value from anyone in a wide variety of other mail order businesses.

A case history may familiarize you with a company or a field. It may orient you to a medium of advertising such as TV or direct mail. Outside the Case History Sampler, a taped speech or lecture, a magazine article or book referred to will often go into one or more case histories. Exposure to research material of one type may lead to added know-how in other areas. Varied exposure stimulates ideas you won't otherwise get. You learn of techniques and methods, opportunities and pitfalls that you otherwise wouldn't. You multiply all the experience you can personally obtain in a lifetime.

The following case histories are arranged by types of business so that you can quickly find them in fields you're interested in. Let's proceed.

CATALOGS—GENERAL
The Big Five—USA

ALDENS, INC., 5000 West Rosevelt Road, Chicago, IL 60607. (312) 854-4384. How it functions; its strategy; how it specialized within broad lines, promotes want items rather than staples. Richard T. Patton, VP, Advertising and Sales Promotion, describes Alden's philosophy. DM magazine; February 1974, Volume 36, #10.

MONTGOMERY-WARD, INC., 2 Montgomery Ward Plaza, Chicago, IL 60671. (312) 467-2000. "Montgomery Ward History," the first U.S. mail order-general catalog firm . . . mimeographed *free* copy. From founding in one 12'x14' room . . . with a list of 163 items on a single page . . . to giant catalog, huge store business, acquisition by Mobil Oil and multibillion dollar sales. Write Public Relations Department.

J. C. PENNEY COMPANY, INC., 1301 Avenue of the Americas, New York, NY 10019. (212) 957-7301. How the last of the big five entered the catalog business years after the first and quickly became number one. Its catalog's first ten years; told by Penney's present Chairman of the Board, Donald V. Seibert. DM magazine; June 1974, Volume 37, #2.

SEARS, ROEBUCK & CO., INC., Sears Tower, Chicago, IL 60684. (312) 875-2500. How Sears uses its biggest sales division, its catalogs, for "total marketing"; to display and sell merchandise at an ever increasing rate; prepare areas to open stores; supplement store's stock; develop specialized businesses; increase number of credit customers; explain future merchandising techniques, John B. Kelly, former VP, Catalog Sales, explains Sears' viewpoint. DM magazine; May 1981, Volume 4, #1. Also on tape, Hoke; # 11-0073 - DM - $10.

SPIEGEL, INC.*, Regency Towers, Oak Brook, IL 60521. (312) 986-8800. Henry A. Johnson, Chairman of the Board, tells how Spiegel is turning into the Bloomingdales of catalogs. See Seminar VII, Chapter 9, this book.

SPIEGEL revises catalog: How Spiegel aims for more affluent customers. DM News 5/15/80.

CATALOGS—GENERAL—OVERSEAS

QUELLE VERSAND, Nuernberger Strasse 127, Fuerst, West Germany. The world's second largest mail order firm; its 50 year history; the story of its founder, Dr. H. C. Gustav Schickedanz. Told in English by Dr. Wolfgang Buhler; on tape, Hoke: # 18-0193 - 1D - $8.

CATALOGS—SPECIALIZED
Consumer Catalogs A - Z

Airline Catalogs

TWA and various: How airline catalogs originated, grew and are now operated, kinds of items and ways of presentation that succeed best for them; the story of K-Promotions, the organization that creates and produces over ten million a year of them . . . at its risk; by VP Paul Elias. DM magazine; October 1977, Volume 40, #6. Also on tape, Hoke: # 17-0191 - JH - $8.

Auto Accessories—Luxury

FAF MOTORCARS INC., 3862 Stephens Court, Tucker, GA 30084. (404) 939-5464. How Ferrari service manuals reprinted and sold by mail led to 64-page catalog of Ferrari service parts and accessories . . . then to Ferrari dealership . . . even to selling new and used Ferraris with mail order methods. Told by co-founder John Apen. DM magazine; February 1978, Volume 40, #10. Also on tape, Hoke; # 17-0492 - JH - $8.

Books

CROWN DIRECT MARKETING, 1 Park Avenue, New York, NY 10016. (212) 532-9200. The catalog that sells consumers more individual books for greater dollar sales than any other. Its story told by Cherie Bagdan, Manager Catalog Sales. DM magazine; January 1981, Volume 43, #9. Also on tape, Hoke: # 10-0589 - LK - $10.

Camper Items - RV

CAMPING WORLD, Beech Bend Road, Bowling Green, KY 42101. (502) 781-2718. How a small store on a family-owned campground branched into mail order; tested, projected, succeeded, expanded to 96-page catalog of 1400 items; then three catalogs yearly, big warehouse, chain of service and installation centers. Founder David Garvin tells the story; DM magazine; October 1978, Volume 41, #6. On tape, Hoke; # 18-0363 - JH - $8. Story updated in 1980 by President Garvin; on tape, Hoke; # 10-0213 - LK - $10.

Children's Specialties

WINTERBROOK CORP., Primrose Lane, Laconia, NH 03246. The start and first year of "Just for Kids," catalog in color featuring merchandise for children; the first results, projection, weeding out losers in lists tested; plans, experiments, outcome; strategy decisions how next to proceed; told by President Russel Sabanek. On tape, Hoke; # 18-0236 - JH - $8.

Coins

BOWERS & RUDDY*, 6922 Hollywood Boulevard, Los Angeles, CA 90028. Biggest coin business in world, highest average sale, subsidiary of General Mills. See story on Seminar V, Chapter 2, page 200, this book.

Duck Decoys - Handcrafted

BAY COUNTRY WOODCRAFTS, Oak Hall, VA 23416. (804) 824-5626. Co-founder "Rick" Hornick tells how two brothers started a business in a basement, creating beautifully finished and colored decoys; struggled for ten years to sell them via stores; then succeeded with a mail order catalog, until it mailed over two million copies yearly. DM magazine; June 1981, Volume 44, #2. Also on tape, Hoke; #11-0193 - PH - $10.

Fashion

AVON FASHIONS*, 9 West 57th Street, New York, NY 10019. (212) 593-4017. Its first president, William Willets, tells how it started and grew to $100,000,000 a year in sales (now larger). "Overview," Chapter 12, page 23, this book.

CHESAPEAKE BAY TRADING COMPANY, P. O. Box 5879, Pikesville, MD 21208. (301) 363-1976. Founder Burton Banks tells how he used know-how, as a former slacks manufacturer, and thorough study of direct marketing books and ads to succeed in mail order. He started with denim type clothing . . . "bush" shorts to "gentlemen's jeans" . . . advertised in space ads. He enclosed swatches . . . then a simple catalog; also mailed it out . . . first to 75,000 . . . then to 200,000 . . . then to 750,000. He quadrupled sales in two years, to over two million dollars (now far bigger). On tape, Hoke; #18-0226 and #17-0081 - JH - $8 each.

FRENCH CREEK SHEEP AND WOOL CO., RD 1, Elverson, PA 19520. (215) 286-5700. He had been a teacher. His wife had been a fashion designer. They bought an 18th century farm, with sheep on it. She designed sheepskin coats. He created a simple brochure, ran small space ads to get inquiries. The brochure grew to a 32-page catalog which grossed over $1 million. Eric Flaxenberg, owner, tells story in DM magazine; March 1979, Volume 41, #11. Also on tape, Hoke; #18-0406 - JH - $8.

THE PERUVIAN CONNECTION, Canaan Farm, Tonganoxie, KS 66086. (913) 845-2750. A free write-up in the New York Times forced an importer of Peruvian alpaca merchandise (which only sold wholesale) to send out catalogs to thousands of inquiries received. The catalog expanded to offer luxury alpaca sweaters, blankets, ceramics, gifts. Sales quadrupled in four years. Anne Hurlbut, proprietress, explains how. DM magazine, May 1981, Volume 44, #1. Also on tape, Hoke; #10-0616 - LK - $10.

THE TALBOTS*, 175 Beal Street, Hingham, MA 02043. (617) 749-7600. It's the successful fashion catalog with the suburban look for working women . . . and a General Mills subsidiary. See Seminar V, Chapter 2, page 200, this book.

Film Distribution

How a thousand dollar mail order investment led to a 44 million dollar a year film distribution company. It sells by mail order rolls of film in the U.S., Canada, England and France. Founder Martin Faber tells the story. DM magazine; October 1973, Volume 36, #6.

Garden Items—Orchids

THE BEALL COMPANY, P. O. Box 467, Vashon Island, WA 98070. (206) 463-9151. A catalog with no color, no pictures, no drawings; not on computer; not mailed bulk rate; simply describes each of about 150 different varieties, 30 - 50 new each issue . . . ten times a year. Frank Shride, manager orchid division, tells how it profitably sells hobbyists, more each year. DM magazine; October 1979, Volume 42, #6. Also on tape, Hoke; #18-0224 - JH - $8.

HANES ORCHIDS OF DISTINCTION*, 6264 North Bion Avenue, San Gabriel, CA 91775. (213) 287-8945. How John Hanes planned for retirement 28 years before he did . . . later became a mail order moonlighter with his hobby of hybridizing the Paphiopedilum and selling to hobbyists, then retired and sells by mail order world-wide. See Seminar V, Chapter 3, page 205, this book.

Gifts

COUNTRY CURTAINS, INC., Main Street, Stockbridge, MA 01262. (413) 298-5565. How the Fitzpatricks, husband and wife, bought the Red Lion Inn, launched a catalog selling curtains and other decorative products . . . and made it in mail order. DM magazine; December 1975, Volume 38, #8.

LILLIAN VERNON*, 510 South Fulton Avenue, Mt. Vernon, NY 10550. (914) 699-4131. Founder Lillian Katz tells how she started with $450 ad for monogrammed belt, converted to catalog business, built it to $40 million yearly . . . see Seminar I, Chapter 4, this book.

I strongly recommend that you read "Search for New Customers and Merchandise," by her. DM magazine, March 1977, Volume 39, #11. She tells more of her success and business on tape, Hoke; # 18-0358 - DW - $8, and # 10-0480 - LK - $10. Son and VP, Fred Hochberg, detailed the operation in a great lecture at New York University Direct Marketing course; On tape, Hoke; #19-0307 - NY - $12.

The New York Times, April 26, 1978, tells her story in "A Business Made to Order by Mail," by George Dullea. Check if your library has the issue on microfilm.

Gourmet Foods: Confections, Dried Fruit, Nuts

HOUSE OF ALMONDS, 5300 District Blvd., Bakersfield, CA 93309. (805) 835-6561. California Almond Orchards, Inc., founded it . . . to sell almonds and nuts by mail order. Sales were $49,000 the first year, passed $1 million a year, continued to grow. Mailing list went from 3,000 to 500,000. Now it's all a division of Tenneco. Ron Zell, General Manager, tells the story of the first ten years of mail order; how mail order led to opening one retail store after another. DM magazine; April 1975, Volume 37, #12. Also on tape, Hoke; # 10-0402 - LK - $7.

Gourmet Foods: Cheese

NEW ENGLAND CHEESEMAKING SUPPLIES, Main Street, Ashfield, MA 01330. (413) 628-3808. Ricki and Robert Carroll were school teachers who owned several goats and one cow and had trouble securing the cheesemaking equipment and supplies they wanted and learned to make it themselves. They made their own, taught others, quit their jobs and went into the mail order business . . . with classified and small display ads to get inquiries, and simple catalog. Their story is told in the DM News, October 15, 1981.

Gourmet Foods: Processed Food

PFAELZER BROTHERS, 4501 West District Boulevard, Chicago, IL 60632. (312) 927-7100. How the mail order gift division of Armour Processed Meat Co. repositioned its catalog and tripled its sales in three years, and how it laid the groundwork. Merlin Fliehe, General Manager of Pfaelzer and executive of its agency, HNK&P Direct, tell the story; on tape, Hoke; # 10-0499 - CM - $10, and # 19-0379 - LK - $8.

OMAHA STEAKS INTERNATIONAL, 4400 South 96th Street, Omaha, NE 68127. (402) 297-9310. Frederick J. Simon, Executive VP, tells how a catalog sells hospitality dinners by mail; on tape, Hoke; # 17-0115 - DM - $10.

Handmade Home Furnishings

PUCKIHUDDLE PRODUCTS, LTD., Oliverea, NY 12462. (914) 254-5553. Shortly after Larry and his wife, Nat Bauer,

started their catalog of handmade items . . . in 1972 . . . American Home did a life-style article on their project. Over 20,000 catalog inquiries came in. The uniqueness of the handmade items pulled in sales. The venture has prospered. Larry Bauer tells of the problems, excitement and success of the first seven years. DM magazine; July 1980, Volume 43, #3. Also on tape, Hoke; # 10-0130 - LK - $10.

Handmade Items

OLD GUILFORD FORGE, On the Green, Guilford, CT 06437. (203) 453-2731. The story of a sick catalog business "on its knees and staggering" . . . selling hand-made forged hardware items, fireplace tools and manufactured home accessories . . . and how new owners made it well so that it has since prospered. Thomas Romano, President, tells what kind of items he cut out, what items did best, gives full details of changes, and how results improved. On tape, Hoke; # 10-0478 - LK - $10.

Hobbies—Crafts: Model Steam Engines

CALDWELL INDUSTRIES, 4468 Zarahemla Drive, Salt Lake City, UT 84117. How $47 ad for a steam engine model kit, run in the 3,000 circulation magazine, "Live Steam," started it . . . how this led to a 60-page newsprint catalog, a book club, organized trips to England, many other related products, co-op promotion with Heathkit, Edmund Scientific and others. Founder John Matlock tells it all. DM magazine; August 1975, Volume 38, #4. Also on tape, Hoke; # 15-0279 - PH - $8.

Home Security

MOUNTAIN WEST ALARM, 4215 North Sixteenth Street, Phoenix, AZ 85016. (602) 263-8831. 1400 items in 68-page catalog did estimated $2.6 million in 1980, up from $77,000 in 1971 . . . the launch year. John Sanborne, President, says it's growing 30% a year . . . selling door switches, wiring, simple controls, bells, sirens—reliable merchandise do-it-yourselfers can install and repair. Mails 700,000 catalogs a year. John Sanborne explains it all; on tape, Hoke; # 10-0620 - LK - $10.

Jewelry Making

ALPHA FACETING COMPANY, 1225 Hollis Street, Bremerton, WA 98310. (206) 373-3302. It took eleven years to develop from a hobby to a moonlighting mail order business in the basement; then it grew to a 220-page catalog of 1900 items for making jewelry. It included stones, equipment, findings, instructions for hobbyists and was sent to collectors and "rock shops". How Charlene Botema's company first grossed over $1,000,000 a year. On tape, Hoke; # 18-0071 - JH - $8.

Jewelry Making—Metalwork

ATLAS PRESS COMPANY, 2019 North Pitcher Street, Kalamazoo, MI 49007. (616) 345-7155. The first two years of a manufacturer's mail order catalog offering metal cutting tools to home hobbyists along with related items. Mailings made, average orders received, overall results. How conflict with trade was avoided; growth strategy. Interview with John Klok, Merchandise Manager, in DM magazine; March 1979, Volume 41, #11. Also on tape, Hoke; # 18-0525 - JH - $8.

Needlecraft—Hooked Rugs

MARY MAXIM, 2001 Holland Avenue, Port Huron, MI 48060. (313) 987-2000. President and owner, Larry McPhedrain, tells how his firm started in mail order following up 400 inquiry names and later expanded to mailing 7 million catalogs, one for needlecraft and one for hooked rugs . . . The principles and methods that caused success; DM magazine; October 1977, Volume 40, #6. Also on tape, Hoke; # 17-0302 - JH - $8.

Tom Jensen of Mary Maxim tells how to plan and produce catalog promotion for profit; on tape, Hoke; # 18-0286 - CD - $8.

Old House Renovation

THE RENOVATOR'S SUPPLY INC., Millers Falls, MA 01349. (413) 659-3542. It was launched with 50,000 black and white catalog mailing to Old House Journal list. It offered 400 items including old materials, tools to work with them, reproductions, even advice; 19 months later it sent out 100,000 catalogs. Then 2 months later it went to color. This was so successful that 4 months after that 280,000 and 3 months after that one million were mailed. By then the catalog contained 900 items. Interview Chris Frado, Advertising Director, on tape, Hoke; # 11-0508 -DV - $10.

Outdoor Products

EDDIE BAUER, INC.*, 1737 Airport Way South, Seattle, WA 98134. A sporting goods store owner developed a better shuttlecock, for badminton. He then invented a down-padded jacket, later a down-padded sleeping bag. He sold them successfully by mail order . . . later created a mail order catalog . . . and then sold out. How General Mills acquired Eddie Bauer, Inc., expanded it. In this book, in Seminar V, Chapter 2, on page 4. In DM magazine and on tape President James Casey gives far more detail; how changing life styles affect product mix, advertising, everything; how mail order and store sales help each other, with no conflict; spells out operations, growth methods, control, ways of selling, number of catalogs, frequency and timing of mailings. DM magazine; February 1979, Volume 41, #10. Also on tape, Hoke; # 18-0531 - JH - $8, and # 10-0318 - MN - $10, D.M. Day, Minn., MN.

L. L. BEAN, INC., Casco Street, Freeport, ME 04033. (207) 865-4761. A better hunting shoe started its founder, Mr. L. L. Bean, in mail order sales. Bean then led his business into a 12½ million dollar operation. Space ads, 24-hour retail store, and in-house lists were keys to success. President Leon Gorman tells how. DM magazine; January 1973, Volume 35, #8.

From 1973 under Leon Gorman, L. L. Bean became the most successful outdoorsman catalog and one of the most exciting success stories in direct marketing. Gorman built on the base of the founder, above all on customer satisfaction. Bean grew big while appearing to be small . . . a plain and simple New England firm. Gorman insisted on selling the steak, not the sizzle. In ten years, he multiplied sales over fifteen times. William Henry, Advertising Director, tells the story. DM magazine; July 1980, Volume 43, #3. Also on tape, Hoke; # 11-0228 - 1X - $10.

The Growth of L. L. Bean, Inc. Half-page story in Sunday N.Y. Times, August 31, 1980. Check your library microfilm department.

THE ORVIS COMPANY, INC., Route 7, Manchester, VT 05254. (802) 362-3622. How Lee Perkins bought an old, small mail order firm, but famous for its quality fishing and hunting catalog . . . then multiplied its size . . . selling profitably to serious sportsmen fine products. Lee tells what it took; in DM magazine; March 1977, Volume 39, #11.

P & S SALES, P. O. Box 45095, Tulsa, OK 74145. (918) 622-7970. President Bob Sturgis tells how a simple, black and white catalog succeeded in selling modestly priced products to sportsmen over a 25-year period . . . starting with two-step mailing to magazine and inquiries . . . then by mailing to customers and prospects; use of special offers, fliers; serious traps to avoid; what not to sell. On tape, Hoke; # 19-0354 - LK - $8.

SPORTSMAN'S GUIDE, OLEN COMPANY, INC., 1415 Fifth Street South, Hopkins, MN 55343. (612) 933-3050. Its start

as a one-shot moonlighting venture . . . selling deer hunter patches in one step, with small ads in sports publications; its development of a 12-page black and white brochure as package insert . . . showing other patches, T-shirts, belt buckles; the mailing of a brochure to 15,000 Sportsman's Guide customers; its gradual, successful expansion of brochure to 48-page catalog . . . the two owners in partnership with their former boss. Interview on tape, Hoke; # 18-0332 - JH - $8.

VOYAGEUR'S LTD.*, P. O. Box 512, Shawnee Mission, KS 66201. (913) 764-7755. Jack Scaritt left a secure career as a chemist with a Fortune 500 company . . . to sell products he invented for outdoorsmen; how he sold by mail order; how, as a result, he succeeded with a retail store and sold it; how he then manufactured his products for the trade, but sold them by mail order instead of using reps. "Overview," Chapter 13, page 26, this book.

Products for Pet Owners

RALSTON—PURINA, Checkerboard Square, St. Louis, MO 63188. (314) 982-3877. Ralston-Purina has gone into the mail order business. Its Checkerboard Catalog first sold pet accessories, mainly for the dogs and cats. But when it tested offering clothing and gifts—with a pet motif—for people . . . people bought products for people more than for pets. Adding chickens, horses and other farm animals in product design was more profitable than just cats and dogs. DM News; September 15, 1981, gives the story, the dollars, the numbers; what worked, what didn't; which outside mail order services Ralston had contracted for performed satisfactorily; for which functions Ralston found it necessary to set up inside . . . after outside services did not perform satisfactorily.

Science Products

EDMUND SCIENTIFIC CO., 7082 Edscorp Building, Barrington, NJ 08007. (609) 547-3488. The successful marketing to a very specialized, highly sophisticated field of an astonishingly popular catalog . . . offering optics, telescopes, microscopes, electronic and other scientific items; how mail order started the firm, sold consumers; brought business from educational institutions, industrial firms and retail stores, even led to Edmund's starting a factory outlet store. Stephen Lett, Marketing VP, describes catalog evolution. On tape, Hoke; # 19-0208 - PC - $8; Philadelphia DM Club, 4/18/79.

Robert Edmund, President, tells the story of its biggest growth period when sales multiplied eleven times. On tape, Hoke; # 19-0456 - HM - $8; HMC, Newsweek, 10/11/79.

Robert Edmund, President, and Leon Parker, VP, describe the basic process; the realities requiring decisions; the entire operation from financial planning through catalog production; key elements needed. On tape, Hoke; # 11-0410 - NY - $15; NYU, 11/10/81.

Also read "Edmund Scientific's Formula Works for Several Different Marketplaces," by Sandra Friedlander, ZIP magazine, October 1980.

Woodworking

ALBERT CONSTANTINE & SONS, INC., 2050 Eastchester Road, Bronx, NY 10461. (212) 792-1600. Founded in 1812, the firm sold exotic woods by the carload. In 1932, Albert and Gertrude Constantine began to sell to craftsmen by mail order, cutting wood to size desired.

The first catalog was two mimeogaphed pages. In 1933, it jumped to 24 pages. By 1982, it was 102 pages (for $1). There are hard woods, veneers and inlay kits; special tools, books and hardware; marquetry kits and supplies (no other firm offers them). a 24-page tabloid goes out quarterly, filled with wood-working tips and products. 295,000 catalogs go out once yearly.

Response from catalogs and tabloids averages 10%. In 1982, the average order was $35. Catalogs are also sent to schools for a much higher average order (as high as $5,000). Sales were running at $3 million yearly including $1 million from two retail stores. On tape, Hoke; #12-0100 - KH - $10.

CATALOGS—SPECIALIZED
Multiple Catalogs

CML GROUP

It is a catalog conglomerate... How it was put together; the story of Carroll Reed, Sturbridge Yankee Workshop, Sierra Designs, Gokeys and Mason & Sullivan... all in the leisure field and CML acquired; how the companies operate, how CML manages them overall; judges catalogs to acquire, avoids mass-market mail order; interview with Charles M. Leighton, Board Chairman; DM Magazine, January 1974; Volume 36, #9; also on tape, Hoke; #18-0089 - DM - $8.

GENERAL MILLS*, Post Office Box 1113, Minneapolis, MN. 55440. (612) 540-4341.

How General Mills acquired, manages and succeeds with five catalog houses... The Talbots; Henry Harris Stamp Co.; Bowers & Ruddy (coins); Eddie Bauer; LeeWards Creative Crafts; see Seminar V, Chapter 2, this book.

HANOVER HOUSE INDUSTRIES, INC., 340 Poplar Street, Hanover, PA 17337. (717) 637-2271.

Seasonal catalogs have difficulties. Volume is irregular. In busiest season, employees are new, and green. Overhead is higher per dollar of sales. President Harold Schwartz overcame these problems, by expansion. He launched or acquired one new catalog after another... each with a separate identity, in different fields—in gardening, sports, for working women. He combined operating with gift and fashion catalogs. How he did... traded up to higher average sales... set up employee incentives... multiplied sales... jumped profits... became the specialty catalog man for all seasons. On tape, Hoke; #19-0073 - PC - $8.

CATALOGS—SPECIALIZED
Business and Industry Mail Order

Brushes—Specialized

BRAUN BRUSH COMPANY, 434 Albertson Avenue, Albertson, NY 11507. (516) 741-6000. How President Max Cheney created ten segmented "families" of industrial brushes, each for a specialized market... highly specialized brushes not generally available... with a separate simple catalog for each "family"'-and turned a declining business into a winner. DM magazine; September 1979, Volume 42, #5. Also on tape, Hoke; # 19-0072 -JH - $8.

Business Forms

QUILL CORPORATION, 100 South Schelter Road, Lincolnshire, IL 60069. (312) 634-4850. Founder Jack Miller explains Quill's success with catalog of 5500 business forms and related items; how orders are processed super fast, mostly 8 - 32 hours by use of automation, training of employees from first day, constant checking at each step, sums up five elements that lead to increased sales and profits. On tape, Hoke; # 11-0146 - MW - $10; MWDMA, Minneapolis, MN, 2/11/81.

Chemicals

REVERE CHEMICAL CORPORATION, 30875 Carter Street, Cleveland, OH 44134. (216) 248-0606. Catalog offering industrial products so successful Revere had to enlarge quarters to serve 100,000 customers from list of 150,000 names. Interview with Ed Baker and Jack Serringer, in DM magazine; October 1973, Volume 36, #6.

First Aid Kits and Supplies

A. J. MASUEN COMPANY, 11 Central Avenue, Le Mars, IO 51031. (712) 546-4124. How Al Masuen started selling door-to-door, then traveled 17 states for 39 years... and how mail order then quintupled sales over previous high; his catalog's first five years selling to schools, industries, municipalities, meat and poultry plants. Al describes his operation in detail in DM magazine; May 1979, Volume 42, #1. Also on tape, Hoke; # 18-0330 - JH - $8.

Moving Equipment

MATER COMPANY, 2775 North 32nd Street, Milwaukee, WI 53210. (414) 445-4066. He started carrying appliance dollies to prospects in back of a used hearse. His business grew to require a 55,000 square foot building. 95% of the business came from his catalog. How it became a thirteen million dollar mail order business selling conveyors, dollies, lift trucks. Founder Eugene Mater interviewed in DM magazine; May 1980, Volume 43, #1. Also on tape, Hoke; # 19-0530 - LK - $8.

Office Furniture

FRANK EASTERN CO., 625 Broadway, New York City, NY 10012. (212) 677-9100. Founder Stan Frank tells how he started in 1946, sold casters to office buildings after school, full-time after graduation; then added salesmen, opened store, ran ads, sold on telephone... and then created full-line catalog, updated three times yearly—his biggest source of business and helping all other sources to grow faster. On tape, Hoke; # 10-0298 - LK - $7.

Office Supplies

GINNS, 00 Broad Street, Richmond, VA 23219. (804) 649-0571. The launch of a 64-page, two thousand item catalog after 100 years in office supplies and growth to 13-store chain, step by step. What happened and results... average order and reorder. How the catalog evolved into "store". DM magazine; Part I: April 1978, Volume 40, #12; Part II: May 1978, Volume 41, #1. Also on tape, Hoke; # 18-0040 - JH - $8.

IBM DIRECT, IBM CORP.*, 400 Parsons Pond Drive, Franklin Lakes, NJ 07417. (201) 848-2157. IBM's mail order sales reps; its surprisingly simple, pragmatic and successful mail order operation; its experience can help smaller companies to make effective use of direct marketing and of salesmen to get leads and to sell. See Seminar VIII, Chapter 2, this book.

CATALOGS—SPECIALIZED
Miscellaneous

Key Catalog Firms, a round-up of interviews; Direct Marketers Catalog: Their Successes; January 18, 1982; $1.; Crain Communications Inc., 708 Third Avenue, New York, NY 10021. (212) 986-5050.

Variety of Catalog Launches, a report citing money needed before turning corners; interviews with founders: "Catalog Sales is a High Stakes Venture", September, 1979; $1.50; Venture Magazine Inc., 35 West 45th Street, New York, NY 10036.

Different Success Stories: "Catalog Firms Go Specialty; May, 1981; $1.75; Venture Magazine Inc., 35 West 45th Street, New York, NY 10036; (212) 840-5580.

CATALOGS—SPECIALIZED
Retailer Catalogs

Clothing

"BRITCHES OF GEORGETOWNE," 1321 Leslie Avenue, Alexandria, VA 22301. (703) 548-0200. "Britches" started with one store featuring "updated classics" in men's wear. Mail order ads then succeeded and led to a mail order catalog. It grew and helped "Britches" expand to 12 stores. Interview with Rick Hindin; DM magazine; August 1978, Volume 41, #4. On tape, Hoke; # 18-0269 - JH - $8.

Cookware

WILLIAMS-SONOMA, 5750 Hollis Street, Emeryville, CA 96408. (415) 652-1555. An alumnus of Horchow Collection became president of a four-store chain specializing in professional type cookware for the home. He selected products, ran stores and created a mail order catalog. It built sales volume in three years equal to all four stores. This increased sales in stores and made it possible to double number of stores. Interview with Gerard Dirkx, President, in DM magazine; June 1978, Volume 41, #2. Also on tape, Hoke; # 18-0013 - JH - $8.

Department Stores

BLOOMINGDALES, 1000 Third Avenue, New York, NY 10022. (212) 223-7111. Doreen McCurley, former Vice President, Direct Response Marketing, tells how Bloomingdales made its mail order/retail marriage work; in detail; what special catalogs are sent out and when, use of credit cards, building a mail order list, use of toll-free calls, going outside trading area. How Bloomingdales got its first 100,000 mail order customers. How it cut one catalog size over 28% while increasing sales over 80%: possible future strategy in use of electronic mail order media. DM magazine; September 1980, Volume 43, #5. On tape, Hoke; # 10-0414 - LK - $10.

SAKOWITZ, INC., 1111 Main Street, Houston, TX 77001. (713) 759-1111. This family-owned, 8-store group in Houston made department store history, with a mail order Christmas catalog mailed nationally. It combined showmanship, unique merchandise and occasional extravagant luxury items. It created dramatic mail order success, while trading up store image and jumping store sales. Robert Sakowitz tells story. DM magazine; January 1981, Volume 43, #8. On tape, Hoke; # 18-0083 - RA - $8.

Gifts

THE VERY THING, Box 549, Crozet, VA 22932. "RTI" (804) 456-8181. Mrs. Jane Ewald is the owner of a prestigious country inn. In it, she started a gift shop, The Very Thing . . . and experimented successfully selling gifts by mail order. She then brought out a catalog and moved mail order operations to a low-cost neighborhood, renovating an old house. She selected conservative items with style, designer items. She then designed her own item, exclusively hers . . . and then more. She tells the story of her catalog's first growth and success (since then far greater). On tape, Hoke; # 18-0115 - JH - $8.

THE SCOTTISH LION, North Conway, NH 03860. (603) 356-6381. Jack Hurley owns it . . . and its gift shop, which sells Scottish merchandise. How the gift shop started a mail order catalog; its first three years; how it operates . . . and subsidizes the innkeeper out of season. Interview in DM magazine; April 1978, Volume 40, # 12. Also on tape, Hoke; # 17-0503 - JH - $8.

THE WILDCAT VALLEY COUNTRY STORE, Jackson, NH 03846. (603) 383-9612. Twenty-three years after starting, it

brought out a mail order catalog, first in tabloid newspaper format offering country store merchandise. The catalog was test-mailed to a list of 3,000 visitors to inns in the area. The mailing was so successful it was expanded to 100,000 names and then to 200,000. It went to full-color, traded up the merchandise, increased prices. Kurt Bahr tells the story of the successful three-year evolution into a sophisticated mail order business. On tape, Hoke; # 10-0431 - LK - $7.

Jewelry

MERRIN JEWELRY COMPANY, INC., 724 Fifth Avenue, New York, NY 10022. (212) 582-3303. How it grew . . . from its start in a 20' x 20' office in New York City to its first $5 million a year volume; the step-by-step development of its successful mail order division; the showmanship and ability of owner Joseph Merrin created its growth. DM magazine; August 1979, Volume 42, #4.

Marine

GOLDBERG MARINE, 202 Market Street, Philadelphia, PA 19106. (215) 627-3700. After almost 30 years in operating marine stores only, the three Goldberg brothers started a catalog. Mail order now accounts for 70% of business. How they obtained 200,000 mail order customers; how they built a 248-page mail order catalog, then a 72-page sales catalog . . . two million copies a year in total. Interview with Richard Goldberg and Al Urban in DM magazine; March 1981, Volume 43, # 11. Separate interviews with Charles Goldberg; on tape; Hoke; # 17-0339 - JH - $8; and # 10-0465 - LK - $10.

Men's Clothes

BROOKS BROTHERS*, 346 Madison Avenue, New York, NY 10017. (212) 682-8800. How a retailer created a mail order profit center operating semi-autonomously, as though another Brooks store; how its mail order catalog operations differ from those of its stores. Seminar IX, Chapter 7, this book.
The typical store catalog yields no measurable results, says Alfred E. Schmidt, Jr., V.P. Brooks Brothers; how Brooks does measure results, has built a "business within a business" mailing 15 million catalogs in 1982. How Brooks did it. A great lecture on tape, Hoke; # 12-0004 - NY - $15.

Read also interview with Al Schmidt. He tells the history of the Brooks Brothers catalog and describes operations in detail. DM magazine; November 1981, Volume 44, #7.

Museum Shops

METROPOLITAN MUSEUM OF ART*, Fifth Avenue & 82nd Street, New York, NY 10028. (212) 879-8500. Some aspects of its mail order operation described in this book in "Making a Career in Museum Mail Order"; Seminar V, Chapter 11. Also read "How Direct Marketing Revolutionized New York's Metropolitan Museum of Art", Thomas Hoving, former Director; DM magazine; July 1979, Volume 42, #3. On tape, Hoke; # 10-0091 - DM - $10.

Museum Mail Order

Museums that have failed, broken even and succeeded in mail order, covered case by case. DM News; February 15, 1981.

Sportswear

FUN WEAR BRANDS 141 East Elkhorn Avenue, Estes Park, CO 80517. (303) 586-3361. Norman (Pep) Petrocine owns three stores selling quite different lines. One features "rugged sportswear"; one features backpacking clothing and accessories; one summer resort-wear and is open summers only. Pep tells of the mail order formulas he found to match with his stores; the kind of catalog he created . . . when he mails; how mail order became 40%

of his volume and evened out overall business year-round, while controlling overall growth. Interview on tape, Hoke; # 18-0359 -JH - $8.

CONTINUING MAIL ORDER SALES
Clubs

Book Clubs

BOOK-OF-THE-MONTH-CLUB, INC., 485 Lexington Avenue, New York, NY 10017. (212) 210-8440. David Soskin, its former VP of Marketing, (later president of Soskin-Thompson Associates), describes how BOMC makes profitable mail order decisions; results from direct mail vs. from space; changes in use of direct mail; best time to mail; coupon placement; element testing. Interview on tape, Hoke; # 17-0390 - CM - $8.

DOUBLEDAY & CO., INC.* 245 Park Avenue, New York, NY 10167. (212) 953-4561. Its founding by Frank Doubleday; how his son, Nelson Doubleday, first started in mail order . . . later founded the first Doubleday clubs; beginning years of the clubs. Seminar I, Chapter 10, this book.

How DOUBLEDAY'S* book clubs grew . . . from the 1930's to the end of the 1960's, recalled by Milton Runyon, retired executive vice president. Seminar II, Chapter 1, this book.

How DOUBLEDAY* expanded its clubs, refined its methods, and operated through 1981. Robin Smith, former president all Doubleday book clubs, interviewed. Seminar VIII, Chapter 6, this book.

"The Sphinx called Doubleday," an analysis of the publishing giant . . . in detail; The New York Times, Sunday, July 15, 1979. Check your library.

"The Doubleday Story," the longest story I've seen on any individual company in the Sunday business section of The New York Times, November 19, 1972; still fascinating. Check your library.

Record and Tape Clubs

CBS COLUMBIA HOUSE*, 1211 Avenue of the Americas, New York, NY 10036. (212) 975-5311. Success . . . in clubs, in mail order . . . by know-how; when to get in, how to start expanding, when to get out. See Overview, Chapter 12, pages 24-25, this book.

RCA MUSIC SERVICE, 1133 Avenue of the Americas, New York, NY 10036. (212) 930-4000. David Heneberry, former president (now president of T-L-K Advertising), cites RCA experience in mail order clubs and mail and TV single offers; explains techniques, fulfillment methods, credit hazards; analyzes direct marketing strategies, the difference between short and long-term profits. Much applies to any form of mail order. On tape, Hoke; # 16-0001 - NY - $12.

Grapefruit Club

FRANK LEWIS FRUIT CO.*, 100 N. Tower Road, Alamo, TX 78516. (512) 787-5971. A grapefruit farmer started in mail order by writing to two hundred people. How he went on to succeed modestly; how his son later mastered mail order . . . and sold with great success ruby red grapefruit . . . in huge volume, through an automatic shipment club plan. See Seminar II, Chapter 9, this book.

CONTINUING MAIL ORDER SALES
Continuity Programs

COSMETIQUE BEAUTY CLUB, INC., 5320 North Kedzie Avenue, Chicago, IL 60625. (312) 583-5410. How the world's biggest cosmetic continuity program got its first three and a half million members in six years, using a personalized mail program,

June Posen, President, explains what members need and want; then offers them unique programs to fill those needs and wants. DM magazine; December 1980, Volume 43, #8.

GREYSTONE PRESS*, 250 West 57th Street, Suite 519, New York, NY 10107. (212) 765-0606. The birth of the continuity program in the U.S. to sell hard cover books. John Stevenson's extraordinary success with it in selling books and records. Seminar IV, Chapter 1, this book.

GROLIER, INC.*, Sherman Turnpike, Danbury, CT 06816. (203) 797-3500. Former board chairman Elsworth Howell tells how it taught children to read better, faster . . . by mail order with the help of Dr. Suess. How Howell built 150 million dollars in mail order sales for Grolier, starting from zero. See Seminar VI, Chapter 5, this book.

TIME-LIFE BOOKS, INC.*, 777 Duke Street, Alexandria, VA 22314. (703) 960-5110. How Jerry Hardy founded it; the success of the first years, continuity program by program. Seminar V, Chapter 1, this book.

Rhett Austell who took over from Jerry Hardy, continues the story of programs introduced while he was publisher. Walter Roher tells the story of his years as publisher. Then Roger Lourie who in 1980, when he left, was director of New Product Development, brings the story up to date. Seminar VII, Chapter 1, this book.

Editorial Segmentation

How switching the #1 volume offered changed the Life Encyclopedia of Gardening from a set too marginal to promote to a hit; how adapting copy to regional areas and focusing on regional problems hit the jack pot for TIME-LIFE BOOKS. John Canova, V.P. Sales, explains. Not dated although in Direct Marketing Magazine; December 1973, Volume 36, #8.

WESTERN PUBLISHING,* Subsidiary of Mattell Toy Co., 1220 Mount Avenue, Racine, WI 53404. (414) 639-6331. Consultant James Hinckley IV tells of Western's success with continuity programs . . . expanding "Sesame Street Readers' Program"; how it develops new programs. Overview, Chapter 12, this book.

CONTINUING MAIL ORDER SALES
Insurance

SIGNATURE FINANCIAL MARKETING INC.* (subsidiary of Montgomery Ward), 2020 Dempster Street, Evanston, IL 60202. (312) 570-5000. How President Dick Cremer conceived it, created it and built it to its first $150 million yearly . . . largely by offering specialized insurance policies to Ward customers via inserts in Ward bills. Seminar III, Chapter 3, this book.

"Innovation: Ward's Key to successful Mail Order Venture." President Dick Cremer tells the story of Montgomery Ward's beginnings and growth . . . and of Signature Financial Marketing Inc. . . . selling insurance and other services. DM magazine; April 1980, Volume 42, #12.

How Signature Financial Marketing used Montgomery Ward's credit customer list with astounding success to skyrocket growth for new direct response division. A fascinating story in detail by Dick Cremer. DM magazine; February 1979, Volume 41, #10. Also on tape, Hoke; # 18-0395 - HM - $8.

BENEFICIAL STANDARD CORP., 3700 Wilshire Boulevard, Los Angeles, CA 90010. (213) 381-8011. Its subsidiary, Direct Marketing Corp. of America, sells insurance by mail order . . . using third party sponsorship of famous, trusted department stores. Interview DMCA executives; DM magazine; February 1979, Volume 41, #10; also on tape, Hoke; # 19-0253 - CD - $12.

OLD AMERICAN INSURANCE COMPANY*, 4900 Oak Street, Kansas City, MO 64141. (816) 753-4900. It has made insurance direct marketing more and more of a science. Martin Baier, VP of Marketing, explains how it built its 20 million house list; how often it mails; how it works with list brokers; its list selection methods; its various offers; far more. Seminar IX, Chapter 2, this book.

In much more detail Martin Baier explains the complex segmentation methods proven profitable by OLD AMERICAN: DM magazine; January 1976, Volume 37, #10.

J. C. PENNEY FINANCIAL SERVICES DIVISION, 800 Brooksedge Blvd., Westerville, OH 43081. 800-848-8860. How it successfully sells casualty insurance via mail and phone. W. A. Joseph, DM magazine; November 1978, Volume 41, #7.

Also read: "13 year old insurance arm of nation's third largest retailer saved parent company from red ink last quarter," New York Times, Business Day Column, 8-26-80.

CONTINUING MAIL ORDER SALES
Periodicals

BASSMASTER, Bass Anglers Sportsman Society, P. O. Box 17900, Montgomery, AL 36141. (205) 272-9530. How it got launched, got its first 300,000 members . . . built a successful magazine for fishermen . . . acquired another . . . went into a variety of products and services it offers to members. Helen Sevier, VP Marketing, tells the story. On tape, Hoke; # 19-0401 -LA - $8.

CONTEST NEWS-LETTER*, P. O. Box 1059, Fernandina Beach, FL 32034. (904) 261-4503. First a hobby, it grew to do $5,000,000 a year. It's still by mail order, from home, part-time . . . with only one employee. The founding couple explain. See Seminar I, Chapter 7, this book.

INC. MAGAZINE, 38 Commercial Wharf, Boston, MA 02110. (617) 227-4700. The winning combination that launched it: A compiled list of 400,000 managers, presidents and entrepreneurs had been researched by a Harvard student as part of a college project. INC. arranged to send its first issue with a direct mail wrap-around to all 400,000 names; the wrapper had a mail label, subscription offer card and order card for special charter subscription. Norm Raben, Executive V.P.-Publisher, tells the story . . . how the system developed 200,000 paid circulation while continuing same controlled circulation. On tape, Hoke; # 11-0394 - NE - $10.

THE MOTHER EARTH NEWS, P. O. Box 70, Hendersonville, NC 28739. (704) 693-0211. John and Jane Shuttleworth started it with only $1500 and a kitchen table and sold it for $10,000,000; how it got subscriptions by mail order and grew to 900,000 circulation, and built a big mail order publishing and product business as well. Quest magazine; February/March 1981; Advertising Age; October 19, 1981. Quest is no longer published, but check your library.

THE OLD HOUSE JOURNAL*, 69 A Seventh Avenue, Brooklyn, NY 11217. (212) 636-4514. Its starting pains; the no-risk way publisher Clem Labine discovered to get subscribers; how they renewed because of the quality of "The Journal;" its success and expansion. See Overview, Chapter 10, page 19, this book.

THE READER'S DIGEST ASSOCIATION, INC., 200 Park Avenue, New York, NY 10166. (212) 972-4000. Pleasantville, NY 10570. (914) 769-7000. Francis E. Ronnenberg, VP and Circulation Director, tells how the magazine with the most subscribers in the world gets them. On tape, Hoke; # 19-0211 - CM - $8.

The reasons for Reader's Digest's success-gaining subscriptions by mail order told by Victor Ross, Managing Director, Reader's Digest Association Ltd., England. On tape, Hoke; # 19-0096 - DM - $6.

RODALE PRESS INC., 33 East Minor Street, Emmaus, PA 18049. (215) 967-5171. J. I. Rodale, an electronic manufacturer, had a strong interest in health . . . and in good food which he believed came only from good land and good farms. He started a small publishing business, largely as a hobby. His son, Robert Rodale, developed and expanded it into a hugely successful enterprise . . . building on the strong beliefs he shared with his father . . . and his use of scientific mail order methods. Among other magazines, Rodale publishes Prevention and Organic Gardening. Its book publishing has grown to 1,700,000 books sold annually. An interview with Robert Rodale and executives in DM magazine; October 1980, Volume 43, #6. A splendid story. "The Rodale Press Story," is further told by President Bob Teufel, on tape, Hoke; # 11-0327 - FL - $10.

Bob Teufel's NYU lecture in the fall of 1981 gives an in-depth account of Rodale Press methods to get subscriptions via direct mail, on radio and TV and in space ads as well as using direct mail inserts and co-ops; how Rodale has grown to over $100 million a year in sales; what works best for Rodale, magazine by magazine; how Rodale creates a direct mail piece; the kind of words it avoids; valuable. On tape, Hoke; # 11-0408 - NY - $15.

SAVVY MAGAZINE, 111 8th Avenue, New York, NY 10011. (212) 255-0990. The first test issue of this money know-how magazine for women was inserted in New York and New West in April 1977. A mailing of 275,000 pieces was made in September. It pulled 4%. A 5,000,000 mailing rolled out in January 1980. Editor-Publisher Judith Daniels tells the story and future growth plans; on tape, Hoke; # 10-0291 - WD - (Women's D.R. Group) -$10.

SCIENCE 82, 1101 Vermont Avenue, N.W., Washington, D.C. 20005. (202) 842-9500. This magazine's subscribers provided the working capital and a positive cash flow. Its circulation multiplied almost ten times in a year. Two words added to one letter increased response over 30%. Former general manager Owen Lipstein tells how, and much more. On tape, Hoke; # 11-0504 -WM - $7.

THE VEGETARIAN TIMES*, P. O. Box 570, Oak Park, IL 60303. (312) 848-8120. Its start as a 4-page newsletter for a $17 investment and growth to a 84-page Time sized magazine and to its first 50,000 circulation. See Overview, Chapter 13, page 26, this book.

THE WALL STREET JOURNAL*, 22 Cortlandt Street, New York, NY 10007. (212) 285-5000. Its first zooming growth from a 37,000 circulation of investors (it later achieved the largest daily circulation of any U.S. newspaper); told by direct marketing consultant Larry Chait. See Seminar III, Chapter 8, this book.

CONTINUING MAIL ORDER SALES
Newsletters

Little Periodicals Proliferate

Filling special needs; report on newsletters; The Wall Street Journal, December 24, 1979; write: The Wall Street Journal, Editorial Dept., 22 Cortlandt Street, New York, NY 10048. (212) 285-5000.

Newsletters

Why they exist; successes in varied areas; start-ups. July/August 1979 issue by David Gilman. D&B Reports, 99 Church Street, New York, NY 10007. (212) 285-7679.

Subscribing to Profits

Stories of entrepreneurs who launched newsletters; advice from founders. August 1979 issue; $1.50; write: Venture Magazine Inc., 35 West 45th Street, New York, NY 10036. (212) 840-5580.

CONTINUING MAIL ORDER SALES
Continuing Directories

DIRECT MARKETING MARKETPLACE*, Hilary House Publishers, Inc. Hewlett Harbor, NY 11557. (516) 295-2376. Ed Stern got the idea for it, published it, made it a necessity for direct marketers. He sold subscriptions by direct marketing and continues to make it bigger every year. Seminar III, Chapter 6, this book.

FACTORY OUTLET SHOPPING GUIDE*, Box 239, Oradell, NJ 07649. (201) 384-2500. How a New Jersey couple first shopped at factory outlet stores, then made a list of them; how they gave the list to friends, then published it . . . selling it by mail order. How they expanded it to regional editions, began to sell through stores and continue to sell the guides by mail order. Overview, Chapter 13, page 27, this book.

CONTINUING MAIL ORDER SALES
Miscellaneous

Portrait Studios

OLAN MILLS INC., 4325 Amnicola Highway, Chattanooga, TN 37406. (615) 622-5141. How it sells almost five million portrait sittings a year by phone . . . often year after year to the same people. Fred Tregaskis of Olan Mills outlines its phone marketing program. Olan Mills has 700 studios, mostly in shopping centers. It has 200 travelling studios covering small cities. Its average sale is $12 to $14. Olan Mills found that the Metromail system of applying census and demographic information works well. It selects households that have incomes in range from 65% to 125% of each state's median income. It finds mornings (9 to 12 noon) and evenings (5 to 8 PM) the best. The most productive hour is 6 to 7 PM. Olan Mills makes no afternoon calls. Credit card use varies, but the highest area is Washington, D.C., where 70% of calls are made by credit card. On tape, Hoke; # 11-0582 - SL - $10.

TWO-STEP MAIL ORDER

Automotive Products

DOMUS, VW Village*, Kansas City, MO 64108. An offshoot of a Volkswagen service agency began to sell, by mail order two-step, conversion kits to turn "bugs" into pick-up trucks. How, at no risk, it got a bonanza of qualified leads, then converted to orders. See Overview, Chapter 10, page 18, this book.

Collectibles

ANTIQUE MAPS—RICHARD & JO-ANN CASTENS*, Wading River, NY 11792. (516) 929-6820. How they turned a hobby of collecting antique maps into a moonlighting business, selling to collectors, and built it from scratch to over $500,000 yearly . . . with no employees, part-time, from home. See Seminar II, Chapter 7, page 11, this book.

AIRPLANE SLIDES—RODERICK K. PENFIELD*, Satterly Road, East Setauket, NY 11734. (516) 941-4447. The hobby of a pilot to collect photographs of every possible model of every airline became a moonlighting and then retirement business, selling slides to collectors from home, with no employees, by two-step . . . getting inquiries and converting them. See Seminar V, Chapter 3, page 4, this book.

POTTERY—DAVE RAGO*, P. O. Box 3592, Station E, Trenton, NJ 08629. (609) 585-2546. Young success in old pottery. . . 19th century American . . . as a collector-dealer . . . by mail order; its moonlighting start, in college. Seminar II, Chapter 7, page 94, this book.

PLATE COLLECTING—VIOLET KRISPIEN*, 8 Burrwood Court, East Northport, NY 11768. (516) 368-8184. A retired dietician with a hobby of collecting plates began to sell them from home, built a business largely by mail order, made it succeed and sold out at a good figure - all within 3½ years. See Seminar II, Chapter 7, page 2, this book.

Correspondence Schools and Camera Equipment

NATIONAL CAMERA, INC., Englewood, CO 80110. One subsidiary is The Camera House Study School. The other is The National Camera Equipment Catalog. For each business ads are run in publications asking for inquiries and direct mail follow-up sent to each inquiry. Over 1000 students take the home study course. Over 60 take a classroom course. The catalog gets 130,000 inquiries a year resulting in about 4,000 purchases. Photograph magazines pull best; direct mail not as good to get leads. Interview with Ann McLendon, V.P.; on tape, Hoke; # 18-0225 -JH - $8.

Garden Items

LORD & BURNHAM GREENHOUSES, 2 Main Street, Irvington, NY 10533. (914) 591-8800. Inquiries produced by ads and converted by mail built the business . . . and how this mail order method was adapted to sell vs. key local dealer: The ad gets inquiry which goes to dealer who converts to sale. Andrew Ratskoff, Consumer Products Manager, explains. DM mgazine; February 1980, Volume 42, # 10. Also on tape, Hoke; # 19-0372 -LK - $8.

Hobbies—Crafts

NEEDLEWORK—THE HUCKERY*, P. O. Box 59, Malverne, NY 11565. (516) 599-4143. Pat Schatz turned her hobby of Swedish huck weaving into business offering the biggest collection of designs, first in retail store, then by mail order, partially and then entirely; how she gets inquiries without risk and converts them to sales. See Overview, Chapter 10, page 17, this book.

"NEEDLE-EASE" MICHELE SELDEN*, 81 Uplands Drive. West Hartford, CT 06107. An electronic engineer, "Tony" Selden and his wife Michele, discovered problems of needlecrafters and then developed products to solve them. They tell how they sold by mail order, first to individuals . . . then to dealers and jobbers, almost without promotional risk. See Overview, Chapter 10, page 16, this book.

Outdoor Products

EARLY WINTERS LTD., 110 Prefontaine Place South, Seattle, WA 98104. (206) 622-5203. It began in a basement in 1972 as manufacturers of an expedition mountaineering tent of its own design. Sales climbed to $8 million yearly in less than ten years. In 1976, a plain black and white brochure featuring a new tent of waterproof, yet breathable, fabric allowing condensation to escape, pulled $70,000 in orders. An expanded mail order schedule featured a whole line of tents, outdoor rainwear, other products. Soon the catalog contained packs, sleeping bags, even jogging accessories. President Bill Nicolai and Ron Zimmerman, VP Marketing, tell it all: DM magazine; July 1981, Volume 44, #3. Also on tape, Hoke; # 11-0302 - NV - $10.

FROSTLINE KITS, 12376 Frostline Circle, Thornton, CO 80241. (303) 451-5600. Dale Johnson had some mail order experience, $5,000 and space in his basement . . . where he cut materials for making outdoor wear. He tells how he started with a brochure and mail order ads and built to $13.5 million in the first 12 years (he's grown much more since). Dale tells the toughest part of making it: the best market, how the growth came, how mail order made possible the first 18 stores nationwide. On tape, Hoke; # 18-0317 - JH - $8.

Stencils
ADELE BISHOP, INC.*, Box 557, Manchester, VT 05254. (802) 362-3537. How an interior decorator's hobby created an improved way of stenciling for hobbyists and a growing mail order business, by two-step. See Seminar VII, Chapter 2, this book.

Telescopes
QUESTAR CORP.*, RD #1, New Hope, PA 18938 (215) 862-5277. A hobby of studying stars and wildlife led to a better telescope for hobbyists . . . and a lifetime business selling by two-step mail order; what made it succeed. See Seminar III, Chapter 14, this book.

Tools
SHOPSMITH INC., 750 Center Drive, Vandalia, OH 45377. (513) 898-6070. How direct marketing built a $50 million business with a five-tools-in-one woodworking machine . . . that did not sell in stores without demonstration and which direct mail alone failed to sell by mail order. Then TV ads and exhibits got inquiries. They were followed up by direct mail and then qualified by telephone. To close sales, appointments were made to see demonstrations at temporary exhibits in shopping malls. Shopsmith's own woodworking magazine and plans increased use of machine by owners. Three catalogs a year mailed to owners offered allied products and accessories. Larry Blank, Shopsmith-senior vice president, explains how this synergy worked. On tape, Hoke; #11-0554 - CM - $10. Also in DM magazine, February 1982.

MAIL ORDER OFFER STREAM
Case Histories

Art Prints
*The Tall Ships**
The race to sell prints before late becomes too late. Seminar IV, Chapter 10, this book.

Books
WM. H. WISE & CO.*, 34 Exchange Place, Building #2, 6th Floor, Jersey City, NJ 07302. (201) 864-5200. How President John Crawley Sr. saved it; in hardest times, with the offer stream technique, how he sold more how-to books by mail order than ever before. Seminar III, Chapter 1, this book.

AMERICAN HERITAGE PUBLISHING CO., INC.*, 10 Rockefeller Plaza, New York, NY 10020. (212) 399-8900. Consultant Dick Benson tells of the days when working under publisher James Parton, a small creative group pioneered new methods of selling (far more successfully) higher-priced, quality books. Seminar VI, Chapter 11, this book.

Business and Industry
HEWLETT-PACKARD*, W. 120 Century Road, Paramus, NJ 07652. (201) 265-5000. Consultant Bob Kestnbaum tells how it successfully launched its scientific pocket calculators by mail . . . and then converted to store distribution. Seminar VII, Chapter 12, this book.

Cameras, Projectors, Related Products
BELL & HOWELL CO., INC.*, 7100 McCormick Blvd., Lincolnwood, IL 60645. (312) 673-3300. Consultant Maxwell Sroge, formerly Director of Sales, recalls its classic, high-ticket mail order success. This offer, more than any before, interested Fortune 500 companies in mail order. Seminar V, Chapter 12, this book.

Collectibles
THE BRADFORD EXCHANGE, 9333 Milwaukee Avenue, Chicago, IL 60648. (312) 966-2770. It began in 1973 selling by mail order limited editions of plates and collectibles. In six years sales reached $40 million, by sending out 30 million mailing pieces. Interview with founder J. Roderick Mac Arthur, DM magazine; May 1978, Volume 41, #1; also on tape, Hoke; # 17-0216 - JH - $8.

THE FRANKLIN MINT*, Franklin Center, PA 19091 (215) 459-6000. Founder Joe Segel tells how it started, got up to its first $100,000,000 a year in sales; Seminar I, Chapter 6, this book.

Brian G. Harrison, President, tells more of the story of the world's leading producer of collectibles and operator of world's largest private mint. On tape, Hoke; # 19-0284 - PC - $6.

Charles Wickard explains how Franklin Mint first established advertising strategy for each country as it expanded overseas sales country by country. DM magazine; December 1976, Volume 39, #8.

Read the interview with Chairman of the Board, Charles L. Andes, in the New York Times, 11-11-79, regarding broadened sales directions. Read also financial review of Franklin Mint; New York Times, 12-31-79, as well as annual reports Franklin Mint for each year up to acquisition by Warner Communications in fall 1980. Check your library.

Francis Margulies, Executive Vice President, tells how Franklin Mint - with one 3,000,000 mailing - obtained $90,000,000 commitment sales. On tape, Hoke; # 14-0137 - SE - $6.

Diamonds to Dealers
BERMONT DIAMOND COMPANY, 665 Fifth Avenue, New York, NY 10022. 800-223-7914 / 212-751-8900. Bermont provides high-rated dealers with access to tens of thousands of diamonds . . . without stocking. It supplies lists by shape, carat, size, color, grade and suggested retail price. The customer can select from literature diamonds to consider. The dealer can then order on 800 phone number. Bermont sends selection by registered mail. President Monroe Osterman and Consultant Jim Prendergast tell how spending $16,000 on two mailings to 6,000 best stores produced $238,000 in sales. On tape, Hoke; # 19-0038 - PH - $8.

Financial Services
THE DREYFUS CORPORATION*, 767 Fifth Avenue, New York, NY 10022. (212) 935-3000. How in a year and a half, with Jerry Hardy as president, it sold a billion dollars of financial fund investments by direct marketing; Seminar V, Chapter 1, this book.

General Merchandise—Unusual
CHARTER PUBLISHING CO., INC.*, (formerly Downe Communications), 641 Lexington Avenue, New York, NY 10022. How Ed Downe started as a moonlighter with a one inch ad; how he came up with a constantly growing stream of innovative mail order offers; how he built a $250,000,000 business, sold out and retired . . . in his forties. Seminar VI, Chapter 8, this book.

Garden Tools
GARDEN WAY, INC., Freedom, NH 03836. Its executives explain how it started from scratch and built sales of garden tools

and related products to its first $62 million a year (now bigger). Its history, techniques and philosophy; its emphasis on product integrity and relaxed sell. On tape, Hoke; # 19-0117 - DM - $8.

Gifts

AMERICAN EXPRESS CARD DIVISION, American Express Plaza, New York, NY 10004. (212) 323-3900. Sandra Meyer, VP, American Express Communication Division, tells how it built mail order sales to over 900,000 annually at close to $100 average order; how it views opportunities, problems and the future in mail order. On tape, Hoke; # 10-0619 - IX - $10; and Direct Marketing magazine, March 1981, Volume 43, #11.

For an even more complete and detailed report on its mail order operations read the interview with Bob Meyers, VP, American Express Card Division, in DM magazine; October 1981, Volume 44, #6.

Men's Clothing Specialties

HABAND, INC., 265 North 9th Street, Paterson, NJ 07530 (201) 942-2600. Founder Max Habernickel tells its story . . . from a moonlighting venture, started with $50, selling ties mail order, to a $50 million business, mailing over 30 million pieces annually and heavy space advertising. DM magazine; December 1976, Volume 39, #8.

VAN HEUSEN COMPANY, 1290 Avenue of the Americas, New York, NY 10019. (212) 541-5200. It's Van Heusen's mail order arm and Baker Street Shirtmakers started in mail order with the "aviation shirt." Every ad in four tests made money. Repeat ads kept doing well. Using an 800 number increased results 10%. Ads ran 12 months a year. Ads grew to full pages, testing classical dress and traditional Oxford shirts. The business computerized. Executives saturated themselves in direct marketing how-to.

The average order became $40., with three shirts per order. Big multiple orders began to increase. Baker Street started to use direct mail, successfully mailing to prestige lists. It went profitably from a single shirt to alternating ten shirts to 30 shirts, and then to a shirt brochure. Advertising expenditures passed a million dollars a year using 55 upscale publications in addition to direct mail. Inquiries came in at about a dollar a name in advertising cost. And Van Heusen executives feel this is just the beginning. On tape, Hoke; # 11-0658 - PH - $10. Interview DM magazine; January 1982, Volume 44, #9.

Nuts and Bolts

DRI INDUSTRIES, INC., 11105 Hampshire Avenue South, Bloomington, MN 55438. (612) 944-3530. President Paul Harmon tells how DRI started; how it sold a 99¢ assortment of nuts and bolts in a plastic bag as its media offer to generate names, sold 2,000,000 20-box cabinets of a wide variety of fasteners; how syndicated offers got oil companies, banks and publishers to sell nuts and bolts; got over 1,000,000 customers; how it got them to repeat. On tape, Hoke; # 11-0048 - SC - $12.

Photofinishing

NASHUA PHOTO PRODUCTS, Nashua Group, 44 Franklin St., Nashua, NH 03061. (603) 880-2938. How it secures first-time customers; what it does to convert them to repeat buyers; how the Nashua mail order strategy created a huge mail order business. Interview with John R. Mapley, Marketing Director, Mail Order; on tape, Hoke; # 10-0501 - NE - $10.

Specialty Merchandise

FINGERHUT CORPORATION, 4400 Baker Road, Minnetonka, MN 55343. (612) 932-3237. Fingerhut became the most profitable per-dollar division of American Can Corporation. But just a few years before, it had big difficulties resulting from too fast expansion . . . lost $1,000,000 in fiscal 1974 and $5,000,000 in 1975. Al Kaules, Media Director, tells the fascinating story how it made a $13 million turnaround. On tape, Hoke; # 17-0376 - CM -$8. Also in DM magazine; February 1979, Volume, 41, #10. Another story on Fingerhut . . . how it uses computer technology to increase profits while better satisfying customers and treating them like individuals.

Women's Stockings

L'EGGS PRODUCTS, DIV. HANES CORP, Box 2495, Winston-Salem, NC 27102. (919) 725-7493. It sells hosiery and panty hose through mass retailers. How it began also to sell by mail order discontinued stockings at regular prices; got its first 400,000 mail order customers; pulled 15% with following offers to its mail order list; how selling by mail order helped L'EGGS store sales; on tape, Hoke; #10-0500 - PH - $10. 1980 Henry Hoke Award winner - DM magazine; November 1980; Volume 44, #7.

TANDY CORPORATION, RADIO SHACK*, 1800 One Tandy Center, P.O. Box 17180, Fort Worth, TX 76102. (817) 390-3700. When Tandy was a small leather findings jobber . . . a stream of leather-craft offers gave Tandy its first real jump in sales, working cash to start stores, and information where to start them. Vice Chairman of the Board, James West, tells the story. "Overview," Chapter 12, this book.

Reference Section VI
Mail Order's Helpers

Direct Marketing's Growth Industry
Its Support System of Experts,
Services and Suppliers

Helping mail order grow is a growth industry . . . more profitable, more secure, with a brighter future than in most fields.

Anita Bagnoli and Martin Sass met at Huber Hoge. They learned the mail order business, graduated from Hoge, went on to work in direct marketing for Hoge alumni and got married. Then they got their big idea, the U.S. MONITOR SERVICE which they own and operate.

It's a network of exclusive agents. Decoy names with addesses of agents are supplied to clients who put the names on their mailing lists. These names are unknown to anyone but U.S. Monitor, its agents and clients.

Mailings are carefully checked by agents for date of arrival, spelling of label and whether all pieces are correctly enclosed; also printing quality and whether received at all. Most important of all, agents watch for and note any unauthorized use of the list. Agents date when received and forward to U.S. Monitor each piece which is noted and forwarded the same day to clients. Where desired, U.S. Monitor analyzes and summarizes for clients. It's a flourishing and growing service with close to 500 clients and is located at 86 Maple Avenue, New City, NY 10956. (914) 634-1331. It is one of many quite new kinds of businesses created by the needs of direct marketers. But many businesses in many established fields find new profitable volume from direct marketers.

Printers do . . . and advertising agencies . . . and media of every kind. So do manufacturers and importers . . . and computer companies and service businesses . . . and specialists, experts and authorities in related fields. The list business is tied to it. Fortune 500 companies and cottage industries do. Maybe you can . . . if your training, talent and background fit . . . if the business you own or are an executive in has the capability or can develop it. To find out, bone up on direct marketing. All through this book are stories how those in the support system started working with mail order people, grew as a result—and succeeded. Each story can help direct marketers and also help others to do business with direct marketers.

Many articles and talks by experts, consultants and executives of services and suppliers are referred to in the following pages. Each gives more background on part of the support system and each helps direct marketers. Only some of those in any area of the support system are covered here, often only a smattering. To get the names of more, consult "The Direct Marketing Marketplace" directory, at your business library.

For example, direct marketing advertising agencies, often called direct response advertising agencies, are growing faster than general agencies. The following stories concern them.

Direct Response Agencies
DM News; Special Feature Section, September 15, 1981.
Direct Response Advertising Agencies
DM News; Special Feature Section; December 15, 1980. Selection, payment, desirable size, budgeting of campaigns for clients by agencies, technological changes in agency operation and direct marketing; the merging of direct response and general agencies.

Contributors include Stan Rapp, of Rapp & Collins; Alvin Eicoff, President of A. Eicoff & Co., and Robert Sawyer, Sr. VP of NW Ayer.

BBD&O Direct* 380 Madison Avenue, New York, NY 10017. 212-356-5000. Its start in April 1982; its founding president, Ed Nash, his career; its organizational plan, method of staffing and philosophy; Seminar VI, Chapter 12, this book.

Clark Direct Marketing* 801 Second Avenue, New York, NY 10017. 212-661-9230. It specialized in the educational field, then for magazine publishers. First in direct mail, then for general media. How computer modeling helped its clients; and its growth. Seminar VII, Chapter 5, this book.

Grey Direct* 777 Third Avenue, New York, NY 10017. 212-546-1800. It's a subsidiary of Grey Advertising, one of the top ten general agencies. George Wiedemann is president. How it started from scratch with six employees, succeeded the first year in attracting talent and accounts; its growth strategy and positioning plan. Seminar VI, Chapter 7, this book.

Also read the story of Grey Direct's launch and interview with George Wiedemann and key executives in the DM News; October 15, 1981.

Kobs & Brady Advertising, Inc.* 625 North Michigan Avenue, Chicago, IL 60611. 312-944-3500. President Jim Kobs tells how he and Tom Brady started it, built it with speed and succeeded for clients; practical advice from Kobs to help anyone in direct marketing. Seminar IX, Chapter 1, this book.

Ogilvy & Mather Direct Response, Inc.* 675 Third Avenue, New York, NY 10017. 212-986-6900. How David Ogilvy's lifelong love affair . . . with mail order . . . helped his clients sell just about anything better . . . him become world-famous . . . his agency, Ogilvy & Mather, to grow to 143 offices worldwide with close to $2 billion yearly billing, and its direct marketing agency subsidiaries to bill over $150,000,000. Seminar VIII, Chapter 10, this book.

Smith-Hemmings-Gosden* 3360 Flair Drive, El Monte, CA 91731. 213-571-6600. It's the biggest in the West. It has most of its accounts all over the U.S. and is one of the biggest U.S. direct marketing agencies. Freeman Gosden, Jr., its managing partner, tells of the agency's growth, philosophy and way of working. Seminar III, Chapter 13, this book.

Maxwell Sroge International, Inc.* 4825 N. Scott Street, Schiller Park, IL 60176. 312-671-4670. How Maxwell Sroge started his first job in mail order, became director of sales for Bell & Howell, responsible for its entrance into direct marketing; how he became a consultant, opened an advertising agency, expanded into a variety of direct marketing activities . . . and launched one Fortune 500 company after another into mail order. Seminar V, Chapter 12, this book.

Stone & Adler, Inc.* 150 North Wacker Drive, Chicago, IL 60606. 312-346-6100. Co-founder Bob Stone tells of his Depression start; his years of studying mail order; the beginnings of direct marketing; his early jobs; first clients how he and Aaron Adler started Stone & Adler with $500 each; its rise; how it functions. In Seminar II, Chapter 4.

Throckmorton Associates, Inc.* 152 Madison Avenue, New York, NY 10016. 212-689-9230. The biggest direct response agency founded by a woman, Joan Throckmorton; her career, its start, growth, success, philosophy, way of working with clients. See Seminar IV, Chapter 13, this book.

Wunderman, Ricotta & Kline, Inc.* 575 Madison Avenue, New York, NY 10022. 212-909-0100. How it became the biggest direct marketing agency and then an important part of Young &

Rubicam, the biggest general advertising agency. Seminar IX, Chapter 11, this book.

Zimmerman Marketing, Inc., 342 Madison Avenue, New York, NY 10017. 212-697-0011. Caroline Zimmerman is founder and president as well as a top author. She is also an able business-woman, a talented media buyer and very creative. She cites examples where her agency's copy has outpulled current mailing pieces and ads of major direct marketers. On tape, Hoke; # 19-0264 - HM - $8.

Executives of other direct response agencies (listed below) have written many of the articles and made many of the speeches and talks referred to in this reference section.

Ahrend Associates, Inc. 79 Madison Avenue, New York, NY 10016. 212-685-0033.

Barry Blau & Partners, 462 Danbury Road, Wilton, CT 06897. 203-762-8643.

Chapman Direct Marketing, Inc., 415 Madison Avenue, New York, NY 10017. 212-758-8230.

A. Eicoff & Co., 520 North Michigan Avenue., Chicago, IL 60611. 312-944-2300.

A. Eicoff & Co., 675 Third Avenue, New York, NY 10017. 212-883-9500.

The Emerson Marketing Agency, Inc., 44 East 29 Street, New York, NY 10016. 212-260-5280.

McCaffrey & McCall Inc., 575 Lexington Avenue, New York, NY 10022. 212-421-7500.

McCann-Erickson March, Inc., 485 Lexington Avenue, New York, NY 10017. 212-286-0460.

Rapp & Collins, Inc., 475 Park Avenue South, New York, NY 10016. 212-725-8100.

Schwab/Beatty, Div. Marsteller, Inc., 866 Third Avenue, New York, NY 10022. 212-752-6500.

Soskin/Thompson Associates, Div. of J. Walter Thompson Co., 420 Lexington Avenue, New York, NY 10017. 212-210-8000.

TLK Direct Marketing, 605 Third Avenue, New York, NY 10016. 212-972-9000.

Guy L. Yolton Advertising, Inc., 6073 Arlington Blvd., Falls Church, VA 22044. 703-237-8550.

This book does not presume to cover the gamut of qualified advertising agencies doing a fine job for direct marketers. I've simply written stories about some of them and reviewed speeches and articles by executives of others.

The Consultants*

Perhaps the fastest growing part of mail order's growth industry is the consulting field. There are consultants for starting, acquiring, selling, growing; for advertising and its subdivisions; for shipping or mailing, computerization, hiring, planning or research . . . for the big, small and those in between. You name it and you can hire a consultant for it, by the year, month, hour, job—sometimes even based on results.

Why do so many direct marketers use so many consultants? Sometimes for reassurance but more often for real need. Growth and proliferation keep making direct marketing more complex . . . constantly accelerated by technological change. The biggest and smartest direct marketers don't have the money, the staff or the time to specialize in every area. They increasingly call in specialists as consultants.

Many of these same consultants write articles and give talks which are available in back issues and tapes and which pass on quite valuable specialized expertise. Some I write about in this book. But those I write about and whose articles and talks I recommend are but a sample of the many more available. Articles and tapes by any of these others can be assembled in your own custom direct marketing course. But first, the following may help you. Each has written articles or given speeches I recommend in this book.

John Henry Achziger, Chairman, John Henry Achziger, Inc. c/o Worldbook Childcraft Complex, Merchandise Mart Plaza, Chicago, IL 60654. (312) 245-3068. Telephone marketing expert. One of the best.

Herbert Ahrend, President, Ahrend Associates, Inc., 79 Madison Avenue, New York, NY 10016. (212) 685-0033. Plans, advises; writes promotion; strong on books, clubs, magazines, business to business, two-step mail order, solo direct mail.

Shell Alpert, President, Shell Alpert Direct Marketing, 444 Lakeview Court, Langhorne, PA 19047. (215) 752-3433. Writes, gives seminar, consults, particularly on creating direct mail.

Win Barnes, President, Win Barnes Kross, Inc., 12801 Foothill Blvd., San Fernando, CA 91342. (213) 361-1296. Research for direct marketing; particularly experienced in working with focus groups.

Richard V. Benson, President*, The Benson Organization, Inc., 5 Water Oak-Amelia Island Plt., Amelia Island, FL 32034. (904) 261-0121. Specializes in books, clubs, continuity programs but mostly magazine subscriptions; some products; suggests the offers; makes the plan; gets the creative people, selects the media. Concentrates on direct mail. Seminar VI, Chapter 11.

Robert C. Blattberg, Professor of Marketing and Statistics, Graduate School, of Business, University of Chicago, 1101 East 58 Street, Chicago, IL 60637. (312) 753-4259. He is a professor of mathematics, statistics and economics who works 14 hours a day. Direct marketers call on him to help set up tests that will be statistically reliable; also to help interpret results and to double-check projections. Seminar VIII, Chapter 3

Arthur Blumenfield, President, Blumenfield Marketing Inc., 300 Broad Street, Stamford, CT 06901. (203) 359-2080. Veteran specialist in use of computers for direct marketers. Advises on when to computerize and how; selection of equipment, pro-gramming; what to do with inside computers and when to use outside computer services. Seminar I, Chapter 8.

Len Carlson, President, Lenca Inc., 9595 Wilshire Blvd., Suite 1010, Beverly Hills, CA 90212. (213) 273-6098. Founded, succeeded with and sold out one catalog; advises others on every aspect; strong on finding and developing new items, particularly imports from everywhere.

Lawrence G. Chait, 430 West Merrick Road, Suite N., Valley Stream, NY 11580. (516) 825-2699. Circulation background Time, Inc., Wall Street Journal; headed his own top direct marketing agency; handled wide variety of direct marketing accounts, all media. Strong on planning, creative—particularly in direct mail. Seminar III, Chapter 8.

Thomas Conlon, President, D. L. Blair, 185 Great Neck Road, Great Neck, NY 11021. (516) 487-9200. Conlon mastered use of promotions to increase sales working on P & G account at Benton & Bowles. Blair is the biggest firm running biggest sweepstakes for advertisers. Conlon advises direct marketers how to use sweepstakes to increase orders, cut advertising cost per sale. Seminar VI, Chapter 10, this book.

Ray Considine, President, Considine & Associates, 521 S. Madison Avenue, Pasadena, CA 91101. (213) 449-4210. Strongly experienced in two-step mail order, getting leads for salesmen, and fund raising.

Henry Cowen, President, The Cowen Group, Inc. 205 East Main Street, Huntington, NY 11743. (516) 673-0099. His copy sold tens of millions of subscriptions, insurance policies, books and varied merchandise. He trained his son and son-in-law to be top writers. A fine team. Strong in direct mail. Seminar III, Chapter 12.

C. Richard Cryer, V.P., Marketing Development, Scholastic Inc., 50 West 44th Street, New York, NY 10036. (212) 944-7700. An expert; especially in every phase of book club operation.

John Jay Daly, President, Daly Associates, Inc., 918 Sixteenth Street, North West, Suite 702, Washington, D.C. 20006. (202) 659-2925. Government and public relations of direct marketers. He trained with the DMMA and works for the biggest.

Stanley J. Fenvessy*, President, Fenvessy Associates, Inc., 745 Fifth Avenue, New York, NY 10151. (212) 751-3707. The systemizer of mail order. His specialty is fulfillment, pleasing customers, lowering costs, saving personnel and square foot space used; increasing productivity per person. Praised for his practical approach. Seminar IX, Chapter 3.

Wendell Forbes*, 87 Peaceable Road, Ridgefield, CT 06877. (203) 438-4527. At Time Inc. he learned the trade of securing magazine subscriptions... in many ways... in big volume... at lower cost. He co-developed dramatic new computer methods to analyze the value of different sources of subscriptions based on conversion and renewals over a period of years. He trained many leaders, continues to teach many and is a most trusted consultant in magazine marketing. Seminar IV, Chapter 11.

Orlan Gaeddert*, Orlan Gaeddert Research, 34-47 80th Street, Jackson Heights, NY 11372. (212) 426-8024. Another Time, Inc. alumnus. At Time he applied statistical science (he has an MBA majoring in statistics in marketing) to set up tests, analyze results, make projections scientifically. Now a consultant, he uses this for his clients. Seminar V, Chapter 9.

Rene Gnam, President, Rene Gnam Consultation Corp., P. O. Box 6435, Clearwater, FL 33518. (813) 536-5556. Creates ads, direct mail, gives seminars and consults; plans and executes complete direct response ad campaigns.

Gordon W. Grossman*, President, Gordon W. Grossman, Inc., 606 Douglas Rd., Chappaqua, NY 10514. (914) 238-9387. At Reader's Digest he was in on over 10,000 mail order tests, became director of Direct Marketing. He is strong in direct mail but in all media as well. He is a pioneer in the use of TV-supported telephone marketing, is often consulted on list and media selection by publishers and other direct marketers. Seminar IV, Chapter 2.

Jerome S. Hardy, 420 Lexington Avenue, Room 2304, New York, NY 10017. (212) 687-2592. Eminently successful as Director of Mail Order Sales of Doubleday, as founder of Time-Life Books, as former president of Dreyfus Fund and for his clients. Strong in planning, financing, launching and developing clubs, continuity programs, magazines, financial services, anything in direct marketing. Seminar V, Chapter 1.

Roy Hedberg, President, Hedberg & Associates. Inc., 3606 Terrace View Dr., Encino, CA 91436. (213) 789-2079. Top catalog specialist; experienced in "big 5" and specialized catalogs.

Richard Hodgson*, 1433 Johnny's Way, Westtown, PA 19395. (215) 399-0962. World's most famous authority on direct mail. Strong in catalogs; a printing expert; prolific copywriter; knows international mail order; has worked on wide variety of products. Seminar VII, Chapter 3.

Robert Kaden*, President, Goldring & Co., Inc., 919 North Michigan Avenue, Chicago, IL 60611. (312) 440-5252. He learned market research at major agencies, became president and acquired interest in Goldring, then multiplied its size. Goldring does research for Sears, Wards, Spiegel, the DMMA, many direct marketers; asks responders why they did, non-responders why they didn't; researches people's reactions to possible changes in product offer. Seminar III, Chapter 7.

Robert Kestnbaum*, President, R. Kestnbaum & Company, 221 North LaSalle Street, Chicago, IL 60601. (312) 782-1351. A Harvard MBA. He was president of Bell & Howell's mail order division. As a consultant he helped Hewlett-Packard, American Express, IBM and many other Fortune 500 firms to launch profitably mail order divisions. Strong in planning, controls, finance, marketing... particularly active in direct mail, catalogs, inserts, solos ... emphasizes use of computers. Seminar VII, Chapter 12.

James Kobak*, President, James Kobak, Inc., 774 Hollow Tree Ridge Road, Darien, CT 06820. (203) 655-8764. Another Harvard MBA. He headed J. K. Lasser & Company Accountants. He advised on reorganization of Young & Rubicam and the DMMA. His specialty is working on launches, merger, acquisitions, reorganizations of magazines. He emphasizes direct marketing as a tool to profitably gain subscriptions. Seminar II, Chapter 8.

Philip Kotler*, Professor Marketing, J. L. Kellogg School of Management, Northwestern University, Nathaniel Leverone Hall, 2001 Sheridan Road, Evanston, IL 60201. A great professor of marketing and author of marketing text books; a consultant who declines most assignments. He concentrates on long-term future planning for biggest companies and only accepts direct marketers or clients for such commitments. Seminar IV, Chapter 5.

Ed McLean, Ed McLean Direct Marketing, Ghent, NY 12075. (518) 392-9788. A direct mail star; he has worked for biggest publishers and varied accounts; sold his own items; gives seminars all over the world. Strong in all phases of the creative advertising process.

Betty Anne Noakes*, 251 East 51 Street, Apt. 14 J, New York, NY 10022. (212) 688-6840. She learned direct marketing and how to write copy at Reader's Digest, Canada. She worked for the biggest consulting firm in direct marketing a number of years ago. She has been a consultant and written copy for leading book clubs, magazine and book publishers. Seminar IV, Chapter 6.

Pierre A. Passavant*, President, Passavant Direct Marketing, P. O. Box 1206, Middletown, CT 06457. (203) 346-3003. He was director of catalog sales for J. C. Penney, VP of Direct Marketing for Gerber Insurance and Zerox Educational Systems. He gives wonderful seminars for the DMMA. His strength is creative, analytical and organizational . . . quite varied. He's devoting more time to consulting. Seminar V, Chapter 7.

Murray Raphel, President Murray Raphel Advertising, 1012 Atlantic Avenue, Atlantic City, NJ 08401. (609) 348-6646. A store owner, shopping mall operator, retail showman, skilled user of direct mail, top consultant ... particularly on applying direct marketing to retailing.

Sig Rosenblum, P.O. Box 1552-E, Southampton, NY 11968. (516) 283-2284. He closed a highly successful New York City advertising agency because he preferred the one-to-one consultant lifestyle. Great copy, prolific ideas, sound plans, all media. His greatest strength is creating convincing letter campaigns.

Maxwell C. Ross*, President, Maxwell C. Ross & Company, 3 Crown Center, 2440 Pershing Rd., Kansas City, MO. (816) 471-5200. The man who wrote a billion letters. He learned how at LOOK magazine, went on to sell insurance for Old American Insurance, became a consultant for accounts as varied as Pepperidge Farms, insurance companies and magazines. Creates winning copy or plans of entire campaigns. Seminar I, Chapter 12.

Thomas Ryan*, Thomas E. Ryan, Inc., 1 North Street, Hastings-on-Hudson, NY 10706. (914) 478-0890. He trained at Time Inc. in marketing research. He has since worked for clients such as Smithsonian. He has strong views on effective use of research by direct marketers. Seminar VI, Chapter 3.

Paul Sampson, Box 100, Freedom, NH 03836. (603) 539-4080. He co-founded a top direct mail lettershop. Was chairman of the DMMA, chairman of Garden Way, has given seminars all over, teaching basic and advanced direct marketing. Strong on direct mail—from planning to creative through production.

Eugene Schwartz*, 1160 Park Avenue, New York, NY 10028. (212) 876-6255. He's a Hoge alumnus, a prolific writer, and an author. His copy launched the Boardroom newsletter, consistently pulls for Rodale Press, Inc. and Prevention Magazine, sells books, cosmetics, many items, but he accepts almost no new clients. Seminar VIII, Chapter 8.

David Shepard, President, David Shepard Associates, Inc., 2 Micole Court, Dix Hills, NY 11746. (516) 271-5567. Strong in book clubs and continuity programs.

Christopher Stagg, 26150 Hidden Hills Road, Salinas, CA 93908. (408) 659-4997. He was born into advertising. A superlative direct mail writer, particularly for magazines, books, clubs, continuity programs.

Andrew Svenson, Jr.*, President, Andrew Svenson Company, Inc. 3767 Prairie Dunes Drive, Sarasota, FL 33583. (813) 921-3359. He started at Doubleday, was responsible for selling $60 million of books a year at Meredith Publishing, became a consultant. He is strong on syndication of book offers from one publisher to another and on launching book departments for magazine publishers. Seminar IX, Chapter 4.

John Tighe, Copywriter, 72 West 85th Street, New York, NY 10024. (212) 873-2520. Quite varied experience; strong record selling merchandise, book clubs, continuity programs, services.

There are many more consultants. These are a sample. The bigger direct marketing gets the more skills it calls upon. Today there are consultants specializing in mergers and acquisitions, others in accounting and law, more in mathematics, organization, and more in computer applications. Perhaps the most versatile consultant organization I can think of is Maxwell Sroge*. You name it, Mac will do it. See his story in Seminar V, Chapter 12, this book.

You may already have expertise direct marketing can use. You begin to apply it for direct marketers and do so profitably. As you do, you may learn more of direct marketing problems than your colleagues, find more solutions, become an expert . . . and end up a consultant.

List Businesses

An activity overwhelmingly important to direct marketers and an exciting growth area to go into is the list business.

The road to success in mail order has been the increasing use of segmentation . . . selecting more precisely all the time whom to sell for what items and services. The center of all this has been the list business which has contributed to and benefitted from the process. The excitement and opportunity keeps attracting more new talented people.

The talent for list selection now available helps create for each client a custom circulation, as though for a new specialized magazine. The result has been that despite skyrocketing postage and paper cost, direct mail keeps increasing in volume . . . and all phases of the list business . . . brokerage, management, consulting and compiling. The stories here concern only a few of the experts in these activities, but do give an indication of the potentials and problems of the list business.

The DM News ran a Special Feature Section entitled "The List Business," on August 15, 1982. I suggest reading it. In this book the following stories on individual list businesses of different sizes and types may be useful. If interested in the field I suggest that you reread the following stories in this book (and check all reference sections for material concerning anyone in the list business).

ED BURNETT CONSULTANTS, INC.*, 2 Park Avenue, New York, NY 10016. (212) 679-0630 / 800-223-7777. Ed Burnett is president. He has trained many in the list business. He originated the concept of list management and contributed greatly to unique compiling of business list. He runs outstanding seminars and can teach all of us much. Seminar III, Chapter 9, this book.

COMPUTER DIRECTIONS GROUP*, 40 East 34th Street, New York, NY 10016. (212) 725-1555. The biggest combination of list businesses. Subsidiaries include Woodruff-Stevens, Inc. in list management and Names Unlimited in list brokerage. It keeps starting more subsidiaries each specializing in different list areas. Founder Stan Woodruff is the driver and planner, along with some talented executives. His career, its start, many activities and successes . . . and his advice for anyone starting in direct marketing . . . Seminar VI, Chapter 6, this book.

DEPENDABLE LISTS, INC.*, 257 Park Avenue South, New York, NY 10010. (212) 677-6760. How Jack Oldstein built it by helping new entrepreneurs in widely varied fields grow . . . using his list know-how . . . and made it the world's biggest list broker. Seminar II, Chapter 5, this book.

DIRECT MEDIA, INC.*, 90 South Ridge Street, Port Chester, NY 10573. (914) 937-5600. Founder Dave Florence tells how his career started; how he launched Direct Media; how it grew to one of the largest list brokers in the business. It's a lesson how to make big money with a no-risk start and quiet expansion in a simple way. Seminar IV, Chapter 8, this book.

GEORGE-MANN ASSOCIATES, INC.*, 403 Mercer Street, P. O. Box 930, Hightstown, NJ 08520. (609) 443-1330. How George Sharoff (a Hoge alumnus) and his brother Manny started this list management business . . . by offering to computerize at its risk lots of new clients; the growth and success of George-Mann. Seminar IX, Chapter 5, this book.

THE KLEID COMPANY, INC.*, 200 Park Avenue, New York, NY 10166. (212) 599-4140. The longest established major list firm, founded by Lewis Kleid, a great direct marketing pioneer and authority. From the beginning, Kleid worked for aristocrats of mail order. Rose Harper worked for him, learned from him. Her accounting experience and numbers know-how helped her select lists more scientifically for clients and launch new direct marketers. This helped the Kleid Company to succeed more and more as a consultant, broker and list manager. It also helped her acquire the firm . . . and triple its size. Seminar I, Chapter 3, this book.

W. S. PONTON COMPANY, INC.*, 1414 Hawthorne Street, Pittsburgh, PA 15201. (412) 782-2360. It's the oldest list company in the U.S. How Harvey, and his wife Geri, Rabinowitz took it over when it was defunct . . . started from scratch at home . . . ran the business their own way, with no overhead, collecting payment before delivering names . . . and compiled "rich lists" to prosper . . . Seminar VIII, Chapter 5, this book.

The DM News has run two interesting stories on Ponton: The first is "Advance Pay Cuts Sales Volume by 65%: why W. S. Ponton sticks to it—and makes money." DM News; 12/15/79. The second is "Increased Action for High Rollers", DM News; June 1980.

Service Businesses

Service businesses for direct marketing keep proliferating. In this book I describe a number of them. I try to indicate the opportunities and problems in building such a business as much as to show the services they perform. If you are in or considering going in any service business for direct marketers, the following stories in this book may be of interest.

There are many companies serving direct marketers who combine services. Some start at performing one service and then end up performing another.

Metromail Corporation*, 901 West Bond Street, Lincoln, NE 58521, (402) 475-4591, is a huge business combining lists and statistical research, the biggest lettershop in the world and much more. I tell the story of Metromail; of Bill Howe, its president, its 60 million names; its position among the big three mass compilers; its new analysis techniques that can dramatically improve mail order results. See Seminar V, Chapter 13, this book.

Tyme Letter Service Corporation, 250 Hudson Street, New York, NY 10013, (212) 691-4444, is a printer as well as a lettershop. Lincoln Graphic Arts, a leading Long Island printer, formerly owned a lettershop.

Angelo R. Venezian, Inc.*, 10-64 Jackson Avenue, Long Island City, New York, NY 11101, (212) 784-0500, is primarily a list broker but owns a lettershop specializing in very small jobs, invaluable for tests. "Ask Angelo" was the greatest solution to get the best authoritative answer when Angelo Venezian was vice president of circulation at McGraw-Hill Magazines. Since then Angelo Venezian has built a business in list brochures and related activities, specializing in business, technical and professional firms . . . largely by consulting free with those selling these fields . . . particularly magazine and newsletter publishers. His story and a good deal of helpful advice from him; Seminar V, Chapter 4, this book.

Fulfillment Houses

Fulfillment Corporation of America*, 205 West Center Street, Marion, OH 43302. (614) 383-5231. It works for magazines, does everything to service the subscribers but mail the magazines: bills, collects, banks, corresponds, reports. President John P. Courtney

tells why it started, ups and downs, exactly what it does. Seminar VII, Chapter 8, this book.

Printers are computerizing, and computer service businesses are going into computer and laser printing, largely for direct marketers. In Seminar VIII, Chapter 9, I tell the story of Leo Yochim, pioneer of computer letters, and of the start, growth and success of Printronic Corporation of America, 10 Columbus Circle, New York, NY 10019, (212) 247-8800, of which he is president.

Scientists are getting into mail order . . . even atomic scientists. In "Egg Head Mail order," Seminar II, Chapter 3, I tell the story of MAGI*, Mathematical Applications Group, Inc., 3 Westchester Plaza, Elmsford, NY 10523, (914) 592-4646; a group of mathematicians and physicists who first worked with computers in nuclear projects . . . but then came up with a better way to eliminate duplicates in mailing lists.

Lettershops/Mailing Houses

All through the U.S. are lettershops and mailing houses which work overwhelmingly for direct marketers. In this book I describe how several started, grew and prospered. I write about problems as well as successes. I tell stories of these two in detail:

Hy-Aid, Inc.*, 6 Commercial Street, Hicksville, NY 11801; (516) 433-3800. It ships books and items for biggest direct marketers. It started with four employees in a basement. It now employs 350 at peak . . . in an industrial park. Founder Dick Levinson tells its story. Seminar IV, Chapter 3, this book.

The Mailmen*, 15 Enter Lane, Hauppauge, NY 11788. (212) 986-4862 - NYC tie line. It mails up to 1,000,000 a day. A trip through it; what it does; founder Lee Epstein's career; some advice to those starting out. Seminar VI, Chapter 2, this book.

Printers

An important segment of mail order's support system is the printing field. Numerous printers work for direct marketers. Many diverse specialties have been developed, particularly for mail order. It would take a far larger book than this to list them all. A bigger and bigger percentage of total sales of biggest printers are to direct marketers. More and more medium size printers are becoming increasingly dependent on sales to mail order people. Small printers are finding a place making more and more smaller tests for direct marketers. Those who specialize most in direct marketing get business from direct marketers. The following describes the facilities of a few of them.

Special Feature Section: Direct Response Printers, Graphics and Color Services
A report, firm by firm on facilities, clients and history of each. DM News; 2/15/80.

JOHN BLAIR & CO.*, 9 West 57th St., New York, NY 10019. (212) 838-9191. Blair succeeded as a sales representative firm . . . first for radio stations, then TV stations . . . and then as a broadcast station owner. It then purchased several major printing groups and formed Blair Graphics. Blair Graphics has continually developed new print media for direct marketers and has had considerable success with the new technology it invested in. It tells how it then used broadcast profits to buy printing technology to help direct marketers. Seminar IV, Chapter 9, this book.

LINCOLN GRAPHICS ARTS, INC.*, 475 Park Avenue South, New York, NY 10016. (212) 532-4004. It is a moderate sized quality printer. It has had increasing success working for direct marketers. I write of the beginnings of Lincoln Graphics; of the joining together of its present four partners, their mail order background; its growth. Its vice president, Nat Ross . . . the unofficial dean of direct marketing. Two partners tell the story of printing technology vs. postage inflation; holding down printing prices while improving quality. Seminar VII, Chapter 11, this book.

Many help but most help comes from self-education. To accelerate this, there exists a unique self-education network. Reference Section VII lists some of its component parts.

Reference Section VII
Mail Order's
Self-Education Network

Lists of courses, clubs and Days . . .
of magazines and newsletters . . .
seminars . . . associations . . . shows

In this book, stories on each tell how, far more than in most fields, mail order is knit together. There are good courses available. Clubs give courses for little more than the cost of a meal. The Direct Marketing Days assemble bargain collections of course lectures. The magazines and newsletters report, inform, teach. The associations prod. The shows expand teaching to maximum. You can take or leave any part of it all . . . meet others in the field . . . exchange know-how . . . form friendships.

Let's examine Mail Order's Self-Education Network.

The Direct Marketing Courses

They're starting up all over. They're hard to keep track of. Universities, colleges, community colleges and graduate schools are adding them. Many institutions are including them in their continuing schools of education for adults. Many are available in early evening hours, some on weekends and some at lunch time. Some are credit and some non-credit courses.

Some direct marketing courses are organized and run by direct marketing clubs (and one advertising club). Large direct marketers often aid in organizing them. Much of the cost of courses their employees take is paid by them, often 100%. One course often leads to several more . . . basic to advanced . . . general to specific . . . and one subject to another.

Another trend is for general marketing courses to include coverage of direct marketing. Many feel that almost all basic

marketing courses anywhere will soon include more and more direct marketing.

Some courses start and stop. Others go on year after year. At any one time its hard to determine how many there are. At press time, estimates indicated that over 70 credit and non-credit marketing courses were available. Tuition fees vary and keep changing with inflation, so much so that sometimes even professors conducting the courses aren't sure of latest fees. It often takes a bit of detective work to find out whether a course given last year is being given this year, as well as plans for new courses.

What is the difference between a seminar and a course? I've considered small groups conducted by one, two or three and lasting for one to three-and-a-half days as seminars. I've considered larger groups being taught over a period of a number of weeks by one or more lecturers as a course. I've considered an intensive all day, every day, five-day saturation of lectures, by a variety of instructors, as a course.

Tuition for most courses range from $200 or more to as low as $60 to $70 and averages over $100. But that is changing and rising fast and I'm not always including price (or specific dates and time) in the following listing which is merely a sampling of what was available at press time.

Courses with an asterisk are described more fully in Seminar IV, Chapter XII, the Direct Marketing Courses. Names of individuals marked with an asterisk can be looked up in the index for a story concerning them.

To get latest information about courses in your area, check the nearest direct marketing club or Direct Marketing Magazine, DM News or ZIP magazine . . . or best of all the Direct Mail/Marketing Educational Foundation, 6 East 43rd Street, New York, NY 10017; (212) 689-4977.

The following courses are representative of courses available:

CALIFORNIA

California State University, LA
Mail Order/Marketing; Dr. William A. Cohen; 9 sessions; 4 hours; 6:10-10:00 PM; once weekly; spring/fall; $132; School of Business Economics, Department of Marketing, 5151 State University Drive, Los Angeles, CA 90032. (213) 224-2811 or (213) 224-0111.

Direct Marketing Club of Southern California, LA
Direct Marketing; Freeman Gosden, Jr.*; 6 to 8 sessions; 6:30-10:00 PM; once weekly; fall/winter; $95; DMCSC, c/o Hooven Business Mail, 1801 South Hill, Los Angeles, CA 90015. (213) 747-0241.

Fashion Institute of Design & Merchandising
Direct Mail Advertising; Mary E. Norton; 12 sessions; once weekly; days; quarter semester; full year offering; rolling admission; $250; FIDM, Merchandising Department, 818 West Seventh Street, Los Angeles, CA 90017. (213) 624-1200.

University of California, LA (Extension)
Direct Response Marketing & Direct Mail Advertising; 12 sessions; 3 hours; evenings; once weekly; fall; $105; Business and Management Office, Box 24901, Los Angeles, CA 90024. (213) 825-7031; Dean's Office (213) 825-5603.

COLORADO

University of Northern Colorado, Greeley
Direct Mail Advertising; Wayne W. Melanson; 10 sessions; one hour; once weekly; alternating days and evenings by semester;

spring; $96; UNC, School of Business, Department of Journalism, Greeley, CO 80639. (303) 351-2726 or (303) 351-1890.

ILLINOIS

Printing Industries Institute, Chicago
Direct Marketing; Larry Nieminski (Allstate Insurance); 8 weeks; 2½ hours; 6:00-8:30 PM; one evening weekly; $187, members $140; fall; PII, 200 East Ontario Street, Chicago, IL 60611. (312) 751-0440, ext. 32.

Roosevelt University, Chicago
Two great courses: 15 sessions; 3 hours; days; spring/fall; over $300; *Direct Marketing I; Direct Marketing II;* 15 sessions; 3 hours; evenings; spring/fall; over $350; Dr. Kenneth Mangun; RU, Walter E. Heller College of Business Administration, 430 South Michigan Avenue, Chicago, IL 60605. (312) 341-3722 or (312) 341-3848.

University of Illinois, Urbana/Champaign
Written Persuasion (direct mail copy); John Maguire, professor, writer and consultant on direct marketing and a particular authority on business and industrial direct marketing; 48 sessions; 1 hour; 3 times weekly, days; spring/fall; over $280; UI, College of Liberal Arts, English Department, Division of Business & Technological Writing; Urbana/Champaign, IL 60801. (217) 333-4135 or (217) 333-1000.

INDIANA

St. Joseph's College, Rensselaer
Direct Marketing; Professor Walter Scherb; 48 sessions; 50 minutes; 1:00-2:00 PM; 3 times weekly; spring/fall; $351; SJC, Department of Business Administration; Box 927, Rensselaer, IN 47978. (219) 866-7111.

MICHIGAN

Western Michigan University, Kalamazoo
Direct Mail Marketing; Zane Cannon; 3 hours; one evening weekly; fall; $80; WMU, College of Business, Department of Marketing, Kalamazoo, MI 49008. (616) 383-1600.

MISSOURI

University of Missouri, Columbia
Direct & Mail Order Advertising; Robert Haverfield; 16 sessions; 1½ hours; twice weekly; days; fall; $127; UM, Journalism Department, 102 Neff Hall, P.O. Box 838, Columbia, MO 65205. (314) 882-7471.

University of Missouri, Kansas City
Marketing Channel Systems; Elements of the Marketing Concept; Marketing Research; Martin Baier; three fine courses; 12 sessions each; 3 hours each; twice weekly; evenings; UM, School of Continuing Education, Department of Marketing, 5100 Rockhill Road, Kansas City, MO 64110. (816) 753-4900 or (816) 276-2205.

NEW YORK

Baruch College, New York City
Direct Mail and Direct Response Advertising; Dr. Stan Ulanoff; 15 weeks; 1:00-2:15 PM; twice weekly; fall/spring; $135; BC, Department of Marketing/Advertising, 17 Lexington Avenue, New York, NY 10010. (212) 725-3295 or (212) 725-7172.

Hofstra University, Hempstead
Direct Mail Marketing; Bob Jurick; 10 sessions; 7:30-9:30 PM; one evening weekly; fall/spring; $115; HU, Division of Continuing Education, Center for Business Studies, Hempstead, NY 11550. (516) 560-3245/3286. Ask for Mrs. Anita Pescow. Or call (516) 560-0500.

Nassau Community College, Garden City
Everything You Wanted to Know About the Mail Order Business; Jack Mandel; guest lecturers; 4 sessions; 3½ hours; 6:30-10:00 PM; once weekly; fall; spring; $70; NCC, Department of Continuing Education, Stewart Avenue, Garden City, NY 11530. (516) 222-7500.

St. John's University, Queens Campus
Principles of Direct Marketing; Dr. Herbert Katzenstein, professor of marketing; every summer; 5½ weeks; Monday-Thursday; 2 hours; 4 times a week; $321; also, fall; 15 weeks; twice weekly; days; and fall; 15 weeks; twice weekly; evenings 6:00-7:20 PM. Grand Central & Utopia Parkways, Jamaica, NY. (212) 969-8000.

State University of New York, College at Old Westbury
Direct Marketing; Dr. Al Mickens, department head; 12 sessions; 5:30-7:30 PM; once weekly; spring; $140; SUNY, Department of Business Studies, Old Town Lane, Westbury, NY 11568. (516) 876-3000.

New School for Social Research, New York City
Direct Marketing; John Pahmer; (president of New York's Hundred Million Club); 6:00-8:00 PM; once weekly; winter; $135; NSSR, Business Department, 66 West 12th Street, New York, NY 10011. (212) 741-5600.

New York University, New York City
Direct Marketing; Direct Mail & Mail Order; the first and splendid direct marketing course; Nat Ross, father of it all; top guest lecturers; 10 sessions; 6:00-8:00 PM; one evening weekly; spring/fall; $210; NYU Management Institute, 326 Shimkin Hall, New York, NY 10003. (212) 598-2100.

New York University, New York City
Direct Marketing; Concepts, Strategies, Techniques; James W. Prendergast; 12 weeks; spring; 6:00-8:30 PM; $240; Norman Thomas Center, 111 East 33rd Street, New York, NY 10003. (212) 598-2100 or (212) 598-1212.

New York University, New York City
Direct Marketing; Direct Mail & Mail Order; advanced course; one week saturation, all day, Monday through Friday; 8:15 AM to 6:00 PM; in-depth; one great specialist after another all day, all week; July; $240; NYU: School of Continuing Education, Division of Liberal Studies, Norman Thomas Center, 2 Park Avenue, Room 21, New York, NY 10003. (212) 598-2371 or (212) 598-1212.

Parsons School of Design, New York City
Mailing Lists; two courses conducted by Edith Gould, Sr. VP of Sales, Zeller & Letica, Inc.: one course is one evening weekly and one is a noon session weekly; spring/fall; $90.

Direct Response Advertising; conducted by Curtis Reilly, Account Supervisor, Ogilvy & Mather Direct Response; 12 weeks; once weekly; 5:25-7:50 PM; fall; just under $200.

Mail Order; conducted by Charles Gardner, Managing Partner, Alternatives In Marketing; 12 sessions; once weekly; 5:25-7:50 PM; fall; just under $200; all courses given at PSD, Midtown Campus, 560 Seventh Avenue, New York, NY 10018. (212) 741-7576.

OHIO

Youngstown State University
Direct Mail Advertising; Dr. Frank Seibold, Eugene Sekeres; once weekly; 1½ hours; evenings; $95; YSU, Department of Advertisng & Public Relations, 410 Wick Avenue, Youngstown, OH 44555. (216) 742-3077 or (216) 742-3000.

OKLAHOMA

Central State University, Edmond
Direct Mail/Marketing Design; for those in graphics, photography and layout; Dr. Hall Duncan; 32 sessions; 2 hours; twice weekly; 5:30-7:30 PM; third quarter; $32; CSU, Art Department, 100 North University Drive, Edmond, OK 73034. (405) 341-2980, ext. 212 or 201.

PENNSYLVANIA

Temple University, Philadelphia
Profitable Direct Marketing Methods; 6 Mondays; 3 hours each; evenings; fall/spring/summer; $165; Center for Professional Development, School of Business Administration, Temple University, 201 Speakman Hall, Philadelphia, PA 19122. (215) 787-7833 or (215) 787-7000.

WEST VIRGINIA

Bethany College, West Virginia
Direct Mail Marketing; James W. Carty, Jr.; 14 weeks; 2 hour sessions; twice weekly; spring; $160; or, 7 weeks; 4 times weekly; 2 hours each; days; BC, Department of Communications, Bethany, W.VA 26032. (304) 829-7000.

WISCONSIN

University of Wisconsin, LaCrosse
Direct Response; John Jenks; 17 sessions; 50 minutes each; 3 times weekly; fall; $66; UW, Deparment of Mass Communications, LaCrosse, WI 54601. (608) 785-8371.

For students of business courses at college, junior college, a university or business graduate school, there is a possible free direct marketing course. It is open to a limited number of very qualified students as follows:

Collegiate Institute*
Free transportation, hotel, meals, seminar to qualified business course students. Top experts teach for nothing and pay their own expenses. Top companies sponsor. A phenomenon. Only top few students recommended by their professor and selected by panel qualify. The Direct Mail/Marketing Education Foundation, 6 East 43rd Street, New York, NY 10017; (212) 689-4977.

There is one basic and low-cost correspondence course offered by the AMA and another very complete and advanced one offered by the DMMA.

Fundamentals of Direct Mail Marketing
Design, copy, format, list selection, segmentation; creating and maintaining house lists; testing; evaluation; basic 20-hour self-study course; $65. Extension Institute, American Management Association, 135 West 50th Street, New York, NY 10020; (212) 586-8100.

Direct Marketing Career Development Program
George Wiedemann; textbook, workbook, exam; 4 tape cassettes. Successful Direct Marketing methods by Bob Stone; catalogs of direct marketing books and cassettes; $375. Direct Mail/Marketing Association, 6 East 43rd Street, New York, NY 10017; (212) 689-4977.

Here's the perfect subject for a correspondence course on audio tape:

How To Market By Telephone
Demonstrates the telephone as a marketing tool; 10 hours of listening; explains applications, cost effectiveness; tells how to start . . . define buyer, find list success, product sales; shows techniques; tells how to write a pre-planned script, select and train telephone sales force; make prospecting calls, sales calls, take orders . . . evaluate results. It covers formats, equipment, new technology; workbook, cassettes; $144; Extension Institute, American Management Association, 135 West 50th Street, New York, NY 10020. (212) 586-8100.

Here's the first video-taped correspondence course on direct marketing:

Direct Mail/Marketing
Ed Burnett's Pace University Course, taped on four video cassettes; introduction to and structure of direct mail business; compiled lists, consumer and business; mathematics of direct mail; copy, offer and package; course can be used over and over; $450; DM News, Video Tape Department, 19 West 21st, New York, NY 10010. (212) 741-2095.

Direct Marketing Club Listings*

Clubs are often the first introduction to direct marketing. The following refers you back to the more detailed story on them in this book and then lists them by localities.

Membership cost is very low. Lunches and dinners are inexpensive. Talks by top experts are free. Excellent to meet those in direct marketing, exchange information, make friends . . . learn and get contact for career and business. Seminar I, Chapter 9, this book.

It's sometimes hard to locate the clubs. Almost all have no permanent offices. Contact is in care of the president (often different each year) at his or her place of business. Employees there may be new and unfamiliar with the club, particularly after the presidency of the club passes on to someone at some other firm. If the numbers we give you seem obsolete, ask for the secretary to the president of the firm at the number. Often you'll get the new number and person to call right away.

Otherwise, call Direct Marketing, DM News, ZIP Magazine . . . or DMMA, Information Central. Patience and fortitude. Meanwhile, here are addresses as we went to press.

ARIZONA

Phoenix
The Phoenix Direct Marketing Club, c/o Otto Meyer, P.O. Box 8756, Phoenix, AZ 85066. (602) 974-8058/(602) 268-5237.

CALIFORNIA

Los Angeles
Direct Marketing Club of Southern California, c/o Hooven Business Mail, 1801 South Hill Street, Los Angeles, CA 90015. (213) 747-3735.

San Diego
San Diego Direct Marketing Club, c/o James Rosenfield, P.O. Box 1027, Solana Beach, CA 92075. (714) 296-2204.

San Francisco
San Francisco Advertising Club, DM Department, 681 Market, Suite 898, San Francisco, CA 94105. (415) 986-3878.

DISTRICT OF COLUMBIA

Washington, D.C.
Direct Marketing Club of Washington, D.C., 608 "H" Street SW, Washington, DC 20004. (202) 347-MAIL.

FLORIDA

Fort Lauderdale
FDMA Gold Coast Direct Marketing Club, 800 West Oakland Park Blvd., Ft. Lauderdale, FL 33311 (Suite 309), Attention: Kathy. (305) 561-9667.

Tampa
Florida Direct Marketing Association, c/o Direct Response Services, 5444 Bay Center Drive, Suite 131, Tampa, Fl 33609. (813) 870-1806.

ILLINOIS

Chicago
Chicago Association of Direct Marketing (CADM), 221 North LaSalle Street, Chicago, IL 60601. (312) 346-1600.

MASSACHUSETTS

Boston
The New England Direct Marketing Association, Boston Envelope Co., Inc., 150 Royal Street, Canton, MA 02021. (617) 828-6100.

MICHIGAN

Detroit
Direct Marketing Association of Detroit, c/o Ellen Shook, 606 Michigan Building, Detroit, MI 48226. (313) 961-9720.

MINNESOTA

Minneapolis
Midwest Direct Marketing Association (MDMA), 537 Plymouth Building, 12 South 6th Street, Minneapolis, MN 55402. (612) 338-3361; (612) 371-7576.

MISSOURI

Kansas City
Direct Marketing Club of Kansas City, c/o NCR, P.O. Box 281, Shawnee Mission, MO 64141. (816) 531-0538.

St. Louis
Direct Marketing Club of St. Louis; c/o Bill Shoss, c/o Shoss Association, Inc., 1401 S. Brentwood Blvd., St. Louis, MO 63144. (314) 961-7620.

NEW YORK

Long Island
Lond Island Direct Marketing Association (LIDMA), c/o Bernard Lande, 260 Duffy Avenue, Hicksville, NY 11802. (516) 944-9081.

New York City
Hundred Million Club of New York, c/o Accredited Mailing Lists, Inc., 3 Park Avenue, New York, NY 10016. (212) 889-1180.

OHIO

Cleveland
Cleveland Advertising Club, The Cleveland Plaza, Cleveland, OH 44115. (216) 241-4807.

PENNSYLVANIA

Philadelphia
Philadelphia Direct Mail Club, Inc., P.O. Box 1074, Philadelphia, PA 19105. (215) 232-6711.

TEXAS

Dallas/Fort Worth
Direct Marketing Club of North Texas, c/o Richard Braun, National Business Lists, 3321 Towerwood, Suite 103, Dallas, TX 75234. (214) 241-5061.

Houston
Houston Direct Mail/Marketing Club, c/o John Glazier, 360 Garden Oaks Boulevard, Houston, TX 77018. (713) 691-0668.

The Direct Marketing Days* Listing

I suggest you reread Seminar VII, Chapter 6, on them. Almost every direct marketing club has one. Contact nearest club to you for information. Direct Marketing Day in New York is manned, set-up and operated by an organization of volunteers. Contact Hoke Communications, Inc., 224 Seventh Street, Garden City, NY 11530; (516) 746-6700, or in New York: (800) 645-6132. Some of the best known Direct Marketing Days are:

Direct Marketing Day in New York*
Dramatic! Eye opener, updater; the book clubs, the magazine circulation champs, biggest direct marketers . . . the agencies, services, writers, printers, all the media are here. Big, varied, educational 8-ring circus, 4,000 attend.

CADM Direct Marketing Days in Chicago, IL
Chicago is the mother of mail order. Here are giant catalogs, huge insurers, more kinds of mail order than anywhere. Its masters teach us all; talent is brought in from everywhere. Exciting, encyclopedic, latest know-how; biggest event of the direct marketing club with most educational activities.

Direct Marketing Day in Los Angeles, CA
Started later, but with California energy direct marketers have made this show grow faster—with help of great creative people who live here; bringing top talent too. Good teaching show. Put on by Direct Marketing Club of Southern California. (L.A. Conference on Direct Marketing, CA).

New England Direct Marketing Day in Boston, MA
Home of many successful specialty catalogs. Modern fund raising and list brokerage started here. Smaller, more intimate. Lots of one-to-one know-how sharing. Good mini-seminar. Put on by Direct Marketing Association of New England, Boston, MA.

San Diego Direct Marketing Days
A bigger attendance than other cities its size. A very strong program. Top talent lecturers come here. Excellent.

Some other Direct Marketing Days with a strong following are:

Detroit, MI
Direct Marketing Association of Detroit.

Dallas - Fort Worth (at the airport)
North Texas Direct Marketing Club.

Kansas City Direct Marketing Days
Direct Marketing Club of Kansas City.

Minneapolis
Midwest Mail/Marketing Association Direct Marketing Day (MDMA).

Philadelphia Direct Marketing Day
Philadelphia Direct Mail Club, Inc.

St. Louis, MO
Direct Marketing Club of St. Louis.

Washington, D.C. Direct Marketing Day
Direct Marketing Club of Washington, D.C.

And in Canada there is:
Toronto Direct Marketing Day

If you're a student or professor taking or giving business courses in college or graduate business schools, you might be interested in the following. But few qualify.

Direct Marketing Career Days
Sponsored by Direct Marketing Days, clubs and conferences are often in co-operation with the Direct Mail/Marketing Educational Foundation. From a dozen or so to over a hundred students and professors from college and university business courses are invited guests at local DM Days. A DM Career Day has even been brought to the campus of St. John's University, NYC. Students and professors are often individually invited to DM club events. Business course students! Ask your professors or contact the Direct Mail/Marketing Educational Foundation, 6 East 43rd Street, New York, NY 10017; (212) 689-4977.

In New York City a one-day event similar to a Direct Marketing Day is:
The Direct Marketing Symposium
A saturation day of top talent talks, panels, mini-seminars; New School for Social Research, 66 West 12th Street, New York, NY 10011; (212) 741-5600; or contact: Hoke Communications.

Here's a final suggestion. Before attending a Direct Marketing Day, reread Seminar VII, Chapter 6, this book . . . *The Direct Marketing Days - How to saturate yourself in mail order.*
P.S. Incidentally, most Direct Marketing Days are in March or April, with some in February or May. Cost is usually $110 to $125, including lunch, and quite a bargain.

Magazines and Newsletters
Helpful to Direct Marketers

Those starred (*) have individual stories concerning them in this book. The three trade magazines of direct marketing are:

Direct Marketing*
It's published by Hoke Communications, Inc. How Henry Hoke started it, "Pete" Hoke transformed it and Hank Hoke helps "Pete" build it. How the Hoke operation is run like a radio station, publishes magazines and newsletters and offers 6,000 tapes of direct marketing speeches by authorities. Seminar I, Chapter 2, this book.
Monthly magazine; emphasizes case history interviews and transcribed and edited talks and lectures of leaders in direct marketing. Packed with know-how, a continuing course; $30 yearly; Hoke Communications Inc., 224 Seventh Street, Garden City, NY 11530. (516) 746-6700.
Back articles of DM magazine referred to in Reference Section IV and V are: $2.00 (minimum) for one article, $1.50 ea., if more than one. The Hoke tapes referred to in Sections IV and V are:

$ 7 per 30 min. tapes
$10 per 60 min. tapes
$12 per 90 min. tapes
$15 per 2 hour tapes

The DM News*
"We seek, investigate and report the stories behind the mail order stories," says Adrian Courtenay III, publisher. How it started; its publisher's philosophy; its unique, special issue sections with reports on special areas of direct marketing. Seminar II, Chapter 11, this book.
Monthly; in tabloid newspaper format; covers direct marketing; emphasizes marketing, advertising agencies, media list field; $24 yearly. DM News, 19 West 21st Street, New York, NY 10010; (212) 741-2095. Back issues, $1 each when available. If not, they are available on microfilm. For price write University Microfilms, Ann Arbor, MI 48100.

ZIP Magazine*
How its editor-publisher, Ray Lewis, created a personality profile of tomorrow's direct marketing executives, as they will become . . . and then created ZIP's format, reporting, research and content for them. ZIP's start; the editorial changes that got it into the black; its special areas of strength; how it can help you. Seminar VII, Chapter 4, this book.
Magazine published 10 times yearly. Covers direct marketing, mailing by direct mail; feature articles on areas of activity, new developments. Emphasis on lists, mailing, fulfillment; $24 yearly. North American Publishing Co., 401 N. Broad Street, Philadelphia, PA 19108; (215) 574-9600. Back issues $3 each, photocopies of articles $1 each. Order from ZIP, 545 Madison Avenue, New York, NY 10022; (212) 371-7800.

Newsletters on the field keep starting, as the following indicates:

Newsletters About Mail Order*
Too many to read . . . some too good to miss. An appraisal of the best. Seminar VII, Chapter 10, this book.

This is the most read newsletter on direct marketing:
Friday Report*
Weekly; covers every major occasion and event in direct marketing; highlights within days most important talks, lectures. Reports new developments and the views of "Pete" Hoke; personal; worthwhile. $92 yearly. Hoke Communications, Inc., 224 Seventh Street, Garden City, NY 11530. (516) 746-6700.

Another excellent newsletter for bigger firms on all direct marketing is:
Non-Store Marketing Report*
Twice monthly, covers all non-store distribution, mainly mail order. Well written, useful; $135 yearly. Maxwell Sroge Publishing Inc., 731 North Cascade Avenue, Colorado Springs, CO 80903. (303) 633-5556.

There are a number of newsletters on specific areas of direct marketing. One fine one on catalogs is:
Catalog Marketer Newsletter
Bi-monthly; excellent coverage of many aspects of profitable operation of mail order catalogs. Useful for those in or considering starting catalog businesses. $115 yearly; Maxwell Sroge Publishing Inc.

A very well written newsletter on 800 telephone marketing is:
AIS 800 Report
Twice monthly; covers all aspects of toll-free marketing via an 800 number; taped telephone commercials proven profitable, outside service vs. in-house operation; techniques, equipment;

$99 yearly. Advertising Information Service, 353 Lexington Avenue, New York, NY 10016. (212) 683-9070.

There are some extremely good list newsletters. Some are:

Immediate Release
The Kleid Company newsletter; beautifully written by President Rose Harper; pleases, teaches; published from time to time; free. Write: The Kleid Company, 200 Park Avenue, New York, NY 10017. (212) 599-4140.

List Marketing Newsletter
Simple, outstanding articles on one subject after another concerned with mail order via direct mail. $24 per year, single issue $5. Dependable Lists Inc., 257 Park Avenue South, New York, NY 10010. (212) 677-6760.

Here's one for those in mail order who are sophisticated users of statistical research:

Data User News
Monthly newsletter of the Census Bureau; informs on censuses; surveys planned; estimates and projections in preparation; also highlights of statistics from other government agencies; conferences and workshops; covers new Census Bureau reports and guides; state and other organizations offering statistical services; reports new computer technology and latest statistical methods; $14 a year. Superintendent of Documents, U.S. Government Printing Office, Washington, D.C. 20402; (202) 275-2051.

Heavy mailers might consider the following:

Postal World
Bi-weekly magazine for volume mailers. Emphasizes how to save money: use of pre-sort, when it pays; which very light paper stock to select; mailing heavily just before postal rate increases (Postal World even warns you in time); first class vs. third in certain situations; $158. Postal World, 8701 Georgia Ave., Silver Springs, MD 20910; (301) 589-8875.

If you publish a newsletter or would like to try this:

Newsletter on Newsletters
How to start, write, promote, succeed with a newsletter; $54 yearly. The Newsletter Clearinghouse, 44 West Market Street, P.O. Box 311, Rhinebeck, NY 12572; (914) 876-2081.

One magazine anyone in mail order should consider is:

Direct Magazine
Bi-monthly consumer magazine about shipping by mail, for mail order buffs: news; items, bargains, new catalogs; $12 yearly. Direct Magazine, 60 East 42nd Street, Suite 1825, New York, NY 10165; (212) 883-1995.

Direct marketers of gifts should consider this magazine:

"Made in Europe"
160 pages or more, illustrated, much color; monthly import guide: Continuous trade fair in print; features primarily giftware; several thousand items a year shown in advertising and editorial pages, with source addesses; prices given in U.S. dollars. 12 issues yearly, each in 3 geographic areas; no single copy sales; 1 year $40, 3 years $90. USA: "Made in Europe," 150 Green Street, Brooklyn, NY 11222; (212) 383-8100.

For direct marketers concerned with major advertising, this magazine can help:

Advertising Age
Weekly newspaper of marketing. Special issue on DM once yearly. Occasional articles on DM. Most important for those in media, in the advertising agency business and in major company advertising departments; $40 yearly. Crain Communications, Inc., 740 Rush Street, Chicago, IL 60611. (312) 649-5215.

Here's a newsletter free to those mailing in volume:

Memo to Mailers
Monthly; write: U.S. Postal Service, P.O. Box 600, La Plata, MD 20646.

Two publications widely read by fund raisers are:

FR Weekly (Newsletter)
Same approach for fund raisers as Friday Report for general direct marketers; $78 yearly; Hoke Communications Inc., 224 Seventh Street, Garden City, NY 11530; (516) 746-6700.

Fund Raising Management*
Monthly magazine of direct marketing know-how applied to fund raising. $30 yearly. Hoke Communications Inc.

One newsletter on mail order overseas is:

International Direct Marketing Letter
One year's subscription $50; IDM, 8716 Plymouth Street, Suite 2, Silver Springs, MD 20901. (301) 588-3959.

There's one newsletter just on mail order selling to schools:

Direct Response Marketing to Schools
Monthly; Bob Stimolo, former senior product manager of Xerox Education Publications, is publisher. If you'd like to sell by mail order to schools, read it. $69 yearly; Market Research Institute, P.O. Box 160, Chester, CT 06412; (203) 526-9690.

The Seminar Selector

See Seminar VIII, Chapter 1, for an overview of leading seminars and how they operate.

Please note that the cost of seminars is constantly rising and that those giving seminars alternate subjects, dropping one here and there and introducing another, and often reviving one of several years previous. Listed here are a number of seminars with their attendance fees at the time this book went to press. Usually, I do not list cities but do tell where to write for latest changes of subject, personalities, dates and places. Often there are new excellent seminars at modest cost, and at no cost (given by services and suppliers). It is wise to check the various magazines on direct marketing for any such events.

The Direct Marketing Days usually include mini-seminars but sometimes longer ones. For instance: San Diego Direct Marketing Day has offered a day-long seminar with Jim Prendergast for $85. New England Direct Marketing Day has featured several free seminars on direct response copy with Paul Butterworth.

An asterisk (*) follows the title of any seminar listed when the personality conducting it is featured in the story in this book. Simply refer to that name in the index.

As noted elsewhere in this book, full-length DMMA seminars are not taped but mini-seminars of the same personalities are. A number are listed in our section on tapes and articles. The following seminars are among those put on by the Direct Mail/Marketing Association. For latest information and rates, and news of their newest seminars, write: DMMA, 6 East 43rd

Street, New York, NY 10017, or phone: (212) 689-4977. Savings for members are so great that if you attend several, you probably can get most of the cost of a membership by joining the DMMA and getting the member discount.

Basic Direct Mail Marketing Institute*

Conducted by Paul Sampson and Dick Hodgson*. Described in detail in this book, Seminar VIII, Chapter 1, page 307. Excellent; $775; for four days, scheduled in various key cities coast to coast; DMMA.

1001 Ideas for Direct Mail Users

Dick Hodgson in all-day marathon covers basic technique and new approaches: discusses sweeps, tokens, stamps, contests, rub-off devices, personalization, publishers' letters, recordings, color, die-cuts, teasers, reprints and preprints, pop-ups, specialty envelopes; dimensionals; copy, newsletters, mini-catalogs; blow-ups; certificates, special printing and binding techniques; continuity programs, clubs; much more; highly praised; several key cities; $250.

The Basic Theories Behind Direct Marketing

Martin Baier*, the practical scholar of direct marketing, explains; marketing concept, system and research, consumer behavior, market segmentation, channels of distribution; offers ad promotion planning; decision making procedure; value of a customer; revenue vs. costs, actual vs. forecasted results; much more; highly praised. Various cities. DMMA. $440.

Advanced Seminars in Direct Marketing

Pierre Passavant*; mailing lists; copy and art; math and finance; three of one day each; highly praised; number of days or people: $250/one; $475/two; $650/three; various cities; DMMA.

Direct Marketing and Strategic Planning

Richard Shaver; explanation of decision-making processes; formatting strategic information; finding leverage, isolating targets, bridges from objective to strategy; finding and using obstacles to trigger strategy; leverage of competitive advantages to catapult response. You join one core group and work out a "live" direct marketing situation. It covers concept, offer components, copy; graphics, sound, film; direct mail, phone, space; multi-media, scheduling, timing; tracking, budgets and forecasts. Three days, $575; various cities; DMMA.

Catalog Institute

Richard Hodgson*; covers role of catalogs, basics, determining markets, merchandise selection, budgeting, design and copy; prediction and distribution; lists, action devices, ideas; back end, bottom line, evaluation. Highly praised; 4 days, $775; various cities; DMMA.

Merchandising Mail Order Products

Len Carlson, who has found and created hundreds of mail order catalog hits explains: product selection and development; psychological reasons why people buy; developing your own checklist of consumer problems; product and service life cycle; how to learn from failures; how to research new product ideas and market prospects at low cost; pros and cons of sophisticated product testing; values and pitfalls of selling your existing product overseas. Important! Occasional one shot; DMMA.

Mail Order Catalogs

Richard Hodgson*; right merchandise selection, planning and budgeting; design and copy; lists; action devices; back end, bottom line; 3½ days, $725; worth it; various cities; DMMA. Exciting one-day seminars never offered before—in New York, Chicago, Atlanta (two per city); $250 each.

Managing For Fulfillment Excellence*

Conducted by Stanley Fenvessy*, Robert Bonner and Robert Earley of Fenvessy Associates and Peter Rozaker, a systems consultant. See Seminar IX, Chapter 3, for story on Fenvessy. Every key step covered. Highly praised. $320; DMMA.

Outward Bound Telephone Marketing

John Henry Achziger; management decisions; applications; campaign strategy; marketing plans; costing; creating scripts; layout of sales center, equipment; hiring and training of personnel analyzed. New York and Chicago. $440.; DMMA.

Inbound Telephone Marketing

John Henry Achziger; characteristics; what to expect; how to combine with other media for maximum impacts; television and telephone, space advertising and phone, catalog and phone; in-house vs. outside services; 800 vs. local and collect; traffic management, spreading peaks and valleys; hiring and training people; equipment; budgeting; planning; future; New York and Chicago; $440.; DMMA.

School for Magazine Marketing

Wendell Forbes, master of subscription marketing, gives thorough orientation; clarifies scope and variety of subscription direct marketing from trial offer to last renewal letter; splendid; usually at Tarrytown Hilton, Tarrytown, NY; 3 days; $440.; DMMA.

The DMMA's various Councils also run workshops typical of which is the following:

Direct Marketing to Business and Industry

Four hour workshop session; once yearly in a different city; run by DMMA Business Industrial Council.

A quite important seminar in New York City only is the following:

Tools and Techniques for Direct Mail Marketing Management

Nat Ross* and Arlene Minick, V.P. of Kleid Company moderate; top pros; 8:15 to 5 PM one day saturation; advanced seminar; January; $160; New York University, School of Continuing Education, Division of Liberal Studies, Room 21, 2 University Place, New York, NY 10003. (212) 598-2371.

NYU also conducts the following seminar in NYC and in other cities.

Telephone Marketing

New York University, School of Continuing Education; 2 days; various cities; contact NYU Conference Center, 360 Lexington Avenue, New York, NY 10017. (212) 953-7262.

There are highly successful executives and consultants with unusual talent for conducting seminars or participating in them. But usually their own careers prevent them from being continually available. This means that some of the best seminars come and go. A seminar this year may not be scheduled by the time you read this book. But sometimes those most successful keep carving out time to give seminars or do so every several years.

Jim Kobs, who puts on extremely effective seminars has less time to do so as Kobs & Brady keeps growing. He gave some fine 2-day seminars with Peter Spaulder sponsored by the Philadelphia Direct Marketing Club. The cost of each seminar was $350. To find out future scheduling write: School of Business Administration, Temple University, 13th & Montgomery, Philadelphia, PA 19122. (215) 787-7833.

There are a number of direct marketing seminars just for specific fields. An excellent one on the mail order book business is the following:

Direct Mail and Direct Response Selling
For book publishers; how to manage; Andrew Svenson* conducts; in various cities; one day, $195; contact: Institute for Publishing Professionals, 701 Westchester Avenue, White Plains, NY 10604.

Two effective seminars on the list field are put on at Pace Institute in New York City each year and occasionally in other cities by Paul Goldner and Ed Burnett with whom Paul is associated. For schedule and latest rates write: Ed Burnett Consultants, 2 Park Avenue, New York, NY 10016. (212) 679-0630.

Effective Computer Use In Mailing List Processing
Paul Goldner; overview, basics; creating, maintaining and augmenting a list on computers; mailing list selection, data banks; computer and laser letters; postal requirements; merge-perge, unduplicate, statistics, demographics, psychographics; in-house- vs. service bureaus; computer selection - micro, mini, midi, maxi; more, in-depth; one day, usually back-to-back to Ed Burnett seminar in various U.S. cities; $200. either day; $350. for both.

Effective List Marketing*
The key to direct marketing profits; Ed Burnett*; see story in this book, Seminar III, Chapter 9. In key cities, intensive, full day, excellent; one day; $200, or $350 with Goldner seminar.

Direct marketing clubs usually put considerable effort into arranging seminars for members. Some seminars come from other areas. Others are local but often feature nationally known authorities who live there.

The following are two of several seminars the Long Island Direct Marketing Association (LIDMA) puts on; usually in Westbury, 20 miles from New York City. For latest rates, dates and news of the LIDMA seminar write: Long Island Direct Marketing Association, 260 Duffy Avenue, Hicksville, NY 11802, or phone Gloria Schude at Research Project (516) 481-4410.

Mailing Seminar
Long Island processes 18% of the nation's bulk mailings. Top people in every aspect are club members and join together in an afternoon and evening one day saturation session. Excellent from concept to production to list selection. Usually in May. Contact LIDMA.

Mini-Computer Mini-Course
Hardware, software, user's problems; do's, don'ts, interplay. The frustrated complain. The experts explain. Thorough, helpful, needed. Once Yearly; 4 hours; usually in fall; LIDMA.

For years all over the U.S. and the world Ed McLean has put on excellent seminars in direct mail copy. He's done fine ones on magazine circulation renewals for the Circulation Managers Association. For his future seminar plans write: Ed McLean, Thistle Hill, Ghent, NY 12075; (518) 828-9791.

Rene Gnam has been an effective writer of successful mail order copy for biggest magazines and a consultant for medium sized mail order firms as well as big. The following is his very useful seminar on direct mail.

Direct Mail Response
How to plan, create, design and produce effective direct mail; mailing list selection, usage, frequency; key U.S. cities; $245 one day to $675 three days. Write: Rene Gnam Consultation Corp., P.O. Box 6435, Clearwater, FL 33518. (813) 536-5556.

Shell Alpert writes a column for ZIP magazine, consults for clients, has been in his own mail order business and from time to time puts on seminars of which the following is one.

Recognizing Opportunities in Direct Mail
Shell Alpert tells how: various cities; one day; $125. Contact: Shell Alpert, Direct Marketing, Langhorne, PA 19047. (215) 752-3433.

One seminar I'd really like to save up for is this one:

Catalog Marketing
Advanced conference; the art of creating deluxe catalogs. Learn like a millionnaire how to sell the rich, in a VIP boot camp, from Jo Von Tucker. For 20 years she contributed mightly to the creation, presentation, production and profitability of some of the most upscale successes. Now she shows how.

The psychology of item selection and display; of color, styling, wording needed; the photography and art, typography and layout required; how glossy or sleek to be; provocative ways to pull highest ticket order from the wealthy. Four nights; three intensive working days; spring $1,700. (includes single deluxe hotel accomodations); Hyatt Baja Hotel, Cabo San Lucas, Mexico. Benefitting the Direct Mail/Marketing Educational Foundation; Jo Von Tucker & Associates, 3525 Cedar Springs, Dallas, TX 75219. (214) 528-9210.

Most seminars train the rising managers-to-be of the big. Small entrepreneurs also often attend. But one that some big and quite a few small attend is the following:

How To Start a Newsletter
Since 1970 this seminar has helped newcomers start newsletters. How to find market, select mailing lists; the principles of direct mail; creating promotions; fulfillment, renewals, editorial content and production; designing your newsletter. Good panelists explain, answer questions. Usually in New York City twice yearly. $145. The Newsletter Clearinghouse, 44 West Market Street, Rhinebeck, NY 12572. (914) 876-2081.

Direct Marketing for Retailers
Symposium 1½ days; $350.; NYC; National Retail Merchants Association, 100 W 31st Street, New York, NY 10001; (212) 244-8780.

Many big firms not in mail order are integrating direct marketing methods with their sales forces. The following is a seminar to help.

Building Sales Through Inquiries
Top authorities explain how to use reader inquiries to save on selling expense while increasing sales volume. How they set up systems; bugs, pitfalls, problems to avoid; how to save time and costs to get your own system going; questions to ask suppliers; how to train sales force to use system and follow-up leads more effectively. $115.; Advertising Research Foundation, 3 East 54th Street, New York, NY 10022. (212) 751-5656.

More and more big and small firms use telephone marketing. They do so to aid salesmen, save the time of salesmen, and to maximize mail order results from inquiries secured via advertising - as a form of 2-step mail order - for them, here's another seminar.

Selling by Telephone
Basic, thorough; various cities; spring and fall; one day; $95. Contact: Reuben H. Donnelley, 825 Third Avenue, New York, NY 10022. (212) 972-8266.

Here's one for big and small magazines.

Customer Service
Fulfillment Management Association; spring; New York City. Contact: Dorothy Forier, 250 West 55th Street, New York, NY 10019; (212) 262-7997.

The smallest moonlighter wants to save money on producing ads and to improve presentation. The biggest mail order company wants to train advertising art and production people to do so. Here's a basic one on paste-ups.

Paste-Up Workshop
One day; various cities; spring and fall; techniques to prepare paste-ups, print photos, alterations; use of tools and materials; Correcting and handling copy; $120; Idea Seminars, P.O. Box 369, Omaha, NE 60101. (800) 228-7272 toll free.

And here's something more complete for those who work for printers, agencies and advertising departments.

Art & Production Seminars
Excellent on the following: Basic layout and paste-up; clip art -how to use it; typography in design; photodesign; newsletter design. Step-by-step; concepts and execution. Two and three day seminar on each, $295. to $415.; substantial discounts for multiple seminars or attendance; scheduled in key U.S. cities yearly. Write for catalog: Dynamic Graphics Educational Foundation, 6707 N. Sheridan Rd., P.O. Box 1901, Peoria, IL 61656; (309) 691-0428.

And here's one for people who work for mailing houses or in the mailing department of companies which mail in quite large volume.

Mail Room Training
How to operate Philipsburg, Kirk Rudy inserting machines and Cheshire labelling machines; two days, various cities; $195. The Institute of Continuing Education, Mail Advertising Service Association, 7315 Wisconsin Avenue, 818-E, Bethesda, MD 20814; (301) 654-7030.

The more mail order proliferates the more direct marketing seminars do for new problems and new opportunities. The DMMA runs the DMMA Washington Symposium with detailed information on current postal matters—from rates to volume discounts to ZIP code area changes.

There are even direct marketing seminars for professors of marketing . . . put on occasionally by the Direct Marketing Educational Foundation. Professors of college and graduate business courses who are interested attend at no cost.

Direct Marketing Institute For University and College Professors
3½ days; strategy, planning, lists and projects, testing, offers, copy and graphics; launching new products, multimedia; plans; lists/list management: direct response insurance and financial series; catalogs, telephone marketing: broadcast space advertising, new media; Direct Mail Marketing Educational Foundation, 6 East 43rd Street, New York, NY 10017. (212) 689-4977.

If you mail now in volume and are interested in electronic mail here's an excellent free seminar.

ECOM First Class Mail
Electronic Computer Originated Mail: how to layout, space, head; character codes used; sample letter layout sheets, examples of coding; features, procedures; user telecommunications hardware, service required; whom to deal with and where to reach them; free seminar, U.S. Postal Service. Ask your post office for office of nearest MSC Manager - Postmaster.

Associations That Aid Direct Marketers

Those starred (*) are described in stories in this book. The most important to anyone in mail order is the Direct Mail/Marketing Association* about which much is written in this book. Its address is:

DMMA, 6 East 43rd Street, New York, NY 10017
Telephone: (212) 689-4977

Regarding the many information services of the DMMA described in this book, I advise non-members to consider buying books and attending one or two seminars. To attend a number of seminars or any conference, you're better off to join. The saving on members' discounts is substantial. As far as the DMMA Manual is concerned, I advise non-members not to buy individual sections. If you're interested in a number of sections, I recommend that you join and get the entire manual free.

In considering whether to join the DMMA and, if so, when you're ready to join, you might look again at the following two stories of a number in this book which concern the DMMA:

Guiding Direct Marketing's Growth*
The story of Robert DeLay and how for 20 years, as president of the Direct Mail/Marketing Association, he has been a driving force to multiply and greatly expand its services, in its growth and that of direct marketing. What he's done can help you. Seminar I, Chapter 11, this book.

The Direct Mail/Marketing Association*
What the DMMA does for members. Seminar II, Chapter 2, this book.

An elite organization of slightly more than a hundred members, located in New York City, has national impact. It's the Direct Marketing Idea Exchange. The following describes it.

The Direct Marketing Idea Exchange*
How it was founded, operates; the high calibre of speakers at its lunches. Nat Ross . . . its guiding force. Seminar III, Chapter 4, this book.

There are two other organizations which started in New York in a small way, have grown in a major way and are becoming national in scope. One is particularly helpful to creative people and the other to women executives in all areas of direct marketing. They are:

The Direct Marketing Creative Guild*
516 Fifth Avenue, NYC 10036; (212) 909-0206. How it helps creative people start, get better jobs, increase earnings; its New York based activities and those with national impact. Seminar VI, Chapter 9, this book.

The Women's Direct Marketing Group*
P.O. Box 5134, FDR Station, NYC 10150. (212) 765-6500, Ext. 356. How women help each other rise in direct marketing with their own organization; how it started; its services; the outstanding women who have helped it grow; its success in New York and national expansion plans. Seminar V, Chapter 5, this book.

There are a number of associations important to those concerned with specific areas of direct marketing. These are:

Association of Direct Marketing Agencies (ADMA), 342 Madison Avenue, New York, NY 10173; (212) 687-2100.

Associated Third Class Mail Users (ATCMU), 1725 K Street, N.W., Suite 607, Washington, D.C. 20006; (202) 296-5232.

Direct Mail Fundraisers Association Inc., 111 East 59th Street, New York, NY 10022; (212) 840-0711.

Direct Marketing Computer Association, 750 Zeckendorf Boulevard, Garden City NY 11530; (516) 877-1400.

Fulfillment Management Association, 250 West 55th Street, New York, NY 10019; (212) 262-7997.

Direct Marketing Credit Association (DMCA), c/o Prentice Hall, Inc. Englewood Cliffs, NJ 07632; (201) 592-3143.

Envelope Manufacturers Association, 1 Rockefeller Plaza, New York, N.Y. 10020; (212) 245-5885.

Graphic Communications Association (printers), 1730 N. Lynn, Arlington, VA 22209; (703) 841-8160.

Mail Advertising Service Association International, (lettershops and associated services), 7315 Wisconsin Ave., 818-E, Bethesda, MD 20814; (301) 654-7030.

NRMA/National Retail Merchants Association, 100 West 31st Street, New York, NY 10001; (212) 244-8780.

National Society of Fund Raisers, 235 East 31st Street, New York, NY 10016; (212) 532-4500.

Newsletter Association of America, 1008 National Press Building, Washington, D.C. 20045; (202) 347-5220.

Parcel Shippers Association (formerly Parcel Post Association) 1211 Connecticut Avenue, N.W., Washington, D.C. 20036; (202) 296-3690.

U.S. Electronic Mail Association, Harvard Square, Box 43, Cambridge, MA 02138; (617) 542-0100.

Direct Marketing Show and Conference* Listings

Starred shows are described in Seminar III, Chapter 2, this book. The following are shows to consider.

DMMA Annual Conference and Trade Show*
The big one! Like a week of biggest Direct Marketing Days. Fall. Alternates each year to one of various cities.

DMMA Government Affairs Conference*
The larger your firm gets in direct marketing the more concerned you'll be with how to deal with government and the more important this becomes. Washington, D.C.

DMMA List Day*
The scope and variety of a big Direct Marketing Day but just on lists; summer, usually in New York City.

DMMA Spring Conference
Excellent program; half the attendance of the Annual Conference. A good working show. Alternates each year to one of various cities.

DMMA International Conference
Direct Marketing Management Conference, usually in February, Monte Carlo, Monaco; attracts representatives from many countries.

For information on any of the above, contact Direct Mail/Marketing Association, Conference Department, 1730 "K" Street NW, Suite 905, Washington, D.C. 20006. (202) 347-1222.

International Direct Marketing Symposium
Experts from 40 countries update the international direct marketing community. The first major European Direct Marketing show; very big; Montreux, Switzerland. For details write: Hoke Communications Inc. in U.S.A. (224 Seventh Street, Garden City, NY 11530; (516) 746-6700).

Pan Pacific Direct Marketing Symposium
Mail order is growing fast from Japan to Australia. This show is becoming more important for world direct marketing. Usually in Sydney, Australia. In U.S. contact: Hoke Communications, 224 Seventh Street, Garden City, NY 11530. (800) 645-6132.

NAA International Newsletter Conference
Spring, Washington, D.C.; 5 days. Fundamentals, launching, promotion, accounting; production, editorial, management; computer use, new technology; extra sales, ways to save and improve profits; $350; Newsletter Association of America, 1008 National Press Building, Washington, D.C. 20045; (202) 347-5250.

Information Utilities (NYC)
Executive conference on electronic media ... videotex ... teletex, .. interaction cable TV ... videodiscs ... teleshopping ... home banking and finance . . . electronic publishing . . . satellite broadcasting . . . impact of electronic media on mail order; spring. Contact: Online Inc., 11 Tannery Lane, Weston, CT 06883; (203) 227-8466.

Videotex Conference and Exhibition
Newest developments, latest applications around the world in Videotex. The Conference alternates annually between New York and Toronto. Three saturation days. Canada $695 vs. US $585. Online Conferences Ltd., Argyle House, Northwood Hills, HA 6 ITS Middlesex, UK. Phone: Northwood (09274) 28211 -International phone: 44-9274-2811. Telex: 923 498.

Merchandise Shows—USA

Trade shows are a great help to mail order firms, but mostly to those already established which seek additional items related to those already successful.

The dream of a mail order newcomer is that going to a trade show is like picking up an item at a drug store or supermarket. Just pick it up, run an ad, and make money. This is seldom done.

Exhibitors at trade shows seek dealers and distributors at normal discounts giving needed profit margins. They try to avoid exclusives. They're busy and wish to concentrate on the kind of customers they seek. The conventional margin they offer is usually insufficient for mail order. Yet some seek mail order business. Some are more flexible than others.

My suggestion is that newcomers, particularly, reread Seminar I, Chapter 4, the story of Lillian Katz, and how she buys items. For a mail order firm to get the right item, at the right price, on the right basis, at a trade show is a sales problem. Discounts offered vary widely by fields. Needed discounts for mail order vary by the mail order situation. A catalog may work with a bit lower discount structure than a solo direct mailer. A package insert of a related product which you ship your customer will work with least discount. But the quest is always for more margin without sacrifice of quality.

This can best be done in other ways than by shopping at trade shows. It's particularly difficult to get items at a trade show unique enough, with margin enough and exclusive enough to have a good chance for a new mail order business. But it's still sometimes done. Let's consider specific fields and shows appropriate for them.

Books

Most book clubs sell fiction and most continuity plans non-fiction. Almost all other mail order firms sell non-fiction, chiefly how-to ... in sets or single volumes. Success for all starts with title selection. The ability to recognize a title that will sell by mail is more frequent after the fact. Original publishers sometimes don't, and are therefore cooperative towards anyone who can, successfully sell books via mail order.

It's not easy, sophisticated direct marketers frequently fail in tests. Most beginners fail . . . but many try. Yet moonlighters originate a surprising number of successful mail order titles. Tiniest moonlighters sometimes select a number of how-to titles in one specialized area . . . type out a description of each, photocopy a crude catalog which they offer via classified ads . . . and succeed. Sometimes they get such titles from remainder houses at a fraction of original costs.

Biggest publishers are not geared to promote in such small ways. Smallest publishers often lack know-how. Both seek those who can sell by mail and will sometimes give needed margins in discounts offered, reprint rights and even exclusivity via mail order. Most first mail order tests of books are arranged by mail and phone. Personal meetings then help. For the most book contacts in the shortest time consider this:

The ABA Convention & Trade Show
Once annually; late spring. Alternates among various cities; 4 days; free; huge show. Over 10,000 how-to titles sold to some degree by mail controlled by over 1,000 exhibitors; including principal remainder houses; American Booksellers Association, 122 East 42nd Street, New York, NY 10168. (212) 867-9060.

Consumer Electronics

Computerized everything; does almost anything; high technology creates, marketing sells; mail order often launches; often not the manufacturer, sometimes the small. New items are constantly sought by entrepreneurs and entrepreneurs by makers of new items. Its getting harder for the small. The big deal more with the big.

Yet the small start, innovate and succeed as well as fail. Moonlighting programmers create software for arcade games and home computers. Small software catalogs and small catalogs for video tapes and new video discs start up. New groupings of consumer electronics in new small catalogs sometimes succeed and get big. The excitement is for the new. Small and big rush in . . . as in a gold rush. And here is where there's first crack for somebody at most brand new items in the field.

The National Consumer Electronics Show
Big, exciting, confusing and tiring, but a possible bonanza; twice annually; winter, Las Vegas; summer, Chicago; 4 days; free but business card required; Consumer Electronic Industries Association, 2001 "I" Street, NW, Washington, D.C. (202) 457-4919.

Every successful mail order business develops its own personality, usually quickly. It's then important to keep each item it buys in character. This determines desirable shows to attend, particularly in fashion mail order. For a fashion catalog with a boutique image appealing to the young and budget minded the following is a show to consider.

National Fashion & Boutique Show
Innovative; big; twice annually; New York in spring; Los Angeles in fall; 1,200 exhibitors, 35,000 attend; free, but business card required. For information contact National Fashion & Boutique Show, 71 West 35th Street, New York, NY 10001. 800-225-4278.

Gifts

Gift catalogs range from mass to class. Each seeks items in character, with maximum appeal and lowest price in relation to sales. Biggest and most mass catalogs seek to develop items, have them made under contract exclusively, and to import items directly. All seek exclusives. Mass catalogs often seek gifts in mass merchandise shows. Most catalogs seek small but stable manufacturers who will give maximum discounts on unadvertised or lightly advertised products. Above all, they seek hits already successful by mail order for someone just starting to project.

The gift shows were originally geared for gift shops and department store gift departments. Catalogs appealing to equivalent customers do best at gift shows. There are gift shows in Boston, Atlanta, Dallas and other cities. Select one near you. These are the two biggest.

Chicago Gift Market
Very large; twice annually; winter and summer; 1,100 exhibitors; 15,000 attendees. Advance registration; free; business card required. Merchandise Mart, Chicago, IL 60654. (312) 527-4141.

New York Gift Show
The biggest; twice yearly; winter, summer; 900 exhibitors; 20,000 attendees; free; business card required; New York Coliseum (Convention Center 1984 on). For information write: Little Brothers Shows, 261 Madison Avenue, New York, NY 10016. (212) 986-8000.

Hardware

Even nuts and bolts have been mail order hits when offered in unusual variety and groupings. Hard-to-find tools have been strong in mail order in special catalogs. For mail order firms which seek hardware, here's an important show.

National Hardware Show
Another big one; once yearly; August; 2,500 exhibitors; 20,000 items; 25,000 attend; free; business card required; Chicago, McCormick Place; American Hardware Manufacturer's Association, 117 E. Palatine Road, Palatine, IL 60067.

Housewares

They include many new small appliances ideal for mail order via demonstration on TV, solo mailing pieces and in catalogs. Department stores often launched such items. Now often mail order does. Housewares range from some garden items to earthenware and decorative placques. For the mail order firm that fits, here is an important show.

National Housewares Expo
Geared to department stores in price and character of merchandise; twice yearly; winter, summer; huge; over 1,900 exhibitors; almost 20,000 items; 60,000 attend; free with business card; National Housewares Manufacturer's Association, 1324 Merchandise Mart, Chicago, IL 60654. (312) 644-3333.

Marine

Big yachts don't sell by mail. But to sell them there are regional boat shows all over which also include many accessories and marine items sometimes sold by mail. Get the latest list, addresses and information on all important regional shows from Boating Magazine, Ziff-Davis Publishing Co., One Park Avenue, New York, NY 10016. (212) 725-3970.

The following are three important marine shows:

International Marine Trade Show
Biggest boat trade show; annually; fall; for boat dealers. Big range of accessories. Almost 1,000 exhibitors. Close to 30,000 attend. McCormick Place, Chicago, IL. Free; business card required; for information contact National Marine Manufacturer's Association, 401 North Michigan Avenue, Chicago, IL 60611 (312) 836-4777.

National Boat Show

Biggest boat consumer show. Annually; January; highly publicized; TV promoted; over 400,000 attendance by public. Open with two trade days; free with business card; 4 floors of big boats with lots of little items here and there. Always plenty of new marine items. For information contact the New York Coliseum, Columbus Circle, New York, NY (212) 757-5000.

Miami International Boat Show

Getting bigger every year. If you're in marine mail order and in Florida in February, attend it. Quite a few marine items made in the south often are exhibited here before they are nationally. There's a big national representation too. Once yearly. Trade days first at no cost if you show business card. For information write: Miami International Boat Show, 6358 Manor Lane, South Miami, FL 33143. (305) 666-0661.

Premiums

The trend in them has been to trade up; to higher quality, to high priced self-liquidators to quality incentive merchandise for sales organizations and to dealers. Many of the same items are suited to mass mail order firms who regularly attend these premium shows.

National Premium/Incentive Show

Each year in the spring in New York, New York Coliseum (Convention Center 1984 on); each fall in Chicago, McCormack Place. Great variety; lots of new items. For information concerning New York show contact Thalheim Exposition Management Corp., 98 Cutter Mill Road, Great Neck, NY 11021. (212) 357-3555. For Chicago show information contact Hall-Erickson Inc., Managing Directors, 7237 Lake Street, River Forest, IL 60305. (312) 366-1733.

Sporting Goods

There's a lot of it sold by mail but mostly in specialized areas of sporting goods. There are specialized sport shows for each speciality. The following is the biggest general show. There are a number of similar big regional shows. A big proportion of exhibits at all of them are team sports and guns. But there's much more. Consider this one.

The NSGA Annual Convention & Show

Biggest in the world; once yearly; winter; 4 days; alternates Chicago (McCormick Place), and other key cities. Small registration fee to dealers. For information write: National Sporting Goods Association, 717 North Michigan Avenue, Chicago, IL 60611. (312) 944-0205.

Toys

Demonstration TV, catalogs, direct mail solos and inserts and space ads all sell toys by mail. It's getting harder but with right items is still profitable. The search for a mail order toy often starts at the toy shows. This is the biggest.

International Toy Fair

Mammoth; once a year; winter; 4 days; New York Convention Center; from fanciest electronic to basics; free to dealers with business card. For information contact Toy Manufacturer's of America, 200 5th Avenue, New York, NY 10010. (212) 675-1141.

Various

Specialized mail order is growing faster than general mail order. Smallest beginners who succeed usually do so in areas too small and specialized for the big. The big seek specialized areas that are growing fast and are capable of volume. Both are apt to go to more specialized trade shows for items.

Fishing tackle products are found at the show in Chicago and alternating cities of the American Fishing Tackle Manufacturer's Association, with very little shown at the NSGA Show. Golf, tennis and ski equipment manufacturers are at the NSGA but even more so at their own individual shows.

There are several thousand mail order stamp companies only interested in stamp shows. Mail order coin companies only desire numismatic shows. Industrial direct marketers may look for the Plant Maintenance Show. The Hobby Show and Needlework Show each have trade attendees interested in no other. There are specialized garden shows, miniature furniture shows and craft shows. Each is perfect for the kinds of mail order firm suited. There are small mail order ventures selling equipment to bee keepers, big ones who sell only by mail to schools, and lots who sell stationery.

For virtually every trade, sport and hobby show, every business and professional show, there are mail order firms specializing in the field which benefit by attending. The solution is to look in the appropriate section of one of the media manuals described in Reference Section III, preferably at a library. Find a magazine in the desired field. Telephone it and ask for the editorial department. Then ask for latest information about the show for that field. Ask your library for the Trade Show and Convention Guide.

There are shows every week in leading cities. Each exhibit center in that city can give a list of upcoming shows. There are many more mass shows. There's the National Mail Order Show in New York, mostly for lower priced items. There's the National Back to School Merchandise Show in New York with cameras, luggage, and educational supplies. There's the Variety Merchandise Show and the National Merchandise Show, both huge, in New York and filled with mass items. Sometimes when the biggest show in the field is continually overbooked, an overflow show starts usually with new companies and new products sometimes suited to mail order.

And when you're finished in the U.S. you can consider the great trade shows of Europe and then all over the world. Check the Trade Commission of individual key countries for lists, dates and information on trade shows. If you can't locate the Trade Commission, try the nearest Consulate, and if you can't find that write the Embassy in Washington of each major country.

The Book Remainder Houses

For mail order newcomers a dream recurs ... of a mail order product supplier with item after item to select from, each a proven success, to be advertised for instant, sure profit.

To find a new product that makes money often seems more like searching for a needle in a haystack. But, surprisingly, books are occasionally found in remainder houses which do sell profitably by mail order, sometimes at the original retail price, yet can be bought at so low a price as to make possible an ample gross profit margin. Remainder books are those of a printing remaining in stock unordered by regular customers and these are sold at a distress price to a "remainder house."

Yet a mail order operator may uncover a special market, one the original publisher never effectively approached, if at all. It might be via a highly specialized magazine or equivalent broadcast audience. It might be by running the tiniest of ads flagging a particular group to highly suitable books and asking for inquiries. Sometimes the simplest of descriptions of each book mailed to inquirers will produce profitable orders.

In this field, as in all mail order, the least knowledgeable are most apt to lose. Success more often comes when the books offered are related to books or items already successfully sold by mail order. Newcomers have least chance. Yet remainder houses have helped launch many new mail order ventures. The following are some leading book remainder houses.

A. & W. Promotional Books (Division of A. & W. Publishers), Inc.
A major firm; specializes in books that respond to promotion. 95 Madison Avenue, New York, NY 10016; (212) 725-4977.

Book Sales Inc.
Big; great variety; President Arnold Hausner has personally worked with many mail order entrepreneurs, often from the start. 110 Enterprise Avenue, Secaucus, NJ 07094; (201) 864-6341 or 679-9191.

Marboro Books, Inc.
The first remander house to aggressively promote through coop ads, catalogs, its own stores and catalog. Great range with exact figures how each of thousands of titles has responded to mail order. 205 Moonachie Road, Moonachie, NJ 07074; (201) 440-3800.

Outlet Book Company
The biggest remainder house; biggest volume of sales by mail order; publishes most widely distributed remainder catalog; has most data on mail order results in advertising of remainders. A great source! President Alan Mirkin understands and cooperates with mail order people. One Park Avenue, New York, NY 10010; (212) 532-9200.

Quality Books, Inc.
Wide variety of remainder books. 400 Anthony Trail, Northbrook, IL 60062; (312) 498-4000.

Book World Promotions.
Text, technical, business, general. 87-93 Christie Street, Newark, NJ 07100; (201) 589-7877.

CFP Books, Inc.
General interest and specialized books. 468 Park Avenue South, New York, NY 10016; (212) 725-5672.

X-S Books Inc.
Text, technical, business. 675 Dell Road, Carlstadt, NJ 07072; New York City Showroom, 432 Park Avenue South, New York, NY 10016; (212) 532-0588.

Bookthrift, Inc. (a Simon & Schuster subsidiary);
Remainders, imports, bargain books. Often has excellent specialty books, excellent for specialized mail order. One West 39th Street, New York, NY 10018; (212) 221-4610.

This concludes Reference Section VII, the Help Source Guide, and the book.

INDEX
To Overview and Seminars

SUMMARY
UNTIL WE MEET
AGAIN

And so we're finished. Thanks for reading my book.

You may wonder how much time it would take to refer to material listed and how much time would be left to apply it. Let me tell you what we do at our business. It has worked for us and might for you.

This book took four years to research and write. It required several of our people to help me . . . pretty much full time. Different people rotated. Needed time was taken away from the business. The project cost much out-of-pocket money. Yet, it has already paid off for us as a kind of basic research.

Over my business lifetime I have trained many people. I gave them whatever mail order knowledge I had gained. Some did quite well. But now I can also give people what others have been teaching me.

I've been fortunate to have talked, for this book, to some people loaded with know-how. I tried to cover each important direct marketing development, particularly new areas. The people I interviewed are very smart. Each told me direct marketing experiences new to me. Each conveyed a unique way of thinking. Each told of key decisions arrived at. Each described what had worked best when. Some old friends told me things they never had before. One question I asked each was who and what had influenced them most. If it was a book and I hadn't read it, I then did. If it was a living individual, I called up and interviewed him or her. From each I got more. The process went on and on. I read faster and faster, more and more, transcripts of speeches, booklets, reports, articles, books. I listened to tapes. I took tens of thousands of pages of notes of what these bright people said to me.

Meanwhile, those who worked with me on the project got interested. I'd pass along and recommend most interesting material to each for the specific ambitions each had. Others in this office wanted to learn what we were learning. My son Cecil and my wife, Fritzi, became interested. I gave each material important for the work each was doing. Soon I was passing on and recommending one type of material to a copy trainee, another for one in media, and so on.

My wife is Prussian. I said, let's create an army of officers as Prussia did at the time of Napoleon. Let each here who is ambitious learn. We'll all learn together.

We have found that learning from others extended and multiplied our own know-how. We're a young crew. I have age and experience but have learned to learn and that it's never too late to learn. I advise. The others do. I try to have perspective, to observe what's going on elsewhere, to suggest trying ourselves what is working for others. We're doing things we never did before, thanks to the book project.

During this period we've had dramatic growth. Such success as we've had has had many causes . . . the right products at the right time . . . Fritzi's frugality . . . Cecil's creativity, planning and execution . . . other talented associates . . . a lot of hard work. But an important added factor has been the extension of know-how, the trying of new methods which has come from the book project.

Our business is still not big, but it has multiplied—and our mail order operations most of all. The result is creating more opportunity for those associated with us.

And in comparing the young people of our new Huber Hoge with successful Hoge alumni over the years, I'm proud of those now coming up . . . of the copy written, the media decisions made, the pride in quality presentation, but above all of the constant desire to learn. This book has become our training course. We try to be selective. No one person attempts to study all, but each selects and regularly learns more of that which is suited to his or her work.

I think this plan will work for you. One day, perhaps, we'll meet and exchange know-how. The best place to reach me is: Cecil C. Hoge Sr., President, Huber Hoge & Sons Advertising Inc., 104 Arlington Avenue, St. James, NY 11780; (516) 724-8900.